Prentice-Hall Psychology Series

JAMES J. JENKINS, *Editor*

READINGS
in the
PSYCHOLOGY
of
LANGUAGE

READINGS in the PSYCHOLOGY of LANGUAGE

edited by

Leon A. Jakobovits
University of Illinois

and

Murray S. Miron
Syracuse University

Prentice-Hall, Inc. / Englewood Cliffs, New Jersey

Library of Congress Catalog Card Number: 67–20935

Printed in the United States of America

Current printing (last digit):
10 9 8 7 6 5 4 3 2 1

Prentice-Hall International, Inc., LONDON
Prentice-Hall of Australia, Pty. Ltd., SYDNEY
Prentice-Hall of Canada, Ltd., TORONTO
Prentice-Hall of India Private Ltd., NEW DELHI
Prentice-Hall of Japan, Inc., TOKYO

Preface

The problems of choice for a volume of this kind are, to state it cautiously, difficult. The nascent concern of the psychologist for matters linguistic has filled our journals with worthy material far greater in quantity than could ever be included in a volume of manageable size. As a consequence, with acceptance of the exigencies of choice, we have selected material on the basis of our evaluation of its usefulness to those within and outside the field as a survey of the theory and experimentation in the psychology of language. We have done so with remorse for that excluded and debate for that included.

It is our hope that the student psychologist and his colleagues from the related disciplines interested in the behavioral approach to language will find the easy access that reprinting provides a material aid in his teaching and research. As teachers ourselves, our motivation for an enterprise such as this one is, at the very least, an expression of our desire to use the book for such a purpose. Reprinting of published material, with all its selective lacunae, can after all only be justified by convenience. We are modestly hopeful that many students and teachers will find this volume useful on that account.

As to what the psychology of language, or psycholinguistics, may be, we are not content by default to offer the rather empty and oft quoted definition that it is the study of the relations between messages and the characteristics of the humans who select and interpret those messages. More specifically, it has been characterized as the study of the relationships between the processes of encoding and decoding as these relate states of messages to states of communicators. Obviously this defines a field of study sufficiently broad to include most of what we call human behavior. Messages need not be restricted to verbal communications. Encoding and decoding processes involve all behavioral and sensory manifestations. States of communicators include maturational, dispositional, personality and intellectual characteristics, to list only a few. Thus this definition might embrace studies of the pottery designs of different tribal societies, the interactions between inmates of a prison community, the relations between musical notation systems and composers, or comparisons of the programming languages preferred by computer users. What it is that sets apart psycholinguistics as a separate subset discipline distinct in its own right remains as difficult to specify as when the above definition was first proposed some fifteen years earlier.

Practically, the field has been limited to those aspects of symbolic activity required to produce and understand natural languages. The psycholinguist of recent years has been increasingly concerned with the translation of the competence models of the descriptive linguist into the performance models of the behavior theorist. The linguist has provided a wealth of detail about what it is we must know in order to comprehend or implement an utterance. The psychologist for his part provides the principles of behavior modification and acquisition. The psycholinguist seeks to understand how language controls behavior, verbal and non-verbal both, and how the language-user comes to know what linguistic theory indicates he must know.

This book assumes as its credo the more restrictive definition. There has been a dramatic shift from viewing verbal behavior as sequences of isolated units to viewing it as organized, hierarchal patterns simultaneously manipulated. This shift, which characterizes most of the contributions in this book, is both overdue and refreshing. Psychology viewed from a psycholinguistic vantage point may at last have come of age. From our rat-infested laboratories we are reaching for that aspect of human behavior which is least animal-like—symbolic behavior. That is what this book is about.

In an area as volatile as that of language, it is unreasonable to assume that the editors of this book are always in complete agreement on all of the theoretical issues. In point of fact, it is such disagreement that forms the basis of the structure of this volume. From the principle that honest and rational disagreement serves to best clarify issues, in each of the areas one point of view is immediately followed by another. As with the selections themselves the editors espouse somewhat different approaches to the problem. The student should be aware of the biases which may be implicit or explicit in the introductory material. The first editor has prepared the introduction to Part Three and the second editor those of Parts One and Two. They are identified only to avoid the embarrassment of forcing one to defend in the face of possible disagreement the other's errors in judgment.

That which is not in error is probably best attributed to those whose assistance in preparing this book was so freely given. We thank James Jenkins, Donald Dulaney, and Charles Osgood for their invaluable reactions to the selections; Mr. Michael Mery and Mrs. Cheryl Elsea for their assistance in preparing the manuscript for the printers and, of course, all of the contributors whose work is this book.

L. A. J.
M. S. M.

Contents

PART ONE

Some Major Theoretical Formulations 1

The Psychologist Looks at Language O. HOBART MOWRER 6

Behavior Theory and the Social Sciences CHARLES E. OSGOOD 51

Mentalism in Linguistics JERROLD J. KATZ 73

Methodological Preliminaries NOAM CHOMSKY 85

On Understanding and Creating Sentences CHARLES E. OSGOOD 104

Thinking B. F. SKINNER 128

Review of Skinner's Verbal Behavior NOAM CHOMSKY 142

Some Preliminaries to Psycholinguistics GEORGE A. MILLER 172

PART TWO

Experimental Approaches to Language 181

Studies in the Psychological Correlates of the Sound System of American English
JOSEPH H. GREENBERG and JAMES J. JENKINS 186

Some Psychological Studies of Grammar GEORGE A. MILLER 201

Some Perceptual Consequences of Linguistic Rules
GEORGE A. MILLER and STEPHEN ISARD 219

On Learning the Grammatical Order of Words
MARTIN D. S. BRAINE 232

On the Acquisition of Syntax: A Critique of "Contextual Generalization" T. C. BEVER, J. A. FODOR and W. WEKSEL 257

On the Basis of Phrase Structure: A Reply to Bever, Fodor, and Weksel MARTIN D. S. BRAINE 274

Is Linguistics Empirical? T. G. BEVER, J. A. FODOR and W. WEKSEL 285

Word Association and the Acquisition of Grammar ROGER BROWN and JEAN BERKO 294

Hesitation Phenomena in Spontaneous English Speech HOWARD MACLAY and CHARLES E. OSGOOD 305

The Psychological Reality of Linguistic Segments J. A. FODOR and T. G. BEVER 325

Studies in Aphasia: Background and Theoretical Formulations JOSEPH M. WEPMAN, LYLE V. JONES, R. DARRELL BOCK and DORIS VAN PELT 333

Stuttering Behavior and Learning: A Preliminary Theoretical Formulation GEORGE J. WISCHNER 342

PART THREE

The Problem of Meaning 355

An Approach to the Problem of Symbolic Representation: Nonverbal and Verbal BERNARD KAPLAN 363

Semantic Differential Technique in the Comparative Study of Cultures CHARLES E. OSGOOD 371

The Structure of a Semantic Theory JERROLD J. KATZ and JERRY A. FODOR 398

The Atomization of Meaning DWIGHT BOLINGER 432

An Analysis of Meaning CLYDE E. NOBLE 449

Meaning and m*: Correlated but Separate* ARTHUR W. STAATS and CAROLYN K. STAATS 461

Syntactic Position and Rated Meaning MICHAEL G. JOHNSON 472

The Principle of Associative Symmetry SOLOMON E. ASCH and SHELDON M. EBENHOLTZ 480

On the Relation Between the Probability of a Word as an Association and in General Linguistic Usage DAVIS HOWES 517

Changes with Age in the Verbal Determinants of Word-Association
SUSAN M. ERVIN-TRIPP 530

Mediated Generalization and the Interpretation of Verbal Behavior: I. Prolegomena
CHARLES N. COFER and JOHN P. FOLEY, JR. 541

Mediation in Paired-Associate Learning
NAN E. MCGEHEE and RUDOLPH W. SCHULZ 561

Words, Meanings and Concepts JOHN B. CARROLL 567

On Some Factors in the Organizational Characteristics of Free Recall
CHARLES N. COFER 587

Verbal Mediating Responses and Concept Formation
ALBERT E. GOSS 604

READINGS in the PSYCHOLOGY of LANGUAGE

PART ONE

Some Major Theoretical Formulations

In this, the first section of this book, are brought together several disparate and often antagonistic lines of thought. Roughly grouped, we can place the behaviorist psychologies of Mowrer, Osgood, and Skinner against the rationalist principles of Chomsky and Katz, with Miller in something of a middle ground between the two groups. While the behaviorist generally has minimized the importance of native endowment in the use of language, the rationalist assigns greater and greater importance to the specific nature of the species-linked talents required. For the behaviorist, the principles of learning, notably those involving conditioning, with slight extensions are as applicable in the explanation of language as they are in the development of limb flexion in the dog. The rationalist, on the other hand, continually argues the complexity of language and the inevitableness of some assumptions about specific innate capacities, other than the behaviorists' general principle of learning adaptability.

Beyond this, Chomsky in his review of Skinner's attempt to demonstrate the nature of the minimum extensions of traditional behavioral theory to language, has explicitly questioned the very givens of the behaviorists' approach. It is not the task of the editors to defend either position in a volume of this kind; rather we shall attempt to show the nature and extent of the controversy as presented by the readings chosen.

The conflict appears to concern the nature of the thing it is we wish to explain and what it is that constitutes adequate explanation. While Chomsky and Miller fasten upon the marvelous intricacy and complexity of abstraction involved in language, Mowrer and Skinner, notably, view it as much more mundane. Whereas Chomsky favors the rationalist approach over the empirical, Mowrer and Osgood search for explanations derived from observation and procedural formulae.

In the first of these papers Mowrer argues for the empiricists' position that all of language is reducible to a set of common object referents. Thus, the meaning of words is given by the arbitrariness of associationistic principles governing the conditioning of mediating responses, the fractional

r_m's of Osgood's theory, attached to neutral vocal noises or established signs. His position with respect to sign learning has been attacked on the grounds that the mediating response is too vaguely specified to carry the theoretical weight assigned to it (cf. Fodor, 1965). Every mediating response evoked by a learned sign must be distinct in total configuration from every other mediating response, and, consequently, the question must be raised as to how this distinctiveness is selected out of the total reactions to significants with which the sign is paired. With respect to an explanation of the simple, regular, active, declarative utterance as a conditioning device, it has been argued that the explanation is at once too restrictive and inadequate, at that, for even the restrictive case. For example, we need to know how it is that a speaker understands that in the utterance, "Tom asked Bill to get him," *Bill* functions as both the object and subject, or, that in Miller's sentence, "The car Tom stole won," how it is we are to label the parts in order to establish the proper ordering for conditioning to operate. No aspect of the form of the words gives us any clue as to their function in the sentence. Even word order in the absence of function markers will not suffice for explaining our understanding of "A thief Tom is not" and not understanding "A short Tom is not."

Let us hasten to observe, however, that Mowrer was writing at a time when the knowledge of the complexities of language was not well appreciated by psychologists. Thus, we find Miller much later apologizing for arguing complexity but arguing it nonetheless.

Skinner's functional analysis of verbal behavior as socially reinforced operants is a molar kind of taxonomy of the relationships between controlling stimuli and linguistic responses. The particular chapter chosen is included here to remind the student that the distinction between the mediation theorists and the "strict S-R' ists" is after all illusory. The difference between Osgood, for example, and Skinner is much more subtle and basic than the postulation of mediating events. It is, rather, the difference between a mentalistic and an empirical approach. In this regard, some critics now consider Osgood as closer to the "mentalism" of linguists such as Chomsky or Katz than to his behaviorist colleagues, such as Skinner.

Osgood's paper on the social sciences sets out the motivation for introducing an additional complexity to the "empty organism" of S-R psychology. For apparently very compelling reasons, he argues that the mediation approach is necessary to account for much of ordinary behavior and is the *sine qua non* of verbal behavior. Although it is difficult to find anyone who holds a strictly S-R view (even Skinner argues for mediating events in his chapter on thinking), those tempted to reason in this manner should be dissuaded by Osgood's arguments. Using the magical seven principles of behavior theory plus mediation as the link, Osgood sets out to explain Miller's seven aspects of human language. If there is any aspect of language which is prime on this list, it is that an utterance bears no simple relation to either the stimulus form or its component parts. The Katz article, although directed against taxonomic linguistics, might as well have served as a polemic against the taxonomy of the behaviorist. Emphasis upon the concepts of behaviorism, mechanism, operationalism, and physicalism characterizes the approaches to language advocated by Mowrer, Skinner, and Osgood. While Osgood feels compelled to justify the inclusion of the mentalistic device of mediation and show how it is in actuality quite physicalistic, Katz, arguing that there is a lack of physical basis for much of language, seeks to include much more without apology. Throughout his book Skinner seeks a taxonomy of functional relations between physical observables. Mowrer argues for the physicalism of conditioned connections between parts of sentences. In contrast Miller seeks explanation in the operation of rules, the discovery of which is given as a species-specific mental trait of man. What appears to emerge is an argument over the degree of complexity the theorist is compelled to assume in order to explain, not merely predict, language behavior. Katz, Chomsky, and Miller wish to attribute much more to the user of a language than do Osgood, Mowrer, and Skinner.

The "new psycholinguists" (Miller, 1964) are cautioning their colleagues that the facts accumulated within the traditional area of psychology known as verbal learning should not be confused with an understanding of language. Elaborate analyses of the theoretical predictions already in hand for this area (e.g., Osgood, 1953; Gibson, 1940; Underwood and Schulz, 1961; Goss and Nodine, 1965) indicate that we know quite a bit about such learning. But, it is argued, unsupported extensions of the principles applicable to laboratory exercises must not be accepted as adequate explanation. The learning of isolated orthographic combinations of finite dimensions is not, it seems, very revealing for an explanation of a novel connected utterance. As Chomsky has expressed in his evaluation of Skinner, language cannot be learned in any trivial sense of "learned." It seems obvious to these critics that the principles of conditioning, even supplemented by increasingly higher orders, will not suffice. The behaviorist is understandably reluctant to discard hastily the power of associationism, and yet the linguist continually reiterates the complexity of the behavior such simple principles will be required to cover. Even in the learning of the lexicon of his language, the child shows remarkable generative powers. Morphological extensions of the kind that Brown and Berko (see part 2) have investigated indicate the internalization of very abstract rules. To be sure, a theoretical explanation based upon discrimination training and generalization with social reinforcement can be invoked, but the transformationist fears that such explanations overlook the essential demonstration of the existence and primacy of rules in language. The fact that children and adults alike make mistakes in the application of such rules cannot be used as evidence against their validity. Psychology has long practiced the same distinction the modern linguist makes between competence and performance. Even allowing the validity of an explanation of the acquisition of morphological rules on the basis of stimulus generalization following discrimination training, the transformationist argues that such explanatory principles fail or become vacuously vague when applied to the more complex problems of notions like subject and object or the appreciation of the difference between "John is eager to please" and "John is easy to please."

The behaviorist seeks a model for the language user. Clearly this must be a much more complex task than that of the grammarian. Not only must the psychologist show how the form of the language affects behavior but, in addition, how it is that behavior itself is initiated and controlled. Osgood in his latest theoretical paper of this section has tried to show how the notions of the transformationist might be combined with those of the behaviorist. Assuming a set of formative rules, Osgood postulates hierarchies of behavioral contingencies probabilistically available to the organism as the determinants of resultant action. Thus, he superimposes on the generative rules of the transformationist a finite state model explaining the behavioral consequences of such rules. Osgood argues that although Chomsky elsewhere shows the inadequacy of the finite stochastic model as a theory of language, such a model is adequate as explanation of behavior. As Carroll (1959) has pointed out and for that matter Chomsky as well, a theory of behavior must take into account the finite limitations imposed by memory and mortality of the human user of language. The student is cautioned, however, to try to keep distinct theories of language structure and theories of the structure of language users. Put trivially, Chomsky seeks a model to explain the understanding of a sentence that may never be uttered, i.e., never realized in behavior. Osgood seeks a model for what has been realized. Hence Osgood (or Skinner) searches the past associations between constituent elements of experienced sentences at every level of their linguistic description for probabilistic determinants of the likelihood of future utterances. He assumes as given the capacity to label and analyze the constituent elements of these utterances, leaving the formulation of the rules for such to the grammarian. Thus, in this sense, no conflict exists between the grammarian and the psychologist. The conflict arises when the capacities actualized in behavior are minimized, when the theories of behavior seek to explain something less than what the linguist regards as essential to language capacity. The anonymous psychologist with his biased and inadequate definition of language cited by Miller is not altogether atypical of the simplistic physicalism that some psychologists display when talking about language. It is then, after all, a state of mind which is at issue.

References

CARROLL, J. B., "An Operational Model for Language Behavior," *Anthropological Linguistics,* 1 (1959), 37–54.

CHOMSKY, N., *Syntactic Structures.* The Hague: Mouton, 1957.

FODOR, J. A., "Could Meaning Be an r_m ?", *Journal of Verbal Learning and Verbal Behavior,* 4 (1965), 75–81.

GIBSON, E. J., "A Systematic Application of the Concepts of Generalization and Differentiation to Verbal Learning," *Psychological Review,* **47** (1940), 196–229.

GOSS, A. E., and C. F. NODINE, *Paired-Associates Learning*. New York: Academic Press, 1965.

MILLER, G. A., "The Psycholinguists: On the New Scientists of Language," *Encounter,* 23 (1964), 29–37.

OSGOOD, C. E., *Method and Theory in Experimental Psychology.* New York: Oxford University Press, Inc., 1953.

UNDERWOOD, B. J., and R. W. SCHULZ, *Meaningfulness and Verbal Learning*. Philadelphia: J. B. Lippincott Co., 1960.

The Psychologist Looks at Language[1]

O. HOBART MOWRER[2]

Writing in 1933, Leonard Bloomfield was prompted to remark that "psychologists generally treat language as a side issue" (6, p. 512). This observation was amply justified, for a survey of 100 introductory textbooks in psychology, published in this country during the first three decades of this century, reveals that in only 27 is there a discussion of language as such; and in most of these instances the discussion is, at best, incidental and sketchy.[3]

This neglect of language is especially remarkable when one considers how much of the waking life of human beings is spent in talking, listening, writing, reading, or using the subvocal equivalents thereof in thinking. In part, this neglect was certainly an expression of the then prevalent structuralistic emphasis. With its stress upon "the study of consciousness per se," structuralism saw language mainly as the tool or vehicle for describing states of consciousness, and hardly ever as something interesting and important in its own right. But this neglect was also fostered by behaviorism, as the most vigorous and outspoken form of functionalism. If, for the structuralist, language was merely the means of revealing or expressing one's

1 Presented, in abridged form, as the presidential address at the sixty-second annual convention of the American Psychological Association.

2 The list of references at the end of this paper very inadequately indicates the writer's indebtedness to others. Besides those specifically mentioned, various other persons have given generously of their knowledge and critical assistance, in conversation and through correspondence. The writer warmly thanks colleagues and students both in his own department and elsewhere for their helpfulness. Special thanks are due to Dr. Charles E. Osgood, Mr. William G. Perry, Jr., Dr. Fillmore H. Sanford, and Dr. Laurance F. Shaffer for reading and very usefully criticizing a preliminary draft of this paper.

3 Cf. McCarthy's remark that "In 1930 scarcely more than an isolated paragraph or two on language was to be found in textbooks on psychology" (40, p. 495). Three rather striking exceptions are Judd's *Psychology* (33), published in 1907; Hollingworth's *Psychology, Its Facts and Principles* (27), 1928; and Rexroad's *General Psychology* (62), 1929. All three of these books devote entire chapters to the topic of language and make distinctive contributions. An indication of the awakening of interest in language on the part of psychologists is the fact that the May issue of the *Psychological Bulletin* for 1929 was entirely devoted to this topic (1).

O. Hobart Mowrer, "The Psychologist Looks at Language," The American Psychologist, 9, No. *11 (November, 1954), 660–694. Reprinted by permission of the author and the publisher.*

inner life, for the behaviorist it ceased to be scientifically important even in this role; and such attempts as were made within this framework to deal with language objectively lacked vitality because of the seemingly necessary rejection of the whole problem of meaning.[4]

However, within the last two decades the picture has changed. During this period, one psychologist became so enthusiastic about the study of language that he once announced that "any one who is working on anything else is just wasting his time!" And scores of other psychologists have acquired similar convictions and have researched and written significantly in this field. Publications by Boder (7), Bousfield (8), Carroll (11), Cofer (12), Dollard (17), Fairbanks (18), Grummon (25), Johnson (32), Lewis (36), McCarthy (39), George Miller (44), Neal Miller (45), Osgood (55), Pronko (60), Razran (61), Roback (63), Sanford (64), Skinner (69), Tomkins (79), and Werner (84) are representative of the versatile and intensive inquiry and logical analysis which psychologists are now carrying on in the thriving domain of psycholinguistics.

It cannot be our purpose here to review the very solid accomplishments of recent workers in this area. Rather shall we devote ourselves to a consideration of some of the exciting questions about the psychology of language which are still incompletely answered but which can now, thanks to work already done, be formulated in more precise and, possibly, more productive ways.

[4] It should perhaps be said, in anticipation of the discussion which is to follow, that there seems now in the making a sort of *rapprochment* between that conception of psychology which accented consciousness and that which restricted itself to the study of behavior. As our objective investigation of living organisms has progressed, we have found it necessary to take subjective events, such as drives, perceptions, and other constructs, or "intervening variables," increasingly into account. This "neobehaviorism" (cf. Carroll, 11, pp. 71–73), while stemming directly from classical behaviorism, gives promise of providing a more powerful form of scientific analysis than did either introspectionism or behaviorism, in their original forms (cf. Mowrer, 51; Tomkins, 79).

I. SIGNS AND SENTENCES

The term "language" has been used in varied contexts. We hear of the language of animals, the language of nature, the language of love. Scientifically, what does the term mean or, more precisely, what can we most usefully make it mean?

Since the actual historical origin of language is lost beyond any hope of recovery, we are left with only more or less plausible surmises, or fictions. My favorite fiction in this connection is one that has the advantage of giving us, by implication, also a good working definition of language. In his book, *Man, An Autobiography,* George Stewart, professor of English at the University of California, goes about the problem in this way. He supposes that a sound like "Ouch" may have developed as a half-reflexive reaction to sudden pain. And then, says Man, speaking autobiographically:

> After awhile, when a creature had as good a brain as mine, [such] sounds would be more standardized, and their meanings fitted to the situation. Thus, "Ouch!" might be used playfully, when the individual felt no real pain, or it might warn a child not to pick up a bee (71, pp.31–32).
>
> Again, [says Man], something which could start more for playfulness than for "use" might soon come to be of value in other ways. When the band was foraging, one of them might signal his position by calling "Coo!" like a dove, to let the others know where he was.
>
> Eventually came the union of the noun-idea and the verb-idea. It may be that a woman came back without her companion, and much troubled. All attempts at gesture failed to tell what had happened. In desperation, naturally enough and yet with a stroke of genius, she cried, "Coo-ouch!" Then they knew that he who was called Coo had been taken with a sudden pain. Such a combination of two ideas was more than mere expression of personal feeling, and more also than

mere pointing-out of an individual. It was the setting of two ideas into a new relation, and thus the begining of real language (pp. 32–33).

The foregoing passages are the relevant ones for our immediate purposes, but they are followed by a brief paragraph which I cannot resist also quoting. The author goes on to say:

I like to think that the mothers may first have made and practiced language, and that for some generations the fathers still sat around merely grunting while the mothers chattered happily. At least I notice that girl-babies are still quicker to speak than boy-babies, and that they grow up in general to be more fluent talkers.[5] Besides, there has always been in language a great deal of an illogical and emotional quality. I might say, "Women invented language, but men invented grammar" (p. 33).

With the male ego thus saved, let us return to our inquiry. What Professor Stewart has done here, following Grace DeLaguna (15) and others, is to make the phenomenon of *predication,* i.e., the combination of two (or more) signs into a so-called sentence, the bedrock of true language development. Certainly anyone who has been present when a child starts, as we say, "putting words together" knows what a momentous event it is. I shall never forget when my own first child, a little girl, met me at the door one evening and excitedly exclaimed: "Pammy-kitty! Pammy-kitty!" I knew that our daughter had visited our little neighbor, Pammy, that afternoon. Therefore, "Pammy-kitty" clearly said, "Pammy (has a) kitten," and the enthusiasm which accompanied the statement also implied the qualifying phrase, "which is really quite wonderful."[6]

No, there can be no doubt that the act of putting words together in novel and informative combination is of enormous importance, both in the history of the race and in the development of each individual. And the product, which we call the sentence, can usefully serve as the central fact in our definition and analysis of language. However, an instructive complication at once arises, namely, the existence and relatively frequent use of the so-called one-word sentence.[7] And with this we are back where we started, so to say, at single, non-combined signs.

It is certainly a common-place observation that small children, well before they start speaking in formal sentences, communicate quite effectively—though, as we shall see, with definite limitations—by means of single words. And even at the adult level, we often make single words function as full sentences, in what Skinner (69) has called "mands," i.e., demands, commands, exclamations, etc. But if we look closely at these so-called one-word sentences, we discover an interesting characteristic, namely that they always, or at least commonly, *imply* something else and thus *function,* in a restricted way, as a two-sign complex or true sentence. "Mands," it seems, always refer to or imply, some thing or person which is physically present at the moment. Thus, if a baby says, "Bottle," it implies, "*I* want bottle"; and if an adult cries, "Stop," he implies, "Discontinue what *you* are now doing." Or, to revert to

---

[5] Stewart might also have observed that women are still the first language teachers of both boy and girl infants. On the basis of an analysis of language published elsewhere (49), it seems likely that very few, if any, children learn to speak from their fathers, save in the most exceptional circumstances. See Thompson (75, pp. 366–367).

[6] Wyatt (88) has noted and analyzed some 26 of the sentences first used by a little girl whom she systematically observed. She concludes: "The first appearance of these phrases was quite striking. At fifteen and a half months it seemed absolutely impossible for Nana to put words together. . . .Then suddenly, overnight, so to speak, the faculty to put words together or to produce two words in succession, emerged (age sixteen months)" (p. 29).

[7] *Webster's New Collegiate Dictionary* speaks of *"full sentences,* as distinguished from *minor sentences,* which generally consist of a completive word or phrase" (90, p. 771). Fowler says that where the subject or the predicate of a sentence is "understood," one has an "elliptical sentence" (21, p. 523).

the passage quoted from Stewart, the "Ouch" which the primitive man (or woman) uttered as a child was about to pick up a bee implied the bee and said, in effect, "Take care! *That object* is dangerous, will cause—pain." We may say, therefore, that although a single word or phrase can tell us something (and thus function as language) with respect to *something physically present,* it cannot tell us anything about what Hull has aptly referred to as "the not here and the not now" (28, p. 524). To say anything about a physically or temporally remote thing, event, or person we must represent it symbolically—there is, apparently, no other option; and this involves a *second* sign, or term, to which conventionally—and probably for very sound psychological reasons (see Sections II and III)—we give first place in the two-sign sequence. Thus, as Stewart so insightfully observes, language comes into its own only with the development of the "noun-idea," i.e., when sentences have "sign" subjects as opposed to "thing" subjects. And as we shall see in a later section, this is a feat which no infrahuman organism seems to have achieved, and one which it takes even the human organism a little while to get the hang of.[8]

In summary of our inquiry thus far, we may say, then, that the transition from the use of single signs to multisigns or language proper is, in some ways, insignificant but in other ways truly momentous: It enables us to go from the concrete to the abstract, from the here-and-now to the "not here, not now." Our next major task is to clarify and expand this assumption and to indicate in more detail just how the grammatical unit or complex which we call the sentence works.[9]

[8] This analysis helps explain why it is that some writers (e.g., Hunter, 30; Hollingworth, 27) make language equivalent to *any* use of signs. As we have seen, if the "subject" of a sentence is physically present, a single sign can serve to "complete" the sentence. Thus, without careful scrutiny, single and combined signs may appear to serve essentially the same function. But the one-sign sentence has, as we have seen, the serious disadvantage of restricting communication to the here-and-now. For communication concerning the there-and-then, we must go to the two-sign sentence as a minimum. Cf. McCarthy (40, pp. 544–551) for a discussion of the "one-word sentence" in small children. A few pages later, McCarthy, citing various investigators, makes the point that it is only when the child's speech becomes more complex that it also becomes "abstract." She says: "Lewis [36] brings out that at first the language of the child is concerned exclusively with the immediate situation in which it is spoken and that gradually it begins to deal with things that are absent. This matter of reference to things absent has also been emphasized by both K. and C. Bühler [9, 10]. Lewis relates the child's use of past and future tenses to the functions of his earlier undifferentiated speech. It is because of the child's use of speech as an instrument to draw others into his social circle that he begins to speak of absent things and events" (40, p. 557). "Ames [2] reports that children first speak of the present, then of the future, and that references to the past occur later" (p. 558). Of course, by prearrangement, a single stimulus (like the lantern in the Old North Church of Boston) can be made to convey—or, perhaps more accurately, *confirm*—a highly complex message. But such "code" stimuli, by their very nature, cannot be combined, in nonprearranged ways, with other signs; they thus fall outside the realm of language as we shall here consider it.

[9] There remains, however, an incidental problem which ought to be discussed in the present context in at least a preliminary way. It pertains to the problem of the "parts of speech." In the foregoing, we have made the subject-predicate relationship, or "predication," the essence of language. And we have seen that this approach demands a minimum of two signs. The question is: Do these two signs, the so-called subject and predicate, differ in any intrinsic or scientifically meaningful way? Subjects are commonly thought of as "nouns" and predicates as "verbs" And it is certainly true that, in English—with the exception of a few words like "lightening," which can be either a noun or a verb—we can quickly identify a word (if it is not some other "part of speech") as one or the other. However, no less a student of linguistics than Whorf (86, p. 6), on the basis of comparative data, questions the validity of the noun-verb distinction; and several examples which will be given later in this paper, as well as the "Pammy-kitty" sentence already cited, suggest that there is not a one-to-one relationship between subjects and "nouns" and

II. WHAT DO SENTENCES DO?

In the preceding discussion we have asked and in at least a preliminary way answered, the question: What is the *nature* of a sentence? We have tried, that is to say, to determine what sentences, scientifically considered, *are*. In the present section an attempt will be made to discover what sentences *do*, i.e., how they *work*, psychologically speaking.

There is a very widespread assumption, which we will later have occasion to question, that in the process of spoken or written communication we, somehow, transfer meanings from mind to mind. To communicate, it is suggested, is to make something common, shared; and this something is meaning, understanding, thought, knowledge, ideas, information. One writer puts the matter this way. He says that language, broadly speaking, is characterized by a "transfer of meaning." It is the device "by which men have conveyed significant messages to one another since the dawn of history." "Meaning may be transferred by devices that have nothing to do either with the spoken language or with its written counterpart, and this basic proposition few will be so hardy as to deny" (58, p. 10).

Another writer says:

> When the day arrived on which one person could make such movements, gestures, or grimaces as would lead another person to avoid or to accept an object, that is to say, when a meaning could be transferred to one mind from another, language was created (24, pp. 207–208).

And yet another says:

> The philosophy of language, we may then say, to begin with, is concerned with *the evaluation of language as a bearer of meanings, as a medium of communication and as a sign or symbol of reality* (81, p. 37).

And to this the same writer later adds:

> On the question as to what linguistic fact is not, linguists are in general agreed. They are also agreed upon what it is that constitutes positively linguistic fact. The *sine qua non* of language is precisely the *meaning* of which the sounds, the motor processes and tactual sensations, are the bearers (p. 66).

The first of the writers just cited is a linguist, the second a psychologist, and the third a philosopher. We thus see how widely accepted is the notion that the basic function of language is to *transfer* or *bear* meanings from person to person, from mind to mind.[10]

It is not hard to understand how this conception of language has arisen; and, as we shall see later, there is a certain limited sense in which it is undoubtedly correct. But in another, perhaps more basic sense, this notion seems to be wide of the mark and to have been a barrier to the development of a psychology of language with real "power."[11]

predicates and "verbs" (see McCarthy, 40, p. 530). If the general psychological approach to the phenomenon of language suggested in this paper proves valid, it may provide a new frame of reference in which to re-examine the whole question of speech parts. (Cf. Fries, 22, ch. V–VIII; see also Section X of the present paper.)

[10] The three quotations cited are from books published, respectively, in 1949, 1924, and 1939. In Greenough and Kittredge's book, *Words and Their Ways in English Speech*, published in 1906, we find the same general thesis formulated thus: "Language is the expression of thought by means of words" (23, p. 2). And even in Fries's otherwise very adventurous book, *The Structure of English: An Introduction to the Construction of English Sentences*, published in 1952, we find the author saying that he does not "deny that the chief business of language is to communicate meanings of various kinds" (22, p. 8).

[11] Contemporary "information theory," in the manner of Shannon and Weaver (67), seems to be based, at least obliquely, upon the person-to-person-transfer-of-meaning notion. Perhaps this is why some of the original promise of the theory has not been fulfilled. Wilson (87) has recently summed up the situation by saying: "As the previous discussion has indicated, information theory's chief contribution to the study of language is a set of descriptive measures and a unit, the *bit*, which are much more broadly applicable than

Let us explore now, instead, the proposition that in communication we are not transferring meanings from person to person so much as we are transferring meanings *from sign to sign* within a given person, within a single mind. Said a little differently, the suggestion is that in order for us to communicate effectively with another person, he must already *have* the meanings with which we shall be dealing and that in the communicative act we are, for the most part, merely changing the signs to which particular meanings are attached, merely shifting or transferring meanings from one sign to another. One person, by the use of appropriate words or other signs, can *arouse,* or "call up," particular meanings in the mind of another person; but he does not transfer or implant them there. The communicative act, in its most salient and significant aspect, lies rather in the combination, juxtaposition, or association of the meanings thus aroused *in novel, "informative" ways.*

A rudimentary sentence will illustrate this notion. Let us assume that John is telling Charles that: *Tom is a thief.*[12] It is clear, is it not, that for the intended effect to be produced by this sentence, Charles must already know Tom and must know about thieves and thievery. In other words, Charles must already have meanings attached to the words, *Tom* and *thief.* What, then, is the function of the sentence, "Tom is a thief"? Most simply and most basically, it appears to be this. "Thief" is a sort of "unconditioned stimulus"—we shall later want to qualify this term, but for the moment it will suffice—a sort of "unconditioned stimulus" which can be depended upon to call forth an internal reaction which can be translated into, or defined by, the phrase, "a person who cannot be trusted," one who "takes things, steals." When, therefore, we put the word, or sign, "Tom" in front of the sign "thief," as shown in Fig. 1, we create a situation

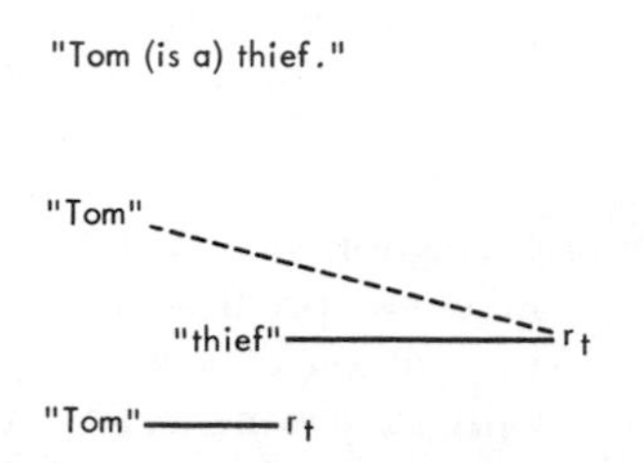

Fig. 1: Diagram illustrating how the sentence, "Tom is a thief," can be recast in the vernacular of conditioning theory.

from which we, as psychologists, can predict a fairly definite result.[13] On the basis of the familiar principle of conditioning, we would expect that some of the reaction evoked by the second sign, "thief," would

to language processes themselves. It serves chiefly, therefore, as a quantitative tool for describing language processes. It is not a theory of information in the usual sense, nor does it provide us with a theoretical model which can provide hypotheses about or explain the phenomena of human language communication" (p. 24).

12 Lest there be any ambiguity about the identity of the particular Tom here referred to, let it be said that he is Tom, the Piper's Son, of fable and song.

13 In the above analysis the copula and indefinite article are omitted on the assumption that, in a present indicative sentence, they are really unessential. Support for this position is provided by the following excerpts from a recent letter from Professor Gregory Razran. He says: "The Russian equivalent of the English, 'I am a thief,' is 'Ya Vor.' The copula is always omitted in modern Russian in the present indicative, but is not omitted in Czech and Polish. The copula was not omitted in Old Slavic. Yet it would be incorrect to attribute such omissions to modern developments, since such copulas are also absent in ancient Hebrew. Moreover, . . . such copulas may also be omitted in Latin and Sanskrit (one may say in Latin, 'Ego fur sum,' as well as, for emphasis, 'Ego fur.'). As far as I know, Slavic languages have neither a definite nor an indefinite article, while Hebrew has a definite but not an indefinite article. The indefinite article in Teutonic and Romance languages seems to have developed from 'one,' as notice their identity in German, French, Spanish, and Italian, and, I believe, also in Old English. However, there is the differentiation of 'a' and 'an' from 'one' in modern English."

get shifted to the first sign, "Tom," so that Charles, the hearer of the sentence, would thereafter respond to the word, "Tom," *somewhat as he had previously responded to the word, "thief."* Thus, in the Stewart example of the prehistoric woman saying "Coo-ouch," some of the quality of "ouchness" presumably gets attached to the word, "Coo," and in the case of the little girl saying "Pammy-kitty," the hearer likewise comes to make some part of the "kitty" reaction to "Pammy."

Although the notion that the essence of language involves predication, i.e., the temporal conjunction of something called a *subject* with something called a *predicate,* is ancient and widespread,[14] there has recently been considerable tendency to replace it with the view that single words and sentence do not differ basically. In their book, *The Meaning of Meaning* (54), published in 1923, Ogden and Richards, while accepting the hypothesis that words *arouse* but do not "convey" or "bear" meanings,[15] nevertheless take the position that a sentence is just a complex sign. They say:

> Thus the reference of "larks sing," since it has two components, will differ from that of "larks" just as do "soaring larks" or "lark pie," being also dual references. This difference is therefore unessential, though most complex references do in fact use the propositional form (p. 259).

In his *Signs, Language, and Behavior* (47), Morris says:

> The fifth criterion requires that language signs be combinable with each other in certain ways and not in others, and that these combinations form a complex sign.... Hull has suggested that such combinations are to be explained in terms of simultaneous and temporal stimulus patterning, since "...In reading, each letter is a complex visual pattern, each word is a complex pattern of these letter patterns, and each sentence is a temporally patterned sequence of printed word patterns" (p. 58).

And more recent and more explicit still is the following formulation by Dollard and Miller (17):

> As has already been pointed out, a person can learn to respond to specific combinations of stimuli or relationships among them and to make different responses to the same cues in different contexts. This is called patterning. A person's responses to the words that he hears someone else speak obviously involve patterning. Thus a parent will respond quite differently to the following two reports containing the same words in different sequences: "Jim hit Mary" and "Mary hit Jim." This is an exceedingly simple example. Although scarcely a beginning has been made toward the study of language from the point of view of learning theory, it is obvious that man's great innate capacity and rigorous social training have produced marvelously intricate and subtle patterning in his responses to spoken language (p. 100).[16]

14 "Thus Sapir is voicing a view very prevalent among philologists, when he writes, 'There must be something to talk about and something must be said about this subject of discourse once it is selected.... The subject of discourse is a noun....No language wholly fails to distinguish noun and verb" (54, p. 260). "For centuries it has been insisted that, for completeness, every sentence must have a word representing a person, place, or thing, and also a word 'asserting' or 'saying something' about that person, place or thing. There must be a 'subject' and a 'predicate' " (22, p. 14).

15 Malinowski wrote an essay entitled "The Problem of Meaning in Primitive Languages" which Ogden and Richards published as part of their book and which Osgood (55), in discussing the notion that words "carry" meanings from person to person, cites as follows: "Malinowski aptly dubbed this naive conception the 'bucket theory' of meaning—words like little buckets are assumed to pick up their loads of meaning in one mind, carry them across intervening space, and dump them in another mind. 'This attitude in which the word is regarded as a real entity, containing its meaning as a Soul-box contains the spiritual part of a person or thing, is shown to be derived from the primitive, magical uses of language and to reach right into the most important and influential systems of metaphysics. Meaning, the real "essence" of a word, achieves thus Real Existence in Plato's realm of Ideas...' " (41, p. 680).

16 The notion that language is just a form

The notion under examination in the present paper is different. It is that the sentence is, preeminently, a *conditioning device,* and that its chief effect is to produce new associations, new learning, just as any other paired presentation of stimuli may do. This position is congruent with the traditional notion that predication is the essence of language and may indicate, perhaps more precisely than purely linguistic research has done, the basic nature of this phenomenon. [17]

This notion is presented here in a frankly exploratory manner, as a hypothesis which others are invited to consider and test against the prevailing concepts and facts of their particular specialties. The remainder of this paper will be concerned with an examination and elaboration, both theoretical and empirical, of this hypothesis from a psychological point of view, with special reference to learning theory.[17a]

---

of interpersonal stimulation and response is undoubtedly a product of the era of behaviorism; and it achieved one of its earliest, clearest, and most influential formulations in the writings of Bloomfield (6). In a chapter on "The Use of Language," Bloomfield says: "Language enables one person to make a reaction (R) when another has the stimulus (S). In the ideal case, within a group of people who speak to each other, each person has at his disposal the strength and skill of every person in the group. ...The division of labor, and, with it, the whole working of human society, is due to language" (p. 24). Thus a person with a need or wish may respond either by trying to deal with the need himself ("practical action"), or he may try to stimulate someone else to do it for him ("linguistic substitute reaction"). The latter situation Bloomfield represents as follows: S (first person's problem or need)→r (speech reactions) →s (speech as heard by another person) →R (the instrumental response or work done for the first person by the other person). Here the recipient of the speech stimulus is what Courtney (13), in discussing the child-mother relationship, has called a "mediator" (not to be confused with "mediating response," Sections III and IV). While widely accepted (see Fries, 22, ch. III), this conception of language seems greatly oversimplified: it ignores the phenomenon of predication (making a sentence basically the same as a stimulus) and bypasses the whole problem of meaning, knowledge, information, i.e., mediate as opposed to immediate behavior, predispositions to action as opposed to direct response.

[17] In thus emphasizing predication, the writer does not exclude the possibility that word combinations not involving predication (in the English sense of that term) may function as sentence equivalents. Consider this observation by Wyatt: "At the age of sixteen and a half months [Nana] said *bighorsy,* pronouncing it like one word. She then began to take the word 'big' out of the compound and to combine it with other words: *big hat, big bag,* and so on" (88, p. 29). One cannot escape the feeling that *big hat* and even *bighorsy* may be roughly equivalent, functionally, to "The hat is big," "The horse is big." Wyatt further observes that "Sapir has proved that in all known languages juxtaposition is the simplest, most economical method of binding words together and of bringing them into some relation to each other, without attempting an inherent modification of these words. 'The very process of juxtaposing concept to concept, symbol to symbol, forces some kind of relational *feeling,* if nothing else, upon us. Words and elements, once they are listed in a certain order, tend not only to establish some kind of relation among themselves but are attracted to each other in greater or in less degree' " (88, p. 31). Perhaps it should be said that in the present paper we are examining the psychological implications of *one form* of word "juxtaposition," namely the propositional or subject-predicate form. Whether other forms of juxtaposition involve different psychological principles is at present an open question (see Section X).

[17a] Since this paper went to press, the writer has discovered a very closely related, but unelaborated, conception of the communicative process. In a recent paper by Carpenter (10a), entitled "A theoretical orientation for instructional film research," we find brief reference to the "releasor-organizer hypothesis," which is "that the signals, signs, and symbols of sound motion pictures function principally as releasors and organizers of meanings and responses in human subjects" (p. 42). The releasing function of signs is said to be "both dependent (or interdependent) on the stimulation and on the activated brain processes ('engrams') of the experiencing subjects. Thus, it may be reasoned that the functions of signals, signs, and symbols is to *release responses in subjects.* ...Signs and symbols *do not transmit* meanings; they release meaning when and only when the subjects respond. The characteristics of these responses relate closely to personal life history differences" (pp. 42–43). The author continues: "The

III. THE CONCEPT OF MEDIATION

Perhaps the most generally accepted criterion as to whether a sentence has or has not done its work is this: If, as a result of hearing or reading a sentence, an individual's behavior, on some future occasion, with respect to some person, thing, or event not present when the sentence occurred, is different from what it would otherwise have been, then that sentence may be said to have been "understood" and to have functioned effectively. If, for example, John tells Charles, in the absence of Tom, that Tom is a thief and if, when Charles subsequently encounters Tom, he reacts toward him with distrust and apprehension, communication has clearly taken place.

But this criterion of linguistic action poses an interesting problem for the behavioral scientist. As psychologists, we are all quite familiar with situations in which an organism learns, or is taught, to react to a sign more or less as if it were the thing or event signified. In the vernacular of the conditioning laboratory, the organism, after conjoint exposure to the conditioned stimulus and the unconditioned stimulus, reacts to the CS somewhat as if it were the UnCS. Or, as we may equivalently say, the meaning of the UnCS "moves forward" and becomes anticipatory.

This phenomenon seems to occur in language, true enough, as when the predicate meaning of a sentence "moves forward" and gets connected to the sentence subject. But in language something else, of a different nature, is also involved. This is the remarkable, and indeed somewhat paradoxical, phenomenon of an organism, after exposure to a sentence, reacting to some thing, event, or person as if it were the corresponding sign or symbol which was the subject of the sentence. In other words, the new meaning attached, by means of predication, to the sign constituting the subject of a sentence has a tendency to shift or transfer "back," so to say, to the thing, event, or person which the subject of the sentence represents, or "stands for." This is a phenomenon to which comparatively little attention has been given but which can be satisfactorily accounted for on the basis of well-known principles.

Let us note, first of all, that what we are positing here is something quite different from so-called backward conditioning. This is fortunate, for backward conditioning is a questionable, controversial type of event, whereas the phenomenon with which we are here concerned seems, as phenomenon, not to be in the least questionable. We are, however, in need of a precise explanation. Let us begin by making a more detailed diagrammatic analysis of the sentence, "Tom is a thief." In Fig. 1 we have already seen how the familiar principle of conditioning can explain the fact that some part of the reaction evoked by the word "thief" gets connected to the word "Tom," but we have not as yet said anything about the sequence of events whereby "Tom" and "thief" originally acquired their meanings. As Fig. 2 shows, the word "Tom" acquired its meaning by being associated with, and occurring in the context of, Tom as a real person. Tom

---

releasor concept of signs and symbols must be supplemented by the related *organizer* concept. Previously learned 'engrams' may be modified by new stimulation, and even new *related* elements may be 'imprinted.' New relationships may be shown, and old responses modified by film mediated stimulation. The results are conceived to consist principally of the *reorganization* of previously learned neural-organic patterns which intervene between film stimulation and the subsequent actions or reactions of the individual" (p. 43). The notion that signs release, or arouse, meanings *in* rather than "bear" them *to* another individual, as stated by Carpenter, is identical with the position taken in the present analysis. The "organizer" conception, while stated in somewhat different terms, is also believed to be essentially congruent, at a relatively abstract level, with the theory of sentence function as here developed. Whether the notion of "reorganization" can, without injustice, be analyzed in terms of conditioning and mediation (see next section) or whether more holistic principles are required (see Section X) is uncertain.

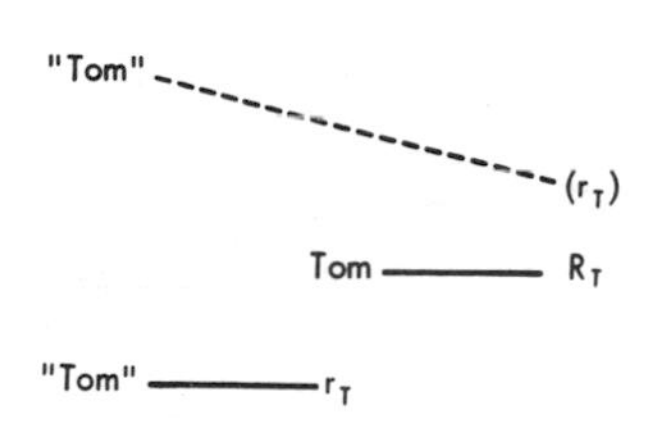

Fig. 2: Schematic indication of the way in which the word, "Tom," through the process of conditioning, comes to denote, mean, or imply a certain person, Tom.

himself has elicited in John and Charles and others who have had first-hand contact with him a reaction which we can label, R_T, of which r_T, is a component. And as a result of the paired presentation or concurrence of "Tom" the word and Tom the person, the component, or "detachable," reaction, r_T, gets shifted from the latter to the former.[18]

And similarly for the word, "thief." As indicated in Fig. 3, this word is likewise

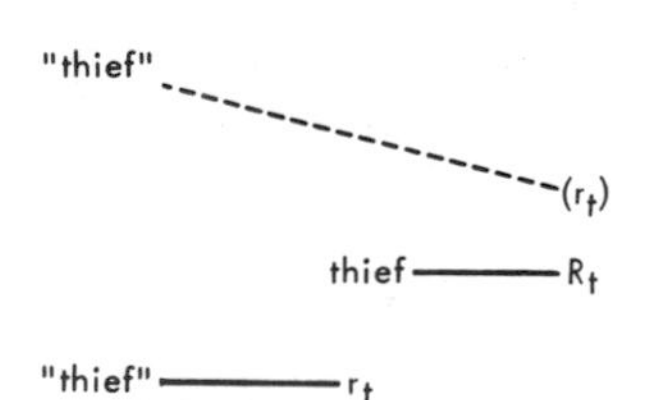

Fig. 3: Replication of Fig. 2 showing how the word, "thief," acquires its distinctive meaning.

presumed to have acquired its distinctive meaning by having been used in the presence of, or to have been, as we say, "associated with," actual thieves. Therefore, when we make the sentence, "Tom (is a) thief," it is in no way surprising or incomprehensible that the r_t reaction gets shifted, as originally shown in Fig. 1, from the word, "thief," to the word, "Tom." This is seemingly a straightforward instance of second-order conditioning: By first-order conditioning some part of the total reaction elicited by real thieves gets shifted to the word, "thief," and by second-order conditioning of the type provided by the sentence, this same reaction, with some attenuation or weakening, gets further transferred or shifted to the word "Tom."

Our analysis thus far is, however, either incomplete or faulty, for if language worked precisely as suggested, it would pretty obviously not do what we want it to do and what, a good deal of the time, it manifestly does. If language worked as thus far indicated, the sentence, "Tom is a thief," would serve merely to *change the meaning of "Tom,"* so that when Charles, as the recipient of this sentence, subsequently heard this word, it would remind him less or perhaps not at all of Tom but rather of thieves. It would, in other words, become just a synonym for the word, "thief," and we would have simply an instance of *reconditioning,* a procedure whereby the noise, "Tom," would lose its old meaning and acquire a new, different one. This type of conditioning, or reconditioning, would, pretty obviously, not serve our communicative needs at all and would soon lead to utter chaos.[19] Clearly,

[18] It may be helpful to think of the R_T reaction, mentioned above, and the so-called "detachable component," r_T, as analogous, respectively, to the total reaction produced by an electric shock in a rat and the reaction produced by a stimulus which is merely a sign of shock. Shock produces sensations of pain and also fear; but it is only the latter which gets conditioned, or "detached," and occurs anticipatorily, to a mere signal or sign of shock.

[19] Some premonition of what this might be like, on a general scale, is suggested by the experience which many persons report of sometimes repeating two or three times (either to themselves or aloud) some word whose meaning is not very well established and finding that the word "loses its meaning," more or less completely. The word becomes, so to say, "blank," a mere empty sound. The problem which language theory manifestly poses for us in this connection is that of determining how it is that a word, as the subject of a sentence, can take on some of the denotation, or at least connotation, of the predicate of the sentence and still retain its original meaning. (But see Section IV.)

something essential is missing here; but, fortunately, the difficulty is easily remedied.

In drawing a diagram of conventional type to represent conditioned-response learning, we are likely to represent the UnCS and the response it elicits and then, in adding the CS, to say something like this: "This is an originally neutral stimulus. Oh, to be sure, it probably evokes some reaction, but for our purposes it is not important." Thus we end with a drawing something like that shown in Fig. 4.

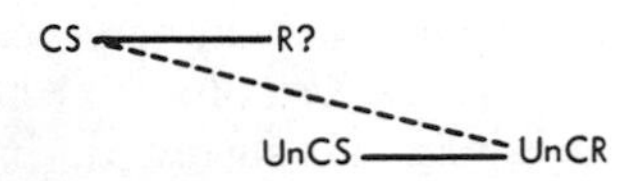

Fig. 4: Conventional conditioning diagram, indicating the common neglect of the reaction originally produced by the conditioned stimulus.

But if we are to succeed in making conditioning theory account for the basic facts of language, we must manifestly proceed a little differently at this point. As already indicated, particularly in Fig. 2, the subject, or "CS," in our specimen sentence has, by assumption, a very definite reaction potential or meaning, which we have designated as r_T. Let us, therefore, redraw Fig. 1 and, instead of ignoring r_T, let us give it rightful recognition in the diagram. Figure 5 is the result.

Assuming now, as we reasonably may, that the "Tom"—r_T connection is a relatively stable one, we will expect the conditioning outcome shown at the bottom of Fig. 5. Instead of r_t, the thief-meaning, getting connected *directly* to the word, "Tom," and more or less replacing the r_T reaction, we may infer that r_t will get conditioned rather to the reaction—or, more accurately, to the stimuli or sensations produced by the reaction—which the word "Tom" produces, namely r_T. This internal reaction, or meaning, thus becomes what Lumsdaine (38), Foley and Cofer (20), Osgood (56), and others have recently called a *mediating response,* and

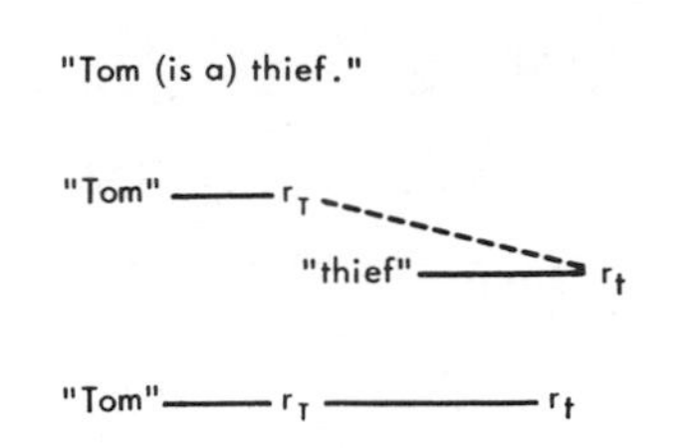

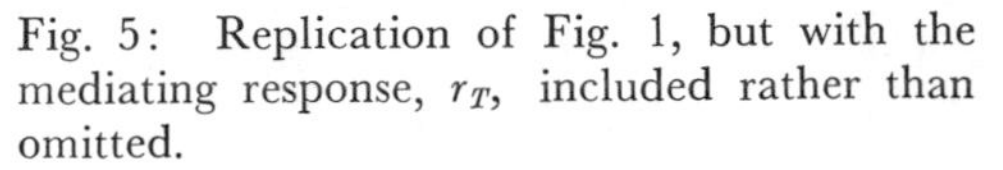

Fig. 5: Replication of Fig. 1, but with the mediating response, r_T, included rather than omitted.

its importance is indicated by the felicity with which it delivers us from the difficulties into which a too simple, too abbreviated analysis of language in terms of conditioning plunges us.

If our specimen sentence worked as Fig. 1 implies, i.e., if the thief-meaning, r_T, then there would be only one apparent way in which the thief-meaning could get transferred to Tom as a person, namely for Tom-the-person, when encountered, to elicit in Charles *a labeling reaction,* which would involve his saying, at least subvocally, the word, "Tom," which in turn would then elicit the thief-meaning, r_t (see Fig. 6). While this hypothesis is logically ten-

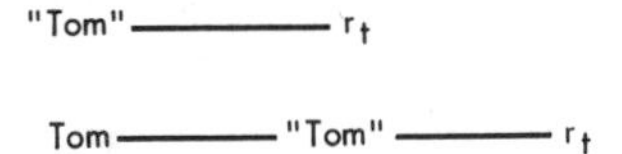

Fig. 6: A possible, but not entirely satisfactory, conception of how a meaning acquired by a word ("Tom") can get transferred to the thing or person (Tom) represented by the word.

able and may in some cases correspond to reality, it has, as will be shown in the next section, rather limited applicability. Moreover, a different way of looking at the same problem is immediately available which seems much less restrictive.[20]

[20] Dollard and Miller (17, see especially ch. VI) have developed in considerable detail the notion of response generalization and transfer (as well as discrimination) through "labeling." However, they agree that such generaliza-

We have already posited (see Fig. 2) that the meaning reaction, r_T, which gets connected to the word, "Tom," is a component of R_T, which is the reaction or reaction complex evoked by Tom himself; and we have also posited (see Fig. 5) that the sentence, "Tom (is a) thief," will cause the thief-meaning, r_t, to get connected to r_T. Therefore, when Tom-the-person is subsequently encountered by Charles, he will elicit in him the R_T reaction, of which r_T is a part, which will in turn elicit the thief-meaning, r_t. Q.E.D. This mechanism for the occurrence of semantic generalization or meaning transfer from sign to thing is shown schematically in Fig. 7 and is characterized by

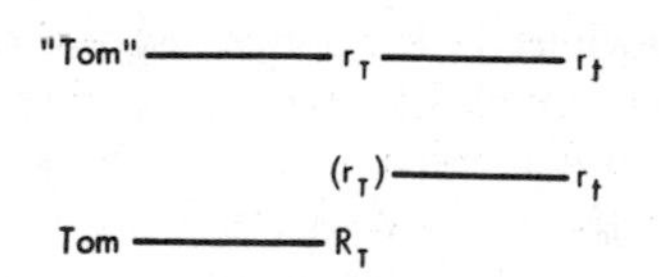

Fig. 7: Indication of how r_T, in the example given, functions as a "mediating response." Cf. Fig. 5 and Fig. 2.

relative simplicity yet also possesses, seemingly, considerable generality and explanatory vigor. In the next section we shall look for other than logical evidence to support such a notion.[21]

tion may occur on the basis of "labeling or other cue-producing responses" (p. 105). Thus they do not exclude as a possibility the mechanism which is to be emphasized in the following discussion.

21 Interestingly enough, this hypothesis has at least verbal similarity to the "identical-elements" theory of "transfer of training" as advanced by Thorndike (77) and others. A mediating reaction, such as r_T in the above example, is an "identical element" in the reaction produced by both the word, "Tom," and the person, Tom. Therefore, if, by means of the Tom-is-a-thief sentence, we get a new meaning-reaction, r_t conditioned to r_T as elicited by the word, "Tom," we will expect it to generalize to r_T as elicited (in the context of the total R_T) by the person, Tom.

IV. VERBAL AND NONVERBAL EXAMPLES OF RESPONSE MEDIATION

As Osgood has remarked, the concept of mediation is not devised "solely to meet the needs of semantics; it is the application of a general theory of learning to this particular class of phenomena" (55, p. 696). Two of the experiments which are most relevant in this connection have been concisely summarized by Osgood as follows:

> Fortunately [he says] there are cases in which the mediation process is specifiable with some accuracy. Shipley [68] paired a faint light with a sudden tap on the cheek, which elicited winking; then the tap was paired with shock to the finger, eliciting withdrawal; on subsequent tests, the light flash (never paired with shock) evoked finger withdrawal. Since this did not occur unless the light and tap had initially been paired, any sensitization explanation is ruled out...It becomes evident that the only difference between this experiment and those on sensory conditioning lies in the specificity of the mediating reaction—here, the winking movement (55, pp. 461–462).

This experiment is schematized in Fig. 8 and provides a nice example of how it is that a response, in this case the eye blink, can, so to say, "carry" another response, finger flexion, from one stimulus (tap on cheek) to another (light) without the latter having ever been used either as a conditioned or an unconditioned stimulus for the elicitation of the flexion response. This, in essence, is the mechanism posited in the preceding section to explain how it is that, in a sentence, a meaning conditioned to another meaning, i.e., to the mediating response, can generalize or transfer back to the object represented by the sign that elicits the mediator or, more precisely, to the *response* elicited by that object.[22]

22 It should be noted, however, that the Shipley experiment does not provide an exact parallel of what happens in language. There the new meaning is acquired by the mediating reaction as produced by a word (conditioned

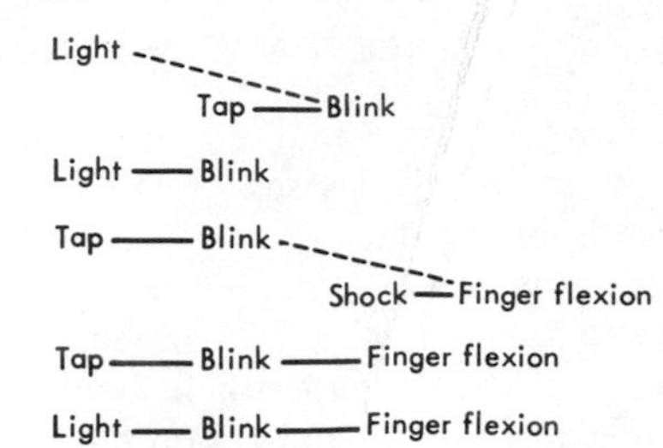

Fig. 8: An example of response mediation discovered, rather accidentally, by Shipley (68). The assumption is that in the second stage of conditioning (lines four and five), the finger flexion gets attached, not directly to the tap stimulus, but to the response (blink) produced by the tap (see next to last line). (More precisely said, the finger flexion gets conditioned to the proprioceptive and other stimuli produced by the blink—or to the central equivalents of the blink. See text.) And since light, as a result of the first stage of conditioning, is also capable of producing the blink reaction, it follows that the light, through the intermediation of the blink, will produce finger flexion (see last line), even though the light itself has never been paired with tap, the unconditioned stimulus for finger flexion.

However, since the Shipley experiment was done without reference to the mediation hypothesis and with no particular attention being paid to the blink reaction in the second stage of conditioning, it is important to ask, as does Osgood:

But did this mediating winking reaction actually occur? [By way of reply, this writer goes on to say:] Lumsdaine [38; cf. pp. 230 ff. in Hilgard and Marquis, 26] has repeated Shipley's experiment with detailed graphic recording. His records indicate that, in most cases the light *did* elicit a winking movement which was closely followed by finger withdrawal. There were some cases, however, in which the withdrawal reaction antedated the eyelid movement, and this suggests that the winking movement may be only an overt index of the actual mediation process. This is what would be expected according to the mediation hypothesis: in the original training, the light (sign) was presumably becoming associated with the fractional anticipatory portions of the reaction to tap-on-cheek (stimulus-object), and it is this mediation process which is more or less faithfully indexed by the overt winking (55, p. 462).

Elsewhere in his book, Osgood (see also Cofer and collaborators [12]) cites a number of other instances of response mediation, reported mainly by Russian investigators, in which responses conditioned to words readily generalized to the objects they represent and in which responses conditioned to objects generalized to cognate words. Against the background of these findings, it is not surprising to discover, as Razran (61) has, that a salivary response conditioned to one word, e.g., "style," will readily generalize to another word, viz., "fashion," which is physically very different but which elicits much the same meaning or mediating reaction. In fact, this investigator found that considerably more generalization of conditioning (59% as opposed to 37%) occurred on the basis of similarity of meaning (synonyms) than on the basis of similarity of sight or sound (homophones, e.g., in the present instance, to a word like "stile"). That some transfer occurred on both bases suggests that, in the Razran experiment, the salivary response was conditioned not only to the meaning reaction produced by the word "style" but also, to some extent, directly to the word itself. To the extent that this occurred we may say that saliva-

stimulus) and generalizes to the thing (unconditioned stimulus); whereas, in the Shipley experiment, the new response (figure flexion) is conditioned to the mediating reaction (blink) as produced by the tap (unconditioned stimulus) and generalizes to the light (conditioned stimulus). Experiments cited later in this section show that "semantic generalization" of conditioned reactions occurs from thing to cognate word as well as from word to thing. But ordinarily, in language, we are more concerned with the latter occurrence than with the former. For the Shipley paradigm to have been strictly parallel to this type of generalization, finger flexion should have been conditioned to blink as elicited by light (a conditioned stimulus) so that the flexion could have generalized to the tap (or unconditioned stimulus).

tion replaced the meaning response previously attached to this word, i.e., its meaning was *changed;* but this was not the only, or even the main effect, since transfer on the basis of the mediation mechanism was greater.

No, the notion of response mediation—Hull (28) spoke of "pure stimulus acts," Hilgard and Marquis (26), of "intermediate responses"—is by no means invented "to meet the needs of semantics." It is a common and well-established phenomenon whose centrality in language can hardly be doubted and which apparently can alone explain, broadly yet simply, how it is that what we learn through sentences can generalize, or transfer, despite absence of any sensory similarity or continuum, both to other words of similar meaning and also to the realities thereby denoted.[23]

In concluding this section, it may be useful to emphasize a distinction which is implicit in the foregoing but which may have become somewhat obscured in the course of the discussion. We have seen, first of all, that the basic function of the subject-predicate unit which we call a sentence is to condition the predicate meaning so that it will later be connected to and elicited by the subject meaning. This we have referred to, somewhat elliptically, as a transfer of meaning from sign to sign, as opposed to mind to mind. And in the consideration of semantic generalization we have likewise spoken of transfer. What needs to be particularly noted here is that the kind of "transfer" involved in the two cases is different: in the first instance it involves transfer in the sense of *conditioning* and, in the second instance, in the sense of *generalization.* The two phenomena can be easily confused if something of an effort is not made to keep them distinct.[24]

V. FURTHER ANALYSIS OF THE SENTENCE AS A CONDITIONING DEVICE

The essence of the argument advanced up to this point is that the subject-predicate complex which we call a sentence is, in effect, simply an arrangement for conditioning the meaning reaction produced by the predicate to the interoceptive stimulation aroused by the meaning reaction elicited by the subject. The following laboratory paradigms will help put this way of thinking about language function into a broader, more systematic perspective.

Let us assume that our objective is to train a rat not to eat a certain preferred food. Cheese is such a food for rats, which they will readily take even though fully satiated on such a well-balanced ration as Purina Laboratory Chow. The most direct

23 A psychologist can hardly think about response mediation as it functions in language without also being reminded of at least some of the phenomena implied by the word "insight." In the published report of one of the first experiments in which response mediation was unequivocally demonstrated, the author, N. E. Miller (45), while making no reference to language, speaks repeatedly of "insight" and "foresight" (see also May, 43; Nygaard, 53; and Mowrer, 52, ch. 5 and 11). For a consideration of insight with special reference to "transfer of training," see Thompson (75, p. 165); see also the discussion of language and the syllogism, Section VIII. For experiments and theoretical discussions bearing on the problem of "latent learning" but which are also relevant to the concept of mediation, see Tolman and Gleitman (78) and Strain (72).

24 It may be useful at this point to refer back to Fig. 8. There is a temptation to think of the experiment there represented as merely an instance of higher order conditioning. But it is something different. It involves "transfer" in the sense of generalization: because both tap-on-cheek and, after conditioning, light can be used to elicit the blink reaction, if finger flexion gets conditioned to the blink reaction as elicited by the tap, finger flexion will generalize to blink as elicited by light as well. Incidentally, we may add that if one takes the position that a sentence is a conditioning device, it is understandable why the reactions of a human subject, in a conditioning experiment, can often be dramatically altered by "instructions." They constitute a form of anterior conditioning, so that the subject is no longer "naive."

way, and the one to be first considered here, of teaching chow-satiated rats not to eat cheese is to punish them while in the process of eating or starting to eat the forbidden food. It goes without saying that by using a harmless source of pain like electric shock it is possible in this way to make cheese itself, as well as the actions involved in taking and eating it, so fear-producing that rats will turn away from it instead of moving toward and taking it. This procedure for accomplishing a purely heuristic objective is represented diagrammatically in Fig. 9 and is, of

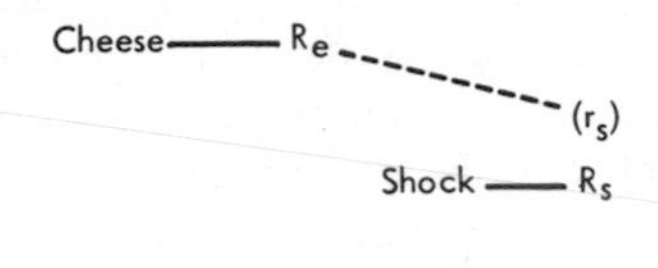

Fig. 9: A "thing-thing" conditioning sequence, or "sentence." R_e is the eating reaction elicited by the cheese (and hunger), and R_s is the total reaction elicited by the shock, of which r_s is the "detachable component," *fear*. Since r_s gets conditioned to R_e (or, more exactly, to its proprioceptive "backlash"), R_e tends to get inhibited as shown in the lower line of the diagram. (There is also some fear conditioned to the cheese itself, but for simplicity of analysis, this connection is not represented and, for present purposes, is not relevant. For support, derived from experimentation with human subjects, for this kind of analysis, see Razran [61]).

course, analogous to the practice, not uncommonly employed in child training, of catching the child, as we say, "in the act" and administering some sort of primary punishment forthwith.

While the most direct and in some ways most efficient way of inhibiting a particular form of behavior, the procedure just described—which we shall refer to as a "thing-thing sentence"—is only one of four ways in which the same objective can, at least in principle, be achieved.

The second of these involves what we may call a "thing-sign sentence." Let us suppose that we take naive rats and first pair a tone with electric shock a few times (Fig. 10). Now let us present cheese and

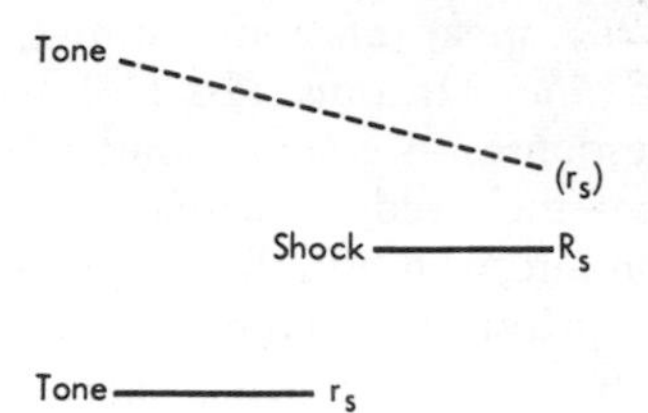

Fig. 10: Conventional procedure for conditioning a fear reaction, r_s to tone.

as the rat starts to take it, we sound the tone (Fig. 11). This involves the use of what may be called *secondary,* or fear,

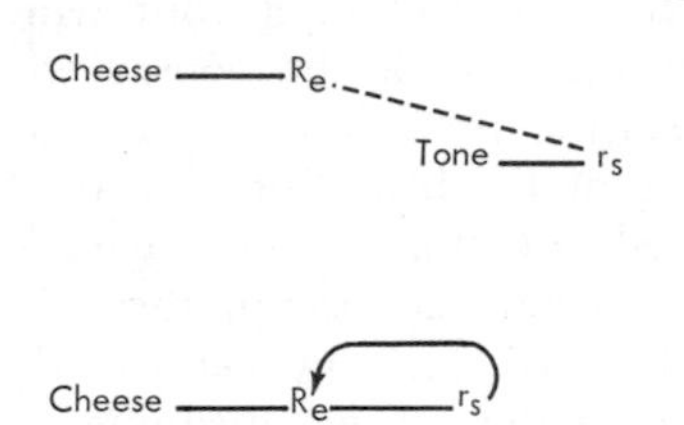

Fig. 11: Illustration of how cheese eating can be inhibited by paired presentation of cheese and a fear-eliciting tone.

punishment and will serve only a little less effectively than does primary punishment to inhibit the act with which it is associated. A recent study by Bixenstine (4) shows that this means of controlling behavior can be used quite effectively with rats; and it is clearly parallel to the parental practice of warning, or "speaking to," a child when engaged, or about to engage, in some disapproved action. This procedure, as I have suggested, may be conveniently dubbed a thing-sign sentence.

Next there is a procedure which we may, in the same vein, call a "sign-thing" sentence. Suppose we have paired a blinking light a good many times with the presentation of cheese so that it elicits a confident "expectation" of cheese and appropriate anticipatory movements (Fig. 12). If the rat is placed on a grill-like floor and if cheese is presented vertically on the end of a stylus a little to one side of the rat and the blinking light is presented a few seconds in advance of the cheese, the rat will soon start making horizontal pendular, or "groping," movements in anticipation of the presentation of the food. (Albino and therefore partially blind rats have been used in this study and are probably better, for this particular experiment, than rats with pigmented eyes.)

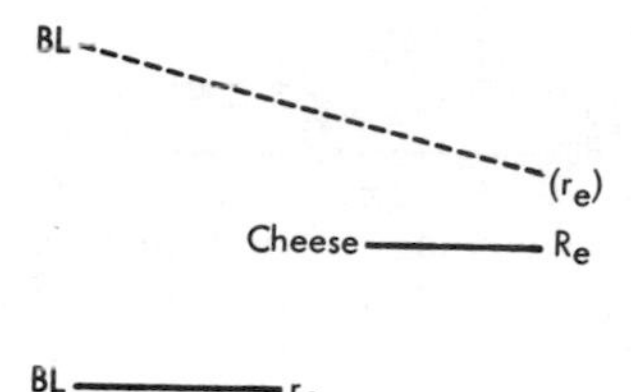

Fig. 12: Procedure for getting a part (r_e) of the total eating reaction (R_e) elicited by cheese conditioned to a blinking light (BL).

A sharp discrimination between the experimental situation with and without the blinking light is necessary and is achieved by leaving the animals in the situation for relatively long periods of time between presentations of the blinking light and cheese. In other words, the sign value of the experimental situation as such is thus pretty thoroughly extinguished. For reasons to be mentioned shortly, such a clear-cut discrimination is necessary in this type of investigation.

If we now present the blinking light, which elicits the "searching" or "groping" head movements, and follow it with shock, we will expect these movements to be punished and to be inhibited, as suggested in Fig. 13.[25] And since the same movements are part of the total response called forth by cheese itself, we will expect this training to generalize to cheese, as shown in Fig. 14. It will be seen that we are here employing exactly the same assumptions about the role of mediating reactions advanced in earlier parts of this paper and that the situation is parallel to one in which a parent reinstates verbally some form of misbehavior and then administers primary punishment.[26]

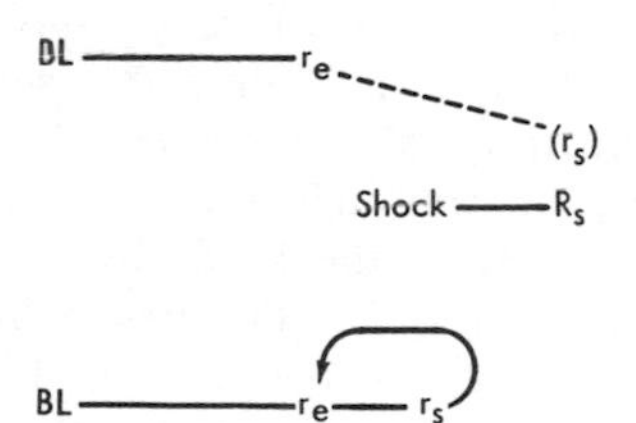

Fig. 13: Procedure for getting fear attached to the anticipatory, food-seeking response (r_e), which is produced by the blinking light (see Fig. 12).

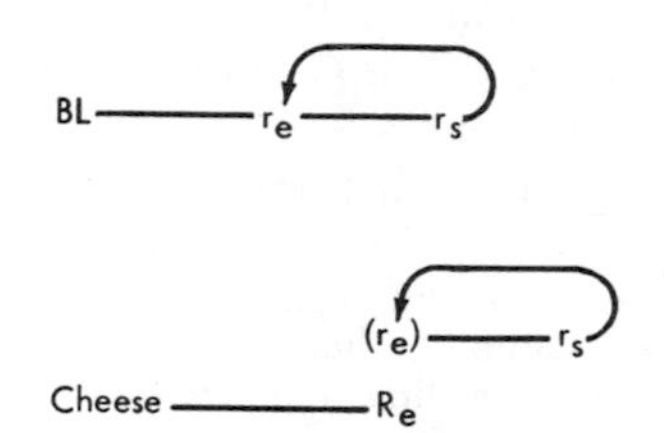

Fig. 14: Indication of how it is that inhibitory tendencies acquired at the symbolic level (see top line) generalize, through the mediating response r_e, to the "reality" level (bottom line).

[25] The reason, alluded to above, why the head movements need to be conditioned quite specifically to the situation-plus-blinking-light is that if they occur also with any frequency to the situation-alone, then any attempt to determine, in a control group, the effect of administering a shock not combined with the BL would be invalidated; an animal might be in the act of making the head movements, "spontaneously," just as the shock came on, which would produce an effect not greatly different from that obtained where the BL and shock are paired.

[26] Passing reference should be made here to the nature of meaning, or mediating, re-

Finally, we come to a procedure which parallels what is presumably involved in language proper, a "sign-sign" sentence. Let us assume that our subjects have had the kinds of training shown in Fig. 10 and 12 and then the kind shown in the upper part of Fig. 15. The first behavioral result we would expect from this type of sign-sign conditioning is that the anticipatory, exploratory responses formerly elicited by the blinking light (r_e) will be inhibited (lower line, Fig. 15), because of the fear that has gotten attached to them. And as a further consequence, we would expect this inhibitory effect to generalize to the behavior produced by the thing represented by the blinking light, namely cheese. This would involve the now familiar mechanism of response mediation, as already shown in Fig. 14. Exploratory experiments give empirical support for the foregoing inferences.[27]

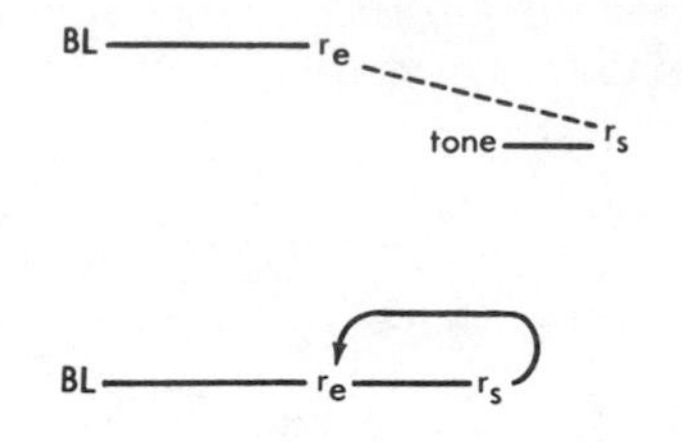

Fig. 15: Diagram showing how fear (r_s) is connected, by a "sign-sign" sentence, to the anticipatory food reaction, r_e, and tends to inhibit it.

Here we seem to fulfill the criterion of true language: By means of a two-sign complex, or sentence, namely BL-tone, we cause a living organism to be so modified, in the absence of something (cheese), that when it later encounters that thing it behaves differently from the way it would have behaved without the intervening training.[28] The parallel to our earlier

sponses as conceived of in this paper. In the foregoing example, there is presumably no harm in so regarding the groping head and neck movements. However, there is probably more to the meaning that the BL has acquired than just this: it has very likely also acquired the capacity to produce certain autonomic responses, such as salivation, and perhaps purely subjective or "central" effects for which there are no peripheral counterparts. That the latter may be the case is at least suggested by Lumsdaine's finding, discussed by Osgood in the excerpts quoted in Section IV, to the effect that mediation can take place without the occurrence of the overt response (eye blink) which, as Osgood says, is the "index" of the subjective, central counterpart. (Parenthetically, we may note that Osgood and Suci [56] have shown that the largest part of the variance in the meaning of words, as determined by the semantic-differential method, represents an "evaluative" factor, that of "good" and "bad," thus suggesting that much of the meaning which signs acquire involves arousal of either the parasympathetic or the sympathetic divisions of the autonomic nervous system.)

27 However, the results thus far obtained have been somewhat ambiguous because of lack of objective quantification of some of the variables involved. The writer plans shortly to repeat the experiment, with an improved methodology.

28 The demonstrations reported in the foregoing pages suggest a number of other problems to be investigated. For example, let us consider that of "word order." It has been repeatedly shown that if we want a response to take on either the secondary reinforcing or the secondary motivating properties provided by a so-called unconditioned stimulus (i.e., by a primary reward or a punishment), it is necessary to have the response precede, rather than follow, this stimulus. Similarly we find that in most languages of the world, subject precedes predicate, as the analysis of language function here presented would demand. This is generally true of English and other Indo-European languages and is, apparently, absolutely required in Chinese. On the other hand, there are languages, such as Latin and Hebrew, in which word order seems relatively unimportant. At first glance, it might appear that these exceptions invalidate our whole analysis. But there is a redeeming feature of Latin and Hebrew: these languages are highly "inflected," i.e., the principal words have special prefixes and suffixes to indicate "distinctions of case, gender, number, tense, person, mood, voice, etc." (90, p. 430). More specifically, and more importantly for our purposes, the status of subject or predicate is indicated by the device of inflection rather than by position. If, therefore, a person gets a word with a "tag" on it indicating that it is going to be the predicate of a subject not yet given, what he seems to do is to "store" this word (or group of words) until

analysis of the English sentence, "Tom is a thief," or "Tom, thief," will be evident. In both cases we see once again, and perhaps more clearly than before, that what we call a sentence is basically a device for producing associative shifting, or conditioning, but that in order for the sentence completely to fulfill its intended function there must also be the phenomenon of response mediation (Fig. 14), whereby the new meaning which thus gets connected to the sentence subject can generalize, or transfer, to the thing thus symbolized.

VI. DO ANIMALS HAVE LANGUAGE?

This question has been often asked and variously answered. If we agree to accept what, in the preceding section, has been called a "thing-thing sentence" as language, then animals may clearly be said to use and understand language. If, for example, an old dog does not want a younger one to eat food from his bowl, all he has to do to communicate this point of view is to bite the younger dog as he eats from or moves toward the bowl.

And it is also clear that some animals "have language" in the sense of their being able to use thing-sign sentences. If, for example, the old dog once or twice growls at the pup before biting him, the growl alone can be subsequently used, now by second-order conditioning, to attach fear to particular objects or actions. Indeed, such thing-sign sentences seem to be very common in the animal world. Anyone who has observed a mother hen with baby chicks will recall two striking instances. When the hen has discovered food, she makes quick clucking sounds which seem to say, "...is good,...is here,...is good." Here the "subject" of the "sentence" is the food itself, and the predicate is provided by the rapid clucking. Similarly, when any large bird is sighted in the sky, the hen utters a cry which seems to mean, "...is dangerous,...will hurt you." But once again the subject has to be physically present. The hen apparently has no sign for food or for hawks and is, therefore, unable to "tell" her chicks anything about them when they are not present. This means that the hen cannot make either sign-thing or sign-sign sentences. She cannot, in other words, speak "abstractly."[29]

But perhaps the illustrations cited do not do full justice to language in animals. Perhaps other species are more accomplished in this regard. Since language and social development are often linked together, perhaps the so-called "social insects" have transcended the limitations

he gets the subject and then mentally "tacks it on" (but see Section X). Another interesting though rather incidental consideration is this: suppose that, as in the paradigms described above, blinking light is associated with the presentation of cheese and then a punishment (either primary or secondary) is associated with the cheese and the act of eating it. Question: Will the fear thus attached to the cheese and the act of eating generalize, through response mediation, "back" to the blinking light? This matter could be put to experimental test, but commonplace observation and studies cited in Section IV suggest that the answer is "yes." When a person has had a painful, unpleasant experience, he may be heard to say, "Oh, don't remind me of that. I don't even want to *talk* about it." This sort of comment certainly suggests that there is "semantic generalization," not only from sign to thing, but also from thing to sign.

[29] We may, in fact, give the hen too much credit when we assume that she employs thing-sign sentences. All depends upon whether we can properly regard the clucking and the alarm cry as "signs." If these sounds have, for baby chicks, instinctive "meanings"—and there is some indication that they do—then we cannot call them signs if by the term "sign" we mean a stimulus the reaction to which has been acquired through conditioning. In the event that baby chicks do react to these noises instinctively, then the "sentences" cited are reduced, in effect, to the thing-thing variety. Yet there is something obviously vicarious, or "meaningful," about the use of these noises. Perhaps, for want of a better solution to the problem at the moment, we can say that the noises are "signs" or have "significance" through "racial" rather than individual learning.

which we have just noted. Fortunately, Karl von Frisch has meticulously studied and beautifully described for us what he calls the "language" of bees. In reporting on an experiment in which sugar water is placed a few meters from a bee hive with special provision for observing activity in the hive, von Frisch says that it takes some little while before the first bee locates the sweetened water. Then bees, all from the same hive, shortly start arriving in large number. "Evidently," says von Frisch, "this bee must have announced its discovery at home" (83, p. 53). How, precisely, is this done? Von Frisch continues:

After she has returned to the hive, our marked bee is first seen to *deliver most of the sugar-water to other bees. Then* she begins to perform what I have called a round dance (p. 55, italics added).

During the dance, the bees near the dancer become greatly excited; they troop behind her as she circles, keeping their antennae close to her body. Suddenly one of them turns away and leaves the hive. Others do likewise, and soon some of these bees appear at the feeding place. After they have returned home they also dance, and the more bees there are dancing in the hive, the more appear at the feeding place. It is clear that the dance inside the hive reports the existence of food (p. 56).

Later investigation showed that the round dance is used by bees to indicate the presence of food within a radius of 50 to 100 meters from the hive, without reference to direction. It is, in short, an invitation or command to go out and "cruise" around the hive. Food sources beyond 100 meters, on the other hand, are reported by means of what von Frisch calls "wagging dances," which indicate, apparently with considerable precision, both distance and direction. Here we shall not be concerned with the intricacies of the latter, but rather with the fact that in the case of both the round dance and the wagging dance, the returning bee brings some of the newly discovered food and *distributes it to other bees*. This behavior is of special importance for purposes of language analysis, for it suggests that, for all its ability to execute sentence predicates, sometimes of remarkable complexity, the bee has no signs for sentence subjects and has to use a bit of the thing itself for this purpose. Therefore, unless I misunderstand the import of all of von Frisch's work, one may conclude that even the industrious and ingenious bee has not, in any basic sense, transcended other animals with respect to language function: it, too, is limited to "sentences" of the thing-sign variety.[30]

But what of the "talking birds"? To indicate how remarkable their vocal performances can be, let me play for you a recorded excerpt from the vocalizations of a Shell Parakeet, or "Budgie," called "Blueboy."[31] (*Recording.*) In this record-

[30] It has not been possible for the writer to survey the literature on "language" in the other social insects. Schneirla (66) summarizes the known facts for ants as follows: "For ants, no adequate evidence supports the notion that the arousal of secondary ants by the finder involves a 'code' effect in the sense that she 'deliberately' offers a descriptive or indicative (i.e., symbolic) representation of what she has encountered and where it may be found" (p. 261). Schneirla does, however, cite a finding, reported by Eidmann, that "In...tests with *Myrmica laevinodis* housed in artificial nests, when a returned finder ant entered the nest compartment with food and made excited antennal contacts with workers there, the secondary ants upon emerging were able to follow the route of the finder more or less successfully and presently reach the food source" (p. 260). Here we find communicative behavior very similar in general pattern to that reported for bees by von Frisch. But further observations by Eidmann indicate that the source of food is found by the other ants by backtracking (through olfactory cues) on the trail left by the finder, rather than on the basis of specific directions. Different species of ants seem to handle problems of communication in different ways; but in no case does there seem to be any evidence that they have mastered the "noun idea," and such "predicates" as they employ seem more primitive, less refined than those which von Frisch has reported for bees.

[31] This recording is reproduced with the kind permission of Mr. and Mrs. G. William Smith, Hickman Mills, Missouri, owners and trainers of "Blueboy."

ing you have heard not only many different words and phrases and short sentences, but also the complete first stanza of "Mary Had a Little Lamb." Here, in terms of physical sounds, we have three relatively long sentences, which are unmistakably of the sign-sign type. But it seems most unlikely that, for example, the sentence, "Its fleece was white as snow," means to the parakeet anything at all like what it means to us. In other words, although parakeets and many other types of birds are capable of learning to "parrot" long verbal sequences, there is no indication that they are thus doing anything more than amusing themselves or trying to entertain and thus keep close to them some beloved human being.[32]

In summary, then, we may say that the "talking birds" can reproduce but cannot *use,* in the proper sense of that term, true sentences; and we have also seen that rats can "understand" a simple but authentic sentence.[33] But we have no indication that these creatures will ever compose a genuine two-sign sentence. As will be seen in the next section, it is a simple matter for a rat to learn to produce, by pressing a Skinner bar, a blinking light once this stimulus has come to signify food; and rats can also squeal to pain, thus warning other rats of danger.[34] Therefore, it is conceivable that a rat, if properly motivated, could, in the presence of another rat or a human being, make the light blink by pressing the bar and then squeal. This stimulus sequence would clearly say, "Cheese (is) dangerous." But in a study reported jointly with Palma and Sanger (52), it has been shown that the rat cannot squeal "voluntarily" (i.e., in response to a sign or signal of pain), and even if this were possible, it is still unlikely that these organisms would ever be motivated to reproduce the blinking light and the squeal in sequence, purely for communicative purposes.[35]

That man, or protoman, was able to develop true language must have been contingent upon a combination of unique and unusually fortunate circumstances. His vocalizations had to have been released from reflexive control—something that has not yet happened to our nearest kin among the apes—and to have attained a degree of flexibility that is matched probably only in certain of the birds. He had also, as Stewart has indicated, to get the "noun idea"; and finally, he had to have achieved enough social organization to make "helping others," through speech, a rewarding activity.[36] Susanne Langer has, I think, caught the spirit of what the advent of human speech has meant, in these words:

[32] Evidence presented elsewhere (49, ch. 24) indicates that the talking birds can, however, as the fanciers say, "form associations," i.e., certain words, phrases, or sentences will be regularly cued off by particular situations or objects. They can also "ask for" desired food or favors. However, the generalization apparently stands that they cannot use sentences in their fully developed, abstract, creative sense.

[33] Many dog owners believe these animals can understand sentences. It would be interesting to make a study of this belief against the background of the analysis of language presented in this paper.

[34] This is not to say that the squealing constitutes an "intentional" form of communication. It probably occurs reflexly, and other rats respond to it reflexly ("instinctively") or on the basis of conditioning resulting from their having heard themselves squeal while in pain. For further consideration of the latter mechanism, see Section VII.

[35] Professor Charles Elliott, of the department of speech at Northwestern University, has suggested the interesting possibility of making a series of Skinner bars available to a rat, depression of each of which would produce, through the medium of tape recordings, some word. For example, one bar would permit the rat to "say" *water,* another *food,* etc. This ingenious arrangement would circumvent the limitations imposed by lack of versatility and voluntary control of vocalization in the rat (dog, chimpanzee, and other species) and might make possible a number of very useful investigations.

[36] The notion that language is used to "help others" calls attention to two quite different conceptions of its function. One common view of language is that it is used primarily as a means of helping oneself; this view is discussed in the latter part of Section II (see especially

Not higher sensitivity, not longer memory or even quicker association sets man so far above other animals that he can regard them as denizens of a lower world: no, it is the power of using symbols—the power of *speech* —that makes him lord of the earth (34, p. 20).

By means of this phenomenon, man's whole behavior-pattern has undergone an immense change from the simple biological scheme, and his mentality has expanded to such a degree that it is no longer comparable to the minds of animals (p. 24).

Language is, without a doubt, the most momentous and at the same time, the most mysterious product of the human mind. Between the clearest animal call of love or warning or anger, and a man's least trivial *word,* there lies a whole day of Creation—or in modern phrase, a whole chapter of evolution (p. 83).

If these sentences perhaps overdramatize the advent and importance of language as it has been developed in and by human beings, they nevertheless vividly remind us of its centrality in human mentality and experience in a way which more prosaic statements may fail to do.

And Wyatt (88) has summarized her observations on language and personality development in the young child as follows:

A learning process of constantly increasing complexity, taking from five to six years of the child's early life, is necessary for [the acquisition of language] and this learning process itself is part and parcel of the individual's ego development (p. 32).

The continuous process of identifying and structuring reality, through the use of words, emerges as one of the foremost factors in ego development (p. 37).

But this symbolic transformation of bits of reality into language, serves the child in more than one area. Not only can immediate events become identified and thus meaningful and coherent for the child; the same fascinating occurrence can be repeated indefinitely, even after the actual stimulation has passed. With the help of words, sensations and their feeling tone can be *remembered* and *recalled* at will (p. 39).

Thus, language at this early stage has already a variety of functions: to structure reality and thus to protect the child against overwhelming sensory-motor stimulation; to recall experiences; to express wishes and desires; to make people do things for the child; to communicate with other people. In addition language become the outstanding vehicle for the "working through" of difficult, painful or anxiety-producing situations, a mechanism well known to child therapists (p. 40).

Nana, at the age of a year and a half, was able to provide for herself such a symbolic working-through arrangement. With the help of the most powerful symbolic magic: *words,* she was able to deal with frustration and anxiety: *Mommy backsoon, Mommy backsoon* (p. 40; see also Section IX).

VII. THE ORIGIN AND ACQUISITION OF WORDS

In the present section we shall be concerned with the question of how words originated and how, once in use by others, they are learned by children.[37] More spe-

footnote 16). Here language is seen as serving mainly to coerce or cajole someone else into doing something useful for the speaker (or writer). By contrast, there is the view that language is the medium by which "gifts" are bestowed upon others; we are said to "give them information," which *they* will find useful. In fact, perhaps the best general definition of "education" (see Section VIII) is that it is a means whereby one person (usually through language) helps another solve some problem more quickly than he himself could do on an unaided (trial-and-error) basis. Ontogenetically, the "selfish" use of language comes first and the "altruistic" use later; perhaps this was also true historically. But in any event we can say that both uses of language presuppose considerable social cooperation.

[37] How it is that small children get around to combining words into true sentences, instead of using them singly or merely in phrases, is only a little less of a riddle than is the question of how protoman first developed this form of behavior. Of course, it is conceivable that, in the case of children, sentence making is in some way "learned from" their elders. But it is also possible that this trick is, by each child, independently "discovered." The issue could be put to test by finding a few parents who

cifically and narrowly, we shall be concerned here with the question of how words are learned, not in the sense of their comprehensibility or meaning, but in the sense of production and reproduction. Although it has taken a bit of doing to get the theory of word meaning straight, this aspect of the language problem now seems well on its way toward solution: words are, in the main, arbitrary signs which acquire their sign-ificance, or meaning, through conditioning. However, the problem of the acquisition and use of words as overt forms of behavior, to which we are here addressing ourselves, is more difficult and, as of the present, less well understood.

The question of where and how man got his words, especially those whose origins lie far back in racial experience, has occasioned more interest and speculation, probably, than any other single aspect of the whole language problem. In fact, so much attention was being paid to this matter in Europe during the eighteenth and nineteenth centuries that the French Academy of Science passed a rule formally excluding any more communications on this topic from its transactions. Here no attempt will be made to review or evaluate the many ingenious suggestions which have emerged in this connection; they are, in fact, so generally known to this audience that enumeration or description is unnecessary. Instead, I shall speak only about two or three notions that seem to lend themselves especially well to laboratory investigation.

One aspect of the problem of the origin of words which is of special interest here has to do with the tendency, under favorable conditions, for instrumental acts, or "habits," to become foreshortened into mere behavior tokens, or "gestures." I shall always remember the following experience with the little girl mentioned earlier in this paper. Having learned to sit alone on the floor when about six months of age, she would occasionally cry to be picked up; and often, in anticipation of such action on the part of her parents, she would hold up her arms flexed in preparation for being lifted. One day she was seen looking hopefully in the direction of her father, arms flexed, but not crying. She was picked up, and her mother's cooperation was elicited in seeing what would happen if we let this gesture replace crying as a signal for being taken up. Being more effortful, apparently, the crying quickly gave way to the arm flexing; and, then, this response itself underwent further involution. Soon the little girl was lifting only her right arm, and finally she would just hold up the right hand or forefinger.

The tendency for actions which an experimenter has arbitrarily defined as "correct" in a problem-solving situation to deteriorate has been commented on by various writers. As early as 1896, Thorndike (76), having taught cats and dogs to lick or scratch themselves as a means of getting out of a problem box, remarked: "There is in all these cases a noticeable tendency, of the cause of which I am ignorant, to diminish the act until it becomes a mere vestige of a lick or scratch" (p. 28). And some forty years later, Lorge (37), having performed a similar type of experiment, wrote:

> In addition to reducing the time required to make these responses followed by rewards irrelevant to them, the animals *short-circuited* these responses. With successive trials, the responses became more perfunctory and stereotyped. The "face washing" changed from a vigorous wash to a rapid movement of both forelegs to the face; the "scratch" changed

---

would be willing to speak only single words in their infant's presence and see if children so reared would, unaided, "invent" the sentence. However, in view of the anxiety which most parents feel about their children's "learning to speak"—not to mention the responsibility and concern of the experimenter—such an investigation would not be feasible unless it was reasonably certain that children thus deprived could later be taught to make sentences in the event they did not spontaneously originate them.

to a rapid flexion of the hind-leg to the flank, only remotely reminiscent of the first response to irritation (p. 110).

This "strain toward inertia," a phrase used by Sumner and Keller (73), or tendency toward economy of effort can be observed to special advantage under the circumstances shown in the following motion picture. (*Movie.*) Here we see how readily an initially complete instrumental response, involving a rat's going about two feet from a food trough to push a Skinner bar and then returning thereto for the food thus produced, will, if given an opportunity, deteriorate, first in the sense of the bar pressing turning into mere bar touching; then the rat will begin running well down toward the bar but turning around and going back to the trough without touching the bar; then these "loops" are seen to get shorter and shorter; until, finally, the rat, after finishing a pellet of food, will merely move his head around and "glance" in the direction of the bar. Thus, he may be said merely to give us the "nod" to indicate his wish for another pellet.[38]

It goes without saying that in order for gesturing to replace fully instrumental behavior, there must be, somewhere in the situation, a second organism which is able and willing to do some of the first organism's work for it, on the basis of a mere sign or "command."[39] In the present instance, this second organism was the experimenter, who took over the function of activating the food delivery mechanism which had previously been done by the rat's bar pressing. Thus, what was originally a fully instrumental action, involving only the rat and the physical world, was changed into a *social situation* and what was originally an instrumental act became a *social act* involving, minimally, two organisms.[40]

The protracted helplessness of the human infant and the necessity for the mother to display, in response to signs, what Courtney (13) has called mediating behavior creates a strong natural predisposition for human beings to be inveterate sign users. Because of this long period of dependence and indulgence, perhaps it is not too much to suppose that we spend a good deal of our lives trying, by means of signs, to get others to do things for us or, at least, cooperate with us. Infantile helplessness very likely gave the human race one of its most powerful pushes to-

38 The writer is indebted to Mr. William G. Perry, Jr., for the following comments concerning the foregoing paragraphs. He says: "I keep wondering if the word 'deteriorate' does not obscure positive aspects of this process. I even think of the word 'refined.' The animal could be said to *abstract* from all the business of face-washing or scratching the element now instrumental for other purposes. The whole process could be thought of as one of 'discovery' depending on what behavior units one happened to be thinking in. We say of a rat in a Skinner box that he engages in many exploratory acts and finally learns to isolate bar pressing, let us say, to get food. But if we had considered each of the exploratory trips down and around the box as an act, we could then say that the act 'deteriorates' to 'mere' bar pressing. Does the rat conceive of behavior or 'acts' in the same size units as we do? Is not the discovery and isolation (i.e., learning) of the instrumental response the obverse of 'the law of least effort'?" (personal correspondence).

39 This statement, unless slightly qualified, may be misleading. Obviously, a machine of the right kind could replace the second organism in a situation of the kind described. All that would be required of it, essentially, is that it have a "distance receptor," such as a microphone or photoelectric "eye," capable of "picking up" the gesture act and converting it into an "order" to apparatus capable of the required "work."

40 The writer also recalls the development of an interesting gesture on the part of a mynah bird. When offered food, this bird was sometimes not able to determine if she liked it or not merely from its appearance, so would have to take it into her mouth and taste it. If she did not like it, she would then shake her beak vigorously back and forth in order to eject the food. On numerous occasions it was observed that when this mynah was offered food previously found objectionable, she would shake her head *as if* it were in her mouth. Here we see perhaps an ancient historical root of the corresponding human gesture of negation. Cf. Darwin (14).

ward both language and sociality, generally speaking.

The Law of Least Action, as Wheeler (85) called it, which we have seen exemplified in the foregoing discussion, is a very pervasive behavior principle, whose special applications in certain areas of language have been documented in detail by Zipf (89). However, it has a major limitation with respect to our present concern. We find that the signs most commonly employed in human communication are not gestures, which are visually transmitted, but rather the particular noises we call words.[41] And since a great many instrumental actions are essentially silent to begin with, we cannot very plausibly look upon words as condensations, or foreshortened versions, of originally fully instrumental, nonsocial behaviors.[41a] Some words may very well have originated as copies of sounds associated with particular actions, as, for example, the word, "patter," to represent or suggest running. But even here the responses involved in saying "patter" have nothing in common with the responses involved in actually "pattering," so even in this case we must look for a different principle.

Fortunately, such a principle is not hard to find, or to illustrate in the laboratory. As is well known, any sound (or other stimulus) which is associated with primary satisfaction tends to acquire secondary reinforcing properties. Therefore, as I have tried to show more fully elsewhere (49, 50; see also Miller and Dollard, 46, pp. 81, 139, and 277), if a living organism can itself reproduce such a sound, or a reasonable approximation thereof, the particular responses involved will get secondarily, or "autistically," reinforced and will tend to become a part of the organism's response repertoire. For other organisms with similar background experiences, such sounds, when thus reproduced, will have much the same meaning as the sources by which they were originally produced and may thus serve for signaling or even symbolic purposes (see Section IX). As I have indicated in the studies cited, such a notion accounts relatively well for what we know about word learning by babies (and also by "talking birds") from adults who already have command of these sounds;

[41] Perhaps the most elaborate visual sign and gesture language known in historical times was the *Lingua franca* of the American Indians. In comparison with any known spoken language it was, however, apparently very awkward and inefficient.

[41a] At the risk of overcomplicating an argument which is already far from simple, the writer is tempted to inject the following thought at this point. Granted that words probably did not stem directly from the foreshortened instrumental acts which we call gestures, there is still a sense in which language is a *substitute* for grosser, more effortful action. In fact, one of the powerfully reinforcing things about language is that it so often, and so effectively, *saves us trouble,* the trouble of going somewhere else and doing something ourselves which another person, who is already *there,* can more economically *do for us.* (Being "somewhere else" may be interpreted either geographically or in terms of special skills which only a few acquire because of the "long road" of experience and learning that is involved in mastering them.) When we think of how much "lost motion" is thus avoided, i.e., how much more we can accomplish ("get out of life") if we are "in contact" with others at more or less remote points in space (or who have specialized skills) than we could if we had to "go and do" everything for ourselves, the implications of language become almost overwhelming; and we see, especially clearly, how intimate and indispensable a role it plays in creating and perpetuating what we call *society,* or "sociality," both transversely and longitudinally, through space and through time. These remarks will recall what has already been said in footnote 16 and, at the same time, indicate that there is at least a superficial inconsistency between the conception of language as a means of social coordination and control and the view, more especially stressed in this paper, that the main function of the sentence is to produce second-order conditioning in others, which will then be generalized to the referent, or significate, of the sentence subject. In the one case we are primarily interested in *"getting action"* and, in the other, in *giving information.* How these two aspects of language process, both of which seem real enough, are systematically related invites separate—and probably quite extended!—study.

and it also provides, as just suggested, a not improbable conception of how prehistoric man may, in turn, have acquired at least certain verbal forms from nature. Of the various classical theories of word origination, the one most closely related to this scheme is obviously the "onomatopoetic" or so-called "bow-wow" theory.[42]

This conception of word genesis can be illustrated in a crude but probably valid way as follows: Suppose that just before or as we give a laboratory rat a bit of food, we sound a tone of standard pitch and intensity. This tone, as we know from numerous studies, will take on secondary reinforcing properties. And if the rat could, with its own vocal cords, make a noise reasonably like the tone, we would predict, on the basis of principles already cited, that it would soon begin to do so. Unhappily, in view of the severe limitations on vocalization in the rat which have already been mentioned, we cannot expect this to happen. However, if we place the electronic oscillator used by the experimenter in producing the tone at the disposal of the rat, on the basis of movements which the rat can easily make, we should not be in the least surprised if the rat, under these circumstances, is disposed to "make" the sound. So let us, after the rat is well trained with respect to tone associated with food, make a Skinner bar available, depression of which will have the same action, with respect to producing the tone, as the telegraph key previously used by the experimenter. Figure 16 shows the behavior of a hungry rat toward such a bar during a 20-minute period, in the course of which bar pressing produced no food, but the "promise" of it in the form of the tone and the secondary reinforcement it had acquired from prior pairings with food.[43]

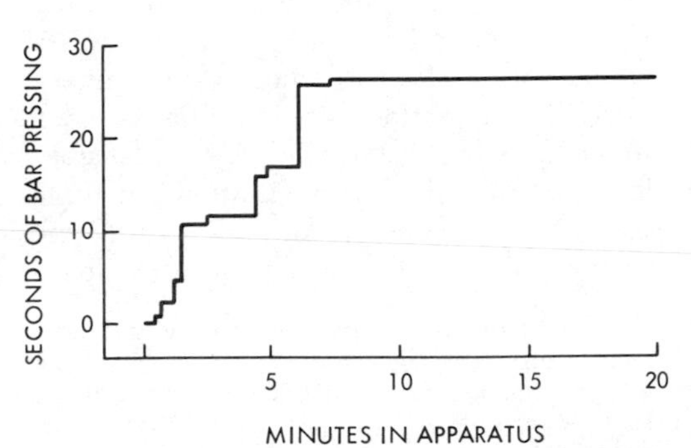

Fig. 16: Graphic record of bar pressing by rat, where this performance produced a tone which had been previously associated with food. The bar-pressing "habit" was thus learned solely on the basis of the secondary reinforcement provided by the tone. As the secondary reinforcement extinguished, the animal ceased to press the bar. In this situation the experimenter may be said first to have made the signal to the rat as a means of indicating that it was going to get food. The rat, when given an opportunity to push a bar which turned on the tone, made the signal "back" to the experimenter, but the experimenter did not respond (cf. Fig. 17).

42 A particularly rich source of sounds which might then be transformed into "words" are those which living organisms characteristically make during consummatory behavior of any kind. This possibility was called to the writer's attention under the following circumstances. A number of rats were being fed, seriatim (but at rather long intervals), in separate compartments so constructed that they could not see each other but could easily hear any noises which the other rats made. The particular manner of feeding involved inserting food up into each animal's compartment, "under its nose," so to say, on the end of a small metal rod, between the bars constituting the floor grill of the compartment. While eating, the rat would hold the rod in its front paws and inadvertently "rattle" it against the grill bars. Because this "rattling"—which itself sounds as if it might have had an onomatopoetic origin—accompanied eating, it became a "sign" to which the rats not having the rod responded with much interest and apparent anticipation. It rather clearly had come to "mean" *food*, and one could imagine that in a comparable situation involving prehistoric men such a sign might well have supplied the model for some vocal reproduction.

43 For experimental indication that a rat will push a bar thus "baited" more often than a bar which does not produce a secondarily

How energetically a rat, trained in the manner just described, will continue using the tone as a *signal to the experimenter,* if the experimenter will only cooperate, is suggested in Figure 17. Here will be seen what happens if, when the rat pushes the bar and produces the tone, another organism responds to it as a sign that the rat wants food—and obliges.[44] A stimulus which was originally made by the environment to the rat is thus "taken over" by the rat and "made back" to the environment; and if another organism will respond thereto, it becomes a "social act," or true sign.[45] Of course, on the basis of trial-and-error learning alone, without the presence of a signal of any sort, a rat would eventually learn to press the bar if it produced food. But the precipitous nature of the learning shown in Fig. 17 suggests, and experimentation reported elsewhere (49, ch. 11) confirms, that the intermediation of a stimulus with previously acquired secondary reinforcing properties produces a performance markedly superior to what can be expected on the basis of trial and error alone.

In summary, the foregoing analysis suggests that although there is a pervasive tendency for instrumental behavior to degenerate into gestures, such contractions do not seem to have provided a common basis for spoken words. A more likely hypothesis is that sounds naturally associated

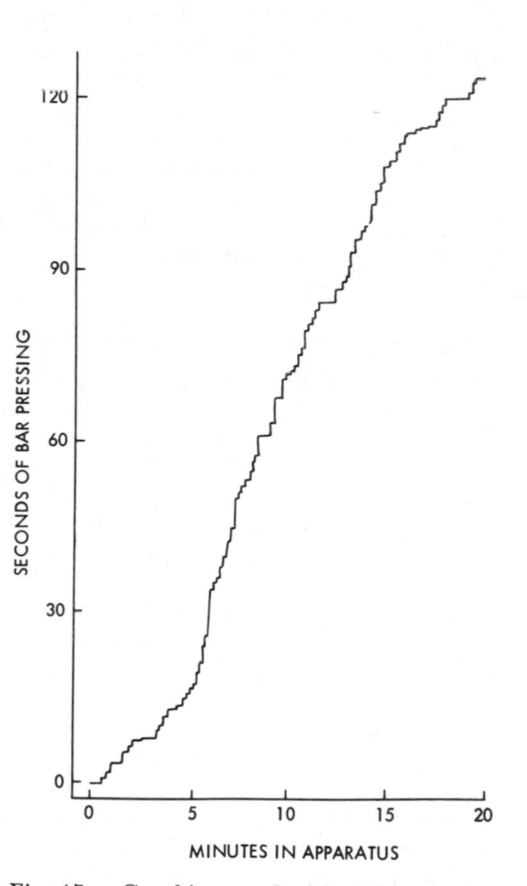

Fig. 17: Graphic record of bar pressing by a rat where this performance produced a tone previously associated with food, and caused the experimenter to provide food. After several trials, there was something like an "insight" (see upward inflection of curve at about 5 minutes). As the animal become satiated, toward the end of the recording, the rate of responding declined. In this record we see what happens if an organism learns the meaning of a signal, is then permitted to make that signal, and some other organism responds appropriately thereto. See text for discussion of possible bearing of this demonstration on the question of where human beings first got the noises they used as words and how infants learn to speak.

reinforcing stimulus, see Jenkins (31). This phenomenon of an organism being prompted to reproduce a stimulus with secondary reinforcement is pretty clearly related to, but probably not strictly identifiable with, food hoarding in nonhungry rats, as described by various writers (e.g., Marx, 42).

44 The reader may be struck by a crude analogy between the performances shown in Fig. 16 and 17 and the two stages of language development in the child as proposed by Piaget (59): the "ego-centric" stage, wherein the child "talks to himself," and the stage of social communication, wherein the child talks to someone else.

45 A somewhat parallel instance is reported by Hollingworth (27), as follows: Having trained a pet terrier to "sit up" on command, with food as a reward, Hollingworth observed that the dog was soon "sitting up" on its own initiative, now not as an act of obedience but as a way of "begging," i.e., signaling its desire for food.

with gratifying experiences were, by the mechanisms indicated, "copied" by proto-man and thus gave rise to at least the beginnings of language as we know it today.[46]

Perhaps it should be added that what is said here is not intended as in any sense providing a completely adequate theory of the origin of articulate speech. But it is a way of thinking about the problem of word origin which meshes comfortably with learning theory and has, apparently, also some plausibility with respect to what we know about language itself.

VIII. LANGUAGE, LOGIC, THOUGHT, KNOWLEDGE, AND CULTURE TRANSMISSION

First of all, I want to disavow, if I can, some of the pretentiousness seemingly implied by the title of this section. The various broad topics included here will not be discussed in any comprehensive or systematic way at all, but only as they immediately relate to the particular conception of language process which has been developed in this paper.

Logicians, and philosophers generally, have long been concerned with language. Here we shall not attempt to review their very interesting and substantial contributions to this field.[47] Instead, I wish only to call attention to a rather striking bearing which the present discussion has upon the nature and function of the syllogism, or at least one type of syllogism. Let us revert, again, to the by now well-worn specimen sentence, "Tom is a thief." If one thinks about this sentence in the context of some of the earlier sections of this paper, one sees that, functionally, it is the minor premise of an implicit syllogism of the following sort:

(Thieves cannot be trusted.)
Tom is a thief.
(Therefore, Tom cannot be trusted.)

Consideration of the sentence as a conditioning mechanism suggests this logical form; and when made explicit, this form throws new light upon sentence function as here conceived. What the foregoing syllogism does, pretty clearly, is to change the definition or class membership of Tom from that of supposedly honest men to that of dishonest ones. The definition or meaning of a thief is a person who cannot be trusted, and this definition is given in the implied major premise. The sentence, "Tom is a thief," which appears here as the minor premise, serves to transfer a known person, Tom, into the category of men who cannot be trusted. This is what happens likewise in the simpler, cruder conditioning that has been so extensively studied in the laboratory: here the conditioned stimulus (directly, without the benefit of mediation) similarly takes on some of the attributes of the unconditioned stimulus. Thus, if X is followed by Y and Y is "bad" (e.g., painful), then X also becomes "bad," whereas if Y is "good" (relieving, pleasurable), then X likewise becomes "good."

In our paradigm sentence, we see that the subject, "Tom," has a specific, idiosyncratic reference whereas the key word in the predicate is a concept, with a generic denotation. How generally this situation holds is something to be further explored; but it fits well with the assumption that the principal function of the sentence is, so to say, to *reclassify*, or "modify," the subject, i.e., to change our expectations with respect to it. This is apparently best done when we put the more specific sign first and the more gen-

46 The mechanism whereby "bad" sounds were copied and used as words is obviously different and, probably, more complex. This problem invites further inquiry. See Stewart's references (Section I) to the word "ouch"; also footnotes 34 and 40.

47 See, for example, Max Black's *Language and Philosophy, Studies in Method* (5) and Section I, "Language, Meaning and Truth," in *Readings in Philosophical Analysis* (19), edited by Herbert Feigl and Wilfrid Sellars.

eral sign second. Certainly, in our example, it would not mean much to reverse the subject-predicate order and say, "A thief is Tom," unless, of course, we meant, "A thief, is Tom," which is merely a poetic or whimsical form which, I suspect, we quickly translate back into the standard sequence, "Tom (is a) thief."

I am sure that what has been said in the preceding paragraphs could be considerably expanded or perhaps corrected by either a logician or a grammarian, and I advance these thoughts only as illustrating the way in which a learning theory analysis of language ramifies.

Likewise, what I would like to say here about the nature of *thought* will be avowedly incomplete and no more than suggestive. Let me begin with an example. A few weeks ago, I took home to my seven-year-old son a box of small blocks and other scrap lumber from our departmental machine shop. I knew the box, after the blocks were taken out, ought to be returned to the shop and so took it back to the psychology building; but, at the time, the shop was locked so I put the box in a storage room—and, then, forgot about it for several days. Later, at home, I remembered the box and thought, "Machine-shop door, box. Machine-shop door, box." In more elaborate terms I was, I suppose, saying to myself something like this: "The next time I pass the *machine-shop door* I must remember to get and return that *box* to the shop." Later, when walking down the hall on the way to my office, I passed the door, was reminded of the box, got it, and returned it to its accustomed place.

What I had done, evidently, was to condition myself in advance to the door, by using a symbol thereof, so that it would cue off the reaction of getting and returning the box. I had, in other words, in the absence of the door (and the box, too, for that matter)—i.e., in the realm of the "not here, not now"—conditioned myself so that the door, on the basis of generalization from symbol to thing, would bring to mind, or re-mind me, that I ought to do a particular thing. In effect, I had "talked to myself" and produced a result apparently quite comparable to that which we have here made the basic criterion of objective sentence formation and interpersonal communication.

I would not hold that this is the only or even the most typical pattern which thinking takes. Certainly planning and the consideration of alternatives would have to be carefully examined in this connection and may turn out to involve something rather different. More formal reasoning, e.g., that involved in mathematics, may also depart more or less critically from this pattern. However, enough has been said to suggest that in at least some types of thinking, there is a process of self-stimulation and response, involving the subject-predicate relationship, which is similar to that involved in interpersonal stimulation and behavior alteration of the kind achieved by objectively expressed sentences. In other words, in the light of the present analysis of sentence psychology, it now appears that we can "talk to ourselves" as well as to others and achieve thereby much the same outcome, namely, that of so affecting (conditioning) an organism (oneself) in the presence of a mere symbol for something that when that thing itself is later encountered, there will be a manifest change in behavior with respect to that thing.[48]

[48] What we know about the role of *repetition* in language corresponds moderately well with common facts from the conditioning laboratory. A signal and an electric shock usually have to be paired at least twice before an animal such as the rat seems to "get the connection"—it's as if the chances are too great that one conjoint occurrence may be mere coincidence, so that the reality of the relationship has to be established by at least a second conjunction of the two stimuli. Small children seem to learn very quickly that a sentence twice repeated—"Pammy-kitty, Pammy-kitty"—is more effective than a single repetition thereof. When we are trying to *remember* something, through a process such as described above, the association is also usually repeated

To say that one "knows" or "has knowledge" of something is, broadly speaking, certainly equivalent to saying that one has *learned something*.[49] Vinacke (81) puts the matter well when he refers to learning as the "internalization of experience." It is, in other words, a process whereby living organisms establish a correspondence between what is in the external world and what is inside their heads. By means of sensory processes, the immediate, contemporaneous environment is, momentarily, internalized; that is to say, stimuli are converted into transitory sensations. On the other hand, what gets internalized through learning is events *through time,* or sequential regularities, and the results are relatively permanent. I. A. Richards once remarked that he thought learning, in the end, would turn out to be related in some rather precise way to causality. We are now perhaps closer than before to seeing the cogency of this conjecture. In all forms of learning we know that contiguity of events favors learning and that as their propinquity lessens the likelihood of our "making connections" or "forming associations" progressively diminishes. We know, too, that causation is more likely to be immediate than delayed so that the contiguity principle is well calculated to capture causal connections and encapsulate, or "store," in the brain a sort of replica of the sequential as opposed to the purely sensory aspects of reality.

To date, psychologists have given relatively little thought to the bearing which learning theory manifestly has for epistemology or the "problem of knowledge."[50] But now that we are looking more intently at language, with special reference to underlying learning mechanisms, there may be a revival of interest along these lines.[51] What is said here can at best be merely illustrative of the type of development which may be expected in this connection.

Perhaps one of the reasons that psychologists and epistemologists have not "gotten together" more than they have is the fact that psychologists have been, in the main, content to study stimuli as signals, whereas students of the theory of knowledge have been centrally interested in symbolization. Perhaps we are now in a position to suggest something of a *rapprochement* here. Many writers have noted and stressed the difference between signals, or natural signs, so-called, and symbols, which are referred to as "artificial signs." John Dewey, in his *Logic—The Theory of Inquiry* (16), puts the distinction this way:

> It is by agreement in conjoint action of the kind already described, that the word "smoke" stands in the English language for an object of certain qualities. . . . To such cases of representation the word "artificial sign" applies. When it is said that smoke as an actual existence points to, is evidence of, an existential fire, smoke is said to be a natural sign of fire. Similarly, heavy clouds of given

at least two times, as a minimum. This is not to deny that single repetitions of sentences often "do the trick," but we have no way of knowing how often this is because the recipient "picks up" the sentence, so to say, and fixes and confirms it by subvocal rehearsal (cf. discussion of the concept of "congruity" in Section X).

[49] "Instinct," insofar as it may be regarded as an established fact, can be thought of, perhaps, as a kind of "innate knowledge," "racial learning," "built-in habits." Somewhat the same view can be taken with respect to reflexes.

[50] A probable reason for this is the implied subjectivity of such concepts as "knowledge" and "knowing." Conspicuous among the relatively rare references to this problem by psychologists is Hull's "Knowledge and Purpose as Habit Mechanisms" (28). Among philosophers who have considered the learning-knowledge issue may be cited Urban (81) and Morris (47), the former taking a generally guarded attitude concerning the possibility of a *rapprochement* between epistemologists and learning theorists, while the latter is more hopeful. See particularly Morris' sections on "Belief and Knowledge" (pp. 108–111) and "The Limits of Significance and Knowledge" (pp. 111–114); see also note 6, p. 262.

[51] See Berlyne's just published paper, "Knowledge and Stimulus-Response Psychology" (3).

qualities are a natural sign of probable rain, and so on (p. 51).[52]

This distinction is sometimes further elaborated by pointing out that natural signs, or signals, are "followed by" something, whereas artificial signs, or symbols, "stand for" something and are therefore not, ordinarily, "followed by" that thing.[53] Thus, the whistle of an approaching train is a signal that it will shortly "be along." But, on the other hand, when I now utter the word, "train," we have no expectation that the referent of this symbol will shortly come roaring into this hall.

Most psychologists have not, I suspect, taken this distinction very seriously, inclined, as they are, to assume that all signs, be they so-called signals or symbols, acquire their significance, or meaning, in basically the same way, namely through conditioning. It now appears that any kind of sign, natural or arbitrary, can in principle function as either a signal or as a symbol and that the signalizing as opposed to the symbolizing function is determined, not by the nature of the stimulus itself, nor by the nature of the antecedent learning, but *by context,* by what *happens to* the anticipatory response, or meaning, which a particular sign elicits. If a sign is followed by its significate (Tolman's terminology is very apt here), its meaning is merely confirmed or, in learning terms, "reinforced." Here all the sign has done is to signalize the immanence of its referent. But if, on the other hand, a sign is presented, arouses a meaning response, and is then followed by some thing or event, or by a sign thereof, which is *different from the thing or event implied by the first sign,* then a wholly different outcome can be predicted. The sign-significance-significate sequence of the first sign is not reinforced, but instead the sign arouses its significance, to which is then attached, by conditioning and in the manner indicated in preceding sections, a new meaning, or significance, of some sort. This process we have, for better or for worse, here made the essence of language function, as exemplified in both the sign-thing sentence and the sign-sign sentence (Section V). Only when a sign is thus used is it, at least by present definition, a symbol. In short, then, it is the usage or treatment given a sign and not any inherent characteristic that seemingly determines whether it will merely signal or symbolize.

In the laboratory paradigm previously described, we have seen that, during the first stage of training, the blinking light, as far as the rat was concerned, was a "natural sign" or signal that cheese would "be along" shortly. Under these circumstances, the rat, if it could, might have paraphrased our common statement about smoke and fire by saying, "Where there's blinking light, there's cheese," since, up to this point, cheese has only and always followed the blinking light. But we found that we could also make the blinking light, which had previously been just a signal, perform as a symbol if we changed its context, so that it was followed, not by cheese, but by shock or a sign of shock, i.e., tone.

At this point we are in a position to look again, more insightfully perhaps, at the question of what nouns do and what predicates do. Stewart suggests that the "verb idea," because it is somehow simpler, developed first and that the "noun idea" was harder to come by.[54] Perhaps our laboratory paradigm can make this

[52] This example might have been more apt if Dewey had compared smoke, as a sign of fire, with the word "fire," rather than the word, "smoke." However, the intended distinction is probably clear enough, as stated.

[53] For a more extended treatment of this distinction, see Langer's *Philosophy in a New Key* (34), especially Chapters 2 and 3.

[54] This is not to say that "verbs," as a grammarian would define them, necessarily came before "nouns" historically or that they do in infant development. It merely says, what seems to be borne out by observation of animals, that predication was first practiced with things present and that "nomination," in the sense of saying something about things *not present* was historically and is, in the child, a later accomplishment. As we have seen, a "noun" may serve very acceptably as a predicate or "verb idea."

surmise more concrete. As we have seen, it is the capacity of the "noun," or first of two signs which minimally constitute a sentence, to produce a mediating response that makes language, in the highest sense, possible. The predicate meaning gets attached, we conjecture, to the nominative meaning and in this way performs the most useful type of communicative service. Considered in one way, the second sign in such a sentence also has a mediating function, i.e., in the example under discussion, the tone "mediates," "implies," "represents," or "stands for" the electric shock. But there is a difference between what happens to the predicate meaning and the nominative meaning in a sentence: the predicate meaning goes essentially unmodified by its conjunction with the nominative meaning, whereas the reverse is not true; the nominative meaning, or at least a part of it, gets attached thereto. Just as it is the reaction to the so-called conditioned stimulus, rather than the reaction to the unconditioned stimulus, that gets modified in ordinary conditioning, it likewise seems that it is the reaction to the nominative sign, rather than the reaction to the predicate sign, that gets modified in the extraordinary type of conditioning that is produced by the sentence. Perhaps the same thought is implied by grammarians when they say that a sentence, or statement, is made "about" the subject, not about the predicate. (But see Section X.)

What remains to be said, by way of completing this section, about culture transmission or "education" can be brief. The whole burden of the foregoing analysis has been to show how it is that language makes it possible for its users to have *vicarious experience,* to learn through and from the learning of others—and this, as I see it, is the essence of education. Culture, in both its technological and socially regulatory aspects, is what our forebears have been taught and have confirmed or modified on the basis of their own experience, which they then pass on to us, and which we, in turn, transmit to our children and students. While the power of example, as opposed to precept, is not to be underrated, yet there seems to be no serious dissent from the assumption that this continuous, never-ending flow of knowledge and belief which we call culture occurs mainly through the medium of language and that without it, the cultural stream would quickly shrink to the veriest trickle.[55]

Language, as we know, can be a treacherous device. It can be knowingly perverted, and even its most well-intentioned users can be deceived by it. But for all its hazards, it is clearly indispensable for the human enterprise. However deeply one may empathize with some of the educational problems which the Progressive Education Movement was designed to solve, it is now pretty generally conceded that children do not and cannot learn all or even a very sizable fragment of what they, as our cultural heirs, must learn, solely on the basis of *direct* experience. The indirect, vicarious experience which is brought to children by means of language so greatly expedites both their personal and intellectual development that only by generous recourse to it can we impart to the young, in one or two short decades, the legacy of human history, its trials, tragedies, techniques, and triumphs.[56]

[55] However essential language is to the process of culture transmission as here conceived, it obviously has other very important functions, notable among which is culture diffusion (or what may be called "horizontal" or "transverse," as opposed to "longitudinal," transmission), social coordination, organization, and cooperation, and, in a somewhat lighter vein, interpersonal entertainment and enrichment of individual life through shared experience or fantasy. But these other functions, as far as language is concerned, seem to involve no new principle and need not, therefore, be more specifically considered at this time. All language, in the sense of telling another something he did not previously know, may be said to be "education."

[56] Some of the phraseology employed in the foregoing, especially with reference to education as a process of *transmitting* experience,

IX. WORD MAGIC, GENERAL SEMANTICS, AND PSYCHOTHERAPY

Word magic, so-called, in both its primitive and contemporary forms, has been repeatedly examined by scientific writers and scholars and, almost universally, deplored.[57] Such treatment has probably been largely deserved, but in some ways it may have been wide of the mark. It will be our purpose here to take another look at this phenomenon and to suggest a somewhat modified interpretation.

Language is certainly magical in the sense of being wonderful and remarkable. But what has been called "word magic" can be at least partially defended in a more specific way. The charge that is most commonly made against it is that it involves an equating, or confusing, of words with the things they represent. We have been repeatedly reminded, especially in recent years, that "the word is not the thing," but the approach to language and its operation which has been followed in this paper suggests that, in one rather important respect, a word and its referent, a sign and its significate, are indeed "the same." They are the same, or equivalent, in the sense that they produce, at least to some degree, *the same response.* If such were not the case, it would be difficult to see how words otherwise perform the services which we commonly expect of and receive from them.

Therefore, in view of this very real equivalence, or communality, it should perhaps neither surprise nor too much distress us if, when impotent to deal otherwise with certain aspects of experience, human beings sometimes turn to a substitutive manipulation of these intractable realities at the level of symbolization. I do not wish to defend or justify this type of behavior or deny that dangers are involved in this practice, but neither should we overlook an element of plausibility and naturalness therein. If we can take the name of a person, for example, "Tom," and by attaching certain other words to it alter the way in which Tom himself will be perceived and reacted to by others, then in a very real way we have affected or influenced the real Tom, by merely manipulating his symbolic representation. Thus, in everyday life we engage in a form of behavior which is only a step removed from so-called word magic and which probably creates a universal disposition to resort to it in extremity.

Concern over the ways in which language function can go awry, though given much current emphasis by the General Semantics Movement, is, of course, very ancient. Even contemporary phraseology is older than we may sometimes suppose.

---

may seem inconsistent with the reservations expressed in earlier sections with respect to the notion that words perform their main function in conveying, bearing, or transferring meanings from person to person. Given a careful definition of terms, I believe there is no inconsistency in the position that we transmit or transfer "experience" but do not transfer "meanings." A sentence says, in effect, "This goes with that." (For example, the sentence "Tom is a thief" says that thievishness "goes with" Tom.) But, as already suggested, the "this" and the "that" have to be "known," must already "have meaning" for the individual who is on the "receiving" end. Once our hearer knows Tom and has the concept of thief, then we can truly transmit to him our own experience (which may have been either directly or vicariously derived). But this is not to say that words "convey" or "bear" meanings. They merely *arouse* them and then *associate* them in novel ways. Perhaps a part of the dilemma on which the Progressive Education Movement foundered can be resolved by noting that meanings are indeed best established on the basis of direct experience, but that, once meanings are well founded in reality, knowledge and intellectual development can be vastly extended by the use of sentences. A part of the effort of the Progressivists was directed, probably quite adaptively, toward helping children get more substantial meanings for words so as to avoid the "empty verbalism" which otherwise occurs when statements involving poorly understood words are heard or uttered. But to avoid "verbalism" altogether is to abandon as precious a tool as man has ever fashioned.

[57] For a scholarly, yet relatively restrained discussion of word magic, see Schlauch (65, pp. 13–18, 278–280).

For example, we find Lionel Trilling, in an essay on "The Sense of the Past," writing as follows:

> Nearly a century ago Dickens said that he was tired of hearing about "the tyranny of words" (he used that phrase); he was, he said, less concerned about the way words abuse us than the way we abuse words. It is not words that make our troubles, but our own wills. Words cannot control us unless we desire to be controlled by them. And the same is true of the control of systematic ideas (80, p. 189).

Basically the complaint which general semanticists make with respect to language is the same as that which we have just considered under the rubric of word magic. But the charge is made somewhat more specific and technical in that we are warned against the danger of "overgeneralizing," in fact, against the danger of generalizing at all. Words, we are told, never adequately or accurately represent reality, and we must constantly be on guard against letting them too much color and control our perception of and reactions to the real world. Language, in short, is a sort of web which we spin between ourselves and the true essence of things, and we must constantly struggle to keep from becoming hopelessly enshrouded therein.

Perhaps the best safeguard against such genuine hazards as language involves is a sound understanding of what language is and does. In earlier sections of this paper, we have seen that generalization, or "transfer of training," is an indispensable feature of the communicative act and that language, in its highest development, is extraordinarily useful and that without it, human culture, personality, and mentality would be very far from what, with the aid of language, they have in fact become. However desperate or deplorable the human scene may seem, either historically or contemporaneously, we can hardly condemn or reject language without also taking an essentially nihilistic attitude toward human existence and human aspirations generally. Jonathan Swift, with humor as well as logic, defended language against its detractors in his day by having his illustrious traveler, Dr. Gulliver, visit the University of Lagado, where he was taken on a tour and shown various research projects, including the following:

> We next went to the school of languages, where three professors sat in consultation upon improving that of their own country.
>
> The first project was to shorten discourse, by cutting poly-syllables into one, and leaving out verbs and participles; because, in reality, all things imaginable are but nouns.
>
> The other project was a scheme for entirely abolishing all words whatsoever; and this was urged as a great advantage in point of health as well as brevity. For it is plain, that every word we speak is, in some degree, a diminution of our lungs by corrosion; and consequently contributes to the shortening of our lives. An expedient was therefore offered, "that since words are only names for things, it would be more convenient for all men to carry about them such things as were necessary to express a particular business they are to discourse on." And this invention would certainly have taken place; to the great ease as well as health of the subject, if the women, in conjunction with the vulgar and illiterate, had not threatened to raise a rebellion unless they might be allowed the liberty to speak with their tongues after the manner of their forefathers; such constant irreconcilable enemies to science are the common people. However, many of the most learned and wise adhere to the new scheme of expressing themselves by things; which has only this inconvenience attending it, that if a man's business be very great, and of various kinds, he must be obliged, in proportion, to carry a great bundle of things upon his back, unless he can afford one or two strong servants to attend him. I have often beheld two of these sages almost sinking under the weight of their packs, like peddlers among us; who, when they met in the street would lay down their loads, open their sacks, and hold conversation for an hour together; then put up their implements, help each other to resume their burdens, and take their leave.
>
> But for short conversations, a man may carry implements in his pockets, under his arms, enough to supply him; and in his house,

he cannot be at a loss. Therefore the room where company meet who practice this art, is full of all things ready at hand, requisite to furnish matter for this kind of artificial converse (74, pp. 174–175).[58]

And Susanne Langer speaks well for our time when she says:

> As long as sense was supposed to be the chief factor in knowledge, psychologists took a prime interest in the organs that were the windows of the mind, and in the details of their functioning; other things were accorded a sketchier and sometimes vaguer treatment. If scientists demanded, and philosophers dutifully admitted, that all true belief must be based on sense-evidence, then the activity of the mind had to be conceived purely as a matter of recording and combining; then intelligence had to be a product of impression, memory, and association. But now, an epistemological insight has uncovered a more potent, howbeit more difficult, factor in scientific procedure—the use of symbols to attain, as well as to organize, belief. Of course, this alters our conception of intelligence at a stroke. Not higher sensitivity, not longer memory or even quicker association sets man so far above other animals that he can regard them denizens of a lower world: no, it is the power of using symbols—the power of *speech*—that makes him lord of the earth. So our interest in the mind has shifted more and more from the acquisition of experience, the domain of sense, to the *uses* of sense-data, the realms of conception and expression (34, p. 20).

And in response to disparaging evaluations of language by Pitkin, Richet, Chase, and others, Dr. Langer asks this pointed question:

> How can an instrument develop in the interests of better practice and survive, if it harbors so many dangers for the creature possessed of it? How can language increase a man's efficiency if it puts him at a biological disadvantage beside his cat? (p. 27).

Yet we must concede that our world is grievously afflicted with political, economic, social, and psychological ills. And merely to vindicate language in this connection is not to banish these problems and the confusion and misery they entail. Surely, great tolerance and forebearance are due all honest efforts to understand and improve man's condition, however fumbling they may presently be. Which brings us, finally, to that realm in which psychologists are trying to make such contribution as they can to social and psychological health. It would be beyond the scope of our topic if we attempted this evening in any comprehensive way to deal with the many intricate questions involved in the theory and practice of psychotherapy, but since language plays so central a role in therapeutic interaction we may take at least a brief look at it in this context.

It has been many times remarked that what one does in the name of psychotherapy is contingent upon what one regards as the essential nature and genesis of the psychoneurotic state. If we can accept one widespread view thereof, the role of language in therapy should be quite simple and straightforward. Many otherwise diverse schools of thought share the common assumption that the neurotic is a person with unrealistic fears, and on the basis of this assumption the treatment of choice calls for an attempt to extinguish or otherwise undo the adventitious or misguided learning which brought these fears into being. How can this best be done and, more particularly, done through the medium of language?

On the basis of the conception of language process which has been sketched in this paper, an answer to the problem, when posed in this fashion, is immediately forthcoming. If, by means of sentences, we can condition living organisms to fear things by merely attaching fear to symbols, it would quickly stand to reason that we could likewise *lessen* the fears which they have of things (or actions or impulses) by lessening the fears elicited by the corresponding symbols. If, in other words,

[58] The writer thanks Professor Max Black of Cornell University for calling this passage to his attention.

fear will generalize, as our earlier analysis indicates, from sign to significate, extinction of fear which is achieved at the level of signs ought also to carry over to the realities which they represent.[59] Much psychotherapeutic endeavor is apparently rationalized on the basis of this type of inference.

But there is at least a reasonable doubt as to whether the foregoing conception of neurosis is valid, or at least universally so, and if it is not, we can hardly expect therapeutic efforts, based upon it, to be as effective as we would like them to be. The commonly held view implies that psychopathology arises because the afflicted person, through a kind of deception or misrepresentation, has been malconditioned by others and that therapy involves, in essence, little more than deconditioning. But a different view can, with some empirical justification, be put forward, at least tentatively, to the effect that neurosis is indeed related to deception but that it is less a question of an individual's having been deceived than of his having learned and practiced this device, himself. If this be so, there is, alas, no very evident or simple way in which the condition can, by purely verbal means, be banished. Where there is reasonable doubt about the truth of a proposition, the injurious effects of its having been taught to an individual can, it would seem, be relatively easily reversed. But once the exploitative, self-protective strategies which the act of deception makes possible have been learned, replacing them by personal consistency, honesty of report, and consideration for others is not, as parents and teachers generally know to their sorrow, an easy thing.

Or, let the problem be put more broadly. It is again generally agreed that the neurotic is a person who has "too much guilt." But there is a central issue here which we have not yet fully examined, much less resolved. One view holds that the excess of guilt encountered in neurosis stems from a too strict training of the individual with respect to certain inherent needs and their gratification. But it is still an open question, is it not, whether the neurotic suffers because he is thus overtrained or because he has not "lived up" to certain reasonable and necessary standards held by the social group of which he is a part. And there is, as a consequence, the cognate question as to whether therapy should be directed toward getting rid of "guilt" in the sense of lessening the individual's predisposition or capacity to experience it *or* toward helping him modify such attitudes and action *as give rise to it*.

The problem, thus phrased, impales us on the horns of a broadly philosophical, but nonetheless urgently practical, dilemma: Shall we assume that this is an "imperfect world" and that life in it is largely a matter of compromise and "getting by" or shall we assume, with the Judeo-Christian ethic, that although social and moral perfection is never attained by man, its steadfast pursuit is the one thing that can make life meaningful and, on occasion, joyous? If we assume that guilt and neurosis arise from too high standards and too strenuous efforts at social and moral perfection, then, we can see a clear and simple rationale for therapy through the medium of words. But if we assume that guilt and neurotic conflict arise, not from an excess of character and good conduct, but from personal shortcomings and imperfections, then the therapeutic task becomes—both for the individual who is trying to help himself and for others—as complex, as

[59] This deduction could be put to laboratory test by taking rats which have been taught, by direct conditioning, to fear eating cheese and seeing if this fear could be reduced by extinguishing the fear aroused by a (previously learned) cheese sign, e.g., a blinking light. (This experiment was suggested to the author by Dr. Joel R. Davitz.) On the basis of what we otherwise know about "semantic generalization" (see Section IV), it seems likely that positive results would be obtained.

challenging, and, at times, as discouraging, as education, experience, and human existence itself.

As we have seen, the conception of language which has emerged from earlier sections of this paper provides, theoretically at least, a relatively straightforward rationale for treating neurosis, if one makes certain assumptions about the nature thereof. The fact that therapy is generally a more arduous enterprise, with less certain outcome, than this type of thinking would imply suggests either that our understanding of the mechanisms of language is considerably less adequate than we now imagine or, a possibility that should also be considered, that some of our common assumptions about the causation and nature of neurosis perhaps need to be open-mindedly reappraised.

With psychologists generally, I believe in scientific method and in the naturalistic approach to life and its problems; but it is conceivable that when we come to such profound issues as we encounter in neurosis, our science has not as yet given us all the answers or, indeed, enabled us to ask all the right questions.

Here we are dealing, surely, with issues as deep and as broad as life itself. And if, as yet, our accomplishments in this area are meager, it need not be an occasion for undue discouragement, but rather a reason for modesty, tolerance, and renewed dedication to the scientific and humane pursuit of knowledge and understanding in all things.

X. CREDIBILITY, CONGRUITY, AND OTHER COMPLICATIONS

As the preceding sections indicate, the particular interpretation of language process in terms of learning theory which has been developed in the earlier parts of this paper has considerable generality. But it would be premature to imply universality. The paradigm sentence to which frequent reference has been made is an extremely simple one. Its simplicity arises in part from the fact that it involves an intransitive verb, and a rather special one at that. So we should ask, at the very least, what the situation is when a sentence involves a transitive verb.

For example, suppose that we say, "Tom robbed the bank." Here we have, in addition to the subject, and as part of the predicate, something which grammarians call an *object*. And it is at once apparent that in saying, "Tom robbed the bank," we are—or at least may be—conveying information, or "news," not only about *Tom* but also about a particular *bank*. This sentence not only tells us that Tom is a bank robber; it can also tell us that the bank in question has been robbed.

A moment's reflection will indicate that a sentence such as this one, on the other hand, may not actually convey any new information at all about the so-called object. It may already be known that the bank has been robbed, and the question may merely be: Who did it? The sentence, "Tom robbed the bank," may therefore say no more than, "Tom did it." In this case, much the same sort of analysis as has been made of the original paradigm sentence would seem to apply likewise to this new one.

But it cannot be denied that the sentence, "Tom robbed the bank," *may* convey genuine news about the bank as well as about Tom. In such a case, our attitudes and perhaps also our actions will be modified both with respect to Tom and to the bank. The preceding discussion offers no very apparent way of explaining how it is that the bank, so to say, "gets into the (communicative) act."

One possibility is that "Tom robbed the bank" is really a compressed version of two separate sentences: "The bank has been robbed; (and it is believed or known that) Tom did it." Whether this type of reductionism is supportable must be determined by further research. For the present, suffice it to say that Osgood and Tannenbaum (57) believe that it is not. In a paper now in press, these writers point out that there is varied evidence for believing that an assertion such as, "Communists favor strong labor unions," sometimes changes the recipient's attitude toward labor unions more than it does his attitude toward Communists. This is the familiar technique of "guilt (or goodness) by association," so often used in propaganda and advertising. But how it works, in terms of precise psychological mechanisms, is uncertain. It is clearly illicit to reason:

Communists favor strong labor unions.
Communists are bad.
Therefore, strong labor unions are bad.

Using precisely the same logic form, one might say:

Communists are bad.
Communists favor fresh air.
Therefore, fresh air is bad.

In the latter case, the inference, "fresh air is bad," would almost certainly not be drawn; but in the former case, an illicit inference is by no means so unlikely. This remarkable fact prompts Osgood and Tannenbaum to posit what they call the *principle of congruity,* which says (in a manner reminiscent of Lecky's concept of self-consistency [35]) that the tendency to accept or reject an assertion is a function of whether it is consistent or inconsistent with respect to other beliefs or attitudes already held. Thus, since hardly anyone is opposed to fresh air, upon hearing that Communists favor it, most persons would be likely to reply, "So what?" But if one does not like labor unions and is, so to say, "hungry" for criticisms thereof, the assertion that Communists favor them may produce a marked effect. If, on the other hand, one believes in labor unions, he is likely to dismiss such an assertion with the remark, "The person making that assertion is obviously a propagandist (or worse), and not to be taken seriously."[60]

In light of the manifest complexities here involved, it is not surprising that Osgood and Tannenbaum, in concluding their paper, remark:

> No attempt has been made to integrate this particular theoretical model with more general psychological theory. The principles used here bear a close resemblance, superficially at least, to those of general gestalt theory. . . . But one could also translate this model into the terms of a modern, mediational learning theory. . . . We feel no urge at this time to attempt such detailed translations (57).

The Osgood-Tannenbaum paper serves usefully to remind us how quickly we approach the unknown in psycholinguistics as soon as we depart from a circumscribed problem or conceptual model. But the complications thus introduced are not wholly unanticipated. In the laboratory it has been repeatedly shown that conditioning is often a very delicate and, indeed, unpredictable affair, depending in highly intricate ways upon the organism's past experience, situational context, subtle cues, and so forth.[61] In advancing conditioning

60 Here we encounter, at least tangentially, the little explored problem of credibility. We know that the conditioning involved in communication does not occur entirely automatically; we always "consider the source." Advertisers and propagandists know that pure repetition is not without effect, but we tend to give "weight" to or to "discount" what we hear or read depending upon the degree of confidence we have in a particular speaker or writer. To complicate matters even further, we observe that our attitudes toward a given communicator tend to be influenced by whether we "like" what he says, regardless of how valid it may be. The bearer of good tidings is always welcome, whereas a person whose messages are characteristically adverse is likely to be dubbed "Bad News," and shunned.

61 These complexities are such as to have prompted one recent writer (70) to go so far as to suggest that conditioning itself is an artifact. While the present writer does not believe this to be the case, the article cited is a sober reminder of the still tentative and debatable nature of our knowledge in this important area.

theory as a possible means of explaining the phenomenon of sentence predication, one is not, therefore, wholly unprepared to find that language often operates in subtle and, on occasion, baffling ways. At present it is therefore uncertain whether such complexities as those instanced by Osgood and Tannenbaum can be handled only within the framework of gestalt psychology or can be resolved by increasing refinement of stimulus-response learning theory.

(Since this paper was written and set in type, the author has received a very helpful suggestion from his colleague, Professor Wilbur Schramm. Let us revert to the paradigm sentence, "Tom is a thief." The assumption tacitly made earlier in this paper is that the conjunction of "Tom" and "thief," in this order, will change one's conception of Tom considerably (especially if Tom has previously been regarded as an honest man), and will change one's conception of thieves not at all—just as conjunction of a conditioned stimulus and an unconditioned stimulus, of the type commonly employed in the laboratory, is presumed to change the reaction made to the CS, but not the reaction made to the UnCS. In fact, the very term "unconditioned," or "unconditional," as applied to the latter stimulus, carries with it an implication of invariance with respect to the reaction it evokes. But the notion proposed by Dr. Schramm suggests that we have been perhaps too much influenced by laboratory conditioning practices in thinking about the language problem. Here is the argument. Obviously r_t (i.e., the thief-meaning) reaction is a *composite:* it is a "concept," derived or abstracted from the entire population of persons we have known (or possibly read or heard about) who have been labeled *thieves*. Now these persons obviously have characteristics other than their thievishness; and if, by means of the statement, "Tom is a thief," we add Tom to this population (see Section VIII)—and if Tom is for us in any way unique or "special," as, for example, a well-loved friend or son, brother, or father—then the very fact that the category, "thief," now includes for us such a person *changes the category* and, *ergo,* alters—perhaps quite radically—the r_t reaction which we make to the word, "thief."

(This reasoning is, at least to the writer, compelling and also illuminating. It enables us to see, for example, why laboratory experience has not prepared us for this type of insight: we have not worked with "conditioned stimuli" which, prior to pairing with an unconditioned stimulus, already have powerful meanings. Deliberately we select, for this purpose, stimuli which, as we say, have been "previously neutral," i.e., relatively meaningless. Yet we have seen [Sections III and IV] that, in order for the sentence, as a conditioning device, to *work,* we must grant pre-established and definite meaning to the subject [first sign] as well as to the predicate [second sign]. Otherwise we have no "mediating response" and no satisfactory way of accounting for semantic generalization or transfer.

(Dr. Schramm's suggestion also seems to offer promise of a way of interpreting such effects as Osgood and Tannenbaum cite, without, however, impugning the essential logic of the earlier sections of this paper. Within the proposed framework, we can still think of the sentence as essentially a conditioning mechanism, with major change ordinarily occurring to the sign [and its significate] about which the predicate "says something." But we can now also see how, as in the "Tom is a thief" sentence, the meaning of the predicate term may also get modified—and this without assuming "backward conditioning." Dr. Schramm's proposal is thus a very welcome refinement and extension of the conception of sentence function here proposed, not, it seems, in any way a refutation. This proposal "feels" as if it has various other interesting and useful implications, but they cannot be further explored at this time.)

Caution and circumspection with respect to any interpretation of language in terms of presently extant learning theory are also suggested by what grammarians refer to as the formal structure of a language. Charles Fries's book, *The Structure of English, An Introduction to the Construction of English Sentences* (22), presents this intriguing problem in both its traditional and a more novel form. A few sentences from this work will indicate the general nature and scope of the problem. The author says:

> In the usual approach to the grammatical analysis of sentences one must know the total meaning of the utterance before beginning any analysis (p. 54).
>
> It is the devices that signal structural meanings which constitute the grammar of a language. *The grammar of a language consists of the devices that signal structural meanings.*
>
> The contrast between the older traditional procedure of grammatical analysis and the approach used here lies in the fact that the conventional analysis starts from the undifferentiated total meaning of an utterance and raises the question, "What names apply to various parts of this meaning" whereas our analysis starts from a description of the formal devices that are present and the patterns that make them significant and arrives at the *structural meanings as a result of the analysis.* From a practical point of view we are concerned, too, with the utterances in which clear grammatical signals are not present, and thus *when* and *why* the structural meanings of any utterance become ambiguous (pp. 56–57).

Bereft of the numerous examples which Fries gives to support and clarify his thesis, the foregoing quotations are necessarily abstract and perhaps not too meaningful. But they nevertheless suggest a whole spectrum of problems to which the learning theorist has thus far given hardly a passing glance. In the paradigm sentence, "Tom is a thief," we have deliberately selected a proposition with a minimum of "grammatical signals," and even these (with the exception of word order and word form) we have stripped away in the interests of analysis. One can hardly think of a more exciting, yet arduous, scientific undertaking than would be involved in a joint exploration by grammarians and learning theorists of the innumerable psychological functions which, over countless centuries, have become imbedded in the structural forms of the world's major and minor languages. In light of the challenge and magnitude of this task, the suggestions put forward in the present paper seem crude and preliminary in the extreme.

In a philosophy course which the author once took as an undergraduate, the instructor told of having spent an evening during his just past vacation on the veranda of a little mountain cottage belonging to an old prospector, during the course of which a huge boulder suddenly came crashing down the mountain, barely missing the cottage. As the dust and echoes died away in the valley below, the prospector slapped his knee and quipped: "By cracky, the world ain't made *yit!*" Despite the extreme antiquity of human language, despite the long and painstaking study that has been made of it, and despite the increasingly intensive work done during the past half century on the psychology of learning, we are still, surely, a goodly distance from the day when it can be said that the riddles of language and its psychological understructure and overtones have been completely solved.

XI. SUMMARY

Within the past half century, substantial progress has been made with respect to the "science of signs." However, there has been comparatively little interest in, or accomplishment with respect to, what may be called the psychology of the sentence. For a long time philosophers have talked and written about propositions, or sentences, from an epistemological point of view; and grammarians have also had their own special concerns in this connection. But consideration of the sentence from the standpoint of general behavior principles is apparently a new but not unpromising development.

The following statements, drawn from the sections with which they are numbered to correspond, give a summary view of the present paper:

I. Despite apparent exceptions, the sentence is composed minimally of two units, a sign which functions as subject and another sign which functions as predicate. So-called one-word sentences seem always to imply or presuppose some event, thing, or person immediately present. Only when *both* subject and predicate are represented by means of signs does language, in its true and highest form, come into existence.

II. The prevailing notion has been that sentences, like single signs, serve to convey meanings, ideas, understandings from speaker to hearer, writer to reader. The basic assumption examined in the present paper is that what the sentence does, instead, is to shift or transfer meanings, not from person to person, but from sign to sign within the mind of the recipient. This is accomplished, it seems, by the familiar principle of conditioning: the sentence subject is analogous to the conditioned stimulus and the predicate to the unconditioned stimulus. What a sentence therefore does, in essence, is to provide an opportunity for the meaning elicited by the sentence predicate to get connected to the sentence subject.

III. We are familiar, in the conditioning laboratory, with the phenomenon of a reaction originally elicited by a thing getting transferred, or shifted, to a sign which has been associated with that thing. And we are also familiar, in so-called higher order conditioning, with the phenomenon of a reaction getting shifted from one sign to another sign. But in the case of language, if the foregoing analysis is correct, something else is also involved: a new reaction, or meaning, which has gotten connected to the first sign, or subject, of a sentence then gets "shifted," or "transferred," to the thing, person, or event represented by that sign. Unelaborated conditioning theory has no provision for explaining this sort of process. However, by positing a "mediating reaction," i.e., a reaction which is produced by the subject of a sentence (and also by the referent of the subject), and by assuming that the meaning reaction produced by the predicate of a sentence gets conditioned, not directly to the sentence subject but to this mediating response, then the phenomenon of "semantic generalization," as it has been called, can be readily accounted for.

IV. Fortunately, in psychological literature there are a number of instances, involving both motor and verbal responses, of response mediation. Some of these are cited and serve to show that the concept of mediation, as employed in this paper, has not been invented as a theoretical convenience for present purposes only.

V. A series of laboratory paradigms suggests that the effects produced by a true sentence, or *sign-sign* sequence, can also be produced by three other lower orders of "sentence," a *sign-thing* sentence, a *thing-sign* sentence, and a *thing-thing* sentence. These are all more or less effective conditioning devices and can be used to produce much the same end result. However, as previously shown, the "sign-sign" sentence has certain important practical advantages which set it apart from the other three "sentences," or conditioning procedures.

VI. A survey of communication in animals suggests that in all instances they are restricted to thing-thing and thing-sign "sentences." In no case do we find clear evidence of animals using signs as the first element, or subject, in interorganismic conditioning. As indicated earlier, only man has apparently mastered the "noun-idea" and thus become capable of "abstract" speech. Sentences uttered by so-called "talking birds" seem to represent mere chain associations and have a very low order of communicative function.

VII. This section is primarily concerned with the old question of the "origin of language," historically considered. Because of the tendency for overt, instrumental behavior to telescope, or "deteriorate," into *gestures* (if another organism will respond to them as signs and do the work originally performed by the complete instrumental response), there is a temptation to infer that language developed out of these diminutive acts. There are, however, persuasive reasons for believing that this was not the actual course of language development. It seems more probable that natural sounds, associated with primary sources of reinforcement, took on secondary reinforcing value and so, when more or less accidentally reproduced by man, were repeated and, because of their occurrence in nature, had for others a pre-established meaning and readily lent themselves to communicative purposes. A laboratory paradigm is used to illustrate this conception of word origin and acquisition.

VIII. This section, entitled "Language, Logic, Thought, Knowledge, and Culture Transmission," is long and cannot be summarized here except in a highly general way. As already indicated, the total sequence involved in language is apparently as follows. Part of the reaction made to some thing, person, or event gets transferred, by conditioning, to a sign. (This is the process whereby infants come to *understand,* or "know the meaning of," words.) By means of a sentence (that is, higher order conditioning), the meaning reaction produced by one sign (the sentence predicate) gets connected to the meaning reaction produced by the other sign (the sentence subject). From here, for reasons previously considered, the predicate meaning reaction generalizes to the thing, person, or event which this other sign represents. We may therefore say that, in the complete communicative act, what happens is that a part of the reaction produced by one thing, person, or event gets transferred to, or "rubbed off on," some other thing, person, or event. In other words, we start with "things" and we end with "things": and signs, as employed in sentences, are devices for transferring some of the "reaction potential" of one thing to another thing.[62] In short, language is a device whereby another person, on the basis of experience with one reality, may be made to react (at least attitudinally) somewhat differently toward another reality, *without any new direct experience with that reality.* We thus see why language is said to provide "vicarious experience," and why it is, also, that this vicarious experience, or learning, may be either valid or false, helpful or misleading. In this connection the matter of symbolizing as opposed to signalizing is also considered.

IX. Word magic, so-called, has often been deplored and its irrationality emphasized. However, the present analysis of language indicates that, contrary to common claim, the word *is* the thing, if by this we mean that the word and the thing are the same, or equivalent, in the sense that they both produce somewhat the same reaction; for the meaning of a word is, as we have seen, a part of the response produced by the thing or event which the word signifies. This being true, it follows that if neurosis is primarily an unjustified fear of things (actions, impulses), then extinction of the fear elicited by the symbols of such things ought to generalize and have a therapeutic effect. Consideration of this problem to even the limited extent that is here possible suggests that both neurosis and its alleviation are more complicated matters.

X. This paper can be properly criticized on the ground that the central theoretical analysis has been based in large measure upon a simple, declarative, present-tense sentence with a transitive verb.

[62] One thus sees perhaps new justification for the position taken by some writers that language is entirely, or at least largely, metaphorical. "The *wind* is like *ice,*" we say; or, "This *man* is strong as an *ox.*" However, this suggestion must be further scrutinized before much credence can be given to it.

Perhaps no apology is needed for having examined the simple before proceeding to the complex. But the question must at least be raised as to whether the theory of language process here evolved is valid only for such simple sentences or whether it can also encompass, for example, sentences within transitive verbs. Preliminary inquiry shows that when a sentence has an "object," as well as a "subject," numerous complications arise, including those of formal grammatical structure cues, context, credibility, and intrapsychic congruence. As of the present, it is not apparent whether these complexities can be handled within the framework of stimulus-response theory or call for principles more nearly like those adduced by gestalt psychologists.

The domain of psycholinguistics offers enticing vistas for further exploration and research.

References

1. ADAMS, S., *et al.* (Special language number.) *Psychol. Bull.*, 1929, **26**, 241–340,

2. AMES, LOUISE B. The development of the sense of time in the young child. *J. genet. Psychol.*, 1946, **68**, 97–125.

3. BERLYNE, D. E. Knowledge and stimulus-response psychology. *Psychol. Rev.*, 1954, **61**, 245–254.

4. BIXENSTINE, V. E. Secondary drive as a neutralizer of time in integrative problem solving. Unpublished doctor's thesis, Univer. of Illinois, 1953.

5. BLACK, M. *Language and philosophy, studies in method.* Ithaca, N. Y.: Cornell Univer. Press, 1949.

6. BLOOMFIELD, L. *Language.* New York: Holt, 1933.

7. BODER, D. P. The DRQ as a measure of tension in personal documents. Unpublished manuscript, Illinois Institute of Technology, 1951.

8. BOUSFIELD, W.A., & BARCLAY, W. D. The application of Zipf's analysis of language to sequences of restrictive responses. *J. genet. Psychol.*, 1951, **44**, 253–260.

9. BÜHLER, CHARLOTTE. *The first year of life.* New York: Day, 1930.

10. BÜHLER, K. *The mental development of the child.* New York: Harcourt, Brace, 1930.

10a. CARPENTER, C. R. A theoretical orientation for instructional film research. *Audio-visual communication review*, 1953, **1**, 38–52.

11. CARROLL, J. B. *The study of language.* Cambridge: Harvard Univer. Press, 1953.

12. COFER, C. N., *et al.* Mediated generalization and the interpretation of verbal behavior. I-V. *Psychol. Rev.*, 1950, **49**, 513–39; *J. exp. psychol.*, 1943, **32**, 168–175; **32**, 266–269; **33**, 188–200; **33**, 299–309.

13. COURTNEY, P. D. Identification and learning: a theoretical analysis. Unpublished doctor's dissertation, Harvard Univer., 1949.

14. DARWIN, C. *The expression of the emotions in man and animals.* London: J. MURRAY, 1872.

15. DELAGUNA, GRACE. *Speech: its function and development.* New Haven: Yale Univer. Press, 1927.

16. DEWEY, J. *Logic—the theory of inquiry.* New York: Holt, 1938.

17. DOLLARD, J., & MILLER, N. E. *Personality and psychotherapy.* New York: McGraw-Hill, 1950.

18. FAIRBANKS, G. Systematic research in experimental phonetics: I. A theory of speech mechanism as a servosystem. *J. Speech Hearing Disorders,* 1954, **19**, 133–139.

19. FEIGL, H., & SELLARS, W. (Eds.). *Readings in philosophical analysis.* New York: Appleton-Century-Crofts, 1949.

20. FOLEY, J. P., JR., & COFER, C. N.

Mediated generalization and the interpretation of verbal behavior: II. Experimental study of certain homophone and synonymous gradients. *J. exp. Psychol.*, 1943, **32**, 168–175.

21. Fowler, H. W. *A dictionary of modern English usage*. London: Clarendon Press, 1926.

22. Fries, C. C. *The structure of English—an introduction to the construction of English sentences.* New York: Harcourt, Brace, 1952.

23. Greenough, J. B., & Kittredge, G. L. *Words and their ways in English speech.* New York: Macmillan, 1906.

24. Griffith, C. R. *General introduction to psychology.* New York: Macmillan, 1924.

25. Grummon, D. L. An investigation into the use of grammatical and psychogrammatical categories of language for the study of personality and psychotherapy. Unpublished doctor's dissertation, Univer. of Chicago, 1950.

26. Hilgard, E. R., & Marquis, D. G. *Conditioning and learning.* New York: D. Appleton-Century, 1940.

27. Hollingworth, H. L. *Psychology, its facts and principles.* New York: D. Appleton, 1928.

28. Hull, C. L. Knowledge and purpose as habit mechanisms. *Psychol. Rev.*, 1930, **37**, 511–525.

29. Hull., C. L. *Principles of behavior.* New York: D. Appleton-Century, 1943.

30. Hunter, W. S. *Human behavior.* Chicago: Univer. of Chicago Press, 1928.

31. Jenkins, W. O. A temporal gradient of derived reinforcement. *Amer. J. Psychol.*, 1950, **63**, 237–243.

32. Johnson, W. Studies in language behavior. I. A program of research. *Psychol. Monogr.*, 1944, **56**, No. 2 (Whole No. 255) 1–15.

33. Judd, C. H. *Psychology—general introduction.* New York: Scribner's 1907.

34. Langer, Susanne K. *Philosophy in a new key.* New York: Pelican Book, 1942.

35. Lecky, P. *Self-consistency: a theory of personality.* New York: Island Press, 1947.

36. Lewis, M. M. *Infant speech: a study of the beginnings of language.* New York: Humanities Press, 1951.

37. Lorge, I. Irrelevant rewards in animal learning. *J. comp. Psychol.*, 1936, **21**, 105–128.

38. Lumsdaine, A. A. Conditioned eyelid responses as mediating generalized finger reaction. *Psychol. Bull.*, 1939, **36**, 650 (Abstract).

39. McCarthy, Dorothea. The language development of the preschool child. Minneapolis: Univer. of Minnesota Press, 1930. (*Institute of Child Welfare Monogr. Ser.*, No. 4.)

40. McCarthy, Dorothea. Language development in children. In L. Carmichael (Ed.), *Manual of Child psychology.* New York: Wiley, 1954. Pp. 492–630.

41. Malinowski, B. The problem of meaning in primitive languages. In C. K. Ogden & I. A. Richards, *The meaning of meaning.* Supplement I. New York: Harcourt, Brace, 1938.

42. Marx, M. A stimulus response analysis of the hoarding habit in the rat. *Psychol. Rev.*, 1950, **57**, 80–91.

43. May, M. A. Experimentally acquired drives. *J. exp. Psychol.*, 1948, **38**, 66–77.

44. Miller, G. A. *Language and communication.* New York: McGraw-Hill, 1951.

45. Miller, N. E. A reply to 'Sign-gestalt

or conditioned reflex?" *Psychol. Rev.*, 1935, **42**, 280–292.

46. Miller, N. E., & Dollard, J. *Social learning and imitation.* New Haven: Yale Univer. Press, 1941.
47. Morris, C. *Signs, language, and behavior.* New York: Prentice-Hall, 1946.
48. Morris, C. W. Foundations of the theory of signs. *Int. Encycl. Unif. Sci.*, 1938, No. 1, 63–75.
49. Mowrer, O. H. *Learning theory and personality dynamics.* New York: Ronald, 1950.
50. Mowrer, O. H. The autism theory of speech development and some clinical applications. *J. Speech Hearing Disorders*, 1952, **17**, 263–268.
51. Mowrer, O. H. Learning theory: historical review and reinterpretation. *Harv. educ. Rev.*, 1954, **24**, 37–58.
52. Mowrer, O. H., Palma, Florence, & Sanger, Marjorie D. Individual learning and "racial experience" in the rat, with special reference to vocalization. *J. genet. Psychol.*, 1948, **73**, 29–43.
53. Nygaard, J. Unpublished research. See Osgood (55).
54. Ogden, C. K., & Richards, I. A. *The meaning of meaning.* New York: Harcourt, Brace, 1923.
55. Osgood, C. E. *Method and theory in experimental psychology.* New York: Oxford Univer. Press, 1953.
56. Osgood, C. E., & Suci, G. J. Factor analysis of meaning. *J. exp. Psychol.*, in press.
57. Osgood, C. E., & Tannenbaum, P. H. The principle of congruity in the prediction of attitude change. *Psychol. Rev.*, in press.
58. Pei, M. *The story of language.* New York: J. B. Lippincott, 1949.
59. Piaget, J. *The language and thought of the child.* (Trans. by M. Warden.) New York: Harcourt, Brace, 1926.
60. Pronko, N. H. Language and psycholinguistics: a review. *Psychol. Bull.*, 1946, **43**, 189–232.
61. Razran, G. H. S. A quantitative study of meaning by a conditioned salivary technique (semantic conditioning). *Science, N.S.*, 1939, **90**, 89–90.
62. Rexroad, C. N. *General psychology.* New York: Macmillan, 1929.
63. Roback, A. A. *Destiny and motivation in language.* Cambridge, Mass.: Sci-Art Press, 1954.
64. Sanford, F. H. *Speech and personality. Psychol. Bull.*, 1942, **39**, 811–845.
65. Schlauch, Margaret. *The gift of tongues.* New York: Modern Age Books, 1942.
66. Schneirla, T. C. Basic correlations and coordinations in insect societies, with special reference to ants. *Colloques Internationaux du Centre National de la Recherche Scientifique.* XXXIV. Structure et physiologie des sociétés animales. Paris: March, 1950.
67. Shannon, C. E., & Weaver, W. *The mathematical theory of communication.* Urbana: Univer. of Illinois Press, 1949.
68. Shipley, W. C. An apparent transfer of conditioning. *Psychol. Bull.*, 1933, **30**, 541. (Abstract)
69. Skinner, B. F. *Verbal behavior.* William James Lectures, 1947. (To be published by The Harvard University Press.)
70. Smith, K. Conditioning as an artifact. *Psychol. Rev.*, 1954, **61**, 217–225.
71. Stewart, G. R. *Man, an autobiography.* New York: Random House, 1946.
72. Strain, E. R. Establishment of an avoidance gradient under latent-

learning conditions. *J. exp. Psychol.*, 1953, **46**, 391–399.

73. SUMNER, W. G., & KELLER, A. G. *Science of society.* New Haven: Univer. Press, 1927.

74. SWIFT, J. *Gulliver's travels.* New York: E. P. Dutton, 1909.

75. THOMPSON, G. G. *Child psychology, growth trends in psychological adjustment.* Boston: Houghton Mifflin, 1952.

76. THORNDIKE, E. L. Animal intelligence. *Psychol. Monogr.* 1898, 2, No. 4 (Whole No. 8).

77. THORNDIKE, E. L. *Educational psychology.* New York: Teachers Coll., Columbia Univer., 1925.

78. TOLMAN, E. C., & GLEITMAN, H. Studies in learning and motivation: I. Equal reinforcements in both end-boxes, followed by shock in one end-box. *J. exp. Psychol.*, 1949, **39**, 810–819.

79. TOMKINS, S. S. Consciousness and the unconscious in a model of the human being. Unpublished manuscript.

80. TRILLING, L. The sense of the past. In *The liberal imagination.* Garden City, N. Y.: Anchor Books, Doubleday, 1953. Pp. 179–193.

81. URBAN, W. M. *Language and reality—the philosophy of language and the priciples of symbolism.* New York: Macmillan, 1939.

82. VINACKE, W. E. *The psychology of thinking.* New York: McGraw-Hill, 1952.

83. VON FRISCH, K. *Bees, their vision, chemical sense, and language.* Ithaca, N. Y.: Cornell Univer. Press, 1950.

84. WERNER, H. Change of meaning: a study of semantic processes through the experimental method. *J. gen. Psychol.*, 1954, **50**, 181–208.

85. WHEELER, R. H. *The science of psychology.* New York: Crowell, 1929.

86. WHORF, B. L. Science and linguistics. Notions about talking and thinking which compose a system of natural logic, go wrong in two ways; how words and customs affect reasoning. In *Collected papers on metalinguistics.* Washington, D. C.: Department of State, Foreign Service Institute, 1952. Pp. 3–7.

87. WILSON, K. In C. E. Osgood & T. A. Sebeok (Eds.), *Psycholinguistics—a survey of theory and research problems.* Bloomington: Univer. of Indiana Press, 1954. (Indiana University Publications in Anthropology and Linguistics, Memoir 10.)

88. WYATT, GERTRUDE L. *Speech and interpersonal relations.* Glencoe, Ill.: Free Press, in press.

89. ZIPF, G. K. *Human behavior and the principle of least effort.* Cambridge, Mass.: Addison-Wesley Press, 1949.

90. *Webster's new collegiate dictionary.* Springfield, Mass.: G. & C. Merriam Co., 1951.

Behavior Theory and the Social Sciences[1]

CHARLES E. OSGOOD

The evolution of behavioral theory can be largely described in terms of what is assumed to happen between "stimulus" and "response." In any case these supposed events are generally not directly observable—they take place within a black box. Nineteenth-century psychologists filled the black box with "faculties," "motives," and "instincts." Early behaviorists refused to speculate about its contents altogether. Later behaviorists gradually introduced hypothetical "intervening variables," whose supposed nature and assumed relations became the identifying marks of various psychological theories and schools.

The recent focusing of interest on the symbolic process and attempts at constructing an "exact" theory of such processes provide an opportunity of combining in psychology the rigorous methods of natural science with the characteristic non-physical content of psychological phenomena.

Psychology has a rather unique position among the sciences. It is at once the most social of the biological sciences and the most biological of the social sciences. As the science of behavior—particularly human behavior—it claims and maintains active interest in much of what is equally the domain of neurology and physiology and in much of what is equally the domain of sociology and anthropology. And its practitioners reflect this Janus-faced orientation; some of us are quite indistinguishable from neurophysiologists, and indeed prefer their meetings to our own, and others of us consort almost exclusively with cultural anthropologists. Despite fractionation of both the field and the individual, this duality of interest may have certain advantages; whereas principles of human behavior may aid our understanding of problems in the social sciences, so may the nature of these problems impel reanalysis and modification of behavior theory.

CERTAIN RELATIONS BETWEEN THE BEHAVIORAL SCIENCES

One indication of the validity of a principle is the vigor and persistence with which it is opposed. This holds for the

[1] Originally prepared for the Conference on Analytic Systems conducted by the Department of Political Science, Northwestern University, 1955.

Charles E. Osgood, "Behavior Theory and the Social Sciences," Behavioral Science, *1, No. 3 (July, 1956), 167–185. Reprinted by permission of the author and publisher.*

rather old-fashioned notion of the hierarchy of sciences, that the principles of chemistry are reducible to physics, that the principles of biology are reducible to physio-chemistry, and so on. There is today very strong resistance to this sort of reductionism, particularly among social scientists, and they may be right, but reductionism is nevertheless a fruitful point of view. Fruitful, that is, as a guide in theorizing, not as a restriction on such activity.

Let us look for a moment at theory in psychology from this viewpoint. The psychologist, when he is functioning as a psychologist, is limited to observing what goes into the organism (which he calls *stimuli*) and what comes out (which he calls *responses*). Between these two observation points lies a no-man's-land of speculation; this region is the nervous system, also referred to these days as "the black box." Now the psychologist's task is to explain and predict relations between and among his two sets of observables, stimuli and responses, and to do this he must make certain assumptions about what goes on in the black box. In other words, psychological *theory,* as contrasted with psychological observation, is made up of hunches about how the nervous system operates. This is true for every psychological principle, whether it be a simple association postulate by the behaviorist or a field interaction postulate by the gestaltist. These assumptions about the nervous system may be explicit or may remain implicit, but they are being made nevertheless. One criterion of psychological theory, then, is compatibility with what is known about neurophysiology; other things equal, a theory that is consistent with such knowledge is better than one that is not—but this is only one criterion.

It seems that the same logic holds for the relation between psychology and the more social sciences. In this case, behavior principles become the great unknown, about which the economist, sociologist, or political scientist necessarily makes assumptions when he postulates general principles or laws operating at his own level, explaining and predicting relations among *his* observables. When the economist states laws, for example, he is setting up some kind of "economic man," who perhaps behaves rationally and is motivated by self-interest. When the linguist describes certain general laws governing language change over space and time, he is making assumptions about how individual language users learn and modify the myriad habits of hearing and speaking. When the sociologist generalizes about status and role in a society, surely he is also assuming something about how individual human beings perceive, learn, are motivated, and come in conflict.

For the most part, as in psychological theorizing, I imagine that these assumptions about the principles of behavior, the more molecular science in this case, remain implicit. In fact, the social scientist is sometimes quite shocked at the inappropriateness of his assumptions when they are made explicit—as when labor-management people discovered that economic self-interest was by no means the only, or even strongest, motivation of workers. It would seem useful to make the assumptions of social science theory as explicit as possible so that their compatibility with what *is* known about human behavior can be examined. The greater this compatibility—again, we must stress "other things equal" —the better the theory. And let me hasten to add that this does not mean that theories at a molar level must be limited to what is known at the more molecular level. Quite to the contrary, just as the psychologist is always far beyond the neurophysiologist in the assumptions he must make about the nervous system, so is the social scientist far beyond the psychologist in the assumptions *he* must make about human behavior. Only when molar assumptions prove to be flatly contrary to what is known molecularly does the molar principle lose tenability. And, as a matter of fact, what seem to be necessary assumptions for psychological science often provide an impetus and direction to the research of neurophysiologists, and this appears to be true for the impact of the other social sciences upon psychology as well.

BEHAVIOR THEORY—AN OVERVIEW

Behavior theory, then, in the broadest sense is made up of hunches about how the nervous system operates to generate the lawful relations we observe among and between stimuli and responses. Over the past century we can trace a gradual refinement in the rules of procedure whereby psychologists make and test these hunches, and this trend toward increased rigor in theorizing has been paralleled by similar development in other social sciences.

In nineteenth-century psychology the characteristic procedure in theorizing was simply to postulate a new entity or mechanism whenever some new regularity was discovered. Whenever something needed explaining, a new explanatory device was stuck inside the black box, and it rapidly became chock-full of ill-assorted and ill-digested demons. For every nameable phenomenon of human behavior a different "faculty" would be posited to explain it; for every nameable motive, a different "instinct" would be listed as its explanation. And, at least for communicating with his patients, Freud had big, flat-footed superegos stomping around on red-slippery ids, while cleverly anxious little egos tried to arbitrate. Thus, as suggested in Figure 1, the little black box was filled with a

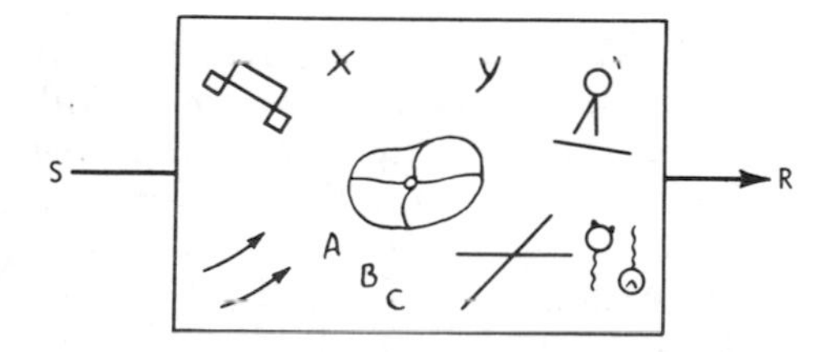

Fig. 1: The black box.

wondrously diverse collection of explanatory devices, just about as many as there were things to be explained. This could fairly be called "junkshop psychology." While it had the advantage of free exercise of often brilliant intuition, it had the disadvantage of complete lack of parsimony and consequent confusion.

In direct revulsion against this brand of theorizing, a group of American behaviorists around the turn of the century went to the other extreme, claiming that the psychologist was better off if he made no assumptions whatsoever about what went on in the black box. The group included Weiss, Kantor, Watson, and somewhat later, Skinner (13). This viewpoint toward theory has come to be known as "empty organism psychology." According to this view, as shown in diagrammatic fashion, in Figure 2 there is absolutely

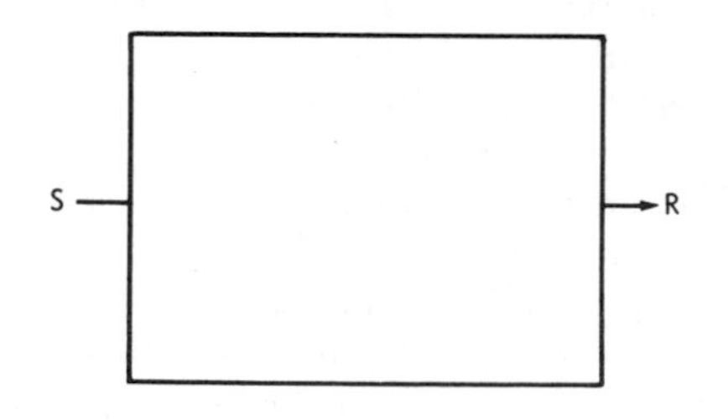

Fig. 2: Empty organism psychology.

nothing in the region between S and R, and what *is* there is none of the psychologist's business! This objective viewpoint was a healthy antidote for the loose mentalism which had preceded it, and it came to characterize American psychology. It led to increased emphasis on the details of accurately measuring stimuli and recording responses, to the establishment of dependable empirical laws relating input and output events, and to a general suspicion of unobservable explanatory devices, like "ideas," "purposes," and "feelings." But it also led psychologists to limit their interest to problems that could be handled in this simple mold—which automatically eliminated most phenomena of peculiarly human significance. The rat replaced the human as the standard subject in psychological research.

Most contemporary behaviorists could be characterized as "frustrated empty-boxers." Armed with a minimum but effective set of principles—really a set of empirical generalizations gleaned from systematic observations of S-R functions—they set out to explain and predict behavior in general. It soon became obvious, even with rats as subjects, that something had to be put back into the black box, that some intervening variables had to be postulated between S and R in order to explain our observations. But the contemporary behaviorist was more sophisticated about theory construction than his nineteenth-century forebear and, furthermore, he was under constant critical pressure from his objectively oriented colleagues. Therefore (*a*) he tried to put as little back into the box as possible, e.g., to postulate as few intervening variables as possible, and (*b*) he tried to anchor these hypothesized constructs to antecedent and subsequent observables as firmly as he could. What he has done, in effect, is to postulate an intervening response-like process which produces self-stimulation, e.g., *a two-stage mediation process,* as shown in Figure 3. In other words,

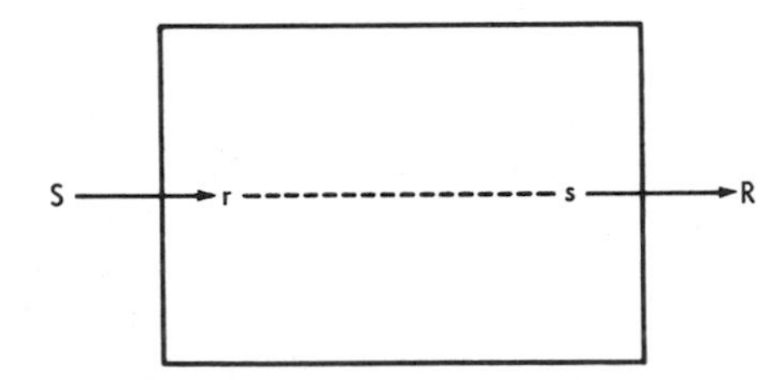

Fig. 3: Two-stage mediation process.

"mediation psychology" sets up within the organism a replica of the S-R model, and it assumes that the same laws governing single-stage S-R processes apply to both stages of the mediation model. This is the essence of Hull's (5) "pure-stimulus-act," a response whose sole function is to provide the organism with distinctive self-stimulation (and which Hull identified, interestingly enough, with symbolic processes); it is the ubiquitous "movement-produced-stimulus" of the mechanist, Guthrie, with which he extricates himself from most tight empirical corners; and Tolman's "expectancy" or "hypothesis" in rats can, I think, be shown to be functionally the same process. Later I shall try to show how the postulation of a mediation process increases the explanatory power of learning theory.

Although the gestalt psychologists have been more concerned with perception than with learning, at the level of higher mental processes like problem solving, insight, and concept formation they have certainly come into competition with the behavioristically inclined people. Using principles of organization developed in connection with perceptual studies, they have tried to interpret processes like insight as sudden restructurings of the perceptual field of the organism. This kind of behavior theory, since it seems to involve interactions among sensory processes, has been called "S-S psychology" and might be diagrammed as shown in Figure 4. Some writers

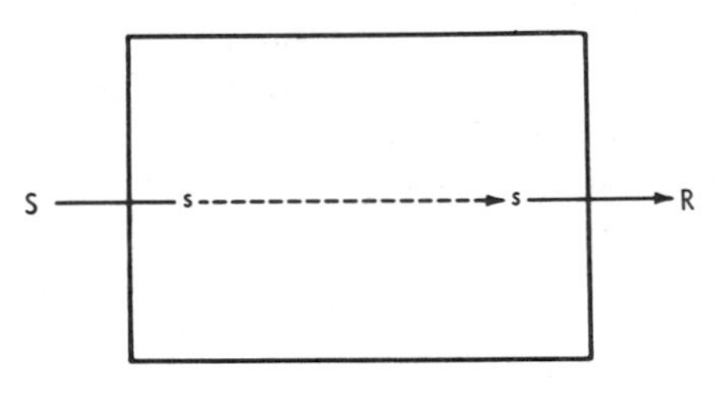

Fig. 4: S-S psychology.

have put Tolman's (15) kind of theory in this category, because he deals with associations between signs (S_1) and their significates (S_2), but I think his view is essentially a variant of S-R behaviorism. In passing it should be noted that behavioristic S-R conceptions have had practically nothing to say about perception itself, and this is certainly an important part of behavior-in-general.

Under the pressure of trying to handle language phenomena, I have found it necessary to put something else back into the black box. Along with symbolic, representational processes (which I think can be handled with the two-stage mediation model), language behavior also includes the most complex integrations of both perceptual processes and motor skill processes. On both input (decoding) and output (encoding) sides of the equation, as shown in Figure 5, I think we must

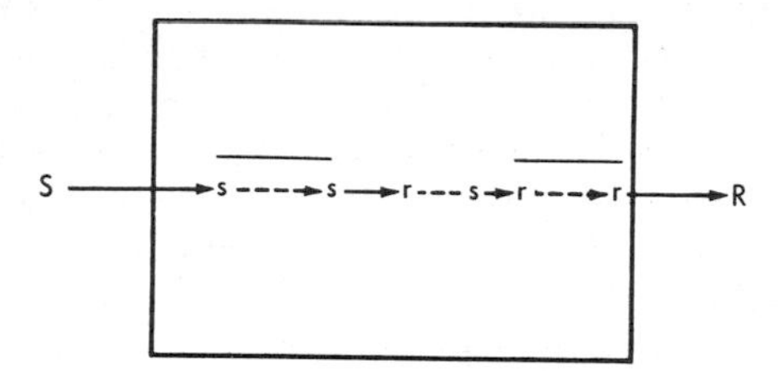

Fig. 5: Central integration among neural events.

postulate *central integration* among neural events. We need something of this kind to handle standard perceptual phenomena like closure as well as standard motor phenomena like the execution of skilled movements at a rate far greater than could be explained by S-R feedback mechanisms. We might call this model "integration-mediation psychology." But we have been leaping ahead much too quickly here; let us back-track a bit to the simple "empty organism" model and see what basic principles appear to govern S-R relations.

BASIC PRINCIPLES OF S-R BEHAVIOR THEORY

Although learning theorists disagree among themselves somewhat as to the language to be used, and occasionally as to the necessity of certain postulations, the basic principles described below would find pretty wide acceptance. They all deal in one way or another with the formation of *associations* among input and output events by organisms and thus reflect our heritage from philosophical Associationism —except that the events associated are stimuli and responses rather than ideas. They all may also be viewed as fundamental assumptions psychologists make about how the nervous system both organizes and is organized by behavioral experience.

1. Contiguity. In general, *the closer in time the occurrence of a stimulus event and a response event, the greater the increment in their association.* It is the time interval between a stimulus and a response, not two stimuli, with which this principle is concerned. Although it is true that in *conditioning* procedure we vary the time interval between the to-be-conditioned (or to-be-associated) stimulus (CS) and the unconditioned (or already-associated) stimulus (US), this is simply to guarantee sufficient contiguity between CS and the R which US controls. Some such principle as this is necessary on common-sense grounds; all events that occur in a lifetime are not associated indiscriminately. Its operation is also clearly evident in all experimental data on learning; the more we separate in time the S-R events to be associated, the more difficult it becomes to form the association, e.g., to get this S to elicit this R predictably. Degree of associativeness is probably a negatively accelerated decreasing function of time interval and limited to short time periods in the pure case. A number of assumptions about the nervous system are implicit in this psychological principle: (*a*) that the neural correlates of motor events are capable of becoming dependent on those of sensory events; (*b*) that these neural correlates must persist or reverberate over at least short intervals of time; and (*c*) that to become "associated," the sensory and motor correlates must be simultaneously active and somehow brought into propinquity in space. The latter notion really depends upon the underlying assumptions of materialistic, natural science.

2. *Summation.* Common-sense observation reveals certain consistencies and predictabilities in the stream of behavior: when the postman approaches the door, your dog can be expected to bark; when someone gives your child a present, he can be expected to say "Thank you." We call such predictable regularities *habits.* We also note that these habits can vary in *strength,* which we index by observing the probability with which R follows S, the amplitude of R given S, and the latency or speed with which R follows S. Furthermore, this *habit-strength* seems to increase with repetition or practice. As a general principle we may state that *successive increments in the association of a stimulus event with a response event summate to yield habit strength.* It seems reasonable that the strength of any habit should have a limit or asymptote, and empirical data do show that with large numbers of repetitions the increments per trial become imperceptible. Habit strength is an increasing negatively accelerated function of the number of repetitions. Here again the psychologist makes assumptions about neurophysiology—perhaps that at the synapses linking the neural correlates of sensory and motor events certain progressive and cumulative changes in conductivity can occur.

3. *Generalization.* Now, it is one of the fortunate things about behavior as we observe it that having learned to make a particular response in a particular situation we do not have to completely relearn this habit if the situation changes slightly, nor do we have to accomplish the behavior with precisely the original movement. Having learned to say "Thank you" in the home, your child is likely to employ the same social grace elsewhere; having learned to walk normally, we can usually hobble about pretty well with a sore ankle. It appears that habits spread or generalize among similar stimuli and similar responses. There is also a logical necessity for postulating a generalization principle.

Our habit principle says that successive increments in the association of a stimulus and a response summate; yet if there is one thing we know about behavior it is that precisely the same stimulus and response are never repeated. How, then, can there be summation among unique events? The following principle takes account of common-sense observation and the apparent paradox: *the habit-strength generated between a stimulus event and a response event generalizes to other stimulus and other response events, the amount of such generalized habit strength being a function of* (a) *the similarity between directly associated events and non-associated events and* (b) *the strength of the original association.* Laboratory evidence is consistent with such a principle; if we train a rat to jump in the air to a 1000-cycle tone, by pairing this tone repeatedly with shock, and then test with other tones of varying frequency, results like those shown in Figure 6 are typically obtained—the more

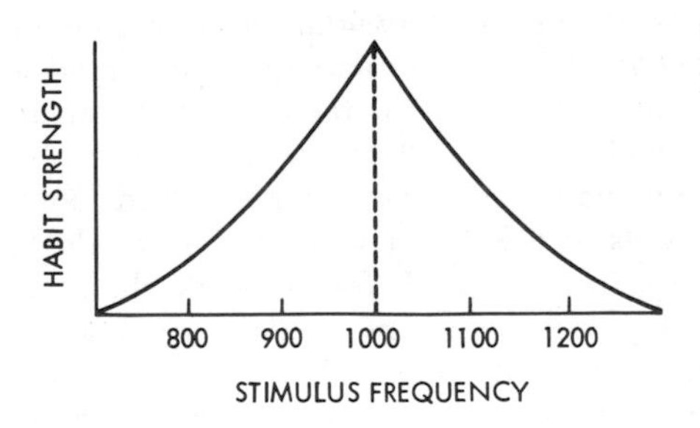

Fig. 6: An example of generalization.

similar the test tone to the conditioning tone, the greater the amplitude (speed, probability) of generalized jumping. This principle assumes that, in both sensory and motor nervous systems, the neural correlates of similar events are closer together than those of less similar events, and both sensory and motor projection systems do seem to display just such an organization.

4. *Motivation.* The mere fact that a

set of associations or habits have been learned does not guarantee that they will be utilized. Place a satiated rat at the starting point of a well-learned maze and he will probably groom himself or go to sleep rather than running; place a highly motivated worker on the job and he will usually produce more than a poorly motivated worker. Learning theorists phrase this general law of behavior somewhat as follows: *motivation combines multiplicatively with habit-strength to yield performance.* In other words, if either the motivation level or the learned habit-strength is zero, the probability of the behavior in question becomes zero; and further, this implies that within limits, at least, we can trade or exchange motivation for learning and maintain a constant output—a highly motivated student with poor training may equal in performance a poorly motivated student with good training. In the laboratory we usually index drive level operationally by the number of hours' deprivation of food or water in the case of hunger and thirst drives, by physical intensity of shock in pain drive, by the measured amount of testosterone in the blood in sex drive, and so on; with human subjects we usually depend upon such indirect indices as the subject's verbal statements, what he tells us about himself, or even, quite circularly, upon how energetically he performs.

5. *Reinforcement.* It is commonplace in the home as well as in the animal laboratory that subjects learn better when they are rewarded than when they are not. In fact, in the laboratory as well as outside of it, unrewarded or unreinforced associations tend to get weaker despite repetition, a process we call *extinction.* Some psychologists, so-called "effect" theorists like Thorndike (14) and Hull (6), have incorporated this basic empirical fact about behavior in a postulate; others accept the phenomenon but think it can be derived from other principles, for example, a sheer contiguity theorist like Guthrie (3). Since this paper is not the place for arguing fine points of theory—and, indeed, the amount of evidence that would have to be evaluated is prohibitive—I shall merely state the reinforcement principle in its usual form: *the size of the increment in association between a stimulus event and a response event varies inversely with the time interval between association and a reinforcing state of affairs and directly with the amount of reinforcement.* If a rat is learning to press a bar in order to obtain food pellets, (*a*) the greater the delay in receiving pellets the more trials it takes to reach a criterion of performance and (*b*) the smaller the size of the pellet the longer it will take. What actually constitutes this "reinforcing state of affairs"? Some theorists, like Hull, specify reduction in the intensity of a drive (hunger, thirst, pain, anxiety, and so on) as the essential condition. A possible neurophysiological correlate of reinforcement has appeared in some recent experiments at McGill—when performance was accompanied by electrical stimulation of a certain brain region in animal subjects, learning occurred; when stimulation of this region was eliminated, learning failed to take place and old habits were extinguished. What relation this may bear physiologically to drive states and their reduction I do not know.

6. *Inhibition.* Now, let us look at two paradoxes. The first, already mentioned briefly, is *extinction.* Suppose a rat has already learned to press a bar to obtain food pellets that roll down into a cup in what we call a Skinner box. Suddenly, without the rat's knowledge, we shut off the supply of pellets. For some period of time, the rat will persist in pressing the bar because he has both a learned habit and is hungry; but the rate of pressing will gradually go down until he fails to press the bar for some criterion interval, say 5 minutes, and we say he has extinguished. This in itself is paradoxical, because there is nothing in our principles so far to account for this behavior—a motivated or-

ganism is reacting to a stimulus (pressing the bar) repeatedly, S is being followed by R, yet the habit seems to be getting weaker. Why, you may ask, do we not simply postulate that unreinforced associations are weakened by repetition? If we do this, we run into another paradox, called *spontaneous recovery*. Let us now take our extinguished rat out of the Skinner box and let him rest overnight in his home cage; the next morning we put him back in the Skinner box again and, lo and behold he is busily pressing the bar again. If we claimed that the habit had been lost during the previous extinction, then it would appear that a habit could be learned spontaneously without reinforced repetitions, which would be contrary to our principles! These paradoxical phenomena are well documented, and it is situations like these that "put the pressure" on theorists.

To handle this type of situation we may postulate an inhibition principle: *the execution of any response produces an increment of inhibition toward making that response, such inhibition increasing with the effortfulness of the response and dissipating spontaneously with rest.* During learning the effects of reinforcement counteract these work-produced decrements, unless the rate of responding is too great, but as soon as reinforcements cease to be given, inhibitory tendencies mount to a point where the animal stops responding, i.e., extinction. During rest in his home cage, the work-produced inhibition dissipates and in the morning the learned habit appears again spontaneously. But haven't we explained too much and gotten ourselves into another paradox? If what we have said were literally true, animals would never be able to unlearn habits, and this doesn't jibe with facts—the recovery from successive extinctions actually becomes less and less. As a matter of fact, we can handle this without any new principles. Since the fatigue sensations accompanying work-produced inhibition constitute an unpleasant drive state, and since rest involves spontaneous reduction in this drive state, we have the necessary reinforcement conditions for new learning. During the later stages of extinction, whenever the subject stops reacting and rests while still in the situation, he is actually learning *not* to press the bar and this response-of-not-responding is being reinforced by fatigue-drive reduction. This inhibitory habit subtracts directly from the previous excitatory one and constitutes the permanent unlearning produced by extinction operations.

7. Selection. We are all familiar with situations involving response conflict. Approaching a divided staircase, we experience a momentary ambivalence as to turning left or right; warned not to touch the freshly baked and frosted cake, but seeing it right there before our eyes, we can remember oscillating between approach and avoidance. In general, *whenever two or more responses have been associated with the same stimulus, the reaction having the momentarily strongest habit strength will occur.* If the reactions in question are compatible, of course (like smiling and shaking hands), then both may occur simultaneously. When a number of incompatible reactions are associated with a common stimulus, we speak of a *divergent hierarchy*; this is a response competition situation, and probabilities of alternatives depend on contextual factors and the strengths of motives associated with each. When a number of stimuli are associated with a common reaction, we speak of a *convergent hierarchy*; this is a facilitative, transfer situation and follows the principle of generalization already discussed.

These seven principles are by no means exhaustive, they are not worded precisely as any particular theorist might state them, and they are not the exact assumptions made by any particular theorist, but they do seem to represent a set of basic notions which are common in one form or another to most psychologists who deal with learning. Let us analyze a few standard learning situations.

Maze learning. The maze is one instance of a general category we refer to as *instrumental learning*; the subject must make the correct series of responses before reinforcement is given, and hence the correct responses are "instrumental" in obtaining reward. Figure 7 diagrams a

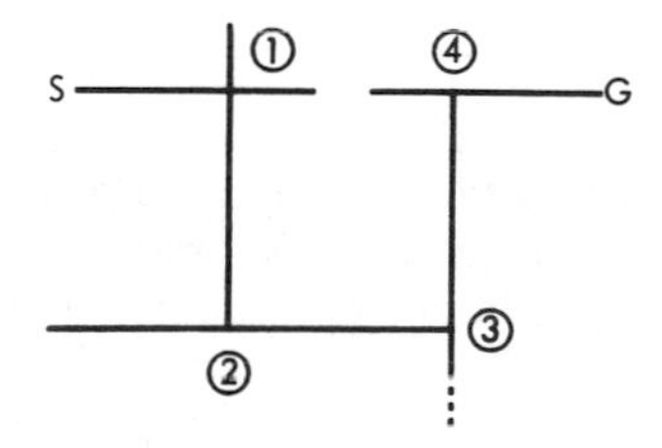

Fig. 7: A multiple T maze.

multiple-T maze, where *S* is the starting point, *G* is the goal box where a food reward is found, and the encircled numbers refer to successive choice points. At each such choice point we have a stimulus situation and two alternative reactions, turning left or right. We shall assume that our subjects are highly motivated. Now we may ask a series of questions of Nature and predict from theory what her answer will be. (*a*) *What will be the order of eliminating errors?* Prediction: other things equal, errors will be eliminated first at the choice point nearest the goal and work back progressively toward the starting point. Why? The closer an S-R association to the point of reinforcement, the greater the increment in habit-strength. Although the animal always gets to the goal, any wrong response necessarily causes a longer delay in obtaining reward, and hence the ratio always favors the correct choice. (*b*) *How will increasing the physical similarity between choice points* 3 *and* 4 *affect errors at choice point* 3? Prediction: increased similarity will increase errors at choice point 3. Why? In (*a*) above we have deduced that the right-turning response at 4 will tend to be learned earlier than the left-turning response at 3; the greater the similarity of choice points 3 and 4, the greater will be the generalization of the right-turning response from 4 back to 3, where it is an error. Since this "error" is also followed by reinforcement, it will be strengthened and compete more successfully with the correct reaction at 3. (*c*) *What effect upon errors at choice point* 3 *will lengthening the blind alley there have?* Prediction: the longer the blind, the more quickly it will be eliminated. Why? Two principles combine to yield this prediction: in the first place, the longer the blind the greater the delay in reinforcement and hence the more favorable the ratio of strengthening the correct reaction; in the second place, running a long blind produces more extinctive inhibition, which would be used to explain the fact that the rat runs less and less far into the blind as trials continue.

Classical conditioning. Pavlov (12) studied a learning situation in which one stimulus, which was not originally capable of eliciting a response, became gradually capable of doing so if it was paired with another stimulus which regularly and reliably produced this response. Figure 8

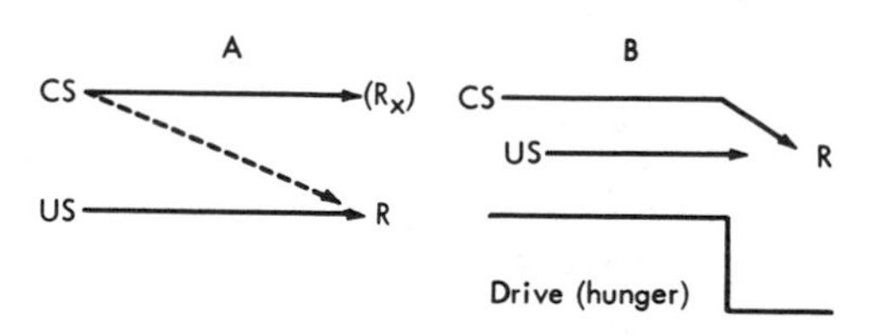

Fig. 8: A diagram of classical conditioning.

diagrams the relations assumed in conditioning in two ways, first descriptively (*A*) and then interpretively (*B*) according to the principles we have been discussing. A typical case would be that in which a dog subject learns to salivate to a tone (CS), food powder blown into the mouth being the unconditioned stimulus (US) and amount of saliva secreted being the reaction measured (R). The model given as *A* makes it appear as if this were a different "kind" of learning, simple substitution of one stimulus for another. The model given as *B* assumes that the dog must be hungry (motivated) in order to be conditioned and that the US (food powder) has a dual function, both in reliably eliciting the correct response of salivating (an unconditioned reflex in this case) and in providing reinforcement (reduction in hunger drive). Thus in conditioning, according to this view, we have contiguity between CS and R, motivation, reinforcement, and evidence for summation into habit-strength, in that the probability of the tone eliciting salivation is shown by experiment to increase with the number of repetitions. We may ask some additional questions: (*a*) *Does ease of conditioning vary with the time interval between CS and US?* Prediction: from some optimal interval (about .5 sec., presumably dependent on nervous system functioning), ease of conditioning will decrease as interval between CS and US (and hence interval between CS and R) increases. This phenomenon is regularly observed. (*b*) *What will happen as the pitch of the tone is varied?* Prediction: the less similar in frequency any test tone from the tone used during conditioning, the less will be the amount of saliva secreted (generalization). This phenomenon is regularly observed. (*c*) *What occurs if the US is discontinued?* Prediction: since reinforcement is no longer given, but the reaction keeps occurring, inhibition develops and the magnitude of the salivary reaction will decrease. This is known as extinction of a conditioned reaction.

Discrimination. Now, suppose that in the situation we have just been describing one tone is always associated with the giving of food powder (S_A) and another tone is always associated with the withholding of food powder (S_B). As shown in Figure 9, the habit-strength associated with the positive stimulus must generalize along the pitch continuum. Similarly, we assume that the inhibitory tendency associated with the negative stimulus must generalize (e.g., generalization of a response of not-responding). If we apply principle 7

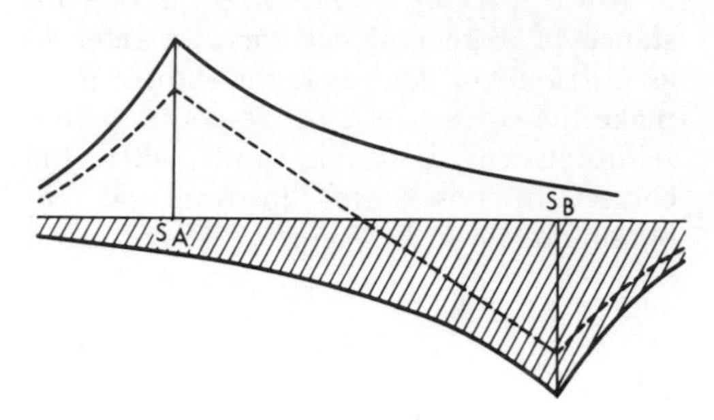

Fig. 9: Discrimination.

(selection among competing R's according to momentary habit-strength) to each point along the continuum, we in effect plot the resolution of these two gradients (dashed line). Wherever the resolution is above the base line, there will be that degree of excitatory tendency; wherever the resolution is below the base line, there will be that degree of inhibitory tendency. What this operation does in effect is to narrow the range of generalization, i.e., produce discrimination. As can be seen, it could be predicted that the more similar the two tones, the more difficult it should be to obtain discrimination, and this is precisely what is observed. To climb out into the world of everyday affairs again, it would be predicted, for example, that a man hired to reject unpainted plaques in an assembly line would have a harder job if the paint were white than if it were red.

INSUFFICIENCY OF THE SINGLE-STAGE S-R MODEL

Employed with ingenuity, even such a minimal set of tools as these can be effective in predicting and interpreting over a considerable range of behavioral phenomena. But there are some gross insufficiencies with this single-stage S-R model, particularly when one tries to handle typically human activities. For one thing, the entire problem of *perceptual organization* seems to be omitted, since it involves relations among input events, S-S integrations; for another, the development and use of *motor skills* is omitted, to the extent that such behavioral phenomena involve R-R integrations; and finally, in its unextended form, the single-stage S-R model is incapable of handling *symbolic processes,* which are so characteristic of human behavior. The reader should keep in mind, however, that in pointing out these insufficiencies of the S-R model I am not claiming that its basic principles are thereby invalid—to the contrary, in dealing with the symbolic processes, at least, the same general principles will be assumed to operate.

Perceptual organization. Our sensory, receiving systems are so planned by Nature that points on the receptor suface (e.g., the retina of the eye) are mapped in more or less point-for-point correspondence onto the sensory cortex in the brain. In other words, activity in certain sensory portions of the brain is isomorphic with the stimulus events affecting our receptors. This first stage in reception is called *projection.* Furthermore, the transmission characteristics of this projection system have been shown to be unaffected by experience, e.g., unmodifiable through learning. But it has also been shown that beyond this first projection level, point-for-point correspondence breaks down, and organization on the basis of learning replaces organization on the basis of innate "wired in" isomorphism. What is the nature of this "perceptual learning"? A very simple principle of *sensory integration* on the basis of sheer frequency can be postulated here (cf., Hebb, 4) : *the greater the frequency with which stimulus events* A *and* B *have been paired in input experience, the greater will be the tendency for the central neural correlates of one,* a, *to activate the central correlates of the other,* b. If the frequency of stimulus pairing is very high, the occurrence of one may become a sufficient central condition for evoking the central correlate of the other (evocative relation); if the frequency of stimulus pairing is less, the occurrence of one will merely "tune up" or prepare occurrence of the other (predictive relation). This principle obviously makes certain assumptions about the nervous system, specifically, that nerve cells more central than the projection system which are in fibrous contact and are caused to be simultaneously active somehow increase their capacity to fire one another.

One behavioral manifestation of the working of this sensory integration principle can be seen in the well-documeted phenomena of *closure.* We typically inspect our environment with rapid samplings and the sensory information must be sketchy, yet we perceive wholistic, complete forms; experimentally, an incomplete circle can be flashed on a screen briefly and most observers will report seeing the completed form— the given signals are sufficient to evoke the central correlates of those which are missing in a familiar form. Similar effects have been observed in language decoding: when printed words are flashed briefly on a screen, a highly regular inverse relation is found between the duration of the flash necessary for perception of a word and its frequency-of-usage in printed materials like magazines and books; the same relation is found for the auditory intelligibility of spoken words. In general, on the sensory side of behavior, it appears that the original chaos of sensations which William James postulated for the newborn infant is gradually molded into a world of perceived forms on the basis of sheer frequency of stimulus pairing in experience.

Motor skill. On the final output side of behavior we also find a "wired in" isomorphic projection system between motor cortex and muscle elements; this motor projection system is also unmodifiable through experience. But just as in the sensory system, the nervous tissues in the motor cortex more central to the motor projection system seem capable of being organized on the basis of sheer frequency of response pairing and sequencing. We can formulate a principle of *motor integration* or programming: *the greater the frequency with which response events* A *and* B *have been paired in output experience, the greater will be the tendency for the central neural correlates of one,* a, *to activate the central neural correlates of the other,* b. Again, extremely high frequency of response pairing or sequencing will result in completely evocative units (like the syllables in spoken language) and lesser frequencies will result in merely predictive integrations (like the grammatical sets or expectancies in language). S-R behaviorists have usually tried to explain motor skills like shoe tying, typing, and piano playing in terms of proprioceptive feedback—each muscle movement in a sequence produces proprioceptive self-stimulation which becomes the cue for the next response in the series—but measurements on the maximum rate of nerve fiber conduction show that there just simply isn't enough time for such control in rapidly executed skills like playing a cadenza.

The merely predictive sensory and motor integrations are interesting because they provide an experience-based stability in both decoding (receiving) and encoding (expressing) activities of the organism. Sight of a falling object is predictive of a certain striking noise; hearing Lowell Thomas say "So long..." is predictive of hearing "...until tomorrow"; seeing a piece of ice and one's hand reaching toward it is predictive of cold sensations—and in all such cases one's shock of surprise is great when these predictions occasionally are not borne out (indeed, if the lack of confirmation is not clear and intense enough, we often misperceive in accordance with what is expected). On the motor side, lighting a cigarette is predictive of blowing the match out; saying "*either* he will..." is predictive of saying "*or* he..."; unbuttoning one's shirt is predictive of peeling it off—one is usually aware of a sense of incompletion when, for some reason, such integrated sequences are interrupted. In other words, there is a syntax of perceiving and behaving just as there is for hearing and speaking a language, and this syntax seems to depend on the formation of S-S and R-R associations or integrations, as I have called them.[2]

Symbolic processes. The unextended S-R model uses certain hypothetical constructs, like habit-strength and inhibition, to make possible summary statements about a wide range of phenomena, but it does not use intervening variables—its principles concern relations between external S and external R. There are many observations we make of stimulus-response relations, however, which require the postulation of intervening variables; these observations fall generally in the category of symbolic or representational processes and, although they are certainly more characteristic of human behavior, they can also be observed in primitive form in subhuman species. Before we try to extend our principles to cover such phenomena, let us review some of the evidence that seems to require such extension.

We may look first at some evidence in rat behavior. In the typical *avoidance training* situation a buzzer sounds a few seconds before a strong shock is delivered to the animal's food-pads; in the course of reacting agitatedly to shock, the rat hits upon the correct response, perhaps turning a ratchet-wheel which eliminates the shock; after some number of trials, the rat will come to react to the *buzzer* in a way that takes account of the coming shock, e.g., will turn the ratchet-wheel before the shock comes on. In an operational sense, we could say that the rat has foresight, that it anticipates the shock, that the buzzer has become a *sign* of shock. To demonstrate that the buzzer has indeed acquired a danger significance for the rat, we can now remove the ratchet-

[2] A more detailed analysis of such sensory and motor integrations is given in a paper by this writer prepared for the Colorado Symposium on Cognition (10).

wheel and substitute a hanging chain; without ever being shocked at all in this new situation, the rat can learn to pull the chain if that act turns off the buzzer; he will be galvanized into vigorous activity by the persisting buzzer (*acquired or symbolic drive*) and will learn the new act on the basis of eliminating this anxiety-producing sound (*acquired or symbolic reinforcement*). Perhaps more striking is this demonstration of "intelligent transfer" in the rat: Initially these animals are subjected to unavoidable shock in a little pen, the experimental group having a buzzer paired with the shock and the control group also hearing the buzzer but not paired with the shock—all they can do is freeze and crouch in this situation; then both groups are trained to escape a shock in a different apparatus by running and leaping over a barrier, until they do this immediately when they feel the shock come on; finally, both groups are tested by suddenly sounding the buzzer—the experimental animals immediately run and leap the barrier *to the buzzer* whereas the control animals do not. Since the buzzer-sound has never been single-stage associated with running and leaping, we must infer that the buzzer excites *some intervening process* which is associated with this response, e.g., some shock-representing process. Many other sources of evidence from animal behavior could be cited, delayed reactions when cues are eliminated, problem solving, learning from sheer observation, and so on, but this will have to suffice.

Nearly all the phenomena we consider peculiarly human depend upon symbolic mechanisms. A simple but typical example is *semantic generalization:* a subject is shocked whenever the word JOY appears among lists of other words; some response, such as finger-flexion or electrodermal skin reaction, is recorded; then a list of test words is presented, and we find that the subject makes a generalized reaction to words like GLEE and FUN, but not to words like BOY or TOY—and this despite the fact that the latter are physically more similar to JOY than the former. It is clear that some symbolic, meaningful process, common to JOY and GLEE but not to JOY and BOY, must be mediating the transfer of reaction. Another impressive demonstration of the necessity of postulating a two-stage process in human learning, when you think of it, is the simple fact that we humans can be tremendously modified in our attitudes and subsequent behavior by merely watching a TV program like the Army-McCarthy hearings—yet at the time S is given no observable R is made. Similarly, a man can spontaneously initiate complex instrumental responses, smiling, walking out of his study, talking about a thousand-and-one things, without any observable appropriate S being present. And needless to say, the entire structure of language behavior, upon which any adequate understanding of social science must be based, is quite incomprehensible when viewed within a single-stage S-R framework, because within such a framework questions of significance, meaning, and intention can only be sidestepped.

REPRESENTATIONAL MEDIATION PROCESSES IN BEHAVIOR

We have come upon a number of facts about both animal and human behavior which cannot be handled with a single-stage S-R model. This means that we must make some additional assumptions about what goes on in the black box. In keeping with the law of parsimony, we wish to make as few assumptions as possible, and yet be able to incorporate the relevant phenomena. In order to account for S-S relations (perceptual organization) and R-R relations (motor skill), it seemed possible to cover the ground by simply postulating neural integration among the central correlates of sensory and motor signals respectively on the basis of sheer frequency of input or output pairing. What is the least amount of additional baggage needed to handle symbolic processes? In effect, we shall break our single-stage process into two stages by postulating a learned, self-stimulating, response-like process as an intervening variable. The first stage, which we shall call *decoding,* will be the association of external stimuli with these internal, symbolic responses; the second stage, which we shall call *encoding,* will be the association of the self-stimulation (produced by these symbolic reactions) with external responses. The great advantage of this solution is that, since each stage is itself an S-R process, we can simply transfer all the conceptual machinery of single-stage S-R psychology into this new model without new postulation. The critical problem, of course, is to anchor this intervening variable firmly to both antecedent and consequent observables, e.g., objective stimulus and response variables. This mediation theory is treated more fully elsewhere (9).

Development of representational mediators

We start with the fact that certain stimulus patterns have a "wired in" connection with certain behavior patterns (unconditioned reflexes) and additional stimuli have acquired this capacity (conditioned reflexes). Food powder in the mouth regularly and reliably elicits a complex pattern of food-taking reactions (including salivating, swallowing, and the like); a shock to the foot-pads regularly and reliably elicits a complex pattern of escape reactions (leaping, running, urinating, autonomic "fear" reactions, and the like). What I shall call a *significate,* then, is any stimulus which, in a given situation, regularly and reliably produces a predictable response pattern. For the naive organism, there are multitudes of stimuli which do *not* have such characteristics—a buzzer-sound does not reliably produce escape behavior like the shock does; the sound of a metronome does not reliably produce food-taking behavior like food-powder-in-the-mouth does. And for the human infant, the visual image of its bottle or the breast does not initially produce sucking, salivating, and the like. Our problem really is this: how can neutral, meaningless stimuli like these become meaningful *signs* for the organisms affected by them?

A moment's thought convinces us that ordinary single-stage conditioning does not provide a satisfactory answer—the reactions made to signs of objects (CS) are almost never the same as those made to the objects themselves (US), even for the rat subject. When the buzzer sounds in the avoidance situation, the rat behaves in such a way as to take account of the shock, not as it would to the shock itself; when the human hears the word FIRE, he behaves in a way appropriate to the whole situation including this sign, not as he would to the object referred to. But if we look into the so-called conditioning situation more carefully, we can, I think, see an answer to our problem. Many experiments on the details of the conditioning process combine to support the following conclusion: not all components of the total unconditioned reaction are conditionable to, appear in, the conditioned reaction equally; rather, certain "light-weight" components, like autonomic reactions (changed heart-rate, glandular secretion, etc.) and minimal muscular and postural adjustments (tensing, lip-licking, etc.) tend to be elicited by the CS long before the "heavy-weight" components like paw-lifting, chewing, running and the like. Incidentally, this could have been predicted from single-stage principles—"heavy-weight" reactions will involve greater amounts of work-produced inhibition.

The diagram in Figure 10 represents the formation of a representational mediation process, which we may phrase as a principle in the following way: *Whenever a neutral stimulus is contiguous with a significate, and this occurs sufficiently close to a reinforcing state of affairs, the neutral stimulus will acquire an increment of as-*

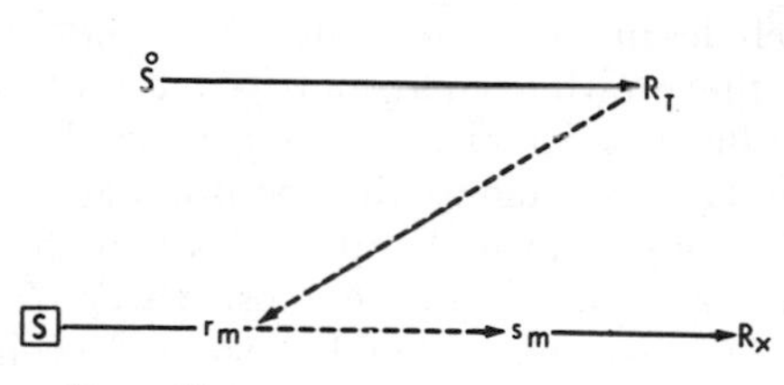

Fig. 10: Formation of a representational mediation process.

sociation with some portion of the total behavior elicited by the significate as a representational mediation process. This stimulus-producing response process (r_m) is *representational* because it is part of the very same behavior produced by the significate itself (R_T)—thus the buzzer becomes a sign ([S]) of shock (Ṡ) rather than a sign of any of a multitude of other things. It is *mediational* because the self-stimulation (s_m) produced by making this intervening reaction can become associated with a variety of instrumental acts (R_x) which "take account of" the object signified—the anxiety state generated by the buzzer may serve as a cue for turning the ratchet which eliminates the shock.

Now, with this principle in mind, let us look back at some of the symbolic phenomena which proved embarrassing to the single-stage conception. In avoidance training, shock reliably produces total escape behavior; being regularly paired with buzzer, or the traces of the buzzer sound, this initially neutral stimulus acquires some distinctive portion of the total behavior to shock (here, what we call an *anxiety reaction*); the self-stimulation from this mediator also becomes associated with the instrumental act of ratchet-turning. That this mediator has an impelling danger significance (symbolic punishment) is shown by the fact that a new instrumental act, like pulling the hanging chain, can be learned simply on the basis of turning off this stimulus. We could fairly say that this buzzer-sound has acquired a new *meaning* for the rat, has become a sign of something other than itself. The learning of meanings is central in human behavior, of course, so we look at semantic generalization in terms of this model. Prior to the experiment itself, we assume that our subject has learned the meanings of JOY, GLEE, BOY, and so forth. JOY and GLEE, as arbitrary social signs, occurred in similar total situations, in which intense pleasant reactions were taking place; therefore these signs will be associated with representational portions of these reactions. BOY will be associated with quite different mediation processes, we assume. Now, since the quality of self-stimulation depends entirely upon the reactions producing it, it follows that the s_m produced by JOY (and conditioned to a new reaction in the experiment) must be more similar to that produced by GLEE than that produced by BOY; therefore it follows from the generalization principle (applied to our stage 2, encoding) that the new reaction conditioned to JOY will transfer more to GLEE than to BOY.

As illustrated in this last analysis, the most important role of representational processes in behavior is as the common element in mediated generalization and transfer. It is this, I think, which gives the tremendous flexibility we observe in the behavior of higher animals, particularly humans. Figure 11 diagrams this mediating role. Whenever a set of stimuli are associated with the same significate, and hence with the same total behavior pattern, they must become a hierarchy of

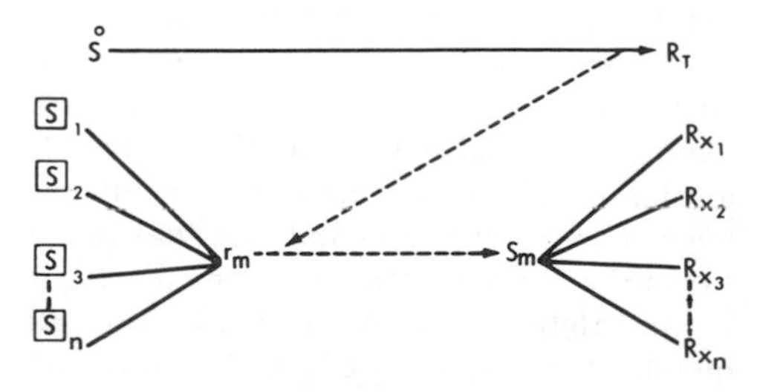

Fig. 11: Mediating role of representational process.

signs associated with the same representational process and hence have the same significance. Thus, for the rat, the sight and smell of the food pellet, the cup in which it is found, the click which announces its delivery, and so forth all become more or less equivalent signs of food reinforcement; thus, for the male human, a lace handkerchief, the smell of perfume, words like "pretty" and "nice" become partially equivalent signs of the feminine goal object. Similarly, on the other side of the behavioral equation, this common mediation process as a form of self-stimulation becomes associated with a hierarchy of overt instrumental acts. To situations which have in common a danger significance, the rat has learned to run, to crouch and freeze, to squeak, to turn a ratchet, and so on; in similar situations, the human has learned to run also, to plead verbally, to "talk his way out," and so forth. Selection among such a divergent hierarchy of responses depends upon both the absolute habit-strength of the alternatives and the contextual cues present (e.g., the human is more likely to "talk his way out" when in a locked room than when in an open field). Note the remarkable increase in flexibility such a mechanism provides: Once a novel stimulus has been associated with an established mediator (e.g., a flickering light is made a sign of shock), it immediately takes command over the entire hierarchy of instrumental acts already associated with this mediator (e.g., the rat will operate the ratchet to turn off this flickering light without new training). Similarly, once a new instrumental act has been associated with an established mediator, it immediately becomes available to all members of the class of signs having the same significance.

This analysis leads one to draw a distinction between what might be called primary and secondary learning. *Primary learning* would involve the original formation of sensory integrations (perceptions), motor integrations (skills), and representational processes (meanings); such learning is the daily work and play of the growing child, and what evidence we have indicates that this primary learning is extremely time-consuming and laborious (albeit happily dealt with as natural "play" for the most part). *Secondary learning* would involve nothing more than associative reshuffling of signs with mediators and of mediators with instrumental acts. This kind of learning is characteristic, I think, of the mature or sophisticated organism. One type of secondary learning, as shown in Figure 12,

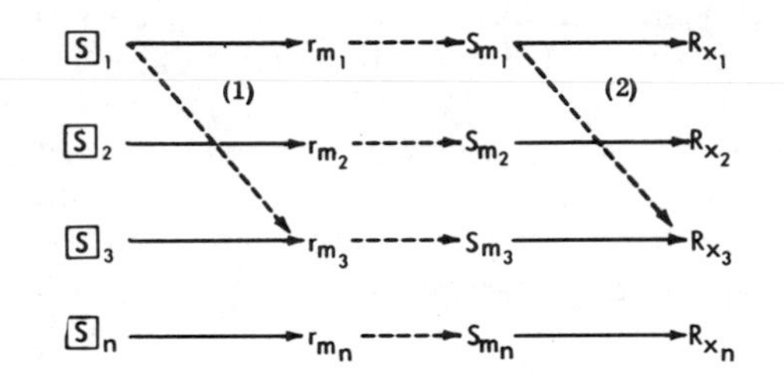

Fig. 12: Secondary learning: (1) Change in significance of a sign. (2) Change in instrumentation.

is *change in significance of a sign*: Most so-called conditioning experiments are of this sort; a dog for whom a whistle has already some significance (seldom investigated, actually) must come to associate this stimulus with a food-taking significance, indexed by salivation. A young lad for whom an officer's uniform has one significance, based on movie-going experience, comes to modify this significance somewhat after being drafted (in passing, note the relation of this analysis to status and role conceptions in sociological theory). Another type of secondary learning is *change in instrumentation*. As we have seen, the rat may be induced to modify its overt responses to a buzzer-sound (from running to ratchet-wheel turning) without changing the previously learned danger significance of this sound. The maturing human changes radically his instrumental responses to his mother and father, to his peers and superiors, as he shifts through childhood, adolescence, and maturity, without necessarily changing the significance of these people to him; similarly, he learns to behave differently to danger signals, food signals, and so on; on the other hand, the changes in his behavior to females of his species probably involve simultaneous changes in both significance and instrumentation. What is suggested, in other words, is that the average mature individual (human or animal) engages in very little "new" learning, very little in the way of forming new perceptual integrations, new skills, or even new meanings—he has the familiar physical and social world pretty well organized with respect to himself—rather, what learning he does do is concerned with occasionally shuffling relations among established perceptions, meanings, and skills, and most of us do precious little of this.

This leads rather directly into the problem of *psychological units*. As compared with the linguist, for example, the psychologist has done a very unsatisfactory job of defining his stimulus and response units on the purely descriptive level. Linguists agree among themselves quite well upon the identification of both the molecular units of messages (phonemes) and the molar units (morphemes), but it would be difficult to find two psychologists who, observing the same situation and activity, could agree on their identifications and classifications of stimuli and responses. I think we can take a hint from the linguist here, for, in actuality, he is dealing with a particular segment of the psychological domain, language, which is simultaneously both responses from one individual and stimuli for another. The linguist identifies two major levels of units: *phonemes* (which are meaningless in themselves but serve as basic discriminanda) and *morphemes* (which are meaningful units). Correspondingly, in behavior in general we have sensory and motor integrations ("phonemes") as the fine, molecular units of input and output as well as "situations" and "acts" ("morphemes"), but how are the latter to be defined?

Here again, methodologically, we can take a hint from the linguist. He classifies as "the same" all segments in messages which have the same *meaning* or significance in the code (thus the physically different endings of *walk-ed, add-ed,* and *play-ed* in spoken language are all members of the same past-tense morpheme), without inquiring into *what* this meaning may be per se. Now, it seems that the representational mediation process in behavior makes possible a similar definition of molar units in psychology. I would say that all members of the class of physically different stimuli which are associated with a common representational process (e.g., have the same significance to the organism) are "the same" as molar situations; thus, a welcoming smile, "Hi!" "Good to see you again," and the like are functionally equivalent situations in the social interaction matrix. Similarly, I would say that all members of the class which are mediated by a common representational process (e.g., express the same intention for the organism) are "the same" as molar actions; thus, a tight-lipped glare, a muttered oath directed at someone, a clenched fist, and the like are functionally equivalent acts in the social interaction matrix.

This type of learning theory analysis places a premium on developing methods of indexing representational states, e.g., measuring meaning, particularly in human organisms. Some research over the past few years has been directed chiefly along these lines (11). Dealing with language responses themselves—which, after all, are supposed to be "expressions of meaning" —attempts were made to discover a limited number of basic factors or dimensions along which meaningful reactions vary and hence can be measured. Several fairly large-scale factor analyses have already been done, and the same first three factors have appeared in each case: an *evaluative* factor, a *potency* factor, and an *activity* factor. A number of semantic measuring instruments have been devised, for specific problems on the basis of these factors, and these applications have been successful so far. It is assumed that these factors, derived in judgmental situations, are representative of at least some of the major ways in which representational mediation processes in human beings can vary.

ANALYSIS OF SOME BASIC SOCIAL MECHANISMS

It is a truism that the social behavior of human individuals is learned. The tremendous variation in personality and culture across the continents testifies to this fact. To the extent that the learning principles discovered by psychologists are valid, they should be operating in the complex matrix of social life, always conditioned, of course, by the particular situations of each culture. And if the analysis in the preceding few pages has been adequate, the most characteristic mode of learning at this level will be in terms of a two-stage process: learning of significances for signs and learning of instrumental acts which express intentions.

Assign learning—concepts, stereotypes, and symbols

In complex societies most signs representing categories and relationships are highly abstract, far removed from the earthy behaviors in which we presume meanings have their origins. We may refer to signs of this abstract sort as *assigns*, e.g., their meanings are literally assigned through repeated association with simpler signs having direct behavioral reference. An experiment recently completed will serve to illustrate this point (2). The problem was to demonstrate that the meaning acquired by a nonsense item, MEBLU, was predictable from the frequency of association of this item with simple adjectives. Subjects read a brief article, presumably taken from the *National Geographic Magazine*, in which they saw references to "the brawny Meblu" several times, "the excitable Meblu" twice, and "the friendly Meblu" only once; other groups of subjects encountered this hypothetical Meblu tribe with other adjectives and with different frequencies of association. In all cases the measured meaning of MEBLU shifted from neutral meaninglessness in a direction and to an extent predictable from the meanings of the common adjectives with which it had been associated.

Suppose now an individual is exposed repeatedly, and more or less exclusively, to the *Chicago Tribune*: He experiences the initially meaningless stimulus ALIEN in such contexts as "Aliens are *not* to be *trusted*," "Our national life is being *poisoned by* alien ideologies," and "We should *deport* these *dangerous* aliens." The resulting connotation of ALIEN is predictable from the meaningful contexts in which it appears. The important thing to consider is that most of the linguistic signs with which we deal in the mass media—Eisenhower, Fixed Farm Supports, the U. N., desegregation, and so on ad infinitum—acquire their meanings as assigns rather than through direct behavioral experience.

The notion of *stereotype* is that of a common meaning or significance attached to a class of people, not necessarily similar physically, this common significance serving to mediate a class of instrumental actions, variable with the total situation but all reflecting the common meaning of the class. Thus "stereotype" is a special case of the mediation model described in Figure 11. On the decoding side, the identification of a particular individual as a member of the stereotype (e.g., the evocation of the appropriate mediation process) usually depends upon certain combinations of cues—skin color, shape of nose, certain gestures, certain dialectic deviations in speech, and so on—but the use of the appropriate linguistic label, in the newspaper, by someone else, is also sufficient to elicit the common mediation process. Since we all use stereotypes—indeed, categorizing of this sort is the essence of concept formation or "coding" of our world—the real problem concerns the *nature* of the mediation process or meaning. Either based upon direct behaviors as shown in Figure 11 (e.g., living in a race-conscious neighborhood where gang warfare along national lines occurs), or more often based upon assign learning through the words used by parents, friends, and the media we acquire such meanings—NEGROES may be conceived as friendly, kind, and submissive or as dangerous, cruel, and aggressive depending upon such learning conditions. The classes of instrumental behaviors associated with stereotypes will necessarily reflect such significances, but will vary with the total situation in which the stereotype is experienced—Mr. A may hire a Negro for a menial job but avoid sitting next to him on the train, for example. The learning of such contextually dependent behaviors presumably depends upon the differential rewards and punishments delivered by those other individuals in the learner's environment (parents, superiors, etc.) who have prestige for him and with whom he identifies.

Abstract *symbols* play an important role in society. We have our flags, our ceremonial robes, and our briefcase in the hand. The distinguishing characteristic of the symbol is that it is a stimulus pattern which, already having its own specific representational process, is used to signify something else. For example, perception of a briefcase in a man's hand, as a visual pattern, specifically signifies a container for papers and the like; but above and beyond this specific denotation is its symbolic significance of "professional man." I suspect that we are dealing here with a rather direct process of transfer of meaning through association. Let's look at the hypothetical development of *money* as a symbol: The young child early learns to recognize nickels, dimes, and quarters, as well as paper bills, as objects having certain characteristics, round and rollable, hard and jingly, tearable and foldable and so on. But the nickel, let us say, is later used in exchange for an ice cream cone, and part of the ice cream cone significance (including its gratifying aspects) comes to occur in anticipatory fashion when nickels are held in the hand. If this were all that nickels were good for, they would presumably become a symbol of ice cream cones and nothing else. But later still another nickel is exchanged for candy, another for a ride on a bus, another to pay "protection" from the local bully. What do all these situations have in common? About the only thing is generalized gratification, getting something desired at the moment. As a result of such a learning sequence, one would expect money to acquire a very general "pleasure" and "security" significance, e.g., a very abstract symbol.

Imitation and identification

Another basic problem for social science is the transmission of culture (e.g., ways of perceiving and behaving in specified situations) from one generation to another. Deliberate training, of course, plays an important role, but much of the transmission is on a more informal, *imitative* basis. As Miller and Dollard (8) describe it, the dependent individual, not knowing the critical cues himself, learns to match his behavior to that of a model, an individual who does know the critical cues. For example, the older of two brothers in a family knows that heavy footsteps on the stairs signify the arrival of father (often with a little present of candy or toys); he runs to the door; the little toddler in the family happens to imitate the older brother, responding to his running behavior by doing the same

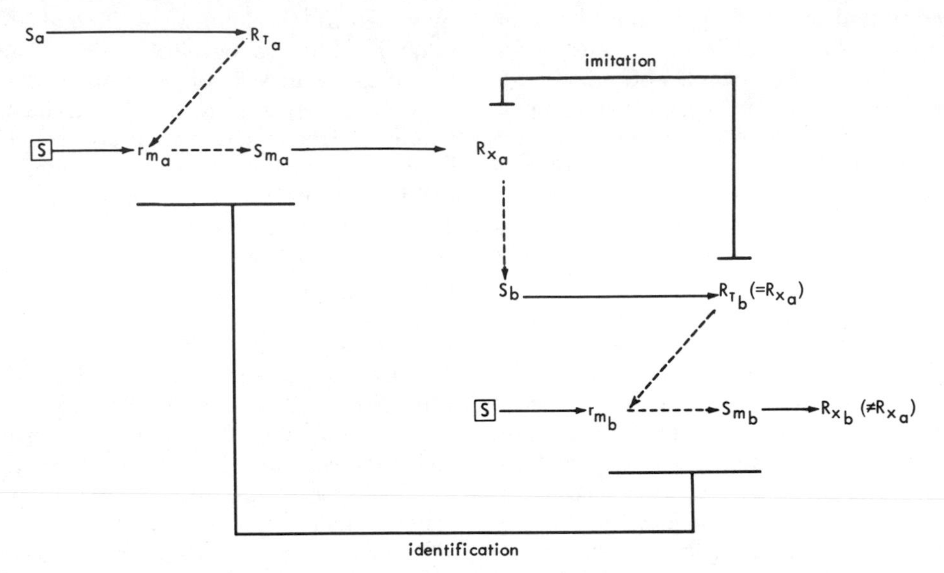

Fig. 13: The sign-learning process.

thing; both are rewarded with candy gumdrops. After a number of rewarded experiences of this kind, the younger individual will develop a generalized imitative set, a readiness to match his overt behavior with others in situations where he does not know the significance of the cues. Note that the prestige of the model here determines the probability of imitation, but this prestige in turn presumably depends upon rewarding associations.

But in many cases—most cases in adult behavior—what we observe is not simple imitation of the overt behavior but rather "appropriate" behavior in terms of the interpreted attitudes or meanings of the model. The teen-age son does not imitate his father's behavior toward girls. Not only has he had no opportunity to observe such behavior on his father's part, but times have changed and also courting customs. Rather he behaves "like his father might in this situation." When I see a person strike his thumb with a hammer, I do not behave like he does, but rather as I might behave in the same experienced situation, e.g., I "put myself in his shoes" and behave accordingly. We refer to this as identification of one person with another. But how does it operate?

Again we must use our two-stage model. Based on imitation of overt behaviors, e.g., of parent by child, the dependent individual acquires meanings of situations, people, activities, etc. that are similar to those of the model. Given such similarities in the significance of cues, the dependent individual will then behave in ways that are equivalent to those of the model, e.g., express the same intention, even though not identical and not based on direct imitation. Figure 13 illustrates the nature and development of such identifying behavior according to this type of theory. Subscript *a* refers to the model and subscript *b* to the dependent individual. Note that imitation refers to the identity of behavior to certain objects and identification to the similarity of meanings (representational processes) resulting. Thus, having imitated the authoritarian behavior of his father toward women in the family, the child develops a significance of women like that of his father, this condescending significance determining subsequent behaviors on his part to girls-in-general which, while not imitated from his father, are "like what he might do in such situations" (7). The broader import of such an analysis is that when some individuals in a society (followers) identify with another (leader), they do so on the basis of shared meanings for situations and then proceed to interpret situations as the model does and hence behave in ways equivalent to those of the model, e.g., quite literally "putting oneself in the place of another (interpretively) and behaving accordingly!"

Personality traits and culture traits

Allport (1) has defined a personality trait, in essence, as that which renders equivalent classes of situations and classes of behaviors for an individual. Thus, for a person with an "inferiority complex," any competitive situation signifies threat and he responds by avoidance, by "big talk," by compensating with some other activity in which he excels and so on, depending upon the particular context. Similarly, a person with a "stingy" trait perceives situations like requests for loans from him, sharing the tip at a meal, and spending money for presents in similar ways and behaves toward these situations in equivalent ways, e.g., ways which have in common the avoidance of giving things up. Looking at Figure 11 again, it can be seen that this mediated generalization and transfer model applies here as well; a class of signs have acquired a common significance to the individual and this common significance mediates a class of equivalent instrumental actions.

Now, when the members of a society *share,* as a result of common experience and training, a mediational mechanism such as shown in Figure 11, I think we may speak of a *culture trait.* If, for example, members of a given society agree in perceiving spirits in natural objects like trees and lakes and agree in behaving appropriately toward these objects by ceremonial avoidance of some, giving offerings to others, talking about them with animistic terms, and so on, we have a *shared significance which renders equivalent a class of stimulus situations and a class of behaviors,* and thus, in my terms, a culture trait. At a more molecular level, all of the lexical items of a language can be thought of as culture traits. The concept "red" is a common cognitive reaction to a class of functionally equivalent stimuli, as is the concept "dog," the concept "happy" and so on. I do not know whether this conception of a culture trait is consistent with sociological theory or not, but it does offer a hand-hold for analysis of the formation of such shared significances and behaviors.

SUMMARY

Starting quite frankly from the notion of the hierarchy of the sciences, this paper has tried to show how psychology, as a sort of Janus-faced discipline between the biological and social sciences, both implies certain neurophysiological conceptions and is implied by certain social science conceptions. The basic principles of simple S-R psychology were described and then shown to be insufficient (but not necessarily invalid) for an analysis of characteristically human behavior. A two-stage, mediational model was then suggested, a model which emphasizes both the decoding of situational significances and the encoding of intentions instrumentally. The implications of such a model for the observed flexibility of human behavior, for a distinction between "primary" and "secondary" learning, and for the problem of psychological units were drawn. Finally, a very superficial and sketchy application of this type of psychological theory to a few socially relevant mechanisms, like stereotyping, identification, and culture traits, was made by way of illustration.

References

1. Allport, G. W. *Personality: a psychological interpretation.* New York: Holt, 1937.

2. Dodge, J. Predicting the meanings of assigns from the measured meanings of signs with which they are associated. Unpublished doctoral thesis, University of Illinois, 1955.

3. Guthrie, E. R. *The psychology of learning.* New York: Harper, 1935.

4. Hebb, D. O. *The organization of behavior: a neurophysiological theory.* New York: Wiley, 1939.

5. Hull, C. L. Knowledge and purpose as habit mechanisms. *Psychol. Rev.*, 1930, **37**, 511–525.

6. Hull, C. L. *Principles of behavior: an introduction to behavior theory.* New York: Appleton-Century-Crofts, 1943.

7. Lazowick, L. M. On the nature of identification. *J. abnorm. soc. Psychol.*, 1955, **51**, 175–183.

8. Miller, N. E., & Dollard, J. *Social learning and imitation.* New Haven: Yale Univ. Press, 1941.

9. Osgood, C. E. *Method and theory in experimental psychology.* New York: Oxford Univ. Press, 1953.

10. Osgood, C. E. A behavioristic analysis of perception and meaning as cognitive phenomena. *Symposium on cognition.* University of Colorado, 1955.

11. Osgood, C. E., Suci, G. J., & Tannenbaum, P. H. *The measurement of meaning.* Urbana: Univ. of Illinois Press, in press.

12. Pavlov, I. P. *Conditioned reflexes.* London: Oxford Univ. Press, 1927.

13. Skinner, B. F. *The behavior of organisms: an experimental analysis.* New York: Appleton-Century-Crofts, 1938.

14. Thorndike, E. L. *Animal intelligence: experimental studies.* New York: Macmillan, 1911.

15. Tolman, E. C. *Purposive behavior in animals and man.* New York: Appleton-Century-Crofts, 1932.

Mentalism in Linguistics*

JERROLD J. KATZ

Linguists who conceive of their science as a discipline which collects utterances and classifies their parts often pride themselves on their freedom from mentalism. But freedom from mentalism is an inherent feature of the taxonomic conception of linguistics, for, according to this conception, a linguist starts his investigation with observable physical events and at no stage imports anything else.

We may expand on this inherent freedom from mentalistic commitment as follows. Utterances are stretches of physical sound. Since the primary data for a taxonomic linguistic investigation is a set of utterances elicited from informants or obtained from texts, the linguist begins with observable physical events, sounds or inscriptions. At the first stage of classification—the cataloguing of phonemes on the basis of these stretches of sound or some grouping of them—the linguist erects classes of significant sounds. At the next stage he forms classes of sequences of phonemes, thus producing a catalog of the morphemes of the language. Finally he classifies sequences of morphemes as sentential constituents of various types. Even if at some point the linguist should also consider an aspect of the speaker himself (such as his intuitive judgments about well-formedness) or an aspect of the speaker's environment (such as what he is referring to), such consideration is restricted to just those aspects that are capable of being observed by anyone who cares to carry out the same investigation. Therefore, on the taxonomic conception of linguistics, there is nowhere from the beginning to the end of a linguistic investigation, any appeal to mental capacities or mental processes. Alternatively, the taxonomic conception is a very narrow form of reductionism, which holds that every linguistic construction, at any level, reduces ultimately, by purely classificational procedures, to physical segments of utterances.

This philosophy of linguistics is never

* This work was supported in part by the U. S. Army, Navy, and Air Force under Contract DA36-039-AMC-03200(E); in part by the U. S. Air Force, ESD Contract AF 19 (628)–2487; and in part by the National Science Foundation (Grant G-16526), the National Institutes of Health (Grant MH-04737-03), and the National Aeronautics and Space Administration (Grant NsG-496). This paper, although based on work sponsored in part by the U. S. Air Force, has not been approved or disapproved by that agency.

Jerrold J. Katz, "Mentalism in Linguistics," Language, **40,** *No. 2 (1964), 124–137. Reprinted by permission of the author and publisher.*

explicitly defended in current literature, because the linguists who hold it generally assume that Bloomfield long ago conclusively refuted mentalism.[1] Hence a taxonomic linguist considers it unnecessary to put forth arguments of his own against this doctrine. When he criticizes other linguists for subscribing to a mentalistic philosophy of linguistics or for adopting a mentalistic theory of linguistic structure, he relies on Bloomfield's critique of mentalism for support.

But when we look at Bloomfield's critique of mentalism and compare the doctrine he criticized with the doctrines that modern taxonomic linguists criticize for being mentalistic, we find, curiously enough, that the most influential of the latter turn out not to be the kind of doctrine that Bloomfield attacked. Bloomfield criticized, not mentalism in the contemporary sense of this term, but a highly theologized conception of mentalism, which very few who regard themselves as mentalists would have any desire to call their own. Typical of Bloomfield's criticism of mentalism is this:[2]

> The *mentalistic* theory...supposes that the variability of human conduct is due to the interference of some non-physical factor, a *spirit* or *will* or *mind*...that is present in every human being. This spirit, according to the mentalistic view, is entirely different from material things and accordingly follows some other kind of causation or perhaps none at all.

Here and in similar statements, Bloomfield makes it clear that he is criticizing mentalism because it renders prediction and explanation of linguistic behavior in terms of causal laws completely impossible. Since Bloomfield's critique applies only to a theologized version of mentalism, it follows that taxonomic linguists are not justified in appealing to Bloomfield's 'refutation' to support their criticism of a version of mentalism according to which mental capacities and processes are subject to causal laws. Indeed, such a version of mentalism is wholly compatible with the doctrine Bloomfield called 'mechanism.'

There is, however, another feature of Bloomfield's discussion of mentalism which, though it can hardly be construed as a refutation of anything, does provide the taxonomic linguist with some basis in Bloomfield's work for his polemic against a nontheological version of mentalism. This feature is Bloomfield's endorsement of the empiricist viewpoint on scientific methodology. In this vein, he writes,[3]

[1] For obvious reasons, Bloomfield's own version of Bloomfieldian antimentalism is taken as my point of departure. But I could just as easily have taken any one of the many antimentalist positions found in the tradition of American behaviorist linguistics—for instance, with Twaddell's view of the psychological reality of linguistic concepts as expressed in his influential paper *On defining the phoneme* = *Language monographs* no. 16 (1935). There Twaddell writes:
'It is a work of supererogation to try to restate what Bloomfield has so well stated. For the sake of completeness, though, it may be justifiable to recapitulate the general principles which invalidate any "mental" definition of the phoneme.

'Such a definition is invalid because (1) we have no right to guess about the linguistic workings of an inaccessible "mind", and (2) we can secure no advantage from such guesses. The linguistic processes of the "mind" as such are quite simply unobservable; and introspection about linguistic processes is notoriously a fire in a wooden stove. Our only information about the "mind" is derived from the behavior of the individual whom it inhabits. To interpret that behavior in terms of "mind" is to commit the logical fallacy of "explaining" a fact of unknown cause by giving that unknown cause a name, and then citing the name x as the cause of the fact. "Mind" is indeed a summation of such x's, unknown causes of human behavior.'

Other particularly explicit statements of the antimentalist viewpoint against which I intend to argue include C. F. Hockett, 'Biophysics, linguistics, and the unity of science', *American scientist* 1948, 558–72; and a work as recent as R.M.W. Dixon, *Linguistic science and logic* (The Hague, 1963).

[2] L. Bloomfield, *Language* 32 (New York, 1933).

[3] Bloomfield, 'Linguistic aspects of science', *International encyclopedia of unified science* 1.231 (Chicago, 1938).

...we can distinguish science from other phases of human activity by agreeing that science shall deal only with events that are accessible in their time and place to any and all observers (strict *behaviorism*) or only with events that are placed in coordinates of time and space (*mechanism*), or that science shall employ only such initial statements and predictions as lead to definite handling operations (*operationalism*), or only terms such as are derivable by rigid definition (*physicalism*).

The charge against mentalism made by those who cite Bloomfield in support of their dismissal of mentalism, then, is that mentalistic theories deal with events that do not meet the methodological demands of behaviorism, mechanism, operationalism, and physicalism. They believe the charge to be justified because they believe that a theory of linguistic structure which deals with such events is based on bad scientific methodology.

It is extremely important to note that Bloomfield goes on to say,[4]

...These several formulations [behaviorism, mechanism, operationalism, and physicalism], independently reached by different scientists, all lead to the same delimitation, and this delimitation does not restrict the subject matter of science but rather characterizes its method.

Bloomfield is here at pains to stress that the empiricist viewpoint on scientific methodology does not restrict the range or kind of phenomena that a scientist can describe and explain. The present paper denies just this claim. Against it, I argue two points. First, the taxonomic linguist's criticism of mentalistic theories for being based on bad scientific methodology fails through the inadequacy of the empiricist viewpoint on which it depends. That is, I shall argue that the empiricist viewpoint does not deserve to be the standard by which any conception of linguistics or any other science is judged. Second, a mentalistic theory is better than a taxonomic one because the delimitation imposed by the empiricist viewpoint, and accepted by taxonomic linguists, so severely restricts the character of a taxonomic theory that the range and kind of linguistic phenomena for which such a theory can account is considerably narrower than the range and kind that a mentalistic theory can handle. If these two points are both established, there should be an end to the criticizing of linguistic theories for being mentalistic; and, more significantly, there should be an end to taxonomic theories themselves.

One may formulate the controversy between taxonomic linguistics and mentalistic linguistics in terms of the following opposition. The linguist who adopts a causal conception of mentalism is contending that purely linguistic theories cannot succeed in predicting and explaining the facts of linguistic performance without making reference to the mental events, capacities, and processes of speakers, i.e., that linguistic theories must contain concepts which enable linguists to formulate the principles of mental operation that underlie speech. On the other hand, the linguist who adopts the taxonomic conception of linguistics is contending that purely linguistic theories can succeed in predicting and explaining the facts of linguistic performance.

It might appear that there is no way to settle this controversy short of some abstruse examination of the philosophical principles underlying the taxonomic and mentalistic positions, but this is false. The dispute can be settled simply by determining whether a taxonomic or a mentalistic theory is, in principle, better able to account for what is known about the general facts of linguistic phenomena. This determination can be made by showing that a mentalistic theory accounts for everything that a taxonomic theory accounts for, and, in addition and with no extension of the theory, for many things that the taxonomic theory must fail to account for. This is the spirit of Chomsky's criticisms of theories of grammar constructed within

[4] Ibid. 231.

the taxonomic framework.[5] Unfortunately, Chomsky's arguments are often not taken in this way but are taken rather as trying to establish a new kind of taxonomic system.

The basic point of Chomsky's criticisms is that the failure of a taxonomic theory to handle the full range of facts about linguistic structure is due to the failure of such theories to concern themselves with mental capacities, events, and processes. The point which has been missed by those who interpret his arguments as trying to establish a new kind of taxonomic system is that only by introducing mentalistic concepts into our theories do we provide ourselves with the conceptual machinery which makes it possible to account for the full range of linguistic facts.

The general form of Chomsky's criticism of taxonomic linguistics is summarized as follows. The best kind of theory is one which systematizes the widest range of facts; hence a mentalistic theory is better than a taxonomic one because the former can handle any fact that the latter can handle, whereas the latter is unable to handle many kinds of facts that the former handles easily and naturally. The difference in the facts that these theories can handle is a direct function of the difference in the conceptual machinery they contain.

If it is to be shown that mentalism thus succeeds where taxonomic linguistics fails, it will be necessary to clarify certain features of the mentalist conception of linguistic theories. In particular, it must be made clear just what a mentalist means when he says that reference to mental states is a necessary aspect of any adequate linguistic theory, and just what status he intends mentalistic concepts to have. Unless his meaning is clarified, it will remain unclear whether it is the reference to mental states that is responsible for the margin of explanatory power by which mentalistic theories excel taxonomic theories. Unless the status of his concepts is clarified, it will remain open for the taxonomic linguist to claim that, although the mentalist says that his reference to mental states is a reference to things or events within the causal realm, the actual way in which this reference is made gives no clue how mental states might stand as causal antecedents of physical events like vocalization and speech sounds. These matters must be clarified in such a way that those who construe Chomsky's arguments as seeking to establish a new kind of taxonomic system cannot claim that the machinery in Chomsky's theories which produce the margin of explanatory power by which they are more empirically successful have no psychological reality but are merely new kinds of data-cataloguing devices.

First, how can mental events like those referred to in mentalistic linguistic theories be links in the causal chain that contains also vocalizations and sound waves? To explain how speakers are able to communicate in their language, the mentalist hypothesizes that, underlying a speaker's ability to communicate, there is a highly complex mechanism which is essentially the same as that underlying the linguistic ability of other speakers. He thus views the process of linguistic communication as one in which such mechanisms operate to encode and decode verbal messages. The aim of theory construction in linguistics is taken to be the formulation of a theory that reveals the structure of this mechanism and explains the facts of linguistic communication by showing them to be behavioral consequences of the operation of a mechanism with just the structure that the formulated theory attributes to it.

The step of hypothesizing such a mechanism in the process of theory construction in linguistics is no different from

[5] Cf. N. Chomsky, 'A transformational approach to syntax' and 'Current issues in linguistic theory', *The structure of language: Reading in the philosophy of language,* ed. by J. Fodor and J. J. Katz (Englewood Cliffs, N. J., 1964).

hypothetical postulation in theory construction in any other branch of science where some component of the system about which we wish to gain understanding is inaccessible to observation. The linguist can no more look into the head of a fluent speaker than a physicist can directly observe photons or a biologist directly inspect the evolutionary events that produced the human species. The linguist, like the physicist and biologist, can only achieve scientific understanding by constructing a model of the system which contains a hypothesis about the structure of the components of the system that are not observable. If the logical consequences of the model match the observable behavior of the system and would not do so without the hypothesis, the scientist may say that this hypothesis accounts for the behavior of the system in terms of the behavior of the unobservable but causally efficient component. If the model is the simplest one which enables the scientist to derive all the known facts and predict previously unknown ones as effects of the hypothesized component, he can assert that his model correctly pictures the structure of the system and its unobservable components. In this way, a linguist can assert that his theory correctly represents the structure of the mechanism underlying the speaker's ability to communicate with other speakers.

This mechanism is, according to the mentalist linguist, a brain mechanism, a component of a neural system. It is inaccessible to observation in the sense that, even if the linguist could look inside a speaker's head, he would be unable to figure out the structure of the mechanism from the electrochemical events going on there. But, as I have just pointed out, this limitation does not doom the linguist's program of discovering the nature of the speaker's ability to communicate in language. Hence it cannot be taken as grounds for supposing that a linguistic theory is not about a brain mechanism and its concepts are not about mental states. It is perhaps because, from the behaviorist viewpoint, this observational inaccessibility of the neural mechanism represents the boundary of the subject matter of linguistics, that taxonomic linguists have denied that theoretical concepts in a linguistic theory can have psychological reality. It would certainly explain why they have confined themselves to the corpus of elicitable utterances, behavioral responses to such utterances, and observable features of the context in which utterances occur, and why they have refused to regard the internal psychological properties of speakers as part of the subject matter of a linguistic theory.

Of course, the view that the reality of theoretical concepts in linguistics is mentalistic yet (in principle) irreducible to brain states, is a form of psychophysical dualism that a linguist should be reluctant to accept. But holding that brain states are observationally inaccessible and, at the same time, that linguistic constructions have an underlying psychological reality does not commit one to accepting such a dualism.

Let us suppose that the linguist constructs a theory by inferring hypothetically the characteristics of the mechanism underlying linguistic communication. His inference begins by positing a mechanism of which the observable events of linguistic communication are causal consequences. He invents a theory about the structure of this mechanism and the causal chain connecting the mechanism to observable events, to explain how these internal causes produce linguistic communication as their effect. Now it is clear that the linguist, though he claims that his theory describes a neurological mechanism, cannot immediately translate the theory into neurological terms, i.e. into talk about synapses, nerve fibers, and such. But—and this is the crucial point in showing that the mentalist is not a psychophysical dualist—this failure to have a ready neurological translation means only that he cannot yet specify what kind of physical realization of his theoretical description is inside the speaker's head. Since linguistics and neurophysiology are independent fields, it does not matter for the linguist what kind of physical realization is there. For the purpose of linguistic investigation, it is immaterial whether the mechanism inside the speaker's head is in reality a network of electronic relays, a mechanical system of cardboard flip-flops and rubber bands, or, for that matter, a group of homunculi industriously at work in a tiny office. All of these possibilities, and others, are on a par for the linguist as physical realizations of this mechanism, so long as each is isomorphic to the representation of linguistic structure given by the theory of the language. The critical distinction is, then, between an abstract, formal characterization of linguistic structure—the theory itself—and a physical system of some kind which instances this structure.[6] Discovering what kind of a physical system in the human brain instantiates the representation of structure given by a linguistic theory is the task of the neurophysiologist. The linguist's task is to provide a theory which represents the structure that any physical system must possess if it is to be capable of linguistic communication as we know it.

The theoretical constructions used by a mentalist linguist in building his theories are intended by him to have psychological reality. They do not, for the linguist, require translation into neurophysiological terms, even though reference to mental states is construed as reference to brain states. This is why the events to which the mentalist's constructions refer can stand as links in the causal chain that contains vocalizations and sound waves as other links.

Why, now, do mentalistic linguistic theories excel taxonomic linguistic theories in descriptive and explanatory power, and why must mentalistic concepts be given credit for this excellence?

The three fundamental questions with which a synchronic description of a particular language deals are these:

(1) What is known by a speaker who is fluent in a natural language? That is, what facts about his language underlie his ability to communicate with others in that language?

(2) How is such linguistic knowledge put into operation to achieve communication? That is, how does a speaker use such linguistic knowledge to convey his thoughts, opinions, wishes, demands, questions, emotions, and so on to other speakers?

(3) How do speakers come to acquire this ability? That is, what innate dispositions and developmental processes are responsible for transforming a nonverbal infant into a fluent speaker?

An answer to (1) may be referred to as a 'linguistic description'.[7] A linguistic description has three components: syntactic, phonological, and semantic. If the linguistic description is a mentalistic theory, the syntactic component is a generative system which enumerates strings of minimally syntactically functioning units (which may be called formatives), together with a description of their syntactic structure. These structural descriptions, the output of the syntactic component in a linguistic description, are the input to both the phonological component and the semantic component. These two components are interpretative systems: the former interprets the abstract, formal descriptions of the syntactic structure of sentences as representations of vocal sound by assigning them a phonetic shape; the latter interprets them as meaningful messages. That is, the semantic component converts the outputs of the syntactic com-

6 Cf. H. Putnam, 'Minds and machines', *Dimensions of mind,* ed. by S. Hook (New York, 1960).

7 For further discussion of this concept cf. J. J. Katz and P. Postal, *An integrated theory of linguistic descriptions* (Cambridge, Mass., 1964).

ponent into the messages that the sentences communicate to those who understand the language. The phonological and semantic components have no systematic connection with each other: one is concerned with pronunciation and the other with conceptualization.

An answer to (2) consists of at least two procedures. One is a 'sentence recognition procedure', whose function is to assign to any given perceived utterance a phonetic representation, a syntactic description, and a semantic interpretation. The function of the other procedure is to choose an appropriate syntactic structure for any message that the speaker wishes to communicate and to provide a phonetic representation for that structure; it is a 'sentence production procedure'. Together, the two procedures determine how the knowledge of the language embodied in the linguistic description is used by a speaker to understand and produce sentences.

An answer to (3) is a theory of language acquisition. Such a theory explains how a nonverbal infant who is exposed in the normal way to a sample of sentences and nonsentences, and perhaps other data as well, comes to possess a linguistic description and procedures of sentence recognition and sentence production.

The first of the three questions is logically prior to the others. We must know what linguistic facts a speaker knows before we can say how those facts enable him to communicate and before we can say how he acquired them: linguistic description must precede inquiry into the nature of language use and acquisition. But this logical priority does not mean that the attempt to answer (2) and (3) must wait for a full answer to (1); rather, it means that substantive contributions toward an answer to (1) must be available in order that attempts to answer (2) and (3) can begin. Furthermore, it means—and this is critical—that the kind of answer that will be given, or sought, for (2) and (3) is determined by the kind of answer which is given or sought for (1). Since (2) is, in the same sense, logically prior to (3), the same applies to these two.

The basic fact about languages that a full answer to (1) must account for is that speakers can understand indefinitely many sentences never before encountered by them. So ubiquitous and commonplace is this fact that its theoretical significance is often missed: the very fact that almost every sentence we encounter is heard for the first time keeps us from fully appreciating how amazing it is that a fluent speaker is able to understand new sentences. But if we think about learning a foreign language, the theoretical significance of this feat becomes apparent immediately. We do not credit a person with mastery of a foreign language if he is only able to understand those sentences which he has been previously taught. The test of fluency is whether he can understand sentences that he has not been taught. The theoretical significance of understanding new sentences is that this ability is the test of whether one has mastery of a natural language.

To account for this feat in answering (1), the grammar must take the form of a system of rules which describe the structure of every sentence that a speaker would (in the absence of linguistically irrelevant psychological limitations) understand if he were to encounter it. Such rules must describe an infinite set of sentences because in a natual language there is no longest sentence. Given a sentence composed of n formatives, there is always another composed of $n + r$ formatives, formed from the first by various syntactic procedures, for instance by replacing a noun by a noun and a modifier which contains another noun, itself replaceable by a noun and a modifier, and so on. There will, of course, be a point at which still longer sentences cannot be either produced or understood by normal speakers in normal situations; but this limitation has to do with perceptual limits, the finite bound on memory storage, human mortality, and other linguistically inessential considerations. If we mistakenly identify these speech limitations with a finite-length limitation on what qualifies as a grammatical sentence of the language, we are forced to the absurd conclusion that, as such limitations are weakened (say, by the use of paper and pencil), either a new language is being used or the old one has undergone radical change.

This shows that a taxonomic grammar which describes only the sentences in a corpus fails to be empirically adequate: infinitely many grammatical sentences are left undescribed. Some taxonomic grammars are intended to describe the full set of sentences—that is, to segment and classify not only the sentences in a corpus but also of those that might be elicited and those that are of the same syntactic form as the elicited and elicitable sentences. But this should not obscure the theoretically more significant fact that such grammars are nonetheless put forth as data-cataloguing systems, the data being strings of syntactically well-formed formatives. Accordingly, their rules have no psychological reality, and cannot be construed as accounting for the knowledge that a speaker has which enables him to understand new sentences of his language. Furthermore, such rules cannot be the basis for an answer to (2), since an answer to (2) must relate the speaker's knowledge of the structure of sentences to procedures for applying this knowledge. For the same reason, such rules cannot be the basis for an answer to (3), since an answer to (3) is an input-output device which explains how a sample of sentences and nonsentences as input gives as output a linguistic description and procedures of sentence production and sentence recognition.

To show that a mentalistic theory of linguistic communication can succeed in answering (1), (2), and (3), and why mentalistic concepts are essential in giving it that power, we require an overall model which shows how the mechanism of linguistic communication operates in an actual situation. Such a model represents the most rudimentary form of the theory of linguistic communication which mentalists seek to construct, and is thus a first approximation toward an exact formulation of that theory in its fully sophisticated form. It should be stressed, however, that even as a first approximation such a model shares with the fully elaborated and precise theory the character and status of a hypothetically inferred theoretical construction.

Given that both speaker and hearer are equipped with a linguistic description and procedures for sentence production and recognition, we can reconstruct the communication situation in these terms. The speaker, for reasons that are biographically but not linguistically relevant, chooses some message he wants to convey to the hearer. He selects some thought he wishes to express to him, some command he wants to give him, or some question he needs to ask him. This message is, we may assume, in whatever form the semantic component of his linguistic description uses to represent the meaning content of thoughts, commands, questions, or the like. The speaker then uses the sentence production procedure to obtain an abstract syntactic structure having the proper conceptualization of his thought, command, or question as its semantic interpretation. This procedure helps him find a sentence that is suitable to the circumstances by rejecting all syntactic structures which, though they bear the proper semantic interpretation, are for sentences that are too long, syntactically too complicated, too pedantic, etc. After he has a suitable syntactic structure, the speaker utilizes the phonological component of his linguistic description to produce a phonetic shape for it. This phonetic shape is encoded into a signal that causes the speaker's articulatory system to vocalize an utterance of the sentence. The sound waves of which these utterances consist are transmitted through the air and, after they reach the hearer's auditory system, are converted into a signal which is decoded into a phonetic shape. On the basis of that shape the hearer's sentence recognition procedure then provides a syntactic structure. That is, the procedure converts the signal produced by hearing the utterance into a phonetic shape whose physical realization is what reached the ear, and recovers the syntactic structure that the speaker originally chose as a formalization of his message. Once the hearer is in possession of this syntactic structure, he employs the semantic component of his linguistic description to obtain its semantic interpretation. He thus represents to himself the same message that the speaker wished to convey to him, and communication has taken place.

Although this model is phrased as if the processes described were conscious, no such assumption is involved. It is not an essential feature of mentalism that the processes postulated by the mentalist as going on inside a speaker's head should be open to the speaker's conscious awareness. This point alone ought to remove one source of opposition to mentalism in modern linguistics.

Within the framework of the above model of linguistic communication, every aspect of the mentalistic theory involves psychological reality. The linguistic description and the procedures of sentence production and recognition must correspond to independent mechanisms in the brain. Componential distinctions between the syntactic, phonological, and semantic components must rest on relevant differences between three neural submechanisms of the mechanism which stores the linguistic description. The rules of each component must have their psychological reality in the input-output operations of the computing machinery of this mechanism. The ordering of rules within a component must, contrary to the claims of Bloomfield and many others,[8] have its psychological reality in those features of this computing machinery which group such input-output operations and make the performance of operations in one group a precondition for those in another to be performed.

There are two further points concerning the superiority of a mentalistic theory. First, since the psychologist and the mentalistic linguist are constructing theories of the same kind, i.e. theories with the same kind of relation to the neurophysiology of the human brain, it follows that the linguist's theory is subject to the requirement that it harmonize with the psychologist's theories dealing with other human abilities and that it be consistent with the neurophysiologist's theories concerning the type of existing brain mechanisms. A linguistic theory that meets this requirement will have a wider range of facts into whose explanation it can enter and so will be a better theory than one which is otherwise equivalent to it in explanatory power. Such a theory enters into the explanation of many of those psychological theories with which it harmonizes. Theories of perception, theories of memory, of thinking, of learning, and other psychological theories leave open various questions about the effect of language on these processes and the effect of these processes on language; only a mentalistic theory of linguistic structure can hope to answer them. Further, by subjecting a linguistic theory to this requirement we make it more easily testable. For the requirement enables us to refute a linguistic theory if we can find psychological theories or facts that are inconsistent with it or neurophysiological accounts

[8] This, then, is the answer to Hockett's question about how to construe ordering otherwise than historically; cf. 'Two models of linguistic description', *Word* 10.233 (1954): '...if it is said that the English past tense form *baked* is "formed" from *bake* by a "process" of "suffixation", then no matter what disclaimer of historicity is made, it is impossible not to conclude that some kind of priority is being assigned to *bake* as against *baked* or the suffix. And if this priority is not historical, what is it?'

which describe brain structure in a way that precluded the linguistic theory from being isomorphic to any of the structures in the human brain. Again, a fruitful requirement like this can only be imposed on a mentalistic theory.

Second, a mentalistic theory also can provide a psychological reality for linguistic universals. Instead of linguistic universals being treated simply as common features of the linguistic description of every language, as they are in the the taxonomic view, the fact that such common features are universal, i.e. are necessary features of natural languages, is explained in terms of the psychology of human language learners, the one constant feature among all the individual differences between speakers of different natural languages, and all the differences between the situations in which they learn to speak. One clear-cut sense of psychological reality for linguistic universals is that proposed by Chomsky.[9] According to Chomsky's account, there are two kinds of linguistic universals, substantive and formal. The formal universals are specifications of the form of the rules that appear in each of the components of any empirically successful linguistic description of a natural language; the substantive universals are theoretical terms which enter into the formulation of the rules of particular linguistics descriptions. Chomsky's hypothesis is that the child is innately equipped with a language-learning device that contains such linguistic universals and a simplicity principle; the latter enables him to acquire the simplest linguistic description of the form determined by the linguistic universals which accords with the sample of utterances he is exposed to. Linguistic universals thus have psychological reality as part of the internal structure of the innate mechanism responsible for a child's acquisition of a language. Such a hypothesis, if true, explains why there should be a certain structure and content found in every language: they are found in every language because they are implanted by the innately given language-learning device that makes the acquisition of a natural language possible for normal humans.

Finally, why must this kind of psychological reality be attributed to the concepts of a mentalistic theory? Why can they not be regarded as mere fictions or as new kinds of data-cataloguing devices?

Bloomfield presents a particularly clear statement of the view against which I will argue. He writes,[10]

> We can describe the peculiarity of these plurals [*knives, mouths,* and *houses*] by saying that the final [f, θ, s] of the underlying singular is replaced by [v, ð, z] before the bound form is added. The word 'before' in this statement means that the alternant of the bound form is the one appropriate to the substituted sound; thus, the plural of *knife* adds not [-s], but [-z]: 'first' the [-f] is replaced by [-v], and 'then' the appropriate alternant [-z] is added. The terms 'before', 'after', 'first', 'then', and so on, in such statements, tell the *descriptive order*. The actual sequence of constituents, and their structural order...are a part of the language, but the descriptive order of grammatical features is a fiction and results simply from our method of describing the forms; it goes without saying, for instance, that the speaker who says *knives,* does not 'first' replace [f] by [v] and 'then' add [-z], but merely utters a form (*knives*) which in certain features differs from a certain other form (namely, *knife*).

Bloomfield says that the speaker 'merely utters a form (*knives*)'. I have argued that in order to answer the three fundamental questions of linguistics, this is not enough; it is necessary to explain why the speaker says this rather than *knifes*. The mentalist, I have argued, explains this fact of English pluralization by crediting the speaker of English with a linguistic description that contains both the kind of rules and the kind of ordering restriction that Bloomfield mentions. The mentalist asserts that an English speaker says

9 Chomsky, review of *Verbal behavior* by B. F. Skinner, *Lg.* 35.26–58 (1959).

10 Bloomfield, *Language* 213.

knives rather than *knifes* because sentences whose underlying syntactic form is... *knife* + *pl*... are produced by using such rules and ordering restrictions to pass from this syntactic form to its phonological realization *knives*. Presumably Bloomfield's answer to this would be that one need not treat such rules and ordering restrictions as psychologically real; they may be regarded as fictions and still enable us to correctly predict the way in which speakers of English pluralize.

Here is the crux of the issue. It is true that these features of the grammar may be regarded as fictions and still enable us to predict the facts of English pluralization; but what is required for prediction and what is required for explanation are two different things. A few examples show this quite dramatically. Suppose I have a betting system for the races that never fails to pick the winner. The system may be based on numerology, astrology, geneaology, or what have you. Suppose, further, that my system predicts that a certain horse will win in the third race, and he does. If any basis for correctly predicting an event is also an acceptable explanation for the event once it has occurred, then we are forced to the absurd conclusion that the horse won because my system predicted it. Again, suppose I predict that Jones will be sick because he drank my home brew, and it is known that 95 per cent of those who drink it become sick: is it an explanation of Jones's illness that he drank my home brew? Obviously not, since to explain why Jones became sick we must explain how he differs from the 5 per cent who can drink home brew without becoming sick.[11] The crucial question, then, is why we cannot explain linguistic facts if we treat the rules and ordering restrictions of a linguistic description as simply convenient fictions.

As described above, the mentalist explains the facts about a speaker's and hearer's linguistic performance in terms of a model that reconstructs the process by which a message is transmitted from the speaker to the hearer through the speaker's encoding the message in the form of an utterance and the hearer's decoding that utterance back to the speaker's original message. Such a model explains why an utterance has a certain linguistic property, and what function that property has in the process of communication, by locating the property in the causal chain which links the utterance on one side to the neurophysiological mechanisms that perform the encoding and articulation, on the other side to those that accomplish the perception and decoding. But if, with the taxonomic viewpoint, we interpret any of the elements of the mentalist's description of the process of communication as merely fictions, rather than references to neurophysiological links in such a causal chain, the whole explanation collapses. For that interpretation would amount to the claim that there are gaps in the causal chain. If there are gaps, we cannot account for the causal antecedents of a linguistic property and of its effects. The Bloomfieldian mode of interpreting features of a linguistic description is like contending that the pressure of a gas on the walls of its container is the effect of molecules striking the walls, and at the same time denying that a molecule is a real physical object. The hypothesis of a mechanism of linguistic communication, with the kind of structure attributed to it by an optimal linguistic description, can explain how linguistic communication takes place only if the mechanism and all its features have the same ontological status as the utterance itself. The hypothesized mechanism must be capable of affecting the articulatory system of a speaker so as to produce an utterance, and capable of being affected by the output of his receptor system when stimulated by an utterance. This

[11] Cf. S. Bromberger, *The concept of explanation* (dissertation, Harvard University, 1960), for the first set of convincing examples of this kind to be proposed.

implies, however (to stress it again), no commitment for the mentalist to any particular kind of physical realization for the linguistic description, except that whatever is inside the speaker's head must be capable of causal connection with the physical sounds that serve as the vehicle of linguistic communication.[12]

The taxonomic linguist assumes that only his conception and treatment of linguistics saves the linguist from countenancing such occult mental entities as a 'spirit' and 'soul'. The truth is, rather, that mentalism also—in the only sense of 'mentalism' for which any serious claim to validity is made—avoids those occult entities. Both taxonomic and mentalist linguists deal exclusively with physically real events and structures. Both leave it to other sciences to determine the exact nature of the physical reality of the phenomena they theorize about. Just as the taxonomic linguist must leave it to the physicist to tell him about the physical reality of sound waves, and (if he is behavioristically inclined) to the physiologist to tell him about the physical reality of muscular contractions and glandular secretions, so the mentalist linguist must leave it to the neurophysiologist to tell him about the neurophysiological realization of his abstract linguistic description.

The actual difference between the taxonomic and the mentalistic conceptions of linguistics lies in what linguistic theories built on each of these conceptions can accomplish by way of answering questions (1), (2), and (3). We have found that the taxonomic linguist confines linguistic investigation to stating those facts about the structure of a natural language which can be formulated within the framework of a classificational system, while the mentalist goes far beyond this in seeking a full answer to all three questions. This difference is important: it justifies us in rejecting the taxonomic conception in favor of the mentalistic one. Taxonomic linguistics can only describe the utterances of a language; mentalistic linguistics not only can do this but can also explain how speakers communicate by using the utterances, and how the ability to communicate is acquired. Instead of the taxonomic linguist having a just complaint against the mentalist for appealing to occult entities, the mentalist has a just complaint against the taxonomic linguist for excluding from linguistics, a priori and arbitrarily, just what it is most important for this science to do. The freedom from mentalism inherent in the taxonomic conception of linguistics is its inherent weakness.

12 For a general discussion of the fictionalist view of scientific theories cf. Katz, 'On the existence of theoretical entities', in preparation.

Methodological Preliminaries

NOAM CHOMSKY

1. GENERATIVE GRAMMARS AS THEORIES OF LINGUISTIC COMPETENCE

This study will touch on a variety of topics in syntactic theory and English syntax, a few in some detail, several quite superficially, and none exhaustively. It will be concerned with the syntactic component of a generative grammar, that is, with the rules that specify the well-formed strings of minimal syntactically functioning units (*formatives*) and assign structural information of various kinds both to these strings and to strings that deviate from well-formedness in certain respects.

The general framework within which this investigation will proceed has been presented in many places, and some familiarity with the theoretical and descriptive studies listed in the bibliography is presupposed. In this chapter, I shall survey briefly some of the main background assumptions, making no serious attempt here to justify them but only to sketch them clearly.

Linguistic theory is concerned primarily with an ideal speaker-listener, in a completely homogeneous speech-community, who knows its language perfectly and is unaffected by such grammatically irrelevant conditions as memory limitations, distractions, shifts of attention and interest, and errors (random or characteristic) in applying his knowledge of the language in actual performance. This seems to me to have been the position of the founders of modern general linguistics, and no cogent reason for modifying it has been offered. To study actual linguistic performance, we must consider the interaction of a variety of factors, of which the underlying competence of the speaker-hearer is only one. In this respect, study of language is no different from empirical investigation of other complex phenomena.

We thus make a fundamental distinction between *competence* (the speaker-hearer's knowledge of his language) and *performance* (the actual use of language in concrete situations). Only under the idealization set forth in the preceding paragraph is performance a direct reflection of competence. In actual fact, it obviously could not directly reflect competence. A record of natural speech will show numerous false starts, deviations from rules, changes of plan in mid-course,

Reprinted from Aspects of the Theory of Syntax, *Chapter 1, pp. 3–27, by Noam Chomsky by permission of the M. I. T. Press, Cambridge, Massachusetts, and the author.*

and so on. The problem for the linguist, as well as for the child learning the language, is to determine from the data of performance the underlying system of rules that has been mastered by the speaker-hearer and that he puts to use in actual performance. Hence, in the technical sense, linguistic theory is mentalistic, since it is concerned with discovering a mental reality underlying actual behavior.[1] Observed use of language or hypothesized dispositions to respond, habits, and so on, may provide evidence as to the nature of this mental reality, but surely cannot constitute the actual subject matter of linguistics, if this is to be a serious discipline. The distinction I am noting here is related to the *langue-parole* distinction of Saussure; but it is necessary to reject his concept of *langue* as merely a systematic inventory of items and to return rather to the Humboldtian conception of underlying competence as a system of generative processes. For discussion, see Chomsky (1964).

A grammar of a language purports to be a description of the ideal speaker-hearer's intrinsic competence. If the grammar is, furthermore, perfectly explicit—in other words, if it does not rely on the intelligence of the understanding reader but rather provides an explicit analysis of his contribution—we may (somewhat redundantly) call it a *generative grammar*.

A fully adequate grammar must assign to each of an infinite range of sentences a structural description indicating how this sentence is understood by the ideal

[1] To accept traditional mentalism, in this way, is not to accept Bloomfield's dichotomy of "mentalism" versus "mechanism." Mentalistic linguistics is simply theoretical linguistics that uses performance as data (along with other data, for example, the data provided by introspection) for the determination of competence, the latter being taken as the primary object of its investigation. The mentalist, in this traditional sense, need make no assumptions about the possible physiological basis for the mental reality that he studies. In particular, he need not deny that there is such a basis. One would guess, rather, that it is the mentalistic studies that will ultimately be of greatest value for the investigation of neurophysiological mechanisms, since they alone are concerned with determining abstractly the properties that such mechanisms must exhibit and the functions they must perform.

In fact, the issue of mentalism versus antimentalism in linguistics apparently has to do only with goals and interests, and not with questions of truth or falsity, sense or nonsense. At least three issues are involved in this rather idle controversy: (*a*) dualism—are the rules that underlie performance represented in a nonmaterial medium?; (*b*) behaviorism—do the data of performance exhaust the domain of interest to the linguist, or is he also concerned with other facts, in particular those pertaining to the deeper systems that underlie behavior?; (*c*) introspectionism—should one make use of introspective data in the attempt to ascertain the properties of these underlying systems? It is the dualistic position against which Bloomfield irrelevantly inveighed. The behaviorist position is not an arguable matter. It is simply an expression of lack of interest in theory and explanation. This is clear, for example, in Twaddell's critique (1935) of Sapir's mentalistic phonology, which used informant responses and comments as evidence bearing on the psychological reality of some abstract system of phonological elements. For Twaddell, the enterprise has no point because all that interests him is the behavior itself, "which is already available for the student of language, though in less concentrated form." Characteristically, this lack of interest in linguistic theory expresses itself in the proposal to limit the term "theory" to "summary of data" (as in Twaddell's paper or, to take a more recent example, in Dixon, 1963, although the discussion of "theories" in the latter is sufficiently vague as to allow other interpretations of what he may have in mind). Perhaps this loss of interest in theory, in the usual sense, was fostered by certain ideas (e.g., strict operationalism or strong verificationism) that were considered briefly in positivist philosophy of science, but rejected forthwith, in the early nineteen-thirties. In any event, question (*b*) poses no substantive issue. Question (*c*) arises only if one rejects the behaviorist limitations of (*b*). To maintain, on grounds of methodological purity, that introspective judgments of the informant (often, the linguist himself) should be disregarded is, for the present, to condemn the study of language to utter sterility. It is difficult to imagine what possible reason might be given for this. We return to this matter later. For further discussion, see Katz (1964*c*).

speaker-hearer. This is the traditional problem of descriptive linguistics, and traditional grammars give a wealth of information concerning structural descriptions of sentences. However, valuable as they obviously are, traditional grammars are deficient in that they leave unexpressed many of the basic regularities of the language with which they are concerned. This fact is particularly clear on the level of syntax, where no traditional or structuralist grammar goes beyond classification of particular examples to the stage of formulation of generative rules on any significant scale. An analysis of the best existing grammars will quickly reveal that this is a defect of principle, not just a matter of empirical detail or logical preciseness. Nevertheless, it seems obvious that the attempt to explore this largely uncharted territory can most profitably begin with a study of the kind of structural information presented by traditional grammars and the kind of linguistic processes that have been exhibited, however informally, in these grammars.[2]

The limitations of traditional and structuralist grammars should be clearly appreciated. Although such grammars may contain full and explicit lists of exceptions and irregularities, they provide only examples and hints concerning the regular and productive syntactic processes. Traditional linguistic theory was not unaware of this fact. For example, James Beattie (1788) remarks that

> Languages, therefore, resemble men in this respect, that, though each has peculiarities, whereby it is distinguished from every other, yet all have certain qualities in common. The peculiarities of individual tongues are explained in their respective grammars and dictionaries. Those things, that all languages have in common, or that are necessary to every language, are treated of in a science, which some have called *Universal* or *Philosophical* grammar.

Somewhat earlier, Du Marsais defines universal and particular grammar in the following way (1729; quoted in Sahlin, 1928, pp. 29–30):

> Il y a dans la grammaire des observations qui conviennent à toutes les langues; ces observations forment ce qu'on appelle la grammaire générale: telles sont les remarques que l'on a faites sur les sons articulés, sur les lettres qui sont les signes de ces sons; sur la nature des mots, et sur les différentes manières dont ils doivent être ou arrangés ou terminés pour faire un sens. Outre ces observations générales, il y en a qui ne sont propres qu'à une langue particulière; et c'est ce qui forme les grammaires particulières de chaque langue.

Within traditional linguistic theory, furthermore, it was clearly understood that one of the qualities that all languages have in common is their "creative" aspect. Thus an essential property of language is that it provides the means for expressing indefinitely many thoughts and for reacting appropriately in an indefinite range of new situations (for references, cf. Chomsky, 1964, forthcoming). The grammar of a particular language, then, is to be supplemented by a universal grammar that

[2] This has been denied recently by several European linguists (e.g., Dixon, 1963; Uhlenbeck, 1963, 1964). They offer no reasons for their skepticism concerning traditional grammar, however. Whatever evidence is available today seems to me to show that by and large the traditional views are basically correct, so far as they go, and that the suggested innovations are totally unjustifiable. For example, consider Uhlenbeck's proposal that the constituent analysis of "the man saw the boy" is [*the man saw*] [*the boy*], a proposal which presumably also implies that in the sentences [*the man put*] [*it into the box*], [*the man aimed*] [*it at John*], [*the man persuaded*] [*Bill that it was unlikely*], etc., the constituents are as indicated. There are many considerations relevant to the determination of constituent structure (cf. note 7); to my knowledge, they support the traditional analysis without exception against this proposal, for which the only argument offered is that it is the result of a "pure linguistic analysis." Cf. Uhlenbeck (1964), and the discussion there. As to Dixon's objections to traditional grammars, since he offers neither any alternative nor any argument (beyond the correct but irrelevant observation that they have been "long condemned by professional linguists"), there is nothing further to discuss, in this case.

accommodates the creative aspect of language use and expresses the deep-seated regularities which, being universal, are omitted from the grammar itself. Therefore it is quite proper for a grammar to discuss only exceptions and irregularities in any detail. It is only when supplemented by a universal grammar that the grammar of a language provides a full account of the speaker-hearer's competence.

Modern linguistics, however, has not explicitly recognized the necessity for supplementing a "particular grammar" of a language by a universal grammar if it is to achieve descriptive adequacy. It has, in fact, characteristically rejected the study of universal grammar as misguided; and, as noted before, it has not attempted to deal with the creative aspect of language use. It thus suggests no way to overcome the fundamental descriptive inadequacy of structuralist grammars.

Another reason for the failure of traditional grammars, particular or universal, to attempt a precise statement of regular processes of sentence formation and sentence interpretation lay in the widely held belief that there is a "natural order of thoughts" that is mirrored by the order of words. Hence, the rules of sentence formation do not really belong to grammar but to some other subject in which the "order of thoughts" is studied. Thus in the *Grammaire générale et raisonnée* (Lancelot *et al.*, 1660) it is asserted that, aside from figurative speech, the sequence of words follows an "ordre naturel," which conforms "à l'expression naturelle de nos pensées." Consequently, few grammatical rules need be formulated beyond the rules of ellipsis, inversion, and so on, which determine the figurative use of language. The same view appears in many forms and variants. To mention just one additional example, in an interesting essay devoted largely to the question of how the simultaneous and sequential array of ideas is reflected in the order of words, Diderot concludes that French is unique among languages in the degree to which the order of words corresponds to the natural order of thoughts and ideas (Diderot, 1751). Thus "quel que soit l'ordre des termes dans une langue ancienne ou moderne, l'esprit de l'écrivain a suivi l'ordre didactique de la syntaxe française" (p. 390); "Nous disons les choses en français, comme l'esprit est forcé de les considérer en quelque langue qu'on écrive" (p. 371). With admirable consistency he goes on to conclude that "notre langue *pédestre* a sur les autres l'avantage de l'utile sur l'agréable" (p. 372); thus French is appropriate for the sciences, whereas Greek, Latin, Italian, and English "sont plus avantageuses pour les lettres." Moreover,

> le bons sens choisirait la langue française; mais...l'imagination et les passions donneront la préférence aux langues anciennes et à celles de nos voisins...il faut parler français dans la société et dans les écoles de philosophie; et grec, latin, anglais, dans les chaires et sur les théâtres;...notre langue sera celle de la vérité, si jamais elle revient sur la terre; et...la grecque, la latine et les autres seront les langues de la fable et du mensonge. Le français est fait pour instruire, éclairer et convaincre; le grec, le latin, l'italien, l'anglais, pour persuader, émouvoir et tromper: parlez grec, latin, italien au peuple; mais parlez français au sage. (pp. 371–372)

In any event, insofar as the order of words is determined by factors independent of language, it is not necessary to describe it in a particular or universal grammar, and we therefore have principled grounds for excluding an explicit formulation of syntactic processes from grammar. It is worth noting that this naïve view of language structure persists to modern times in various forms, for example, in Saussure's image of a sequence of expressions corresponding to an amorphous sequence of concepts or in the common characterization of language use as merely a matter of use of words and phrases (for example, Ryle, 1953).

But the fundamental reason for this

inadequacy of traditional grammars is a more technical one. Although it was well understood that linguistic processes are in some sense "creative," the technical devices for expressing a system of recursive processes were simply not available until much more recently. In fact, a real understanding of how a language can (in Humboldt's words) "make infinite use of finite means" has developed only within the last thirty years, in the course of studies in the foundations of mathematics. Now that these insights are readily available it is possible to return to the problems that were raised, but not solved, in traditional linguistic theory, and to attempt an explicit formulation of the "creative" processes of language. There is, in short, no longer a technical barrier to the full-scale study of generative grammars.

Returning to the main theme, by a generative grammar I mean simply a system of rules that in some explicit and well-defined way assigns structural descriptions to sentences. Obviously, every speaker of a language has mastered and internalized a generative grammar that expresses his knowledge of his language. This is not to say that he is aware of the rules of the grammar or even that he can become aware of them, or that his statements about his intuitive knowledge of the language are necessarily accurate. Any interesting generative grammar will be dealing, for the most part, with mental processes that are far beyond the level of actual or even potential consciousness; furthermore, it is quite apparent that a speaker's reports and viewpoints about his behavior and his competence may be in error. Thus a generative grammar attempts to specify what the speaker actually knows, not what he may report about his knowledge. Similarly, a theory of visual perception would attempt to account for what a person actually sees and the mechanisms that determine this rather than his statements about what he sees and why, though these statements may provide useful, in fact, compelling evidence for such a theory.

To avoid what has been a continuing misunderstanding, it is perhaps worth while to reiterate that a generative grammar is not a model for a speaker or a hearer. It attempts to characterize in the most neutral possible terms the knowledge of the language that provides the basis for actual use of language by a speaker-hearer. When we speak of a grammar as generating a sentence with a certain structural description, we mean simply that the grammar assigns this structural description to the sentence. When we say that a sentence has a certain derivation with respect to a particular generative grammar, we say nothing about how the speaker or hearer might proceed, in some practical or efficient way, to construct such a derivation. These questions belong to the theory of language use—the theory of performance. No doubt, a reasonable model of language use will incorporate, as a basic component, the generative grammar that expresses the speaker-hearer's knowledge of the language; but this generative grammar does not, in itself, prescribe the character or functioning of a perceptual model or a model of speech production. For various attempts to clarify this point, see Chomsky (1957), Gleason (1961), Miller and Chomsky (1963), and many other publications.

Confusion over this matter has been sufficiently persistent to suggest that a terminological change might be in order. Nevertheless, I think that the term "generative grammar" is completely appropriate, and have therefore continued to use it. The term "generate" is familiar in the sense intended here in logic, particularly in Post's theory of combinatorial systems. Furthermore, "generate" seems to be the most appropriate translation for Humboldt's term *erzeugen*, which he frequently uses, it seems, in essentially the sense here intended. Since this use of the term "generate" is well established both in logic and in the tradition of linguistic theory, I can see no reason for a revision of terminology.

2. TOWARD A THEORY OF PERFORMANCE

There seems to be little reason to question the traditional view that investigation of performance will proceed only so far as understanding of underlying competence permits. Furthermore, recent work on performance seems to give new support to this assumption. To my knowledge, the only concrete results that have been achieved and the only clear suggestions that have been put forth concerning the theory of performance, outside of phonetics, have come from studies of performance models that incorporate generative grammars of specific kinds—that is, from studies that have been based on assumptions about underlying competence.[3] In particular, there are some suggestive observations concerning limitations on performance imposed by organization of memory and bounds on memory, and concerning the exploitation of grammatical devices to form deviant sentences of various types. The latter question is one to which we shall return in Chapters 2 and 4. To clarify further the distinction between competence and performance, it may be useful to summarize briefly some of the suggestions and results that have appeared in the last few years in the study of performance models with limitations of memory, time, and access.

For the purposes of this discussion, let us use the term "acceptable" to refer to utterances that are perfectly natural and immediately comprehensible without paper-and-pencil analysis, and in no way bizarre or outlandish. Obviously, acceptability will be a matter of degree, along various dimensions. One could go on to propose various operational tests to specify the notion more precisely (for example, rapidity, correctness, and uniformity of recall and recognition, normalcy of intonation).[4] For present purposes, it is unnecessary to delimit it more carefully. To illustrate, the sentences of (1) are somewhat more acceptable, in the intended sense, than those of (2):

(1) (i) I called up the man who wrote the book that you told me about
(ii) quite a few of the students who you met who come from New York are friends of mine
(iii) John, Bill, Tom, and several of their friends visited us last night

(2) (i) I called the man who wrote the book that you told me about up
(ii) the man who the boy who the students recognized pointed out is a friend of mine

The more acceptable sentences are those that are more likely to be produced, more easily understood, less clumsy, and in some sense more natural.[5] The unacceptable sentences one would tend to avoid and

[3] Furthermore, it seems to me that speech perception is also best studied in this framework. See, for example, Halle and Stevens (1962).

[4] Tests that seem to determine a useful notion of this sort have been described in various places—for example, Miller and Isard (1963).

[5] These characterizations are equally vague, and the concepts involved are equally obscure. The notion "likely to be produced" or "probable" is sometimes thought to be more "objective" and antecedently better defined than the others, on the assumption that there is some clear meaning to the notion "probability of a sentence" or "probability of a sentence type." Actually, the latter notions are objective and antecedently clear only if probability is based on an estimate of relative frequency and if sentence type means something like "sequence of word or morpheme classes." (Furthermore, if the notion is to be at all significant, these classes must be extremely small and of mutually substitutable elements, or else unacceptable and ungrammatical sentences will be as "likely" and acceptable as grammatical ones.) But in this case, though "probability of a sentence (type)" is clear and well defined, it is an utterly useless notion, since almost all highly acceptable sentences (in the intuitive

replace by more acceptable variants, wherever possible, in actual discourse.

The notion "acceptable" is not to be confused with "grammatical." Acceptability is a concept that belongs to the study of performance, whereas grammaticalness belongs to the study of competence. The sentences of (2) are low on the scale of acceptability but high on the scale of grammaticalness, in the technical sense of this term. That is, the generative rules of the language assign an interpretation to them in exactly the way in which they assign an interpretation to the somewhat more acceptable sentences of (1). Like acceptability, grammaticalness is, no doubt, a matter of degree (cf. Chomsky, 1955, 1957, 1961), but the scales of grammaticalness and acceptability do not coincide. Grammaticalness is only one of many factors that interact to determine acceptability. Correspondingly, although one might propose various operational tests for acceptability, it is unlikely that a necessary and sufficient operational criterion might be invented for the much more abstract and far more important notion of grammaticalness. The unacceptable grammatical sentences often cannot be used, for reasons having to do, not with grammar, but rather with memory limitations, intonational and stylistic factors, "iconic" elements of discourse (for example, a tendency to place logical subject and object early rather than late; cf. note 32, Chapter 2, and note 9, Chapter 3), and so on. Note that it would be quite impossible to characterize the unacceptable sentences in grammatical terms. For example, we cannot formulate particular rules of the grammar in such a way as to exclude them. Nor, obviously, can we exclude them by limiting the number of reapplications of grammatical rules in the generation of a sentence, since unacceptability can just as well arise from application of distinct rules, each being applied only once. In fact, it is clear that we can characterize unacceptable sentences only in terms of some "global" property of derivations and the structures they define—a property that is attributable, not to a particular rule, but rather to the way in which the rules interrelate in a derivation.

This observation suggests that the study of performance could profitably begin with an investigation of the acceptability of the simplest formal structures in grammatical sentences. The most obvious formal property of utterances is their bracketing into constituents of various types, that is, the "tree structure" associated with them. Among such structures we can distinguish various kinds—for example, those to which we give the following conventional technical names, for the purposes of this discussion:

(3) (i) nested constructions
(ii) self-embedded constructions
(iii) multiple-branching constructions
(iv) left-branching constructions
(v) right-branching constructions

The phrases A and B form a nested con-

---

sense) will have probabilities empirically indistinguishable from zero and will belong to sentence types with probabilities empirically indistinguishable from zero. Thus the acceptable or grammatical sentences (or sentence types) are no more likely, in any objective sense of this word, than the others. This remains true if we consider, not "likelihood," but "likelihood relative to a given situation," as long as "situations" are specified in terms of observable physical properties and are not mentalistic constructs. It is noteworthy that linguists who talk of hardheaded objective study of use of sentences in real situations, when they actually come to citing examples, invariably describe the "situations" in completely mentalistic terms. Cf., e.g., Dixon (1963, p. 101), where, in the only illustrative example in the book, a sentence is described as gaining its meaning from the situation "British Culture." To describe British culture as "a situation" is, in the first place, a category mistake; furthermore, to regard it as a pattern abstracted from observed behavior, and hence objectively describable in purely physical terms, betrays a complete misunderstanding of what might be expected from anthropological research.

For further discussion, see Katz and Fodor (1964).

struction if A falls totally within B, with some nonnull element to its left within B and some nonnull element to its right within B. Thus the phrase "the man who wrote the book that you told me about" is nested in the phrase "called the man who wrote the book that you told me about up," in (2i). The phrase A is self-embedded in B if A is nested in B and, furthermore, A is a phrase of the same type as B. Thus "who the students recognized" is self-embedded in "who the boy who the students recognized pointed out," in (2ii), since both are relative clauses. Thus nesting has to do with bracketing, and self-embedding with labeling of brackets as well. A multiple-branching construction is one with no internal structure. In (1iii), the Subject Noun Phrase is multiple-branching, since "John," "Bill," "Tom," and "several of their friends" are its immediate constituents, and have no further association among themselves. In terms of bracketing, a multiple-branching construction has the form [[*A*][*B*]...[*M*]]. A left-branching structure is of the forrn [[[...]...]...]—for example, in English, such indefinitely iterable structures as [[[[*John*]'*s brother*]'*s father*]'*s uncle*] or [[[*the man who you met*] *from Boston*] *who was on the train*], or (1ii), which combines several kinds of left-branching. Right-branching structures are those with the opposite property—for example, the Direct-Object of (1i) or [*this is* [*the cat that caught* [*the rat that stole the cheese*]]].

The effect of these superficial aspects of sentence structure on performance has been a topic of study since almost the very inception of recent work on generative grammar, and there are some suggestive observations concerning their role in determining acceptability (that is, their role in limiting performance). Summarizing this work briefly, the following observations seem plausible:

(4) (i) repeated nesting contributes to unacceptability

(ii) self-embedding contributes still more radically to unacceptability

(iii) multiple-branching constructions are optimal in acceptability

(iv) nesting of a long and complex element reduces acceptability

(v) there are no clear examples of unacceptability involving only left-branching or only right-branching, although these constructions are unnatural in other ways—thus, for example, in reading the right-branching construction "this is the cat that caught the rat that stole the cheese," the intonation breaks are ordinarily inserted in the wrong places (that is, after "cat" and "rat," instead of where the main brackets appear)

In some measure, these phenomena are easily explained. Thus it is known (cf. Chomsky, 1959*a*; and for discussion, Chomsky, 1961, and Miller and Chomsky, 1963) that an optimal perceptual device, even with a bounded memory, can accept unbounded left-branching and right-branching structures, though nested (hence ultimately self-embedded) structures go beyond its memory capacity. Thus case (4i) is simply a consequence of finiteness of memory, and the unacceptability of such examples as (2ii) raises no problem.

If (4ii) is correct,[6] then we have evi-

[6] That it may be true is suggested by several (for the moment, quite untested) observations. For example, in Chomsky and Miller (1963, p. 286) the following example is cited: "anyone who feels that if so many more students whom we haven't actually admitted are sitting in on the course than ones we have that the room had to be changed, then probably auditors will have to be excluded, is likely to agree that the curriculum needs revision." This contains six nested dependencies (along with other dependencies that go beyond nesting) with no self-embedding. Though hardly a model of felicitous style, it seems fairly comprehensible, and not extremely low on the scale of acceptability. In comparison, self-embedding of degree two or three seems to disturb acceptability

dence for a conclusion about organization of memory that goes beyond the triviality that it must be finite in size. An optimal finite perceptual device of the type discussed in Chomsky (1959*a*) need have no more difficulty with self-embedding than with other kinds of nesting (see Bar-Hillel, Kasher, and Shamir, 1963, for a discussion of this point). To account for the greater unacceptability of self-embedding (assuming this to be a fact), we must add other conditions on the perceptual device beyond mere limitation of memory. We might assume, for example, that the perceptual device has a stock of analytic procedures available to it, one corresponding to each kind of phrase, and that it is organized in such a way that it is unable (or finds it difficult) to utilize a procedure φ while it is in the course of executing φ. This is not a necessary feature of a perceptual model, but it is a rather plausible one, and it would account for (4ii). See, in this connection, Miller and Isard (1964).

The high acceptability of multiple-branching, as in case (4iii), is easily explained on the rather plausible assumption that the ratio of number of phrases to number of formatives (the node-to-terminal node ratio, in a tree-diagram of a sentence) is a rough measure of the amount of computation that has to be performed in analysis. Thus multiple coordination would be the simplest kind of construction for an analytic device—it would impose the least strain on memory.[7] For discussion, see Miller and Chomsky (1963).

Case (4iv) suggests decay of memory, perhaps, but raises unsolved problems (see Chomsky, 1961, note 19).

Case (4v) follows from the result about optimal perceptual models mentioned earlier. But it is unclear why left- and right-branching structures should become much more severely. The matter is worth studying, since a positive result concerning (4ii) would, as noted, support a conclusion about organization of memory which is not entirely obvious.

[7] It has sometimes been claimed that the traditional coordinated structures are necessarily right-recursive (Yngve, 1960) or left-recursive (Harman, 1963, p. 613, rule 3i). These conclusions seem to me equally unacceptable. Thus to assume (with Harman) that the phrase "a tall, young, handsome, intelligent man" has the structure [[[[*tall young*] *handsome*] *intelligent*] *man*] seems to me no more justifiable than to assume that it has the structure [*tall* [*young* [*handsome* [*intelligent man*]]]]. In fact, there is no grammatical motivation for any internal structure, and, as I have just noted, the assumption that there is no structure is also supported on grounds of acceptability, with extremely weak and plausible assumptions about organization of memory. Notice that there are cases where further structure might be justified (e.g., [*intelligent* [*young man*]] or, perhaps [*YOUNG* [*intelligent man*]], with contrastive stress on "young"), but the issue is rather whether it is always necessary.

The same is true if we consider the very different type of Adjective-Noun construction that we find in such phrases as "all the young, old, and middle-aged voters" (for an interesting discussion of these various kinds of modification relations, see Ornan, 1964). Here, too, neither the structure [[*young, old*] *and middle-aged*] nor [*young* [*old and middle-aged*]] has any justification.

Similarly, it is surely impossible to assume, with Yngve, that in the phrase "John, Mary, and their two children" the structure is [*John*] [[*Mary*] [*and their two children*]], so that "John" is coordinated with "Mary and their two children," the latter being analyzed into the coordinated items "Mary" and "their two children." This is entirely counter to the sense. Notice, again, that conjunction *can* have this structure (e.g., "John, as well as Mary and her child"), but surely it is false to claim that it *must* have this structure.

In these cases all known syntactic, semantic, phonetic, and perceptual considerations converge in support of the traditional view that these constructions are typically coordinating (multiple-branching). Notice also that this is the weakest assumption. The burden of proof rests on one who claims additional structure beyond this. There are various ways of justifying assignment of constituent structure. For example, in such a phrase as "all (none) of the blue, green, red, and (or) yellow pennants," if one wanted to argue that "blue, green, red" is a constituent (i.e., that the structure is left-branching), or that "green, red, and (or) yellow" is a constituent (that the structure is unnatural after a certain point, if they actually do.[8]

One might ask whether attention to less superficial aspects of grammatical structure than those of (3) could lead to somewhat deeper conclusions about performance models. This seems entirely possible. For example, in Miller and Chomsky (1963) some syntactic and perceptual considerations are adduced in support of a suggestion (which is, to be sure, highly speculative) as to the somewhat more detailed organization of a perceptual device. In general, it seems that the study of performance models incorporating generative grammars may be a fruitful study; furthermore, it is difficult to imagine any other basis on which a theory of performance might develop.

There has been a fair amount of criticism of work in generative grammar on the grounds that it slights study of performance in favor of study of underlying competence. The facts, however, seem to be that the only studies of performance, outside of phonetics (but see note 3), are those carried out as a by-product of work in generative grammar. In particular, the study of memory limitations just summarized and the study of deviation from rules, as a stylistic device, to which we return in Chapters 2 and 4, have developed in this way. Furthermore, it seems that these lines of investigation can

---

right-branching), then he would have to show that these analyses are required for some grammatical rule, that the postulated intermediate phrases must receive a semantic interpretation, that they define a phonetic contour, that there are perceptual grounds for the analysis, or something of this sort. All of these claims are patently false in this case, and the other cases mentioned here. Thus no semantic interpretation can be assigned to "old and middle-aged" in "young, old, and middle-aged voters" or to "green, red, or yellow" in "none of the blue, green, red, or yellow pennants" or to "Mary and their two children" in "John, Mary, and their two children"; the phonetic rules explicitly preclude such constituent analysis; there are no grammatical rules that require these analyses; there are no perceptual or other arguments to support them. It seems difficult, then, to see any grounds for objecting to the traditional analysis and insisting on additional intermediate categorization, in such cases as these.

[8] Yngve (1960, and several other papers) has proposed a different theory to account for certain observations such as those of (4). Beyond the obvious condition of finiteness of memory, his theory assumes also that order of generation is identical with order of production—that the speaker and hearer produce sentences "from top-to-bottom" (they first decide on the major structures, then the substructures of these, etc., leaving to the very end of the process the choice of lexical items). Under this highly restrictive additional assumption, the optimal perceptual device mentioned earlier is no longer constructible, and left-branching and multiple-branching, as well as nesting and self-embedding, contribute to "depth" in Yngve's sense, hence to unacceptability. To support this hypothesis, it would be necessary to show (*a*) that it has some initial plausibility, and (*b*) that left-branching and multiple-branching in fact contribute to unacceptability exactly as do nesting and self-embedding. As to (*a*), I see no plausibility at all to the assumption that the speaker must uniformly select sentence type, then determine subcategories, etc., finally, at the last stage, deciding what he is going to talk about; or that the hearer should invariably make all higher-level decisions before doing any lower-level analysis. As to (*b*), the hypothesis is supported by no evidence at all. The examples given by Yngve all involve nesting and self-embedding and hence are irrelevant to the hypothesis, since the unacceptability in this case follows from the assumption of finiteness alone without the additional assumption of "top-to-bottom" production for speaker and hearer. Furthermore, the hypothesis is contradicted by the observation (4iii) that multiply coordinated structures (cf. note 7) are the most acceptable (rather than the least acceptable, as predicted and that left-branching structures are far more acceptable than nested structures of equal "depth," in Yngve's sense. It also fails to explain why examples of type (4iv), such as (2i), though very low in "depth," are still unacceptable.

However, Yngve makes one important point in these papers, namely, that some transformations can be used to decrease nesting, hence to reduce the perceptual load. This suggests an interesting argument as to why grammars should contain transformational rules. Some additional weight to this argument is given by the discussion of performance models involving transformational grammars in Miller and Chomsky (1963, Part 2).

provide some insight into performance. Consequently, this criticism is unwarranted, and, furthermore, completely misdirected. It is the descriptivist limitation-in-principle to classification and organization of data, to "extracting patterns" from a corpus of observed speech, to describing "speech habits" or "habit structures," insofar as these may exist, etc., that precludes the development of a theory of actual performance.

3. THE ORGANIZATION OF A GENERATIVE GRAMMAR

Returning now to the question of competence and the generative grammars that purport to describe it, we stress again that knowledge of a language involves the implicit ability to understand indefinitely many sentences.[9] Hence, a generative grammar must be a system of rules that can iterate to generate an indefinitely large number of structures. This system of rules can be analyzed into the three major components of a generative grammar: the syntactic, phonological, and semantic components.[10]

The syntactic component specifies an infinite set of abstract formal objects, each of which incorporates all information relevant to a single interpretation of a particular sentence.[11] Since I shall be concerned here only with the syntactic component, I shall use the term "sentence" to refer to strings of formatives rather than to strings of phones. It will be recalled that a string of formatives specifies a string of phones uniquely (up to free variation), but not conversely.

The phonological component of a grammar determines the phonetic form of a sentence generated by the syntactic rules. That is, it relates a structure generated by the syntactic component to a phonetically represented signal. The semantic component determines the semantic interpretation of a sentence. That is, it relates a structure generated by the syntactic component to a certain semantic representation. Both the phonological and semantic components are therefore purely interpretive. Each utilizes information provided by the syntactic component concerning formatives, their inherent properties, and their interrelations in a given sentence. Consequently, the syntactic component of a grammar must specify, for each sentence, a *deep structure* that determines its semantic interpretation and a *surface structure* that determines its phonetic interpretation. The first of these is interpreted by the semantic component; the second, by the phonological component.[12]

9 It is astonishing to find that even this truism has recently been challenged. See Dixon (1963). However, it seems that when Dixon denies that a language has infinitely many sentences, he is using the term "infinite" in some special and rather obscure sense. Thus on the same page (p. 83) on which he objects to the assertion "that there are an infinite number of sentences in a language" he states that "we are clearly unable to say that there is any definite number, *N*, such that no sentence contains more than *N* clauses" (that is, he states that the language is infinite). Either this is a blatant self-contradiction, or else he has some new sense of the word "infinite" in mind. For further discussion of his remarks in this connection, see Chomsky (in press).

10 Aside from terminology, I follow here the exposition in Katz and Postal (1964). In particular, I shall assume throughout that the semantic component is essentially as they describe it and that the phonological component is essentially as described in Chomsky, Halle, and Lukoff (1956); Halle (1959*a*, 1959*b*, 1962*a*); Chomsky (1962*b*); Chomsky and Miller (1963); Halle and Chomsky (1960; forthcoming).

11 I assume throughout that the syntactic component contains a lexicon, and that each lexical item is specified in the lexicon in terms of its intrinsic semantic features, whatever these may be. I shall return to this matter in the next chapter.

12 In place of the terms "deep structure" and "surface structure," one might use the corresponding Humboldtian notions "inner form" of a sentence and "outer form" of a sentence. However, though it seems to me that "deep structure" and "surface structure," in the sense in which these terms will be used here, do correspond quite closely to Humboldtian

It might be supposed that surface structure and deep structure will always be identical. In fact, one might briefly characterize the syntactic theories that have arisen in modern structural (taxonomic) linguistics as based on the assumption that deep and surface structures are actually the same (cf. Postal, 1964*a*, Chomsky, 1964). The central idea of transformational grammar is that they are, in general, distinct and that the surface structure is determined by repeated application of certain formal operations called "grammatical transformations" to

---

"inner form" and "outer form," respectively (as used of a sentence), I have adopted the more neutral terminology to avoid the question, here, of textual interpretation. The terms "depth grammar" and "surface grammar" are familiar in modern philosophy in something roughly like the sense here intended (cf. Wittgenstein's distinction of *"Tiefengrammatik"* and *"Oberflächengrammatik,"* 1953, p. 168); Hockett uses similar terminology in his discussion of the inadequacy of taxonomic linguistics (Hockett, 1958, Chapter 29). Postal has used the terms "underlying structure" and "superficial structure" (Postal, 1964*b*) for the same notions.

The distinction between deep and surface structure, in the sense in which these terms are used here, is drawn quite clearly in the Port-Royal *Grammar* (Lancelot *et al.,* 1660). See Chomsky (1964, pp. 15–16; forthcoming) for some discussion and references. In philosophical discussion, it is often introduced in an attempt to show how certain philosophical positions arise from false grammatical analogies, the surface structure of certain expressions being mistakenly considered to be semantically interpretable by means appropriate only to other, superficially similar sentences. Thus Thomas Reid (1785) holds a common source of philosophical error to lie in the fact that

> in all languages, there are phrases which have a distinct meaning; while at the same time, there may be something in the structure of them that disagrees with the analogy of grammar or with the principles of philosophy. . . . Thus, we speak of feeling pain as if pain was something distinct from the feeling of it. We speak of pain coming and going, and removing from one place to another. Such phrases are meant by those who use them in a sense that is neither obscure nor false. But the philosopher puts them into his alembic, reduces them to their first principles, draws out of them a sense that was never meant, and so imagines that he has discovered an error of the vulgar [pp. 167–168].

More generally, he criticizes the theory of ideas as based on a deviation from the "popular meaning," in which "to have an idea of anything signifies nothing more than to think of it" (p. 105). But philosophers take an idea to be "the object that the mind contemplates" (p. 105); to have an idea, then, is to possess in the mind such an image, picture, or representation as the immediate object of thought. It follows that there are two objects of thought: the idea, which is in the mind, and the thing represented by it. From this conclusion follow the absurdities, as Reid regards them, of the traditional theory of ideas. One of the sources of these absurdities is the failure of the philosopher to attend "to the distinction between the operations of the mind and the objects of these operations. . . although this distinction be familiar to the vulgar, and found in the structure of all languages. . ." (p. 110). Notice that these two senses of "having an idea" are distinguished by Descartes in the Preface to the *Meditations* (1641, p. 138). Reid's linguistic observation is made considerably earlier by Du Marsais, in a work published posthumously in 1769, in the following passage (pp. 179–189):

> Ainsi, comme nous avons dit *j'ai un livre, j'ai un diamant, j'ai une montre,* nous disons par imitation, *j'ai la fièvre, j'ai envie, j'ai peur, j'ai un doute, j'ai pitié, j'ai une idée,* etc. Mais *livre, diamant, montre* sont autant de noms d'objects réels qui existent indépendamment de notre manière de penser; au lieu que *santé, fièvre, peur, doute, envie,* ne sont que des termes métaphysiques qui ne désignent que des manières d'êtres considérés par des points de vue particuliers de l'esprit.
>
> Dans cet exemple, *j'ai une montre, j'ai* est une expression qui doit être prise dans le sens propre: mais dans *j'ai une idée, j'ai* n'est dit que par une imitation. C'est une expression empruntée. *J'ai une idée,* c'est-à-dire, *je pense, je conçois de telle ou telle manière. J'ai envie,* c'est-à-dire, *je désire; j'ai la volonté,* c'est-à-dire, *je veux,* etc.
>
> Ainsi, *idée, concept, imagination,* ne marquent point d'objets réels, et encore moins des êtres sensibles que l'on puisse unir l'un avec l'autre.

In more recent years, it has been widely held that the aims of philosophy should, in fact, be strictly limited to "the detection of the sources in linguistic idioms of recurrent misconstructions and absurd theories" (Ryle, 1931).

objects of a more elementary sort. If this is true (as I assume, henceforth), then the syntactic component must generate deep and surface structures, for each sentence, and must interrelate them. This idea has been clarified substantially in recent work, in ways that will be described later. In Chapter 3, I shall present a specific and, in part, new proposal as to precisely how it should be formulated. For the moment, it is sufficient to observe that although the Immediate Constituent analysis (labeled bracketing) of an actual string of formatives may be adequate as an account of surface structure, it is certainly not adequate as an account of deep structure. My concern in this book is primarily with deep structure and, in particular, with the elementary objects of which deep structure is constituted.

To clarify exposition, I shall use the following terminology, with occasional revisions as the discussion proceeds.

The base of the syntactic component is a system of rules that generate a highly restricted (perhaps finite) set of *basic strings*, each with an associated structural description called a *base Phrase-marker*. These base Phrase-markers are the elementary units of which deep structures are constituted. I shall assume that no ambiguity is introduced by rules of the base. This assumption seems to me correct, but has no important consequences for what follows here, though it simplifies exposition. Underlying each sentence of the language there is a sequence of base Phrase-markers, each generated by the base of the syntactic component. I shall refer to this sequence as the *basis* of the sentence that it underlies.

In addition to its base, the syntactic component of a generative grammar contains a *transformational* subcomponent. This is concerned with generating a sentence, with its surface structure, from its basis. Some familiarity with the operation and effects of transformational rules is henceforth presupposed.

Since the base generates only a restricted set of base Phrase-markers, most sentences will have a sequence of such objects as an underlying basis. Among the sentences with a single base Phrase-marker as basis, we can delimit a proper subset called "kernel sentences." These are sentences of a particularly simple sort that involve a minimum of transformational apparatus in their generation. The notion "kernel sentence" has, I think, an important intuitive significance, but since kernel sentences play no distinctive role in generation or interpretation of sentences, I shall say nothing more about them here. One must be careful not to confuse kernel sentences with the basic strings that underlie them. The basic strings and base Phrase-markers do, it seems, play a distinctive and crucial role in language use.

Since transformations will not be considered here in detail, no careful distinction will be made, in the case of a sentence with a single element in its basis, between the basic string underlying this sentence and the sentence itself. In other words, at many points in the exposition I shall make the tacit simplifying (and contrary-to-fact) assumption that the underlying basic string *is* the sentence, in this case, and that the base Phrase-marker is the surface structure as well as the deep structure. I shall try to select examples in such a way as to minimize possible confusion, but the simplifying assumption should be borne in mind throughout.

4. JUSTIFICATION OF GRAMMARS

Before entering directly into an investigation of the syntactic component of a generative grammar, it is important to give some thought to several methodological questions of justification and adequacy.

There is, first of all, the question of how one is to obtain information about the speaker-hearer's competence, about his knowledge of the language. Like most facts of interest and importance, this is neither presented for direct observation nor extractable from data by inductive procedures of any known sort. Clearly, the actual data of linguistic performance will provide much evidence for determining the correctness of hypotheses about underlying linguistic structure, along with introspective reports (by the native speaker, or the linguist who has learned the language). This is the position that is universally adopted in practice, although there are methodological discussions that seem to imply a reluctance to use observed performance or introspective reports as evidence for some underlying reality.

In brief, it is unfortunately the case that no adequate formalizable techniques are known for obtaining reliable information concerning the facts of linguistic structure (nor is this particularly surprising). There are, in other words, very few reliable experimental or data-processing procedures for obtaining significant information concerning the linguistic intuition of the native speaker. It is important to bear in mind that when an operational procedure is proposed, it must be tested for adequacy (exactly as a theory of linguistic intuition—a grammar—must be tested for adequacy) by measuring it against the standard provided by the tacit knowledge that it attempts to specify and describe. Thus a proposed operational test for, say, segmentation into words, must meet the empirical condition of conforming, in a mass of crucial and clear cases, to the linguistic intuition of the native speaker concerning such elements. Otherwise, it is without value. The same, obviously, is true in the case of any proposed operational procedure or any proposed grammatical description. If operational procedures were available that met this test, we might be justified in relying on their results in unclear and difficult cases. This remains a hope for the future rather than a present reality, however. This is the objective situation of present-day linguistic work; allusions to presumably well-known "procedures of elicitation" or "objective methods" simply obscure the actual situation in which linguistic work must, for the present, proceed. Furthermore, there is no reason to expect that reliable operational criteria for the deeper and more important theoretical notions of linguistics (such as "grammaticalness" and "paraphrase") will ever be forthcoming.

Even though few reliable operational procedures have been developed, the theoretical (that is, grammatical) investigation of the knowledge of the native speaker can proceed perfectly well. The critical problem for grammatical theory today is not a paucity of evidence but rather the inadequacy of present theories of language to account for masses of evidence that are hardly open to serious question. The problem for the grammarian is to construct a description and, where possible, an explanation for the enormous mass of unquestionable data concerning the linguistic intuition of the native speaker (often, himself); the problem for one concerned with operational procedures is to develop tests that give the correct results and make relevant distinctions. Neither the study of grammar nor the attempt to develop useful tests is hampered by lack of evidence with which to check results, for the present. We may hope that these efforts will converge, but they must obviously converge on the tacit knowledge of the native speaker if they are to be of any significance.

One may ask whether the necessity for present-day linguistics to give such priority to introspective evidence and to the linguistic intuition of the native speaker excludes it from the domain of science. The answer to this essentially terminological question seems to have no bearing at all on any serious issue. At most, it determines how we shall denote the kind of research that can be effectively carried out in the present state of our technique and understanding. However, this terminological question actually does relate to a different issue of some interest, namely the question whether the important feature of the successful sciences has been their search for insight or their concern for objectivity. The social and behavioral sciences provide ample evidence that objectivity can be pursued with little consequent gain in insight and understanding. On the other hand, a good case can be made for the view that the natural sciences have, by and large, sought objectivity primarily insofar as it is a tool for gaining insight (for providing phenomena that can suggest or test deeper explanatory hypotheses).

In any event, at a given stage of investigation, one whose concern is for insight and understanding (rather than for objectivity as a goal in itself) must ask whether or to what extent a wider range and more exact description of phenomena is relevant to solving the problems that he faces. In linguistics, it seems to me that sharpening of the data by more objective tests is a matter of small importance for the problems at hand. One who disagrees with this estimate of the present situation in linguistics can justify his belief in the current importance of more objective operational tests by showing how they can lead to new and deeper understanding of linguistic structure. Perhaps the day will come when the kinds of data that we now can obtain in abundance will be insufficient to resolve deeper questions concerning the structure of language. However, many questions that can realistically and significantly be formulated today do not demand evidence of a kind that is unavailable or unattainable without significant improvements in objectivity of experimental technique.

Although there is no way to avoid the traditional assumption that the speaker-hearer's linguistic intuition is the ultimate standard that determines the accuracy of any proposed grammar, linguistic theory, or operational test, it must be emphasized, once again, that this tacit knowledge may very well not be immediately available to the user of the language. To eliminate what has seemed to some an air of paradox in this remark, let me illustrate with a few examples.

If a sentence such as "flying planes can be dangerous" is presented in an appropriately constructed context, the listener will interpret it immediately in a unique way, and will fail to detect the ambiguity. In fact, he may reject the second interpretation, when this is pointed out to him, as forced or unnatural (independently of which interpretation he originally selected under contextual pressure). Nevertheless, his intuitive knowledge of the language is clearly such that both of the interpretations (corresponding to "flying planes are dangerous" and "flying planes is dangerous") are assigned to the sentence by the grammar he has internalized in some form.

In the case just mentioned, the ambiguity may be fairly transparent. But consider such a sentence as

(5) I had a book stolen

Few hearers may be aware of the fact that their internalized grammar in fact provides at least three structural descriptions for this sentence. Nevertheless, this fact can be brought to consciousness by consideration of slight elaborations of sentence (5), for example: (i) "I had a book stolen from my car when I stupidly left the window open," that is, "someone stole a book from my car"; (ii) "I had a book stolen from his library by a professional thief who I hired to do the job", that is, "I had someone steal a book"; (iii) "I almost had a book stolen, but they caught me leaving the library with it," that is, "I had almost succeeded in stealing a book." In bringing to consciousness the triple ambiguity of (5) in this way, we present no new information to the hearer and teach him nothing new about his language but simply arrange matters in such a way that his linguistic intuition, previously obscured, becomes evident to him.

As a final illustration, consider the sentences

(6) I persuaded John to leave

(7) I expected John to leave

The first impression of the hearer may be that these sentences receive the same structural analysis. Even fairly careful thought may fail to show him that his internalized grammar assigns very different syntactic descriptions to these sentences. In fact, so far as I have been able to discover, no English grammar has pointed out the fundamental distinction between these two constructions (in particular, my own sketches of English grammar in Chomsky, 1955, 1962*a*, failed to note this). However, it is clear that the sentences (6) and (7) are not parallel in structure. The difference can be brought out by consideration of the sentences

(8) (i) I persuaded a specialist to examine John
(ii) I persuaded John to be examined by a specialist

(9) (i) I expected a specialist to examine John
(ii) I expected John to be examined by a specialist

The sentences (9i) and (9ii) are "cognitively synonymous": one is true if and only if the other is true. But no variety of even weak paraphrase holds between (8i) and (8ii). Thus (8i) can be true or false quite independently of the truth or falsity of (8ii). Whatever difference of connotation or "topic" or emphasis one may find between (9i) and (9ii) is just the difference that exists between the active sentence "a specialist will examine John" and its passive counterpart "John will be examined by a specialist." This is not at all the case with respect to (8), however. In fact, the underlying deep structure for (6) and (8ii) must show that "John" is the Direct-Object of the Verb Phrase as well as the grammatical Subject of the embedded sentence. Furthermore, in (8ii) "John" is the logical Direct-Object of the embedded sentence, whereas in (8i) the phrase "a specialist" is the Direct-Object of the Verb Phrase and the logical Subject of the embedded sentence. In (7), (9i), and (9ii), however, the Noun Phrases "John," "a specialist," and "John," respectively, have no grammatical functions other than those that are internal to the embedded sentence; in particular, "John" is the logical Direct-Object and "a specialist" the logical Subject in the embedded sentences of (9). Thus the underlying deep structures for (8i), (8ii), (9i), and (9ii) are, respectively, the following:[13]

(10) (i) Noun Phrase — Verb — Noun Phrase—Sentence
(*I—persuaded—a specialist—a specialist will examine John*)
(ii) Noun Phrase — Verb — Noun Phrase—Sentence
(*I—persuaded—John—a specialist will examine John*)

(11) (i) Noun Phrase—Verb—Sentence
(*I—expected—a specialist will examine John*)
(ii) Noun Phrase—Verb—Sentence
(*I—expected—a specialist will examine John*)

In the case of (10ii) and (11ii), the passive transformation will apply to the embedded sentence, and in all four cases other operations will give the final surface

[13] These descriptions are not fully accurate. In fact, the sentential complement in (10) should, more properly, be regarded as embedded in a Prepositional-Phrase (cf. Chapter 3); and, as Peter Rosenbaum has pointed out, the sentential complement of (11) should be regarded as embedded in the Noun-Phrase Object of "expect." Furthermore, the treatment of the Verbal Auxiliaries in (10) and (11) is incorrect, and there are other modifications relating to the marking of the passive transformation, to which we shall return in the next chapter.

forms of (8) and (9). The important point in the present connection is that (8i) differs from (8ii) in underlying structure, although (9i) and (9ii) are essentially the same in underlying structure. This accounts for the difference in meaning. Notice, in support of this difference in analysis, that we can have "I persuaded John that (of the fact that) Sentence," but not "I expected John that (of the fact that) Sentence."

The example (6)–(7) serves to illustrate two important points. First, it shows how unrevealing surface structure may be as to underlying deep structure. Thus (6) and (7) are the same in surface structure, but very different in the deep structure that underlies them and determines their semantic interpretations. Second, it illustrates the elusiveness of the speaker's tacit knowledge. Until such examples as (8) and (9) are adduced, it may not be in the least clear to a speaker of English that the grammar that he has internalized in fact assigns very different syntactic analyses to the superficially analogous sentences (6) and (7).

In short, we must be careful not to overlook the fact that surface similarities may hide underlying distinctions of a fundamental nature, and that it may be necessary to guide and draw out the speaker's intuition in perhaps fairly subtle ways before we can determine what is the actual character of his knowledge of his language or of anything else. Neither point is new (the former is a commonplace of traditional linguistic theory and analytic philosophy; the latter is as old as Plato's *Meno*); both are too often overlooked.

A grammar can be regarded as a theory of a language; it is *descriptively adequate* to the extent that it correctly describes the intrinsic competence of the idealized native speaker. The structural descriptions assigned to sentences by the grammar, the distinctions that it makes between well-formed and deviant, and so on, must, for descriptive adequacy, correspond to the linguistic intuition of the native speaker (whether or not he may be immediately aware of this) in a substantial and significant class of crucial cases.

A linguistic theory must contain a definition of "grammar," that is, a specification of the class of potential grammars. We may, correspondingly, say that *a linguistic theory is descriptively adequate* if it makes a descriptively adequate grammar available for each natural language.

Although even descriptive adequacy on a large scale is by no means easy to approach, it is crucial for the productive development of linguistic theory that much higher goals than this be pursued. To facilitate the clear formulation of deeper questions, it is useful to consider the abstract problem of constructing an "acquisition model" for language, that is, a theory of language learning or grammar construction. Clearly, a child who has learned a language has developed an internal representation of a system of rules that determine how sentences are to be formed, used, and understood. Using the term "grammar" with a systematic ambiguity (to refer, first, to the native speaker's internally represented "theory of his language" and, second, to the linguist's account of this), we can say that the child has developed and internally represented a generative grammar, in the sense described. He has done this on the basis of observation of what we may call *primary linguistic data*. This must include examples of linguistic performance that are taken to be well-formed sentences, and may include also examples designated as nonsentences, and no doubt much other information of the sort that is required for language learning, whatever this may be (see pp. 31–32). On the basis of such data, the child constructs a grammar—that is, a theory of the language of which the well-formed sentences of the primary linguistic data constitute a small sample.[14]

[14] It seems clear that many children acquire first or second languages quite successfully even

To learn a language, then, the child must have a method for devising an appropriate grammar, given primary linguistic data. As a precondition for language learning, he must possess, first, a linguistic theory that specifies the form of the grammar of a possible human language, and, second, a strategy for selecting a grammar of the appropriate form that is compatible with the primary linguistic data. As a long-range task for general linguistics, we might set the problem of developing an account of this innate linguistic theory that provides the basis for language learning. (Note that we are again using the term "theory"—in this case "theory of language" rather than "theory of a particular language"—with a systematic ambiguity, to refer both to the child's innate predisposition to learn a language of a certain type and to the linguist's account of this.)

To the extent that a linguistic theory succeeds in selecting a descriptively adequate grammar on the basis of primary linguistic data, we can say that it meets the condition of *explanatory adequacy*. That is, to this extent, it offers an explanation for the intuition of the native speaker on the basis of an empirical hypothesis concerning the innate predisposition of the child to develop a certain kind of theory to deal with the evidence presented to him. Any such hypothesis can be falsified (all too easily, in actual fact) by showing that it fails to provide a descriptively adequate grammar for primary linguistic data from some other language—evidently the child is not predisposed to learn one language rather than another. It is supported when it does provide an adequate explanation for some aspect of linguistic structure, an account of the way in which such knowledge might have been obtained.

Clearly, it would be utopian to expect to achieve explanatory adequacy on a large scale in the present state of linguistics. Nevertheless, considerations of explanatory adequacy are often critical for advancing linguistic theory. Gross coverage of a large mass of data can often be attained by conflicting theories; for precisely this reason it is not, in itself, an achievement of any particular theoretical interest or importance. As in any other field, the important problem in linguistics is to discover a complex of data that differentiates between conflicting conceptions of linguistic structure in that one of these conflicting theories can describe these data only by *ad hoc* means whereas the other can explain it on the basis of some empirical assumption about the form of language. Such small-scale studies of explanatory adequacy have, in fact, provided most of the evidence that has any serious bearing on the nature of linguistic structure. Thus whether we are comparing radically different theories of grammar or trying to determine the correctness of some particular aspect of one such theory, it is questions of explanatory adequacy that must, quite often, bear the burden of justification. This remark is in no way inconsistent with the fact that explanatory adequacy on a large scale is out of reach, for the present. It simply brings out the highly tentative character of any attempt to justify an empirical claim about linguistic structure.

To summarize briefly, there are two

---

though no special care is taken to teach them and no special attention is given to their progress. It also seems apparent that much of the actual speech observed consists of fragments and deviant expressions of a variety of sorts. Thus it seems that a child must have the ability to "invent" a generative grammar that defines well-formedness and assigns interpretations to sentences even though the primary linguistic data that he uses as a basis for this act of theory construction may, from the point of view of the theory he constructs, be deficient in various respects. In general, there is an important element of truth in the traditional view that "the pains which everyone finds in conversation...is not to comprehend what another thinketh, but to extricate his thought from the signs or words which often agree not with it" (Cordemoy, 1667), and the problem this poses for speech perception is magnified many times for the language learner.

respects in which one can speak of "justifying a generative grammar." On one level (that of descriptive adequacy), the grammar is justified to the extent that it correctly describes its object, namely the linguistic intuition—the tacit competence—of the native speaker. In this sense, the grammar is justified on *external* grounds, on grounds of correspondence to linguistic fact. On a much deeper and hence much more rarely attainable level (that of explanatory adequacy), a grammar is justified to the extent that it is a *principled* descriptively adequate system, in that the linguistic theory with which it is associated selects this grammar over others, given primary linguistic data with which all are compatible. In this sense, the grammar is justified on *internal* grounds, on grounds of its relation to a linguistic theory that constitutes an explanatory hypothesis about the form of language as such. The problem of internal justification—of explanatory adequacy—is essentially the problem of constructing a theory of language acquisition, an account of the specific innate abilities that make this achievement possible.

On Understanding and Creating Sentences*

CHARLES E. OSGOOD

The writing of this paper began in the spring of 1963 specifically for my presidential address before the American Psychological Association in September of that year. By mid-summer—with some 100 pages completed and obviously another 100 to go—it became obvious that this was to be more in the order of a little book than an hour-or-so address. The address as given represented a compromise between summarizing the fuller materials for my psycholinguist colleagues and trying to say something of significance to the other (perhaps 90 per cent) of the psychologists in the audience. As is often the way with compromises, neither goal was probably attained, and needless to say the style of the paper reflects its original purpose.

If I were writing this paper today, there is much that would be modified. The sections dealing with linguistics per se *would be up-dated to include materials from and implications of significant papers by Chomsky, Fodor, Katz, Miller, and others not then available to me (e.g., in the Fodor and Katz collection, 1964; the* Handbook of Mathematical Psychology, *1963; and in Chomsky's most recent book,* Aspects of a Theory of Syntax, *1965). The general characteristics of my own model of the language user (speaker-hearer) would not be modified to any great extent, but I would now have much more to say about the notion of meaning as a simultaneous bundle of distinctive semantic features—how such features relate to componential* r_m *'s, how they can be inferred from the rules of combination of words in phrases and sentences, and how this notion appears to converge with the most recent ideas of Chomsky on subcategorization and selection rules in the grammar. But then, I am sure we would all like to rewrite our earlier attempts rather than see them appear reprinted in collections in all their innocence.*—Charles E. Osgood

* Address of the President to the Seventy-First Annual Convention of the American Psychological Association, Philadelphia, September 1, 1963.

Charles E. Osgood, "On Understanding and Greating Sentences," American Psychologist, 18 *(1963), 735–751. Reprinted by permission of the author and publisher.*

References

Chomsky, N., *Aspects of the Theory of Syntax.* Cambridge; Mass.: M.I.T. Press, 1965.

Fodor, J. A., and J. J. Katz, eds., *The Structure of Language: Readings in the Philosophy of Language.* Englewood Cliffs, N. J.: Prentice-Hall, Inc., 1964.

Luce, R. D., R. R. Bush, and E. Galanter, eds., *Handbook of Mathematical Psychology.* New York: John Wiley & Sons, Inc., 1963.

It was exactly a decade ago that Hobart Mowrer (1954) offered this Association his Presidential Address on "The Psychologist Looks at Language." At the core of his paper was the insightful proposition that "in communication we are not transferring meanings from person to person so much as we are transferring meanings *from sign to sign* within a given person, within a single mind [p. 663]." And he went on to say that "The communicative act, in its most salient and significant aspect, lies... in the combination, juxtaposition, or association of the meanings thus aroused *in novel, 'informative' ways* [pp. 663–664]." The means for accomplishing this was the *sentence,* and Mowrer proposed that, psychologically, the sentence is essentially a conditioning device. Many, many words about words have flowed through the psychological literature in the decade since then, and it seems necessary, as well as appropriate, to take another look at the psychology of the sentence.

Toward the close of his address, Hobart Mowrer also had this to say:

> One can hardly think of a more exciting, yet arduous, scientific undertaking than would be involved in a joint exploration by grammarians [linguists] and learning theorists of the innumerable psychological functions which, over countless centuries, have become imbedded in the structural forms of the world's major and minor languages [p. 690].

What with linguists like Roman Jakobson, Joseph Greenberg, and Noam Chomsky to the left of me and with psychologists like Fred Skinner, Jack Carroll, Jim Jenkins, and Roger Brown to the right of me—not to mention George Miller, who is usually ahead of me—I feel that I have been rather in the thick of psycholinguistics. This paper is my attempt to meet a challenge from the linguists that has become completely explicit in the past few years: *Can our psychological theories incorporate and render comprehensible the way human beings understand and create sentences?* If not, then our theories are at best insufficient and at worst erroneous.

THE PROBLEM

So that you will appreciate the nature of the problem, I must ask you to return with me, for just a little while, to grammar school. We will start with a simple, unanalyzed string of words—The man hits the colorful ball—and trace through a series of increasingly powerful linguistic models designed to analyze them and define their sentence-hood.

We may begin with the finite state grammar, a model generally familiar to psychologists. Since sentences have a way of proceeding sequentially (or from left to right on the printed page), it seems intuitively reasonable that each succeeding word should be probabilistically dependent upon the preceding words, and hence that a Markov-type sentence generating machine should be sufficient. The probabilities at each transition point would depend upon the machine's previous experience with sentences, this experience providing both its lexicon and its rules of transition (or grammar). The lin-

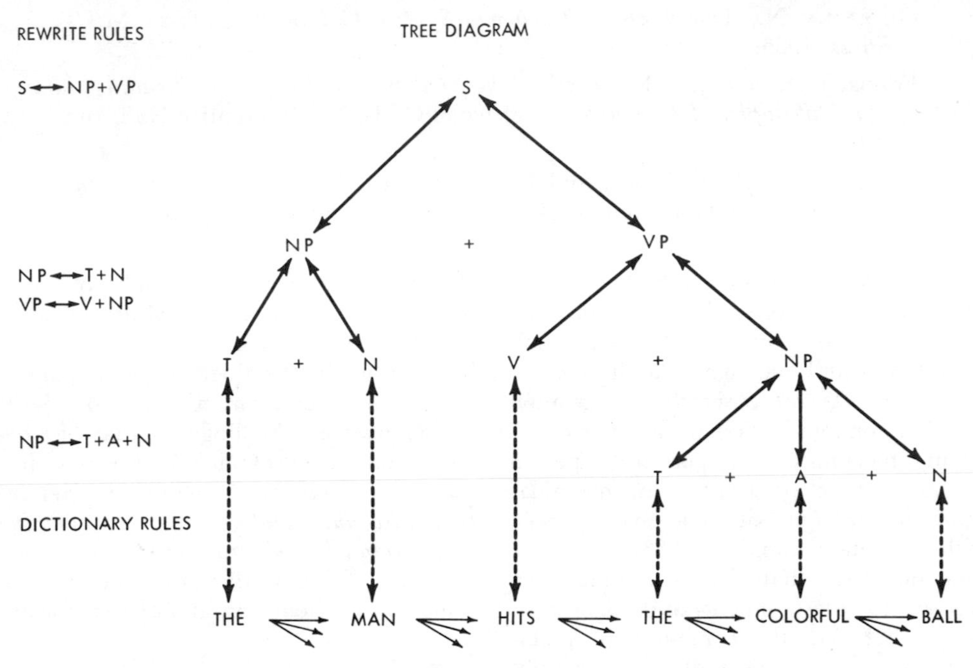

Fig. 1: Illustration of phrase structure analysis.

guist Chomsky (1957) has argued that such a finite-state generator could not produce the potentially infinite set of grammatical sentences, including novel ones, that characterizes any natural language, and Miller, Galanter, and Pribram (1960) have pointed out that, assuming an ordinary vocabulary and an upper limit of 20 words per sentence, it would take a childhood lasting 100 years to be exposed just once to each of the possible sentences. Chomsky also demonstrates that a Markov-type generator could not handle the potentially infinite imbedding that characterizes sentences in natural languages, as for example in the sentence *The man who said that I know that John is the one who left the party that we had earlier is here*—a difficult but by no means inconceivable utterance.

A model that seems to resolve these difficulties, and the one commonly employed by linguists, is the phrase structure grammar. As shown in Figure 1, our sample sentence (S) is first resolved into its immediate constituents, a noun phrase (NP) plus a verb phrase (VP), these in turn are resolved into their immediate constituents, and so on—gradually generating a hierarchically organized "tree." Now you are certainly convinced that you're back in grammar school! This is nothing other than what we once studied under the name of "parsing" or "diagraming" a sentence. But there is more to this than meets the eye.

Note first that each shift from one level to the next can be represented by a rewrite rule, and each rewrite rule is restricted to a linear segregation or amalgamation of the units at the subordinate level. Note second that such grammatical trees, as contrasted with the Markov model, clearly specify "what goes with what" along the terminal strings (thus *the man* or *the colorful ball* form wholes, whereas *hits the* definitely does not). Finally, note that the rewrite rules are of quite different kind than what I have called the dictionary rules: The rewrite rules are analogous to the principles in a scientific theory, with the symbols (S, NP, V, etc.) serving as the theoretical constructs; but the dictionary rules are like those of identification, where we assign construct status to events in the real world in order to operate on them in the theory. Thus the sentence *A boy rings an ancient bell* is equivalent in grammatical theory to the sentence we have diagramed here.

Contrary to usual linguistic practice, in which the rewrite arrows and sequences within the tree are unidirectional (left-to-right and up-to-down), I have deliberately shown bidirectional arrows. The linguist's way of doing things reflects his too exclusive concern with the speaker, I think —that is, with generating or encoding sentences. The listener, in the position of interpreting or decoding sentences, begins with strings of words, combines them into large units and, finally, understands the sentence as a whole. In other words, sentence creators start at the trunk and end with the leaves, whereas sentence understanders begin with the leaves and hopefully end up at the trunk. At the very bottom of this diagram I have suggested the humble status of the finite state sentence generating model.

Is this phrase structure model sufficient for linguistic purposes? The problem is one of efficiency, simplicity, and elegance. Not only does this grammar require a different representation for every modification of each basic sentence, but, since no account is taken of the derivational history of sentences, it cannot disambiguate ambiguous sentences like *The shooting of the hunters was terrible*—without knowing whether this sentence was derived from *the hunters shoot* or from *they shot the hunters,* we do not know whether to say "They should practice more" or "They should have been wearing red jackets!" Chomsky's major contribution to linguistics has been his elaboration of the rationale for a transformational grammar. One set of transformation rules will carry our diagramed kernel sentence into the passive (*The colorful ball is hit by the man*); another set carries it into negation (*The man does not hit the colorful ball*); a combination of these two sets of rules carries it into a passive-negation construction (*The colorful ball is not hit by the man*); and so forth. The power of this theory lies in its capacity to generate an infinite set of grammatical sentences, and no ungrammatical ones, from a minimally finite set of kernels and a minimally finite set of transformations.

But what about meaning? Linguists have had relatively little to say about semantics; indeed, one could fairly say that they have avoided it like the plague. The most rigorous attempt to apply linguistic methods to the semantics of sentences of which I am aware is to be found in a recent paper by Katz and Fodor (1963) titled "The Structure of Semantic Theory." Their basic proposition is that *semantics equals linguistic description minus grammar.* What does grammar leave for semantics? In the first place, we note that any grammar will provide identical structural descriptions for sentences that obviously differ in meaning (*Man bites dog* versus *Dog bites man,* for example) and different descriptions for sentences that are the same in meaning (*The dog bit the man* versus *The man was bitten by the dog*). There are also sentences that are structurally unambigous but semantically ambiguous, like *He will get the case* (of beer? at law? in the railroad station?), sentences that are structurally unambiguous but semantically anomalous, like *He was aware of the subliminal stimulus* (I realize that a number of psychologists have failed to recognize the anomaly here!), and sentences that are paraphrases of each other and yet structurally different, as the sentence *She is my mother-in-law* is to *She is my wife's mother.*

What, according to Katz and Fodor, are the necessary components of a semantic theory, i.e., necessary for an understanding of the fluent native speaker's ability to interpret sentences? The first component is a dictionary—the grammar of a language cannot account for differences in interpretation that depend solely upon substitution of lexical alternatives within otherwise identical frames. It means something quite different to say *A scorpion bit me* than to say *A mosquito bit me*. The second necessary component is a set of projection rules which take account of relations between words in the sentence and between syntactic structure and meaning alternatives—a dictionary usually provides more semantic alternatives for a word than are possible in the context of the given sentence.

Now let us return to the sample sentence diagramed in Figure 1 and subject it to semantic analysis *à la* Katz and Fodor. Such a sentence, along with its structural description as diagramed, is the input and a semantic interpretation is the output. Since we are dealing with the interpretation (decoding) of this sentence we proceed upward, successively amalgamating the branches under each node. The structural analysis predetermines the grammatical alternatives we select from the dictionary—thus *man* (N) rather than *man* (V) and *hits* (V) rather than *hits* (Npl)—but it does not select semantic alternatives within the same form class. Combining the two dictionary alternatives for *colorful* ("abounding in contrasting bright colors" versus "having distinctive character") with the three dictionary meanings of *ball* ("large assembly for the purpose of dancing" versus "having globular shape" versus "solid missile for projection by engine of war"), and applying a semantic rule which eliminates anomalous compounds, Katz and Fodor retain four viable amalgamations of *the* + *colorful* + *ball*. Looking up *hits* in our dictionary, and following only the grammatical path marked V (verb), we find two alternatives: "collides with an impact" versus "strikes with a blow or a missile." Combining these alternatives with the four viable alternatives for *the colorful ball* and again using a rule of anomaly, all alternatives using *ball* in the sense of "large assembly for the purpose of dancing" are eliminated. The final combination of *the man* with *hits the colorful ball* does nothing further to disambiguate this sentence, and Katz and Fodor conclude (*a*) that this sentence is not semantically anomalous and (*b*) that it is four ways semantically ambiguous.

I have gone through this rather laborious analysis to make two critical points: First, *semantic analysis of this type takes no account of the varying probabilities of alternative interpretations.* I take it to be intuitively obvious that the four alternatives here differ markedly in the probability of what was intended by the speaker or writer, and this can be shown by paraphrasing the alternative readings:

1. *the man strikes the colorful round object with a blow* (very high probability);
2. *the man collides with the colorful round object* (conceivable, but it would have to be a pretty big ball!);
3. *the man strikes the colorful solid missile with a blow* (conceivable, but not probable in this day and age);
4. *the man collides with the colorful solid missile* (all one could say to this would be, "What, is Tom Thumb drunk again?").

Second, *semantic analysis of this type is unable to select among ambiguities and resolve them.* If such an inocuous sentence as *The man hits the colorful ball* is open to no less than four unresolvable interpretations, I suspect that the vast majority of sentences we encounter in everyday life would remain ambiguous after analysis—and if this were the best fluent speakers and listeners could do, communication would be in an even worse state than it is now.

The reason for this sorry state of affairs, of course, is precisely what Katz and

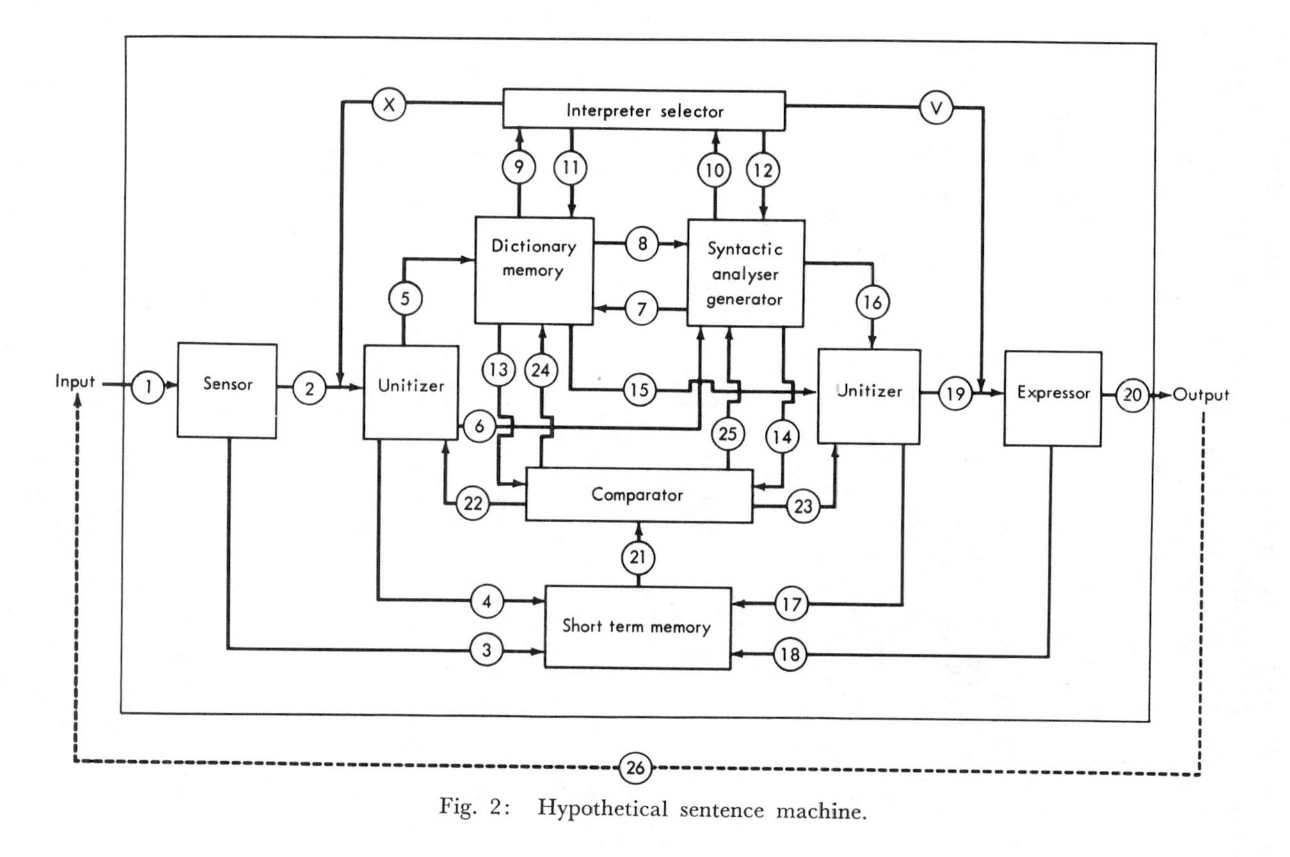

Fig. 2: Hypothetical sentence machine.

Fodor must leave out in order to make their analysis rigorous in the linguistic sense—knowledge on the part of users of a language about the nature of their world and about the momentary situational, motivational, and linguistic contexts in which particular sentences occur.

I have asked my colleagues in linguistics and computeristics what would be the minimum equipment required for a sentence understanding and creating machine. The result of this inquiry is shown in Figure 2. It is just a bit overwhelming. I am not going to lead you along the paths of this flow diagram—it would take too much time—but I would like you to note the types of equipment needed: For sentence decoding we need SENSORS, UNITIZERS, SHORT-TERM MEMORIES, DICTIONARY MEMORIES, SYNTACTIC ANALYZERS, COMPARATORS, and INTERPRETERS; for sentence *encoding* we would need SELECTORS, DICTIONARIES, SYNTACTIC GENERATORS, COMPARATORS, UNITIZERS, and EXPRESSORS. Computer models of this kind are exercises in problem setting rather than problem solving. Terms like DICTIONARY, UNITIZER, COMPARATOR, and SYNTACTIC GENERATOR merely point to processes that must be accounted for in any psychological theory, rather than providing explanations in and of themselves—and besides, I think we can do the job more economically.

NEO-BEHAVIORISM AND PSYCHOLINGUISTICS

So let me turn now to a bit of psychological theory. I will be very brief about it, both because I have presented these ideas *in extenso* elsewhere (cf. Osgood, 1955, 1956, 1957, 1963), and because I am eager to get on with the psychology of the sentence. In complete agreement with B. F. Skinner (1957), I believe that an adequate theory of language behavior must be a learning theory, but that we neither wish nor require any special theory for language. The goals of psycholinguistic theory include those of linguistics—since, after all, the rules of grammar are part of the lawfulness of human behavior—but must go beyond to encompass relations between linguistic and nonlinguistic events (semantics and pragmatics). We will consider several models of behavior in general, each of increasing complexity—a complexity forced by the criterion of sufficiency.

Of course, there are differences between linguistic and psychological approaches to language that go beyond the question of inclusiveness. It was the linguist Ferdinand de Saussure who first made the oft-cited distinction between *la langue* and *la parole*. *La langue* refers to language as an abstract system; *la parole* refers to language as actualized speech events. The linguist is characteristically interested in the former, the psychologist in the latter. Chomsky's conception of the grammar of a language as a theory which will generate an infinite set of sentences that are grammatical and none that are ungrammatical is clearly in the realm of *la langue*. When one listens to spontaneous speech with an ear toward how things are being said rather than what is being said, however, it appears that well-formed, grammatical sentences are an exception to the rule. Here is a literal transcription from the taped spontaneous speech of someone whom I consider to be a normally fluent speaker of English:

> As far as I know, no one yet has done the // in a way obvious now and interesting problem of / doing a // in a sense a structural frequency study of the alternative / syntactical ///[a] in a given language, say, like English, the alternative /[a] possible structures, and how // what their hierarchical / probability of occurrence structure is.

Lest some of my colleagues in psycholinguistics suspect this might be an excerpt from their speech, let me hasten to say that this was a bit of my own verbal behavior at a Social Science Research Council conference on content analysis.

If one wishes to travel over a terrain, and he builds a kiddie-car to do it in, this is fine if it gets him everywhere he wants to go efficiently and economically. In fact, it is then a most parsimonious device. So when I refer to Skinner's single-stage behaviorism as a "kiddie-car model" I am not being derogatory—merely descriptive. In his book *Verbal Behavior,* Skinner (1957) sets himself the task of describing the antecedent conditions which determine the emission of verbal responses, that is, lawful dependency relations between classes of stimuli and classes of responses (operants). That his is a very mechanistic and deterministic conception of man's highest achievement is not the issue. The question is one of sufficiency. There are some psychological peaks and linguistic jungles which the kiddie-car simply cannot negotiate.

There is the securely documented phenomenon known as semantic generalization: Having learned a novel response to the word JOY (for example, lifting the forefinger to escape shock), the normal adult speaker of English will promptly transfer this response to the word GLEE—but not to the physically more similar word BOY. The basis for the transfer is obviously similarity of meaning, but there is no place for such symbolic processes in Skinner's behaviorism. There is also the phenomenon of semantic satiation which Wallace Lambert and Leon Jakobovits (1963) are busily pinning down: When subjects rapidly repeat the words CANOE or NEGRO, semantic profiles for these words shrink toward meaninglessness; but equally massed repetition of the nonsense syllables NÚKA or GRONÍ (which have the same overt response form as CANOE or NEGRO) produces no semantic satiation. And then there are the jungles of grammar and syntax, which Skinner tries to explore armed with little more than the autoclitic (a special form of intraverbal operant); according to Chomsky's (1959) incisive review, this excursion is a monumental failure.

The *two*-stage mediation model had its origins in Hull's notion of the "pure stimulus act," an act whose function is to produce distinctive self-stimulation rather than to be instrumental in itself. At that time, 1930, Hull noted that such a mechanism could serve as the basis for symbolic processes, but he did not fully explore this possibility himself. Along with many others, I have proposed the mediation model as the characteristic, rather than the exceptional, case in behavior, and I have tried to use it as the basis for a psychological theory of meaning. We might dub this the "horse-and-buggy model"—at least it has the advantage of putting the driver inside.

The essential nature of mediation can be understood in terms of Figure 3. *Whenever some originally neutral stimulus* (sign-to-be), [S], *is repeatedly contiguous with another stimulus* (significate), $\dot{S}$, *which regularly and reliably elicits a particular pattern of total behavior,* R_T, *the neutral stimulus will become associated with some portion,* r_m, *of this total behavior as a representational mediation process.* This is a conditioning postulate with a significant difference—namely, that the mediating reaction to the sign is not the same as the reaction to the significate, but rather consists of those most readily conditionable, least effortful, and least interfering components of the total original reaction. Such a process is representational because it is part of the very same behavior made to the thing signified; it is mediational because the distinctive self-stimulation, s_m, can become associated selectively with various instrumental acts, R_X, which are

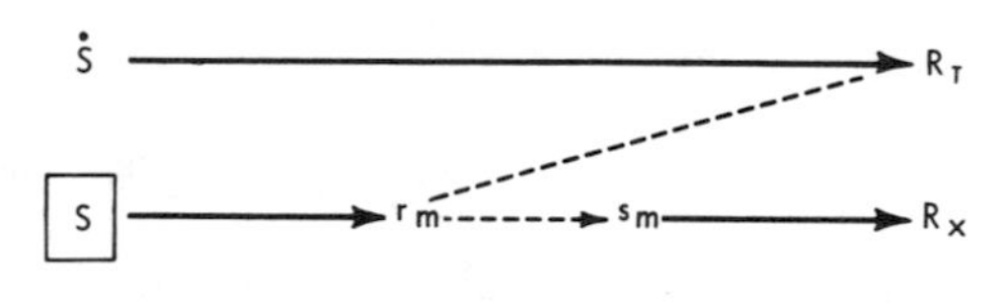

Fig. 3: Two-stage mediation model

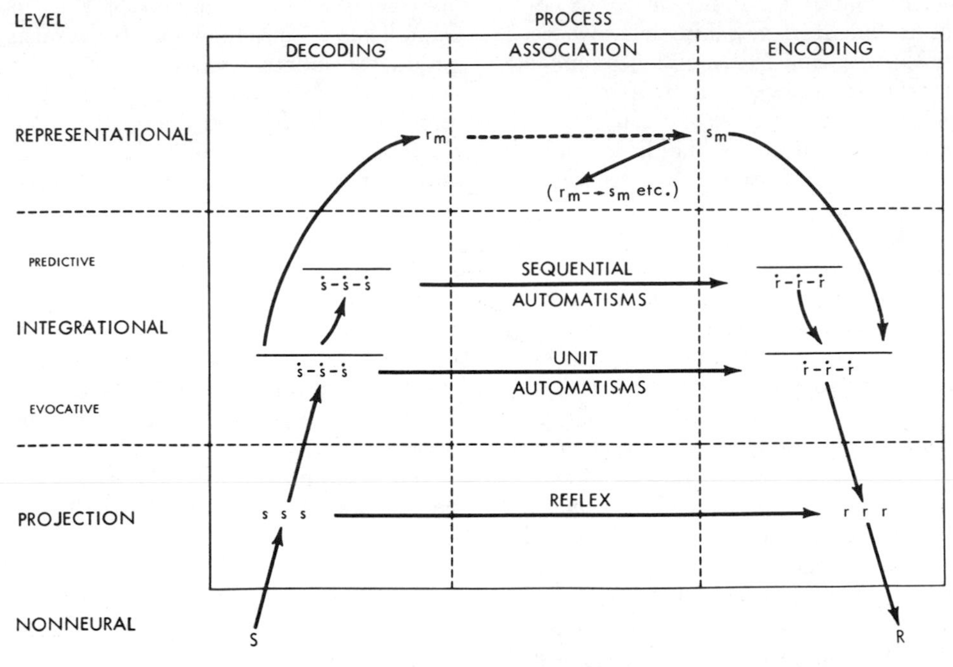

Fig. 4. Three-stage mediation-integration model.

appropriate to, or take account of, the thing signified.

What has been done here, in effect, is to break the behavior sequence between overt S and overt R into two independently variable parts, decoding habits and encoding habits. All of the conceptual machinery of single-stage S-R theory—generalization, inhibition, and the like—is assumed to apply to each of the stages of the mediation model. This separation greatly increases the explanatory power of behavior theory: The phenomena of semantic generalization and semantic satiation are readily incorporated, and we have the beginnings of a theory of meaning and the symbolic processes. But there are at least two regions where this horse-and-buggy model cannot travel. The first of these is the territory of perceptual organization, long the stronghold of Gestalt theory and the Waterloo of S-R theory. The second is the territory of motor skill organization. In both cases we appear to be dealing with closure and integration phenomena, either of S-S or R-R nature, and no strictly S-R model will suffice.

Therefore, let us investigate the possibilities in a *three*-stage mediation-integration model. At the APA meetings last year, two of our award winning members, J. J. Gibson (1963) and Donald Hebb (1963), agreed on the need to separate sensation from perception but also on the identification of perception with meaning. Let me suggest that on both input and output sides we are dealing with a three-level system, as suggested in Figure 4. On the input side, the lowest level, which I shall call *sensory,* begins with the receptors and ends with sensory signals at the termini of the projection systems, providing a faithful mirror of "what is." The second level, which I shall term *perceptual,* begins with these patterns of sensory signals and ends with the most probable integration of their more central correlates as determined by redundancies in past experience—thus, a mirror of "what ought to be." The third level, which I shall call *meaningful*, begins with these meaningless sensory integrations and ends with the most probable representational mediation processes with which they have been associated—a mirror of "what it signifies" in terms of past experience with behavioral outcomes. Similar analysis of behavioral output yields *execution* (projection), *skill* (integrational), and *intention* (meaningful) level.

What now requires some explication is the integration level. Let me borrow, rephrase, and simplify a notion developed by Hebb (1949) in his analysis of cell assemblies and phase sequences, and call it the Integration Principle: *The greater the frequency with which stimulus events* (S-S) *or response events* (R-R) *have been paired in input or output experience of the organism, the greater will be the tendency for their central correlates to activate each other.* One critical variable here is redundancy among input or output events; another is frequency; yet another is temporal contiguity. But I think this is all—motivation and reinforcement seem to have nothing to do with the formation of S-S or R-R integrations.

All of the extensive literature relating visual and auditory thresholds for words to their frequencies of usage testifies to the role of frequency—high frequency and contiguity yield evocative integrations (units which display closure) whereas lower frequency or less contiguity yield merely predictive integrations which help to override the "noise" in everyday decoding and encoding. A recent experiment by Vernon Tyler (1962) tested the assumption that sensory integrations are formed independently of reinforcement; results were as predicted.

This model must appear quite complicated in comparison with most S-R theories. I'm afraid complexity is the price we must pay for sufficiency. However, since I am by no means convinced that even this "monster" is sufficiently complex to handle language behavior, I merely dub it "the Model-T Ford theory." Also, I realize that there are many who will conclude that, despite the fancy chrome and the three-tone horn, this is still just the little old kiddie-car at heart. In a sense this is true, and that is as it should be. The question before us is whether this souped-up kiddie-car will enable us to navigate the domain of The Sentence.

DECISION AND CONTROL IN BEHAVIOR

Now I want to discuss the problem of decision and control in behavior. It will be useful for us to think in terms of two quite different types of hierarchies: sequential hierarchies (horizontal, left-to-right), relating antecedent to subsequent events; and simultaneous hierarchies (vertical, up-to-down), relating subordinate events to supraordinate events. The former are clearly Markovian or probabilistic in nature; the latter clearly are not.

Viewed in the abstract, there are two different kinds of sequential hierarchies, convergent and divergent: A pure convergent hierarchy exists when multiple antecedent events are associated with a single subsequent event; a pure divergent hierarchy exists when a single antecedent event is associated with multiple subsequent events. As we know from transfer and interference studies, convergent hierarchies are facilitative whereas divergent hierarchies are competitive. But behavior does not transpire in the abstract, of course, and in practice convergent and divergent hierarchies involving the same sets of events operate simultaneously. Let me make two simple, and I hope clarifying, assumptions here: *First, "decision" in behavior is simply selection of the momentarily most probable alternative within any divergent hierarchy.* There is nothing necessarily "cognitive" or "volitional" involved; it is a probabilistic business going on at all levels in decoding, associating,

		Ψ Correlate	ℒ Decoding	ℒ Encoding	Ψ Correlate
MEANINGFUL	Temporal pattern	Interpretations	SENTENCES	SENTENCES	Intentions
		Kernel amalgamation	(PHRASES)	(PHRASES)	Kernel differentiation
	Spatial pattern	Meanings	WORDS	WORDS	Meanings
MEANINGLESS	Temporal pattern	Forms	WORDS	WORDS	Forms
		?	(MORPHEMES)	(MORPHEMES)	?
		Perceptual skill components	PHONEMES	SYLLABLES	Motor skill components
	Spatial pattern	Sensory signals	DISTINCTIVE FEATURES	DISTINCTIVE FEATURES	Motor signals

Fig. 5: Units of decoding and encoding.

and encoding. *Second, "control" over behavior is simply the way in which combination and patterning within convergent hierarchies modify the momentary probabilities of dependent alternatives.* This, too, is a strictly probabilistic business, having nothing to do with "purpose" or "will," except as these notions may be redefined in these terms. It is the way context influences outcomes at choice points throughout the behavior system.

The notion of simultaneous, vertical hierarchies of units within units within units has been about as foreign to psychologists as the notion of probabilistic sequential hierarchies has been to linguists. The only psychologists I know who have made full use of the notion of hierarchical "trees" in a general theory of behavior are Miller, Galanter, and Pribram (1960) in their book on *Plans and the Structure of Behavior,* but this conception is consistent with the way complex operations are programed on a computer and with the phrase structure grammar employed by linguists. The problem is to identify the functional units at each level of organization. One of the rules of the game is that the units at each supraordinate level must be exhaustively divisible into units at all subordinate levels, with no leftover pieces, and vice versa.

The two inner columns in Figure 5 present what I think are the minimum and sufficient levels of units in language decoding and encoding. Units which do not seem to have psychological reality—regardless of their linguistic reality and usefulness—are bracketed. Psychological correlates of each unit are suggested in the outer columns. A major division is indicated between meaningful and meaningless levels of organization, and within each a distinction is made between spatially and temporally patterned events. Thus phonemes at the meaningless level and words at the meaningful level are represented as simultaneous "bundles" of distinctive, differentiating features.[1]

There are several rather radical proposals embodied in this diagram. One is that the units of decoding and encoding are not necessarily the same—the syllable, for example, is plainly evident in speaking but seems to have no representation in listening. Another is that the morpheme, so crucial in linguistic analysis, is psychologically nonexistent; compare *boys* with *noise*—the former is two morphemes, [boy] + [s-pl.] and the latter is one, yet there is no sense of the morpheme boundary in the former case. Perhaps the most radical suggestion is the double role given the *word*—incidentally, a unit which linguists have great trouble defining even if native speakers do not. Here the humble word is shown as Janus faced; at meaningless levels it serves as the most inclusive unit whereas at meaningful levels it serves as the minimal unit. I will have more to say on this anon.

Now we are in position to reconsider the Markov versus Chomsky controversy. The Markovian model of language behavior provided a happy meeting ground for information theorists and learning theorists, and the past decade has witnessed an outpouring of descriptive and experimental demonstrations of the stochastic nature of language behavior at all levels. Yet, you will recall, Chomsky demonstrated the insufficiency of the Markov model on several logical grounds, and many of his adherents have interpreted "insufficient" to mean "erroneous." Actually, the evidence for nonchance, transitional dependencies in language behavior is impressive and neither trivial nor irrelevant; it must also be taken into account in any complete psycholinguistic theory.

I detect what I believe are two ambiguities in Chomsky's (1957) arguments. The first is what I shall call the unilevel fallacy: Many of his criticisms of the Markovian model involve the tacit assumption that stochastic processes operate only on one level of units at a time—usually on the terminal strings of grammatical trees, i.e., the word level. There is nothing about the model itself that sets this restriction. The second is what I shall call the decision fallacy: Chomsky's generative grammar, even in its full-blown transformational form, says nothing whatsoever about decision making. For example, what determines whether the speaker will select a simple kernel sentence form or transform it into a passive or a question form? As a matter of fact, such decisions are what Chomsky (1959) himself has termed the "optional rules of grammar"; not only are these options by no means trivial, as Chomsky agrees, but they appear to be precisely the points of articulation between the Markovian and Chomskian models.

Figure 6 suggests how sequential (probabilistic) and simultaneous (unitizing) hierarchies can be integrated. You will recognize this as the "tree" diagram with which we began, but with some modifications and additions. Divergent sequential hierarchies have been substituted for the +'s in the old diagram, to indicate that what follows what within the noun phrase or within the verb phrase is in part optional and therefore probabilitistically determined. Both an antecedent sentence

[1] The figure is not quite accurate with regard to phonemes.

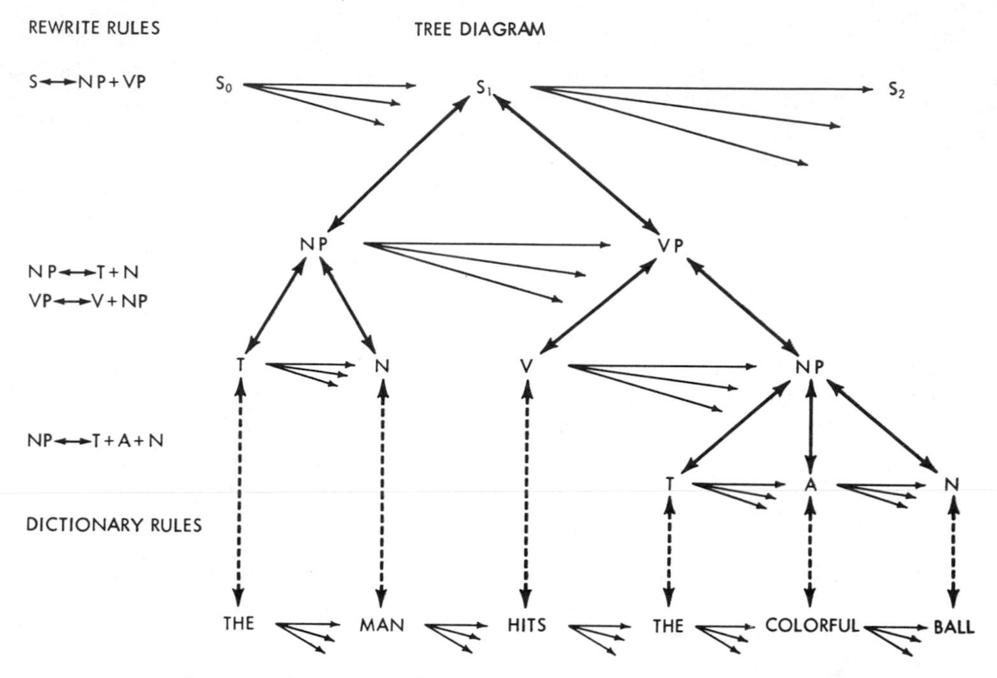

Fig. 6: Integration of sequential and simultaneous hierarchies.

(S_0) and a subsequent sentence (S_2), which could have been produced either by the same or a different speaker, have been added, to indicate that sentences as wholes do not appear out of nowhere but rather are themselves linked probabilistically to other units at their own level. Transitional decisions at supraordinate levels modify the probabilities of units at subordinate levels, but only partially; not that the noun class of *man* in the diagramed sentence is jointly dependent upon its vertical relation to NP and its horizontal relation to T.

A very recent experiment by Neal Johnson (1963) is particularly a propos here. He had subjects learn sentences of the two grammatical types shown in Figure 7. In the first, linguistic analysis would locate one major juncture between *boy* and *saved;* in the second, there would be a minor break between *house* and *across* and a major one between *street* and *is.* Johnson predicted that probability of transitional error in recall would be greater across phrase boundaries than within. The bars in this figure give the relative probabilities of errors at each word-to-word transition. Note, first, that as predicted sentence Type (a) has one peak of transitional error between *boy* and *saved* whereas sentence Type (b) has a minor peak between *house* and *across* and a major peak between *street* and *is.* But note, second, that within each phrase there is an almost linear decrease in transitional errors running from left to right. These data appear to confirm rather strikingly the idea that simultaneous and sequential hierarchies combine in the understanding and creating of sentences.

COMPONENTS OF A THEORY OF THE SENTENCE

Now I would like to suggest three essential components or processes in a psy-

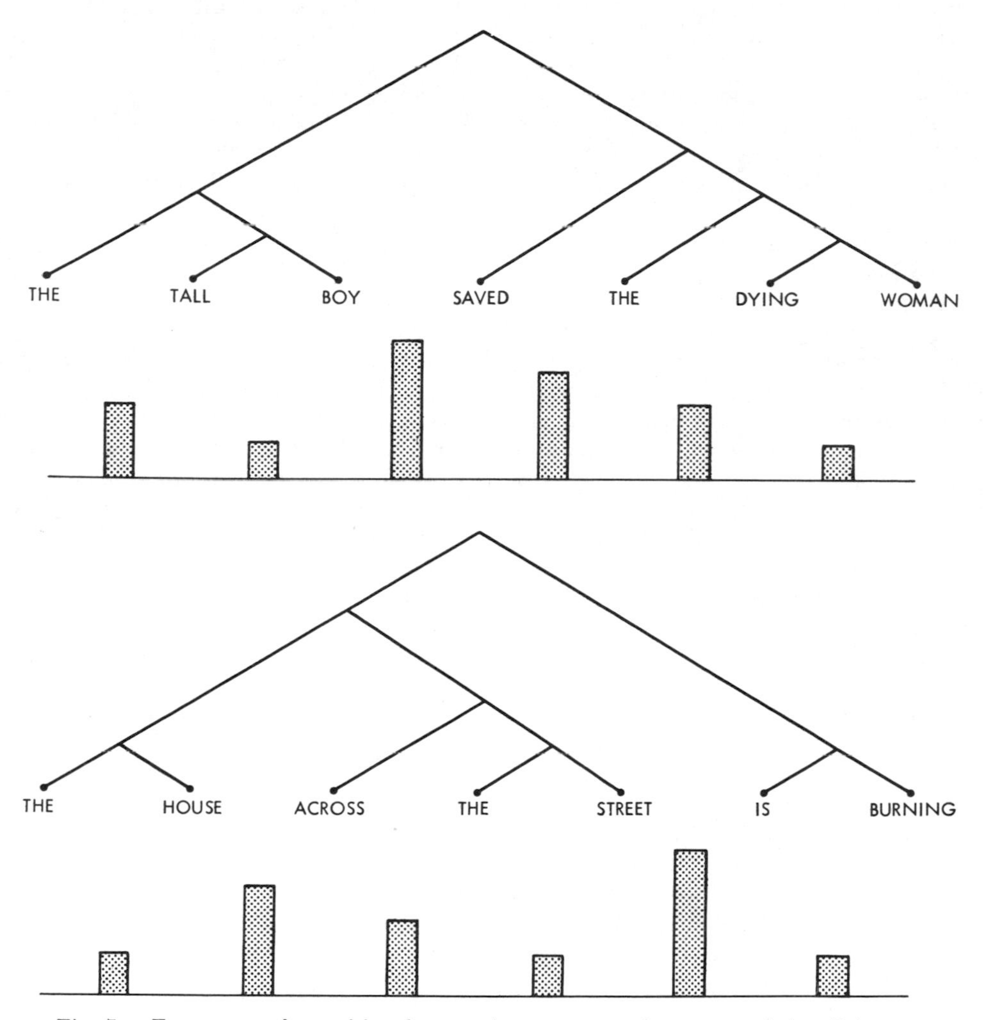

Fig. 7: Frequency of transitional errors in two types of sentences (after Johnson, 1963).

chological theory of the sentence. Although I will give them fancy names for communication purposes, this will be no special theory of language behavior, since in each case I shall try to show that these functions require nothing more, mechanismwise, than is available in the three-stage, mediation-integration model of behavior in general.

First, we have the Word Form Pool. The term "pool" has at least two metaphorical usages: (*a*) as a reflecting surface on which ephemeral patterns can be displayed and (*b*) as a supply of entities or the place where they are stored. I intend to convey both of these notions simultaneously. What I have termed the sensory and motor integration systems are modifiable in terms of the redundancy, frequency, and contiguity of their inputs and outputs respectively; thus they can come to "mirror" in their own neural organization regularities in the past experience of the organism. Being convergent, probabilistic systems, they have the additional, most important property of closure—sketchy input information is internally elaborated into the most probable wholes. By virtue of the reverberatory property of cell assemblies, these systems provide a "reflecting surface" on which the elements for sentence building can be displayed; they are thus functionally equivalent to the notion of "temporary storage" as used by those who think in terms of computers. They are also "unitizers" of input or output, by virtue of the closure property.

But what *are* the units at this level? Given the principles by which the integration systems work, the units must tend toward the largest segments of language that are (*a*) highly redundant, (*b*) very frequent in occurrence, and (*c*) within the temporal limits of cell-assembly reverberation. Some short sentences (like *How do you do* and *What do you know*) and many trite phrases will fit these requirements, but most *words* in a person's active vocabulary obviously do. *I am therefore led to propose the word as the characteristic unit of perceptual forms in language.* The morpheme fits neither the requirements nor the data—witness the fact that the tachistoscopic threshold for MOTHER is lower than that for either of its morphemic components, [MOTH] and [ER], despite the fact that their total frequency of occurrence must be higher since they appear in many words besides MOTHER.

What about my assertion that word units in the Form Pool are meaningless? First note that the lawful relation between threshold duration and frequency of usage only obtains when all instances of the same form, regardless of meaning, are summed. The word form TAKE is given no less than 69 meanings in *Webster's Collegiate Dictionary,* yet there is no sensory clue as to its particular meaning when it is flashed on the screen. Second, note that in semantic satiation the subject must repeatedly and discriminately perceive the word form and vocalize the form, as a single-stage "texting operant" in Skinner's terms, yet it is the meaning that satiates, not the "texting." The meaningless status of words at this level implies that the number of discriminable units in the Word Form Pool can be much smaller than the number of meaningful words in a speaker's vocabulary. There will be only one *play,* one *player,* one *plays* and so forth; the grammatical fact that *plays* can be either noun plural or verb and the semantic fact that *play* can be in the theatre or the backyard has no relevance in the Word Form Pool, but this *is* the focus for the next stage in sentence understanding and creating.

Let us turn, then, to the Semantic Key Sort. A little demonstration will help us bridge the gulf between form and meaning. I am going to give you a perfectly meaningful and grammatical sentence that you may have a bit of trouble understanding: LIGHT LIGHTS LIGHTLY LIGHT LIGHT LIGHTS. I imagine few readers could give a satisafctory paraphrase. The reason is that each of the three word-form units is ambiguous as to both grammatical and semantic coding. But now let me provide a paraphrase along with a situational context: It is a balmy summer evening, we are sitting in a Japanese garden, and I say, PALE FLAMES GENTLY ILLUMINATE AIRY LANTERNS, or, LIGHT LIGHTS LIGHTLY LIGHT LIGHT LIGHTS. As a form in the Word Pool, LIGHT could activate any combination of three grammatical codings (N, V, or A) each with some five semantic codings, yielding at least 15 high-probability alternatives. Disambiguation requires independent representation of these alternatives and probabilistic selection among them.

Imagine now a very large box of edge-punched key sort cards. There must be one card for each discriminable usage. Thus, whereas there was only one *play* in the Word Form Pool, in the Semantic Key Sort there will be $play_1$ (verb, to frolic), $play_2$ (verb, to act), $play_3$ (verb, to wager), $play_{11}$ (noun, recreation), $play_{12}$ (noun, drama), $play_{13}$ (noun, game event), $play_{111}$ (adjective, make-believe),

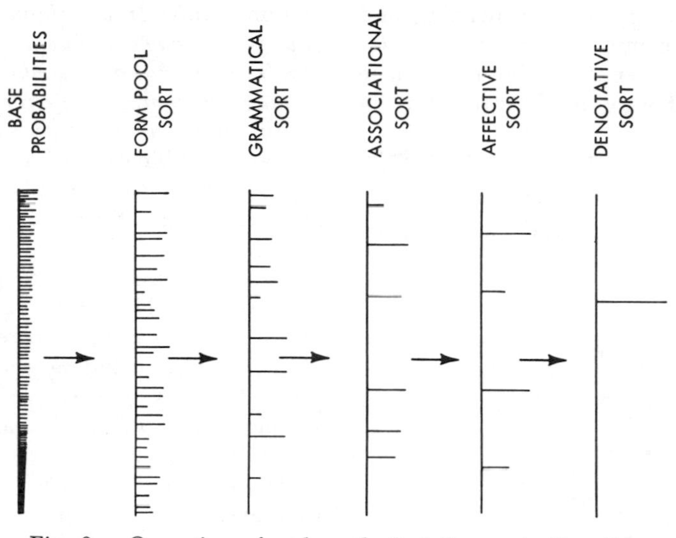

Fig. 8: Operation of a hypothetical Semantic Key Sort.

and so on through many more discriminable interpretations and intentions. I have only indicated grammatical and semantic (denotative) coding, but the cards would also have to have "fields" for gross affective coding and associative coding. And finally—or perhaps we should say first—each card would have to be coded for its representation in the Word Form Pool, since this exercises a major selective effect. Let me hasten to point out that, although my analogy with a key sort implies a physical place of storage (as do terms like "dictionary" or "permanent memory"), the actual behavioral model will deal with semantic selection as a process, involving multiple usage of (hopefully) a relatively small number of components.

But first let's see how such a Semantic Key Sort might operate. Figure 8 illustrates a series of sortings, even though I'm sure they would be simultaneous for maximum efficiency. I assume that the cards would be ordered according to their base probabilities of usage, but given the large number of items having at least some probability, the differences here would be very small. Now imagine that our human computer scans this sentence, *The play got rave reviews in "Variety" this week,* and word forms *the* and *play* appear first in the Pool. The "needle" for the meaningless form *play* selects all cards coded appropriately, this representing a great reduction in uncertainty. Utilizing the unfolding grammatical information in the Word Form Pool, here the T——V frame, the grammatical N needle sorts the *play* cards again, and all that are not nouns drop out. The needle sensitive to the REVIEW-*play* associative coding reduces the probabilities of *play* as in gambling, games, or puns; affective needles do their work; and finally the discriminative denotative needles, sensitive to the restrictive effects of *the, review,* VARIETY, and *this week* select that one *play* card punched for "specific dramatic product, contemporary."

Now, since I do *not* think semantic coding would actually operate this way, let me return to behavior theory. I will use the affective meaning system as a model, not because it is the most important system for sentence understanding and creating but because I think I know more about it. We have been able to demonstrate three bipolar factors or dimensions which account for a large share of the variance in affective meaning and appear to be common to all people, regardless of differences in both language and culture. Figure 9 illustrates how a

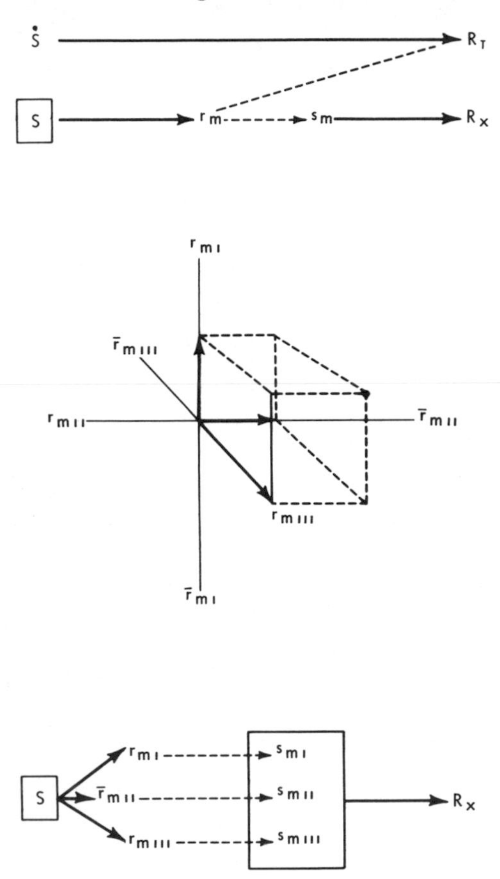

Fig. 9: Differentiation of the affective meaning of a concept in terms of three bipolar components.

concept (represented by the black dot) must project simultaneously onto all of the dimensions. Now, as shown in the diagram, if in theory we identify each bipolar factor with an independent, reciprocally antagonistic reaction system, then we have here three independent affective components of meaning. In other words, representational mediation processes (r_m) are assumed to be just as complexly componential as the total behaviors from which they are derived. My general suggestion is this: *In a fashion strictly analogous to the way a phoneme is defined as a bundle of simultaneous phonetic features, so may a meaning be defined as a bundle of simultaneous semantic features.* And just as recombination of a relatively small number of distinctive phonetic features generates a relatively large number of phonemes, so may recombination of semantic features generate large numbers of meanings. The problem is to identify all of the semantic features, or components, of r_m, including the grammatical ones. Needless to say, we are far from solving this problem, particularly for denotative meaning.

Is there any support for my assumption that grammatical distinctions are at base semantic in nature? Although the trend in contemporary linguistics has been to enforce an absolute separation between grammar and meaning, no less an authority than Roman Jakobson (1959) states approvingly that "It was clear to Boas that any difference of grammatical categories carries semantic information." For some grammatical categories the semantic information is clear (for example, when we hear the plural [-s] morpheme on a concrete noun, we look for more than one of it), but for others it is less so (for example, what is the semantic of *to* in the infinitive form *to go?*). In any case, it is clear that grammatical coding would have to operate on clues available in the strings of meaningless word forms, including affixes, function words, word orders, and guesses about ambiguous items. Tannenbaum and Stolz (1963) have reported recently that a computer programed to assign grammatical form classes to strings of words in newspaper English on just this basis does so as well as college sophomores!

The notion of a semantic "field" or "sphere" is familiar to historical linguists, to philologists, and to psychologists who have worked with aphasic patients. Semantic change over time seems to operate componentially (psychologically, a special case of mediated generalization), and aphasics seem to make errors on a similar basis (e.g., saying *violin* for *trumpet, smoke* for *pipe,* and so on)—in other words, shifts appear to be stepwise within the same semantic sphere. In a more experimental vein, Pollio (1963) had subjects produce serial associations and then compared rapid versus slow "bursts" in terms of both the associative overlap among the words involved and their mean distances in semantic profiles. He found that the more closely related words are in either associative or affective meaning, the more likely they are to appear together in rapid bursts. Research by Arthur and Caroline Staats on verbal operant conditioning (cf. Staats, Staats, Finley, & Minke, 1961) and by Susan Ervin (1961, 1963) and James Deese (1962) on word association also suggests that common semantic coding is the basis for formation of verbal response classes. It would appear, then, that rather than a deck of key sort cards in any permanent memory or "dictionary" we have a system for multiple, simultaneous, differential coding of words, and it is this which gives them meaning.

The third component of a psychological theory of the sentence is what I shall call a Cognitive Mixer—but this, too, is really a process. Let us return to Hobart Mowrer's (1954) notion of the sentence as a conditioning device and his now-classic example, *Tom is a thief.* Mowrer saw the predicate, *thief,* functioning as the unconditioned stimulus, and the subject, *Tom,* functioning as the conditioned stimulus. There are several difficulties with this formulation:

1. It doesn't explain how we understand momentarily the meaning of the novel utterance *Tom is a thief,* without necessarily believing it, on a single presentation or trial.

2. It doesn't take grammatical structure into account—simple conditioning in the sentence *Tom is a perfect idiot* should lead to cancellation of the *Tom is perfect* and *Tom is an idiot* effects.

3. It doesn't account for the fact that the predicate may be modified as much as or more than the subject, as in the sentence *President Kennedy favors a test-ban treaty.*

But Mowrer's essential insight—that a sentence communicates by producing a dynamic interaction in the mind of the receiver—remains as valid now as it was a decade ago. The problem is to specify the nature of the interaction.

In 1955 Percy Tannenbaum and I (Osgood & Tannenbaum, 1955) proposed the Congruity Hypothesis as means of explaining some very systematic data on attitude change. The underlying notion was that, since the meaning system can do only one thing, assume only one "posture" at a time (cf. meaning as a simultaneous "bundle" of semantic components), *if* this meaning system is driven in two or more directions at once it must reach a compromise on every factor or component. The formal statement is as follows: *Whenever two signs are related by an assertion, the mediating reaction characteristic of each shifts toward congruence with that characteristic of the other, the magnitude of the shift being inversely proportional to the intensities of the interacting reactions.* In other words, more meaningful items have greater "pulling power." Note that the signs must be related by "an assertion"—which is our entrée to grammatical structure and the fundamental notion of the sentence as a propositionalizing device. But assertions can be perceptual as well as verbal; the sight of TOM DIPPING HIS HAND IN THE TILL is just as much an assertion as the sentence *Tom is a thief.* And note, finally, that assertions may be either associative or dissociative; the impact upon *Tom* must be quite different in the sentence *Tom is a thief* than it is in the sentence *Tom is not a thief* (which, incidentally, is another count against the simple conditioning model).

The general hypothesis states that meaning shifts are always toward congruence—but what or where is congruence? It is intuitively evident that the assertion *Tom is a thief* is already congruous to the policeman who caught him with his hand in the till, but not to Tom's mother; there should be no shift in meaning in the first case, but a cruel if momentary cognitive twist toward semantic fusion of *Tom* and *thief* in the mother's mind. It is also intuitively apparent that the assertion *Tom is not a thief* would already be congruent to his mother, but incredibly incongruent to the officer who had just taken Tom's hand out of the till; here there should be no meaning shift produced in the mother, but a gasping if momentary cognitive effort toward semantic dissolution of the meanings of *Tom* and *thief* on the part of the earnest officer of the law. Our general principle can be extended formally as follows: *Whenever two signs are related by an assertion, they are congruent to the extent that their mediating reactions are equally intense, either in the same* (compatible) *direction of excitation in the case of associative assertions or in opposite* (reciprocally antagonistic) *directions in the case of dissociative assertions.* Thus cognitive interaction is fusive for associative assertions and dissolusive for dissociative assertions.

In a paper bearing the intriguing title, "Computer Simulation of 'Hot Cognition'," Robert Abelson (1963) criticizes the Congruity Hypothesis on the ground that it makes meaning change complete and inexorable and, through repeated fusions, must leave people "adrift in a sea of neutrality." It certainly is true that if word meanings were completely at the mercy of "instant conditioning," one's semantics would be reduced to a hopeless, meaningless shambles by the end of a paper like this—if it is not anyhow for other reasons! But Abelson fails to note that dissociative assertions tend to push meanings outward—the wily politician keeps pushing himself off from such stable evils as Communism, Sin, and Higher Taxes. In fact, I think there is a general pressure toward polarized opposition, simple flip-flop binaries being easier to deal with cognitively than finely graded distinctions. Going back to my key sort analogy, I assume that an assertion pulls a couple of cards from the deck, which are already semantically punched, cognitive interaction produces some momentary compromise, which is necessary for sentence understanding, and then the cards are replaced in the file—slightly indented by the momentary collision but not permanently repunched. Of course, if the same assertion is repeated again and again—as was the case with *Fifth-Amendment Communist* during the heyday of Senator McCarthy—then repeated indenting yields permanent repunching, or meaning change.

Now we are in position to inquire into the dynamics of phrase interpretation. In 1956, for the rather practical purposes of content analysis, Sol Saporta, Jum Nunnally, and I (Osgood, Saporta, & Nunnally, 1956) applied the Congruity Hypothesis to gauging attitudes from message materials, by what we called "evaluative assertion analysis." Each complex sentence had to be transformed by a set of rules into an exhaustive set of "kernel assertions," all of the subject-copula-object form and together being semantically equivalent to the original sentence. Although we did not realize it then, since this was in the pre-Chomskian era, we had fallen into a kind of transformational grammar—by no means as elegant as Chomsky's formal system and different in several crucial respects, but crudely serviceable for psycholinguistic purposes.

Take for illustration the fairly complex sentence *the clever young thief was severely sentenced by the rather grim-faced judge* given in the following display:

S

THE CLEVER YOUNG THIEF WAS SEVERELY SENTENCED BY THE RATHER GRIM-FACED JUDGE

Kernel Assertions

[THE THIEF] [WAS] [CLEVER]
[THE THIEF] [WAS] [YOUNG]
[THE JUDGE] [WAS] [RATHER GRIM FACED]
[THE JUDGE] [SENTENCED SEVERELY] [THE THIEF]

As shown, under assertion analysis this sentence breaks down into the following kernels: [*the thief*] [*was*] [*clever*]; [*the thief*] [*was*] [*young*]; [*the judge*] [*was*] [*rather grim faced*]; [*the judge*] [*sentenced severely*] [*the thief*]. You can judge for yourself whether or not these kernels preserve the total meaning of the original sentence, albeit in primitive, childlike form. Now note that there are two basic types of phrases implicit in my bracketing—between-bracket phrases (like *the thief was clever*) and within-bracket phrases (like *rather grim faced*). My proposal here is this: *There are two essentially different types of phrase analyzing processes psychologically—qualifying operations* (between brackets) *and quantifying operations* (within brackets)*—and each follows a different rule of cognitive interaction, the former homeostatic and the latter multiplicative.* Examples of qualifying phrases, and their transformations, would be: *Castro's Cuba* (Cuba belongs to Castro); *volatile Castro* (Castro is volatile); *American promises* (promises are American); *dependable promises* (promises are dependable). Interactions here should be predictable from the Congruity Hypothesis. Examples of quantifying phrases would be: V × AUV (*used to steal,* which weakens the assertion); V × AV (*works hard,* which strengthens the assertion); N × Q (*some men,* which reduces the intensity of men); A × AV (*very kind,* which intensifies the adjective). Interactions here should follow a multiplicative function.

Is there any evidence for these speculations? Interactions of the qualifying type (between brackets) were investigated by Tannenbaum (cf. Osgood & Tannenbaum, 1955); assertions like *The Chicago Tribune condemns Modern Art* were imbedded in news type messages, and meaning changes for sources and concepts were predicted from the Congruity Hypothesis—results were as predicted. Osgood and Ferguson (cf. Osgood, Suci, & Tannenbaum, 1957) predicted the meanings of adjective/noun combinations (like *listless nurse, sincere scientist, and average husband*) from the meanings of their components (*listless, sincere, nurse, scientist,* and so forth) with reasonable success, except that there was evidence for adjective dominance and negative polarization.

Interactions of the quantifying type have been studied by Norman Cliff (1959), using intensive adverb/adjective combinations like *somewhat evil, quite ordinary,* and *very charming,* and by Edmund Howe (1963), using probabilistic adverb/adjective combinations like *possibly evil, probably ordinary,* and *certainly charming;* both types of combination were found to obey a multiplicative function. Howe went further and combined probabilistic and intensive modes of quantifying (e.g., *certainly quite angry*); he concluded that "the data satisfactorily indicate. . . that content-free adverbs of the two classes used here systematically combine with each other [with] predictable multiplicative effects upon adjectives." Of course, there are many other types of phrases that require such quantitative analysis, but a pattern seems to be emerging.

Finally, let us look at the cognitive resolution of sentences as wholes. It was Hobart Mowrer's insight, as well as Edward Sapir's, that sentences "interpret" their subjects. Sapir referred to the sentence as being essentially a "topic" plus "commentary." If this is the case, then understanding a sentence psychologically should be a series of phrase resolving interactions terminating in a final resolution of the basic kernel sentence, thereby yielding a uniquely modified meaning of the subject or "topic" of the sentence. So let us now see what, in theory, should happen to our sample sentence as it unreels in the meaningless Word Form Pool. I shall assume that "storage" in the Word Form Pool is limited in duration and that the meaning system can do only one thing at a time—and therefore that phrases will tend to be resolved as units in the order of their appearance. I shall also assume that within-bracket (quantifying) phrases are resolved prior to between-bracket (qualifying) assertions whenever the same sentential material is involved.

A hypothetical series of operations upon inputs from the Word Form Pool which generate semantic modifications as outputs is shown in the following display:[2]

	Input	*Operation*	*Output*
(1)	THE CLEVER YOUNG. . .	—	—
(2)	THIEF WAS. . . [CLEVER]	$N_1^0 \overset{+}{\rightarrow} A_1^0$	N_1^1
(3)	[N_1^1] [YOUNG]	$N_1^1 \overset{+}{\rightarrow} A_2^0$	N_1^2
(4)	[N_1^2] [WAS] SEVERELY. . .	—	—
(5)	[N_1^2] [WAS] [SEVERELY] SENTENCED BY. . .	$V_1^0 \times AV_1^0$	V_1^1
(6)	[N_1^2] [V_1^1] THE RATHER. . .	—	—
(7)	[N_1^2] [V_1^1] [THE] [RATHER] GRIM-FACED. . .	$A_3^0 \times AV_2^0$	A_3^1
		+	
(8)	[N_1^2] [V_1^1] JUDGE	$N_3^0 \rightarrow A_3^1$	N_2^1
(9)	[N_1^2] [V_1^1] [N_2^1]	$N_2^1 \overset{+}{\rightarrow} N_1^2$	N_2^2
(10)	N_2^2 = the momentary meaning of JUDGE		

The then *clever* then *young* (1) appear as meaningless word forms which serve to elicit sequentially their corresponding bundles of semantic features. Until *thief* appears there is no cognitive interaction, since no qualitative or quantitative assertion has been formed—hence *clever* and *young* are stored temporarily. *The thief was clever* (2) resolves into *thief* once modified [N_1^1] and *The thief* (once modified) *was young* (3) resolves into *thief* twice modified [N_1^2] which is temporarily stored—but presumably now a rather dynamic thief! Sensory integrations in the Word Form Pool are continuing to be formed; *severely* (4) is differentiated but no interaction is required, and then *sentenced by* appear (5)—promptly yielding the multiplicative V × AV resolution, which is stored [V_1^1]. Occurrence of *the* and *rather* (6) produce no dynamics, but *grim-faced* (7) generates another multiplicative A × AV resolution. In Stage (8), *judge was grim faced* is resolved. Now, in Stage (9), we have stored noun *thief* twice modified, verb phrase *was sentenced by* once modified, and noun *judge* once modified. This is the final assertion to be resolved, and I make the dubious assumption (as Chomsky does) that passives must be transformed to actives—hence, that *judge* is the real "topic" of the sentence.

2 Subscripts indicate specific items; superscripts indicate operations already performed; brackets indicate items in temporary storage; → indicates qualifying operation; × indicates quantifying operation; + indicates associative assertion.

This final qualifying assertion resolves into *judge* twice modified—which is the momentary meaning or "image" of *judge* communicated by this sentence.

Does all this seem extraordinarily, perhaps even frighteningly, complicated? Of course it does. But one would not expect Man's unique and highest achievement—sentence understanding and creating—to be exactly simple. The question is whether such complexity is necessary and sufficient to handle the phenomenon, and I suspect my model is not complex and subtle enough. However, it should be kept in mind that the computer program for even a simple operation, such as generating a finite series of numbers according to some rule, looks pretty complicated—yet the computer, once programed, can complete the entire operation within less than a second. The human brain is a pretty efficient computer, too.

THE QUESTION OF SUFFICIENCY

By way of concluding, let me return to the question of sufficiency. I have no illusions whatsoever about what I have presented here being a complete theory of the sentence. For one thing, I have said less about creating sentences than I will say in an extended version; for another, space limitations have forced me to cut out much of the substantiating data. But even with these items added, my account would remain nothing more than a sketch of what I consider to be some of the essentials in a very complicated process.

Psycholinguists are now busily filling in details of the sketch—an architect's version of a sentence interpreting and generating machine. And there are many architects. George Miller, both in his Presidential Address before the Eastern Psychological Association last year (1962) and in his more recent paper at the International Congress in Washington, has described some extremely significant experiments—one, for example, demonstrating that we can measure the increased time required for sentence understanding as the number of grammatical transformations is increased. In our own laboratory at the Institute of Communications Research, George Kent and Merrill Garrett are following up a lead given them by Ladefoged and Broadbent (1960)—that the apparent occurrence of a "click" given to one ear is displaced toward the syntactic boundaries of a sentence being fed simultaneously into the other ear; Kenneth Forster is trying to separate the contribution of syntactic variables from both grammatical and semantic sequential dependencies, by using nonsense sentences like *the siths who ouberelled the entis theatly esiled the ongel raton,* under both serial learning and whole learning conditions. And this, of course, is only a small part of the role.

The thing we must avoid, I think, is "explaining" sentence understanding and creating by simply putting a new homunculus in our heads—in this case, a little linguist in every brain. It is true that speakers produce novel sentences all the time, but the semantic *and* the grammatics cannot both be simultaneously novel, or we fail to comprehend. What is novel is the combination, and this is a familiar psychological problem. It is also true that sentences may be ambiguous without syntactic analysis—witness the sentence *They are cooking apples.* But also note the fact that the speaker is never ambiguating (except when he is deliberately punning, i.e., using a metalanguage) and the hearer is never ambiguated in ordinary discourse (he sees the cooks stirring the apples). If the only claim for a little linguist in our heads were disambiguation, then I am sure we are not in trouble—because the very contextual factors the linguist must leave out are the psychologist's strength in dealing with language "as she is spoke." Let us therefore strive for psychological theories of the sentence which are part of our theories of behavior in general.

References

ABELSON, R. P. Computer simulation of "hot cognition." New Haven: Yale University, 1963. (Mimeo)

CHOMSKY, N. *Syntactic structures.* The Hague: Mouton, 1957.

CHOMSKY, N. Review of B. F. Skinner, *Verbal behavior. Language,* 1959, **35,** 26–58.

CLIFF, N. Adverbs as multipliers. *Psychol. Rev.,* 1959, **66,** 27–44.

DEESE, J. On the structure of associative meaning. *Psychol. Rev.,* 1962, **69,** 161–175.

ERVIN, S. M. Changes with age in the verbal determinants of word-association. *Amer. J. Psychol.,* 1961, **74,** 361–372.

ERVIN, S. M. Correlates of associative frequency. *J. verbal Learn. verbal Behav.,* 1963, **1,** 422–431.

GIBSON, J. J. The useful dimensions of sensitivity. *Amer. Psychologist,* 1963, **18,** 1–15.

HEBB, D. O. *The organization of behavior: A neurophysiological theory.* New York: Wiley, 1949.

HEBB, D. O. The semiautonomous process: Its nature and nurture. *Amer. Psychologist,* 1963, **18,** 16–27.

HOWE, E. S. Probabilistic adverbial qualification of adjectives. *J. verbal Learn. verbal Behav.,* 1963, **1,** 225–242.

HULL, C. L. Knowledge and purpose as habit mechanisms. *Psychol. Rev.,* 1930, **37,** 511–525.

JAKOBSON, R. Boas view of grammatical meaning. *Amer. Anthropologist,* 1959, **61,** 139–145.

JOHNSON, N. F. Linguistic models and the functional units of language. Unpublished manuscript, University of Ohio, 1963.

KATZ, J. J., & FODOR, J. A. The structure of a semantic theory. *Language,* 1963, **39,** 170–210.

LADEFOGED, P., & BROADBENT, D. Perception of sequence in auditory events. *J. exp. Psychol.,* 1960, **12,** 162–170.

LAMBERT, W. E., & JAKOBOVITS, L. A. The case for semantic satiation. Montreal: McGill University, 1963. (Mimeo)

MILLER, G. A. Some psychological studies of grammar. *Amer. Psychologist,* 1962, **17,** 748–762.

MILLER, G. A., GALANTER, E., & PRIBRAM, K. H., *Plans and the structure of behavior.* New York: Holt, 1960.

MOWRER, O. H. The psychologist looks at language. *Amer. Psychologist,* 1954, **9,** 660–694.

OSGOOD, C. E. A behavioristic analysis of perception and meaning as cognitive phenomena. *Symposium on cognition. University of Colorado, 1955.* Cambridge: Harvard Univer. Press, 1957.

OSGOOD, C. E. Behavior theory and the social sciences. *Behav. Sci.,* 1956, **1,** 167–185.

OSGOOD, C. E. Motivational dynamics of language behavior. In M. R. Jones (Ed.), *Nebraska Symposium on Motivation: 1957.* Lincoln: Univer. Nebraska Press, 1957.

OSGOOD, C. E. Psycholinguists. In S. Koch (Ed.), *Psychology: A study of a science.* New York: McGraw-Hill, 1963.

OSGOOD, C. E., SAPORTA, S., & NUNNALLY, J. C. Evaluative assertion analysis. *Litera,* 1956, **3,** 47–102.

OSGOOD, C. E., SUCI, G. J., & TANNENBAUM, P. H. *The measurement of meaning.* Urbana: Univer. Illinois Press, 1957.

OSGOOD, C. E., & TANNENBAUM, P. H. The principle of congruity in the prediction of attitude change. *Psychol. Rev.,* 1955, **62,** 42–55.

POLLIO, H. R. Some semantic relations among word-associates. *Amer. J. Psychol.*, 1963, in press.

SKINNER, B. F. *Verbal behavior.* New York: Appleton-Century-Crofts, 1957.

STAATS, A. W., STAATS, C. K., FINLEY, J. R., & MINKE, K. A. Mediating responses in the operant conditioning of word classes. Technical report No. 21, 1961, 2794(02), Office of Naval Research.

TANNENBAUM, P. H., & STOLZ, W. S. Markov chains in the grammatical structure of English. Madison: University of Wisconsin, 1963. (Mimeo)

TYLER, V. O., JR. Sensory integration with and without reinforcement. *J. exp. Psychol.*, 1962, 63, 381–386.

Thinking

B. F. SKINNER

The place of verbal behavior in group co-ordination is often discussed in speculating about the origin of language. As soon as men began to work together in hunting, fishing, building shelters, or making war, situations must have arisen in which rudimentary verbal responses would be of use.[1] In a co-operative fishing enterprise, for example, one man might be in a position to see the fish while another could pull the net. Any response which the former might make to the fish would improve the timing of the latter, possibly with advantages for both. Comparable co-ordinating functions are easily discovered in the behavior of a well-developed verbal community.

Plausible advantages are not, as such, an explanation of the origin and maintenance of verbal behavior, but they point to the reinforcing contingencies which are. Verbal behavior extends both the sensory powers of the listener, who can now respond to the behavior of others rather than directly to things and events, and the power of action of the speaker, who can now speak rather than do. If, as a result of a division of labor, the wise-but-weak can control the uninformed-but-strong, their combined accomplishments may exceed anything possible for either alone. Co-operative enterprises are not always for the benefit of all parties, but the interlocking contingencies necessary to sustain verbal behavior prevail even in the extremely unsymmetrical relation of master and slave.

Verbal behavior must have become much more valuable, both to the group as a whole and severally to its members, when responses began to be transmitted from one man to another. "Word-of-mouth" transmission became possible with the development of echoic and intraverbal behavior, while the invention of writing and the subsequent development of textual behavior permitted an even more effective mode. The "speaker" who leaves an enduring record of his behavior can affect "listeners" in distant places and times, and these in turn profit from the special points of vantage of the remote "speaker." The achievement of the transmission of verbal behavior is seen today in codes of law, books of wisdom, formularies, and religious writings, which amplify almost without limit the effects of the behavior

[1] See Malinowski's appendix to *The Meaning of Meaning* of Ogden, C. K. and Richards, I. A.

which originally produced them, and in histories, biographies, diaries, and experimental reports, which give the reader an almost unlimited contact with the environments of other men.

Emergence of Other Functions

A useful division of labor is not the only achievement of verbal behavior. Other functions must soon have emerged from the mands and tacts (and the corresponding nonverbal and verbal responses of the listener) which were first effective in facilitating group co-ordination. The special effects discussed in Chapter 6* would soon have become possible, with results which we see epitomized in literature when a particular work arouses the reader emotionally or entertains him in various ways. These collateral reactions of listeners must soon have altered the behavior of speakers. Moreover, as soon as the listener also became an accomplished speaker, verbal behavior could arouse *verbal* reactions in him—delighting him with humorous or stylistic effects in multiple causation, prompting and probing his behavior in persuasion or thoughtful stimulation, and so on.

These additional uses of verbal behavior do not result from an extension of sensory or motor power. They may or may not have a bearing on group co-ordination. They are most interesting when a group is not involved—when, in short, a man talks to himself. Once a speaker also becomes a listener, the stage is set for a drama in which one man plays several roles. The initial advantages for group co-ordination are missing, but there are compensating gains. This has been recognized traditionally when the behavior of a speaker with respect to himself as listener, particularly when his behavior is not observable by others, is set aside as a special human achievement called "thinking."

An account of verbal behavior is not complete until its relation to the rest of the behavior of the organism has been made clear. This can be done conveniently by discussing the problem of thinking.

Covert Verbal Behavior

If someone who is sitting quite still is asked *What are you doing?*, he may reply *Nothing, I'm just thinking.* In the terminology of the layman (and of many specialists) thinking is often simply opposed to doing. But as a living organism a man is behaving in some sense while "doing nothing," even though his behavior may not be easily observed by others or possibly even by himself. We do not discuss these activities effectively because they are almost always accessible only to the "thinker" and useful verbal responses to them cannot easily be developed. Some progress has been made in improving public observation through the instrumental amplification of small-scale behavior, but the problem of explaining the normal occurrence of such behavior remains.

In a sense verbal behavior which cannot be observed by others is not properly part of our field. It is tempting to avoid the problems it raises by confining ourselves to observable events, letting anyone extend the analysis to his own covert behavior who wishes to do so. But there would then be certain embarrassing gaps in our account. In intraverbal chaining, for example, necessary links are sometimes missing from the observable data. When someone solves a problem in "mental arithmetic," the initial statement of the problem and the final overt answer can often be related only by inferring covert events. We also have to account for verbal behavior which is under the control of covert speech—which reports it (Chapter 5) or qualifies it with autoclitics (Chapter

* *The reader is referred to Chapter 6, "Special Conditions Affecting Stimulus Control," in* Verbal Behavior, *pp. 147–171, for the complete discussion of "special effects" resulting from the reinforcement of a speaker or writer.* (Eds.)

12). Covert behavior has also had to be considered in discussing grammar (Chapter 13), sentence composition (Chapter 14), editing (Chapter 15), and other topics of Part V.* Some discussion of its dimensions is therefore required.

Covert behavior often seems to be like overt except that it occurs on a smaller scale. If we recite the alphabet while speaking and whispering alternate letters, it is easy to observe the voicing which makes the difference: *A-b-C-d-E-f-G-h*. . . . If we whisper every other letter while saying the rest silently, we observe what appears to be a comparable difference between overt and covert forms: *a*-( )-*c*-( )-*e*-( )-*g*-( ). . . . But the silent response may recede to very subtle dimensions. The muscular involvement demonstrated by mechanical or electrical amplification can often be detected by trying to "think" such a response as *bubble, bubble* while holding the mouth as wide open as possible. But this can often be done, especially after a little practice, and there are other difficulties in assuming that covert behavior is always executed by the muscular apparatus responsible for the overt form. Experienced public speakers, especially those who say the same thing many times, appear to "think" one verbal response while saying another aloud, and one sometimes appears to read aloud mechanically while carrying on, say, a "fantasied" conversation. Small-scale muscular activity is also not very plausible in representing incipient verbal behavior. *I was going to say*. . . may be followed by a response which has not been previously emitted, even subaudibly. A rapid speaker may compose a sentence to provide for a response which has yet to be executed, and it is difficult to explain this by assuming rapid silent rehearsal. We break off an unhappy remark before damage is done and, though we may complete it subaudibly, evidently before it has actually occurred.

We do not need to make guesses about the muscular or neural substratum of verbal events. We account for the probability or strength of a suppressed or manipulated response as we account for the probability of any behavior. In an instance of editing, for example, we observe that behavior which is ordinarily followed by a given response is suddenly interrupted. The fact that it is "ordinarily" so followed is a behavioral fact concerning past occurrences of the response under given circumstances. Physiological processes mediate the probability of covert and overt responses alike, as they undoubtedly mediate all the relations disclosed in a functional analysis of behavior, but we can talk about both forms of response "when they are not being emitted" without identifying physiological mediators. The data which give rise to the notion of covert speech can be dealt with as such with the degree of rigor prevailing elsewhere in a science of verbal behavior at the present time.

Other questions, however, remain to be answered. Why should a response become covert at all? Operant behavior almost always begins in a form which affects the external environment, for it would not otherwise be reinforced. (Exceptions are certain responses which are automatically reinforced by the organism itself.) Why does it not remain overt?

Behavior becomes covert when, in the first place, its strength drops below the value needed for overt emission. It may be weak because the controlling variables are deficient. When we say *I thought that was Jones (but I see it is not)*, we actually emit the response *Jones*; but we are describing a previous covert instance which was weak because the stimulus was inadequate. If the response *Jones* had been weak because it was poorly conditioned or partially forgotten, the report might have taken the form *I thought his name was Jones*.

* *The author-noted chapter references will provide the reader with a full discussion of the relevant issues. Part V includes Chapters 15 through 19.* (EDS.)

Covert behavior may be strong, however, as shown by the fact that it will appear at the overt level under other circumstances. The covert response is simply the easiest or, for any reason, the likeliest at the moment. The energy level of nonverbal behavior usually declines so long as the reinforcing contingencies are maintained. When Thorndike reinforced a cat for licking its paw, the movement grew slighter and slighter until it could scarcely be detected.[2] The reinforcing contingencies could not be maintained beyond that point. (We might say that the cat could not be reinforced for "thinking" about licking its paw.) But a considerable reinforcement survives in covert *verbal* behavior when the speaker is his own listener. One important consequence of our definition is that, when talking to oneself, it is unnecessary to speak aloud and easier not to. A response which is subaudible for reasons of convenience will become audible if an advantage is to be gained. We speak aloud to ourselves upon occasion—for example, when the audible response improves intraverbal chaining. In the solution of a difficult problem, mathematical or otherwise, we resort to overt responses, vocal or written. For the same reason such covert behavior as counting money or adding figures is likely to become overt in the presence of distracting stimuli.

Covert speech is not, however, wholly or perhaps even primarily a labor-saving practice. As we have seen, verbal behavior is frequently punished. Audible behavior in the child is reinforced and tolerated up to a point; then it becomes annoying, and the child is punished for speaking. Comparable aversive consequences continue into the adult years. Punishment is not always in the nature of reproof, for speech which is overheard may have other kinds of undesirable effects, such as giving away a secret. The privacy of covert behavior has a practical value. So long as a verbal response is emitted primarily for its effect upon the speaker himself, it is best confined to that audience. (The content of autistic verbal behavior is often significant to the therapist just because it is relatively free of the control exercised by a punishing audience.)

That avoidance of punishment is a more likely explanation than convenience is shown by the fact that covert behavior returns to the overt level when a punishing audience is no longer in control though convenience has not been altered. Many people who live alone gradually come to talk to themselves aloud. In the presence of other people the return to the overt level may take time, for the nonpunishing character of an audience cannot be established in a moment. It is usually hard to induce people to "think aloud"—that is, to emit in the presence of an external audience behavior which is primarily controlled by the speaker himself. The extent of the special control exerted by the private audience is seen in the fact that overt behavior in the absence of an external listener frequently generates anxiety or other emotional effects. Many people are embarrassed when using a dictating machine for the first time, or when rehearsing a speech aloud in an empty room. A full release of previously covert behavior at the audible level may come very slowly. The noncensuring audience provided by the psychoanalyst is not immediately effective, though overt speech of otherwise punishable form may eventually appear.

There are, then, important variables which determine whether a response will be overt or covert. But they do not greatly affect its other properties. They do not suggest that there is any important distinction between the two levels or forms. Nothing is gained, therefore, by identifying thinking with subaudible talking. This was done in certain early behavioristic analyses, apparently in an effort to find replacements for the so-called mental processes. The traditional view that an idea occurs first and that the speaker then

[2] Thorndike, E. L., *Animal Intelligence* (New York, 1898).

expresses it in words had to be discarded. The actual precursors of speech are, as we have seen, the independent variables of which it is a function, but these are for the most part outside the organism and hence not very plausible replacements for ideas as inner causes. It was tempting to suppose that the speaker "thought about what he was going to say" in the simple sense of saying if first to himself. But the covert response, if it occurs, is in no sense the cause of the overt. The full force of the expression of ideas cannot be carried by a mere sequence of covert and overt responses.

Other "mental processes" rejected in a behavioristic analysis are not easily replaced by covert verbal behavior, but their traditional prestige no doubt contributed to the need to find inner replacements. Some of these are exemplified when a speaker acquires or retains a response (the mental processes of "learning" and "memory"), responds differently to different stimuli ("discrimination"), reacts with one response-form rather than another ("differentiation"), responds in a given way to a new stimulus bearing some resemblance to the old ("generalization," "metaphor," or "analogical thinking"), responds under the control of a single property or a special set of properties of a stimulus ("abstraction"), arrives at a constructed response through a controlled intraverbal chain ("reasoning"), and so on. These are not *behaviors,* covert or overt. They are controlling relations or the changes in probability which result from changes in such relations.

The theory that thinking was merely subaudible speech had at least the favorable effect of identifying thinking with behaving. But speech is only a special case of behavior and subaudible speech a further subdivision. The range of verbal behavior is roughly suggested, in descending order of energy, by shouting, loud talking, quiet talking, whispering, muttering "under one's breath," subaudible speech with detectable muscular action, subaudible speech of unclear dimensions, and perhaps even the "unconscious thinking" sometimes inferred in instances of problem solving. There is no point at which it is profitable to draw a line distinguishing thinking from acting on this continuum. So far as we know, the events at the covert end have no special properties, observe no special laws, and can be credited with no special achievements.

THE SPEAKER AS HIS OWN LISTENER

A better case can be made for identifying thinking with behaving which automatically affects the behaver and is reinforcing because it does so. This can be either covert or overt. We can explain the tendency to identify thinking with covert behavior by pointing out that the reinforcing effects of covert behavior *must* arise from self-stimulation. But self-stimulation is possible, and indeed more effective, at the overt level.

When a man talks to himself, aloud or silently, he is an excellent listener in the sense of Chapter 10.* He speaks the same language or languages and has had the same verbal and nonverbal experience as his listener. He is subject to the same deprivations and aversive stimulations, and these vary from day to day or from moment to moment in the same way. As listener he is ready for his own behavior as speaker at just the right time and is optimally prepared to "understand" what he has said. Very little time is lost in transmission and the behavior may acquire subtle dimensions. It is not surprising, then, that verbal self-stimulation has been regarded as possessing special properties and has even been identified with thinking.

* *That is, the same variables affect "both." The reader is referred to Chapter 10 "Supplementary Stimulation" in* Verbal Behavior, *pp. 253–292.* (Eds.)

Simple Soliloquy

The speaker's own verbal behavior automatically supplies stimuli for echoic, textual, or intraverbal behavior, and these in turn generate stimuli for further responses. The result is the "soliloquy"—as exemplified in its dramatic use and in some stream-of-consciousness writing. It is not essentially productive thinking. Unexpected twists may turn up, but subsequent soliloquizing is modified only slightly, if at all, as a result. Dashiell[3] has analyzed Hamlet's *To be or not to be* in this spirit. An intraverbal connection between *die* and *sleep* leads to another between *sleep* and *dream,* and *dream* then strengthens an incipient response which is broken off with *Aye, there's the rub.* Regardless of the respectability of the connections, such a "train of thought" is a mere intraverbal or self-echoic linkage and scarcely to be distinguished from a "flight of ideas."

Thinking is more productive when verbal responses lead to specific consequences *and are reinforced because they do so.* Autistic behavior is a step in this direction. The verbal fantasy, whether overt or covert, is automatically reinforcing to the speaker as listener. Just as the musician plays or composes what he is reinforced by hearing, or as the artist paints what reinforces him visually, so the speaker engaged in verbal fantasy says what he is reinforced by hearing or writes what he is reinforced by reading. This is the realm of the verbal daydream and of much poetry, fiction, and other forms of literature. The writer composes verbal stimuli which arouse (in himself and, incidentally, in others) emotional or other kinds of responses, or serve as prompts or probes to permit him to behave verbally when he would otherwise remain silent for lack of energy or wit or because of punishing circumstances. The writer constitutes within himself an adequate community for the sustained production of literary behavior, and he may continue to write for a long time with no further contribution from the external community. The practices of the inner community often drift toward disturbing idiosyncrasies, however, as the work of such a poet as Emily Dickinson suggests.

[3] Dashiell, J. F., *Fundamentals of Objective Psychology* (Boston, 1928).

Verbal Behavior Having Practical Effects Upon the Speaker as Listener

Aside from autistic or artistic behavior, verbal responses may be automatically reinforced by practical consequences. These may follow even when the speaker is his own listener. Although he cannot extend his own sensory or motor powers, many of the substantial mediating contingencies which generate and maintain verbal behavior continue in force.

A self-mand is not as useless as it may at first appear. A man may enjoin himself to get out of bed on a cold morning, to stop when he has made a mistake, or to be sure to remember an errand. These are not wholly magical mands. The verbal response comes first because it has less aversive consequences than the behavior manded. *Get up!,* for example, is easier to execute than getting out of bed and less likely to be followed by a cold shock. It may be strong by induction from instances in which we have induced other people to get up, and it may be effective if it increases the likelihood of our getting out of bed by induction from behavior with respect to other speakers. It might be supposed that self-mands supported only by induction would eventually suffer extinction as the two audiences are more sharply discriminated, but there are continuing sources of reinforcement. Let us suppose that a man is learning to hunt under circumstances in which it is advantageous to stand quite still (in order to let the quarry approach) in spite of a strong inclination to reduce the distance more quickly by advancing. An instructor generates the correct behavior by saying *Stand still!*, and the would-be hunter may achieve the same effect by manding his own behavior. He may have acquired the verbal response at an earlier date—perhaps from a book—or it may have been more readily learned on the spot as a briefer and more sharply defined response than "standing still." In any case the hunter who can tell himself *Stand still*! is probably at an advantage in controlling himself effectively in the field. The result may continue to reinforce verbal behavior in the form of self-mands.

The possibility that the speaker may respond to his own *verbal* stimuli in echoing himself or reading notes he has written has already been pointed out. He may also respond to his own intraverbal stimuli, as in opening a combination lock by following the directions he gives himself by reciting the combinations as an intraverbal chain.

A man may usefully "speak to himself" or "write to himself" in the form of tacts. Thus, from some momentary point of vantage he may compose a text which he then responds to as a reader at a later date. Daybooks, diaries, memoranda, and similar devices bridge the temporal gap between behavior and controlling variables. The ultimate behavior may be verbal or nonverbal. The self-tact has an immediate effect in helping the speaker identify or clarify the situation to which it is a response. A confusing international situation falls into a standard pattern with the official declaration *This is war*. One's behavior with respect to a vaguely familiar person changes when his name can at last be recalled. Faced with an unfamiliar object in a hardware store, one can marshal appropriate behavior (and dismiss a possibly aversive state of puzzlement) if one can say, even tentatively, *It's a can-opener*. Categorizing responses are especially effective in this way. The zoologist hitting upon the proper classification of an unfamiliar insect, the young mother identifying the behavior of her child as an example of a pattern described by a psychologist, or the business man deciding that a chart shows that the time has come to buy a particular stock, all show substantial changes in behavior as a result of categorizing responses. *Nomina si nescis, perit et cognitio rerum*.

The automatic clarification produced by the tact is no doubt supported by self-instruction. The speaker's future behavior will be different, although the response is not necessarily emitted again. In thinking out a difficult problem, we may reaffirm certain key relationships or re-identify relevant facts, especially when these tend to be forgotten or obscured by other matters, even though the categorizing effect has already been felt. Thus, in solving a detective-story crime we may find ourselves insisting that a character is guilty in spite of a small but conclusive bit of evidence to the contrary. As we drift again and again toward the wrong conclusion, we may re-instruct ourselves: *No! No! It CAN'T be Billingsly. Billingsly was in the conservatory talking to the gardener*. We are not telling ourselves anything we did not know, but we are altering the *extent* to which we know it, and we make it less likely that we shall emit other responses placing Billingsly at the scene of the crime.

Although the speaker may find his own responses useful when they have the form of tacts, the special consequences which destroy the purity of the relation (Chapter 6) are likely to be operative. Since automatic reinforcement need not respect the contingencies which prevail in the external verbal environment, controlling relations can be "stretched" at will, beginning perhaps with a slight exaggeration but leading eventually to fiction and lying. The verbal behavior of people who live alone and talk mostly to themselves often seems "queer" to the occasional external listener. The speaker, as his own audience, has come to control a special subdivision of his verbal repertoire, distorted by special effects. The public contingencies may need replenishment, although some automatic correction will occur if the intrusion of irrelevant consequences destroys eventual practical advantages.

The special characteristics of verbal behavior having multiple sources of strength prevail when the speaker is his own listener and provide other reasons for talking to oneself. Indeed, they may be especially marked because of the optimal correspondence in verbal strength between the speaker and listener in the same skin. The autoclitics and the grammatical and syntactical ordering of verbal behavior in composition are imposed upon verbal behavior primarily for their effects upon the speaker himself, and the principal activity in editing may be specifically attributed to such effects, particularly when they result from earlier punishment. The special conditions under which editing is at a minimum and verbal behavior therefore "released" may be ultimately reinforcing to induce such conditions.

Another source of automatic reinforcement is seen in "problem solving," where the speaker generates stimuli to *supplement* other behavior already in his repertoire. He prompts and probes his own behavior, as in recalling a half-forgotten name or teasing out an effective classifying response. He may do this because he has been reinforced for similar behavior by other listeners, but automatic practical consequences may supply the necessary contingencies. Scientific behavior "pays off" even when the scientist is talking to himself. Thus, it is often automatically reinforcing to calculate the odds at poker rather than to play according to accidental reinforcements. It is often automatically reinforcing to count a number of objects rather than estimate them. It is automatically reinforcing to use a watch (a special kind of text) rather than trust to one's own "sense of time." It is automatically reinforcing to use special mnemonics or algorithms in the construction of new verbal behavior rather than trust to the miscellaneous intraverbals of the moment.

Verbal self-supplementation plays an important role in decision making. A man escapes from an aversive indecision by tossing a coin. Having set up the substitutability of *Go!* for *Heads* and *Stay!* for *Tails,* he constructs one or the other of these texts (by tossing the coin), reads it, makes the appropriate substitution, and responds to the resulting mand.

The Freudian dynamisms describe activities which are automatically reinforcing, usually because they permit one to avoid or escape from aversive consequences due to previous punishment. Many are verbal, and some almost necessarily so. "Rationalizing" is an example. Men are generally punished for hurting others but are permitted to hurt in special cases—for example, in punishing undesirable behavior or bringing bad news which cannot be concealed. The community distinguishes between two classes of rather similar behavior, punishing only one of them. As a result, when an emotional situation disposes a man to hurt someone, a member of the unpunished class of injurious responses is most likely to emerge. That is to say, men are more likely to punish or carry bad news to those whom they do not like. When the two classes of behavior are not easily distinguished, as is often the case, a man is less likely to be punished by the external community or to suffer the conditioned aversive stimulation of "guilt" if he can characterize his behavior as belonging in the unpunished class: *I spanked him "for his own good."*

Another sort of rationalization consists of characterizing an event as positively reinforcing when it is more likely to be aversive. We may suffer less from an unfortunate event by calling it a blessing in disguise. Boswell reports that Dr. Johnson was aware of the process:

> Sir, all the arguments which are brought to represent poverty as no evil, show it to be evidently a great evil. You never find people laboring to convince you that you may live very happily upon a plentiful fortune.

As these examples suggest, verbal behavior which is reinforced because it alters subsequent behavior in the speaker is often of ethical significance. The troublesome expressions *ought* and *should* can be interpreted as describing contingencies of reinforcement. When we say *The young man ought to have said "No"*, we assert that there were consequences of saying *No,* not further identified, which were reinforcing. Perhaps *No* would have saved him from aversive labor or injury. In the ethical case, where saying *No* is the "right" thing to do, the response might have prevented group censure or brought praise. When, then, a man tells himself *I ought to say "No,"* he is asserting that *No* would have certain reinforcing consequences (not further specified). His response differs from the self-mand *Say "No"* in the source of its power. The mand exploits an old paradigm of controlling relations which may ultimately lose its effectiveness, but the response containing *ought* identifies or clarifies a more lasting reinforcing contingency and may successfully increase its effect on the speaker. The vicar of society within the individual, the Freudian superego or the Judaeo-Christian conscience, is essentially verbal. It is the "still small *voice."*

A "resolution" is a sort of mand upon oneself which masquerades as a tact. *I am not going to smoke for the next three months* is not a response to a future event. Its value in self-control lies in the fact that it can be made now when appropriate contingencies, possibly involving aversive events, are powerful, whereas "not smoking for three months" requires three months for its execution, during which time the underlying deprivation or aversive stimulation may change. The resolution creates a set of conditions under which smoking is particularly punished (as "breaking a promise") either by the speaker himself or by others. The effect is greater if the resolution is publicly announced or, better, conspicuously posted during the period in which it is in force.

The following example of sustained self-stimulating verbal behavior exemplifies many of these points. It is a direct transcription of the responses a nine-year-old girl made to herself while practicing the piano. The behavior was overt, but of the sort which would have receded to the covert level with a little more punishment. The transcription begins after several minutes at the piano. A mistake is made. *No, wait!* (Plays correctly and reaches end of piece.) *Hah!* (Plays a few bars of a new piece.) *Let's see. Is that right? I'll do it once more.* (Finishes the piece.) *Ah, now I can study on something else.* (Looks at new piece.) *That's written in the key of G.* (Plays and sings words at same time. Finishes and looks at clock.) *That takes one minute. One minute to play that whole song.* (Starts another piece, and makes mistake.) *All right, now I'll start the whole thing over.* (Makes another mistake.) *I'll have to start all over again.* (Difficult piece. Emits a few *Gosh's.* Works on difficult passage. Presses finger on correct key.) *Oh, my finger, it hurts so much! But I'm going to MAKE it work!* (Forces finger against key again. Looks at finger.) *Hah! Makes beautiful designs on it.* (Notices clock.) *Wowee! I've taken some of my other things' time.* (Looks at another piece.) *Aw, I can't do that!* (Notices clock.) *Just a minute.* (Takes up clock.) *I'm putting it back five minutes. There! Got a lot more time to practice.* (Plays, notices clock again.) *Hey! Don't! Don't do that. You're going too fast.* (Adjusts clock.) *Better. Five minutes.* (Plays and makes mistake.) *Aw!* (Looks at clock.) *Come ON!* (Adjusts clock. Calls out to father in next room.) *Daddy, I'm making this clock go slowly —I don't have time to practice. I turned it around an hour. I've got so much time to practice.*

In this example of "thinking aloud" mands like *No, wait, Just a minute,* and *Is that right?* accompany behavior of stopping and looking, which they may have some effect in strengthening. The resolutions *I'll do it once more* and *I'll have to start all over again* precede the behavior which they appear to describe. They may or may not strengthen it, but they clarify each act as an instance of "starting all over because of a mistake." The tact *That's written in the key of G* is probably helpful in strengthening appropriate nonverbal behavior. *My finger, it hurts so much* can scarcely be useful in the same way and seems to be a mere comment—emitted because of the special strength of the stimulus. The juxtaposition of *I'm putting it back five minutes* and *Got a lot more time to practice* may strengthen further behavior toward the clock. A similar pair of responses occur later, and turning the clock back an hour may be the result of the clarification of the connection between moving the clock and having more time to practice. The magical mand addressed to the clock *Don't do that! You're going too fast!* may also contribute to the behavior of turning the clock back. There is very little intraverbal chaining in the sample because it is intimately connected with concurrent nonverbal behavior. The chaining is from verbal to nonverbal and back again. The example is closer to productive verbal thinking for this reason.

There are good reasons, then, why a speaker also conditioned by the verbal community as a listener should turn his verbal behavior upon himself. The result is close to "thinking" in many traditional senses of the term. Such behavior can, of course, be subtle and swift, especially because the speaker is optimally prepared for his own speech as listener. But all the important properties of the behavior are to be found in verbal systems composed of separate speakers and listeners. A necessary connection between verbal thinking and self-stimulation might be said to arise from the fact that, in the strictest sense of our definition, any behavior which is reinforced because it modifies subsequent behavior in the same individual is necessarily verbal regardless of its dimensions. The reinforcement is "mediated by an organism," if not strictly another organism, and responses which do not have the usual dimensions of vocal, written, or gestured behavior may acquire some of the characteristics of verbal behavior. The refinement of the definition given in Chapter 8,* however, permits us to maintain such a distinction as that between visual and verbal fantasy, for example, by excluding the former from the verbal category. In any case, although self-stimulating behavior may be in some sense necessarily verbal, verbal behavior need not be self-stimulating. When Plato asks, then, "Is not thought the same as speech with this exception: thought is the unuttered conversation of the soul with herself?", we must decline to allow the exception.

Thought as Verbal Behavior

Are we to be content with the rest of Plato's phrase: "thought is the same as speech"? Disregarding the distinction between overt and covert and the possibility that verbal behavior may be especially effective upon the speaker himself, are we to conclude that thinking is simply verbal behavior? Admittedly, this has been an appealing notion. "He gave man speech, and speech created thought, which is the measure of the Universe."[4] Some version of the doctrine has been actively propounded by behaviorists as a solution to the psychological problem of knowledge, and by logical positivists for their own epistemological purposes. Much earlier, in *The Diversions of Purley*,[5] John Horne

* *The refinement to which Skinner here refers involves the restriction that verbal behavior be confined to that behavior that has an effect upon the behavior of another individual only because that other individual has been conditioned* "precisely in order to reinforce the behavior of the speaker." (Eds.)

[4] Shelley, Percy Bysshe, *Prometheus Unbound*.

[5] Tooke, John Horne, *The Diversions of Purley* (London, 1857).

Tooke attacked British empiricism in the same spirit:

> Perhaps it was for mankind a lucky mistake, for it was a mistake, which Mr. Locke made, when he called his book "An Essay on Human Understanding," for some part of the inestimable benefit of that book has, merely on account of its title, reached to many thousands more than, I fear, it would have done, had he called it (what it is merely) a *Grammatical* Essay, or a Treatise on *Words,* or on *Language*. . . .
>
> . . . I only desire you to read the Essay over again with attention, and see whether all that its immortal author has justly concluded will not hold equally true and clear, if you substitute the composition [association], &c. of terms, wherever he has supposed a composition [association], &c. of ideas.[6]

Tooke and others who have advocated this solution have been preoccupied with a kind of human behavior which, because it is verbal, possesses certain properties relevant to the problem of thinking. It is tempting to suppose that other peculiarly verbal properties will solve the problem as a whole. But this is evidently not the case. The results of thinking are often quite surprising and apparently impossible to explain. We can sympathize with the urge to find an explanation at the earliest possible moment and with the belief that the process will be found to have a touch of the mysterious or even miraculous. Covert behavior is an appealing modern substitute for thought processes because of its difficult dimensions, and verbal behavior which is self-stimulating is also a promising candidate because of the fact that it *can* be private and that after a long period of working alone the thinker may emit astonishingly effective behavior. (It has always been easy for "thinkers" to claim special powers.)

Verbal behavior, quite apart from its covert or overt form or from the identity of the listener upon whom it is effective, also has some of the magic we expect to find in a thought process. It is relatively free of environmental conditions and temporal restrictions. Faced with a piece of music at the piano, we can react nonverbally to its being in the key of G (for example, by playing it correctly) but we cannot do this all at once. The verbal response *That's in the key of G* is quick and clear-cut, and it achieves an immediate result by clarifying the situation and heightening the probable effectiveness of the nonverbal behavior to follow. A unitary response to something which takes place over a period of time or in more than one place is almost necessarily verbal, and it seems to transcend great obstacles in achieving this result. When we solve a practical problem verbally, we construct a guide to a nonverbal solution; but before we have made use of it, we have found the *whole* solution at once in verbal form. Responses which are concerned with number illustrate the same point. If there is an act which is equivalent to, or identical with, "thinking of one hundred," it is the verbal response *one hundred.* Whether it is constructed by counting a hundred objects or in some other way (when it is under the control of other variables), it seems to transcend the awkward numerosity of one hundred things.

A verbal response makes it possible to "think about" *one* property of nature at a time. Since there is no practical response appropriate to all instances of red, the abstract tact *red* is an evidently unique

[6] Compare also the following passage (written, as is most of the book, in the form of a dialogue):

"B—What difference then do you imagine it would have made in Mr. Locke's Essay, if he had sooner been aware of the inseparable connexion between words and knowledge; or, in the language of Sir Hugh, in Shakespear, that 'the lips is *parcel* of the *mind?*'

H—Much. And amongst many other things, I think he would not have talked of the *composition* of *ideas;* but would have seen that it was merely a contrivance of Language: and that the only composition was in *terms;* and consequently that it was as improper to speak of a *complex idea,* as it would be to call a constellation a complex star: And that they are not ideas, but merely *terms,* which are general and *abstract*. . . ."

verbal accomplishment. The response *fox* is abstract in this sense, in spite of the fact that it refers to an object which is usually called concrete, and our reaction to the fact that one has said *fox* may be nothing more than our own verbal response *fox,* particularly if we possess no useful practical behavior with respect to foxes. A piece of music may lead us to say *I think that's Mozart,* and there is little more to be done to the music of Mozart *as such.* Locke[7] himself was aware of this function of terms. "In mixed moods," he says, "it is the name that ties the combination together and makes it a species." Thus, without the term *triumphus* we might have had descriptions of what "passed in that solemnity: but yet, I think, that which holds those different parts together, in the unity of one complex idea, is that very word annexed to it; without which the several parts of that would no more be thought to make one thing, than any other show. . . ." For Locke, however, the term merely supported the idea for which it stood.

These are important and distinctive functions of verbal behavior, but they are nevertheless not relevant to a definition of thinking. Nor are certain other accidental reasons why this solution has been so often reached. Those who have looked at themselves thinking have frequently seen *verbal* behavior. Led by prevailing philosophies to search for inner thought processes, they have naturally been impressed by the convenience of execution of covert verbal behavior—as contrasted, say, with nonverbal parallels such as turning a cartwheel or driving a car "silently," where the co-ordination of movement normally involves the physical environment. Verbal behavior is also easy to see because it is relatively easy to describe. We can report *I said to myself "That's ridiculous"* much more readily than we can describe covert nonverbal behavior evoked under the same circumstances. A verbal conclusion "comes to one," or "is reached," in a relatively conspicuous way.

But not all covert behavior is verbal. Most people can turn some sort of elliptical cartwheel privately, and we discover that we are driving from the back seat when, in an emergency, we break into overt behavior and press our feet against the floor to stop the car. The layman's use of *I think* covers nonverbal behavior. *I think I shall be going* can be translated *I find myself going, I seem to be going,* or *I am on the point of going.* It would be awkward to interpret this by saying that the behavior of going gives rise to the verbal response *I am going* and that this is qualified by the response *I think.* Covert nonverbal behavior is described, as it is in the less committal *It occurs to me to go.* Nonverbal "ideas" and "thoughts" are common in descriptions of problem solving. In *The thought (or idea) occurred to me to try the door* the speaker is reporting the appearance of a nonverbal act.

Thought as Behavior

The simplest and most satisfactory view is that thought is simply *behavior*—verbal or nonverbal, covert or overt. It is not some mysterious process responsible for behavior but the very behavior itself in all the complexity of its controlling relations, with respect to both man the behaver and the environment in which he lives. The concepts and methods which have emerged from the analysis of behavior, verbal or otherwise, are most appropriate to the study of what has traditionally been called the human mind.

The field of human behavior can be conveniently subdivided with respect to the problems it presents and the corresponding terms and methods to be used. A useful distinction may be made between reflexes, conditioned or otherwise, and the operant behavior generated and maintained by the contingencies of reinforcement in a given environment. Tradition

[7] Locke, John, *Essay on Human Understanding.*

and expedience seem to agree in confining the analysis of human thought to operant behavior. So conceived, thought is not a mystical cause or precursor of action, or an inaccessible ritual, but action itself, subject to analysis with the concepts and techniques of the natural sciences, and ultimately to be accounted for in terms of controlling variables.

The emphasis upon controlling variables is important. A practical consequence is that such a scientific account implies a technology. There is no reason why methods of thinking and of the teaching of thinking cannot be analyzed and made more effective. But there is a more immediate theoretical issue. Nothing is gained by regarding thought as behavior in the sense of a mere *form* of action. We cannot move very far in the study of behavior apart from the circumstances under which it occurs. Bertrand Russell has tried to improve upon a merely formal analysis, but he has never been fully successful because the methods available to the logician are not appropriate to the study of behavior. Consider, for example, the following passage from *An Inquiry into Meaning and Truth:*[8]

> Thought, in so far as it is communicable, cannot have any greater complexity than is possessed by the various possible kinds of series to be made out of twenty-six kinds of shapes. Shakespeare's mind may have been very wonderful, but our evidence of its merits is wholly derived from black shapes on a white ground.

Russell might have gone a step further and reduced all of Shakespeare's "mind" to a series of dots and dashes, since the plays and poems could be sent or received in that form by a skilled telegraphist. It is true that evidence of the "merits of Shakespeare's mind" is derived from black shapes on a white ground, but it does not follow that thought, communicable or not, has no greater "complexity." Shakespeare's thought was his behavior *with respect to his extremely complex environment.* We do not, of course, have an adequate record of it in that sense. We have almost no independent information about the environment and cannot infer much about it from the works themselves. In discussing Shakespeare's thought, then, we merely guess at a plausible set of circumstances or deal with our own behavior in responding to the works. This is not very satisfactory, but we cannot improve the situation by identifying thought with mere form of behavior.[9]

An emphasis upon form obscures the significance of behavior in relation to controlling variables. It is obvious that two forms of response constitute very different "thoughts" if they are emitted under different circumstances. Moreover, some apparent instances of verbal behavior, satisfying all the formal criteria, may not be "thoughts" at all. Thus, accidental arrangements of anagrams or sentences constructed by the random manipulation of printed words are not records of verbal behavior, although they may be read as texts. It may serve some purpose in logic to say that "For any sentence, however long, we can construct a longer sentence by adding 'and the moon is round,' " but the resulting sentences could be accounted for in relation to trivial variables which do not warrant our calling them verbal. A similar neglect of the controlling relation is seen in Russell's remark "It is difficult to describe a statement without making it." Emitting a response having the form of a statement as an echoic response or hypostatical tact is not to be confused with emitting the same form of response under the kinds of circumstances which permit us to call it a statement.

This concern with form has left the study of the content of thought in an

[8] Russell, Bertrand, *An Inquiry into Meaning and Truth* (New York, 1940), p. 413.

[9] Molière carried the formalistic argument one step nearer the ridiculous. All that is most beautiful in literature, one of his characters argues, is to be found in the dictionaries. "It is only the words which are transposed."

unsatisfactory state, but the "facts," propositions," and other "referents of statements" find an adequate representation among our controlling variables. The functional relations between behavior and the environment are usually complex and very often confusing, but we are not in doubt as to their dimensions or the techniques with which they may be studied. We can disregard the troublesome dissection of human thought into the familiar pattern of (1) a *man* possessing (2) *knowledge* of (3) a *world*. Men are part of the world, and they interact with other parts of it, including other men. As their behavior changes, they may interact more effectively, gaining control and power. Their "knowledge" is their behavior with respect to themselves and the rest of the world and can be studied as such.

The "effects of language on thought" must, of course, be restated. If it is "impossible to express a given idea" in a given language because a necessary term is lacking, we have only to say that the contingencies arranged by a given verbal community fail to respect a possible variable. If it is difficult "to express the same idea in two languages," we have merely to say that the reinforcing practices of two verbal communities differ. Any sort of behavior may be confusing and ineffective. The subtle contingencies of reinforcement arranged by a verbal community easily miscarry: a tact may be extended beyond warrant, an important autoclitic may be omitted, incompatible responses may result from faulty constructions. From the point of view of the listener, verbal behavior may fall far short of the nonverbal circumstances under which it arose; the thing itself may seem very different from the description of the thing. There is *indescribable* beauty in the sense in which there are colors which cannot be named in a given language. There are *ineffable* thoughts in the sense that contingencies in a nonverbal environment generate behavior which has no parallel among verbal responses. All behavior, verbal or otherwise, is subject to Kantian a priori's in the sense that man as a behaving system has inescapable characteristics and limitations.

When we study human thought, we study behavior. In the broadest possible sense, the thought of Julius Caesar was simply the sum total of his responses to the complex world in which he lived. We can study only those of which we have records. For obvious reasons, it is primarily his verbal behavior which has survived in recorded form, but from this and other records we know something about his nonverbal behavior. When we say that he "thought Brutus could be trusted," we do not necessarily mean that he ever said as much. He behaved, verbally and otherwise, as if Brutus could be trusted. The rest of his behavior, his plans and achievements, are also part of his thought in this sense.

It is a salutary consequence of this point of view to accept the fact that the thoughts of great men are inaccessible to us today. When we study great works, we study the effect *upon us* of surviving records of the behavior of men. It is *our* behavior with respect to such records which we observe; we study *our* thought, not theirs. Fortunately, the contemporary thinker can be subjected to a different kind of analysis. So far as a science of behavior is concerned, Man Thinking is simply Man Behaving.

There is nothing exclusively or essentially verbal in the material analyzed in this book. It is all part of a broader field—of the behavior of a most complex creature in contact with a world of endless variety. For practical purposes a special field has been set apart in terms of characteristics imparted to it by special controlling variables. It is in terms of these variables—of the contingencies arranged by the verbal community—that verbal behavior can be defined and analyzed.

Review of Skinner's Verbal Behavior

NOAM CHOMSKY

Rereading this review after eight years, I find little of substance that I would change if I were to write it today. I am not aware of any theoretical or experimental work that challenges its conclusions; nor, so far as I know, has there been any attempt to meet the criticisms that are raised in the review or to show that they are erroneous or ill-founded.

I had intended this review not specifically as a criticism of Skinner's speculations regarding language, but rather as a more general critique of behaviorist (I would now prefer to say "empiricist") speculation as to the nature of higher mental processes. My reason for discussing Skinner's book in such detail was that it was the most careful and thoroughgoing presentation of such speculations, an evaluation that I feel is still accurate. Therefore, if the conclusions I attempted to substantiate in the review are correct, as I believe they are, then Skinner's work can be regarded as, in effect, a reductio ad absurdum *of behaviorist assumptions. My personal view is that it is a definite merit, not a defect, of Skinner's work that it can be used for this purpose, and it was for this reason that I tried to deal with it fairly exhaustively. I do not see how his proposals can be improved upon, aside from occasional details and oversights, within the framework of the general assumptions that he accepts. I do not, in other words, see any way in which his proposals can be substantially improved within the general framework of behaviorist or neobehaviorist, or, more generally, empiricist ideas that has dominated much of modern linguistics, psychology, and philosophy. The conclusion that I hoped to establish in the review, by discussing these speculations in their most explicit and detailed form, was that the general point of view is largely mythology, and that its widespread acceptance is not the result of empirical support, persuasive reasoning, or the absence of a plausible alternative.*

If I were writing today on the same topic, I would try to make it more clear than I did that I was discussing Skinner's proposals as a paradigm example of a futile tendency in modern speculation about language and

B. F. Skinner, Verbal Behavior *(New York: Appleton-Century-Crofts, Inc., 1957), pp. viii, 478. Reviewed by Noam Chomsky in* Language, **35**, *No. 1 (1959), 26–58. Reprinted by permission of the author and publisher.*

mind. I would also be somewhat less apologetic and hesitant about proposing the alternative view sketched in Sections 5 and 11—and also less ahistorical in proposing this alternative, since in fact it embodies assumptions that are not only plausible and reasonably well-confirmed, so it appears to me, but also deeply rooted in a rich and largely forgotten tradition of rationalist pyschology and linguistics. I have tried to correct this imbalance in later publications (Chomsky, 1962, 1964, 1965; see also Miller et al., *1960; Katz and Postal, 1964; Katz, 1965; Fodor, 1965; Lenneberg, 1966).*

I think it would also have been valuable to try to sketch some of the reasons—and there were many—that have made the view I was criticizing seem plausible over a long period, and also to discuss the reasons for the decline of the alternative rationalist conception which, I was suggesting, should be rehabilitated. Such a discussion would, perhaps, have helped to place the specific critique of Skinner in a more meaningful context.
—NOAM CHOMSKY

References

CHOMSKY, N., "Explanatory Models in Linguistics," in *Logic, Methodology and Philosophy of Science*, ed. E. Nagel, P. Suppes, and A. Tarski. Stanford; Calif.: Stanford University Press, 1962.

———, *Current Issues in Linguistic Theory*. The Hague: Mouton and Co., 1964.

———, *Cartesian Linguistics*. New York: Harper & Row, Publishers, 1966.

FODOR, J., "Could Meaning Be an 'r_m'," *Journal of Verbal Learning and Verbal Behavior,* 4 (1965), 73–81.

KATZ, J. and P. POSTAL, *An Integrated Theory of Linguistic Description.* Cambridge, Mass.: M. I. T. Press, 1964.

LENNEBERG, E., *Biological Bases of Language.* (In press.)

MILLER, G. A., E. GALANTER, and K. H. PRIBRAM, *Plans and the Structure of Behavior.* New York: Holt, Rinehart & Winston, Inc., 1960.

1. A great many linguists and philosophers concerned with language have expressed the hope that their studies might ultimately be embedded in a framework provided by behaviorist psychology, and that refractory areas of investigation, particularly those in which meaning is involved, will in this way be opened up to fruitful exploration. Since this volume is the first large-scale attempt to incorporate the major aspects of linguistic behavior within a behaviorist framework, it merits and will undoubtedly receive careful attention. Skinner is noted for his contributions to the study of animal behavior. The book under review is the product of study of linguistic behavior extending over more than twenty years. Earlier versions of it have been fairly widely circulated, and there are quite a few references in the psychological literature to its major ideas.

The problem to which this book is addressed it that of giving a 'functional analysis' of verbal behavior. By functional analysis, Skinner means identification of the variables that control this behavior and specification of how they interact to determine a particular verbal response. Furthermore, the controlling variables are to be described completely in terms of such notions as stimulus, reinforcement, deprivation, which have been given a reasonably clear meaning in animal experimentation. In other words, the goal of the book is to provide a way to predict and control verbal behavior by observing and manipulating the physical environment of the speaker.

Skinner feels that recent advances in the laboratory study of animal behavior permit us to approach this problem with a certain optimism, since 'the basic processes and relations which give verbal behavior its special characteristics are now fairly well understood . . . the results [of this experimental work] have been surprisingly free of species restrictions. Recent work has shown that the methods can be extended to human behavior without serious modification' (3).[1]

It is important to see clearly just what it is in Skinner's program and claims that makes them appear so bold and remarkable. It is not primarily the fact that he has set functional analysis as his problem, or that he limits himself to study of 'observables', i.e. input-output relations. What is so surprising is the particular limitations he has imposed on the way in which the observables of behavior are to be studied, and, above all, the particularly simple nature of the 'function' which, he claims, describes the causation of behavior. One would naturally expect that prediction of the behavior of a complex organism (or machine) would require, in addition to information about external stimulation, knowledge of the internal structure of the organism, the ways in which it processes input information and organizes its own behavior. These characteristics of the organism are in general a complicated product of inborn structure, the genetically determined course of maturation, and past experience. Insofar as independent neurophysiological evidence is not available, it is obvious that inferences concerning the structure of the organism are based on observation of behavior and outside events. Nevertheless, one's estimate of the relative importance of external factors and internal structure in the determination of behavior will have an important effect on the direction of research on linguistic (or any other) behavior, and on the kinds of analogies from animal behavior studies that will be considered relevant or suggestive.

Putting it differently, anyone who sets himself the problem of analyzing the causation of behavior will (in the absence of independent neurophysiological evidence) concern himself with the only data available, namely the record of inputs to the organism and the organism's present response, and will try to describe the function specifying the response in terms of the history of inputs. This is nothing more than the definition of his problem. There are no possible grounds for argument here, if one accepts the problem as legiti-

1 Skinner's confidence in recent achievements in the study of animal behavior and their applicability to complex human behavior does not appear to be widely shared. In many recent publications of confirmed behaviorists there is a prevailing note of skepticism with regard to the scope of these achievements. For representative comments, see the contributions to *Modern learning theory* (by Estes et al.; New York, 1954); Bugelski, *Psychology of learning* (New York, 1956); Koch, in *Nebraska symposium on motivation* 58 (Lincoln, 1956); Verplanck, Learned and innate behavior, *Psych. rev.* 52.139 (1955). Perhaps the strongest view is that of Harlow, who has asserted (Mice, monkeys, men, and motives, *Psych. rev.* 60.23–32 [1953]) that 'a strong case can be made for the proposition that the importance of the psychological problems studied during the last 15 years has decreased as a negatively accelerated function approaching an asymptote of complete indifference.' Tinbergen, a leading representative of a different approach to animal behavior studies (comparative ethology), concludes a discussion of 'functional analysis' with the comment that 'we may now draw the conclusion that the causation of behavior is immensely more complex than was assumed in the generalizations of the past. A number of internal and external factors act upon complex central nervous structures. Second, it will be obvious that the facts at our disposal are very fragmentary indeed'—*The study of instinct* 74 (Oxford, 1951).

mate, though Skinner has often advanced and defended this definition of a problem as if it were a thesis which other investigators reject. The differences that arise between those who affirm and those who deny the importance of the specific 'contribution of the organism' to learning and performance concern the particular character and complexity of this function, and the kinds of observations and research neccessary for arriving at a precise specification of it. If the contribution of the organism is complex, the only hope of predicting behavior even in a gross way will be through a very indirect program of research that begins by studying the detailed character of the behavior itself and the particular capacities of the organism involved.

Skinner's thesis is that external factors consisting of present stimulation and the history of reinforcement (in particular the frequency, arrangement, and withholding of reinforcing stimuli) are of overwhelming importance, and that the general principles revealed in laboratory studies of these phenomena provide the basis for understanding the complexities of verbal behavior. He confidently and repeatedly voices his claim to have demonstrated that the contribution of the speaker is quite trivial and elementary, and that precise prediction of verbal behavior involves only specification of the few external factors that he has isolated experimentally with lower organisms.

Careful study of this book (and of the research on which it draws) reveals, however, that these astonishing claims are far from justified. It indicates, furthermore, that the insights that have been achieved in the laboratories of the reinforcement theorist, though quite genuine, can be applied to complex human behavior only in the most gross and superficial way, and that speculative attempts to discuss linguistic behavior in these terms alone omit from consideration factors of fundamental importance that are, no doubt, amenable to scientific study, although their specific character cannot at present be precisely formulated. Since Skinner's work is the most extensive attempt to accommodate human behavior involving higher mental faculties within a strict behaviorist schema of the type that has attracted many linguists and philosophers, as well as psychologists, a detailed documentation is of independent interest. The magnitude of the failure of this attempt to account for verbal behavior serves as a kind of measure of the importance of the factors omitted from consideration, and an indication of how little is really known about this remarkably complex phenomenon.

The force of Skinner's argument lies in the enormous wealth and range of examples for which he proposes a functional analysis. The only way to evaluate the success of his program and the correctness of his basic assumptions about verbal behavior is to review these examples in detail and to determine the precise character of the concepts in terms of which the functional analysis is presented. §2 of this review describes the experimental context with respect to which these concepts are originally defined. §§3–4 deal with the basic concepts 'stimulus', 'response,' and 'reinforcement', §§6–10 with the new descriptive machinery developed specifically for the description of verbal behavior. In §5 we consider the status of the fundamental claim, drawn from the laboratory, which serves as the basis for the analogic guesses about human behavior that have been proposed by many psychologists. The final section (§11) will consider some ways in which further linguistic work may play a part in clarifying some of these problems.

2. Although this book makes no direct reference to experimental work, it can be understood only in terms of the general framework that Skinner has developed for the description of behavior. Skinner divides the responses of the animal into two main categories. *Respondents* are purely reflex responses elicited by particular stimuli. *Operants* are emitted responses,

for which no obvious stimulus can be discovered. Skinner has been concerned primarily with operant behavior. The experimental arrangement that he introduced consists basically of a box with a bar attached to one wall in such a way that when the bar is pressed, a food pellet is dropped into a tray (and the bar press is recorded). A rat placed in the box will soon press the bar, releasing a pellet into the tray. This state of affairs, resulting from the bar press, increases the *strength* of the bar-pressing operant. The food pellet is called a *reinforce*; the event, a reinforcing event. The strength of an operant is defined by Skinner in terms of the rate of response during extinction (i.e. after the last reinforcement and before return to the preconditioning rate).

Suppose that release of the pellet is conditional on the flashing of a light. Then the rat will come to press the bar only when the light flashes. This is called *stimulus discrimination.* The response is called a *discriminated operant* and the light is called the *occasion* for its emission; this is to be distinguished from elicitation of a response by a stimulus in the case of the respondent.[2] Suppose that the apparatus is so arranged that bar-pressing of only a certain character (e.g. duration) will release the pellet. The rat will then come to press the bar in the required way. This process is called *response differentiation.* By successive slight changes in the conditions under which the response will be reinforced it is possible to shape the response of a rat or a pigeon in very surprising ways in a very short time, so that rather complex behavior can be produced by a process of successive approximation.

A stimulus can become reinforcing by repeated association with an already reinforcing stimulus. Such a stimulus is called a *secondary reinforcer.* Like many contemporary behaviorists, Skinner considers money, approval, and the like to be secondary reinforcers which have become reinforcing because of their association with food etc.[3] Secondary reinforcers can be *generalized* by associating them with a variety of different primary reinforcers.

Another variable that can affect the rate of the bar-pressing operant is drive, which Skinner defines operationally in terms of hours of deprivation. His major scientific book, *Behavior of organisms,* is a study of the effects of food-deprivation and conditioning on the strength of the bar-pressing response of healthy mature rats. Probably Skinner's most original contribution to animal behavior studies has been his investigation of the effects of intermittent reinforcement, arranged in various different ways, presented in *Behavior of organisms* and extended (with pecking of pigeons as the operant under investigation) in the recent *Schedules of reinforcement* by Ferster and Skinner (1957). It is apparently these studies that Skinner has in mind when he refers to the

[2] In *Behavior of organisms* (New York, 1938), Skinner remarks that 'although a conditioned operant is the result of the correlation of the response with a particular reinforcement, a relation between it and a discriminative stimulus acting prior to the response is the almost universal rule' (178–9). Even emitted behavior is held to be produced by some sort of 'originating force' (51) which, in the case of operant behavior is not under experimental control. The distinction between eliciting stimuli, discriminated stimuli, and 'originating forces' has never been adequately clarified, and becomes even more confusing when private internal events are considered to be discriminated stimuli (see below).

[3] In a famous experiment, chimpanzees were taught to perform complex tasks to receive tokens which had become secondary reinforcers because of association with food. The idea that money, approval, prestige, etc. actually acquire their motivating effects on human behavior according to this paradigm is unproved, and not particularly plausible. Many psychologists within the behaviorist movement are quite skeptical about this (cf. fn. 23). As in the case of most aspects of human behavior, the evidence about secondary reinforcement is so fragmentary, conflicting, and complex that almost any view can find some support.

recent advances in the study of animal behavior.[4]

The notions 'stimulus,' 'response', 'reinforcement' are relatively well defined with respect to the bar-pressing experiments and others similarly restricted. Before we can extend them to real-life behavior, however, certain difficulties must be faced. We must decide, first of all, whether any physical event to which the organism is capable of reacting is to be called a stimulus on a given occasion, or only one to which the organism in fact reacts; and correspondingly, we must decide whether any part of behavior is to be called a response, or only one connected with stimuli in lawful ways. Questions of this sort pose something of a dilemma for the experimental psychologist. If he accepts the broad definitions, characterizing any physical event impinging on the organism as a stimulus and any part of the organism's behavior as a response, he must conclude that behavior has not been demonstrated to be lawful. In the present state of our knowledge, we must attribute an overwhelming influence on actual behavior to ill-defined factors of attention, set, volition, and caprice. If we accept the narrower definitions, then behavior is lawful by definition (if it consists of responses); but this fact is of limited significance, since most of what the animal does will simply not be considered behavior. Hence the psychologist either must admit that behavior is not lawful (or that he cannot at present show that it is—not at all a damaging admission for a developing sceince), or must restrict his attention to those highly limited areas in which it is lawful (e.g. with adequate controls, bar-pressing in rats; lawfulness of the observed behavior provides, for Skinner, an implicit definition of a good experiment).

Skinner does not consistently adopt either course. He utilizes the experimental results as evidence for the scientific character of his system of behavior, and analogic guesses (formulated in terms of a metaphoric extension of the technical vocabulary of the laboratory) as evidence for its scope. This creates the illusion of a rigorous scientific theory with a very broad scope, although in fact the terms used in the description of real-life and of laboratory behavior may be mere homonyms, with at most a vague similarity of meaning. To substantiate this evaluation, a critical account of his book must show that with a literal reading (where the terms of the descriptive system have something like the technical meanings given in Skinner's definitions) the book covers almost no aspect of linguistic behavior, and that with a metaphoric reading, it is no more scientific than the traditional approaches to this subject matter, and rarely as clear and careful.[5]

[4] Skinner's remark quoted above about the generality of his basic results must be understood in the light of the experimental limitations he has imposed. If it were true in any deep sense that the basic processes in language are well understood and free of species restrictions, it would be extremely odd that language is limited to man. With the exception of a few scattered observations (cf. his article, A case history in scientific method, *The American psychologist* 11.221–33 [1956]), Skinner is apparently basing this claim on the fact that qualitatively similar results are obtained with bar-pressing of rats and pecking of pigeons under special conditions of deprivation and various schedules of reinforcement. One immediately questions how much can be based on these facts, which are in part at least an artifact traceable to experimental design and the definition of 'stimulus' and 'response' in terms of 'smooth dynamic curves' (see below). The dangers inherent in any attempt to 'extrapolate' to complex behavior from the study of such simple responses as bar-pressing should be obvious, and have often been commented on (cf. e.g. Harlow, op.cit.). The generality of even the simplest results is open to serious question. Cf. in this connection Bitterman, Wodinsky, and Candland, Some comparative psychology, *Am. jour. of psych.* 71.94–110 (1958), where it is shown that there are important qualitative differences in solution of comparable elementary problems by rats and fish.

[5] An analogous argument, in connection with a different aspect of Skinner's thinking, is

3. Consider first Skinner's use of the notions 'stimulus' and 'response'. In *Behavior of organisms* (9) he commits himself to the narrow definitions for these terms. A part of the environment and a part of behavior are called stimulus (eliciting, discriminated, or reinforcing) and response, respectively, only if they are lawfully related; that is, if the 'dynamic laws' relating them show smooth and reproducible curves. Evidently stimuli and responses, so defined, have not been shown to figure very widely in ordinary human behavior.[6] We can, in the face of presently available evidence, continue to maintain the lawfulness of the relation between stimulus and response only by depriving them of their objective character. A typical example of 'stimulus control' for Skinner would be the response to a piece of music with the utterance *Mozart* or to a painting with the response *Dutch.* These responses are asserted to be 'under the control of extremely subtle properties' of the physical object or event (108). Suppose instead of saying *Dutch* we had said *Clashes with the wallpaper, I thought you liked abstract work, Never saw it before, Tilted, Hanging too low, Beautiful, Hideous, Remember our camping trip last summer?,* or whatever else might come into our minds when looking at a picture (in Skinnerian translation, whatever other responses exist in sufficient strength). Skinner could only say that each of these responses is under the control of some other stimulus property of the physical object. If we look at a red chair and say *red,* the response is under the control of the stimulus 'redness'; if we say *chair,* it is under the control of the collection of properties (for Skinner, the object) 'chairness' (110), and similarly for any other response. This device is as simple as it is empty. Since properties are free for the asking (we have as many of them as we have nonsynonymous descriptive expressions in our language, whatever this means exactly), we can account for a wide class of responses in terms of Skinnerian functional analysis by identifying the 'controlling stimuli'. But the word 'stimulus' has lost all objectivity in this usage. Stimuli are no longer part of the outside physical world; they are driven back into the organism. We identify the stimulus when we hear the response. It is clear from such examples, which abound, that the talk of 'stimulus control' simply disguises a complete retreat to mentalistic psychology. We cannot predict verbal behavior in terms of the stimuli in the speaker's environment, since we do not know what the current stimuli are until he responds. Furthermore, since we cannot control the property of a physical object to which an individual will respond, except in highly artificial cases, Skinner's claim that his system, as opposed to the traditional one, permits the prac-

---

given by Scriven in *A study of radical behaviorism=Univ. of Minn. studies in philosophy of science,* Vol. 1. Cf. Verplanck's contribution to *Modern learning theory* (283–8) for more general discussion of the difficulties in formulating an adequate definition of 'stimulus' and 'response'. He concludes, quite correctly, that in Skinner's sense of the word, stimuli are not objectively identifiable independently of the resulting behavior, nor are they manipulable. Verplanck presents a clear discussion of many other aspects of Skinner's system, commenting on the untestability of many of the so-called 'laws of behavior' and the limited scope of many of the others, and the arbitrary and obscure character of Skinner's notion of 'lawful relation'; and, at the same time, noting the importance of the experimental data that Skinner has accumulated.

[6] In *Behavior of organisms,* Skinner apparently was willing to accept this consequence. He insists (41–2) that the terms of casual description in the popular vocabulary are not validly descriptive until the defining properties of stimulus and response are specified, the correlation is demonstrated experimentally, and the dynamic changes in it are shown to be lawful. Thus, in describing a child as hiding from a dog, 'it will not be enough to dignify the popular vocabulary by appealing to essential properties of "dogness" or "hidingness" and to suppose them intuitively known.' But this is exactly what Skinner does in the book under review, as we will see directly.

tical control of verbal behavior[7] is quite false.

Other examples of 'stimulus control' merely add to the general mystification. Thus a proper noun is held to be a response 'under the control of a specific person or thing' (as controlling stimulus, 113). I have often used the words *Eisenhower* and *Moscow*, which I presume are proper nouns if anything is, but have never been 'stimulated' by the corresponding objects. How can this fact be made compatible with this definition? Suppose that I use the name of a friend who is not present. Is this an instance of a proper noun under the control of the friend as stimulus? Elsewhere it is asserted that a stimulus controls a response in the sense that presence of the stimulus increases the probability of the response. But it is obviously untrue that the probability that a speaker will produce a full name is increased when its bearer faces the speaker. Furthermore, how can one's own name be a proper noun in this sense? A multitude of similar questions arise immediately. It appears that the word 'control' here is merely a misleading paraphrase for the traditional 'denote' or 'refer'. The assertion (115) that so far as the speaker is concerned, the relation of reference is 'simply the probability that the speaker will emit a response of a given form in the presence of a stimulus having specified properties' is surely incorrect if we take the words 'presence', 'stimulus', and 'probability' in their literal sense. That they are not intended to be taken literally is indicated by many examples, as when a response is said to be 'controlled' by a situation or state of affairs as 'stimulus'. Thus, the expression *a needle in a haystack* 'may be controlled as a unit by a particular type of situation' (116); the words in a single part of speech, e.g. all adjectives, are under the control of a single set of subtle properties of stimuli (121); 'the sentence *The boy runs a store* is under the control of an extremely complex stimulus situation' (335); '*He is not at all well* may function as a standard response under the control of a state of affairs which might also control *He is ailing*' (325); when an envoy observes events in a foreign country and reports upon his return, his report is under 'remote stimulus control' (416); the statement *This is war* may be a response to a 'confusing international situation' (441); the

[7] 253 f. and elsewhere, repeatedly. As an example of how well we can control behavior using the notions developed in this book, Skinner shows here how he would go about evoking the response *pencil*. The most effective way, he suggests, is to say to the subject 'Please say *pencil*' (our chances would, presumably, be even further improved by use of 'aversive stimulation', e.g. holding a gun to his head). We can also 'make sure that no pencil or writing instrument is available, then hand our subject a pad of paper appropriate to pencil sketching, and offer him a handsome reward for a recognizable picture of a cat.' It would also be useful to have voices saying *pencil* or *pen and*...in the background; signs reading *pencil* or *pen and*...; or to place a 'large and unusual pencil in an unusual place clearly in sight'. 'Under such circumstances, it is highly probable that our subject will say *pencil*.' 'The available techniques are all illustrated in this sample.' These contributions of behavior theory to the practical control of human behavior are amply illustrated elsewhere in the book, as when Skinner shows (113–4) how we can evoke the response *red* (the device suggested is to hold a red object before the subject and say 'Tell me what color this is').

In fairness, it must be mentioned that there are certain nontrivial applications of 'operant conditioning' to the control of human behavior. A wide variety of experiments have shown that the number of plural nouns (for example) produced by a subject will increase if the experimenter says 'right' or 'good' when one is produced (similarly, positive attitudes on a certain issue, stories with particular content, etc.; cf. Krasner, Studies of the conditioning of verbal behavior, *Psych. bull.*, Vol. 55 [1958], for a survey of several dozen experiments of this kind, mostly with positive results). It is of some interest that the subject is usually unaware of the process. Just what insight this gives into normal verbal behavior is not obvious. Nevertheless, it is an example of positive and not totally expected results using the Skinnerian paradigm.

suffix *-ed* is controlled by that 'subtle property of stimuli which we speak of as action-in-the-past' (121) just as the *-s* in *The boy runs* is under the control of such specific features of the situation as its 'currency' (332). No characterization of the notion 'stimulus control' that is remotely related to the bar-pressing experiment (or that preserves the faintest objectivity) can be made to cover a set of examples like these, in which, for example, the 'controlling stimulus' need not even impinge on the responding organism.

Consider now Skinner's use of the notion 'response'. The problem of identifying units in verbal behavior has of course been a primary concern of linguists, and it seems very likely that experimental psychologists should be able to provide much-needed assistance in clearing up the many remaining difficulties in systematic identification. Skinner recognizes (20) the fundamental character of the problem of identification of a unit of verbal behavior, but is satisfied with an answer so vague and subjective that it does not really contribute to its solution. The unit of verbal behavior—the verbal operant—is defined as a class of responses of identifiable form functionally related to one or more controlling variables. No method is suggested for determining in a particular instance what are the controlling variables, how many such units have occurred, or where their boundaries are in the total response. Nor is any attempt made to specify how much or what kind of similarity in form or 'control' is required for two physical events to be considered instances of the same operant. In short, no answers are suggested for the most elementary questions that must be asked of anyone proposing a method for description of behavior. Skinner is content with what he calls an 'extrapolation' of the concept of operant developed in the laboratory to the verbal field. In the typical Skinnerian experiment, the problem of identifying the unit of behavior is not too crucial. It is defined, by fiat, as a recorded peck or bar-press, and systematic variations in the rate of this operant and its resistance to extinction are studied as a function of deprivation and scheduling of reinforcement (pellets). The operant is thus defined with respect to a particular experimental procedure. This is perfectly reasonable, and has led to many interesting results. It is, however, completely meaningless to speak of extrapolating this concept of operant to ordinary verbal behavior. Such 'extrapolation' leaves us with no way of justifying one or another decision about the units in the 'verbal repertoire'.

Skinner specifies 'response strength' as the basic datum, the basic dependent variable in his functional analysis. In the bar-pressing experiment, response strength is defined in terms of rate of emission during extinction. Skinner has argued[8] that this is 'the only datum that varies significantly and in the expected direction under conditions which are relevant to the "learning process".' In the book under review, response strength is defined as 'probability of emission' (22). This definition provides a comforting impression of objectivity, which, however, is quickly dispelled when we look into the matter more closely. The term 'probability' has some rather obscure meaning for Skinner in this book.[9] We are told, on the one hand,

[8] Are theories of learning necessary?, *Psych. rev.* 57.193–216 (1950).

[9] And elsewhere. In his paper Are theories of learning necessary?, Skinner considers the problem how to extend his analysis of behavior to experimental situations in which it is impossible to observe frequencies, rate of response being the only valid datum. His answer is that 'the notion of probability is usually extrapolated to cases in which a frequency analysis cannot be carried out. In the field of behavior we arrange a situation in which frequencies are available as data, but we use the notion of probability in analyzing or formulating instances of even types of behavior which are not susceptible to this analysis' (199). There are, of course, conceptions of probability not based directly on frequency, but I do not see how any of these apply to the cases that Skinner has in mind. I see no way of inter-

that 'our evidence for the contribution of each variable [to response strength] is based on observation of frequencies alone' (28). At the same time, it appears that frequency is a very misleading measure of strength, since, for example, the frequency of a response may be 'primarily attributable to the frequency of occurrence of controlling variables' (27). It is not clear how the frequency of a response can be attributable to anything BUT the frequency of occurrence of its controlling variables if we accept Skinner's view that the behavior occurring in a given situation is 'fully determined' by the relevant controlling variables (175, 228). Furthermore, although the evidence for the contribution of each variable to response strength is based on observation of frequencies alone, it turns out that 'we base the notion of strength upon several kinds of evidence' (22), in particular (22–8): emission of the response (particularly in unusual circumstances), energy level (stress), pitch level, speed and delay of emission, size of letters etc. in writing, immediate repetition, and—a final factor, relevant but misleading—over-all frequency.

Of course, Skinner recognizes that these measures do not co-vary, because (among other reasons) pitch, stress, quantity, and reduplication may have internal linguistic functions.[10] However, he does not hold these conflicts to be very important, since the proposed factors indicative of strength are 'fully understood by everyone' in the culture (27). For example, 'if we are shown a prized work of art and exclaim *Beautiful!*, the speed and energy of the response will not be lost on the owner.' It does not appear totally obvious that in this case the way to impress the owner is to shriek *Beautiful* in a loud, high-pitched voice, repeatedly, and with no delay (high response strength). It may be equally effective to look at the picture silently (long delay), and then to murmur *Beautiful* in a soft, low-pitched voice (by definition, very low response strength).

It is not unfair, I believe, to conclude from Skinner's discussion of response strength, the 'basic datum' in functional analysis, that his 'extrapolation' of the notion of probability can best be interpreted as, in effect, nothing more than a decision to use the word 'probability', with its favorable connotations of objectivity, as a cover term to paraphrase such low-status words as 'interest', 'intention', 'belief', and the like. This interpretation is fully justified by the way in which Skinner uses the terms 'probability' and 'strength'. To cite just one example, Skinner defines the process of confirming an assertion in science as one of 'generating additional variables to increase its probability' (425), and more generally, its strength (425–9). If we take this suggestion quite literally, the degree of confirmation of a scientific assertion can be measured as a simple function of the loudness, pitch, and frequency with which it is proclaimed, and a general procedure for increasing its degree of confirmation would be, for instance, to train machine guns on large crowds of people who have been instructed to shout it. A better indication of what Skinner probably has in mind here is given by his description of how the theory of evolution, as an example, is confirmed. This 'single set of verbal responses. . . is made more plausible —is strengthened—by several types of construction based upon verbal responses in geology, paleontology, genetics, and so on' (427). We are no doubt to interpret the terms 'strength' and 'probability' in this context as paraphrases of more familiar locutions such as 'justified belief' or 'warranted assertability', or something of

preting the quoted passage other than as signifying an intention to use the word 'probability' in describing behavior quite independently of whether the notion of probability is at all relevant.

[10] Fortunately, 'In English this presents no great difficulty' since, for example, 'relative pitch levels. . .are not. . .important' (25). No reference is made to the numerous studies of the function of relative pitch levels and other intonational features in English.

the sort. Similar latitude of interpretation is presumably expected when we read that 'frequency of effective action accounts in turn for what we may call the listener's "belief" ' (88) or that 'our belief in what someone tells us is similarly a function of, or identical with, our tendency to act upon the verbal stimuli which he provides' (160).[11]

I think it is evident, then, that Skinner's use of the terms 'stimulus', 'control', 'response', and 'strength' justify the general conclusion stated in the last paragraph of §2 above. The way in which these terms are brought to bear on the actual data indicates that we must interpret them as mere paraphrases for the popular vocabulary commonly used to describe behavior, and as having no particular connection with the homonymous expressions used in the description of laboratory experiments. Naturally, this terminological revision adds no objectivity to the familiar 'mentalistic' mode of description.

4. The other fundamental notion borrowed from the description of bar-pressing experiments is 'reinforcement'. It raises problems which are similar, and even more serious. In *Behavior of organisms,* 'the operation of reinforcement is defined as the presentation of a certain kind of stimulus in a temporal relation with either a stimulus or response. A reinforcing stimulus is defined as such by its power to produce the resulting change [in strength]. There is no circularity about this: some stimuli are found to produce the change, others not, and they are classified as reinforcing and non-reinforcing accordingly' (62). This is a perfectly appropriate definition[12] for the study of schedules of reinforcement. It is perfectly useless, however, in the discussion of real-life behavior, unless we can somehow characterize the stimuli which are reinforcing (and the situations and conditions under which they are reinforcing). Consider first of all the status of the basic principle that Skinner calls the 'law of conditioning' (law of effect). It reads: 'if the occurrence of an operant is followed by presence of a reinforcing stimulus, the strength is increased' (*Behavior of organisms* 21). As 'reinforcement' was defined, this law becomes a tautology.[13] For Skinner, learning is just change in response strength.[14] Although the statement that presence of reinforcement is a sufficient condition for learning and maintenance of behavior is vacuous, the claim that it is a necessary condition may have some content, depending on how the class of reinforcers (and appropriate situations) is characterized. Skinner does make it very clear that in his view reinforcement is a necessary condition for language learning and for the continued availability of linguistic responses in the adult.[15] However, the looseness of the term 'reinforcement' as Skinner

11 The vagueness of the word 'tendency', as opposed to 'frequency', saves the latter quotation from the obvious incorrectness of the former. Nevertheless, a good deal of stretching is necessary. If 'tendency' has anything like its ordinary meaning, the remark is clearly false. One may believe strongly the assertion that Jupiter has four moons, that many of Sophocles' plays have been irretrievably lost, that the earth will burn to a crisp in ten million years, etc., without experiencing the slightest tendency to act upon these verbal stimuli. We may, of course, turn Skinner's assertion into a very unilluminating truth by defining 'tendency to act' to include tendencies to answer questions in certain ways, under motivation to say what one believes is true.

12 One should add, however, that it is in general not the stimulus as such that is reinforcing, but the stimulus in a particular situational context. Depending on experimental arrangement, a particular physical event or object may be reinforcing, punishing, or unnoticed. Because Skinner limits himself to a particular, very simple experimental arrangement, it is not necessary for him to add this qualification, which would not be at all easy to formulate precisely. But it is of course necessary if he expects to extend his descriptive system to behavior in general.

13 This has been frequently noted.

14 See, for example, Are theories of learning necessary? 199. Elsewhere, he suggests that the term 'learning' be restricted to complex situations, but these are not characterized.

15 'A child acquires verbal behavior when

uses it in the book under review makes it entirely pointless to inquire into the truth or falsity of this claim. Examining the instances of what Skinner calls 'reinforcement', we find that not even the requirement that a reinforcer be an identifiable stimulus is taken seriously. In fact, the term is used in such a way that the assertion that reinforcement is necessary for learning and continued availability of behavior is likewise empty.

To show this, we consider some example of 'reinforcement'. First of all, we find a heavy appeal to automatic self-reinforcement. Thus, 'a man talks to himself... because of the reinforcement he receives' (163); 'the child is reinforced automatically when he duplicates the sounds of airplanes, streetcars...' (164); 'the young child alone in the nursery may automatically reinforce his own exploratory verbal behavior when he produces sounds which he has heard in the speech of others' (58); 'the speaker who is also an accomplished listener "knows when he has correctly echoed a response" and is reinforced thereby' (68); thinking is 'behaving which automatically affects the behaver and is reinforcing because it does so' (438; cutting one's finger should thus be reinforcing, and an example of thinking); 'the verbal fantasy, whether overt or covert, is automatically reinforcing to the speaker as listener. Just as the musician plays or composes what he is reinforced by hearing, or as the artist paints what reinforces him visually, so the speaker engaged in verbal fantasy says what he is reinforced by hearing or writes what he is reinforced by reading' (439); similarly, care in problem solving, and rationalization, are automatically self-reinforcing (442–3). We can also reinforce someone by emitting verbal behavior as such (since this rules out a class of aversive stimulations, 167), by not emitting verbal behavior (keeping silent and paying attention, 199), or by acting appropriately on some future occasion (152: 'the strength of [the speaker's] behavior is determined mainly by the behavior which the listener will exhibit with respect to a given state of affairs'; this Skinner considers the general case of 'communication' or 'letting the listener know'). In most such cases, of course, the speaker is not present at the time when the reinforcement takes place, as when 'the artist...is reinforced by the effects his works have upon...others' (224), or when the writer is reinforced by the fact that his 'verbal behavior may reach over centuries or to thousands of listeners or readers at the same time. The writer may not be reinforced often or immediately, but his net reinforcement may be great' (206; this accounts for the great 'strength' of his behavior). An individual may also find it reinforcing to injure someone by criticism or by bringing bad news, or to publish an experimental result which upsets the theory of a rival (154), to describe circumstances which would be reinforcing if they were to occur (165), to avoid repetition (222), to 'hear' his own name though in fact it was not mentioned or to hear nonexistent words in his child's babbling (259), to clarify or otherwise intensify the effect of a stimulus which serves an important discriminative function (416), etc.

From this sample, it can be seen that the notion of reinforcement has totally lost whatever objective meaning it may ever have had. Running through these examples, we see that a person can be reinforced though he emits no response at all, and that the reinforcing 'stimulus' need not impinge on the 'reinforced person' or need not even exist (it is sufficient that

relatively unpatterned vocalizations, selectively reinforced, gradually assume forms which produce appropriate consequences in a given verbal community' (31). 'Differential reinforcement shapes up all verbal forms, and when a prior stimulus enters into the contingency, reinforcement is responsible for its resulting control....The availability of behavior, its probability or strength, depends on whether reinforcements *continue* in effect and according to what schedules' (203–4). Elsewhere, frequently.

it be imagined or hoped for). When we read that a person plays what music he likes (165), says what he likes (165), thinks what he likes (438–9), reads what books he likes (163), etc., BECAUSE he finds it reinforcing to do so, or that we write books or informs others of facts BECAUSE we are reinforced by what we hope will be the ultimate behavior of reader or listener, we can only conclude that the term 'reinforcement' has a purely ritual function. The phrase 'X is reinforced by Y (stimulus, state of affairs, event, etc.)' is being used as a cover term for 'X wants Y', 'X likes Y', 'X wishes that Y were the case', etc. Invoking the term 'reinforcement' has no explanatory force, and any idea that this paraphrase introduces any new clarity or objectivity into the description of wishing, liking, etc., is a serious delusion. The only effect is to obscure the important differences among the notions being paraphrased. Once we recognize the latitude with which the term 'reinforcement' is being used, many rather startling comments lose their initial effect—for instance, that the behavior of the creative artist is 'controlled entirely by the contingencies of reinforcement' (150). What has been hoped for from the psychologist is some indication how the casual and informal description of everyday behavior in the popular vocabulary can be explained or clarified in terms of the notions developed in careful experiment and observation, or perhaps replaced in terms of a better scheme. A mere terminological revision, in which a term borrowed from the laboratory is used with the full vagueness of the ordinary vocabulary, is of no conceivable interest.

It seems that Skinner's claim that all verbal behavior is acquired and maintained in 'strength' through reinforcement is quite empty, because his notion of reinforcement has no clear content, functioning only as a cover term for any factor, detectable or not, related to acquisition or maintenance of verbal behavior.[16] Skinner's use of the term 'conditioning' suffers from a similar difficulty. Pavlovian and operant conditioning are processes about which psychologists have developed real understanding. Instruction of human beings is not. The claim that instruction and imparting of information are simply matters of conditioning (357–66) is pointless. The claim is true, if we extend the term 'conditioning' to cover these processes but we know no more about them after having revised this term in such a way as to deprive it of its relatively clear and objective character. It is, as far as we know, quite false, if we use 'conditioning' in its literal sense. Similarly, when we say that 'it is the function of predication to facilitate the transfer of response from one term to another or from one object to another' (361), we have said nothing of any significance. In what sense is this true of the predication *Whales are mammals*? Or, to take Skinner's example, what point is there in saying that the effect of *The telephone is out of order* on the listener is to bring behavior formerly controlled by the stimulus *out of order* under control of the stimulus *telephone* (or the telephone itself) by a process of simple conditioning (362)? What laws of conditioning hold in this case? Furthermore, what behavior is 'controlled' by the stimulus *out of order*, in the abstract? Depending on the object of which this is predicated, the present state of motivation of the listener, etc., the behavior may vary from rage to pleasure, from fixing the object to throwing it out, from simply not using it to trying to use it in the normal way (e.g. to see if it is really out of order),

16 Talk of schedules of reinforcement here is entirely pointless. How are we to decide, for example, according to what schedules covert reinforcement is 'arranged', as in thinking or verbal fantasy, or what the scheduling is of such factors as silence, speech, and appropriate future reactions to communicated information?

and so on. To speak of 'conditioning' or 'bringing previously available behavior under control of a new stimulus' in such a case is just a kind of play-acting at science. Cf. also footnote 43.

5. The claim that careful arrangement of contingencies of reinforcement by the verbal community is a necessary condition for language learning has appeared, in one form or another, in many places.[17] Since it is based not on actual observation, but on analogies to laboratory study of lower organisms, it is important to determine the status of the underlying assertion within experimental psychology proper. The most common characterization of reinforcement (one which Skinner explicitly rejects, incidentally) is in terms of drive reduction. This characterization can be given substance by defining drives in some way independently of what in fact is learned. If a drive is postulated on the basis of the fact that learning takes place, the claim that reinforcement is necessary for learning will again become as empty as it is in the Skinnerian framework. There is an extensive literature on the question of whether there can be learning without drive-reduction (latent learning). The 'classical' experiment of Blodgett indicated that rats who had explored a maze without reward showed a marked drop in number of errors (as compared to a control group which had not explored the maze) upon introduction of a food reward, indicating that the rat had learned the structure of the maze without reduction of the hunger drive. Drive-reduction theorists countered with an exploratory drive which was reduced during the prereward learning, and claimed that a slight decrement in errors could be noted before food reward. A wide variety of experiments, with somewhat conflicting results, have been carried out with a similar design.[18] Few investigators still doubt the existence of the phenomenon. Hilgard, in his general review of learning theory,[19] concludes that 'there is no longer any doubt but that, under appropriate circumstances, latent learning is demonstrable.'

More recent work has shown that novelty and variety of stimulus are sufficient to arouse curiosity in the rat and to motivate it to explore (visually), and in fact, to learn (since on a presentation of two stimuli, one novel, one repeated, the rat will attend to the novel one);[20] that rats will learn to choose the arm of a single-choice maze that leads to a complex maze, running through this being their only 'reward';[21] that monkeys can learn object discriminations and maintain their performance at a high level of efficiency with visual exploration (looking out of a

[17] See, for example, Miller and Dollard, *Social learning and imitation* 82–3 (New York, 1941), for a discussion of the 'meticulous training' that they seem to consider necessary for a child to learn the meanings of words and syntactic patterns. The same notion is implicit in Mowrer's speculative account of how language might be acquired, in *Learning theory and personality dynamics,* Chapter 23 (New York, 1950). Actually, the view appears to be quite general.

[18] For a general review and analysis of this literature, see Thistlethwaite, A critical review of latent learning and related experiments, *Psych. bull.* 48.97–129 (1951). MacCorquodale and Meehl, in their contribution to *Modern learning theory,* carry out a serious and considered attempt to handle the latent learning material from the standpoint of drive-reduction theory, with (as they point out) not entirely satisfactory results. Thorpe reviews the literature from the standpoint of the ethologist, adding also material on homing and topographical orientation (*Learning and instinct in animals* [Cambridge, 1956]).

[19] *Theories of learning* 214 (1956).

[20] Berlyne, Novelty and curiosity as determinants of exploratory behavior, *Brit. jour. of psych.* 41.68–80 (1950); id., Perceptual curiosity in the rat, *Jour. of comp. physiol. psych.* 48.238–46 (1955); Thompson and Solomon, Spontaneous pattern discrimination in the rat, ibid. 47.104–7 (1954).

[21] Montgomery, The role of the exploratory drive in learning, ibid. 60–3. Many other

window for 30 seconds) as the only reward;[22] and, perhaps most strikingly of all, that monkeys and apes will solve rather complex manipulation problems that are simply placed in their cages, and will solve discrimination problems with only exploration and manipulation as incentives.[23] In these cases, solving the problem is apparently its own 'reward'. Results of this kind can be handled by reinforcement theorists only if they are willing to set up curiosity, exploration, and manipulation drives, or to speculate somehow about acquired drives[24] for which there is no evidence outside of the fact that learning takes place in these cases.

There is a variety of other kinds of evidence that has been offered to challenge the view that drive-reduction is necessary for learning. Results on sensory-sensory conditioning have been interpreted as demonstrating learning without drive-reduction.[25] Olds has reported reinforcement by direct stimulation of the brain, from which he concludes that reward need not satisfy a physiological need or withdraw a drive stimulus.[26] The phenomenon of imprinting, long observed by zoologists, is of particular interest in this connection. Some of the most complex patterns of behavior of birds, in particular, are directed towards objects and animals of the type to which they have been exposed at certain critical early periods of life.[27] Imprinting is the most

papers in the same journal are designed to show that exploratory behavior is a relatively independent primary 'drive' aroused by novel external stimulation.

22 Butler, Discrimination learning by Rhesus monkeys to visual-exploration motivation, ibid. 46.95–8 (1953). Later experiments showed that this 'drive' is highly persistent, as opposed to derived drives which rapidly extinguish.

23 Harlow, Harlow, and Meyer, Learning motivated by a manipulation drive, *Jour. exp. psych.* 40.228–34 (1950), and later investigations initiated by Harlow. Harlow has been particularly insistent on maintaining the inadequacy of physiologically based drives and homeostatic need states for explaining the persistence of motivation and rapidity of learning in primates. He points out, in many papers, that curiosity, play, exploration, and manipulation are, for primates, often more potent drives than hunger and the like, and that they show none of the characteristics of acquired drives. Hebb also presents behavioral and supporting neurological evidence in support of the view that in higher animals there is a positive attraction in work, risk, puzzle, intellectual activity, mild fear and frustration, etc. (Drives and the CNS, *Psych.* rev. 62.243–54 [1955]). He concludes that 'we need not work out tortuous and improbable ways to explain why men work for money, why children learn without pain, why people dislike doing nothing.'

In a brief note (Early recognition of the manipulative drive in monkeys, *British journal of animal behaviour* 3.71–2 [1955]), W. Dennis calls attention to the fact that early investigators (Romanes, 1882; Thorndike, 1901), whose 'perception was relatively unaffected by learning theory, did note the intrinsically motivated behavior of monkeys', although, he asserts, no similar observations on monkeys have been made until Harlow's experiments. He quotes Romanes (*Animal intelligence* [1882]) as saying that 'much the most striking feature in the psychology of this animal, and the one which is least like anything met with in other animals, was the tireless spirit of investigation.' Analogous developments, in which genuine discoveries have blinded systematic investigators to the important insights of earlier work, are easily found within recent structural linguistics as well.

24 Thus J. S. Brown, in commenting on a paper of Harlow's in *Current theory and research in motivation* (Lincoln, 1953), argues that 'in probably every instance [of the experiments cited by Harlow] an ingenious drive-reduction theorist could find some fragment of fear, insecurity, frustration, or whatever, that he could insist was reduced and hence was reinforcing' (53). The same sort of thing could be said for the ingenious phlogiston or ether theorist.

25 Cf. Birch and Bitterman, Reinforcement and learning: The process of sensory integration, *Psych. rev.* 56.292–308 (1949).

26 See, for example, his paper A physiological study of reward in McClelland (ed.), *Studies in motivation* 134–43 (New York, 1955).

27 See Thorpe, op.cit., particularly 115–8 and 337–76, for an excellent discussion of this phenomenon, which has been brought to prominence particularly by the work of K. Lorenz (cf. Der Kumpan in der Umwelt des Vogels,

striking evidence for the innate disposition of the animal to learn in a certain direction, and to react appropriately to patterns and objects of certain restricted types, often only long after the original learning has taken place. It is, consequently, unrewarded learning, though the resulting patterns of behavior may be refined through reinforcement. Acquisition of the typical songs of song birds is, in some cases, a type of imprinting. Thorpe reports studies that show 'that some characteristics of the normal song have been learnt in the earliest youth, before the bird itself is able to produce any kind of full song'.[28] The phenomenon of imprinting has recently been investigated under laboratory conditions and controls with positive results.[29]

Phenomena of this general type are certainly familiar from everyday experience. We recognize people and places to which we have given no particular attention. We can look up something in a book and learn it perfectly well with no other motive than to confute reinforcement theory, or out of boredom, or idle curiosity. Everyone engaged in research must have had the experience of working with feverish and prolonged intensity to write a paper which no one else will read or to solve a problem which no one else thinks important and which will bring no conceivable reward—which may only confirm a general opinion that the researcher is wasting his time on irrelevancies. The fact that rats and monkeys do likewise is interesting, and important to show in careful experiment. In fact, studies of behavior of the type mentioned above have an independent and positive significance that far outweighs their incidental importance in bringing into question the claim that learning is impossible without drive-reduction. It is not at all unlikely that insights arising from animal behavior studies with this broadened scope may have the kind of relevance to such complex activities as verbal behavior that reinforcement theory has, so far, failed to exhibit. In any event, in the light of presently available evidence, it is difficult to see how anyone can be willing to claim that reinforcement is necessary for learning, if reinforcement is taken seriously as something identifiable independently of the resulting change in behavior.

Similarly, it seems quite beyond question that children acquire a good deal of their verbal and nonverbal behavior by casual observation and imitation of adults and other children.[30] It is simply not true

parts of which are reprinted in English translation in Schiller (ed.), *Instinctive behavior* 83–128 (New York, 1957).)

[28] Op.cit. 372.

[29] See e.g. Jaynes, Imprinting: Interaction of learned and innate behavior, *Jour. of comp. physiol. psych.* 49.201–6 (1956), where the conclusion is reached that 'the experiments prove that without any observable reward young birds of this species follow a moving stimulus object and very rapidly come to prefer that object to others.'

[30] Of course it is perfectly possible to incorporate this fact within the Skinnerian framework. If, for example, a child watches an adult using a comb and then, with no instruction, tries to comb his own hair, we can explain this act by saying that he performs it because he finds it reinforcing to do so, or because of the reinforcement provided by behaving like a person who is 'reinforcing' (cf. 164). Similarly, an automatic explanation is available for any other behavior. It seems strange at first that Skinner pays so little attention to the literature on latent learning and related topics, considering the tremendous reliance that he places on the notion of reinforcement; I have seen no reference to it in his writings. Similarly, Keller and Schoenfeld, in what appears to be the only text written under predominantly Skinnerian influence, *Principles of psychology* (New York, 1950), dismiss the latent-learning literature in one sentence as 'beside the point', serving only 'to obscure, rather than clarify, a fundamental principle' (the law of effect, 41). However, this neglect is perfectly appropriate in Skinner's case. To the drive-reductionist, or anyone else for whom the notion 'reinforcement' has some substantive meaning these experiments and observations are important (and often embarrassing). But in the Skinnerian sense of the word, neither these results nor any conceivable others can cast any doubt on the claim that

that children can learn language only through 'meticulous care' on the part of adults who shape their verbal repertoire through careful differential reinforcement, though it may be that such care is often the custom in academic families. It is a common observation that a young child of immigrant parents may learn a second language in the streets, from other children, with amazing rapidity, and that his speech may be completely fluent and correct to the last allophone, while the subtleties that become second nature to the child may elude his parents despite high motivation and continued practice. A child may pick up a large part of his vocabulary and 'feel' for sentence structure from television, from reading, from listening to adults, etc. Even a very young child who has not yet acquired a minimal repertoire from which to form new utterances may imitate a word quite well on an early try, with no attempt on the part of his parents to teach it to him. It is also perfectly obvious that, at a later stage, a child will be able to construct and understand utterances which are quite new, and are, at the same time, acceptable sentences in his language. Every time an adult reads a newspaper, he undoubtedly comes upon countless new sentences which are not at all similar, in a simple, physical sense, to any that he has heard before, and which he will recognize as sentences and understand; he will also be able to detect slight distortions or misprints. Talk of 'stimulus generalization' in such a case simply perpetuates the mystery under a new title. These abilities indicate that there must be fundamental processes at work quite independently of 'feedback' from the environment. I have been able to find no support whatsoever for the doctrine of Skinner and others that slow and careful shaping of verbal behavior through differential reinforcement is an absolute necessity. If reinforcement theory really requires the assumption that there be such meticulous care, it seems bset to regard this simply as a reductio ad absurdum argument against this approach. It is also not easy to find any basis (or, for that matter, to attach very much content) to the claim that reinforcing contingencies set up by the verbal community are the single factor responsible for maintaining the strength of verbal behavior. The sources of the 'strength' of this behavior are almost a total mystery at present. Reinforcement undoubtedly plays a significant role, but so do a variety of motivational factors about which nothing serious is known in the case of human beings.

As far as acquisition of language is concerned, it seems clear that reinforcement, casual observation, and natural inquisitiveness (coupled with a strong tendency to imitate) are important factors, as is the remarkable capacity of the child to generalize, hypothesize, and 'process information' in a variety of very special and apparently highly complex ways which we cannot yet describe or begin to understand, and which may be largely innate, or may develop through some sort of learning or through maturation of the nervous system. The manner in which such factors operate and interact in language acquisition is completely unknown. It is clear that what is necessary in such a case is research, not dogmatic and perfectly arbitrary claims, based on analogies to that small part of the experimental literature in which one happens to be interested.

The pointlessness of these claims becomes clear when we consider the well-known difficulties in determining to what extent inborn structure, maturation, and learning are responsible for the particular form of a skilled or complex performance.[31] To take just one example,[32] the

reinforcement is essential for the acquisition and maintenance of behavior. Behavior certainly has some concomitant circumstances, and whatever they are, we can call them 'reinforcement'.

31 Tinbergen (op.cit., Chapter VI) reviews some aspects of this problem, discussing the

gaping response of a nestling thrush is at first released by jarring of the nest, and, at a later stage, by a moving object of specific size, shape, and position relative to the nestling. At this later stage the response is directed towards the part of the stimulus object corresponding to the parent's head, and characterized by a complex configuration of stimuli that can be precisely described. Knowing just this, it would be possible to construct a speculative, learning-theoretic account of how this sequence of behavior patterns might have developed through a process of differential reinforcement, and it would no doubt be possible to train rats to do something similar. However, there appears to be good evidence that these responses to fairly complex 'sign stimuli' are genetically determined and mature without learning. Clearly, the possibility cannot be discounted. Consider now the comparable case of a child imitating new words. At an early stage we may find rather gross correspondences. At a later stage, we find that repetition is of course far from exact (i.e. it is not mimicry, a fact which itself is interesting), but that it reproduces the highly complex configuration of sound features that constitute the phonological structure of the language in question. Again, we can propose a speculative account of how this result might have been obtained through elaborate arrangement of reinforcing contingencies. Here too, however, it is possible that ability to select out of the complex auditory input those features that are phonologically relevant may develop largely independently of reinforcement, through genetically determined maturation. To the extent that this is true, an account of the development and causation of behavior that fails to consider the structure of the organism will provide no understanding of the real processes involved.

It is often argued that experience, rather than innate capacity to handle information in certain specific ways, must be the factor of overwhelming dominance in determining the specific character of language acquisition, since a child speaks the language of the group in which he lives. But this is a superficial argument. As long as we are speculating, we may consider the possibility that the brain has evolved to the point where, given an input of observed Chinese sentences, it produces (by an 'induction' of apparently fantastic complexity and suddenness) the 'rules' of Chinese grammar, and given an input of observed English sentences, it produces (by, perhaps, exactly the same process of induction) the rules of English grammar; or that given an observed application of a term to certain instances it automatically predicts the extension to a class of complexly related instances. If clearly recognized as such, this speculation is neither unreasonable nor fantastic; nor, for that matter, is it beyond the bounds of possible study. There is of course no known neural structure capable of performing this task in the specific ways that observation of the resulting behavior might lead us to postulate; but for that matter, the structures capable of accounting for even the simplest kinds of learning have similarly defied detection.[33]

primary role of maturation in the development of many complex motor patterns (e.g. flying, swimming) in lower organisms, and the effect of an 'innate disposition to learn' in certain specific ways and at certain specific times. Cf. also Schiller, *Instinctive behavior* 265–88, for a discussion of the role of maturing motor patterns in apparently insightful behavior in the chimpanzee.

Lenneberg (*Language, evolution, and purposive behavior*, unpublished) presents a very interesting discussion of the part that biological structure may play in the acquisition of language, and the dangers in neglecting this possibility.

32 From among many cited by Tinbergen, op.cit. (this on page 85).

33 Cf. Lashley, In search of the engram, *Symposium of the Society for Experimental Biology* 4.454–82 (1950). Sperry, On the neural basis of the conditioned response, *British journal of animal behaviour* 3.41–4 (1955), argues that to account for the experimental results of Lashley and others, and for other

Summarizing this brief discussion, it seems that there is neither empirical evidence nor any known argument to support any SPECIFIC claim about the relative importance of 'feedback' from the environment and the 'independent contribution of the organism' in the process of language acquisition.

6. We now turn to the system that Skinner develops specifically for the description of verbal behavior. Since this system is based on the notions 'stimulus', 'response', and 'reinforcement', we can conclude from the preceding sections that it will be vague and arbitrary. For reasons noted in §1, however, I think it is important to see in detail how far from the mark any analysis phrased solely in these terms must be and how completely this system fails to account for the facts of verbal behavior.

Consider first the term 'verbal behavior' itself. This is defined as 'behavior reinforced through the mediation of other persons' (2). The definition is clearly much too broad. It would include as 'verbal behavior', for example, a rat pressing the bar in a Skinner-box, a child brushing his teeth, a boxer retreating before an opponent, and a mechanic repairing an automobile. Exactly how much of ordinary linguistic behavior is 'verbal' in this sense, however, is something of a question: perhaps, as I have pointed out above, a fairly small fraction of it, if any substantive meaning is assigned to the term 'reinforced'. This definition is subsequently refined by the additional provision that the mediating response of the reinforcing person (the 'listener') must itself 'have been conditioned *precisely in order to reinforce* the behavior of the speaker' (225, italics his). This still covers the examples given above, if we can assume that the 'reinforcing' behavior of the psychologist, the parent, the opposing boxer, and the paying customer are the result of appropriate training, which is perhaps not unreasonable. A significant part of the fragment of linguistic behavior covered by the earlier definition will no doubt be excluded by the refinement, however. Suppose, for example, that while crossing the street I hear someone shout *Watch out for the car* and jump out of the way. It can hardly be proposed that my jumping (the mediating, reinforcing response in Skinner's usage) was conditioned (that is, I was trained to jump) precisely in order to reinforce the behavior of the speaker. Similarly for a wide class of cases. Skinner's assertion that with this refined definition 'we narrow our subject to what is traditionally recognized as the verbal field' (225) appears to be grossly in error.

7. Verbal operants are classified by Skinner in terms of their 'functional' relation to discriminated stimulus, reinforcement, and other verbal responses. A *mand* is defined as 'a verbal operant in which the response is reinforced by a characteristic consequence and is therefore under the functional control of relevant conditions of deprivation or aversive stimulation' (35). This is meant to include questions, commands, etc. Each of the terms in this definition raises a host of problems. A mand such as *Pass the salt* is a class of responses. We cannot tell by observing the form of a response whether it belongs to this class (Skinner is very clear about this), but only by identifying the controlling variables. This is generally impossible. Deprivation is defined in the bar-pressing experiment in terms of length of time that the animal has not been fed or permitted to drink. In the present context, however, it is quite a mysterious notion. No attempt is made here to describe a method for determining 'relevant conditions of deprivation' independently of the 'controlled' response. It is of no help at all to be told (32) that it can be

---

facts that he cites, it is necessary to assume that high-level cerebral activity of the type of insight, expectancy, etc. is involved even in simple conditioning. He states that 'we still lack today a satisfactory picture of the underlying neural mechanism' of the conditioned response.

characterized in terms of the operations of the experimenter. If we define deprivation in terms of elapsed time, then at any moment a person is in countless states of deprivation.[34] It appears that we must decide that the relevant condition of deprivation was (say) salt-deprivation, on the basis of the fact that the speaker asked for salt (the reinforcing community which 'sets up' the mand is in a similar predicament). In this case, the assertion that a mand is under the control of relevant deprivation is empty, and we are (contrary to Skinner's intention) identifying the response as a mand completely in terms of form. The word 'relevant' in the definition above conceals some rather serious complications.

In the case of the mand *Pass the salt,* the word 'deprivation' is not out of place, though it appears to be of little use for functional analysis. Suppose however that the speaker says *Give me the book, Take me for a ride,* or *Let me fix it.* What kinds of deprivation can be associated with these mands? How do we determine or measure the relevant deprivation? I think we must conclude in this case, as before, either that the notion 'deprivation' is relevant at most to a minute fragment of verbal behavior, or else that the statement 'X is under Y-deprivation' is just an odd paraphrase for 'X wants Y', bearing a misleading and unjustifiable connotation of objectivity.

The notion 'aversive control' is just as confused. This is intended to cover threats, beating, and the like (33). The manner in which aversive stimulation functions is simply described. If a speaker has had a history of appropriate reinforcement (e.g. if a certain response was followed by 'cessation of the threat of such injury—of events which have previously been followed by such injury and which are therefore conditioned aversive stimuli') then he will tend to give the proper response when the threat which had previously been followed by the injury is presented. It would appear to follow from this description that a speaker will not respond properly to the mand *Your money or your life* (38) unless he has a past history of being killed. But even if the difficulties in describing the mechanism of aversive control are somehow removed by a more careful anlaysis, it will be of little use for identifying operants for reasons similar to those mentioned in the case of deprivation.

It seems, then, that in Skinner's terms there is in most cases no way to decide whether a given response is an instance of a particular mand. Hence it is meaningless, within the terms of his system, to speak of the *characteristic* consequences of a mand, as in the definition above. Furthermore, even if we extend the system so that mands can somehow be identified, we will have to face the obvious fact that most of us are not fortunate enough to have our requests, commands, advice, and so on characteristically reinforced (they may nevertheless exist in considerable 'strength'). These responses could therefore not be considered mands by Skinner. In fact, Skinner sets up a category of 'magical mands' (48–9) to cover the case of 'mands which cannot be accounted for by showing that they have ever had the effect specified or any similar effect upon similar occasions' (the word 'ever' in this statement should be replaced by 'characteristically'). In these pseudo mands, 'the speaker simply describes the reinforcement appropriate to a given state of deprivation or aversive stimulation'. In other words, given the meaning that we have been led to assign to 'reinforcement' and 'deprivation', the speaker asks for what he wants. The remark that 'a speaker appears to create new mands on the analogy of old ones' is also not very helpful.

Skinner's claim that his new descriptive

[34] Furthermore, the motivation of the speaker does not, except in the simplest cases, correspond in intensity to the duration of deprivation. An obvious counter-example is what Hebb has called the 'salted-nut phenomenon' (*Organization of behavior* 199 [New York, 1949]). The difficulty is of course even more serious when we consider 'deprivations' not related to physiological drives.

system is superior to the traditional one 'because its terms can be defined with respect to experimental operations' (45) is, we see once again, an illusion. The statement 'X wants Y' is not clarified by pointing out a relation between rate of bar-pressing and hours of food-deprivation; replacing 'X wants Y' by 'X is deprived of Y' adds no new objectivity to the description of behavior. His further claim for the superiority of the new analysis of mands is that it provides an objective basis for the traditional classification into requests, commands, etc. (38–41). The traditional classification is in terms of the intention of the speaker. But intention, Skinner holds, can be reduced to contingencies of reinforcement, and, correspondingly, we can explain the traditional classification in terms of the reinforcing behavior of the listener. Thus a question is a mand which 'specifies verbal action, and the behavior of the listener permits us to classify it as a request, a command, or a prayer' (39). It is a request if 'the listener is independently motivated to reinforce the speaker'; a command if 'the listener's behavior is... reinforced by reducing a threat'; a prayer if the mand 'promotes reinforcement by generating an emotional disposition'. The mand is advice if the listener is positively reinforced by the consequences of mediating the reinforcement of the speaker; it is a warning if 'by carrying out the behavior specified by the speaker the listener escapes from aversive stimulation'; and so on. All this is obviously wrong if Skinner is using the words 'request', 'command', etc., in anything like the sense of the corresponding English words. The word 'question' does not cover commands. *Please pass the salt* is a request (but not a question), whether or not the listener happens to be motivated to fulfill it; not everyone to whom a request is addressed is favorably disposed. A response does not cease to be a command if it is not followed; nor does a question become a command if the speaker answers it because of an implied or imagined threat. Not all advice is good advice, and a response does not cease to be advice if it is not followed. Similarly, a warning may be misguided; heeding it may cause aversive stimulation, and ignoring it might be positively reinforcing. In short, the entire classification is beside the point. A moment's thought is sufficient to demonstrate the impossibility of distinguishing between requests, commands, advice, etc., on the basis of the behavior or disposition of the particular listener. Nor can we do this on the basis of the typical behavior of all listeners. Some advice is never taken, is always bad, etc., and similarly with other kinds of mands. Skinner's evident satisfaction with this analysis of the traditional classification is extremely puzzling.

8. Mands are operants with no specified relation to a prior stimulus. A *tact*, on the other hand, is defined as 'a verbal operant in which a response of given form is evoked (or at least strengthened) by a particular object or event or property of an object or event' (81). The examples quoted in the discussion of stimulus control (§3) are all tacts. The obscurity of the notion 'stimulus control' makes the concept of the tact rather mystical. Since, however, the tact is 'the most important of verbal operants', it is important to investigate the development of this concept in more detail.

We first ask why the verbal community 'sets up' tacts in the child—that is, how the parent is reinforced by setting up the tact. The basic explanation for this behavior of the parent (85–6) is the reinforcement he obtains by the fact that his contact with the environment is extended; to use Skinner's example, the child may later be able to call him to the telephone. (It is difficult to see, then, how first children acquire tacts, since the parent does not have the appropriate history of reinforcement). Reasoning in the same way, we may conclude that the parent induces the child to walk so that he can make some money delivering newspapers.

Similarly, the parent sets up an 'echoic repertoire' (e.g. a phonemic system) in the child because this makes it easier to teach him new vocabulary, and extending the child's vocabulary is ultimately useful to the parent. 'In all these cases we explain the behavior of the reinforcing listener by pointing to an improvement in the possibility of controlling the speaker whom he reinforces' (56). Perhaps this provides the explanation for the behavior of the parent in inducing the child to walk: the parent is reinforced by the improvement in his control of the child when the child's mobility increases. Underlying these modes of explanation is a curious view that it is somehow more scientific to attribute to a parent a desire to control the child or enhance his own possibilities for action than a desire to see the child develop and extend his capacities. Needless to say, no evidence is offered to support this contention.

Consider now the problem of explaining the response of the listener to a tact. Suppose, for example, that B hears A say *fox* and reacts appropriately, looks around, runs away, aims his rifle, etc. How can we explain B's behavior? Skinner rightly rejects analyses of this offered by Watson and Bertrand Russell. His own equally inadequate analysis proceeds as follows (87–8). We assume (1) 'that in the history of [B] the stimulus *fox* has been an occasion upon which looking around has been followed by seeing a fox' and (2) 'that the listener has some current "interest in seeing foxes"—that behavior which depends upon a seen fox for its execution is strong, and that the stimulus supplied by a fox is therefore reinforcing'. B carries out the appropriate behavior, then, because 'the heard stimulus *fox* is the occasion upon which turning and looking about is frequently followed by the reinforcement of seeing a fox'; i.e. his behavior is a discriminated operant. This explanation is unconvincing. B may never have been a fox and may have no current interest in seeing one, and yet may react appropriately to the stimulus *fox*.[35] Since exactly the same behavior may take place when neither of the assumptions is fulfilled, some other mechanism must be operative here.

Skinner remarks several times that his analysis of the tact in terms of stimulus control is an improvement over the traditional formulations in terms of reference and meaning. This is simply not true. His analysis is fundamentally the same as the traditional one, though much less carefully phrased. In particular, it differs only by indiscriminate paraphrase of such notions as denotation (reference) and connotation (meaning), which have been kept clearly apart in traditional formulations, in terms of the vague concept 'stimulus control'. In one traditional formulation a descriptive term is said to denote a set of entities and to connote or designate a certain property or condition that an entity must possess or fulfill if the term is to apply to it.[36] Thus the term *vertebrate* refers to

[35] Just as he may have the appropriate reaction, both emotional and behavioral, to such utterances as *The volcano is erupting* or *There's a homicidal maniac in the next room* without any previous pairing of the verbal and the physical stimulus. Skinner's discussion of Pavlovian conditioning in language (154) is similarly unconvicing.

[36] Mill, *A system of logic* (1843). Carnap gives a recent reformulation in Meaning and synonymy in natural languages, *Phil. studies* 6.33–47 (1955), defining the meaning (intension) of a predicate 'Q' for a speaker X as 'the general condition which an object y must fulfill in order for X to be willing to ascribe the predicate "Q" to y'. The connotation of an expression is often said to constitute its 'cognitive meaning' as opposed to its 'emotive meaning', which is, essentially, the emotional reaction to the expression.

Whether or not this is the best way to approach meaning, it is clear that denotation, cognitive meaning, and emotive meaning are quite different things. The differences are often obscured in empirical studies of meaning, with much consequent confusion. Thus Osgood has set himself the task of accounting for the fact that a stimulus comes to be a sign for another stimulus (a buzzer becomes a sign for food, a word for a thing, etc.). This is clearly (for linguistic signs) a problem of denotation.

(denotes, is true of) vertebrates and connotes the property 'having a spine' or something of the sort. This connoted defining property is called the meaning of the term. Two terms may have the same reference but different meanings. Thus it is apparently true that the creatures with hearts are all and only the vertebrates. If so, then the term *creature with a heart* refers to vertebrates and designates the property 'having a heart'. This is presumably a different property (a different general condition) from having a spine; hence the terms *vertebrate* and *creature with a heart* are said to have different meanings. This analysis is not incorrect (for at least one sense of meaning), but its many limitations have frequently been pointed out.[37] The major problem is that there is no good way to decide whether two descriptive terms designate the same property.[38] As we have just seen, it is not sufficient that they refer to the same objects. *Vertebrate* and *creature with* a *spine* would be said to designate the same property (distinct from that designated by *creature with a heart*). If we ask why this is so, the only answer appears to be that the terms are synonymous. The notion 'property' thus seems somehow language-bound, and appeal to 'defining properties' sheds little light on questions of meaning and synonymy.

Skinner accepts the traditional account in toto, as can be seen from his definition of a tact as a response under control of a property (stimulus) of some physical object or event. We have found that the notion 'control' has no real substance, and is perhaps best understood as a paraphrase of 'denote' or 'connote' or, ambiguously, both. The only consequence of adopting the new term 'stimulus control' is that the important differences between reference and meaning are obscured. It provides no new objectivity. The stimulus controlling the response is determined by the response itself; there is no independent and objective method of identification (see §3 above). Consequently, when Skinner defines 'synonymy' as the case in which 'the same stimulus leads to quite different responses' (118), we can have no objection. The responses *chair* and *red* made alternatively to the same object are not synonymous, because the stimuli are called different. The responses *vertebrate* and *creature with a spine* would be considered synonymous because they are controlled by the same property of the object under investigation; in more traditional and no less scientific terms, they evoke the same concept. Similarly, when metaphorical extension is explained as due to 'the control exercised by properties of the stimulus

---

The method that he actually develops for quantifying and measuring meaning (cf. Osgood, Suci, Tannenbaum, *The measurement of meaning* [Urbana, 1957]) applies, however, only to emotive meaning. Suppose, for example, that A hates both Hitler and science intensely, and considers both highly potent and 'active', while B, agreeing with A about Hitler, likes science very much, although he considers it rather ineffective and not too important. Then A may assign to 'Hitler' and 'science' the same position on the semantic differential, while B will assign 'Hitler' the same position as A did, but 'science' a totally different position. Yet A does not think that 'Hitler' and 'science' are synonymous or that they have the same reference, and A and B may agree precisely on the cognitive meaning of 'science'. Clearly it is the attitude toward the things (the emotive meaning of the words) that is being measured here. There is a gradual shift in Osgood's account from denotation to cognitive meaning to emotive meaning. The confusion is caused, no doubt, by the fact that the term 'meaning' is used in all three senses (and others). [See Carroll's review of the book by Osgood, Suci, and Tannenbaum in this number of LANGUAGE.]

37 Most clearly by Quine. See *From a logical point of view* (Cambridge, 1953), especially Chapters 2, 3, and 7.

38 A method for characterizing synonymy in terms of reference is suggested by Goodman, On likeness of meaning, *Analysis* 10.1–7 (1949). Difficulties are discussed by Goodman, On some differences about meaning, ibid. 13.90–6 (1953). Carnap (op.cit.) presents a very similar idea (§6), but somewhat misleadingly phrased, since he does not bring out the fact that only extensional (referential) notions are being used.

which, though present at reinforcement, do not enter into the contingency respected by the verbal community' (92; traditionally, accidental properties), no objection can be raised which has not already been levelled against the traditional account. Just as we could 'explain' the response *Mozart* to a piece of music in terms of subtle properties of the controlling stimuli, we can, with equal facility, explain the appearance of the response *sun* when no sun is present, as in *Juliet is [like] the sun.* 'We do so by noting that Juliet and the sun have common properties, at least in their effect on the speaker' (93). Since any two objects have indefinitely many properties in common, we can be certain that we will never be at a loss to explain a response of the form *A is like B,* for arbitrary A and B. It is clear, however, that Skinner's recurrent claim that his formulation is simpler and more scientific than the traditional account has no basis in fact.

Tacts under the control of private stimuli (Bloomfield's 'displaced speech') form a large and important class (130–46), including not only such responses as *familiar* and *beautiful,* but also verbal responses referring to past, potential, or future events or behavior. For example, the response *There was an elephant at the zoo* 'must be understood as a response to current stimuli, including events within the speaker himself' (143).[39] If we now ask ourselves what proportion of the tacts in actual life are responses to (descriptions of) actual current outside stimulation, we can see just how large a role must be attributed to private stimuli. A minute amount of verbal behavior, outside the nursery, consists of such remarks as *This is red* and *There is a man.* The fact that 'functional analysis' must make such a heavy appeal to obscure internal stimuli is again a measure of its actual advance over traditional formulations.

9. Responses under the control of prior verbal stimuli are considered under a different heading from the tact. An *echoic operant* is a response which 'generates a sound pattern similar to that of the stimulus' (55). It covers only cases of immediate imitation.[40] No attempt is made

[39] In general, the examples discussed here are badly handled, and the success of the proposed analyses is overstated. In each case, it is easy to see that the proposed analysis, which usually has an air of objectivity, is not equivalent to the analyzed expression. To take just one example, the response *I am looking for my glasses* is certainly not equivalent to the proposed paraphrases: 'When I have behaved in this way in the past, I have found my glasses and have then stopped behaving in this way', or 'Circumstances have arisen in which I am inclined to emit any behavior which in the past has led to the discovery of my glasses; such behavior includes the behavior of looking in which I am now engaged.' One may look for one's glasses for the first time; or one may emit the same behavior in looking for one's glasses as in looking for one's watch, in which case *I am looking for my glasses* and *I am looking for my watch* are equivalent, under the Skinnerian paraphrase. The difficult questions of purposiveness cannot be handled in this superficial manner.

[40] Skinner takes great pains, however, to deny the existence in human beings (or parrots) of any innate faculty or tendency to imitate. His only argument is that no one would suggest an innate tendency to read, yet reading and echoic behavior have similar 'dynamic properties'. This similarity, however, simply indicates the grossness of his descriptive categories.

In the case of parrots, Skinner claims that they have no instinctive capacity to imitate, but only to be reinforced by successful imitation (59). Given Skinner's use of the word 'reinforcement', it is difficult to perceive any distinction here, since exactly the same thing could be said of any other instinctive behavior. For example, where another scientist would say that a certain bird instinctively builds a nest in a certain way, we could say in Skinner's terminology (equivalently) that the bird is instinctively reinforced by building the nest in this way. One is therefore inclined to dismiss this claim as another ritual introduction of the word 'reinforce'. Though there may, under some suitable clarification, be some truth in it, it is difficult to see how many of the cases reported by competent observers can be handled if 'reinforcement' is given some substantive meaning. Cf. Thorpe, op.cit. 353 f.; Lorenz, *King Solomon's ring* 85–8 (New York, 1952);

to define the sense in which a child's echoic response is 'similar' to the stimulus spoken in the father's bass voice; it seems, though there are no clear statements about this, that Skinner would not accept the account of the phonologist in this respect, but nothing else is offered. The development of an echoic repertoire is attributed completely to differential reinforcement. Since the speaker will do no more, according to Skinner, than what is demanded of him by the verbal community, the degree of accuracy insisted on by this community will determine the elements of the repertoire, whatever these may be (not necessarily phonemes). 'In a verbal community which does not insist on a precise correspondence, an echoic repertoire may remain slack and will be less successfully applied to novel patterns'. There is no discussion of such familiar phenomena as the accuracy with which a child will pick up a second language or a local dialect in the course of playing with other children, which seem sharply in conflict with these assertions. No anthropological evidence is cited to support the claim that an effective phonemic system does not develop (this is the substance of the quoted remark) in communities that do not insist on precise correspondence.

A verbal response to a written stimulus (reading) is called 'textual behavior'.

Other verbal responses to verbal stimuli are called 'intraverbal operants'. Paradigm instances are the response *four* to the stimulus *two plus two* or the response *Paris* to the stimulus *capital of France*. Simple conditioning may be sufficient to account for the response *four* to *two plus two*,[41] but the notion of intraverbal response loses all meaning when we find it extended to cover most of the facts of history and many of the facts of science (72, 129); all word association and 'flight of ideas' (73–6); all translations and paraphrase (77); reports of things seen, heard, or remembered (315); and, in general, large segments of scientific, mathematical, and literary discourse. Obviously the kind of explanation that might be proposed for a student's ability to respond with *Paris* to *capital of France*, after suitable practice, can hardly be seriously offered to account for his ability to make a judicious guess in answering the questions (to him new) *What is the seat of the French government?,...the source of the literary dialect?,...the chief target of the German blitzkrieg?*, etc., or his ability to prove a new theorem, translate a new passage, or paraphrase a remark for the first time or in a new way.

The process of 'getting someone to see a point', to see something your way, or to understand a complex state of affairs (e.g. a difficult political situation or a mathematical proof) is, for Skinner, simply a matter of increasing the strength of the listener's already available behavior.[42] Since 'the process is often exemplified by relatively intellectual scientific or philosophical discourse', Skinner considers it 'all the more surprising that it may be reduced to echoic, textual, or intraverbal supplementation' (269). Again, it is only the vagueness and latitude with which the notions 'strength' and 'intraverbal response' are used that save this from absurdity. If we use these terms in their

---

even Mowrer, who tries to show how imitation might develop through secondary reinforcement, cites a case, op.cit. 694, which he apparently believes, but where this could hardly be true. In young children, it seems most implausible to explain imitation in terms of secondary reinforcement.

41 Though even this possibility is limited. If we were to take these paradigm instances seriously, it should follow that a child who knows how to count from one to 100 could learn an arbitrary 10 × 10 matrix with these numbers as entries as readily as the multiplication table.

42 Similarly, 'the universality of a literary work refers to the number of potential readers inclined to say the same thing' (275; i.e. the most 'universal' work is a dictionary of clichés and greetings); a speaker is 'stimulating' if he says what we are about to say ourselves (272); etc.

literal sense, it is clear that understanding a statement cannot be equated to shouting it frequently in a high-pitched voice (high response strength), and a clever and convincing argument cannot be accounted for on the basis of a history of pairings of verbal responses.[43].

10. A final class of operants, called *autoclitics*, includes those that are involved in assertion, negation, quantification, qualification of responses, construction of sentences, and the 'highly complex manipulations of verbal thinking'. All these acts are to be explained 'in terms of behavior which is evoked by or acts upon other behavior of the speaker' (313). Autoclitics are, then, responses to already given responses, or rather, as we find in reading through this section, they are responses to covert or incipient or potential verbal behavior. Among the autoclitics are listed such expressions as *I recall, I imagine, for example, assume, let X equal* . . ., the terms of negation, the *is* of predication and assertion, *all, some, if, then,* and, in general, all morphemes other than nouns, verbs, and adjectives, as well as grammatical processes of ordering and arrangement. Hardly a remark in this section can be accepted without serious qualification. To take just one example, consider Skinner's account of the autoclitic *all* in *All swans are white* (329). Obviously we cannot assume that this is a tact to all swans as stimulus. It is suggested, therefore, that we take *all* to be an autoclitic modifying the whole sentence *Swans are white. All* can then be taken as equivalent to *always,* or *always it is possible to say.* Notice, however, that the modified sentence *Swans are white* is just as general as *All swans are white.* Furthermore, the proposed translation of *all* is incorrect if taken literally. It is just as possible to say *Swans are green* as to say *Swans are white.* It is not always possible to say either (e.g. while you are saying something else or sleeping). Probably what Skinner means is that the sentence can be paraphrased '*X is white* is true, for each swan X'. But this paraphrase cannot be given within his system, which has no place for *true*.

Skinner's account of grammar and syntax as autoclitic processes (Chapter 13) differs from a familiar traditional account mainly in the use of the pseudoscientific terms 'control' or 'evoke' in place of the traditional 'refer'. Thus in *The boy runs,* the final *s* of *runs* is a tact under control of such 'subtle properties of a situation' as 'the nature of running as an *activity* rather than an object or property of an object'.[44] (Presumably, then, in *The attempt fails, The difficulty remains, His anxiety increases,* etc., we must also say that the *s* indicates that the object described as the attempt is carrying out the activity of failing, etc.) In *the boy's gun,* however, the *s* denotes possession (as, presumably, in *the boy's arrival,. . . story, . . . age,* etc.) and is under the control of

[43] Similarly, consider Skinner's contention (362–5) that communication of knowledge or facts is just the process of making a new response available to the speaker. Here the analogy to animal experiments is particularly weak. When we train a rat to carry out some peculiar act, it makes sense to consider this a matter of adding a response to his repertoire. In the case of human communication, however, it is very difficult to attach any meaning to this terminology. If A imparts to B the information (new to B) that the railroads face collapse, in what sense can the response *The railroads face collapse* be said to be now, but not previously, available to B? Surely B could have said it before (not knowing whether it was true), and known that it was a sentence (as opposed to *Collapse face railroads the*). Nor is there any reason to assume that the response has increased in strength, whatever this means exactly (e.g. B may have no interest in the fact, or he may want it suppressed). It is not clear how we can characterize this notion of 'making a response available' without reducing Skinner's account of 'imparting knowledge' to a triviality.

[44] 332. On the next page, however, the *s* in the same example indicates that 'the object described as *the boy* possesses the property of running.' The difficulty of even maintaining consistency with a conceptual scheme like this is easy to appreciate.

this 'relational aspect of the situation' (336). The 'relational autoclitic of order' (whatever it may mean to call the order of a set of responses a response to them) in *The boy runs the store* is under the control of an 'extremely complex stimulus situation', namely, that the boy is running the store (335). *And* in *the hat and the shoe* is under the control of the property 'pair'. *Through* in *the dog went through the hedge* is under the control of the 'relation between the going dog and the hedge' (342). In general, nouns are evoked by objects, verbs by actions, and so on.

Skinner considers a sentence to be a set of key responses (nouns, verbs, adjectives) on a skeletal frame (346). If we are concerned with the fact that Sam rented a leaky boat, the raw responses to the situation are *rent, boat, leak,* and *Sam.* Autoclitics (including order) which qualify these responses, express relations between them, and the like, are then added by a process called 'composition' and the result is a grammatical sentence, one of many alternatives among which selection is rather arbitrary. The idea that sentences consist of lexical items placed in a grammatical frame is of course a traditional one, within both philosophy and linguistics. Skinner adds to it only the very implausible speculation that in the internal process of composition, the nouns, verbs, and adjectives are chosen first and then are arranged, qualified, etc., by autoclitic responses to these internal activities.[45]

This view of sentence structure, whether phrased in terms of autoclitics, syncategorematic expressions, or grammatical and lexical morphemes, is inadequate. *Sheep provide wool* has no (physical) frame at all, but no other arrangement of these words is an English sentence. The sequences *furiously sleep ideas green colorless* and *friendly young dogs seem harmless* have the same frames, but only one is a sentence of English (similarly, only one of the sequences formed by reading these from back to front). *Struggling artists can be a nuisance* has the same frame as *marking papers can be a nuisance,* but is quite different in sentence structure, as can be seen by replacing *can be* by *is* or *are* in both cases. There are many other similar and equally simple examples. It is evident that more is involved in sentence structure than insertion of lexical items in grammatical frames; no approach to language that fails to take these deeper processes into account can possibly achieve much success in accounting for actual linguistic behavior.

11. The preceding discussion covers all the major notions that Skinner introduces in his descriptive system. My purpose in discussing the concepts one by one was to show that in each case, if we take his terms in their literal meaning, the description covers almost no aspect of verbal behavior, and if we take them metaphorically, the description offers no improvement over various traditional formulations. The terms borrowed from experimental psychology simply lose their objective meaning with this extension, and take over the full vagueness of ordinary language. Since Skinner limits himself to such a small set of terms for paraphrase, many important distinctions are obscured. I think that this analysis supports the view expressed in §1 above, that elimination of the independent contribution of the speaker and learner (a result which Skinner considers of great importance, cf. 311–2) can be achieved only at the cost of eliminating all significance from the descriptive system, which then operates at

[45] One might just as well argue that exactly the opposite is true. The study of hesitation pauses has shown that these tend to occur before the large categories—noun, verb, adjective; this finding is usually described by the statement that the pauses occur where there is maximum uncertainty or information. Insofar as hesitation indicates on-going composition (if it does at all), it would appear that the 'key responses' are chosen only after the 'grammatical frame'. Cf. C. E. Osgood, unpublished paper; Goldman-Eisler, Speech analysis and mental processes, *Language and speech* 1.67 (1958).

a level so gross and crude that no answers are suggested to the most elementary questions.[46] The questions to which Skinner has addressed his speculations are hopelessly premature. It is futile to inquire into the causation of verbal behavior until much more is known about the specific character of this behavior; and there is little point in speculating about the process of acquisition without much better understanding of what is acquired.

Anyone who seriously approaches the study of linguistic behavior, whether linguist, psychologist, or philosopher, must quickly become aware of the enormous difficulty of stating a problem which will define the area of his investigations, and which will not be either completely trivial or hopelessly beyond the range of present-day understanding and technique. In selecting functional analysis as his problem, Skinner has set himself a task of the latter type. In an extremely interesting and insightful paper,[47] K. S. Lashley has implicity delimited a class of problems which can be approached in a fruitful way by the linguist and psychologist, and which are clearly preliminary to those with which Skinner is concerned. Lashley recognizes, as anyone must who seriously considers the data, that the composition and production of an utterance is not simply a matter of stringing together a sequence of responses under the control of outside stimulation and intraverbal association, and that the syntactic organization of an utterance is not something directly represented in any simple way in the physical structure of the utterance itself. A variety of observations lead him to conclude that syntactic structure is 'a generalized pattern imposed on the specific acts as they occur', and that 'a consideration of the structure of the sentence and other motor sequences will show...that there are, behind the overtly expressed sequences, a multiplicity of integrative processes which can only be inferred from the final results of their activity'. He also comments on the great difficulty of determining the 'selective mechanisms' used in the actual construction of a particular utterance.

Although present-day linguistics cannot provide a precise account of these integrative processes, imposed patterns, and selective mechanisms, it can at least set itself the problem of characterizing these completely. It is reasonable to regard the grammar of a language *L* ideally as a mechanism that provides an enumeration of the sentences of *L* in something like the way in which a deductive theory gives an enumeration of a set of theorems. ('Grammar', in this sense of the word, includes phonology.) Furthermore, the theory of language can be regarded as a study of the formal properties of such grammars, and, with a precise enough

46 E.g. what are in fact the actual units of verbal behavior? Under what conditions will a physical event capture the attention (be a stimulus) or be a reinforcer? How do we decide what stimuli are in 'control' in a specific case? When are stimuli 'similar'? And so on. (It is not interesting to be told e.g. that we say *Stop* to an automobile or billiard ball because they are sufficiently similar to reinforcing people [46].)

The use of unanalyzed notions like 'similar' and 'generalization' is particularly disturbing, since it indicates an apparent lack of interest in every significant aspect of the learning or the use of language in new situations. No one has ever doubted that in some sense, language is learned by generalization, or that novel utterances and situations are in some way similar to familiar ones. The only matter of serious interest is the specific 'similarity'. Skinner has, apparently, no interest in this. Keller and Schoenfeld (op.cit.) proceed to incorporate these notions (which they identify) into their Skinnerian 'modern objective psychology' by defining two stimuli to be similar when 'we make the same sort of *response* to them' (124; but when are responses of the 'same sort'?). They do not seem to notice that this definition converts their 'principle of generalization' (116), under any reasonable interpretation of this, into a tautology. It is obvious that such a definition will not be of much help in the study of language learning or construction of new responses in appropriate situations.

47 The problem of serial order in behavior, in Jeffress (ed.), *Hixon symposium on cerebral mechanisms in behavior* (New York, 1951).

formulation, this general theory can provide a uniform method for determining, from the process of generation of a given sentence, a structural description which can give a good deal of insight into how this sentence is used and understood. In short, it should be possible to derive from a properly formulated grammar a statement of the integrative processes and generalized patterns imposed on the specific acts that constitute an utterance. The rules of a grammar of the appropriate form can be subdivided into the two types, optional and obligatory; only the latter must be applied in generating an utterance. The optional rules of the grammar can be viewed, then, as the selective mechanisms involved in the production of a particular utterance. The problem of specifying these integrative processes and selective mechanisms is nontrivial and not beyond the range of possible investigation. The results of such a study might, as Lashley suggests, be of independent interest for psychology and neurology (and conversely). Although such a study, even if successful, would by no means answer the major problems involved in the investigation of meaning and the causation of behavior, it surely will not be unrelated to these. It is at least possible, furthermore, that such notions as 'semantic generalization', to which such heavy appeal is made in all approaches to language in use, conceal complexities and specific structure of inference not far different from those that can be studied and exhibited in the case of syntax, and that consequently the general character of the results of syntactic investigations may be a corrective to oversimplified approaches to the theory of meaning.

The behavior of the speaker, listener, and learner of language constitutes, of course, the actual data for any study of language. The construction of a grammar which enumerates sentences in such a way that a meaningful structural description can be determined for each sentence does not in itself provide an account of this actual behavior. It merely characterizes abstractly the ability of one who has mastered the language to distinguish sentences from nonsentences, to understand new sentences (in part), to note certain ambiguities, etc. These are very remarkable abilities. We constantly read and hear new sequences of words, recognize them as sentences, and understand them. It is easy to show that the new events that we accept and understand as sentences are not related to those with which we are familiar by any simple notion of formal (or semantic or statistical) similiarity or identity of grammatical frame. Talk of generalization in this case is entirely pointless and empty. It appears that we recognize a new item as a sentence not because it matches some familiar item in any simple way, but because it is generated by the grammar that each individual has somehow and in some form internalized. And we understand a new sentence, in part, because we are somehow capable of determining the process by which this sentence is derived in this grammar.

Suppose that we manage to construct grammars having the properties outlined above. We can then attempt to describe and study the achievement of the speaker, listener, and learner. The speaker and the listener, we must assume, have already acquired the capacities characterized abstractly by the grammar. The speaker's task is to select a particular compatible set of optional rules. If we know, from grammatical study, what choices are available to him and what conditions of compatibility the choices must meet, we can proceed meaningfully to investigate the factors that lead him to make one or another choice. The listener (or reader) must determine, from an exhibited utterance, what optional rules were chosen in the construction of the utterance. It must be admitted that the ability of a human being to do this far surpasses our present understanding. The child who learns a language has in some sense constructed the grammar for himself on the basis of his observation of sentences and nonsentences (i.e. corrections by the verbal community). Study of the actual observed ability of a speaker to distinguish sentences from nonsentences, detect ambiguities, etc., apparently forces us to the conclusion that this grammar is of an extremely complex and abstract character, and that the young child has succeeded in carrying out what from the formal point of view, at least, seems to be a remarkable type of theory construction. Furthermore, this task is accomplished in an astonishingly short time, to a large extent independently of intelligence, and in a comparable way by all children. Any theory of learning must cope with these facts.

It is not easy to accept the view that a child is capable of constructing an extremely complex mechanism for generating a set of sentences, some of which he has heard, or that an adult can instantaneously determine whether (and if so, how) a particular item is generated by this mechanism, which has many of the properties of an abstract deductive theory. Yet this appears to be a fair description of the performance of the speaker, listener, and learner. If this is correct, we can predict that a direct attempt to account for the actual behavior of speaker, listener, and learner, not based on a prior understanding of the structure of grammars, will achieve very limited success. The grammar must be regarded as a component in the behavior of the speaker and listener which can only be inferred, as Lashley has put it, from the resulting physical acts. The fact that all normal children acquire essentially comparable grammars of great complexity with remarkable rapidity suggests that human beings are somehow specially designed to do this, with data-handling or 'hypothesis-formulating' ability of unknown character and complexity.[48] The study of linguistic structure may ultimately lead to some significant insights into this matter. At the moment the question cannot be seriously posed, but in principle it may be possible to study the problem of determining what the built-in structure of an information-processing (hypothesis-forming) system must be to enable it to arrive at the grammar of a language from the available data in the available time. At any rate, just as the attempt to eliminate the contribution of the speaker leads to a 'mentalistic' descriptive system that succeeds only in blurring important traditional distinctions, a refusal to study the contribution of the child to language learning permits only a superficial account of language acquisition, with a vast and unanalyzed contribution attributed to a step called 'generalization' which in fact includes just about everything of interest in this process. If the study of language is limited in these ways, it seems inevitable that major aspects of verbal behavior will remain a mystery.

[48] There is nothing essentially mysterious about this. Complex innate behavior patterns and innate 'tendencies to learn in specific ways' have been carefully studied in lower organisms. Many psychologists have been inclined to believe that such biological structure will not have an important effect on acquisition of complex behavior in higher organisms, but I have not been able to find any serious justification for this attitude. Some recent studies have stressed the necessity for carefully analyzing the strategies available to the organism, regarded as a complex 'information-processing system' (cf. Bruner, Goodnow, and Austin, *A study of thinking* [New York, 1956]; Newell, Shaw, and Simon, Elements of a theory of human problem solving, *Psych. rev.* 65.151–66 [1958]), if anything significant is to be said about the character of human learning. These may be largely innate, or developed by early learning processes about which very little is yet known. (But see Harlow, The formation of learning sets, *Psych. rev.* 56.51–65 (1949), and many later papers, where striking shifts in the character of learning are shown as a result of early training; also Hebb, *Organization of behavior* 109 ff.) They are undoubtedly quite complex. Cf. Lenneberg, op. cit., and Lees, review of Chomsky's *Syntactic structures* in *Lg.* 33.406 f. (1957), for discussion of the topics mentioned in this section.

Some Preliminaries to Psycholinguistics[1]

GEORGE A. MILLER

The success of behavior theory in describing certain relatively simple correlations between stimulation and response has encouraged experimental psychologists to extend and test their theories in more complicated situations. The most challenging and potentially the most important of these extensions, of course, is into the realm of linguistic behavior. Consequently, in recent years we have seen several attempts to characterize human language in terms derived from behavioristic investigations of conditioning and learning in animals. These proposals are well known, so I will make no attempt to summarize them here. I will merely say that, in my opinion, their results thus far have been disappointing.

If one begins the study of a new realm of behavior armed with nothing but hypotheses and generalizations based on experience in some quite different area, one's theoretical preconceptions can be badly misleading. Trivial features may be unduly emphasized, while crucially important aspects may be postponed, neglected, or even overlooked entirely. These hazards are particularly dangerous when we generalize across species, or from nonverbal to verbal behavior.

The impulse to broaden the range of phenomena to which our concepts can be applied is commendable. But when this enthusiasm is not guided by a valid conception of the new phenomena to be explained, much intelligent enterprise can end in frustration and discouragement. Human language is a subtle and complex thing; there are many aspects that, if not actually unique, are at least highly distinctive of our species, and whose nature could scarcely be suspected, much less extrapolated from the analysis of nonverbal behavior.

It was with such thoughts in mind that I decided to take this opportunity to summarize briefly seven aspects of human language that should be clearly understood by any psychologist who plans to embark on explanatory ventures in psycholinguistics. The ideas are familiar to most peo-

[1] This paper is based on research supported in part by funds granted by the Advanced Research Projects Agency, Department of Defense, Contract No. SD-187; by Public Health Service Research Grant No. MH-08083 from the National Institutes of Health; by National Science Foundation, Contract No. GS-192; and by Carnegie Corporation of New York Grant No. 8-3004, to the Center for Cognitive Studies, Harvard University.

George A. Miller, "Some Preliminaries to Psycholinguistics," *American Psychologist,* **20** (1965), 15–20. Reprinted by permission of the author and publisher.

ple working in the field, who could no doubt easily double or treble their number. Nevertheless, the seven I have in mind are, in my opinion, important enough to bear repeating and as yet their importance does not seem to have been generally recognized by other psychologists.

Without further apologies, therefore, let me begin my catalogue of preliminary admonitions to anyone contemplating language as a potential subject for his psychological ratiocinations.

A POINT OF VIEW

It is probably safe to say that no two utterances are identical in their physical (acoustic and physiological) characteristics. Nevertheless, we regularly treat them as if they were. For example, we ask a subject to repeat something we say, and we count his response as correct even though it would be a simple matter to demonstrate that there were many physical differences between his vocal response and the vocal stimulus we presented to him. Obviously, not all physical aspects of speech are significant for vocal communication.

The situation is more complicated than that, however. There are also many examples—homophones being the most obvious—where stimuli that are physically identical can have different significance. Not only are physically different utterances treated identically, but physically identical utterances can be treated differently. It may often happen that the difference in significance between two utterances cannot be found in any difference of a physical nature, but can only be appreciated on the basis of psychological factors underlying the physical signal.

The problem of identifying significant features of speech is complicated further by the fact that some physical features are highly predictable in nearly all speakers, yet have no communicative significance. For example, when a plosive consonant occurs initially, as in the word *pen*, American speakers pronounce it with aspiration; a puff of air accompanies the *p* (which you can feel if you will pronounce *pen* holding the back of your hand close to your lips). When *p* occurs as a noninitial member of a consonant cluster, however, as in *spend*, this puff of air is reduced or absent. The same phoneme is aspirated in one position and unaspirated in the other. This physical feature, which is quite reliable in American speech, has no communicative significance, by which I mean that the rare person who does not conform is perfectly intelligible and suffers no handicap in communicating with his friends. Facts such as these, which are well known to linguists, pose interesting problems for psychologists who approach the acquisition of language in terms of laboratory experiments on discrimination learning.

In order to discuss even the simplest problems in speech production and speech perception, it is necessary to be able to distinguish significant from nonsignificant aspects of speech. And there is no simple way to draw this distinction in terms of the physical parameters of the speech signal itself. Almost immediately, therefore, we are forced to consider aspects of language that extend beyond the acoustic or physiological properties of speech, that is to say, beyond the objective properties of "the stimulus."

Since the concept of significance is central and unavoidable, it is important to notice that it has two very different senses, which for convenience, I shall call "reference" and "meaning."

For example, in most contexts we can substitute the phrase, "the first President of the United States" for "George Washington," since both of these utterances refer to the same historical figure. At least since Frege's time, however, it has been customary to assume that such phrases differ in meaning even though their referent is the same. Otherwise, there would be no point to such assertions of identity as "George Washington was the first President of the United States." If meaning and reference were identical, such an assertion would be as empty as "George Washington was George Washington." Since "George Washington was the first President of the United States" is not a pointless assertion, there must be some difference between the significance of the same "George Washington" and of the phrase "the first President of the United States," and, since this difference in significance is not a difference of referent, it must be a difference in something else—something else that, for want of a better name, we call its meaning.

This distinction between reference and meaning becomes particularly clear when we consider whole utterances. An utterance can be significant even though it might be extremely difficult to find anything it referred to in the sense that "table" refers to four-legged, flat-topped piece of furniture, etc. Sentences are meaningful, but their meaning cannot be given by their referent, for they may have none.

Of course, one might argue that psycholinguists should confine their attention to the significance of isolated words and avoid the complexities of sentences altogether. Such an approach would be marvelously convenient if it would work, but it would work only if words were autonomous units that combined in a particularly simple way. If the meaning of a sentence could in some sense be regarded as the weighted sum of the meanings of the words that comprise it, then once we knew how to characterize the meanings of individual words, it would be a simple matter to determine the meaning of any combination of words. Unfortunately, however, language is not so simple; a Venetian blind is not the same as a blind Venetian.

Perhaps the most obvious thing we can say about the significance of a sentence is that it is not given as the linear sum of the significance of the words that comprise it. The pen in "fountain pen" and the pen in "play pen" are very different pens, even though they are phonologically and orthographically identical. The words in a sentence interact.

In isolation most words can have many different meanings; which meaning they take in a particular sentence will depend on the context in which they occur. That is to say, their meaning will depend both on the other words and on their grammatical role in the sentence. The meanings to be assigned to word combinations can be characterized in an orderly way, of course, but not by some simple rule for linear addition. What is required is an elaborate description of the various ways in which words can interact in combination.

As soon as we begin to look carefully at the relations among words in sentences, it becomes obvious that their interactions depend on the way they are grouped. For example, in sentences like, "They are hunting dogs," one meaning results if we group "are hunting" together as the verb, but another meaning results if we group "hunting dogs" together as a noun phrase. We cannot assign meanings to words in a sentence without knowing how the words are grouped, which implies that we must take into account the syntactic structure of the sentence.

Moreover, when we consider the psychology of the sentence, the problem of productivity becomes unavoidable. There is no limit to the number of different sentences that can be produced in English by combining words in various grammatical fashions, which means that it is impossible to describe English by simply listing all its grammatical sentences. This fairly obvious fact has several important implications. It means that the sentences of English must be described in terms of *rules* that can generate them.

For psychologists, the implication of this generative approach to language is that we must consider hypothetical constructs capable of combining verbal elements into grammatical sentences, and in order to account for our ability to deal with an unlimited variety of possible sentences, these hypothetical constructs must have the character of linguistic rules.

Language is the prime example of rule-governed behavior, and there are several types of rules to consider. Not only must we consider syntactic rules for generating and grouping words in sentences; we must also consider semantic rules for interpreting word combinations. Perhaps we may even need pragmatic rules to characterize our unlimited variety of belief systems. Only on the assumption that a language user knows a generative system of rules for producing and interpreting sentences can we hope to account for the unlimited combinatorial productivity of natural languages.

Rules are not laws, however. They can be broken, and in ordinary conversation they frequently are. Still, even when we break them, we usually are capable of recognizing (under appropriate conditions) that we have made a mistake; from this fact we infer that the rules are known implicitly, even though they cannot be stated explicitly.

A description of the rules we know when we know a language is different from a description of the psychological mechanisms involved in our use of those rules. It is important, therefore, to distinguish here, as elsewhere, between knowledge and performance; the psycholinguist's task is to propose and test performance models for a language user, but he must rely on the linguist to give him a precise specification of what it is a language user is trying to use.

Finally, it is important to remember that there is a large innate component to our language-using ability. Not just any self-consistent set of rules that we might be able to invent for communicative purposes could serve as a natural language. All human societies possess language, and all of these languages have features in common—features that are called "language universals," but are in fact prelinguistic in character. It is difficult to imagine how children could acquire language so rapidly from parents who understand it so poorly unless they were already tuned by evolution to select just those aspects that are universally significant. There is, in short, a large biological component that shapes our human languages.

These are the seven ideas I wished to call to your attention. Let me recapitulate them in order, this time attempting to say what I believe their implications to be for psycholinguistic research.

SOME IMPLICATIONS FOR RESEARCH

1. Not all physical features of speech are significant for vocal communication, and not all significant features of speech have a physical representation. I take this to imply that the perception of speech involves grouping and interpreting its elements and so cannot be simply predicted from studies of our ability to discriminate among arbitrary acoustic stimuli. Such studies can be useful only in conjunction with linguistic information as to which distinctions are significant. Linguists seem generally agreed that the absolute physical characteristics of a particular phone are less important than the binary contrasts into which it enters in a given language. It is noteworthy that after many decades of acoustic phonetics, we are still uncertain as to how to specify all the physical dimensions of the significant features of speech, particularly those that depend on syntactic or semantic aspects of the utterance.

2. The meaning of an utterance should not be confused with its reference. I take this to imply that the acquisition of meaning cannot be identified with the simple acquisition of a conditioned vocalization in the presence of a particular environmental stimulus. It may be possible to talk about reference in terms of conditioning, but meaning is a much more complicated phenomenon that depends on the relations of a symbol to other symbols in the language.

3. The meaning of an utterance is not a linear sum of the meanings of the words that comprise it. I take this to imply that studies of the meanings of isolated words are of limited value, and that attempts to predict the meaning of word compounds by weighted averages of the meanings of their components—an analogy with the laws of color mixture—cannot be successful in general. In Gestalt terminology, the whole is greater than (or at least, different from) the sum of its parts.

4. The syntactic structure of a sentence imposes groupings that govern the interactions between the meanings of the words in that sentence. I take this to imply that sentences are hierarchically organized, and that simple theories phrased in terms of chaining successive responses cannot provide an adequate account of linguistic behavior. Exactly how concepts are combined to produce organized groupings of linguistic elements that can be uttered and understood is a central problem for psycholinguistics.

5. There is no limit to the number of sentences or the number of meanings that can be expressed. I take this to imply that our knowledge of a language must be described in terms of a system of semantic and syntactic rules adequate to generate the infinite number of admissible utterances. Since the variety of admissible word combinations is so great, no child could learn them all. Instead of learning specific combinations of words, he learns the *rules* for generating admissible combinations. If knowledge of these rules is to be described in our performance models as the language user's "habits," it is necessary to keep in mind that they are generative habits of a more hypothetical and less abstract nature than have generally been studied in animal learning experiments.

6. A description of a language and a description of a language user must be kept distinct. I take this to imply that psycholinguists should try to formulate performance models that will incorporate, in addition to a generative knowledge of the rules, hypothetical information-storage and information-processing components that can simulate the actual behavior of language users. In general, limitations of short-term memory seem to impose the most severe constraints on our capacity to follow our own rules.

7. There is a large biological component to the human capacity for articulate speech. I take this to imply that attempts to teach other animals to speak a human language are doomed to failure. As Lenneberg has emphasized, the ability to acquire and use a human language does not depend on being intelligent or having a large brain. It depends on being human.

In science, at least half the battle is won when we start to ask the right questions. It is my belief that an understanding of these seven general propositions and their implications can help to guide us toward the right questions and might even forestall ill-considered forays into psycholinguistics by psychologists armed only with theories and techniques developed for the study of nonverbal behavior.

A CRITIQUE

I have now stated twice my seven preliminary admonitions. In order to make sure that I am being clear, I want to repeat it all once more, this time in the form of a critical analysis of the way many experimental psychologists write about language in the context of current learning theory.

For the purposes of exposition, I have chosen a sentence that is part of the introduction to the topic of language in a well-known and widely used textbook on the psychology of learning. After remarking that, "language seems to develop in the same way as other instrumental acts," the author says:

> Certain combinations of words and intonations of voice are strengthened through reward and are gradually made to occur in appropriate situations by the process of discrimination learning.

This, I believe is fairly representative of what can be found in many other texts. I have chosen it, not because I bear any malice toward the author, but simply because I think that all seven of my admonitions are ignored in only 27 words. Let me spell them out one by one.

First, since infants are not born with a preconception of what words are, they could hardly be expected to begin acquiring language by uttering combinations of words. Perhaps the author was not thinking of infants when he wrote this sentence. If he had been, he would probably have written instead that, "Certain combinations of *sounds* and intonations of voice are strengthened through reward and made to occur by the process of discrimination learning." In either case, however, he ignores my first admonition that not all physical features of speech are significant and not all significant features are physical.

A child does not begin with sounds or words and learn to combine them. Rather, he begins by learning which features are significant, and progressively differentiates his utterances as he learns. It is conceivable, though not necessary, that he might acquire those significant distinctions that have some physical basis "by the process of discrimination learning," but it would require an extensive revision of what we ordinarily mean by discrimination learning in order to explain how he acquires significant distinctions that are not represented in the physical signal, or why he acquires those features (such as aspiration only on initial plosives) that are not significant and are not systematically rewarded or extinguished.

Second, as I have already admitted (too generously, perhaps), it is possible to argue that a referential relation might be established between a visual input and a vocalization "by the process of discrimination learning." I deny, however, that it is reasonable to speak of acquiring meaning in this way.

Exactly what should be included in the meaning of a word is open to debate, but any interpretation will have to say something about the relation of this word's meaning to the meanings of other words and to the contexts in which it occurs—and these are complicated, systemic interrelations requiring a great deal more cognitive machinery than is necessary for simple discrimination. Since the author says specifically that *words* are acquired by discrimination learning, and since words have meaning as well as reference, I can only assume that he has ignored my admonition not to confuse reference and meaning. Perhaps a more accurate interpretation, suggested by the phrase "occur in appropriate situations," would be that he has not really confused reference and meaning, but has simply ignored meaning entirely. In either case, however, it will not do as a basis for psycholinguistics.

There is unfortunate ambiguity in the phrase, "Certain combinations of words and intonations of voice." I am not sure whether the author meant that each word was learned with several intonations, or that we learn several intonations for word combinations, or that we learn both to combine words and to modulate the pitch of our voice. Consequently, I have been forced to cheat on you by examining the context. What I found was no help, however, because all the formal propositions referred simply to "words," whereas all the examples that were cited involved combinations of words.

Perhaps I am being unfair, but I think that this author, at least when he is writing on learning theory, is not deeply concerned about the difference between words and sentences. If this distinction, which seems crucial to me, is really of no importance to him, then he must be ignoring my third admonition that the meaning of words are affected by the sentences in which they occur.

My fourth admonition—that the syntactic structure of a sentence imposes groupings that govern the interactions between the meanings of its words—is also ignored. No matter how I interpret the ambiguous phrase about, "Certain combinations of words and intonations of voice," it must be wrong. If I read it one way, he has ignored the problem of syntax entirely and is concerned only with the conditioning of isolated word responses.

Or, if I put a more generous interpretation on it and assume he meant that combinations of words are strengthened and made to occur by discrimination learning, then he seems to be saying that every word and every acceptable combination of words is learned separately.

By a rough, but conservative calculation, there are at least 10^{20} sentences 20 words long, and if a child were to learn only these it would take him something on the order of 1,000 times the estimated age of the earth just to listen to them. Perhaps this is what the word "gradually" means? In this interpretation he has clearly violated my fifth admonition, that there is no limit to the number of sentences to be learned, and so has wandered perilously close to absurdity. Any attempt to account for language acquisition that does not have a generative character will encounter this difficulty.

Sixth, from the reference to responses being "strengthened" I infer that each word-object connection is to be characterized by an intervening variable, along the lines of habit strength in Hull's system. This is a rather simple model, too simple to serve as a performance model for a language user, but it is all our author has to offer. As for keeping his performance model distinct from his competence model, as I advise in my sixth admonition, he will have none of it. He says—and here I restort to the context once more—that language "is a complex set of responses [*and*] also a set of stimuli." It may be defensible to talk about speech as a set of responses and stimuli, but what a language user knows about his language cannot be described in these performance terms.

A language includes all the denumerable infinitude of grammatical sentences, only a tiny sample of which ever have or ever will occur as actual responses or stimuli. The author would blush crimson if we caught him confusing the notions of sample and population in his statistical work, yet an analogous distinction between speech and language is completely overlooked.

Finally, we need to make the point that the kind of reinforcement schedule a child is on when he learns language is very different from what we have used in experiments on discrimination learning. No one needs to monitor a child's vocal output continually and to administer "good" and "bad" as rewards and punishments. When a child says something intelligible, his reward is both improbable and indirect. In short, a child learns language by using it, not by a precise schedule of rewards for grammatical vocalizations "in appropriate situations." An experimenter who used such casual and unreliable procedures in a discrimination experiment would teach an animal nothing at all.

The child's exposure to language should not be called "teaching." He learns the language, but no one, least of all an average mother, knows how to teach it to him. He learns the language because he is shaped by nature to pay attention to it, to notice and remember and use significant aspects of it. In suggesting that language can be taught "by the process of discrimination learning," therefore, our author has ignored my final admonition to remember the large innate capacity humans have for acquiring articulate speech.

In summary, if this sentence is taken to be a description of the fundamental processes involved in language acquisition, it is both incomplete and misleading. At best, we might regard it as a hypothesis about the acquisition of certain clichés or expressive embellishments. But as a hypothesis from which to derive an account of the most obvious and most characteristic properties of human language, it is totally inadequate.

This completes the third and final run through my list of preliminaries to psycholinguistics. If I sounded a bit too contentious, I am sorry, but I did not want to leave any doubt as to why I am saying these things or what their practical implications for psycholinguistic research might be.

My real interest, however, is not in deploring this waste of our intellectual resources, but in the positive program that is possible if we are willing to accept a more realistic conception of what language is.

If we accept a realistic statement of the problem, I believe we will also be forced to accept a more cognitive approach to it: to talk about hypothesis testing instead of discrimination learning, about the evaluation of hypotheses instead of the reinforcement of responses, about rules instead of habits, about productivity instead of generalization, about innate and universal human capacities instead of special methods of teaching vocal responses, about symbols instead of conditioned stimuli, about sentences instead of words or vocal noises, about linguistic structure instead of chains of responses—in short, about language instead of learning theory.

The task of devising a cognitive production model for language users is difficult enough without wearing blinders that prevent us from seeing what the task really is. If the hypothetical constructs that are needed seem too complex and arbitrary, too improbable and mentalistic then you had better forgo the study of language. For language is just that—complex, arbitrary, improbable, mentalistic—and no amount of wishful theorizing will make it anything else.

In a word, what I am trying to say, what all my preliminary admonitions boil down to, is simply this: Language is exceedingly complicated. Forgive me for taking so long to say such a simple and obvious thing.

PART TWO

Experimental Approaches to Language

The separation of this and the preceding section is clearly artificial. Experimentation on language processes, normal or deviant, does not take place in a theoretical vacuum. It proceeds in all instances from either an implicit or explicit theoretical framework which gives it both meaning and direction. The papers reprinted in this section represent both the behavioral and the recent transformational approaches to language sketched in the earlier selections. The purpose of this section is to acquaint the student with the kinds of experimental attacks which have been made upon some of the theoretical issues discussed in the preceding section. Additionally, they add considerable clarification to the issues themselves. Indeed, what may merely be abstruse as theory often becomes sanguinely pertinent when phrased as an experimental prediction. Conversely, what may appear obvious in normal language, and consequently assumed as given, frequently is crucial to an understanding of disordered language. The existence of specific syndromes of language disability casts considerable light upon the essentials of linguistic ability. Thus the disabilities are of concern not so much for what results may accrue to our knowledge about such disorders *per se,* as desirable as that may be, but for what they may tell us of normal language acquisition and use.

The search for correspondence between theory and behavior is an inescapable part of the scientific method. We have few better means for determining the worth of a theory. Further, the reification of constructs in terms of psychological utility assures us that we are by that amount accurate in our speculations.

The paper by Greenberg and Jenkins is an excellent example of this process. The phonological regularities discussed in the Chomsky and Miller selection of the preceding section are here explored in terms of subjects' reactions to novel phoneme configurations. The authors' success in predicting subject reactions indicates that the speaker of a language must refer the novel phonemic pattern to his internalized awareness of the phonological structure of his language. The psychologist, in fact, has become increasingly aware in recent years of the operation of such sound structure contingencies and their importance for the understanding of the processes underlying the learning and retention of verbal material. Underwood and Schulz (1960), for example, in a recent volume reporting the results of a carefully contrived series of experiments in verbal learning, conclude that pronuncibility is a key variable in predicting such learning. Greenberg and Jenkins' investigation of distinctive features, moreover, shows that these elemental markers proposed by Jakobson, Fant, and Halle (1963) for the linguistic specification of the phoneme are, as well, valid predictors of the speakers' judgments of phonemic similarity. Clearly, such psychological validity for one of several competing and otherwise equally efficient theoretical constructs is an important criterion for choice among them.

The next two articles by Miller and Miller and Isard extend the experimental approach to language beyond its phonological structure to the higher units of organization. The first of these articles, delivered as the presidential address before the Eastern Psychological Association in 1962, represents one of the earliest attempts on the part of a psychologist to utilize the linguistic model of the transformational grammarian as a tool for the study of speech behavior. Although the collection of reaction times for the assessment of the validity of transformations is admittedly primitive, the conception of the decision processes assumed necessary for an appreciation of the speakers' understanding of language is novel and indicative of the newer trend in psycholinguistics. This article presents an account of the significance of the phrase structure and transformational components of language. The import of both articles is clear. Speech perception is dependent upon a complex set of hierarchically organized interdependencies which are well characterized by the transformationist approach. The results of these experiments must lead to the conclusion that the user of the language is well aware of the relations between sentence types and of their constituent structures, although such awareness may not be possible in the form of explicit expression. Miller argues that a conception of the sentence as composed of probabilistically connected linear segments is incompatible with the data of these experiments. He substitutes a conception in terms of rule-like principles which organize the speech signal into related structural components. Such a model supposes the user of a language to be an active decision maker rather than a passively dependent receiver (see also Miller, Gallanter, and Pribram, 1960). According to such a model each utterance must be referred to a generated description and compared for acceptable match before understanding can take place. Miller's work further suggests that the retention of verbal material is based upon the storage of a simplified and regular representation, corresponding in the case of language to what has been called the "kernel," plus a marker or markers indicating how the needed material can be recreated by the application of a set of already learned rules. Obviously such a model would increase the potential capacity of the human storage system far beyond the limits imposed by a system requiring the establishment of specific linear dependencies between the units of the materials to be retained.

How it is that structural units might be acquired by the human user of language is explored in the paper by Braine. Through the use of artificially constructed languages showing certain positional constraints on its elements, Braine is trying to demonstrate that some form of what he calls context generalization could account for the ability to learn the syntactic components of sentential material. The Brown and Berko paper of this section represents an attempt to show the correctness of the assumption that the child is learning the category membership rules of the lexical items of his language. From a machine-like reproducer of the sequential dependencies between lexical units which mirror the input experience to which he has been exposed, the child gradually comes to organize his associations into classes of syntactically substitutive units. This tendency can be characterized as an increasing freedom from the stimulus characteristics of the speech signals he is exposed to and an increase in the abstract structural organization which is characteristic of adult speech.

Whereas the primary stimulus generalization models assume shared physical features as the principle organizing class membership, the characteristic absence of such common physical features for syntactic categories makes such a principle weak as a reasonable theory of their acquisition. Some sort of positional context rule, however, has been postulated to provide the basis for an abstract mediator of syntactic category membership. Braine explores the nature of such a mechanism in his analysis of how such context generalization might operate to produce a syntactic description. Although he concludes in this article that the approach is restricted to the regular and simple constructions characterized as kernels, later work on transformations has led him to extend these principles. He concludes from his later experiments that "One can view the conception of a transform language as a sort of equilibrium state resulting from the interplay of different generalizing tendencies. When a learner is exposed to verbal arrays which exemplify more than one sentence-type, he will learn features which distinguish the sentence-types, and also other features which lead to the importation of material from one sentence-type into another. As a result of these distinguishing and assimilatory tendencies, the language learned will often tend to a state in which the sentence-types are distinguished but in which the sentences of one type are a 'projection or mapping' of the sentences of another." The lengthy interchanges between Braine and Bever, Fodor and Weksel are perhaps the finest clarification of the differences in approach of many behavior theorists and grammarians. Such arguments of theory and method abound in the history of science, and, like this one, they invariably work to achieve far deeper understanding than the superficial acrimony suggests. At least three major points are at issue: 1) how does one apply the parsimony rule to select among competing theoretical explanations, 2) how is deep structure, not given to experience, learned if at all required, and 3) is linguistics, after all, empirical? This last should not be confused with whether or not linguistics is a science; the theory of language which Chomsky has proposed clearly is scientific in a very deep and far-reaching sense. It seeks an explanation of a peculiarly human capacity. What is at issue is whether or not such a theory accrues to some automatic process of data classification. The confusion regarding the "kernel" of language is so widespread that it deserves additional emphasis. Many of the behavior theorists, only casually interested in language, probably have used as their source material Miller's exposition of the transformation position as contained in his earlier American Psychological Association address reprinted in this volume. Miller perhaps too clearly suggests in that article that the kernel is the set of simple declarative sentences. Even if Chomsky's earlier exposition might have been mistakenly construed as indicating such a position, his later writings (see his 1965 chapter of Part 1) clearly indicate otherwise. Miller proposed a theory of language behavior based upon a notion of psychological deformation of the active sentence. Chomsky argues for a theory of language competence based upon deformation of abstract deep structure of sentential components never realized in speech.

The following two articles, that by Maclay and Osgood and that by Fodor and Bever, both reiterate by example the importance of phrase structure in the decisions required for language understanding and production. The normal hesitations and non-fluencies of speech are not randomly determined; the loci are predictable from a knowledge of both the synthetic categories to which the verbal units belong and the structural organization of the utterance into large phrase units. If phrase boundaries represent decision points in the spontaneous, encoding behavior of the speaker as shown by Maclay and Osgood, Fodor and Bever have shown that they are also decision points in the decoding of speech. While the encoder uses the phrase boundary to select and process his intentions, these same intervals represent relaxation hiatuses in decoding. Hence the decoder will show a tendency to displace an intrusive signal to a point in the speech sequence in which he can attend to it, while the encoder is maximally loaded during this same interval evidencing non-fluencies of one kind or another. Both studies, however, indicate that all of the behavior of the encoder or decoder cannot be explained by the phrase structure boundaries alone. Both agree that individual lexical boundaries and other unexplained loci are also present. What emerges then is a model of the human processing system which appears to contain decision choices for syntactic categories which are organized into higher-order phrase sequences which in turn display still higher-order organizational dependencies.

Although a considerable amount of work has been done on the determination of the loci of stuttering behavior with respect to syntactic categories or word classes, unfortunately nothing is available which explores the role of phrase structure as a predictor of stuttering. One would assume that the effects found by Maclay and Osgood in spontaneous normal speech would be characteristic of the stutterer as well. The paper by Wischner here reprinted, however, omits any mention of structural aspects of the stutterer's speech. The emphasis upon individual lexical choices as the determinant of stuttering behavior is in general characteristic of the approach which has been current in the field. As a behavioristic interpretation of the nature and etiology of stuttering it is a clear application of the deductions offered by behavior theory. That orientation is, however, clearly quite different from the approach represented by most of the other selections of this section. Whether or not it is an adequate characterization is an empirical question which will have to await the determination of the adequacy of prediction the generative position affords for the incidence of stuttering behavior.

Aphasia, perhaps more than any other disability, has immediate and direct relevance to the development of a theory of language. Involving as it does the processes of symbol manipulation, it is rich in implications for the nature of the capacities involved in language. The model proposed by Wepman, *et al.*, posits the existence of modality-specific capacities as well as organizational levels. Cases involving disabilities which are specific to the visual or auditory modalities affecting largely the ability to encode or decode verbal material have been observed. Further such disabilities within a given modality can impair the use of syntactic categories or phrase organization, apparently more or less independently. Although other theorists, notably Schuell and Jenkins (1959), have emphasized the general linguistic loss in aphasia, the model proposed in the selection here chosen is not necessarily antithetical to such a position. Given general and widespread loss of capacity for symbol manipulation as a result of brain damage, it is still possible to observe relatively prominent specific disabilities. The demonstration of an ability to deal with phrase structure or syntactic categories as a viable clinical syndrome, of course, adds directly to the validity of a model which supposes such processes as essential to the characterization of normal language (see Osgood and Miron, 1963).

References

JAKOBSON, R., C. G. M. FANT, and M. HALLE, *Preliminaries to Speech Analysis: The Distinctive Features and Their Correlates.* Cambridge, Mass.: The M.I.T. Press, 1963.

MILLER, G. A., E. GALLANTER, and K. H. PRIBRAM, *Plans and the Structure of Behavior.* New York: Holt, Rinehart & Winston, Inc., 1960.

OSGOOD, C. E., and M. S. MIRON, *Approaches to the Study of Aphasia.* Urbana, Ill.: University of Illinois Press, 1963.

SCHUELL, HILDRED, and J. J. JENKINS, "The Nature of Language Deficit in Aphasia," *Psychological Review,* 66 (1959), 45–67.

UNDERWOOD, B. J., and R. W. SCHULZ, *Meaningfulness and Verbal Learning.* Chicago: J. B. Lippincott Co., 1960.

Studies in the Psychological Correlates of the Sound System of American English

JOSEPH H. GREENBERG
and JAMES J. JENKINS

I. MEASURING LINGUISTIC DISTANCE FROM ENGLISH[1]

It is a linguistic commonplace that the sequences of phonemes in English, as probably in all languages, are subject to powerful constraints. For initial and final consonant sequences rules have been formulated by a number of linguists.[2] One of the consequences of these rules as formulated by these writers, is that they allow for the generation of many sequences which do not occur in English, e.g. */strib/. It is reasonable to hypothesize that such a sequence will elicit a response from English-speaking subjects different from that of an existent sequence, e.g. /strʌk/ but different also from such a sequence as */gvsurs/ which cannot be generated from rules of English consonant sequences. One would conjecture that on some psychological dimension of strangeness or distance from English */strib/ would be located between /strʌk/ and */gvsurs/. Indeed we are likely to be dealing with a dimension more complex than a three-point scale consisting of existing sequences, generatable sequences and non-generatable sequences. Consider, for example, the sequence */stwip/. Here the prevocalic sequence of three consonants conforms to the general rule of sequence /s/, unvoiced stop (in this case /t/) and liquid or semivowel (in this case /w/). However, it is less close to the pattern of English than the above-mentioned */strib/. This is because /stw-/ does not occur as an initial sequence in any English word although it

[1] These studies were begun at the Center for Advanced Studies in the Behavioral Sciences, Stanford, in 1959, where both authors were Fellows for the academic year, 1958–59. We are indebted to the Social Science Research Council which enabled us to carry out joint research at the University of Minnesota during the summer of 1960 and to the Psychology Department of that university for the use of its facilities.

[2] L. Bloomfield, *Language* (New York, 1933), pp. 127–138; B. Whorf, "Linguistics as an Exact Science," *Technology Review,* XLIII (1940), 61–63, 80–83, reprinted in *Language, Thought and Reality,* ed John B. Carroll (Cambridge, Mass., 1956), pp. 220–232.

Joseph H. Greenberg and James J. Jenkins, "Studies in the Psychological Correlates to the Sound System of American English," *Word,* **20,** No. 2 (August, 1964), 157–177. Reprinted by permission of the authors and publisher.

can be analogically deduced from, say, *skr-*:*skw-* = *str-*:*x*, where *skr-*, *skw-* and *str-* all occur. Here we have, so to speak, a combination which is not as possible as */strib/ but more possible than */gvsurs/. We would predict, therefore, that it should take a correspondingly intermediate position on our hypothetical scale of nearness to English.

Faced with the present problem, the reaction of the psychologist and linguist is characteristically different. The psychologist immediately thinks of experiments and subject reactions. The linguist reaches for pencil and paper and works for refinement of definition based on logico-mathematical manipulation of the structure of existent forms in the language. These two procedures are logically independent. The possibility of devising a mathematical scale based on the structure of English, to be presently described; and then measuring subject reactions on the basis of psychological dimensions such as those just mentioned, makes this an area of possible psycholinguistic investigation. Much as in classical psychophysics, we have an objectively derivable dimension which can be investigated in relation to its psychological correlates.

A common linguistic procedure which might be employed here is substitution. Thus, for example, */lʌt/ is close to English because we can reach existent English words by single substitutions in each position, e.g. *but, let, luck*. In the case of *stwip*, we can get 'strip' by substituting *r* for *w*, but since no existent word begins with *stw-* it is clear that no substitutions in the fourth or fifth position can give an English word. However, if we move to substitutions in two places simultaneously, we can, for example, by substituting *-kr-* for *-tw-* get *scrip* whereas such measures will still be of no avail in sequences such as *gvsurs*. It is clear that length plays a role also. The longer the sequence, the more difficult it becomes to produce English words by substitutions. It seems advisable, therefore, to hold the factor of length constant. For the experiments described here, sequences of four phonemes all of the form *CCVC* were chosen. If we have a sequence of length n, we can substitute from zero up to n at a time and each such number of substitutions can be done in $\binom{n}{i}$ ways where i takes on values from 0 to n. The total will, of course, be 2^n, in this case 16. By zero substitution we will mean leaving the word as it is, in which case it will only qualify if it already exists in English. At the other end of the scale any sequence of four whatever can become English by substitution in all places simultaneously. Since we wish our scale to reflect distance so that the larger numbers will be given to words farther from English we will subtract the total number of successful substitutions from 17. In this way a word which can only become English by a single type of substitution, that is in all four places, will have a rating of $17 - 1 = 16$ and a word which exists in English will allow of all 16 substitutions and have the value $17 - 16 = 1$. To illustrate with a syllable used in Experiment A, /klæb/ was rated as 2, that is, as very close to English, in the following way. In this table, the first column gives the number of simultaneous substitutions, the second column the number of ways $\binom{n}{i}$ in which this can be done and the third column the number of these which give English words.

Table 1

A	*B*	*C*	
0	1	0	
1	4	4	(e.g. slab, crab, club, clam)
2	6	6	
3	4	4	
4	1	1	

The total in column C is 15 and the rating of /klæb/ is $17 - 15 = 2$. The identity substitution is allowed. Thus any existent word automatically receives all possible substitutions. Substitution by zero is not allowed. For example, by substituting zero in the second place of *klæb* we would get *kæb*. Usually it make no difference to the rating which decision is taken in regard to identity and zero substitution.

The linguist then devised a list of 24 sequences of the form *CCVC* designed to sample the sixteen-point scale just described. This list, hereafter referred to as List 1, contained the following items. The linguistic substitution scale will hereafter be referred to as S.

Table 2

Syllable No.	*S*	*Syllable No.*	*S*	*Syllable No.*	*S*
1. stɪk	1	9. klɛb	4	17. žwup	12
2. græs	1	10. swæč	4	18. ðyʌŋ	12
3. spɛl	1	11. srʌm	5	19. vrüɣ	13
4. trʌk	1	12. θlæs	5	20. žlöp	13
5. slʌk	2	13. θwæǰ	8	21. ðgɪx	16
6. swɪt	2	14. trʊg	8	22. zbüɣ	16
7. klæb	2	15. træx	9	23. mböl	16
8. brʌd	2	16. žrɪk	9	24. mzœç	16

Experiment A, designed as a preliminary exploration, was carried out at the Center for Advanced Study in the Behavioral Sciences in the early months of 1959. The words of List 1 were recorded by the linguist on a Revere tape recorder in two random orders.

Each syllable was pronounced twice with a three-second delay between repetitions and an interval of fifteen seconds between the last occurrence of each word and the first occurrence of the next word. The technique used was free magnitude estimation. Each of the six subjects was tested individually.[3] The instructions were as follows:

This is an experiment on the relationship of one-syllable foreign words to English. You will hear each of these words repeated two times, so that you can hear each word clearly. Some of these words are from languages that are very close to English, some not so closely related, and some from languages that are very distant from English.

Your task will be, when you hear one of these words, to give me a number, as a judgment as to how far this seems to be from being an English word. Use this first word and score as a basis for your next judgment. If that seems to be twice as far from English, you would give me a number that is twice as large. If the word seems to be half as far from English, give a number that is half as large. It it is ten times as far, give a number that is ten times as large, and so on. Remember, you can use any system of numbers. Just choose some numbers that you feel comfortable with. Are there any questions?

Let's try a word to see how it will go. (Put on tape for one word.)

How far would you say that is from English?—That's fine. Now if the next word seems to be twice as far away, you would say——. If it is half as far away, you would say——. If it is ten times as far away,——. O.K.?

Let's try it from the beginning and run through the sequence.

(Put the tape on for all 24 words and record the responses.)

Now I would like to have some personal information. (Personal questionnaire administered.)

We will now go through the list in a different order. You can change your scale if you like, but that is not necessary, and it does not matter if you do not give the same response to the same words. The reason we repeat the list of words is to help you get more familiar with the procedure and to get away from any order effects that might exist due to chance pairings of different words.

(Continue the tape and leave it on for the rest of the experiment.)

An overall impression of the results of Experiment A can be gathered from Figure 1, in which the results of the two trials for the six subjects are given. For the abscissa, the values are those of the linguistic rating scale S as described above. The set of 24 words are divided into six groups of four words each with the mean values 1, 2, 4.5, 8.5, 12.5, and 16, respectively. The ordinate values are the means of each set of four words on the magnitude estimation scales for the six subjects. The mean for each word is the mean of the six subjects, with each subject's ratings equated at a mean of 50. The result is,

[3] For those unacquainted with free magnitude estimation, the instructions for subjects which follow should provide sufficient indication.

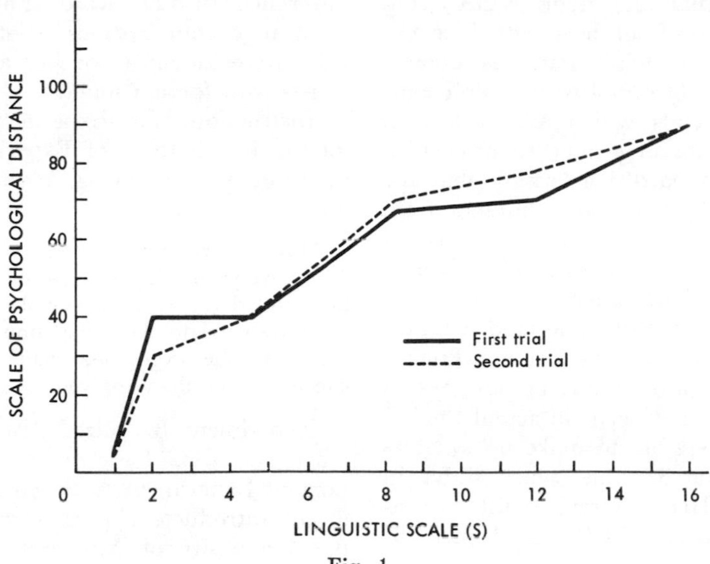

Fig. 1

except for a threshold effect at the value of 1 of the linguistic rating, very nearly linear. For the second trial, a line $D_{50} = 20.75 + 4.14\ S$ very nearly coincides with four of the six points. The values of these means for each of the two trials is as follows:

Table 3

S	*First trial*	*Second Trial*
1	8.21	7.81
2	39.24	29.03
4.5	39.09	39.33
8.5	62.40	64.76
12.5	64.47	72.22
16	86.77	86.99

The means for individual words of List 1 for the second trial is as follows:

Table 4

Word	*S*	*Means*
1. stɪk	1	6.60
2. græs	1	10.35
3. spɛl	1	7.17
4. trʌk	1	7.17
5. slʌk	2	33.08
6. swɪt	2	22.63
7. klæb	2	21.7
8. brʌd	2	38.55
9. klɛb	4	42.53
10. swæč	4	32.48
11. srʌm	5	62.58
12. θlæš	5	19.70
13. θwæǰ	8	70.43
14. trʊg	8	42.12
15. træx	9	72.92
16. žrɪk	9	73.58
17. žwʊp	12	64.28
18. ðyʌŋ	12	66.07
19. vrüγ	13	77.82
20. žlöp	13	80.73
21. ðgɪx	16	106.95
22. zbüγ	16	89.93
23. mböl	16	67.25
24. mzœç	16	83.82

Quite large deviation from the expected result may be noted for a few individual words, notable *θlæš* ranked as closer to English than was hypothesized and *brʌd* and *srʌm* farther away. It turned out that several subjects had misheard *θlæš* as *flæš* 'flash' on a recording of only mediocre fidelity. The deviation away from English in the items brʌd and srʌm are both possibly attributable to the fact that the linguist, a New York City native, has an *r* sound which is different from that of Midwestern and Far Western speakers and that his vowel ʌ is farther back than that of most dialects of American English.

A discussion of the results of this experiment as described by the linguist to a Linguistics Department Seminar at Columbia University raised the issue of foreign sounds as against English sounds in the judgment of the subjects. It was pointed out that such items as *zbüγ* contained two non-English sounds. The objection might be boldly stated as follows: Subjects are confronted with stimuli some containing sounds which are in English and some containing some sounds which are not. It is hardly surprising that the latter are judged as more different from English. Of course this will not account for the consistent difference of judgment in the intermediate range.

Since the linguistic scale used will give the same result for words with non-English sounds or English sounds in positions in which they do not occur in actual English words, it is possible to make up syllables with the same S value which differ in this respect. Hence a revised list, hereinafter to be called List 2, was devised for the subsequent experiment.

The words of List 2 are as follows:

Table 5

	Word	*S*		*Word*	*S*
1.	stɪk	1	13.	θwæǰ	8
2.	græs	1	14.	trUg	8
3.	spɛl	1	15.	træx	9
4.	trʌk	1	16.	žrɪk	9
5.	slʌk	2	17.	čwUp	12
6.	swɪt	2	18.	ðyʌŋ	12
7.	klæb	2	19.	zml̩p	13
8.	brʌd	2	20.	vrüγ	13
9.	klɛb	4	21.	ðgöh	16
10.	swæč	4	22.	ðgɨx	16
11.	srʌm	5	23.	zbüγ	16
12.	knæp	5	24.	zgr̩γ	16

In this list, *θlæš* of List 1, which, as was noted, was misheard as *flæš*, has been replaced by *knæp* (item 12) and new items 17, 19, 21 and 24 have been so constructed that of the two items with S = 12, number 17 has one non-English sound while 18 has none, of the two items with value 13, number 19 has no non-English sound while number 20 has one, and of the four items with value 16, two (22, 23) have two non-English sounds while two (21, 24) have only one such sound. Subsequent experiments using List 2 showed that this made no significant difference. In other words, English sounds in strange combinations or strange positions were judged to be just as foreign as words with foreign sounds.

Instructions for Experiment A were identical with those of Experiment B except for the following additional paragraph:

> O.K. we will hear the list one more time. Again, you can change your numbers if you like, and don't worry if you do not give the same response to the same stimuli. This is a check on the experiment and the ordering effects, rather than for your reliability.

Experiment B utilized List 2 and employed the same basic design and instructions as Experiment A. Seventeen students in an introductory psychology course at the University of Minnesota were individually tested. This time an Ampex recording of high fidelity was used and there were three trials instead of two as in Experiment A. As before, each word was said twice with a three-second interval between repetitions and a 15-second interval between words. The last trial was taken for analysis as being most free of experimental artifacts, but the data are very similar for all three trials.

The results of this experiment were very similar to those of Experiment A (see Table 7). Again, if the words are grouped in sets of four, the result is very nearly linear with a threshold effect for words in English (S = 1). For Trial 3 the results are as follows with the individual rating scales once more equated, with their means at 50:

Table 6

S	*Means of ME Ratings*
1	3.145
2	28.955
4.5	35.478
8.5	56.198
12.5	71.146
16	102.417

The coefficient of linear correlation based on values for individual words between the S scale value and the magnitude estimation means for Trial 3 was .94. The means for individual words obtained on the third trial of Experiment B were as follows:

Table 7

Word No.	*S*	*Means*
1	1	2.90
2	1	3.06
3	1	2.90
4	1	3.71
5	2	29.16
6	2	25.10
7	2	28.15
8	2	33.40
9	4	32.92
10	4	29.25
11	5	46.12
12	5	33.90
13	8	63.19
14	8	41.16
15	9	62.14
16	9	67.59
17	12	87.97
18	12	46.49
19	13	66.62
20	13	84.63
21	16	82.68
22	16	111.87
23	16	98.57
24	16	111.56

Experiment C once more utilized List 2. However, instead of free magnitude estimation, an 11-point rating scale was used. The purpose here was to evaluate the reliability of free magnitude estimation as a rating technique by the use of the more commonly employed rating scale as well as to test further the nature and reliability of the phenomena investigated in Experiments A and B. Experiment C used 15 subjects at the University of Minnesota and as in Experiment B there were three trials. The same recording was used as in Experiment B. The instructions to the subjects were as follows:

This is an experiment sponsored jointly by Dr. Joseph Greenberg, a linguist at Columbia University, and Dr. James Jenkins of our department. We are interested in developing a measure of the degree of differences that exist between languages. This experiment is designed to see how people perceive differences between languages. I am going to present some words to you with the tape recorder. Some of these words are common English words; some are from languages closely related to English, some not so closely related to English; some distantly related, and some that are very, very distantly related to English. All of these words are short, one syllable words, and they will each be presented two times, so that you will be sure to hear them clearly.

Now this is what I would like you do:

Look at the booklet I handed you. Write your name and trial 1 on the top line. You will notice that there are numbers going down the page, and by each number there is a line that is numbered from one to eleven. When you hear a word you are to decide how close it is to being an English word. If you think it is an English word you are to circle the mark above the number one. If you think it is as far from English as it can possibly be you are to circle the mark over the eleven, if it is relatively near English circle the smaller numbers, and if it is relatively far from English circle the larger numbers. Try to make use of the whole scale. Are there any questions? If not I'll play the first word to see how it goes.

If there are no further questions I will play the list throughout. Listen to the number of the word and then listen to the word repeated twice, rate the word accordingly and wait for the next word.

Second time

Turn the page to a new rating scale and number this trial two. You are now going to hear the list in a different order. Now you have an idea of the range of stimuli, and therefore your responses may change accordingly. Do not attempt to rate a word a certain way because that is the way it was rated the last time.

Third time

Number the next rating scale trial three. This is a still different order of the same words. Listen carefully and rate appropriately.

Now we would like you to fill out the information blank on the last page. If you do not know the answer of any of the ques-

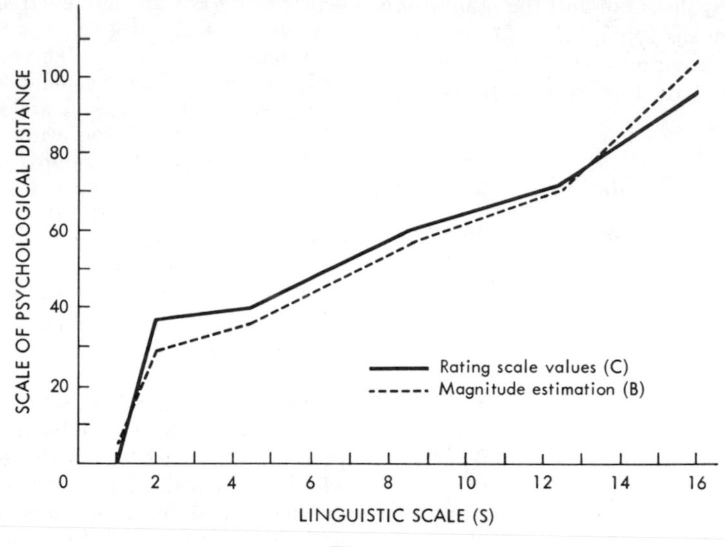

Fig. 2

tions, just leave it blank. But please answer honestly.

The results of C were extremely close to those of Experiment B, as shown in Figure 2. The coefficient of correlation between rating scale medians and magnitude estimation medians was + .98. The correlation between the results of C (medians) and linguistic measure S was + .95, insignificantly different from the value + .94 for the results of B and the linguistic measure as mentioned earlier. The rank order correlation between the rating scale of Experiment C and magnitude estimation of Experiment B was + .94. The correlation between the rating-scale median and means for the third trial was + .99 indicating essential identity of the measures for scaling purposes.

If the first category on the rating scale is assigned a value of zero and each successive interval increases by one unit, the mean rating scale value is 4.86. The results may then be compared to the magnitude estimation values by multiplying by 10.30. While such a comparison is crude, since it makes no assumptions about the nature of the scales whatsoever, it can be seen that it yields good agreement. Table 8 gives the resulting values for the rating scale experiment.

Table 8

1	0.00	13	51.50
2	0.00	14	46.66
3	0.00	15	65.92
4	0.07	16	72.10
5	43.98	17	87.86
6	26.78	18	57.68
7	29.56	19	74.88
8	37.80	20	66.64
9	39.14	21	93.42
10	35.74	22	96.10
11	50.78	23	89.92
12	35.02	24	98.16

The finding that the magnitude estimation procedure and the category rating scale produce virtually identical results is of more general importance than is superficially apparent. Psychophysical scales may be divided into two general classes which Stevens has termed "prothetic" and "metathetic".[4] The first class seems to characterize continua having to do with

[4] S. S. Stevens, "On the Psychophysical Law," *Psychological Review,* LXIV (1957), 153–181.

how much (loudness, length, numerousness, duration, etc.) while the second seems typical of continua concerned with *what kind* and *where* (visual position, angular inclination, proportion, pitch, etc.). Category scales of the first class of stimuli are usually of quite different form from magnitude estimation scales. For the second class, the two forms of scaling tend to agree, as they do in this case. One of the implications of this finding is that the perceptual sensitivity of the subjects is uniform across the entire length of the scale as opposed to being highly sensitive for small departures from English and less and less sensitive for differences between very distant "words" as one might initially suppose to be the case. The writers believe that the agreement of the scaling methods and the linear relation which both bear to the linguistic scale constitute indirect evidence for the correspondence of the psychological comparison process and the linguistic substitution analysis which led to the development of the scale. Subjects appear to match this substitution procedure when asked to make distance or category ratings and match it equally well at all points on the continuum tested. This consideration leads directly to the next study.

Experiment D, the last of the group, was a word association test with the 24 words of List 2 as the stimuli. The test was given at the University of Minnesota in June 1960 to 117 subjects. The time allowed each subject for writing down the associations was 15 seconds. The instructions for Experiment D were as follows:

You are about to participate in one of the Minnesota studies in verbal behavior. This particular study is sponsored by Professor James Jenkins of the Psychology Department here and Professor Joseph Greenberg, Professor of Linguistics at Columbia.

Please put your name, age, sex, and date on the cover of the blue books that have been passed out to you. Now open the book and put a number 1 in the middle of the first line of the first page. About halfway down the first page put the number 2. Then fold back the page and put a three on the back of the first page. Continue numbering in this manner until you reach 24.

I have on this tape recorder a list of words. Some of these words are English, but most of them are from foreign languages so you probably have never heard them before. The speaker will give the number of each word, and then he will say the word two times. When you hear the word you are to write down as many other words as this one makes you think of in the time allowed. The words that you write down might be things, places, ideas, events, or whatver you happen to think of when you hear the key word.

For example, the speaker might say, 'Number one, horse, horse.' You might think 'horse-cow,' write 'cow,' then you might think 'horse-race,' write 'race' below 'cow.' Be sure to think back to the original word after each word you write down because the test is to see how many words *that* word makes you think of. A good way to do this is to think of the key word over and over as you write. In the example above we do *not* want you to respond to 'horse': 'cow,' 'calf,' 'leg,' 'arm,' a chain of associations, but respond to the stimulus word 'horse' itself.

Another stimulus word might be 'ketch,' in which case you might write 'ketchup,' or 'boat,' or you might not think of any word before the speaker gives the next number. In that case you are to leave the space blank. But work as rapidly as you can in the interval given and get ready for the next word when the speaker gives the number. Are there any questions?

The mean number associates for each word across all the subjects is given in the following table:

Table 9

Word No. (List 2)	*S*	*Associates*
1	1	2.68
2	1	3.05
3	1	2.62
4	1	3.14
5	2	1.83
6	2	2.25
7	2	2.22
8	2	2.22
9	4	1.72

Word No. (*List* 2)	*S*	*Associates*
10	4	1.91
11	5	1.96
12	5	2.45
13	8	1.44
14	8	1.74
15	9	1.85
16	9	1.58
17	12	1.52
18	12	1.91
19	13	1.37
20	13	1.58
21	16	1.95
22	16	1.76
23	16	1.35
24	16	1.06

Correlations between these results and those of Experiments B and C which likewise utilized List 2 were as follows: The coefficient of linear correlation between the median number of associations and medians of the magnitude estimation results of Experiment B was − .86; with the rating-scale medians of Experiment C it was − .75. Rank-order correlations between the inverse order of number of associations and the rank of magnitude estimation medians was + .81; with the rating scale medians + .80.

As was to be expected, the correlations here are somewhat lower than that between magnitude estimation and rating scales, since the latter two require the same judgment by the subject. At the same time, that high correlations would be obtained was hypothesized on the basis of a general meaningfulness dimension such as has appeared in psychological investigation of both nonsense syllables and real words varying in frequency of usage.[5] The three most popular associates to each of the syllables of List 2 are given below:

1. stɪk : tree 27; wood 19; hit 14
2. græs : green 85; lawn 30; soft 10
3. spɛl : words 34; word 28; write 17
4. trʌk : car 33; truck 18; road 17
5. slʌk : slug 22; mud 12; slow 10
6. swɪt : sweat 39; sweet 39; swift 20
7. klæb : clap 23; hands 12, clam 11
8. brʌd : bread 48; brother 42; blood 26
9. klɛb : club 28; clip 14; cliff 9
10. swæč : switch 26; swatch 14; hit 14
11. srʌm : strong 19; sarong 12; strum 10, guitar 10
12. knæp : nap 31; canoe 17; knapsack 9
13. θwæj : thatch 23; thrash 20; whip 5
14. trʊg : truck 22; trudge 13; true 12
15. træx : track 41; trash 16; train 7
16. žrɪk : jerk 12; giraffe 9; shriek 7
17. çwʊp : whip 8; hoop 8; whoops 6; whoop 6
18. ðyʌŋ : young 54; old 13; girl 8; boy 8
19. zmlp : milk 26; smooth 19; smoke 9
20. vrüɣ : room 16; broom 11; rim 5
21. ðgöh : girl 21; good 15; go 8
22. ðgɪx : baby 26; good 22; girl 9
23. zbüɣ : German 10; bird 6; book 6
24. zgrɣ : girl 19; good 10; go 8

The following additional observation may be made in regard to the results of Experiment D. It was noted earlier in reference to Experiment A, that the greater than hypothesized linguistic distance from English of two syllables, *brʌd* and *srʌm*, might be attributable to the relative strangeness of the *r* and *ʌ* sounds of the linguist's New York speech to subjects of Midwestern or Far Western speech background. This seems to find some confirmation in the fact that in Experiment D, 18 subjects, as noted above, responded to /trʌk/ with the association 'truck' whereas, e.g. no subject responded to the stimulus /spɛl/ with 'spell'.

Examination of the actual responses of subjects to the 24 stimuli shows that a very large number of responses were single substitutions, or, for words with lower S values, multiple sound substitutions, including zero substitutions. For example, among the responses to */swɪt/* as a stimulus were: *wit* 2; *quit* 2; *sit* 1; *spit* 1; *slit* 1; *sweat* 39; *sweet* 39; *swat* 17; *Swiss* 1; *swish* 2; *swim* 4; *swig* 2; *switch* 17; *swing* 3; and even a non-existent **swip* 1, besides a large number obviously mediated by one

[5] For a discussion of meaningfulness see B. J. Underwood and R. W. Schulz, *Meaningfulness and Verbal Learning* (Philadelphia: Lippincott, 1960).

of the foregoing. It seems then that the high agreement found between the S scale and subject reactions is to be attributed largely to the fact that subjects do in fact substitute and that S is a measure of the possibilities offered by substitutional procedures. At the same time reliable differences are found among words having the same S ratings. It may be hypothesized that, in large part, these differences may be explained in terms of three other related factors. First, it should be noted, that in calculating S a single substitution is all that is required in order to score a plus for any one of the 2^n possibilities. Thus, of two words with the same S rating, one might have total substitutional possibilities greater than the other. Second, those substitutions are more frequent in which the sound substituted in the response is phonetically similar to the sound of the stimulus. Thus, among the substitution responses to /swɪt/ listed above, the possible substitution *skit* with *k* for *w* does not occur, whereas *spit* and *slit* do. In these two latter examples, *p* resembles *w* as being bilabial and both *w* and *l* are sonants. On the other hand, *k* has no basis of similarity with *w* other than sheer consonantality. A third factor is certainly associational strength of the substituted form. In principle it should be possible to evolve a finer measure than S, in which the associational strength and phonetic similarity of individual substitutions are taken into account and which might explain some of the remaining variance.

Finally, it may be noted that in a few cases there was undeniable mediation by the graphic form although the immediate stimulus was purely auditory. This was particularly noteworthy in the case of the stimulus /knæp/. It is clear that the responses with initial *n* which were favored were those which are spelled *kn-*. It even led to misspellings with *kn-* of words whose standard spelling begins with *n-* or even with *gn-*, e.g. *knat* 3; *knap* 2; *knick* 5; *knip* 1. In a further study to be reported elsewhere, in which methods similar to those already discussed are applied to the meaningfulness values of nonsense syllables, it will appear that auditory mediation of the visual stimulus presented to subjects in the usual nonsense syllable experiments carried out by psychologists is of fundamental significance.

II. DISTINCTIVE FEATURES AND PSYCHOLOGICAL SPACE

The results of the preceding paper, with its unusually high intercorrelations between successive applications of free magnitude estimation and between free magnitude estimation and other techniques, encouraged the application of this technique in further instances. A series of experiments was carried out in the summer of 1960, with students at the University of Minnesota as subjects designed to explore the psychological correlates of distinctive features in phonology. These experiments involved the method of paired comparisons. In this method, from a set of *n* stimuli all possible non-identical pairs are presented in both orders. Thus if the original set contained three basic stimuli A, B, C, the following six sets of paired stimuli would result: AB, BA, AC, CA, BC, CB. It is evident that the number of pairs resulting from *n* basic stimuli will be $2 \times \binom{n}{2}$. Thus with the six basic stimuli employed in the experiments reported in this section there were $30 = 2 \cdot \binom{6}{2} = 2 \cdot \frac{6 \cdot 5}{1 \cdot 2} = 30$ sets of paired stimuli. Since the addition of further members to the basic set increases in number of paired stimuli at an increasing rate, it is not feasible to present, for example, the entire consonantal or vocalic system of a language such as English since it presents an excessively difficult and time-consuming task for the subject.

The basic stimuli chosen were the six consonants p, b, t, d, k, g, since these constitute a neatly structured subsystem of the overall sound system of English. The actual stimuli in the four experimental runs to be described were oral and/or visually presented instances of these consonants with a following *a,* e.g. *pa,* or with [a] in oral presentation. The subjects were asked to assign a number as a measure of distance between PA and BA.

The following are some of the questions to which such a series of experiments might furnish answers. Are pairs which differ in two features consistently rated as more distant from each other than those which are only one feature apart (e.g. PA–GA vs. PA–KA)? Among those which are one feature apart, are pairs agreeing in manner rated as closer or more distant than those which agree in position (e.g. PA–KA vs. PA–BA)? Is the greater articulatory distance between the peripheral labial and velar position as against labial-alveolar and velar-alveolar distance reflected in the results (e.g. PA–TA vs. PA–KA)?

In the first experiment (A), five subjects were presented with the set of 30 paired stimuli as described above in three different random orders on three successive trials. In this, as in the other experiments of this series, only the results of the third trial were employed in formulating the results statistically. In experiment A subjects were presented with the stimuli on tape and recorded their distance estimates in a space beside the written representation of what they heard. There were thus both aural and visual stimuli.

The instructions for experiment A were as follows:

This is one of a series of studies in the psychology of language sponsored by Professor James Jenkins in our department and Professor Joseph Greenberg of the Department of Anthropology at Columbia University. The aim of this research is to knit together the sciences of psychology and linguistics. We regard it as important research and would appreciate your wholehearted cooperation.

We are interested in your impressions as to how much speech sounds differ.

I am going to ask you to listen to some syllables on the tape recorder and I shall ask you to give an estimate in numbers as to how different the sounds are. This, of course, is subjective and there are no right or wrong answers. We just want to know how far apart *you* think the sounds are.

I know that this is an unusual task, so in order to clarify what I would like you to do, I will give you an analogous situation. See the dots on this sheet of paper? (Hold up sheet with six randomly arranged dots.) They would be representative of bacteria seen through a microscope, just dots on paper, or galaxies viewed through a giant telescope. If I were to ask you to tell me how far apart these two dots are (pointing), and did not give you any more information, you could say any number you chose, 5 10, 36, 100, etc. But if I then asked you to give me a number estimating how far apart *these two* are (pointing to two dots twice as far apart as first two), in relation to your first number, you would be more restricted. If your first number had been 5, you would probably now say 10 or 11. If the first were a 10, you would probably say 20. Now look at these two (pointing to two dots about half as far apart as the initial pair). If my first were 5, I would probably say 2 or 2½. If the first were 10, I would say about 5, and so on. For this distance (pointing again), I would probably say about the same as my first value.

You see how it works? If they are twice as far apart, give them a number twice as big, if ten times as far apart, a number ten times as big, half as far apart would warrant a number half as big, and so forth.

What we would like in *this* experiment is this: When you hear the first pair of syllables, give them a number as to how far apart they sound to you, your own subjective judgment. If the next pair sounds twice as far apart, give a number twice as large; half as far apart, give a number half as large, and so on.

We are not interested in how different the letters look, or how far apart they are in the alphabet, but how different the sounds of the syllables seem to be in your estimation. You may worry that your scale is changing or that you have forgotten what you said before, and so on. Don't let this worry you; you can do this task better than you think you can. And you will get better and better as we go along.

Are there any questions at this point?

Before we begin the actual rating, I would like you to be familiar with the speaker's voice. The syllables that are to be used in the actual rating are listed on this sheet in alphabetical order. (Hand out paper.) Just circle the syllable as it is spoken. Any questions?

(Gives familiarization list.)

Now the speaker will say the syllables in pairs, and he will repeat the syllables once. You are to listen carefully, give the first pair a number representing how far apart they sound to you, and use this judgment as a basis for later ones.

Write the number of your estimate on dashed line immediately following the listed pair of syllables. The cardboard shield with the window in it will allow you to concentrate on one pair at a time. Just slide it down and make your responses through the window.

(Present first randomization.)

This part of the experiment is like the last except that the order of the pairs is different. You have warmed up to the procedure and know what it is like. You can shift your scale or have it remain the same, whichever you prefer.

(Present second randomization.)

Now, one more time through the list in a new order and we will be through.

The accompanying sheet for experiment A had the following form:

1. pa ba ——
2. ga pa —— etc.

In experiment B there were likewise five subjects and the procedures were the same as for experiment A except that there was no visual presentation; only identifying numerals each followed by a blank space were on the instruction sheet in place of the numerals followed by the syllable pair followed by a blank space. The results would presumably be more free of orthographic effects but the subject was more likely to mishear the syllables. The instructions for experiment B were exactly like those for experiment A, already given, except that the third paragraph from the end, beginning "Write the number of your estimate on the dashed line..." was replaced by the following:

Write the number of your estimate on this paper after the number of the syllable pair read.

Since a preliminary comparison of the results of experiments A and B indicated considerable variability among subjects, particularly in the case of B, it was decided to repeat the procedures of B on another group of five subjects in order to increase the size of the sample. This repetition is called here experiment C and is identical with experiment B except for the identity of the subjects.

Finally, for the same reason as in the first group of experiments, namely to investigate the reliability of magnitude estimation by comparison with other methods, five subjects were used in essentially the same experiment but with a rating scale substituted for magnitude estimation as the technique. This set is here called experiment D. The instructions for D were as follows:

This is one of a series of experiments in the psychology of language sponsored by Professor James Jenkins in our department and Professor Joseph Greenberg of the Department of Anthropology at Columbia University. The aim of this research is to knit together the sciences of psychology and linguistics. We regard it as important research and would appreciate your wholehearted cooperation.

We are interested in your impression as to how speech sounds differ.

I am going to ask you to listen to some syllables on the tape recorder and I shall ask you to rate on this scale (holding sample scale up) how similar the consonants of the syllables sound to you. The vowel is always the same; it is merely to carry the sound of the consonant.

This task is, of course, subjective. There are no right or wrong answers. We just want to know how far apart *you* think the sounds are.

Before we begin the actual rating, I would like you to be familiar with the speaker's voice. All of the syllables to be used in the actual rating are listed in this sheet in alphabetical order. (Hand out paper.) Just circle the syllable as it is spoken. Are there any questions?

(Familiarization list is presented here. Subject has a list of 30 items, each of which lists the six syllables. As each item is spoken he circles the correct syllable.)

(Hand out rating sheets.)

Now the speaker will read the syllables in pairs. You are to listen carefully and rate on this sheet by circling the colon above the similarity rating you would like to give the speech sounds. Are there any questions?

(Present the first list of pairs on the tape.)

This part of the experiment is like the first except that the order of presentation is different. Do not try to give a response just because you gave that response before. Just rate how similar the sounds are.

(Present second randomization.)

We will go through the list one more time in a different order and then we will be through.

(Present third randomization.)

The instruction sheet for experiment D had the following appearance:

1.	:	:	:	:	:	:
	extremely similar	decidedly similar	pretty similar	somewhat similar	slightly similar	not similar
2.	:	:	:	:	:	:
	extremely similar	decidedly similar	pretty similar	somewhat similar	slightly similar	not similar

As can be inferred from these instructions, experiment D resembled B and C in that there was no visual stimulus.

As with the group of experiments reported in the first paper of this series, it was, of course, necessary to calibrate the differing scales of individual subjects on the free magnitude estimation experiments A, B, C, and to calibrate the results of free magnitude estimation with those of the rating scale of experiment D. In this present instance, instead of equating all the results to an arbitrary mean, statistical comparisons were based on the rank order of distance estimates. This seemed adequate since the subjects generally restricted themselves to a narrow interval in magnitude estimation and to generally equal intervals.

For each pair of syllables differing in order only, e.g. pa-ta and ta-pa, the two raw scores were averaged to give a single measure of distance. For each subject these 15 scores were ranked, the smallest number representing the smallest judged distance being assigned the number 1. For the rating scale, the number 1 was assigned as raw score for the judgment 'very similar' implying the smallest distance and each successive point on the scale received the next larger natural number up to 6 for the judgment 'not similar'. As with the magnitude estimation data, these scores were averaged for each pair of syllables differing in order only and the 15 resultant scores ranked with the lowest receiving rank order 1.

The set of raw scores, i.e. actual numerical judgments for one subject in experiment A, will serve as an illustration of the method employed.

Table 1

	p	b	t	d	k
b	6,5	—	—	—	—
t	6,4	6,7	—	—	—
d	7,7	3,5	5,6	—	—
k	4,5	5,4	3,4	4,7	
g	5,6	3,5	3,7	4,4	4,4

For example, this subject rated the distance between *ka* and *ta* as 3 when presented in that order but as 4 when presented in the order *ta* followed by *ka*.

For this subject, the pair *ka-ta* was rated as closest (average of the two orders 3.5) and this pair was therefore given the rank order 1. The next closest judgment, 4, was given both for DB and BG. The usual procedure in cases of tied ranks was followed. The sum of the ranks 2 and 3 were averaged so that both DB and BG received a rank of 2.5. A similar procedure was employed for the rating scale experiment (D) utilizing the numbers 1 to 6 for raw scores as described above.

That the subject found this a more difficult task than the rating of distance from English in the first set of experiments is shown by the lower intercorrelations among the four experiments as set forth in Table 2.

Table 2

	A	B	C	D
A	—	.6923	.6170	.7640
B	.6923	—	.7216	.2880
C	.6170	.7216	—	.1715
D	.7640	.2880	.1715	—

A correlation of .514 or greater is significant at the 5% confidence level and of .641 at the 1% level. Thus the results of A (magnitude estimation with aural-visual presentation) correlates significantly at the 5% levels with all the others and B and C correlate with each other and with A while D (rating scale) only correlates significantly with A. This suggests that future tests with larger samples should concentrate on the techniques employed in test A, the only test involving aural-visual stimuli.

The results of these tests show great internal consistency from the linguistic point of view. As a point of departure we may take the rank of each pair of syllables when averaged across the 20 subjects in the four experiments. Thus if a particular pair had been rated as closest by every subject, it would receive an average rank of 1, if last, an average rank of 15. These average results ranked in turn in order of average judgment of closeness are to be found in Table 3. Alongside of these results are the averages for five subjects in experiment A only, since this was the method which correlated most highly with the others. The column gives the rank order of the averages for experiment A, which differs in some respects from the results of an overall pooling of the results of the four experiments.

Measures summarizing the relative importance of agreements or disagreements in particular features can be easily obtained by averaging the above results. For example, a measure of the importance of agreement in point of articulation can be obtained by averaging the distance measures of the pairs PB, TD and KG; agreement in possession of the voicing feature by averaging the results for BD, BG and DG. Again the measure of alveolar-labial distance as against alveolar-velar distance can be measured by averaging the distances of the set TP, TB, DP and DB against those of the set TK, TG, DP and DG etc. Results for a number of such factors of agreement or contrast are shown in the following table:

Table 3

	Total averages	*Rank order*	*Test A averages*	*Rank order*
BD	3.225	1	3.3	1
GD	4.750	2	3.8	2
PB	5.850	3	5.9	3.5
KG	6.075	4	7.9	7.5
BG	6.500	5	5.9	3.5
PT	6.575	6	6.0	5
KT	7.575	7	6.1	6
TD	8.000	8	7.9	7.5
PD	9.475	9	9.5	11
PK	9.975	10	10.0	12
TB	10.025	11	11.1	13
TG	10.150	12	9.1	9
KD	10.275	13	11.7	14
KB	10.350	14	9.2	10
PG	10.600	15	12.2	15

Table 4

	Total for all experiments	*Experiment A only*
A		
1. agreement in presence of voicing	4.825	4.333
2. agreement in non-voicing	8.042	7.366
3. agreement in presence or absence of voice	6.433	5.849
4. agreement in point of articulation	6.642	7.233
B		
5. alveolar-labial contrast	7.325	7.475
6. alveolar-velar contrast	8.187	7.675
7. labial-velar contrast	9.356	9.325
C		
8. difference in one feature	6.503	6.266
9. difference in two features	10.146	10.466

The following are the main conclusions which emerge from an examination of the above results. 1. Sounds agreeing in all but one feature are consistently judged as closer than those differing by two features. 2. Distances between points of articulation are ranked as follows: labial-alveolar, alveolar-velar, labial-velar, conforming fairly closely to articulatory facts. 3. Agreement in voicing is a much greater factor in judgments of similarity than agreement in lack of voicing. In fact, it is the most important factor of all those measured in the experiment. This perhaps not unexpected result presumably reflects the greater psychological weight of marked as against unmarked features and, it might be conjectured, would hold at least as strongly for agreement in nasality as against agreement in non-nasality.

A schematic representation of the "psychological" space of p, t, k, b, d, g, is portrayed in Figure 3.

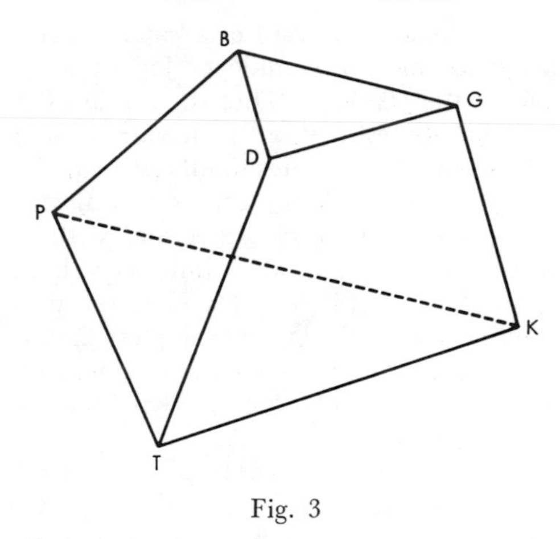

Fig. 3

In general, the linguistic coherence of the results obtained by this series of experiments suggests that it would be useful to extend them to other sets of consonants or vowels, employing the technique of experiment A on a larger sample of subjects.

Some Psychological Studies of Grammar[1]

GEORGE A. MILLER

Language is a topic that psychologists have long discussed from many points of view. We have treated it as a system of cognitive categories, as a medium for self-expression or for persuasion, therapy, and education, as a tool for ordering and controlling our other mental operations, and in many other ways. The approach I want to take here, however, is to regard language as an extremely complicated human skill. My aspiration is to examine that skill in detail in the hope of learning something more about what it consists of and how it functions.

When psychologists talk about language as a skill they frequently emphasize problems of *meaning*. Learning what different utterances mean is, of course, a fundamental skill that any user of a language must acquire. But meaning is too large a problem to solve all at once; we are forced to analyze it into more manageable parts. Consequently, there is in psychology a long tradition of defining meaning in terms of *reference*—in terms of an arbitrary association between some referrent and a vocal utterance—and then reducing reference in turn to a simple matter of *conditioning*. In that way many difficult problems of human language are transformed into simpler processes that can be studied in lower animals as well as in man, so the general similarities, rather than the specific differences between linguistic and other skills are emphasized.

I have no quarrel with that approach as long as we recognize that it treats only the simplest 1% of the psycholinguistic problem, and that our crucially important human skill in arranging symbols in novel and useful combinations is largely ignored by the successive reduction of language to meaning to reference to conditioning.

Our combinatorial power, which is so characteristically human, provides the psychological foundation for something that linguists usually call "grammar." I use the term defiantly, for I am fully aware that it is a grim and forbidding subject. It still reeks of the medieval trivium of grammar, logic, and rhetoric; it still reminds us vividly of all those end-

[1] Presidential address delivered before the Eastern Psychological Association in Atlantic City, New Jersey, April 27, 1962. The preparation of this document was supported in part by the National Science Foundation (NSF G-16486).

George A. Miller, "Some Psychological Studies of Grammar," *American Psychologist*, **17** (November, 1962), 748–762. Reprinted by permission of the author and publisher.

less and incomprehensible rules that our teachers tried to drum into us in grammar school. I wish I could gloss over it with some euphemism about "communication theory" or "verbal behavior," but, alas, I have no honest alternative but to admit that it is grammar that concerns me. It is grammar that is so significantly human, so specific to our species, so important for psychologists to understand more clearly. I do not in any sense wish to criticize psychological studies of the referential process, or of the intricate associative network that supports the referential process. My goal is rather to persuade psychologists, by argument and illustration, that there is much more to our linguistic skills than *just* the referential process. I do not see how we are going to describe language as a skill unless we find some satisfactory way to deal with grammar and with the combinatorial processes that grammar entails.

In order to illustrate what our linguistic skills are, I need to draw on certain basic concepts of modern linguistics. Fortunately, modern linguists have a somewhat different conception of grammar—a more scientific conception—that your English teacher had years ago. If I can communicate this newer conception of grammar well enough, perhaps it will revive some spark of interest that you may still have.

Consider a brief sample of the scientific approach to grammar. Let us choose a sentence so simple that we can have no trouble in analyzing it or in understanding the principles of analysis that are being used. Interesting sentences are much more complicated, of course, but the same principles are involved.

Take the sentence *Bill hit the ball.* To native speakers of English it is intuitively obvious that this sequence of words has a kind of structure, that some pairs of adjacent words are more closely related than others. For instance, *the ball* feels like a more natural unit than, say, *hit the.* One way to express that fact is to say that it is very easy to substitute a single word for *the ball,* but it is difficult to think of a single word for *hit the* that would not change the underlying structure of the sentence.

Table 1

Illustrating Constituent Analysis of a Simple Sentence

<table>
<tr><td>1</td><td>Bill</td><td>hit</td><td>the</td><td>ball</td></tr>
<tr><td>2</td><td>Bill</td><td>hit</td><td colspan="2">it</td></tr>
<tr><td>3</td><td>Bill</td><td colspan="3">acted</td></tr>
</table>

<table>
<tr><td rowspan="2">Bill</td><td rowspan="2">hit

V</td><td>the
T</td><td>ball
N</td></tr>
<tr><td colspan="2">NP_2</td></tr>
<tr><td>NP_1</td><td colspan="3">VP_1</td></tr>
</table>

On the first line at the top of Table 1 is the original sentence, *Bill hit the ball.* On line 2 is the derived sentence, *Bill hit it,* which is formed by substituting *it* for *the ball.* On line 3 there is another substitution—*acted* instead of *hit it*—and so we obtain the sentence *Bill acted.*

This process, in one form or another, is called "constituent analysis" by modern linguists (Harris, 1946; Nida, 1948; Pike, 1943; Wells, 1947). As described so far, it may sound as though it depends on your perseverance in searching for alternative words to substitute for each constituent. We can generalize the procedure, however, by introducing specific names for the various kinds of constituent units. Such a use of names is indicated in the lower half of the table. *The* is an article (symbolized *T*) and *ball* is a noun (symbolized *N*); together they form a noun phrase (symbolized *NP*). The verb *hit* combines with the noun phrase to form a verb phrase (symbolized *VP*). And, finally, the initial noun phrase *Bill* combines with the verb phrase to form a grammatical sentence. Thus each type of constituent has its own name.

As soon as we try to deal abstractly

with grammatical sentences, we become involved with these kinds of structured patterns. Obviously, we need some formal system to keep track of them. Several theoretical possibilities are currently available.

One way to deal with the constituent structure of a sentence is to use what linguists have come to call a *generative grammar* (Chomsky, 1956). The central idea was first developed for combinatorial systems in the study of formal logic (Post, 1936, 1944). Starting from a basic axiom, we apply rules of formation that permit us to rewrite the axiom in certain acceptable ways until we have finally derived the desired sentence. If the rules are formulated properly, only the grammatical sentences will be derivable; all other sentences will be ungrammatical.

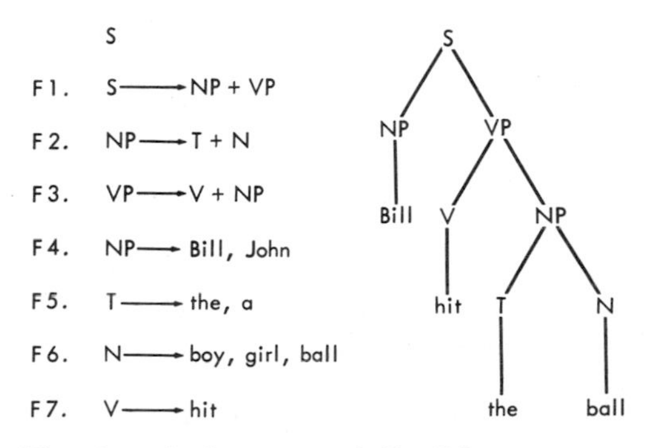

Fig. 1: A fragment of English grammar, phrased in terms of rewriting rules, illustrating a generative grammar.

Figure 1 illustrates how a small fragment of English grammar might be expressed in this manner. The basic axiom is *S*. The rewriting rules F1–7 permit us to form the sentence *Bill hit the ball* in a sequence of steps. First *S* is rewritten as *NP* + *VP*, according to rule F1. Then we can rewrite *NP* as *Bill* according to rule F4. Since there is not any rule available for rewriting *Bill*, we are forced to stop at this point. We can, however, rewrite *VP* according to rule F3, thus getting *Bill* + *V* + *NP*. In this way we can proceed as indicated by the tree graph on the right until the desired sentence is derived. Note that the diagram of the derivation corresponds to the constituent structure that we saw in Table 1.

The set of rewriting rules on the left of Figure 1 can be conveniently referred to as the grammar, and the set of sentences that the grammar generates defines the language. It is an important feature of this kind of grammar that there are terminal symbols, symbols that cannot be rewritten, and these comprise what we ordinarily recognize as the vocabulary of the language. According to this way of representing it, the vocabulary is included in the grammar.

Most people, when they encounter a generative grammar for the first time, get an impression that it means we must always form our sentences from axiom to terminal symbols, that we must always decide what phrases we want before we can decide what words we want to use. That is not a necessary assumption, however. These rules of formation, and the trees that represent the structures of the grammatical sentences, are purely formal devices for representing word groupings. How a sentence is actually manufactured or understood by users of the language—what particular cognitive processes he performs—is not a linguistic problem, but a psychological one.

Just to suggest how the same structural properties can be formalized in a different manner, therefore, consider briefly something that linguists have come to call a *categorial grammar* (Bar-Hillel, 1953; Lambek, 1958). This alternative was also borrowed from symbolic logic. (Cf. Ajdukiewicz, 1935.) According to this way of thinking about grammar, all the words and constituents must be classified into syntactic categories—corresponding roughly to what you may once have learned to call *parts of speech*—that, like chemical elements, are characterized by the ways they can combine with each other. I can make the reasoning clear most quickly, I think, by an example. In

a	t
ball	t\n
Bill	n
boy	t\n
girl	t\n
hit	(n\s)/n
John	n
the	t

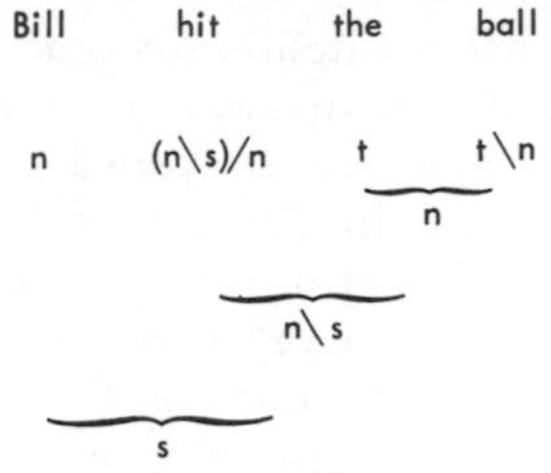

Bill hit the ball

n (n\s)/n t t\n

n

n\s

s

Fig. 2: A fragment of English grammar, phrased in terms of rules of cancellation, illustrating a categorial grammar.

Figure 2 on the left is a small segment of the English vocabulary, alphabetized as it would be in any proper dictionary. Listed after each entry are a set of symbols that indicate the syntactic categories that the word belongs to. In order to use those category markers you must understand a simple fact about the way they cancel, namely, that left and right cancellation are distinct. The word *ball* belongs to the category $t \backslash n$ (read "t under n") and has the characteristic that when a member of t is placed to its left the ts cancel, much as in ordinary algebra, leaving simply n. According to this way of representing the grammar, each word in the sentence is first replaced by its category symbol, then the category symbols are combined by left and right cancellation in all possible ways. If any result includes the single symbol s, then we know that we are dealing with a grammatical sentence; the order of cancellations indicates its underlying constituent structure. In the case of *Bill hit the ball,* the successive cancellations are shown on the right half of Figure 2.

There are obvious differences between categorial grammars and generative grammars. A categorial grammar starts with the words and works toward a single symbol that represents a grammatical sentence; a generative grammar seems to move in the opposite direction. Notice also that the categorial system seems to have all its grammatical rules included in the dictionary, whereas the generative system does just the opposite and includes the dictionary in its grammatical rules. In spite of these superficial differences, however, it has been possible to show—by stating each type of system precisely and studying its formal properties—that they are equivalent in the range of languages that they are capable of characterizing (Bar-Hillel, Gaifman, & Shamir, 1960).

That is enough grammatical theory for the moment. It is time now to stop and ask whether there are any psychological implications to all this. Are these systems of rules nothing more than a convenient way to summarize linguistic data or do they also have some relevance for the psychological processes involved? If human speech is a skilled act whose component parts are related to one another in the general manner that the linguists have been describing, what measurable consequences can we expect to find? What measurable effects would such skills have on our other psychological processes?

First, we might ask if there is any solid empirical evidence for the psychological reality of syntactic categories. One clear implication of these linguistic hypotheses would be that we must have our memory for the words of our language organized according to syntactic categories. Is there any evidence that such an organization exists? There is, of course. For example, psychologists who work with word associations have always claimed—although until recently they have done relatively little to explore the claim—that responses from adult subjects on a word-association test have a marked tendency to be members of the same syntactic category as are the stimuli that evoke them (Ervin, 1961). Certainly there is *some* lawful relation between the syntactic category of the stimulus word and the syntactic category of the response word, but exactly what the relation is may not be quite as simple as originally advertised. James Deese has recently begun to study the syntactic dimensions of word associations in considerable detail; in a few years we may be in a much better position to discuss these relations.

As further evidence for the psychological reality of syntactic categories, recall that our syntactic categories affect the way we memorize and remember new verbal materials. Here again everybody knows this relation exists, but few studies have tried to exploit it. One example should indicate what I have in mind. Murray Glanzer (1962) has shown that in learning paired associates it is clearly easier for us to learn associations between nonsense syllables and content words (nouns, verbs, adjectives, adverbs) than it is to learn associations between nonsense syllables and function words (pronouns, prepositions, conjunctions). That is to say, YIG-FOOD and MEF-THINK can be associated more readily than TAH-OF and KEX-AND, etc.

Of particular interest in Glanzer's studies, however, was the fact that function words become easier to learn when they are placed in contexts that seem more suitable to them. For instance, when triplets consisting of syllable-word-syllable were used, then TAH-OF-ZUM and KEX-AND-WOJ are learned faster than are YIG-FOOD-SEB and MEF-THINK-JAT. The point, of course, is that in the triplet context the function words are more readily bound to the nonsense syllables because they seem to form natural syntactic constituents in that context.

Where do syntactic categories come from? The development of these categories is currently a matter of great concern and excitement to several psychologists. Here again I will mention only one example, just to indicate the sort of thing that is going on. In a effort to discover how children learn the syntactic categories, Martin Braine (in press) has recently used very simple artificial languages to explore a process he calls "contextual generalization." Contextual generalization resembles stimulus generalization, where the verbal context plays the role of the stimulus. Will a verbal response learned in one context generalize to other contexts? If so, the process might help to explain how children learn the syntactic categories. Braine has his subjects learn a few of the nonsense sentences in the artificial language, then tests generalization to other sentences that the learners have not seen before.

There are limits to what we can explain with a notion such as contextual generalization. Some of its inadequacies may become apparent below when we consider transformational aspects of grammar. However, this is not the time and I am not the person to review Braine's work in detail. I mention it merely to persuade you that the psychological problems posed by these simple grammatical concepts are indeed well defined and that with a little patience and ingenuity it is even possible to coax them into the psychological laboratory.

One unavoidable fact about nonsense materials, however, is that they are nonsense; and artificial languages are inescapably artificial. I believe that the case for the psychological reality of these grammatical conventions might be strengthened if we would focus on the process of comprehension, rather than on the processes of learning and memory. In order to phrase the matter in a strong form, consider the following proposition: *We cannot understand a sentence until we are able to assign a constituent structure to it.*

Perhaps the simplest way to illustrate what I have in mind is to examine a sentence that is syntactically ambiguous. In Figure 3 we have an example of the sort that linguists like to consider: *They are eating apples* is really two sentences,

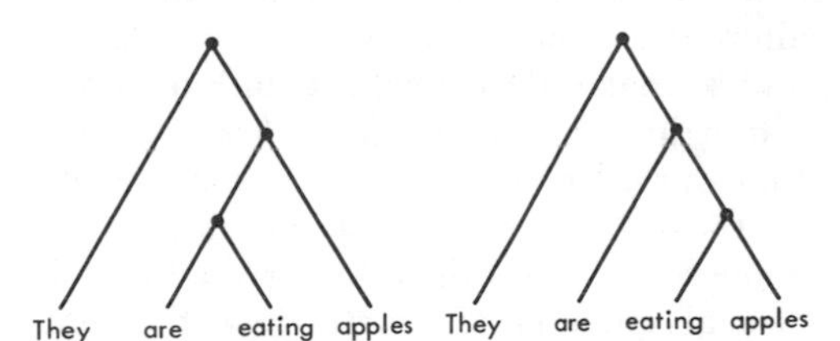

Fig. 3: Syntactic ambiguity arises when two different sentences are expressed by the same string of words.

even though both of them consist of exactly the same sequence of words. The sentence on the left would answer the question, *What are your friends doing?* The one on the right would answer the question, *Are those apples better for eating or for cooking?* On the basis of the linear sequence of words alone, however, we cannot tell which meaning is intended. Somehow, from the context, we must decide which syntactic structure is appropriate. Until we have decided on its structure, however, the sentence is ambiguous and we cannot completely understand its meaning. Thus, the proper functioning of our syntactic skill is an essential ingredient in the process of understanding a sentence. Again I emphasize that the problem of meaning involves a great deal more than the matter of reference.

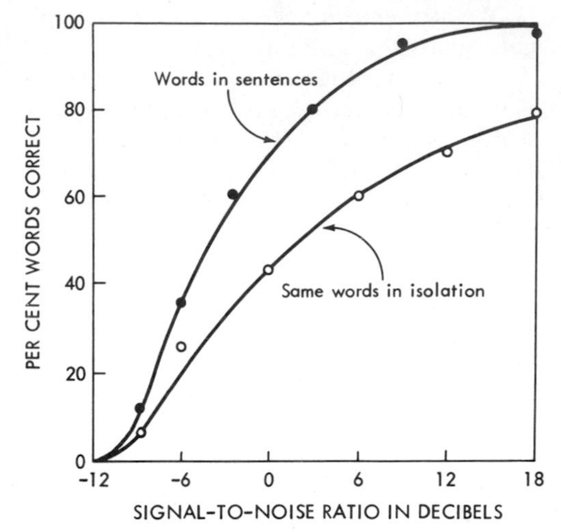

Fig. 4: The effect of sentence context on the intelligibility of words (from Miller, Heise, & Lichten, 1951).

For still another example of the psychological significance of syntactic structure let me draw on some of my own research on the perception of speech. Several years ago I participated in an experimental study showing that words can be perceived more accurately when they are heard in the context of a sentence than when they are pronounced separately as individual items on a list of test words (Miller, Heise, & Lichten, 1951). Those results are shown graphically in Figure 4, where the percentage of the words that were heard correctly is plotted as a function of the signal-to-noise ratio. As you can see, the same words were heard more accurately in sentences than in isolation.

In 1951 when we first reported this observation we argued that a sentence context serves to narrow down the set of alternative words that the listener expects, and so makes the perceptual task of recognition just that much easier. I still believe that our original explanation was correct, as far as it went. But it did not go far enough. It left open the psychologically crucial question of exactly *how* the sentence context reduced the variety of alternatives.

Words in sentences are often slurred and pronounced carelessly, yet we found they were more accurately perceived; an explanation in terms of reduced alternatives might account for that, of course. But words in sentences also run together. A listener must segment the ongoing flow of sound in order to discover the word units, yet this extra operation seemed to be no burden; the explanation in terms of reduced alternatives says nothing at all about this extra operation of segmentation. And, perhaps, worst of all, the explanation seemed to imply that a listener makes separate, successive decisions about the identity of the separate, successive words he is hearing in the sentence. Since words can be spoken at a rate of two or three per second, the rate at which successive sets of alternative words must be conjured up, recognized, and replaced by the listener is really quite remarkable. In short, the more I thought about how the sentence context exerts its helpful influence, the more complicated it seemed.

In order to explore the matter further, therefore, we performed the following experiment (Miller, 1962): First, we drew up a list of 25 monosyllabic English words and divided it into five sublists of

Table 2

FIVE SUBVOCABULARIES USED TO EXPLORE THE PERCEPTUAL EFFECTS OF GRAMMATICAL CONTEXT

1	2	3	4	5
Don	Brought	His	Black	Bread
He	Has	More	Cheap	Sheep
Red	Left	No	Good	Shoes
Slim	Loves	Some	Wet	Socks
Who	Took	The	Wrong	Things

five words each, as shown in Table 2. These sublists are constructed in such a way that if you chose any words successively from sublists 1, 2, 3, 4, and 5, they will form a grammatical English sentence. The subjects in this experiment spent an entire summer with me—four afternoons a week—listening to these 25 words in the presence of a masking noise. To say they knew the lists perfectly is a gross understatement; before the summer was over we all were thoroughly sick of them.

We tested four separate conditions. The first two conditions provided a kind of control. In one case, successive words were selected from the entire set of 25 words in random order. In the second case, successive words were selected in random order from one of the five sublists of five words. The words were spoken in groups of five and heard by the listeners against a background of random masking noise. The listeners' responses were spoken aloud and individually recorded, so the tests did not need to be delayed in order to allow time for the listeners to write down their responses. As we had expected, the words were easier to recognize when they occurred as one of 5 alternatives than when they were one of 25 alternatives. Those two control conditions provided the calibration we needed for the two remaining experimental conditions.

In the third test condition, words were chosen from the subgroups successively so as to form grammatical sentences: *Don has no wet things,* for example. And in the fourth test condition, the order of the subgroups was reversed, so that the sequence of words was not grammatical: *things wet no has Don,* for example. Since these backward strings were based on exactly the same sublists of alternatives as were the sentences, we called them pseudosentences.

Our question, of course, was whether there would be any difference between the intelligibility of the sentences and the intelligibility of the pseudosentences. The answer was both yes and no. When we paused between successive strings of five words and gave the listeners a chance to think about what they had just heard, there was no difference; sentences and pseudosentences gave the same results, and both were the same as the results for the 5-word sublists.

When the test was speeded up, however, by eliminating the pauses between successive sentences, a difference appeared. Under time pressure we got the results shown in Figure 5. On the left the word intelligibility scores are plotted as a function of the signal-to-noise ratio for all four test conditions. The sentences and the 5-word vocabularies give one function; the pseudosentences and the 25-word vocabularies give another. On the right are the corresponding functions obtained when the scoring unit was the entire sentence, rather than the individual words.

The results with pseudosentences demonstrated that when time is short and words do not follow a familiar grammatical pattern, subjects are unable to exploit a narrower range of alternatives. They do not have time to hear each word separately, decide what it was, then anticipate the next set of alternatives, listen to the next word, etc. At slow speeds they had time to make separate decisions about each word, but not at the more rapid speeds that would be characteristic of normal, conversational speech. All they could do with the rapid pseudosentences was to treat the successive words as if they were chosen randomly from the larger set of 25 alternatives.

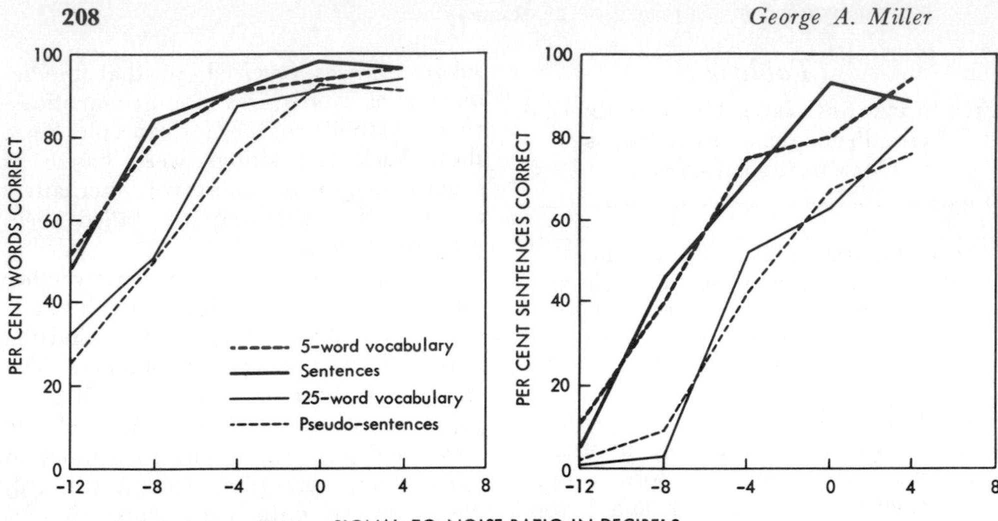

Fig. 5: Word intelligibility (left) and sentence intelligibility (right) scores indicate that under time pressure grammatical contexts facilitate speech perception and ungrammatical contexts do not, even though the number of different words involved is not altered by the context (after Miller, 1962).

Thus it is possible to show that the sentence context does indeed serve to narrow the range of alternative words, but the mechanism involved seems to be more complicated than we had originally imagined. In addition to reducing the variety of competing alternatives, the sentence context also enables us to organize the flow of sound into decision units larger than individual words—perhaps into units similar to the linguist's constituents—and so to make our perceptual decisions about what we are hearing at a slower and more comfortable rate.

In short, I am arguing that in ordinary conversation the functional unit of speech perception is usually larger than a single word or a single morpheme and more nearly the size and shape of a syntactic constituent. As long as we studied speech perception by using lists of words spoken in isolation, the existence of those larger units was not apparent. As soon as we begin to combine words into continuous sequences, however, we discover that the familiar grammatical sequences form unique and distinctive patterns of words. And that, of course, is just what a linguistic theory of syntactic structures would lead us to expect.

The experiment I have just described argues for the existence of perceptual units larger than a single word. It does not, however, argue in favor of any particular type of structure underlying those larger units. That is, it does not show that some form of grammatical structure must be preferred to, say, a Markovian structure of the kind that communication theorists talk about (Shannon, 1948, 1951).

In order to illustrate the psychological reality of these syntactic structures, we must consider the critical feature that these grammatical systems admit, but that Markovian structures do not—namely, the possibility of unlimited self-embedding (Chomsky, 1959). Again I will draw upon my own research, but now in the field of verbal learning and verbal memory.

One important feature of the grammatical rules that linguists have proposed is that they are recursive. That is to say, there is no limit to the number of times that the same rule can be applied in the derivation of a sentence. In general, three different kinds of recursiveness are permitted by our grammatical rules. In Figure 6 we see syntactic structures illustrating each of the three types: left-recursive, right-recursive, and self-embedding. All three are characterized by the fact that a given type of constituent—labeled "A" in this figure—can appear as a part of itself; where it appears—at the left end, at the right end, or in the middle—determines the type of recursiveness. In English, for example, a left-recursive construction would be *The obviously not very well dressed man is here,* or *John's father's car's roof's color is red.* Right-recursive structures can be strung out at great length; a famous example is *This is the cow with the crumpled horn that tossed the dog that worried the cat that killed the rat that ate the malt that lay in the house that Jack built.* This same sentence can be rephrased, however, to illustrate a self-embedded construction. We can build up the self-embedded version step by step:

The rat ate the malt,
The rat that the cat killed ate the malt,
The rat that the cat that the dog worried killed ate the malt,
The rat that the cat that the dog that the cow tossed worried killed ate the malt, etc.

It is fairly clear that even though the self-embedded version is perfectly grammatical, it is far more complicated psychologically—harder to understand and to remember—than the right-recursive version.

There are some relatively profound reasons why this should be the case. A language that could be characterized entirely in terms of right-recursive rules could be described in terms of a Markov process (Chomsky, 1956; Chomsky & Miller, 1958). The possibility of unlimited self-embedding, however, means that a Markov system is too simple to serve as a grammar for a natural language. Of more practical significance, however, is the fact that self-embedding by its very nature places heavier demands on the temporary storage capacity of any device

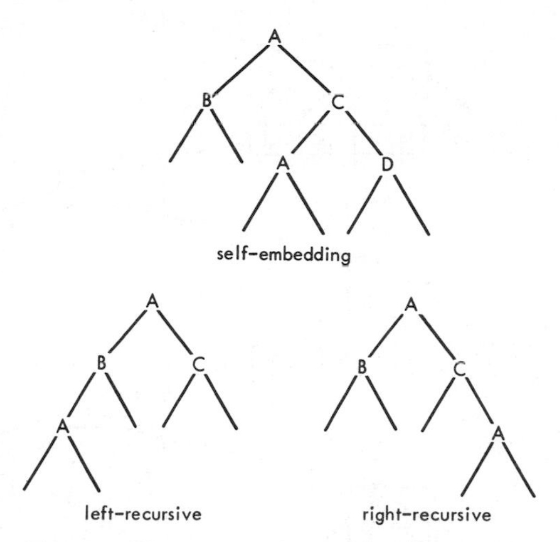

Fig. 6: Illustrating three types of recursive rules that permit an element of type A to be part of an element of type A.

that attempts to cope with it—far heavier than do either left-recursive or right-recursive constructions. And, since our temporary memory is quite limited, we can experience great difficulty following grammatical rules in this type of syntactic structure.

In order to explore this matter we can take some sentences with very complicated syntactic structure and ask people to repeat them. For example, one sentence I have worked with is diagramed in Figure 7:

The race that the car that the people whom the obviously not very well dressed man called sold won was held last summer.

Then, as a control, the same words were arranged in a right-branching structure:

The obviously not very well dressed man called the people who sold the car that won the race that was held last summer.

I read such sentences as these to college students who tried to repeat them as accurately as possible.

As you would expect, on the basis of almost any theory of verbal learning that

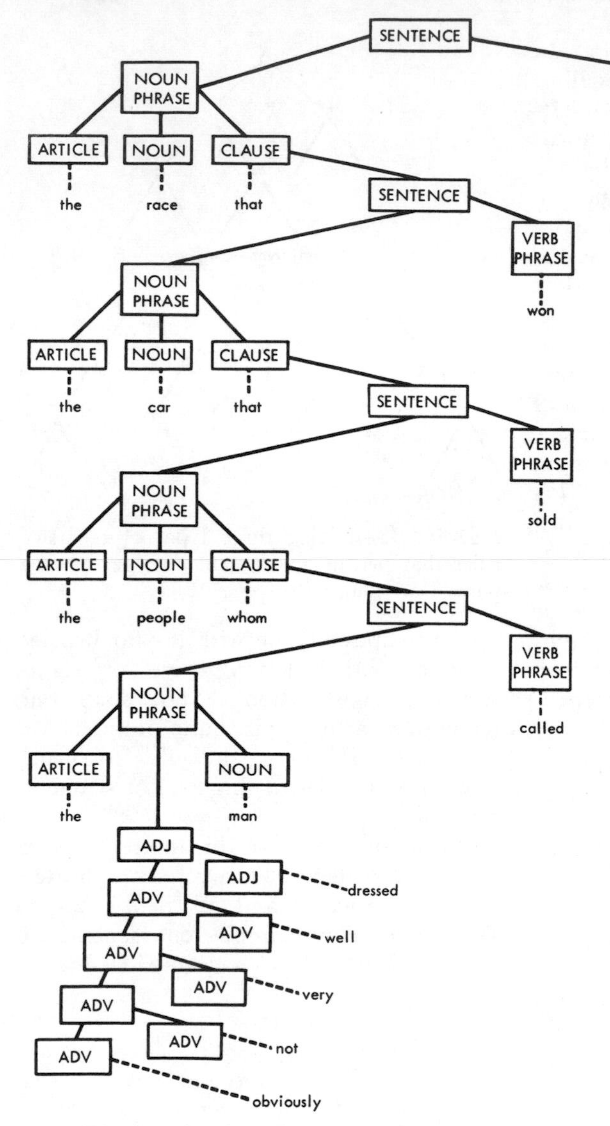
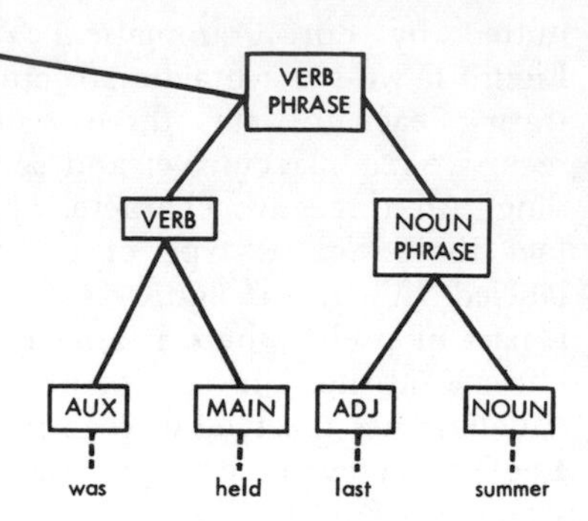

Fig. 7: Syntactic structure of the self-embedded sentence, "The race that the car that the people whom the obviously not very well dressed man called sold won was held last summer."

I can imagine, right-recursive sentences are easier for English-speaking people to repeat and to memorize than are self-embedded sentences. I will not summarize the quantitative results, but I think that some of the qualitative results are amusing. For example, after hearing the self-embedded sentence only once, subject may say:

The race—that the car—that the clearly not so well dressed man—saw—sold one—last summer?

The subjects who respond in this way are quite interesting; their intonation is characteristic of the recitation of a list of unrelated phrases, not the utterance of a sentence. And I was also interested to note that the number of items on the list would usually be about six or seven, close to the span of immediate memory for those subjects (Miller, 1956).

The second time such a subject hears the same sentence he may still recite it as though it were a list, but with somewhat more accurate recall of the individual items. By the second or third time through, however, there may be an "Aha!" experience, and from then on he tries to give it a normal, sentence intonation.

These examples should indicate why I believe that sentences are not just arbitrary chains of vocal responses, but that they have a complex inner structure of their own. How we perceive them, understand them, and remember them depends upon what we decide about their structure. Just as we induce a three-dimensional space underlying the two-dimensional pattern on the retina, so we must induce a syntactic structure underlying the linear string of sounds in a sentence. And just as the student of space perception must have a good understanding of projective geometry, so a student of psycholinguistics must have a good understanding of grammar.

There is much more to grammar, however, than just the system of syntactic categories and constituent structure. Let me lapse once again into linguistics long enough to introduce the transformational rules of grammar (Chomsky, 1956, 1957; Harris, 1952a, 1952b, 1957). Go back to the simple sentence *Bill hit the ball.* But now observe that there are a large number of other sentences that seem to be closely related to it: the negative, *Bill didn't hit the ball;* the passive, *The ball was hit by Bill;* various interrogative forms, *Did Bill hit the ball?, What did Bill hit?, Who hit the ball?,* and so on.

Linguists disagree about the best way to describe these different kinds of relations among sentences. One opinion is that we learn "sentence frames" that we keep filed away in a sort of sentence-frame dictionary. The declarative, interrogative, affirmative, negative, active, passive, compound, complex, etc., sentence frames are all supposed to be learned separately and to have no intrinsic relation to one another. A second opinion agrees with the first in seeing no intrinsic relations among the various types of sentences, but argues that there are too many different frames to learn them all separately. The advocates of this second view say that there must be rules, similar to those we have just been discussing, that the talker can use actively to manufacture a grammatical frame as it is needed. But, according to this view, there is one set of rules for manufacturing active, declarative, affirmative sentences, another set of rules for manufacturing passive, declarative, affirmative sentences, etc.

On the other side of the argument are linguists who wish to describe the relations among these sentences in terms of explicit rules of transformation. One version of this view, which I favor, says that we do indeed have a scheme for manufacturing simple, active, declarative sentences, but we can apply rules of transformation to change them from active to passive, or from declarative to interrogative, or from affirmative to negative, or to combine them, etc. This transformational scheme shortens the statement of a grammar considerably, since many rules need be stated only once and need not be repeated for each separate type of sentence. And once you have admitted such rules to your grammar you quickly discover many uses for them.

Transformational rules are both complicated and powerful, however, so many linguists are reluctant to use them. There has been some esthetic disagreement about which kind of simplicity is more desirable in a linguistic theory. Is it better to have a long list of short rules, or a short list of long rules?

The arguments among linguists—who seem to rely heavily on their linguistic intuitions, on logical counterexamples, and on appeals to the economy and elegance of simplicity—can get rather bitter at times. And it is by no means obvious a priori that the most economical and efficient formal description of the linguistic data will necessarily describe the psychological process involved when we actually utter or understand a grammatical sentence. In the hope of providing a more experimental foundation to the argument, therefore, we have recently begun to test some of the psychological implications of a transformational linguistic theory. Our efforts to explore this aspect of linguistic skill are still tentative, however, so the two examples to be mentioned below are still in the enthusiastic stage and subject to revision as more data accumulate. But they will serve to support the main point, that an experimental approach to these matters is both possible and (potentially) rewarding.

Perhaps the simplest way to study grammatical transformations experimentally would be to tell a person what transformation to perform, then give him a sentence, and measure how long it takes him to make the transformation. We intend to explore the transformation process in just that way, but at the moment we are not prepared to report on the results. Instead, therefore, let me tell you about a more indirect method—a sentence-matching test—that Kathryn Ojemann McKean, Dan Slobin, and I have been using.

Our first assumption is that the more complicated a grammatical transformation is, the longer it will take people to perform it. The purpose of the test is to give subjects a set of sentences to transform and to see how many of them they can complete in a fixed interval of time. Of course, there is much more that we would like to know about the transformation than just how long it takes, but at least this is one way to begin.

One form of the test that we have used contains 18 basic, or kernel sentences: all of the sentences that can be formed by taking *Jane, Joe,* or *John* as the first word, *liked* or *warned* as the second word, and *the small boy, the old woman,* or *the young man* as the final phrase. In addition, we used the corresponding sets of 18 sentences that can be produced from those kernels by negative, passive, and passive-negative transformations. Thus, for example, *Joe liked the small boy* appears in the set of kernels; *Joe didn't like the small boy* appears in the set of negatives; *The small boy was liked by Joe* appears in the set of passives; and *The small boy wasn't liked by Joe* appears in the set of passive-negatives.

A test is constructed by taking two of these four sets of 18 sentences and asking people to pair them off. Take as an example the test that requires people to match passive sentences with their corresponding passive-negative forms. The test sheet looks something like Table 3. Half of the pairs are arranged with the passive sentences on the left, half with the passive-negative sentences on the left. This produces two lists, a left-hand list and a right-hand list, which are presented to the subject. Similar tests can be constructed for all the other pairs of sentence types.

Before the two lists of sentences are presented, the subject studies a sample pair of sentences that illustrates the desired transformation, and he prepares himself to perform the same transformation (or its inverse) on the test sentences. When the signal is given to start, he begins with the first sentence at the top of the left column, identifies its type and decides whether the transformation or its inverse is called for, performs the indicated transformation (or its inverse), searches for the transformed sentence in the right-hand column, then places the number of the transformed sentence to the left of the original sentence in the left-hand column. He continues in this way down the left-hand list until, at the end of one minute, he is instructed to stop. This general strategy is shown in Figure 8 by a flow chart.

As a control condition, six further tests

Table 3

EXAMPLE OF A SENTENCE-MATCHING TEST DESIGNED TO STUDY TRANSFORMATIONS BETWEEN AFFIRMATIVE-PASSIVE AND NEGATIVE-PASSIVE SENTENCES

—The old woman was warned by Joe	1. The small boy wasn't warned by John
—The small boy wasn't liked by Joe	2. The old woman wasn't warned by Jane
—The young man was liked by John	3. The young man was warned by Jane
—The old woman wasn't liked by Joe	4. The old woman wasn't warned by Joe
—The young man wasn't warned by Jane	5. The old woman was liked by John
—The small boy was liked by Jane	6. The small boy wasn't liked by John
—The young man wasn't liked by Jane	7. The young man wasn't warned by John
—The old woman was warned by Jane	8. The old woman was warned by John
—The small boy wasn't warned by Joe	9. The young man wasn't warned by Joe
—The small boy was warned by John	10. The small boy was warned by Jane
—The young man was warned by John	11. The small boy was warned by Joe
—The small boy wasn't warned by Jane	12. The small boy wasn't liked by Jane
—The small boy was liked by John	13. The young man wasn't liked by John
—The young man wasn't liked by Joe	14. The young man was liked by Jane
—The young man was warned by Joe	15. The old woman was liked by Joe
—The old woman was liked by Jane	16. The old woman wasn't liked by Jane
—The old woman wasn't liked by John	17. The small boy was liked by Joe
—The old woman wasn't warned by John	18. The young man was liked by Joe

required no transformations at all; the sentences in the left column were simply matched with the identical sentences in the right column (where the right column was the same one used in the corresponding experimental test). From these measurements on the identity transformation, therefore, we could estimate how long subjects required to read down the right-hand column, find the sentence they wanted, and write its number in the appropriate space. We assume that on these control tests the subject's strategy is just the same as on the experimental tests, except that the steps enclosed in dotted lines in Figure 8—the transformational steps—can be omitted. Therefore, we can subtract the time spent searching and writing from the total time, and so can obtain an estimate of the time required to recognize, analyze, and transform the sentences.

We knew, of course, that subtracting reaction times involves some of the oldest pitfalls in psychology, and we would not have been terribly surprised if the results had been meaningless. Fortunately, we got fairly large and (we believe) sensible differences for the various kinds of transformations.

Consider what you might expect to get on the basis of various theories that grammarians have talked about. Linguists who look upon the four different sentence types as four separate, coordinate, and independent sentence frames would probably expect that moving between any two of them should be about as difficult as moving between any other two. This line of reasoning is depicted in Figure 9, where the letters indicate the various kinds of sentences—kernels, negatives, passives, and passive-negatives—and the lines between them indicate all the possible relations between them. A grammatical theory that says that all sentence frames are coordinate would assign the same difficulty to every one of those connecting lines. It is just one step from any type of sentence to any other type of sentence.

On the other hand, a transformational theorist would like to reduce those six direct relations to a pair of transformations: one for the affirmative-negative aspect and one for the active-passive aspect. This line of reasoning leads to

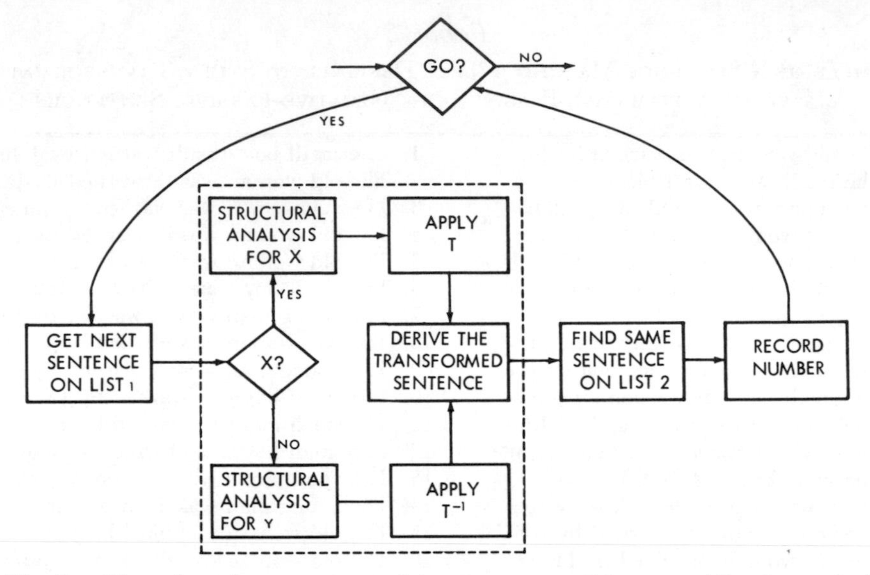

Fig. 8: Flow chart for strategy used in sentence-matching test. (On the control tests—identity transform—the operations inside the dashed line could presumably be omitted.)

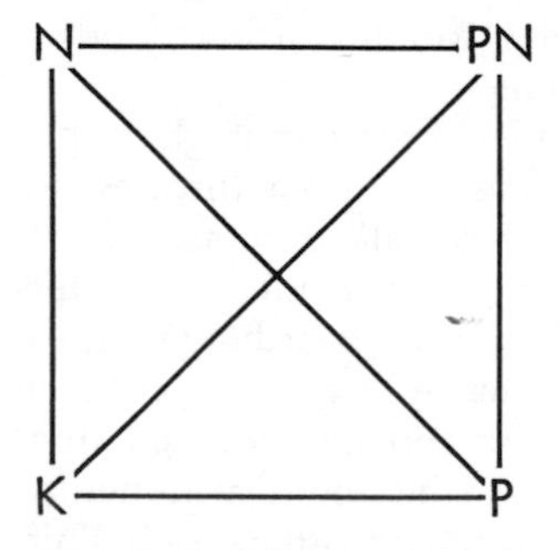

Fig. 9: Graph indicating six pairs of sentence types that can be formed with kernel sentences (K), negatives (N), passives (P), and passive-negatives (PN).

Figure 10, where the lines indicate the direct results of applying a grammatical transformation. In this view of things, two steps are required to go between kernels and passive-negative sentences, or between passives and negatives. Therefore, a transformational theory leads us to expect that these diagonal relations will take longer to perform than the simpler, one-step relations.

Some data are given in Table 4. For each type of test, Table 4 gives the average number of sentences that our 60 subjects were able to transform and/or locate in one minute. The reciprocals give the time per sentence for the average subject. And in the right-hand column is the result we are looking for—the estimates (in seconds) of the time it took to perform the grammatical transformations.

It is apparent that some tests were easier than others. Look at the pattern: the top two of these estimated times involve only a negative transformation or its inverse; they seem to occur rather quickly. The second pair of these estimated times involves only the passive transformation or

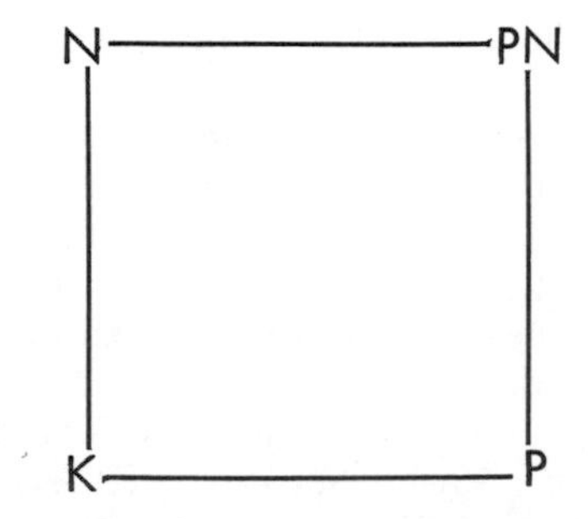

Fig. 10: Graph indicating one-step transformations.

Table 4

THE MEAN NUMBERS OF SENTENCES MATCHED CORRECTLY IN ONE MINUTE, WITH TRANSFORMATIONS (EXPER.) AND WITHOUT (CONTR.), IS USED TO ESTIMATE THE AVERAGE TRANSFORMATION TIME PER SENTENCE ($N = 60$)

Test condition	*Mean number of sentences correct*		*Time for average subject (secs.)*		*Estimated transformation times (secs.)*
	Exper.	Contr.	Exper.	Contr.	
K:N	7.5	8.7	8.0	6.9	1.1
P:PN	5.5	6.4	10.5	9.3	1.2
K:P	8.1	10.1	7.4	5.9	1.5
PN:N	6.7	8.5	8.9	7.1	1.8
K:PN	6.9	10.0	8.7	6.0	2.7
N:P	5.6	8.4	10.7	7.2	3.5

its inverse; these are slightly longer, which would agree with one's intuitive impression that the passive is a more complicated transformation. And, finally, the bottom two estimated times involve both the negative and the passive transformations; on the average, they are the slowest of all.

In their gross outline, therefore, these data support the transformational theorists. In their fine detail, however, they raise several interesting questions. Before we spend too much effort answering them, however, we had better make sure the data are correct. At the present time, therefore, we are trying to perfect our measuring instrument in order to obtain results accurate enough to test in detail some of the available linguistic theories about the transformational process.

There are, of course, many other psychological methods that we might use to test the validity of a transformational theory of grammar. One that I believe holds considerable promise has been proposed by Jacques Mehler; he has only begun to explore it, but already the results look interesting. His idea was to present a list of sentences for people to learn and to score the results in terms of the syntactic errors that they made. For example,

The typist has copied the paper is a kernel sentence;
The student hasn't written the essay is a negative sentence;
The photograph has been made by the boy is a passive sentence;
Has the train hit the car? is a query;
The passenger hasn't been carried by the airplane is a passive-negative sentence;
Hasn't the girl worn the jewel? is a negative query;
Has the discovery been made by the biologist? is a passive query; and
Hasn't the house been bought by the man? is a passive-negative query.

Other sets of sentences can easily be generated, of course, by permuting the kernels with the various transformations.

Mehler presents such a list of sentences—without the syntactic comments, of course—to his subjects, who then try to write them out word for word. He gives them five trials, scrambling the order on each trial.

The first question, of course, is whether or not subjects make any syntactic errors in this situation. Mehler's preliminary results are shown in Figure 11. Errors have been grouped into three main classes: (*a*) errors of omission, (*b*) syntactic errors, and (*c*) other types of errors (which includes the introduction of extraneous words and the confusion of two different sentences). As you can see from the figure, the probability that a sentence will be

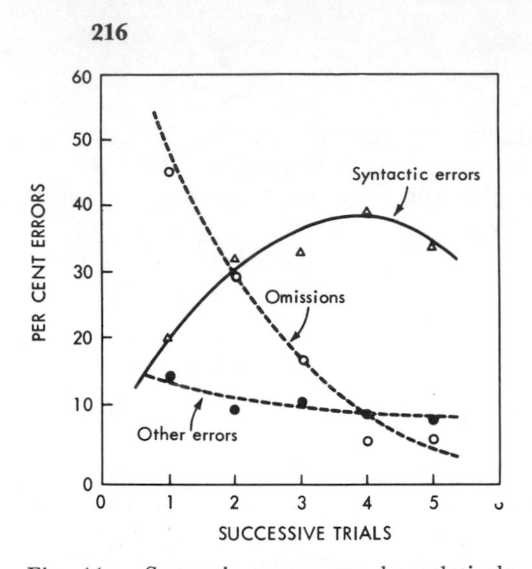

Fig. 11: Syntactic errors can be relatively common in the free recall of sentences that are of different types.

completely missing in recall decreases very rapidly, and the probability of semantic confusion is low and relatively constant. The bulk of the errors that people make on this task are of a syntactic nature—they recall the sentence, but they alter its syntactic form.

For several years now I have held rather stubbornly to the opinion that there is an operation called "recoding" that frequently plays an important role in remembering verbal materials. Let me develop this opinion into a specific hypothesis about Mehler's experiment.

The hypothesis is that what people remember is the kernel sentence, but that when you ask them to recite the original sentence exactly, they supplement their memory of the kernel with a footnote about the syntactic structure. This variant of Woodworth's "schema-plus-correction" method of recoding turns *Hasn't the girl worn the jewel?* into the kernel sentence *The girl has worn the jewel,* plus some kind of implicit code that—if remembered correctly—enables the subject to make the necessary grammatical transformations when he is called upon to recite the original sentence.

The relations among the eight types of sentences that Mehler uses are indicated in Figure 12. The lines connect the types of sentences that would become confused if the subject remembered incorrectly just one of the three transformations that he has to keep track of. If my recoding hypothesis was correct, of course, I would expect most of the syntactic errors to involve just one of the three transformations, and two and three step errors would be relatively less frequent.

Before Mehler's data were analyzed I had expected to find a strong shift toward the recall of kernels. There is some tendency for people to favor kernel sentences when they recall, but it is insignificant and probably would not have been noticed at all if we had not been looking for it. What seems to happen, however, is actually simpler than I had expected. The subjects quickly get the impression that about half the sentences are negative, half are passives, half are questions; in recall, therefore, they try a little probability matching. If a transformation is forgotten, it is not simply omitted; instead, a guess is made, based upon the overall impression of how often each transformation should be applied.

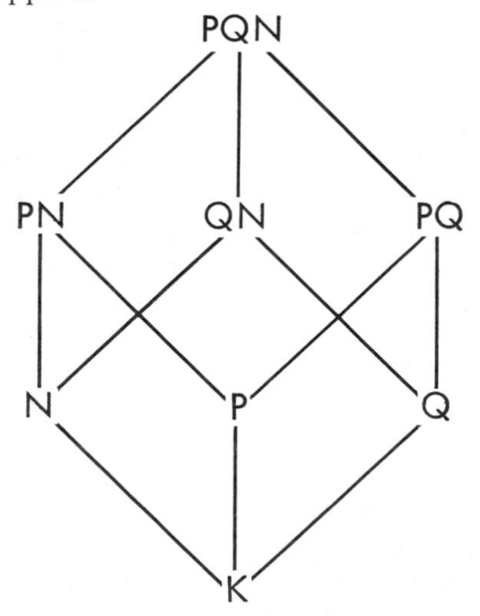

Fig. 12: Graph indicating relations among eight types of sentences formed by negative (N), passive (P), and interogative (Q) transformations.

The upshot of this argument was that I constructed a very simple hypothesis, based on this kernel-plus-code idea, plus an absurd but convenient assumption that each of the four elements necessary for correct recall—that is to say, the kernel and the three transforms—was recalled independently of the other three. Thus the probability of a correct recall would be simply the product of the probabilities of recalling each of the four components, and the probability of one syntactic error would be the product of the probability of recalling the kernel and the probability of getting two transformations right and one wrong, and so forth. The simple result of this line of reasoning is the following equation. Given these definitions: k = probability of recalling the kernal; $p = 1 - q$ = probability of recalling transform; m = number of transforms to be recalled; P_i = probability of recall with i syntactic errors; then, on the assumption of independent recall of the kernels and the séveral transformations, we have:

$$P_i = k \binom{m}{m-i} p^{m-i} q^i$$

Now by lumping together all of Mehler's 15 subjects on all trials for all sentences, we can estimate the necessary probabilities and then see if the assumption of independence will predict the observed distribution of errors. The results are shown in Table 5. The estimated probability of recalling the kernel was 0.66. The estimated probabilities for getting each of the transformations correct were all very close to 0.80, so that a single value was used for all three. And when we put these parameter values into the equation for P_i, we obtain fairly good agreement between data and hypothesis. Or to state the matter more carefully, on the basis of Mehler's preliminary evidence, we cannot reject the hypothesis that sentences were recoded and that each of the four components of the kernel-plus-code was remembered correctly or incorrectly independently of the others.

Table 5

Distribution of Syntactic Errors in Free Recall of Sentences

Errors: i	0	1	2	3
Calculated P_i	0.34	0.25	0.06	0.01
Obtained P_i	0.36	0.20	0.09	0.01

Here again our work has only begun and so my report of it is still colored by all the natural enthusiasm and prejudices that seem to accompany every programmatic statement. My colleagues and I now see syntactic structure as an important variable to explore. The logicians and linguists are currently defining the theoretical issues with great precision, so that the full range of our experimental and psychometric methods can be brought to bear. I am enthusiastically convinced that such studies have an important contribution to make to the science of psychology.

In the course of this work I seem to have become a very old-fashioned kind of psychologist. I now believe that mind is something more than a four-letter, Anglo-Saxon word—human minds exist and it is our job as psychologists to study them. Moreover, I believe that one of the best ways to study a human mind is by studying the verbal systems that it uses. But what I want most to communicate here is my strong conviction that such a program is not only important, but that it is also possible, even now, with the relatively crude and limited empirical weapons that we have already developed. In the years ahead I hope we will see an increasing flow of new and exciting research as more psychologists discover the opportunities and the challenge of psycholinguistic theory and research.

References

Ajdukiewicz, K. Die syntaktische Konnexität. *Stud. phil.*, 1935, 1, 1–27.

BAR-HILLEL, Y. A quasiarithmetical notation for syntactic description. *Language,* 1953, 29, 47–58.

BAR-HILLEL, Y., GAIFMAN, C., & SHAMIR, E. On categorial and phrase-structure grammars. *Bull. Res. Council Israel,* 1960, 9F, 1-16.

BRAINE, M. D. S. On learning the grammatical order of words. *Psychol. Rev.*, in press.

CHOMSKY, N. Three models for the description of language. *IRE Trans. Inform. Theory*, 1956, IT-2, 113–124.

CHOMSKY, N. *Syntactic structures.* 's-Gravenhage: Mouton, 1957.

CHOMSKY, N. On certain formal properties of grammars. *Inform. Control,* 1959, 2, 137–167.

CHOMSKY, N., & MILLER, G. A. Finite state languages. *Inform. Control*, 1958, 1, 91–112.

ERVIN, S. M. Changes with age in the verbal determinants of word-association. *Amer. J. Psychol.*, 1961, 74, 361–372.

GLANZER, M. Grammatical category: A rote learning and word association analysis. *J. verbal Learn. verbal Behav.*, 1962, 1, 31-41.

HARRIS, Z. S. From morpheme to utterance. *Language*, 1946, 22, 161–183.

HARRIS, Z. S. Discourse analysis. *Language*, 1952, 28, 1–30. (a)

HARRIS, Z. S. Discourse analysis: A sample text. *Language*, 1952, 28, 474–494. (b)

HARRIS, Z. S. Co-occurrence and transformation in linguistic structure. *Language*, 1957, 33, 283–340.

LAMBEK, J. The mathematics of sentence structure. *Amer. math. Mon.*, 1958, 65, 154–169.

MILLER, G. A. The magical number seven, plus or minus two. *Psychol. Rev.*, 1956, 63, 81–97.

MILLER, G. A. Decision units in the perception of speech. *IRE Trans. Inform. Theory*, 1962, IT-8, 81–83.

MILLER, G. A., HEISE, G. A., & LICHTEN, W. The intelligibility of speech as a function of the context of the test materials. *J. exp. Psychol.*, 1951, 41, 329–335.

NIDA, E. A. The analysis of immediate constituents. *Language*, 1948, 24, 168–177.

PIKE, K. L. Taxemes and immediate constituents. *Language,* 1943, 19, 65–82.

POST, E. L. Finite combinatory processes: Formulation I. *J. symb. Logic*, 1936, 1, 103–105.

POST, E. L. Recursively enumerable sets of positive integers and their decision problems. *Bull. Amer. Math. Soc.*, 1944, 50, 284–316.

SHANNON, C. E. A mathematical theory of communication. *Bell Sys. tech. J.*, 1948, 27, 379–423.

SHANNON, C. E. Prediction and entropy of printed English. *Bell Sys. tech. J.*, 1951, 30, 50–64.

WELLS, R. S. Immediate constituents. *Language*, 1947, 23, 81–117.

Some Perceptual Consequences of Linguistic Rules[1]

GEORGE A. MILLER
and STEPHEN ISARD

Miller, Heise, and Lichten (1950) have reported that content words (nouns, verbs, adjectives, adverbs) are more intelligible when heard in the context of a grammatical sentence than when scrambled and spoken in isolation as items on a list. They attributed this difference to a contextual reduction in the numbers of alternative words among which a listener must choose as he hears the successive words in the sentence; they found that, other things being equal, the smaller the set of alternative words, the easier it was to identify any particular word. Exactly how a listener uses the grammatical context to reduce the number of alternative words, however, was left as an open question. In the present paper an attempt is made to phrase that question more precisely.

Presumably, anyone who speaks a natural language knows (tacitly, at least) that successive words in that language are normally chosen subject to certain constraints; to violate those constraints is to invite misunderstanding and failure of communication. The constraints are usually classified according to their origins in the *grammatical, semantic,* or *pragmatic* rules of the language. These rules must be known and respected by all users of the language, talkers and listeners alike.

The present study is based on the assumption that in order to understand a spoken sentence it is necessary to process the received acoustic signal according to these linguistic rules and that perception is more accurate when this processing can be performed in its habitual fashion. That is to say, the linguistic rules will normally serve to limit the number of alternatives from which a listener must choose.

Grammatical rules are of two types, phonological and syntactic. In the experiments to be discussed here we will ignore phonological rules, because the same words are always used and only their verbal context is manipulated. The acoustic stimulus is, of course, critically important for the accurate perception of speech, but

[1] This research was supported in part by funds granted by Public Health Service Research Grant No. M-05120-02 from the National Institutes of Health, by the National Science Foundation Grant No. NSF G-16486, and by the Carnegie Corporation of New York, to Harvard University, Center for Cognitive Studies. We are indebted to Professor N. Chomsky for valuable comments and criticisms of this work.

George A. Miller and Stephen Isard, "Some Perceptual Consequences of Linguistic Rules." Reprinted by permission from *Journal of Verbal Learning and Verbal Behavior,* 2 (1963), 217–228.

simple acoustic differences cannot be used to explain the perceptual effects to be reported. We are, therefore, interested here principally in the syntactic component of the grammar.

An adequate characterization of syntax must, among other things, provide for every sentence a description of the possible phrase structures underlying the string of words that comprise it (cf. Chomsky, 1957). For example, the syntactic rules must specify that the sentence, *A boy hit the ball,* consists of a noun phrase, *A boy,* followed by a verb phrase, *hit the ball.* The noun phrase in turn is made up of an article, *A*, and a noun, *boy*; the verb phrase consists of a verb, *hit,* and another noun phrase, *the ball.* Thus, the structural description of the total sentence can be indicated by parentheses; (*A boy*) (*hit* (*the ball*)), where it is understood that each subunit is of a particular syntactic type. An important step in understanding any sentence is the determination of its phrase structure (Miller, 1962).

Only certain classes of words can be substituted into the various positions in a sentence, so a listener's response at each position can be limited to a choice from the appropriate class, rather than from the total vocabulary of English. For a listener to be able to take advantage of these syntactic constraints, however, he must first infer the phrase structure of the sentence. If a sentence is grammatical but so complicated syntactically that the listener cannot easily grasp its phrase structure (e.g., *The race that the car that the people whom the obviously not very well dressed man called sold won was held last summer*), it will be difficult for him to exploit the syntactic rules and he will be unable to use his knowledge of English syntax to simplify his perceptual decision.

Semantic rules also play a role in limiting the class of words from which a listener makes his choice. For example, *The boy spoke a triangle* is grammatical, but semantically anomalous. A listener might expect to hear that the boy *spoke a sentence,* or that he *drew a triangle,* but *spoke a triangle* violates semantic rules known (and usually accepted) by all native speakers of English. An adequate semantic theory must incorporate a dictionary that lists, for each word (or morpheme) of the language, all of the syntactic functions and all of the senses of that word, plus some indication of the linguistic contexts in which each sense is appropriate. The theory must also include rules for using the dictionary, i.e., rules for selecting senses that are mutually appropriate when the words enter into grammatical compounds. In the anomalous construction mentioned above there would be no sense of the verb *spoke* that would be appropriate for combination with any of the various senses of the noun *triangle,* so no compound sense could be attached to their concatenation; if such an utterance actually occurred, we could understand it only by generalizing one or more of the senses involved. In ordinary speech, however, we will often find several senses for words that are mutually appropriate; in such cases, the semantic theory must account for the resulting ambiguity of the sentence (cf. Kaplan, 1950; Joos, 1958; Katz and Fodor, 1963). Presumably, a speaker makes use of such semantic rules for combining the senses of his words into a meaningful sentence, so a listener who knows the rules is able further to limit the set of alternative words from which his perceptual choice must be made.

Pragmatic rules are difficult to formulate precisely, since they may involve nonlinguistic information about the context in which a sentence is uttered, about factors governing the degree of belief the listener would assign to the sentence (cf. Martin, 1959), etc. Since the tests to be discussed here do not involve structured sequences longer than a single sentence, however, and since the artificiality of the experimental situation tends to evoke a temporary suspension of disbelief on the part of our listeners, we are probably safe in ignoring constraints imposed by pragmatic rules. In ordinary conversations, however, they play a very important role in limiting the sequences of words that a listener can expect to hear and understand.

We assume that these linguistic rules are normally involved in understanding the various verbal utterances we hear each day. In the following experiments, however, it is not general understanding that is tested, but the more specific function of speech perception, as measured by *S*'s ability to repeat what he is listening to. The strategy employed is systematically to violate some linguistic rules and to ask whether or not such violations make the perceptual task more difficult. We expect to find that if a sentence is understandable (conforms to all the linguistic rules), it will also be relatively easy to hear.

CONSTRUCTION OF TEST MATERIALS

In order to illustrate how we can generate strings of words that obey some linguistic rules while violating others, let us consider a particular example. The following two grammatical sentences have the same phrase structure:

(1) *The odorless liquid became a filthy mess.*

(2) *The academic lecture attracted a limited audience.*

Note that, although the phrase structure of these two sentences is identical, they are not syntactically equivalent; a difference is indicated by the fact that we can form the passive of (2), but not of (1). Thus, *become* and *attract* must belong to two different syntactic categories. In general, however, such differences will not concern us here, since no transformations are applied to our test sentences.

Now consider what happens when some of the words in (1) are substituted for words in (2), where the substitution is limited to words appearing in the same position in the structure. To be definite, suppose we form two new strings of words by choosing alternate words from (1) and (2):

(3) *The academic liquid attracted a limited mess.*

(4) *The odorless lecture became a filthy audience.*

Most people find sentences formed in this manner to be surprising, even mildly amusing. They appear to be grammatical sentences, yet they are clearly not subject to some of the constraints normally imposed on sentences. What constraints have been violated? The phrase structure has not been altered, so the more obvious aspects of syntax remain unchanged. They are, of course, highly improbable, but so are (1) and (2). It is not likely that a listener would have heard any of these sentences before we present them to him. The probabilities, insofar as the listener would be able to estimate them on the basis of the very finite sample of sentences he has heard before, are effectively the same (zero) for all four sentences.

What, then, is odd about (3) and (4)? We will contend here that their unusual character is attributable to the fact that they violate the standard semantic rules of English. This contention needs to be examined in some detail. Certainly it is true that some semantic integrity exists: *became a filthy audience* and *attracted a limited mess* seem relatively unobjectionable, and anyone who would accept *the colorless lecture* as meaningful might be persuaded that *the odorless lecture* is not beyond the bounds of metaphor. Nevertheless, when they are combined as in (3) and (4) the total result is semantically anomalous.

The violation of semantic rules can be illustrated most simply for the pair of words, *academic liquid,* so we will consider it explicitly.

First, we assume that the listener has been able to discover the syntactic structure of the sentence and so recognizes that *academic* is an adjective modifying the noun *liquid.* In attempting to assign a sense to their union, therefore, he is constrained by this syntactic information. He must consider only those senses of *academic* that are associated with the adjectival use of this word, and he must combine one or more of those senses with the senses of *liquid* when *liquid* is used as a noun.

Next, consider the senses that these two words can have. If we possessed an adequate semantic theory of English, its dictionary would provide the following information (or something closely resembling it). As an adjective, *academic* has two principal senses: (i) belonging to or associated with a college or university, and (ii) not expected to be of immediate practical value. Roughly speaking, sense (i) is appropriate whenever the adjective modifies a noun that denotes an adult, human being (*an academic writer*), or an intellectual activity (*an academic lecture*), or a symbol of intellectual activity (*an academic degree*), or a social activity (*an academic procession*), or some real property (*an academic building*). Sense (ii) can be invoked whenever the adjective modifies a noun that denotes an intellectual activity (*an academic argument*). As a noun, the word *liquid* has but one sense. It denotes a physical substance (nonhuman) in a fluid state.

Finally, we must assume the operation of some simple rule for selecting the senses of *academic* that are appropriate when it is used to modify *liquid*. Fortunately, we need not try to state that rule explicitly, for it is obvious that regardless of how it is stated there would be no sense of *academic* suitable when this adjective modifies a noun denoting a physical substance. The noun *liquid* fails to select either of the two senses of the adjective *academic*. Thus we conclude that *academic liquid* is an anomalous combination of words.

Does this conclusion imply that *academic liquid* could never occur in a meaningful English sentence? Not at all. We are discussing linguistic rules, not natural laws. It is perfectly possible to create *ad hoc* senses of a word that are appropriate in particular contexts, but that would not be sufficiently general to merit inclusion in a standard dictionary. We can easily construct an example using these same two words: First, we ask whether the noun *liquid* might have its sense generalized sufficiently to provide an appropriate context for some one of the various senses of the adjective *academic*. It is probably too great a generalization to expect *liquid* to denote either a person or a human activity, but we might generalize it rather naturally to denote some real property, since many physical objects are in fact the property of someone or other. This extension of ordinary usage might be accomplished by providing a context in which *liquid* was clearly defined to be something, say ink, that was the property of a college or university. Following this line we might be led to say something about *the academic liquid that filled the university's inkpots.* In this context the words *academic liquid* do not seem semantically anomalous because an additional semantic rule is provided implicitly by the phrase itself.

For convenience we shall refer to such sentences as semantically anomalous or, more briefly, *anomalous.* What we have, therefore, is a method for systematically generating sentences that are syntactically admissible but semantically anomalous by simply interchanging words that appear in the same syntactic positions in different sentences.

Fifty anomalous sentences were constructed for the purposes of the present experiments. The exact procedure for constructing them can best be communicated by an example. Begin with the following five grammatical sentences which all have the same structural description:

Gadgets simplify work around the house.
Accidents kill motorists on the highways.
Trains carry passengers across the country.

Bears steal honey from the hive.
Hunters shoot elephants between the eyes.

Excluding *the,* which appears in the same position in every sentence, there are five important words in each of the five sentences. We can, therefore, construct a new string of words by taking the first word from the first sentence, the second word from the second sentence, etc., until we obtain the anomalous sentence:

Gadgets kill passengers from the eyes.

By continuing in this fashion until we have used all the words, we also obtain:

Accidents carry honey between the house.
Trains steal elephants around the highways.
Bears shoot work on the country.
Hunters simplify motorists across the hive.

In this way we can construct five anomalous sentences from the five original grammatical sentences. With minor exceptions, anomalous sentences so constructed had the same syntactic structure as the original sentences; the exceptions involved occasional differences in the use of plurals.

In addition to the anomalous sentences, ungrammatical strings of words were also produced by haphazardly permuting the positions in order to destroy their syntactic structure. This procedure gives:

Around accidents country honey the shoot.
On trains hive elephants the simplify.
Across bears eyes work the kill.
From hunters house motorists the carry.
Between gadgets highways passengers the steal.

Ten such sets of five sentences were produced and recombined in this manner, so that altogether there were 50 grammatical sentences, 50 anomalous sentences, and 50 ungrammatical strings of words. Each of the ten sets of five grammatical sentences employed a different phrase structure.

A word of warning should be added here for the reader who contemplates constructing such sentences for his own purposes. It is a simple matter to write five grammatical sentences all having the same structural description, but some ingenuity is required to insure that when the words are recombined the results will all be more or less anomalous. This task is simplified if high-frequency words are avoided. *Thing, they, be, good, that, etc.,* are quite promiscuous about the company they will keep; they have such a wide variety of different senses that it is difficult to find words to go with them that will exclude all their possible meanings. Less frequent, yet not unfamiliar words have fewer senses and so are more likely to produce anomalies when they are combined freely with one another.

TESTS OF SENTENCE INTELLIGIBILITY

The first experimental question that was posed using these three classes of sentences concerned their relative intelligibility in the quiet. If a listener's knowledge of linguistic rules facilitates his perception of speech, one would expect that ungrammatical strings, which violate both semantic and syntactic rules, would be the most difficult to repeat, and that grammatical sentences which obey both semantic and syntactic rules would be the easiest. This expectation was borne out by the following study.

The 150 sentences constructed in the manner described above were mixed together in haphazard order and recorded on magnetic tape by one of the authors (GAM). They were spoken at a rate of about 2 words per sec, with only a brief pause for breath between successive sentences. The recording was played over a high-fidelity system into Permoflux PDR-8 earphones at a sound pressure level of approximately 100 db re 0.002 dyne/cm^2. The *S*s were asked to "shadow"—to repeat aloud immediately afterward—exactly what the talker was saying, and their speech was recorded on standard office dictating machines. Eight *S*s participated. They were given approximately 20 min of experience in listening to speech through earphones and in using the dictating equipment before the experiment began. One group of four worked simultaneously and then, since it might have been possible for them to overhear one another, four additional *S*s were run individually; when no systematic differences were found in their performance, the data for all eight were pooled. Responses were scored both for the number of principal words (five per sentence) and for the number of complete sentences that were repeated exactly.

The sentence scores were: 88.6% of the grammatical sentences, 79.3% of the anomalous sentences, and only 56.1% of the ungrammatical strings were repeated exactly. These differences, based on a sample of 400 observations for each type of sentence, are statistically significant. In order for a sentence to be counted as correct every word—all function words as well as the five principal words—had to be repeated correctly. The ungrammatical strings, which included the function words in ungrammatical positions, would be expected to show the largest number of errors due to mistakes in repeating or omitting these "little" words, and that was in fact the case. If we revise the scoring procedure, therefore, to admit as correct any sentences in which the five principal words were correct (but some function words may have been incorrect), the scores rise to 89.4, 81.1, and 61.1% for the grammatical, anomalous, and ungrammatical strings, respectively. We can conclude, therefore, that the differences in intelligibility among these three types of sentences cannot be attributed simply to an inability to hear the function words out of their normal syntactic contexts. The differences are more fundamental than that.

If we consider the scores for the principal words, we find that 97.5% of the words in grammatical sentences were heard correctly; 95.8% of the words in anomalous sentences were heard correctly; and 88.3% of the words in the ungrammatical strings were heard correctly. These scores, each based on a sample of 2000 observations, may seem more homogeneous than the sentence scores. However, if we consider the probability of hearing a sentence to be simply the product of the probabilities of hearing five successive words correctly, then we can predict the sentence scores by taking the fifth power of the probabilities for the individual words. The sentence scores predicted in this fashion are 88.1, 80.7, and 53.7, respectively, in fair agreement with the sentence scores actually observed.

Analysis of the data indicated that, in spite of the preliminary training period, there was significant improvement in the *S*s' performance as the experiment progressed. If we consider only the first ten sentences of each type that the *S*s heard, their sentence scores for grammatical, anomalous, and ungrammatical strings were 85.7, 68.6, and 35.7%, respectively. For comparison, the scores on the last 30 sentences of each type were 91.5, 82.7, and 62.1%, respectively. Unfortunately, no data are available from this experiment concerning the changes in information processing responsible for this improvement.

EFFECTS OF A MASKING NOISE

A second study concerned the relative intelligibility of these three types of sentences when heard in the presence of masking noise. The results confirm those obtained in the preceding experiment and extend them to conditions in which even the most acute listeners are forced to make many mistakes in their attempts to repeat what they hear.

The conditions of the experiment were as before, except that now the output of a noise generator was mixed with the speech signal before it was amplified and let to the *S*'s earphones. The spectrum of the noise was tailored to match the long-term spectrum of speech; this spectrum provides a very efficient masking signal. Five different noise intensities were used, ranging from +15 to −5 db relative to the level of the speech. The noise was sufficiently intense that the *S*s heard very little of what was going on in the room around them; thus it was possible to run tests with groups of *S*s simultaneously. Two groups were run, totalling six *S*s altogether.

During the first ten of the 150 test sentences the speech-to-noise ratio was set at +15 db; beginning with the 11th sentence the noise intensity was increased so that S/N = + 10 db; on the 21st sentence it was again increased so that S/N = +5 db; and so on, until on the 51st the noise dropped back to S/N = + 15, at which point the same sequence of intensities was repeated; beginning the 101st sentence, the sequence was repeated again.

Sentence intelligibility scores are shown graphically in Fig. 1, where the per cent of the sentences repeated exactly is plotted as a function of the speech-to-noise ratio for each type of sentence. (The results from the preceding experiment on unmasked speech are also plotted in Fig. 1.) The superior intelligibility of the grammatical sentences is even clearer here than in the preceding experiment. At S/N = 0 db, for example, 63% of the grammatical sentences were repeated correctly, but only 3% of the ungrammatical strings. Clearly, grammatical sentences are more resistant to noise interference (by about 10 or 12 db) than are ungrammatical. Anomalous sentences were heard more accurately than ungrammatical ones, which we take to mean that syntactic rules do play a part in the perception of sentences, but were heard less accurately than the normal sentences, which we take to mean that semantic rules also play a part.

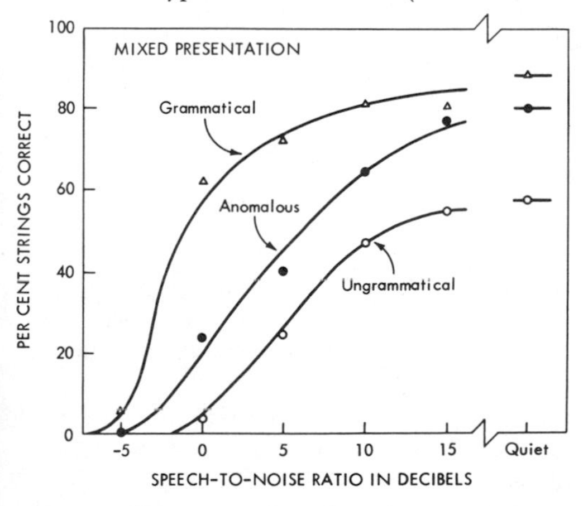

Fig. 1: Per cent strings heard correctly as a function of speech-to-noise ratio when the three types of test strings are presented in mixed order.

The word scores for this same experiment are shown graphically in Fig. 2.

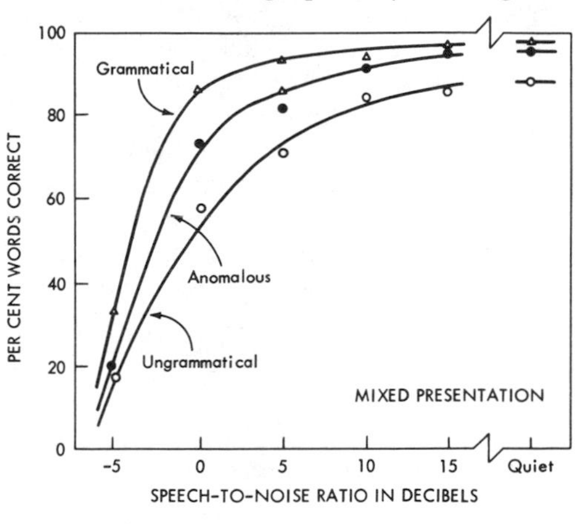

Fig. 2: Per cent words heard correctly as a function of speech-to-noise ratio when the three types of strings are presented in mixed order.

When the results are analyzed in this way the differences between the three types of sentences look less impressive, perhaps, than they do in Fig. 1. Here again, however, sentence scores are close to the fifth power of the word scores.

This experiment also revealed an effect of learning to hear speech in the presence of noise as the experiment progressed. The effect is small, however, relative to the size of the differences among the three types of sentences.

EFFECTS OF PREPARATORY SET

The experiments described above were both conducted with all three types of sentences mixed haphazardly together. Listeners did not know until they heard it which type of sentence to expect. In the following study, however, the three types have been separated and individual tests conducted on each, so that *S*s were able to set themselves optimally for the type of material they were asked to repeat.

Because there are six different orders in which three types of sentences can be presented, six different groups of four *S*s each were used. The listening conditions described above for the masking experiment were used again; for each set of 50 sentences, the speech level was lowered 5 db after every 10th sentence.

The sentence scores obtained for the three types of test materials under these conditions (where results from all 24 *S*s are pooled) are shown graphically in Fig. 3 as a function of the speech-to-noise ratio.

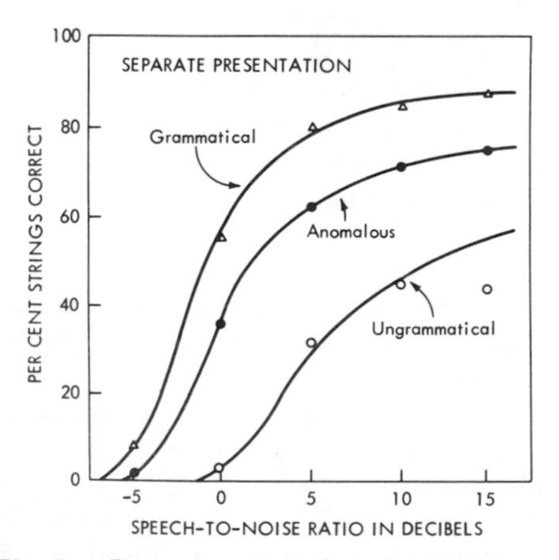

Fig. 3: Per cent strings heard correctly as a function of speech-to-noise ratio when each type of test material is presented separately.

Performance under these conditions is slightly improved over what it was when the sentences were presented in a mixed order; this is true for all three types of test materials, but the improvement is noticeably greater for anomalous sentences than for either grammatical or ungrammatical ones. Presumably, therefore, under the mixed conditions of presentation there was a certain degree of mutual interference among sentence types. The *S*s were set to hear normal sentences, and this set actually interfered with their ability to hear anomalous sentences; when this customary set was not adopted, in the separate presentations, interference did not occur and the anomalous sentences were more easily recognized.

Word scores obtained with separate presentation of the three types of materials are shown in Fig. 4. Here again it is quite

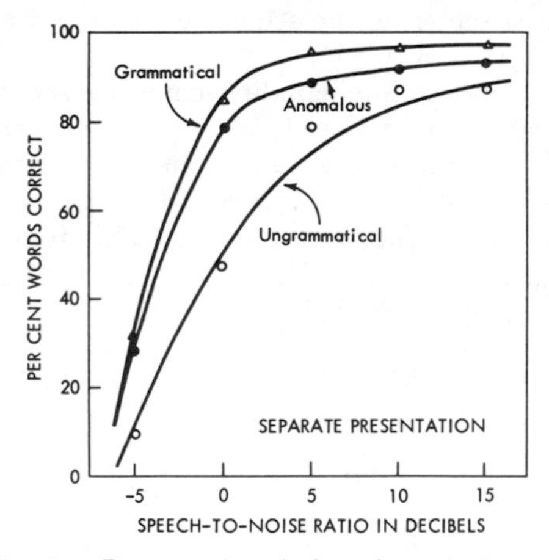

Fig. 4: Per cent words heard correctly as a function of speech-to-noise ratio when each type of test material is presented separately.

clear that the anomalous sentences are almost as audible as the normal sentences when *S*s are set to perceive them.

There is some evidence of a learning effect, which is again most noticeable for ungrammatical strings, but it is difficult to evaluate because, due to the experimental design, the learning effects are confounded with the decreasing speech-to-noise ratio. It seems safe to conclude, however, that learning to listen to these sentences in noise has a small effect relative to the differences attributable to syntactic and semantic conformity.

DISCUSSION

The general conclusion that these experiments appear to support is that linguistic rules of a non-phonological sort do indeed have measurable effects on our ability to hear and repeat sentences. Moreover, both syntactic and semantic rules are effective, since grammatically acceptable but semantically anomalous sentences are intermediate in difficulty, falling below the normal sentences but above the ungrammatical strings in terms of the measures of perceptual accuracy that we have employed. A complete psycholinguistic description of speech perception, therefore, must take into account the syntactic and semantic rules of the language—and perhaps a number of nonlinguistic, pragmatic rules as well. A description along the general lines suggested by Halle and Stevens (1962) would be perfectly compatible with the results we have observed here.

Because these various types of rules are so numerous and intricate, it is sometimes convenient simply to ignore them and to summarize their cumulative effect in terms of probabilities. This was the approach suggested by Shannon (1948), who characterized a message source as a Markov process and proposed measures for the average uncertainty (the "information") a listener would have about the future of a message on the basis of its history.

In the present study one feels intuitively that grammátical sentences are more probable (and so convey less information) than anomalous sentences, which in turn are more probable (and less informative) than ungrammatical strings. Since a higher signal-to-noise ratio is needed to transmit messages that convey more information, this argument would seem to account for the observed results.

It is not possible to discredit this Markovian model in terms of our present data, although one might expect a Markovian theorist to be at least mildly puzzled that anomalous sentences (in which successive pairs of words are often quite unusual and improbable) are heard as readily as they are. The real reasons for rejecting a Markovian formulation of linguistic rules are based on other considerations (Chomsky, 1956). Valuable as the statistical approach may be for communication engineering, it does not provide a useful basis for a psycholinguistic theory of the actual information processing that is performed by a language user.

Savin (1962) has pointed out that the argument that perceptual accuracy is a simple function of stimulus probability, independent of what the stimulus might be, provides a poor explanation of perceptual data even for isolated words. For grammatical strings of words it is completely useless. When we deal with five-word sentences, the average probabilities involved are on the order of 10^{-10}. That is to say, for even short sentences the probabilities are infinitesimally small that a listener would have heard them before. (Indeed, much of the usefulness of language as a means of communication derives from this very fact.) His ability to use sentence context, therefore, cannot be simply based on response probabilities derived inductively from previous listening to sentences; presumably it is derived from an intimate (though tacit) knowledge of linguistic rules. And any attempt to derive the probabilities for five-word (or longer) sentences from experience with two and three-word sequences will be quite inadequate when confronted with the long and complicated patterns of syntactic dependencies that frequently occur in actual speech and writing.

One's intuitive impression that some strings of words should be more probable than others cannot be taken as the basis for a psycholinguistic theory of sentence perception. On the contrary, such impressions are derived from one's knowledge of linguistic rules and can only be accounted for by a precise linguistic statement of those rules, plus a psychological account of how a native speaker-listener uses them. Our perceptual theory must, therefore, make room to accommodate such linguistic rules.

An appeal to rules rather than to Markov processes, of course, raises theoretical issues that are both subtle and ubiquitous in the social sciences. It is quite obvious that such rules are not universal laws of nature; linguistic rules describe socially accepted linguistic practices. Sometimes the rules are put forward as normative, as specifying what good usage ought to be, but that is not the intent of most descriptive linguists, nor do we wish to advocate it here. Linguistic rules need not be normative; it is perfectly possible to consider them simply as a definition of the linguistic practices of a given community, just as the rules of chess are a nonnormative definition of the game of chess. Nevertheless, the question remains open whether a descriptive science, such as psychology aspires to be, can incorporate systems of rules into a framework provided by the more traditional form of scientific laws. Although such issues carry us well beyond the immediate scope of the present research, it may be useful to conclude with a few remarks on the larger context in which the controversy of rules vs. probabilities is embedded.

Toward a system of linguistic rules, as toward all social practices, there are two contrasting attitudes one can assume; Hart (1961) has called them "internal" and "external" points of view. The external view of a system of socially accepted rules is the view that a disinterested outsider might take of the practice. According to it, rules of practice are simply codified summaries of habitual behavior, useful principally to predict what may happen in any situation to which they apply. The rules are imagined to play much the same descriptive role as is played, say, by the differential equations of physics.

There are important differences, however, between predictive equations and rules of practice. As Rawls (1955) has pointed out, it is difficult to imagine that particular habits develop first and only later come to be codified as rules, because without rules of practice there is no way to know which bodily movements are to be counted as instances of the practice. The skills involved in stealing bases, for example, cannot become habitual until the rules of baseball have defined what is meant by stealing bases. Rules of practice are, therefore, logically prior to any particular behavior specified by the practice.

A person who wishes to participate in any particular social practice, who wishes to play the game, is expected to assume an internal view of it, and to accept certain obligations toward the other players. To the participants a rule is not merely a prediction of what is likely to follow—it is a reason for it. Particular actions are justified in terms of the rules. Of course, the rules in turn may be justified on other grounds; in the case of language, perhaps, on utilitarian or pragmatic grounds of free expression and mutual intelligibility. But it is important to note that it is the rules, not particular actions taken in compliance with the rules, that must be justified or "reinforced" by the general consequences of the practice.

Psychologists, as descriptive scientists dedicated to a search for causal relations, generally feel more comfortable with predictions than with obligations, and generally prefer the disinterested view of an outsider to the committed view of a participant. There is a danger, however, that these preferences may lead us to overlook the internal point of view, even to legislate it out of existence, and to pretend that the rules mean nothing more to participants than they would to outsiders. How to avoid this mistake—how to recognize civilized man as an inveterate rule-follower and incorporate his addiction to social practices into a descriptive science—is an old and difficult issue for psychological theorists. Presumably, the psychologist's descriptive task is to understand why some practices develop rather than others, to understand how a participant acquires his knowledge of the practice, and to understand the limits on his ability to obey his own rules. This is obviously a large undertaking, but without some kind of two-level theory including both descriptive laws and rules of practice it is not clear how psycholinguistic phenomena, and many others of a similar nature, can be incorporated into scientific psychology.

SUMMARY

Three experiments on the auditory perception of grammatical, anomalous, and ungrammatical sentences are interpreted to mean that both syntactic and semantic rules are normally involved in the perception of sentences.

APPENDIX: MATERIALS USED IN INTELLIGIBILITY TESTS

Grammatical Sentences

1. A witness signed the official legal document. A jeweler appraised the glittering diamond earrings. A magazine exposed the shocking political corruption. A storm prevented the annual company picnic. A knight slew the ferocious fire-breathing dragon.

2. Sloppy fielding loses baseball games. Romantic poetry describes eternal love. Spilled ink leaves ugly spots. Total chaos follows nuclear attacks. Instant coffee saves wasted minutes.

3. Colorless cellophane packages crackle loudly. Fragrant yellow roses bloom annually. Foreign political ideas spread dangerously. Healthy young babies sleep soundly. All angry wildcats fight furiously.

4. The book explained the complicated mathematical formula. The club elected the worst possible officers. The bolt fastened the heavy oak door. The President advocated the controversial health bill. The musicians played the gay lilting waltz.

5. The academic lecture attracted a limited audience. The odorless liquid became a filthy mess. The wealthy child attended a private school. The Holy Bible inspired a deep reverence. The transparent wrapper fitted a chocolate bar.

6. The newly opened restaurant needed customers. The nationally advertised cigarette caused cancer. The cleverly disguised criminal fooled everybody. The brightly colored toys pleased children. The gently falling snow covered streets.

7. The clock was built by a Swiss watch maker. The crowd was awed by a daring lion tamer. The event was foretold by a Gypsy fortune teller. The blaze was extinguished by a volunteer fire fighter. The trash was removed by a lazy garbage collector.

8. Union leaders call sudden strikes. Bright flies lure rainbow trout. Loud parties wake sleeping neighbors. Tropical jungles challenge hardy explorers. Compact cars use cheaper gasoline.

9. The sticky humid weather frayed tempers. The popular young actor signed autographs. The frenzied Latin rhythm aroused passions. The old gray mare ate hay. The secret miracle ingredient worked wonders.

10. Gadgets simplify work around the house. Accidents kill motorists on the highways. Trains carry passengers across the country. Bears steal honey from the hive. Hunters shoot elephants between the eyes.

Anomalous Sentences

1. A witness appraised the shocking company dragon. A jeweler exposed the

annual fire-breathing document. A magazine prevented the ferocious legal earrings. A storm slew the official diamond corruption. A knight signed the costly political picnic.

2. Sloppy poetry leaves nuclear minutes. Romantic ink follows wasted games. Spilled chaos saves baseball love. Total coffee loses eternal spots. Instant fielding describes ugly attacks.

3 Colorless yellow ideas sleep furiously. Fragrant political babies fight loudly. Foreign young wildcats crackle annually. Healthy angry packages bloom dangerously. All cellophane roses spread soundly.

4. The book elected the heavy health waltz. The club fastened the controversial lilting formula. The bolt advocated the gay mathematical officers. The President played the complicated possible door. The musicians explained the worst oak bill.

5. The academic liquid attended a deep bar. The odorless child inspired a chocolate audience. The wealthy Bible fitted a limited mess. The Holy wrapper attracted a filthy school. The transparent lecture became a private reverence.

6. The newly advertised criminal pleased streets. The nationally disguised toys covered customers. The cleverly colored snow needed cancer. The brightly falling restaurant caused everybody. The gently opened cigarette fooled children.

7. The clock was awed by a Gypsy fire collector. The crowd was foretold by a volunteer garbage maker. The event was extinguished by a lazy watch tamer. The blaze was removed by a Swiss lion teller. The trash was built by a daring fortune fighter.

8. Union flies wake hardy gasoline. Bright parties challenge cheaper strikes. Loud jungles use sudden trout. Tropical cars call rainbow neighbors. Compact leaders lure sleeping explorers.

9. The sticky young rhythm ate wonders. The popular Latin mare worked tempers. The frenzied gray ingredient frayed autographs. The old miracle weather signed passions. The secret humid actor aroused hay.

10. Gadgets kill passengers from the eyes. Accidents carry honey between the house. Trains steal elephants around the highways. Bears shoot work on the country. Hunters simplify motorists across the hive.

Ungrammatical Strings

1. A legal glittering the exposed picnic knight. A diamond shocking the prevented dragon witness. A political annual the slew document jeweler. A company ferocious the signed earrings magazine. A fire-breathing official the appraised corruption storm.

2. Loses poetry spots total wasted. Describes ink attacks instant baseball. Leaves chaos minutes sloppy eternal. Follows coffee games romantic ugly. Saves fielding love spilled unclear.

3. Sleep roses dangerously young colorless. Fight ideas soundly angry fragrant. Crackle babies furiously cellophane foreign. Bloom wildcats loudly yellow healthy. Spread packages annually political all.

4. Explained the officers bold health gay the. Elected the door President lilting complicated the. Fastened the bill musicians mathematical worst the. Advocated the waltz book possible heavy the. Played the formula club oak controversial the.

5. Attracted wrapper the reverence private odorless a. Became lecture the bar deep wealthy a. Attended liquid the audience chocolate Holy a. Inspired child the mess limited transparent a. Fitted Bible the school filthy academic a.

6. Needed advertised cleverly the toys streets. Caused disguised brightly the snow customers. Fooled colored gently the restaurant cancer. Pleased falling newly the cigarette everybody. Covered opened nationally the criminal children.

7. The built a was tamer fortune blaze by lazy. The awed a was teller fire trash

by Swiss. The foretold a was fighter garbage clock by daring. The extinguished a was collector watch crowd by Gypsy. The removed a was maker lion event by volunteer.

8. Call flies neighbors hardy compact. Lure parties explorers cheaper union. Wake jungles gasoline sudden bright. Challenge cars strikes rainbow loud. Use leaders trout sleeping tropical.

9. Tempers young rhythm ate secret the. Autographs Latin mare worked sticky the. Passions gray ingredients frayed popular the. Hay miracle weather signed frenzied the. Wonders humid actor aroused old the.

10. Around accidents country honey the shoot. On trains hive elephants the simplify. Across bears eyes work the kill. From hunters house motorists the carry. Between gadgets highways passengers the steal.

References

Chomsky, N. Three models for the description of language. *IRE Trans. Infor. Theory,* 1956, IT-2, 113–124.

Chomsky, N. *Syntactic structures.* The Hague: Mouton, 1957.

Halle, M., and Stevens, K. Speech recognition: A model and a program for research, *IRE Trans. Infor. Theory,* 1962, IT-8, 155–159.

Hart, H. L. A. *The concept of law.* Oxford: Oxford Univer. Press, 1961.

Joos, M. Semology: A linguistic theory of meaning. *Studies in Linguistics,* 1958, 13, 53–70.

Kaplan, A. An experimental study of ambiguity and context. Rand Corporation Report P18, 1950. (Reprinted in *Mechanical Translation,* 1955, 2, 39–46.)

Katz, J. J., and Fodor, J. A. The structure of semantic theory. *Language,* 1963, 39, 170–210.

Martin, R. M. *Toward a systematic pragmatics.* Amsterdam: North-Holland Publ., 1959.

Miller, G. A. Some psychological studies of grammar. *Amer. Psychologist,* 1962, 17, 748–762.

Miller, G. A., Heise, G. A., and Lichten, W. The intelligibility of speech as a function of the context of the test materials. *J. exp. Psychol.,* 1951, 41, 329–335.

Rawls, J. Two concepts of rules, *Phil., Rev.,* 1955, 64, 3–32.

Savin, H. The word frequency effect and errors in the perception of speech. Ph.D. dissertation, Harvard University, 1962.

Shannon, C. W. A mathematical theory of communication. *Bell Syst. Tech. J.,* 1948, 27, 379–343.

On Learning the Grammatical Order of Words

MARTIN D. S. BRAINE[1]

The possibility is examined that grammatical structure is acquired by "contextual generalization"— a type of generalization which results from a S's learning the position of a unit in a sequence. Several experiments, in which S's learn miniature artificial languages, demonstrate and explore certain aspects of this type of generalization in verbal learning. From the experiments a theory of the learning of grammatical structure is developed. Confrontation of the theory with facts about the structure of natural languages, especially English, suggests that it may be tenable, provided its scope is narrowed in ways discussed, and provided that an additional assumption is made—that as well as learning the locations of units, Ss form paired associates whose foci are closed-class morphemes, i.e., articles, auxiliaries, affixes, etc.

[1] The writer is indebted to the Superintendent of Schools, and to the Principals of Woodlin and Rosemary Hills elementary schools, of Montgomery County, Maryland, for their cooperation in making available subjects and school facilities for Experiments I—IV. For Experiment V a similar debt is owed to James Hymes of the University of Maryland nursery school.

Just how virtually every human child contrives to learn his native language probably constitutes the most arresting mystery in psychology. A salient feature of the development is the relative rapidity with which the complexity of sentence structure increases during the initial period of acquisition. The purpose of the present paper is to explore the potentialities of the concept, "contextual generalization," for explaining the acquisition of grammatical structure, especially those aspects of grammatical structure which have to do with word order (which constitute much of the grammar in English).

For verbal learning, contextual generalization may be defined informally as follows: when a subject, who has experienced sentences in which a segment (morpheme, word, or phrase) occurs in a certain position and context, later tends to place this segment in the same position in other contexts, the context of the segment will be said to have generalized, and the subject to have shown contextual generalization.

Thus defined, contextual generalization falls within the general rubric of stimulus and response generalization. One speaks

Martin D. S. Braine, "On Learning the Grammatical Order of Words," *Psychological Review,* 70 (1963), 323–348. Reprinted by permission of the author and publisher.

of "stimulus generalization" when a subject, who has learned to make a certain response to a stimulus S_1, later makes the same response to a new stimulus S_2 which is like S_1. In stimulus generalization, the mediating property (the way in which S_2 is like S_1) is usually conceived to be some intrinsic property of S_1 and S_2, e.g., color, shape, etc. Similarly, in response generalization, the mediating property of R_1 and R_2 is usually thought of as some intrinsic property of the responses. Although the properties mediating generalization are usually intrinsic ones, there seems to be no particular reason why this should be so, and contextual generalization appears to be a special case where the mediating property is an extrinsic one, namely, temporal location in an utterance.

There are various suggestions in the literature that learning word order is similar to learning the associative connections manifest in word association tests. According to an early view of Miller (1951), "controlled associations are quite similar to the choice of successive words in speech [p. 186]." Consistently with this idea, Miller leaned heavily on the concepts of "contextual constraint" and "transitional probability"—"By grammatical habits we mean the operations of contextual constraints upon the sequence of symbols [p. 185]." While these concepts have been shown to be relevant to some verbal learning and memory experiments, no one has tried to develop these ideas to the point at which they can be taken seriously as a theory of the learning of grammatical structure. Perhaps this failure reflects the difficulties of such an enterprise.

A central difficulty of a theory based on learned associations between words is its clumsiness in handling generalization phenomena that obviously occur in verbal behavior. Thus, if we are told, for example, that PEOPLE KIVIL EVERY DAY, we are likely to deduce the existence of a verb TO KIVIL, and to accept sentences like GEORGE KIVILS as grammatical. Similarly, sentences like IRON FLOATS, or COLORLESS GREEN IDEAS SLEEP FURIOUSLY (Chomsky's 1957 example), would probably be recognized as having the structure of English even though it is doubtful that any of the words have ever previously been associated with each other in the experience of most English speakers; certainly such sentences would be considered more grammatical than WE ARE GOING TO SEE HIM IS NOT CORRECT TO CHUCKLE LOUDLY AND DEPART FOR HOME, in which the associational bonds between the words are quite strong (Miller, 1951, p. 81). It seems obvious therefore that there must exist generalization mechanisms in language learning whereby a word learned in one context generalizes to another context, even though no associations may have previously formed between the word and its new context.

In any explanation of the learning of grammatical structure it seems to the writer that some such generalization mechanism will have to occupy a central position. The present paper explores whether contextual generalization is a serious candidate for this role.

The paper is divided into two parts. The first part reports a series of experiments in which children learn some miniature artificial languages with nonsense syllables as words. Contextual generalization is first demonstrated as a phenomenon, and then various problems associated with the concept are explored. From the experiments, the general lines are sketched of a theory of the learning of grammatical structure based on contextual generalization—based, that is, on the notion that "What is learned" are primarily the proper locations of words in sentences.

Although experiments with artificial languages provide a vehicle for studying learning and generalization processes hypothetically involved in learning the natural language, they cannot, of course, yield any direct information about how the natural language is actually learned. The adequacy of a theory which rests on findings in work with artificial languages will therefore be judged by its consistency with data on the structure and development of the natural language. In the second part of the paper an attempt is made to confront the theory developed with known facts about the grammatical structure of natural languages, especially English, so as to discover the limitations of the theory, the stumbling blocks it faces, and the resources it can draw upon to meet the stumbling blocks.

EXPERIMENT I: THE A+P LANGUAGE WITH WORD CONSTITUENTS

This experiment demonstrates, for a very simple language, that the position of a word in a verbal array can be the "functional stimulus" mediating generalization.

Method

Description of the language. There were two classes of words, A words and P words, and sentences were always two words long and consisted of an A word followed by a P word. The words were low-association value nonsense syllables. KIV, JUF, and FOJ were the A words, and BEW, MUB, and YAG the P words. Two words of each class were used during the initial learning, and the third was introduced in generalization trials.

Procedure. The subject was told that he was going to play a sort of word game in which he would learn a bit of a new language which might seem strange because he would not know what any of the words meant. The words (written on 1.5 × 3 inch cards) were shown to him and a consensus about their pronunciation was reached.

The "language" was taught through a series of sentence-completion problems. A word was presented on the ledge of a board, either preceded or followed by a vacant position; A words were always presented on the left, and P words on the right of the vacant position. In each problem, the subject was given two words, one of each class, to choose from to complete the sentence by placing his selection in the vacant position. Before each problem the subject was asked "Do you remember how this one goes?" or "How do you think this one should go?" If he chose the correct word he won a poker chip (eight poker chips were worth a chocolate); if he chose wrongly he was shown the correct answer. After each problem, the correct sentence was read aloud by him, and repeated by the experimenter.

In the initial learning two A words (KIV and JUF) and two P words (BEW and MUB) were used. Four sentences can be formed from these, and eight sentence-completion problems can be constructed since each sentence can be formed either by filling in the first word or by filling in the last word. The initial learning had two stages. Four of the eight problems were first selected and were presented in random order until learned to a criterion of seven successive correct responses (not including the first presentation of the first problem, which was used to demonstrate the procedure to the subject). Then the remaining four problems were presented once each, followed by all eight problems in random order until correct responses to seven successive presentations were made.

After the initial learning four generalization problems were each presented once to discover whether the subjects had registered the positions of the words used in the initial learning. A new A or P word was presented, with the alternatives always being words used in the initial learning. The generalization problems were (with the alternatives in parenthesis): FOJ—(KIV,BEW);—YAG (MUB, KIV); —YAG (JUF, BEW); FOJ—(MUB, JUF).

Subjects. The subjects were 16 children aged 9–6 to 10–5, 8 boys and 8 girls. Nonreaders were excluded.

Results

The initial learning was accomplished quite rapidly, two subjects making no errors whatever following the initial demonstration problem. As a demonstration of contextual generalization, the main interest of the experiment lies in the performance on the generalization problems. In 78% of these problems the subjects filled the vacant position with the word that had occupied this position in the initial learning. Using the binomial expansion, one would expect by chance that, among 16 subjects, 5 subjects would respond correctly on either all four or three of the four generalization problems, 6 subjects on two problems, and 5 subjects on one problem or none. The obtained figures were 12, 4, and 0 subjects, respectively. The tendency to respond correctly is highly significant ($\chi^2 = 15.5$, $df = 2$, $p < .001$).

A vacant second position was filled in correctly in 91% of the problems (13 subjects correct on both problems, and 3 subjects on one or none), as compared with 66% for a vacant first position (8 subjects on both problems, and 8 subjects on one or none). Tested by chi square for correlated proportions, the difference between the positions is not statistically significant.

After the generalization problems, the subjects who had correctly completed at least three of the four sentences were asked why they picked the one they did. The two most frequent explanations were "It sounded right," and "I remembered" (when asked *what* they remembered these subjects said they did not know—further questioning usually elicited that they had not realized that all the sentences in the generalization problems were new). Only one subject said anything to indicate that he had noticed the constant positions of the words. These explanations suggest that the subjects responded unwittingly to the positional cue and that this cue was temporal rather than spatial in nature, and auditory rather than visual (i.e., the temporal position of the word in the sentence when read aloud or rehearsed subvocally, rather than its left or right position in the visual display). Further evidence for this is provided in a later experiment.

Conclusion

The results indicate that subjects who have experienced sentences in which words occur in a certain position and context tend to place these words in the same positions in new contexts. Such behavior indicates the learning of an association of words with their positions, the context generalizing. A suggestion as to the mechanism of contextual generalization is contained in the subjects' explanations of their responses: perhaps the repeated experience of a certain word in a certain position makes it sound familiar, and therefore sound "right," in this position, even though the original context be changed.

Discussion

Extrapolating from the above conclusion, it is possible to hazard a guess about the infant's learning of grammatical word order. Perhaps he constantly hears the same expressions recurring in the same positions in his verbal environment; these therefore come to sound familiar and therefore "right" to him in these positions, and consequently in his own language he reproduces the same positional relationships. Such a theory would make the learning of grammatical word order a special case of "Gibsonian" perceptual learning (Gibson & Gibson, 1955), i.e., a process of auditory differentiation, or of becoming familiar with, the temporal positions of expressions in utterances. Perceptual learning is usually assumed to be a rather primitive process and there is therefore no reason to suppose that it demands much in the way of intellectual capacity in the learner. Learning of this sort would therefore satisfy at least one requirement of any process postulated to be involved in first language learning, namely, that it not require intellectual capacities obviously beyond the reach of the 2-year-old.

The most immediate problem in the above line of thought concerns the definition of position. In the learning of a language more complex than the one used in this experiment, two closely related questions arise. One question concerns whether it is the absolute positions of expressions (e.g., first, second, etc.) that are learned, or the positions of expressions relative to other expressions. A less obvious but probably more important question concerns the nature of the elements that fill positions. It is perhaps most natural to assume that the word is the principal element whose position is learned. If the word is the only element whose position is learned, then for English, position must be defined relatively and not absolutely, since almost any English word can occur in any absolute position in a sentence. However, some exploratory work suggested that the relative positions of words were rather difficult to learn. It seemed, therefore, that it might be fruitful to question the assumption that there is anything inevitable about the word as the sole or principal element whose position is learned.

An alternative assumption is that the elements are hierarchically organized: a sentence would be assumed to contain a hierarchy of elements in which longer elements (e.g., phrases) contain shorter elements (e.g., words) as parts, with the positions that are learned always being positions within the next larger element in the hierarchy. A hierarchy of elements would require that expressions of any length can be elements whose position is learned; words (or morphemes) would be merely the smallest elements in the hierarchy. At each level in a hierarchical scheme position could be defined either absolutely or relatively. A simple example of a hierarchical scheme in which position is defined absolutely is provided by binary fractionation. In this scheme a sentence contains just two positions, a first and a last, and each expression in these positions can itself contain two positions, a first and a last, and each resulting expression is potentially divisible in turn in like manner, etc. It may be noted that this method of defining position seems relevant to English structure, e.g., the verb in English generally constitutes the first part of the last section of a sentence. A hierarchical organization of elements is assumed in immediate constitutent analysis in structural linguistics (cf. Chomsky, 1957).

EXPERIMENT II: THE A+P LANGUAGE WITH PHRASE CONSTITUENTS

This experiment was designed to investigate whether the ease and effectiveness of learning is related to the way in which position is defined for the subject. The learning of the same language was compared under conditions (*a*) when words were the units and the positional cues were relative, and (*b*) when phrases (either one or two words long) were the units and the positional cues were absolute —first and last. It was expected that Condition *b* would prove simpler. The initial learning procedure was designed to match that of Experiment I, so that the learning scores could be compared with those for the apparently simpler language of Experiment I.

Method

Description of the language. The language was that of Experiment I, except that an additional word (GED) always preceded two of the three A words (JUF and FOJ), and another additional word (POW) always followed one of the P words (BEW). Sentences could thus vary from two to four words in length, and the A and P words were sometimes first and second, and sometimes second and third; the relative ordinal positions were, however, the same as in Experiment I, i.e., A words (KIV, JUF, and FOJ) always immediately preceded P words (BEW, MUB, and YAG).

An alternative way of specifying this

language is to say that any of three A phrases (KIV, GED JUF, GED FOJ) could be followed by any of three P phrases (BEW POW, MUB, YAG). When described in this way the grammar is an exact replica of the grammar taught in Experiment I, but with phrases instead of words as the immediate constituents.

Procedure. The procedure had four parts: initial learning, second learning, learning test, and recall test. To match Experiment I, the initial learning used only two A terms (KIV, and JUF preceded by GED) and two P terms (BEW followed by POW, and MUB). Using a sentence completion procedure as before, the language was taught in two ways. For one group of subjects (Group 1) only the position of the A or P word was left vacant in a problem, and the choices available for sentence completion were always an A and a P word. (For this group the two new words GED and POW never had to be filled in.) For another group of subjects (Group 2), the sentences were presented in each problem lacking the whole A or P phrase (i.e., either one or two words as the case might be), and the choices available for completing the sentence were always a whole A and P phrase. (When the choices were of unequal length, these subjects of course were not given any cues as to the length of the sentence to be constructed.) The initial learning was exactly parallel to the initial learning in Experiment I: to every sentence completion problem used then there corresponded a problem for each group in this experiment, and the order of administration of problems and the learning criteria were the same. Subjects who failed to complete the initial learning in 60 trials were not included in the remaining parts of the experiment.

The purpose of the second learning was to introduce and provide practice with the A term (FOJ preceded by GED) and the P term (YAG) not used in the initial learning. Nine problems combined these new items with previously used words or phrases, and with each other; in a further six problems, each A and P word (or phrase) occurred twice, once as the correct alternative and once presented in the sentence for completion. In the second learning, as in the initial learning, Group 1 filled in A and P words only, and Group 2 the full A or P phrase.

In the learning test, each of the eight sentence completion problems of the initial learning were administered in turn to both groups with only the A and P words to be filled in. For Group 1 the learning test was simply a repetition of the same eight problems they had already learned to criterion.

In the recall test, the eight words of the language were handed to the subjects and they were asked to try to make a complete sentence of the language that they remembered. The request was repeated until they had offered four sentences.

Subjects. In each group there were 12 children, aged 9–7 to 10–7, 6 boys and 6 girls. Nonreaders were excluded.

Results

The first three lines of Table 1 show the learning scores for the two groups and for the subjects of the previous experiment. Since some subjects failed to reach the learning criterion, the scores are expressed in terms of the median and range. It can be seen that there is no difference between Group 2 and the subjects of Experiment I in either trials-to-learn, or errors.

Using the nonparametric Mann-Whitney sum-of-ranks test, it was found that Group 2 learned in fewer trials ($z = 2.7$, $p < .01$), and made fewer errors ($z = 1.7$, $p < 0.5$ for the one-tailed hypothesis), than Group 1.

In the eight problems of the learning test, there was only one error among the 12 subjects of Group 2, whereas 6 of the 10 subjects in Group 1 who took the test made one error apiece $\chi^2 = 4.5$, $p < .05$). Subjects who had learned by filling

Table 1

LEARNING AND ERROR SCORES IN THE VARIOUS EXPERIMENTS

Experiment	*N*	*Percent subjects learning*	*Trials to learn Mdn and range*	*Number errors Mdn. and range*
I	16	100	10.5 (0–28)	4 (0–7)
II: 1	12	83	24 (5–60 +)	5 (2–20+)
II: 2	12	100	9.5 (2–20)	3.5 (1–9)
III	24	100	11 (0–40)	3 (0–14)
IV: 1	6	33	50 + (29–50+)	20 + (10–20+)
IV: 2	14	64	32 (4–50+)	9 (3–20+)
V	12	100	13 (0–55)	4.5 (0–18)

in the whole A or P phrase therefore knew the relative positions of the individual words of the phrase even better than the subjects who had been trained to fill in the individual words.

In the recall test the subjects of Group 1 constructed an average of 2.6 sentences, as against 3.1 for Group 2. The results favor Group 2, as predicted, but the difference is not significant ($t = 1.2$). The difference between the groups might well have been greater if the experimenter had not foolishly limited the subjects to four sentences, thus imposing a ceiling on the recall scores to the probable detriment of the group with the higher mean score! It should also be remembered that the two worst subjects in Group 1 were excluded from the recall test because they failed to complete the initial learning.

Discussion

The similarity between the learning scores for Group 2 and for the language of Experiment I indicates that it matters little whether the elements in first and last position are words or variable length phrases (one or two words).

The results also indicate that the same language is learned more easily and effectively when the response units are phrases of variable length and the positional cues are first and last, than when the response units are words and the positional cues are provided by the relative positions of the words to each other. This result is probably due to the greater informational economy of a first-last dichotomy; that is, to learn the absolute positions of the phrases fewer items of information would have to be registered than to learn the positional relationships between the words taken individually. Consider, for example, the complexity of a relative definition of the position of BEW: BEW precedes POW; it follows either KIV, JUF, or FOJ, whichever of these appear; and it occurs next but one after GED, when GED is present. Obviously it is much simpler to take BEW POW as a unit and state only that this occurs last. (Within a hierarchical scheme the position of BEW could then be specified as the first member of a BEW-POW unit.)[2]

The results of this experiment therefore suggest that learning is easier with a simple definition of position, and that a variable length element does not impair learning. Such a result would be expected under the assumption that position can be defined through a hierarchical scheme,

[2] One way (which would apply only to a language more complex than the one taught here) in which the complexity of a relative definition of position could be reduced, would be to arrange that a few elements recur in a very large number of sentences of the language. The subject might quickly learn to recognize these elements and they might then serve him as reference points in the sentence; the positions immediately preceding or following such elements would then be defined in a fairly simple manner. The familiar element would, so to speak, serve as a "tag" (cf. the discussion of "closed-class" morphemes, below).

since a hierarchical scheme permits a simple definition of position, but does so at the cost of a complex element.

EXPERIMENT III: THE A+PQ AND AB+P LANGUAGES

The experiment was designed to explore the learning of locations in a language with a hierarchy of elements. Suppose a grammar in which a double binary fractionation of sentences is possible (i.e., not only a division of the sentence into an A and a P phrase, but also a further subdivision of at least one of the phrases into two parts). Such a grammar would be exemplified in a language with four A phrases, a_1, a_2, a_3, a_4 (not necessarily of equal length), any of which may precede any of four P phrases, p_1q_1, p_2q_2, p_1q_2, p_2q_1. The P phrase has internal structure, consisting of a P word (p_1 or p_2) followed by a Q word (q_1 or q_2). With such a language, it was predicted that the subjects would not only associate phrases with their position within the sentence, but also associate words with their position within the phrase—contextual generalization should occur both between and within phrases.

For the above language, between-phrase generalization would be demonstrated in essentially the same way as in Experiment I. At a certain point in the learning, an A and a P phrase (e.g., perhaps a_4 and p_2q_1), not yet experienced by the subject, would be introduced and presented in problems of the form $a_4(\ \ )$ and $(\ \ )p_2q_1$. If the subject has registered the positions of the A and P phrases in the previous learning, he should complete these sentences correctly, to form, e.g., $a_4p_1q_1$, $a_1p_2q_1$.

However, the more complex grammar brings a new factor up for consideration, not present in Experiment I. In a language in which some of the phrases have internal structure, the component phrases of most new sentences will be formed by joining words not previously combined, and not represent new additions to the vocabulary. When new phrases are recombinations of familiar elements, any associations of a paired-associate type, which may have formed during the previous learning, will have an opportunity to facilitate generalization. In the case of the language outlined, where only one phrase has internal structure, such associations could facilitate solution only of generalization problems in which the unstructured phrase is to be filled in. Thus in problems of the form $a_4(\ \ )$, in which the structured phrase has to be filled in, a_4 is a new addition to the vocabulary so that no associations can have formed to it; whereas in problems of the form $(\ \ )p_2q_1$, associations could have formed between the familiar unstructured A phrases to be filled in and the words p_2 and q_1 of the phrase presented. Analysis of performance on such generalization problems may therefore give some indication of the extent of associative effects in this kind of generalization.

Within-phrase generalization would be demonstrated in problems of the form $a_np_3(\ \ )$ and $a_n(\ \ )q_3$, where a_n is any A phrase (familiar), and p_3 and q_3 are new words. If, in the previous learning, the subject has registered the positions of the P and Q words in the P phrase, he should complete the sentences correctly, to form, e.g., $a_np_3q_1$, $a_np_1q_3$. Since a_n can be any of the four A phrases, a generalization problem of the above form, e.g., $a_np_3(\ \ )$, can be replicated four times, with a_1, a_2, a_3, a_4 serving in turn as the A phrase; in each replication a correct response will construct the same P phrase (e.g., p_3q_1) in the context of a different A phrase. One can therefore ask whether the association of words with their within-phrase positions is demonstrated on the first problems, and also whether there is an increase in generalization with successive A phrase contexts. An increase might be due either to an increase in the strength of association of the word with its within-phrase position or to between-phrase contextual generalization of the new P phrase from one A phrase to another.

Method

Description of the languages. The two languages are defined in Table 2. In the AB + P language the structured phrase was in first position, in the A + PQ language in second position.

Procedure. The procedure had five parts: initial learning, second learning, between-phrase generalization test, third learning, and within-phrase generalization tests. Since the languages are mirror images, the procedure will be described only for the A + PQ language; the procedure for the AB + P language was an exact analogue—read A in place of P, B in place of Q, and P in place of A in the following description.

The initial learning was an exact problem-by-problem analogue of that used in the two previous experiments. KIVIL and OB ORDEM were the A phrases, and MERVO SOM (p_1q_1) and YAG EENA (p_2q_2) the P phrases. The subjects always filled in the whole phrase, in the same way as Group 2 in the previous experiment. The initial learning, then, was comparable to the first experiments, two A phrases and two P phrases with, as yet, no elaboration of internal structure.

The second learning introduced a new A phrase (a_3: REMIN GICE) and a new P phrase (p_1q_2: MERVO EENA). The first nine problems combined these new phrases with the previously used ones and with each other; then a random assortment of problems constructible from the six phrases were learned to a criterion of seven successive correct responses. The second learning thus introduced a new A term, unrelated to the previous A terms; the P term, however, was systematically generated by the combination of elements from the previously learned P terms.

The between-phrase generalization test consisted of six problems presented once each. The problems introduced a new A phrase unrelated to previous A phrases (a_4: NOOT) and a new P phrase generated by recombination of elements (p_2q_1: YAG SOM). These were presented three times each in the positions appropriate to their class, and in each problem a different one of the previously used phrases had to be filled in. In the three problems in which YAG SOM was the phrase presented, the incorrect choice was always MERVO EENA (because otherwise the subjects might well solve these problems by adopting the hypothesis that the same word could not occur twice in a sentence).

In the third learning 15 problems constructible from the eight phrases were presented, most of which contained the two phrases just introduced in the generalization test. The purpose of the third learning was to familiarize the subjects with these new phrases.

The within-phrase generalization problems differed from all previous parts of the procedure in that sentences were presented lacking one word only, and in that subjects had to choose from three instead of two alternatives (because there were three parts of speech). Preceding the first generalization problem there were three "buffer" problems with these characteristics which contained no new words. There were 16 within-phrase generalization problems; these were arranged in four sets, each set comprising four prob-

Table 2

A + PQ LANGUAGE

A Phrase	*P Phrase*	
KIVIL (a_1)	MERVO (p_1)	SOM (q_1)
OB ORDEM (a_2)	YAG (p_2)	EENA (q_2)
REMIN GICE (a_3)	LECK (p_3)	WIMP (q_3)
NOOT (a_4)		

Note.—A p_nq_n sequence constitutes a P phrase, and an A phrase followed by a P phrase is a sentence. The AB + P language is obtained by interchanging A and P phrases of the A + PQ language.

lems. In two problems of each set, the P phrase presented was p_3 (LECK) followed by the space to be filled in; in the other two problems it consisted of q_3 (WIMP) preceded by the blank; the choices were always a P word, a Q word, and a word selected from one of the A phrases; each of p_1, p_2, q_1, q_2 were correct once. In the first set of problems the A phrase used was always a_1, in the second set a_2, in the third a_3, and in the fourth a_4. Thus, in the first set the problems were: KIVIL LECK—(ORDEM, SOM, MERVO); KIVIL—WIMP (YAG, EENA, REMIN); KIVIL—WIMP (SOM, GICE, MERVO); KIVIL LECK—(ORDEM, YAG, EENA). In the second, third and fourth sets of problems, in addition to replacement of the A phrase, the order of presentation of problems containing particular P phrases was varied, as also were the wrong alternatives. To give the subjects additional experience of the sentences used in each set of generalization problems before going on to the next set, between sets the subjects were given eight problems made up from the four sentences introduced in the set just completed. In these practice problems, the whole A or P phrase had to be filled in, as in the earlier learning.

If two sessions were required to complete the procedure, the break between sessions always occurred during the second learning.

Subjects. Twenty-four children, aged 9–11 to 11–1, served as subjects. Each language was learned by 6 boys and 6 girls. Nonreaders were excluded.

Results

Table 1 shows the initial learning scores for the 24 subjects, who were treated as a single group since the scores were very similar for the two languages. It can be seen that the scores are almost exactly the same as those found in Experiment I and for Group 2 in Experiment II.

In 74% of the between-phrase generalization problems, the subjects filled the vacant position with the phrase which had occupied this position in the previous learning. Using the binomial expansion, one would expect that among 24 subjects, 8.25 subjects would be correct on either zero, one, or two of the six problems, 7.5 subjects correct on three problems, and 8.25 subjects correct on four, five, or six problems. The obtained figures were 2, 3, and 19 subjects ($\chi^2 = 21.8$, $p < .0001$). Since, as described in the procedure, three of the problems had the same wrong alternative (MERVO EENA), there was the possibility that subjects might have solved some of these by avoiding this couplet. This possibility is ruled out by the fact that the subjects made slightly fewer errors on the first of the three problems than on the other two, and also that they did not make more than the average number of errors on the one problem on which this couplet was correct.

It will be remembered that in the AB + P language the structured phrase was in first position, and in the A + PQ language in final position. The 12 subjects who learned the AB + P language correctly placed the structured phrase in first position in 83% of the 36 relevant problems (3 problems per subject); they correctly placed the unstructured phrase in final position in 69% of the problems. The corresponding figures for the subjects who learned the A + PQ language were 75% for the unstructured phrase in first position, and 69% for the structured phrase in final position. These four percentages do not seem to differ from each other.

On the first set of within-phrase generalization problems the subjects filled 68% of the vacant positions with the words that had previously occupied these positions (as against the 33% expected by chance). Among 24 subjects one would expect from the binomial expansion that 14.2 subjects would make errors on all or all but one of the four problems, and that 9.8 subjects would make two or more correct responses. The obtained figures were 4 and 20, and the difference is highly significant ($\chi^2 = 18.0$, $p < .0001$). Despite the small number of subjects for each language, the tendency to respond according to word position on the first set of within-phrase generalization problems is significant for each language individually (by a similar chi square test using Yates' correction).

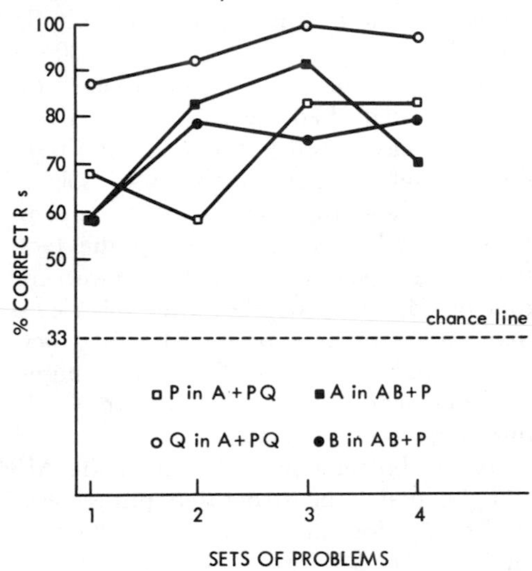

Fig. 1: Proportion of sentences in each set of four within-phrase generalization problems in which a given position was correctly filled (e.g., the open squares indicate how often the P position in the A + PQ language was filled with a P word).

In Figure 1 the results on all four sets of within-phrase generalization problems are presented, showing for each set the proportion of times that a given within-phrase position was correctly filled. It can be seen that correct responses occurred somewhat more frequently on the later sets than on the first, suggesting that some generalization from one sentence context to another occurred over and above the within-phrase generalization manifested by the better-than-chance success on the first set. Comparing the within-phrase positions with each other, Figure 1 suggests that the tendency to associate a word with its position may be greatest for the Q position in the A + PQ language (i.e., for the last word in the sentence), and about the same for the remaining three positions.

When asked how they knew what to pick, three subjects said something about position (e.g., "I don't know exactly; this one usually starts it"); the remaining subjects showed no insight. The most frequent answer made some reference to the sound of the sentence (e.g., "I don't know; I just put it because it sounds right"); a number of subjects said that they "remembered," and it was obvious that most subjects were quite unaware that many of the new sentences were new. One subject said she "tried them all out and picked the one that made the most sense"!

Discussion

The similarity of the initial learning scores to those in Experiment I, and for Group 2 in Experiment II, indicates that ease of learning is not related to such factors as number of words per phrase, number of syllables per word, exact phonetic or lexical constitution of the words, etc., at least within the limits that these factors were varied. Similarly, the results on the between-phrase generalization problems confirm and extend the observations of Experiment I, in that they provide evidence that phrases as well as words tend to become associated with the sentence positions in which they recur, and thus to generalize to fresh contexts. Both these findings indicate that, within fairly wide limits, the constitution of the elements in first and last position is not an important variable for either learning or generalization.

It was noted in the introduction to the experiment that paired-associate links, formed between phrases and parts of phrases during learning, might act to facilitate solution of the between-phrase generalization problems in which the unstructured phrase was to be filled in. However, no evidence was found for such a facilitative effect, since the unstructured phrase was not filled in correctly more often than the structured phrase.

The results on the within-phrase generalization problems indicate that during learning the component words of the structured phrase become associated with their positions within the phrase. This finding confirms the assumption that elements can be hierarchically structured for the subject, that is, the locations with which expressions become associated can be locations within longer expressions whose location in the sentence is also learned.

This experiment completes the experiments which explore ways in which the structure of the verbal array may define positions for the subject. In Experiment IV the question of the role of the oral-auditory cycle in this kind of learning is given further consideration.

EXPERIMENT IV: POSITIVE AND NEGATIVE INSTANCES

It was suggested earlier that the relevant positional cue was the temporal position of the word in the sentence as spoken, and not the left-right position in the visual display. It was also suggested that, since only the correct sentences were read aloud, the subjects had much more opportunity to become familiar with the sound of the correct sentences, their experience of ungrammatical sentences being confined entirely to subvocal rehearsal of the wrong answers to problems. In choosing between the alternatives on a given problem, the subjects would therefore be able to rehearse each alternative and select the one that sounded "right," i.e., familiar. Even in the subvocal rehearsal it is likely that the correct alternative would be rehearsed more often than the incorrect one, since if the subject happened to try the correct alternative first it would sound right, and the incorrect alternative might not then be rehearsed.

In ordinary discrimination-learning experiments, matters are usually arranged so that the subject has equal experience with both the positive and negative stimuli. In the previous three experiments, if the subjects' method of solution has been correctly interpreted, there was very unequal experience with correct and incorrect sentences, exposure to positive instances greatly predominating. First language learning by infants, it may be noted, occurs through exposure to positive instances almost exclusively.

The following modifications of the procedure used in Experiment I were made both to test the above interpretation of the subjects' method of solution, and also to explore the possible importance for language learning of the distinction between learning to discriminate positive from negative instances, and learning primarily through exposure to positive instances. It was predicted that learning would be seriously impaired if the training procedure were altered so that the subjects had nearly equal familiarity with correct and incorrect sentences. Two procedures were designed, each modifying Experiment I in a slightly different way. The language in each case was the A + P language with word constituents, described for Experiment I.

First Modification

Procedure. The preliminary instructions, the rewards, the learning criteria, the sequence of presentation of problems, and the actual words used in each problem were exactly the same as in Experiment I. The difference lay in the fact that each problem was not presented as a sentence completion problem; instead the correct and incorrect sentences involved in a problem were each written on separate cards, and were presented to the subject one on his left and one on his right. He was instructed to read each one aloud and then to point to the one which "could be said in this language." He was told whether he was right, but neither sentence was read aloud following his response.

Six children, aged 9–6 to 10–7, served as subjects.

Results. The results are shown in Table 1 (Row IV: 1). Only two subjects reached the learning criterion, and both these required more trials and made more errors than any subject in Experiment I. This procedural modification obviously impairs learning very severely indeed.

Second Modification

Procedure. While the preceding modification probably gave the subjects equal exposure to the sound of the correct and incorrect sentences, it also altered the visual display, and the precise nature of the response demanded of the subject. The modification now described maintained the same visual display and the same response as in Experiment I.

The procedure was an exact duplicate of that in Experiment I, except that in each problem before completing the sentence, the subject read aloud the sentences which would be produced by substituting each alternative in turn in the vacant position. After completing the sentence he was told whether he was correct, and if incorrect was shown the correct sentence, but he did not then read it aloud. If he read it aloud spontaneously he was told not to; the experimenter did not read the sentence aloud either. After a 2-second pause the next problem was set up.

Since each problem terminated with the correct sentence exposed visually to the subject, and since literate subjects have a tendency to read to themselves written words they see, there was probably somewhat more exposure (subvocal) to the correct than to the incorrect sentences. However, there was certainly far less differential exposure than in Experiment I.

The subjects were 14 children, aged 10–1 to 10–10.

Results. The results are again shown in Table 1 (Row IV: 2). While the impairment of learning appears to be a trifle less serious with this procedure than with the preceding one, learning is obviously greatly impaired relative to the procedure used in Experiment I. For both trials-to-learn and errors, the difference is highly significant ($p < .001$, and .0001, respectively, by the Mann-Whitney sum-of-ranks test).

Discussion

Since the difference between the second modification and the procedure used in Experiment I involved only the reading of the sentences, the results strongly support the previous interpretation of the basis of the subjects' responses. That is, the relevant cue was the temporal position in the spoken sentence, and as learning progressed words or phrases came to sound familiar in the positions in which they recurred. The subjects were then able to respond correctly in generalization problems by picking the alternative which made the sentence "sound right."

It may be added that the deleterious effect on grammatical judgments of self-exposure to negative instances is a phenomenon within ordinary experience. For example, if a foreigner asks whether DIFFERENT TO, DIFFERENT THAN, or DIFFERENT FROM is correct in English, or whether a sentence like THE CHILD SEEMS SLEEPING is any less correct than THE BOOK SEEMS INTERESTING, one is usually much more confident of the answer if one responds at once than if one repeats each alternative 20 times before responding. The very act of repeating the ungrammatical (or less grammatical) sequence a number of times seems to make it momentarily "sound right," and thus removes the usual basis for the judgment.

EXPERIMENT V: THE A+P LANGUAGE WITH 4-YEAR-OLDS

Experiments I—III were all performed with children about 10 years old. Since the theory developed claims to have relevance to first language learning, it assumes that the phenomena under study also occur readily in much younger children. Experiment V was designed to examine this assumption. An attempt was made to repeat Experiment I with preschool subjects making only such procedural changes as were necessitated by their illiteracy.

Method

Procedure. The following modifications were made to the procedure used in Experiment I with the older children. (*a*) Instead of nonsense syllables, animal noises served as the "words" of the language; "sentences" were thus sequences like MOO MEOW, OINK QUACK, etc. (*b*) Instead of being written each word was graphically represented by a picture of the animal or of its head, with the mouth open as if to talk. (*c*) The sentences were "read" from top to bottom rather than from left to right, i.e., a sentence was completed by placing a word (picture) in the vacant position above or below the presented word; this modification was introduced because it was thought that preschool children would more easily adopt a consistent top-to-bottom than left-to-right direction of reading. (*d*) A correct response was rewarded with a raisin, and if the subject wished he could exchange four raisins for an M & M candy. (*e*) There were several sessions rather than one; these were kept short and second and subsequent sessions always began with one presentation of each of the first four problems; responses to these problems were not tallied if the subject had met the learning criterion on these problems in prior sessions.

Before the training began, a consensus, determined by the experimenter, was reached for each picture as to "what the animal said." Then the first problem was presented several times over and used as a vehicle for teaching the children to read the pictures smoothly in the top-bottom sequence; on subsequent problems if the child had difficulty reading the sequence after his response, he was helped until he had read it at least once smoothly.

In addition to the above, a further modification had to be introduced. On problems in which the word presented (e.g., MOO) was in top position, the child was instructed before his response: "Does it go Moo. . . , or Moo. . .?"; during the first brief pause the experimenter indicated one alternative with the end of his pencil, and during the second the other alternative. When the word presented (e.g., QUACK) was in bottom position, the instruction was "Does it go. . .QUACK, or . . .QUACK?" with similar indication of the alternatives. The purpose of the instruction was to encourage some sort of rehearsal of the alternative sentences. It was necessary because a picture appears to elicit vocal or subvocal rehearsal of a particular word less readily than does the written word. The experimenter was careful not to give voice or gestural cues which could guide the subject to the correct response.

Subjects. The subjects were 12 nursery-school children, aged 4–2 to 5–0.

Results

The learning scores are shown in Table 1. All subjects learned[3] and it can be seen that the median scores for both errors and trials to learn are very similar to those of the older subjects of Experiment I. Although the upper end of the

[3] The procedure proved not to be well adapted to some 4-year-olds. The initial teaching, the preliminary instruction to each problem, and the requirement of reading the picture sequences involved controls on the subjects' behavior which tended to arouse their opposition. This was generally handled by keeping the sessions brief, but nevertheless four subjects refused to cooperate after experiencing only one or two sessions. These subjects are omitted from the results (they were not learning more slowly than the others when they stopped).

range is higher, two subjects completed the initial learning without any errors whatever, just as in Experiment I. On 75% of the generalization problems the subjects filled the vacant position with the word that had occupied this position in the previous learning. This figure is close to the figure of 78% found in Experiment I. Vacant first and second positions were filled in about equally often. One subject gave a crude but accurate statement of the principle involved.

While the procedure necessarily differs in too many ways from that of Experiment I to permit firm conclusions to be drawn from the comparison, it can nevertheless be stated that the preschool subjects did not find this task substantially more difficult than the older subjects found the analogous task in Experiment I. Moreover, contextual generalization occurred in both age groups. While a comparison of age groups on a relevant task which involved neither reading nor simulation of reading in either group would be more satisfactory, the results nevertheless provide prima facie evidence of age-group similarities in the learning processes involved.

GENERAL DISCUSSION

The remainder of the paper will consider how far a theory based on contextual generalization may provide a plausible account of the learning of the grammatical structure of natural languages, particularly English. As developed in the preceding experiments the theory consists of three proposals. (*a*) "What is learned" are the locations of expressions in utterances. (*b*) Units (i.e., expressions whose position is learned) can form a hierarchy in which longer units contain shorter units as parts, the location that is learned being the location of a unit within the next-larger containing unit, up to the sentence. (*c*) The learning is a case of perceptual learning—a process of becoming familiar with the sounds of expressions in the positions in which they recur.[4]

With respect to Proposal (*b*), probably the simplest hierarchial scheme is provided by the binary-fractionation model. This model, in which position is defined through successive first-last dichotomies, is the one used in the design of Experiments II and III, and can serve as a basis for discussion where a specific model is required.

One direct way in which the theory might be examined is by collecting data on the development of grammatical structure. The first word combinations of three children 18–24 months old studied by the writer have been shown to have a characteristic structure which was interpreted as indicating that what had been learned was that each of a small number of words belonged in a particular position in a word combination (Braine, 1963). Occasional reference to the subsequent development of these children will be made in the discussion.

The discussion will be concerned with some obvious facts about the structure of natural languages, English especially, which raise difficulties for the theory proposed. Each difficulty will be discussed in turn. Since it is hardly to be expected that the learning of all of the many kinds of grammatical regularities that exist will

[4] Certain cues not involved in the experiments could facilitate the learning of position in natural languages. In English, for example, various suffixes are associated with many nouns and verbs (e.g., -MENT, -ATION, -NESS, etc., and -ATE -IZE, etc.). Also, many of the more frequent nouns (especially those without suffices) are correlated with "object-like" features in the external world, and many verbs with "process-like" features. That quite young children know these correlates has been demonstrated by Brown (1957). Where they covary with position, all such cues, although only probabilistic, should facilitate the learning of the locations of expressions. (In the experiments it is likely that learning and generalization would have been markedly assisted if the words belonging in a given position had been "tagged" in some way, e.g., by giving them all the same ending.)

prove amenable to interpretation in terms of the above proposals, a purpose of the discussion will be to determine the range of phenomena to which the theory can hope to apply, and suggest ways of extending its scope.

Contrasting Word Order

Of the conceivable arrangements of any given set of morphemes, usually only a few are grammatically possible (e.g., THE MAN, is possible in English, whereas MAN THE. is not); the word-order is said by linguists to be "restricted" to those that can occur (e.g., Harris, 1951, p. 184). When two (or more) arrangements are grammatically possible, sometimes the two orders are equivalent (e.g., BOYS AND GIRLS, GIRLS AND BOYS), in which case the order is said to be "free"; more often the two orders are non-equivalent (e.g., GEORGE HIT JOHN, JOHN HIT GEORGE, or THE CHILD IS INSIDE THE CAR, THE CAR IS INSIDE THE CHILD), in which case the orders are said to "contrast."

In mastering distinctions associated with contrasts between word orders, the child probably learns to respond to relationships quite different from any suggested so far in this paper. For example, in English both the sequences Noun + INSIDE, and INSIDE + Noun can occur; to use them appropriately the child must presumably learn to place INSIDE before the word for the container and after the word for the contained object. One of the children the writer has studied uttered both verb-noun and noun-verb sequences at about 24 months of age, but he had apparently not learned that the agent of an action goes before the verb, and the object of the action typically after it, so that where English word order contrasts, his word order was free. Thus, among Gregory's utterances one finds CARRY MOMMY (where Mommy is to do the carrying), COMES ELEVATOR, TRUCK FIX, FALL DOWN RABBIT, as well as the normal English word order, e.g., DADDY FIX, MOMMY COMES, etc. Apparently the agent—action sequence is not necessarily primitive in the English sentence but can develop, at least in some children, as a polarization of a sequence which is initially more or less random. In a similar way one finds Gregory saying INSIDE DOCTOR Z--- (meaning that Dr. Z--- is inside his office), POCKET INSIDE, as well as the normal order, e.g., CANDY INSIDE, INSIDE POCKET.

It seems clear that the theory developed is not relevant to the learning of contrasts between word orders, and that its scope must be confined to the learning of restrictions on word order. This exclusion from the theory may be quite far-reaching: it seems probable that features of English word order which have to do with the difference between transitive and intransitive verbs, and with the distinction between the prepositional and adverbial use of words like INSIDE, ON, OFF, DOWN, etc. (e.g., THE CAR OUTSIDE, OUTSIDE THE CAR, or THE LIGHT [IS] ON, ON THE TABLE) may not develop until the appropriate contrasts have been learned.

Cues to the "Middle" of Utterances

If, as claimed, children learn the sentence-positions of words and phrases, they must have some way of identifying where in the sentence the initial phrase ends and the next phrase begins. In the experiments described, the boundary was clearly defined by the procedure: the subjects filled in the entire first or last phrase. (In the one experiment where this was not true, learning was impaired.) But what cues define borders between constituents for the 2-year-old learning the natural language?

One can only speculate about possible answers to this question. Two major types of cue offer themselves for consideration. The first have to do with intonation. By "intonation" is meant the variety of phenomena referred to by such terms as "stress," "pitch," "juncture," "off-glide," "on-glide," "contour," "superfix," "intonation pattern," etc. Just how much information about utterance structure is given by intonation is currently a matter of controversy in the linguistic literature. According to Trager and Smith (1951, pp. 67–77), the segmentation of an utterance into parts, and of the parts into parts, is almost completely specified by features of intonation. If this is true, most of the necessary information about the location of the boundaries between positions is contained within an utterance as spoken. However, the extent of the correlation between intonation phenomena and grammatical structure has been seriously questioned (e.g., Bolinger, 1957). Moreover, Trager and Smith's analysis assumes the existence of 12 phonemes which have to do with stress, pitch, and juncture. Recent work indicating that pitch and not intensity is the main cue to stress (Bolinger, 1958) would appear to put this phonemic analysis in jeopardy. It is doubtful, however, that anyone would claim that intonational phenomena provide no information about the partition of utterances.

That intonation does provide information about segmentation is shown by the following demonstration. A five-word nonsense sentence, OB ORDEM KIVIL MERVO EENA was recorded several times over, spoken in two ways. In one case the sentence was spoken with definite primary stress on the first syllables of the second and last words; in the other case stresses were placed on the third and last words; care was taken that there should be no special pause between any pair of words. Five people on the institute staff listened to each form of the sentence and wrote down a five-word English sentence which seemed to them grammatically similar to the model. It was predicted that the sentence would be heard as composed of two parts, with the point of division located immediately following the word carrying the first main stress. Despite the crudity of the stimuli, the prediction was consistently borne out. In half the sentences a subject-predicate division was placed at the predicted mid-point (e.g., THE LÁDY/GOES INTO TÓWN, THE ALGEBRA CLÁSSROOM/SEATED TWÉNTY); in four sentences an initial prepositional phrase was separated off (e.g., FOR SWÉETENING/SHE PREFERRED SÚGAR, IN THIS ÓRDER/WORDS FLÝ); in the remaining sentence the midpoint divided the predicate-phrase (THEY ARE GÓING/RIGHT AWÁY—with a pronoun subject in English the first main stress tends to shift forward). If the length of the juncture between words, as well as the location of the first main stress, were manipulated, it may well be that the subjects could be led to be more consistent in the type of division they hear.

In addition to intonational phenomena, a role in defining the immediate constituents may well be played by the closed-class morphemes (i.e., articles, prepositions, auxiliary verbs, etc.—these classes are called "closed" because they contain only a small number of morphemes which change relatively slowly in the history of a language, whereas the "open" classes, i.e., nouns, verbs, and adjectives, contain enormous numbers of members and show a relatively fast turnover historically). Computer programs which analyze grammatical structure rely completely on the closed-class morphemes (Klein & Simmons, 1961). How much use the child makes of them probably depends on his level of development, since some of the closed-class morphemes tend to develop relatively late. However, even in the early stages of development when the child may not differentiate them clearly, they may nevertheless provide boundary markers for the utterance constituents. In ordinary conversation these morphemes are typically unstressed and poorly differentiated phonetically (cf./wɔnəgow/for WANT TO GO,/əpiysəkukiy/for A PIECE OF COOKIE, /ɔlə/for ALL THE, etc.); conceivably they may serve in the early stages to provide a noise-filled physical separation between the stressed (and therefore phonetically clearer) meaning-bearing open-class words in the utterances the child is exposed to. Some support for this speculation is provided by one of the children studied by the writer at 24–27 months of age. Steven used two elements like these morphemes: one, which will be written UH, usually took the phonetic form /ə/; the other, which will be written DI consisted of /d/ followed by a front or central vowel. Although they were devoid of meaning, definite rules seemed to govern Steven's use of these elements. Both could occur at the beginning or middle of almost any utterance; when one of them occurred at the middle of the utterance, it seemed to mark the boundary between immediate constituents. Thus, in the corpus of Steven's utterances at this time there is a sequence UP UH TOP (i.e., "up on top"), and another UP TOP UH BETTY (i.e., "up on top of Betty"), where UH appears to have shifted forward to the phrase division. Similarly, there is BETHY DI SLEEPY BED (i.e., "Bethy's asleep in bed"), and NO UH DADDY SLEEPY (i.e., "Daddy's not asleep," or, "I don't want Daddy to sleep"), where there is again a shift to the phrase division. While Steven was the only one of the three children studied to develop elements of this kind, his apparent use of them as boundary markers may indicate how very young children tend to hear some closed-class morphemes, even if they do not incorporate them in their own speech in this way.

Positional Regularities in English?

Since colloquial English constitutes both the terminal point of the child's own development and the verbal environment in which he develops, a theory which proposes that what is learned are the locations of words must suppose that rigid rules define what parts of speech can occur in what phrase- and sentence-positions in ordinary English grammar.

In discussing the extent to which such a correlation exists, it is convenient to follow recent work in linguistics which divides English grammar into two parts. According to Harris (1957) and Chomsky (1957), the grammar of a language can be hierarchized into an elementary part, called the "kernel" of the language, and a second part which consists of a set of transformational rules for deriving complex sentences from simple ones. The kernel grammar contains the definitions of the main parts of speech and describes rules for constructing simple declarative statements without complex noun or verb phrases. The transformational rules then carry these kernel sentences into other sentences, or into phrase or clause segments of sentences, which could not be derived in the kernel grammar. Thus from the kernel of English one could generate THE MAN IS BITING THE DOG. The transformational rules would then show how to turn this into the passive, or into the negative, or into any of several questions (e.g., WHY IS THE MAN BITING THE DOG?), or into a relative clause (e.g., . . . WHO IS BITING THE DOG. . .), or into a noun phrase (e.g., THE MAN'S BITING THE DOG, as subject perhaps of IS CAUSE FOR SUPPRISE), etc.

Obviously no set of rules defining the positions of words and phrases in simple declarative sentences like THE LIGHT IS ON or GEORGE WALKED ACROSS THE STREET, will also fit the part-of-speech positions in complex sentences of transformational origin like SHE FOUND THEM HELPING THE MAN MAKE IT GO with its successive noun-verb sequences, or THE BOY'S PUSHING THE LAWNMOWER WOKE THE BABY where the arrangement of words in the initial noun phrase is more like that of a normal sentence than of an ordinary noun phrase. Correlations of parts of speech and sentence positions must therefore be discussed separately for kernel sentences and for the derived transforms. Within the simple declarative kernel sentence there appears to be a standard arrangement of words and phrases which is normal for this type of sentence. (Whether this arrangement actually shows the detailed correlations of words and phrases with positions which is required by the theory proposed will be considered in the next section.) Similarly, in each types of transform there seem to be definite rules governing the positional arrangements of parts of speech which is standard for that type of transform. For example, all interrogatives are constructed according to a plan which is standard for interrogatives; similarly questions beginning with WHAT, WHERE, WHY, WHEN, HOW, WHO have a common arrangement; relative clauses follow one of two main arrangements according to whether the pronoun is object or subject of its verb; transforms which occupy noun positions in other sentences follow one of several standard arrangements (e.g., THE BOY'S PUSHING THE LAWN-MOWER, THE LIGHT'S BEING ON, HIS BRAKING THE CAR AT THAT MOMENT, etc., or THE READING OF BOOKS, THE ACTING OF PLAYS, etc., or FOR THE LIGHT TO BE ON, FOR HIM TO BRAKE THE CAR AT THAT MOMENT, etc., and several other forms); the same is true for the several other types of transform. In general, therefore, within the kernel and within each of the various types of transform there is a standard arrangement of parts of speech; the various standard arrangements are, however, all different from each other.

One way to formulate this state of affairs would be to regard English not as a unitary language, but as a family of sublanguages. The sentences in some of the sublanguages are complete English sentences; in others they do not occur alone, being merely clauses or phrases of English. The sublanguages differ in that the sequential arrangement of morphemes in each sublanguage is peculiar to that sublanguage. The languages have in common the fact that they all share the same vocabulary, and that any class of words which constitutes a part of speech in one sublanguage constitutes a part of speech in all the others. Moreover there are sentence-by-sentence correspondences between the sublanguages: to every sentence in each of the transformations there corresponds a sentence in the kernel (e.g., to JOHN WAS HIT BY GEORGE in the passive transformation, there corresponds GEORGE HIT JOHN in the kernel). However, the converse, that to every sentence in the kernel there corresponds a sentence in each transformation, is not true since many of the transformations are defective vis-a-vis the kernel (e.g., there are no passive transforms of kernel sentences containing the verb TO BE or intransitive verbs). The kernel therefore has a privileged status since the sentences in each sublanguage apparently constitute a mapping of some large group of sentences of the kernel (cf. Harris, 1957, Footnote 61). It is worth noting that the changes in arrangement made in the various transformations are usually rather minor ones, and much of the normal word order of the kernel grammar tends to be retained (e.g., in the interrogative there is merely an inversion of subject and auxiliary verb; noun transforms like THE BOY'S PUSHING THE LAWNMOWER differ little in arrangement from the kernel sentences to which they correspond, i.e., THE BOY WAS PUSHING THE LAWNMOWER, etc.).

In attempting to account for the child's learning of this intricate set of structures, it seems to the writer that it would be sound strategy to aim first at finding an explanation for the learning of the kernel of the language, i.e., for the learning of the structure of the simple declarative English sentence. This constitutes enough of a problem already. Moreover, any proposed theory which fails to account for the learning of the kernel will, a fortiori, fail to account for the learning of the structure of the language as a whole. If a viable account of the learning of the kernel can be found, then the fact that all the sublanguages have so very much in common (the same vocabulary and parts of speech, and many of the same word arrangements) suggests that there may be some hope of treating the learning of the other sublanguages as a problem in transfer of training. In any case the remainder of this discussion will consider only whether the proposals advanced earlier can be worked into a defensible account of the learning of the kernel grammar.

Even with the scope of the proposals narrowed in this way, there still remains the problem that the verbal environment in which the child learns contains both kernel and transforms, and therefore does not consistently present to him the same parts of speech in the same positions. It is difficult to evaluate this problem. On the one hand, it is noticeable that adults tend to simplify their language when speaking to very young children; also, since transforms usually change the normal word order in minor ways, it is probably true that most stretches of speech exemplify the normal positional arrangements more than they distort them. On the other hand, in the early stages of development the positional relationships in the child's own language obviously do not simply mirror the relationships in the adult English around him, but must be related to them in a much more complex manner. Almost nothing is known about the sequence in which various structures of English develop, so there is no point in discussing this question further.

Contingencies between Positions

Even as a theory of the learning of the kernel grammar, the proposals advanced are insufficient. The fundamental stumbling block is that the parts of speech which can occur in one position are frequently contingent on what part of speech occurs in some other position. Another way of expressing this difficulty is to say that the proposals advanced predict more generalization than actually occurs in natural languages. Thus, if four parts of speech, A, B, C, and D, occur in sequences AB and CD, the theory predicts that sequences AD and CB should also occur, by generalization. Yet such unlimited generalization of context often fails to occur in natural languages.

The concept of a primary phrase. The above difficulty arises in part because the proposals advanced make no provision that sentences be segmented so that generalization only occurs between comparable units. Consider the predicate phrases in such sentences as GEORGE IS THROWING, GEORGE IS READING, GEORGE IS THROWING ACCURATELY, GEORGE IS READING THE BOOK. According to the binary fractionation model, in the first two sentences, the first predicate position is occupied by IS and the second position by THROWING or READING; in the other two sentences the first predicate position has IS THROWING or IS READING, and the second position ACCURATELY or THE BOOK. If the content of the first position in one case is recombined with that of the second position in the other case one obtains such predicate phrases as IS ACCURATELY, IS READING THROWING. As they stand, the proposals can be interpreted to predict that such recombinations would occur by generalization. To avoid such absurdities the theory clearly has to regard the predicate division of GEORGE IS THROWING into IS + THROWING as somehow less important than the predicate division of GEORGE IS READING THE BOOK into IS READING + THE BOOK. The simplest way to accomplish this is to set up a distinction between "primary phrases" and "components of phrases" (i.e., morphemes): IS THROWING, THE BOOK, ACCURATELY are "primary phrases," each having component morphemes (e.g., IS, THROW, -ING; ACCURATE, -LY). The proposals advanced must contain two levels, and must state specifically that it is the locations of expressions which are primary phrases, or whose parts are primary phrases, that are learned, and that within each type of primary phrase the locations of the component morphemes are also learned. With the proposals thus modified, one could say that the first part of a sentence is a noun phrase, and that the second part is either a verb phrase, or has as its first component a verb phrase. A statement of this kind is not possible unless a primary phrase such as a verb can be treated as a single unit, regardless of whether it is THROWS, THROW, IS THROWING, HAS THROWN, HAS BEEN THROWING.

Primary phrases typically consist of an open-class morpheme (e.g., noun, verb) together with one or more closed-class morphemes (e.g., article, auxiliary verb). Since the closed-class morphemes tend to be specific to the primary phrases to which they belong (e.g., articles to noun units, -LY to adverbial units), and tend to recur much more frequently than the open-class morphemes, they could serve as cues to "mark" or "tag" primary phrases. They would then facilitate the learning of the locations of primary phrases.

Some support for the concept of a primary phrase unit is provided by Glanzer (1962), who has shown that in paired-associate learning, although associates are learned more readily to open- than closed-class words in isolation, the opposite is true when the words are embedded in a nonsense syllable context. For example, although OF is a more difficult associate than FOOD, TAH OF ZUM is easier than YIG FOOD SEB. Glanzer interprets the results to indicate that closed-class words are incomplete units when isolated from context.

The notion of a primary phrase also receives some confirmation in the stress sequences in English, since the normal English intonation seems generally to mark with some degree of strong stress the principal word of each primary unit in simple sentences (e.g., OUR NÉIGHBOUR IS RÉADING THE RÍOT-ACT QUITE VOCÍFEROUSLY TO HIS CHILDREN IN THE GÁRDEN).

One new problem is created by the concept of a primary phrase: one now has to enquire what makes the phrase a unit. What, if the metaphor will be forgiven, provides the psychological cement which binds the morphemes of a primary phrase more closely to each other than to other components of an utterance? Discussion of this question is temporarily deferred.

Contingencies still incompatible with the proposals. Even when utterances are treated as segmented into primary phrases in the above manner, there are still very many cases where the occupancy of one position is contingent on the occupancy of other positions. Thus, in many English dialects, a small class of verbs (e.g., IS, BECOME, SEEM) yield predicate phrases consisting of verb + adjective, whereas following other verbs one usually finds adverbs (e.g., THE WIND BECAME VIOLENT, but THE WIND BLEW VIOLENTLY; THE OPPOSITION SEEMED SKILLFUL, but THE OPPOSITION OBJECTED SKILLFULLY). The widespread phenomenon of grammatical agreement constitutes another kind of contingency between positions. Consider, for example, the case of the arbitrary gender distinction in French. Masculine and feminine articles, and endings elsewhere in the sentence, occur in the same positions as each other; according to the theory as it now stands, their contexts should generalize feminine articles and endings occurring in association with masculine nouns and vice versa. A French child instructed according to the theory should get thoroughly confused. Since French children apparently contrive not to be, there is clearly something lacking in the proposals advanced. Within primary phrases a contingency of one morpheme on the presence of another in the same unit is particularly frequent. There is, for instance, the contingency between certain prepositions and verbs (e.g., TEAR UP, THINK OVER), or between certain words and noun-making particles (e.g., INVOLVEMENT, but DEPEND-ENCE). Such contingencies become very elaborate in the varied declensions and conjugations of highly inflected languages. Thus, to write a computer program which would produce Latin verb forms, one would have to proceed more or less by setting up paired lists A and a, B and b, C and c, . . . etc.; on list A would be the first conjugation stems, and on List a the first conjugation endings; Lists B and b, C and c, D and d would cover the second, third, and fourth conjugations, and Lists E and e, F and f, . . . Z and z would take care of the irregular forms. A long disjunctive instruction would be required stating that a verb consists of a pair of items either from A and a, or from B and b, or C and c, . . . or Z and z. According to the theory proposed, such an intricate system should be very difficult to learn: the stems and endings should both generalize in the course of learning with the result that the whole complex system should collapse into simple structure—one set of stems and one set of endings; it would, according to the theory, be simpler that way. Yet apparently it was not. It is, of course, possible that the Roman child did overgeneralize in this way at some point in his development, much as English speaking children occasionally form participles like SINGED and BROKED; but such generalizations must clearly have been relatively transitory and easily corrected, otherwise the language itself would presumably have been less stable.

There are therefore two central problems which cannot be handled by the theory as it now stands: the contingencies between the contents of different positions, and the question as to what causes the morphemes of a primary phrase to "go together" as a unit.

Learning contingencies. Let us add to the theory the assumption that the subjects learning a language tend to form associations—similar to those studied in paired-associate experiments—between morphemes of the language, and let us see if the addition of this assumption can provide a solution to the above problems. The assumption itself is not an extravagant one. That English-speaking subjects do indeed form such associations is amply demonstrated by the work of Miller and Selfridge (1950) and others.

The notion that learned paired associations between morphemes play a role in learning grammatical structure can only be plausible under certain circumstances. If one is forced to assume that every member of one of the large open classes of morphemes becomes associated with every member of another such class, the sheer number of associations posited becomes astronomical, and the assumption therefore implausible. If, however, one can assume that the foci of associative bonds are typically members of the closed morpheme classes (i.e., articles, prepositions, plural -s, pronouns, auxiliary verbs, verb endings -ING, -ED, etc., adverbial -LY, noun and verb suffixes -MENT, -ENCE, -IZE, etc.), the assumed number of paired associates learned, though still large, is very considerably less large. If the validity of the law of exercise is assumed, i.e., that the strength of an associative link is proportional to the frequency of occurrence of the pair, then, given the fact that the most frequently occurring morphemes are members of the closed classes, it is inevitable that these morphemes should become the foci of associational links. From the law of exercise one would predict that the strongest associative bonds should form between closed-class morphemes, as, for instance, between prepositions and articles (e.g., NEAR THE, OF A, IN SOME), or between auxiliaries and verb endings (e.g., IS —ING, HAS —ED, HAS —EN); links somewhat less strong should occur between closed- and open-class morphemes—thus an association of some strength might be expected to be learned between the articles and virtually all the nouns in an English speaker's vocabulary, and between the auxiliary and verb endings and the verb stems. Paired-associate links of negligible strength would be expected to form between pairs of open-class words, except for a few pairs—few in proportion to the total number of possible pairs—which recur together frequently for ecological rather than grammatical reasons (e.g., DRIVE-CAR, DRINK-COFFEE).[5]

Most cases of contingencies between positions can be schematized more or less as follows. One of two (or more) words, or classes of words may occupy the first position in a construction. Let us call these A′ and A″. These are followed by a word class, P, which is in turn followed by elements x and y, the choice of x or y being contingent on whether A′ or A″ occurs in first position. That is, if an A′ occurs then x occurs, if an A″ then y, giving grammatical sequences A′Px, A″Py; the elements x and y thus "agree" with the earlier part of the utterance. It is possible, of course, for x and y to precede P, in which case the formulae would read A′xP, A″yP, with the covarying elements contiguous. In terms of the theory one must assume that in the course of learning contingencies of this nature a paired-associate link forms between x and every A′, and between y and every A″. If A′ and A″ are members of a closed word class, as is often the case (e.g., pronouns each individually linked with particular verb endings x, y, . . .), the assumption seems to the writer reasonably plausible since the number of associations assumed is quite limited, and the amount of practice enormous. Frequently A′ and A″ are not completely different words but are distinguished only by accompanying closed-class elements. Thus A′ may take the form Af or fA and A″ the form Ag or gA, where f and g are closed-class morphemes, either affixes or separate elements like articles or auxiliaries. The formulae then take the form AfPx, AgPy (or fAPx, gAPy). Gender in French, and the singular-plural distinction in English and a large number of languages seem to be examples of this type.[6] The only associative linkages which need be assumed are between f and x, and g and y.

The theory has now developed all the ideas necessary for understanding grammatical frames (e.g., in English a grammatical frame consists of an arrangement of closed-class morphemes and dashes, such as THE— — S — LY, which completely determines the parts of speech going in each vacant position). If a part of a language fulfills the formulae fAPx, gAPy, and if it is assumed that the dependencies of fA and gA units on first position and of Px and Py units on second position are learned in addition to the paired associates f-x, g-y, then it is clear that the frames f — — x, g — — y will determine the parts of speech occupying the blanks.

From the assumption that children learn both positional regularities and paired associations between morphemes, it is possible to deduce the conditions under which overgeneralization would be expected to occur in the course of learning declensions and conjugations. Such errors would depend on the relative rates of learning positional regularities and associations If the positional regularities are learned more rapidly, children should pass through a stage where "errors" such as

[5] The recent finding (Glanzer, 1962) that closed-class words elicit a greater variety of responses than open-class words in free word association, appears to support these contentions. However, it is not certain that free association data are germane, since there may be factors of set operative in free association experiments, which lead subjects to prefer responses based on meaning (e.g., perhaps, BLACK-WHITE) to responses that reflect directly learned verbal contingencies (e.g., perhaps, SLACK-BOARD).

[6] It is here assumed that the absence of an ending which is frequently present can itself serve as the focus of an association. Structural linguists frequently treat the absence of an element as itself an element; thus, in the same way that BOYS is analyzed as BOY + -S, many grammarians analyze BOY as BOY + ϕ, where ϕ is the "zero ending" associated with the singular. The notion that the absence of a frequently present cue can itself serve as a cue does not seem objectionable psychologically. The English concord can thus be schematized as NϕVs or NsVϕ (N = noun, V = verb, ϕ = zero ending); this exemplifies the text formula.

SINGED and BROKED are common. The relative paucity of inflexions in English gives the English-speaking child less scope for errors of this nature than children learning some other languages; it would be interesting, for example, to know the extent and kinds of overgeneralizations that the elaborate case systems and conjugations of Russian or Finnish give rise to in the children of these countries. Guillaume (1927) provides some data on the development of the verb inflections in French. According to Guillaume, initially verbs tend not to be inflected: one form is used regardless of context. For example, in the case of the verb *TENIR*, of which the three most used forms are *TENIR*, *TENU*, and *TIENT* (or *TIENS*—*TIENS* and *TIENT* are, of course, phonetically identical), only *TIENT* may be used, e.g., *IL A TIENT* instead of *IL A TENU*. At a somewhat later stage the verb is inflected but overgeneralizations are frequent—Guillaume cites the infinitive *TIENDRE* (instead of *TENIR*), the participle *ÉTEINDÉ* (instead of *ETEINT*), the imperfects *PRENDAIS*, *TIENDAIS* (instead of *PRENAIS*, *TENAIS*). Of particular interest is the fact that alternative incorrect instances of the same form are uttered in quick succession by the same child. Thus one child is reported as using both the participles *BUVE* and *BUVU* (instead of *BU*, from *BOIRE*) indiscriminately at one period; similarly, both *OUVRI* and *OUVERT*, *PRIS* and *PRENDU*, are reported as occurring in the same or successive utterances. If positional regularities (e.g., learning to place *-É*, *-I*, or *-U* at the end of the verb stem) are learned more rapidly than paired-associates (e.g., associations of particular endings *-É*, *-I*, or *-U* with particular verb stems) are formed, then it would be predicted that such forms as *BUVÉ* and *BUVU* might both occur temporarily without a marked preference for one or the other being shown.[7]

If cases exist where associations are formed more rapidly than the positional regularities are learned, a different kind of error would be expected—one in which there is some inversion of the normal order of morphemes. Invented English examples might be FALL-DOWNED, or HANG-UPING.

The notion that associations form between pairs of morphemes may also provide an answer to the question raised earlier as to what makes the morphemes of a primary phrase go together as a unit. If the strength of an associational link between morphemes is a function of the proximity of the morphemes in the sentence as well as of the frequency of their joint occurrence, it would follow that in the great majority of utterances each open-class morpheme will be more strongly associated with the other morphemes of the primary phrase in which it occurs than with morphemes outside the phrase.

Conclusion

The preceding discussion indicates that the line of thought developed from the experiments described certainly cannot provide a general theory of the learning of grammatical word order. However, the

[7] It would probably be wrong to view the learning of conjugations as simply an associating of particular stems with particular endings. In the Indo-European languages conjugations tend to have a characteristic thematic stem vowel. Thus in French the stems of two conjugations end with a thematic -E or -I in many forms, and the "-RE" verbs have a terminal consonant (cf. the futures DONN-E-R-AI, FIN-I-R-AI, VEND-ϕ-R-AI). In Latin thematic long vowels -Ā, -Ē, -Ī were characteristic of three conjugations and in the remaining conjugation a consonantal (or short vowel) stem was thematic. It would follow from the general line of thought presented that these thematic vowels (or their absence) should permit a considerable economy in the number of associations learned, since often it need only be assumed that associations form between the radical and the thematic vowel on the one hand, and between the vowel and those endings specific to a conjugation on the other. In Latin the three long-vowel conjugations sometimes shared endings which were not possessed by the other conjugation, so that one might speculate that the length of the stem vowel itself may have been a focus for associations, permitting a further reduction in the total number of associations to be learned.

gross facts of English structure reviewed appear to be compatible with a modified version of the theory, restricted in scope. The necessary restrictions in scope are the limitation of the theory to the learning of the kernel grammar (although further study may permit extension to transformations), and the exclusion of the learning of contrasts between word orders.

As modified the theory proposes: (*a*) "What is learned" are the locations of units, and associations between pairs of morphemes. (*b*) The location learned is the location of a unit within the next-larger containing unit of a hierarchy of units. There are hierarchies at two levels: within sentences the units are primary phrases and sequences of primary phrases; within primary phrases the ultimate units are morphemes. (*c*) The learning of locations is a case of perceptual learning—a process of becoming familiar with the sounds of units in the temporal positions in which they recur.

References

Bolinger, D. L. Intonation and grammar. *Lang. Learn.*, 1957, 8, 31–38.

Bolinger, D. L. A theory of pitch accent in English. *Word*, 1958, 14, 109–149.

Braine, M. D. S. The ontogeny of English phrase structure. The first phase. *Language*, 39, 1963, 1–13.

Brown, R. W. Linguistic determinism and the part of speech. *J. abnorm. soc. Psychol.*, 1957, 55, 1–5.

Chomsky, N. *Syntactic structures.* The Hague: Mouton & Co., 1957.

Gibson, J. J., & Gibson, Eleanor J. Perceptual learning: Differentiation or enrichment? *Psychol. Rev.*, 1955, 62, 32–41.

Glanzer, M. Grammatical category: A rote learning and word association analysis. *J. verbal Learn. verbal Behav.*, 1962, 1, 31–41.

Guillaume, P. Le développement des éléments formels dans le langage de l'enfant. *J. Psychol. norm. pathol.*, 1927, 24, 203–229.

Harris, Z. S. *Methods in structural linguistics.* Chicago: Chicago Univer. Press, 1951.

Harris, Z. S. Co-occurrence and transformation in linguistic structure. *Language*, 1957, 33, 283–340.

Klein, S., & Simmons, R. F. Automated analysis and coding of English grammar for information processing systems. *Sys. Develpm. Corp. Rep.*, 1961, SP-490.

Miller, G. A. *Language and communication.* New York: McGraw-Hill, 1951.

Miller, G. A., & Selfridge, J. A. Verbal context and the recall of meaningful material. *Amer. J. Psychol.*, 1950, 63, 176–185.

Trager, G. L., & Smith, H. L., Jr. An outline of English structure. *Stud. Linguist. occas. Pap.*, 1951, No. 3.

On the Acquisition of Syntax:

A Critique of "Contextual Generalization"[1]

T. G. BEVER, J. A. FODOR
and W. WEKSEL[2]

It has been recently suggested that the child's assimilation of the syntax of simple sentences can be attributed to a process of "contextual generalization" whereby information about the ordinal position of words and phrases is transferred from sentences the child has observed to new sentences. The theoretical and experimental bases for this claim are examined in the present paper. It is argued that such a process could not, in principle, account for what children learn about the structure of or relations between the sentences of their language. It is further argued that the experiments which purportedly demonstrate the existence of contextual generalization are, in fact, equivocal.

Introduction

There is a wide gap between the view of language current in linguistics (cf. Chomsky, 1957; Fodor & Katz, 1964; Lees, 1960) and the view of the language-using organism implicit in psychological theories of learning. The reason for this is clear. Neither the methods nor the results of recent work on grammar are fully compatible with the methodological and theoretical tenets prevalent in psychology.

The present paper examines the work of Braine (1963). This work has been selected for analysis because Braine attempts to assimilate insights provided by current linguistic theories while retaining an approach typical of psychological in-

1 This work was supported in part by the United States Army, Navy, and Air Force under Contract DA 36–039-AMC-03200(E); in part by the National Science Foundation (Grant GP-2495); the National Institutes of Health (Grants MH-04737-04 and MPM-16, 760); the National Aeronautics and Space Administration (Ns G-496); the United States Air Force (ESD Contract AF 19 [628–2487]).

2 Thomas Bever is a Junior Fellow, Society of Fellows, Harvard University.

William Weksel was a National Science Foundation Postdoctoral Fellow during the preparation of this manuscript.

We wish to thank Margaret Bullowa and her staff for their kindness in making available to us the data discussed in Footnote 4.

T. G. Bever, J. A. Fodor, and W. Weksel, "Theoretical Notes on the Acquisition of Syntax: A Critique of 'Contextual Generalization,'" *Psychological Review,* **72,** No. 6 (1965), 467–482. Reprinted by permission of the authors and publisher.

quiries into syntax. The inadequacies of Braine's position thus suggest a number of respects in which such theories resist translation into the vocabulary of learning theory. In particular, since Braine's position differs only in details from that of such other learning theorists as Jenkins and Palermo (1964), the arguments we shall present apply to their work *mutatis mutandis*.

According to Braine, "the acquisition of grammatical structure, especially those aspects of grammatical structure which have to do with word order...[p. 323]" is to be explained by appeal to a process of *contextual generalization*. Contextual generalization is informally defined as a process whereby an individual who learns the position of a word or a phrase in the sentence he hears "tends to place this segment in the same position in other contexts [p. 323]." Thus, "'What is learned' are primarily the proper locations of words in sentences [p. 324]."

Braine clearly recognizes that the ability to deal with novel sentences constitutes a major part of the child's linguistic competence. It is thus central among the phenomena that a theory of language learning must explain. Braine takes the ability to construct and comprehend novel sentences to be a special case of transfer of training based upon stimulus and response generalization. Specifically, contextual generalization is identified as a case of perceptual learning, "a process of auditory differentiation, or, of becoming familiar with, the temporal positions of expressions in utterances [p. 326]."

ARGUMENTS FOR CONTEXTUAL GENERALIZATION

Braine notes the inadequacy of a theory of syntax acquisition based on associative relations between lexical items. Such a theory cannot account for the ability of speakers to recognize the grammatical structure of nonsense material. Thus, a nonsense syllable, *kivil*, is recognized as a nonce verb in:

1. People kivil every day.

That is, 1 is recognized as syntactically well formed despite the lack of associative connections between the words.

Such examples show that the speaker's ability to exploit syntactic relations does not depend upon forming associative bonds between lexical items. Therefore, Braine argues, the speaker's information about syntactic structure primarily concerns the grammatical properties of *locations* in sentences. Thus, the child learns such facts as: The first position in a simple English sentence is characteristically the noun position; the second position is characteristically occupied by a verb. Since the syntactic properties of a position do not, by definition, depend on the lexical item or phrase that appears in that position, novel material in a given location is perceived as having the grammatical properties characteristic of that location. Thus *kivil* is recognized as a verb in 1 because it appears in the position assigned the verbal element in such sentences as:

2. The boys eat the rabbits.
3. The boys do eat the rabbits.

For Braine, then, the syntactic properties of a segment are determined by the locations in which it occurs. A verb is defined as a word which characteristically appears in the second position in simple sentences, a noun is a word which characteristically appears in the first position in simple sentences, etc. To learn the syntactic properties of a word is primarily to learn the positions in which it can occur. In particular, given the positions a word can occupy in one sentence, we can often predict the positions which it may occupy in new sentences. From the fact that *eat* occupies the second position in 2, we can predict that it will occupy the homologous position in 4.

4. The wolves eat the rabbits.

Syntax assimilation thus consists of generalizing information about the positions in which a word is observed to occur. The correct use of a given word in a given position in new sentences is a consequence of such processes of generalization.

Braine holds that a description of word order accounts for much of the grammar of English and, consequently, that a theory which accounts for the learning of positions will have considerable explanatory power. Braine admits, however, that learning syntactic relations cannot consist solely of learning the appropriate relative positions of words and phrases. First, Braine points out, knowledge of relative positions would contribute little to the mastery of languages in which syntactic relations are expressed by inflection rather than order. Second, the notion of a position must be construed sufficiently abstractly so that a given sentential position can be occupied either by a word or by a phrase. (Notice, for example, that the "second" position in 3, i.e., the position functionally equivalent to the one occupied by "eat" in 2, is filled by the phrase "do eat.") Some explanation is required for the fact that phrases may exhibit positional privileges analogous to those exhibited by single words. In short, an explanation is needed of how phrases can act as syntactic units.

To accommodate inflection as a syntactic device and to account for the integrity of the phrase, Braine resorts to a limited associationism. He postulates associative bonds between "closed-class" morphemes (e.g., inflections) and "open-class" morphemes such as nouns and verbs. For example, Braine would presumably hold that the phoneme "s" at the end of a noun is associated with the lack of a phoneme "s" at the end of a following verb and conversely. Such associations hold for simple declarative sentences like:

5. The boy eats the rabbits.
6. The boys eat the rabbits

Braine believes that the formation of associations, augmented by position learning, is adequate to explain how the syntax of simple declarative sentences is learned. In effect, Braine considers such sentences to be sequences of "primary phrases." Primary phrases are themselves sequences of open- and closed-class morphemes connected by associative bonds. "The location learned is that of a unit within the next-larger containing unit of a hierarchy of units. There are hierarchies at two levels: within sentences the units are primary phrases and sequences of primary phrases; within primary phrases the ultimate units are morphemes [p. 348]."

Braine is aware that the information that certain sequences of linguistic elements behave as units and that such units can appear only in specified positions in simple sentences does not exhaust the speaker's knowledge of syntax. There are many different kinds of sentences allowing nearly all possible orders of words and primary phrases. Thus, if we take into account *all* the types of sentences in which it may occur, there are indefinitely many permissible locations of a linguistic unit (see examples, sentences 35–41). A list of the positions available to a linguistic unit could at best specify its behavior in only a circumscribed part of the language. Yet it is only the learning of such a list that contextual generalization could explain.

Braine meets this objection by restricting the scope of this theory to the assimilation of the grammatical properties of simple declaratives. He maintains this restriction is not arbitrary since simple declaratives have psychological and linguistic characteristics which justify postulating special processes for their assimilation. Braine thinks simple declaratives may predominate in the child's verbal environment, thus forming the primary models from which the child's knowledge of his language is extrapolated. Second, Braine claims recent work in linguistics divides grammar into two parts.

According to Harris (1957) and Chomsky (1957), the grammar of a language can be hierarchized into an elementary part, called the "kernel" of the language, and a second part which consists of a set of transformational rules for deriving complex sentences from simple ones. The kernel grammar contains the definitions of the main parts of speech and describes rules for constructing simple declarative statements...[p. 340].

Thus, if we can explain the acquisition of simple declarative sentences, we have accounted for the basic component of the grammar. The remaining portion—the complex sentences produced by transformation—is to be described as a set of *sublanguages,* one sublanguage for each type of sentence (passive, relative, question, etc.). Rather than attempting to study English in its full complexity, Braine concludes "...it seems that it would be sound strategy to aim first at finding an explanation for the learning of the kernel of the language, i.e., for the learning of the structure of the simple declarative English sentence. This constitutes enough of a problem already [p. 342]."

Finally, Braine argues that perceptual learning, of which contextual generalization is a special case, is a primitive process which does not demand much in the way of intellectual capacity of the learner. Contextual generalization would therefore satisfy at least one requirement on any process involved in first-language learning, namely, that it "not require intellectual capacities obviously beyond the reach of the 2-year-old [p. 326]."

If the learning of syntax is the generalization of the ordinal positions in which linguistic units appear, it is evident that the initial stage must consist in the perceptual isolation of such units. Braine claims that an argument for the feasibility of contextual generalization is that the boundaries of such units can be identified with certain specifiable properties of the speech signal.

Braine proposes two sorts of cues the child could use to identify these boundaries. One is "intonation": The stress, rhythm, and pitch patterns of sentences are assumed to be acoustic features which communicate information about segmentation. The other is the position of closed-class morphemes which, Braine holds, tends to delimit phrases.

We now turn to a discussion of these arguments. We first consider the claim that simple declaratives ought to receive special treatment. Second, we investigate whether the linguistic character of simple declaratives can be selected by reference to the syntactic properties of sentential positions. Third, we ask how much of the relation between simple declaratives and other types of sentences can be expressed by such a specification. Fourth, we consider broader issues raised by Braine's treatment of inflection, intonation, and perceptual isolation of units. Finally, we discuss his experimental techniques and results.

THE ROLE OF DECLARATIVE SENTENCES

Because he believes that a theory of the simple declarative sentences explains the basic part of the grammar and that such sentences predominate in the child's linguistic environment, Braine holds an account of the learning of simple declaratives is important even if it does nothing else. We shall return to the question of the kernel grammar presently. Let us first consider the claim that the verbal environment of the child exhibits a preponderance of grammatical simple declaratives.

It is clear that normal speech among adults does not exhibit any statistical bias towards fully grammatical simple declarative sentences. On the contrary, adult speech is usually ungrammatical (cf. Maclay & Osgood, 1959), and there is little evidence that adults engage in a careful limitation of their linguistic output when conversing with children.[3] More-

[3] Brown and Bellugi (1964) do find a relatively large proportion of fully grammatical utterances in their recordings of mothers' speech to children. They do *not,* however, find that

over, the verbal environment of children includes utterances produced by adults conversing among themselves, utterances produced by siblings with little command of the language, utterances heard on radio and television, etc. These diverse sources presumably form a heterogeneous verbal environment.

Even if simplified speech predominates in the child's verbal environment, there is no reason to suppose that the environment is unusually rich in simple declaratives. Analyses we have made of the speech of mothers taped during conversations with their children fail to support that hypothesis.[4] On the contrary, of a total of 432 utterances, 258 were fully grammatical. Of these, only 46 were simple declaratives.

Of course the character of the verbal environment plays a major role in language acquisition. It determines which language, vocabulary, style, and accent the child learns. *What is unknown, however, is which features of the verbal environment are critical for such learning.* There is, at present, no reason to believe that the learning of English is facilitated by a preponderance of simple declaratives in the child's sample of his language. Nor is there any reason to suppose that such a bias normally obtains.

We turn now to the question of whether the simple declarative has any formal or linguistic peculiarities to which its claim for special psycholinguistic status might be referred.

Braine makes a mistake that has unfortunately been common in psychological investigations concerned with generative grammar.[5] He supposes there exists a base or kernel grammar producing all and only simple declaratives and that the transformational operations producing complex sentences are defined over the declaratives generated by this base component. If this *were* the case, one might plausibly maintain that the status of the simple declarative as the underlying *linguistic* form justifies a parallel psycholinguistic precedence.

Braine is correct in asserting that there is a base form from which all syntactically related sentences are directly or indirectly derived. It is also true that base form is produced by a set of rules whose formal properties distinguish them from other rules in a generative grammar. *But it is not true that the base form is the simple declarative sentence.* The kernel grammar does *not* produce simple declarative sentences; it does not produce *any* sentences. Rather, the kernel grammar produces abstract structures that are transformed into a variety of different sentence types of which the simple declarative is one. In particular, the kernel sentence discussed by Chomsky (1957) should not be con-

simple declaratives are preponderant among such utterances. On the contrary, in the only sample of their data they present (a sample which they say is "rather representative"), only one of the six sentences produced by the mother is of the simple declarative type.

[4] The data were supplied by Margaret Bullowa and her staff at the Massachusetts Mental Health Center. The total represents 38 half hours of recorded conversation between three mothers and their children taped at ages ranging from 6 to 30 months. Six transcripts were selected for analysis, greater weight being given the recordings made at 20 months than those made at 6 months.

Neither our judgments of grammaticality nor sentential type were checked for interjudge reliability. While some degree of latitude may be involved in judgments of the former kind, the criteria for the latter are reasonably objective. It is clear that there is need for an extensive survey of the verbal environment of the child; the data we have cited are intended only as preliminary.

[5] For examples of discussions in which this mistake appears to have been made, see Miller (1962); Miller, Galanter, and Pribram (1960); Osgood (1963); and Mehler (1963). All these assume that linguistics assigns a privileged status to the simple declarative. For example, Miller's (1962) discovery that it takes less time to find the passive corresponding to an active than to find the passive corresponding to a question is *not* explained by appeal to the linguistic fact that the active is the underlying form in the production of the passive and the question. There is no such linguistic fact.

fused with these abstract structures. Kernel sentences differ from sentences of other types solely in that they are the consequence of applying only obligatory transformations to the kernel structure. Kernel sentences are thus in no sense the source for, or underlying form of, sentences of other syntactic types.[6]

Since the misunderstanding of the kernel notion has been widespread, it is worth indicating some of the linguistic considerations that militate against supposing the simple declarative to be the underlying form from which other sorts of sentences are derived. Consider the passive construction. We might attempt to derive 7*b* from 7*a* by a rule like that given in 8.

7*a*. The boy chases the dog.
7*b*. The dog is chased by the boy.

8. If NP_1 Verb NP_2 is a declarative sentence, and if NP_2 is the object of the verb, then NP_2 is Verbed by NP_1 in the corresponding passive.[7]

But now, consider 10, the result of applying 8 to 9:

9. The boy chases the dogs.
10. *The dogs is chased by the boy.

a string which is not grammatical for many dialects since the number of the verb should be determined by the subject. To avoid 10, Rule 8 must be split into two rules:

8*a*. NP_1 V $NP_2 + sg \rightarrow NP_2$ is V + ed by NP_1.
8*b*. NP_1 V $NP_2 + pl \rightarrow NP_2$ +s are V + ed by NP_1.

However, consider 12 and 14, the result of the application of 8*a* to 11 and 13 respectively.[8]

11. The boy is chasing the dog.
12. *The dog is is chasing ed by the boy.
13. The boy chased the dog.
14. *The dog is chased ed by the boy.

Just as the difference in the number of the object required us to adopt different passive rules for 7*a* and 9, so two more rules, 8*c* and *d*, will be required to passivize 11 and 15:

15. The boy is chasing the dogs.

8*a*. NP_1 is V ing $NP_2 + sg \rightarrow NP_2$ + sg is being V ed by NP_1.
8*d*. NP_1 is V ing $NP_2 + pl \rightarrow NP_2$ + pl are being V ed by NP_1.

and similarly for 13 and 16.

16. The boy chased the dogs.

8*e*. NP_1 V + ed $NP_2 + sg \rightarrow NP_2$ + sg was V + ed by NP_1.
8*f*. NP_1 V + ed $NP_2 + pl \rightarrow NP_2$ + pl were V + ed by NP_1.

In general, if we derive passives from

[6] That this has always been Chomsky's view is clear from a reading of *Syntactic Structures.* That Harris does not hold the simple declarative to be the base form follows from the fact that the notion of a derivation plays no role in Harris' theory. The mappings Harris (1957) employs in transformational analysis are characteristically symmetrical, hence there can be no questions of identifying an underlying syntactic form.

[7] We shall adhere to the notational conventions employed by linguists. In particular, ungrammatical strings will be preceded by *. ϕ stands for the zero number of a linguistic class (the plural of the English word "sheep" is thus "sheep + ϕ"). The following abbreviations will also be employed: NP for Noun Phrase, T for Article, VP for Verb Phrase, S for Sentence, N for Noun, V for Verb, sg for the singular morpheme, pres for the present-tense morpheme, pl for the plural morpheme, Det for determiner. Be will be used to designate any inflection of the verb "to be."

[8] If 8*a* can be allowed to interpret *is chasing* as a V at all, then it produces the incorrect form *12; if it cannot, then another new rule is required to produce 19 from 11. In all the examples in this paper, we do not claim to present the unique solutions and rules, either for those formulations which we show to be essentially incorrect or for those that are essentially correct. All the rules are considered out of the context of a presumed full grammar. *In* that context they might appear somewhat differently—but the distinctions and characteristics with which we are concerned will remain unchanged.

their corresponding actives, a different passive rule is required for each choice of object number and verb tense. For five tenses and two numbers there are at least 10 rules required to derive the simple passive from declarative sentences. Furthermore, even these 10 rules will not serve to derive the passive of more complicated sentences. For example, we will need special rules for:

16*a*. Does the boy chase the dog?
16*b*. Is the boy being chased by the dog?
17*a*. Why does the boy chase the dog?
17*b*. Why is the dog chased by the boy?

and so on.

In each of the cases we have discussed, the problem clearly arises from the attempt to derive the passive from its corresponding declarative. This difficulty would be avoided were it possible to define the transformation which rearranges the subject and object phrases so that it applies prior to the attachment of tense and number to the verb. In this way we specify the operations on the noun and verb relevant to passivization *without reference to the particular choice of tense and number they exhibit in a given sentence*. This rule is easily formulated:

18. NP_1 aux V NP_2 is rewritten as NP_2 aux be + Past part. V by NP_1.

However, it can be applied to generate all passives only if suitable abstract representations of sentences are provided as its domain. For example, the passive sentence, 19:

19. The dogs are being chased by the boy.

has, as its corresponding active, Sentence 15. Yet, if 19 is to be generated by an application of Rule 18, 15 cannot be its source, since 15 does not possess the formal properties required of strings in the domain of 18. No definite sense can therefore be given to the notion of applying 18 to 15. Rather, the source for 19 is the abstract illustrated in Figure 1.[9]

It can be demonstrated that derivations employing Rule 18 can account for the examples we have investigated so far. This means, in effect, that we have eliminated the proliferation of passive rules by insuring that inflections of number and tense are not specified by the passive rule. To do this, however, we have had to assume that the underlying form from which the passive derives is not a corresponding active but rather an abstract structure never realized in speech. Since analogous considerations show that the active itself is merely one of the deformations of this underlying structure, there would appear to be nothing in the linguistic theory of the derivation of English sentences which would justify assigning a special status to active declarative sentences.

[9] Of course, the result of 18's application to the structure in Figure 1 is *not* an actual sentence. The full derivation of Sentence 19 from the structure represented in Figure 1 is accomplished in at least three steps: (*a*) Rule 18 converts it into the string (constituent structure is not marked here) *the dog pl pl pres be+ing be+Past part. chase by the boy sg sg;* (*b*) an affix-attachment rule (affix, V→V+affix) *then* applies to produce the string *the dog pl be+pl+pres be+ing chase+Past part. by the boy sg sg;* (*c*) morphophonemic "spelling" rules convert this into Sentence 19 (see the paragraph following 33 in this paper and Chomsky, 1957, for other examples of affix movement and sentence derivations). The concept of the abstract and concrete level in sentences is a formal representation of many intuitions: for example, the difference between "logical" and "apparent" grammatical relations, the description of relations among sentences, and so on (see Fodor & Katz, 1964, for various discussions). Notice that by having the affix-attachment rule follow the passivization rule, 18, we avoid formally the multiplication of passive rules. Thus, this analysis is a formal account of the intuition that "passive" sentence is a unitary notion, and the intuition that it is the number of the apparent subject of the verb which determines verb number in English, not the number of the underlying or "logical" subject (see the section on inflection and Footnote 10 in this paper).

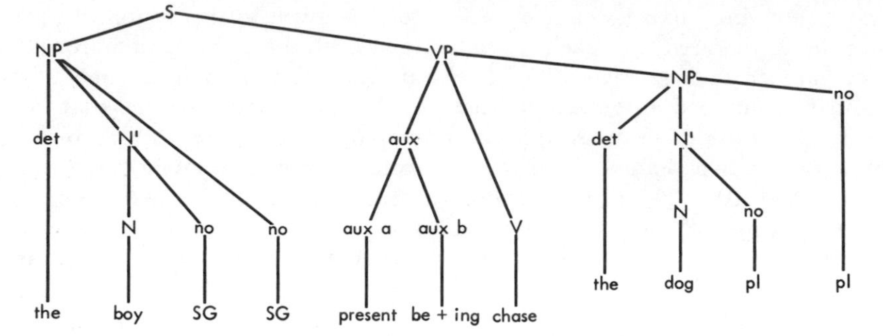

Fig. 1: Tree diagram of the underlying (untransformed) structure of the sentence: "The boy is chasing the dog."

CONTEXTUAL GENERALIZATION AND THE LEARNING OF POSITION

Suppose, however, that we grant Braine's assumption that there is some point to a special theory of the psychological processes underlying the learning of the syntax of declaratives. We must ask how much of the character of such sentences emerges from an analysis of the order relations among their constituents. We shall see that very little of the speaker's knowledge of the syntactic structure of simple declaratives can be attributed to having learned such relations.

To see how little of the syntax of a simple declarative is expressed by order, it is only necessary to consider sentences whose grammatical structure is not so expressed. Thus a speaker who knows that 20 and 21 are sentences also knows that while 22 is perfectly good English, there is something wrong with the syntax of 23.

20. The kangaroo cost 10 dollars.
21. The child blew the kazoo.
22. The kazoo was blown by the child.
23. *Ten dollars was cost by the kangaroo.

This example is particularly embarrassing for Braine, since 20 and 23 exhibit precisely the sort of positional relations on the basis of which contextual generalization is supposed to operate. That is, since both "10 dollars" and "the kazoo" appear postverbally, and since "The kazoo" appears preverbally in 22, the operation of contextual generalization ought to permit the preverbal appearance of "Ten dollars" in 23. The ungrammaticality of 23 suggests that there must be a difference between "blow" and "cost." Though this difference is not revealed by their positional privileges in simple declaratives, it is decisive for determining how passivization operates in sentences in which they occur.

A similar case is the following:

24. John phoned Jane up.
25. John phoned up Jane.
26. John phoned her up.
27. *John phoned up her.

Since "up" appears in the fourth and third positions respectively in 24 and 25, and since it appears in the fourth position in 26, Braine's theory predicts that place generalization requires its occurrence in 27. This prediction is incorrect. On the contrary, it is a necessary condition upon the grammaticality of sentences of the form:

28. John phoned up X.

that X not be a pronoun. Hence, if we are able to formulate the rule which permits 25 but precludes 27, we must take account not only of the ordinal positions of the words in those strings, *but also of the syntactic classes to which the words belong.*

These examples are a consequence of

a quite general fact: *the types of expression that can appear at a given ordinal position in a simple declarative sentence are extremely heterogeneous.* This fact is of the utmost importance for an evaluation of Braine's theory. For it entails that contextual generalization is an inadequate mechanism for extrapolating the grammatical regularities the child observes in his language. Many types of expression can appear at a given sentential position. Hence sentences exhibiting precisely the same ordinal relations among their segments may nevertheless be of different syntactic types. Since the operation of contextual generalization requires only that features of order be common to conditioned stimulus and generalized stimulus, it follows that we cannot infer that String S is a sentence whenever there exists a sentence, S′, related to S in a way that satisfies the conditions for contextual generalization.

To put it slightly differently, the examples just discussed demonstrate that some of our information about the syntactic character of simple declaratives cannot be expressed in terms of location information; rules which determine the interrelations among simple declaratives and the relations between simple declaratives and other sorts of sentences distinguish between expressions that can appear in a given location.

The similarity between Braine's view and that of Jenkins and Palermo (1964) is most evident at this point. Jenkins and Palermo apparently hold that the syntactic structure of a sentence can be expressed by a sequence of markers representing the classes of which the words comprising the sentence are members. Thus, they remark that "...the ideas we want to present here are of two sorts: *sequence* and *class* [p. 164]" and that

"Colorless green ideas sleep furiously" is a sentence in English not because it is true, or sensible, or interpretable by the listener, but because it is a "correct" assembly of classes appropriately modulated (*i.e.,* they are the right general classes of entries properly modified to take their places in the particular sequence).... The critical question, then, is seen to be that of the organization of the elements into classes [p. 164].

It is thus evident that Jenkins and Palermo's view of syntax is simply a weaker version of Braine's. For while Jenkins and Palermo acknowledge only sequences of class markers (and inflection), Braine has noticed the necessity of providing some psychological mechanism to account for the phrase structure of such sequences.

In short, there is no basis for Jenkins and Palermo's belief that the employment of mediational paradigms affords a breakthrough in the study of syntax assimilation. Though the formation of word classes can perhaps be accounted for by such paradigms, they throw no light whatever upon the assimilation of even such relatively superficial syntactic features as phrase structures. It goes without saying that appeals to them are utterly unilluminating on the question of how the child learns the deep syntactic structures with which this paper is primarily concerned.

THE DERIVATION OF ORDER

Thus far we have noted one sense in which order is a relatively unimportant feature of syntactic structure even in English, where inflection is not widely used: Identity of order relations is compatible with considerable differences in syntactic form. There is a more important point which also stems from Braine's failure to distinguish between underlying and surface structure. Often a correct formulation of the rules determining syntactic structure requires distinguishing between the order of lexical items in the sentence and in the underlying representation from which the sentence is derived. While contextual generalization might conceivably account for learning the former, it is patent that it could not account for the learning of the latter.

For example, in our discussion of the passive we treated *be* + *ing* as a unit in the underlying representation of sentences like 15. There are intuitive and formal advantages to this treatment. It permits us to account for the intuition that *be* + *ing* functions as a semantic unit indicating a particular mode of the main verb. Moreover, treating these morphemes as a single item permits us to account for the fact that such strings as:

29*a*. *The man is chase the dog.
29*b*. *The man chasing the dog

are not sentences: If *be* + *ing* is represented as a lexical unit, one of the morphemes comprising that unit cannot be selected without also selecting the other.

Cases in which simplicity of representation and linguistic intuition require an underlying order differing from the order of elements in the manifest sentence are found throughout English. Thus in sentences 24–27, the underlying form of the verb must be *phone* + *up*, since English restricts the particles that can accompany certain verbs. Thus we have no

30*a*. *John phoned down the girl.
30*b*. *John phoned the girl down.

Similarly, 31*a*, but not 31*b*, is grammatical.

31*a*. They looked the house over.
31*b*. *They looked the house in.

To account for such examples and for the fact that the verb-particle sequence forms a semantic unit, such sequences are recorded in the underlying form as *verb* + *particle*. But notice that, though the particle precedes the object in the *underlying* representation of 27, a mandatory transformation of that underlying structure permutes the particle and the object whenever the latter is a pronoun. Hence the underlying form of 27 has a different order from its manifest form. Moreover, this underlying order is *never* directly reflected in an actual sentence.

Finally, even the very simplest sentences derive from an underlying form in which the order of the elements differs from the manifest order. Consider:

32. The child runs.

The terminal portion of the tree representing the underlying structure of this sentence is:

33. Det N sg pres V.
∅ə/čaild/run.

The tense marking (present) precedes the verb phrase in the underlying structure in order to permit a uniform treatment with more complicated sentences. In the manifest sentence, the tense marker is always attached to the first verbal element in the verb phrase whether that element is an auxiliary, modal, or compound verb. This is accomplished for complicated expansions of the auxiliary by a rule which permutes the tense marker with the adjacent verbal element to the right. If the tense and verb order for 32 were not as represented in 33, 32 would constitute an exception to this rule and would thus require a complication of the grammar (cf. Chomsky, 1957, and Footnote 9).

This indirect relation between the order of elements in the underlying form and their order in the manifest sentence poses serious problems for *any* theory of syntax learning. It is clear that the child never encounters manifest models of the underlying sentence order. Adults do not utter such sequences as:

34. ∅ə čaild s run.

We have seen, however, that in a formalization of English grammar 34 represents a step in the derivation of 32. Hence, if the child who learns English learns the rules governing the syntax, it follows that he *must learn to manipulate underlying structures, for which his verbal environment provides him with no explicit models*. It is evident that contextual generalization, simply because it *is* a variety of generalization, cannot account for such learning.

"SUBLANGUAGES"

We have seen that relatively little of the syntactic character of simple declarative sentences can be expressed in terms of the manifest order of their constituents. We now ask how much of the syntactic relations between simple declarative and other types of sentences can be expressed in those terms. We maintain that the behavior of a linguistic unit in complex sentences cannot be captured by a theory which represents its syntactic properties by a list of the positions it is capable of occupying. There are two reasons for this, one of which Braine acknowledges; the other has escaped him.

It is clearly possible to construct complicated sentences exhibiting almost any order of syntactic constituents. Thus in Sentence 15, Braine would presumably distinguish three major positions occupied, respectively, by *the boy, is chasing,* and *the dogs.* The relations between these three positions are however, very flexible. Consider:

35. The dogs are being chased by the boy.
36. It is the dogs the boy is chasing.
37. What is being chased by the boy are the dogs.
38. What the boy is chasing are the dogs.
39. It is the dogs that are being chased by the boy.
40. Chasing them is what the boy is doing to the dogs.
41. Chasing the dogs is what the boy is doing.

Far from it being the case, as Braine suggests, that transformation tends to produce relatively minor variations in order, examples 35–41 show that order is the syntactic property transformation is least likely to preserve.

Braine is aware that relative order is preserved only within sentences of the same syntactic type. This leads him to suggest that natural languages should be thought of as systems of "sublanguages," distinguished by a characteristic constituent order. This suggestion is defective in a number of ways. First, if sublanguages are specified solely by the ordinal relations of their constituents, there must be an infinity of sublanguages since sentences in a natural language may be arbitrarily long, and every pair of sentences which differ in length will ipso facto differ in constituent order at some level. It is thus logically impossible that the child should master his language by learning one sublanguage after another.

The preceding demonstrates what was shown above on purely syntactic grounds: The differences between types of sentences cannot, in general, be specified in terms of differences in constituent orders since sublanguages cannot be defined in those terms.

This can be seen most strikingly in the ambiguity of such sentences as:

42. The office of the president is vacant.

where the lexical items and order of constituents *at all levels* are the same on both readings despite the fact that any reasonable analysis of English into sublanguages must assign 42 to two sublanguages, because it can be questioned in two quite different ways (cf. 43 and 44):

43. Where is the office of the president?
44. Who held the office of the president?

There are other examples which illustrate the impossibility of exploiting constituent order to capture relations between syntactically different types of sentences: 45 is related to 46 rather than to 47 while the reverse holds for 48.

45. John is easy to please.
46. They please John.
47. John pleases them.
48. John is eager to please.

Since, however, the constituents of 45 and 47 are ordered in precisely the same way, we cannot appeal to order to explain the relations between the sublanguages these sentences belong to.

These examples reflect a fact that must be evident to anyone who has seriously considered the problem of describing the syntactic structure of a language like English: Very few of the interrelations between types of sentences are expressed by similarities and differences of manifest order. Rather, a theory which marks such interrelations must do so in terms of highly abstract constructs such as the phrase analyses and transformational histories underlying sentences. Linguistic evidence shows that no simpler apparatus explains intersentential relations that are intuitively evident to native speakers. It follows that Braine's attempt to specify sublanguages and their interrelations in terms of constituent order can be of no serious explanatory value.

INFLECTION

We now turn to some of the broader issues raised by Braine's theory. The first arises from difficulties implicit in Braine's assumption that the processes employed in learning order languages are different in kind from those employed in learning inflected languages.

The search for the mechanism of syntax acquisition is, presumably, a search for species-specific capacities common to all children. An adequate theory of syntax acquisition must explain the ability of a child to learn any language to which he happens to be exposed. It follows that a theory of language learning which makes essential reference to linguistic features specific to a particular language or group of languages is necessarily suspect. However, one of Braine's arguments for contextual generalization rests on the fact that constituent order is a major device for expressing syntactic structure in English. It is thus notable that, whatever the relevance of word order to English, there exists a host of languages in which surface order is far less constrained (Russian and German, for example). The notion that contextual generalization is essential for the learning of syntax is thus incompatible with the assumption that the language-learning mechanisms are independent of the peculiarities of particular languages. Rather, Braine's position requires either that the child has different mechanisms with which to learn different languages (contextual generalization for English but not for Russian) or that he has a universal mechanism which, however, is biased to learning certain languages. The first of these suggestions is unparsimonious and not easily reconciled with the fact that languages *do* exhibit a number of important universal properties, suggesting a corresponding pretuning of the language-learning mechanisms (cf. Lenneberg, 1964). The second assumption is tantamount to the naïve view that some languages are "harder" than others. It can be maintained only in face of the fact that there exists no evidence that children find languages in which position is constrained easier to learn than languages in which it is not. Indeed, there exists no evidence that children find *any* natural language harder to learn than any other. (Compare the well-known differences in the assimilability of formally different types of writing systems.) In short, it is presumably the commonalities, not the differences, between natural languages that provide us with insight into the mechanisms underlying their assimilation.

In fact, the distinction between underlying and manifest sentence structure resolves the difficulty posed by the existence of inflection and order as alternative means for expression of syntactic relations. The difference between an "ordering" language and an "inflected" language *is one which concerns the manifest sentence only:* The structure of the underlying forms is similar in both types of languages as are the kinds of transformations which apply to the underlying representations.

In general the rules which determine

inflection are formulated with reference to the order and function of elements in an underlying representation of a sentence. This underlying order may, of course, be deformed by the operation of later rules. For example, in Latin, the manifest sentences:

49*a*. *Puer amat eam.*
49*b*. *Eam amat puer.*
49*c*. *Amat puer eam.*
49*d*. *Puer eam amat.*
49*e*. *Eam puer amat.*
49*f*. *Amat eam puer.*

all share the same underlying form:

50. *puer* + sg pres + *am ea* + sg.

ea has the accusative attached because it is in the object position in the underlying form, while *eo*, because it is in subject position, remains nominative. Subsequent transformations in Latin allow freedom of order in the manifest sentence, while preserving inflections of case and number attachment acquired in the underlying string.

The inflection of words in manifest sentences thus depends on the order of elements in their underlying representations. Inflection is *a direct reflection of the structural relations in the underlying form.* We have already seen that languages which constrain manifest order do so as a way of exhibiting underlying structural relations. Thus, the difference between inflecting and order language is a matter of how the underlying relations are reflected in the speech signal.[10]

[10] In fact, the most important difference between "ordering" and "inflecting" languages concerns the order in which syntactic rules are applied in generating sentences. Thus, derivations in "inflecting" languages tend to apply the rules which determine inflection (e.g., affix movement in Footnote 9) before the rules that rearrange constituents (e.g., passivization in Rule 18). In "order" languages the reverse is typically the case. "Order" languages express underlying relations in the order of elements in the manifest sentence.

We are indebted to M. D. S. Braine for pointing out an error in our original example from Latin.

In both cases, however, the same types of rules apply to abstract representations which underlie the manifest sentences. In both cases, it is primarily the assimilation of the rules for generating these underlying structures and for deforming them into manifest sentences that a theory of language learning must explain. A theory which affords such an explanation would ipso facto provide a *uniform* treatment of the learning of inflected and uninflected languages.

PERCEPTUAL SEGMENTATION AND INTONATION

We have argued that the generalization of position does not account for the learning of syntax. We now consider Braine's claim that the discrimination of acoustic properties of speech signals accounts for the learning of segmentation.

According to Braine, normal speech indicates its segmentation by stress, pitch, juncture, intonation pattern, etc. Braine reports brief experiments in which a nonsense utterance was spoken with differing stress patterns. Subjects were asked to respond with sentences which seemed grammatically similar. The major syntactic division in the response corresponded to the boundary following the stressed nonsense word. Braine concludes that stress and intonation are capable of transmitting structure.

Beyond doubt, extra stresses or artificially introduced pauses can induce structure in a random sequence. In natural speech, however, it is extremely difficult to determine the physical parameters which signal structural units. They cannot be simple pauses, for often large constituent breaks are not marked by pauses while relatively minor ones are coincident with large acoustic gaps. Physical intensity is directly related to "stress" only in the case of special emphasis, and "intonation" often does not correspond to the actual pitch of the voice fundamental. Indeed, it is the rule that the acoustic analogue of linguistic percepts is either found to be extremely complex or is not found at all. Though pauses, stress, sound units, intonations, etc. are *heard* as objective features of the flow of speech, it appears that these percepts are, in fact, the result of some elaborate manipulation of the acoustic data. In the case of stress and pauses in English it is clear that they are usually a function of the syntactic structures underlying the speech signal as well as its acoustics.[11]

If, however, such perceptual correlates of structure as stress, pause, and intonation have no simple acoustic analogues, it is pointless to argue that the child's learning of segmentation consists of the discrimination of stress, pause, and intonation. For the problem then arises of how the child *learns to hear* stress, pause, and intonation correctly. Insofar as perception of the correlates of segmentation is the result of complicated integrations of the acoustic signal with the syntax, the child cannot be capable of perceiving them before he has learned to analyze syntactic structure.

This difficulty raises doubts about the description of language learning according to which the child first isolates individual speech sounds and then groups them successively into words, phrases, and simple sentences. For example, it is widely accepted in the literature that the child effectively masters the intonation pattern of his language *before he has learned any words at all.*[12] Since intonation is intimately related to syntactic structure, this indicates that the order of assimilation of syntactic structures is unlikely to be the one mentioned above. Instead, it suggests that derived constituent structure may be among the earliest syntactic information assimilated.

In short, the correct interpretation may be not that the perceived location of pause, stress, and intonation are the child's clue to the analysis of structure, but rather that the prior analysis of structure is what determines where the child learns to hear pause, stress, and intonation. Nor is the possibility of some intermediate position excluded.

EXPERIMENTATION ON CONTEXTUAL GENERALIZATION

We have considered some inadequacies of explanations of syntax assimilation that appeal to contextual generalization. However, Braine has shown that subjects *can* learn miniature artificial languages whose constituents are nonsense words by position generalization. This may appear to provide a foundation for theories of language learning in which contextual generalization plays an important role. However, Braine's results are equivocal. A brief discussion of his experimental techniques is therefore in order.

There is some danger in applying results garnered in the study of the learning of artificial languages by latency-aged children to the learning of first languages by preschoolers. First, it is possible that the psychological processes mediating the learning of first languages are pretuned for the assimilation of systems having quite specific formal properties. If this is correct, very little will be revealed about these processes by studying the assimilation of artificial languages whose structure is arbitrarily different from that of natural languages.

Second, as Thorpe (1961) has suggested, the learning of language may be one of the capacities for which

> there... exist specific brain mechanisms ready to be activated during and only during a par-

[11] For a theoretical analysis of the relation between syntactic structure and stress see Chomsky and Miller (1963). Lieberman (in press) has shown experimentally that the perception of intonation and stress is dependent on a knowledge of the syntactic structure.

[12] See Jakobson (1941), Grégoire (1937), and McCarthy (1954). Jakobson has described this period of intonation imitation (around 1–1½ years) as the period when the child "speaks without words."

ticular period of the life span of the child and...if they are not properly activated at the right time subsequent activation is difficult or impossible, resulting in permanent disabilities in later life [p. 200; cf. also Penfield & Roberts, 1959].

This speculation supports the widely held view that adults learn second languages in a manner essentially different from the way children learn first languages.

Braine has attempted to control for this source of error by replicating the simpler of his experiments with a population of 4-year-olds. The point is not, however, that very young children may be incapable of contextual generalization. It is rather that there may be language-learning processes operative in younger children which do not occur in older ones. Braine controls for the former but not the latter of these possibilities.

We now consider the details of Braine's experiments. It is essential to Braine's argument to demonstrate the existence of contextual generalization among phrases as well as words. We have seen that Braine defines the notion of a position in such a way that it may be occupied by a word in one sentence and by a phrase in another.

Braine's experiments are thus divided into two groups. The first demonstrates contextual generalization in a language whose sentences are all of the type shown in Figure 2, where A and P are classes of single (nonsense) words, and a and p are items drawn from those classes.

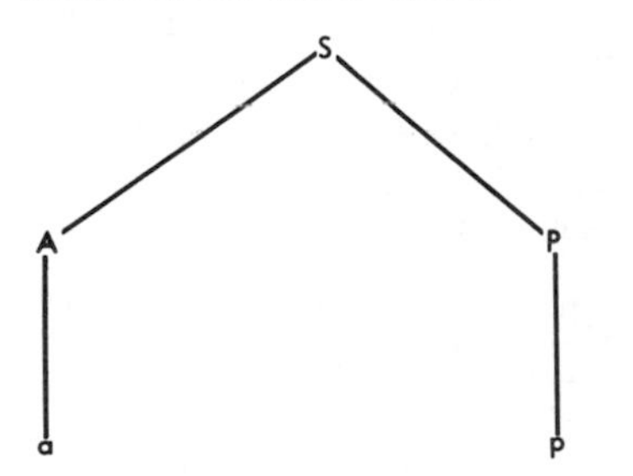

Fig. 2: Tree diagram of the alleged structure of nonsense sentences in Braine's a + p language.

Braine's second experiment purports to show that contextual generalization can also function when the constituents are phrases. Here Braine uses language in which sentences are said to be either of the types shown in Figures 3 or 4.

But Braine provides no support for the analyses of the String axp in Figures 3 and 4 beyond the remark that, in the

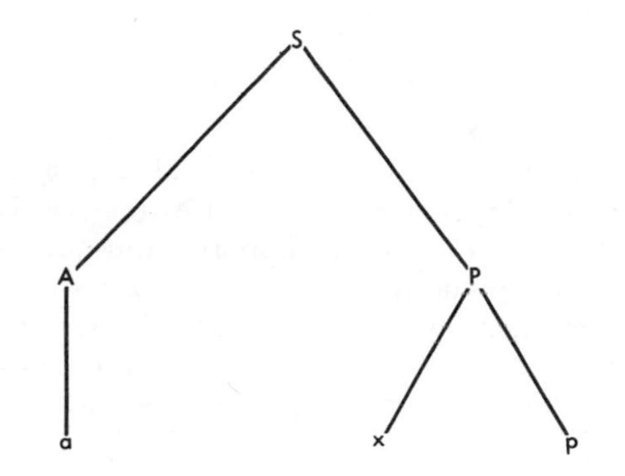

Fig. 3: Tree diagram of the alleged structure of the nonsense sentences in Braine's a + xp language.

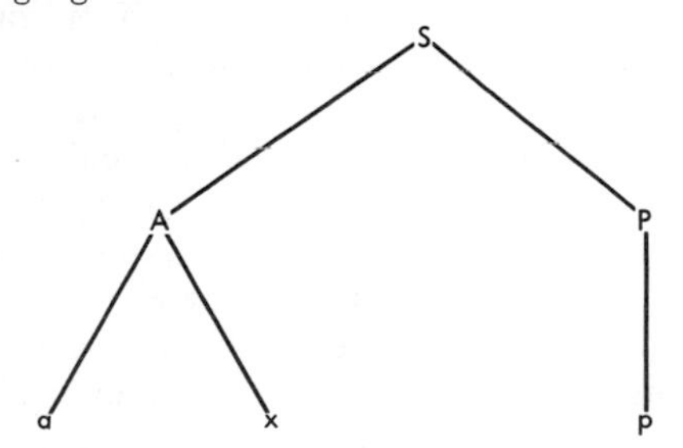

Fig. 4: Tree diagram of the alleged structure of the nonsense sentences in Braine's ax + p language.

situations where ax was intended to have phrase status, a and x were presented together, while in the situation where xp was intended to have phrase status, x and p were presented together.

In short, Braine's experimentation is at least compatible with the interpretation that what his subjects *learned* were strings with the structure exhibited in Figure 5. So long as this interpretation remains open, Braine can hardly claim that his experiments demonstrate contextual gene-

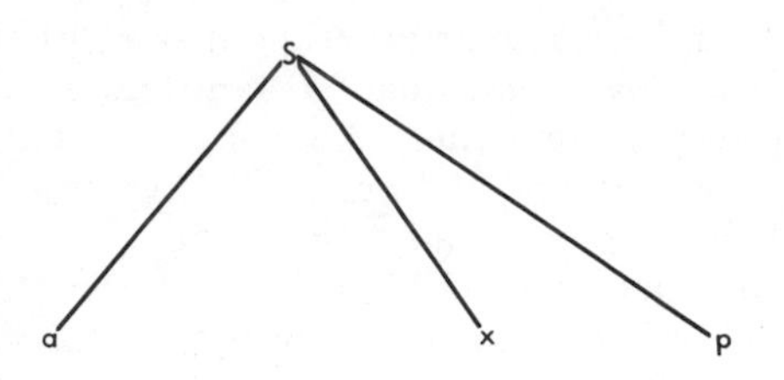

Fig. 5: A possible alternative structure for sentences allegedly belonging either to a + xp or to ax + p languages.

ralization among phrase-length constituents.

In experiments with artificial languages consisting of a finite set of strings, it is extremely difficult to support claims about the psychological reality of abstract structures like phrases. In natural languages, appeals to the intuitions of speakers concerning the appropriate segmentation of sentences constrain phrase analyses to some extent. More important, formulation of the rules for transformation and stress imposes certain requirements upon the phrase-structure analysis since the phrase structure articulates the domain to which these rules apply. In the case of the artificial languages Braine studies, neither of these considerations holds. Speakers do not have structural intuitions about artificial language, and no language which consists of a finite set of strings requires phrase-structure rules in its grammar, for any such language can be enumerated by a simple list. If, therefore, it is suggested that Braine's subjects may not have analyzed the stimulus material in the way Braine wanted them to, it is difficult to see what reply he could make.

The difficulty may have stemmed from Braine's belief that the process responsible for the perceptual integrity of the phrase is association. On that view, co-presentation of pairs of nonsense syllables would perhaps tend to establish such pairs as phrases. The fact that the pairs of items intended to be perceived as phrases were presented together would thus help to justify the analysis provided in Figures 3 and 4.

The claim that the integrity of the phrase is mediated by processes of association is, however, totally untenable. Phrases in natural language can exhibit grammatical dependencies across strings of arbitrary length. It is thus inconceivable that the psychological unity of phrases could be attributed to associative bonds between the elements. Conversely, the suggestion that the basis of phrase integrity is associationistic in short phrases but that some different and unknown psychological mechanism operates in longer phrases is too evidently ad hoc to merit consideration.

References

Braine, M. D. S. On learning the grammatical order of words. *Psychological Review,* 1963, 70, 323–348.

Brown, R., & Bellugi, U. Three processes in the child's acquisition of the syntax. *Harvard Educational Review,* 1964, 34 (2), 133–151.

Chomsky, N. *Syntactic structures.* The Hague: Mouton, 1957.

Chomsky, N., & Miller, G. Introduction to the formal analysis of natural languages. In R. Luce, R. Bush, & E. Galanter (Eds.), *Handbook of mathematical psychology.* Vol. 2. New York: Wiley, 1963. Pp. 269–323.

Fodor, J., & Katz, J. (Eds.) The structure of language. In, *Readings in the philosophy of language.* Englewood Cliffs, N. J.: Prentice-Hall, 1964. Pp. 479–518.

Grégoire, A. *L'Apprentissage du langage.* Liège, Belgium: l'Université de Liège, 1957.

Harris, Z. Co-occurrence and transformation in linguistic structure. *Language,* 1957, 33 (3), 283–340.

Jakobson, R. *Kindersprache, Aphasie und allgemeine Lautgesetze.* Uppsala, Sweden: Uppsala Universität, 1941.

Jenkins, J., & Palermo, D. Mediation

processes and the acquisition of linguistic structure. In Ursula Bellugi & R. W. Brown (Eds.), *The acquisition of language.* Chicago: Univer. Chicago Press, 1964. Pp. 141–169.

LEES, R. The grammar of English nominalizations. *International Journal of American Linguistics,* 1960, 26 (Pt. 2), 205–220.

LENNEBERG, E. The capacity for language acquisition. In J. Fodor & J. Katz (Eds.), *Readings in the philosophy of language.* Englewood Cliffs, N. J.: Prentice-Hall, 1964. Pp. 579–608.

LIEBERMAN, P. On the acoustic basis of the perception of intonation by linguists. *Word,* 1965, 21, in press.

MACLAY, H., & OSGOOD, C. Hesitation phenomena in spontaneous English speech. *Word,* 1959, 15, 19–44.

MCCARTHY, D. Language development in children. In L. Carmichael (Ed.), *A manual of child psychology.* (2nd ed.) New York: Wiley, 1954. Pp. 429–630.

MEHLER, J. Some effects of grammatical transformations on the recall of English sentences. *Journal of Verbal Learning and Verbal Behavior,* 1963, 2, 346–351.

MILLER, G. A. Some psychological studies of grammar. *American Psychologist,* 1962, 17, 748–762.

MILLER, G. A., GALANTER, E., & PRIBRAM, K. H. *Plans and the structure of behavior.* New York: Holt, Rinehart & Winston, 1960.

OSGOOD, C. E. On understanding and creating sentences. *American Psychologist,* 1963, 18, 735–751.

PENFIELD, W., & ROBERTS, L. *Speech and brain mechanisms.* Princeton: Princeton Univer. Press, 1959.

THORPE, W. H. Sensitive periods in the learning of animals and men. In W. H. Thorpe & O. L. Zangwill (Eds), *Current problems in animal behavior.* Cambridge: Cambridge Univer. Press, 1961. Pp. 194–224.

On The Basis of Phrase Structure:

A Reply to Bever, Fodor, and Weksel

MARTIN D. S. BRAINE

On Bever et al.'s central contention, the linguistic evidence seems insufficient to show that the order of elements in the simple declarative sentence is a deformation of the order in the underlying string: The deformation appears to be imposed by the choice of a particular phrase-structure model, rather than a fact about English. While undoubtedly insufficient and imprecise, the writer's proposals on grammar acquisition seem to have more potentialities than Bever et al. allow. Too little is known for it to be argued that they are inconsistent with the character of the verbal environment. Limitations of the proposals in respect to the learning of word classes and several other issues raised by Bever et al. are discussed.

The arguments of Bever, Fodor, and Weksel (1965b) will be discussed in the order in which they were presented.

THE VERBAL ENVIRONMENT

Bever et al. begin by saying that I (Braine, 1963) claim "the verbal environment of the child exhibits a preponderance of grammatical simple declaratives [p. 470]," and they cite data to the contrary. Their data also indicate that the child is exposed to many ungrammatical utterances, although there appears to be some disagreement with Brown and Bellugi (1964) on this point.

I did not claim that children were mainly exposed to simple declaratives, and it greatly distorts my conception to think that a simple count of the number of simple declaratives in adult speech is relevant to it. Information about positional and contingency relations in simple sentences is abundantly exemplified in many transforms (as well as in many "not-fully-grammatical" utterances). As one among many examples that could be cited, consider the similarity in verb-phrase structure between passives and sentences with adjective predicators (e.g., *George was served—George was sensible*): The same auxiliary structure (*has been, would be, might have been, being,* etc.) occurs with past participles and with adjectives. Experience with the verb structure of one

Martin D. S. Braine, "On the Basis of Phrase Structure: A Reply to Bever, Fodor, and Weksel," *Psychological Review,* 72, No. 6 (1965), 483–492. Reprinted by permission of the author and publisher.

sentence type could hardly fail to transfer to the other type. In general, it seems to me that too little is known about the verbal environment and the child's response to it to build much of an argument for or against my proposals.

The conflicting data on the prevalence of ungrammatical utterances raise some question as to the criteria of grammaticality used. It seems important to distinguish at least three kinds of not-fully-grammatical utterances: (*a*) incomplete sentences where the speaker hesitates or changes his mind in midsentence—these are likely to be grammatical between hesitations, (*b*) correctly constructed phrases (isolated noun phrases, prepositional phrases, etc.) which expose the major components of sentences to the learner uncluttered by context and may be important in the learning of the segmentation of sentences, as well as in the learning of the internal structure of the phrases themselves, (*c*) radically ungrammatical utterances with the appearance of being random combinations of words (e.g., *To went school he* for *He went to school*). It is primarily this last category, which seems very infrequent, that might be expected to handicap learning.

MANIFEST AND UNDERLYING STRUCTURE

The next argument is central to the critique. It has two parts: Bever et al. claim I made a mistake in supposing (*a*) that there is "a base or kernel grammar producing all and only simple declaratives," and (*b*) that "the transformational operations producing complex sentences are defined over the declaratives generated by this base component [p. 471]." It should be carefully noted that (*b*) is only very tangentially relevant to my article. My discussion of transformations was too brief to be more than approximate, and its main purpose was to show that the existence of transformations did not contradict my proposals concerning simple declaratives. Yet most of the arguments of Bever et al. relate to (*b*) rather than (*a*). In particular, their long discussion of the passive transformation, associated with sentences 7*a*–19, is relevant only to the question of what the passive transformation is a transformation of. Bever et al. argue that certain rules (e.g., the subject-verb concord) apply to both active and passive, so that much duplication would be avoided in a grammar if these rules applied *after* the transformation was made. This argument says nothing about the relation between the kernel grammar and simple declarative sentences. Bever et al. implicitly admit its irrelevance when they say "analogous considerations show that the active itself is merely one of the deformations of this underlying structure [p. 473]." Whether the simple declarative is a "deformation" of an underlying terminal string thus turns on what these unstated "analogous considerations" are. It is difficult to take issue with unstated arguments. The discussion below relates to English, for which I am fairly clear about what the analogous considerations are.

I know of only one place in the generative grammar literature where a direct argument is made that transformations are involved in the generation of the simple declarative English sentence—that is Chomsky's (1957, pp. 38–42) argument relating to the auxiliary verb structure. Chomsky makes it clear that the validity of his argument turns on the question of whether discontinuous constituents are permissible in a phrase-structure grammar. He concludes: "In the auxiliary verb phrase we really have discontinuous elements, e.g., . . .*have*. . .*en* and *be*. . .*ing*. But discontinuities cannot be handled within [phrase-structure] grammars [p. 41]." Whether or not a phrase-structure (kernel) grammar can permit discontinuities is a technical question about the form of such grammars. Since Bever et al. rest so much of their case on the argument that the simple declarative sentence does not reflect the order of elements in the underlying string, it is necessary to examine their conception of a phrase-structure grammar in detail.

Phrase-structure grammars employ symbols representing morpheme and phrase classes (conventionally written in capital letters) and symbols representing morphemes (conventionally written lowercase). Rules are of the form $\varphi \rightarrow \psi$ (to be read "φ may be rewritten as ψ"), where φ and ψ are strings of symbols. There is a privileged symbol, S (= "sentence"), and the first rewriting rule applied in generating a sentence is of the form S → . . . ; each rewriting rule permits one capital letter to be rewritten, and the rewriting rules are successively applied until all capital letters have been rewritten, leaving a string of morphemes which is the sentence or "terminal string" generated. The grammars defined in this manner comprise a large family of possible models. Different types of models in the family are specified by defining kinds of rewriting rules that are permitted (see Chomsky, 1963, for a description of several types). The permissibility of discontinuous rules turns on whether it is required in expansion rules $A \rightarrow \psi$ that ψ be a continuous string. Discontinuous rules drop this requirement to the extent of permitting such expansions as $A \rightarrow \lambda \ldots \mu$, where the ellipsis indicates that λ and μ straddle the element on the right of A. Thus, a pair of rules, $X \rightarrow AY$, $A \rightarrow \lambda \ldots \mu$, generates strings of the form $\lambda Y \mu$ in which the components are Y and $\lambda \ldots \mu$. A grammar which forbids discontinuous rules is obliged to generate such a string in two stages: Phrase-structure rules, $X \rightarrow AY$ and $A \rightarrow \lambda\mu$, generate terminal strings with the order $\lambda\mu Y$, and a transform then permutes the order $\lambda\mu Y$ into $\lambda Y \mu$. Such a grammar is forced to impose on the language a distinction between manifest structure ($\lambda Y \mu$) and "underlying structure" ($\lambda\mu Y$). It is now known that certain kinds of discontinuities, which include those that appear in simple English sentences, can be tolerated in phrase-structure grammars (Matthews, 1963; Yngve, 1960).[1] The recent work makes it clear that Chomsky's (1957, p. 41) statement that "discontinuous rules cannot be handled within [phrase-structure] grammars" is wrong. The use of models which do not admit discontinuities is controversial within linguistics.[2] Discontinuous constituents have been widely used by grammarians outside the generative grammar school (e.g., Bloch, 1946; Harris, 1951; Wells, 1947).

In their section, "The Derivation of Order," (which continues the argument begun in their earlier section, "The Role of Declarative Sentences") Bever et al. cite as evidence for the distinction between manifest and underlying order the phrases *be chasing* and *phone her up*. Both these are of the $\lambda Y \mu$ form. A grammar which forbids representing the constituents in the form *be...ing* and *phone...*

[1] Yngve's discontinuous rules are of the form $A \rightarrow \lambda \ldots \mu$, with the restriction that sentences are to be generated from left to right. Matthews defines a much wider class of discontinuities. The requirement of left-to-right generation could probably be dropped, although specification of an order of application of rules is necessary. (In the above example, if $Y \rightarrow WZ$, then the rule sequence $X \rightarrow AY$, $A \rightarrow \lambda \ldots \mu$, $Y \rightarrow WZ$ generates $\lambda WZ \mu$, and the rule sequence $X \rightarrow AY$, $Y \rightarrow WZ$, $A \rightarrow \lambda \ldots \mu$ generates $\lambda W \mu Z$: Failure to specify an order of application would leave the terminal order vague.) Specification of an order among rules is a normal practice in grammars without discontinuities (Bach, 1964). Matthews shows that, with the left-to-right restriction, grammars with discontinuous rules generate context-free languages; without this restriction they generate context-sensitive languages.

[2] Unfortunately, the argument over discontinuous rules has taken place not over whether such rules exist and what their precise form is but rather as part of the larger argument that transformational grammars are necessary (e.g., Harman, 1963; Postal, 1964). The likelihood that both transformational and discontinuous rules exist has received little discussion.

up must necessarily generate the orders *be* + *ing* + *chase* and *phone* + *up* + *her;* having generated the items in the wrong order, it is of course necessary to permute them into the actual order. The entire argument associated with sentences 29*a*–34 rests on a particular choice of phrase-structure model.

This distinction between manifest and underlying structure in kernel sentences creates a special kind of methodological difficulty in assessing the validity of generative grammars. A full grammar contains both a phrase structure and a transformational component. If the terminal strings generated by the phrase structure are permitted to be arbitrarily different from any actual sentence structures, there are no independent data against which the phrase structure and the transformational rules can be separately tested. Since transformational rules provide an extraordinarily powerful tool for mapping one system into another, the grammarian can write the phrase-structure kernel partly on the basis of his convenience, free to correct any poor fit with the manifest structure of the language by using transforms to reshuffle the elements. This methodological looseness makes it impossible to accept empirical claims about the properties of phrase-structure grammars of natural languages. (For example, the similarity in structure between ordering and inflected languages, reported by Bever et al. in their section, "Inflection," may not reflect a linguistic universal, but rather the prior decision to treat a certain kind of phrase-structure description as convenient.)

In general, in order to establish the existence of "deformations" in simple declaratives, Bever et al. would have to show that there are no feasible forms of phrase-structure model which would permit transformational grammars to be written so that only the identity transform intervened between the phrase structure and the morphophonemic rules. No one has yet attempted to make such a difficult argument. Instead, it seems to have been assumed that, if transformational rules are to be used at all, then there is no motive for not exploiting them, leaving the detailed character of phrase-structure grammars to be settled, in part, according to the grammarian's convenience. It is doubtful, however, that the distinction between manifest and underlying structure in kernel sentences is ultimately convenient even to the grammarian, for the methodological reasons noted above. The distinction is certainly not convenient psychologically: The assumption that the learner learns structures to which he was never exposed would indeed pose "serious problems for *any* theory of syntax learning [p. 476]," as Bever et al. note.

THE SCOPE OF THE PROPOSALS

The next argument, associated with sentences 20–28, is that my proposals account for very little of the structure even of simple declarative sentences. Although my article did not claim sufficiency, my proposals seem to account for more of the structure of the simple declarative than Bever et al. allow.

The assertion that the theory must fail for sentences 24–28 reflects an over-simplistic interpretation of the theory. Positions learned are those determined by the immediate constituent analysis; I never remotely suggested they were a simple 1-2-3-4 ordinal series. *John phoned Jane up* contains two main parts—*John* and *phoned Jane up; phoned Jane up* contains two parts—*phoned. . .up* and *Jane.* Presumably English speakers learn that verb units often contain verb-particle sequences with the particle frequently contingent on the verb (*phone up* but not *phone down, think over* but not *think across,* etc.), and they also learn that noun phrases sometimes follow the verb-particle sequence (*phone up the girl*) and sometimes occur between these two parts of the verb unit (*phone the girl up*). They may also learn that a short list *him, her, it, us,* etc. always go between the verb and the particle.[3]

Sentences 20–23 are not apposite for several reasons. First, Bever et al. seriously misunderstand my proposals: They assume I postulate that if a list of items occurs in a certain position, and one member of the list occurs in some nonhomologous position, then the entire list will occur in both positions. This is a stronger generalization mechanism than I proposed. Second, the anomaly in 23 presumably lies in the verb phrase *was cost,* not in the occurrence of *ten dollars* as subject. Third, my article specifically excluded the learning of transforms, so that neither 22 nor 23 are appropriate examples; my proposals could capture the structure of passives only insofar as they are similar to predicate phrases with adjective heads (cf. *The kazoo was blown by the child; The coffee was hot on the stove*).

Since it appears that Bever et al. have misunderstood the proposals, I must try to restate them more clearly and clarify their limitations. The discussion includes some recent thinking. The proposals are that what is learned are the temporal positions of units in verbal arrays and contingencies between morphemes. The position learned is the position of a unit within the next-larger containing unit of a hierarchy of units. Position within a unit may be defined absolutely (e.g., first) or relatively to a reference point (e.g., before *f*, first after *f*, second after *f*, where *f* is some frequently occurring morpheme—learning of such positions is shown in Braine, 1965b). Contingent morphemes need not be adjacent. All these positional and contingency relationships assumed to be learned could be represented by rewriting rules; for example, the rules $X \rightarrow fAB$, $X \rightarrow gAC$, $A \rightarrow a_1, a_2, \ldots$, $B \rightarrow b_1, b_2, \ldots$, $C \rightarrow c_1, c_2, \ldots$ represent that X phrases are prefixed by either f or g, that the a_i occur in second position, and that the b_i and c_i occur next-but-one after f and g, respectively. An adequate notation would presumably be a phrase-structure system of some kind. (The insufficiency of a finite-state notation is shown in Braine, 1965a.) A phrase-structure grammar is essentially a system for representing hierarchically organized positional relationships, and my proposals posit that it is these positional relations that are learned.

Although the theory appears to provide a sufficient basis for the learning of the treelike structures of a phrase-structure grammar, its handling of the learning of word classes requires examination. The theory implies some special limitations on the learning of unmarked word lists (i.e., word lists which are not correlated with particular function morphemes). The learner should have two kinds of difficulties with unmarked word lists: registering that (*a*) two such lists occurring at homologous locations are different lists, and that (*b*) one list occurring at two nonhomologous locations is the same list. The nature of the problem may be illustrated by considering a pair of rules of the form $X \rightarrow AB$, $X \rightarrow CD$, where A, B, C, and D are arbitrary lists of words. Exposed to such a system, the learner should readily learn which words go first and which second, but he has no way of distinguishing A items from C items, or B items from D items; thus, he should confuse the subsystems. (There is laboratory evidence for such confusion—Smith,

[3] More probably, however, they learn a stress correlate for the construction. Bever et al. make a mistake about English structure when they assert that "it is a necessary condition upon the grammaticality of sentences of the form:

28. John phoned up X.

that X not be a pronoun [p. 474]." Pronouns can occur after the particle when they are strongly stressed (*THAT woman! John phoned up HER!*). There appears to be some requirement that the terminal unit in this construction have at least secondary stress; pronouns are not normally as strongly stressed, and this may be the reason the terminal placement is avoided.

1965.) For the subsystems to be distinguished, either the classes have to be marked (e.g., $X \rightarrow A'B'$, $X \rightarrow C'D'$, $A' \rightarrow fA$, $B' \rightarrow gB$, $C' \rightarrow hC$, $D' \rightarrow kD$), or else the subsystems have to be marked (e.g., $X \rightarrow fAB$, $X \rightarrow gCD$, where the list positions are differentiated as "first after f," "second after f," etc.).

It follows from the above considerations that the kind of phrase-structure system for which my proposals are adequate is one which permits only one unmarked word list at any given location and which restricts the circumstances in which an unmarked list can occur at two nonhomologous locations.[4] A property of this sort may be called an "indexing" restriction, since such a grammar provides, in effect, an overt indexing system for its vocabulary lists. An indexing restriction would explain the purpose of function morphemes: Perhaps the human subject needs function morphemes to index classes and distinguish their locations. It is important to observe that a phrase-structure model which introduces classes as arbitrary lists of words (as in rules like N → *man, ball,* . . ., V → *hit, take,* . . .), and which imposes no restrictions on how the lists may be distributed in the rules, assigns to the human subject an *unlimited* capacity to learn and retain long lists of unrelated items occurring in complex positional relationships to each other without becoming confused. At the most general level, the question involved here is whether characteristics of human learning and long-term memory place any essential limitations on the form of a grammar. No limitations are built into the context-free and context-sensitive models (Chomsky, 1963) assumed by Bever et al., and these models do not distinguish function morphemes and lexicon. I would urge that laboratory studies of the learning of semantically empty systems can make an important contribution to the investigation of subjects' abilities to handle lists of unrelated words. A promising method for such studies is suggested elsewhere (Braine, 1965a; cf. also Smith, 1963, 1965).

[4] To state this restriction precisely, much more experimental work is required: Locations can be partially homologous, and the circumstances in which lists occurring at partially homologous locations tend to be learned as the same list, or as different lists, have to be determined by experiment.

Covert Categories

Despite the plausibility of some kind of indexing restriction, it is a fact that languages contain structures in which the same position can be occupied by two or more classes which are not differentially marked. Bever et al. are correct in pointing out that this sort of structure poses a problem for my proposals. These "covert categories," as they were called by Whorf (1956), may ultimately be based on semantic properties or relations. This notion would be consistent with the thinking behind my theory: Class markers provide a device for making heterogeneous items similar (they all "go with" the marker); however, when items are already similar by virtue of a semantic property or relation of some sort, it would be readily understandable that the overt marker might not be needed—the covert semantic marker would suffice to index the list. Covert semantic markers undoubtedly exist. Proper names provide an obvious example: A speaker hearing an exotic name for the first time presumably does not need to hear it used in noun positions in sentences in order to know its grammatical category. Unfortunately, semantic correlates are rarely so transparent. More often, although the class has a set of nuclear members which clearly have a common property, it also contains many words without the property. For example, Whorf (1956) says of some covert noun subclasses in Navaho:

> Some terms belong to the round (or roundish) class, others to the long-object class, others fall into classes not dependent on

shape. . . . I doubt that such distinctions are simply. . . recognitions of. . . objective differences. . . . One must learn as a part of learning Navaho that "sorrow" belongs in the round class [p. 91].

Since the speaker has to learn not only that round versus long is the basis of classification but also that "sorrow" is to "count as" round, it follows that a semantic-correlate theory of covert categories gives the correlate the status of a mediator in the sense of Jenkins and Palermo (1964).

Bever et al. are mistaken in asserting that the ideas of Jenkins and Palermo are "simply a weaker version of Braine's [p. 475]."[5] Bever et al. point out that Jenkins and Palermo have little to say about phrase structure, and the difficulties faced by mediation theory in explaining position learning have been indicated by Smith (1965). However, Jenkins and Palermo do provide a reasonable thory of word-class formation that is at least theoretically capable of explaining covert categories. Their ideas are complementary to mine and not a weaker competitor. It is important to note, however, that my proposals imply a restriction on the scope of the four-stage stimulus equivalence paradigm: It should not be demonstrable without some semantic support for the equivalence classes.

SECONDARY ISSUES

Transformations and "Sublanguages"

My article was mainly concerned with phrase structure, and the brief overview on transformations was not intended as a precise statement about English, but rather as a general line of thought as to how a quest for what is learned might approach these aspects of English structure. English clearly does present a number of parallel phrase and sentence forms of the kind described as sublanguages. What might be learned in learning transformations is difficult to discuss in part because the transformation concept itself seems unclear. The unclarity appears in at least three ways. First, it seems impossible to deduce from Chomsky's (1961) definition of a transformational grammar what features should be built into a verbal learning experiment in order to ensure that a subject is faced with the task of learning a transformation; laboratory study is therefore difficult. Second, it seems likely that a resolution of Putnam's (1961, p. 41) criticism, that Chomsky's definition of a transformational grammar is "much too wide," will affect the character of such grammars. Third, there are serious unresolved difficulties associated with the phrase structure of the products of transformation (Bach, 1964, pp. 70–78; Chomsky, 1955); discussing these, Chomsky (1962) has said candidly: "All answers I have seen so far are ad hoc. . . .I think. . . there is some important insight that is still lacking [p. 158]." Transformations are surely destined to be further clarified, and detailed discussion of their learning may have to wait upon the clarifications. Meanwhile, the difficulty of the laboratory study of transformations provides a pragmatic reason for concentrating on phrase structure.

Inflection

There is no truth whatever, nor warrant in my article, for the statement that I assume "that the processes employed in learning order languages are different in kind from those employed in learning inflected languages [p. 477]." Of course a theory of grammar acquisition should explain a child's ability to learn any language. However, I doubt that the Latin speaker learned what Bever et al. say he learned.

The major cues in Latin are based on relative position. The subject of the sen-

[5] Incidentally, it is inappropriate of Bever et al. to attribute to Jenkins and Palermo a belief that the employment of mediational paradigms affords "a breakthrough" in the study of syntax. This term was not Jenkins and Palermo's.

tence is the element which occurs immediately before the nominative-case suffix; the object is the element immediately before the accusative-case suffix; the verb is the element to which suffixes comprising tense, mood, voice, aspect, and person morphemes are attached, etc. It is the learning of these kinds of relative positional relationships which has to be explained in giving an account of the learning of the grammar of an inflected language like Latin. It is not apparent why my viewpoint would have more difficulty with Latin-like languages than with English.

The analysis of Latin provided by Bever et al. leads to curious problems. If the "underlying strings" generated in the phrase structure have a rigid word order, then it must be assumed that the learner learns this order, even though no such order is visible in the language. It is difficult to see how the learner could learn this, or why one should want to postulate that he does. The analysis is not made more plausible by assuming that the learner also learns permutation rules governing the movements of the contents of various positions to other positions. Moreover, the suffixes, which are clearly the cues defining the major grammatical positions, enter only peripherally into the formulation. I know of no generative grammar of Latin that has yet been published, and it may not even be certain that a feasibly simple grammar can be written in the manner suggested by Bever et al. Simple Latin sentences can contain more than three words. Six words have 720 possible orders, and eight have 40,320; even allowing for the rarity of some of these possible orders, a very large number of permutation transforms would presumably be required merely to generate the kernel sentences.

Intonation

I did not claim "that the discrimination of acoustic properties of speech signals accounts for the learning of segmentation [p. 479]." I suggested only that intonational cues might be helpful, a possibility Bever et al. admit.

Experimentation

With regard to my Experiment III, it is true, as several people have pointed out to me, that the segmentations are not inherent in the "languages" but are determined by the experimental procedure. Throughout the training phases, A and PQ phrases (in the A + PQ system) are presented as stimulus units in sentence-completion problems of the form $a_i \ldots (a_j, p_iq_i)$ and $\ldots p_iq_i$ $(a_ip_jq_j)$; it is assumed that this presentation of the phrases as units during training is sufficient to define the sentences as having two parts, an A phrase and a PQ phrase. The results of Experiment II provide some support for this assumption.

The reconstructive-memory technique (Braine, 1965a) seems superior to the sentence-completion procedure as a method for studying grammar acquisition. An important reason for dissatisfaction with the sentence-completion procedure is not that it fails to specify the segmentation, but rather that it *does* specify it. It is greatly preferable that the subject be required to discover the segmentation for himself. I have little doubt that the learning of positions within phrases can be demonstrated to the satisfaction of Bever et al.

Bever et al. raise objections to laboratory learning studies. However, their thought that young children may have especially rich capacities for grammar acquisition ("pretuned") is relevant only if it is assumed that these capacities do not operate in the laboratory; people who have speculated about the possibility of such capacities seem to believe that they endure until adolescence (Bellugi & Brown, 1964, p. 139), well past the age when laboratory work becomes feasible. I am unable to follow the second objection, that useful laboratory work is extremely difficult with artificial languages consisting of a finite set of strings. Their point that "any such language can be enumerated by a simple list [p. 481]" would be appropriate only if subjects learned a list of sentences as a list. On the contrary, memory for a list of patterned strings is primarily a reconstructive process and not a learning of a large number of individual items (Braine, 1965a; Smith, 1965). Subjects learn regularities in pattern that the strings exhibit, and "recall" is in large part a reconstruction of strings which have the regularities that the subject has registered. Thus, laboratory studies yield information about the pattern properties or "structural descriptions" learned.

In conclusion, I would like to return to what seems to me the fundamental issue at stake in this interchange: whether the order of elements in simple sentences reflects the order in the underlying string. It seems a very natural psychological approach to grammar to regard grammar acquisition as a learning of the patterned regularities in sentences, and my proposals are initial suggestions as to the bases of some kinds of regularities. This approach promises to be fruitful. However, Bever et al. are arguing that this approach is precluded because the learner is often never exposed to the pattern properties which must be assumed to be learned. Before accepting this argument, I would urge that psychologists examine the linguistic evidence for a distinction between manifest and underlying structure in kernel sentences very closely indeed.[6]

[6] (This footnote was added in proof following receipt of Bever et al.'s. (1965a) rejoinder.) I see that Bever et al. now allow that it would be possible to write a grammar of English in which there would be no distinction between manifest and underlying structure in simple declaratives but claim that such a grammar would involve an unnecessarily complex system. They seem to assume that I would agree, since their section, "The Moral," accuses me of "playing fast and loose with simplicity constraints [p. 497]." I think that it is simply untrue that a phrase-structure analysis permitting discontinuous rules must lead to the kinds of complexities they claim: They do not appear to have investigated the potentialities of such an analysis thoroughly enough. Specifically, while they have seen that the affix-permutation rule (Chomsky, 1957, p. 39, Rule 29–ii; 1962, p. 141, Rule 12) would no longer be needed in the generation of simple declaratives, they have failed to see that it would not be needed elsewhere in the grammar either. This rule is the one which introduces the distinction between manifest and underlying structure into the auxiliary verb phrase, and the possibility of its total elimination (a gain in "simplicity" in the transformational part of the grammar) is one of the reasons for thinking that English contains discontinuous rules. Bever et al. say: "Of course the facts might have shown that the discontinuous phrase-structure rules are the appropriate linguistic analysis. To show this, the facts would have to be (at least) *that no sentence constructions require a transformational rule for affix movement* which can also be utilized by the simple declarative [p. 496; italics mine]." Since the italicized clause is true, the facts argue that discontinuous rules are *an* appropriate analysis. (Incidentally, there are independent objections to the affix-movement rule—see Bach, 1964, p. 81. The rule is not well formed because the symbol, "Affix," is introduced ad hoc, and reformulation is not simple.)

A word on "simplicity": It is possible to agree with Bever et al. that simplicity is an important consideration in scientific theorizing and still to reject their use of simplicity arguments. I am troubled by two main difficulties of principle.

1. Detailed measurement of simplicity (e.g., by means of a rule count, or other metric) must presuppose a particular form of grammatical model—it is doubtfully meaningful to count rules which are not of the same type. Competing grammars which differ in form (i.e., in the kinds of rules permitted) cannot therefore be compared in simplicity, except at the gross "intuitive" level that is usual in comparing scientific theories. While some very general questions (e.g., whether a phrase-structure grammar is adequate for the entire language) can be settled by simplicity considerations, because the differences in simplicity in the resulting grammars are great, it is hard to see that more detailed questions about the kinds of rules used in natural languages can be settled in this way. It follows that Bever et al. never confronted my original methodological point; if the component parts of a grammar are not separately responsive to data, and if simplicity considerations become inconclusive beyond a certain level of detail, then how are questions about the form of grammars settled, if not by convenience?

References

BACH, E. *An introduction to transformational grammars.* New York: Holt, 1964.

BELLUGI, URSULA, & BROWN, R. (Eds.) *The acquisition of language. Monographs of the Society for Research in Child Development,* 1964, 29 (1, Whole No. 92), 1–192.

2. There is a major question about the domain over which simplicity should be taken. Should the domain comprise only the possible grammars of a language (as Bever et al. assume), or should it also include possible accounts of the acquisition of the grammars? If there is a possibility that the simpler of two possible grammatical solutions might require the more complex acquisition theory, then the domain over which simplicity is taken cannot be restricted to grammar alone and must include acquisition theory—otherwise the grammarian merely purchases simplicity at the psychologist's expense. The difficulty is well illustrated in Bever et al.'s main argument: They contest my proposals on the ground that simple English sentences contain a distinction between manifest and underlying structure; however, they acknowledge that a grammar could be written in which there is no such distinction, but claim that such a grammar should be rejected on grounds of complexity. Nevertheless, they allow that the grammatical solution containing the distinction might require a more complex acquisition theory (it would pose "serious problems for *any* theory of syntax learning"—1965b, p. 476). Thus, even on their own calculations, they cannot claim a *net* gain in simplicity for their analysis. In general, simplicity arguments are inherently question begging when they are used to constrain theories which are outside the domain over which simplicity is taken.

If the existence of a distinction between manifest and underlying kernel structure is to be settled by simplicity calculations (which seems undesirable), then surely the gain in simplicity accruing to an acquisition theory for taking the underlying structure as overt in simple sentences would likely be so great that it would more than compensate for an increase in grammatical complexity involved in writing the grammar so that the underlying structure was overt. And it has not been shown that there must be an increase in grammatical complexity. (Ultimately, it would seem parsimonious to identify grammatical simplicity with ease of acquisition.)

BEVER, T. G., FODOR, J. A., & WEKSEL, W. Is linguistics empirical? *Psychological Review,* 1965, 72, 493–500. (a)

BEVER, T. G., FODOR, J. A., & WEKSEL, W. On the acquisition of syntax: A critique of "contextual generalization." *Psychological Review,* 1965, 72, 467–482. (b)

BLOCH, B. Studies in colloquial Japanese: II. Syntax. *Language,* 1946, 22, 200–248.

BRAINE, M. D. S. On learning the grammatical order of words. *Psychological Review,* 1963, 70, 323–348.

BRAINE, M. D. S. The insufficiency of a finite state model for verbal reconstructive memory. *Psychonomic Science,* 1965, 2, 291–292. (a)

BRAINE, M. D. S. Learning the positions of words relative to a marker element. Washington, D. C.: 1965. (Mimeo) (b)

BROWN, R., & BELLUGI, URSULA. Three processes in the child's acquisition of syntax. *Harvard Educational Review,* 1964, 34, 133–151.

CHOMSKY, N. Transformational analysis. Unpublished doctoral dissertation, University of Pennsylvania, 1955.

CHOMSKY, N. *Syntactic structures.* The Hague: Mouton, 1957.

CHOMSKY, N. On the notion "rule of grammar." In R. Jakobson (Ed.), *Structure of language and its mathematical aspects, Proceedings of the 12th Symposium in Applied Mathematics.* Providence, R. I.: American Mathematical Society, 1961. Pp. 6–24.

CHOMSKY, N. A transformational approach to syntax. In A. A. Hill (Ed.), *Third Texas conference on problems of linguistic analysis in English.* Austin: Univer. Texas Press, 1962. Pp. 124–158.

CHOMSKY, N. Formal properties of grammars. In R. D. Luce, R. R. Bush, & E. Galanter (Eds.), *Handbook of mathe-*

matical psychology. Vol. 2. New York: Wiley, 1963. Pp. 323–418.

Harman, G. H. Generative grammars without transformation rules: A defense of phrase structure. *Language,* 1963, 39, 597–616.

Harris, Z. S. *Methods in structural linguistics.* Chicago: Chicago Univer. Press, 1951.

Jenkins, J., & Palermo, D. Mediational processes and the acquisition of linguistic structure. In Ursula Bellugi & R. Brown (Eds.), *The acquisition of language. Monographs of the Society for Research in Child Development,* 1964, 29 (1, Whole No. 92), 141–169.

Matthews, G. H. Discontinuity and asymmetry in phrase structure grammars. *Information and Control,* 1963, 6, 137–146.

Postal, P. Constituent structure: A study of contemporary models of syntactic description. *International Journal of American Linguistics,* 1964, No. 30. (Monogr. Suppl. Part III)

Putnam, H. Some issues in the theory of grammar. In R. Jakobson (Ed.), *Structure of language and its mathematical aspects, Proceedings of the 12th Symposium in Applied Mathematics.* Providence, R. I.: American Mathematics Society, 1961. Pp. 25–42.

Smith, K. H. Recall of paired verbal units under various conditions of organization. Unpublished doctoral dissertation, University of Minnesota, 1963.

Smith, K. H. Mediation and position learning in the recall of structured letter pairs. *Psychonomic Science,* 1965, 2, 293–294.

Wells, R. Immediate constituents. *Language,* 1947, 23, 81–117.

Whorf, B. L. *Language, thought, and reality: Selected writings.* Cambridge, Mass.: Technology Press, 1956.

Yngve, V. A model and an hypothesis for language structure. *Proceedings of the American Philosophical Society,* 1960, 104, 444–466.

Is Linguistics Empirical?

T. G. BEVER, J. A. FODOR,
and W. WEKSEL

This paper continues the discussion of issues raised by Braine's theory of "contextual generalization." The arguments for analyzing the English declarative as transformationally generated are discussed at length. Broader issues about the nature of confirmation of claims made by grammars are also considered. It is argued that while the direct experimental verification of such claims is often not feasible, considerations of simplicity and generality can provide adequate grounds for their empirical confirmation or disconfirmation.

Braine's (1965) reply to our (1965) paper successfully clarifies the two major issues between us. The first of these concerns a detail of the grammar of English: Braine claims (and all generative grammarians have denied) that the simple declarative sentence has a special linguistic character in that it has no transformations in its derivational history. The second issue concerns the possible bases for confirming or disconfirming particular claims about the character of the grammatical analysis of a class of sentences. In our critique we argued that the special status Braine seeks for simple declaratives can be obtained only at the price of the ad hoc decision to treat them in isolation from the rest of the types of sentences in the language. This is equivalent to saying that a grammar which treats declaratives as nontransformational is inherently more complex than a grammar which does not. The methodological issue between us is that Braine does not accept such arguments as supplying even prima facie confirmation of the transformational characterization of declaratives. Braine apparently holds that each decision in the construction of a grammar must be susceptible to direct experimental confirmation or else be considered a mere artifact of the linguistic description, adopted "at the convenience of the linguist." It seems to us that Braine is certainly wrong on both points. On one hand the grammar that Braine proposes for simple declaratives is thoroughly unacceptable; on the other hand to accept Braine's view of confirmation would be to make linguistic science (or, for that matter, any other kind of science) impossible. We shall discuss these points in reverse order.

T. G. Bever, J. A. Fodor, and W. Weksel, "Is Linguistics Empirical?", *Psychological Review*, 72, No. 6 (1965), 493–500. Reprinted by permission of the authors and publisher.

Progress in linguistic analysis of natural language has depended on the careful separation of the theory of the language (*"langue"* or "competence") from the theory of the use of language (*"parole"* or "performance"). In this way the linguist has insulated himself from the fact that the variables determining the character of speech behavior reflect features other than the formal structure of the spoken language. For instance, the fact that some sentences are difficult to say, to remember, or to understand is obvious. Evidently, such facts are the consequence of interactions between linguistic variables and variables of memory, perception, motor integration, etc. To fail to so represent these facts would render impossible the representation of *either* the systematic character of language *or* the systematic character of speech behavior.

To avoid this consequence, linguistic analysis does not accept as pertinent to the characterization of *language* all facts that are pertinent to the characterization of verbal behavior. Only certain types of information about language are considered, for example, whether a sequence is intuitively grammatical, its relations to other sentences, the units of which it is constructed, etc. Such information is quite real and as palpable as any other psychological data; that *all* facts about speech are not considered in linguistic analysis does not reduce the scientific objectivity of those that *are* considered. A theory that can explain the latter phenomena is in fact a sound, *empirically supported* part of the total theory of language behavior. The linguist and psychologist seek to discover how the theory of the language, which explains one restricted set of data, is embedded within the theory of the speaker of a language, which explains speech behavior in general.

It is not at all surprising that the analysis of speech behavior should proceed from two empirical and theoretical sources. Indeed, distinguishing among the different kinds of data that constitute superficially homogeneous phenomena is absolutely universal in scientific explanations; it occurs wherever considerations of simplicity and explanatory power require that the observations be represented as interaction effects. Consider, for example, the analysis of a block sliding down an inclined plane. There are two kinds of variables that interact to determine the block's behavior—first, the forces acting downward on the body and determining the acceleration for an ideal system; second, the reactive forces (e.g., friction) due to the character of the particular body and plane under study. The observed behavior is susceptible of systematic explanation only on the view that it is the product of interactions between distinct systems.

Since the theory of verbal performance is directly concerned with the behavior of speakers, it may often be subject to fairly direct experimental examination. The theory of competence, on the other hand, is concerned with the formulation of the linguistic information underlying verbal behavior. The speaker's competence is only reflected in his behavior via the kinds of performance variables mentioned above. The direct experimental verification of the theory of competence is correspondingly difficult.

This is not to say that the theory of competence is in any sense conventional or arbitrary. For, its support rests not only on occasional experimental confirmation but also on considerations of theoretical simplicity and power, fruitfulness, availability for integration with theories of performance variables, and so on. It must be reemphasized that this relative inaccessibility to experimental manipulation is not specific to theories of linguistic competence. On the contrary, it is obvious that the more a scientific theory concerns itself with the fundamental mechanisms underlying the observables, the less susceptible it is to direct experimental test.

SOME EMPIRICALLY BASED FORMAL DECISIONS

We now consider some of the points where Braine feels that the form of the grammar is at the grammarian's (and his) arbitrary disposal. In each case we try to show that the particular claim about grammar we made in our original critique is responsive to some compelling facts about natural language. In any given instance it is, of course, possible to argue that the facts we invoke are wrong or that they might be accounted for in some more economical fashion. But it is *not* possible to claim that the form of the grammar is arbitrary. We will take the points in the order they appear in Braine's reply and omit discussion of Braine's new data or proposals and of the accuracy of our reading of his original paper.[1]

THE NONPRIVILEGED STATUS OF SIMPLE DECLARATIVE SENTENCES

We argued that declarative sentences have neither linguistic nor psychological preeminence and that the underlying constituent structure of simple declarative sentences is itself an abstract object, just as in the case of the passive and all other constructions. Braine counters with several arguments indicating that we did not suggest evidence for this and that the only evidence he can think of relies on arbitrary decisions about the form of grammar:

> [1.]...their long discussion of the passive transformation...is relevant only to the question of what the *passive* transformation is a transformation of.... This argument says nothing about the relation between the kernel grammar and simple declarative sentences [p. 484; emphasis ours].

2. The only argument he can recall in favor of an abstract underlying constituent structure (UCS) for simple declaratives is the treatment of discontinuous elements; he claims this is an artifact of an arbitrary decision about the form of grammar.

"Whether or not a phrase-structure (kernel) grammar can permit discontinuities is a *technical* question about the form of such grammars [p. 484; emphasis ours]." In particular, our claim that such constructions as *be chasing* are evidence for the distinction between manifest and underlying order is spurious: "These are of the $\lambda \ldots \mu$ form [p. 485]." Braine suggests earlier that such discontinuities can be treated by a phrase-structure rule, $X \rightarrow \lambda \ldots \mu$, where it is a formal convention that μ permutes with the next rightmost element. For example, this sequence of phrase-structure rules would give the phrase *be chasing* as an output of the underlying phrase structure:

VP → aux V; aux → be...ing; V → chase.

> A grammar which forbids representing the constituents in the form *be...ing*...must necessarily generate [the order] *be* + *ing* + *chase* [and we presume John + sg + pres + run] and...having generated the items in the wrong order, it is of course necessary to permute them into the actual order. *The entire argument associated with [these structures] rests on a particular choice of phrase-structure model* [p. 485; emphasis ours].

3. Braine then laments the alleged lack of basis for any decisions between "competing" phrase structure and transformational solutions of descriptive problems in syntax.

> If the terminal strings generated by the phrase structure are permitted to be arbitrarily different from any actual sentence structures, *there are no independent data against which the phrase structure and the transformational*

[1] If we misunderstand Braine (1963) on some points in our critique, we apologize to him and to the reader and suggest that they both satisfy themselves that our misunderstandings were based on misreading. In this paper we quote Braine directly whenever possible. We do not utilize any linguistic discoveries made after 1957; recent theoretical modifications do not affect Braine's theory nor its incorrectness.

rules can be separately tested...the grammarian can write the phrase-sentence kernel *partly on the basis of his convenience,* free to correct any poor fit with the manifest structure of the language by using transforms to reshuffle elements. This methodological looseness makes it impossible to accept empirical claims about the properties of phrase-structure grammars of natural languages [p. 485; emphases ours].

4. Braine claims, in summation, that we did not show that the simple declarative sentence has a distinct abstract form underlying it, and he asserts that to show it we...

...would have to show that there are no feasible forms of phrase-structure model which would permit transformational grammars to be written so that only the identity transform intervened between the phrase structure and the morphophonemic rules [p. 485].

Our replies can in some instances be quite brief.

1. Braine's argument on page 484 is simply wrong. On grounds of simplicity, *any* argument which shows that the underlying constituent structure for one sentence type is generated by a particular kind of phrase-structure rules is prima facie an argument that all sentence types have such rules underlying them. A grammar does not treat certain sentence types to the exclusion of others, and there is no reason to believe that a child does either.

2. It is difficult to understand what Braine can mean by the claim that the explanation of discontinuities is a "technical question." He correctly assesses the literature as showing that linguistic formalisms could provide either phrase-structure or transformational solutions. When nonequivalent explanations of the data compete, we must surely decide between them by asking which formalism accounts for the facts under consideration with the greatest economy and generality. If this makes the question of how discontinuous constituents are to be explained "technical," then *all* questions of scientific theory are technical, since considerations of simplicity and generality underlie the solution of all such questions.

It is true that the use of discontinuous phrase-structure expansions could adequately generate number agreement and appropriate placement of the affix *ing* in the simple declarative sentence. But that is *all* it could do. The arguments in our critique showed that for other constructions (e.g., passive, negative passive, question passive, cleft-sentence passive, negative-question passive, etc.) the affix-movement rule must *follow* the passive rule, which itself follows the development of the base structure. Thus, the affix-movement rule needed for these constructions *cannot* be in the phrase structure and is consequently a transformation. Indeed, since the same transformation is formally capable of accounting for number agreement and affix permutation in the simple declarative as well as other constructions, we have a clear choice between two types of grammar. One grammar uses a discontinuous phrase-structure rule for number attachment in the declarative and a transformation for number attachment in all other constructions. The other grammar employs only the transformation. Clearly the latter grammar must be preferred since it explains the facts with less duplication and with a more restricted form of grammar.

Of course the facts *might* have shown that the discontinuous phrase-structure rules *are* the appropriate linguistic analysis. To show this, the facts would have to be (at least) that *no* sentence constructions require a transformational rule for affix movement which can also be utilized by the simple declarative. That is, the transformational solution *could* have been invalidated by the character of English, and thus the decision to reject the discontinuous phrase-structure solution is not based on the "grammarian's convenience," but on the facts of the language.

3. It is hard to imagine what the "independent data" might be that could "separately" confirm any linguistic analysis since the theoretical decisions themselves are based on all presently available empirical considerations extractable from the language.

Perhaps we can additionally support the decision to treat number agreement (and affix-movement phenomena) with one transformation by an appeal to the reader's intuition about some previously unconsidered facts. Is it not the case that the subject-verb number agreement (and formation of *be* + *ing*) is the same sort of relation in these two sentences?

They were running.

They were being served.

The analysis proposed by Braine generates these two subject-verb agreements by two distinct *kinds* of processes,[2] and we might expect that if this analysis were true, different intuitions about the nature of the agreements could be informally or experimentally extracted from native speakers. In fact, we have no reason to believe that such differences exist. Number agreement seems to be a psychologically unitary process in English. This is reflected in the formal analysis to which the linguistic facts led us.

4. In short, although there *is* probably a "feasible" form of grammar in which the underlying and derived constituent structures of simple declaratives would be identical, this analysis is blocked for English on empirical grounds. We have shown briefly that at very least such a solution would involve an unnecessarily complex system since there is a simpler analysis which accounts for the relevant facts. In this way we show that Braine's claim that there is a "base" or "kernel" grammar producing all and only simple declaratives to be *logically* possible but empirically unacceptable.

THE MORAL

We have argued that there is strong empirical support for the claim that declaratives have abstract underlying structures and that this support derives primarily from considerations of the simplicity and generality of grammatical rules. In conclusion it may be pointed out that, though it is true that a suitable complication of the grammar would permit Braine to treat simple declaratives as the only untransformed structures, it must be added that similar complications would permit that treatment *for any other sentence type*. There is no more reason for complicating the grammar in order to render declarative sentences uniquely nontransformational than there is for complicating the grammar in order to render passives, questions, negatives, imperatives, etc. uniquely nontransformational. The difficulty with playing fast and loose with simplicity constraints is that, once having started, it is hard to find a way to stop.

THE EXCLUSION OF TRANSFORMATIONS

Braine states that the "...main purpose [of my discussion of transformations] was to show that [their] existence did not contradict my proposals concerning simple declaratives [p. 484]." And later (p. 486), "my [proposal] specifically excluded the learning of transforms...my proposals could capture the structure of passives only insofar as they are similar to predicate phrases with adjective heads (cf. *The kazoo was blown by the child; The coffee was hot on the stove.*)" Furthermore he states that the fact that many transforms *appear* similar to simple declarative sentences explains why it is reasonable to assume that simple declaratives

2 Discontinuous phrase structure for the first, transformational for the second.

are learned separately by the child, even though there is no evidence that they preponderate in the child's verbal environment:

I did not claim that children were mainly exposed to simple declaratives. . . . Information about positional and contingency relations in simple sentences is abundantly exemplified *in many transforms*. . . consider the similarity in verb-phrase structure between passives and sentences with adjective predicators (e.g., *George was served—George was sensible*). . . . Experience with the verb structure of one sentence type could hardly fail to transfer to the other type [p. 483; emphases ours].

This line of argument appears to involve Braine in a hopeless dilemma. To wit, if the child cannot exclude transformations, then our objections in the critique and in this reply obtain; if the child *can* isolate and reject transforms from consideration, then he must already know the grammar *including its transformational component:* Transformational information is required to distinguish between declaratives and other types of sentences.

This dilemma runs deep. If the child cannot yet tell whether an *apparent* declarative sentence actually is one, how does he know when to transfer experience from one putative declarative to another? It is undeniable that many sentences other than declaratives appear in the declarative-like form "NP VP." How does the child know which such sentences are *sufficiently* "like" true declarative to permit relevant transfer of training unless he already has transformational information? How can "experience with one type. . . transfer to another" sentence of the same type unless the child can see that they *are* of the same type? That is, he must have the transformational information required to distinguish between real and apparent declaratives. Furthermore, *how does the child know what kind of experience to generalize?* Surely if everything the child knows about

George was served.

generalized to

George was sensible.

the child should expect the sentence

**Somebody sensibled George.*

to parallel

Somebody served George.

THE DISCRIMINATION OF HOMOLOGOUS SEQUENCES AND "COVERT CATEGORIES"

Several different problems for Braine's earlier and present proposals are manifestations of Braine's inability to answer the question: How are sentence types differentiated when they have similar word-class orders? (See our critique for examples.)

Braine says, ". . . the kind of phrase-structure system for which my proposals are adequate is one which permits only one unmarked word list at any given location and which restricts the circumstances in which an unmarked list can occur at two nonhomologous locations [p. 487]." He proposes that this requirement be met by an "indexing restriction" partially carried by "function words" which "index classes and distinguish their locations [p. 487]."[3] But, he notes, this is not an adequate solution: ". . . it is a fact that languages contain structures in which the same position can be occupied by two or more classes which are not differentially marked. Bever et al. are correct in pointing out that this sort of structure poses a problem for my proposals [pp. 487–488]."

As a solution, Braine invokes the use of "covert categories" which he presumes to be "semantic." Words that are otherwise undifferentiated in a particular sentence type thus must have an "internal" analysis which differentiates them.

We, of course, agree with this proposal since it reduces to the tautology that what-

[3] Since Braine's first paper, rules for the introduction of lexical items into underlying structures have been shown to be substitution transformations (Chomsky, 1965; Matthews, 1963) and not phrase-structure rules. His argument at the end of his section, "The Scope of the Proposals," is therefore unsound.

ever *really* is different ought to be described. But the tautology is useless unless a theory for providing correct internal analyses is also forthcoming, and Braine's own discussion suggests how unlikely it is that such analyses can be formulated in semantic terms. In fact, generative grammars do provide differing types of words in homologous position with distinct analyses; they do so largely by the use of transformations which can distinguish between items that have similar privileges of occurrence but which differ in the base structures from which they derive. Consider first a nontransformational case—proper names (an example proposed by Braine): Presumably there are different internal analyses for the lexical items "George" and "butter" which allow the sentences

George is nice.
Butter is nice.

and the sentence

The butter is nice.

but block the otherwise contextually generalizable

The George is nice.

But what internal markers differentiate the participle in these sentences?

Making mistakes can be annoying.
Recurring mistakes can be annoying.

What "markers" allow

Many mistakes were made.

but block

**Many mistakes were recurred.*

The analysis which differentiates the participles successfully must refer to the underlying constituent structure, namely to the fact that "make" occurs with an object permissible in the UCS (and that "mistakes" is that object) and that "recur" does not (so that "mistakes" is the subject in the UCS).[4]

In short, we agree with Braine's proposal that words and homologous sentence types are differentiated by characteristics *not directly observable in the sequences themselves.* In addition we propose that differences in transformational derivation are necessary to provide the explanation for many of these "covert" distinctions. So far as we can see, Braine has provided no reason whatever for rejecting this suggestion.

THE "UNCLARITY OF TRANSFORMS"

Braine states: "What might be learned in learning transformations is difficult to discuss in part because the transformation concept itself seems unclear [p. 488]." The "unclarity" appears in at least two general ways: (*a*) "...it seems impossible to deduce from Chomsky's (1961) definition...what features should be built into a verbal learning experiment in order to ensure that a subject...[learns] a transformation [p. 488]"; (*b*) grammars are too strong and their character will change as they become refined. Rules for derived constituent structure are not well understood.

Regarding (*a*), it seems to us fantastic to require that experiments should be *deducible* from theories. Regarding (*b*), the questions in grammatical theory which await theoretical and empirical elucidation do not place in jeopardy the answers which we do have.

ON LABORATORY EXPERIMENTATION WITH PRIMITIVE ARTIFICIAL LANGUAGE

In our critique we suggested that experiments on artificial languages are

[4] Notice that this exactly characterizes the distinction between "transitive" and "intransitive" verbs, although this distinction is not apparent in the surface structure of the sample sentences. We could decide that such notions as *transitive, intransitive,* and so on should be represented as "covert features" of lexical items without reference to the UCS. This possibility is empirically rejected because it would not eradicate an abstract level from the grammar, and it would result in duplication in the surface phrase marker of the distinctions already made in the UCS. It is never difficult to construct a theory *more* complicated than the simplest one currently available.

equivocal with respect to natural language. It is inconclusive to show that the subjects learn the intended structure when exposed to a relatively small number of instances either in artificial or natural language since the structure that must be assumed for natural languages is determined by the need to supply a simple, uniform treatment for a large variety of sentences of very specific formal character. Finally there is no reason to believe that simple phrase-structure artificial languages are on a psychological continuum with natural language.

Braine counters in his reply that he has other evidence indicating that the subjects did learn the assumed structure. He also points out that it is silly to assume that a child loses his natural language-learning capacity when he enters a laboratory.

Of course we were only questioning the *experiment's* capacity to bring out the child's ability. There is no support for the assumption that the experiment with this restricted "language" elicits the mechanisms employed in learning natural language. Evidence that these languages do not elicit first-language learning mechanisms can be found in the recent work of Wales and Grant.[5] They repeated Braine's Experiment III with adults and obtained exactly the same results. This means either that adults learn languages in the same way as children or that the experiment is not tapping the language ability indigenous to the child.[6]

[5] Wales, personal communication, 1965.

[6] It seems to us unlikely *on any account* that adults learn languages in the same manner as children do. This does not depend on an assumption of "innateness" for language learning in children, nor must it reject the possibility that "proactive inhibition" explains the adult's difficulty with language learning. Whatever view you hold, it is obvious that an adult with 20-years experience in Language X will learn Language Y differently from a child that has had only 2- or 3-years active experience in X. The fact that children and adults yield identical experimental results thus indicates that the experiment is not stimulating first-language learning mechanisms in children.

THE CONFLICT BETWEEN LINGUISTIC ANALYSIS AND CURRENT LEARNING THEORY

In our critique, we suggested that current models of learning are in fact incompatible with the empirically based results of linguistic theory. Braine is sensitive to this, and he implicitly uses it as an argument *against* certain features of linguistic analysis; in particular, he is bothered by the concept of an "abstract" underlying constituent structure for which no explicit representation appears.

> The distinction [between manifest and underlying structure in kernel sentences] is certainly not convenient psychologically: The assumption that the learner learns structures to which he is never exposed would indeed pose "serious problems for *any* theory of syntax learning [p. 486]."
>
> ...the fundamental issue at stake in this interchange [is] whether the order of elements in simple sentences reflects the order in the underlying string.... Bever et al. are arguing that
>
> ...the learner is often never exposed to the pattern properties which must be assumed to be learned. Before accepting this argument, I would urge that psychologists examine the linguistic evidence for a distinction between manifest and underlying structure in kernel sentences very closely indeed [p. 490].

We of course agree, and we have tried to expand and clarify the empirical basis for the decision (*a*) that *all* sentences have an abstract structure underlying them and (*b*) that this structure is not isomorphic with the simple declarative sentence. The essential themes of our discussion have been: (*a*) Related parts of a language cannot be considered in isolation; (*b*) decisions concerning the form of grammar are based on determining which formalism explains the facts of the language with the least duplication and the most generality.

The psychological role of the underlying constituent structure has not been carefully studied except insofar as it is an integral part of the account of grammatical sentences themselves. Though linguistic evidence of this latter sort is not in any sense arbitrary or equivocal, we do feel that the exact form of the empirical extensions of the underlying constituent structure into other aspects of language behavior requires thorough psychological investigation. Part of that study will no doubt include experimental effects of UCS upon the recall, perception, or learning of sentences. A crucially important part of that study must center on *how* the child goes about learning structures for which there are no explicit models.

There are those who agree with Braine that this is impossible either in fact or in principle. As the empirical basis for assuming an abstract underlying structure in language becomes broader and the explanatory power of that assumption becomes deeper, *we recommend to all psychologists that they seriously question the adequacy of any theory of learning that cannot account for the fact that such structures are acquired.*

References

Bever, T. G., Fodor, J. A., & Weksel, W. On the acquisition of syntax: A critique of "contextual generalization." *Psychological Review*, 1965, 72, 467–482.

Braine, M. D. S. On learning the grammatical order of words. *Psychological Review,* 1963, 70, 323–348.

Braine, M. D. S. On the basis of phrase structure: A reply to Bever, Fodor, and Weksel. *Psychological Review,* 1965, 72, 483–492.

Chomsky, N. Topics in the theory of generative grammar. In T. A. Sebeok (Ed.), *Current trends in linguistics.* Vol. 3. *Linguistic theory.* New York: Humanities Press, 1965.

Matthews, G. H. Discontinuity and asymmetry in phrase structure grammars. *Information and Control,* 1963, 6, 137–146.

Word Association and the Acquisition of Grammar

ROGER BROWN
and JEAN BERKO [1]

Every natural language is a system. From knowledge of one part it is possible to anticipate correctly many other parts. The linguistic scientist studies some finite set of utterances (his linguistic "corpus") in search of the recurrent elementary units and patterns of combination that will generate the infinite set of utterances belonging to the language. Every child, in learning his first language, does much the same thing with the difference that he does not explicitly formulate most of the rules that govern his language behavior. A child is not, in his first few years, exposed to all possible utterances belonging to the community language but only to that small sample brought to him by his family, his friends, and television. Exposure to this sample, however, teaches him to understand and to produce utterances not actually experienced but implied by what has been experienced. The child may begin as a parrot imitating what others say, but he will end as a poet able to say things that have not been said before but which will be grammatical and meaningful in his community. This is the terminal achievement which a theory of language acquisition must explain.

The linguistic scientist describes language systems at several levels: the *phonological* level of distinctive sound elements and their permissible combinations; the *morphological* level of elementary meaningful forms (*morphemes*) and their combination to make words; the *syntactic* level of sentence creation from words. We have described elsewhere (2) these three levels and have reported two studies (1, 3) concerning the acquisition by children of morphology and syntax. The present study is concerned with syntax and, more

[1] This research was done while Dr. Berko held Public Health Service Postdoctoral Research Fellowship MF 9261 from the Division of Research Grants of the National Institutes of Health, and the research was facilitated by a Supply Grant accompanying that fellowship. Grateful acknowledgment is made of this support and also of the generous cooperation of the staff and students of the Michael Driscoll School in Brookline, Massachusetts.

Roger Brown and Jean Berko, "Word Association and the Acquisition of Grammar," *Child Development,* **31,** (1960), 1–14. Reprinted by permission of the author and The Society for Research in Child Development, Inc.

particularly, with the child's utilization of the English parts-of-speech.

The linguistic scientist defines the parts-of-speech in purely syntactic or formal terms. He has shown that the English teacher's semantic definitions (e.g., "a noun is the name of a person, place, or thing") are imprecise approximations to the underlying but less obvious syntactic facts. The noun, in descriptive linguistics, is a class of words having similar "privileges of occurrence." Nouns are words that can follow articles and can occur in subject and object positions and, in this respect, are distinct from such other classes of words as the verb, adjective, and adverb. The fact that the words of any language fall into classes of approximate syntactic equivalents is of great interest to the student of language acquisition because it suggests one of the ways in which the lawful flexibility of speech is developed. A new word is ordinarily introduced to a child in a sentence, and this sentence will often serve to identify the part-of-speech to which the new word belongs. If the parts-of-speech have been internalized, this would mean that one vast array of sentence positions is available for the new word and other arrays are not. From the fact that *X* is a noun one can anticipate all of the grammatically acceptable uses of *X* and set aside all of the unacceptable uses. Is there evidence that children learn to operate with the parts-of-speech? We suspect that such evidence is to be found in certain well-established facts concerning word association.

Since the experiment of Woodrow and Lowell (7), it has been known that the word associations of children show consistent difference from the associations of adults. Woodworth (8) offers as examples of these differences the words appearing in Table 1. Woodrow and Lowell and others after them have conceptualized these differences in terms that are primarily semantic. Children are said to give more "contiguity" responses and more "whole-part" responses while adults are said to give more "coordinate," "contrast," and "similarity" responses. In several cases Woodrow and Lowell desert their semantic concepts and speak of "adjective-noun" associations and "verb-object" associations (both of which are more common in children's than in adult's responses). These classifications by parts-of-speech suggest a very general formal principle which contrasts the word associations of children and adults, a principle which so far as we know was first suggested by Ervin (4). The associative responses of adults belong to the same part-of-speech as the stimulus word more often than do the associative responses of children. We shall speak of the adult type of association as homogeneous-by-part-of-speech (abbreviated Hmg.) and the child's type as heterogeneous-by-part-of-speech (Htg.).

Looking again at the examples of Table 1, we see that the response favored by adults is almost invariably Hmg. while that favored by children is Htg. Many of the largest differences found in the Woodrow and Lowell study conform to this syntactic principle though they were not so classified by the authors. In addition to these data from the past there are recent findings of Ervin (4) who used a list of common words belonging to various parts-of-speech with groups of children in kindergarten and the first, third, and sixth grades. She found large increase with age in Hmg. responses to nouns, verbs, prepositions, adjectives, and adverbs. What is the significance of this apparently reliable developmental trend in word association?

There are, of course, many kinds of association that can link one word with another; similarity or contrast of referents, spatio-temporal contiguity of referents, and high transition probabilities between words are obvious possibilities. Similarity and contrast and contiguity between referents would sometimes lead to Hmg. responses (e.g., *table-chair*) and sometimes to Htg. responses (e.g., *table-eat*). Immediate transitions of high probability

Table 1

WORD ASSOCIATIONS FROM ADULTS AND CHILDREN

Stimulus	*Response*	*1000 Children*	*1000 Men and Women*
Table	Eat	358	63
	Chair	24	274
Dark	Night	421	221
	Light	38	427
Man	Work	168	17
	Woman	8	394
Deep	Hole	257	32
	Shallow	6	180
Soft	Pillow	138	53
	Hard	27	365
Mountain	High	390	246
	Hill	91	184

will very seldom exist between two words of the same part-of-speech, and so such pairs as *dark-night, deep-hole,* and *soft-pillow* are Htg. Elaborating a suggestion of Ervin's (2), we propose that the word associations of very young children are governed by such principles as we have cited but that, with increasing age, another principle of association begins to operate which has the effect of increasing the number of Hmg. responses.

From the time that a child begins to use phrases his speech repertoire will manifest the morphological structure that is a universal characteristic of adult speech in any language. The same meaningful forms (morphemes and words) occur in a variety of contexts; not all forms can occur in all contexts but some forms can occur in some of the same contexts. From these morphological universals it follows that words resemble one another in the degree to which they have similar privileges of occurrence. This syntactic similarity is always objectively present in speech involving phrases but probably it takes considerable time and maturity to analyze out syntactic similarity. The appreciation of syntactic similarity is, however, prerequisite to the ability to form meaningful and grammatical sentences that are not imitated from someone else. Suppose a child has learned that such words as *house, barn, table,* and *fence* can all occur in such positions as: "See the ——"; "I own a ——"; "The —— is new"; and "This —— is mine." If now he hears for the first time such a sentence as "See the *car*" in which *car* is a new word, he can be prepared to say "I own a *car*"; "The *car* is new"; and "This *car* is mine." Of course, the particular sentence uttered on a given occasion depends on semantic and motivational factors but the universe of sentences from which the particular can be drawn is established by the syntactic kinship linking *car* with *house, barn, table,* and *fence*.

Modern methods of teaching second or foreign languages begin, as does first language learning, with the repetition of phrases which recombine a limited set of meaningful elements. In second language learning, as in first, there comes a time when the student "creates" a phrase by realizing the syntactic implications of the material practiced. This is often accomplished nowadays by implicit induction without any explicit tuition in syntactic rules, and that is exactly the way it is accomplished by all children who become full participants in a first language.

Syntactic similarity is a matter of degree. The parts-of-speech are simply very large and very useful classes of approximate combinational equivalents. Animate nouns are more closely equivalent than nouns in general, and transitive verbs are more closely equivalent than verbs in general. Such popular adult word associations as *bright-dark* are not only semantic antonyms; they are also adjectives having highly similar privileges of occurrence. *Bright* has more sentence contexts in common with *dark* than with such another adjective as *virtuous*. It is our general hypothesis that, as utilization of syntax develops in children, syntactic similarity in words becomes an increasingly important determinant of word association and that the developmental trend from Htg. responses toward Hmg. responses is a manifestation of this great step forward into syntactic operations. We have undertaken to test this hypothesis by relating the child's tendency to give Hmg. word associations to his ability to make correct grammatical use of new words after hearing them in a couple of sentences.

METHOD

We worked with four groups of 20 subjects each. In each group there were equal numbers of male and female subjects. Groups I, II, and III were students from, respectively, the first, second, and third grades of the Michael Driscoll School in Brookline, Massachusetts. The Driscoll School is a public school in a middle-income residence area. Children in a given group were all taken from the same classroom and simply drawn in the order of the seating arrangement until 20 had served. The fourth group (Group Ad.) consisted of 20 adults, students or staff at M.I.T., who responded to an advertisement asking for subjects.

Word Association Test

This test consisted of 36 stimulus words such that there were six words representing each of six parts-of-speech. The words were selected because all have high frequency in the speech of American elementary-school children (6) and because in earlier studies they yielded large differences between the associations of children and adults. The words were presented in a constant order to all subjects.

Verbs in English may be subdivided into transitive and intransitives. Intransitive verbs can appear without an object (e.g., "We *laugh*") while transitives almost always occur with some sort of object (e.g., "We *sent* something"). For the present experiment the transitives and intransitives were treated as two parts-of-speech, and there were six words representing each of them.

Nouns in English can be separated into "count nouns" and "mass nouns." The names are suggested from a distinction of reference; count nouns usually name bounded objects (e.g., *table, house*) while mass nouns name extended substances (e.g., *milk, sand*). However, there is also a clear syntactic distinction; count nouns in the singular can be preceded by *a* while mass nouns cannot (e.g., *a table* but not *a sand*) and, in addition, count nouns, when preceded by *some*, appear in the plural whereas mass nouns appear in the singular (e.g., *some tables* but *some milk*). On the present list of stimulus words there were six mass nouns and six count nouns.

In addition to the two varieties of noun and two varieties of verb, there were six adjectives and six adverbs on the list. The complete list is as follows:

Count Nouns (C.N.): table, house, foot, needle, apple, doctor.

Mass Nouns (M.N.): milk, water, sand, sugar, air, cheese.

Adjectives (Adj.): dark, soft, cold, white, sweet, hard.

Transitive Verb (T.V.): to send, to bring, to find, to take, to hit, to invite.

Intransitive Verbs (I.V.): to skate, to come, to live, to laugh, to stand, to walk.

Adverbs (Adv.): quickly, slowly, sadly, now, softly, gently.

Many English words belong to more than one part-of-speech. It is possible in English to *table* a motion and to *foot* a bill but *table* and *foot,* in the vast majority of their occurrences, function as nouns and, when presented in isolation as stimulus words, are apprehended as nouns by most English-speaking adults. The words on the present list belong primarily to one part-of-speech though they may have secondary membership in others. The verbs were presented as infinitives with preceding *to* so that their verbal character would be clear.

Usage Test

The general plan of this test was to introduce to *S* a new word (actually a pronounceable nonsense syllable) by using it in two sentences. The two sentences were adequate to place the word in one of six parts-of-speech: the count noun, mass noun, transitive verb, intransitive verb, adjective, or adverb. After this introduction to the word, *S* was asked to use it in sentences of his own creation, and these were scored as correct if the new word was used as it ought to be in view of the part-of-speech implied by the introductory sentences.

As "new words" 12 nonsense syllables were used: *wug, boff, latt, roog, stog, huft, nass, sib, bik, rik, nare,* and *pilk.* There were 12 problems in all with two syllables assigned to each of the six parts-of-speech. The syllables were rotated through all 12 problems so that there was no regular association between any syllable and any particular problem. The syllable *wug* will be used here to indicate the general character of the presentations.

For each problem, *S* was shown a colorful picture of either a girl, a boy, a man, a woman, a cat, or a dog, and *E* read text of the following kind: "Do you know what a *wug* is? This is a picture of a little girl thinking about a *wug*. Can you make up what that might mean?" This was the presentation identifying *wug* as a count noun. Where *wug* was to be identified as an intransitive verb, *E* would say: "Do you know what it means to *wug*? This is a picture of a little boy who wants to *wug*." With *wug* as mass noun there would be such sentences as: "This is a cat thinking about some *wug*." With wug as transitive verb such a sentence as this was used: "This is a woman who wants to *wug* something." Where *wug* was to be identified as an adverb, *E* spoke of a dog thinking of doing something *wuggily.*

There were two problems for each part-of-speech and a different syllable for each problem. There were two identifying sentences for each problem and, in the case of the adjectives and adverbs, the appended suffixes *-y* and *-ly*. The pictures gave no clue to the meaning of the new word and were only included to interest the child and keep his attention. The figures in the pictures were always simply thinking about the new word, not demonstrating its meaning.

Procedure

E was introduced to the children in a class by the teacher, and the class was told that each member would have a chance to look at some pictures and play some games. The children were interviewed individually either in the corridor outside the classroom or in an unused classroom. The Word Association Test was presented first with the remarks: "This is a game called 'say a word.' Have you ever played 'say a word'? Well, this is the way it works. I'm going to say a word and I want you to listen to my word and then say another word, not my word but a different word. Any word is all right so long as it's the first word that comes into your head when you hear my word. Are you ready?"

When the word associations had been recorded, *E* brought out the picture cards and said: "Now we're going to play a making-up game. How are you at making things up? Pretty good? Well, let's see." The problems were presented so as to go through all parts-of-speech once before repeating any of them.

The procedure with adults was the same except that *S* knew he was participating in an experiment on language and *E* did not call either part a game. In explanation of the brightly colored pictures and rather childish text, the adults were told that the tests had been designed for use with children as well as with adults.

Scoring

Scoring on the Word Association Test involves assigning response words to a part-of-speech; scoring on the Usage Test involves determining from *S*'s use of a new word the part-of-speech to which *S* has implicitly assigned the new word. Because English words can belong to more than one part-of-speech and because single sentences employing a new word do not always unequivocally indicate the part-of-speech membership of the new word, there were sometimes problems in scoring.

On the Free Association Test those response words that were marked with characteristic suffixes (adjectives and adverbs) or with the *to* of the verbal infinitive could be confidently classified. With most potentially doubtful responses membership in one part-of-speech is so much more common than membership in another that it was safe to assign the word this primary membership. Where there was some doubt, however, *E* asked *S* to use the response word in a sentence and, in doing so, *S* revealed the part-of-speech he had in mind. It was necessary for *E* mentally to score the responses as they were elicited so that he could resolve scoring problems where necessary.

On the Usage Test *S* sometimes translated the new word into a conventional English word. When told that a man was thinking about some *wug* and asked to "tell what that might mean," *S* sometimes provided a familiar word as a translation, saying for instance, "He is thinking about some *milk*." In such a case the part-of-speech membership of the familiar equivalent was scored and would be correct, in the present instance, as *milk* is a mass noun and that is the part-of-speech implied for *wug*. Where the translation word was not clearly of one part-of-speech, *E* encouraged *S* to "say some more about it."

In other cases *S* interpreted the Usage Test as calling for use of the new word in a sentence and so might provide: "The man has some *wugs* for breakfast every day." In such a case the part-of-speech was inferred from the sentence and, in the present instance, would be scored incorrect as *wug* has been used as a count noun. Not every sentence is unequivocal in this regard, and so it was sometimes necessary to urge *S* to say a little more.

RESULTS

There were 36 stimulus words on the Free Association Test, six words for each of six parts-of-speech. Each of the 36 response words (or phrases) was scored as Hmg. or Htg. with reference to its stimulus word, and so for every subject there was a possible maximal score of six Hmg. responses for each of six parts-of-speech. There were 12 new words on the Usage Test, two words for each of six parts-of-speech. Each of the new words was scored Hmg. or Htg. according to the agreement between the part-of-speech implied by the introductory sentences and the part-of-speech implied by *S*'s use or translation of the new word. For each *S*, therefore, there was a possible maximal score of two Hmg. responses on each of six parts-of-speech. After the rules of scoring had been developed by one judge, another judge independently scored 10 complete protocols (360 response words on word association and 120 new words on usage) from the rules. The two scorings agreed perfectly except for three instances where more information should have been elicited, and so it appears that this is essentially an objective scoring problem with no difficulties in the reliability sphere. The mean Hmg. scores for each part-of-speech and each age group appear in Table 2.

A two-way analysis of variance with 20 cases in each cell was carried out for the Free Association means and another for the Usage means. The results are summarized in Tables 3 and 4. Both age and part-of-speech account for large amounts of variance. In addition, there is a significant interaction between the two variables, and it can be seen in both the Free Association and Usage means that the increase with age of Hmg. responses is far less for count nouns than for the other parts-of-speech.

We are not primarily interested in the effects of age and of part-of-speech and so will not compare the 24 individual means for each test. It, is, however, worth noting the extraordinary uniformities in Table 2. The individual means have been

Table 2

MEAN HMG. SCORES ON FREE ASSOCIATION AND USAGE FOR EACH PART-OF-SPEECH AND EACH AGE GROUP

			FREE ASSOCIATION				
Group	*C.N.*	*Adj.*	*I.V.*	*T.V.*	*Adv.*	*M.N.*	*Total*
Ad.	5.10	5.00	4.80	4.45	4.95	2.35	4.44
3rd	4.65	3.65	3.40	2.95	1.95	2.40	3.17
2nd	4.55	3.90	2.75	2.40	2.25	1.90	2.96
1st	3.95	1.25	1.60	1.40	.80	1.20	1.70
Total	4.56	3.45	3.14	2.80	2.49	1.96	3.07

			USAGE				
Group	*C.N.*	*Adj.*	*I.V.*	*T.V.*	*M.N.*	*Adv.*	*Total*
Ad.	1.85	1.75	1.70	1.60	.95	1.20	1.51
3rd	1.45	1.65	1.65	1.75	.55	.55	1.27
2nd	1.55	1.50	1.20	1.10	.70	.45	1.08
1st	1.20	.75	.90	.90	.45	.10	.72
Total	1.51	1.41	1.36	1.34	.66	.58	1.15

Table 3

ANALYSIS OF VARIANCE FOR FREE ASSOCIATION MEANS

Source	*Sum of Squares*	*df*	*Variance Estimate*
Age (rows)	453.6167	3	151.2056
Parts-of-Speech (columns)	321.2167	5	64.2433
Interaction	84.6833	15	5.6456
Individual differences (within cells)	1345.3500	456	2.9503
Total	2204.8667	479	

Interaction $F = 1.91; p < .05$.
Age $F = 26.78; p < .001$.
Parts-of-Speech $F = 11.38; p < .001$.

Table 4

ANALYSIS OF VARIANCE FOR USAGE MEANS

Source	*Sum of Squares*	*df*	*Variance Estimate*
Age (rows)	40.0896	3	13.3632
Parts-of-Speech (columns)	67.2688	5	13.4538
Interaction	11.1673	15	.7445
Individual differences (within cells)	208.5556	456	.4574
Total	327.0813	479	

Interaction $F = 1.63$; p about .05.
Age $F = 17.95$; $p < .001$.
Parts-of-Speech $F = 18.07$; $p < .001$.

arranged in the order of the grand means of the rows (age groups) and columns (parts-of-speech). When this is done for Free Association, there are only three reversals of one position each in the age order, only four reversals of one position, and a single reversal of two positions in the part-of-speech data. The same sort of ordering of the Usage means results in only three reversals of one position each in the age order, only one reversal of three positions, and one reversal of two positions in the part-of-speech order. There is clear confirmation in this table of the increase with age of Hmg. responses found by Ervin (4) and also clear evidence that the count noun and adjective function in child speech in advance of other parts-of-speech. Finally, ordering the Free Association and Usage cell means in the order of their grand means results in identical age and part-of-speech orders (except for a reversal of the Adv. and M.N. columns) in the two sets of data. This is a good first indication of the covariation in free association and usage which is the effect predicted by our hypothesis. We proceed to a more detailed presentation of the evidence for this effect.

It would have been possible to compute correlations between the individual scores on usage and the individual scores on free association for each part-of-speech and each age group. We examined these scores and saw that the correlations would be very small, probably because the usage scores can only range from zero to two and because this small sample of usage from each *S* is not a very reliable measure of *S*'s grammatical skills. We decided to work instead with the means of Table 2 which yield a greater range of scores and a more reliable estimate of grammatical skill in a kind of *S*. The rank-order correlation between the 24 means from the Free Association Test and the 24 means from the Usage Test is .84, and this is a relationship significant at far better than the .001 level.

Contributing to the rank-order correlation of all 24 means is the tendency for usage and free association scores to increase with age as well as the tendency for scores on the six parts-of-speech to covary for usage and free association. Insofar as the correlation is generated by the former factor, it is possible that we have nothing more here than a tendency for all sorts of language performance scores to move together with increasing age towards adult values. We are interested in something more particular than this. We want to know whether the increasing tendency to give Hmg. responses in free association can be interpreted as evidence of the developing organization of vocabulary into parts-of-speech which define correct grammatical usage for new words. We shall have better ground for this interpretation if correlations exist with the age variation

Table 5

RANK ORDER CORRELATIONS BETWEEN FREE ASSOCIATION AND USAGE HMG. SCORES

Rho for all paired means, $N = 24$	.84	$p < .001$
Rho for grand means of the parts-of-speech, $N = 6$	.94	$p = .01$
Rho for Adults, $N = 6$	.83	$p = .05$
Rho for 3rd grade, $N = 6$	.46	$p = .40$
Rho for 2nd grade, $N = 6$	.94	$p = .01$
Rho for 1st grade, $N = 6$	.83	$p = .05$
Combined p value for adults, 3rd grade, 2nd grade, 1st grade		$p = .0002$

taken out. One way of accomplishing this effect is to correlate the grand means (across all age groups) for the six part-of-speech columns for free association and usage. This rank order *rho* is .94 and even with only six cases that value is significant at about .01. Another way of testing for this relationship is to correlate the six paired means for each of the four age groups. The results appear in Table 5 (together with the previously mentioned *rhos*); three are significant and one is not. The p values for these four samples can be combined to yield a single p value for the relationship of free association to usage. Mosteller and Bush (5) suggest transforming the individual p values into normal deviates, summing them, and dividing the sum by the square root of the number of observations. The resultant value is itself a normal deviate with a p of about .0002. It seems very certain, therefore, that Hmg. scores for free association are related to Hmg. scores for usage.

DISCUSSION

The change with age in both free association and usage is very striking when one examines individual protocols. For free association, consider the stimulus words *to send.* One first grade child responds *away,* another *letter,* another *a card,* another *mail,* etc. In response to this same word adults give: *to receive, to get, to deliver, to bring, to mail, to fetch.* Both the child responses and the adult responses are semantically related to the stimulus word, and the one set does not seem to be any more so than the other. The difference lies with the fact that the child responses are phrase completions (words that commonly follow the stimulus) while the adult words would almost never follow *to send* in an English sentence but are very closely matched with it in that they are transitive verbs. More specifically, the adult responses are transitive verbs naming human actions which ordinarily have some small inanimate thing as object. This further similarity is semantic but, in addition, involves a closer syntactic match than would be true for transitive verbs in general.

Consider now the sort of thing that happens on the Usage Test with a nonsense syllable intended to be a transitive verb. One first grade child was told: "This is a cat who wants to *niss* something. Can you make up what that might mean?" The child replied: "The cat wants a fish. A *niss* is a fish." To this same problem an adult responded: "The cat wants to catch something. To *niss* is to catch." The child seems to have put together knowledge about cats and the sound of *niss* to come up with a count noun—*fish.* He was not troubled by the fact that this translation violates the part-of-speech membership of *niss.* When *E* says "to *niss* something," that should exclude the possibility of saying "A *niss* is a fish," but, for this child, it does not. Apparently the first grade children paid little attention to the formal marks of the syntactic potentialities of *niss.* The adult, on the other hand, principally attended to these marks. In many cases the translations provided by adults seem to have been suggested by the sound of the new word even as *niss* suggested *fish* to the first grader. However, when this happened with adults, it was almost always within the limits of the class of words suggested by the syntactic cues. In general, then, both the free association results and the usage results seem to be manifestations of the developing organization of vocabulary into syntactic classes.

As the analyses of variance have demonstrated, both age and part-of-speech are highly significant determinants of the number of Hmg. responses on both the Free Association and Usage tests. These two variables may perhaps be conceptualized as a single determinant—the amount of experience with words belonging to a part-of-speech. Experience of words in all six parts-of-speech is bound to increase with age, and Hmg. responses on all parts-of-speech clearly do increase with age. In addition, however, we note in Table 2 that the count noun and the adjective produce more Hmg. responses across all age levels than do the other parts-of-speech. While we do not know of any exact tests of the frequency of occurrence in English of words belonging to the various parts-of-speech, it seems to us that no test is needed to persuade the native speaker that count nouns and adjectives are more common than intransitive verbs or transitive verbs or adverbs or mass nouns. This is to say that at any given age a speaker of English is likely to have had more experience of count nouns and adjectives than of the other parts-of-speech we have studied.

The count noun has always the highest number of Hmg. responses and, indeed, does not change greatly in this respect from the first grade to adulthood because it is already at a near peak level in first graders. The count noun is, of course, the kind of word adults regularly undertake to teach children, for these are the names of denotable things: a *man*, a *dog*, a *car*, a *bike*. Surely speakers of English have greater experience of words in this class than of words in any other class.

The low number of Hmg. responses generally obtained for mass nouns requires a special comment. The Htg. responses given to mass nouns were usually count nouns, i.e., members of the same major part-of-speech. There is a good reason why these two varieties of noun were not usually distinguished even by adults. Mass nouns in English can always be used as count nouns. Ordinarily one says *some sand, some water, some marble* but one can say *some sands, some marbles*, and even *some waters*. The difference is that in the former cases a quantity of a uniform substance is suggested while in the latter case varieties or subspecies of some category of substances are suggested. This syntactic overlap seems to result in an overlap on the word association and usage tasks.

We have suggested that degree of experience of words in a part-of-speech is the basic determinant of the degree to which that part-of-speech functions in free association and usage. The significant sort of experience might be the number of words belonging to the part-of-speech or the variety of sentences for each word or the number of occurrences for each sentence. Probably all of these kinds of experience are close correlates in the natural situation. There are many different count nouns in English; there are many different sentences for most count nouns; and there are many sentences involving count nouns that occur very frequently. Without deliberate experimental manipulation of experience it probably will not be possible to determine the relative importance of these factors.

SUMMARY

It is a reliable finding that the response words provided by adults in a word association test usually belong to the same parts-of-speech as the respective stimulus words. There are fewer of these homogeneous-by-part-of-speech responses with young children; the tendency to associate words within a part-of-speech increases with age. *The present paper suggests that this change in word associations is a consequence of the child's gradual organization of his vocabulary into the syntactic classes called parts-of-speech.* To test the degree to which *S* has accomplished this latter grammatical task, a Usage Test was designed. In this test a new word was used in a couple of sentences which sufficed to indicate the part-of-speech to which the new word belonged. After hearing these sentences, *S* was asked to create some sentences of his own using the new word, and his performance was scored correct if it employed the word in ways permitted by its part-of-speech membership. Four groups of *S*s (adults and first, second, and third grade children) were given a Word Association Test (consisting of stimulus words belonging to six different parts-of-speech) and also a Usage Test (consisting of new words assigned to the same six parts-of-speech). The Word Association Test was scored for homogeneous responses within each part-of-speech and the Usage Test for correct usage in accordance with each part-of-speech. It was found that scores on both tests regularly increased with age and that scores on the two tests were closely related to one another. It was concluded that the formal change in word association and the ability to make correct grammatical use of new words are two manifestations of the child's developing appreciation of English syntax.

References

1. Berko, Jean. The child's learning of English morphology. *Word,* 1958, 14, 150–177.
2. Berko, Jean, & Brown, R. Psycholinguistic research methods. In P. Mussen(Ed.), *Handbook of research methods in child development.* New York: Wiley, in press.
3. Brown, R. Linguistic determinism and the part of speech. *J. abnorm. soc. Psychol.,* 1957, 55, 1–5.
4. Ervin, Susan M. Grammar and classification. Paper read at Amer. Psychol. Ass., New York, September, 1957.
5. Mosteller, F., & Bush, R. R. Selected quantitative techniques. In G. Lindzey (Ed.), *Handbook of social psychology.* Vol. I. Cambridge, Mass.: Addison-Wesley, 1954. Pp. 289–334.
6. Rinsland, H. D. *A basic vocabulary of elementary school children.* New York: Macmillan, 1954.
7. Woodrow, H., & Lowell, F. Children's association frequency tables. *Psychol. Monogr.,* 1916, 22 No. 97.
8. Woodworth, R. S. *Experimental psychology.* New York: Holt, 1938.

Hesitation Phenomena in Spontaneous English Speech

HOWARD MACLAY
and CHARLES E. OSGOOD

This paper reports an exploratory investigation of hesitation phenomena in spontaneously spoken English. Following a brief review of the literature bearing on such phenomena, a quantitative study of filled and unfilled pauses, repeats, and false starts in the speech of some twelve participants in a conference is described. Analysis in terms of both individual differences and linguistic distribution is made, and some psycholinguistic implications are drawn, particularly as to the nature of encoding units and their relative uncertainty. A distinction between non-chance statistical dependencies and all-or-nothing dependencies in linguistic methodology is made.

INTRODUCTION

Although references to pause and silence occur frequently in the literature of structural linguistics, very little research of the kind undertaken here has been carried out. A brief examination of three important works will illustrate the customary treatment of pause and hesitation in language description.

In his list of the phonemes of Chicago Standard English, Bloomfield (1933, p. 92)* includes [,], which he describes as being "...placed between primary symbols, the pause, often preceded by rising pitch, that promises continuation of the sentence: *John, the older boy, is away at school....*" This is a *pause-pitch* or *suspension-pitch* phoneme which consists of a rise in pitch before a pause within a sentence. A later comment (p. 185) by Bloomfield suggests that the pausal component of this phoneme is a useful, but not a necessary part, of the criterion for its identification.

Harris (1951, p. 174) uses pause in the same general way, as an index of juncture:

12.52. Intermittently Present Pause. We may also find in some languages that loose contact

* All bibliographic references are identified at the end of the article.

Howard Maclay and Charles E. Osgood, "Hesitation Phenomena in Spontaneous English Speech," *Word,* 15 (1959), 19–44. Reprinted by permission of the authors and publisher.

and division between breath-groups of phonemes occur sometimes (though not always) at morpheme boundaries, but practically never within a morpheme... except as intermittently present features in the utterance. They are free variants, and do not occur every time morpheme boundary occurs. But in some occurrences of the morpheme sequence those pauses would constitute observable evidence of morpheme boundary.

In many cases, however, these pauses come at points containing phonemic junctures. At these points in the utterance we find segments which occur only at utterance boundary or at points of intermittently present pause, and which are phonemicized into junctures or into sequences of some phoneme plus juncture. We can then say that the pause (when it occurs) is an occasionally-occurring free variant of the phonemic juncture.

Probably the most explicit and systematic employment of pausal phenomena as an element in linguistic analysis is seen in Bloch's work on Japanese (1946), where he states (p. 201):

1.2. All pauses within a sentence are preceded by level intonation. Every such pause is *facultative:* repeated utterances of the same sentence (by the same speaker or different speakers) will show the pause sometimes present, sometimes absent, without any change in meaning. The presence or absence of pauses within a sentence depends partly on stylistic factors (with more pauses in emphatic or affective speech), partly on the tempo and care of utterance.

However, some facultative pauses are more constant than others, appearing more consistently in repeated instances of the same sentence. It is enough to distinguish two *ranks* of facultative pauses: *higher* (more constant), marked with a semicolon; and *lower* (less constant), marked with a comma.

Bloch also defines a "minimal pause group" which provides one of the criteria for defining words in Japanese. An interesting aspect of Bloch's discussion is the ranking of pauses on the basis of frequency in a given environment and the implication that they are not randomly distributed with respect to linguistic forms.

It seems fair to conclude that pausal phenomena, while they are often mentioned by linguists, function essentially as non-significant events which may serve to identify linguistically relevant units, such as junctures located at the boundaries of phonemes, morphemes, words, phrases, and sentences. The physical character of pause as the term is used by linguists is seldom specified. While it is likely that many of the instances of pause that are referred to in linguistic description overlap with the hesitation types defined below, there is one basic difference between pause and hesitation: hesitations, as we define them, refer to events that are relatively gross and easily observable, while the juncture-pauses of linguistic theory are quite short in duration and much harder to observe and record. In addition, hesitations often interrupt the flow of speech while juncture pauses do not.[1] Thus, under "hesitation" we also include the phenomena which classical rhetoric called aposiopesis and anacolouthon. To quote Bloomfield again (p. 186):

Often enough non-linguistic factors interfere with construction; what the speaker has said is nevertheless meaningful, provided he has already uttered a free form. In *aposiopesis* the speaker breaks off or is interrupted: *I thought he* ——. In *anacolouthon* he starts over again: *It's high time we—oh, well—I guess it won't matter.* When a speaker hesitates, English and some other languages offer special parenthetic *hesitation-forms,* as [r] or [ɛ] in *Mr.—ah—Sniffen* or *Mr.—what you may call him—Sniffen* or *that—thingamajig—transmitter.*

This statement defines two of the hesitation types described below—*False Start* and *Filled Pause.*

Bloomfield's observation that non-linguistic factors are operating here agrees with our results, and leads us to the psychological side of the question. Although possessing a long tradition of research on verbal behavior, experimental psychologists have usually preferred to rely on

[1] This distinction is taken from Lounsbury, in Osgood and Sebeok (1954), p. 98.

normalized written material and have therefore shown little or no interest in the hesitations present in spoken language. Various sorts of speech deviation have, however, been the concern of clinical psychologists, especially psychoanalysts, for many years. Freud has devoted a good deal of attention to the interpretation of speech slips, which include the forgetting of words, the replacement of intended words by others, and transpositions of sounds and words (see, e.g., Freud, 1938). He has offered psychoanalytic explanations of these phenomena, and psychotherapists have often observed that a sudden onset of hesitations, extended silences and speech disturbances in general indicates that an anxiety-provoking area in the patient has been touched.

In a recent series of studies, George Mahl (1956*a*, 1956*b*, 1957)[2] has attempted to specify more exactly the relation between the speech disturbances and level of anxiety in both clinical interviews and stressful role-playing situations. He has established eight "disturbance" categories: (1) "ah"; (2) sentence correction; (3) sentence incompletion; (4) repetition of words; (5) stutter; (6) intruding incoherent sound; (7) tongue slip (neologisms, transpositions, etc.); (8) omission of words or parts of words.[3] He has also developed three speech disturbances ratios: *general*, which is the number of disturbances divided by the number of words in an utterance; *ah*, which is the number of instances of category 1 divided by the number of words; and *non-ah*, which is the number of instances of categories 2–8 divided by the total number of words. He finds that the *non-ah* ratio correlates positively with degree of anxiety as judged by a trained observer and the *ah* ratio correlates negatively, whereas the *general* ratio is independent. He presents anecdotal material which indicates that "the vast majority of the speech disturbances are 'unintended' and escape the awareness of both speakers and listeners, in spite of their very frequent occurrence." He also finds "striking individual differences in the frequency of speech disturbances, and in the relative predilections for the individual categories of disturbance." We have preferred to call our measures "hesitations" rather than "disturbances," but the overlap with Mahl's categories is obvious, and our results accord very well with his where direct comparisons are possible.

Another research program bearing closely on our work is that being conducted by Frieda Goldman-Eisler (1954*a*, 1954*b*, 1955, 1957, 1958*a*, 1958*b*). She has studied the rate of speech production, hesitation pauses, speech-breathing and their interrelationships under various conditions, particularly the psychiatric interview. Among her significant observations are the following: (1) Variability in total speech rate proves to be mainly a function of the time spent in hesitation pauses and not in time spent in articulation. (2) Short utterances are much more variable in speech rate than long utterances, a high degree of stability within the individual being found for utterances longer than 100 syllables. (Our samples are mostly 100 *words* or longer, hence well within the range of stable rate.) (3) Interruptions in the flow of speech are occasioned by both breathing pauses and by hesitation pauses; the former seem to vary more with emotionality and the latter more with cognitive processes, e.g., prevocal formulation of utterances, word finding and the like. (4) Most relevant to this study is Goldman-Eisler's report (1958*b*) that hesitation pauses anticipate sudden increases in information or uncertainty in the message being produced (1958*a*, p. 67):

[2] See also G. Mahl (1958).

[3] These equate as follows with our hesitation types: "ah" is equivalent to our Filled Pause; sentence correction equates with our Retraced False Start; sentence incompletion is equivalent to our Non-Retraced False Start; repetition plus stutter corresponds to our Repeat. Categories 6, 7, and 8 have no counterparts in our analysis, and Mahl used nothing strictly equivalent to our Unfilled Pause (although he has studied extended silences).

> ...the close relation found to exist between pauses and information on the one hand and fluency of speech and redundancy on the other, seems to indicate that the interpolation of hesitation pauses in speech is a necessary condition for such an increase.... Fluent speech was shown to consist of habitual combinations of words such as were shared by the language community and such as had become more or less automatic. Where a sequence ceased to be a matter of common conditioning or learning, where a speaker's choice was highly individual and unexpected, on the other hand, speech was hesitant.

Our own findings point to very much the same general conclusion.

Lounsbury has discussed hesitation phenomena along highly similar lines (in Osgood and Sebeok, 1954, pp. 98–101). Three of his hypotheses are worth repeating since our results bear directly on them.

> HYPOTHESIS 1: Hesitation pauses correspond to the points of highest statistical uncertainty in the sequencing of units of any given order.
>
> HYPOTHESIS 2: Hesitation pauses and points of high statistical uncertainty correspond to the beginning of units of encoding.
>
> HYPOTHESIS 3: Hesitation pauses and points of high statistical uncertainty frequently do not fall at the points where immediate-constitutent analysis would establish boundaries between higher-order linguistic units or where syntactic junctures or 'facultative pauses' would occur.

Hypotheses 1 and 3 are testable, and we offer some evidence on them in this paper. Hypothesis 2 has an element of circularity, in that no independent method of defining encoding units has been developed. However, the implication of the hypothesis is that it should be possible to identify functional psycholinguistic units of encoding through analysis of hesitation phenomena.

PROCEDURE

This study is based on analysis of a sample of slightly over 50,000 words taken from a conference held at the University of Illinois in 1955. The selection of the sample was non-random in that it included almost all of the relatively longer utterances in the text, those under 80 words being omitted. The final corpus consists of 163 utterances by 13 male speakers, all professional people, with a mean utterance length of 309 words. The data were tape recorded and transcribed in normal English orthography by secretaries who were instructed to produce as literal a transcription as possible. They were told to avoid any "cleaning up" of the text and asked to preserve everything said by each speaker regardless of their opinion as to its grammatical accuracy. This resulted in what might be called a "semi-literal" text, in that it lies somewhere between a rigorous phonemic transcription and the usual normalized orthographic version of spoken English. This compromise arose primarily from the nature of the study. It seemed wise to sacrifice depth for breadth in an exploratory investigation, with the hope that any significant relations that might have been affected by this procedure could be checked in future studies using a fully adequate linguistic transcription.

Four Hesitation Types were defined.

1. REPEATS (R): All repetitions, of any length, that were judged to be non-significant semantically. In the utterance, *I I saw a very very big boy, I* is repeated but *very* is not, since in the latter case the repetition intensifies *big* and thus changes the meaning, while this is not the case for *I*. We assume that the utterance with or without the repeated *I* would be judged the "same" in meaning by English speakers, while utterances with one as against two occurrences of *very* would be judged "different." A REPEAT can vary from a single phoneme to an extended stretch that could, theoretically, be of any length but actually does not exceed four or five words in this corpus.

2. FALSE STARTS (FS): All incomplete or self-interrupted utterances. *I saw a very* ...is an incomplete utterance with FS

following *very*, while *I saw a very big// a very small boy* is a self-interrupted utterance with FS following *big*. The second case represents an instance of RETRACED FS and the first an instance of NON-RETRACED FS. This distinction is made on the basis of whether or not the speaker backed up in an attempt to correct one of the words he had already used. Intonational patterns and word order are the major linguistic cues in the identification of this type.

3. FILLED PAUSES (FP): All occurrences of the English hesitation devices [ɛ, æ, r, ə, m]. Of these alternatives [ə] is by far the most frequent in our data.

4. UNFILLED PAUSES (UP): These were marked when there was judged to be an abnormal hesitation in speech that could not be referred to the three previous categories. UP has two major forms: silence of unusual length and non-phonemic lengthening of phonemes. This is necessarily a matter of judgment on the part of listeners (here, the authors) familiar with the pace and style of a particular speaker. What may be clearly noted as an instance of Unfilled Pause for one speaker would not be so judged for another speaker, say, with a slower rate of delivery.

On the whole, these four categories refer to variations in speech that have not been the explicit concern of linguists, although Unfilled Pauses would certainly include many instances of Bloch's facultative pause. False Starts seem to cover much the same ground as is included in the terms aposiopesis and anacolouthon.

A word of caution should be entered concerning the references to intonation, non-phonemic length and other linguistic correlates of the hesitation types. These are after-the-fact interpretations; the actual scoring involved judgments that were not explicitly based on these considerations. The authors, as native speakers of English, attempted to categorize and locate the hesitations that seemed to be present in the text. Scoring was based on the tape recording with the written text being used as a guide and a frame-work within which the scores might be placed. Preliminary preparation of the judges was limited to a general discussion of the types and a one-hour session in which a sample text was jointly scored.

After each author had independently scored a semi-literal transcription, a final text was obtained by combining the two ratings and counting only those hesitations where both judges agreed as to type and location. This means that some hesitations which actually occurred were not included, but it also makes it highly probable that all hesitations upon which the analysis is based really did occur at the points indicated. Very high product-moment correlations (r) were found between the independent ratings for utterance totals (R: + 94; FS: + 98; FP: +99; UP: +88). Specific correlations based on agreements and disagreements at each point presumably would have been lower. These latter, and more accurate, reliability estimates could not be obtained due to the impossibility of stating the number of cases where *neither* judge had indicated a hesitation. This uncertainty led to the conservative decision to consider only instances of complete agreement. In addition to the frequency of each type of hesitation per utterance, the speed in words per minute of each utterance was calculated.

In the following sample taken from the final text, R is indicated by underscoring the items repeated, FS by //, FP by /ᵃ and UP by /.

> As far as I know, no one yet has done the // in a way obvious now and interesting problem of / doing a // in a sense a structural frequency study of the alternative / syntactical ///ᵃ in a given language, say, like English, the alternative /ᵃ possible structures, and how // what their hierarchal / probability of occurrence structure is. Now, it seems to me you <u>w-w-will</u> need that kind of data as base line from which to judge or study deviations —in particular style in the clinical situation and so on. If we get this // now in other

words, if you find that in the clinic, say in the /ª protocol of a patient, that the distribution of these /ª alternative structures are precisely what they are in ordinary /ª communications, then there's no evidence that this, at least i-is a / relevant variable for the clinical situation. On the other hand, if, knowing that standard sort of thing for English / speakers, /ª then you find you get oscillations about that in different stages of therapy and so on, then it becomes, I think, very very very relevant. For example, a // if under // I was speaking to you, George, the // at supper last night, I think. If /ª you find that /ª at each point, say, in English structure you have an alt- // several alternatives, some of which are highly probable / in ordinary English sentences, syntactical sequences of, for example, /ª adjective, noun, verb /ª vs. a a de-dependent phrase inserted, and so on. But these have / differing probabilities of occurrence in ordinary English. Now, if you find, for example, that in high points of anxiety and stress in the therapy situation that he / shifts into very simple ones—I mean ones that are of a higher // much higher probability, whereas when he's being intellectual, if you will, and / resisting, you tend to get /ª relatively low probability / sequences, you see. (Subject D, Utterance 10).

RESULTS

Linguistic Distribution of Hesitation Types

Method of analysis. We have made a preliminary attempt to state the distribution of the four hesitation types with respect to English word classes as described by Fries (1952).[4]

Fries classifies English words on the basis of their occurrence in relation to other words rather than on semantic grounds. For example, one class of words can be established by first listing the following three sentence contexts or frames:

Frame A: The —— is/was good.
Frame B: The —— remembered the ——.
Frame C: The —— went there.

We then place in one class all the words which can be inserted in one or more of the blanks and still form a grammatical English sentence. The following sentences illustrate this procedure: The *coffee* was good. The *man* was good. The *clerk* remembered the *tax*. The *husband* remembered the *food*. The *team* went there. The *dog* went there. We would therefore conclude that *coffee, man, clerk, tax, husband, food, team* and *dog* are members of the same class, along with a great many other English words, of course, that could be inserted in these frames. A word such as *the,* however, cannot be placed in these frames and thus must be placed in a different class established by other frames. Each English word class is similarly defined in terms of occurrence within a set of frames.

Obviously, the class described has much in common with the traditional class of nouns defined semantically. For those who may be unfamiliar with Fries' system, we present below the nearest traditional equivalent of his classes. It cannot be too strongly emphasized that the overlap is far from complete, and our analysis depends entirely on the description by Fries and not on the traditional classification. We have also followed Fries in making a distinction between the four major classes (which we call "lexical") and the "function" word classes.

In some of the tables which follow, Fries' Class 1 has been arbitrarily split into 1p, which contains subject personal pronouns (*I, you, he, she, it, we, they*), and 1, which includes the remaining members of this class. In addition, the Function Word classes G, H, K, L, M, N, and O are grouped in one category entitled "other function words" in Table 1.

If we are to describe the distribution of hesitation types we must first locate them relative to the sequences of words in our corpus. The overwhelming majority of Filled and Unfilled Pauses are located at word boundaries and their oc-

[4] The summary of Fries' system which follows is for the benefit of readers who have not been trained in linguistics.

	Fries' Classes	*Traditional Classes*
Lexical Words	1	Nouns
	2	Verbs
	3	Adjectives
	4	Adverbs
Function Words	A	Articles, Possessive Pronouns, Numbers, etc.
	B	Verb Auxiliaries
	C	"not"
	D	Adjective and Adverb Modifiers
	E	Connectives
	F	Prepositions
	J	Words uniting phrases in a single sentence.

Table 1

DISTRIBUTION OF FALSE STARTS AND REPEATS BY WORD CLASSES

Fries' Word Class	*1p*	*1*	*2*	*3*	*4*	*A*	*B*	*C*	*D*	*E*	*F*	*J*	*Other Function Words*	*Total*
FS	53	200	150	73	42	121	57	10	15	7	54	18	17	817
R	123	67	87	37	6	247	66	7	9	38	172	67	46	972

Probability that difference in distribution of FS and R is due to chance by x^2: $< .001$.

currences can therefore be described as falling generally between words of any class.

"you tend to get /ª relatively low probability / sequences..." (Subject D, Utterance 10.)

The Filled Pause (/ª) here is located between a class 2 word, *get*, and a class D word, *relatively*, while the Unfilled Pause (/) falls between two class 1 words, *probability* and *sequences*.

Repeats cannot reasonably be located between words, and we have therefore associated each Repeat with the class of the words or parts of words repeated.

"...a measure of the / of the structure of English, the probabil-probabilistic structure of /ª English language..." (Subject D, Utterance 4.)

The first Repeat involves two words, *of* (class F) and *the* (class A), while the second is associated with the class 3 word *probabilistic*. In the scoring of this part of the utterance, classes F, A, and 3 would each be given one association with the Repeat hesitation type.

The most convenient way of describing the distribution of False Starts is in terms of the class of the word immediately preceding the break. We adopt this convention for purposes of comparison with the other types. Most False Starts do occur at word boundaries, but many occur at morpheme boundaries within words and some even within morphemes, as the following examples illustrate:

False Start (//) at word boundary:

"...And the next one would // might be that the the receiver of the action becomes initiator..." (Subject 1, Utterance 3.)

False Start at morpheme boundary within word:

"...whenever anyone mentions communism-capital // capitalism, communism comes up..." (Subject A, Utterance 3.)

False Start within morpheme:

"...if you were to select your samples differently and to /ª to consider the conte- //

the larger context from which you select this 250 word sample..." (Subject B, Utterance 7.)

In the last example we concluded that the False Start follows the class 1 word, *context*. We determine that the phonetic sequence [kánte?] is class 1 by the presence of the class A word *the* preceding it and the use of the full word *context* in the retracing which follows the False Start. A clear decision as to the class of the words preceding False Starts is often not possible when the break comes early in the word and no retracing follows, for example:

"...We disregard the structure; we simply take /ᵃ as our unit /ᵃ w- // more or less the whole interview..." (Subject E, Utterance 5.)

On the basis of our semi-literal transcription we might guess that the speaker intended *whole* before the False Start, but an examination of the tape shows that the sound preceding the break was the voiced semivowel /w/ rather than the phoneme /h/ which begins *whole*. In cases of this kind no score was recorded.

A second type of ambiguity arises when the phonemic shape of the word preceding the False Start can be recognized but its class affiliation is uncertain due to a lack of following context, e.g.,

"...I think I have // this is a tool..." (Subject 7, Utterance 1.)

The *have* could be either class B (verb auxiliary) or class 2 (verb). In this case one score was given to each of the possible classifications.

False starts and repeats. The hesitation types differed distributionally in several respects. Table 1 compares the total distributions of False Starts and Repeats with respect to 11 of Fries' classes. The distributions of the two hesitation types are significantly different from each other by Chi-square test over the 13 divisions of Table 1 at a level beyond .001. Repeats typically involve class 1p words (subject personal pronouns), class A (articles, possessive pronouns, numbers), class F (prepositions), and class J (words uniting phrases); False Starts typically involve class 1 words (nouns), class 2 (verbs), class 3 (adjectives), and class 4 (adverbs). Table 2 presents a direct test of the hypothesis that Repeats and False Starts are reciprocally distributed with respect to lexical vs. function words. The Chi-square value for this test is significant at the .001 level. Using a chance estimate based on the fact that 42% of a random sample of our corpus were function words, we find that False Starts tend to occur with lexical words (.01 level) and Repeats with function words (.001 level) more often than would be expected by chance. One aspect of these distributions warrants special comment: subject personal pronouns (1p, classified by Fries with lexical nouns) appear to function with respect to hesitation phenomena like function words rather than lexical items.

The instances of Retraced False Starts offer some interesting data on speech

Table 2

Distribution of False Starts (FS) and Repeats (R) by Lexical vs. Function Words

	FS	*R*
Lexical Words	518	320
Function Words	299	652
Total	817	972

Probability that differences are due to chance (chi-square test):

FS vs. R < .001

FS vs. Chance < .01

R vs. Chance < .001

Table 3

FALSE STARTS: AMOUNT OF RETRACING BY WORD CLASSES

Fries' Word Class	*I* *Retracing Includes Only Corrected Words*	*II* *Retracing Includes Preceding Words*	*I* / *I + II*
1p	8	4	.667
1	10	39	.204
2	15	34	.306
3	2	12	.143
4	0	4	.000
Lexical Totals	*35*	*93*	*.273*
A	48	7	.873
B	2	13	.133
D	5	0	1.000
F	28	1	.966
Function-Word Totals	*83*	*48*	*.634*

Probability that lexical vs. function-word difference is due to chance (x^2): $< .001$.

behavior. Every retracing that involved a correction of the word immediately preceding the break was examined. The word corrected was classified by Fries' system, with only those cases where the class determination was clear being included. The question is this: will the amount of retracing vary with the class of the corrected word, so as to include in the retrace function words just antecedent to corrected lexical items? A two-way distinction was established: retracings involving only the corrected word (I) and retracings involving words preceding the corrected word which were not themselves corrected (II). Given the sentence, *I never saw such a man // woman,* the False Start occurs after the class 1 word, *man*, and the retracing includes only the word corrected (case I). In the sentence, *I never saw such a man // a woman,* the False Start occurs in the same place, but the retracing includes the function word, *a*, which is repeated without correction (case II). Table 3 presents the relevant data. It is clear that there is a statistically significant tendency (.001 level) for retraced corrections of lexical items to include antecedent words (almost always function words), whereas retraced corrections of function words seldom include antecedent items. Two exceptions may be noted: again, subject personal pronouns operate more like function words; and class B words (verb auxiliaries) operate more like lexical items. If we assume that speakers will retrace to a boundary of an "encoding unit,"[5] these results suggest one kind of a unit as containing a function word followed by a lexical word.

Repeats. These tend to involve function words rather than lexical items, as has been shown. We may also ask what classes of words they just precede: do speakers tend to repeat items just antecedent to lexical items? Combining all repeats for speakers A through E, we find that 74% of them just precede a lexical item; this proportion is significantly different from chance, based on the relative frequency of lexical items (58%). It thus appears that Repeats tend to be distributed in a way similar to that of pauses (see below). A final question we ask about Repeats is this: How much of the utterance do they typically include? Again combining the data from our major speak-

[5] On the problem of "encoding units" see pp. 40f. below; see also Osgood and Sebeok (1954), pp. 50–73, and Sarah C. Gudschinsky, "Native Reactions to Tones and Words in Mazatec," *Word* XIV (1958), 338–345.

ers (A through E), we find that 7% of all repetitions include only a single phoneme, 4% a single syllable, 1% a single morpheme (which is not a word), 71% a single word, and 17% two or more words. It is clear that Repeats characteristically involve the single word, occasionally several words, but only rarely units smaller than the word. This, again, seems to have implications for the nature of encoding units.

Hesitation pauses. The first question with which we are concerned is whether or not hesitation pauses of both types are distributed at random in spontaneous speech and, if not, what are the determinants of their distribution. A second question concerns the relation between Filled Pause and Unfilled Pause: are they essentially in free variation, or are their distributions complementary to each other? Rather than attempting to collect and analyze all of the pauses occurring in this large corpus, a sample of sixteen word sequences or frames that occurred relatively frequently in the data was selected for detailed analysis. These sequences would usually be defined as phrases in a linguistic description. Table 4 lists the sequences chosen, according to Fries' class-

Table 4

DISTRIBUTION OF FILLED (FP) AND UNFILLED PAUSES (UP) OVER SELECTED SEQUENCES

*Sequence Type**	*Example*		*Positions* 1	2	3	4	5	*Totals*
A1	*1*the*2*house*3*	FP	98	61	55			214
		UP	50	74	61			185
		total	148	135	116			
F1	*1*at*2*home*3*	FP	37	80	112			229
		UP	44	64	42			150
		total	81	144	154			
B2	*1*will*2*go*3*	FP	42	52	50			144
		UP	18	73	46			137
		total	60	125	96			
A11	*1*the*2*manor*3* houses*4*	FP	7	6	5	17		35
		UP	5	13	7	4		29
		total	12	19	12	21		
AA1	*1*the*2*three*3* houses*4*	FP	7	3	3	5		18
		UP	4	3	5	3		15
		total	11	6	8	8		
A31	*1*the*2*red*3* houses*4*	FP	24	24	19	35		102
		UP	17	36	35	19		107
		total	41	60	54	54		
FA1	*1*to*2*these*3* houses*4*	FP	40	32	35	57		164
		UP	50	34	66	33		183
		total	90	66	101	90		
F11	*1*of*2*manor*3* houses*4*	FP	3	14	2	16		35
		UP	5	6	4	1		16
		total	8	20	6	17		
F21	*1*of*2*going*3* home	FP	3	7	1	2		13
		UP	3	7	5	2		17
		total	6	14	6	4		
F31	*1*across*2*wide*3* streets*4*	FP	11	35	12	22		80
		UP	7	18	13	6		44
		total	18	53	25	28		

*In terms of Fries' classes.

Sequence Type	*Example*		*Positions* 1	2	3	4	5	*Totals*
BB2	*1*may*2*have*3* gone*4*	FP	7	1	9	10		27
		UP	2	1	14	9		26
		total	9	2	23	19		
A331	*1*the*2*big*3*fat*4* man*5*	FP	2	3	3	1	4	13
		UP	1	3	4	7	5	20
		total	3	6	7	8	9	
AD31	*1*one*2*very*3*big*4* man*5*	FP	5	5	0	4	2	16
		UP	1	5	1	7	0	14
		total	6	10	1	11	2	
FA11	*1*under*2*the*3* manor*4*house*5*	FP	4	3	4	4	7	22
		UP	3	4	5	3	2	17
		total	7	7	9	7	9	
FA31	*1*under*2*the*3* big*4*house*5*	FP	14	8	13	11	16	62
		UP	14	16	32	17	7	86
		total	28	24	45	28	23	
F331	*1*under*2*heavy*3* white*4*sheets*5*	FP	1	5	2	3	2	13
		UP	3	2	2	2	3	12
		total	4	7	4	5	5	

ification of the word classes included, and presents the frequencies of Filled Pauses (FP), Unfilled Pauses (UP), and their totals occurring in each of the possible inter-word positions, both at the boundaries of these phrases and within them. Illustrative words are given for each sequence. These data are summed over speakers; individual differences in the distribution of pauses have not been analyzed, but casual inspection does not indicate that they are of any magnitude.

Lounsbury's first hypothesis was that hesitation pauses will tend to occur at points of highest uncertainty in spontaneously produced utterances. Since, as Fries notes, there are many more members (alternatives) in his lexical classes than in his function-word classes, we should expect pauses of both types to occur more frequently before lexical words than before function words. Table 5 provides a test of this hypothesis. According to chance, it is assumed, pauses would occur equally in each possible position; actually, both Filled Pauses and Unfilled Pauses are found to occur significantly more frequently before lexical words than before function words (.02 and .001 level, respectively, by Chi-square test). Lounsbury's third hypothesis was that hesitation pauses would often occur at points within phrases where immediate-constituent analysis would not establish syntactical junctures. Inspection of the data in Table 4 shows this to be clearly the case. If we assume that syn-

Table 5

Distribution of Filled and Unfilled Pause by Word Class Following Pause

	Filled Pause	*Unfilled Pause*
Lexical Words	418	525
Function Words	360	290
Total	778	815

Probability that differences are due to chance (chi-square tests):
Filled Pause vs. Unfilled Pause < .001
Filled Pause vs. Chance < .02
Unfilled Pause vs. Chance < .001

tactical junctures do not occur within a phrase, then it is obvious that many pauses of both types do not function syntactically. As a matter of fact, approximately half (47%) of all pauses occur within the phrases rather than at their boundaries. Table 6 provides further evidence for the non-chance distribution of hesitation pauses—in this case, for constructions of specific types for which sufficient data for testing were available.

Are Filled and Unfilled Pause in free variation or in complementary distribution with respect to each other? The answer is, clearly, neither. Although both types are about equally likely to occur in any of the phrase sequences studied (*Totals* column, Table 4), they are not equally likely to occur in any of the positions within phrases. Table 5 demonstrates that Filled Pause is relatively more likely to appear before function words, while Unfilled Pause is relatively more likely to appear before lexical words, this difference in distribution being significant at the .001 level by Chi-square test. Table 6 indicates that in particular sequence types, where sufficient data were available for analysis, distributions of Filled and Unfilled Pauses may be significantly different. In phrases of the type *will go* (Fries' B2), we find FP before *will* and UP before *go*; in phrases of the type *the red houses* (Fries' A31), we find FP at the external boundaries and UP within the phrase; in phrases like *to these houses* (Fries' FA1), FP again tends to occur at the external boundaries and UP most often before the lexical items; in F31 phrases like *across wide streets*, the same trend is noted, as is also the case for FA31 phrases like *under the big house*. In other words, for those constructions that can be analyzed statistically, Filled Pauses occur more frequently at phrase boundaries and Unfilled Pauses at word boundaries within phrases. It should be noted that these are statistically significant tendencies, not cases of absolute complementary distribution in the linguistic sense.

Individual Differences in Hesitation Phenomena

Differences between speakers can be described in terms of both variation between individuals on particular measures and variation within individuals across all measures (e.g., profiles). Table 7 summarizes the data used for these comparisons; speakers are ordered according to their mean rates of speaking in words per minute. The numbers of utterances on which the mean speeds and hesitation types are based varied considerably, as can be seen in the table. We shall limit our discussion mainly to those speakers (A through E) who contributed 15 or more utterances of sufficient length for analysis. It may be noted that for the group as a

Table 6

CHI-SQUARE TESTS ON DISTRIBUTION OF FILLED AND UNFILLED PAUSES OVER EIGHT SELECTED SEQUENCES

*Sequence**	*Filled Pause/Chance*	*Unfilled Pause/Chance*	*Filled/Unfilled*
A1	.001*	.001	.10
F1	.001	.001	.10
B2	.01	.70	.001
A11	.10	.02	.10
A31	.01	.20	.01
FA1	.01	.05	.01
F31	.20	.01	.05
FA31	.05	.50	.001

*In terms of Fries' classes.

Each cell indicates probability that difference is due to chance.

Table 7

SPEED OF SPEAKING (WORDS/MINUTE) AND RATES PER 100 WORDS OF HESITATION TYPES

*Speaker**	*N of Utter-ances*	*Mean Words per Minutes*	*Mean Rates/100 Words* *R*	*FS*	*FP*	*UP*	*Totals (R, FS, FP, UP)*
3	4	181	.19	.47	1.88	2.53	5.35
D	38	177	1.39	2.12	2.48	3.58	10.20
8	10	173	1.55	1.16	3.30	1.84	8.77
7	8	163	2.17	1.65	3.10	2.01	9.34
4	5	162	.60	.94	1.54	2.65	6.16
6	3	153	1.70	2.13	2.77	5.74	13.19
A	16	149	1.79	1.91	3.80	3.40	11.64
2	8	144	2.50	1.85	2.96	5.27	13.22
B	22	143	2.21	1.28	6.41	1.80	12.26
1	7	140	3.26	1.34	5.35	2.91	13.61
E	15	136	1.38	1.90	7.21	2.68	13.60
C	21	134	1.45	1.30	3.06	4.51	10.78
5	6	122	1.68	1.18	6.41	4.44	14.50
Grand Means		152	1.68	1.48	3.87	3.34	10.97

R—Repetitions; *FS*—False Starts; *FP*—Filled Pauses; *UP*—Unfilled Pauses.
*Speakers having 15 or more utterances of sufficient length are designed by letters, the others by numbers.

whole, with a few minor exceptions, Filled and Unfilled Pauses occur more frequently as hesitation types than do Repeats or False Starts.

Significant differences between speakers appear for all of the measures made. SPEED OF TALKING: Only one of the 21 utterances by the slowest speaker (C) is as fast as the fastest speaker's (D) median; reciprocally, only one of the 38 utterances by the fastest speaker is as slow as the median rate for the slowest speaker. REPETITIONS: Only three of the 15 utterances by the least repetitious speaker (E) exceed the median of the most repetitious speaker (B), and reciprocally two of the 22 utterances by the most repetitions speaker are below the median for the other. FALSE STARTS: Only two of B's utterances have as many false starts as D's median; eight of D's 38 utterances are below B's median, however. FILLED PAUSES: None of D's 38 utterances have as many filled pauses as E's median level; reciprocally, none of E's 15 utterances have as few filled pauses as D's median. UNFILLED PAUSES: None of B's 22 utterances have as many unfilled pauses as C's median rate and, reciprocally, only one of C's 21 utterances shows as few unfilled pauses as B's median. These median tests indicate that, for the five speakers on whom we have sufficient data, differences on these measures are highly characteristic.

Table 8 gives the correlations across all subjects for these measures. The low and non-significant correlations between the hesitation types indicate that Repetition, False Start, Filled Pause, and Unfilled Pause are essentially independent variables across subjects. The higher correlations of total hesitations with the two types of pauses than with the other phenomena merely reflects the greater frequencies of the former. The fact that there is a very significant negative correlation between speed of talking and total hesitations might be explained away as simply reflecting the fact that speakers who pause more often must produce fewer words per minute. This proves not to be the case,

Table 8

PRODUCT-MOMENT CORRELATIONS OF VARIABLES ACROSS SUBJECTS†

	R	*FS*	*FP*	*UP*	*Total Hesitation*
Speed	−.121	−.078	−.712**	−.385	−.795**
R		+.027	+.112	+.032	+.181
FS			+.032	+.111	+.148
FP				−.157	+.720**
UP					+.478*

* = $.05 > p > .01$ ** = $.p < .01$

† For meaning of abbreviations, see Table 7.

however—at least not within the range of variation in our speakers. For when we recompute words per minute, counting all hesitations as words (i.e., "ah"-pause equaling a word, etc.), the correlation between original and recomputed speeds of speaking is + .98. Therefore we conclude that fast speakers tend to be "better" speakers in the sense that they make significantly fewer hesitation errors of the types measured here.

It is always possible that correlations based on a group of subjects may wash out important relations within subjects taken individually. As a check on this possibility, rank correlations (*rho*) were computed for the five subjects on whom we had enough utterances to make this procedure meaningful. Inspection of Table 9 shows that these variables are related within individuals pretty much as they are across subject averages. The correlations among the hesitation types (R/FS, R/FP, R/UP, FS/FP, FS/UP, and FP/UP) tend to be small in magnitude, different in sign, and averaging toward zero, whereas correlations between speed and pauses of both types (and hence also total errors) are consistently negative as before.

Within these generally consistent relations across speakers there may be uniquely individual tendencies, however. Subjects A and E, for example, show negative correlations of considerable magnitude between False Starts and Unfilled Pauses, as if a sufficient amount of pausing eliminated the conditions for making false starts. Subject B shows a definite tendency to increase False Starts and Unfilled Pauses as his speed of talking increases in utterances, this being in contrast to the other speakers. Furthermore, as Mahl has shown for psychiatric interviews, there may be considerable variation within an

Table 9

RANK CORRELATIONS OF VARIABLES WITHIN SUBJECTS*

Variables	*A*	*B*	*C*	*D*	*E*
Speed/R	+.13	−.11	+.07	+.11	−.09
Speed/FS	+.06	+.39	+.08	+.03	−.01
Speed/FP	−.70	−.59	−.24	−.63	−.54
Speed/UP	−.46	+.17	−.48	−.65	−.52
R/FS	+.36	+.11	−.13	+.09	+.34
R/FP	+.22	+.12	+.07	−.09	−.28
R/UP	−.19	.00	−.17	−.17	+.02
FS/FP	−.12	+.08	−.19	−.21	+.21
FS/UP	−.40	+.15	−.08	−.01	−.56
FP/UP	+.23	−.24	+.09	−.23	−.03
Speed/Total	−.56	−.39	−.40	−.55	−.74

* For meaning of abbreviations, see Table 7.

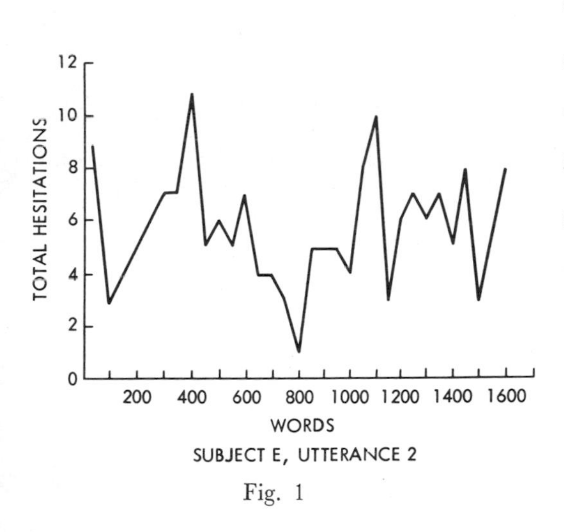

Fig. 1

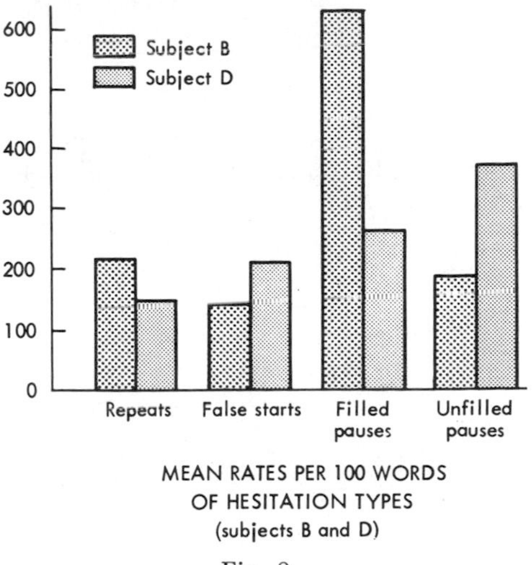

Fig. 2

extended utterance for a single speaker. Figure 1 plots total hesitations in successive 50-word units for a 1600-word utterance by speaker E; variations from as low as 1/50 to as high as 11/50 are shown, and they seem to follow a non-random course. However, we have not in this study attempted to relate such variations either to the content of utterances or to the states of speakers.

It can also be shown that the relative "preference" for hesitation phenomena of different types varies consistently between individuals. Figure 2 compares profiles for speakers B and D. B's utterances are characterized by a relatively large number of filled pauses and repeats (and a rather slow pace), whereas D's utterances show comparatively more unfilled pauses and false starts (and a rapid pace). Table 10 presents coefficients of concordance (Kendall's w) for the rankings from zero to 1.00, measures the extent to which the ranking of the hesitation types over his various utterances is consistent within the individual speaker. W is significant beyond the .01 level in every case, indicating that individuals—however they may order the types—tend to do it the same way for all of their utterances. Table 10 (like Figure 2) also shows that different speakers rank these hesitation types in different ways. In other words, the relative "preference" for hesitation phenomena of different types may be considered an aspect of individual *style* in speaking.

Table 10

COEFFICIENTS OF CONCORDANCE (w) FROM RANKS ASSIGNED TO HESITATION TYPES

Subject	w	*Probability that w is due to chance*	*Average ranking of Hesitation Types** 1	2	3	4
A	.33	<.01	FP	UP	FS	R
B	.73	<.01	FP	R	UP	FS
C	.64	<.01	UP	FP	R	FS
D	.40	<.01	UP	FP	FS	R
E	.60	<.01	FP	UP	FS	R

* For meaning of abbreviations, see Table 7.

DISCUSSION

Interpretive Summary of Findings

The spontaneous utterances analyzed in this study display consistent differences between speakers, in both the absolute frequencies of False Starts, Repeats, Filled Pauses, and Unfilled Pauses, and in the relative "preference" for these types of hesitation phenomena. However, types of hesitation phenomena are uncorrelated (i.e., independent) both across speakers and across utterances for the same speaker. The negative relations obtained between speed of talking and hesitation phenomena, even when these phenomena are treated as words in counting words per minute, suggest that there are overall differences between individuals in ability to speak spontaneously. The consistency of individual differences demonstrates that hesitation phenomena may be studied as an attribute of individual style in spontaneous encoding.

Analysis of the linguistic distribution of these hesitation phenomena shows that whereas False Starts typically involve lexical items (blocking after a lexical choice and returning to correct it), Repeats typically involve function words and occur antecedent to lexical items. Repeats thus tend to occur in the same locations as pauses and presumably serve the same function—providing time for selection among diverse lexical alternatives. Repeats are most frequently (71%) of a single word or several words, but rarely (only 12% of cases) of smaller units than the word. When a False Start is retraced, the retracing usually includes the function word or words immediately prior to and associated with that lexical item. Although both Filled Pauses and Unfilled Pauses occur more frequently before lexical than before function words—testifying to the greater uncertainty at these points—and occur within phrases as often as at their boundaries, these two types of pauses are not free variants with respect to positions of occurrence. Filled Pauses occur relatively more frequently before function words and at phrase boundaries; Unfilled Pauses, on the other hand, occur more frequently before lexical words and within syntactic phrases. However, these two types of pauses are not in complementary distribution linguistically, since either type *can* occur in any position where the other occurs and does so frequently.

Linguistic and Psycholinguistic Criteria of Structure

Linguists have typically regarded the data of their science as being confined to those aspects of vocal activity that can be precisely described with a finite number of discrete categories. (See Joos, 1950, for a discussion of this point.) According to this view hesitations fall in a non-linguistic (phonetic) area. We may add, however, that they are "outside" language in a way that other phonetic data are not. These latter, while they may be regarded as continuous phenomena, are systematically related to language structure, since continuous variations in phonetic quality may be translated into discrete phonemic categories by means of linguistic discovery methods. Hesitations are not pre-linguistic in this sense; they function as auxiliary events which help to identify and circumscribe linguistic units, rather than as part of the raw data for which a structural statement must account. The fact that they serve this function shows a recognition of their non-random relation to linguistic forms. We may ask whether a structural statement should account for statistically relevant hesitations as it now does for continuously varying phonetic qualities. A definition of hesitations as part of the raw data of a linguistic description would focus attention on a number of problems concerning the role of statistical methods in a field that has preferred to rely on a discrete 'either-or' approach.

If we define *structure* as a list of elements and statements about the permissible relations among them it may be that the most acceptable compromise will involve reliance upon discrete assumptions to define units (this would exclude hesitations from the list of elements) and continuous statistical assumptions to state their rules of combination and distribution. It is also possible that statistical methods and criteria could be extended to the identification of phonemes and morphemes and this procedure would include hesitations as linguistic units. Yet another resolution would be to consider as linguistically determined only phenomena that are obligatory in a language code, all other non-randomness being considered to be psycholinguistically determined. Linguistic determinants will inevitably control a substantial part of the message—phonetic content, ordering of phonemes and morphemes, and sequences of word classes and phrase types are largely dictated by the rules of grammar. On the other hand, the selection of alternative constructions and of particular lexical items must be explained primarily on non-linguistic grounds. Hesitation phenomena are clearly related to the dynamics of grammatical and lexical selections. Such a classification does not imply that the formal properties of language are independent of psychological processes in language users; to the contrary, obligatory features represent the extreme case of cultural control in behavior.

Implications for the Nature of Psycholinguistic Units

Although the final output of spontaneous speech is necessarily linear or unidimensional through time, this does not mean that the psycholinguistic process underlying it is a simple unit-by-unit sequencing. Carroll (1953) suggested a hierarchical process, in which selection of larger units at "higher" levels is followed by selection of smaller units at "lower" levels, the smaller units filling in the larger constructions. More recently, Chomsky (1957) has challenged the entire notion of the unreeling of speech as a Markov process. Does the study of pausal and other hesitation phenomena provide us with any insight into the nature of psycholinguistic units and their selection?

Depending on which measure we pick, we seem to get a different picture of the functional units of encoding. Repeats characteristically involve whole, single words (suggesting the word as a unit at some level of analysis), yet they usually affect a function word and appear before lexical choices. When False Starts are retraced, it is usually a lexical item that is corrected, but the speaker also includes the closely associated function words in his retracing. This would suggest that at some level of organization the encoding unit is phrase-like, a lexical core with its tightly bound grammatical context. In at least superficial contradiction to this, however, is the fact that pauses of both types tend to occur just before lexical choices and thus often *between* the function-word context and the lexical core (e.g., *in the / house*). Yet—finally—statistical analysis of the distribution of Filled vs. Unfilled Pauses clearly shows that the former tend to coincide with the syntactical junctures at phrase boundaries, while the latter fall within phrases.

What implications for the nature of the "encoding" (speaking) process can we draw from these data? In the first place, the data as a whole suggest that the speaker is operating with units at least as large as the word, not smaller. But words always involve grammatical as well as lexical selection: e.g. (*walk/-* vs. *walk/s* vs. *walk/ing* etc.) versus (*play/-* vs. *play/s* vs. *play/ing* etc.). We must therefore infer something like a "mixer" just prior to the final common path of output. It is as if we had available at some lower level of encoding a "pool" of heavily practiced, tightly integrated word and phrase units, but selection from this pool requires simultaneous lexical and grammatical determinants. Secondly, the evidence as a whole suggests at least two levels of organization in encoding, which we may call lexical (or semantic) and grammatical (or structural). The best evidence for two such levels or classes of determinants is the fact that the speaker often begins a phrase and then pauses just before the lexical choice within that phrase, as if he had made a structural choice before fully selecting the precise lexical item from the many alternatives available. The statistically significant, if imperfect, complementary distribution between the "ah" and silence pauses also implies some such distinction between levels of selection.

What about the distinction between Filled Pause and Unfilled Pause? We suggest that the main distinction lies in *the duration of the non-speech interval.* Let us assume that the speaker is motivated to keep control of the conversational "ball" until he has achieved some sense of completion. He has learned that unfilled intervals of sufficient length are the points at which he has usually lost this control—someone else has leapt into his gap. Therefore, if he pauses long enough to receive the cue of his own silence, he will produces some kind of signal ([m, ər], or perhaps a repetition of the immediately preceding unit) which says, in effect, "I'm still in control—don't interrupt me!" We would thus expect Filled Pauses and Repeats to occur just before points of highest uncertainty, points where choices are most difficult and complicated. We have also noted that Filled Pauses tend to occur at the junctures of larger syntactical units, presumably where constructional decisions as well as decisions as to *what* to say, content-wise, are being made. This assumption that "ah"-type pauses are reactions of the speaker to his own prolonged silences at points of difficult decision is consistent with our finding that these two pause-types are merely statistically, not absolutely, different in distribution. A difficult choice *can* occur almost anywhere, although it is more likely at points where both structural and content alternatives are being juggled.

We have the picture, then of the speaker operating simultaneously on two levels of choices, lexical and grammatical. These are merged in the final selection of word and phrase units that are highly practiced skills, reflecting both types of determinants. The larger the unit being "programmed," the more complex the transformation in Chomsky's sense, or the less probable the sequence, the more prolonged the non-speech interval and hence the greater the tendency for an "ah" or a repetition. Since structural choices typically involve fewer alternatives than lexical choices, the speaker will often initiate a construction before he has completed his lexical decisions—with the result that he may pause slightly in the middle of phrases before such lexical items. Since he is monitoring the sense of his utterances more than their structure, and because errors of sense are more likely than errors of form, he will often halt after a lexical "miss," retrace, and correct it—but the unit of retracing is that of the skill sequence, and this typically includes the function-word context along with the lexical core. Speakers differ in how they manage the complex variables in spontaneous speech. Some slow down to avoid False Starts and syntactical disorder, using "ah's" and repetitions to hold on to the conversational line; others pause (silently) only where lexical difficulties force them to, rather recklessly committing False Starts and only extricating themselves from syntactical impasses by sheer disregard for the rules. This overall picture may be quite wrong, of course, but it seems consistent with the hesitation phenomena we have observed.

Directions for Further Research

Our findings are consistent both with Lounsbury's predictions about where hesitation phenomena should occur and with Goldman-Eisler's reported observations and interpretations. However, the interpretation that such phenomena occur at points of high uncertainty, because they appear more before lexical items than before function words, is rather inferential. Also unsupported is our view that more Filled Pauses and Repeats occur before points of higher uncertainty than do Unfilled Pauses. These matters can be tested by comparing the Thorndike-Lorge frequencies of the lexical items following pauses with a random sample of lexical items following structurally similar points where pauses did *not* occur, and by comparing the frequencies of lexical items following Unfilled Pauses with those following Filled Pauses and Repeats. We have not yet made the necessary analyses.

It is clear from the work of Mahl that the motivational and emotional states of speakers will influence the frequency of hesitation phenomena and perhaps their distribution. Apart from the interview situation, clinical and otherwise, in which Mahl has worked, it should be possible to study the effects of conversational stress (e.g., implied support or criticism from the audience), of status differences between speaker and listener, of the amount of planning or rehearsal of an utterance, and so forth. These phenomena can also be studied from the point of view of the listener. Presumably the hesitations that slow the speaker at points of uncertainty also permit the listener to catch up, as well as serving to stress the less predictable items. Debate coaches will often encourage their charges to "rough up" their presentations when the season is about half over. It is also possible that natural-appearing pauses and other hesitation phenomena influence the listener's connotative judgment of the speaker, e.g., of the speaker's "sincerity." Similarly, novelists will sometimes introduce pauses (symbolized orthographically by *um, er,* etc.) into the speech of a character to convey impressions that are not easily transmitted by the lexical content.

The periodicity of hesitation rate suggested by Figure 1 is of some interest, although we can at present do no more than speculate on the variables at work. Mahl has pointed to anxiety as one source of variation. If anxiety is a tension-producing phenomenon, vocalization is likely to be tension-reducing. This implies that a subject in an anxiety state as he begins to talk will show an initially high rate of hesitations followed by a decreasing rate as speech continues. The level of hesitations may increase again as a result of external factors or as a consequence of the content of his own utterances. An example of this, to which the authors can testify, is the extreme difficulty of talking about hesitation phenomena without having one's own disturbance rate rise rapidly. Changing transitional probabilities during an extended utterance would be another factor. The alternatives available to the speaker are likely to become more and more dispersed as he exhausts the familiar things to be said about any particular topic, and as he moves into areas of low probability words and sequences he will need more time for selection. When he switches topics, he may gain a new statistical foothold. This tendency is probably reinforced by the stylistic requirement of educated English to search for synonyms rather than to repeat previously used words. On the basis of comparison of a few curves like that in Figure 1, we suspect that subjects differ considerably in the periodicity of their hesitation rates, but what the correlates of these differences may be (e.g., intelligence, personality variables, communication strategy), we do not know.

References

BLOCH, B. (1946). "Studies in Colloquial Japanese. II: Syntax," *Language* 22.-200–248.

BLOOMFIELD, L. (1933). *Language* (New York).

CARROLL, J. B. (1953). *The Study of Language* (Cambridge, Mass.).

CHOMSKY, N. (1957). *Syntactic Structures* (The Hague).

FREUD, S. (1938). "The Psychopathology of Everyday Life," in *The Basic Writings of Sigmund Freud* (New York).

FRIES, C. G. (1952). *The Structure of English* (New York).

GOLDMAN-EISLER, F. (1954*a*). "A Study of Individual Differences and of Interaction in the Behavior of Some Aspects of Language in Interviews," *Journal of Mental Science* 100.177–197.

GOLDMAN-EISLER, F. (1954*b*). "On the Variability of Speed of Talking and on Its Relation to the Length of Utterances in Conversations," *British Journal of Psychology* 45.94–107.

GOLDMAN-EISLER, F. (1955). "Speech-Breathing Activity—a Measure of Tension and Affect During Interviews," *ibid.*, 46.53–63.

GOLDMAN-EISLER, F. (1957). "Speech Production and Language Statistics," *Nature,* Vol. 28, December, p. 1497.

GOLDMAN-EISLER, F. (1958*a*). "Speech Production and the Predictability of Words in Context," *Quarterly Journal of Experimental Psychology* (in press).

GOLDMAN-EISLER, F. (1958*b*). "Speech Analysis and Mental Processes," *Language and Speech* 1.59–75.

HARRIS, Z. S. (1951). *Methods in Structural Linguistics* (Chicago).

JOOS, M. (1950). "Description of Language Design," *Journal of the Acoustical Society of America* 22.701–708.

MAHL, G. (1956*a*). "Disturbances in the Patient's Speech as a Function of Anxiety." Paper read to the Eastern Psychological Association.

MAHL, G. (1956*b*). "'Normal' Disturbances in Spontaneous Speech." Paper read to the American Psychological Association.

MAHL, G. (1957). "Disturbances and Silences in the Patient's Speech in Psychotherapy," *Journal of Abnormal and Social Psychology* 42.3–32.

MAHL, G. (1958). "The Instrumental Model and Relevant Research Methods," in *Trends in Content Analysis,* I. D. Pool, ed. (in press).

OSGOOD, C. E. and SEBEOK, T. A., eds. (1954). *Psycholinguistics: a Survey of Theory and Research* (Baltimore).

The Psychological Reality of Linguistic Segments[1]

J. A. FODOR
and T. G. BEVER

Experimentation with the subjective location of clicks heard during speech supports the following conclusions:

(a) Clicks are attracted towards the nearest major syntactic boundaries in sentential material. (b) The number of correct responses is significantly higher in the case of clicks located at major segment boundaries than in the case of clicks located within segments. (c) These results are consistent with the view that the segments marked by formal constituent structure analysis in fact function as perceptual units and that the click displacement is an effect which insures the integrity of these units. (d) The distribution of acoustic pauses in the sentential material does not account for the observed distribution of errors. (e) There is a slight tendency to prepose responses to clicks in sentences. This tendency is reversed during later stages of the experimental session. Both these effects are asymmetrical for the two ears.

[1] This work was supported in part by the U.S. Army, Navy, and Air Force under Contract DA 36-039-AMC-03200(E); in part by the National Science Foundation (grant GP-2495), the National Institutes of Health (grant MH-04737-04), the National Aeronautics and Space Administration (Ns G-496) and the U. S. Air Force (ESD Contract AF 19 (628)-2487; and, in addition by National Institute of Mental Health grant MPM 17,760. The authors wish to thank Professor H.-L. Teuber for making available the experimental facilities for this work and Mr. M. Garrett for his advice and criticism.

Linguistic models provide an analysis of sentences into segments of a number of different types. For example, the grammar of a language specifies the sequence of sound segments which constitute the sentences of that language. At this level, a sentence is represented by a sequence of phonetic symbols.

In addition, a grammar provides an analysis of the structure which underlies the acoustic pattern exhibited by a phonetic description. It does so, in part, by providing a *constituent analysis* for each sentence. The constituent analysis is a representation of the more abstract segments of which a sentence is composed. It

J. A. Fodor and T. G. Bever, "The Psychological Reality of Linguistic Segments," *Journal of Verbal Learning and Verbal Behavior,* 4 (1965), 414–420. Reprinted by permission of the authors and publisher, Academic Press, Inc., New York.

is with the psychological reality of the segmentations such analyses assign to sentences that we shall be concerned in this paper.

Consider the sentence "That he was happy was evident from the way he smiled." In addition to specifying an appropriate phonetic representation, an adequate grammar of English must provide a correct account of the syntactic relations between that sentence and such sentences as "He was happy," "It was evident," "He smiled in a certain way," etc. It must also correctly predict the stress pattern the sentence exhibits. To achieve these purely linguistic goals, the grammar must analyze this sentence into roughly the following constituents: *that he was happy; he was happy; was happy; was evident from the way he smiled; evident from the way he smiled; from the way he smiled; the way he smiled; the way; he smiled.* This analysis may be expressed by a notation in which each constituent of the sentence is enclosed by parentheses: (((that) ((he) ((was) (happy)))) ((was) ((evident) ((from) (((the) (way)) ((he) (smiled))))))).

The question arises whether the units marked off by such segmentation correspond in any direct way to the perceptual units into which sentences are articulated by speakers and hearers. A number of techniques are available for experimentally determining the segmentation of a complex percept. The simplest of these is a direct appeal to the intuitions of the perceiver. Very often, the *S*'s reports of the preferred segmentation of a speech stimulus appear to be fairly stable for adult speakers of a language.

A more subtle way of establishing the segments of a complex percept exploits the tendency of a perceptual unit to preserve its integrity by resisting interruptions. The *E* introduces an appropriate form of interfering stimulation which the *S* is required to locate relative to the perceptual object. A segmentation is established by demonstrating a reliable tendency for the subjective locations of the interfering stimuli to cluster. The points at which such clusters occur are identified as the boundaries of the segmental units comprising the perceptual object.

A recent attempt to investigate perceptual units in speech by employing this sort of technique was made by Ladefoged and Broadbent (1960). They argued that the unit of speech perception must be longer than a single speech sound (phone), just as the perceptual unit in reading is clearly longer than a single letter. To test that hypothesis, they devised an experiment calculated to reveal the perceptual units of speech. The *S*s listened binaurally to sentences and to strings of digits spoken in English. Each string and each sentence had an extraneous sound (a click) superimposed on it. The *S*'s task was to note the word during which the extraneous sound occurred. It was assumed that switching from processing verbal to processing nonverbal material would be controlled, in part, by the segmentation of the speech and not solely by an intrinsic attention span; i.e., that switching would take place at the boundaries of units. Thus Ladefoged and Broadbent predicted that the magnitude of errors in placing the clicks is a measure of the size of perceptual units.

With eight sentences and ten random digit strings, Ladefoged and Broadbent found that location errors often displace the noise *beyond* the boundaries of the word in which it is objectively positioned; that all *S*s tend to locate the noise prior to its objective position whether in sentences or in random material; and that errors in noise location are larger for sentential material than for digit sequences.

Ladefoged and Broadbent's attempt to apply to linguistic material experimental techniques for establishing segmentation thus produced suggestive results: the unit of speech perception probably does not correspond to the phone and is larger in sentences than in random sequences of words. But they failed to yield a definite answer to the question: to what extent do the larger units into which sentences are segmented for purposes of linguistic analysis correspond to the perceptual units involved in speech recognition?

The experiments which will now be presented are concerned with the following hypothesis. (*H*) *The unit of speech perception corresponds to the constituent.*

This hypothesis supports certain predictions about the effects of the integrity of segments in the sort of experimental situation investigated by Ladefoged and Broadbent. It was seen above that a given word boundary in a sentence may mark a coincidence between the boundaries of any number of constituents. If, as has been supposed, interfering stimuli tend to be displaced to or towards the boundaries of perceptual units, and if *H* is true, there ought to be a demonstrable tendency for clicks presented simultaneously with sentences to be heard at the boundaries of the constituents in which they are objectively located. Moreover, the larger the number of overlapping constituents in which the click is objectively located, the stronger should be the tendency for *S*s to displace it to the common boundary of those constituents. For example, the tendency to displace the noise from its objective position at B to the position between B and C ought to be greater in structures like ((A) (B)) (C) than in structures like (A) (B) (C). For, to perceive the noise in its objective position in the former would interrupt two units, while to perceive it in its objective position in the latter would interrupt only one. Correspondingly, in structures of the former kind, the tendency to hear the noise between B and C ought to be stronger than the tendency to hear it between A and B, since hearing it after B would interrupt no segments while hearing it prior to B would interrupt one.

In short, the assumption that *H* is true, together with the assumption that perceptual units in speech resist interruption, leads to the following experimental prediction: (*H′*) *Noise heard during speech should tend to shift perceptually towards the boundaries of constituents. This shift should occur in such fashion as to minimize the number of constituents the noise is perceived as interrupting.* Thus, for example, a click objectively placed in the final syllable of "happy" in the sentence "That he was happy was evident from the way he smiled" should tend to migrate toward the following boundary, since that boundary represents the termini of three constituents in addition to the word "happy" itself.

Predictions based on *H′* in fact receive some support from a reanalysis of Ladefoged and Broadbent's results for the five sentences for which they provide summaries of their data. Such an examination shows first that, in the case of four of the five sentences, the noise is displaced either into the boundary preceding its objective position or into the boundary following its objective position, depending upon which boundary marks the terminus of the larger number of constituents. Second, the only sentence for which *S*s tend to displace the superimposed noise towards the end was the one in which the boundary marking the terminus of the larger number of constituents *followed* the actual position of the superimposed sound. These results appeared to supply sufficient support for *H′* to warrant more extensive experimental investigation. The following experiment was therefore undertaken.

METHOD

Materials

Twenty-five sentences containing only one boundary at which a relatively large number of constituents are coterminous and five sentences containing two such boundaries were each recorded nine times on one track of a stereophonic recording tape. Sentences ranged in length from 8 to 22 words, with the average length 13.1 words. In each sentence, one boundary was designated the *zero position*. In all cases where a sentence had a single major boundary, it was chosen as zero. In the five other cases, one of the two major boundaries was chosen arbitrarily.

On the second track of each of the nine copies of each sentence, one capacitor-discharge click was recorded. The intensity of the clicks was approximately equal to the most intense speech sound and the duration was about 25 msec. One of the nine copies had the click placed contemporaneously with the *zero position.* A second, third, and fourth copy respectively had clicks contemporaneous with the first, second, and third syllables *posterior* to the zero position. Finally, an eighth, and ninth copy respectively had clicks in the word boundaries prior and posterior to the zero position. The distance between these last two positions and the zero position therefore varied when measured in syllables, but was always unity when measured in words. Thus for the sentence discussed above, the nine click locations were:

That he was happy was evident from
−3 a −2 −1 0 +1 b +2 +3
the way he smiled

where letters designate clicks located in boundaries other than the major one.

It should be noticed that, since the objective locations of the clicks were balanced on either side of the major boundary, any response bias would be self-cancelling. The prediction derived from *H′* was that errors in the location of clicks objectively prior to the major boundary would be towards the end of the sentence and conversely for clicks objectively following the major boundary. Any general directional biases in click placement would therefore tend to reduce the degree of confirmation of *H′* for one-half of the response, but would strengthen it for the other half.

Subjects

Nine experimental groups, consisting of four right-handed undergraduates each, heard one copy of the original 30 sentences. The order of sentence presentation and the click location in the sentences heard by a particular group were determined randomly. Thus each group heard approximately the same number of clicks in each position relative to the major break, although in different sentences and in different orders.

Procedure

The *S*s were presented with the stimulus material through headphones, the sentence in one ear and the click in the other. Each group had two *S*s in each of the orientations of the headphones (viz., click left and sentence right as opposed to click right and sentence left). This orientation was not varied over the 30 sentences. The *S*s were instructed to write the entire sentence and to indicate graphically where in the sentence they thought the click had occurred. They were also given an opportunity to indicate one of three levels of confidence in the correctness of each of their responses.

Scoring

H′ predicts that errors should be in the direction of the major break or into the major break, but not beyond it. Thus, for example, a −3 click if marked by *S* as in a, −2, −1, or 0, confirms *H′*, but if marked in + 1, b, + 2, or + 3 it does not. Although it is not clear that such "overshoot" responses should be counted at all, as a conservative measure these will be scored as errors tending to *dis*confirm *H′*. Responses were scored to the nearest syllable or to the nearest constituent boundary, whichever was relevant.

RESULTS

Of 1080 responses, 22 were not scored because the sentence was incorrectly transcribed by *S*. The 120 responses to clicks objectively located in the "0" position are not directly subject to *H′*, since they are already in the deep break and cannot be attracted towards it. Of the remaining 938 responses to clicks objectively located in the eight nondeep break position, 749 or 80% were errors. The number of errors did not increase with the length of the sentence and no correlation was discovered between the degree of confidence reported by *S*s and the objective accuracy of their performance. (Although they follow all the effects discussed below, the five sentences with two major breaks are hereafter omitted from the data, because the zero position in each was chosen arbitrarily.)

For the sentences with one major syntactic break, *H′* predicted the direction of displacement for 66% of the erroneous responses. That is, errors in locating clicks objectively preceding the major break (−3, −2, −1, a) followed the objective click position. Errors in locating clicks objectively following the major break (+1, +2, +3, b) preceded the objective click position. Specifically, 53 responses beyond the deep break from the objective click position and 115 responses away from the deep break were scored as errors (not confirming *H′*). There were 414 responses towards or into the deep break which were scored as confirming *H′*. The hypothesis was confirmed for all the sentences (reject *H′*, $p < .01$ by sign test two-tailed) and for each of the 36 *S*s (reject *H′*, $p < .01$). It was also confirmed for each of the eight click positions other than '0' (reject *H′*, $p < .01$ by one-tailed test). None of the *S*s, sentences, or click positions yielded results confirming *H′* for less than 60% of the errors.

A subsidiary experimental prediction derivable from *H′* is that clicks whose objective location is in a major syntactic break, i.e., in the '0' position, would be located more accurately than clicks whose objective position is within segments. This follows from the assumption that a substantial proportion of the displacement is attributable to the tendency to maintain the integrity of segments as perceptual units. This prediction was in fact confirmed by the data. Significantly more of the correctly located clicks were objectively in the deep break position than in any other of the nine positions (independence rejected by x^2 − test, $p < .025$ for the "+1", and $p < .01$ for all others).

Analysis of the absolute location of the incorrect responses was also carried out to determine their distribution by position. The analysis exhibited the predicted tendency to displace clicks into the zero position. More than 35% of *all* erroneous responses were into the major boundary, and more than 60% of all erroneous responses (including the "over-shoots") were either in the major boundary or in the syllables immediately preceding or following it. It should be noted, however, that the exact significance of this result depends upon one's prior assumptions about the probability distribution of the perceived clicks if no structural effects were operative. While any particular assumption about this distribution would be difficult to justify, it is clear that the observed differences between the zero position and all others could not be accounted for on a null hypothesis.

DISCUSSION

The above data appear to demonstrate that the major syntactic break plays an important role in determining the subjective location of noise perceived during speech. They would thus appear to provide grounds for the acceptance of hypotheses *H′* and *H*.

It remains possible, however, that the factors determining the direction of displacement of the clicks were only indirectly related to the formal constituent structure of the sentences. In an unpublished experiment, Garrett (1964)[2] has shown that relatively long pauses introduced at a selected point in a string of spoken digits will tend to attract interfering noise. That is, noise superimposed upon the spoken

[2] Unpublished paper.

digits will tend to be heard in the position objectively occupied by the acoustic pause. Also Bolinger and Gerstman (1957) showed that in isolation the ambiguous phrase *light-house* keeper, is assigned a structure depending on the relative duration of the pauses between the individual words. Garrett's and Bolinger and Gerstman's results show that *in the absence of any other cues and isolated from sentences* acoustic pauses are capable of inducing a particular structural organization. It might thus be hypothesized that the constituent breaks in spoken sentences invariably have slight acoustic pauses associated with them, and that the duration of each such pause corresponds to the importance of the corresponding constituent break. It could then be maintained that the effect of constituent structures upon click displacement is attributable to the acoustic pauses in the sentence and not to the underlying constituent structure.

The difference between the interpretation of the present data as directly due to the effect of constituent structure and the interpretation which holds that it is attributable to pausal phenomena that are themselves distributed in accordance with the constituent structure is of considerable importance. If it is actual acoustic pauses that are critical, then it may be claimed that the division of the sentence into perceptual units is accomplished by markers in the physical signal which delineate their boundaries. If, on the other hand, these units are *not* usually marked in the physical signal, then it must be the hearer who imposes an articulation into perceptual units upon the speech signal. On this view, the hearer *contributes* the perceptual structure to the physical signal on the basis of his knowledge of the constituent structure rules of his language. Hence, what is at issue between the two interpretations is the difference between an "active" and a "passive" theory of speech perception.

To answer this question the 25 sentences with one major constituent break were analyzed with a pen oscilloscope. When analyzed in this way, many of the sentences did not exhibit *any* acoustic pause at the point associated with the major boundary (though they do exhibit such pauses at other locations). In the sentence "That he was happy was evident from the way he smiled," for example, there is no acoustic pause discoverable at the break between "happy" and "was."

The 25 sentences were categorized according to whether or not there was a discoverable acoustic pause at the major break. Sentences exhibiting no such pause were analyzed to determine whether there was a measurable drop in energy. To be sure that all acoustic pauses would be included, those attributable to phonetic effects, such as the influences of stop-consonants, were included in the scoring. Nevertheless, only eight sentences showed full acoustic pauses at the major breaks; six had a severe drop in intensity, but not to zero. Seven sentences had a mild intensity drop and four exhibited no pause and no intensity drop.

If it is true that the perceptual organization of speech and the click displacement in sentences are due to acoustic pauses, the four groups above should show a decreasing agreement with H'. That is, the eight sentences with observable pauses should give better results on H' than the four sentences with no intensity drop. The results indicate that this did not occur. Where the per cent energy drop is 100, 81% of the responses confirm H'; where the per cent energy drop is 51–99, 57.5% of the responses confirm H'; where the per cent energy drop is 1–50, 76.5% of the responses confirm H'; where the per cent energy drop is 0, 80% of the responses confirm H'. None of these percentages are significantly different from the average for all sentences. Nor is there any trend among the four groups. From this it is concluded that in full spoken sentences naturally occurring acoustic pauses coinciding with major constituent breaks do not strengthen the role of the breaks in perceptual organization.

In short, some of the sentences exhibit no simple pausal correlate of constituent structure and there is no correlation between the strength of a pause and the strength of the structural effects. Since *all* sentences having one major break show results in the predicted direction, it is evident that the pausal characteristic of the speech signal cannot be the sole factor tending to determine the subjective placement of the clicks.

Ideally, it would be desirable to control not only for pause, but also for other acoustic features which might serve to mark the boundaries of segments. This may be done by using structurally ambiguous sentences as stimulus material. Such sentences may be inserted in contexts which uniquely select one or the other of their possible interpretations. If it can be shown that the displacement of the click is a function of the structure selected, the possibility that acoustic variables determine displacement can be definitely ruled out. For, in the case of ambiguous sentences, the two structures are associated with precisely the same physical signal. Experiments with ambiguous material have been carried out. Their results confirm the hypothesis of the independence of the structure from the acoustics.

Subsidiary Results

The present data suggest that a number of effects other than those predicted by H' contribute to determining the perceived position of the click. In the first place, there was a slight tendency, consonant with the finding of Ladefoged and Broadbent, cited above, to perceive the click earlier than its objective position. Fifty-two per cent of all the erroneous responses were to the left of the objective position of the click, 48% to the right. It is of some interest that the tendency to prepose responses was weaker at the end of the test than at the beginning. Of the erroneous responses to the first 20 sentences presented, 55.5% were preposed, but for the last ten sentences only 47% were preposed (independence rejected at $p < .05$ by x^2). Since order of sentence presentation was randomly varied and the structural prediction for the final ten sentences was balanced, this tendency appears to be a true experience effect.

It is suggested that the failure of some experimenters to replicate the tendency to prepose responses found by Ladefoged and Broadbent is in part attributable to the tendency of that effect to diminish with prolonged experience with the stimulus material. An unpublished paper by Garrett (1964) on the perception of clicks in speech presented binaurally shows no overall tendency for responses to be preposed. Reanalysis of these data reveals, however, a significant tendency to prepose responses for the initial period of the experimental session. This effect is washed out by the later tendency to postpose responses. The fact that Ladefoged and Broadbent's experimental sessions were comparatively short, (8–10 sentences) may thus account for the overall difference between their results and Garrett's and those of others.

It was further discovered that the tendency towards preposed responses is asymmetrical for the two ears. About 43% of the erroneous responses were preposed by *S*s to whom the sentence was presented in the left ear and the click in the right, but 61% of their erroneous responses were preposed by *S*s experiencing the opposite stimulus orientation (independence rejected at $p < .01$ by x^2). The proportions of preposed responses in each of the orientations were also significantly different from the mean (independence from 50% rejected at $p < .01$ by x^2). These data are summarized in Table 1.

A second asymmetry between the two stimulus orientations is related to the

Table 1

PERCENTAGE OF PREPOSED RESPONSES IN TOTAL ERRORS

Part of session	*Right ear*	*Left ear*	*Both ears*
Initial two-thirds	62.5	46.8	55.5*
Final third	58.8	36.3	47.0*
Total	61.3*	43.5*	52.2

Note: The first two column heads refer to the ear in which the *sentence* was heard. Sums marked (*) are not exact averages owing to slight differences in the absolute number of errors in each orientation.

effect of experience. The drop in the frequency of click preposition in the last part of the session appears to have been largely contributed by a shift in the pattern of responses of *S*s hearing the sentence in the left ear and the click in the right (independence of final third rejected at $p < .05$ by x^2). These data on asymmetry between the two orientations are also summarized in Table 1. In brief, the asymmetry of the ears found in this experiment may be functionally characterized in the following way: there is a relative delay of *all* material presented to the right ear. This relative delay increases significantly with experience for those *S*s receiving speech in the left ear.

References

BOLINGER, D., AND GERSTMAN, L. J. Disjuncture as a cue to constructs. *Word,* 1957, 13, 246–255.

LADEFOGED, P., AND BROADBENT, D. E. Perception of sequence in auditory events. *Quart. J. Exp. Psychol.,* 1960, 12, 162–170.

Studies in Aphasia: Background and Theoretical Formulations*

JOSEPH M. WEPMAN, LYLE V. JONES, R. DARRELL BOCK, and DORIS VAN PELT

Language is the symbolic representation of thought and action. It provides us with whatever limited '...light upon the depths of the unknown' (George Eliot) that we have concerning man's inner state. Our studies of language impairment after neural insult have given us some indication of the consequent deviations in thought processes. These have led to the adoption of certain conceptual tools in order to clarify the framework in which our studies have been cast. One of these takes the form of a theory or model to provide an organized picture of certain rather distinct mental functions which appear necessary for language. Another consists of a class of descriptive distinctions of language which have proved successful in linguistics. The application of these tools to the study of individual differences in the language usage of normal and aphasic subjects appears to be a promising approach which should add to our knowledge of human behavior. The purpose of the present communication is to show how these concepts have influenced the form of a new method for assessing the language of aphasic subjects and the psycholinguistic studies we are now pursuing.

Clinical and research interest in aphasia had led to dissatisfaction with the logic of our position concerning the neural processes relative to language and to the

* This article was adapted from a paper read by its senior author at the 11th Congress of the International Association of Logopedics and Phoniatrics, August, 1959, in London, England.

The present communication is a product of the collaboration between the Speech and Language Clinic of The University of Chicago and the Psychometric Laboratory of the University of North Carolina. The research reported was partially supported by grants from the Department of Health, Education, and Welfare through (1) The National Institutes of Health, Neurological Diseases and Blindness Council (Grant B-710), (2) National Institutes of Mental Health (Grants M-1876 and M-1849) and (3) the Office of Vocational Rehabilitation (Grant SP 168A).

Joseph M. Wepman, Lyle V. Jones, R. Darrell Bock, and Doris Van Pelt, "Studies in Aphasia: Background and Theoretical Formulations," *Journal of Speech and Hearing Disorders,* **25,** No. 4 (November, 1960), 323–332. Reprinted by permission of the authors and publisher.

classification of impairment in language subsequent to their disruption. Little relation was seen to exist between either the current theories of neural function or to the categories used by neurologists for describing central nervous system disruption and the language disturbances consequent to them. Therapy for aphasia was largely nonspecific to the disorders as diagnosed. Prognosis was a matter of clinical experience and was also unrelated to the neurological differentiation either in terms of the site or the degree of damage. No reliable data were available on the type or degree of language loss in the various aphasic categories. In fact, these categories were so vague and so grossly stated that attempts to classify recovery in terms of the aphasic process as originally estimated were meaningless. It was this lack of objectivity as well as the inadequacy of our conceptualization of both the aphasic speaker and the norms from which his deviations were established that led to much of our research.

NEUROLOGICAL CONSTRUCTS

The neurological concepts of central nervous system function for language based upon impairment are of two types. The first, the classical viewpoint, is that within the highest level of brain function there exists a series of localized centers, each serving a different aspect of language. From the day of Broca onward, the third prefrontal convolution was held to be the 'center for motor speech' (*1*), while following Wernicke, the second temporal convolution was seen as the 'center for the auditory reception of speech' (*19*). From these and many others came the concept of special centers for each part of the language act. Broca's name was attached to the concept of motor aphasia which later came to mean, in Weisenberg and McBride's terms, 'expressive aphasia' (*15*). Wernicke's name became attached to and synonymous with 'sensory aphasia,' or later 'receptive aphasia' (*15*).

In constrast, a growing group of neurologists and, later, neuropsychologists held that no true centers of speech existed, either sensory or motor (*4, 5, 14*). Rather, varying from the position of Lashley (*8*), who argued for a form of 'equipotentiality' of neural tissue, and the nonlocalization position held by Jackson (*14*) and Head (*7*), there developed the viewpoint that while specialized areas of the brain could be said to subserve specific functions, the language process was better conceived as the product of over-all integration. Additional evidence for this view is to be found in the recent monograph of Penfield and Roberts (*12*). De Barrene summarized the viewpoint most succinctly when he pointed out that '. . . though a certain focal concentration of activity may be present, in all probability the whole cortex participates in these processes (speech, comprehension, reading, writing and thought) . . .' (*3*).

Both the localization and the nonlocalization views have had many adherents; however, aphasia therapists found neither especially helpful in planning therapy. Nevertheless, the concept of the brain functioning as a dichotomized sensory-motor mechanism involving specialized centers became well fixed in the field. Patients were seen as being 'predominantly sensory' or as 'predominantly motor' (*15*) in their language deficits.

At the same time there was a general acceptance of Head's definition of aphasia as a disorder of symbol formulation. No anomaly was seen here, yet one existed. For nowhere in a system divided solely between input and output could symbolic formulation exist as a separate function.

This disparity was recognized when it was seen that many of the language problems presented by the aphasic patients in therapy were not disorders affecting symbol formation but were modality-bound problems of transmission, either along sensory or motor lines. Patients were seen who had no difficulty in formulating symbols when the stimulus reached their levels of conceptualization. In some cases of central auditory deficiency, symbol formulation went on without disturbance following stimulation along retained visual or kinesthetic pathways. Conversely, motor expressive problems in speech were frequently seen in patients who had little or no difficulty formulating the concepts into words, despite apraxic and dysarthric language efforts. It was the recognition of these modality-bound, nonsymbolic problems as differentiated from the symbolic formulation problems which led to an earlier reported concept of aphasia in a communication entitled 'A Theory of Language Disorders Based on Therapy' (*18*).

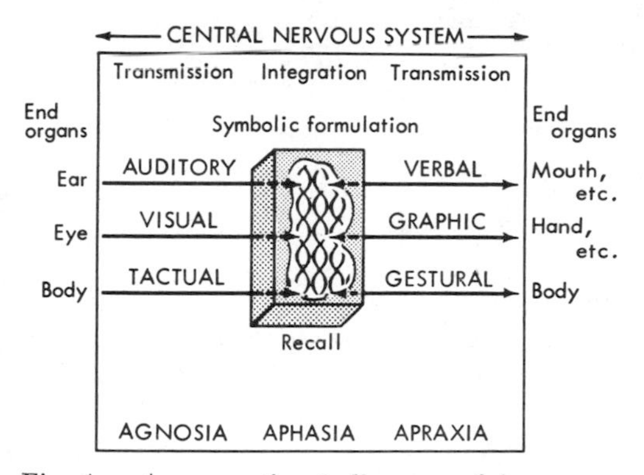

Fig. 1: An operational diagram of language functions in man.

The model presented as Figure 1 was meant to suggest not a duality of language function within the central nervous system, but at least a triad of functions: input transmission leading to integration leading to output transmission. Input and output were seen as being modality-bound, while integration itself had modality-linkage to some degree, but was not bound by it. This permitted the concept of agnosia and apraxia as transmissive, nonsymbolic processes of disruption which should respond to directed therapy. Aphasia was seen as a disruption of integration with little specific modality relationship, and neither a sensory nor a motor problem. Such a concept of process and disruption, it was felt, allowed for Head's definition of aphasia, and yet did not disturb the classical categories of agnosia and apraxia.

Clinical experience proved this to be a valuable distinction. Direct therapy for auditory agnosia, visual agnosia, verbal apraxia and motor agraphia proved valuable, while the more generally conceived stimulation therapies which were non-specific in nature seemed to be more valuable procedures for the aphasic processes. The use of generalized stimulation as opposed to specific training for the aphasias has been presented in an earlier communication (*16*). However, even this concept, which recognized the integrative factor in language as a separate stage between reception and expression, failed to explain many factors evident in aphasic patients and was felt to be out of keeping with much of the new neuroanatomical and neurophysiological research (*6, 9, 12*).

The model presented in Figure 1 failed to show the recognizable role of lower level function in language and the effect of feedback, both internal and external, upon the language process. Many patients were seen who could function imitatively or with normal reflex behavior while still demonstrating conceptual disability. The failure of attempts to restore language utilizing only retained imitative abilities demonstrated the distinction between the lower and higher levels of function. Patients were seen who could imitate but could not function conceptually, while others who could formulate symbols quite adequately and spontaneously could not imitate. At the same time elementary sensory-motor responses at the reflex level were most often recovered first by the patient and apparently without relation to the recovery of either imitative or conceptualized language. Thus, all three levels could function more or less indedendently. To account for these unique bridges across the nervous system from input to output and yet to maintain the tripartite model required a more complex configuration of behavior. Figure 2 shows the present concept, which is a three-level

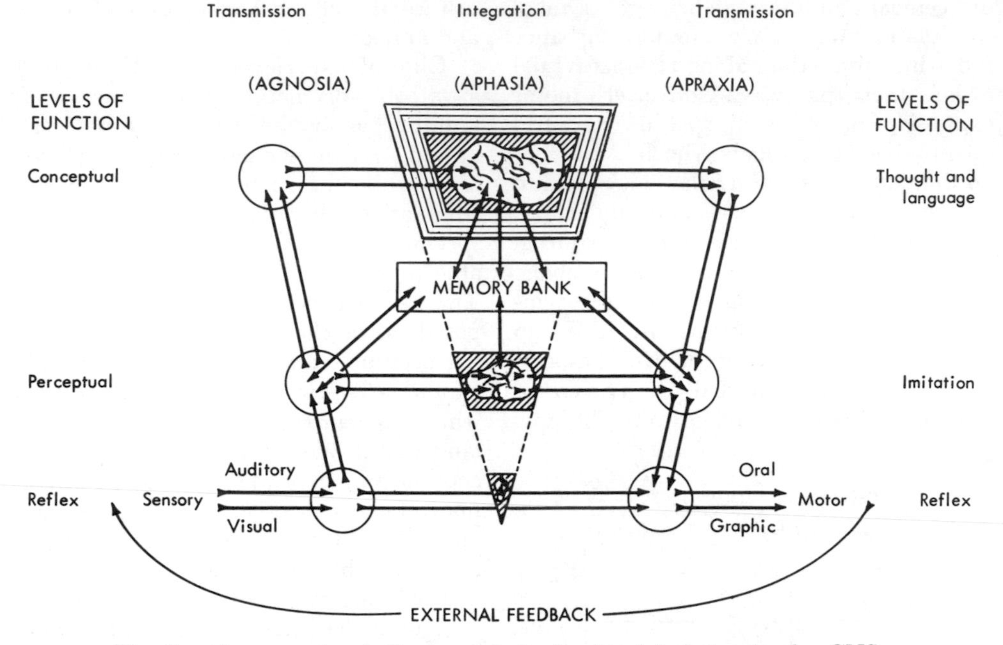

Fig. 2: An operational diagram of the levels of function in the CNS.

operational paradigm for language in the central nervous system. At the lower left is seen the input along the various modalities. At every level, in Osgood's terms, '. . . there exists a hierarchy of alternatives' *(11)*. If the stimulus is directed across the lower line, reflex behavior ensues. No relationship is pictured here between behavior and recall, since reflex action is thought to leave no apparent trace within the system. A degree of central nervous system control is indicated in the central position at this reflex level, where reception is translated into motor acts. While this level is not usually conceived as part of the language mechanism, yet certainly the ability of this level to function communicates specific data to the neurologist, and is frequently his major source of information concerning the intactness of the neural structure.

In the hierarchy of alternatives, when the stimulus is shunted to the next higher level it is seen to be bound to the original receptive modality. Transmission across the system here is seen as the capacity of the organism to transmit percepts which leave their trace on the memory bank but have no meaning to the individual. Across this bridge flows the echoic language of the infant, the parrot, or of any speaking organism.

The central process at this level is seen as providing the necessary transition from the input sign or symbol to the output pattern of expression. Here, the decoding and encoding of messages in terms of previously learned patterns occurs. Here also the internal state of the organism has its effect upon the ability to copy or imitate.

The initial phase of our research, through the use of factor analysis, demonstrated a series of events which were nonconceptual in process but completely bridged the system from input to output. One factor was defined by the ability to repeat auditory stimuli while a second independent factor was defined by the ability to copy printed stimuli. Two additional factors were, in part, also defined as nonconceptual. They were the ability to read aloud and the ability to write words presented aurally. This dependence of response process upon the stimulus modality gave rise to the transmissive concept, shown on the model as separate arrowed lines for each potential modality. The role of recall in these behaviors was evidenced by the correct patterning of responses in terms of previously acquired phonemic, phonetic and orthographic habits. The role of the central process even at this level is seen in the effect that conscious awareness can have on the echoic-imitative act, inhibiting or facilitating it, as the case may be.

Many examples can be called to mind of clinical behavior limited to the lower levels. Thus, it is not uncommon to see patients who can copy what they see without understanding the stimulus in a meaningful way. A child with a mental defect who may be known for his ability to copy or even to recall events which leave no trace of understanding or of concept formation is another example. That recall is a part of this lower level... is also easily demonstrated. Parrots speak in words, using the patterns acquired from previous exposure to these words, yet cannot act on them, and many of us can repeat words of a foreign language but, too often, without meaning.

The highest level of symbol activity appears most prominently in man. Here occurs what the philosopher Cassirer, in speaking of man and his evolutionary change from less differentiated life forms, stated so succinctly, '...(man) has as it were discovered a new method of adapting himself to his environment. Between the receptor system and the effector system, which are to be found in all animal species, we find in man a third link which we may describe as the symbolic system' (2). At this concept-formation level, the modality-bound stimulus is seen to have its effect both upon the memory bank for the arousal of associations and upon the integrative process where incoming stimuli are thought to combine with the associations from the past to form a state of meaningfulness. Here, the internalized emotions play their greatest role; the physical state of the organism, the personality, the intellective ability and the thought processes become concentrated into a new symbolic effort. Meaning invested in diverse symbols and associations becomes transformed into the symbols and symbol sequences of language —the conventional word patterns and grammatical forms which are part of the individual's repertoire of highly overlearned habits. Selection of language symbols may be called the semantic process; articulation of language symbols in discursive expression, the syntactic process. The specific form of expression follows the specific modality selected—speech, writing, or gesture. Stimulation of the process may not always lead to immediate response, but may result in storage of a symbol for use at some later time.

In the factorial analysis referred to earlier an independent 'comprehension' factor was defined which transcends modality and represents higher level symbolic activity.

Aphasia is seen as a disruption of the integrative process after the stimulus is free of its input modality. The defect in language may fall at any point in the process: in the arousal of a meaningful state, in the semantic process of word selection, or in the syntactic process.

The central nervous system is here viewed as a system in both depth and breadth. As Sherrington (*13*) said in speaking of the cerebral cortex, '...(it) is one of several bridges from input to output, though it is of them all the longest way round and the most complex.' Disruptions within the system may affect language in different ways. On the input side, disturbances will be limiting the stimuli that reach the cortex along the specific modality of damage; along the horizontal lines the disruptions will be localized to the process in language for which each level is responsible; along the output lines particular motor acts will be affected. Disruption of the output, whether through impoverishment due to faulty concept formation or faulty transmission at the perceptual level, will have its later effect upon the total behavior as a result of the limitations placed on the restimulation through the feedback process.

Here, both internal and external feedback are seen as playing an important role. Internally, decreased proprioceptive destimulation will lower the accuracy of control and often remove some of the moderation of behavior before it is expressed. Externally, the auditory, visual and other guidance for future action which is so much a part of our constantly guided behavior will be lost. The aphasic patient with auditory agnosia, for example, cannot monitor his oral behavior, cannot guide his expression; the aphasic with visual impairment has greater difficulty maintaining the accuracy of both his writing and his reading. Feedback and its role in the control of our behavior cannot be overemphasized; without it most of our speech attempts would be unintelligible, like the neologistic jargon of certain aphasic patients.

Finally, the essential role of recall to all of our language is seen by the prominence of the memory bank and its interconnections with all stages of the perceptual and the conceptual levels of function. In one sense, all aphasia can be described as a memory defect since the loss of ability to utilize previously learned verbal constructs so frequently typifies the disorder.

The use of the model in conceptualizing aphasia and the disruptions of language seen in our patients has had a ready effect on therapy. The symbolic problems are distinguished from the nonsymbolic ones, and are approached in a different manner. The role of imitation and reflex behavior is relegated to its proper pre-symbolic status. The modality differentiation in the agnosias and apraxias has permitted the development and use of very specific training techniques for this class of defects. The recognition of potentially three different types of aphasics, (1) those who cannot relate in language to a stimulus, internal or external (pragmatic aphasia), (2) those whose problem lies in the semantic act of symbol formation (semantic aphasia) and (3) those whose grammar and syntax is faulty or absent (syntactic aphasia), has led to stimulation therapy specifically prescribed for apparent defect in language process. The essential role of recall in language is recognized and embodied in mnemonic training. Finally, emphasis on the potential of feedback has stimulated a new concept of therapy based on self-correction (*17*).

RESEARCH

These hypothetical constructs were in part developed prior to the present research and in part as the result of discussion following early stages of the research itself. Two lines of investigation have been established. Originally, our research set out to explore the stimulus-response relationship in aphasia along the common modalities of input (auditory, visual) and output (verbal, graphic). The research design necessitated the development of a new test, the Language Modalities Test for Aphasia. By its design, this test explores the ability of aphasic adults to respond to carefully standardized visual and auditory stimuli in speech and writing. By the differential evaluation of erroneous responses to items on the test, evidence has been forthcoming on the symbolic or nonsymbolic nature of the language problems.

The second phase of research deals with the analysis in psycholinguistic terms of the free verbal output of aphasic adults in response to a standard social situation picture (Thematic Apperception Test). It was in the early stages of this phase of research that the need for a model of spoken language from unimpaired adults was recognized. Consequently, a secondary goal was established: to collect from a sample of unimpaired adults spontaneous speech responses to the same social situation pictures. Stratification of the normal sample was based upon (1) socio-economic status plus educational level, (2) sex and (3) age. This sample of carefully transcribed free speech provides anyone wishing to study normal or pathological speech, with a base line for estimating deviations in spoken language.

Each transcript was analyzed statistically to determine the relative incidence of certain elements of language which could be defined in linguistic terms. At the first level of analysis, the incidence of minimal free forms (simple words) was determined and the grammatical function served by the form noted. Also, a phonological (phonemic) analysis was made of all non-English spoken forms.

From the transcripts of the normal subjects, it was possible to establish the expected distribution of the forms, cross-classify by frequency-rank and grammatical function. The defect in each aphasic subject's speech was then characterized in terms of the deviation of his distribution from that expected for normal subjects.

A second level of analysis, which is especially important for characterizing the speech of aphasic subjects with less severe defects, employed phrases and clauses as the elements of analysis. The incidence of certain basic phrase forms in the transcripts was determined and their distributions in normal speech established. By examining the corresponding distribution in the speech of each aphasic subject, defects in speech which involve the grammar and syntax of language, rather than command of words, were characterized. Further methodology for research at this level is now being developed.

The classifications of aphasic subjects which result from this type of analysis are being studied in connection with (1) the etiology of the aphasia and location of insult, (2) responses of the aphasic subjects to the Language Modalities Test for Aphasia, which indicates differences in language defect associated with specific types of stimuli, responses and errors and (3) the progress of the subject in subsequent therapy when such information is available.

If the research results confirm our hypotheses, the following important implications are foreseen: (1) A research tool will have been defined and a methodology developed for studying all forms of disturbance in language formulation, whether the disruption is organic or psychogenic. (2) There will have been established a beginning, at least, toward some understanding of the normal language act by the greater knowledge and finer definition of the organization of languages process. (3) A method will have been established for categorizing aphasic language based upon residual speech as well as upon areas of loss. This has the merit of developing a positive approach to an understanding of the aphasic patient in terms of his retained language abilities rather than in the limited terms of nosological characterization now so widely used. Such a categorization should also lead to the direct planning of a therapeutic program for aphasic patients from the residual speech efforts, something which has been previously lacking. (4) By combining the study of the aphasic adult's residual speech with a study of his retained or disrupted stimulus-response relationship in language it is hoped to provide information relative to the effects of the respective modalities on specific aphasic disturbances.

Further studies are projected using this data and accumulating additional data on (1) other pathological groups, e.g., schizophrenics, (2) further special aphasic groups, (3) groups at different age levels and (4) children in the process of developing speech.

SUMMARY

This paper presents the background and theoretical concepts leading to ongoing clinical procedures and research into disordered language processes. It begins with a brief review of the more important early neurological theories which form the structure for the current emphasis on therapy for aphasia. While these concepts led to static classification systems useful for nosological categorization, they have proven considerably less useful in understanding the language process itself. There was seen to be a need for a modern concept of aphasia which explores the dynamic nature of language as well as the direct structure of therapy.

It was shown in developing the present theory how the oversimplified dichotomy of sensory input leading directly to motor output failed to express the essential integrative process of language formulation. In its place the present concept shows a triad of events in which modality-bound input leads to integration and symbol formulation which in turn leads to modality-bound motor output. A model for this sequence was shown, demonstrating the agnosias and apraxias as transmissive disorders, nonsymbolic in nature, bound by the pathways of reception and expression. The aphasias are shown as disruptions in the symbolic language process. Here the disturbances in the language function are seen to be of at least three presently demonstrable types, tentatively labelled, after Morris (*10*), semantic, syntactic and pragmatic, to correspond to the linguistic differences found in the residual language of brain-injured patients.

The contributions of such a model to operational diagnosis and to the planning of therapy were noted. The direct training procedures for the agnosias and apraxias were contrasted with the indirect stimulative approaches found useful for the aphasias. Changes found in the verbal production of aphasic subjects and described in psycholinguistic terms, when compared with the verbal production of normal speakers, was elaborated and the clinical use that could be made of such data discussed.

References

1. Broca, P., Remarques sur le siege de la faculte du language article suive d'une observation d'aphemia. *Bulletin de la Societe Anatomique de Paris,* Aout, 1861.
2. Cassirer, E., *Essay on Man.* New Haven: Yale University Press, 1944.
3. Dusser de Barenne, J. G., Corticalization of function and functional localization in the cerebral cortex. *Arch. Neurol. and Psychiat.,* Chicago, 1933, 30, 884–901.
4. Freud, S., *On Aphasia.* New York: Int. University Press, Inc., 1953.
5. Goldstein, K., *Language and Language Disturbances.* New York: Grune & Stratton, 1948.
6. Harlow, H., and Woolsey, C. N. (ed.), *Biological and Biochemical Bases of Behavior.* Madison: University of Wisconsin Press, 1958.
7. Head, H., *Aphasia and Kindred Disorders of Speech.* New York: Macmillan, 1926.
8. Lashley, K., *Brain Mechanisms and Intelligence.* Chicago: University of Chicago Press, 1929.
9. Livingston, W. K., Haugen, F. P., and Brookhart, J. M., Functional organization of the central nervous system. *Neurology,* 1954, 4, 485–496.
10. Morris, C. W., Foundations of the theory of signs. *International Encyclopedia of Unified Science,* 1 (2). Chicago: University of Chicago Press, 1938.

11. Osgood, C. E., *Method and Theory in Experimental Psychology.* New York: Oxford University Press, 1953.

12. Penfield, W., and Roberts, L., *Speech and Brain-Mechanisms.* Princeton: Princeton University Press, 1959.

13. Sherrington, C., *The Brain and Its Mechanism.* Cambridge: Cambridge University Press, 1933.

14. Taylor, J. (ed.), *Selected Writings of John Hughlings Jackson.* London: Hodder and Stoughton, 1931.

15. Weisenberg, T., and McBride, K., *Aphasia: a Clinical and Psychological Study.* New York: The Commonwealth Fund, 1935.

16. Wepman, J. M., A conceptual model for the processes involved in recovery from aphasia. *J. Speech Hearing Dis.,* 1953, 18, 4–13.

17. Wepman, J. M., The relationship between self-correction and recovery from aphasia. *J. Speech Hearing Dis.,* 1958, 23, 302–305.

18. Wepman, J. M., and Van Pelt, D., A theory of cerebral language disorders based on therapy. *Folia Phoniatrica,* 1955, 7, 223–235.

19. Wernicke, C., *Der Aphasische Symptomenkomplex.* Breslau, 1874.

Stuttering Behavior And Learning: A Preliminary Theoretical Formulation

GEORGE J. WISCHNER*

The need for some kind of integration of the highly heterogeneous clinical and experimental data in the field of stuttering is generally recognized by those working in this area. Certain recent attempts at unification have been in the nature of a survey of existing facts. The purpose of Reid's discussion (*37*), for example, 'is to survey the generally accepted facts and to interpret some of the persistent questions.' Schuell (*38*) has presented an extensive summary of sex differences in relation to stuttering. Biochemical and physiological investigations of stuttering have been summarized and evaluated by Hill (*20, 21*).

Other attempts at integration (*1, 2, 16*) appear to have been motivated in part by clinical needs. They have consisted of a classification and exposition of stuttering theories and therapies in a form which would make the more important viewpoints and procedures readily available to those engaged in the management of stuttering cases.

A more systematic kind of integration recently has been offered by Hill (*19*), who has presented a discussion of stuttering within Kantor's interbehavioral analysis framework. The present writer elsewhere (*44, 45*) has proposed a systematic consideration of the problem of stuttering within another frame of reference, namely that of behavior or learning theory. The choice of a particular learning frame of reference does not imply that others might not be pursued with profit. It is the writer's bias that the most fruitful learning concepts and principles for the experimental investigation of stuttering stem from conditioning and learning phenomena of the nature of those first studied by Pavlov (*36*) and later further investigated and integrated particularly by Hull (*22*) and his students. This bias has been strengthened by the results of experiments which have

* This article is adapted from a paper presented at the annual meeting of the Midwestern Psychological Association, Detroit, 1950. It is based on a portion of a doctoral dissertation completed at the State University of Iowa under the direction of Professors Wendell Johnson and Kenneth W. Spence.

George J. Wischner, "Stuttering Behavior and Learning: A Preliminary Theoretical Formulation," *Journal of Speech and Hearing Disorders,* 15 (1950), 324–335. Reprinted by permission of the author and publisher.

already been completed as part of a program of research designed to examine the fruitfulness of the application of such concepts and principles to certain stuttering phenomena (*44, 45*). The research program takes as points of departure the following: (1) the adaptation effect in stuttering behavior; (2) the anticipation phenomenon and the roles of expectancy and anxiety in stuttering behavior.

EXPERIMENTAL PROGRAM

Stuttering Adaptation

The adaptation effect in stuttering refers to the progressive reduction in frequency of stuttering behavior with successive readings of the same material. The phenomenon was first reported in a study by Johnson and Knott (*26*). Since this experiment, stuttering adaptation has been noted in a variety of investigations of which those by Harris (*17*), Johnson and Inness (*25*) and Shulman (*39*) are representative.

The present writer has been particularly interested in the course or curve of stuttering adaptation. The curve of adaptation is fairly smooth and is characterized by a relatively sharp drop in the early readings as compared with the later trials. It resembles in appearance the curve of response decrement obtained in connection with the experimental extinction of conditioned and unconditioned responses. A basic group of experiments, some of which have already been completed by this writer and others, have aimed to determine whether one can produce in the stuttering laboratory analogues of certain empirical phenomena observed in conditioning and learning investigations. Although not unequivocal in all studies, results suggest that one may demonstrate in stuttering behavior such analogues as spontaneous recovery (*29, 44, 45*), external inhibition (*45*), disinhibition (*45*) and conditioned inhibition (*46*). Other studies, including projected ones, have been concerned with more complex functional relationships such as the course of successive stuttering adaptations and recovery (*29, 45*), stuttering adaptation as a function of excitant and depressant drugs (*32*), disinhibition as a function of the type of extra stimulation, spontaneous recovery of stuttering behavior as a function of the degree of adaptation, spontaneous recovery of stuttering behavior as a function of the recovery interval, etc.

Expectancy and Anxiety in Stuttering Behavior. The approach to expectancy and anxiety variables in stuttering behavior has been influenced by data in the stuttering literature which represent events on several levels of description. Johnson and his students (*24, 27, 28, 31*), for example, have employed the term expectancy, or anticipation, in a purely descriptive manner to describe the empirical finding that stutterers are able to predict with a high degree of accuracy the words on which they will stutter. The general procedure has been simply to have the stutterer indicate in some fashion, before saying a word, whether or not he expects (anticipates) difficulty with the word. For example, the subject may first underscore such words while reading a passage silently to himself and then read aloud another unmarked copy of the material.

There is some evidence to suggest that stutterers can predict not only the moment of stuttering, but also its duration as judged on a qualitative scale, with descriptive points such as medium, long and severe stuttering (*43*).

Other investigators have concerned themselves with the physiological bases of expectancy. According to Van Riper (*41*), for example, expectancy is no vague abstraction, but 'consists of tiny rehearsal movements and increases in tonus of the musculatures.' In one study (*42*) Van Riper investigated the thoracic breathing of stutterers during the expectancy period and the overt stuttering. He writes as follows:

> Most of the words on which expectancy of block occurred could be distinguished from those which were not feared by the Inspiration-Expiration duration ratio existing immediately subsequent to the exposure of the word. The stutterer saw the word; some cue set off the expectancy, either the association with past stuttering experiences of the first letter, or the meaning of the word, or the word as a word. As this occurred, he prolonged his inspiration, not necessarily taking a longer breath, but merely taking longer to achieve the usual inflation.
>
> When, on the contrary, the word was not feared, expiration was slightly longer in duration and the amplitudes of inspiration and expiration were approximately equal. It is interesting that the duration of expiration during non-expectancy should be longer than in normal silent breathing. This, it is felt, is to be explained in terms of the relief and definite ease felt when the exposed word was seen as 'easy.'

The present experimental attack on the anxiety factor in stuttering has come from several angles. First, it has been extremely valuable to distinguish between *general situation anxiety,* and *specific word anxiety.* These two types of anxiety are similar to those proposed by Van Riper (*40*) and are defined by the antecedent conditions which give rise to them. Stimuli which elicit situational anxiety are essentially nonverbal in character and may include general speech situations of all kinds—the nature of the audience (sex, number, age, relationship to stutterer, such as parent, teacher, minister, etc.) and physical characteristics, such as telephone or microphone. Specific word anxiety is instigated by stimuli which are wholly verbal in character and include specific words and the cues associated with them, such as formal components (beginning consonant, grammatical function, etc.) or meaning. Experiments have been completed which have studied stuttering behavior as a function of general situational anxiety and specific word anxiety with either one held constant or both varied simultaneously (*45*). A study by Dixon (*12*) has been concerned with stuttering frequency and adaptation as a function of the degree of situational anxiety. He found that within each level of anxiety there is an adaptation effect. The primary function of situational anxiety appears to be to fix the height of the adaptation curve.

A study by the author (*45*) suggests that there is an expectancy adaptation phenomenon which resembles the stuttering adaptation phenomenon. In a situation in which stutterers never read the material, but marked the words on which they expected to stutter were they called upon to read it, the frequency of anticipated words (markings) decreased with successive markings of the same material.

Gross (*15*) has reported findings which suggest an anxiety gradient in stuttering behavior. The specific hypothesis tested was that the frequency of stuttering behavior is some function of the time interval between the exposure of a stimulus word and a signal for the stutterer to say the word. It was assumed that at least some words represent danger signals which arouse anxiety; this anxiety is minimal upon presentation of the word and increases gradually with time to some maximum. The longer the time interval between the presentation of the word and the signal to speak, presumably the greater the anxiety and therefore the greater the probability that the word would be stuttered. The results of two separate studies reveal that beyond about one to two seconds the findings tend to support the hypothesis.

A study by Baron (*3*) has utilized the concept of stuttering anxiety as a drive in a prediction concerning the speed of acquisition of a conditioned eyelid response. One group of stutterers was conditioned in the usual manner. A second group was required to speak a word which occurred approximately one-half second following the unconditioned stimulus. The second group conditioned more rapidly and the results are interpreted as supporting a summation theory of drive. The anxiety instigated by having to speak a word is viewed as one component contributing to the total D (drive) in the situation.

THEORETICAL ANALYSIS

The present theoretical analysis of the problem of stuttering has been guided by two major working hypotheses: (1) stuttering behavior is learned, and (2) a basic secondary (acquired) motivational component in stuttering behavior is anxiety or anxiety drive. In other words, stuttering behavior involves a learned anxiety reaction system. There are certain facts and clinical observations concerning stuttering behavior which suggest that it involves an anxiety system which appears to be analogous in many respects to those studied in particular kinds of conditioning and learning experiments. It seems to resemble generally those responses which are originally established on the basis of noxious stimulation and more specifically those which are set up by what Hilgard and Marquis (*18*) have designated as instrumental avoidance training. With this type of training the organism learns to avoid noxious stimulation by reacting appropriately to a signal (conditioned stimulus) which occurs prior to the noxious stimulation. The general condtions for avoidance learning are exemplified in an experiment by Brogden, Lipman, and Culler (*4*). In this investigation animals were trained to run in a revolving cage in response to a buzzer with shock as the unconditioned stimulus. In one group, animals were shocked even when they responded to the buzzer by running. This condition is similar to the classical Pavlovian conditioning procedure where the unconditioned stimulus always follows the conditioned stimulus. In a second group, animals did not receive a shock if they ran in response to the buzzer signal (avoidance training procedure). Hilgard and Marquis (*18*) summarize and interpret the results as follows:

> Guinea pigs which were shocked whether or not they ran continued to show anticipatory agitation at the sound of the buzzer, but after the first few trials the tendency to run did not increase; those shocked only if they did not run developed the habit of running promptly at the sound of the buzzer. Learning in this situation appears to be based in a real sense on the avoidance of the shock. It differs clearly from other types of instrumental training in which the conditioned response is followed by a definite stimulus change—food or the cessation of shock. In instrumental avoidance training the new response is strengthened in the absence of any such stimulus; indeed it is strengthened because of the absence of such a stimulus. Absence of stimulation can obviously have an influence on behavior only if there exists some sort of preparation for or expectation of the stimulation.

Of the extinction of responses based on avoidance training, Hilgard and Marquis say the following:

> It is apparent that the shock cannot be considered an unconditioned stimulus during the later stages of avoidance training. Omission of shock does not produce extinction but instead strengthens the conditioned response. Extinction can be secured only if the dog fails to respond for some reason and thereby 'discovers' that the tone is no longer followed by the shock. After several trials of this sort extinction progresses rapidly.

In avoidance training, then, the successive experiences of the noxious stimulation do not reinforce behavior, and the absence of such stimulation does not lead necessarily to extinction. Avoidance training appears to represent one set of experimental conditions in which the occurrence or non-occurrence of a response seems to be correlated with the presence of a state of expectancy (anxiety) in the organism.

The occurrence or non-occurrence of overt stuttering, as has been seen, also appears to be correlated with the presence or absence of expectancy (anxiety). The assumption that stuttering anxiety is similar to that developed in the learning laboratory raises a number of basic questions. The answers to most of these questions are to be found in research not only in the stuttering area but in broader areas within psychology. The following sections consider these questions as they seem to present themselves within a learning frame of reference.

What are the Current Instigators (Danger Signals) to Anxiety in Stuttering Behavior?

Clinical and experimental evidence indicates rather clearly that the more apparent current instigators to anxiety in the stutterer include speech situations in general and certain words (and the cues associated with them) in particular (*5, 6, 7, 8, 9, 10*).[1] It seems to be a reasonable assumption that for the stutterer anxiety aroused by a word is similar to that evoked by 'danger signals' (conditioned stimuli) employed in learning experiments. It is important to note that the present instigators to anxiety were not originally dangerous in themselves. They are not to be confused with the initial conditions (original instigators) which originally elicited the anxiety. Present danger signals have acquired the capacity to evoke anxiety as a result of a learning process.[2] Their adaptive function is to arouse anxiety in anticipation of the occurrence of noxious stimulation. This anxiety leads to activity to avoid such stimulation.

What is the Stutterer Attempting to Avoid?

The answer to this question would seem to require the specification of the initial conditions (original instigators) which originally evoked the anxiety. An individual clinical approach to the problem of stuttering behavior would imply that the specific initial conditions would need to be determined for each stutterer individually. From a systematic standpoint, it is assumed that these initial conditions, whatever they might be in any particular case, generally constitute painful stimulation.

Johnson (*23*) has presented a theory of the onset and development of stuttering behavior which suggests a more specific hypothesis concerning the nature of the original anxiety-inducing stimulus complex. According to Johnson, a distinction must be made between non-fluency and stuttering. *Non-fluency* refers to the ordinary 'ahs' and 'uhs,' and the hesitations and repetitions which are to be found in the speech of most individuals. Repetitions, it is emphasized, are characteristic of the normal speech of young children and occur in some degree on from 15 to 25 per cent of their words (*11*). Stuttering, says Johnson (*23*), is an avoidance reaction, 'designed to avoid the non-fluency which the individual has learned to fear and dread and expect.' Elsewhere in the same chapter it is stated that stuttering is 'an attempt to avoid the non-fluency that was originally disapproved.'

It seems to be a tenable hypothesis that the original instigators to anxiety in the stutterer are to be found in this original disapproval. Within the present learning frame of reference, however, it would appear to be more accurate to say that the adult stutterer is avoiding, not non-fluency as such, but the original consequences (noxious stimulation) which attended the original non-fluent behavior. These consequences are presumed to center about the behavior of adults in the child's environment, and to arouse painful reactions in the child.

Historically, the sequence of the development of anxiety in the child might be described as follows: The child's nor-

[1] It should be noted that we are concerned here with immediate cues which precipitate a change in anxiety level in the stutterer. Whether stutterers are generally more anxious individuals than non-stutterers is another problem capable of experimental investigation.

[2] The mechanism of stimulus generalization would appear to play a significant role in this connection.

mal non-fluent speech serves as a stimulus to adults (parents, teachers) in his environment to which they respond with disapproval and censure. The reactions of the adults, in turn, have stimulus value for the child and elicit painful reactions in him. These painful reactions become, in turn, response-produced stimulation which evokes a state of anxiety. This anxiety (anticipation of pain) possesses drive properties and motivates the child to activity designed to avoid the noxious stimulation. It is significant that the stimulus cues which are present at this time include persons and words, cues which serve so adequately as instigators to anxiety in the adult stutterer.[3]

How Does the Anxiety Lead to Stuttering Behavior?

The above schematic outline of the development of anxiety in the individual who stutters does not tell us how this anxiety leads to stuttering behavior. After all, not all children who develop anxiety become stutterers. Here is the general problem of symptom choice, the answers to which are yet to be found in experimental investigations of the hypotheses concerning the development and fixation of maladaptive behavior generally.

In those instances where it can be readily demonstrated that the actions of the adult are directly associated with the speech behavior of the child, it seems reasonable that the anxiety may become focalized about the act of speaking. There appear to be at least two alternative hypotheses concerning the relationship between the anxiety and the manifestation of what is recognized as stuttering behavior.

A first hypothesis assumes that although the anxiety is learned, the stuttering behavior itself is not learned, but represents a disorganization of speech behavior consequent upon the state of anxiety which is specific to the speech act. In this connection reference may be made to Mowrer's assumption (*33*) that when anticipatory tensions are very intense and are not greatly diminished by the reactions they help to produce, there may be no learning, but a disintegration of behavior.

A second hypothesis assumes that both the anxiety and the stuttering behavior are learned. It follows Mowrer's formulation (*34*) which postulates that the acquired anxiety is a drive state which motivates the individual to engage in behavior which will lead to escape from the painful stimulation. Those acts which lead to escape are reinforced as a result of the anxiety reduction which accompanies them. In the case of stuttering behavior, it may be that for the child one way of avoiding disapproval (painful stimulation) is not to talk at all. On the other hand, the pressure to communicate is so great that there is generated in the child a conflict between the desire to speak, and the fear of speaking in a certain manner. The child may try, at random, to speak in any one of a number of alternative ways.[4] That pattern of speech will tend to be used most often by the child which is not followed as regularly by punishment (disapproval) on the part of adults about him. That is, the speech behavior which leads to relatively successful avoidance of the anticipated noxious stimulation, and consequently a relatively greater reduction in anxiety, will be more strongly reinforced than the speech behavior which does not lead to equally successful avoidance of the painful stimulation. Why, then, does not the child adopt a 'normal' speech pattern? Perhaps because it is this 'normal' pattern with its normal non-fluencies which has served originally to initiate the anxiety-producing sequence of events.[5]

[3] In the above analysis of the development of anxiety, the sequence of events was assumed to be initiated by non-fluency in the child's speech behavior. It would appear desirable to make the analysis more general by substituting for non-fluency any behavioral pattern exhibited by the child which may lead to a punishing state of affairs.

[4] This random behavior may lead to faulty habits of usage of the speech organs generally.

[5] In those cases where it is difficult to dem-

What Perpetuates Stuttering Behavior?

The issues inherent in this question encompass far more than the stuttering problem alone. One is confronted here with the more general question as to why organisms may sometimes manifest persistent maladaptive or non-integrative behavior. In a recent article concerned with this highly important but complex problem, Mowrer and Ullman (*35*) write:

> Persistent non-integrative behavior, *i.e.*, behavior which has consequences which are usually more punishing than rewarding, remains one of the important unsolved problems in psychology.

It is the intention in this section to offer for consideration certain hypotheses regarding the possible mechanisms underlying the perpetuation of non-integrative behavior, with special reference to the problem of stuttering. Within the present frame of reference stuttering behavior, viewed as an acquired reaction pattern, may be regarded as one type of non-integrative behavior. The specificity and availability of the stuttering response would appear to afford an excellent opportunity for the study of the mechanisms perpetuating such behavior. The hypotheses regarding the nature of these mechanisms which are offered below are to be viewed as first approximations which may be refined on the basis of further analysis and experimentation.

1. It is proposed that the act of stuttering may be specifically reinforced by virtue of its relatively close association with anxiety-tension reduction accompanying the removal of a feared word. It is assumed that a feared word arouses a state of expectancy (anxiety) and that the act of stuttering on the word is reinforced by the tension reduction accompanying the completion of the word on which difficulty is experienced. This hypothesis emphasizes the possibility of a vicious cycle in stuttering behavior in which the completion of the stuttered act results in a reduction of the anxiety-tension evoked by the stumulus word, with consequent reinforcement of the stuttering behavior.

2. That stutterers manifest varied types of avoidance behavior has been shown by Kimmell (30). Some of these avoidances are specific to the speech act itself. For example, many stutterers deliberately develop large vocabularies so that when they come to a feared word, they may substitute another word for it. Other avoidances are associated with speech situations or social situations generally. Stutterers will avoid class recitations, parties, dates, etc. It is assumed that such avoidance behavior is strengthened by an anxiety reduction mechanism. The word or situation arouses the anxiety which leads to behavior to avoid the dangerous stimulus situation. The anxiety reduction accompanying the escape from a feared situation reinforces the behavior which leads to escape.

3. The expectancy phenomenon in stuttering behavior suggests one other possible mechanism of reinforcement which is based, not on tension or anxiety reduction, but on the confirmation of an expectancy (*18*). The mechanism in this case might be described figuratively as a self-verification by the stutterer of his expectation of stuttering.

4. Earlier, reference was made to stuttering behavior as an example of non-integrative behavior which is more punishing than rewarding. Thus far only reinforcing mechanisms in stuttering behavior have been considered. That there are penalties attached to stuttering behavior

---

onstrate specific disapproval by adults of the child's speech behavior, it is more difficult to see how the anxiety becomes attached specifically to speech behavior. In this connection may be noted the stress placed by some writers on the attention-getting value of certain behavioral patterns in childhood. If lack of attention represents a punishing state of affairs which leads to the development of an anxiety system, and this anxiety is reduced by the attention given by adults to a particular type of speech behavior, the latter will tend to be reinforced.

and that the act of stuttering itself is unpleasant would be emphasized by practically all stutterers. So far as the fixation of behavior is concerned, what does occur when an act is followed by both reward and punishment? One of the more recent theoretical treatments of this problem is that by Mowrer and Ullman (*35*). Their hypothesis, which is supported in part by experimental evidence is as follows:

The consequences of a given act determine the future of that act not only in terms of what may be called their quantitative aspects, but also in terms of their *temporal pattern.* In other words, if an act has two consequences —the one rewarding and the other punishing —which would be strictly equal if simultaneous, the influence of those consequences upon later performances of that act will vary depending upon the *order* in which they occur. If the punishing consequence comes first and the rewarding one later, the difference will be in favor of the inhibition. But if the rewarding consequence comes first and the punishing one later, the difference will be in favor of the reinforcement.

According to our earlier analysis of the original development of anxiety in the stutterer, a pattern other than the disapproved (punished) normal non-fluent pattern led to anxiety reduction and therefore consequent reinforcement. This would make it appear that the original stuttering behavior was reinforced by anxiety reduction first although it may have been punished later. The first hypothesis concerning the reinforcement mechanism in stuttering behavior assumed that the stuttering act is reinforced by the tension reduction consequent upon the completion of a stuttered word. It would seem, then, that in the case of stuttering behavior, though there may be both reward and punishment, the initial consequence is probably that of reinforcement due to tension reduction. According to the Mowrer-Ullman hypothesis, this would result in fixation of the non-integrative stuttering behavior.

5. That there may be numerous secondary gains connected with stuttering behavior is pointed out by Fenichel (*13*). One factor mentioned by Fenichel is the pity that may be aroused in others and that may be utilized by the stutterer. Clinical experience reveals a wide variety of material benefits that may accrue to the stutterer without his necessarily being aware of them. Thus there may be 'considerate' teachers who excuse Jimmie from recitation. Or Bill may receive a medical discharge from the Army on the basis of his speech with a disability pension attached. All of these may well serve to reinforce stuttering behavior. It seems important from a therapeutic standpoint to investigate very carefully the possibility of secondary gain in each stuttering case. To accept the stutterer's negative reply at face value to the question, 'Does your stuttering bring any rewards?' is inadequate, since the stutterer very often is not directly aware of the benefits that he might be deriving from his speech behavior.

6. All the above hypotheses regarding the perpetuation of stuttering behavior have involved some kind of reinforcing mechanism. The problem may be approached from a somewhat different point of view by asking, 'What prevents the extinction of stuttering behavior?' An immediate answer is to be seen in the reinforcement of the stuttering behavior by any one or more of the mechanisms proposed thus far. Another possibility is suggested by the previous analogy between stuttering behavior and responses established on the basis of avoidance training in the learning laboratory. The extinction of responses set up by avoidance conditioning is relatively difficult. Such responses can be eliminated only if the animal, for some reason, does not respond to the danger signal, and 'discovers' that there is no shock.

The analogy to stuttering behavior is somewhat as follows: The stutterer has originally established an avoidance reaction with reference to a particular type of speech pattern (presumably one of normal non-fluency) as a result of punishment (disapproval) consequent upon the manifestation of this speech pattern. This avoidance reaction is strengthened in the absence of this punishment by an anxiety-reduction mechanism. For extinction of this avoidance behavior to occur, it would be necessary for the stutterer to manifest the original non-fluent pattern and find that it is no longer followed by punishment. Figuratively speaking, he must exhibit the original speech behavior and learn that 'the electric grill is no longer hot.'

It is interesting in this connection that when a stutterer is asked, 'What are you avoiding?' or 'What do you expect to happen?' he usually gives only vague answers, if any. It may very well be that the adult stutterer may have long forgotten, if he was ever directly aware of, the circumstances surrounding the original instigation to anxiety. From a therapeutic standpoint it may be necessary to determine, by a counseling procedure, what these circumstances might have been. Only then may it be advisable to have the stutterer engage in a non-fluent pattern approximating that which served to initiate the original anxiety-inducing sequence. And only in this way can the stutterer learn that 'the grill is no longer charged'; that whatever he anticipates in fact does not occur.

What Determines the Nature of the Particular Symptoms Entering into the Stuttering Pattern?

It is readily apparent that stuttering patterns vary from one stutterer to another and that for an individual stutterer the pattern may change with time. The basis for this variation, it is believed, is to be found in a learning process. Those symptoms are acquired which are accompanied by reinforcement. Clinical observation indicates that stutterers may consciously utilize certain movements, facial and bodily, because as they say 'they feel it helps them to get the word out.' Such movements ultimately become integrated through continual reinforcement into the total stuttering pattern.[6] The implications of such a view are rather interesting. The stutterer anticipates something, either a 'block' or 'something else,' and he then brings to bear all his resources to help him over this 'something.' These resources include the very devices which are identified by the observer as the stuttering pattern.

SUMMARY

The general nature of a program of research designed as a systematic experimental approach to the problem of stuttering as learned behavior has been outlined. Basic points of departure for the research program are provided by previously reported data concerning the stuttering adaptation effect and the role of expectancy and anxiety in stuttering behavior. One major group of studies has attempted to determine whether one can produce in the stuttering laboratory analogues of certain empirical phenomena observed in conditioning and learning studies such as spontaneous recovery, external inhibition, conditioned inhibition and disinhibition. An allied group of experiments has been concerned with more complex relationships such as the course

[6] Noteworthy in this connection is Froeschels' (*14*) account of the development of accompanying movements, which, although similar to the present formulation, is not systematically related to a reinforcement learning theory. According to Froeschels,

> Accompanying movements probably originate as reflexes. They distract the patient's attention from his speech and thereby break the vicious circle: the patient is able to speak more fluently for the moment. When stutterers become aware of the relief they have accidentally found, they may employ these movements deliberately. After a while, however, a given movement loses its suggestive power. The stutterer, ever resourceful within the confines of his neurosis, usually invents a new movement. In addition, the old one often persists, and may become automatic.

of successive stuttering adaptations and recovery, stuttering adaption as a function of excitant and depressant drugs, the time interval between adaptation and recovery trials, and other variables.

The approach to expectancy and anxiety variables in stuttering behavior has proceeded along various lines. A distinction is made between two kinds of anxiety in stuttering behavior, differentiated, with reference to the stimuli evoking them, into general situational anxiety and specific word anxiety. Research has been concerned with stuttering frequency and adapatation as a function of variation in one kind of anxiety with the other held constant, and with simultaneous variation in both types of anxiety. Other studies have been concerned with the investigation of an anxiety gradient in stuttering behavior and the utilization of stuttering anxiety in a prediction concerning the speed of acquisition of a conditioned eyelid response.

The general working hypothesis that stuttering behavior is a learned anxiety reaction system is presented and elaborated. A major portion of the present article is devoted to a theorctical analysis of the stuttering problem based on this hypothesis. The theoretical approach is pointed up in a discussion centering around the following basic questions: (1) What are the current instigators to anxiety in stuttering behavior? (2) What is the stutterer attempting to avoid? (3) How does the anxiety lead to stuttering behavior? (4) What determines the nature of the particular symptomatic stuttering pattern? (5) What perpetuates stuttering behavior? In connection with the last question several hypotheses regarding the reinforcing factors responsible for the perpetuation of the stuttering response are presented.

References

1. Ainsworth, S. An organized approach to the therapy of stuttering. *JSD,* 1942, 7, 325–328.
2. ——. Integrating theories of stuttering. *JSD,* 1945, 10, 205–210.
3. Baron, M. The effect on eyelid conditioning of a speech variable in stutterers and non-stutterers. Ph.D. Dissertation, State Univ. Iowa, 1949.
4. Brogden, W. J., Lipman, E. A. and Culler, E. The role of incentive in conditioning and extinction. *Amer. J. Psychol.*, 1938, 51, 107–117.
5. Brown, S. F. A further study of stuttering in relation to various speech sounds. *Quart. J. Speech,* 1938, 24, 390–397.
6. ——. The influence of grammatical functions on the incidence of stuttering. *JSD,* 1937, 2, 207–215.
7. ——. The loci of stutterings in the speech sequence. *JSD,* 1945, 10, 181–192.
8. ——. A study of stuttering in relation to word length. *JSD,* 1942, 7, 153–159.
9. ——. Stuttering with relation to word accent and word position. *J. abnorm. soc. Psychol.,* 1938, 33, 112–120.
10. ——. The theoretical importance of certain factors influencing the incidence of stuttering. *JSD,* 1938, 3, 223–230.
11. Davis, D. M. The relation of repetitions in the speech of young children to certain measures of language maturity and situational factors. *JSD,* 1939, 4, 303–318; 1940, 5, 235–246.
12. Dixon, C. The amount and rate of adaptation of stuttering in different oral reading situations. M.A. Thesis, State Univ. Iowa, 1947.
13. Fenichel, O. *The Psychoanalytic Theory of Neurosis*. New York: W. W. Norton, 1945.
14. Froeschels, E. Pathology and therapy of stuttering. In Froeschels, E. (Ed.) *Twentieth Century Speech*

and Voice Correction. New York: Philosophical Library, 1948.

15. Goss, A. An experimental study of an expectancy (anxiety) gradient in stuttering behavior. M.A. Thesis, State Univ. Iowa, 1947.
16. Hahn, E. F. *Stuttering: Significant Theories and Therapies*. Stanford Univ.: Stanford Univ. Press, 1943.
17. Harris, W. E. Studies in the psychology of stuttering: XVII. A study of the transfer of the adaptation effect in stuttering. *JSD*, 1942, 7, 209–221.
18. Hilgard, E. R. and Marquis, D. G. *Conditioning and Learning*. New York: Appleton-Century, 1940.
19. Hill, H. An interbehavioral analysis of several aspects of stuttering. *J. gen. Psychol.*, 1945, 32, 289–316.
20. ——. Stuttering: I. A critical review and evaluation of biochemical investigations. *JSD*, 1944, 9, 245–261.
21. ——. Stuttering: II. A review and integration of physiological data. *JSD*, 1944, 9, 289–324.
22. Hull, C. L. *Principles of Behavior*. New York: Appleton-Century, 1943.
23. Johnson, W. *People in Quandaries*. New York: Harper, 1946.
24. Johnson, W. and Ainsworth, S. Studies in the psychology of stuttering. X. Constancy of loci of expectancy of stuttering. *JSD*, 1938, 3, 101–104.
25. Johnson, W. and Inness, M. Studies in the psychology of stuttering. XIII. A statistical analysis of the adaptation and consistency effects in relation to stuttering. *JSD*, 1939, 4, 79–86.
26. Johnson, W. and Knott, J. R. Studies in the psychology of stuttering. I. The distribution of moment of stuttering in successive readings of the same material. *JSD*, 1937, 2, 17–19.
27. Johnson, W. and Sinn, A. Studies in the psychology of stuttering. V. Frequency of stuttering with expectation of stuttering controlled. *JSD*, 1937, 2, 98–100.
28. Johnson, W. and Solomon, A. Studies in the psychology of stuttering. IV. A quantitative study of expectation of stuttering as a process involving a low degree of consciousness. *JSD*, 1937, 2, 95–97.
29. Jones, E. L. Adaptation and spontaneous recovery in stuttering behavior. Ph. D. Dissertation, State Univ. Iowa, 1950.
30. Kimmell, M. Studies in the psychology of stuttering. IX. The nature and effect of stutterer's avoidance reaction. *JSD*, 1938, 3, 95–100.
31. Knott, J. R., Johnson, W. and Webster, M. J. Studies in the psychology of stuttering. II. A quantitative evaluation of expectation of stuttering in relation to the occurrence of stuttering. *JSD*, 1937, 2, 20–22.
32. Love, W. R. The effect of pentobarbital sodium (nembutal) and amphetamine sulphate (benzedrine) on the severity of stuttering. M.A. Thesis, State Univ. Iowa, 1947.
33. Mowrer, O. H. Preparatory set (expectancy) a determinant in motivation and learning. *Psychol. Rev.*, 1938, 45, 62–91.
34. ——. A stimulus-response analysis of anxiety and its role as a reinforcing agent. *Psychol. Rev.*, 1939, 46, 553–566.
35. Mowrer, O. H. and Ullman, A. D. Time as a determinant in integrative learning. *Psychol. Rev.*, 1945, 52, 61–90.
36. Pavlov, I. P. *Conditioned Reflexes*. (Trans. by G. V. Anrep) London: Oxford Univ. Press, 1927.

37. Reid, L. D. Some facts about stuttering. *JSD*, 1946, 11, 3–12.

38. Schuell, H. Sex differences in relation to stuttering. *JSD*, 1946, 11, 277–298; 1947, 12, 23–38.

39. Shulman, E. A study of certain factors influencing the variability of stuttering. Ph.D. Dissertation, State Univ. Iowa, 1944.

40. Van Riper, C. The effect of devices for minimizing stuttering on the creation of symptoms. *J. abnorm. soc. Psychol.*, 1937, 32, 185–192.

41. ——. The preparatory set in stuttering. *JSD*, 1937, 2, 149–154.

42. ——. Study of the thoracic breathing of stutterers during expectancy and occurrence of stuttering spasm. *JSD*, 1936, 1, 61–72.

43. Van Riper, C. and Milisen, R. L. A study of the predicted duration of the stutterer's blocks as related to their actual duration. *JSD*, 1939, 4, 339–345.

44. Wischner, G. J. An experimental approach to stuttering as learned behavior. *Amer. Psychologist*, 1948, 278–279.

45. ——. Stuttering behavior and learning: A program of research. Ph.D. Dissertation, State Univ. Iowa, 1947.

46. Yensen, E. Stuttering adaptation and the role of cues. M.A. Thesis, State Univ. Iowa, 1947.

PART THREE

The Problem of Meaning

It is said that history repeats itself, and in a sense this is also true of the history of psychology. In the early years of psychology as a science, the study of the mind was the general concern of psychologists. The advent of Behaviorism switched the emphasis to the study of behavior. Nowadays, behavioristic psychologists define their field either in terms of mind or behavior (see, for example, Hebb, 1958). Today, in the age of electronic computers, mentalism is a perfectly acceptable mode of discourse as long as contemporary scientific standards of methodology are used in its investigation. The treatment which the problem of meaning is receiving in contemporary psychological literature reflects this concern with methodology. Major theoretical issues in meaning center as much around its measurement operations as its effect upon behavior.

The first four papers of this section represent four different approaches to the problem of meaning. Kaplan's contribution belongs to a line of thought which makes contact with European psychologists but which is least familiar to American psychologists: Piaget's genetic-developmental theory of perception (see Flavell, 1963), and Werner's "sensory-tonic" theory of perceptual development (see Werner and Kaplan, 1964). The theme of Kaplan's paper concerns the recognition of the importance of symbolic activity in man, pointed up by the suggestion that man would be more properly defined as an *animal symbolicum* rather than an *animal rationale*. To Kaplan, the problem of meaning relates to "man's capacity for transforming simple sensory material into symbolic vehicles—carriers of the finest intellectual and emotional distinctions." He contrasts two views: one, opposed to his, in which "translocation of something 'outside the mind' to a place 'inside the mind'." is accomplished independently of ontogenesis ("agenetic"); the individual gradually comes to perceive "things as they are;" the sign is an arbitrary conditioned stimulus to the referent. The second view, his own, is "genetic;" perception is not the "discovery" of the world but literally its "construction": it is made up by the "knower" and "doer" and intimately related to his genetic development. Perception is tied to symbolization which need not be verbal or conscious: there is no percept without concept. Kaplan recalls the Humboldtian sense of language which "is not restricted to vocal patterns." There is a constant contrast between the developmental approach ("sequence of stages in the relationship between symbolic activity and cognition") which concerns itself with the "physiognomic dynamic universe" and a universe independent of the observer who is supposed to abstract out common elements or conceptions. This preoccupation with genetic-perceptual processes leads him to a preference in research for non-verbal media of expression of symbolization (music, color, visual imagery, bodily movements).

It is interesting to note that Osgood's work on the "semantic differential" as summarized in the second paper of this section, was originally sparked by a similar preoccupation with the problem of "synesthesia" (the relationship between symbolizations across different perceptual modalities; see Osgood, 1953). Since 1952, Osgood and his associates (Osgood, 1952; Osgood, Suci, and Tannenbaum, 1957; Osgood, Archer, and Miron, 1962) have carried out a systematic investigation of meaning viewed as a spatial attribute of signs. According to this view, the meaning of a concept is given by its location in an imaginary "semantic space" such that spatially proximate concepts have similar meanings. The semantic differential is a rating instrument which specifies the dimensionality of the semantic space. In this paper, Osgood reports the results of extensive cross-cultural investigations designed to "discover" the dimensionality of semantic space in various cultures and languages accomplished by himself and his colleagues. The findings point to a consistency of semantic structure as evidenced by factorial invariance of three universal dimensions of meaning: evaluation, potency, and activity.

The third paper in this section represents an approach to the study of meaning strongly influenced by recent new developments in linguistics resulting from writings of Chomsky and his associates (Chomsky, 1957; Katz and Postal, 1964). Katz and Fodor view their contribution mainly as a "metatheory," that is, the characterization of the "abstract form" which a semantic theory of a natural language ought to take. To many linguists today, the striking fact about the use of language is the absence of repetition: "almost every sentence uttered is uttered for the first time." This approach places emphasis upon a characteristic feature of language by which it makes available "an infinity of sentences from which the speaker can select appropriate and novel ones to use as the need arises." The problem then becomes one of specifying the rules of grammar which a speaker must necessarily use in projecting the finite set of sentences he already knows to the infinite set of sentences of the language he is theoretically capable of producing. The solution to this projection problem is, according to this view, the (synchronic) description of a natural language. According to Katz and Fodor, if we subtract from the goals of a description of a language whatever the grammar contributes to the solution of the projection problem, we are left with the goals of a semantic theory. The formula then is: "synchronic linguistic description minus grammar equals semantics." ("Grammar" is used here in the broad sense which includes phonology, morphology, and syntax.) As a concrete illustration of their solution to the problem of semantics, Katz and Fodor attempt a semantic interpretation of the simple English sentence "the man hits the colorful ball." As the reader will note, this "simple" sentence has an amazing number of different possible interpretations.

The Bollinger article that follows provides a wealth of illuminating reactions to the specifics of the influential Katz and Fodor article. Setting aside the details, Bollinger's concern is over the theoretical difficulties inherent in opting for a limited and ungraded set of semantic markers or features with maximally wide applicability. His counter examples explicate the difficulty necessarily encountered in an attempt to isolate some such set of markers and their counterintuitive inadequacy once fixed. It is refreshing to have the delightful persuasiveness of Katz and Fodor's brilliance tempered by Bollinger's insightful critique in juxtaposition. Together these two articles provide perhaps the most serious and different approach to meaning that has emerged to date. Correct or incorrect, in detail or basis, semantic marker theory will undoubtedly influence most of the research and thinking concerning semantic aspects of language for some time to come. (See, for example, Osgood's prefatory statement to his paper "On Understanding and Creating Sentences" in Part 1).

Noble's relatively less involved paper, which follows, has also, nonetheless, been quite influential in recent research on meaning in behaviorist circles. Noble describes his contribution as "a theoretical-experimental analysis of the attribute of meaning in verbal stimulus material." His approach is entirely "intraverbal" in that he defines the meaning of a word in terms of other words with which it is associated. He proposes a "purely empirical concept"—the "*m*" index which refers to the number of associations given by a subject to a word within a predetermined limit of time, usually 60 seconds. Work on the role of "meaningfulness" in verbal learning has been extensive (see, for example, Underwood and Schulz, 1960). The question of the relationship between Noble's *m* and Osgood's semantic differential (SD) is the issue in the paper that follows. Staats and Staats view Noble's *m* as a measure of relationships between words, whereas SD represents to them "word-environmental relationships." They note that the correlation between *m* and polarity (intensity) of SD ratings is positive and substantial. They argue that words which tend to appear in the same (physical) enviroment will form associations between each other (clusters) and will tend to have similar meanings (see also Flavell, 1961, for an analogous view). Thus, the more often a stimulus word is paired with its associates, the stronger become the intraverbal associations between them. In addition, however, the meaning of each of the associates is "conditioned" to the stimulus word; therefore, repeated pairing would result in a correlation between intensity of meaning (polarity on SD) and word-association value (*m*). Nevertheless, it is possible to show that word-association meaning and SD meaning can be "conditioned" separately to nonsense words such that words can have high SD similarity but low overlap of associations. To support the contention that meaning can be conditioned, Staats and Staats present an experiment in the paper that follows in which such a demonstration is given.

"Conditioning of meaning" is also the subject of Johnson's paper which follows, yet his motivation stems from entirely different premises. According to Miller (see his paper in Part 2) active and passive sentences are "transforms" of the same "kernel" sentence. Johnson shows that when nonsense words are imbedded in active and passive sentences in subject and object syntactic positions, the resultant conditioned meaning (SD) which the nonsense words acquire are different. Because active and passive sentences show different distributional properties in meaning, Johnson believes that the transformational notion of a common kernel sentence is untenable. Instead, he interprets his data as supporting a view based on an analysis of amount of uncertainty given by the sentence structure.

The notion that meaning can be investigated by intraverbal associations is quite widespread among psychologists today. This view is perhaps not so different from the position of the early British empiricists who viewed the process of association as the basis for all mental (today we tend to say "cognitive") activity. In the paper that follows, Asch and Ebenholtz reexamine a fundamental tenet of the principle of association, namely its implication that associations are directional. This refers to the notion that if an *A—B* association is formed such that *B* follows *A* in experience, the established relationship will be in the same order, i.e., $A \rightarrow B$. The authors report seven experiments designed in such a way that each succeeding experiment attempts to clarify a point unanswered by those preceding it. The authors conclude that there is no evidence for the directionality of associations. They propose a theory of "associative symmetry," according to which there is an equality between backward and forward associations. Since associative symmetry permits the transition in recall from one term to another in more than one way, it represents greater latitude of cognitive functioning than hitherto believed.

The implications of viewing associations in this new light may be important to an understanding of its role in serial phenomena with which Lashley (1951) was concerned. It remains to be seen to what extent this new theoretical development will be more successful in accounting for the learning and use of grammar which many view as the basic problem in psycholinguistics.

The relationship between word associations and general linguistic usage is reexamined in the paper that follows. Stochastic analyses of language behavior were thoroughly investigated by Zipf (1949) whose work is now considered a classic (see also Miller, 1951). That the word association procedure yields responses comparable in certain stochastic properties to free discourse has been shown in some early work by Skinner (1937), as well as in more recent studies by French psychologists (Moscovici and Ackerman, 1961; Ajuriaguerra *et al.,* 1963). In this paper, Howes clarifies the relationship between associative probability of a word as measured by the Kent-

Rosanoff tables and the probability of emission of a word in general linguistic usage as measured by the Lorge magazine count. The high positive correlation previously suspected is once more corroborated. In addition, Howes is able to show that this relationship is reversed for a fairly small number of words called "interstitial" (conjunctions, articles, prepositions, auxiliaries, pronouns)—words which were systematically excluded from the Kent-Rosanoff stimulus list and which do not occur as associations despite their high occurrence in free discourse.

Part of the process of language learning is the acquisition of word associations. In this next paper, Ervin presents evidence that supports a theory of associations based on training by forward contiguity in speech. Her findings appear stable and have been replicated by Brown and Berko (1960). (For more detailed comparisons across age groups with an association task restricted to adjectival responses, see Di Vesta, 1965.)

The next couple of papers in this section deal with experimental investigations of the effects of meaning and word associations in a variety of cognitive situations related to the use of language. The Cofer and Foley paper, although quite old and admittedly rather dated in outlook (see Cofer's preface to the article), is perhaps the best example of the classic position of the behaviorist with respect to language. Miller might well have been speaking of these authors in "Some Preliminaries to Psycholinguistics" (see Part 1). Although the authors contrast their approach with something they call language morphology, "i.e., language as things—isolated words or syllables," their own views are nonetheless, by modern standards, quite atomistic and avowedly non-mentalistic approaches which, at the time these authors were writing, were all too well accepted as gospel. One needs only to contrast this with Katz's "Mentalism in Linguistics" in Part 1 to see the drastic change which has taken place since 1942. In 1943 these same authors (Foley and Cofer, 1943) published the second part of the paper which provided empirical support of the theory delineated in this reprinted selection. They show that generalization occurs not only from a word to its synonym or homonym but to other words related along lines of relationship even further removed. They suggest that the basis for such generalizations may be in verbal chains such as $A \rightarrow B \rightarrow C$ in which B is a synonym of A and C is a synonym of B, but C is not a synonym of A. This kind of "mediate association" has been investigated for many years (e.g., Peters, 1935; Russell and Storms, 1955). When associative chains are used to study verbal learning its effect is known as "mediated facilitation." The paper by McGehee and Schulz uses a classic design in the study of mediated facilitation as follows: the subject is first given a paired-associate task involving A-B pairs; then he is required to learn an A-D list in which D is related to B through C ($B \rightarrow C \rightarrow D$). By comparing the efficiency of A-D learning to a number of control lists, the amount of the facilitation effect can be assessed. (For an example of generalization of inhibition or "mediated satiation," see Jakobovits and Lambert, 1962.)

The problem of mediated generalization is important in a survey of psycholinguistics, since mediational accounts of grammatical phenomena represent one of the few attempts by psychologists to deal directly with this problem (see Jenkins, 1964; Jenkins and Palermo, 1964; Smith, 1964; Braine, 1963; Skinner, 1957). (For criticisms of the principle of generalization see Chomsky's paper in Part 1 and the recent review by Feather, 1965.)

The paper by Carroll reflects his concern with the relevance of psychological and psycholinguistic theory and experimentation in guiding the teaching of concepts. He views "concepts" as essentially non-linguistic (or "alinguistic") because they are "classes of experience" arrived at by the individual through deduction and induction, independent of symbolic language phenomena. Subsequently, following the learning and socialization process, these concepts are associated with words (meaning).

The next paper, by Cofer, explores the role of meaning in higher processes such as recall, concept formation, and problem solving. Cofer recalls that Thomas Hobbes said, in a discussion of trains of association around 300 years ago, "the mind can lead from almost anything to anything." According to Cofer, it is the word *almost* which is critical in the quotation, and his work represents the search for its further explication. The phenomenon of "clustering in free recall" has received the attention of a number of researchers in the verbal learning area, such as Bousfield, Jenkins, Mandler, Deese, and their students and colleagues. When a subject is asked to recall a set of words previously presented to him in a random order, he tends to recite them by groups, which shows evidence of organization. Cofer examines the evidence available in an attempt to discover the basis of the organization (i.e., association, categorization, synonym, mediation). His question of how do associations and category relations lead the subject to "put this with that" reminds him of the questions the Würzburgers raised over 60 years ago. He gives no adequate answer but his reasoning is worth following.

The last paper, by Goss, treats in considerable detail that perennial problem of the cognitive psychologist—the acquisition and use of conceptual categories clearly of considerable importance in most human functioning. His historical review of the concept of concepts in behavioral tradition is excellent. Part of the road map to the crisscrossing of connections among initiating stimuli, mediating events and terminal responses is provided by the theoretical discussions of Part 1. Mediation is firmly established as a theoretical device and just as firmly criticized. If this presents a confusing state of affairs, the confusion is healthy.

References

Ajuriaguerra, J. De, F. Bresson, P. Fraisse, B. Inhelder, P. Oléron, and J. Piaget, *Problèmes de psycholinguistique.* Paris: Presses Universitaires de France, 1963.

Braine, M. D., "On Learning the Grammatical Order of Words," *Psychological Review,* **70** (1963), 323–348.

Brown, R. W., and Jean Berko, "Word Association and the Acquisition of Grammar," *Child Development,* **31** (1960), 1–14.

Chomsky, Noam. *Syntactic Structures.* The Hague: Mouton, 1957.

Cofer, C. N., and J. P. Foley, Jr., "Mediated Generalization and the Interpretation of Verbal Behavior: I. Prolegomena," *Psychological Review,* **49,** (1942), 513–540.

Di Vesta, F. J., "Developmental Patterns in the Use of Modifiers as Modes of Conceptualization," *Child Development,* **36,** (1965), 185–213.

Feather, B. W., "Semantic Generalization of Classically Conditioned Responses: A Review," *Psychological Bulletin,* **63,** (1965), 425–441.

Flavell, J. H., *The Developmental Psychology of Jean Piaget.* Princeton: D. Van Nostrand Co., Inc., 1963.

———, "Meaning and Meaning Similarity: I. A Theoretical Reassessment," *Journal of General Psychology,* **64,** (1961), 307–319.

Foley, J. P., Jr., and C. N. Cofer, "Mediated Generalization and the Interpretation of Verbal Behavior: II. Experimental Study of Certain Homophone and Synonym Gradients," *Journal of Experimental Psychology,* **32,** (1943), 168–175.

Hebb, D. O., *A Textbook of Psychology.* Philadelphia: W. B. Saunders Co., 1958.

Jakobovits, L. A., and W. E. Lambert, "Mediated Satiation in Verbal Transfer," *Journal of Experimental Psychology,* **64,** (1962), 346–351.

Jenkins, J. J., "A Mediational Account of Grammatical Phenomena," *Journal of Communications,* **14,** (1964), 86–97.

———, and D. S. Palermo, "Mediation Processes and the Acquisition of Linguistic Structure," *Mongraph of the Society for Research in Child Development,* **29,** No. 1 (Serial No. 92) (1964), 141–169.

Katz, J. J., and P. M. Postal, *An Integrated Theory of Linguistic Descriptions.* Cambridge, Mass.: The M.I.T. Press, 1964.

Lashley, K. S., "The Problem of Serial Order in Behavior," in *Cerebral Mechanisms in Behavior,* ed. L. A. Jeffress. New York: John Wiley & Sons, Inc., 1951.

Lambert, W. E., and L. A. Jakobovits, "Verbal Satiation and Changes in the Intensity of Meaning," *Journal of Experimental Psychology,* **60,** (1960), 376–383.

Miller, G. A., *Language and Communication.* New York: McGraw-Hill Book Company, 1951.

Moscovici, S., and W. Ackerman, "Processus d'association et dimensions des signes linguistiques," *Bulletin de Psychologie,* **15,** (1961), 200–222.

Osgood, C. E., *Method and Theory in Experimental Psychology.* New York: Oxford University Press, Inc., 1953.

———, "The Nature and Measurement of Meaning," *Psychological Bulletin,* **49,** (1952), 197–237.

———, W. K., Archer, and M. S. Miron, The Cross-Cultural Generality of Meaning Systems, Progress Report: January 1960–September 1962.

Institute of Communications Research, University of Illinois, 1962. (Mimeographed)

———, G. J. Suci, and P. H. Tannenbaum, *The Measurement of Meaning*. Urbana, Ill.: University of Illinois Press, 1957.

Peters, H. N., "Mediate Association," *Journal of Experimental Psychology,* **18**, (1935), 20–48.

Russell, W. A., and L. H. Storms, "Implicit Verbal Chaining in Paired-Associate Learning," *Journal of Experimental Psychology,* **49**, (1955), 287–293.

———, "The Distribution of Associated Words," *Psychological Record,* **1**, (1937), 71–76.

Smith, K. H., "Grammars and Paradigms: Some Implications for Research," Studies in Verbal Behavior, Report Number 15, Department of Psychology, University of Minnesota, September, 1964. (Mimeographed.)

Underwood, B. J., and R. W. Schulz, *Meaningfulness and Verbal Learning*. Chicago: J. B. Lippincott Co., 1960.

Werner, H., and B. Kaplan, *Symbol Formation.* New York: John Wiley, & Sons, Inc., 1964.

Zipf, G. K., *Human Behavior and the Principle of Least Effort*. Cambridge, Mass.: Addison- Wesley, 1949.

An Approach to the Problem of Symbolic Representation: Nonverbal and Verbal

BERNARD KAPLAN*

During the past fifty years it has become increasingly recognized that symbolic activity is among the most characteristic features of human existence and that the whole development of human culture is based upon man's capacity for transforming simple sensory material into symbolic vehicles—carriers of the finest intellectual and emotional distinctions. So important is symbolic activity in human life that one of the outstanding contemporary philosophers has urged: "Instead of defining man as an *animal rationale,* we should define him as an *animal symbolicum.* By so doing we can designate his specific difference. . . ."[1]

Despite this general recognition of the centrality of symbolic activity to the very definition of man, relatively little work has been undertaken by academic psychologists to clarify the nature of this activity. Even where work has ostensibly been undertaken on the problem of symbolization, it has often been done by those who are theoretically disposed to play down any uniqueness in man's capacities and who are hence inclined to treat symbolization in man on the model of sign-behavior in animals.[2]

PURPOSE

In this paper I shall be primarily concerned with the presentation of a standpoint for inquiring into symbolic activity and into the relations of this activity to other functions—e.g., perceiving, and

* This paper was written during the time that Professor Kaplan was the Principal Investigator on a project dealing with "The Nature of Symbolization and Its Role in Cognition." The project is supported by Grant No. M-3853 from the National Institute of Mental Health.

1 Ernst Cassirer, *An Essay on Man* (New York: Doubleday-Anchor, 1944).

2 See *Ibid.;* Susanne Langer, *Philosophy in a New Key* (Cambridge, Mass.: Harvard University Press, 1942); and Ernest Hilgard, "Psychology after Darwin," in Sol Tax (ed.), *Evolution after Darwin,* Vol. II (Chicago: University of Chicago Press, 1960).

Bernard Kaplan, "An Approach to the Problem of Symbolic Representation: Nonverbal and Verbal," *Journal of Communications,* **11** (1961), 52–62. Reprinted by permission of the author and publisher.

forming concepts. A central feature of this approach is the employment of various nonverbal media in the study of representation. In the course of this exposition, I shall indicate briefly how such media have been and are being used in inquiries carried out from the standpoint which Heinz Werner and I use. This reference will be solely for the purpose of exemplifying some features of the orientation. Systematic and detailed treatment of the studies themselves is reserved for another time and place.[3]

AN ANTITHETICAL APPROACH

Perhaps a useful way to establish the orientation which I propose is to contrast it with another—and antithetical—approach towards some of the major theoretical issues in the area of symbolization. The issues involved are at the very heart of the "problem of knowing"; they concern the interwined relationships of "knower and known," "thought and things," "symbol and referent," etc. With regard to this opposing approach, I do not suggest that it has any single contemporary exponent; it may or may not. I do believe, however, that in essence it underlies many contemporary treatments of symbolization and cognition and that it determines the formulation of problems, the design of experiments, the admission of evidence, etc.[4] Whether or not my belief is justified, I present the approach here primarily as a device for placing in relief the standpoint which I espouse.

Viewed from this other orientation, the objects of our experience exist in an interpersonal and external space in exactly the same form and relationships which they have for us when we perceive them. The knowing of objects is conceived as a more or less direct translocation of something "outside the mind" to a place "inside the mind" without this movement in any way affecting the nature of these objects. In other words, through a process which remains essentially the same during the entire course of ontogenesis, the individual gradually comes to perceive things as they are. Typically tied up with this view of object-perception is a thesis concerning the nature of concept-formation: Concepts or general ideas, it is maintained, are formed through a process of abstraction by means of which the knower selects out of a multiplicity of perceived objects (or their imaged facsimiles) those features which are objectively common to all. The common or identical elements constitute the conception.

In the process of perceiving objects or forming conceptions, symbols are perhaps useful, but not, according to this view, really necessary; after the object is seen or the conception formed, vocal or nonvocal elements may be used to indicate the object or fix the concept "in the mind" (label or tag it, so to speak) but such signs or marks have no role in determining the characteristics of the objects perceived or the notions conceived.[5]

From this opposing standpoint, the relationship between the symbol (sign, conditioned stimulus) and its referent (perceptual object, conceived idea) is perhaps most succinctly expressed in *the principle of arbitrariness*. According to this princi-

[3] Heinz Werner and Bernard Kaplan, *The Symbolic Process: A Developmental Analysis* (in preparation).

[4] In this connection, see the following: Grace A. de Laguna, "Appearance and Orientation," *Journal of Philosophy,* XXXI (1934), 72–77; Thelma Lavine, "Knowledge as Interpretation: An Historical Survey," *Philosophy and Phenomenological Research,* X (1950), 526–540, and XI (1950), 88–103; Stephen C. Pepper, *World Hypotheses* (Berkeley: University of California Press, 1942).

[5] For a critique of this general orientation and its variants, see the following: Ernst Cassirer, *Das Erkenntnisproblem in der Philosophie und Wissenschaft der neueren Zeit,* Vol. I (Berlin: B. Cassirer, 1906), ch. 1; Ernst Cassirer, *Substance and Function* (Chicago: Open Court, 1923), ch. 1; Ernst Cassirer, *Language and Myth* (New York: Dover, 1946), chs. 3, 4 and 6; Ernst Cassirer, *Philosophy of Symbolic Forms,* Vol. I (New Haven, Conn: Yale University Press, 1953).

ple, a material entity becomes a sign or symbol for something else by virtue of a purely external tie between the entity and its referent. This external tie is one of repeated contiguity and/or arbitrary stipulation: the sign is paired with the perceptual object or conception, assigned to it as its "name," and henceforth used in communication to indicate the object or to evoke the concept.[6]

In the main, the standpoint we have just outlined is agenetic: it assumes that the same processes are operative throughout the phylogenetic scale and that no essential difference exists between responding to material elements as signals and taking them as symbols. It therefore maintains that one can, without distortion or oversimplification, study symbolic behavior in rats and parrots as well as in man.[7]

THE ROLE OF SYMBOLIC ACTIVITY IN FORMING CONCEPTS

In contrast to this standpoint stands the orientation which this writer endorses. *First, objects of human perception are permeated through and through with our human activities as knowers and doers.* No direct, unmediated contact with things-in-themselves exists which can in any way be the subject matter of cognition. In other words, perceived objects *as known* are made and not discovered—they are productions or constructions in which the knower's activity plays a constitutive role. From this vantage point, the "given" is indeterminate as to its characteristics and even as to its nature; the specific determination given to presented phenomena varies with different individuals, for the same individual at different times, etc. Furthermore, this determination rests in large part on an underlying activity of schematization, which is indissolubly linked with symbolic activity.[8]

Second, conceptions are rarely formed through the abstraction of objectively identical elements from a manifold of particular percepts. In fact, in a very important sense, conceptions are presupposed in any particular situation where a given sensory event is perceived in one way rather than in another: In Kant's famous aphorism, "Percepts without concepts are blind." Furthermore, conceptions, in order to be grasped, must either be immanent in some particular event or else be represented by some tangible form intended as a symbol.[9] Conceptions are therefore always tied up or interdependent with some symbolic process, although this type of symbolization need not be verbal or in any way overt. Again we contend that probably under all circumstances, but at least in certain phases of cognitive activity, the symbolic process enters into the articulation of conceptions and thus deter-

[6] For a critique of this principle by a linguist-psychoanalyst, see Edouard Pichon, "La linguistique en France: problèmes et méthodes," *Journal de Psychologie,* XXXIV (1937), 25–48.

[7] For a critique of this type of "reductionism," see Hilgard, *loc. cit.;* and T. C. Schneirla, "Levels in the Psychological Capacities of Animals," in Roy W. Sellars, et al. (eds.), *Philosophy for the Future* (New York: The Macmillan Company, 1949).

[8] See Revault d'Allones, "La schématisation," in Georges Dumas (ed.), *Nouveau Traité de Psychologie,* Vol. IV (Paris: Alcan, 1934).

An example of the interpenetration of symbolization and perception is given by A. F. Chamberlain in his report of the following statement by an educated Mohawk Indian: "When I listen [to the whip-poor-will] with my Indian ears, it seems to me utterly impossible to form any other word for the imitation of its notes than *kwa-kor-yeuh,* but when I put on my English ears I hear the bird quite distinctly saying *whip-poor-will."* — "Some Points in Linguistic Psychology," *American Journal of Psychology,* V (1892), 116. In this connection, see also Maurice Grammont, "La psychologie et la phonétique: la phonétique impressive," *Journal de Psychologie,* XXVII (1930), 544–613.

[9] For the role of intentionality in symbolic activity, see Charles Serrus, "L'intention de signification," *Journal de Psychologie,* XXXIII (1936), 321–358; also Roderick Chisholm, "Intentionality and the Theory of Signs," *Philosophical Studies,* III (1952), 56–63.

mines the meaning that ideas have for us in our lives.[10]

The Relationship of Symbolic Vehicles and Referents

As to our view concerning the relationship between symbolic vehicles and referents, Dr. Werner and I distinctly reject both the principle of arbitrariness and the notion that contiguity and convention are the fundamental factors in linking patterns (whether vocal or nonvocal) to referents. At best a partial explanation, this view is limited in that it considers the problem of symbol-referent relationships primarily from the perspective of a detached observer. It therefore concentrates on the obvious fact, externally speaking, that no intrinsic relationship exists between a material entity and the phenomenon which this entity comes to represent in cognition. The external perspective either fails to consider or studiously ignores the role of the subject or symbolizer who utilizes material patterns to represent referents: it thus fails to take into account the most essential factor in symbol-situations—viz., the human being who intends a material entity as a symbol for the representation of an object or the articulation of a conception.[11]

In contradistinction to the opposing viewpoint, our approach is definitely developmental.[12] We maintain that there is a sequence of stages in the relationship between symbolic activity and cognition. In certain respects there is continuity between the earlier and the later phases; in other regards there is discontinuity. Thus, although later stages cannot be reduced to earlier ones, the earlier phases do not drop out when later modes of symbolic activity come into play; rather the genetically earlier phases are subordinated to the more advanced forms and integrated within them. Under conditions where the higher modes of symbolization are impaired or where the normal adult is directed towards some specialized activity, these earlier phases of the symbol-cognition relationship become manifest once again.

It is our belief—especially with respect to the developmentally earlier phases of symbolic activity—that when material entities (e.g., vocalized sound patterns, bodily movements, visual patterns, etc.) or particular objects or events of everyday life are used as symbols for the representation of phenomena of a totally different order, these entities or events are viewed in a markedly different way than that in which they are ordinarily regarded in our

[10] Our standpoint here is closely related to—in some sense, indeed, an extension of—the thesis, initially expressed by von Humboldt and recently taken up by such philosophers as these: Wilbur Urban, *Language and Reality* (New York: The Macmillan Company, 1939); Langer, *loc. cit.;* Cassirer, *Language and Myth* and *Philosophy of Symbolic Forms,* Vol. I. The Humboldtian thesis has also been taken up by such linguists as the following: Edward Sapir in David Mandelbaum (ed.), *Selected Writings of Edward Sapir* (Berkeley: University of California Press, 1949); and Benjamin Lee Whorf, *Four Articles on Metalinguistics* (Washington, D. C.: Foreign Service Institute, 1950). We believe that this thesis becomes warranted only when language is conceived in the original Humboldtian sense as *energeia* (activity) rather than *ergon* (product); in this sense, language activity is not restricted to vocal patterns.

[11] We would therefore say that studies focussing on whether sound patterns of a foreign language may be matched beyond chance expectancies with names for objects or events in our language have been concerned with a secondary and derivative issue. The main issue is not whether there is consensus, but how a subject goes about making a matching—i.e., how he construes the sound pattern and the referent to make any meaningful choice whatsoever. See E. Gombrich, *Art and Illusion* (New York: Pantheon, 1960).

[12] The term *developmental* is used in the sense given it by Heinz Werner, *Comparative Psychology of Mental Development,* 3rd ed. (New York: International Universities Press, 1957) and by H. Werner, "The Concept of Development from a Comparative and Organismic Point of View," in D. B. Harris (ed.), *The Concept of Development* (Minneapolis: University of Minnesota Press, 1957). See also S. Pepper, *op. cit.,* ch. 11; and W. Werkmeister, "Cassirer's Advance Beyond Neo-Kantianism," in Paul Schilpp (ed.), *The Philosophy of Ernst Cassirer* (Evanston: Library of Living Philosophers, 1949).

daily pragmatic-technical commerce with them.[13] By our symbolizing activity, we imaginatively transform these entities and particular events so that they become expressive of that which they are taken to represent.[14] This transformation does not change the material entity *qua* material entity; for the external observer nothing has happened to the material entity which was previously part of the world of existents but which has now become part of the world of symbols; for the symbolizer, however, the material entity has, in certain respects, been brought into the same universe as that of the phenomenon it is taken to represent—a universe analogous to that comprising the object-and-event experiences of early childhood—i.e., a physiognomic dynamic universe.[15]

It is important to stress the difference between early perception and later symbolic representation. In contrast with primitive perception, where no duality exists, symbolization obtains only where there is a duality or tension between symbol and referent. Where such a duality is not maintained, symbol (word) realism is manifested; i.e., the material entity is regarded as consubstantial with the referent and the distinction between the two collapses. The material entity is then treated in the same way as the referent.[16]

In the universe instituted through symbolic activity, the previously "meaningless" patterns—e.g., sounds, lines, movements, or the simple events of everyday life—take on a new coloring and significance: they are invested, so to speak, with a life of their own,[17] which they express in their shapes, contours, and "actions."[18] These features of the patterns *qua* symbols are, to be sure, quite fluid, malleable within limits, etc., but the range of meanings for which they are taken to be adequate is not infinite. In any cognitive activity, these expressive features of the pattern-becoming-vehicle affect the referents with which they are being linked and are affected by them. The symbolizer attempts to bring vehicle and referent into some sort of "fitting" relationship by restructuring the former, by reformulating the latter, or by both; finally, some *modus vivendi* is established.[19]

Advantages of Nonverbal Media for Studies of Symbolic Activity

As I have already mentioned, Werner and I in our research have used nonverbal

---

13 "No representation, however faithful and photographically exact, ever literally reproduces what it represents. The identity between the structural pattern of the representation and the pattern of what is represented, which is essential to representation, is exhibited only when the representation is regarded from the proper standpoint, and this is, of course, not itself contained in the representation."—de Laguna, *op. cit.*, p. 75.

14 Cf. Benedetto Croce, *Aesthetic,* rev. ed., (New York: Noonday, 1956).

15 Cf. Heinz Werner, "A Psychological Analysis of Expressive Language," in H. Werner (ed.), *On Expressive Language* (Worcester, Mass.: Clark University Press, 1955); Heinz Werner, *Comparative Psychology of Mental Development;* and Bernard Kaplan, "Some Psychological Methods for the Investigation of Expressive Language," in Heinz Werner (ed.), *On Expressive Language.*

16 Cf. C. K. Ogden and I. A. Richards, *The Meaning of Meaning* (New York: Harcourt, Brace and Company, Inc., 1923), ch. 2; J. G. Frazer, *The Golden Bough* (ed. T. Gaster) (New York: Criterion, 1959); also Sandor Ferenczi, *Sex and Psychoanalysis* (New York: Basic Books, 1950), ch. 4.

17 Cf. Cassirer, *Language and Myth,* ch. 6.

18 Cassirer discusses this Thou-like character which material entities take on with respect to the problem of the origin of language.

19 See Heinz Werner and Bernard Kaplan, "Symbolic Mediation and Organization of Thought: An Experimental Approach by Means of the Line-Schematization Technique," *Journal of Psychology,* XLIII (1957), 3–25; also Margery Bodansky, "An Experimental and Theoretical Inquiry into the Symbol-Meaning Relationship," M.A. Thesis, Clark University, 1956.

The material pattern through which an individual seeks to realize his unformed conceptions has its say; the resultant product of the confluence and the struggle of unformed meanings with the potential vehicle of representation is often unexpected not merely by the onlooker but also by the producer. The product, in the words of Shakespeare, often is one "not answering the aim/And that unbodied figure of the thought/That gave it surmised shape."

media extensively. Our employment of these media (e.g., line patterns, bodily movements, colors, visual imagery, hypnotically induced dreams, and clay) is based primarily on three considerations. First, our lifelong, habitual, and intimate use of the vocal-sound medium in the development of speech symbols may tend to obscure our vision of the handling of that medium in symbolic activity. This problem is especially likely to exist in the case of sound patterns which have already been structured into symbols—i.e., have become invested with significance. In contrast, the use of nonvocal media, which have not been previously exploited in the service of representation, provides a distance which permits a better view of how the intention to symbolize operates to transform material entities into symbolic vehicles. *One may plausibly argue that certain findings pertaining to the ways in which line patterns or clay blobs are handled in the process of symbolization are, in principle, generalizable to the ways in which sound patterns are handled in the process of being transformed into speech symbols.*[20] After all, vocally produced sound patterns are, from a pragmatic-technical standpoint, no more (and no less) like the events they come to represent than are linear and clay forms.[21]

A second reason for our use of media other than vocal-sound is related to our general thesis that symbolic vehicles play a determining and intrinsic role in cognitive functioning. *A priori,* it is likely that different material media—despite certain generic similarities—are not equally exploitable for the representation or the expression of the innumerable kinds of experiences we undergo: one does not easily express in words what one can express in music and vice versa. Because of these possible differences in the quality and the range of expressivity of different media, it seems to us important to compare and to contrast symbolization of a given kind of experience in various media; doing so allows us to get both a general picture of symbolic activity and a specific understanding of the advantages and the limitations of particular media.

The third reason for using nonverbal media is that they have generally not been structurized into a system of symbols. Individuals obliged to use them for symbolization must begin—as it were—without the advantages and the constraints of an already formed and organized system of vehicles. Through the use of nonverbal means we are enabled to witness, to a far greater extent than would be true otherwise, the early stages in the formation of symbolic vehicles out of a material medium. These observations, by permitting us to make certain inferences as to the early stages in the systematic structuring of any medium, provide some grounds for reconstructing the way in which articulated sounds are formed into speech symbols and systems of such symbols.[22]

ILLUSTRATIONS OF THE USE OF NONVERBAL MEDIA IN STUDYING SYMBOLIZATION

Werner and I have employed nonverbal media as a means of gaining insight into a variety of fundamental problems. Here

[20] Cf. Gombrich, *loc. cit.*

[21] The fundamental similarity of processes underlying the formation of speech symbols and the formation of significant forms in other media has been most extensively elaborated by Croce, *loc. cit.* See also Edward Sapir, *Language* (New York: Harcourt, Brace and Company, 1921), preface.

[22] Since we assume that sounds become symbols only by virtue of the symbolizing activity of a human agent, it is possible that sounds—even with the external forms of words—may be used nonsymbolically. The material pattern itself will not tell us whether a sound pattern is being used symbolically or nonsymbolically. This observation, however, does not negate the fact that some sounds in our everyday discourse are used symbolically. Cf. J. R. Kantor, "Language as Behavior and as Symbolism," *Journal of Philosophy,* XIV (1929), 150–159.

I shall sketch only a few of the studies we have undertaken.

In one study, concerned with the handling of vehicles in the process of representation, we asked subjects to create linear patterns which they felt were adequate for the representation of certain conceptions. For example, we requested them to form a line pattern to represent "an outburst of rage." After a subject had spontaneously produced a linear pattern to represent such a given conception, we asked him to view the pattern he had formed and to note down other conceptions which this pattern might serve to portray. Thus, the symbol produced for the given conception and the extension of this symbol to stand for other conceptions were completely in the hands of the individual subject. After this phase of the experiment was completed, the subject was told to express verbally how the same material pattern—the linear vehicle initially formed—had been used to represent the various conceptions he had listed. In general, we have found that the same material pattern was *imaginatively* restructured—perhaps modified, sometimes elaborated, and occasionally radically changed—in order to portray the different conceptions. In other words, although the pattern was, from the point of view of an external observer, invariant, for the symbolizer it was imaginatively changed so that in each case it sustained for the subject an analogical relationship to the content symbolized.[23] There is no need to emphasize the bearing of such a study on the problem of how an invariant vocal form may be used to represent diverse conceptions at different times.

In another study we investigated the problem of so-called arbitrary stipulation. Here, presenting subjects with certain line patterns, we stipulated that a given design was to be taken as the representation first of one state of affairs and then of another which was contrary or antithetical. For example, we successively decreed that a given line pattern was to be taken as the symbol for "modesty" and as the representation for "arrogance." Again, inquiry showed that the symbolizer did not simply associate the given pattern with the stipulated conception, but rather that he imaginatively transformed the linear pattern so that it fit now one and now the other of the two conceptions. In other words, although an arbitrary relationship between symbol and symbolized was presented, the subject strove to establish a "natural" relationship, analogically based, between the two moments.

The final illustration pertains to the use of nonverbal media for the investigation of primitive forms of cognition. In one of the studies concerned with this problem, we gave subjects the task of representing certain logical relationships in a medium of visual imagery.[24] For example, the subjects were asked to represent such situations as "He paces a great deal if he works hard," "He cries if he is hurt," etc. Typically, it is difficult, if not impossible, to express a conditional relationship in the medium of visual imagery. Insofar as a person does express such relationships, he does so with expressions which are indissolubly fused with the representations of the concrete, tangible features of the given situations.

Through the employment of such media as expressive lines, visual imagery, hypnotically induced dreams, bodily gestures, etc., Werner and I have been able, we believe, to arrive at a clearer picture of the genetically earlier phases in the

[23] The establishment, not the discovery, of an analogical relationship between the vehicle and the referent is characteristic of symbolization in normal adults. A person typically struggles, with varying degrees of success and satisfaction, to form an analogy between the vehicle and the referent; he does not simply *observe* a similarity. Cf. K. Aschenbrenner, "Intention and Understanding," in G. P. Adams et al. (eds.), *Meaning and Interpretation* (Berkeley: University of California Press, 1950).

[24] Cf. I. Meyerson, "Les images," *Journal de Psychologie,* XXVI (1929), 625–709.

symbolic organization of experience.[25] It is our hope that the coordination of findings from experimental studies on nonverbal representation with those from naturalistic studies on the ontogenesis of speech will eventually permit the formulation of the general developmental relationships between the symbolic process and the other activities of human beings.

[25] Cf. Heinz Werner and Bernard Kaplan, "The Developmental Approach to Cognition: Its Relevance to the Psychological Interpretation of Anthropological and Ethnolinguistic Data," *American Anthropologist,* LVIII (1956), 866–880; also Werner and Kaplan, "Symbolic Mediation and Organization of Thought."

Semantic Differential Technique in the Comparative Study of Cultures [1]

CHARLES E. OSGOOD

Most comparisons across cultures are extremely difficult when they concern nonmaterial traits. In part, this is an obvious consequence of the subjective nature of comparisons; in part also, however, this difficulty is attributable to the fact that nonmaterial traits must often be assessed through the medium of language. Indeed, if the Sapir-Whorf psycholinguistic relativity hypothesis were taken literally and considered completely general to all aspects of human cognition, such comparisons would be impossible. The essential point is this: to note differences within any phenomenal domain and order them in any rigorous fashion, one must have certain similarities underlying the phenomena as a frame of reference against which to compare them. Only to the extent that physical objects share such attributes as length, weight, and volume, and to the extent that these attributes can be abstracted and quantified, can comparison be made on anything other than an intuitive basis.

[1] I wish to express my thanks for the contributions of many colleagues, both at Illinois and in many countries around the world, to this cooperative research.

The denotative or referential uses of terms—the way the lexicon carves up the world—appear largely arbitrary and unique to particular languages until the ethnolinguist discovers a framework of semantic components that can be imposed comparably on these phenomena. In closely analogous fashion, our own researches over the past few years provide evidence for a universal framework underlying certain affective or connotative aspects of language. These findings enliven the possibility of constructing instruments for measuring these aspects of "subjective culture" comparably in diverse societies—in effect, circumventing the language barrier. Since the affective reactions people make to symbols and events are important determiners of their overt behaviors with respect to these symbols and events, having comparable means of measuring affective meanings assumes some importance in a world that is rapidly shrinking psychologically, socially, and politically.

A SEMANTIC SPACE

In order to understand the research procedures we have followed and the kinds

Charles E. Osgood, "Semantic Differential Technique in the Comparative Study of Cultures," *American Anthropologist,* **66,** No. 3 (June, 1964), 171–200. Reprinted by permission of the author and publisher.

of cultural data they can provide, it will be useful to begin with a brief presentation of our theoretical model and its measurement implications. Imagine a space of some unknown number of dimensions. This will be our hypothetical semantic space, and we can explore it by analogy with the more familiar color space. Like all self-respecting spaces, this one has an origin, which we define as complete "meaninglessness" (analogous to the neutral grey center of the color space). The meaning of a sign can be conceived as some point in this n-dimensional space, and can thus be represented by a vector from the origin to that point: the length of this vector would index the "degree of meaningfulness" of this sign (like saturation in the color space) and its direction would index the "semantic quality" of this sign (analogous to both hue and brightness in the color space).

To talk about "direction" in any space requires that we have some reference coordinates. Again the analogy with the color space will serve: Just as complementary colors are defined as points equidistant and in opposite directions from the origin in the color space, which when mixed together in equal proportions cancel each other out to neutral grey, so may we conceive of verbal opposites as defining straight lines through the origin of the semantic space. Lexicographers assure us that true verbal opposites do cancel other out semantically, component for component, when "mixed." Imagine now a whole set of different straight-line "cuts" through the semantic space, each passing through the origin and each defined by a pair of opposites. In order to discover the location of concept x in this space, we might play a game of "Twenty Questions" with our subject: it is *beautiful,* not *ugly* (cut no. 1), it is *soft,* not *hard* (cut no. 2), it is *quick,* not *slow* (cut no. 3), and so forth. If these "cuts" were at right angles to each other, and hence independent, then each such binary decision would reduce uncertainty about the location of x by half. Or, if each straight-line "cut" were scaled into seven discriminable steps, as we have done in our work, then each decision would reduce uncertainty of location by 6/7ths, and only three "cuts" would yield a space of 343 discrete regions.

But the assumption of independence (orthogonality) of dimensions demands justification, of course, and we still have the problem of reference coordinates.

Is the up-down, north-south, and east-west of the semantic space to be completely arbitrary, or is there some "natural" built-in structuring of this space analogous to the gravitational and magnetic determinants of geophysical space? These are empirical questions, and the logical tool is some variant of factor analysis. We need to take a large and representative sample of qualitative dimensions defined by verbal opposites, determine their intercorrelations when used by subjects in differentiating a representative sample of concepts, and then see if they do fall into "natural" clusters or factors which can serve as reference coordinates. And one factor analysis is not enough—it is too liable to the happenstances of sampling. Factor analysis becomes a hypothesis, confirming procedure only when analyses of the same domain are replicated, when the rules of sampling this domain are independent of the factors previously discovered, and when, nevertheless, the same factors keep reappearing.

Now let us look at the measurement model. In the typical semantic differentiation task, a subject judges a series of concepts (e.g., *my mother, Chinese, modern art,* etc.) against a series of bipolar, seven-step scales defined by verbal opposites (e.g., *good-bad, strong-weak, fast-slow, hot-cold, fair-unfair,* etc.). The concept is given at the top of each sheet, and the subject judges it against each successive scale by putting his checkmark in the appropriate position, e.g., + 3 *extremely good,* + 2 *quite good,* + 1 *slightly good,* 0 *equally good and bad or neither,* — 1 *slightly bad,* − 2 *quite bad,* and − 3 *extremely bad.* These particular quantifiers have been shown by Norman Cliff (1959) to yield approximately equal degrees of intensity.

When a group of people judge a set of concepts against a set of adjectival scales, representing what we call a "semantic differential," a cube of data is generated. The rows in this cube are defined by the scales, the columns by the concepts being judged, and the "slices" from front to back by the subjects. Each cell represents with a single value how a particular subject rated a particular concept against a particular scale. In analyzing these data we are usually—but not necessarily—interested in the correlations among the scales. We may correlate them across subjects or across concepts; we may collapse the subject dimension of the cube when we are interested in "cultural meanings"; we may run separate analyses for single subjects or classes of subjects (correlating scales across the concepts judged) to determine their individual semantic spaces; or, we may do this for single concepts or classes of concepts (correlating scales across the people judging) to determine the uniqueness of judgmental spaces for concept classes, if such exist. In other words, there are many ways one can slice this semantic space, each appropriate for answering a different kind of question. For the most part, we have employed Pearson product-moment correlation procedures to generate a scale-by-scale matrix of intercorrelations and then subjected this matrix to principal axes factor analysis and varimax rotation.

In the past decade or more, we have made many such factor analyses of data cubes obtained from American speakers of English. Much of this work is summarized by Osgood, Suci, and Tannenbaum (1957). Despite deliberate and independent variations in the sampling of scales, of concepts, and of subjects, three dominant and independent (orthogonal) factors have kept reappearing: an Evaluative Factor (represented by scales such as *good-bad, pleasant-unpleasant,* and *positive-negative*), a Potency Factor (represented by scales such as *strong-weak, heavy-light,* and *hard-solft*), and an Activity Factor (represented by scales such as *fast-slow, active-passive,* and *excitable-calm*). What this means is that there are at least three "directions" in the semantic space which are regions of relatively high density, in the sense of many closely related modes of qualifying, and that these "directions" tend to be orthogonal to each other, in the sense of being independently variable dimensions of meaning. It is also apparent that, contrary to my early expectations, these factors are more reactive in nature than sensory, more broadly affective than discriminatively cognitive, and thus closer to connotative than to denotative aspects of meaning.

In the course of this early work we made many comparisons between groups of people within the English-speaking American culture—between old people and young, between males and females, between students exposed to a new kind of course in international relations and those given the traditional course, between Republicans and Democrats, and even between schizophrenics and normals. The results of all these comparisons can be summarized very simply: in no case have we found significant differences in the underlying dominant factors. Note carefully that this does *not* indicate that the meanings of particular concepts were necessarily the same. Females have a different meaning of the self than do males. Republicans have a very different meaning for *Harry Truman* than do Democrats, and so forth. What this does indicate is that the semantic framework within which these affective judgments are made is constant; the modes of qualifying concepts display the same correlational structure, despite real differences in location of particular concepts within the common framework. Indeed, it is only by virtue of this common frame of reference that differences between people for the same concept and between concepts for the same people can be specified.

THE SEARCH FOR CROSS-LINGUISTIC AND CROSS-CULTURAL GENERALITY

The research described so far has been limited to English-speaking participants in American culture. Although considerable generality of semantic factor structure has been demonstrated for various groups within this particular language/culture composite, the most critical test of generality remains: does the same semantic framework hold for people who speak different languages and enjoy different cultures? Demonstration of such generality would be of considerable scientific interest in and of itself, but, more than this, the existence of such a shared framework would permit us to devise comparable "yard-sticks" for measuring similarities and differences in certain aspects of subjective culture—the affective or emotive aspects.

Prior to the major research effort to be reported here, a number of studies had been carried out designed to assess the generality of affective meaning systems across selected language and culture groups. These included a study by Kumata (1957), comparing Korean bilinguals and Japanese bilinguals and monolinguals with American monolinguals, a study by Triandis and Osgood (1958), comparing Greek and American college students, and one by Suci (1960), comparing several Southwest Indian cultures with Spanish-speaking Americans and Anglos. Even though the details of methods varied, as did the selection of semantic scales and concepts judged—and the same factors nevertheless kept appearing—one dubious aspect of methodology ran through all of these early studies: the samples of scales used were selected either partly or wholly on the basis of results obtained in prior American investigations. Such scales were often simply translated into the languages of the other groups under study. Despite the care with which these translations were carried out (cf. Kumata 1957), the fact that translation served as the vehicle for demonstrating structural similarities in all cases seemed to be the most likely source of bias, if indeed the similarities were artifactual. It was out of this background that we began, in 1960,[2] to apply a design which we hoped would rigorously test the limits of possible generality. To avoid the potential bias of translation, and resultant ethnocentrism, the procedures for selecting modes of qualifying were to be entirely intracultural; each language/culture group must determine its own scales. However, in order to make possible the intercultural comparisons essential for testing the generality hypothesis, the overall methodology of these intracultural samplings had to be carefully standardized. Additionally, it was clear that our design required as heterogeneous a sample of both languages and cultures as could be obtained practically.

The term "practically" here implied several things for us: first, we would work only with literate, "high" cultures in the beginning, since data could be collected more efficiently from groups of subjects in written form; second, we would work with relatively homogeneous samples of young males (12–16 years of age) rather than strive for representative samples of populations, since what is "representative" is very obscure cross-culturally and would, in any case, not be comparable; third, our original sample of six sites, along with the United States as control, would include as many different language families and as gross cultural differences as possible—efficiencies of our data-processing later made it possible to extend our sample to some 16 sites. Table 1 gives the research sites (original set indicated by asterisks), the

[2] From January, 1960, to the present writing, April, 1963, this research has been supported entirely by the Human Ecology Fund, and we here express our gratitude for this assistance.

Table 1

SUMMARY OF LANGUAGE/CULTURE GROUPS COMPRISING TOTAL SAMPLE

Country	*Language*	*Language family*	*Field center*	*Field staff*
*U.S.A.	English	Indo-European	Urbana	Miron, May, Tanaka, Shanmugam
*Finland	Finnish	Finno-Urgic	Helsinki	Allardt, Haavio
*Japan	Japanese	Japanese	Tokyo	Obonai, Asai
*India	Kannada	Dravidian	Mysore	Kuppuswamy Vatsala, Nikam
Netherlands	Dutch	Indo-European	Amsterdam	Jansen, Duijker
Belgium	Flemish	Indo-European	Brussels	Jansen, Nuttin
France	French	Indo-European	Paris	Jansen, Sutter
*Lebanon	Arabic	Semitic	Beirut	Prothro, Diab
Sweden	Swedish	Indo-European	Uppsala	Himmelstrand, Asplund
*Hong Kong	Cantonese	Sino-Tibetan	Hong Kong	Li
*Iran	Farsi	Indo-European	Tehran	Siassi, Minou
Afghanistan	Farsi	Indo-European	Kabul	Majrouh, Sarwari
Yugoslavia	Serbo-Croatian	Indo-European	Belgrade	Tomekovic, Georgievich
India	Hindi	Indo-European	Delhi	Rastogi, Shukla
Poland	Polish	Indo-European	Warsaw	Schaff, Sarapata
Afghanistan	Pashto	Indo-European	Kabul	Majrouh, Ayeen

languages involved, and the names of field staff.

Phase I. Qualifier Selection

Data collection and analysis falls rather naturally into two phases. Phase I involves collection of a large and representative sample of modes of qualifying experience in each language/culture community, on the basis of which to construct a set of bipolar descriptive scales charcteristic of each such community.[3]

A standard list of substantives. It was decided to use a modified word-association procedure to elicit qualifiers in each site—a procedure in which subjects give the first qualifier (adjective, in English) that occurs to them when presented with each substantive (noun, in English). But the requirement of standardization demanded that a common list of substantives be used, ideally involving completely culture-common and culture-fair terms. A pool of 200 substantives was finally drawn from items used in glottochronological studies and purported to be of wide linguistic applicability (Swadesh, 1950; Lees, 1953), from the Kent-Rosanoff list, and from category headings in the Human Relations Area Files Index. Reduction of this pool was accomplished by means of two criteria: *Translation fidelity* was estimated by having the total list translated into Arabic, Cantonese, Finnish, Hindi, Kannada, Japanese, and Persian by panels of approximately 10 English/mother-tongue bilinguals, along with informal back-translation checks; wherever difficulty was encountered in any language, that item was dropped for all languages. *Substantive productivity* was estimated by having the 200 item set administered in Finland and

[3] Phase I actually terminated with a correlational and factorial analysis of the interrelationships among these scales when they are judged against each other (rather than used in differentiating concepts), but since these analyses merely confirm later, more rigorous, tests of the generality hypothesis they will be omitted from this report.

Table 2

THE 100 SUBSTANTIVE STIMULI AS USED IN QUALIFIER ELICITATIONS

1.	House	35.	Work	68.	Thunder
2.	Girl	36.	Story	69.	Truth
3.	Picture	37.	Punishment	70.	Author
4.	Meat	38.	Wealth	71.	Music
5.	Trust	39.	Woman	72.	Sleep
6.	Pain	40.	Cloud	73.	Future
7.	Defeat	41.	Cat	74.	Egg
8.	Book	42.	Poison	75.	Root
9.	Lake	43.	Crime	76.	Sun
10.	Star	44.	Hunger	77.	Dog
11.	Battle	45.	Choice	78.	Money
12.	Danger	46.	Noise	79.	Smoke
13.	Sympathy	47.	Need	80.	Fish
14.	Progress	48.	Hope	81.	Man
15.	Cup	49.	Anger	82.	Wednesday
16.	Courage	50.	Tongue	83.	Chair
17.	Thief	51.	Horse	84.	Guilt
18.	Bread	52.	Marriage	85.	Luck
19.	Love	53.	Game	86.	Peace
20.	Fruit	54.	Color	87.	Hair
21.	Bird	55.	Heart	88.	Food
22.	Snake	56.	Friend	89.	Seed
23.	Heat	57.	Death	90.	Policeman
24.	Map	58.	Knowledge	91.	Father
25.	Husband	59.	Freedom	92.	Fear
26.	Rain	60.	Belief	93.	Pleasure
27.	Tree	61.	Success	94.	Purpose
28.	Stone	62.	Rope	95.	Fire
29.	Tooth	63.	Hand	96.	Doctor
30.	Ear	64.	Mother	97.	Power
31.	Respect	65.	Knot	98.	Window
32.	Laughter	66.	Life	99.	River
33.	Moon	67.	Head	100.	Water
34.	Wind				

the United States; items yielding relatively few qualifier types were eliminated (e.g., the item *blood* was found to yield predominantly a single response, *red,* in both languages, and so was dropped). These procedures enabled us to reduce the substantive list to the 100 items given in Table 2. It should be noted that this list includes a good number of abstract terms, as well as the concrete terms that might be expected. It should also be noted that this is the only point at which translation could in any way affect our results.

Eliciting qualifiers. For a variety of reasons, it is not possible simply to translate English instructions into other languages and expect to get comparable results. For one thing, cultural differences in implicit assumptions about the task exist (e.g., "to say what most people would say" vs. "to give unusual responses"), and we are not sure but what some of these effects are still embodied in our data. For another thing, the linguistic frames which define qualifiers vary with the grammatical structure of each language. Therefore, our ethnolinguist, William Kay Archer, working with field personnel, devised frames in each language presumably as appropriate for that language as the test frames "The——————*Butterfly*" and "The *Butterfly* is——————" are for English.

Given practice with such frames in their own language, 100 young males supplied one qualifier each for each of the items in Table 2. In collating these data, the field workers were instructed to use the same frames for testing dubious items. To facilitate analysis on IBM and ILLIAC computers (and to eliminate the need for translation), orthographic schemes were devised for languages whose alphabetization practices made this necessary. The total "basketful" of approximately 10,000 qualifiers (100 subjects × 100 substantives) obtained in each site, organized in "alphabetized" lists under each substantive, were shipped to Illinois for analysis.

Qualifier selection. After punching onto IBM cards, completely computerized procedures were applied to the qualifier data. These procedures were designed to order qualifier-types in terms of three criteria: (a) maximum overall frequency of usage (salience), (b) maximum diversity of usage (productivity), and (c) minimum correlation in usage (independence). In other words, working "blindly" with standardized computer procedures, we wanted to derive uniquely for each language/culture community a set of terms that would comprise its most characteristic and representative modes of qualifying experience. The first two criteria, frequency and diversity of usage, could be combined into a single index—the H-statistic of information theory; if a qualifier-type (e.g., *good*) should be given by all subjects to all items, it would have the maximum value of H, whereas a qualifier-type that occurred to only one substantive would have an H-value of 0.

When the qualifier-types for each language/culture sample are ranked according to the H-statistic, rather striking similarities are revealed even at this level. Table 3 gives the correlations in rank (here, separately for frequency and diversity indices) of the 40 highest ranking qualifiers, as translated into English in each case. Despite the difficulties of "mapping" one language onto another in translation, these correlations are all positive and highly significant. In other words, the relative importance (frequency and diversity) of various modes of qualifying experience appear to be shared despite differences in both language and culture.

Finally, the distribution of usage across the set of substantives of each qualifier lower in the H-ranked list was correlated with the distribution of every higher-ranked qualifier, using the *phi* coefficient. Where correlations were above a rather stringent criterion, the lower-ranking qualifier was discarded. An illustration will clarify this procedure: suppose that *nice* has a usage profile across the 100 nouns that is highly correlated with *good;* if *good* has a higher H-rank, it is kept and *nice* is discarded. Our purpose here is to eliminate semantically redundant scales and thus maximize the opportunity for independent dimensions to appear in the sample.

Opposite elicitation and scale production. A final list of about 60 qualifiers, ranked according to H (frequency and diversity) and pruned according to semantic redundancy (*phi*-coefficients), is returned to the field staff in each site. They are instructed to use these items as stimuli in eliciting verbal opposites according to a standardized procedure (no difficulties have yet been encountered in this procedure—the notion of, and utilization of, "oppositeness" seems to be a common characteristic of languages). Where certain terms have no agreed upon opposite, or where the opposites are multiple (e.g., homonyms such as *light-dark* and *light-heavy*), rules of procedure are given for either elimination of the term as a scale or further probing. The end result is a list of 50 bipolar scales, representing the highest ranking items remaining after the process. These scales provide the dimensions for concept differentiation in Phase II.

Phase II. Concept-on-scale Factorizations

In this phase the original 100 substantives (Table 2) are judged as concepts against the set of 50 bipolar qualifier scales derived from Phase I by a different,

Table 3

Translation Analysis Elicited Qualifier Intercorrelations

	Frequency							
	English	Arabic	Dutch	Finnish	Kannada	Japanese	French	Flemish
English	1.00	*.53*	*.66*	*.78*	*.76*	*.43*	*.58*	*.65*
Arabic		1.00	.29	.35	.31	.39	.37	.34
Dutch			1.00	.73	.59	.29	.53	.95
Finnish				1.00	.66	.39	.62	.71
Kannada					1.00	.33	.45	.56
Japanese						1.00	.33	.34
French							1.00	.55
Flemish								1.00
	Diversity							
English	1.00	*.64*	*.56*	*.68*	*.70*	*.60*	*.53*	*.56*
Arabic		1.00	.37	.58	.49	.46	.50	.40
Dutch			1.00	.49	.48	.33	.41	.89
Finnish				1.00	.54	.56	.64	.55
Kannada					1.00	.39	.46	.52
Japanese						1.00	.47	.36
French							1.00	.42
Flemish								1.00

but equivalent, group of young males in each country. These data are factored, both uniquely for each group and pan-culturally. On the basis of the common factors derived, short (15 to 18 scales) semantic differentials are selected for each language/culture group for subsequent applied research.

Collection of concept-on-scale data. Since rating 100 concepts on 50 scales is an extremely time-consuming task, the concepts were divided into 10 subsets and each subset of 10 concepts was judged against the total scales by a group of 20 subjects (we have found that the means for groups of this size are highly stable, within about $^1/_3$ of a scale unit). This task thus involved 200 subjects. A 50 (scale) × 100 (concept) × 20 (subject) cube of data was thus generated in each language/culture community. Since we were here interested in cultural meaning systems, not individual, these data cubes were collapsed along the subject dimension by summing and averaging over the 20 subjects for each concept-scale judgment. These data were shipped back to Illinois for analysis.

Analysis of concept-on-scale data. Following the usual transfer of data to IBM cards, the first step was to generate a 50 × 50 scale-by-scale correlation matrix by correlating across the mean judgments for the 100 concepts. This matrix was then factored by the principal component method and usually rotated by the varimax method. This procedure yields a unique solution for each language/culture community, and comparisons can only be made intuitively by inspection of the scales (as translated into English) having high loadings on the factors. Table 4 gives the six highest loading scales for each of the first three factors for six language/culture communities. The first factor in order of magnitude (% variance extracted) is clearly interpretable as *Evaluation* in every case, without any intuitive strain. The second factor in order of magnitude is interpretable either as *Potency* or *Activity,*

Table 4

Principal Component Factors of Full-Scale Instrument as Used in Concept-Scale Task*

American	*Factor I* (45.5%)		*Factor II* (12.0%)		*Factor III* (5.6%)	
	nice-awful	.96	big-little	.81	fast-slow	.64
	sweet-sour	.94	powerful-powerless	.75	noisy-quiet	.56
	heavenly-hellish	.93	deep-shallow	.69	young-old	.55
	good-bad	.93	strong-weak	.68	alive-dead	.55
	mild-harsh	.92	high-low	.64	known-unknown	.48
	happy-sad	.91	long-short	.64	burning-freezing	.36
Dutch	*Factor I* (27.8%)		*Factor II* (17.8%)		*Factor III* (5.9%)	
	pleasant-unpleasant	.95	absorbing-boring	.81	big-little	.70
	cozy-cheerless	.93	changeable-constant	.74	long-short	.66
	pretty-not pretty	.93	active-passive	.72	heavy-light	.63
	happy-unhappy	.92	wild-tame	.71	thick-thin	.57
	good-bad	.91	impressive-not impressive	.70	strong-weak	.56
	beautiful-ugly	.88	exchanging-even	.69	hard-soft	.41
Finnish	*Factor I* (30.8%)		*Factor II* (9.2%)		*Factor III* (7.8%)	
	nice-not nice	.88	agile-clumsy	.68	long-short	.56
	light-gloomy	.88	delicate-sturdy	.63	sharp-dull	.52
	pleasant-unpleasant	.85	capricious-steady	.60	energetic-unenergetic	.50
	sweet-sour	.81	flexible-rigid	.58	large-small	.49
	good-bad	.80	fast-slow	.53	strong-weak	.48
	happy-unhappy	.80	young-old	.53	sturdy-delicate	.47
Flemish	*Factor I* (27.2%)		*Factor II* (8.0%)		*Factor III* (7.8%)	
	agreeable-disagreeable	.90	bloody-not bloody	.69	long-short	.79
	cozy-cheerless	.89	shrewd-naive	.69	big-small	.77
	pleasant-boring	.89	quick-slow	.68	strong-weak	.64
	magnificent-horrible	.89	sharp-blunt	.64	deep-shallow	.60
	beautiful-ugly	.88	active-passive	.64	old-new	.54
	good-bad	.84	violent-calm	.44	old-young	.51
Japanese	*Factor I* (41.0%)		*Factor II* (13.0%)		*Factor III* (8.5%)	
	pleasant-unpleasant	.96	heavy-light	.76	cheerful-lonely	.76
	comfortable-uncomfortable	.95	difficult-easy	.71	colorful-plain	.68
	good-bad	.94	strong-weak	.65	noisy-quiet	.68
	happy-sad	.93	brave-cowardly	.63	active-inactive	.61
	elegant-vulgar	.92	sturdy-fragile	.62	fast-slow	.60
	troublesome-thankful	.93	thick-thin	.60	early-late	.58
Kannada	*Factor I* (30.8%)		*Factor II* (7.2%)		*Factor III* (4.8%)	
	merciful-cruel	.89	many-few	.68	fast-slow	.53
	good-bad	.86	big-small	.68	active-dull	.45
	calm-frightful	.84	huge-small	.68	fatty-slim	.42
	beautiful-ugly	.83	great-little	.54	unstable-stable	.42
	delicate-rough	.82	plenty-little	.54	noisy-quiet	.36
	soft-rough	.79	strong-weak	.44	hasty-considered	.34

*Excluding Flemish; factor coefficients reported for that language were obtained by Varimax rotation.

the former with less intuitive strain than the latter, and the remaining factor is always Potency where the second is Activity, or vice versa. In other words, on such an interpretive basis, the first three factors in every case resemble the Evaluation-Potency-Activity pattern repeatedly found for American English speakers.

To eliminate the problem of intuitive interpretation in comparing two (or more) factorizations, it is necessary to put the variables being compared into the same mathematical space. In the usual two-way factor problem (people against tests), this means that either the subjects must be the same or the tests the same. In our three-way problem (people against concepts against scales) this would mean that one of these sources of variance would have to be the same; this is clearly not the case for our people (different language/culture communities), for our scales (some are translation-equivalent, but many are unique), nor for our concepts (translation equivalent, but no guarantee of semantic identity). However, whereas there exist no possibilities of ordering the data according to people or scales (there is no rationale for pairing), this can be done for the concepts; that is, we can correlate scale x for Americans with scale y for Finns directly, using the means for Americans on x and Finns on y across the 100 pairable translation-equivalent concepts. To the extent that our assumption of common concept meanings is *not* justified, all this can do is reduce the possible magnitude of correlations (by introducing random "noise") and hence work against the hypothesis of factorial similarity.

We have made two types of such "pan-cultural" factor comparisons. The first type involves all of the scales in two language/culture groups (i.e., 100 scales) intercorrelated across the common 100 concepts. So far we have only done this against American English as a common base. Tables 5 and 6 illustrate these results for Finnish and Japanese against English, respectively. Note, first that the common factors of Evaluation, Potency, and Activity are clearly identified in both comparisons; note, second, that rather than a factor being defined by scales in one language (high loadings) and only faintly supported by semantically related scales in the other language (lower loading), here the factors clearly run through scale clusters simultaneously defined by both languages (high loadings tend to alternate across languages). Needless to state, these are most encouraging and convincing results. Limitations on the capacities of our computers make it impossible to throw all scales for all of our 15 or more language/culture communities into a single pan-cultural factor analysis. However, it is possible to take the highest loading scales on each of the major factors derived in single community factor analyses and combine them in a single analysis for all communities. Table 7 shows the results obtained when this is done for seven of our communities where data analysis has proceeded to this stage. Again, there is clear and convincing confluence of semantically similar (in translation to English) scales upon common factors of Evaluation, Potency, and Activity. It is from data such as these that final selection of specific scales for comparable differentials in each language/culture community will be made.

Cross-linguistic and Cross-cultural Similarities: Summary

Before turning attention to cultural differences we will summarize the major cross-cultural similarities found in the "tool-making" Phases I and II. (a) *Salience and productivity of modes of qualifying.* It is evident in our data that, even on the basis of crude and "noisy" translation into English, the modes of qualifying experience that have high *H*-ranks (frequency and diversity of usage) in English also tend to have high rank in other languages. (b) *Qualifier frequency-of-usage*

Table 5

PRINCIPAL COMPONENT FACTORIZATION OF COMBINED ENGLISH AND FINNISH PHASE II TASK

Factor I (36.5%)		Factor II (9.1%)		Factor III (6.7%)		Factor IV (3.7%)		Factor V (3.3%)	
American English		*American English*		*American English*		*American English*		*American English*	
nice-awful	.94	big-little	.83	fast-slow	.65	burning-freezing	.44	dry-wet	.62
sweet-sour	.93	powerful-powerless	.70	noisy-quiet	.51	unknown-known	.42	burning-freezing	.51
heavenly-hellish	.91	deep-shallow	.67	alive-dead	.48	hot-cold	.41	hot-cold	.50
happy-sad	.91	strong-weak	.66	burning-freezing	.36	high-low	.40	known-unknown	.32
good-bad	.91	high-low	.64	young-old	.34	weak-strong	.34	short-long	.31
mild-harsh	.90	long-short	.61	sharp-dull	.32				
beautiful-ugly	.90	heavy-light	.59	hot-cold	.32				
faithful-unfaithful	.88	hard-soft	.46						
clean-dirty	.88	old-young	.45						
helpful-unhelpful	.88	sharp-dull	.44						
useful-useless	.87								
sane-mad	.87								
needed-unneeded	.86								
fine-coarse	.86								
honest-dishonest	.84								
Finnish		*Finnish*		*Finnish*		*Finnish*		*Finnish*	
nice-not nice	.89	sturdy-delicate	.71	agile-clumsy	.70	light-dark	.40	red-blue	.54
light-gloomy	.87	large-small	.65	flexible-rigid	.68	distant-near	.39	hot-cold	.44
pleasant-unpleasant	.87	heavy-light	.54	fast-slow	.67	high-low	.35	steady-capricious	.39
good-bad	.84	strong-weak	.52	lively-subdued	.56	weak-strong	.35	short-long	.35
reassuring-frightening	.79	thick-thin	.46	lively-tired	.50	deep-shallow	.34	shallow-deep	.32
valuable-worthless	.78	long-short	.45	sharp-dull	.49				
ripe-raw	.78	old-young	.42	multicolored-unicolor	.47				
clean-dirty	.78	high-low	.41						
white-black	.77	steady-capricious	.34						
happy-unhappy	.77	brave-timid	.33						
honorable-despicable	.76								
flourishing-barren	.76								
sweet-sour	.76								
right-wrong	.75								
smooth-rough	.70								

Table 6

PRINCIPAL COMPONENT FACTORIZATION OF COMBINED ENGLISH AND JAPANESE PHASE II TASK

Factor I (*40.9%*)		*Factor II* (*10.9%*)		*Factor III* (*6.3%*)		*Factor IV* (*3.9%*)		*Factor V* (*3.9%*)	
American English		*American English*		*American English*		*American English*		*American English*	
nice-awful	.96	powerless-powerful	.76	fast-slow	.65	low-high	.53	serious-funny	.44
good-bad	.93	little-big	.70	noisy-quiet	.56	little-big	.47	burning-freezing	.44
sweet-sour	.93	weak-strong	.68	young-old	.46	short-long	.39	hot-cold	.44
heavenly-hellish	.92	shallow-deep	.56	alive-dead	.41	known-unknown	.36	few-many	.42
happy-sad	.91	short-long	.56	burning-freezing	.38	shallow-deep	.35	weak-strong	.32
mild-harsh	.90	light-heavy	.54	known-unknown	.37	unbroken-broken	.32		
beautiful-ugly	.90	low-high	.51	hot-cold	.36				
helpful-unhelpful	.90	soft-hard	.50						
needed-unneeded	.88	smooth-rough	.48						
clean-dirty	.88	funny-serious	.48						
useful-useless	.88								
faithful-unfaithful	.87								
honest-dishonest	.87								
sane-mad	.86								
safe-dangerous	.86								
Japanese		*Japanese*		*Japanese*		*Japanese*		*Japanese*	
pleasant-unpleasant	.93	light-heavy	.72	cheerful-lonely	.73	plain-colorful	.44	few-many	.56
good-bad	.92	small-big	.67	noisy-quiet	.68	near-far	.40	rare-common	.40
comfortable-uncomfortable	.92	weak-strong	.65	colorful-plain	.65	narrow-wide	.35	late-early	.38
happy-sad	.91	cowardly-brave	.63	active-inactive	.55	sturdy-fragile	.32	slow-fast	.38
elegant-vulgar	.90	fragile-sturdy	.62	red-blue	.53	small-big	.32	difficult-easy	.36
thankful-troublesome	.90	easy-difficult	.61	fast-slow	.53	low-high	.31		
beautiful-ugly	.88	thin-thick	.59	early-late	.50				
necessary-unnecessary	.87	soft-hard	.53						
great-unimportant	.86	simple-complex	.48						
interesting-boring	.86	loose-tight	.47						
wise-foolish	.86								
optimistic-pessimistic	.85								
skillful-unskillful	.80								
great-not great	.80								

Table 7

PAN-CULTURAL FACTOR SCALE ANALYSIS (18 highest loading scales for each pan-cultural factor arranged by culture)

	Factor I (27.7%)		*Factor II (14.9%)*		*Factor III (10.5%)*	
American English	nice-not nice	86	powerful-powerless	69	fast-slow	55
	sweet-sour	81	big-little	62	noisy-quiet	48
	heavenly-hellish	80			young-old	44
					little-big	39
Dutch	pleasant-unpleasant	86	big-little	63	active-passive	61
	pretty-not pretty	83	absorbing-boring	55	absorbing-boring	44
	cozy-cheerless	80	long-short	46		
			changeable-constant	45		
			active-passive	45		
Finnish	nice-not nice	83	energetic-unenergetic	60	agile-clumsy	67
	pleasant-unpleasant	81	dull-sharp	44	capricious-steady	48
	light-gloomy	78	sturdy-delicate	41	delicate-sturdy	42
French	pleasant-unpleasant	83	large-little	75	fast-slow	58
	good-bad	80	strong-weak	66	lively-indolent	55
	likable-repugnant	78	huge-tiny	61	living-dead	44
			indolent-lively	55		
			dead-living	42		
Japanese	comfortable-uncomfortable	83	strong-weak	56	colorful-plain	52
	pleasant-unpleasant	83	heavy-light	40	noisy-quiet	52
	good-bad	82			light-heavy	42
					cheerful-lonely	37
Kannada	calm-frightful	73	big-small	46	fast-slow	37
	merciful-cruel	73			active-passive	36
	good-bad	68				

functions. When the total sample of qualifiers for each language are plotted as lognormal functions (cf., Zipf-type functions), they are found to have very similar slopes, albeit some interesting differences in mean. (c) *Oppositeness.* The functional use of oppositeness in the qualifier realm was clearly present for all languages studied—it did not need to be forced. (d) *Affective factors.* The major hypothesis of this research—that human beings share a common framework for differentiating the affective meanings of signs —is clearly borne out in the data. The dominant factors in the affective meaning system are Evaluation, Potency, and Activity, usually in that order. Whether this system will be found to hold up for non-literate groups remains to be tested in future research, but pilot studies suggest that it will.

EVIDENCE FOR DIFFERENCES IN SUBJECTIVE CULTURE

Differences between language/culture communities that can be drawn from data we are collecting fall into three general categories. First are differences that fall out more or less incidentally from the "tool-making" procedures just described. Despite the over-all similarities stressed above, certain differences between groups are also evident in each phase, and the standardization of procedures enhances the significance of such differences. However, no attempt will be made here to

Table 8

THE 10 HIGHEST *H*-RANKED QUALIFIERS FOR EIGHT LANGUAGE/CULTURE GROUPS

American English		*Lebanese Arabic*		*Dutch*		*Finnish*	
Q	*H*	*Q*	*H*	*Q*	*H*	*Q*	*H*
good	228	large	324	large	519	good	393
big	140	beautiful	241	good	255	big	374
great	091	great	168	beautiful	137	*firm*	185
small	082	severe	122	small	093	small	158
large	076	small	121	much	084	beautiful	119
bad	072	long	104	hard	063	long	097
little	067	strong	088	heavy	059	bad	087
long	063	plentiful	085	long	041	pleasant	067
hard	053	*white*	065	bad	040	*spoiled*	060
strong	043	*red*	058	thick	033	*difficult*	043

Flemish		*French*		*Japanese*		*Indian Kannada*	
Q	*H*	*Q*	*H*	*Q*	*H*	*Q*	*H*
big	425	*tall*	132	big	347	good	336
good	203	good	083	pretty	325	big	172
beautiful	166	deep	048	beautiful	311	slight	115
little	078	*white*	045	*merry*	303	much	093
hard	066	hard	044	fearful	190	*dark*	083
long	061	*black*	037	small	141	*fair*	074
strong	060	fine	036	*glad*	131	severe	072
thick	058	violent	031	strong	123	bad	068
intense	058	pleasant	031	wonderful	116	dreadful	067
bad	053	soft	030	good	110	small	067

give cultural interpretations of these "incidental" differences; this would require more intimate knowledge of the cultures than the present writer possesses. Second, in our future work we plan to apply the short-form differentials derived from the pan-cultural factor analyses to the development of what might be called a "World Atlas of Affective Meanings." This will involve a greatly expanded set of concepts, deliberately selected for their intercultural discriminating power. Third, we plan to undertake a number of pan-cultural comparative studies in particular concept areas, e.g., the self-concept and kin-concepts more generally.

Differences in Existing Data

(1) *H-ranks of qualifiers.* The fact that there are correlations in the .50 to .70 range across the various language-culture communities in modes of qualifying has already been demonstrated (cf., Table 3). Although there is the general semantic correspondence among the top 10 *H*-ranked qualifiers (as translated into English) for the eight groups shown in Table 8, there are also some apparent uniquenesses. Some of these are suggested by italics (e.g., *white* and *red* for Arabic; *firm, spoiled*, and *difficult* for Finnish; *tall, white, black*, and *violent* for French; *merry* and *glad* for Japanese; *dark* and *fair* for Kannada).

Color terms vary in their occurrence and ordering among the first 40 *H*-ranks as shown in Table 9. All seven color terms occur for American English; no color terms occur among the top 40 for Japanese. *White* and *black* are very salient "colors" semantically, both in occurrence and *H*-rank, and among the hues *red* is clearly the most salient; relative emphasis on *white* and *black* is shared by Lebanese,

Table 9

H-RANKS FOR COLOR TERMS OCCURRING AMONG TOP 40 IN RANK

	American	*Lebanese*	*Dutch*	*Finnish*	*Flemish*	*French*	*Japanese*	*Kannada*
white	15	9	34	37	13	4	—	6 (fair)
black	11	11	14	23	19	6	—	5 (dark)
red	12	10	15	21	16	11	—	14
yellow	36	34	—	33	—	—	—	—
green	40	32	—	—	—	—	—	—
blue	21	—	—	38	—	31	—	36
brown	25	—	—	—	—	—	—	—

French, and Kannada-speaking Indians, as against the other groups. Similar comparisons could be made for other qualifier classes.

(2) *Orientation of translation-equivalent scales.* It had been apparent in our earlier studies that semantic differential scales may meet the usual criteria for translation equivalence and yet have quite different affective connotations as evidenced in their factorial orientation. An example from Kumata's (1957) Japanese study was the scale, *rugged-delicate*; this was clearly a Potency scale for Americans, but equally clearly an Evaluative scale (*delicate / good—rugged / bad*) for the Japanese. The implications for international communication, or lack thereof, of such unintended qualifier connotation is obvious. Similar uniquenesses in what qualities connote Evaluation, Potency, or Activity can be found in the present data, despite over-all factorial similarities. The reader is referred back to Table 4. Evaluation is connoted by *elegant-vulgar* (cf., *delicate-rugged* in earlier study) for the Japanese and by *merciful-cruel, delicate-rough,* and *soft-rough* for the Kannada-speaking Indians. Potency is connoted by *high-low* for Americans, by *old-new* and *old-young* for the Flemish-speaking Belgians, by *difficult-easy* for the Japanese, and by *many-few* and *plenty-little* for the Kannada-speaking Indians. Activity is connoted by *noisy-quiet* for Americans, Japanese, and Indians, by *delicate-sturdy* for Finns, by *bloody-not bloody* and *shrewd-naive* for Belgians, and by *fatty-slim* for Indians (note the reversal in direction here from what Americans would predict, e.g., *slim* should be associated with *active,* not *fatty*!). This type of analysis could be extended over the entire data to yield inferences as to what general modes of qualifying have what affective implications in different cultures.

(3) *H-ranks of substantives.* In each language/culture community 100 qualifiers were elicited for each substantive, and one can thereby inquire into the entropy characteristics of the substantives themselves. A substantive to which many subjects gave the same response (e.g., *star*-bright) would have a low *H*-rank and could be called a *culturally stereotyped concept,* whereas one to which subjects tended to give many idiosyncratic responses would have a high *H*-rank and could be called a *culturally amorphous concept.* When the *H*-ranks for substantives were computed for five groups available at that time, and the rank orderings were correlated as had been done with the qualifier-types, it was clear that here there was great diversity: the obtained correlations were .22, .28, .21, and .09 for comparisons of English with Dutch, Afghan Farsi, Iranian Farsi, and Kannada respectively. These values should be contrasted with the .50 to .70 correlations for analogous qualifier ranks.

We may ask which concepts tend to be stereotyped to the same degree across language/culture communities and which tend to display unique culture dependencies in this respect. Table 10 orders the

Table 10

100 Nouns Ranked by Standard Deviation of *H*-Rank

		H-rank							
		American English	*Dutch*	*Afghan Farsi*	*Iranian Farsi*	*Kannada*	*Mean Rank**	*Rank S.D.*	
1.	Star	84	79	85	73	74	79.0	(4)	5.4
2.	Man	19	5	3	1	1	5.8	(1)	
3.	Fish	27	14	7	22	13	16.6	(1)	
4.	Policeman	12	21	1	4	15	10.6	(1)	
5.	Luck	96	75	84	95	100	87.8	(4)	
6.	Chair	38	23	29	45	21	31.2		
7.	Woman	3	29	10	11	29	16.4	(1)	
8.	Love	8	7	37	14	14	16.0	(1)	
9.	Trust	45	68	75	71	54	62.6		
10.	Cloud	76	74	100	100	96	89.2	(4)	13.05
11.	Cup	48	34	11	37	30	32.0		
12.	Punishment	21	56	45	52	43	43.4		
13.	Doctor	49	15	32	17	37	30.0		
14.	Wealth	70	96	77	93	62	79.6	(4)	
15.	Hand	17	6	25	10	44	20.4	(1)	
16.	Sleep	41	42	21	40	65	41.8		
17.	Success	73	59	48	31	45	51.2		
18.	Money	55	72	46	87	68	65.6		
19.	Horse	11	1	41	19	5	15.4	(1)	
20.	Knowledge	53	69	28	42	34	45.2		16.5
21.	Rope	54	84	88	74	53	70.6		
22.	Thief	1	13	26	6	42	17.6	(1)	
23.	Laughter	56	32	36	8	35	33.4		
24.	Snake	57	61	42	58	20	47.6		
25.	Sun	95	55	96	79	70	79.0	(4)	
26.	Map	36	19	15	29	59	31.6		
27.	Meat	46	85	43	56	72	60.4		
28.	Bread	62	65	19	43	40	45.8		
29.	Respect	42	93	69	75	61	68.0		
30.	Danger	100	100	53	82	84	83.8	(4)	19.3
31.	Poison	86	88	64	96	49	76.6	(4)	
32.	Cat	78	80	31	57	50	59.2		
33.	Bird	22	35	40	72	22	38.2		
34.	Lake	31	58	52	89	57	57.4		
35.	Heat	60	49	72	97	95	74.6	(4)	
36.	Head	44	62	58	28	85	55.4		
37.	Egg	29	39	71	59	80	55.6		
38.	Tongue	6	17	34	12	60	25.8		
39.	Smoke	82	41	91	88	94	79.2	(4)	
40.	Story	52	30	61	21	8	34.4		21.9
41.	Dog	7	28	49	50	4	27.6		
42.	Fruit	68	78	89	55	31	64.2		
43.	Anger	51	11	67	20	38	37.4		
44.	Music	58	44	12	9	51	34.8		
45.	Death	34	10	8	3	58	22.6	(1)	
46.	Heart	33	60	2	7	19	24.2	(1)	
47.	Battle	23	26	4	67	39	31.8		
48.	Freedom	64	4	57	38	36	39.8		
49.	Crime	32	25	78	65	69	53.8		
50.	Pain	18	67	62	69	79	59.0		23.7

*Numbers in parentheses indicate mean rank of first or fourth quartile.

Table 10—(Continued)

		H-rank						
	American English	*Dutch*	*Afghan Farsi*	*Iranian Farsi*	*Kannada*	*Mean Rank**	*Rank S. D.*	
51. Sympathy	24	66	80	54	83	61.4		
52. Color	20	50	70	18	17	35.0		
53. Rain	72	47	59	91	28	59.4		
54. Ear	40	52	98	47	78	63.0		
55. Choice	39	94	76	39	52	60.0		
56. Husband	14	37	9	70	41	34.2		
57. Wind	71	90	63	63	23	62.0		
58. Wednesday	43	64	94	41	88	66.0		
59. River	25	36	27	84	27	39.8		
60. Need	85	97	33	81	87	76.6	(4)	25.1
61. Hunger	28	46	68	78	91	62.2		
62. Marriage	61	82	24	24	64	51.0		
63. Hair	81	45	99	35	71	66.2		
64. Author	83	71	30	34	24	48.4		
65. Fire	79	27	82	27	47	52.4		
66. Power	93	70	23	86	67	67.8		
67. Moon	35	99	51	36	75	59.2		
68. Pleasure	77	95	50	32	32	57.2		
69. Water	13	20	6	15	76	26.0		
70. Tree	69	53	74	61	3	52.0		28.5
71. Life	65	3	39	2	56	33.0		
72. Peace	37	8	54	25	81	40.2		
73. Truth	59	31	18	68	92	53.6		
74. Girl	80	86	90	85	18	71.8		
75. Tooth	74	33	93	23	33	51.2		
76. Guilt	2	51	73	64	77	53.4		
77. Future	50	22	97	90	73	66.4		
78. Window	87	77	17	48	25	50.8		
79. Seed	94	38	35	62	11	48.0		
80. Picture	10	91	66	77	46	58.0		30.1
81. Stone	47	24	79	76	7	46.6		
82. Courage	4	76	47	83	66	55.2		
83. Defeat	26	54	5	51	90	45.2		
84. Hope	67	40	20	26	98	50.2		
85. Book	16	92	13	49	26	39.2		
86. Knot	75	12	86	44	89	61.2		
87. Food	90	16	87	33	48	54.8		
88. Purpose	63	87	22	30	97	59.8		
89. Progress	5	83	65	46	12	42.2		
90. Root	88	48	38	5	82	52.2		34.0
91. Work	97	43	44	60	2	49.2		
92. Friend	92	81	60	80	6	63.8		
93. Noise	99	63	56	92	10	64.0		
94. Game	91	9	55	13	16	36.8		
95. Belief	89	2	81	53	86	62.2		
96. Mother	30	73	92	98	55	64.2		
97. Father	9	18	83	94	63	53.4		
98. House	66	98	95	99	9	73.4		
99. Fear	15	89	14	66	93	55.4		
100. Thunder	98	57	16	16	99	57.2		41.2

*Numbers in parentheses indicate mean rank of first or fourth quartile.

100 substantives according to the standard deviation in *H*-ranks across five groups (eventually this will be done across our much larger, total sample). Concepts toward the top of the list display similar degrees of stereotypy across cultures; concepts low in this ranking display marked differences in stereotypy. The actual level of stereotypy is indicated by the *H*-ranks in the table, large ranks indicating high degrees of stereotyping and small ranks, low degrees. Concepts such as *star, luck, cloud, wealth, sun, danger, poison,* and *heat* tend to be stereotyped everywhere; conversely, concepts such as *man, fish, policeman, woman, love, hand, horse, thief,* and *dog* tend to be amorphous (diversely qualified) everywhere.

At the other end of the list in Table 10 we find some very interesting differences: *work* is highly stereotyped in mode of qualifying by Americans (rank 97), but highly amorphous for Indians (rank 2); similarly, the concept *friend* is stereotyped for Americans (rank 92) but amorphous for Indians (rank 6); *belief* is quite stereotyped for all except the Dutch (rank 2); the concepts *mother* and *father* are highly stereotyped for both Farsi-speaking groups, Afghan (ranks 92 and 83) and Iranian (ranks 92 and 94); *house* is a stereotyped notion for the Farsi-speaking groups again (ranks 95 and 99) and the Dutch (rank 98), but clearly amorphous for the Kannada-speaking Indians (rank 9).

It is also suggestive to look comparatively at certain clusters of concepts in terms of degrees of sterotyping. For all groups except Indian, abstract *wealth* is more stereotyped than concrete *money*; for Americans, Dutch, and Indians, the concept *hope* is more stereotyped than the concept *future,* but the reverse holds true for the two Farsi-speaking groups, and to an extreme degree (Afghan from rank 20 for *hope* to rank 97 for *future* and Iranian from rank 26 to rank 90); for all groups except Americans *man* is more diversely qualified than *woman,* while for all groups except Indians *woman* is more diversely qualified than *girl*; if we look at the spread in masculine roles, we find marked differences culturally—with Americans having the smallest spread (*man* 19, *husband* 14, *father* 9), the Dutch fairly small (*husband* 37, *father* 19, *man* 5), the Indians having a much larger spread (*father* 63, *husband* 41, *man* 1) and the two Farsi groups extremely large, Afghans (*father* 83, *husband* 9, *man* 3) and Iranians (*father* 94, *husband* 70, *man* 1)—and note that for the latter three groups with large spreads it is always *father* that is most stereotyped and *man* least; finally, we note that for all groups except Afghan Farsi, *cats* are more stereotyped than *dogs*!

(4) *Polarization of substantives.* The polarization (or affective intensity) of a concept, it will be recalled, is indexed by its distance from the origin of the semantic space. This can be computed either as an average of the *absolute* deviations of judgments of individual subjects from the midpoints of scales, or by the *algebraic* average of the deviations for individual subjects—in which case concepts for which different members of the culture have antagonistic meanings will suffer cancellation in polarization toward zero. The polarization rank data given in Table 11 utilized the second method since we were interested in what might be termed "cultural polarization." Table 11 is analogous to Table 10, in that the concepts are ranked according to the standard deviations among the polarization ranks across five language/culture communities (here, American, Finnish, Flemish, Japanese, and Kannada). Within the body of the table, the most polarized concepts have low ranks and the least polarized, high ranks.

Again we look first at those concepts for which there seems to be agreement across groups in polarization: the concepts *mother, thief, battle, truth, courage, marriage, love, freedom, fruit, bread,* and *heart* have high affective intensities everywhere; the concepts *hand, wednesday, chair, rope, choice, heat, fish, wealth,* and *future* have relatively low affective inten-

Table 11

The 100 Concepts Ranked by Standard Deviation of Polarity

		Polarity Rank							
		American English	*Finnish*	*Flemish*	*Japanese*	*Kannada*	*Mean Rank**	*Rank S. D.*	
1.	Mother	12	14	8	17	9	12.0	(1)	3.7
2.	Hand	70	63	71	60	70	66.8		
3.	Thief	6	4	13	1	12	7.2	(1)	
4.	River	57	62	56	48	49	54.4		
5.	Wednesday	100	99	91	100	84	94.8	(4)	
6.	Chair	80	73	58	75	69	71.0		
7.	Battle	19	3	20	5	19	13.2	(1)	
8.	Truth	35	47	26	25	25	31.6		
9.	Rope	91	70	75	84	66	77.2	(4)	
10.	Courage	38	58	40	27	39	40.4		11.1
11.	Anger	28	40	30	54	51	40.6		
12.	Choice	69	98	74	82	91	82.8	(4)	
13.	Marriage	2	7	10	21	32	14.4	(1)	
14.	Love	4	8	4	33	14	12.6	(1)	
15.	Pleasure	32	52	18	32	35	33.8		
16.	Freedom	1	2	31	9	6	9.8	(1)	
17.	Fruit	36	36	11	35	11	25.8		
18.	Heat	86	61	78	72	99	79.2	(4)	
19.	Moon	26	31	14	49	12	26.4		
20.	Bread	20	15	12	41	44	26.4		15.0
21.	Tooth	40	34	36	65	63	47.6		
22.	Fish	92	55	89	90	83	81.8	(4)	
23.	Smoke	68	37	79	67	58	61.8		
24.	Bird	43	24	53	43	67	46.0		
25.	Hair	77	94	65	85	53	74.8	(4)	
26.	Picture	63	42	88	66	61	64.0		
27.	Star	18	38	34	45	64	39.8		
28.	Head	81	51	46	61	37	55.2		
29.	Cup	72	50	70	36	76	60.8		
30.	Father	16	22	52	14	8	22.4	(1)	17.3
31.	Seed	67	43	47	87	62	61.2		
32.	Window	60	44	60	74	28	53.2		
33.	Cloud	31	67	68	69	41	55.2		
34.	Rain	48	72	69	94	88	74.2		
35.	Knot	99	56	85	99	94	86.6	(4)	
36.	Map	79	49	72	37	73	62.0		
37.	Laughter	30	68	43	58	75	54.8		
38.	Food	39	83	50	40	43	51.0		
39.	Power	56	77	92	93	54	74.4		
40.	Book	62	64	63	71	23	56.6		19.1
41.	Heart	8	5	49	30	7	19.8	(1)	
42.	Man	64	60	66	24	74	57.6		
43.	Death	73	29	32	31	56	44.2		
44.	Cat	85	45	44	81	78	66.6		
45.	Life	52	91	35	62	52	58.4		
46.	Wealth	59	95	55	98	60	73.4		
47.	Danger	66	17	39	15	47	36.8		
48.	Future	55	88	97	50	89	75.8	(4)	
49.	Music	49	21	57	46	5	35.6		
50.	Peace	23	59	6	11	46	29.0		22.8

*Numbers in parentheses indicate mean rank of first or fourth quartile.

Table 11—(Continued)

		Polarity Rank							
		American English	*Finnish*	*Flemish*	*Japanese*	*Kannada*	*Mean Rank**	*Rank S. D.*	
51.	Egg	33	21	61	73	26	42.8		22.9
52.	Poison	53	39	48	6	68	42.8		
53.	Horse	24	13	51	57	4	29.8		
54.	Lake	22	48	54	16	72	42.4		
55.	Trust	21	46	64	38	82	50.2		
56.	Thunder	78	74	80	23	57	62.4		
57.	Purpose	80	92	100	39	71	77.0	(4)	
58.	Water	41	31	3	63	10	29.6		
59.	Friend	11	10	27	64	3	23.0	(1)	
60.	Sun	5	1	1	7	59	14.6	(1)	25.0
61.	Root	90	84	82	53	31	68.0		
62.	Color	45	69	76	77	18	57.0		
63.	Fire	54	32	7	76	33	40.4		
64.	Work	74	79	94	52	27	65.2		
65.	Progress	37	41	62	10	79	45.8		
66.	Defeat	47	26	87	55	86	60.2		
67.	Game	65	80	33	47	13	47.6		
68.	Punishment	75	16	9	51	34	37.0		
69.	Fear	87	33	81	42	90	66.6		
70.	Sympathy	58	27	25	92	45	49.4		27.4
71.	Money	29	54	93	91	81	69.6		
72.	Husband	50	96	45	22	36	49.8		
73.	Stone	74	23	16	78	48	47.8		
74.	Dog	61	9	86	59	44	51.4		
75.	Policeman	46	86	77	70	15	58.8		
76.	Hunger	82	75	21	68	97	68.6		
77.	House	51	87	23	19	21	40.2		
78.	Need	94	100	28	80	92	78.8	(4)	
79.	Belief	13	65	42	44	93	61.4		
80.	Sleep	25	18	17	20	87	33.4		30.0
81.	Ear	34	89	37	95	38	58.6		
82.	Author	89	97	83	83	20	74.2		
83.	Success	44	82	59	2	22	41.8		
84.	Story	89	78	38	79	16	60.0		
85.	Tongue	27	57	95	96	40	63.0		
86.	Woman	14	12	29	89	24	33.6		
87.	Respect	15	71	67	56	1	42.0		
88.	Pain	84	53	24	29	96	57.2		
89.	Snake	95	76	22	28	77	59.6		
90.	Luck	93	66	84	8	65	63.2		33.1
91.	Tree	71	25	90	12	30	45.6		
92.	Noise	96	85	73	18	100	74.4		
93.	Doctor	10	35	98	26	50	43.8		
94.	Meat	42	91	15	86	85	63.8		
95.	Wind	98	81	41	91	17	65.6		
96.	Hope	17	93	96	34	81	64.2		
97.	Girl	7	11	5	88	55	33.2		
98.	Knowledge	3	19	99	13	29	32.6		
99.	Crime	9	6	2	3	98	23.6	(1)	
100.	Guilt	97	28	19	4	95	48.6		44.1

*Numbers in parentheses indicate mean rank of first or fourth quartile.

sities everywhere. Turning to the lower end of the table, we again find some intriguing differences: *respect* has high affective intensity for the Kannada-speaking Indians (rank 1), but relatively little for the Finns (rank 71); *luck* is very polarized in affect for the Japanese (rank 8), but clearly not so for Americans (rank 93); *noise* is polar affectively for Japanese (rank 18), but obviously not so for either Americans (rank 96) or Indians (rank 100); *hope* is a polarized concept for Americans (rank 17), but clearly not so for either Finns (rank 93) or Belgians (rank 96); *crime* is an extremely affective notion for all groups except the Kannada-speaking Indians, where it has a rank of 98; yet *guilt* is not emotionally polarized for Americans along with Indians (ranks 97 and 95), as compared with the Finns (rank 28), the Flemish-speaking Belgians (rank 19) and the Japanese (rank 4).

(5) *Octant allocations of substantives.* The three dominant, orthogonal factors in the common semantic space can be used to define eight octants, e.g., *good, strong,* and *active* (E +, P +, A +), *good, strong,* and *passive* (E +, P +, A −), etc. In a crude anticipation of the profiles that would be presented in a semantic atlas (cf. below), we may inspect the similarities and differences in allocation of concepts to these eight octants across four of our language/culture communities (here, American, Finnish, Flemish, and Japanese). Table 12 shows concept distributions to octants regardless of concept identifications. We note first that there is general agreement cross-culturally in octant densities: evaluatively positive regions (E +) are more densely occupied by concepts than evaluatively negative regions (E −), to an average ratio of 79 per cent to 21 per cent; similarly, positive potency (P +) is more characteristic than negative potency (P −), to an average ratio of 72 per cent to 28 per cent; on the other hand, positive and negative activity are about equally prominent, 46 to 54 per cent. Furthermore, Belgian-Flemish is more similar in concept distribution to American English than are either Finnish or Japanese. The lower portion of Table 12 lists the concepts which fall into the same octants for all four or at least three of this small sample of groups; it should be noted that there are three octants in which no common concepts are found. Whether this unequal utilization of the affective space is characteristic of the human species (e.g., a general "pollyanna" tendency we have noted consistently in our earlier work) or is a happenstance of our particular sample of 100 concepts remains to be determined.

Some of the differences in concept allocation are suggestive of real culture differences; for example: *progress* is *good-strong-active* for all except Finnish, where it is *passive*; similarly, *future* is *good-strong-active* for all except Finnish, where it is *good*, but *weak* and *passive; work* is *good-strong-active* for all but Flemish, where it is *bad-strong-passive,* for some reason; both *friend* and *man* are *good-strong-active* for Americans and Japanese, but *passive* for the Flemish and *weak* for Finns; only for Americans is *policeman good-strong-active,* being *bad-strong-passive* for the Flemish and *bad-strong-active* for the Japanese (unassigned for Finns); *mother* and *father* are both *good-strong-passive* for Americans and Flemish and are both *good-strong-active* for Japanese, but *father* is *good-strong-active* and *mother good-weak-active* for the Finns; the concept of *power* is *good-strong-active* for both Americans and Flemish speakers; but it becomes *passive* for Finns and turns both *bad* and *weak* (but still *active*) for Japanese; and one last set of comparisons —concepts like *defeat, battle, thief, crime,* and *danger* are all *bad-strong-active* for Americans, Belgians, and Finns, but for the Japanese *defeat, thief, crime,* and *danger* are *bad-weak-passive* and *battle* is *good-weak-active.*

All of these comparisons, and those that have preceded, should be taken *cum grano salis* for the present and treated merely as illustrations of the types of differences that might be determined. There are several

Table 12

Concept Distributions by Octants in Four Cultures

	Octant							
Culture	E+ P+ A+	E+ P+ A−	E+ P− A−	E+ P− A+	E− P+ A+	E− P+ A−	E− P− A−	E− P− A+
American	20	48	10	3	14	4	1	0
	16	37	12	3	18	8		
Flemish	16	37	12	3	18	8	3	1
	23	25	9	24	9	2		
Finnish	23	25	9	24	9	2	3	1
Japanese	31	27	8	13	3	0	11	4
Total*	90	137	39	43	44	14	18	6

*Total adds to 391 rather than 400 because a few concepts fell precisely at the midpoints of a factor.

Concepts Commonly Assigned to the Octants by Three or Four of the Four Cultures Examined

	E+, P+, A+	E+, P+, A−	E+, P−, A−	E+, P−, A+	E−, P+, A+
	good strong active	good strong passive	good weak passive	good weak active	bad strong active
Four	Courage Dog Success	Meat Tree Lake Author Symphony Truth Belief Moon Rope Knowledge			Anger Thunder
Three	Progress Husband Laughter Wealth Work Horse Luck Future	House Book Star Sleep Chair Food Window Story	Tooth Seed Tongue Cup Egg	Bird Woman	Defeat Battle Thief Noise Crime Danger Fear

reasons for this: For one thing, although we exercised care in the translations of the list of 100 substantives and the obtained qualifiers, rather slight shifts in denotative mapping could produce marked effects here. For another thing, the samples of language/culture communities upon which these substantive comparisons are being made are still quite small and in no case represent even half of our present total group. Even further, we have not as yet introduced appropriate statistical tests for the significances of the various differences that have been alluded to, since we are waiting for a large sample of our data. Given these caveats, the types of differentiations of subjective culture illustrated seem potentially valuable.

An Atlas of Affective Meanings

The various steps in Phases I and II of the general project provide a great deal of quantitative psycholinguistic information obtained in standardized fashion from subjects in various language/culture groups. For example, we obtain lognormal functions characterizing the over-all distributions of modes of qualifying, entropy indices, reflecting both frequency and diversity of usage, for both qualifiers and substantives, factors and resultant vectors for all scales utilized, locations and polarizations of individual concept meanings for the basic list of 100 substantives, and so forth. Such data derive automatically from the necessary operations of the "toolmaking" phases. To this information we plan to add, particularly, affective meaning profiles (against the final pan-cultural factors) for additional concepts so as to bring the total in the concept-meaning sections of the Atlas to 1,000 translation-equivalent terms.

Comparable information of this sort about languages should have a wide variety of uses. Linguists, psycholinguists, anthropologists and others will be able to make lexical and semantic analyses of such data, e.g., on the comparability of "semantic fields" of the translation-equivalent "nouns" as determined by the overlap in the qualifiers they produce. There is a present trend of interest among linguists in "language universals," and these data should contribute to study of universals in the lexico-semantic aspects of language. The Atlas should also serve as a source of verbal materials having known affective properties for use in many types of cross-cultural psycholinguistic experiments—experiments on human cognition, perception, learning, and so forth. On the more practical side, such an Atlas of Affective Meanings should contribute to more effective international communication. For example, we already know from our Greek study (Triandis and Osgood 1958) that the concept *hospital* has very different affective connotations for Greeks as compared with Americans—for the former it has connotations of warmth and sociability, whereas for the latter it conveys the connotation of cold efficiency (and these differences correlate with cultural customs associated with this institution).

Sampling

In order to make the subject-sample for the new Atlas material (the additional concepts to yield a 1,000 total) comparable with that already obtained in Phases I and II, the subjects will also be young males of junior high school equivalence. Because of the large number of concepts to be included in the Atlas, relatively small subsets (25–30 in a group) will be used for subsets of the concepts (probably about 50, handled in two sessions). For comparison purposes, and for only a subset of the total 1,000 concepts, a mature adult "elite" sample will also be taken. As the Atlas is extended to nonliterate subject groups, it is anticipated that again the subject and concept sample will have to be somewhat modified. The *concept-sample* will include: (a) the basic set of 100 substantives used in Phases I and II, these being "nouns" selected as culture-fair and readily translatable; (b) an additional 500 lexical items (Fries Types I-IV words, e.g., nouns, adjectives, verbs, and adverbs and their functional equivalents in other languages) selected on the basis of frequency-of-usage across language/culture groups (using Thorndike-Lorge type lists for printed material where available, or collecting such data ourselves); and (c) 400 additional concepts selected by the local and foreign staff to tap basic abstractions (life, death, past, present, future, freedom, deity, privacy, law, nation, marriage, disease, health, etc.), occupational stereotypes (farmer, doctor, teacher, soldier, policeman, student, cook, politician, and so forth), national stereotypes (a representative and large sample of nation-names), and various symbols for racial, religious, and other human groupings. The *scale-sample* for Atlas purposes will be the final 15–18 scale form for each language/culture group resulting from the pan-cultural factor analyses of Phase II.

General procedure

The Atlas of Affective Meanings will be organized as sections of tables, each section introduced by some text describing the nature of the tables, how the data were obtained, and some of their possible uses. In order to facilitate expansion as new language/culture groups are added, we plan to make the Atlas loose-leaf in format. Whether this should be printed and published, or simply mimeographed for private distribution, will be decided later when we have a better idea of what the demand for it might be. As presently planned, the sections of the Atlas will be:

(1) tables of qualifiers given to each of the 100 substantives with frequency greater than one, listed in order of frequency;

(2) the over-all qualifier distribution characteristics for each group—lognormal functions, means, and sigmas;

(3) *H*-indices and *H*-ranks for the 200 highest *H* qualifiers;

(4) *H*-indices and *H*-ranks for the 100 substantives used as elicitors;

(5) scale vectors (loadings) in the three-factor space, based on unique factorization (not pan-cultural) for each group;

(6) scale vectors in the three-space defined by pan-cultural factors;

(7) the generalized Semantic Differential (15–18 scale) recommended for use in each language, based on pan-cultural factorizations;

(8) localizations (factor scores), polarizations (distances from origin) and clustering (all other concepts falling within a sphere of constant radial distance, e.g., $D = 2.00$, centered on each concept) of all 1,000 concepts;

(9) distributions of concepts in octants of the space, as derived from above;

(10) other psycholinguistic indices, e.g., Noble's, 1952 *m* values, tables of associative overlap based on Noble's sequential association procedure).

THE NEED FOR AN ADEQUATE MEASURE OF DENOTATIVE MEANING

The research reported above all involves what has been termed the "semantic differential" technique in one form or another. It is now abundantly clear that this method taps only one, restricted (albeit pragmatically important) aspect of meaning. Another important aspect of meaning—indeed, that with which linguists, lexicographers and philosophers have been most concerned—is what I shall call *denotative meaning*. By "denotative" I refer to the descriptive use of signs as contrasted with their emotive or affective use, which appears to be tapped by the semantic differential technique. It is this denotative aspect which leads one to conclude intuitively that "*nail* is more similar to *pebble* than it is to *mouse*," the aspect which presumably underlies the labelling confusions that we regularly observe in anomic aphasics ("That is a... *pipe*—no; a... *match*—no; it's a... *cigarette*—yes, a *cigarette*!") and also the semantic slips of normals ("Patty, where are the pliers—no, I mean nailclippers!").

The problem comes out clearly in the verbal-behavior laboratory when we try to account fully for the phenomena of mediated (or semantic) generalization;

associative bonds between training and test words account for a part of the variance and affective or connotative similarity as indexed by the semantic differential for another part, but there is still a large chunk of variance unaccounted for, and it presumably is that due to what we are calling denotative similarity. An adequate measure should reflect the multidimensional nature of meaning, should yield a quantitative measure of degrees of denotative similarity, should be completely general for all pairs of terms measured, and should meet the usual criteria of reliability, validity, and comparability across subjects and concepts.

Linguistic componential analysis, as applied to restricted semantic domains like kin-terms, provides only a partial answer—precisely because the components appropriate to one area (e.g., male-female, older-younger, blood-marital relation, etc., as applied to kinship) prove to be completely irrelevant to another (e.g., utensils or foodstuffs or modes of transportation). The semantic differential, as usually applied, reflects affective or connotative similarities, but clearly fails to reflect denotative similarities in any consistent fashion (e.g., pairs of terms like *nurse* and *sincerity* or *rabbit* and *melody* or *fate* and *quicksand* may have almost identical locations in affective space).

However, one recent direction of our methodological research holds out some promise. To the question, "Is a *baby large* or *small*?" most people respond *small*. To the question, "Is a railroad *spike large* or *small*?" most people say *large*. Within the class of human organisms, a baby *is* a *small* one, and within the class of nails, a spike *is* a *large* one. The usual semantic differential technique, in which a single stimulus is judged successively on a series of scales, tends to draw out these within-class connotations of signs. In all other psychophysical methods, including the so-called absolute judgment methods, a series of different stimuli (e.g., weights, tones, brightnesses, etc.) are judged against a single scale at a time. Note that if the question becomes, "Is a *baby larger or smaller* than a *spike*?" everyone says *larger*. The general hypothesis, then, is that if a series of concepts, falling into different implicit classes, is judged comparatively on single semantic differential scales one at a time, the scales will tend to be used denotatively to the extent that they have denotative properties. By assessing the dimensionality of the scale-space under these conditions we may be able to generate a denotative semantic space. Such a space will certainly contain many more factors than the affective semantic space. Furthermore, the distances between concepts within this space may provide a usable quantitative index of denotative similarity. The development of a satisfactory quantitative measure of denotative meaning appears to me to be one of the most important problems for contemporary psycholinguistics.

SPECULATIONS CONCERNING GENERALITY

When this research was begun over a decade ago, I had expected that the dimensions of the semantic space would correspond to the ways in which the sensory nervous system divides up the world, e.g., there would be visual brightness, hue and saturation factors, auditory loudness and pitch factors, olfactory factors, and so on. (This result would have been in flat contradiction to my own mediation theory of meaning—according to which meanings are anticipatory portions of the *reactions* we make to signs—although this did not occur to me at the time.) However, the Evaluation, Potency, and Activity dimensions which have reappeared in analysis after analysis are clearly response-like in character rather than sensory.

But these factors are more than simply reactive; they have an *affective* character. The similarity of these factors to Wundt's three dimensions of feeling—pleasantness, strain, and excitement—has been suggested by others.

The highly generalized nature of the affective reaction system—the fact that it is independent of any particular sensory modality and yet participates with all of them—appears to be the psychological basis for the universality of three factors of Evaluation, Potency, and Activity, as well as the basis for synesthesia and metaphor. That is, it appears to be *because* such diverse sensory experiences as a *white* circle (rather than black), a *straight* line (rather than crooked), a *rising* melody (rather than a falling one), a *sweet* taste (rather than a sour one), a *caressing* touch (rather than an irritating scratch) can all share a common affective meaning that one can easily and lawfully translate from one modality into another in synesthesia and metaphor. The labelling of this shared affective response is apparently uncovered in the factor analysis of adjectives.

Speculating still further, I would suggest that this affective meaning system is intimately related to the nonspecific projection mechanisms from the hypothalamic, reticular, or limbic systems and their cortical connections in the frontal lobes. Both are gross, nondiscriminative, but highly generalized systems, and both are associated with the emotional purposive and motivational dynamics of the organism. As yet, only some incidental and entirely inadequate evidence on aphasics supports this last speculation. In a study of a small sample of aphasiac patients, it was found that despite gross disturbances in labelling, sequencing, and other denotative and grammatical tasks, these patients seemed to have no impairment in appropriate affect and made synesthetic judgments essentially like normals on a pictorial (nonverbal) form of the semantic differential.

References

Cliff, N.
1959 Adverbs as multipliers. Psychological Review 66:27–44.

Goodenough, W.
1956 Componential analysis and the study of meaning. Language 32:155–216.

Kumata, H.
1957 A factor analytic investigation of the generality of semantic structure across two selected cultures. Unpublished Ph.D. dissertation, University of Illinois.

Lees, R. B.
1953 The basis of glottochronology. Language 29:113–127.

Lounsbury, F. G.
1956 A semantic analysis of the Pawnee kinship usage. Language 32:158–194.

Murdock, G. P.
1949 Social structure. New York, Macmillan.

Noble, C. E.
1952 An analysis of meaning. Psychological Review 59:421–430.

Osgood, C. E.
1960 The cross-cultural generality of visual-verbal synesthetic tendencies. Behavioral Science 5:146–169.

Osgood, C. E., S. Saporta, and J. C. Nunnally
1956 Evaluative assertion analysis. Litera 3:47–102.

Osgood, C. E., G. J. Suci, and P. H. Tannenbaum.
1957 The measurement of meaning. Urbana, Illinois, University of Illinois Press.

Suci, G. J.
1960 A comparison of semantic structures in American Southwest culture groups. Journal of Abnormal and Social Psychology 61:25–30.

SWADESH, M.
1950 Salish internal relationships. International Journal of American Linguistics 16:157–167.

TRIANDIS, H. C. and C. E. OSGOOD.
1958 A comparative factorial analysis of semantic structures in monolingual Greek and American college students. Journal of Abnormal and Social Psychology 57:187–196.

The Structure of a Semantic Theory

JERROLD J. KATZ
and JERRY A. FODOR

1. INTRODUCTION

This paper[1] does not attempt to present a semantic theory of a natural language, but rather to characterize the form of such a theory. A semantic theory of a natural language is part of a linguistic description of that language. Our problem, on the other hand, is part of the general theory of language, fully on a par with the problem of characterizing the structure of grammars of natural languages. A characterization of the abstract form of a semantic theory is given by a metatheory which answers such questions as these: What is the domain of a semantic theory? What are the descriptive and explanatory goals of a semantic theory? What mechanisms are employed in pursuit of these goals? What are the empirical and methodological constraints upon a semantic theory?

The present paper approaches the problem of characterizing the form of semantic theories by describing the structure of a semantic theory of English. There can be little doubt but that the results achieved will apply directly to semantic theories of languages closely related to English. The question of their applicability to semantic theories of more distant languages will be left for subsequent investigations to explore. Nevertheless, the present investigation will provide results that can be applied to semantic theories of languages unrelated to English and suggestions about how to proceed with the construction of such theories.

We may put our problem this way: What form should a semantic theory of a natural language take to accommodate in the most revealing way the facts about the semantic structure of that language supplied by descriptive research? This question is of primary importance at the present stage of the development of semantics because semantics suffers not from a dearth of facts about meanings and meaning relations in natural languages, but rather from the lack of an adequate theory to organize, systematize, and generalize these facts. Facts about

[1] This work was supported in part by the U. S. Army Signal Corps, the Air Force Office of Scientific Research, and the Office of Naval Research; and in part by the National Science Foundation (Grant G-13903).

Jerrold J. Katz and Jerry A. Fodor, "The Structure of a Semantic Theory," *Language*, **39,** No. 2 (April–June, 1963), 170–210. Reprinted by permission of the authors and publisher.

the semantics of natural languages have been contributed in abundance by many diverse fields, including philosophy, linguistics, philology, and psychology. Indeed, a compendium of such facts is readily available in any good dictionary. But at present the superabundance of facts obscures a clear view of their interrelations, while such theories as have been proposed to account for the facts have, in general, been either too loosely formulated or too weak in explanatory and descriptive power to succeed.

2. THE PROJECTION PROBLEM

A full synchronic description of a natural language is a grammatical and semantic characterization of that language (where the term 'grammatical' is construed broadly to include phonology, phonemics, morphology, and syntax). Hence, a semantic theory must be constructed to have whatever properties are demanded by its role in linguistic description. Since, however, the goals of such description are reasonably well understood and since, in comparison to semantics, the nature of grammar has been clearly articulated, we may expect that by studying the contribution that semantics will be required to make to a synchronic description of a language we can clarify the subject, the form of generalizations, the goals, and the empirical and methodological constraints upon a semantic theory.

A fluent speaker's mastery of his language exhibits itself in his ability to produce and understand the sentences of his language, INCLUDING INDEFINITELY MANY THAT ARE WHOLLY NOVEL TO HIM (i.e. his ability to produce and understand ANY sentence of his language[2]). The emphasis upon novel sentences is important. The most characteristic feature of language is its ability to make available an infinity of sentences from which the speaker can select appropriate and novel ones to use as the need arises. That is to say, what qualifies one as a fluent speaker is not the ability to imitate previously heard sentences but rather the ability to produce and understand sentences never before encountered. The striking fact about the use of language is the absence of repetition: almost every sentence uttered is uttered for the first time. This can be substantiated by checking texts for the number of times a sentence is repeated. It is exceedingly unlikely that even a single repetition of a sentence of reasonable length will be encountered.

A synchronic description of a natural language seeks to determine what a fluent speaker knows about the structure of his language that enables him to use and understand its sentences. Since a fluent speaker is able to use and understand any sentence drawn from the INFINITE set of sentences of his language, and since, at any time, he has only encountered a FINITE set of sentences, it follows that the speaker's knowledge of his language takes the form of rules which project the finite set of sentences he has fortuitously encountered to the infinite set of sentences of the language. A description of the language which adequately represents the speaker's linguistic knowledge must, accordingly, state these rules. The problem of formulating these rules we shall refer to as the projection problem.

This problem requires for its solution rules which project the infinite set of sentences in a way which mirrors the way that speakers understand novel sentences. In encountering a novel sentence the speaker is not encountering novel elements

[2] There are exceptions, such as sentences with technical words that the speaker does not know and sentences too long for the speaker to scan in his lifetime. But these exceptions are of no systematic importance. Analogously, a person's mastery of an algorithm for propositional calculus can be said to exhibit itself in his ability to decide mechanically whether ANY well-formed formula of propositional calculus is a tautology, even though some well-formed formulae are too long for human processing, etc.

but only a novel combination of familiar elements. Since the set of sentences is infinite and each sentence is a different concatenation of morphemes, the fact that a speaker can understand any sentence must mean that the way he understands sentences which he has never previously encountered is compositional: on the basis of his knowledge of the grammatical properties and the meanings of the morphemes of the language, the rules which the speaker knows enable him to determine the maning of a novel sentence in terms of the manner in which the parts of the sentence are composed to form the whole. Correspondingly, we can expect that a system of rules which solves the projection problem must reflect the compositional character of the speaker's linguistic knowledge.[3]

3. SYNCHRONIC LINGUISTIC DESCRIPTION MINUS GRAMMAR EQUALS SEMANTICS

A description of a natural language is, inter alia, a solution to the projection problem for that language. If we are to discover the goals of semantics by subtracting from the goals of a description of a language whatever the grammar contributes to the solution of the projection problem, we must consider the respect in which a grammar is a solution for the grammatical aspect of the projection problem.

Grammars answer the question: What does the speaker know about the phonological and syntactic structure of his language that enables him to use and understand any of its sentences, including those he has not previously heard? They do so by providing rules which generate the sentences of the speaker's language. In particular, these rules generate infinitely many strings of morphemes which, though they are sentences of the language, have never been uttered by speakers.[4] Moreover, a grammar generates the sentences which a speaker is, in principle, capable of understanding in such a way that their derivations provide their structural descriptions. Such descriptions specify the elements out of which a sentence is constructed, the grammatical relations between these elements and between the higher constituents of the sentence, the relations between the sentence and other sentences of the language, and the ways the sentence is syntactically ambiguous together with an explanation of why it is ambiguous in these ways. Since it is this information about a novel sentence which the speaker knows and which enables him to understand its syntactic structure if and when he encounters the sentence, an adequate transformational grammar of a language

[3] A solution to the projection problem is certainly less than a full theory of speech. In particular, it does not provide a theory of speech production (or recognition). The difference between a description of a language and a theory of speech production is the difference between asking for a characterization of the rules of language which a speaker knows and asking for an account of how he actually applies those rules in speaking. Some things left out by the first theory but not by the second are considerations of the psychological parameters of speech production (e.g. limitations of immediate memory, level of motivation), and developmental accounts of the way the child becomes a fluent speaker (by conditioning? by the exploitation of innate mechanisms? by some combination of innate endowment and learning?). Though such problems concerning speech production lie outside the scope of a theory of a language, such a theory is essential to a theory of speech production. It is first necessary to know WHAT is acquired and used before it is sensible to ask HOW it is acquired and used.

[4] This conception of grammar is due to Chomsky. Cf. *Syntactic structures*[2] ('s-Gravenhage, 1962); 'Three models for the description of language', *I.R.E. transactions on information theory:* Vol. IT-2, Proceedings of the Symposium on Information Theory (Sept. 1956). For a bibliography on transformational grammar, see Chomsky, 'On the notion "rule of grammar"', *Structure of language and its mathematical aspects:* Proceedings of symposia in applied mathematics 12.16 fn. 24 (1961).

PARTIALLY solves the projection problem for the language.

A semantic theory of a language completes the solution of the projection problem for the language. Thus, semantics takes over the explanation of the speaker's ability to produce and understand new sentences at the point where grammar leaves off. Since we wish to determine, when we have subtracted the problems in the description of a language properly belonging to grammar, what problems belong to semantics, we must begin by gaining some grasp of how much of the projection problem is left unsolved by an optimal grammar.

One way to appreciate how much of understanding sentences is left unexplained by grammar is to compare the grammatical characterizations of sentences to what we know about their semantic characterizations. If we do this, we notice that the grammar provides identical structural descriptions for sentences that are different in meaning and different structural descriptions for sentences that are identical in meaning. The former will be the case for all morphemically distinct substitution instances of a given sentential type; for example, *The dog bit the man* and *The cat bit the woman.* The latter will be the case for many instances of sentential synonymy; for example, *The dog bit the man* and *The man was bitten by the dog.*[5]

In general, it is obvious that in no sense of meaning does the structural description which the grammar assigns to a sentence specify either the meaning of the sentence or the meaning of its parts. Such considerations must now be made precise in order that we may apply our formula 'linguistic description minus grammar equals semantics' to determine a lower bound on the domain of a semantic theory. Later in this section we will fix an upper bound by determining what problems lie outside the concerns of a complete linguistic description.

Grammars seek to describe the structure of a sentence IN ISOLATION FROM ITS POSSIBLE SETTINGS IN LINGUISTIC DISCOURSE (WRITTEN OR VERBAL) OR IN NONLINGUISTIC CONTEXTS (SOCIAL OR PHYSICAL). The justification which permits the grammarian to study sentences in abstraction from the settings in which they have occurred or might occur is simply that the fluent speaker is able to construct and recognize syntactically well-formed sentences without recourse to information about settings, and this ability is what a grammar undertakes to reconstruct. Every facet of the fluent speaker's linguistic ability which a grammar reconstructs can be exercised independently of information about settings: this is true not only of the ability to produce and recognize sentences but also of the ability to determine syntactic relations between sentence types, to implicitly analyze the syntactic structure of sentences, and to detect grammatical ambiguities. Since, then, the knowledge that a fluent speaker has of his language enables him to determine the grammatical structure of any sentence without reference to information about setting, grammar correspondingly forms an independent theory of this independent knowledge.

We may generalize to arrive at a sufficient condition for determining when an ability of speakers is the proper subject matter of a synchronic theory in linguistics. The generalization is this: IF SPEAKERS POSSESS AN ABILITY THAT ENABLES THEM TO APPREHEND THE STRUCTURE OF ANY SENTENCE IN THE INFINITE SET OF SENTENCES OF A LANGUAGE WITHOUT REFERENCE TO INFORMATION ABOUT SETTINGS AND WITHOUT SIGNIFICANT VARIATION FROM SPEAKER TO SPEAKER, THEN THAT ABILITY IS PROPERLY THE

[5] Moreover, sentences that receive the same structural description may differ in that one is semantically ambiguous or anomalous but the other is not. Compare *The bill is large, The paint is silent,* and *The street is wide,* all of which receive the same structural description from the grammar.

SUBJECT MATTER OF A SYNCHRONIC THEORY IN LINGUISTICS.

The first question in determining the subject matter of a semantic theory is: Can we find an ability which satisfies the antecedent of this generalization, which is beyond the range of grammatical description, and which is semantic in some reasonable sense? If we can, then that ability falls within the domain of a semantic theory.

In order to find such an ability, let us consider a communication situation so constructed that no information about setting can contribute to a speaker's understanding of a sentence encountered in that situation. Any extragrammatical ability that a speaker can employ to understand the meaning of a sentence in such a situation will ipso facto be considered to require semantic explanation.

The type of communication situation we shall consider is the following. A number of English-speakers receive an anonymous letter containing only the English sentence S. We are interested in the difference between this type of situation and one in which the same anonymous letter is received by persons who do not speak English but are equipped with a completely adequate grammar of English. To investigate what the first group can do by way of comprehending the meaning of S that the second group cannot is to factor out the contribution of grammar to the understanding of sentences. We will only investigate aspects of linguistic ability which are invariant from individual to individual within each group. We thus make sure that the abilities under investigation are a function not of idiosyncrasies of a speaker's personal history but only of his knowledge of his language.

Suppose S is the sentence *The bill is large*. Speakers of English will agree that this sentence is ambiguous, i.e. that it has at least two readings. According to one it means that some document demanding a sum of money to discharge a debt

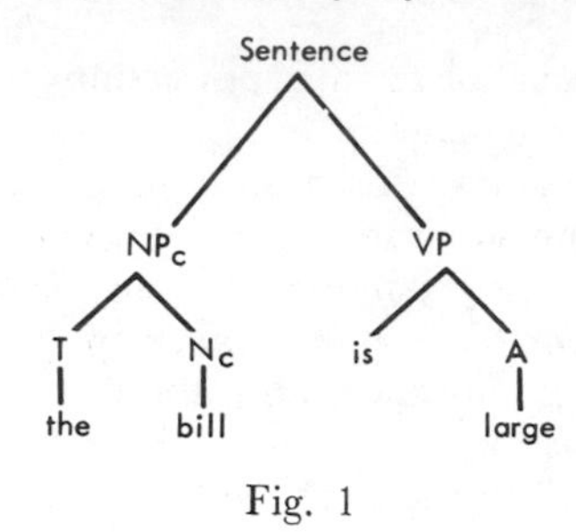

Fig. 1

exceeds in size most such documents; according to the other it means that the beak of a certain bird exceeds in bulk those of most similar birds. However, the fact that this sentence is ambiguous between these readings cannot be attributed to its syntactic structure, since, syntactically, its structure on both readings is as shown in Fig. 1. That is, the group who do not speak English but are equipped with a grammar can say no more about *The bill is large* than what is represented in Fig. 1. Thus, this sentence, which is marked as unambiguous by the grammar, will be understood as ambiguous by a fluent speaker. From this difference between the performances of the two groups, it follows that one facet of the speaker's ability that a semantic theory will have to reconstruct is that he can detect nonsyntactic ambiguities and characterize the content of each reading of a sentence.

Now suppose S is the sentence *The bill is large but need not be paid*. Speakers of English will understand this sentence only on readings in which *bill* means an order to pay a sum of money to discharge a debt. This shows that a speaker can disambiguate parts of a sentence in terms of other parts and thereby determine the number of readings of a sentence. Thus, another facet of the speaker's semantic ability is that of determining the number of readings that a sentence has by exploiting semantic relations in the sentence to eliminate potential ambiguities.

Now let S be the sentence *The paint is silent*. English speakers will as once recognize that this sentence is anomalous in some way. For example, they will distinguish it from such sentences as *The paint is wet* and *The paint is yellow* by applying to it such epithets as 'odd', 'peculiar', 'paradoxical', and 'bizarre'. Though it is clear that the speaker does not have the explicit conceptual machinery to correctly characterize the difference between these sentences, his consistent use of such rough labels shows that he is aware of some sort of linguistic anomaly. But the group who do not speak English and are equipped only with a grammar will regard all these sentences as fully regular, since there is no grammatical basis for distinguishing between them. Hence, another facet of the semantic ability of the speaker is that of detecting semantic anomalies. Correspondingly, a semantic theory will be needed to mark the distinction between semantically anomalous sentences and semantically regular sentences, so far as this distinction is not coextensive with the distinction the grammar makes between ungrammatical and grammatical strings of morphemes.

Finally, whatever sentence the anonymous letter contains, as a rule, speakers of English can easily decide what sentences are paraphrases of it and what are not, in the sense that they can answer the questions. What does the letter say? Does the letter say such-and-such? How can what the letter says be rephrased? This facet of the speaker's ability cannot be referred to his mastery of grammar either, for a person who is equipped with a grammar but who does not speak English will be unable to tell whether or not a sentence is a paraphrase of S. The reasons are simply that there need be no definite grammatical relation between a sentence and its paraphrases, e.g. between *Two chairs are in the room* and *There are at least two things in the room and each is a chair,* and that where a definite grammatical relation obtains between a pair of sentences, neither need be a paraphrase of the other, e.g. *The ball was hit by the man* and *The ball was hit, The man hit the ball* and *The man did not hit the ball.*[6] Thus, still another facet of the speaker's semantic ability which must fall within the domain of a semantic theory is his paraphrasing skill.

We can now tentatively characterize the lower bound on the domain of a semantic theory, since we have found an ability of speakers which cannot be accounted for by grammar, which is semantic in a reasonable sense, and which enables speakers to apprehend the semantic structure of an infinite number of sentences without information about setting and independent of individual differences between speakers. We thus take the goals of a semantic theory to include at least the explication of each facet of this ability and of the interrelations between them.

The speaker's exercise of this ability, which henceforth we shall refer to as THE ABILITY TO INTERPRET SENTENCES, provides empirical data for the construction of a semantic theory, just as the construction of a grammar draws upon empirical data supplied by the exercise of the speaker's ability to distinguish well-formed sentences from ungrammatical strings, to recognize syntactic ambiguity, and to appreciate relations between sentence types. A semantic theory describes and explains the interpretative ability of speakers by accounting for their performance in determining the number and content of the readings of a sentence, by detecting semantic anomalies, by deciding on paraphrase relations between sentences, and by marking every other semantic property or relation that plays a role in this ability.

4. WHAT IS BEYOND THE DESCRIPTIVE SCOPE OF A SEMANTIC THEORY

Having fixed a lower bound on the domain of a semantic theory, our next step must be to fix an upper bound, thus

[6] Cf. *Syntactic structures,* Appendix II, for the transformations which relate these sentences.

uniquely determining the set of problems forming the domain of a semantic theory of a natural language.

Previous conceptions of semantics have usually defined the goals of a semantic description of a natural language in such a way that to achieve them a semantic theory would have to account for the manner in which settings determine how an utterance is understood. We shall now show that to set the goals of a semantic theory this high is to set them too high. Once we have shown that a semantic theory cannot be expected to account for the way settings determine how an utterance is understood, we will have fixed an upper bound on the domain of semantic theories. That is, we will have shown that a semantic theory is a theory of the speaker's ability to interpret the sentences of his language.

The form of a theory of how settings control the understanding of utterances of sentences is as follows. Such a theory is a function F whose arguments are a sentence S; GS, a grammatical description of S; IS, a semantic interpretation of S (where IS is the set of possible readings of S); and C, an abstract characterization of a setting. F(S, GS, IS, C) is

(1) The particular reading in IS that speakers of the language give to S in setting of the type C, or

(2) A n-tuple ($n \geqq 2$) of the reading from IS that speakers of the language give to S if S is ambiguous n-ways in setting of type C, or

(3) The null element if speakers of the language give to S none of the readings in IS when S occurs in settings of type C.

The value of F(S, GS, IS, C) is (1) just in case C fully disambiguates S, i.e. C determines a unique reading from the one or more in IS; it is (2) just in case C fails to fully disambiguate S; it is (3) just in case an occurrence of S in C is token-odd.[7]

An example of each of these cases will clarify this abstract formulation by showing how a theory of this form would explicate the speaker's ability to choose the reading (s) which a setting determines for a sentence occurring in it. As an example of case (1) consider the sentence *The shooting of the hunters was terrible.* This sentence is ambiguous between the reading r_1, on which it means that it was terrible that the hunters were shot, and the reading r_2, on which it means that the marksmanship of the hunters was very bad. This ambiguity will be represented in IS. The theory F must decide which of these readings the sentence bears in settings which disambiguate it, and it must decide in which settings the sentence remains ambiguous. If, then, an utterance of the sentence occurs as an answer to the question *How good was the marksmanship of the hunters?*, i.e. if C represents a situation in which the marksmanship of the hunters is clearly at issue, then, ceteris paribus, the value of F would have to be r_2[8]. Now consider case (2). The ambiguous sentence *He follows Marx,* occurring in a setting in which it is clear that the speaker is discussing intellectual history, cannot bear the reading 'He dogs the footsteps of Groucho'. However, this setting leaves the sentence ambiguous between the readings 'He is a disciple of Karl's and 'He postdates Karl'. Thus, F will have to have these latter two readings as its value for this sentence and this setting as arguments. Finally, as case (3), suppose the sentence *This is the happiest night of my life* is uttered in the middle of the day. Since the sentence is uttered in a setting that lacks conditions which utterances of this sentence presuppose, the occurrence is a case of token-oddity. Thus, for this sentence occurrence F must give the null element as its value, i.e. none of the readings of this sentence in IS are selected by C.

[7] Semantic type oddity is precluded by the assumption that IS contains at least one reading.

[8] In the case where a sentence has exactly one reading in IS, i.e. is unambiguous, that reading must by the theory be assigned to the sentence in each and every normal setting.

This, then, is the form of a theory about the effect of setting upon the way speakers understand sentences. Any particular theory is complete just to the extent that it solves the problems incorporated in this abstract formulation. A complete theory of this kind is more powerful in principle than a theory of the semantic interpretation of sentences in isolation. But a theory of settings must contain a theory of semantic interpretation as a proper part because the readings that a speaker attributes to a sentence in a setting are a selection from among those that the sentence has in isolation. It is clear that, in general, a sentence cannot have readings in a setting which it does not have in isolation. Of course, there are cases in which a sentence may have a reading for some speakers in some setting which it does not have in isolation for all speakers. But these cases are essentially idiomatic in the sense that meaning is determined either by special stipulation (passwords, nonce senses, etc.) or special rule (codes, etc.) or else by special information about the intentions of the speaker. If a theory of the selective effect of setting were required to deal with such cases, no such theory would be possible, because any sentence may be made to mean anything you like simply by constructing the setting to include the appropriate stipulation.[9] Since, then, the readings that a speaker gives a sentence in a setting are a selection from those which it has in isolation, a theory of semantic interpretation is logically prior to a theory of the selective effect of setting.

The abstract formulation given above may be realized in the form of a theory of either of two kinds, depending on how the notion of setting is construed. One kind of theory of setting selection construes the setting of an utterance to be the nonlinguistic context in which utterance occurs, i.e. the full sociophysical environment of the utterance. The other kind takes the setting of an utterance to be the linguistic context in which the utterance occurs, i.e. the written or spoken discourse of which the utterance is a part. We shall consider, in turn, the possibility of constructing a theory of each of these types.

The first kind of theory of setting selection seeks to account for the way in which aspects of the sociophysical world control the understanding of sentences. Differing varieties of this kind of theory may be obtained by varying the aspects of the sociophysical environment of which the rules of the theory are permitted to take account, and by varying the spatiotemporal parameters of the environment. But clearly a necessary condition which any variety of this kind of theory must satisfy is that its construction of setting is so defined that it is able to represent all the nonlinguistic information required by speakers for understanding sentences. So far as a theory fails to satisfy this condition, it is incomplete, since there is then some information which determines the way speakers understand a sentence but which the theory fails to represent as part of the setting of that sentence.

But a complete theory of this kind is not possible in principle; for to satisfy the above necessary condition it would be required that the theory represent ALL the knowledge speakers have about the world. That this is so can be seen from even a few examples which show how nonlinguistic information of any kind may be involved in the understanding of a sentence. Consider (1) *Our store sells alligator shoes* and (2) *Our store sells horse shoes*. In normal settings (e.g. as signs in a store window or as newspaper advertisements), occurrences of (1) will be taken on the reading 'our store sells shoes made from alligator skins' while (2)

[9] Take the following example. Let m be a one-to-one mapping of the set of English sentences onto itself such that the image of each sentence is a sentence which differs from it in meaning. Then the sentence *The sentence S which immediately follows this sentence is to be understood as m(S).* is a setting such that the meaning of a sentence occurring in it is not one of the meanings of that sentence in isolation.

will be taken on the reading 'our store sells shoes for horses'. Notice, however, that (1) is open to the reading 'our store sells shoes for alligators' and (2) is open to the reading 'our store sells shoes made from the skin of horses'. From this it follows that if a theory of setting selection is to choose the correct reading for (1), it must represent the fact that, to date, alligators do not wear shoes, although shoes for people are sometimes made from alligator skin. Conversely, if the theory is to choose the correct reading for (2), it must represent the fact that horses wear shoes, although shoes for people are not usually made from the skin of horses. Other examples illustrate the same point. Compare the three sentences: *Should we take junior back to the zoo? Should we take the lion back to the zoo? Should we take the bus back to the zoo?* Information which figures in the choice of the correct readings for these sentences includes the fact that lions, but not children and busses, are often kept in cages. Three further cases of the same sort are: *Can I put the wall-paper on?* and *Can I put the coat on? Joe jumped higher than the Empire State Building* and *Joe jumped higher than you. Black cats are unlucky* and *People who break mirrors are unlucky.*[10]

The reader will find it an easy matter to construct an ambiguous sentence whose resolution requires the representation of practically any item of information about the world he chooses.[11] Since a complete theory of setting selection must represent as part of the setting of an utterance any and every feature of the world which speakers need in order to determine the preferred reading of that utterance, and since, as we have just seen, practically any item of information about the world is essential to some disambiguations, two conclusions follow. First, such a theory cannot in principle distinguish between the speaker's knowledge of his language and his knowledge of the world, because, according to such a theory, part of the characterization of a LINGUISTIC ability is a representation of virtually all knowledge about the world that speakers share. Second, since there is no serious possibility of systematizing all the knowledge of the world that speakers share, and since a theory of the kind we have been discussing requires such a systematization, it is ipso facto not a serious model for semantics. However, none of these considerations is intended to rule out the possibility that, by placing relatively strong limitations on the information about the world that a theory can represent in the characterization of a setting, a LIMITED theory of selection by sociophysical setting can be constructed. What these considerations do show is that a COMPLETE theory of this kind is impossible.

The second kind of realization of the abstract formulation of a theory of setting selection is one in which the setting of an occurrence of a sentence is construed as the written or spoken discourse of which the occurrence is a part. Such a theory has a strong and a weak version. The strong version requires that the theory interpret a discourse in the same way that a fluent speaker would (i.e. mark the ambiguities that the speaker marks, resolve the ambiguities that the speaker resolves, detect the anomalous strings that the speaker detects, recognize paraphrase relations that the speaker recognizes, and do all this both within and across sentence boundaries). Since, however, in so interpreting a discourse a speaker may need to bring to bear virtually any information about the world that he and other speakers share, the argument given against a

10 We express our gratitude to David Bellugi for referring us to *My little golden book of jokes* (New York, 1961), from which these examples are drawn.

11 We have convinced ourselves of the truth of this claim by making it the basis of a party game. One person supplies a fact, however obscure, and the others try to construct a sentence which that fact disambiguates. The game is not remarkably amusing, but it is surprisingly convincing.

complete theory of selection by sociophysical setting applies equally against the strong version of a theory of selection by discourse. Hence we need only consider the weak version.

The weak version of such a theory requires only that the theory interpret discourses just so far as the interpretation is determined by grammatical and semantic relations which obtain within and among the sentences of the discourse. Thus, such a theory seeks to disambiguate sentences and sequences of sentences in terms of grammatical and semantic relations between these and the sentences which from their setting in a discourse, to determine when an occurrence of a sentence or of a sequence of sentences is rendered anomalous by the sentences which form its setting in a discourse, and to recognize paraphrase relations between pairs of sentences and pairs of sequences of sentences in a discourse.[12]

But it is not at all clear that the weak version of a theory of discourse setting selection has greater explanatory power in these respects than a theory of semantic interpretation, since except for a few types of cases (see below), a discourse can be treated as a single sentence in isolation by regarding sentence boundaries as sentential connectives. As a matter of fact, this is the natural treatment. Consider the two-sentence discourse: *I shot the man with a gun. If the man had had a gun too, he would have shot me first.* The first sentence of this discourse is ambiguous in isolation, but not in this setting. But the problem of explaining this disambiguation is the same as the problem of explaining why the single sentence *I shot the man with a gun, but if the man had had a gun too, he would have shot me first* does not have an ambiguous first clause. This technique of replacing discourses or stretches in discourse by single compound sentences, using sentence connectives in place of sentence boundaries, clearly has a very extensive application in reducing problems of setting selection to problems of semantic interpretation of sentences in isolation. Thus, given a theory of semantic interpretation, little is left for a theory of setting selection to explain.

The fact which underlies this technique is that, in the great majority of cases, the sentence break in a discourse is simply equivalent to the conjunction *and*. (In others it is equivalent to *but*, in others to *for*, in others to *or*, etc.) Sometimes, however, a discourse cannot be directly converted into a compound sentence in this way. For example, the discourse *How are you feeling today? I am fine, thanks.* does not convert to **How are you feeling today and I am fine, thanks.* because the compound sentence is ungrammatical. But the fact that sentences of different types cannot be run together in the obvious way may not pose a serious problem; for it is not at all clear that less obvious conversions will not lead to a satisfactory treatment of such cases within a theory of semantic interpretation. For example, we may convert the discourse just cited into the single sentence *X asked 'How are you feeling today?' and Y replied 'I am fine, thanks.'* If such conversions can be carried out generally, then any problem about disambiguation, detection of anomaly, etc. that can be raised and/or solved in a theory of setting selection can be raised and/or solved by reference to an analogue in the theory of semantic interpretation. But even if such conversions cannot be carried out generally, the most interesting and central cases will still be within the range of a theory of semantic interpretation. Hence, for every discourse there is a single sentence which consists of the sequence of n sentences that comprise the discourse connected by the appropriate sentence connectives and which exhibits the same semantic relations exhibited in the dis-

12 For examples of studies toward a theory of this kind, cf. Z. S. Harris, 'Discourse analysis', *Lg.* 26.1–30 (1952); H. Herzberger, *Contextual analysis* (Princeton University dissertation 1957).

course. But since the single sentence is, ex hypothesi, described by a theory of semantic interpretation, in every case in which a discourse can be treated as a single sentence, a theory of semantic interpretation is descriptively as powerful as a theory of setting selection.

We opened the discussion of theories of setting selection in order to fix an upper bound on the domain of a semantic theory of a natural language. The result of the discussion is that, where such a theory is not reducible to a theory of semantic interpretation, it cannot be completed without systematizing all the knowledge about the world that speakers share and keeping this systematization up to date as speakers come to share more knowledge. A limited theory of how sociophysical setting determines the understanding of an utterance is possible, but even such a theory blurs the distinction between the speaker's knowledge of his language (his linguistic ability) and his knowledge of the world (his beliefs about matters of fact). Therefore, since it is unlikely that anything stronger than a theory of semantic interpretation is possible and since such a theory is clearly an essential part of a linguistic description, it is reasonable to fix the upper bound of a semantic theory of a natural language at the point where the requirements upon a theory of semantic interpretation are satisfied.

5. THE COMPONENTS OF A SEMANTIC THEORY

We must now determine what mechanisms a semantic theory employs in reconstructing the speaker's ability to interpret sentences. We have seen that this ability is systematic in that it enables the speaker to understand sentences he has never heard before and to produce novel sentences that other speakers understand in the way that he understands them. To account for this ability a semantic theory must be so formulated that its output matches the interpretive performance of a fluent speaker. In this section, we describe the form of semantic theories.

It is widely acknowledged and certainly true that one component of a semantic theory of a natural language is a dictionary of that language. The reason for including a dictionary as a component of a semantic theory is based on two limitations of a grammatical description. First, a grammar cannot account for the fact that some sentences which differ ONLY morphemically are interpreted as different in meaning (e.g. *The tiger bit me* and *The mouse bit me*) while other sentences which differ only morphemically are interpreted as identical in meaning (e.g. *The oculist examined me* and *The eye doctor examined me*). Second, a grammar cannot account for the fact that some sentences of radically different syntactic structure are synonymous (e.g. *Two chairs are in the room* and *There are at least two things in the room and each is a chair*) while other syntactically different sentences are not. In each case, the interpretation of the sentences is determined in part by the meanings of their morphemes and by semantic relations among the morphemes. The reason for including a dictionary as a component of a semantic theory is precisely to provide a representation of the semantic characteristics of morphemes necessary to account for the facts about sentences and their interrelations that the grammar leaves unexplained.

What has always been nuclear about a semantic theory is what component(s) it contains besides a dictionary, and how the components of a semantic theory relate to one another and to the grammar. We can find this out by asking in what respects a dictionary and grammar alone are NOT sufficient to match the fluent speaker's interpretations of sentences.

Let us imagine a fluent speaker of English presented with the infinite list of sentences and their structural descriptions generated by a grammar of English. Given an accurate dictionary of English WHICH HE APPLIES BY USING HIS LINGUISTIC ABILITY, the fluent speaker can semantically interpret any sentence on the list under any of its grammatical derivations. He can determine the number and content of the readings of a sentence, tell whether or not a sentence is semantically anomalous, and decide which sentences on the list are paraphrases of each other. Now contrast the fluent speaker's performance with the performance of a machine which MECHANICALLY[13] applies an English dictionary to a sentence in the list by associating with each morpheme of the sentence its dictionary entry. It is clear that the dictionary usually supplies more senses for a lexical item than it bears in almost any of its occurrences in sentences. But the machine will not be able to select the sense(s) which the morpheme actually bears in a given sentence context, except so far as the selection is already determined by the grammatical markers assigned to the morpheme in the derivation of the sentence. (Thus the machine will be able to choose the correct sense of *seal* in *Seal the letter* so far as the choice is determined by the fact that in this sentence *seal* is marked as a verb, and the correct sense of *seal* in *The seal is on the letter* so far as the choice is determined by the fact that in this sentence *seal* is marked as a noun. But the machine will not be able to distinguish the correct sense of *seal* in *One of the oil seals in my car is leaking* from such incorrect senses as 'a device bearing a design so made that it can impart an impression' or 'an impression made by such a device' or 'the material upon which the impression is made' or 'an ornamental or commemorative stamp' and so forth, since all of these senses can apply to nominal occurrences of *seal.*) What the machine is failing to do is to take account of or utilize the semantic relations between morphemes in a sentence. Hence it cannot determine the correct number and content of readings of a sentence. Nor can it distinguish semantically anomalous sentences from semantically regular ones. Since the machine will associate a dictionary entry with each morpheme in a sentence, it does not distinguish cases in which the sense of a morpheme or string of morphemes in a sentence precludes other morphemes in the sentence from bearing ANY of the senses that the dictionary supplies for them. (E.g. the machine cannot distinguish *The wall is covered with silent paint* from *The wall is covered with fresh paint.*) Finally, the machine cannot tell which sentences in the list are paraphrases of each other in any case except the one in which the sentences are of exactly the same syntactic structure and the corresponding words are either identical or synonymous.

The comparison between a fluent speaker and a machine reveals the respects in which a grammar and dictionary by themselves do not suffice to interpret sentences like a speaker of the language. What the fluent speaker has at his disposal that a machine has not are rules for applying the information in the dictionary—rules which take account of semantic relations between morphemes and of the interaction between meaning and syntactic structure in determining the correct semantic interpretation for any of the infinitely many sentences which the grammar generates. Thus, a semantic theory of a natural language must have such rules (which we shall call 'projection rules') as one of its components if it

[13] The qualification 'mechanically' is important: it precluded the employment of linguistic skills not represented by the grammar or the dictionary. It is precisely the possession of such skills that distinguishes the fluent speaker from the nonspeaker equipped with a grammar and a dictionary. Hence, the degree to which the nonspeaker is permitted access to such skills is the degree to which we obscure what must be accounted for. Conversely, by prohibiting their employment, as we do by the qualification 'mechanically', we bring into clear relief the skills that a semantic theory of a natural language must account for.

is to match the speaker's interpretations of sentences.

The central problem for such a theory is that a dictionary usually supplies more senses for a lexical item than it bears in an occurrence in a given sentence, for a dictionary entry is a characterization of EVERY sense that a lexical item can bear in ANY sentence. Thus, the effect of the projection rules must be to select the appropriate sense of each lexical item in a sentence in order to provide the correct readings for each distinct grammatical structure of that sentence. The semantic interpretations assigned by the projection rules operating on grammatical and dictionary information must account in the following ways for the speaker's ability to understand sentences: they must mark each semantic ambiguity that a speaker can detect; they must explain the source of the speaker's intuitions of anomaly when a sentence evokes them; they must suitably relate sentences that speakers know to be paraphrases of each other.[14]

Pictured in this way a semantic theory interprets the syntactic structure which the grammatical description of a language reveals. This conception gives content to the notion that a semantic theory of a natural language is analogous to a model which interprets a formal system. Further, it explicates the exact sense of the doctrine that the meaning of a sentence is a function of the meanings of its parts. The system of projection rules is just this function.

6. THE STRUCTURE AND EVALUATION OF DICTIONARY ENTRIES

We shall here describe the form that a dictionary entry must take in a semantic theory, and discuss how, in an empirical study of the semantics of a natural language, we can evaluate the adequacy of proposed dictionary entries for the lexical items of that language. The next section will describe the form of the projection rules.

From the viewpoint of a semantic theory, a dictionary entry consists of two parts: a grammatical section which provides the part-of-speech classification of the lexical item, and a semantic section which represents each of the distinct senses of the lexical item in its occurrences as a given part of speech. (This leaves out much of what is conventionally found in a dictionary entry, e.g. pronunciation, etymology, chronology. Such information is not relevant to a synchronic semantic description of a language.) For example, the word *play* receives an entry which has grammatical and semantic components as in Fig. 2. The grammatical section classifies the syntactic roles which the lexical item can play in sentences, while the semantic portion supplies one SENSE of the lexical item as the terminal element of each complete distinct descending path through the tree which represents the entry. The sense terminating each path can in turn be analyzed into two parts: a SENSE-CHARACTERIZATION (which appears mandatorily) and a sequence of one or more synonyms (which appears optionally).

The central concept to be studied in this section is that of a sense-characteriza-

[14] The distinction between the dictionary and the rules for its application corresponds, in psychological terms, to a difference between mental processes. The dictionary is something that the speaker learns item by item, more or less by rote, and is constantly learning more of. Knowledge of the rules for applying the dictionary, on the other hand, is gained early and in toto, and comes into play whenever a speaker uses his language. Correspondingly, the use of what is learned in learning a dictionary depends on recalling relatively independent bits of information. The rules involve the exercise of a faculty for coding and decoding linguistic information; they organize whatever systematic, nongrammatical information the speaker has about his language and are thus, in the strongest sense, essential to a knowledge of the language. To know a natural language one MUST know these rules, but one need not know more than a small fraction of its vocabulary.

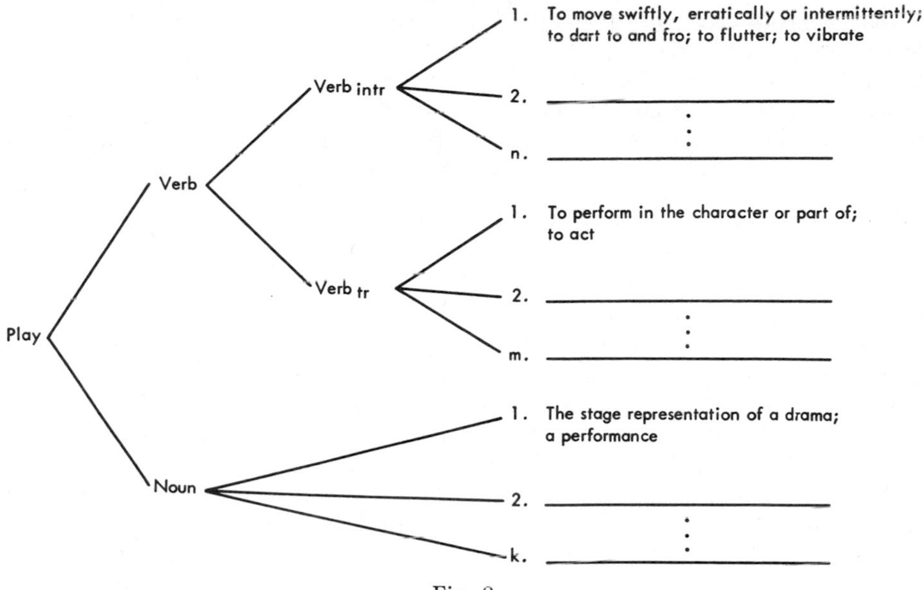

Fig. 2

tion of a lexical item. We can justify our concern with this, to the exclusion of synonyms, on the ground that the concept 'synonymity' can be reconstructed in terms of the concept 'sense-characterization' but not conversely. Therefore, the information about synonyms which a dictionary must provide can be given solely in terms of sense-characterizations. In particular, two lexical items have n synonymous senses if and only if they have n paths in common, and two lexical items are fully synonymous if and only if they have identical entries, i.e. if every path of one is a path of the other. The explicit inclusion of synonyms in a dictionary entry, which is the common practice of conventional dictionaries, is a redundancy introduced to save the user the effort of discovering the synonyms of a lexical item by comparing its sense-characterizations with those of every other item in the dictionary. In short, the practice of listing the synonyms of an item is simply a technique of cross reference. This follows from the fact that it must be a condition upon the adequacy of a dictionary that items which are synonymous in n of their senses have n paths in common.

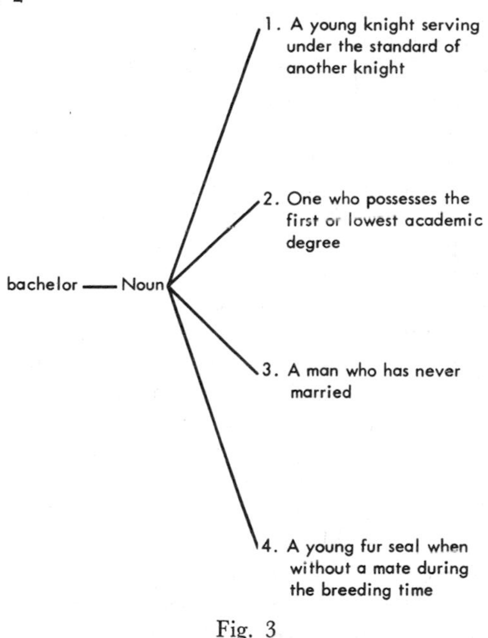

Fig. 3

For the word *bachelor* dictionaries[15] give substantially the entry diagrammed in Fig. 3. However, for reasons which will

[15] Our sources for dictionary information throughout this paper have been *The shorter Oxford English dictionary* and *Webster's new collegiate dictionary.*

presently be made clear, the presentation of dictionary entries in the form exemplified in Figs. 2 and 3 is not adequate for a semantic theory. Instead, we require entries in a form exemplified in Fig. 4. Here the unenclosed elements are GRAMMATICAL MARKERS, the elements enclosed in parentheses are what we shall call SEMANTIC MARKERS, and the expressions enclosed in brackets are what we shall call DISTINGUISHERS. We have already commented upon the function of grammatical markers. The semantic markers and distinguishers are the means by which we can decompose the meaning of one sense of a lexical item into its atomic concepts, and thus exhibit the semantic structure IN a dictionary entry and the semantic relations BETWEEN dictionary entries. That is, the semantic relations among the various senses of a lexical item and among the various senses of different lexical items are represented by formal relations between markers and distinguishers.

It is clear that any lexical information which a conventional dictionary entry can represent can also be represented by an entry in the normal form shown in Fig. 4. It is also clear that any semantic relations which can be reconstructed from an entry of the former type can also be reconstructed from one of the latter. Distinct senses continue to be represented as distinct paths, synonymous senses of a lexical item continue to be represented in terms of identity of paths, and so on. On the other hand, there are semantic relations which can be reconstructed from entries in our normal form but not from entries in the conventional dictionary form. One such relation is that of SEX-ANTONYMY. This relation holds between the members of such pairs of words as *bachelor* and *spinster, man* and *woman, aunt* and *uncle, bride* and *groom, brother* and *sister, cow* and *bull.* What formally characterizes a sex-antonymous pair of words is that the members have identical paths except that where one has the semantic marker (Male) the other has the semantic marker (Female). Since there are indefinitely many important semantic relations which cannot be formally reconstructed from entries in the conventional dictionary, conventional dictionary entries have a serious theoretical disadvantage. But that disadvantage is not the primary reason for introducing our normal form. This is that a formalization of the conventional dictionary entry is required in order to permit a formal statement of the projection rules. We shall go into more detail later.

Semantic markers are the elements in terms of which semantic relations are expressed in a theory. Here there is a strong analogy to grammatical markers, since a grammatical marker (Noun, Verb, Adjective, etc.) is an element in terms of which syntactic relations are expressed. The semantic markers assigned to a lexical item in a dictionary entry are intended to reflect whatever systematic semantic relations hold between that item and the rest of the vocabulary of the language. On the other hand, the distinguishers assigned to a lexical item are intended to reflect what is idiosyncratic about its meaning. Generally speaking, a change in the system of semantic markers has extensive consequences throughout the semantic theory, i.e. such a change radically alters the semantic relations which the theory claims to find between indefinitely many words in the language. But a change in a distinguisher merely alters the relation between one item and its synonyms. For example, if the distinction between the markers (Male) and (Female) were obliterated in a semantic theory of English, not only would every pair of sex-antonyms be represented as synonymous but the indefinitely many other semantic relations involving this distinction would also be incorrectly represented by the theory. In contrast, eliminating the distinguisher [young fur seal when without a mate during the breeding time] would merely prevent a theory from representing one sense of *bachelor* and whatever synonymity relations obtained between that sense of *bachelor* and certain senses of other words.

Branching under a semantic marker is sometimes singulary but very often dyadic or greater.[16] Since every path in a dictionary entry represents a distinct sense of a lexical item, a lexical item whose dictionary entry contains polyadic branching has more than one sense, i.e. it is ambiguous. From the viewpoint of the semantic interpretation of sentences, polyadic branching represents the possibility of sentential semantic ambiguity in any sentence in which the ambiguous lexical item appears. For a necessary condition on the semantic ambiguity of a sentence is that it contain an ambiguous lexical item. But clearly this condition is not also sufficient, since not all sentences containing ambiguous lexical items are themselves ambiguous. Consider the sentence *The stuff is light enough to carry*. The dictionary entry for the word *light* exhibits branching into the semantic markers (Color) and (Weight). Such branching is required to account for the ambiguity of such sentences as *The stuff is light*, *He wears a light suit in the summer*. But since *The stuff is light enough to carry* is unambiguous, it follows that the expression *enough to carry* somehow selects one of the paths in the dictionary entry for *light* and excludes the other(s). Hence, the semantic interpretation of *The stuff is light enough to carry* must explain why the occurrence of *light* in this sentence is understood according to the sense in which *light* is a weight adjective.

In short, if a semantic theory is to predict correctly the number of ways in which speakers will take a sentence to be ambiguous and the precise content of each term of each ambiguity, it must be able to determine every case in which a sentence containing ambiguous lexical items is itself ambiguous and every case in which selection resolves the ambiguities. But this, in turn, amounts to accepting the condition that a dictionary must be so constructed that every case of lexical ambiguity is represented by polyadic branching and that every case of selection can be represented as the exclusion (by some sentence material) of one or more branches. Semantic anomaly can then be construed as the limiting case of selection: the case where there is a lexical item in a sentence whose paths are ALL excluded by selections due to other material in the sentence.

Given the principle that semantic relations are expressed in terms of semantic markers alone, we can see that the primary motivation for representing lexical information by semantic markers will be to permit a theory to express those semantic relations which determine selection and thereby to arrive at the correct set of readings for each sentence. That selection must be represented in terms of semantic markers follows from the fact that selection is a semantic relation between parts of a sentence, together with the principle that all semantic relations are expressed by semantic markers. Thus, the markers in each entry in the dictionary must be sufficient to permit us to reconstruct the operation of the mechanisms of selection in each of the sentences in which the lexical item receiving that entry appears.

Another consequence of expressing semantic relations solely in terms of semantic markers is that distinguishers, when they appear in a path in a dictionary entry, must appear as terminal elements, i.e. there must be no branching under a distinguisher. If branching under a distinguisher were allowed, the theory would posit at least one semantic relation which its dictionary failed to represent by semantic markers, viz. the one between the senses of the lexical item differentiated by that branching.

The distinction between markers and distinguishers is meant to coincide with the distinction between that part of the meaning of a lexical item which is systematic for the language and that part which is not. In order to describe the systematicity in the meaning of a lexical item, it is necessary to have theoretical

[16] In the entries for some lexical items, there will be paths in which the lowest semantic marker dominates nothing, i.e. paths which do not terminate in distinguishers. Such lexical items have special theoretical significance: they are the natural language's representation of semantic categories. Cf. J. J. Katz and J. A. Fodor, 'Categories', unpublished.

constructs whose formal interrelations compactly represent this systematicity. The semantic markers are such constructs. The distinguishers, on the other hand, do not enter into theoretical relations within a semantic theory. The part of the meaning of a lexical item that a dictionary represents by a distinguisher is the part of which a semantic theory offers no general account.

We must now consider the basis on which to decide to represent some lexical information by semantic markers and other lexical information by distinguishers. In the last analysis, the decision can only be justified by showing that it leads to correct interpretation of sentences. What must be explained, therefore, is how such decisions affect the assignment of semantic interpretations and, conversely, how the requirement that a theory assign semantic interpretations correctly affects decisions about the way in which a piece of lexical information is to be represented.

A particular semantic theory of a natural language can REPRESENT only those sentential semantic ambiguities that result from the occurrence of a lexical item for which the dictionary of the theory provides an entry with two or more paths. The degree of semantic ambiguity that a semantic interpretation assigns to a sentence is a function of the degree of branching within the entries for the lexical items appearing in the sentence—branching into markers or into distinguishers, or a combination of both counting equally in determining the degree of ambiguity. On the other hand, a particular semantic theory of a natural language can RESOLVE only those sentential semantic ambiguities which result from the occurrence of lexical material associated with dictionary entries containing two or more paths that differ by at least one semantic marker. This limitation on the power of a semantic theory to resolve ambiguities is a direct consequence of the fact that selection can operate only upon semantic markers. Hence, decisions to represent a piece of lexical information by markers or distinguishers determine in part what semantic ambiguities will be only marked in the semantic interpretation of sentences and which ones will be both marked and resolved.

Such a decision is controlled by two kinds of considerations. Since we wish to construct a semantic theory in such a way that its output matches the performance of a fluent speaker, we want the theory to represent in its semantic interpretations just those ambiguities that the fluent speaker can mark and to resolve just those ambiguities that he can resolve. This will mean that in constructing a theory the lexical information to be represented by markers and by distinguishers will be controlled by our evidence about the disambiguations which a fluent speaker can make. If the dictionary entry for *bachelor* is given as in Fig. 4, every sentence in which this word appears will be represented as ambiguous between the senses given by the paths *bachelor*→noun→(Human)→(Male)→[who has never married], and *bachelor*→noun→(Human)→(Male)→[young knight serving under the standard of another knight]. Since this ambiguity of *bachelor* is represented only by a difference of distinguishers, there is no way that a theory whose dictionary contains this entry can resolve it. But though this is an absolute limitation on such a theory, it is not an absolute limitation on the construction of semantic theories in general. If we notice that fluent speakers do not take such sentences as *The old bachelor finally died* to be ambiguous, we can construct our semantic theory to accommodate this fact simply by taking the lexical information that a bachelor in the second sense is necessarily young to be marker information rather than distinguisher information. This is done by adding the marker (Young) to the marker system and rewriting the dictionary entry for *bachelor* according to Fig. 5.

The other kind of consideration that controls what lexical information is to be included in the system of semantic markers is the desire for systematic economy. The addition of new semantic markers,

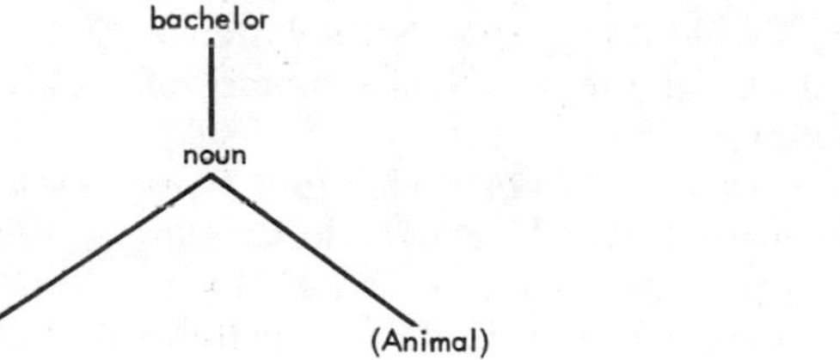

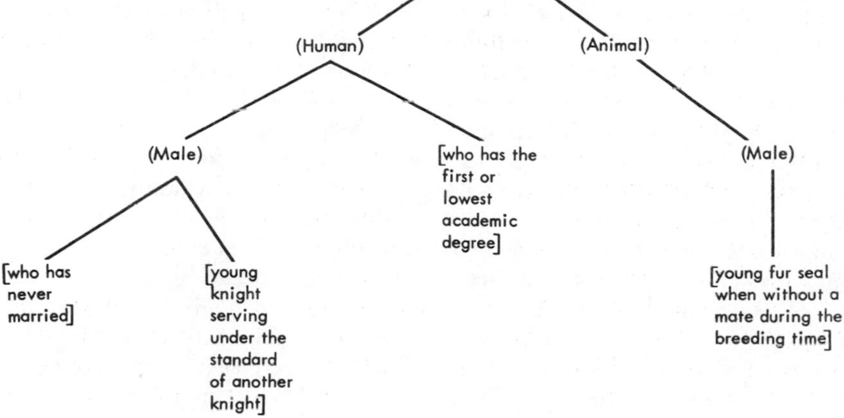

Fig. 4

as in Fig. 5, is for the sake of increasing the precision and scope of a semantic theory, but in so doing it also increases the complexity of the theory's conceptual apparatus. Since allowing more complexity often coincides with greater precision and scope, the decision should be made on the basis of a strategy which seeks to maximize systematic economy: the greatest possible conceptual economy with the greatest possible explanatory and descriptive power. If such decisions are optimally made, there should eventually come a point when increasing the complexity of a semantic theory by adding new markers no longer yields enough advantage in precision or scope to warrant the increase. At that point, the system of semantic

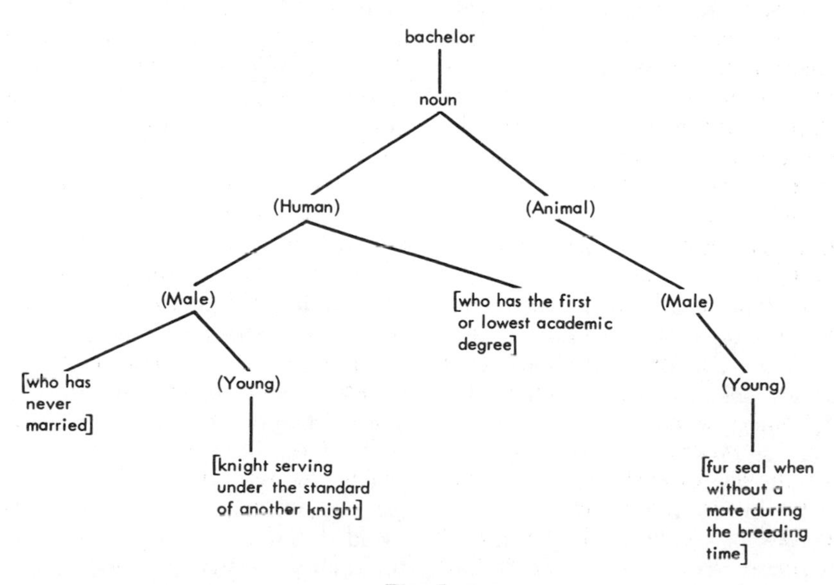

Fig. 5

markers should reflect exactly the systematice features of the semantic structure of the language.

So far we have reconstructed four types of information which conventional dictionaries provide about a lexical item: its part-of-speech classification, the number of its senses, its systematic semantic features, and its idiosyncratic features. There is one further type of information in conventional dictionaries that is relevant to synchronic semantic description: the relation between features of certain combinations into which a lexical item enters and the sense which the item bears in those combinations. For example, consider *The shorter Oxford English dictionary*'s entry for the word *honest*: '...3. of persons: of good moral character, virtuous, upright, ... of women: chaste, virtuous, ...' The phrases 'of persons' and 'of women' are intended to indicate that the senses that follow them apply only under the conditions that they specify. That is, these specifications indicate that if the nominal head which *honest* modifies refers to a person without specification of sex, then *honest* has the meaning 'of good moral character, virtuous, upright', and if the nominal head refers to a woman, then *honest* means EITHER 'of good moral character, virtuous, upright' OR 'chaste, virtuous'. Our reconstruction of this type of dictionary information must follow conventional dictionary procedure as far as it goes, but should go further in that the reconstruction should provide ALL the information necessary to determine selection and exclusion. Where the conventional dictionary, by using devices like the phrases with 'of...', tells us what a word means in certain combinations, our reconstruction must do this systematically and also provide a basis for determining what combinations are semantically acceptable and which ones are not.

For our reconstruction, we shall use left and right angles enclosing a function of syntactic or semantic markers. Such configurations of symbols will be affixed to the terminal element of a path (either the distinguisher or the last semantic marker if there is no distinguisher) and will be construed, relative to the projection rules, as providing a necessary and sufficient condition for a semantically acceptable combination. The angle-enclosed material terminally affixed to the path of a modifier determines the applicability of that path of the modifier to a sense of a nominal head. In particular, a path in the dictionary entry for *honest* will be: *honest* → adjective → (Evaluative) → (Moral) → [innocent of illicit sexual intercourse] ⟨(Human) & (Female)⟩. This is to be construed as saying that an adjectival occurrence of *honest* receives the interpretation (Evaluative) → (Moral) → [innocent of illicit sexual intercourse] just in case the head it modifies has a path containing both the semantic markers (Human) and (Female). How in actual practice a semantic theory utilizes angle-enclosed material to determine selection and exclusion relations in order to obtain semantic interpretations of sentences can only be made clear by the statement of the projection rules.

This concludes the characterization of our normal form for dictionary entries. A dictionary is, then, a list (ordered or not) of the lexical items of the language, each item being associated with an entry in our normal form. The question whether the items are to be words, morphemes, or other units we do not attempt to decide here; but certain considerations are relevant to the decision. The most important is that we choose the unit that will enable us to describe the largest amount of the compositional structure of the language. As a rule, the meaning of a word is a compositional function of the meanings of its parts, and we would like to be able to capture this compositionality. An approach which directs us to choose as lexical units the most compositionally basic units of the language has, moreover, simplicity in its favor. Wherever we can use composition, dictionary entries are avoided. Thus, instead of having an entry for each verb that takes the prefix *de* and a separate entry for *de* plus that verb, we must choose our lexical units so that the dictionary need only contain an entry for *de* and an entry for the unprefiexed form of each verb. This economy can be achieved because combinations of *de*+ verb are compositional wherever the verb is semantically marked as (Process)→ (Reversible).

It will be noticed that the dictionary is so formulated that all semantic properties and relations represented in entries are FORMALLY represented. This is required so that, given a formal statement of the projection rules (i.e. a statement in which the application of rules is defined solely in terms of the shapes of the symbols they apply to, and the operations which the rules effect in producing their output are mechanical), the question what semantic interpretation is assigned to a given sentence can be answered by formal computations without the aid of linguistic intuitions or insights. The need for a formal semantic theory derives from the need to avoid vacuity. A semantic theory is vacuous to the extent that the speaker's intuitions or insights about semantic relations are relied on in order to apply the rules of the theory correctly. Thus, it is uninformative to be told that an English sentence exhibits a semantic relation R just in case it satisfies the condition C, if C is so formulated that we cannot know whether C is satisfied without relying on a speaker's intuitive knowledge of semantic relations like R. A formal theory is ipso facto not vacuous in this respect, since no knowledge about semantic relations in any language is required to determine the correct application of its rules.

Now we turn to the problem of evaluating the adequacy of dictionary entries. It is often assumed that a semantic theory must yield a feasible mechanical procedure which enables the linguist to actually construct a dictionary from information about the verbal behavior of speakers. Every proposal for such a procedure, however, has proved a complete failure; we believe that this is in the nature of the case. We also think that theorists who insist upon a mechanical procedure for deciding whether a putative dictionary entry is optimal have set their aims too high; the practical impossibility of such a decision procedure is also, we believe, in the nature of the case. We shall not argue directly for these claims. We make them primarily to warn the reader against construing the conception of a semantic theory proposed in this paper as either a mechanical discovery procedure or a mechanical decision procedure for dictionary entries.

However, the present paper can be understood as proposing a conception of semantic theory which provides, inter alia, a procedure for determining which of two proposed dictionary entries is the better for a given language. This evaluation procedure, be it noted, differs considerably from what is usually envisioned by semantic theorists. In our conception, a dictionary is only one component of a semantic theory which has as its other component a set of projection rules for semantically interpreting sentences on the basis of the dictionary. Only the theory as a whole can be subjected to empirical test. This means that if a semantic theory gives incorrect interpretations for sentences, one must then decide whether to revise some dictionary entries, some projection rules, or some of each. None the less, there is a derivative sense in which questions of evaluation can be raised about particular dictionary entries. Given projection rules and other dictionary entries that are sufficiently well established, which of two proposed entries yields the best interpretations for sentences? This conception of evaluating dictionary entries differs from the usual one in that it makes evaluation a matter of the degree to which the entry helps achieve the purpose of a dictionary within a theory of semantic interpretation. Semantic theorists usually think of such evaluation as effected by criteria which select the preferable entry simply on the basis of facts about the verbal behavior of speakers, thus overlooking the fact that it is the interpretation of sentences, not the construction of dictionaries, that is the objective of a semantic theory. Because they have overlooked this, their criteria for evaluating dictionary entries are invariably too weak: they fail to utilize systematic constraints on the semantic interpretation of sentences (matching the fluent speaker's ability to determine the number of readings of a sentence, the content of the readings, and their paraphrase relations) in choosing a preferable dictionary entry.

The controls on a semantic theory of a natural language are nothing more than the usual empirical and methodological constraints imposed on any scientific theory; the requirement that a semantic theory match the fluent speaker's ability to interpret sentences is the particular form, in semantics, of the general methodological requirement that a theory accord with the facts. If certain consequences of a semantic theory conflict with the facts (the performance of fluent speakers), various revisions in the dictionary component, in the projection rule component, or in both must be tried out and compared to determine which solution best accommodates the linguistic evidence.

7. THE PROJECTION RULE COMPONENT

A sentence and its grammatical description provide the input to a semantic theory. Its output is a semantic interpretation of each sentence given as input. We may picture the situation as in Fig. 6.

Fig. 6 shows the input to a semantic theory to be a sentence S together with a structural description consisting of the n derivations of S, $d_1, d_2, \ldots, d_n$, one for each of the n ways that S is grammatically ambiguous. The output of the semantic theory is shown as k_1 readings for d_1, k_2 readings for $d_2, \ldots, k_m$ readings for d_n, each reading corresponding to a term of a semantic (nongrammatical) ambiguity of S on some derivation. The schema $\rho_i\ (d_j)$ represents the ith reading of d_j (which the semantic theory supplies).

We can now characterize the notion 'semantic interpretation of the sentence

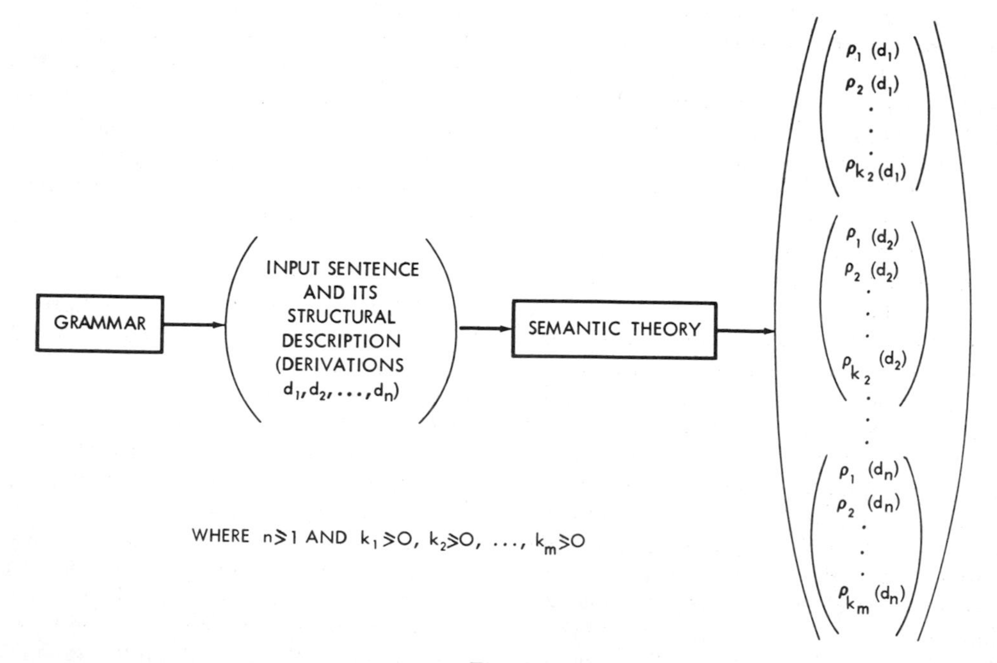

Fig. 6

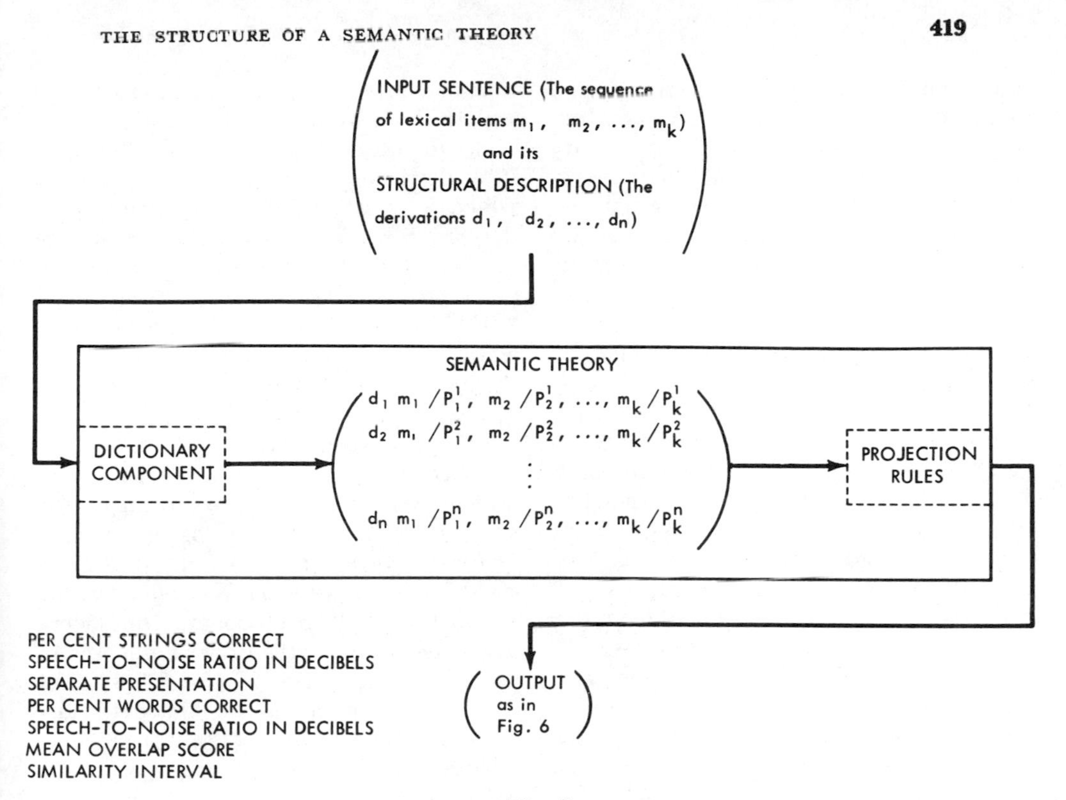

Fig. 7

S' as the conjunction ψd_1 & ψd_2 &...& ψd_n of the semantic interpretations of the n derivations of S. The 'semantic interpretation of S on the derivation d_j' is the output of the dictionary and projection rule components for S on d_j together with the statements about S that can be made on the basis of the following conventions:

(1) If $k_1 + k_2 + \ldots + k_m = 1$, then S is unambiguous.

(2) If $k_1 + k_2 + \ldots + k_m > 1$, then S is $k_1 + k_2 + \ldots + k_m$ ways ambiguous.

(3) If $k_1 + k_2 + \ldots + k_m = 0$, then S is fully anomalous (i.e. anomalous on every derivation).

(4) If the set of readings assigned to the derivation d_j, $\rho_1(d_j)$, $\rho_2(d_j)$, ..., $\rho_{k_i}(d_j)$, has exactly one member, then S is unambiguous on d_j.

(5) If the set of readings assigned to the derivation d_j has more than one member, then S is k_i ways semantically ambiguous on d_j.

(6) If the set of readings assigned to d_j is null, then S is semantically anomalous on d_j.

(7) If S and another sentence P have at least one reading in common, then S and P are paraphrases on that reading.

(8) If S and P have all readings in common, then S and P are full paraphrases.[17]

Fig. 7 schematizes the relation between the dictionary component and the projection rule component. The input to the dictionary component consists of a sentence S represented by a sequence of lexical items $m_1, m_2, \ldots, m_k$ and the set of derivations of S. The symbol 'P_j^i' stands for a

17 For further specification of what semantic features of a sentence can be marked in terms of the output of a semantic theory cf. J. J. Katz, 'Analyticity and contradiction in natural language', to be published in 1963.

finite nonnull set of paths drawn from the dictionary entry for the lexical item m_j in S such that any path in the dictionary entry for m_j is in the set only if the path contains grammatical markers which assign m_j the syntactic role it has on the derivation d_i. The slant line represents the association between a lexical item and a subset of the set of paths in its dictionary entry. The association is effected by the instruction (I) which, together with the dictionary, comprises the dictionary component:

(I) For each pair d_i and m_j, the path p in the entry for m_j is assigned to the set P_j^i if and only if p has as its initial subpath the sequence of grammatical markers $g_1, g_2, \ldots, g_r$ and the derivation d_i contains the path $g_1 \rightarrow g_2 \rightarrow \ldots \rightarrow g_r \rightarrow m_j$.

(I) chooses as relevant to the semantic interpretation of a sentence on a given derivation only those paths from the dictionary entries for each of the lexical items in the sentence which are compatible with the lower-level syntactic structure of the sentence on that derivation. The output of the dictionary component is thus a mapping of a finite nonnull set of paths onto each m_j for each d_i. This output in turn, as Fig. 7 shows, is the input to the projection rules.

We can now give a general picture of the operations whereby the projection rule component converts its input into a semantic interpretation. Each sentence which the grammar makes available for semantic interpretation has associated with it *n* derivations marking the *n* ways in which it is structurally ambiguous. Each derivation marks the constituent structure or the derived constituent structure (if the sentence is generated transformationally) in a way that can be represented by a tree diagram. We shall employ such tree diagrams in the following pages, BUT IT IS TO BE UNDERSTOOD THAT PROJECTION RULES CAN ALSO TAKE ACCOUNT OF INFORMATION ABOUT THE TRANSFORMATIONAL HISTORY OF A SENTENCE WHICH IS NOT REPRESENTED IN A TREE DIAGRAM.

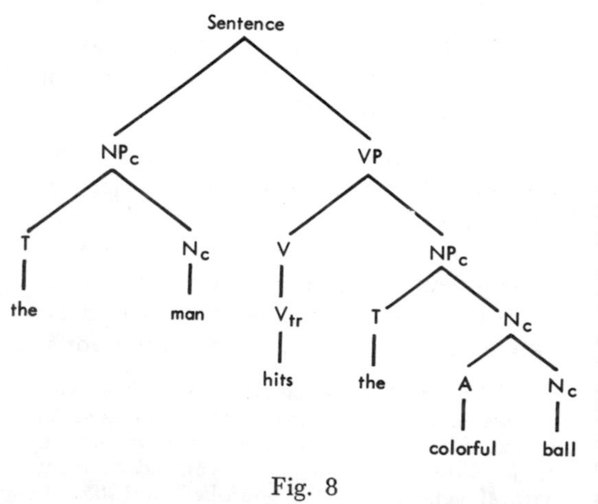

Fig. 8

Fig. 8 gives the derived constituent structure of the sentence *The man hits the colorful ball.*[18] The dictionary component associates sets of paths with such a tree in the manner specified by (I). Thus, after the application of (I), we have the arrangement shown in Fig. 9. The marking of the lexical items *the, man, hits, the, colorful,* and *ball* as Article, Noun concrete, Verb transitive, Article, Adjective, and Noun concrete respectively, which at first glance may seem to have been lost in the application of (I), is actually represented as the common initial subpath of every p in each P_j^i, e.g. P_3 is the set of paths all of whose members begin *hits* $\rightarrow V \rightarrow V_{tr}$.

[18] It can be argued on grammatical grounds that the phrase *the colorful ball* should be represented simply as:

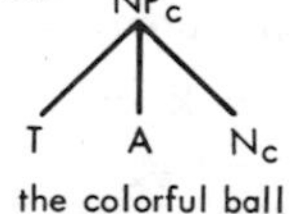

i.e. without the internal syntactic structure it is given in Fig. 9. This representation does not include the information (required by the projection rules) that *colorful* is a modifier of the head *ball.* But the need for this sort of information does not commit us to the assumption that all branching in derived constituent structure trees is binary. For such information can be obtained by examining the transformational history of the sentence. This is a typical case of the way a projection rule can use information taken from the transformational history of the sentences to which it is applied.

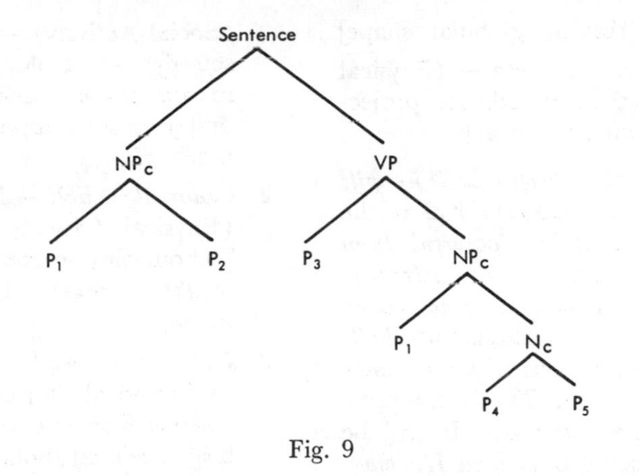

Fig. 9

The general way in which the projection rule component works is by proceeding from the bottom to the top of a constituent structure tree and effecting a series of amalgamations. It starts with the output of (I) and amalgamates sets of paths dominated by a grammatical marker, thus assigning a set of readings to the concatenation of lexical items under that marker by associating the result of the amalgamation with the marker, until it reaches the highest marker 'Sentence' and associates this with a semantic interpretation. The projection rules amalgamate sets of paths dominated by a grammatical marker by combining elements from each of them to form a new set of paths which provides a set of readings for the sequence of lexical items under the grammatical marker. Amalgamation is the joining of elements from different sets of paths under a given grammatical marker if these elements satisfy the appropriate selection restrictions represented by the material in angles.

We now give an example of how a semantic theory of English might interpret a sentence, and in this way exhibit some of the projection rules for English.[19] We choose the sentence *The man hits the colorful ball* under the derivation given in Fig. 8.

The projection rule component receives this sentence and its derivation as input after (I) has operated. (See Fig. 9) The first step for the projection rule component is to amalgamate each set of paths under each of the grammatical markers which immediately dominates ONLY sets of paths, and to associate with the dominating marker the amalgam so obtained. In the case of Fig. 9, the first step is to amalgamate either P_4 and P_5 or P_1 and P_2; the order is immaterial.

Let us first take the amalgamation of P_4 and P_5. The paths comprising the sets P_4 and P_5 are as follows.

P_4

1. *Colorful* → Adjective → (Color) → [Abounding in contrast or variety of bright colors] ⟨(Physical Object) v (Social Activity)⟩
2. *Colorful* → Adjective → (Evaluative) → [Having distinctive character, vividness, or picturesqueness] ⟨(Aesthetic Object) v (Social Activity)⟩

P_5

1. *Ball* → Noun concrete → (Social activity) → (Large) → (Assembly) → [For the purpose of social dancing]
2. *Ball* → Noun concrete → (Physical

[19] It should be made clear that the rules we shall give are not intended as a contribution to a semantic theory of English but only as examples of the type of rules that such a theory would employ.

Object) → [Having globular shape]

3. *Ball* → Noun concrete → (Physical Object) → [Solid missile for projection by an engine of war]

$P_4$1 is the sense of *colorful* in *The gift came in a colorful wrapper*; $P_4$2 is the sense in *No novel is less colorful than Middlemarch, excepting Silas Marner*; $P_5$1 is the sense of *ball* in *The queen danced at the French ambassador's ball*; $P_5$2 is the sense in *Tennis is played with a ball*; $P_5$3 is the sense in *The balls whistle free o'er the bright blue sea.* It will be noticed that the sense of *ball* in *He plays ball better than Babe Ruth* is not represented by a path in P_5, though such a path is to be found in the dictionary entry for *ball.* This is because *ball,* when it means the game, is not a concrete noun; the path which represents that sense is eliminated by (I).

The amalgamation of P_4 and P_5 is accomplished by the following projection rule: (R_1) Given two paths of the form: (1) Lexical $String_1$ → syntactic markers of head → (a_1) → (a_2) → . . . → (a_n) → [1] ⟨set of strings of markers Ω_1⟩; (2) Lexical $String_2$ → syntactic markers of modifier → (b_1) → (b_2) → . . . → (b_m) → [2] ⟨set of strings of markers Ω_2⟩, such that there is a substring σ of the string of syntactic or semantic markers and σ satisfies the condition Ω_2. There is an amalgam of the form: Lexical $String_2$ + Lexical $String_1$ → dominating node marker → (a_1) → (a_2) → . . . → (a_n) → (b_1) → (b_2) → . . . → (b_m) → [[2] [1]] ⟨Ω_1⟩, where any (b_i) is null when ($\exists a_i$) ($b_i = a_i$) and [[2][1]] is [1] when [2] = [1].[20] The amalgam of P_4 and P_5 is the set of derived paths P_6:

P_6

1. *Colorful* + *ball* → Noun concrete (Social Activity) → (Large) → (Assembly) → (Color) → [[Abounding in contrast or variety of bright colors] [For the purpose of social dancing]]
2. *Colorful* + *ball* → Noun concrete → (Physical Object) → (Color) → [[Abounding in contrast or variety of bright colors] [Having globular shape]]
3. *Colorful* + *ball* → Noun concrete → (Physical Object) → (Color) → [[Abounding in contrast or variety of bright colors] [Solid missile for projection by an engine of war]]
4. *Colorful* + *ball* → Noun concrete → (Social Activity) → (Large) → (Assembly) → (Evaluative) → [[Having distinctive character, vividness, or picturesqueness] [For the purpose of social dancing]]

There were six possible amalgamations from the combination of P_4 and P_5, but only four derived paths because, of the possible combinations, only the combination $P_4$2 and $P_5$1 satisfies the selection restriction ⟨(Aesthetic Object) v (Social Activity)⟩. Thus, (R_1) predicts the semantic anomaly of *colorful ball* on the reading where *colorful* has the sense represented by $P_4$2 and *ball* has either the sense represented by $P_5$2 or the sense represented by $P_5$3.

Another example of how (R_1) contributes to the formalization of the distinction between what is semantically acceptable and what is semantically anomalous is the following. The expression *spinster insecticide* would be regarded as anomalous by speakers of English. This can be predicted on the basis of (R_1) and the dictionary entries for *spinster* and *insecticide.* The relevant path for *spinster* contains: *spinster* → Adjective → (Human) → (Adult) → (Female) → [Who has never married] ⟨(Human)⟩. On the basis of this path, (R_1) assigns no reading to the expression *spinster insecticide*—i.e. predicts that the expression is semantically

[20] The reason why Ω_1 appears in the output of (R_1) is that some heads are, in turn, modifiers of other heads; e.g. adjectives are heads for adverbs and also modifiers for nouns: (*light* (*red*)) *ball.* In these cases, the conditions in Ω_1 will be required for selection.

anomalous—because the path for *insecticide* does not contain the semantic marker (Human) which is necessary to satisfy the selection restriction associated with *spinster*.

(R_1) introduces the semantic markers in the path of the modifier just below the string of semantic markers in the path of the head, eliminating from the path of the modifier all semantic material already present in the path of the head, and associating the distinguishers with one another. The operation of (R_1) corresponds closely to our intuitive notions of the nature of attribution. Attribution is the process of creating a new semantic unit compounded from a modifier and a head, whose semantic properties are those of the head, except that the meaning of the compound is made more determinate than that of the head alone by the information which the compound obtains from the modifier. As Lees comments:[21]

> We cannot get along with a single common noun to refer to a familiar common object, but must have at every moment modifiers with which to construct new more complex names to use for all the specific instances of that object which we encounter and talk about. Thus, we cannot, without extensive ambiguity, refer on every occasion to our favorite beverage by means of the single word *coffee;* instead we name its individual instances with such phrases as 'my coffee', 'that cold cup of coffee you left there', 'some fresh coffee on the shelf', 'a new brand of coffee', 'pretty tasteless coffee', 'Turkish coffee' etc. There is no known limitation on the number of distinct objects for which we must at some time or other have distinctive names, and clearly no dictionary is large enough to contain them all, for a great many of the names which we employ have never before been uttered. Like full sentences themselves, there is no longest name, and there must consequently be an infinity of new names available for us to use when and if the need arises.

Though Lees is commenting on the grammar of nominal compounds, what he says applies equally well to their semantics and to the semantics of other modifier-head constructions. It is only because there is a systematic way of understanding the meaning of such constructions in terms of the meanings of their parts, that the infinite stock of strings produced by the grammatical mechanism for creating new modifier-head constructions can be employed by speakers to refer to familiar objects.

As we have just mentioned, the meaning of a compound is more determinate than the meaning of its head alone in respect of the information which the compound obtains from its modifier(s). The word *aunt* is indeterminate as to age (i.e. both the sentences *My aunt is an infant* and *My aunt is aged* are semantically acceptable), but *spinster*, as we have observed above, contains the semantic marker (Adult) in its path. This marker is carried over to the compound when (R_1) operates to produce an interpretation for *spinster aunt*. Thus, *spinster aunt* is made more determinate (with respect to age) than is *aunt*. This shows up in a comparison between the sentences *My spinster aunt is an infant* and *My spinster aunt is aged,* of which the former is contradictory while the latter is not.

The limiting case, where the addition to the compound of semantic material from the modifier is zero, is of considerable theoretical significance. The compound *unmarried bachelor* is a case in point. The erasure clause in (R_1), 'any b_i is null when $(\exists a_i)(b_i = a_i)$ and [[2][1]] is [1] when [2] = [1]', tells us to delete from the path of the modifier any semantic material already represented in the path of the head. Thus, in forming the compound *unmarried bachelor* all the semantic information in the path of the modifier *unmarried* will be deleted so that the derived path for *unmarried bachelor* will contain no more than the semantic material which comes from the path for *bachelor*. The failure of the modifier to add semantic information would appear

[21] R. B. Lees, *The grammar of English nominalizations* xvii–xviii (*IJAL* 26:3, 1960).

to account for the intuition that such expressions as *unmarried bachelor* are redundant and that, correspondingly, such statements as *Bachelors are unmarried* are 'empty', 'tautological', 'vacuous', 'uninformative'. This provides a new explanation of the analyticity of a classical type of analytic truth.[22] Moreover, this feature of the projection rules provides another empirical constraint on a semantic theory: if the theory characterizes an expression or sentence as redundant in the above sense, the theory is confirmed if speakers take the expression or sentence in the appropriate way, and is disconfirmed if they do not.

The next step in the semantic interpretation of *The man hits the colorful ball* is the amalgamation of P_1 and P_2. The entry for *the* in standard dictionaries is exceedingly complex, primarily because the information required to make the correct selections among the various senses of *the* for its sentential occurrences is extremely complicated. We shall have to simplify.

P_1 contains only the path *the* → Noun phrase concrete → Definite Article → [Some contextually definite]. Other paths in the dictionary entry for *the* (those corresponding to the generic senses of the definite article) are not assigned to P_1 by (I) because only the above path contains as its initial subpath the sequence of grammatical markers which dominates *the* in the derivation in Fig. 8.[23] P_2 contains only the path *man* → noun concrete → noun masculine → (Physical Object) → (Human) → (Adult) → (Male). Other paths in the dictionary entry for *man* (those corresponding to the sense of *man* in *Man is occasionally rational* and to the sense in *Every man on board ship was saved except an elderly couple*) do not appear in P_2, the former because in that sense *man* is not a concrete noun and the latter because in that sense *man* is not a masculine noun. The rule which amalgamates P_1 and P_2 is: (R_2) Given two paths of the form: (1) Lexical $String_1$ → syntactic markers of noun → semantic markers of head → [1], (2) Lexical $String_2$ → syntactic markers of article → semantic markers of article → [2] ⟨set of strings of markers Ω⟩, such that there is a substring σ of the string of syntactic or semantic nominal markers and σ satisfies the condition Ω. There is an amalgam of the form: Lexical $String_2$ + Lexical $String_1$ dominating node marker → semantic markers of article → [2] → semantic markers of noun → [1]. The application of (R_2) to P_1 and P_2 produces the derived path: *the* + *man* → Noun phrase concrete → [Some contextually definite] → (Physical Object) → (Human) → (Adult) → (Male). This path is the only member of the set P_7 shown in Fig. 10.

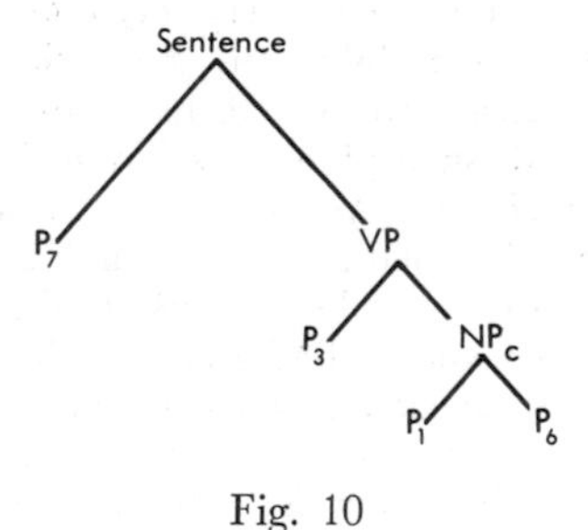

Fig. 10

The amalgamation of P_1 and P_6 works in exactly the same way to yield P_8:

P_8

1. *The* + *colorful* + *ball* → Noun phrase concrete → [Some contextually definite] → (Social Activity) → (Large) → (Assembly) → (Color) → [[Abounding in contrast or

[22] Cf. J. J. Katz, 'Analyticity and contradiction in natural language', to appear in *Readings in the philosophy of language.*

[23] In taking NP_c as part of the sequence of grammatical markers in the dictionary entry for *the,* we are not claiming that *the* is a concrete noun phrase, but only that it occurs as an element of a concrete noun phrase and that, when it does, it has the sense in P_1. This constitutes an extension of the notion of a 'part of speech' classification, but a natural and necessary one.

variety of bright colors] [For the purpose of social dancing]]

2. *The* + *colorful* + *ball* → Noun phrase concrete → [Some contextually definite] → (Physical Object) → (Color) → [[Abounding in contrast or variety of bright colors] [Having globular shape]]
3. *The* + *colorful* + *ball* → Noun phrase concrete → [Some contextually definite] → (Physical Object) → (Color) → [[Abounding in contrast or variety of bright colors [Solid missile for projection by an engine of war]]
4. *The* + *colorful* + *ball* → Noun phrase concrete → [Some contextually definite] → (Social Activity) → (Large) → (Assembly) → (Evaluative) → [[Having distinctive character, vividness, or picturesqueness] [For the purpose of social dancing]]

This leaves us with only that part of the constitutent structure tree shown in Fig. 11 still to be interpreted.

P_3 is as follows.

1. *hits* → Verb → Verb transitive → (Action) → (Instancy) → (Intensity) → [Collides with an impact] ⟨Subject: (Higher Animal) v (Improper Part) v (Physical Object), Object: (Physical Object)⟩[24]
2. *hits* → Verb → Verb transitive → (Action) → (Instancy) → (Intensity) → [Strikes with a blow or missile] ⟨Subject: (Human) v (Higher Animal), Object: (Physical Object), Instrumental: (Physical Object)⟩

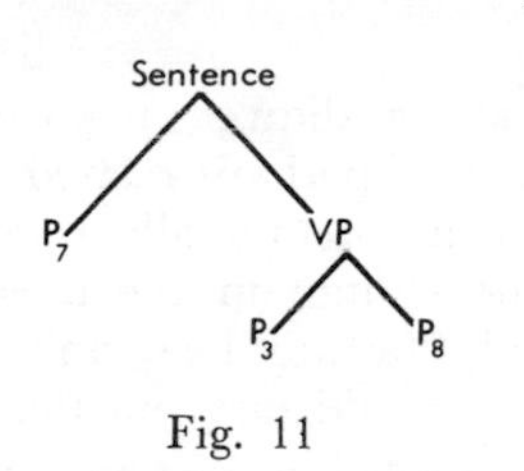

Fig. 11

$P_3$1 is the sense of *hits* in *The rock hits the ground with a thud,* $P_3$2 is the sense in *The man hits the ground with a rock.* It will be noticed that the representation of verbs includes between angles selection restrictions upon the subject, objects, and instrumental of the verb. This information is represented by markers of the form 'Subject: α', 'Object: β', and 'Instrumental: γ', where α, β, and γ represent conditions on the paths associated with subject, objects, and instrumentals respectively.

A few comments on this dictionary entry for *hits* as a transitive verb. We claim no more than rough accuracy for the characterization given. Our interest here, as throughout the paper, is in prescribing the abstract form of a semantic theory, rather than in actually writing one. The characterization of *hits* is intended primarily to illustrate how the results of a linguistic analysis are to be formally presented so that the projection rules can utilize them. But we have tried to make our examples account for the fundamental semantic features. The failure to mark an achievement sense of *hits* is not an oversight. We choose not to mark the special sense of *hits* as an achievement verb because the behavior of *hits* diverges significantly from that of such paradigmatic achievement verbs as *sees* and *hears*. Thus, unlike *He hit the ball intentionally, He saw the picture intentionally* is anomalous (except where it means that he went to see the picture intentionally and *He heard the music intentionally* is anomalous (except where it

[24] Here some explanation is called for. (Instancy) is assigned to verbs representing durationless events. Any sentence whose main verb is marked (Instancy) which is of the form *Subject* + *Verb* + *ed* + *Object* + *for* + *numerical quantifier* + *measure of time* will be understood to mean that the object was verbed more than once. Compare *He hit the ball for three hours* with *He studied the book for three hours.* Next, (Intensity) is assigned to verbs taking adverbs like *hard, soft, gently.* Finally, the marker (Improper Part) is assigned to lexical items that represent wholes which the language contrasts with their parts. The term 'Improper Part' is borrowed from James Thomson.

means that he didn't just overhear the music). This is perhaps related to the fact that one can intentionally miss the ball, though one cannot in the relevant sense intentionally fail to hear the music. If, however, it should turn out that *hits* must be given a special achievement sense, such a sense can be represented within the formalism of the present paper in a straightforward manner.

The projection rule which amalgamates P_3 and P_8 is: (R_3) Given two paths of the form: (1) Lexical String_1 → syntactic markers of main verb → semantic markers → [1] ⟨sets of strings of markers α, β⟩, (2) Lexical String_2 → syntactic markers of object of main verb → Remainder of object path, such that there is a substring of the string of syntactic or semantic markers of the object σ and σ satisfies the condition β, there is an amalgam of the form: Lexical String_1 + Lexical String_2 → dominating node marker → semantic markers of main verb → [1] → String analyzed 'Remainder of object path' ⟨set of strings of markers α⟩. The application of (R_3) to P_3 and P_8 yields P_9, shown in Fig. 12.

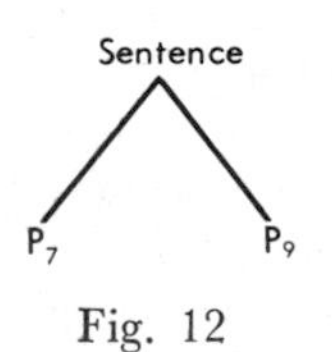

Fig. 12

P_9 contains the following paths:

P_9

1. *hits + the + colorful + ball* → VP → (Action) → (Instancy) → (Intensity) → [Collides with an impact] → [Some contextually definite] → (Physical Object) → (Color) → [[Abounding in contrast or variety of bright colors] [Having globular shape]] ⟨Subject: (Higher Animal) v (Improper Part) v (Physical Object)⟩
2. *hits + the + colorful + ball* → VP (Action) → (Instancy) → (Intensity) → [Collides with an impact] → [Some contextually definite] → (Physical Object) → (Color) → [[Abounding in contrast or variety of bright colors] [Solid missile for projection by engine of war]] ⟨Subject: (Higher Animal) v (Improper Part) v (Physical Object)⟩
3. *hits + the + colorful + ball* → VP → (Action) → (Instancy) → (Intensity) → [Strikes with a blow or missile] → [Some contextually definite] → (Physical Object) → (Color) → [[Abounding in contrast or variety of bright colors] [Having globular shape]] ⟨Subject: (Human) v (Higher Animal)⟩
4. *hits + the + colorful + ball* → VP → (Action) → (Instancy) → (Intensity) → [Strikes with a blow or missile] → [Some contextually definite] → (Physical Object) → (Color) → [[Abounding in contrast or variety of bright colors] [Solid missile for projection by engine of war]] ⟨Subject: (Human) v (Higher Animal)⟩

Finally, the projection rule which operates on P_7 and P_9 to assign a set of readings to 'Sentence' is: (R_4) Given two paths of the form: (1) Lexical String_1 → syntactic markers of verb phrase → Remainder of verb phrase path, (2) Lexical String_2 → syntactic markers of subject → Remainder of subject path, such that there is a substring σ of the string of syntactic or semantic markers of the subject and σ satisfies the condition α. There is an amalgam of the form: Lexical String_2 + Lexical String_1 → dominating node marker → String analyzed 'Remainder of subject path' → String analyzed 'Remainder of verb phrase path' deleting substring ⟨α⟩. The application of (R_4) to P_7 and P_9 yields the set P_{10}:

P_{10}

1. *The + man + hits + the + colorful + ball* → sentence → [Some contextually definite] → (Physical

Object) → (Human) → (Adult) → (Male) → (Action) → (Instancy) → (Intensity) → [Collides with an impact] → [Some contextually definite] → (Physical Object) → (Color) → [[Abounding in contrast or variety of bright colors] [Having globular shape]]

2. *The + man + hits + the + colorful + ball* → Sentence → [Some contextually definite] → (Physical Object) → (Human) → (Adult) → (Male) → (Action) → (Instancy) → (Intensity) → [Collides with an impact] → [Some contextually definite] → (Physical Object) → (Color) → [[Abounding in contrast or variety of bright colors] [Solid missile for projection by an engine of war]]
3. *The + man + hits + the + colorful + ball* → Sentence → [Some contextually definite] → (Physical Object) → (Human) → (Adult) → (Male) → (Action) → (Instancy) → (Intensity) → [Strikes with a blow or missile] → [Some contextually definite] → (Physical Object) → (Color) → [[Abounding in contrast or variety of bright colors] [Having globular shape]]
4. *The + man + hits + the + colorful + ball* → Sentence → [Some contextually definite] → (Physical Object) → (Human) → (Adult) → (Male) → (Action) → (Instancy) → (Intensity) → [Strikes with a blow or missile] → [Some contextually definite] → (Physical Object) → (Color) → [[Abounding in contrast or variety of bright colors] [Solid missile for projection by an engine of war]]

Accordingly, a semantic theory of English containing rules and entries as given above characterizes the sentence *The man hits the colorful ball* as having the following semantic interpretation. The sentence is not semantically anomalous; it is four ways semantically ambiguous on the derivation in Fig. 8; each term corresponds to a reading in P_{10}; it is a paraphrase of any sentence which has one of the readings in P_{10}; and it is a full paraphrase of any sentence that has the set of readings P_{10} assigned to it. The semantic theory interprets the constituent structure tree in Fig. 8 in the way shown in Fig. 13, thus displaying which of the possible combinations of paths at a given node yield derived paths for that node and which possible combinations are blocked.

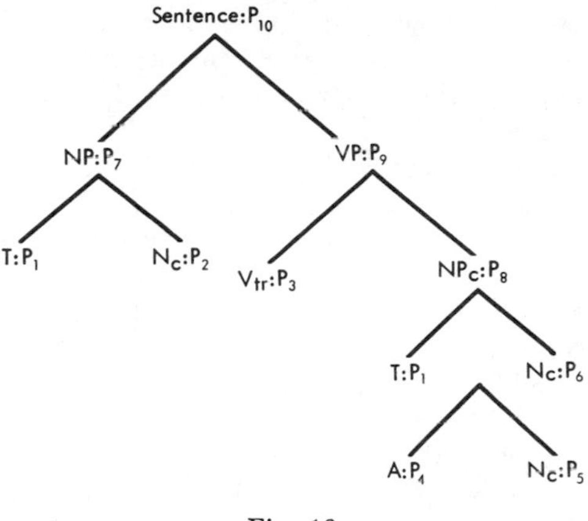

Fig. 13

This completes our example of how a semantic theory of English might interpret a sentence generated by the grammar. Before we conclude our discussion of projection rules, we must consider the question whether the projection rule component will contain types of projection rules different from the type employed above.

What is characteristic of the rules (R_1) through (R_4) is that each rule operates on a part of a partially semantically interpreted constituent structure characterization, amalgamates paths from two sets of paths that are dominated by a particular node, and assigns to that node the set of amalgams as readings for the lexical string that the node dominates. Let us call such rules 'type 1 projection rules'. These rules must assign semantic interpretations to SOME of the sentences generated by the grammar, but they need not be the means by which EVERY sentence receives a semantic interpretation. We can conceive of another type of projection rule (call them 'type 2 projection rules') in the following way. We restrict the application of type 1 projection rules to some formally determined proper subset of the set of sentences. Then we introduce type 2 projection rules to provide a semantic interpretation for every sentence that does not receive a semantic interpretation on the basis of type 1 projection rules. Since those sentences that the grammar produces without the aid of optional transformations, i.e. the kernel sentences, will be semantically interpreted by type 1 projection rules, the type 2 projection rules will assign semantic interpretations to sentences that are constructed with the use of optional transformations. Suppose S has been constructed from a certain set of source sentences by the optional transformation T. A type 2 rule is a rule which operates on the semantic interpretations of these source sentences and on either the derived constitutent structure characterization of S or on the transformation T in order to produce a semantic interpretation of S. Type 2 projection rules should assign semantic interpretations in such a way as to reconstruct the manner in which the meaning of a sentence constructed by the transformation T is a function of the meanings of each of the sentences used by T in S's construction.

The basic theoretical question that remains open here is just what proper subsets of the set of sentences are semantically interpreted using type 1 projection rules only. One striking fact about transformations is that a great many of them (perhaps all) produce sentences that are identical in meaning with the sentence(s) out of which the transform was built.[25] In such cases, the semantic interpretation of the transformationally constructed sentence must be identical to the semantic interpretation(s) of the source sentence(s), at least with respect to the readings assigned at the sentence level. For example, sentences that are related to each other by the passive transformation, e.g. *The man eats cake* and *Cake is eaten by the man*, have the same meaning, except perhaps in instances where quantifiers are involved.[26] Likewise sentence conjunctions, e.g. *The man ate the cake and candy*, which comes from *The man ate the cake* and *The man ate the candy.* Or again, stylistic variants such as *There is something about it that puzzles me, There is about it something that puzzles me,* and *There is something that puzzles me about it.* It would be theoretically most satisfying if we could take the position that transformations never change meaning. But this generalization is contradicted by the question transformations, the imperative transformation, the negation transformation, and others. Such troublesome cases may be troublesome only because we now formulate these transformations inadequately, or they may represent a real departure from the generalization that meaning is invariant under grammatical transformations. Until we can determine whether any transformations change meaning, and if some do, which do and which do not, we shall not know what sentences should be semantically interpreted with type 2 projection rules and how to formulate such rules.

Nevertheless, we can decide the cases that are clear. The set of sentences that will be semantically interpreted using type 1 projection rules includes the sentences produced without the aid of optional transformations. Suppose we permit NO type 2 projection rule for any transformation that we know preserves meaning, and instead introduce the convention that any

[25] For the background of this point cf. Fodor, 'Projection and paraphrase in semantics,' *Analysis* 21:4. 73–7 (1961), and Katz, 'A reply to "Projection and Paraphrase in Semantics"' *Analysis* 22:2.36–41 (1961).

[26] In these instances too, if both active and passive have the same meaning because both are ambiguous.

sentences related by such a transformation T belong to an equivalence class all of whose members receive the same semantic interpretation. Then the facts that there will always be a kernel sentence in such an equivalence class and that every kernel sentence has a semantic interpretation on the basis of type 1 projection rules mean that every non-kernel sentence in such an equivalence class automatically receives the semantic interpretation of its kernel co-member, which makes them all paraphrases as desired.

This treatment is by far the best method of marking paraphrase relations (and other semantic properties) among stylistic variants which result from the operation of a permutation transformation. This method avoids having a special type 2 rule in each such case: such special type 2 rules have no function except to state the empty fact that these transformations do not affect meaning. This method also avoids the use of type 1 rules on a sentence that is produced by a permutation transformation. This is very desirable, because such transformations produce sentences with derived constituent structure characterizations having far less labelled bracketing than the constituent structure characterization of the source sentence, so that what labelled bracketing survives is generally too little for type 1 rules to be able to interpret semantically the derived sentence.

This treatment has the same merits for transformations that permute so as to produce discontinuous elements in the transform and for transformations that delete material. Thus with this treatment we can most simply account for the paraphrase relations between (and other semantic properties of) such pairs as: *John looked up the rule* and *John looked the rule up; Harry plays chess as well as Bill plays chess* and *Harry plays chess as well as Bill.*

The possibility of type 2 projection rules presents two options for the construction of the projection rule component of a semantic theory. Either the projection rule component will consist of type 1 rules alone, or it will contain rules of both type 1 and type 2. Whether type 2 rules will be required, and (if so) to what extent, is a question to which no answer is at present known. The answer involves many considerations, both methodological (conceptual economy, descriptive and explanatory power, etc.) and particular (concerning the structure of individual languages, for instance the degree to which semantic relations between sentences correspond to transformational relations).[27]

8. METATHEORY

We shall here discuss the theoretical perspective from which we have been treating the problem of characterizing the abstract form of a semantic theory—the nature of semantic metatheory. We shall also consider some of the consequences of adopting an explicit metatheory in semantics.

There are two motives for constructing an explicit metatheory for an area in linguistics, and thus for semantics.[28] First,

[27] We can highlight the difference between theories containing only type 1 rules and theories containing rules of both type 1 and type 2 by contrasting the ways that they would deal with relative clause constructions. A theory containing only type 1 rules would determine from the transformational history of a sentence containing such a construction which nominal the relative suppresses, and would then treat the relative clause as an adjectival on that nominal, with amalgamation proceeding in the normal way. A theory containing both types of rules would first provide an interpretation for the matrix sentence and the embedded sentence which underlie the sentence containing the relative clause, and would then convert the semantic interpretations of the source sentences into a semantic interpretation of the sentence containing the relative.

[28] The conception of a metatheory for semantics which is sketched below is adapted from Chomsky's conception of a metatheory for grammar, which he refers to as 'linguistic theory'. Cf. *Syntactic structures,* and *The logical structure of linguistic theory* (microfilm).

the same scientific curiosity which makes us inquire into the semantic structure of individual languages a fortiori makes us interested in what is common to the semantic structure of families of language or of all languages. Hence a metatheory for semantics must be a theory which represents semantic universals. Second, there must be WELL-ESTABLISHED criteria for choosing among different semantic theories for the same language, where each theory is, as far as we can tell, compatible with the available evidence from fluent native speakers. But if a set of such criteria is to be well-established, it must itself be shown to give desirable results with a wide variety of different languages, i.e. it must choose the better semantic theory over the worse consistently from language to language. Hence a semantic metatheory must provide criteria for evaluating individual semantic theories and establish the adequacy of such criteria. We can satisfy both motives if we construct a metatheory which contains an enumeration of the semantic markers from which the theoretical vocabulary of each particular semantic theory is drawn and a specification of the form of the dictionary entries and rules for a semantic theory of a natural language. For the enumeration and the specification provide both a representation of semantic universals and a basis on which to evaluate particular semantic theories. For example, we may adopt the rule that the preferable theory is the one which is rated highest by a metric which compares dictionary entries in the specified form and chooses the theory requiring the smallest number of markers from the enumeration given in the metatheory.

The semantic markers which we have used in our discussions of dictionary entries and projection rules are, of course, only examples. But if we imagine them functioning in a putative semantic theory of English, then the claim for them would have to be that they are drawn from the enumeration of markers provided by the metatheory, just as the claim for the projection rules would have to be that they are in a form specified by the metatheory. In other words, a semantic marker is a theoretical construct which receives its interpretation the semantic metatheory; it is on a par with such scientific constructs as the atom, the gene, valence, and the noun phrase. A marker like (Human) or (Color) is, then, not an English word, but a construct represented by one.

A metatheory for semantics must also exhibit the relations between semantics and other areas of linguistics. We have discussed the relation between grammatical and semantic rules at some length. We now consider the relation between grammatical and semantic markers.

Much confusion has been generated in the study of language by the search for a line between grammar and semantics. This is because students of language who have tried to draw such a line have sought a criterion to determine when a concept expressing something about the structure of a language is syntactic and when it is semantic. But the trouble is that every such criterion seems to be invalidated by concepts which can be regarded, apparently with equal justice, as either syntactic or semantic. There appears to be an overlap between the sets of syntactic and semantic markers; the markers male, female, human, animal, animate, concrete, and abstract appear to fall into this overlap. But the confusion engendered in the search for a line between grammar and semantics is unwarranted: the overlap exists in name only.

This becomes clear once we stop searching for a criterion to decide which markers are properly syntactic and which semantic, and ask instead whether the line between grammatical and semantic makers can be drawn in terms of the theoretical functions they perform.[29] For example, in the grammar the distinction

[29] It is not at all clear that the request for such a criterion is a reasonable one. Would one ask for an analogous criterion to distinguish the concepts of physics from those of chemistry?

between abstract and concrete nouns is drawn in order to construct adequate rules for generating sentences containing nominalizations. According to Lees,[30]

> ...there are certain restrictions on subject/predicate-nominal combinations based on abstractness (as well as perhaps on other lower-order nominal categories). There is a small class of (abstract) nouns which may appear in copula sentences opposite both nominalizations and concrete nominals: The problem is that he went there., The problem is his going there., The problem is his tonsils., etc. for such nouns N_a as *problem, trouble, thing, reason, cause, question,* etc. Nominalizations occur opposite only these latter nouns, while concrete nominals N_c occur opposite either other concretes or one of these latter abstract noun N_a; That he came home is the trouble., but not *That he came home is that she left., or again: His stomach is the cause., His stomach is an organ., but not: *His stomach is his having gone there.

The distinction between mass and count nouns, analogously, is drawn in order to handle the syntactic relations between nouns and their articles and quantifiers. Thus, the mass noun *blood* in the singular takes *the* and *some* but not numerical quantifiers: *The blood was found* but not **One blood was found*; the distinction between animate and inanimate nouns, and between masculine and feminine nouns, has to do (among other things) with pronoun agreement, e.g. *The girl gave her own dress away,* but not **The girl gave his own dress away* or **The girl gave its own dress away.*

On the other hand, semantic markers are introduced to specify something about the meaning of lexical items. Where it appears that a marker is common to both grammar and semantics, there are two distinct markers with the same or similar names. This is most clear from the fact that it is often NOT the case that a lexical item receiving a certain grammatical marker also receives the corresponding semantic marker. If we always assigned a semantic marker where the corresponding grammatical marker is assigned, many lexical items will be given the wrong sense characterization. Grammatically the words *ship, England, fortune,* and *fate* are marked feminine, but clearly they cannot receive the semantic marker (Female) if sentences are to receive the correct semantic interpretations. Again, the words *pain, ache, twinge,* etc. must be marked as concrete nouns, but they cannot be marked as (Physical Object) if we are to account for such anomalies as *The pain weighs three pounds.* Conversely, if we always assigned a grammatical marker where the corresponding semantic marker is assigned, either the grammar will fail to generate some grammatical sentences or it will generate some ungrammatical strings, or else it will fail to assign structure properly. Semantically the nouns *child, baby,* and *infant* must be marked as (Human) to obtain correct sense characterizations and correct semantic interpretations; but if they are marked as human nouns, the grammar will fail to generate such sentences as *The baby lost its rattle.*

Grammatical and semantic markers have, then, different theoretical import. Grammatical markers mark the formal differences on which the distinction between well-formed and ill-formed strings of morphemes rests, while semantic markers give each well-formed string the conceptual content that permits it to be a means of genuine verbal communication. They are concerned with different kinds of selection and they express different aspects of the structure of a language. We can justifiably regard semantic markers as theoretical constructs distinct from the markers employed in grammatical description.

30 Lees, *The grammar of English nominalizations* 14.

The Atomization of Meaning

DWIGHT BOLINGER

History repeats itself, with variations. Two decades ago American structuralists were trying, with indifferent success, to apply to morphology the same analytical techniques that had proved successful in the analysis of sound. For a number of reasons—including the lack of a suitable theory of meaning—the attempt made no headway at a time when phonology was still scoring advances with help from both acoustics and information theory. Morphemics still remains, in current texts on linguistics, a kind of relic of the 1940's. Now we witness a revived attempt from a different direction, but with essentially the same desire: to try out in a new field the techniques that have been developed in an older one. The new field is meaning, the old one is syntax, and the techniques are those of generative grammar. For the moment, morphemics is only slightly involved, but the signs are clear.

The phonological notion that was carried over to morphology was that of the *eme*. The syntactic notion that is being carried over into semantics is that of the *marker*. Syntactic markers are a refinement of the categories of traditional grammar—Noun Phrase, Adjective, Adverb, Determiner, etc.—and are of proved usefulness, as emes were and still are in phonology.

Back of the emes of phonology lay three millennia of strivings to hammer out a system of writing. No linguist would have been apt to 'discover' the phoneme in the year 1930 if he had lacked an alphabet. Here was a body of practical experience where the main thing needed was a linguist's close and analytical attention. On the side of syntax there was also—though rather less diffused in society than alphabetic writing—a large body of traditional grammar with wide agreement on larger matters, from which a scientific grammar could draw. One of the strengths of generative grammar is expressed in the half-truth that it contains 'nothing really new'; it confirms what we felt all along.

The value of a tradition rests in the centuries of winnowing, sifting, selecting, and rejecting on a vast proving ground where practical value is the test of survival, and many hands have performed many experiments of which the ultimate scientific triumph is only the last. Phonology and syntax inherited a limited set of contrasts, an apparatus that was not overburdened with entities. Does semantics inherit anything? If it does—or if not,

Dwight Bolinger, "The Atomization of Meaning," *Language,* **41,** No. 4 (1965), 555–573. Reprinted by permission of the author and publisher.

and the whole thing has to be contrived—are the items limited, or can they be limited, to a manageable number? To answer these questions we must look at the role played by semantic markers in a particular theory, and at their possible hereditary relation, if any, to semantic work that has gone before.

The obvious choice for such an inquiry is the study by Jerrold Katz and Jerry Fodor, 'The structure of a semantic theory',[1] which has been deservedly influential in promoting the notion of the semantic marker. For K-F, 'Semantic markers are the elements in terms of which semantic relations are expressed in a theory' (187), the relational 'atomic concepts' that 'exhibit the semantic structure IN a dictionary entry and the semantic relations BETWEEN dictionary entries' (186). While this puts the case in exclusively decoding terms, and the entire argument is based on how a theory is able to account for the clearing up of ambiguity ('disambiguation' is the term used for this), there are obviously ramifications in other directions, particularly toward the act of encoding. For the moment, what is important is that K-F's statement is concerned exclusively about what a dictionary does or ought to do to enable the rules of the theory—the 'projection rules'—to disambiguate a semantically ambiguous sentence.

Mention of the dictionary suggests that K-F may indeed have in mind a tradition, which is that of lexicography. While they do not claim in so many words that their procedures in setting up definitions are just a refinement of what dictionary-makers have been doing all along, there are some obvious resemblances. We can trace them best by first giving an illustration or two from K-F's treatment.[2]

As an example of one common form of dictionary entry, K-F cite *bachelor*, and diagram it as in Fig. 1. This form, they point out, will not do for a semantic theory, for the characterizations are unsystematic. It must be revised to expose the markers, as shown in Fig. 2. The semantic markers are in parentheses. Brackets enclose the second type of atomic concept, the 'distinguisher', which is the idiosyncratic remainder of a given sense when all the markers have been stripped away. Each sense of the word is exhaustively characterized by tracing the path from grammatical marker (noun) through semantic markers to distinguisher.

The plausibility of this design is of course no accident, for something like it is regularly used in dictionary definitions, even though it did not happen to be used in the definition of *bachelor*. The Merriam-Webster *NID3* defines one sense of *nectar* as 'a sweet liquid that is secreted by the nectaries of a plant'. Presumably this would be traced, along with the other meanings, as in Fig. 3. The markers (Liquid) and (Sweet) are supplied by the dictionary, and serve, respectively, to set off the 'secretion' sense from that of 'a grayish red' and 'any delicious drink'. Probably (Liquid) is too specific (though perhaps needed elsewhere, and so I retain it); I therefore add a superior marker (Material) at the point where the color separates from the other meanings. I am

[1] *Lg* 39.170–210 (1963). Hereafter diminished, in length but not in credit, to K-F.

[2] This is probably the right place to point out that K-F have tried to protect their flank by disavowing any attempt to BUILD a semantic theory. They undertake no more than to sketch an APPROACH to one. If their examples are matched with convincing counterexamples, they will not be abased, but will look for better ones or modify some detail of the theory. This of course assumes that the foundations remain intact: it is hard to make alterations in a house whose frame has to be torn out. But the truth of the matter is that without putting together at least a fair sampling of the structure, one can never know whether the theory will account for more than the particular lexical sets from which the examples are drawn. If from a handful of specimens the theory appears as likely to fail as to succeed, there is no defense in promising to patch it up. In this sense, one cannot excuse a taste because it is only a taste. Until more is presented, everything stands or falls by it, and a theory is as subject to criticism in the light of its examples as a principal is liable to damages for the actions of his agent.

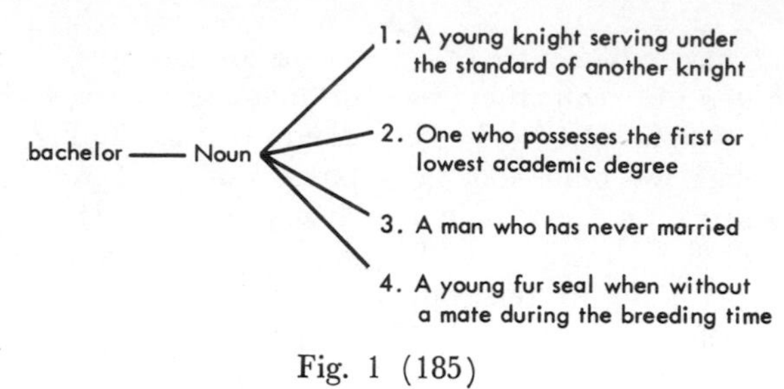

Fig. 1 (185)

not sure that the markers I have chosen would suit K-F, but I think that the illustration is good enough to show that the form of the entry is essentially one of markers and distinguishers.

Having settled that there is a practice in lexicography resembling the semantic analysis proposed by K-F, we can now go on to some of the problems raised by attempting to turn that practice into a theory that will cover the field. There will be time as we go along to ask whether the practice in question is the only one, or even the typical one, to be found in dictionaries, which has theoretical interest.

THE PROBLEM OF DUALISM: I. MARKERS AND DISTINGUISHERS

The dictionary draws no line between markers and distinguishers. This dualism is created by K-F to make it possible to have 'just enough' markers to do the job. A given theory may have more or less, and hence be more or less sensitive to the disambiguations that a fluent speaker is able to make. It is not enough to define *bachelor*, on one of its paths, as noun—(Human)—(Male), if we expect to account for the speaker's ability to discriminate the sense of *The old bachelor finally died* as 'unmarried man' rather than as 'young knight serving under the standard of another knight'. If we require that degree of sensitivity, then we must elevate (Young) to the status of a marker, for markers are, by definition, the semantic atoms through which disambiguations are effected. How far the theory should go is governed by

> . . . a strategy which seeks to maximize systematic economy: the greatest possible conceptual

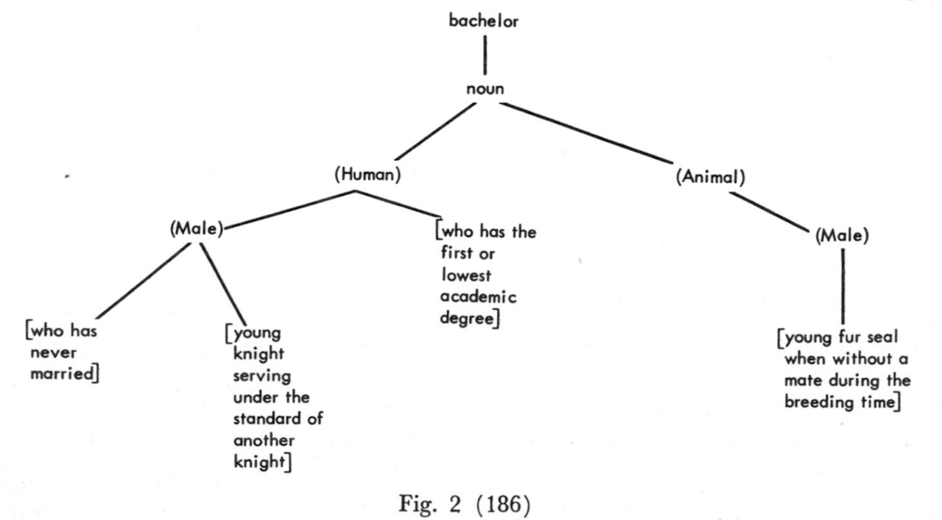

Fig. 2 (186)

economy with the greatest possible explanatory and descriptive power. If such decisions are optimally made, there should eventually come a point where increasing the complexity of a semantic theory by adding new markers no longer yields enough advantage in precision or scope to warrant the increase. At that point, the system of semantic markers should reflect exactly the systematic features of the semantic structure of the language (190).

K-F illustrate the process of extracting a marker from the distinguisher by rediagramming to show the new status of (Young), as in Fig. 4.

While K-F admit the possibility of theories of varying degrees of sensitivity, they also, in the passage just quoted, posit an ideal theory whose 'system of semantic markers should reflect exactly the systematic features of the semantic structure of the language'. It would seem that such a theory would need to handle all the disambiguations that the fluent speaker makes on the analogy of K-F's example (Young). The question then arises whether the distinguisher will not keep receding toward the horizon until it vanishes altogether. Let us see if this in fact does happen when we gather more disambiguations for *bachelor*. I shall give the disambiguating sentences, discuss them, and later rediagram.

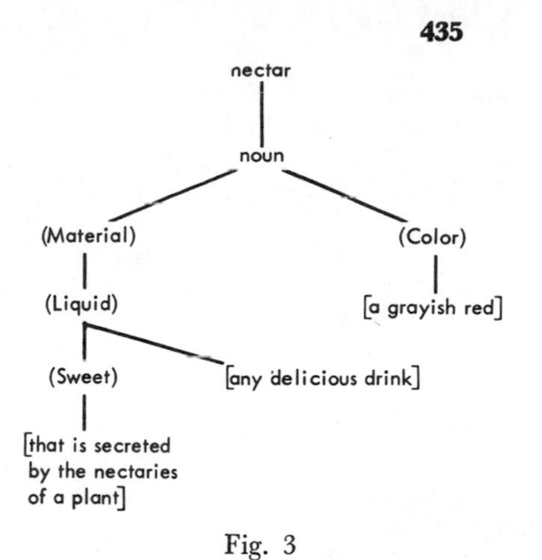

Fig. 3

1. *He became a bachelor.* This rules out the 'man who has never married'—it is impossible to become one who has never done something. We can extract the *-ever* part of *never* from the distinguisher and set up a marker (Nonbecoming).

2. *The seven-year-old bachelor sat on the rock.* The definition 'male who has never married' was deficient. It should have been something like 'adult male who has never married,' and from that expanded distinguisher we now extract the marker (Adult).

3. *Lancelot was the unhappiest of all the bachelors after his wife died.* This seems to justify raising (Unmarried) to

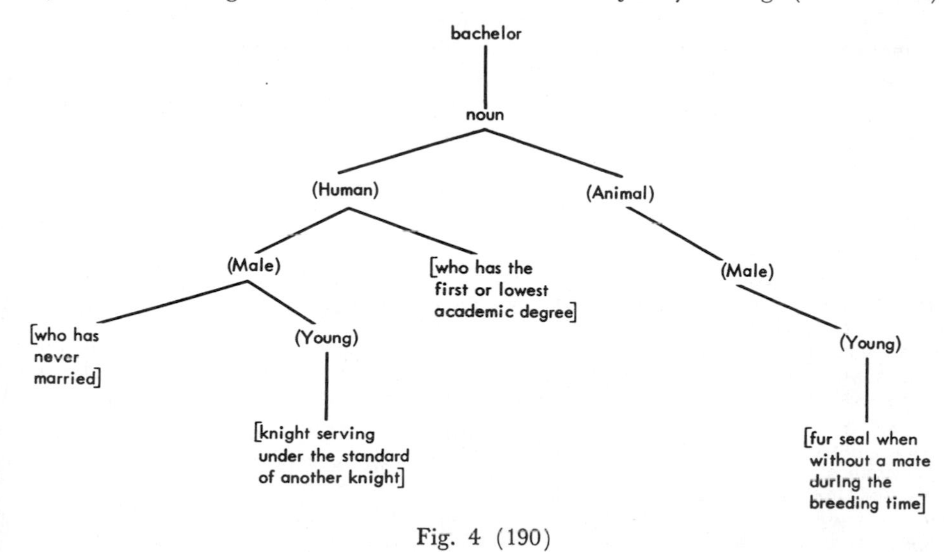

Fig. 4 (190)

marker status and wipes out the distinguisher on one of the branches: *bachelor*—noun—(Human)—(Male)—(Adult)—(Non-becoming)—(Unmarried).

4. *That peasant is a happy bachelor.* Being a peasant is not compatible with being a knight. There must be a marker of status lying around somewhere. A knight has to be of gentle birth. Let us extract (Noble) from the distinguisher (leaving the degree of nobility for the moment undisturbed as still part of the knight's distinguisher).

5. *George is one bachelor who is his own boss.* This eliminates the knight, and turns 'serving under' into another status marker that might be called (Dependent).

6. *George is a bachelor in the service of the Queen.* This again eliminates the knight, and yields a marker that shows the direction of the (Dependency) relationship: it is to the person on the next higher rung of the (Nobility) ladder. I suggest (Proximate), dominated by (Dependent).[3]

7. *Knight banneret Gawain is a bachelor.* This eliminates the lower status of the knight bachelor, and admits (Inferior) as a restriction on (Noble).

8. *At some time in his life every man is a bachelor.* This eliminates both the knight and the B.A., because status has no bearing. We can therefore add a generalized status marker to those two other meanings. I call it (Hierarchic).

9. *A bachelor is expected to fight.* This puts the hierarchy in its proper setting, with a superior marker (Military). There is now no distinguisher left on the knighthood branch; it reads *bachelor*—noun—(Human) — (Male) — (Military) — (Hierarchic) — (Noble) — (Inferior) — (Dependent)—(Proximate)—(Young).

10. *He's studying hard to be a bachelor.* Again there is suggested a possible hierarchic setting of some kind. I will use (Educand).

11. *Employers prefer married men who are at least bachelors; without the degree you hardly have a chance.* This confirms that the general status marker (Hierarchic) should be repeated on this path.

12. *At the age of twenty-five he ceased to be a bachelor, but he never married.* This has to refer to the knight, and points to a marker akin to the (Nonbecoming) that was added to the 'unmarried man' branch: one cannot become an unmarried man, but can cease to be one; one could both become and cease to be a knight bachelor; one can become but not cease to be a bachelor of arts. The position on the academic ladder is therefore (Permanent), and sets off *bachelor* from *sophomore,* for example. As we already have the marker (Inferior) on the knighthood branch, we can add it here and eliminate the distinguisher. The B.A. comes out *bachelor*—noun — (Human) — (Educand) — (Hierarchic)—(Permanent)—(Inferior).

13. *That pet of mine is always nuzzling me and barking and wiggling his flippers.* I include this to show that the system will need, somewhere, to discriminate (Canine) and (Phocine), whence (Phocine) should be extracted from the distinguisher and set up on this path, beneath (Animal). Without going through another series of disambiguations, we can lay down the path *bachelor*—noun—(Animal)—(Phocine) — (Hirsute)[4] — (Male) — (Adult)—(Young)—(Unmated) as an almost complete characterization of the seal by means of markers alone. The re-

[3] The problem of marker dominance is not treated by K-F. Presumably there are set sequences of markers, e.g. (Human) vs. (Animal) must precede (Male) vs. (Female) which in turn must precede (Old) vs. (Young), etc. Otherwise it will be impossible to generalize markers to the point where one like (Inferior), for instance, will serve both for an inferior grade of nobility (when dominated by Noble) and for an inferior academic degree (when dominated by other markers relating to such degrees). A more specific marker will have to be used, increasing the number of markers.

[4] These markers are easily established by following K-F's lead with *old.* Their trick for pulling (Young) out of the distinguisher was

mainder, 'during the mating season,' I shall deal with later.

I have tried to show by this exercise that it is possible to do away with the dualism by converting the distinguisher into a string of markers. It is less awkward theoretically and more satisfying esthetically if this can be done, but for *bachelor* the cost was high—a fivefold increase in the number of markers. It is apparently their unwillingness to pay this price that leads K-F to cling to their dualism, though they recognize that in some definitions no distinguishers are needed; thus (Animal) is not only a marker but also a word, and as a word it will have no distinguisher at the end of the path that corresponds to its meaning as a marker; cf. 187 footnote.[5]

Another fault of distinguishers—at least those in the K-F diagram—is their redundancy. When (Young) is taken out of the distinguisher class and turned into a marker, it is eliminated from the distinguisher. But the latter still contains 'knight', which is necessarily (Human) and (Male). With (Human) and (Male) extracted, what is left should be something like 'member of the lowest nobility' etc., which is distinctly more marker-like in appearance, and invites to the extraction of more markers. Even if distinguishers are kept, they need to be cleaned up. That involves simply examining the terms they contain (e.g. *knight*), looking up their definitions in the dictionary and identifying the markers (Human, Male), and pulling those markers out, canceling the ones that are already spread out on the path of the sense being defined.

The chief fault of the marker-distinguisher dualism, however, is that it does not appear to correspond to any clear division in natural language. For a theory that claims to apply to natural language, having as conspicuous a feature as this with no equally conspicuous objective counterpart is a disadvantage.

Or perhaps K-F have wrought better than they wot, and there is a spot for distinguishers, or something like them, though a bit to one side of where they placed it. Two possibilities occur to me, one embracing certain presuppositions of the theory, the other extraneous but still related to common dictionary practices.

For the first, it is necessary to ask whether, if the theory accounts for human behavior, it must not then take stock of that part of human behavior which provides the sense characterizations that we draw upon as raw material for the theory. Speakers make themselves understood. Understanding presupposes disambiguation. Disambiguation presupposes the processes that make it possible. K-F recognize two such processes—the linguistic one, which employs markers, and the nonlinguistic one, which employs the speaker's knowledge of the world. Here, then, is a possible residue that could form the content of lexical distinguishers. If a sentence like *Henry became a bachelor in 1965* is unambiguous because the speaker knows that knighthood died out a long time ago, *bachelor* in the sense of 'knight' could contain something like 'in the Middle Ages' as its distinguisher, or as part of it. Using the distinguisher in this way would enable the theory to sweep up certain usage labels and other lexical material (for example, the *Rom. antiq.* that heads the *Century* definition of *cohort*) now left out of account. It would be knowledge of the world that is general, of course, not something as personal as a disambiguation of *Bessie*

simply to use its antonym in a sentence: *The* OLD *bachelor finally died*. Similarly, we can take a synonym or an antonym of something in the (Animal) distinguisher, disambiguate with it, and make a new marker: *the phocine bachelor* (establishing Phocine directly), *the hairless bachelor* (establishing Hirsute indirectly), etc.

[5] They also by implication give at least one sense characterization by distinguisher alone. The word *colorful* has as one of its paths (198) 'Adjective—(Color)—[abounding in contrast or variety of bright colors]'. If *colorful* is viewed compositionally in the way that K-F advocate (192), then the only part corresponding to the morpheme *-ful* is 'abounding in', in the distinguisher. The point is not discussed, and there is no way to tell whether it has any significance.

is a bitch in favor of 'canine' rather than 'human' because the hearer knows that the speaker does not use bad language.

This solution has the advantage of reducing two dualisms to one, though the one is still formidable: 'knowledge of one's language' vs. 'knowledge of the world'. It also produces the effect, at some points, of looking through the wrong end of the telescope. A label as comprehensive as *Rom. antiq.* represents a universe of discourse, as powerful a classifying tool as a semantic marker, and a bit large for a distinguisher to swallow. No allowance is made for the universe of discourse in the K-F theory, and I am dubious of the distinguisher as a proper place for it. I am also skeptical about the remaining dualism, and will return to these two matters later.

The second solution incorporates a type of definition which is common in dictionaries but which the K-F outline does not touch upon. It can be illustrated by the two words *sun* and *senate*. In the *ACD* definition for the first, sense 1 is 'the star which is the central body of the solar system', and sense 3 is 'a self-luminous heavenly body'. Sense 1 is a particular case of sense 3. In the definition of *senate*, sense 1 is 'an assembly or council of citizens having the highest deliberative functions', etc.; senses 2 and 3 name particular instances. I see no reason why the level of distinguishers could not be assigned to this point where markers can no longer be used, only lists: '*sun* → *Old Sol, Betelgeuse, Sirius, Alpha Centauri*...' This corresponds to 'NProp → *John, James, Henry, Charles*...' and covers, of course, those dictionary definitions that semantically parallel proper names.

THE PROBLEM OF THE SYMMETRY OF MARKERS

The second theoretical question is the need to keep the markers on all the paths as nearly the same as possible. When we accept a given lexical item as 'a word' we commit ourselves to recognizing some degree of internal organization. If the senses are wildly different we ought to suspect that we are dealing with homonyms—in fact, one dividend of a theory of markers could be a measure of homonymy: below a certain number of markers held in common, two senses could be taken to represent two homonyms, not two distinct paths of the same word. The existence of two markers, or of a marker and a distinguisher, that are similar but not the same ought to raise the suspicion that we have overlooked a hidden identity.

I illustrate with the marker (Young). There is an obvious relationship between (Young) and the characterization 'first or lowest' which K-F deposited in their distinguisher for the A.B. (Young) could be regarded as (Early) on a path leading down from (Annuated). The A.B. is (Early) on a path leading down from (Educand) etc. By spinning the thread a bit finer we reduce (Young) to a marker (Early) that can be shared by an additional path. There is no gain in this from my standpoint since I have already had to add (Inferior) to the knight branch and that takes care of the lowly A.B. as well; but with (Young) as the sole extra marker on the knight branch as K-F had it, there would have been an argument for generalizing it to the A.B. The illustration is not the best to be had, but I give it because it does not involve going beyond the markers that K-F set up.

A better one—involving my added markers—is that between (Unmarried) on the (Human) side and (Unmated) on the (Animal) side. If we disregard the particular mating ceremonies of man and seal (as we would need to disregard them, for example, between a high-church wedding and a common-law marriage), it seems an obvious waste to recognize two markers, and I accordingly reduce them to one, (Unmated).

THE PROBLEM OF LATENT MARKERS

I purposely left one distinguisher on the (Animal) side, 'during the mating season', to illustrate this third theoretical point. Where it was sufficient to designate the human being as (Adult), since human beings do not rut and the whole of their adulthood is characterized by availability for mating, seals do have their season, and (Adult) is not sufficient: one can have a young adult male fur seal without a mate which is still not a bachelor if the time is wrong. 'During the mating season' seems an unlikely candidate for a marker, until we realize that when we call someone—human or animal—a bachelor, we mean that he is without a mate at a time when he is expected to have one: incidentally the whole of adulthood in the human being, incidentally the mating season in the seal. The marker then is (Availability for Mating), or, to use a single appropriate term, (Nubile). If we find that *The migrating bachelors stopped to rest* is unambiguous because we know that the seal's migrating season does not coincide with his mating season, and therefore the bachelors must be human, we are employing our 'knowledge of the world' as we did with *He became a bachelor in 1965*. In other words, (Nubile) can be purified of its temporal associations just as *knight* can, by banishing them to our 'knowledge of the world', and the entry for *bachelor* can now be diagrammed with markers only, as in Fig. 5.

This gives us (Nubile), then, on the (Animal) side. But it is equally appropriate, though unnecessary, on the (Human) side. There it is a latent marker. Shall we add it? This is not a question of CREATING a marker unnecessarily, for it was already required elsewhere. Rather it is a question of how much of the marker system should be made explicit. How cumbersome this would be can be shown by an almost endless number of anomalous sentences: *He walked right through the bachelor* is anomalous because a bachelor is (Solid). *He broke the bachelor in two* is anomalous because a bachelor is (Pliable). *He welded the bachelor* is anomalous because a bachelor is (Organic). These are markers that dominate (Human) and (Animal). If we are to account for the fluent speaker's ability to recognize an anomaly—as well as an ambiguity—

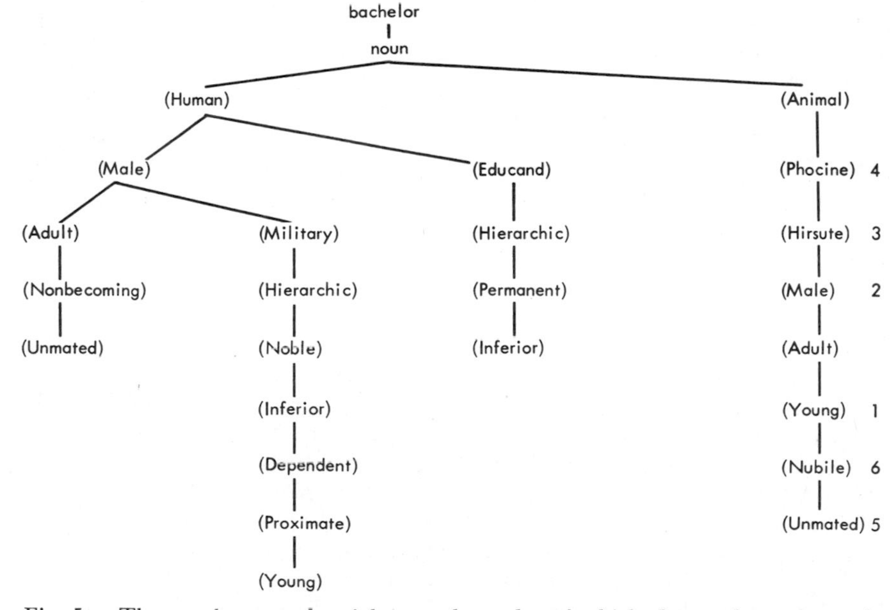

Fig. 5: The numbers on the right are the order of which the markers appear in the dictionary definition: 1 Young 2 Male 3 Fur 4 Seal 5 Without a Mate 6 During the Mating Season.

through the markers at his command, then the number is indeed legion. It spreads laterally downward from an apex which I assume to exist on the analogy of the grammatical S = Sentence—perhaps U for (Universe)? Or G for (God)? This is not as absurd as it sounds. The categories have a distinctly Aristotelian flavor.

There is a difference between a dictionary whose entries are written to account only for disambiguations, and one that must account also for recognitions of anomaly. If the dictionary is to be an auxiliary for a translation machine, where it is fairly safe to assume that no anomalous sentences will be part of the input, then the relatively limited roster of one or two dozen markers per entry may suffice. If it is conceived as a representation of how fluent speakers behave toward anomalies as well as ambiguities, each entry will be interminable. A reasonable solution would be not to use the ordinary dictionary at all, if the model is to serve as a kind of lexical map for a natural language. Instead, it could resemble a thesaurus, where each marker would appear only once, and where each sense of a lexical item would appear as a particular path linking marker to marker.

THE PROBLEM OF ABSTRACT CHARACTERIZATION

The more specific the marker, the greater the number of markers. This follows if we assume that the concepts in our experience are made up largely of shared elements, and are not overly endowed with unique ones or primes. This assumption I think is inherent in a system of markers. Shall we have two markers, (Liquid) and (Gaseous), or one, (Fluid), crossed by two others, (Dense)and (Diffuse)? There is no gain in the latter unless (Dense) and (Diffuse) have uses other than the one of splitting (Fluid) into two halves. If we find that (Diffuse) is useful in characterizing verbs like *scatter, dispel, disseminate,* and (Dense) in characterizing nouns like *crowd, jam, clot,* then there may be an advantage in taking a step back and getting the longer perspective.

The marker (Young) illustrates this point. I have already suggested that it be replaced by (Early), in order to show the symmetrical relationship between the separate paths for *bachelor.* But there is a larger reason. Anything that can be adjusted to a temporal scale can be marked as (Early) or (Late):

	EARLY	LATE
living being (ontogenetic)	young	old
humanity (sociogenetic)	primitive	advanced
perishable product	fresh	stale
other product	new	old
lunar phase	waxing	waning
tide	flood	ebb
fruit	green	ripe
growing thing in general	immature	mature

The interrelations here are shown by various metaphorical transfers, such as *early in life* for *young, early civilizations* for *primitive civilizations, the fresh of the morning* for *the early part of the day, the young moon* for *the crescent phase.* If we are to avoid multiplying markers, then refining them in this way becomes imperative.

Can it be done? It would be rash to assume that it can, until it has been tried on a large scale. The marker theory has to assume that it can, or accept the multiplication of markers.

I am skeptical because I doubt the omnivalence of digits. Certain constructs can be dealt with nicely with a scheme of plusses or minuses like that of distinctive features. A piano, for instance, can be characterized perfectly among musical instruments as + percussion, + keyboard, + string, − wind, + tempered, etc. But a piano is also a piece of furniture, where more gradient things like legs, size, surfaces, inclination (it is not necessary for the instrument to be strictly horizontal or strictly upright), and material become significant.

THE PROBLEM OF GRADIENCE: DEFINITION BY SYNONYM

Dictionary-makers do not shrink from recognizing gradience. One standard way to deal with it is to define by synonymic overlap. This procedure is so foreign to K-F's outlook that they try to deny its existence (185): 'The explicit inclusion of synonyms in a dictionary entry, which is the common practice of conventional dictionaries, is a redundancy introduced to save the user the effort of discovering the synonyms of a lexical item by comparing its sense characterizations with those of every other item in the dictionary. In short, the practice of listing the synonyms of an item is simply a technique of cross reference.' Nothing here about using synonyms to establish the sense characterization itself. Some examples from *NID3*:

detract 3: 'divert, draw'
heavy 5b: 'pregnant, gravid'; 7b: 'dull and confused due to interruption of sleep'; 8f: 'massive, coarse'; 8h: 'steep, acute'; 8i: 'laborious, difficult'

Frequently adjectives are nominalized, as a kind of dodge to avoid the appearance of defining by synonyms. Thus for *petty* 3b: 'reflecting small-mindedness or meanness' (i.e. 'small-minded and mean'); and for *dauntless*: 'marked by courageous resolution' (i.e. 'courageous and resolute'). *NID3* designates its listed synonyms—K-F's 'cross reference'—explicitly, with small capitals; but even these are sometimes pressed into service for a sense characterization. Thus for *encourage* 2: 'to spur on: STIMULATE, INCITE'—three synonyms, two of them explicit. Without the latter two, *encourage* might be taken to apply to a horse; with *stimulate* it is made clear that 'arousal in general' is intended, and with *incite* we learn that the object is normally human, not animal.

When *NID3* uses synonyms to define, there are more often than not two of them: the sense is characterized by an overlap of the semantic ranges of two other terms presumed to be already known, and two are the minimum necessary to have an overlap. Of course it can be argued that this is just a shorthand way of saying 'X has those markers of Y and Z that are not mutually exclusive'—so for (Human) under *encourage*. But with *petty* we have a gradience of pejorativeness: *petty* is more pejorative than *small-minded* but less so than *mean*. Definition by synonyms seems not to be a kind of covert definition by markers, but a definition by the semantic range of individual words. If this kind of definition is necessary, then there is a limit to the use of markers, and K-F have not met the challenge of synonymies by calling them 'redundant'.

THE PROBLEM OF METAPHOR

A complete semantic theory must not only map the markers of all senses but show how markers are added and subtracted to alter the senses of words. One corroboration of a marker theory would be its ability to predict semantic shifts, much as a distinctive-feature theory accounts for phonological shifts in terms of change of one feature at a time. It is premature to look for that kind of corroboration or to put the marker theory to so advanced a test. But a more modest requirement is not out of order: to relate the several senses of a word in terms of their probable derivation one from another, so far as this may affect the choice of markers and the sharing of pathways. One would like to see derived senses represented by closely connected paths. A radical departure from this kind of regularity would suggest that semantic derivation is not amendable to

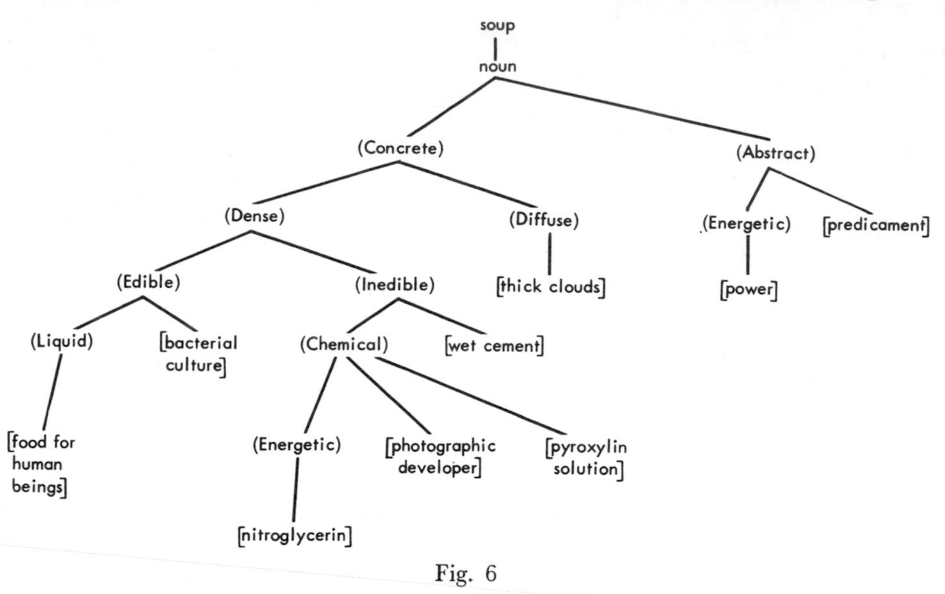

Fig. 6

rule, and this in turn is a threat to formal treatment of semantics as a whole.

I choose as an example the word *soup*, and diagram its senses according to *NID3*, as best I can in the way that I assume K-F would do it. See Fig. 6.

The metaphorical basis of all but one of the senses is immediately apparent. Clouds are compared to the thickness of soup. Chemicals are compared to its consistency and cook's-broth manner of concoction. Bacterial culture is compared to its consistency and edibility. A predicament is compared to the proverbial cartoon of the missionary in the cannibal's cookpot. And power is compared to nitroglycerin which was compared to the food.

From the standpoint of markers, these all represent wide discontinuities. The direct association of predicament and soup kettle spans the widest conceivable gap, that between (Concrete) and (Abstract). So does that of power and nitroglycerin. Looking at these jumps far out of orbit, one can hardly avoid the conclusion of indeterminacy in semantic interrelatedness.

An extreme case is that of thick clouds. Factually, clouds are diffuse. But the intent of calling them soup is to make them appear dense. How, then, does one pick the marker—actually diffuse or metaphorically dense? In shifting its domain from (Dense) to (Diffuse), *soup* 'thick clouds' carries (Dense) along with it, which is just another way of saying that clouds, which cannot be thick, are thick. In a marker theory, which compels us to make all-or-none decisions, this is a dilemma. Markers are atoms. They do not have ranges. A thing is either (Dense) or (Diffuse).

A dictionary is a frozen pantomime. Our problem is only beginning when we consider the pale flowers of that 'nosegay of faded metaphors' that it presses between its pages. A semantic theory must account for the PROCESS of metaphorical invention—all the more so, a theory that stems from generative grammar with its emphasis on creativity. How I make myself understood when I use previously fixed senses that are well known both to me and to my hearer, by a kind of sequence of cancellations, is one thing; how I am understood when I call a chain smoker a fumarole is something else. It is characteristic of natural language that no word is ever limited to its enumerable senses, but carries within it the qualification of 'something like'.

The radical shifts effected by metaphor throw into relief the bold differences between universes of discourse in the totality of language. They raise the question of whether it will ever be possible to attack everything, from slang to technology to science and back again to politics, religion, and the home, with one arsenal of categories.

THE PROBLEM OF SELECTED DATA: CONSTRUCTIVE AND SUBSTANTIVE DEFINITION

Workaday dictionaries do more than one kind of defining. Sometimes they steer it in a more or less marker-like direction, other times by way of overlapping synonyms, others by simile (*cornicle*: a 'horn-shaped' process). Different styles presumably reflect the varying needs of different segments of the lexicon. What will serve for the abstract characterization of *senate* will not serve for the finger-pointing of *Senate*.

This suggests that some kind of survey of the lexicon is needed to determine whether all its entries are really amenable to a single uniform attack. I am inclined to think that K-F's example of *bachelor* is a special kind of word where we 'find' the markers that we have already put in. An *uncle*, similarly, is one who bears a socially defined relationship to *parent* who in turn bears it to an *offspring*—the markers are there because we put them there. It is something different to find markers in anything that has a life history independent of our naming-operations. A bachelor is a bachelor because he is unmarried, and marriage is an arbitrarily defined social ceremony; we impose the conditions. A bird or a fish is something that we take as we find it, and the markers are adjusted like a suit of clothes, often badly. The fit is crude, metaphorical, subject to revision, and above all subject to change as the entity itself grows or decays through time. This distinction is fundamental. A CONSTRUCTIVE definition applies to a social construct, with markers defined a priori. A SUBSTANTIVE definition applies to the hard objects of the natural world. The contrast becomes vivid when we can express it in minimal terms, when the same object can be viewed either way. A recent review criticizes the definition of *to inspect* as 'to examine carefully' on the grounds that *to inspect carelessly* is normal. But *to inspect* is 'to perform the duties of an inspector', and inspectors, viewed substantively, can be careless. From a constructive standpoint, *inspector* as 'one who examines carefully' is perfectly correct. *Inspector, bachelor, cousin, suffrage, baptism, corporal*—these are constructive entries and can be dealt with more or less successfully by means of semantic markers. Matters are less rosy with the lexicon of things.

THE PROBLEM OF DUALISM: II. 'KNOWLEDGE OF THE LANGUAGE' AND 'KNOWLEDGE OF THE WORLD'

He became a bachelor in 1965 was disambiguated by the hearer's grasp of history—he knows that chivalry long since passed from the scene. The speaker's 'knowledge of the world' comes in at the point where two possible theories of disambiguation are pitted against each other, one a theory (the common one) that ambiguities are resolved by the context of situation, the other that they are resolved by rules operating on markers that are part of the linguistic apparatus of a sentence. K-F do not deny the role of the nonlinguistic context in resolving many ambiguities; what they deny is that any tightly constructed theory can be built that will reflect its operation, because it involves too much; nothing less, in fact, than everything we know. The example offered to illustrate the point is *Our store sells alligator shoes* vs. *Our store sells horse shoes*. Our knowledge of the world tells us that alligators do not wear shoes, hence the first of these cannot mean 'shoes for alligators', but that horses do, whence the second probably does not mean shoes made of horsehide. (This ignores the fact that it IS part of our linguistic equipment that *horsehide* contrasts with *horse* and that *horseshoe* is an existing compound while *alligator shoe* is not, but let that pass for the moment.) In other words, we achieve a disambiguation by way of something that is not a semantic marker.

But why is it not a semantic marker? Where do markers like (Animal), (Physical Object), (Young), and (Female) come from if not from our knowledge of the world? What is strange about (Shoe-wearing) as a semantic marker—not as general, surely, as (Female), but general enough? The discalced branch of Carmelite monks is identified by it, and it crops up every now and then as a mark of status, like horse-riding: 'A Methodist, it was said, is a Baptist who wears shoes...'[6]

The immigrant quota protecting markers against a contaminating influx from the outer world is no more secure than the social barrier against the upward migration of distinguishers. Ultimately both dualisms are the same.

THE PROBLEM OF THE MORPHEME

The marker is an atom of content. What are the atoms of form? The selection and justification of the latter, and the bonds between the two sets of entities, are a question that K-F barely touch upon.

To reach it I go afield, from a crossroads of linguistic theory where the signs have, I think, been deceptively posted. I refer to a piece of doctrine that one finds repeated in at least every second or third article on grammar in the past few years, and on which K-F are both explicit and emphatic: 'A fluent speaker's mastery of his language exhibits itself in his ability to produce and understand the sentences of his language, INCLUDING INDEFINITELY MANY THAT ARE WHOLLY NOVEL TO HIM... The striking fact about the use of language is the absence of repetition: almost every sentence uttered is uttered for the first time' (171). K-F then add (171–2),

> In encountering a novel sentence the speaker is not encountering novel elements but only a novel combination of familiar elements. Since the set of sentences is infinite and each sentence is a different concatenation of morphemes, the fact that a speaker can understand any sentence must mean that the way he understands sentences which he has never previously encountered is compositional: on the basis of his knowledge of the grammatical properties and the meanings of the morphemes of the language, the rules which the speaker knows enable him to determine the meaning of a novel sentence in terms of the manner in which the parts of the sentence are composed to form the whole.

If the doctrine of what is 'wholly new' and what is 'familiar' is not to be trivial, there must be some kind of understanding about where the one leaves off and the other begins. In a trivial sense, a stone rolling down a slope and dislodging other stones will form a 'wholly new' pattern with them when they land at the bottom —the novelty is fortuitous. In an almost equally trivial sense, a paragraph of which all has been said before can be juxtaposed to another paragraph of which all has been said before, and the composition will be 'wholly new'. Our attitude toward novelty resembles our curiously puristic notions of 'truth': if anything in a proposition is false, the whole proposition is false; if anything in an utterance is new, the whole thing is new. My example of the two paragraphs may seem extreme, but it must be viewed in the light of K-F's own expansiveness toward the limits of a 'sentence': in making their theory cover all of the linguistic context and exclude all of the situational, they accept the procedure of stringing together unlimited stretches of speech by means of conjunctions: 'replacing discourses or stretches in discourse by single compound sentences'

[6] Richard Hofstadter, *Anti-intellectualism in American life* 60 (New York), 1963.

(180). One actually finds such sentences in the speech of the very young, who have not yet learned the best place to put a stop, or in the speech of adults as a way of fending off interruption. But it should be obvious that 'wholly new' in a sense as inclusive as this is trivial. A speaker sitting at the telephone talking with a friend and at the same time looking out the window might be heard to say, *Jack told me he would be home early, and here he comes up the sidewalk*. If *Jack told me he would be home early* and *here he comes up the sidewalk* have been uttered or heard before, and are hence not new, we cannot claim as new their appearance together when the situation intervenes between them: the man is seen coming up the sidewalk and this serves as a separate stimulus for the speaker—no creation is involved. The only thing potentially 'new' is the *and* between them—a creativity index pretty close to zero. But such an extreme is not what K-F have in mind, as becomes clear from the context in which they use the term 'familiar'. If what is familiar is at the very nethermost level of syntax, the level of the morpheme, then the 'wholly new' does not have to be an inflated sentence but can be any combination of morphemes. And here they err by setting the level too low. There are countless concatenations of morphemes that are familiar, many of them quite large—one intermediate body, with which K-F work and feel no embarrassment in doing so, is that of words. But familiarity reaches much higher. K-F regard the originality of sentences as 'striking'. But what we consider to be striking, what we allow to surprise us, depends on our orientation. I am more inclined to be surprised at the deadly repetitiousness of language. And I am even more surprised at the conformity of linguists to the view that what is 95% old not only in its elements but in much of its internal organization, is to be regarded as 100% new.

To say "X has never been done before" is to claim knowledge beyond human powers. Once we drop our pretensions of omniscience, other ways of viewing disambiguation quickly open up.

I return to the example of *horseshoe,* which I have already quoted from K-F as an instance of possible ambiguity: 'a shoe for a horse' or 'a shoe made out of horse [hide].' The fact that K-F use it is further proof of their fixation on morphemes as the only level to which one can ascribe 'familiarity'. Yet the morphemes in *horseshoe* are only slightly more separable than those in *pretend*, which could be regarded as ambiguous as between 'to tend beforehand' (no more absurd than 'a shoe made of horse') and 'to feign'. *Horseshoe* as it is used by the fluent speaker of English is virtually as univocal as *spree*.

If that is true, we are now free to expand familiarity upward. Any concatenation that repeats itself is familiar. And since concatenations ARE THE SOURCES of the sense characterizations that we carry in our heads—we learn *bachelor* from contexts like *The old bachelor finally got married*—having sense characterizations among which we must disambiguate presupposes them.

Take an example, a special one, special and atypical to about the same degree as *bachelor* (though in a different way), which I choose because it best illustrates the kind of higher-level familiarity which any theory of natural language must recognize: the noun *spell* in the two senses of 'a period of time' and 'an enchantment'.[7] Familiar concatenations for the first are *a spell of warm weather, a cold spell, a hot spell, a rainy spell,* (*He was there*) *for a spell,* etc. Familiar concatenations for the second are *pronounce a spell, cast a spell, under a spell, release from a spell, break the spell* (the last two in the absence of an additional *of hot weather,* for example).

At this point we can argue two ways. We can say, as K-F undoubtedly would say, that *of weather* disambiguates *spell.*

[7] If it is argued that these are 'different entries' because of their etymologies, I would simply get another example. But such an argument would be irrelevant to disambiguation.

Or we can say, as I would say, that there was no ambiguity to begin with: that *spell of weather* is a previously learned unit in the same way that *pretend* is a previously learned unit, and that *of weather* no more disambiguates *spell* than *pre-* disambiguates *tend* by excluding the meaning 'to have a tendency'. The difference of opinion is not one that can be resolved linguistically, but it is one whose philosophical and psychological implications the linguist must face up to. Philosophically, it is the problem of the part and the whole. Psychologically, it is the problem of the point at which integration takes place: do you grasp *A* and *B* in your mind as an integral whole, or do you hold A in your mind and B in your mind and let them operate on each other? If the real linguistic unit is *a spell of warm weather*, learned as a whole (with *spell* abstracted by adult speakers—when you ask them about words—as a kind of homespun lexicographical exercise which is no more functional in the language than folk etymology), then there was never any ambiguity to disambiguate, and *A* and *B*, for the speaker in that particular act of speech (if not for the linguist), was a false division.

The landscape of frozen forms is a jagged one, here and there rising to great heights of morphemes piled on morphemes, in between sinking to levels only one or two morphemes deep. Disambiguation follows a course that skims the top. At no time does it go morpheme by morpheme. A semantic theory adjusted to natural language must somehow reconcile the way in which human beings operate with wholes and at the same time with forms—morphemes—that they have managed to decontextualize from the wholes. Some day, perhaps, with a little more help from psychology, we shall be ready for such a theory.

Meanwhile, how may one characterize the K-F theory? And what may have inspired it?

It is, first, a picture of semantic units whose outlines are sharp. The marker is an absolute. One either is or is not (Male), or (Young), or (Large), or (Evaluative). If we encounter a sfumato effect it is because we have overlooked a marker or two. Allied to this is a sharpness in the lexical units. They are brittle pieces of crystalline structure that may be picked up but not absorbed: 'The dictionary is something that the speaker learns item by item, more or less by rote' (183 footnote). The mental picture to which this gives rise is that of a transaction in which one comes wholly into possession of a piece of property all at once, like buying a parcel of real estate, rather than the gradual EMERGENCE of meaning, for the speaker, through a long process of decontextualization in which a word is only dimly grasped at first, and slowly, as it gains in contexts, cancels its over-extensions one by one. Finally, the lexical units are arbitrary, with no particular relatedness in the system beyond the equally arbitrary sharing of markers, susceptible of being plucked out and replaced with other units without upsetting any internal balances. Fodor, in a recent review, defines the principle of conventionality:[8] 'To say that linguistic symbols are conventional is to say that the integrity of the symbol depends only upon the consensus of speakers; in principle, any vocable could be employed to refer to any

[8] *Lg.* 40.568 (1964).

In principle, probably NO vocable can be replaced by any other without some sort of reverberation in the system. A displacement of just a few rimes would demolish the poetic framework. If the word *too* is replaced, say, by *plethorly*, certain restrictions on the use of *too*, resulting from conflict of homonyms, would disappear (like *excessively*, *plethorly* would remove the asterisk in *Is he nice?—*Yes, too;* also *a *too large group*). If *tiny* is replaced by *perminute*, *teeny* will be left high and dry. If all the one-syllable adjectives are replaced with polysyllables so that the *-er* comparative is lost, certain semantic distinctions that have arisen as a result of the option to use either comparison will be lost along with it. As Householder points out, *Journal of linguistics* 1.18 (1965), there are a number of grammars. The grammar in which it makes no difference whether *tiny* is 'tiny' or *perminute* is only one of them.

object by appropriately altering the linguistic conventions to which speakers adhere.' This is pure Social Contract, an algebraic Rousseauism applied to semantics, and while K-F did not originate it, neither have they modified it. In a framework so rigid there is room neither for the acquisition of meaning as it actually takes place, nor for extensions of meaning as they really happen.

Allied to the sharpness of outline in the lexical unit is its minimalness. K-F subscribe to disarmament down to morphemes. Their messages are printed on movable type, and after each run the forms are broken up and the type is returned to the font. Morphemes are viewed as monads that associate and dissociate by rule, but whose associations leave no trace. Of course K-F know better than this, and would say so; their theory is not intended to account for idioms nor for the blurrings that one finds in any scientific field where it is useful to make one's theoretical START from atomic entities. But if the carry-over of larger units and residual traces have the importance that I believe they have, a lexical monadism will not do. The assumption of the minimal lexical unit is the weakest point in the K-F theory.

As for the inspiration, it is presented as arising from what dictionaries do, but we have seen that dictionaries do more and also do less. There is less of the sort of marker-like definition that lends itself to the K-F formalization. And there are other ways of defining than by a kind of hierarchic referral system. Dictionaries do not exist to define, but to help people grasp meanings, and for this purpose their main task is to supply a series of hints and associations that will relate the unknown to something known. The orderliness and apparent system in a dictionary are more the result of our instinct to be orderly than of any towering need for system based on the subject matter. The dictionary has done its job when it gives the reader a handhold in his own experience—a pair of synonyms, a diagram, a context, a comparison, tied to any convenient reference post, and to be a good practical lexicographer one needs more to be vastly mindful of the possible associations than to be a powerful theorist. *Instanter* is defined in *NID3* wholly by synonyms; *to entangle* is defined by synonyms plus a 'distinguisher' ('to twist or interweave so as to make separation difficult'); *henna* is 'a shrub or small tree', implying that there is a size which neither *shrub* nor *tree* is adequate to describe; one sense of *insignificant* is 'of little size or importance', familiar terms tied to the unfamiliar ones—all these are scarcely more than homely reminders of things we already know. The success of the dictionary is not achieved in disregard of our knowledge of the world, but through it and because of it.

Of course there are dictionaries and dictionaries, and if we do not make the pretension that our picture of the dictionary is a purer version of the lexical manuals that all students are expected to have at their elbows, then we are free to make any kind of dictionary we want, to suit the use to which it is put. Consciously or unconsciously, K-F have a particular operation in mind, and are describing the kind of dictionary that will serve it.

It seems rancorous at this point to hark back to the accusation that the ideal of generativists is to computerize language. On the side of grammar, the argument has been answered: a formal grammar is one that is self-operative, generating by rule, free of outside interference—such a grammar is LIKE a machine, but not born of one.

But there remains a peculiar sense in which what was untrue, or at least overstated, with a generative grammar, is closer to the truth with a formalized semantics. I refer to the pervasive but never quite avowed conviction that the system can be based on a relatively small number of markers.[9] When K-F write (192) that

[9] A bit of wishful thinking that is well founded, as theories go: 'Economy of description' (small inventory of symbols) is one of I. A. Mel'chuk's 'measures of excellence' according to Householder, ibid. 16.

a formal semantic theory must be able to arrive at semantic interpretations 'without the aid of linguistic intuitions or insight', they merely give another name to all those interpretative leverages that they previously excluded as knowledge of the world, which, if included, would make open-ended and unlimited whatever it is in natural language that corresponds to markers. Whereas generative grammar came into being precisely to give a formal footing to grammatical insights, the K-F theory is at pains to exclude certain kinds of semantic insights. If their exclusion makes the theory that much less adequate to explain the behavior of native speakers, then some other motive must lie back of the selection of a few markers out of a vast sea of intuitions. Native speakers need no drastic reduction. A machine, with its relatively low capacity, does. The job of the programmer is to do the best he can with his machine, and a comparatively small number of markers, chosen for their wide application, is the answer. It is not that these have any better theoretical claim to be called markers, but that they happen to carry the heaviest functional load.

If this is true, the theory of K-F is at best a partial theory of the semantics of a natural language, though it may be a very good theory of how to program for mechanical translation.

An Analysis of Meaning[1]

CLYDE E. NOBLE

In response to the Editor's request for a brief reexamination of this topic, here are some remarks on the concepts of "meaning" and "meaningfulness" from the vantage point of 15 years' hindsight.

The theme of my 1952 paper, reprinted in this book, was that a rational quantification of meaningfulness as a psychological attribute ought to be consistent with ordinary linguistic usage of the transitive verb "to mean." Viewing meaning as a logical relation between stimuli (S) and responses (R), I would argue that this relation is: 1) transitive *(if X means Y and Y means Z, then X means Z), 2)* symmetrical *(if X means Y, then Y means X), and 3)* reflexive *(the proposition "X means X" makes empirical sense). Serial relations—those most useful in measurement—are transitive, asymmetrical, and irreflexive. Examples: >, <. "Meaning," in the above sense, is therefore intrinsically nonmeasurable. But this is not necessarily true of "meaning*fulness." *The research objective, as I formulated it around 1948, was to devise an associativity scale characterized by serial relations which would be more objective and reliable than the earlier association-value lists, and which would be linked in a rational manner with the fundamental concepts of contemporary behavior theory. Let me now review the steps in attaining this objective.*

Since my approach to the analysis of verbal learning materials for variations in meaningfulness has been one of emphasizing the connotative rather than the denotative properties of verbal stimuli, it was natural for me to describe items (e.g., nouns, paralogs) which have a large number of con-

[1] This report forms a part of a dissertation submitted to the faculty of the Department of Psychology of the State University of Iowa in partial fulfillment of the requirements for the Ph.D. degree, June 1951. The author is indebted to Prof. Kenneth W. Spence for his advice and criticism. A portion of this paper was read before the Midwestern Psychological Association, April 1951.

The experimental work was conducted during the writer's temporary appointment as research psychologist with the Human Resources Research Center during the summer of 1950. The opinions or conclusions, contained in this report are those of the author. They are not to be construed as reflecting the views or endorsement of the Department of the Air Force.

Clyde E. Noble, "An Analysis of Meaning," *Psychological Review,* 59 (1952), 421–430. Reprinted by permission of the author and publisher.

notations as being "more meaningful" than those which have fewer connotations. Thus, KITCHEN *is more meaningful than* GOJEY, *and* MAN *more so than* XOJ. *The next step was to coordinate (not identify) the psychological concept of association with the logical concept of signification. I took this step when I defined* meaning *as a hypothetical connection between S and R. Meanings were thus construed as being analogous to habit bonds or associative connections. The basic condition for asserting that "S* means *R" is that, in a given subject population, S* sometimes *evokes R. If one considers not only* R_1 *but also* $R_2, R_3, \ldots, R_n$, *then one must deal with the multiple-response-evocation powers of verbal stimuli. Clearly this analysis leads to a frequency criterion of meaningfulness. Based upon this logic, I adopted the symbol* m *as a mnemonic tag for* meaningfulness *and selected as the operational definition of* m *the mean number of continued written associations made by a representative sample of subjects during a standard time interval. This is the "production" method.*

So much for rationale and description. How has m *fared in psychology? Apart from a few misunderstandings of my techniques and intent, the general reaction has been positive. I believe it is fair to say that the* m *scale together with its cousin* m′ *which we developed for consonant-vowel-consonant (CVC) material, has been widely adopted by experimental psychologists. It is also gratifying to observe that the pragmatic value of the associationistic view of meaning is being extended beyond the domain of its first application. Following are some of the probable reasons for its favorable reception. Research in many different laboratories has shown that* m *has a high degree of reliability, measured in terms of product-moment intergroup correlations within and between subject populations. These coefficients have ranged from .96 to .99 and have remained stable over great variations in age and amount of education. From a psychometric point of view the* m *scale has a nonarbitrary origin at zero and an unambiguous unit of measurement, the written associate. Permissible statistical operations upon the scale numerals include those appropriate to ratio scales. In addition to these properties, my colleagues and I have found that* m *is a concept of high validity. It is related by significant correlations to a dozen other psychological variables of empirical and theoretical importance in the field of verbal learning and performance.*

Despite the fact that m *has survived the past decade and a half as a sound, stable, and significant concept, there are still many questions about it that demand answers. To mention just one, the vigorous investigative efforts of a number of talented experimental psychologists have still not solved the puzzle of how and why* m *exerts its facilitative influence on verbal behavior. There are several hypotheses under consideration (e.g., frequency of stimulation, number of associations, statistical dependency, pronounceability), but no one has come up with the final answer yet. The resolution of this research problem looms large as one of the major scientific objectives of the coming years. Somewhere among the laws of learning and transfer, I belive, lies the key which eventually will open this lock.*—CLYDE E. NOBLE

References

Note. For more extended treatments of the role of *m* in human behavior the reader is referred to the following five sources:

GOSS, A. E., and C. F. NODINE, *Paired-Associates Learning*. New York: Academic Press, 1965.

KAUSLER, D. H., Ed., *Readings in Verbal Learning*. New York: The Macmillan Company, 1966.

NOBLE, C. E., "Measurements of Association Value (a), Rated Associations (a'), and Scaled Meaningfulness (m') for the 2100 CVC Combinations of the English Alphabet," *Psychol. Rep.*, **8** (1961), 487–521.

————, "Meaningfulness and Familiarity," in *Verbal Behavior and Learning*, ed. C. N. Cofer and B. S. MUSGRAVE. New York: McGraw-Hill Book Company, 1963. pp. 76–119.

UNDERWOOD, B. J., and R. W. SCHULZ, *Meaningfulness and Verbal Learning*. Philadelphia: J. B. Lippincott Co., 1960.

INTRODUCTION

Intimately related to the production of research data and to the formulation of theory in psychology is the procedure of identifying and quantifying the relevant variables within its various domains. Concerning the field of verbal learning, such writers as Carr (5), Robinson (24), McGeoch (22, 23), Dashiell (8), Melton (19, 20), and Underwood (28) have emphasized the continuing need for this type of analytic research.

The analysis of the attributes of verbal material has, moreover, a more general application. The training of human perceptual and motor skills is often accompanied by verbal instructions intended to facilitate performance on such tasks. One factor which may determine the effectiveness of instructions is the nature of the verbal stimuli which are introduced. For example, particular words may vary in *meaningfulness*. Evidence reviewed in such sources as McGeoch (23), Underwood (28), and Woodworth (31) indicates this to be a potential relevant variable in verbal learning. Historically, however, there has been little agreement on the precise definition of meaning, with the result that few consistent scaling procedures have been developed with which its actual relevance may be evaluated.

The objective of the present study is a theoretical-experimental analysis of the attribute of meaning in verbal stimulus material. Defining operations will be designed in accordance with rational considerations about this concept. In addition, quantitative analysis will provide the scale values necessary to the discovery of accurate functional relationships among this and other better-known psychological variables.

AN ANALYSIS OF MEANING

The many problems of *meaning* have occupied the attention of philosophers and of psychologists for a long time. Some of these problems have been genuine, others spurious. Inasmuch as its necessary and sufficient operations are both logically possible and empirically feasible, it may be shown that at least one of these alleged issues constitutes a genuine problem. Such is the requirement of an analysis of meaning in verbal learning theory.[2]

Within the framework of Hull's (14) behavior theory this is a relatively straightforward task. Consider a stimulus element S_x, a class of conditioned responses R_1, R_2, R_3,. . .R_n, and a class of corresponding habit strengths H_1, H_2, H_3, . . . H_n, forming hypothetical bonds between them. Assume that these Rs have, by virtue of prior training, been connected at various times to S_x, and that, for simplicity, the

[2] For a set of criteria to determine the status of a given problem, *cf.* H. M. Johnson (16). It is of historical interest that Watson's position on the meaning issue in 1925 was that the term was then unnecessary but that, should the need arise, behavioristic definition and explanation could be given (29, p. 201).

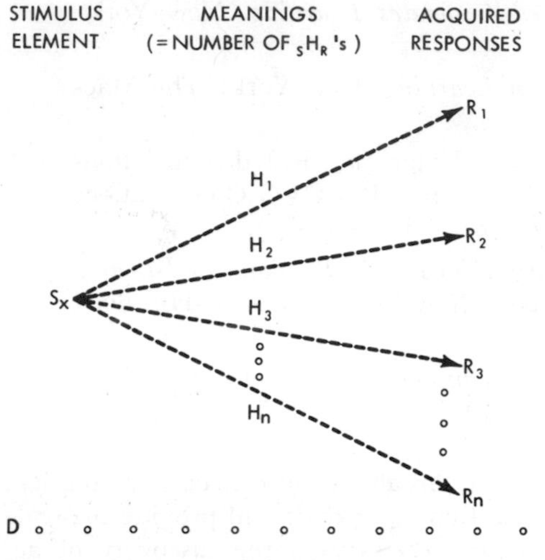

Fig. 1: Schema illustrating the development of stimulus meaning.

*H*s of these connections are severally equal. This hypothetical situation may be represented by the schema in Fig. 1, where the broken-shafted arrows denote learned connections, and where the dotted line following *D* denotes a continuing need or motivational state. It will be seen that this model depicts an ordinary competing response situation, in which each *R* has an equal probability of occurrence (R_p) following the presentation of S_x, and in which, given a wider range of observations, such phenomena as alternation, blocking, and increased reaction latency (R_t) are predictable (*cf.* 15). Should the *H*s be altered considerably in value the principle of competition would still hold, except that to refer to the habit structure under such conditions one would use the term *hierarchy of habits*.

Since, by logical analysis, *meaning* is a relation between terms, let us define the meaningfulness of this *situation* as the number of *H*s subsisting between *S* and the several *R*s taken together. More specifically, the *particular* meanings of S_x are: H_1, H_2, H_3, ... H_n, and different conceptual combinations of these *H*s yield different *numbers* of meanings. In this definition the author presupposes, of course, that the system *S–H–R* is isomorphic with the system *α-means-β*.

Various possible *logical* "meanings" of meaning—e.g., signification, denotation, connotation, equality, equivalence, definitional equivalence, material implication, strict implication—are not at issue here. Throughout the present analysis one must clearly and persistently distinguish between logical and psychological notions about meaning; the former class of notions is conceptual (hypothetical), the latter empirical (categorical). Further, no confusion should result from referring to relations between *S* and *R* as *psychological* (empirical) meanings, since such relations are (a) purely empirical constructs, and (b) presently to be coordinated with an operational index, *m*.

The present analysis does not assert meaning and habit strength to be identical concepts, although they have some common properties. Meanings are postulated to increase in number not as an exponential growth function of the number of *particular S-particular R* reinforcements—as *H* in Hull's theory—but rather as a simple linear function of the number of *particular S-multiple R* connections established. Now in terms of excitatory strength (*E*), where $E \equiv H \cdot D$, a specific "energized" meaning may best be regarded as an unspecified supraliminal value of effective excitatory strength ($\overline{E}$), where $\overline{E} \equiv E - I$. To strengthen $\overline{E}$ beyond the value of the limen (*L*) required for reaction evocation (*R*) may alter R_p, R_a, R_n, or R_t, but the qualitative fact that *S sometimes evokes R* is unaltered. This is the psychological connotation of the assertion: *S means R*.

From an historical point of view it may be interesting to note that the present analysis is formally analogous to certain notions advanced by the British philosophers of the 18th and 19th centuries—especially by Berkeley and by James Mill. Later, from the standpoint of introspectional psychology, Titchener taught that meaning is the conscious context which, under certain conditions, accrues to a "core" of sensory or imaginal content. This is his context "theory" of meaning, which Boring (2, pp. 185, 408) has implemented by suggesting the principle of 'accrual' to be that of association; i.e., learning. In terms of the Titchener-Boring viewpoint, then, *context* (or associated content) $\equiv$ *meaning*. Boring has also attempted to describe Titchener's doctrine in S–R terminology by identifying S with "core" and R with "context" (2, p. 588; 4, p. 18); hence with "meaning." However, since they can be shown to state infeasible demands (*cf.* 16), these and allied considerations—such as whether meaning is "palpable," "unconscious," or only "potential"—are of no scientific concern to modern (behavioristic) psychology.

An interesting approach to a contextual theory of meaning at a more complex level of analysis is provided by the recent paper of Miller and Selfridge (21). Defining meaningfulness in terms of dependent probabilities in successive free-association observations, these investigators have developed lists of varying orders of approximation to the structure of English.

So much for the formal definition of the concept of psychological meaning in terms of habit. Like habit, meaning is here a purely empirical construct. In order to impart significance to this notion—i.e., to relate it systematically to other constructs in behavior theory—it is first necessary to exhibit certain operations by means of which it may be given empirical verification. In other words, one must specify an empirical *index* with which the formal concept of meaning may be placed in correspondence. A few such indices are already available in the field of verbal learning. They are defined by the various operations used for calibrating the "association values" of stimulus items. The work of Cason (6), Glaze (9), Haagen (11), Hull (13), Kreuger (18), and of Witmer (30) represent important contributions to this problem. However, most of these indices are unsatisfactory either because they involved (a) very short response intervals, (b) free association techniques, (c) relative frequency measures, or (d) because their reliabilities were not reported. Since theoretically the number of Rs is proportional to the number of supraliminal $\bar{E}$s, frequency of response is proposed as a rational index of stimulus meaning (m). Therefore, the appropriate association value for the present analysis would be denoted by the central tendency of the frequency distribution of *continued* associations given by Ss per unit time.[3]

Following these considerations an operational index of the attribute of stimulus meaning (m) was sought for each member of a list of 96 dissyllables, as indicated by the following definition:

$$m_s \equiv \frac{1}{N} \sum_{i=1}^{N} R_s, \qquad (1)$$

where $S \equiv$ verbal stimulus; $R \equiv$ unit written response; $N \equiv$ number of subjects.

Procedure

A provisional list of 120 two-syllable nouns was taken from the Thorndike-Lorge tables (26), the principal selection criterion being the G (general) frequency count. These items were drawn with the intention of representing (a) nearly all of the alphabet in the initial letters and (b) an extreme frequency-of-use range. It was hypothesized that frequency of occurrence in the written language would be highly correlated with m and therefore should

[3] *Continued* associations are those which are successively elicited by the same stimulus, as distinguished from *free* or *controlled* associations. The present procedure is analogous to one reported by Cattell and Bryant (7) and called, apparently by Woodworth (31), the *method of continued association*. Krueger (18) later used written responses in determining the association values of nonsense syllables, although the instructions to his Ss would seem to define their responses as *free* associations.

provide a useful approximate ranking of the sample of stimuli to be calibrated.

The words from the Thorndike-Lorge list were supplemented by 18 artificial words which were also dissyllabic and in the form of nouns. They were selected from Dunlap's list (*cf.* 31) or invented by the author. The purpose of including these paralogs was to insure a low-*m* extreme on the final scale, as well as to calibrate such items empirically on a scale continuous with that of actual words.

After a number of arbitrary and systematic rejections, the final list was reduced to 96 items. This list contained approximately 20 per cent paralogs, 35 per cent infrequent items (< 1 per 4 million), and 45 per cent frequent items (> 1 per million). The last two frequency classes are defined by their Thorndike-Lorge relative frequency counts indicated in parentheses. The number 96 was selected because it was associated with a convenient maximum testing time for the prevailing military research schedules at the Human Resources Research Center. The time interval of 60 sec. was chosen because (a) preliminary tests showed that *S*s reported 60 sec. to be an optimal interval, and (b) to insure a reliable time sample of the *S*s' response hierarchy.

The stimulus items were administered in test booklet form with attached answer sheets. A uniform set was maintained by printing only one stimulus per page and by instructing *S* to return to the stimulus each time before responding anew. Furthermore, a given stimulus item was reproduced on each line in an effort to reduce *S*'s inveterate tendency to free-associate. The sequence and order of presentation of the stimuli were varied by shuffling the answer sheets during the assembly of the test booklets. This device served to minimize constant errors due to fatigue, decreasing motivation, and inter-item interaction. After administering a pilot list to 15 *S*s, in order to standardize the procedural variables, the final list of 96 items was given to a sample of 131 basic airmen from two flights undergoing routine classification testing at the Human Resources Research Center. These *S*s were group-tested in four separate units of approximately half-flight size (about 33 men) in order to reduce inter-individual interaction. This source of variance was further reduced by varying the order and sequence of stimuli per *S*, as indicated. Two examiners tested two groups each, and the testing periods were held during the morning hours of two days one week apart. Response periods were of 60 sec. duration per stimulus, with an inter-item interval of 15 sec. Rest periods were given as follows: 5 min. at the end of the first 45 min. of testing, 10 min. at the end of the second 45 min. period, and 5 min. at the end of the next 30 min. period.

Instructions to the *S*s were as follows:

> This is a test to see how many words you can think of and write down in a short time.
>
> You will be given a key word and you are to write down as many *other* words which the key words brings to mind as you can. These other words which you write down may be things, places, ideas, events, or whatever you happen to think of when you see the key word.
>
> For example, think of the word, *KING*. Some of the words or phrases which *KING* might bring to mind are written below:
>
> queen Kingdom
> King Cole England
> ruler imperial
> Sky-King kingfish

*S*s were then given two practice sessions, using as stimuli the words HAM and KOREA. They were permitted to use two-word phrases, slang, long words or short words, provided they were associates of the stimulus words.

Instructions regarding motivation and set were as follows:

> No one is expected to fill in all the spaces on a page, but write as many words as you can which each key word calls to mind. Be sure to think back to the *key* word after each word you write down because the test is to see how many other words the key word makes you think of. A good way to do this is to repeat each key word over and over to yourself as you write.

Table 1

List of Dissyllable Words (Nouns) in Rank Order of Increasing Meaningfulness (m) as Defined by Mean Frequency of Continued Associations in 60 Sec. ($N = 119$)

Rank	*Word Number*	*m-Value*	σ	*Word*	*Rank*	*Word Number*	*m-Value*	σ	*Word*
1	24	0.99	2.05	GOJEY	49	58	2.69	3.43	OVUM
2	53	1.04	1.60	NEGLAN	50	72	2.73	3.24	ROSTRUM
3	49	1.05	1.85	MEARDON	51	84	2.76	2.92	VERTEX
4	8	1.13	1.89	BYSSUS	52	5	2.80	3.27	BODICE
5	4	1.22	1.95	BALAP	53	76	2.89	3.20	TANKARD
6	86	1.22	2.17	VOLVAP	54	60	3.06	3.04	PALLOR
7	77	1.24	2.03	TAROP	55	74	3.21	2.85	SEQUENCE
8	90	1.24	2.20	XYLEM	56	1	3.34	3.34	ARGON
9	41	1.26	2.16	LATUK	57	68	3.36	3.22	RAMPART
10	66	1.26	2.01	QUIPSON	58	35	3.51	3.50	JITNEY
11	25	1.27	2.20	GOKEM	59	17	3.55	3.19	ENTRANT
12	52	1.28	1.96	NARES	60	59	3.62	3.26	PALLET
13	96	1.28	2.19	ZUMAP	61	51	3.64	3.48	NAPHTHA
14	63	1.30	1.98	POLEF	62	62	3.77	3.45	PIGMENT
15	73	1.33	2.06	SAGROLE	63	57	3.91	3.42	ORDEAL
16	55	1.34	2.37	NOSTAW	64	94	4.44	3.19	ZENITH
17	6	1.39	2.12	BODKIN	65	91	4.60	3.82	YEOMAN
18	81	1.50	2.78	ULNA	66	67	4.68	3.13	QUOTA
19	88	1.53	2.05	WELKIN	67	64	5.10	3.45	QUARRY
20	29	1.54	2.84	ICON	68	15	5.13	3.19	EFFORT
21	40	1.55	2.45	KUPOD	69	83	5.32	3.24	UNIT
22	13	1.60	2.46	DELPIN	70	18	5.33	3.46	FATIGUE
23	3	1.71	2.55	ATTAR	71	37	5.47	3.11	KEEPER
24	48	1.73	2.69	MATRIX	72	38	5.52	3.70	KENNEL
25	12	1.74	2.69	DAVIT	73	47	5.61	3.32	MALLET
26	89	1.78	2.77	WIDGEON	74	42	5.94	3.17	LEADER
27	7	1.79	2.65	BRUGEN	75	65	5.98	3.16	QUARTER
28	36	1.82	2.95	KAYSEN	76	69	5.98	3.70	REGION
29	46	1.84	2.85	MAELSTROM	77	28	6.02	3.33	HUNGER
30	79	1.84	2.95	TUMBRIL	78	95	6.15	3.05	ZERO
31	70	1.86	2.85	RENNET	79	30	6.24	3.50	INCOME
32	71	1.90	2.35	ROMPIN	80	82	6.57	3.79	UNCLE
33	22	1.95	2.55	GAMIN	81	92	6.75	4.12	YOUNGSTER
34	19	2.09	3.11	FEMUR	82	80	6.83	3.29	TYPHOON
35	45	2.09	3.42	LOZENGE	83	10	6.88	3.11	CAPTAIN
36	20	2.13	2.77	FERRULE	84	93	7.12	3.75	ZEBRA
37	75	2.14	2.75	STOMA	85	23	7.17	4.48	GARMENT
38	26	2.15	3.09	GRAPNEL	86	85	7.28	4.05	VILLAGE
39	21	2.19	3.25	FLOTSAM	87	31	7.39	3.09	INSECT
40	11	2.26	3.35	CAROM	88	34	7.58	3.69	JEWEL
41	54	2.26	2.65	NIMBUS	89	32	7.70	3.53	JELLY
42	43	2.28	3.06	LEMUR	90	27	7.91	3.86	HEAVEN
43	9	2.41	3.13	CAPSTAN	91	56	7.95	3.66	OFFICE
44	61	2.43	2.88	PERCEPT	92	87	8.12	3.67	WAGON
45	44	2.48	2.96	LICHENS	93	14	8.33	4.21	DINNER
46	33	2.54	3.53	JETSAM	94	50	8.98	4.27	MONEY
47	16	2.59	3.08	ENDIVE	95	2	9.43	4.30	ARMY
48	78	2.63	3.04	TARTAN	96	39	9.61	4.30	KITCHEN

E also gave supplementary motivating instructions during the three rest periods.

The method of recording S's responses was sufficiently objective to require very little evaluation on E's part. However, in terms of the analysis of meaning proposed, it was decided to set up three objective criteria for unacceptable responses. These were:

1. *Illegible responses*: $S_x \rightarrow ?$
2. *Perseverative responses*:

$$S_x \rightarrow R_1\,(s_1) \rightarrow R_1\,(s_1) \cdots$$

3. *Failures of set:* $S_x \nearrow R_1$; $S_x \searrow R_2(s_2) \rightarrow R_{2_2}$, with $R_2(s_2) \nearrow R_{2_1}$ and $R_2(s_2) \searrow R_{2_3}$

This last class of unacceptable responses was further classified into:

(a) *Free or tangential associations*: e.g., LEMUR → Dorothy, Hope, faith, charity. . . .

(b) *Clang or alliterative associations*: e.g., KAYSEN → caisson, Casey, casein, casement. . . .

Finally, a general rule of giving S the benefit of the doubt was adopted. This was occasionally necessary in the case of category 3 above, although free and clang associations were usually easily identified by the three scorers. Of the original 131 Ss tested, 12 protocols were rejected for persistent violations of the criteria cited. This brought the effective sample to 119 Ss.

Results

The index of meaning (m) of a particular stimulus was defined in equation [1] as the grand mean number of (acceptable) written responses given by all Ss within a 60 sec. period. Therefore, the scale values of the stimuli were determined directly by the average response frequencies of the 119 Ss. These m-values with the σ's of their distributions are shown in Table I, ranging in rank order from dissyllables of low response-evocation value (e.g., No. 1: GOJEY) to those of high response-evocation value (e.g., No. 96: KITCHEN). The empirical range is from 0.99 to 9.61. It will be noted that there is no discrete gap between the paralog items and the actual words. In fact, there are a few actual words low on the scale (e.g., No. 4: BYSSUS), while one paralog (No. 32: ROMPIN) appears at the thirdway point. It is also to be noted that response variability tends to increase with increasing m-value.

It was found that the m-values of particular items were quite stable from group to group. Intercorrelations of the four sets of mean m-values per word were carried out among all six combinations of

Table 2

INTERGROUP RELIABILITY COEFFICIENTS (r) FOR m-SCALE BASED ON MEAN m-VALUES FOR FOUR GROUPS OF SS

Group	*I*	*II*	*III*	*IV*	*n*
I	—	—	—	—	27
II	.98	—	—	—	30
III	.98	.98	—	—	30
IV	.96	.97	.98	—	32

N = 119.

groups. These Pearsonian r-values appear in Table II. All are significantly different from zero ($P < 0.01$). Since the sampling distribution of r is skewed for large values, Fisher's Z-transformation was used to estimate the mean intergroup reliability coefficient of the *m-scale*: $\bar{r}_{mm} = 0.975$. It may be pointed out that a between-groups reliability coefficient[4] is the appropriate statistic to compute in this case since it was E's aim to determine the consistency of *different response samples* to the *same stimuli*. A more conventional reliability coefficient—such as one defined by the test-retest, split-half, or the alternate form procedure—would not have evaluated this particular relationship.

[4] Rather than a "reliability" coefficient, some might prefer to call this statistic a coefficient of "objectivity," "agreement," or of "consistency."

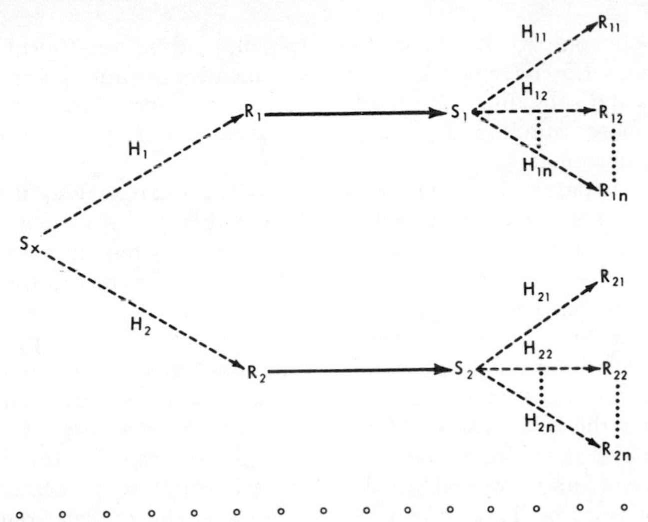

Fig. 2: Schema illustrating the development of more complex degrees of meaning.

Of some interest in this investigation was the extent to which the assumptions of the product-moment correlational method were met. The family of response frequency distributions associated with the stimulus items exhibited skewness at the low-*m* extreme of the scale, but throughout the central and upper portions they were approximately symmetrical. Hence, means were retained as measures of central tendency. When the six intercorrelations of the *m*-scale were plotted, it was found that the requirements of linearity of regression and of homoscedasticity were reasonably satisfied.

DISCUSSION

Meaning. After reviewing the analysis of meaning, one properly may ask whether responses may acquire meanings also, or whether only stimuli do so. As has been indicated, meanings are considered relations between *S*s and *R*s.[5] It is for convenience that, instead of referring to *m*, one speaks of "the meaning of a stimulus" or of "stimulus meaning," just as one speaks of "reinforcing a conditioned response," when more precisely it is the *S–R* connection, or *H*, which strictly is reinforced. To speak of *stimulus* meaning is to imply an asymmetry in the empirical meaning relation. Indeed, common linguistic usage seems to concur that meaning, like causation, be regarded as a property of stimuli rather than of responses.[6]

Under certain conditions, however, it is appropriate to refer loosely to the meaning of a *response*. One such condition would arise if analysis should indicate that a certain class of responses results in proprioceptive stimulation (*s*) to an organism. This is the well-known response-produced stimulus situation, or feedback mechanism. Kinesthesis is perhaps the best example. The descriptive schema outlined in the section on meaning applies equally well, as shown in Fig. 2. Here the situa-

[5] Not all writers would agree to construe meaning thus (*cf.* 2, 3, 4, 17, 27). Some of the divergences of opinion are reflected in the following successive quotations from Boring's 1933 text (3): "The correlation between stimulus and ultimate response *is* a meaning..." (p. 153); "...the data of consciousness are meanings" (p. 222); "...a meaning is a relation" (p. 222); "Meaning is response" (p. 223).

[6] This is not to be interpreted as bearing any relation to the Gestalt doctrine of meaning as immediately given in the external world (*cf.* 17, but simply as a clarification of a familiar idiom.

tion becomes more complex, but no different qualitatively. *H*s develop between initial $R(\rightarrow s)$s and subsequent *R*s, thereby permitting more complex degrees of development of meaning.

The serial anticipation learning situation, for example, fits this schema well in that each successive response functions as a stimulus to the next response in the series, while the verbal stimuli appearing serially in the memory drum aperture serve as secondary reinforcing agents. This type of analysis also suggests an explanatory approach for the relationships Miller and Selfridge (21) have found between reproductive recall and contextual dependencies. The work of Thorndike (25) on "belonging" may be similarly regarded.

The result of this analysis of meaning and its incorporation into learning theory is twofold: (a) it establishes a highly reliable, unequivocal new attribute of variation in learning, and (b) it provides an operational basis for explicating the common-sense notion of "meaning." Thus, if one were to ask a layman what he intended by saying that "home" to him *means*: "family, spouse, children, friends, love," etc., he would doubtless reply, "I think of these things when 'home' is mentioned." It is a simple matter to fit this statement to the model proposed in Fig. 1. A learning theorist would explain that to the auditory (or visual) *S home*, these various verbal *R*s have become conditioned during our imaginary layman's previous experience, and that under appropriate conditions (e.g., adequate *D* level, sufficient reinforcements to each *L*) these *R*s are elicited. The meaning of *S* subsists in the *H*s developed to it—nothing more.[7] A neutral *S*, by the present definitions, is meaning*less*; an *S* conditioned to twenty *R*s is more meaning*ful* (i.e., has more meanings) than is one conditioned to ten, and so on. Speaking quite nontechnically, meanings are habits. And as more habits accrue to a particular stimulus situation, so does its meaningfulness increase.

In the final analysis the index *m*, like *H*, emerges as a statistical concept. It is a function of the number of particular *S*-multiple *R* connections which are formed, and it enjoys an existence independent of the cited operations no more than does any other empirical construct.

In view of its theoretical status and exceptional reliability, the *m*-scale is regarded with especial interest for research in verbal and in perceptual-motor learning. Using the *m*-scale, research may now be directed toward the solution of such current problems as the relationship between difficulty and meaningfulness, the effect of meaningfulness upon reminiscence, and the rôle of verbal instructions in the acquisition of motor skills.

SUMMARY AND CONCLUSIONS

This paper has presented a theoretical-experimental analysis of the attribute of meaning in verbal stimulus material. A word list of 96 dissyllables consisting of nouns and paralogs was presented to a sample of 119 USAF recruits in order to establish a quantitative scale for this attribute. The results of this analysis were as follows:

1. Meaning was formally defined as a relation between *S* and *R*. It was coordinated with Hull's theoretical construct *H* by postulating that meanings increase as a simple linear function of the number of *S*-multiple *R* connections acquired in a particular organism's history.

2. An index of stimulus meaning (*m*) was operationally defined in terms of the

[7] In view of the fact that the class of responses defining the *m*-scale represents a set of individual-difference variables, one should properly denote the meaning relation in this case by the symbol *U* rather than by *H*. From a genetic standpoint, certain learning theorists preserve a distinction between innate or previously-acquired connections (sUr's) and laboratory-established connections (sHr's). However, in Hull's theory both *U* and *H* are considered habit or associational concepts, hence the proposed coordination with meaning is unimpaired. A similar argument holds for conditioned generalized connections ($s\bar{H}r$'s).

mean frequency of continued written associations made by subjects within a 60-sec. time interval.

3. A psychological performance scale of m-values was developed which exhibited a range extending from 0.99 to 9.61. The mean product-moment intergroup reliability coefficient was $\bar{r}_{mm} = 0.975$.

4. The significance of these findings for human learning theory was discussed.

References

1. BERGMAN, G., & SPENCE, K. W. The logic of psychophysical measurement. PSYCHOL. REV., 1944, 51, 1–24.
2. BORING, E. G. *A history of experimental psychology.* New York: D. Appleton-Century Co., 1929.
3. —. *The physical dimensions of consciousness.* New York: D. Appleton-Century, 1933.
4. —. *Sensation and perception in the history of experimental psychology.* New York: D. Appleton-Century, 1942.
5. CARR, H. A. *Psychology: A study of mental activity.* New York: Longmans, Green, 1925.
6. CASON, H. Specific serial learning: a study of backward association. *J. exp. Psychol.,* 1926, 9, 195–227.
7. CATTELL, J. MCK., & BRYANT, S. Mental association investigated by experiment. *Mind,* 1889, 14, 230–250.
8. DASHIELL, J. F. A neglected fourth dimension to psychological research. PSYCHOL. REV., 1940, 47, 289–305.
9. GLAZE, J. A. The association value of non-sense syllables. *J. genet. Psychol.,* 1928, 35, 255–269.
10. GUILFORD, J. P. *Psychometric methods.* New York: McGraw-Hill, 1936.
11. HAAGEN, C. H. Synonymity, vividness, familiarity, and association value ratings of 400 pairs of common adjectives. *J. Psychol.,* 1949, 27, 453–463.
12. HEBB, D. O. *The organization of behavior.* New York: John Wiley & Sons, Inc., 1949.
13. HULL, C. L. The meaningfulness of 320 selected nonsense syllables. *Amer. J. Psychol.,* 1933, 45, 730–734.
14. —. *Principles of behavior.* New York: Appleton-Century, 1943.
15. —. *Elementary theory of individual behavior.* (In preparation.)
16. JOHNSON, H. M. Are psychophysical problems genuine or spurious? *Amer. J. Psychol.,* 1945, 58, 189–211.
17. KÖHLER, W. *The place of value in a world of facts.* New York: Liveright, 1938.
18. KRUEGER, W. C. F. The relative difficulty of nonsense syllables. *J. exp. Psychol.,* 1934, 17, 145–153.
19. MELTON, A. W. The methodology of experimental studies of human learning and retention: I. The functions of a methodology and the available criteria for evaluating different experimental methods. *Psychol. Bull.,* 1936, 33, 305–394.
20. —. Learning. In W. S. Monroe (Ed.), *Encyclopedia of educational research.* New York: Macmillan, 1950, 668–690.
21. MILLER, G. A., & SELFRIDGE, J. A. Verbal context and the recall of meaningful material. *Amer. J. Psychol.,* 1950, 63, 176–185.
22. MCGEOCH, J. A. The vertical dimensions of mind. PSYCHOL. REV., 1936, 43, 107–129.
23. —. *The psychology of human learning.* New York: Longmans, Green, & Co., 1942.

24. ROBINSON, E. S. *Association theory today: An essay in systematic psychology.* New York: Century, 1932.

25. THORNDIKE, E. L. *Human learning.* New York: Century, 1931.

26. —, & LORGE, I. *The teacher's word book of 30,000 words.* New York: Columbia Univ. Press, 1944.

27. TOLMAN, E. C. *Purposive behavior in animals and men.* New York: Century Co., 1932.

28. UNDERWOOD, B. J. *Experimental psychology.* New York: Appleton-Century-Crofts, Inc., 1949.

29. WATSON, J. B. *Behaviorism.* New York: Norton & Co., 1925, 2nd Ed.

30. WITMER, L. R. The association value of three-place consonant syllables. *J. genet. Psychol.*, 1935, 47, 337–359.

31. WOODWORTH, R. S. *Experimental psychology.* New York: Holt, 1938.

Meaning and *m*: Correlated but Separate[1]

ARTHUR W. STAATS
and CAROLYN K. STAATS

The history of psychology is a history of separatism, of clashes of men and theories. Actually, many of the various schools of psychology began as "rebellions," and the field of learning has continued in this tradition. Even as it has been arrayed against other orientations, major efforts within learning have been expended in developing and maintaining separate experimental methods, separate general (philosophical) methodologies, and separate terminologies—even when the empirical referents involved the same principles.

More particularly, there has been such separatism in learning approaches to the study of language. For example, there have been people interested in the instrumental (operant) conditioning of verbal behavior, who many times eschew the experimental results and conceptions of investigators of word meaning and semantic mediation. And, many times these latter investigators reject the importance of operant conditioning in the area of language. A third approach has focused upon verbal learning, including serial and paired associate verbal learning. And this approach has ignored the findings of the former two areas—an action that has largely been reciprocated. To continue with the analysis, another group has been concerned with the mediational properties of word associates. Thus, even though these various approaches spring from the same tradition, they have been theoretical competitors rather than complementing a general learning approach.

This state of affairs is a great disadvantage. The separate growth of the

[1] This article is one of a series of studies, formulated by the first author as the principal investigator of a research project supported under Naval Research Contract No. Nonr-2305 (00), whose general aim is to experimentally test his instrumental and classical conditioning theory of language development and language function.

Arthur W. Staats and Carolyn K. Staats, "Meaning and *m*: Correlated but Separate," *Psychological Review,* **66,** No. 2 (1959), 136–144. Reprinted by permission of the authors and publisher.

experimental results and more importantly the terminologies of the various approaches have retarded the development of a believable conception of language behavior in learning terms. Simplistic learning approaches to language, while productive in their own research realms, have been vulnerable to criticism on general issues by linguists and psycholinguists—that is, it has been relatively easy to pick an example of behavior that the isolated approach could not handle. Obviously, complex language (cognitive) behaviors cannot be accounted for solely on the basis of word associations, word meaning, or operant conditioning principles. Thus, the traditional learning approaches by themselves have been inadequate for dealing with a wide range of human behaviors, and their isolated methods and analyses have not promoted the most rapid progress.

The present author has felt that a learning theory is capable of handling the criticisms of linguists and other cognitive theorists as well as capable of yielding a comprehensive theory of the manner in which language develops and functions. To establish such a theory, however, it is necessary to make an integration of the basic principles of classical and instrumental conditioning and to extend the integration to a detailed consideration of language, utilizing the various relevant learning concepts and experimental findings which are available. Thus, in addition to making extensive use of both the principles of classical and instrumental conditioning, an adequate learning theory must be capable of dealing with verbal learning of the paired associate and serial learning variety, concepts of word meaning and semantic mediation, verbal mediation, the instrumental conditioning of vocalizations, grammatical speech, the reinforcement value of words, and the like, in a manner so that a comprehensive analysis of actual language is made.

Language behavior is not a simple type of repertoire, to be accounted for in terms of a single stimulus-response mechanism, or indeed a few stimulus-response mechanisms. In learning terms, language serves many complex stimulus functions and also involves complex repertoires of responses. A comprehensive learning theory must be concerned with how language is acquired, but also with how the S-R mechanisms, once acquired, function in the individual's adjustment, including his social interactions. Learned language mechanisms are involved in problem solving, thinking, grammatical utterances, mathematical repertoires, intelligence, originality, and so on.

The present author has attempted to provide such an integrated learning theory of language (see Staats, 1957, 1961, 1963, 1964a, 1964b, 1966; Staats and Staats, 1963). The paper to be presented here is one of these attempts to integrate the principles of instrumental and classical conditioning within the context of language. It seemed that here was a case where learning people were interpreting language phenomena in terms of either word associations or word meaning. The author's integrated learning analysis in terms of specific S-R mechanisms suggested that both processes (and both learning principles) were involved. When two word stimuli occur together, each of which controls a word response, the responses should become associated according to the principles of instrumental conditioning. Moreover, if one of the words, for example, elicits a meaning response because of past conditioning, the meaning response should be classically conditioned to the other word.

Although this particular analysis is in a restricted area of study, present-

ing only one facet of a more comprehensive theory, it does indicate the value of an integrated learning approach and detailed S-R analyses, in resolving what erroneously appear to be points of issue in learning approaches to language.—ARTHUR W. STAATS

References

STAATS, A. W. "Learning Theory and 'Opposite Speech,'" *Journal of Abnormal Social Psychology,* **55,** (1957), 268–269.

———, "Verbal Habit-Families, Concepts, and the Operant Conditioning of Word Classes," *Psychological Review,* **68,** (1961), 190–204.

———, "Operant Learning Principles and Communication," in *Human Learning,* ed. A. W. Staats. New York: Holt, Rinehart & Winston. Inc., 1964a.

———, "Conditioned Stimuli, Conditioned Reinforcers, and Word Meaning," in *Human Learning,* ed. A. W. Staats. New York: Holt, Rinehart & Winston, Inc., 1964b.

———, "Verbal Mechanisms in Purpose and Set," in *Human Learning,* ed. A. W. Staats. New York: Holt, Rinehart & Winston, Inc., 1964c.

———, "An Integrated-Functional Learning Approach to Complex Human Behavior," in *Problem Solving: Method, Theory, and Research,* ed. B. Kleinmuntz. New York: John Wiley & Sons, Inc., 1966.

———, and C. K. Staats, *Complex Human Behavior.* New York: Holt, Rinehart & Winston, Inc., 1963.

Noble (1952) has presented a Hullian analysis of meaning and meaningfulness in which meaning is identified as *H,* the relationship between the stimulus word and the response word. Meaningfulness is determined by the number of different *H*s, i.e., a stimulus word is meaningful to the extent that it elicits many response words. In this study, Noble arrived at an index of meaning by measuring the number of word associations made to a given stimulus word in a given period of time. Noble concluded:

Thus, if one were to ask a layman what he intended by saying that "home" to him *means:* "family, spouse, children, friends, love," etc., he would doubtless reply, "I think of these things when 'home' is mentioned."...A learning theorist would explain that to the auditory (or visual) *S home,* these various verbal *R*s have become conditioned ...and under appropriate conditions...are elicited. The meaning of *S* subsists in the *H*s developed to it—noting more (Noble, 1952, p.429).

Bousfield, Cohen, and Whitmarsh (1958) have recently presented a view of meaning which is consonant with Noble's view. They state that perception of a meaningful word involves the elicitation of two types of implicit response. First, the person says the word subvocally. This is called a verbal representational response, R_{vr}. In addition, however, the subject reacts by making another group of implicit verbal associative responses. For example, to the word BLACK, the subject might respond WHITE, DARK, CAT, etc.

These responses may be said to comprise the associative response composite, R_{va} *comp.* Under appropriate conditions the subject may produce the R_{vr} and the R_{va} *comp* explicitly by saying or writing them. Though a definition of meaning is perhaps gratuitous in this discussion, we belive it is useful to identify meaning with the $R_{v\,a}$ *comp*. This definition appears to be consistent with the Hullian interpretation presented by Noble (Bousfield, Cohen, & Whitmarsh, 1958, p. 1).

This approach contrasts with another concept of word meaning which has been developed by other psychologists, e.g., Cofer and Foley (1942), Mowrer (1954), and Osgood (1953). This interpretation, also based on Hullian concepts, states that when a word is contiguously presented with a stimulus object, part of the response elicited by the object may be stably conditioned to the word. This conditioned response becomes the meaning of the word. Osgood has indicated in detail that certain components of the total response elicited by a stimulus object are more readily conditionable (less interfering, less effortful, etc.) and hence are more likely to contribute to the final form of the representational mediation process (i.e., meaning response).

The conditioning of a meaning response can also take place through higher-order conditioning, in which case the US, the stimulus object, is replaced by a word which through prior conditioning already elicits a meaning response. Both of these processes are schematized in Fig. 1. In the upper part of the figure the word BAD is paired with a punishing stimulus. The punishment elicits a number of responses which may be called "unpleasant," or of "negative value." After BAD has been paired with punishment a number of times, the conditionable responses (called "detachable" by Osgood) elicited by the punishment are conditioned to BAD. These responses come to constitute the stable meaning of BAD.

Assuming that the conditioning has been sufficiently strong, contiguous presentation of BAD and another word which has no meaning would result in higher-order conditioning. That is, the meaning response elicited by BAD would be conditioned to some extent to the new CS-word. In an actual life situation, a child might

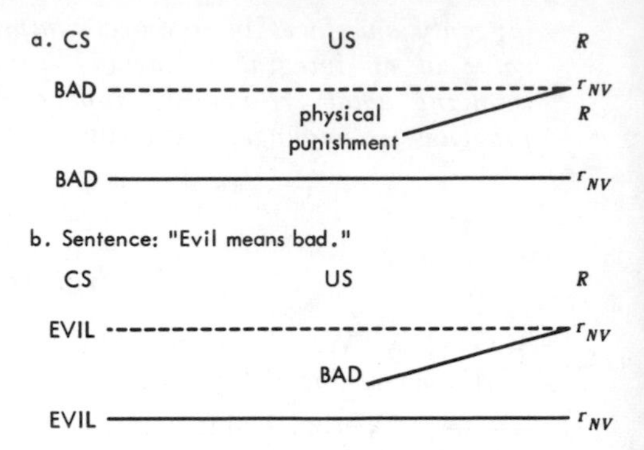

Fig. 1: Diagram *a* depicts first-order conditioning of word meaning. After a number of pairings of BAD, the CS, with punishment, the US, BAD comes to elicit the conditionable (i.e., "detachable") components of the responses elicited by the punishment (symbolized as r_{NV} because of the negative value). The components of the total response which are not stably conditioned are symbolized as *R*. Diagram *b* depicts second-order conditioning of meaning. The negative value meaning responses now elicited by BAD are conditioned to EVIL through contiguous presentation of the two words in the sentence. Although not schematized, it is understood that r_{NV}, as a mediating response, may through the stimuli it produces elicit other overt or implicit responses.

be told "Evil means bad." The negative meaning elicited by BAD would be conditioned to EVIL. This is depicted in Part *b* of Fig. 1.

Recently Osgood, Suci, and Tannenbaum (1957) have taken issue with Noble's approach to meaning. They would accept *m* as a measure of the association value of a stimulus word, but vehemently reject the interpretation that the associations may be thought of as word meaning. They state that a basic distinction exists between the meaning of a sign and its associations. They continue as follows:

This point needs to be labored because one recent writer (Noble, 1952), at least, has seriously proposed that the meaning of a sign is nothing more than the number of different associations between it as a stimulus and other signs as responses. According to Noble, "The index of meaning (*m*) of a particular stimulus was defined. . .as the grand mean number of (acceptable) written responses given by all *S*s within a 60 sec. period.". . .it is his basic notion—that meaning and association can be equated—which is wrong. Does BLACK mean *white* because this is the most common associate? Does NEEDLE mean *sew,* BREAD mean *butter, MAN* mean *woman?* Noble's *m* might be identified as meaningfulness rather than meaning, or better, simply the association value of the stimulus, since this is actually what he is measuring (Osgood, Suci, & Tannenbaum, 1957, pp. 16–17).

Thus, a rather sharp clash of interpretations is enjoined.

RELATIONSHIP BETWEEN THE TWO MEASURES OF MEANING

Osgood et al. insist that meaning of a word is not the same as the word's verbal associates, i.e., the meaning of a word involves a psychological process which is separate from word association processes. However, two recently reported experimental results have shown a relationship between *m* and semantic measures. In the first study, reported by Jenkins and Russell (1956), intensity of meaning, as measured by Osgood's semantic differential, was correlated with Noble's *m*. Intensity of meaning was measured by the extent to which the rating of a word deviated from neutral (4) on a seven-point semantic differential scale.

It was hypothesized here that meaningful words would elicit many extreme ratings on the semantic differential and meaningless words would tend to elicit few such ratings. Accordingly the semantic differential profiles for Noble's concepts were analyzed in terms of their deviations from the neutral scale positions (that is to say, *Ds* were calculated for each profile against a hypothetical profile running through the middle of each scale). The hypothesis was in general well substantiated. The correlation between the size of *D* and Noble's "m" was + .71. This represents the first connecting link between what seemed at the outset to be two entirely different ways of talking about psychological meaning (Jenkins & Russell, 1956, p. 7).

In addition, Noble (1958) has recently presented evidence which supports this result. In his experiment, *m* was correlated with what may be called a measure of intensity of evaluative meaning found by Osgood and Suci (1955). Instead of using a semantic differential scale, Noble had the *S*s rate each word neutral, pleasant, unpleasant, or mixed. A semantic differential scale of pleasant-unpleasant would allow 7 gradations of evaluative meaning, and has no "mixed" category. Nevertheless, Noble's procedure seems to measure evaluative meaning, and the results should be roughly comparable to scoring words on a pleasant-unpleasant semantic differential scale.

Noble found in his study that this type of evaluative rating (which he calls a measure of emotionality) was correlated with *m* .57 ($p = .001$ level of significance). Thus, in this study and the study of Jenkins and Russell, larger *m* measures were associated with more intense meaning.

The question arises, especially in view of the rejection by Osgood et al. of the relevance of Noble's approach to a conception of meaning, of how to account for the relationship of Noble's measure of meaning and Osgood's semantic measures. As Jenkins and Russell imply, the two studies indicate a relationship which demands explanation—if meaning and word associations are to be separately considered. The present paper, in distinguishing meaning and *m,* must explain the relationship between the two. This explanation will also indicate why a word's meaning may be confused with the word's direct verbal associations.

BASIS OF THE RELATIONSHIP BETWEEN *m* AND MEANING

In the conditioning of word meaning it seems likely that both primary and higher-order conditioning are important, i.e., a word gets its meaning through both of the processes represented in Fig. 1. To some extent word meaning is obtained, and maintained, by contiguous presentation with certain primary stimulus objects. In addition, it is suggested that word meaning is conditioned through contiguous presentations with other words. It is this latter occurrence which accounts for the correlation between intensity of meaning and *m* and which, it is thought, results in confusing the two independent psychological processes. A stimulus word gets its meaning, in part, because each time it is paired with another word the meaning of the response word is conditioned to the stimulus word. This also strengthens the associations between stimulus word and response words. For example, if a nonsense syllable was paired with the word "bad" a number of times, direct associations between the syllable and "bad" would be formed. In addition, the meaning response elicited by "bad" would be conditioned to the syllable. Because of this parallelism in development it is easy to consider direct associations, which underlie *m,* and meaning as the same thing. Thus, although *m* and meaning are not the same, the more often a word is paired with its common associates, the stronger become the direct word-word associates and the word-meaning associates, i.e., the same operation strengthens both types of associations.

The stronger the direct associations, the less the latency of response when the stimulus word is presented. Thus, in a given period of time, stronger associations will result in the occurrence of more response words, i.e., the *m* measure will be high when word associates are elicited. In addition, strong word-meaning associations will result in semantic differential ratings which are extreme.

However, if a stimulus word obtains its meaning in part from its word associates, the meaning of a stimulus word must be directly related to the meaning of its response words. Thus, a positive correlation between the meaning of stimulus words and the meaning of their word associates would support the preceding interpretation. To verify the point, the following demonstration was conducted.

SIMILARITY OF THE MEANING OF STIMULUS-WORDS AND THE MEANING OF THEIR WORD-ASSOCIATES

Forty-six students in introductory sociology participated in the experiment.

In the experiment words were required on which semantic differential information was available, as well as information concerning the associates of the words. Jenkins, Russell, and Suci (1957) have provided data on the semantic profiles of 360 words, using different semantic differential scales for the semantic measures. Russell and Jenkins (1954) have also provided word association data on 100 words. Some words appear in both of these studies. For the present study 10 words were chosen on which both data were available from these sources. The criteria for choosing the ten words were: (*a*) that the words be distributed along the "good-bad" evaluative scale, including words which had extreme positive evaluative meaning (mean rating toward 1) and words which had extreme negative evaluative meaning (mean rating toward 7), as well as words which were in between the extremes; (*b*) that word association data be available for the ten words selected. The words chosen are as follows: MUSIC, SWEET, TABLE, MOUNTAIN, DEEP, HARD, ROUGH, ANGER, TROUBLE, SICKNESS.

A folder was prepared which included these ten words and 40 additional words of unsystematic meaning, all arranged in random order. Under each word was a semantic differential scale of good-bad. An example is given below.

MUSIC

good :—:—:—:—:—:—:—: bad

The *Ss* were instructed in rating the meaning of the words.

Three weeks later the same *Ss* rated the meaning of the first twenty word associates of each of the above ten words. The twenty word associates were obtained from Russell and Jenkins (1954). In cases where a word was the associate of more than one of the "evaluative" words it was only listed once. Thus, a folder was used which included the 172 resulting words arranged in random order. The format of this folder was the same as with the first rating task; each word was listed with a "good-bad" scale beneath it. The same instructions were used in administration.

Table 1

MEAN RATINGS OF STIMULUS WORDS AND TWENTY ASSOCIATED WORDS

Word	*Minnesota*	*Arizona State*	*20 Associates (AS)*
Music	1.60	1.56	2.47
Sweet	1.93	1.98	2.74
Table	2.37	2.85	2.75
Mountain	2.73	2.32	2.96
Deep	3.77	3.85	3.20
Hard	4.13	3.91	3.24
Rough	5.00	4.79	3.11
Anger	5.57	5.88	4.50
Trouble	6.10	6.39	4.28
Sickness	6.30	6.56	3.99

Note—On the scales, 1 was "good" and 7 "bad."

In the analysis of the results the mean meaning scores for the original ten words were computed. In addition, the mean meaning score for the 20 associates of each of the ten words was computed. These means are listed in Table 1. The table also includes the mean meaning scores (on good-bad) on the same ten words obtained by Jenkins, Russell, and Suci using University of Minnesota students.

A rank order correlation coefficient was computed between the mean meaning score obtained in this study and the mean meaning scores obtained by Jenkins, Russell, and Suci. The correlation was .99.

The extent of the relationship between the meaning of the stimulus words and the meaning of their word associates was also measured by rank order correlation of their respective mean evaluative meaning scores. The rank order correlation coefficient was .90, which is significant at better than the .01 level. The results support the hypothesis that the meaning of the associates of a stimulus word tends to be the same as the meaning of the word. This gives credence to the hypothesis that m and intensity of meaning are correlated because associating two words conditions the meaning response of one to the other in addition to strengthening associations between the words.

The more often the stimulus word is paired with its associates, the stronger will the direct associations become. At the same time, the meaning of the associates will be more strongly conditioned to the stimulus word, i.e., the stimulus word will acquire more intense meaning. (Studies to be discussed in the next section will give additional support to this interpretation.) Other things equal, contiguous presentations of words will strengthen the associations responsible for high m as well as the associations responsible for intense semantic differential meaning. This effect should not necessarily depend on the frequency of use of a word. It depends on the frequency with which a word is paired with a group of associates which has a certain type of meaning. Words such as "the" no doubt occur extremely frequently with few repeats of any particular word associate. Because of this, "the" would have a great many weak word associates, with many different and probably antagonistic meanings. For this reason it would be thought that "the" would not have strong word associates, nor would it elicit strong meaning responses.

ADDITIONAL DISTINCTIONS IN THE CONCEPTS OF MEANING

The foregoing interpretations and empirical results argue that the verbal associates which words elicit do not account for word meaning. The confusion between these two processes may have arisen because the same operation, paired presentations of words, strengthens both types of associations. However, if word associations and word meaning are really independent processes, it should be possible to find independent operations for their development.

In a recent experiment (A. W. Staats, et. al., 1962), a GSR was conditioned to the word LARGE by pairing the word with noxious stimulation (shock or loud noise—adjusted to be unpleasant for each *S*) as it was presented in a list of words to be learned. After the conditioning the meaning of the word was measured on the semantic differential scale of pleasant-unpleasant. According to the theory of meaning already discussed, part of the "negative" response elicited by the noxious stimuli should be conditioned to LARGE (in the same manner as the GSR) and become, in part, the meaning of the word. This "negative" conditioned meaning response should then mediate the negative rating of LARGE on the semantic differential. The prediction was substantiated—negative evaluative meaning was conditioned to LARGE, without pairing it with other words. In addition, there was a significant correlation between the intensity of the conditioned GSR and the intensity of the conditioned negative evaluative meaning response. There is thus a suggestion that the conditioned GSR and meaning response were part of the same process. Osgood describes an example of the conditioning of negative evaluative meaning which is analogous to this interpretation. In his example, the word SPIDER is paired with the object, a spider, and some of the responses elicited by the spider, including autonomic responses of an aversive nature, are conditioned to the sign. He describes the conditioned autonomic responses as those which "literally confer the unpleasant, connotative meaning of threat upon this word" (Osgood, 1953, p. 696). It may be concluded from the above experimental results that meaning can be conditioned to a word through systematically pairing the word with a nonverbal aspect of the environment.

It might be suggested, however, that nonverbal objects on presentation elicit implicit verbal responses in the individual. Assuming this to be the case in this experimental procedure, if each time shock or sound was presented the *S* said "shock" or "sound," then word associations to LARGE could be formed. Then it might be said that LARGE had gained negative evaluative meaning because it later elicited the words "shock" and "sound." (This, of course, leaves unanswered the question of how "shock" and "sound" have acquired negative meaning.) However, this interpretation does not account for the significant correlation between the intensity of the conditioned GSR and the intensity of the conditioned meaning response. In addition, it seems questionable whether electric shock and an unfamiliar sound, especially in the experimental procedure, would elicit implicit naming responses.

The above experiment was thought to illustrate first-order conditioning of meaning as depicted in the upper part of Fig. 1. In addition, however, several recent studies have shown that meaning may be conditioned through higher-order conditioning (lower part of Fig. 1) independent of strengthening word-word associations. In these experiments a visually presented verbal CS was paired *once each* with 18 *different* auditorily presented words, each word having, however, an identical component of meaning. For example, a nonsense syllable was paired with 18 words like HAPPY, PRETTY, DINNER, and SWEET, which all have what may be called a positive evaluative meaning; and another syllable was paired with words like UGLY, THIEF, AGONY, and DISGUSTING, which have negative evaluative meaning. In addition, four other syllables were each paired in the same manner with 18 different words of no special meaning—yielding a procedure involving six nonsense syllables and 108 different words. Pairing a nonsense syllable only once each with 18 words would yield 18 direct syllable-word associations, all of them weak and mutually inhibitory. On the other hand, the evaluative meaning (either positive or negative) elicited by *each* of the US-words should be strongly conditioned to the syllable with which they were paired. The expected conditioning occurred, even when *S*s who were aware of the systematic pairing of a certain type of word with a nonsense syllable were excluded from the analysis. Meaning, as measured by a semantic differential scale, was conditioned to nonsense syllables (Staats, et. al., 1959; Staats and Staats, 1957), national and proper names (Straats and Staats, 1958), and meaningful words (Staats et. al., 1958). In one experiment (Staats and Staats, 1957), the evaluative, potency, and activity factors of meaning found by Osgood and Suci (1955) were conditioned. A further study of "language conditioning" has indicated that the strength, or intensity, of the conditioned meaning increased as did the number of trials, i.e., number of syllable-meaning pairings (Staats and Staats, 1959), again with a syllable paired only once with any particular word.

Conversely, it should be possible to establish strong direct word-word associations without establishing strong word-meaning associations. This would be possible by selecting US-words (or response-words) which elicit antagonistic meaning responses, e.g., some US-words which elicit positive evaluative meaning and an equal number which elicit negative evaluative meaning. In this case the CS-word (or stimulus word) would be paired with each US-word many times. The result would be strong direct associations between the CS- and US-words, but the meaning of the CS-word should remain neutral, as measured on a semantic differential scale. The positive conditioning would cancel the negative. Similarly, a CS-word could be paired many times with words of neutral meaning (or with nonsense syllables) so that strong direct word-word associations would result. The CS-word would then have a high m, but it would elicit no meaning response, or the meaning response would be neutral as measured on a semantic differential.[2]

The foregoing illuminates a weakness of the interpretation that word meaning is comprised of the word's verbal associates. The conception that word meaning consists of word associates makes no provision for differentiating words in terms of their relationship to different aspects of the environment. While it seems reasonable to state that a word has meaning because it has certain verbal associates, it *is* reasonable because the associates of the word are *meaningful* themselves. The conception becomes unreasonable if the case is considered where the verbal associates are meaningless words, i.e., nonsense syllables. To state that words gain their meaning by eliciting other words leaves all words in the status of nonsense syllables which have been widely associated with one another. It is unreasonable that this process produces meaningful words. No matter how many meaningless associates a nonsense syllable has it will remain meaningless. An illustration of this can be found by imagining a person learning a foreign language solely by pairing (or defining) the foreign words with each other—without ever pairing a foreign word with aspects of the nonverbal environment, or with meaningful words in a familiar language. With sufficient practice the person could in this manner learn many word associations in the foreign

[2] Staats and associates (1963) have experimentally tested this and others of his expectations regarding the independence of meaning and m. The results showed that through the paired presentation of words (in a paired-associate learning task) (1) the meaning of a word could be changed while the word's m was held constant, (2) meaning and m could be varied in a parallel fashion, and (3) a word's m could be changed without changing the word's meaning.

language—but the new language would be meaningless.

A more complete conception of meaning than the theory of word associates must include reference to the systematic pairings of verbal stimuli and various aspects of the environment, and to the properties acquired by the verbal stimuli as a result of this process.

VERBAL GENERALIZATION AND MEANING

Since Bousfield at al. consider meaning to be the composite of associates of a word, they were able to deduce certain hypotheses concerning semantic generalization. A number of studies, summarized elsewhere (Cofer & Foley, 1942; Osgood, 1953), have shown that a response conditioned to a word will generalize to a word of the same or similar meaning. Bousfield et al. conclude that this generalization is mediated, at least in part, by the partial identity of the word associates of two words. They have also provided evidence demonstrating a relationship between the amount of generalization and the degree of identity of word associates. The results of the present study, however, indicate that this relationship may also reflect another variable. Since the word associates in the composites are themselves meaningful words, we may say that they too elicit meaning responses. When two response composites are similar, the meaning responses elicited by the response composites will be similar to one another. Thus, the generalization can also be considered to be due to the mediation of the common meaning responses of the common associates. Including this alternative, semantic generalization may take place on the basis of: (*a*) similarity of meaning responses elicited by two words, (*b*) similarity of the word associates elicited by two words, and (*c*) similarity of the meaning responses elicited by the word associates of the two words. In any situation it may be that each of these factors is contributing to the total generalization.

SUMMARY

Two approaches to meaning were summarized and contrasted. Word meaning may be considered to be the verbal responses made to the word, or word meaning may be a conditioned mediating response, part of the response elicited by the object denoted by the word. The present paper described the latter as meaning and distinguished word meaning from a word's verbal associates. The correlation between intensity of meaning and verbal associate measures which has been reported was seen to be a result of the fact that the same operation strengthens both: the more often a word is paired with its word associates, the stronger the connections between them. In addition, the meaning of the associates is conditioned to the word. This view was supported by showing that the associates of a word tend to have the same meaning as the word.

The two approaches to meaning were discussed further, and it was concluded that words could not gain meaning through verbal associations per se. Originally, it is through systematically pairing words with aspects of the environment that their meaning is gained. The meaning acquired in this process may later be conditioned to other words.

It was also concluded that semantic generalization may be a function of (*a*) similarity of meaning between words, (*b*) similarity of word associates elicited by words, and (*c*) similarity of meaning responses elicited by word associates of words.

References

Bousfield, W. A., Cohen, B. A., & Whitmarsh, G. A. Verbal generalization: A theoretical rationale and an experimental technique. *Tech. Rep. No. 23.* Contract No. Nonr—631 (00) between Office of Naval Research and Univer. of Connecticut, 1958.

Cofer, C. N., & Foley, J. P. Mediated generalization and the interpretation of verbal behavior. I. Prolegomena. *Psychol. Rev.*, 1942, 49, 513–540.

Jenkins, J. J., & Russell, W. A. Annual technical report: Basic studies on individual and group behavior. Contract No. N8 onr-66216 between Office of Naval Research and Univer. of Minnesota, 1956.

Jenkins, J. J., Russell, W. A., & Suci, G. J. An atlas of semantic profiles for 360 words. *Tech. Rep. No. 15.* Contract No. N8 onr-66216 between Office of Naval Research and Univer. of Minnesota, 1957.

Mowrer, O. H. The psychologist looks at language. *Amer. Psychologist*, 1954, 9, 660–694.

Noble, C. E. An analysis of meaning. *Psychol. Rev.*, 1952, 59, 421–430.

Noble, C. E. Emotionality (e) and meaningfulness (m). *Psychol. Rep.*, 1958, 4, 16.

Osgood, C. E. *Method and theory in experimental psychology.* New York: Oxford Univer. Press, 1953.

Osgood, C. E., & Suci, G. J. Factor analysis of meaning. *J. exp. Psychol.*, 1955, 50, 325–338.

Osgood, C. E., Suci, G. J., & Tannenbaum, P. H. *The measurement of meaning.* Urbana: Univer. Illinois Press, 1957.

Russell, W. A., & Jenkins, J. J. The complete Minnesota norms for responses to 100 words from the Kent-Rosanoff Word Association Test. *Tech. Rep. No. 11.* Contract No. N8 onr-66216 between Office of Naval Research and Univer. of Minnesota, 1954.

Staats, A. W., & Staats, C. K. Attitudes established by classical conditioning. *J. abnorm. soc. Psychol.*, 1958, 57, 37–40. (a)

Staats, A. W., Staats, C. K., & Biggs, D. A. Meaning of verbal stimuli changed by conditioning. *Amer. J. Psychol.*, 1958, 71, 429–431.

Staats, A. W., Staats, C. K., & Crawford, H. L. First-order conditioning of word meaning and the parallel conditioning of a GSR. *J. gen. Psychol.*, 1962, 67, 159–167.

Staats, A. W., Staats, C. K., Finley, J. R., & Heard, W. G. Independent manipulation of meaning and *m*. *J. gen. Psychol.*, 1963, 69, 253–260.

Staats, A. W., Staats, C. K., Heard, W. G., & Nims, L. P. Replication report: Meaning established by classical conditioning. *J. exp. Psychol.*, 1959, 57, 64.

Staats, C. K., & Staats, A. W. Meaning established by classical conditioning. *J. exp. Psychol.*, 1957, 54, 74–80.

Staats, C. K., & Staats, A. W. Effect of number of trials on the language conditioning of meaning. *J. gen. Psychol.*, 1959, 61, 211–223.

Syntactic Position and Rated Meaning[1]

MICHAEL G. JOHNSON

Any experimenter who attempts to use meaning as a variable in psychological research must adopt some operational definition of this elusive concept. In doing so, he must deal with the fact that the conclusions which can be drawn from his research may be limited by the particular definition which he adopts. Definitions of meaning which can be operationally applied in experimental situations often have theoretical limitations or ambiguities which leave them open to criticism.

The purpose of the experiments described here was to relate the objective properties of syntactic position to some sort of systematic variation in meaning. This relationship was established using the Semantic Differential as a measure of meaning, but the successful fulfillment of the above-stated purpose is not dependent upon the theoretical generality of the Semantic Differential. It is certainly true that the oppositional character of certain English adjectives, upon which the Semantic Differential is based, is one *of the fundamental aspects of meaning in English. It is this fact, along with the agreement of the present results with those obtained using an entirely different experimental procedure (Clark, 1965), which suggests that the meaning measured in this experiment is more general than the particular operations by which it is defined. It must be pointed out, however, that the Semantic Differential which I used represents a selected subset of all the possible bipolar adjective pairs which might have been used. There are undoubtedly aspects of meaning which these particular adjective pairs are not sensitive to, and which might have been observed had a different set of adjectives been used. I have shown that syntactic position is related to meaning in one way, but it is possible that position may be related to meaning in other ways as well.*—MICHAEL G. JOHNSON

Reference

CLARK, H. H., "Some Structural Properties of Simple Active and Passive Sentences." *Journal of Verbal Learning and Verbal Behavior,* 4 (1965), 365–370.

1 The investigations reported here were supported in part by Public Health Service research grant MH-06550-03, from the National Institute of Mental Health.

Michael G. Johnson, "Syntactic Position and Rated Meaning," *Journal of Verbal Learning and Verbal Behavior,* 6, No.2 (1967). Reprinted by permission of the author and publisher, Academic Press, Inc., New York.

Structural meaning is the part of the total meaning of a sentence signalled by the pattern or arrangement of the individual words which make up the sentence (Fries, 1952). Within the context of structural meaning, one can ask how the position a word occupies in a sentence effects the meaning of that word. Consider, for example, the sentences "The boy hit the ball." and "The ball hit the boy." In both of these sentences the word "boy" refers to (signifies) the same thing, while serving two different functions. It is not entirely clear, however, whether "boy" in the subject position connotes the *same thing* as "boy" in the object position. Similar questions are suggested when words have the same function but occupy different positions, as when one sentence is the passive transform of another. There is, then, a question of the relation between syntactic position and meaning.

In order to study such a relationship a measure of meaning change had to be found in an experimental situation in which context effects (the referential meaning of sentences) can be controlled. The Semantic Differential (Osgood, Suci, and Tannenbaum, 1957) provides a measure of meaning. The experimental technique consists in using nonsense syllables instead of English words in the subject and object positions of simple (noun-verb-noun) active and passive sentences. (The passive subject position is the second noun position in these sentences.) English verbs and articles are retained. The effects of sentence position on meaning can be isolated and measured by properly selecting the verbs used, and by employing suitable counterbalancing measures.

Some hypotheses concerning the outcome of such an experiment were derived from a study of the completion of sentence frames reported by Clark (1965). Clark found that 81.5% of the words which *Ss* chose for the subject position in active sentences were animate nouns, but only 26.7% of the nouns used in the active object position were animate. In passive sentences, 68.3% animate nouns were used in the subject position and 45.8% in the object position. Clark also calculated the variability of the distributions of words used by *Ss* in the different sentence positions, using the informational uncertainty measure *U* (Garner, 1962). He found that a smaller variety of words was used in the active subject position than in the active object position, with the passive positions falling between these two extremes of variability.

These results show that each sentence position has its own characteristic distribution of words associated with it, and these distributions are differentiated by the variety and animateness of the words contained in them. Nonsense syllables used in the subject and object positions of sentences could generalize to the distributions of words normally occupying these positions, and would take on the general properties of these distributions. If this is so, syllables used in the active subject position would be rated more active and potent (animate) on a Semantic Differential than would syllables used in the active object position. The ratings for passive positions would be in the same direction, but less extreme, than those for their active counterparts. Since uncertainty and variance are both measures of variability, it would also be predicted that the variance in the ratings for different sentence positions would show the same pattern as the uncertainties reported by Clark.

Two studies are reported here. The first was concerned with the meanings of subject and object positions in simple active sentences. The second extended the design to include subject and object positions in both active and passive sentences.

EXPERIMENT I

Method

Subjects. The *Ss* were 57 introductory psychology students at Carleton College (Northfield, Minnesota).

Materials. Twelve transitive verbs were selected so that their summed meaning, as measured by loadings on the first three factors yielded by a 20-scale Semantic Differential, was approximately neutral. For example, each highly potent verb was balanced by a low potent verb. The adjective pairs used for these verb ratings were those employed by Jenkins, Russell, and Suci (1958). Three of the verbs selected required an animate subject, four required an animate object, and five could take either animate or inanimate subjects and objects. Six CVC nonsense syllables were selected for low meaningfulness (Noble, 1961) and discriminability. None of the syllables started with the same letter, and the vowel-consonant combinations following the initial letters were different for each syllable. The verbs and syllables were combined to form four lists of 36 sentences of the type "The NIJ hurt the GAQ." Within a list, three of the syllables were used in the subject position and three in the object position. These syllables were paired. This meant that each *S* saw three pairs of syllables repeated several times. The 12 verbs were repeated three times in each list, so that each syllable pair was used once with every verb. The assignment of syllables to subject or object position was counterbalanced over the four lists. Four different randomizations of the verbs were used, and the syllable pairings were different for each list.

Semantic Differential rating scales composed of 15 bipolar adjective pairs were used, with a seven-interval rating scale separating the polar opposites. The pairs (shown in Table 1) were selected to represent each of the three primary factors reported by Osgood, *et al.* (1957)—evaluation, potency, and activity—plus the pairs Subject-Object and Aggressive-Defensive.

Procedure. Data were collected in small groups. The *S*s were given booklets containing one of the sentence lists and six Semantic Differential rating sheets.

Table 1

MEAN SEMANTIC DIFFERENTIAL RATINGS OF SUBJECT AND OBJECT SYLLABLES—EXPERIMENT I

(Each mean represents 171 observations)

Adjective Pair	*Position*	
	Subject	*Object*
Evaluative		
Good-Bad	3.84	3.52
Beautiful-Ugly	4.59	4.09
Wise-Foolish	3.98	4.39
Kind-Cruel	3.95	3.54
Progressive-Regressive	3.48	4.21[b]
Potency		
Hard-Soft	3.51	4.21[a]
Heavy-Light	3.50	4.05[a]
Masculine-Feminine	3.14	3.78[a]
Strong-Weak	3.16	4.34[c]
Potent-Impotent	3.24	4.25[c]
Activity		
Active-Passive	3.01	4.34[c]
Energetic-Inert	3.24	4.22[c]
Fast-Slow	3.49	4.36[b]
Unclassified		
Subject-Object	2.95	4.84[c]
Aggressive-Defensive	3.09	4.16[c]

[a] Significant at .05 level
[b] Significant at .01 level
[c] Significant at .001 level

After *E* read instructions, each *S* studied one list of 36 sentences for 6 min. and then rated the six nonsense syllables on the rating scales. The order in which the syllables were rated was counterbalanced across *S*s. The *S*s did not know that they would be required to rate the syllables until after they had studied the sentences. After all of the syllables were rated, *S*s were asked to "Write down anything you thought of during the experiment which might have affected the way you judged the syllables."

Results

An analysis of variance of the Semantic Differential ratings showed that the difference between the ratings of subject and object syllables was significant, $F(15, 840) = 12.37$, $p < .001$. Since a given rating does not necessarily mean the same thing for all scales, there is no meaningful way to combine the 15 scales for an overall analysis of variance. The above *F*-ratio was obtained from comparing the average variance between positions (within scales) with the average within positions variance (within scales). This is essentially a mixed design in which the scales can be thought of as replications. Table 1 shows the mean ratings of subject and object syllables for each adjective pair. The adjective pairs are grouped according to the factor loading reported by Osgood, *et al.* (1957). The first member of each pair represents the "1" end of the 1–7 rating scale. The significance of differences between subject and object ratings was tested by a two-tailed *t*. The data clearly show that syllables used in the subject position are rated consistently more active and potent than syllables used in the object position. All of the scales which show no significant difference have high loadings on the evaluative factor. The one evaluative scale which does indicate a significant difference (Progressive-Regressive) also had a high loading on the activity factor.

A principle components factor analysis of these data (subject and object matrices were analyzed separately) using a varimax rotation criterion, clearly separated the four non-significant adjective pairs from the 11 significant ones but did not differentiate among the 11 significant pairs. The results of this factor analysis indicate that the general factor "animate-inanimate"—including both activity and potency—is the most useful for the description of the present data.

The comments made after the syllables were rated showed a great deal of variability in the strategies which individual *S*s employed while studying the sentences. Only four of the 57 *S*s indicated that they had made explicit use of the subject-object relation while studying the sentences.

EXPERIMENT II

Method

Subjects. The *S*s were 100 introductory psychology students at The Johns Hopkins University.

Materials. Two nonsense syllables were added to the six used in Experiment I, and were selected according to the same criteria. These eight syllables were combined with the 12 verbs (also from Experiment I) to form four lists of 48 sentences. The lists contained 24 active sentences of the form "The XEK hit the WUQ." and 24 passive sentences of the form "The RIW was comforted by the FOJ." In each list, two syllables were used in one of four positions: active subject (AS), active object (AO), passive subject (PS), and passive object (PO). The syllables were paired, as in the previous experiment, and each syllable was used in a different position in each of the four lists. Within a list, every verb was used twice in each voice (active and passive), and every syllable was used once with every verb—i.e., every syllable pair was used with every verb. Four different randomized orderings of the verbs were used.

The Semantic Differential rating scales were the same as those used in Experiment I, except that the direction of the adjective pairs was randomly assigned. Half of the *S*s rated the syllables in one direction on these randomized scales, and the other half rated the syllables in the reverse direction. This meant, for example, that half of the *S*s rated syllables on a Good-Bad scale, and the other half on a Bad-Good scale.

Procedure. Data were collected in groups of 20 to 30 *S*s. *E* read instructions, then each *S* studied one sentence list for 8 min. and afterward rated each of the eight syllables on the rating scales. The *S*s were not told that they were going to be asked to rate the syllables. After rating the syllables, as in Experiment I, *S*s were asked to comment on anything that might have affected the way in which they rated the syllables.

Results

Table 2 shows the mean Semantic Differential ratings for the four voice-position combinations. Since *S*s rated syllables in both directions on the adjective-pair scales, the means are adjusted so that all of the scales are in the same direction. The first member of each adjective pair (as they are listed) represents the "1" end of the rating scale. The adjective pairs are grouped according to the animate-inanimate factor obtained in Experiment I.

An analysis of variance of the rating scale data showed the effect of subject-object position (within scales) to be highly significant, $F\ (151{,}485) = 73.48$, $p < .001$ The voice by position interaction was also significant, $F\ (151{,}485) = 4.41$, $p < .001$. The design employed here was the same as that used in Experiment I, with the addition of the voice variable. With only three exceptions (which are indicated in Table 3) the predicted linear ordering—AS, PS, PO, AO, in decreasing order of animateness—was maintained on the scales which were sensitive to the animate-inanimate factor. The mean variances for the AS, PS, PO, and AO positions were, respectively, 2.91, 2.94, 3.13 and 3.39. These variances show the same pattern as the uncertainties reported by Clark (1965).

Table 3 indicates the magnitude of differences in ratings. As in Experiment I, the evaluative scales do not consistently

Table 2

MEAN SEMANTIC DIFFERENTIAL RATINGS FOR SUBJECT AND OBJECT POSITIONS IN ACTIVE AND PASSIVE SENTENCES—EXPERIMENT II
(Each mean represents 200 observations)

Adjective Pair	*Act. Subj.*	*Act. Obj.*	*Pass. Subj.*	*Pass. Obj.*
Evaluative				
Good-Bad	3.80	3.88	3.87	3.65
Beautiful-Ugly	4.19	4.11	4.38	4.08
Wise-Foolish	4.01	4.31	3.88	4.15
Kind-Cruel	3.80	3.92	3.96	3.72
Animateness				
Progressive-Regressive	3.15	4.62	3.43	4.48
Hard-Soft	3.23	4.55	3.57	4.54
Heavy-Light	3.52	4.48	3.34	4.50
Masculine-Feminine	2.93	4.19	3.22	4.31
Strong-Weak	2.81	4.68	3.36	4.53
Potent-Impotent	2.87	4.59	3.19	4.49
Active-Passive	2.61	4.78	3.29	4.54
Energetic-Inert	2.93	4.64	3.31	4.45
Fast-Slow	3.12	4.45	3.54	4.34
Subject-Object	2.81	5.00	3.65	4.43
Aggressive-Defensive	3.03	4.70	3.36	4.63

Table 3

DIFFERENCES OF SEMANTIC DIFFERENTIAL RATINGS BETWEEN AND WITHIN VOICE—EXPERIMENT II

Adjective Pair	*AO—AS*	*PO—PS*	*PS—AS*	*AO—PO*
Evaluative				
Good-Bad	.08	−.22	.07	−.23
Beautiful-Ugly	−.08	−.30	.19	−.03
Wise-Foolish	.30	.27	−.13	−.16
Kind-Cruel	.12	−.24	.16	−.20
Animateness				
Progressive-Regressive	1.47	1.05	.28	−.14[a]
Hard-Soft	1.32	.97	.34	−.01[a]
Heavy-Light	.96	1.16	−.18[a]	.02
Masculine-Feminine	1.26	1.09	.29	.12
Strong-Weak	1.87	1.17	.55	.15
Potent-Impotent	1.72	1.30	.32	.10
Active-Passive	2.17	1.25	.68	.24
Energetic-Inert	1.71	1.14	.38	.19
Fast-Slow	1.33	.80	.42	.11
Subject-Object	2.19	.77	.84	.57
Aggressive-Defensive	1.67	1.21	.33	.07

Note—All differences greater than .194 are significant at the .01 level

[a] Exception to predicted AS-PS-PO-AO ordering

differentiate between positions (or voice). The significance of differences was tested by computing the critical difference (Lindquist, 1953) required for significance at the .01 level. A rank correlation coefficient between the magnitude of differences obtained in Experiment I and the AS—AO differences in this experiment is highly significant, $r_s > .99$.

The subjective comments made by the *S*s indicate that no consistent strategy was employed while studying the syllables. Twenty-three of the 100 *S*s reported that they paid some attention to the positions which syllables occupied in the sentences.

DISCUSSION

The results of the two experiments reported indicate that the position a word occupies in a sentence affects the rated meaning of that word. Both of the studies show that nonsense syllables used in the AS position are more active and potent (animate) than those which are used in the AO position. In addition, Experiment II shows that PS syllables are more animate than PO syllables, but that passive positions are more neutral than their active counterparts. Since referential meaning was controlled, only meaning associated with syntactic position can account for these consistent differences. The meanings measured by the Semantic Differential ratings were structural meanings.

The agreement of these results, both the animateness and the variability of the ratings, with those of Clark (1965) suggests that the relationship between sentence position and meaning is symmetrical. The present data show that the grammatic usage of words, at least nouns, plays a part in the determination of their meanings. Clark's data show that the meanings of words determine the uses to which they are put. It seems that both of these sets of data reflect the same properties of English structure and usage. This means that in the present investigations *S*s generalized the nonsense syllables to the class of words normally occupying the positions which they held. The *variability* of the Semantic Differential ratings is then related to how well-defined or diffuse the distributions of words which normally occupy these positions are. This is the same as saying that the variability of the ratings is an index of the information contained in the distributions. Brown and Fraser (1963, p. 193–4) have hypothesized that the information or uncertainty associated with different sentence positions may be reflected in childrens' acquisition of grammar. The same properties may function in adult language behavior as well. The *direction* of the ratings provides more specific information about the actual nature of the words making up these distributions. The data clearly show that these distributions differ along at least one dimension of meaning—animateness.

If this interpretation of the data is correct, if syntactic usage and meaning reflect the same distributional properties of English, then grammar is not, as Chomsky (1957) has suggested, independent of meaning. Perhaps the distributional properties of language can provide a basis for the construction of a general linguistic theory, which would include both grammar and meaning.

The results of the present experiments are not easily understood in terms of a transformational model of language behavior, such as that proposed by Miller (1962). If, as Miller suggests, sentences are understood (recoded) in their kernel form, then a word used in the subject position of a passive sentence should mean the same thing as a word in the subject position of its active kernel. This position is expressed in a more formal way by transformational theorists (Chomsky, 1965; Katz and Postal, 1964) when they argue that singulary transformations (e.g., from active to passive) do not involve meaning change. The present results show that different sentence positions have different structural meanings, and that these meanings are not the same in both active and passive sentences—even for functionally equivalent positions. Since these meanings reflect underlying distributional structures, different sets of words are associated with active and passive sentences (these sets overlap to some extent, of course). This is perhaps one reason for the existence of voice.

In most studies using the Semantic Differential, evaluation emerges as the primary factor. The evaluative factor does not seem to be present in structural meaning, however. Livant (1963) found no evaluative differences between ratings of noun and verb forms of the same word, but did find differences along the activity factor. The present data show that the animate-inanimate component of meaning is one component of meaning that may be structurally determined—i.e. related to the position which words occupy in sentences. Evaluation may serve to differentiate words independent from their syntactic usages.

References

Brown, R., and Fraser, C. The acquisition of syntax. In C. N. Cofer and B. S. Musgrave (Eds.) *Verbal behavior and learning.* New York: McGraw-Hill, 1963.

Chomsky, N. *Syntactic structures.* The Hague: Mouton, 1957.

Chomsky, N. *Aspects of the theory of syntax.* Cambridge: M.I.T. Press, 1965.

Clark, H. H. Some structural properties of simple active and passive sentences. *J. verb. Learn. verb. Behav.*, 1965, *4*, 365–370.

Fries, C. C. *The structure of English.* New York: Harcourt, Brace, 1952.

Jenkins, J. J., Russel, W. A., and Suci, G. J. An atlas of semantic profiles for 360 words. *Amer. J. Psychol.*, 1958, *71*, 688–699.

Katz, J. J., and Postal, P. M. *An integrated theory of linguistic descriptions.* Cambridge: M.I.T. Press, 1964.

LINDQUIST, E. F. *Design and analysis of experiments in psychology and education.* Boston: Houghton Mifflin, 1953.

LIVANT, W. P. A comparison of noun and verb forms on the semantic differential. *J. verb. Learn. verb. Behav.*, 1963, *1*, 357–360.

MILLER, G. A. Some psychological studies of grammar. *Amer. Psychol.*, 1962, *17*, 748–762.

NOBLE, C. E. Measurements of association value (a), rated associations (a′), and scaled meaningfulness (m′) for the 2100 CVC combinations of the English alphabet. *Psych. Rep.*, 1961, Monograph supplement 3-v8.

OSGOOD, E. E., SUCI, G. J., and TANNENBAUM, P. H. *The measurement of meaning.* Urbana, Ill.: The Univ. of Ill. Press, 1957.

The Principle of Associative Symmetry*

SOLOMON E. ASCH and
SHELDON M. EBENHOLTZ

DIRECTION is a pervasive property of experience and action. We experience events as temporally differentiated, as being earlier and later, and as functionally differentiated, in the sense that one leads to the other or causes it. The discrimination of direction is essential to the coherence of experience and action.

Traditionally, the process of association has been invoked in explanation of the directed character of psychological events. One speaks of the formation of an association when two terms, *a* and *b*, have been experienced together, and when subsequently the appearance of one produces the recall of the other. Since recall frequently follows the order of original experience (from *a* to *b*), it seems that association is responsible both for the occurrence and for the order of recall. The concept of association has always referred to the mechanism that connects individual experiences or actions according to the order in which they occur. Although they are logically distinct, the formation of associations and the order of associations have constituted an inseparable problem in the history of psychology. Indeed, it was in this manner that theories of association have attempted, from the days of British empiricism to the present period, to account for the coherence of psychological functioning. This is also clearly evident in the experimental investigation of associations; the accounts of association as a process have tended to be accounts of the formation of sequences of associations.

This has been the theoretical setting for the empirical study of the directionality of associations, or of the problem of "backward association," which has attracted attention since the beginning of experimental investigation. Empirical analysis has appeared to confirm the starting assumption that associative recall generally occurs more readily in the "forward" direction (from *a* to *b*) than in the "backward" direction (from *b* to *a*). Observations of this kind are responsible for the conclusion that the associative process is directed. If the order in which ideas appear, or the order in which responses occur, corre-

* This investigation was supported by grants from the Ford Foundation and the National Science Foundation. We wish to thank Mrs. Sarah Lamont for her assistance in conducting several of the experiments of this investigation.

Solomon E. Asch and Sheldon M. Ebenholtz, "The Principle of Associative Symmetry," *Proceedings of the American Philosophical Society,* **106,** *No.* 2 (1962), 135–163. Reprinted by permission of the authors and publisher.

sponds to earlier experience, and if association is the responsible process, associations must be unidirectional.

Actually the relation between the process of association and the directed character of experience or action is far from clear. Theorists have implicitly included all directional phenomena under the rubric of association, but largely on the blanket assumption that association was the basic process responsible for the effects of past experience. Strictly speaking, however, the concept of association deals with direction at best in a partial way. It handles only the relation of sheer succession, not the host of other relations that imbue psychological events with direction. It treats, for example, the relation of crime and punishment only as temporally differentiated, not in terms of their causal nexus. A first examination shows that there are several quite different senses of direction. One needs to distinguish, for example, first between "functional direction" and "phenomenal direction," the former referring to neural or behavioral direction, and the latter to the experience of these. How the two are related is a factual question; doubtless they often coincide, but this may not be the rule. In turn, it is necessary to discriminate between these and "direction of association"; again it is a factual question whether direction—either in its functional or phenomenal sense—is at all a function of associative processes. In what follows we will confine ourselves to the directional character of associations.

I. THE PROBLEM AND A HYPOTHESIS

The phenomena of association have been generally studied in settings in which direction appears to be an important part of the process. The learner attempts to associate one term with another, *a* with *b*, in a given order.[1] There is, thus, at the outset the distinction between a first and a second term (even when they are objectively simultaneous). Second, the task of association often appears to specify a further functional direction. This is evident when the learner starts from *a* and anticipates *b*. When these conditions are given, the distinction between forward and backward has a clear sense: the former refers to the order followed in experience and action, the latter refers to the reverse of the order in which the learner proceeds. The classical problem of backward association grows out of these conditions. The questions are: Does the formation of an $a \rightarrow b$ association produce necessarily an association in the reverse, or $b \rightarrow a$, direction? If so, are these of equal strength? In short, the question is whether associations are unidirectional or bidirectional, and in the latter case, what their relative strengths are.[2]

These are the questions that we shall be examining. To anticipate the conclusion, we shall propose that association and direction are different in process. More concretely, we shall present evidence for a principle of associative symmetry, which may be stated as follows: *When an association is formed between two distinct terms,* a *and* b, *it is established simultaneously and with equal strength between* b *and* a. The principle asserts (1) that one cannot establish a unidirectional or asymmetrical association between distinct terms, that there are no conditions that will produce an association between *a* and *b* without producing an association of equal strength between *b* and *a*; (2) that

[1] For reasons that will become apparent shortly we shall refrain from referring to the members of an associated pair as "stimulus" and "response" (see p. 137). Instead we shall employ the more neutral designation *a* and *b* to refer to the first and second members of a pair, respectively.

[2] There are different ways of designating the associative property under discussion. An association in one direction may be called unidirectional, asymmetrical, or simply directional. An association in two directions may be called bidirectional, equidirectional, or symmetrical. These respective sets of terms will be used interchangeably in the present paper.

the symmetry of associations is independent of the intention or effort of the learner; and (3) that the relation of symmetry holds for individual associations, not only for populations of instances. These statements further suggest that the relation of symmetry refers to one association, that there is not one association of *a* with *b*, and another of *b* with *a*.

The preceding conclusions go counter to existing interpretations. They contradict the principle that associations are unidirectional, and they question the empirical findings that appear to demonstrate the relative weakness of backward association. Before we turn to the evidence for these formulations it will be necessary to examine the assumptions and procedures underlying the investigation of backward association.

II. A CRITIQUE OF THE STUDY OF BACKWARD ASSOCIATION

Despite continuing evidence to the contrary, many psychologists have distrusted the reality of backward association and have sought to explain away the empirical findings. Nearly all investigators who have addressed themselves to the problem, from the first study of Ebbinghaus down to the present, have found evidence, at times quite strong, for what has been called backward association. (For an exception to the trend, see Trowbridge, 1938.) At the same time it is not unusual for students to report backward association of the same strength as forward association and to qualify the backward effect as "apparent" (Cason, 1924; Hermans, 1936; Murdock, 1956). It is instructive to examine the sources of this skepticism.

A. Assumptions behind the Principle of Associative Asymmetry

There were several reasons for adhering to the principle, which mutually supported each other. Central to all was the tacit assumption that, since the associative situation had unidirectional properties, the associations themselves were unidirectional.

(1) Quite compelling, because least realized, was a phenomenal property of the associative situation. We noted earlier that the associative task as a rule contains a definite directional component; generally the learner attempts to go from *a* to *b*, not from *b* to *a*. This fact creates a naive but powerful presumption that the associative process is equally directed. It is responsible, we believe, for the sense of puzzlement bordering on exasperation that has at times surrounded the analysis of the problem. In discussing the first findings of Ebbinghaus on backward association, Cason once asked: "Why were *backward* associations formed when he seemed to be exercising them only in the *forward* direction?" (1924: 217). As we stated earlier, the relation between phenomenal and functional direction is an empirical question, and cannot be decided on an intuitive basis. It is noteworthy that a phenomenal datum, namely, the impression that the learner is engaging in a unidirectional activity, exerted this potent effect on writers who in principle would have discountenanced such an appeal. The appeal is moreover lacking in force. In principle, phenomenal data cannot decide functional questions, although they can in certain areas provide fruitful hypotheses. This is least likely to be the case, though, with the process of association, which has no phenomenal correlates; there are no experiential signs to indicate whether an association has been formed, or what aspects of a situation have been associated. To conclude, the phenomenal character of associative situations appeared strongly to support the conclusion that association is unidirectional, and barred the way to a consideration of alternatives.

(2) Bolstering the principle of unidirectionality was the conceptualization of association as a stimulus-response connection. A stimulus-response sequence, which

is a sample of action, has a forward direction as an essential characteristic. Action proceeds in a determinate direction; it has a beginning and end, and reversal of it is not only difficult to conceive, but is tantamount to disorganization. The difficulty increases when the classical conditioning situation serves as the model for the action sequence, since the response cannot evoke the stimulus. It was again Cason who formulated the main point: "If we accept the view that an association is between a stimulus and a response, then it would be impossible for the association to function backwards" (1924: 221). We cannot here consider adequately this conceptualization; to us it seems that little is gained and much is obscured by treating linguistic association as an instance of motor action. To do so is to relinquish the most distinct advantage that the study of associations provides, which is to trace the principles of a cognitive process without concurrently introducing the complications that must be faced in the study of motor phenomena.[3]

(3) In the recent period investigators have systematically excluded reference to the neurophysiological correlates of association, but this concern was more prominent in the past. It may therefore suffice to mention that a mechanism adequate to backward association seemed to go counter to usual assumptions. Only forward association appeared in accord with the accepted law of forward neural conduction. This point was also clearly stated by Cason "It would be impossible for such a specific chain of [serial associative] connections to operate backwards, partly because of the law of forward direction across synapses" (1924: 221). It is not necessary to dwell long on this issue; aside from the vagueness of the neurophysiology that was invoked, it is evident that the problem of backward association must be settled first by psychological procedures.

These circumstances make it clear why forward association had all the earmarks of a perfectly orderly phenomenon, and why backward association appeared to be an aberrant effect. Given the principle of asymmetry, one can deal with the empirical fact of backward association only by denying its authenticity. This is, indeed, the interpretation that psychologists tended to adopt. In the main, they proposed that backward association was an artifact, being actually forward association in disguise. The learner, it was proposed, is not completely consistent in maintaining a forward direction during learning. His attention may wander and he may unwittingly change his direction, thus establishing forward associations in the reverse direction. This possibility was raised first in criticism of experimental procedures, such as those of Ebbinghaus, that involved the simultaneous presentation of the materials to be associated. Under these circumstances, it was claimed, the objective possibilities are given for establishing forward associations in both directions. This interpretation had to meet the objection that backward association occurred also under temporally successive conditions. At this point the argument was extended to say that the learner is capable of reversing his direction mentally, even when the terms are not given simultaneously. The evidence for such tendencies was not notably clear. Despite the difficulties in arriving at a decision, Cason concluded: "If practice had been confined entirely to the direction from A to B, then we feel sure that there would not have been the

[3] It is of interest to note that the term "backward conditioning" as it is traditionally used, simply refers to a temporal difference in presentation of the conditioned stimulus and the unconditioned stimulus, and not to the order of occurrence of stimulus and response. There is, therefore, no analogue in classical conditioning procedures to what is meant by backward association in the study of verbal learning processes. It may be possible, however, to study backward association with instrumental or operant behavior sequences. Nevertheless one may still question the validity of the analogue between the procedures of instrumental conditioning and verbal learning.

slightest tendency for stimulus B to call up response A" (1924: 220). The basis for this conclusion was evidently the conviction that associations were unidirectional.

A more empirically oriented interpretation was recently formulated by Underwood (Feldman and Underwood, 1957; Jantz and Underwood, 1958). Without taking a stand on the question of unidirectionality, he proposed (with reference to situations of verbal learning) that backward association is an instance of incidental learning. The reference to incidental learning clearly implies that association proceeds in a forward direction, and that backward association in the strict sense is an artifact. This interpretation, although it does not commit itself explicitly at the theoretical level, must at present be considered a variant of the one described above.[4]

B. Operationalism vs. the Analysis of Process

The above-mentioned grounds for the principle of asymmetry would not have carried much weight if the empirical results contradicted them decisively. The evidence for backward association, although nearly always confirmatory, has, however, varied considerably and apparently unaccountably in strength. At times backward recall has equaled forward recall (Wohlgemuth, 1912; Guthrie, 1933; Hermans, 1936), and there is even one study on record which, within the prevailing view, would have to be interpreted as demonstrating a superiority of backward association (Stoddard, 1929). Most often, however, backward association, although substantial, has been distinctly weaker than forward association (Hermans, 1936; Trowbridge, 1938; Feldman and Underwood, 1957; Jantz and Underwood, 1958; Hunt, 1959). This circumstance served to further doubts about its authenticity.

The differences obtained between forward and backward association are we shall show, largely an artifact, but we must first consider the theoretical analysis upon which our experiments are based and against which the customary findings take on new significance.

We begin with a general point, the conceptualization of an association as a stimulus-response connection. This formulation is more than a conventional manner of speaking; it carries the sense that the stimulus instigates the response, or elicits it. In accordance with this starting point, the index for the presence of an association is the eliciting of a response, and the regularity with which the stimulus elicits it (or the probability of its occurrence) is the index of the strength of an association. This mode of analysis is said to have merit because it "anchors" the phenomenon under observation to clearly specified operations; with it there is no doubt as to what is meant by the term association, or strength of association. It succeeds, however, in doing more: it defines a process totally in terms of a measurement procedure, with the consequence that the measurement is equated with the process, and the distinction between them vanishes. Aside from the serious ontological problems which this approach raises, there is the further consequence that all subsequent questions about the process are reduced to further questions about its measurement. This procedure does an injustice to a valid mode of approach to scientific problems wherein one postulates the properties and characteristics of processes, and proceeds to seek by experimental means to verify the proposed construction.

[4] Yet another and opposed trend of current investigation is to be noted. Some students assume backward association in order to account for certain other effects (e.g., Young, 1959; Primoff, 1938). Others make the assumption of backward association in order to predict various effects (Storms, 1958; McCormack, 1961). This use of backward association as an aid in the understanding of other phenomena has not been accompanied by a direct investigation of the backward association process itself. This state of affairs indicates a further inconsistency of thought concerning the problem.

The exchanging of operations for process carries with it two inherent dangers. On the one hand there is the danger of oversimplification, as when the defining operations do not do full justice to the complexity of the underlying process. The process is then stripped of any properties that cannot be fully coordinated with the defining operations. There is alternately the danger of endowing the process with characteristics that belong solely to the operations of measurement, and that are as such foreign to the underlying phenomena. Admittedly the separation of operation and process is not always practicable; nevertheless, there is much to be lost by a studied avoidance of the distinction.

Let us observe the bearing of this general point upon the present problem. For evidence concerning the formation of associations one must necessarily rely on data of recall. An association is formed at one point of time; the evidence of its presence is obtained subsequently. A process of recall thus necessarily plays a part in the measurement of an association. The significance of the recall process becomes clear when one considers that failure of associative recall is not necessarily identical with loss of association. That failure of recall is often followed, in the absence of intervening practice, by adequate recall tells us convincingly that the association persisted throughout the interval, but that there was interference with its production. At this point, the stimulus-response conceptualization asserts that the associative bond had suffered interference. The strict linking of the production of a response with the condition of the associative bond slights the possibility that an association may be intact and yet fail for reasons connected with the process of recall as such. It ignores the properties of the recall process by confounding it with an unanalyzed measure of association. The consequence of the failure to distinguish between these processes introduces a systematic ambiguity in the study of learning and recall. The following is one illustration, directly pertinent to the present problem.

There is one condition that may interfere with the recall of an association, despite its presence, that is of prime importance in this context. Associative performance is a function not only of the persistence of the association but also of the recall of the terms in question. In what follows we shall assume that the data of past experience differ in ease of recall, or in availability, and that the processes underlying availability are distinct from those of association. Associative recall may, to be sure, fail when the association has suffered change, but also when the term in question cannot be recalled. It now remains only to state one consequence of this assertion in order to see its relevance to the problem of backward association: In order to compare backward with forward association the conditions of recall, or of item availability, must be equated. The studies of backward association have not observed this requirement.

One usual procedure of studying associations is by the method of anticipation. When the task is that of paired-associate learning (or the learning of a set of *a—b* pairs), it is customary to require of *S* that he recall (i.e., anticipate) the *b* term (or the "response" member of the pair), whereas the *a* term (or the "stimulus") must be recognized and at best recited out loud. (In some forms of the anticipation method *S*'s are directed only to anticipate the *b* term.) The test of backward association requires *S* for the first time to anticipate the *a* terms; since he has not had the opportunity to anticipate them previously, it would seem plausible that these items are less available to recall. Thus the study of backward association has not equated the conditions of availability, and often availability has systematically favored forward over backward recall. Investigation has often confounded the effects of availability with the action of associations. This source of error renders many findings in this area equivocal and the interpretations based upon them suspect.

C. A Demonstration of the Availability Function

We shall now provide a direct test of the inference that the typical conditions of associative learning produce systematic differences of availability between the terms entering into association. If confirmed, such a demonstration will make possible the tracing of the effect of availability on the measurement of associative directionality.

Experiment I

If the reasoning stated in the preceding section is correct, there should be clear evidence of superior recall of *b* terms relative to *a* terms under the conditions of paired associate learning by the method of anticipation. In the experiment now to be described, *S*'s learned pairs of nonsense syllables by the method of anticipation. Upon reaching a set criterion of learning, to be described below, they were tested by the method of free recall; that is, they were asked to recall, in any order, all pairs and single items that they could supply. The data of free recall will provide an index of the relative availability of *a* and *b* terms.

Procedure:

Eight pairs of nonsense syllables were learned by the method of anticipation. The first member of each pair appeared alone in the window of the Stoelting memory drum for three seconds, and was followed immediately by the presentation of the entire pair for an additional three seconds. The interval between trials was six seconds. *S* was instructed to pronounce (not to spell) the *a* term out loud when it appeared alone and to anticipate the *b* term. If *S* failed to anticipate or did so incorrectly, he corrected himself by pronouncing the *b* item when it appeared.

There were two groups of *S*'s, sixteen in Group 1 and twelve in Group 2. Group 1 learned to the criterion of a minimum of four out of eight correct on a single trial. Group 2 learned to the criterion of eight correct anticipations on a single trial.[5]

The association value of the pairs ranged from 0 to 47 per cent on the Glaze (1928) list; the members comprising any given pair were identical in association value. The eight pairs were arranged in three different orders; these were presented on successive trials in order to minimize serial learning. One-third of *S*'s began their learning on each of the three different list orders, respectively. One-half of the *S*'s in each group learned pairs with left and right members reversed in comparison with the left and right members given the other half of each group.

Upon reaching their respective criteria *S*'s were instructed to recall as many pairs and single items (in any order) that they could think of. They were encouraged to guess when not certain. A period of two minutes was allowed for this task; it was more than ample for all *S*'s.

When the terms belonging to the same pair were recalled consecutively, they were scored as a correct pair. If both members of a pair were recalled but not consecutively, they were scored as correct single items. A syllable recalled both singly and as a member of a pair was scored only once as a member of a pair.

Results:

1. *Learning to Criterion.* Group 1 reached the criterion (of four out of eight correct anticipations) in an average of 7.3 trials. The average number of trials required of Group 2 to reach the same cri-

[5] The use of groups differing in level of acquisition (and hence practice) serves to lend generality to the obtained effects. It also permits an evaluation of the extent to which differential item availability may be a function of the level of association.

terion was 7.8. Inspection reveals, therefore, that the two groups did not differ in rate of learning.

Group 2 required an average of 17.4 trials to reach the criterion of eight correct anticipations on a single trial. Thus Group 2 received two and one-half times as much practice as Group 1. The choice of criteria for Groups 1 and 2 was therefore quite effective in producing large differences in amount of practice.

2. *Recall of* a *and* b *Terms.* Table 1 gives the mean number of *a* and *b* items recalled correctly in Groups 1 and 2.

In each group mean recall of *b* terms was substantially and significantly higher than of *a* terms. In calculating the statistical significance of the differences between the means of *a* and *b* recalls, we employed the *t*-statistic; for the sample sizes here employed, the *t*-values indicate that differences of the obtained magnitude would occur less than once in a thousand cases by chance. (For Group 1, $t = 4.12$, for Group 2, $t = 4.65$; for both groups $p < .001$.) Group 1 recalled 53.1 per cent of all *a* terms and 74.2 per cent of the *b* terms; the corresponding values for Group 2 were 68.8 and 88.5 per cent. The difference in recall of *a* and *b* terms was of about the same magnitude in both groups.

Table 1

RECALL OF *a* AND *b* MEMBERS: MEAN NUMBER CORRECT AND AS A PERCENTAGE OF MAXIMUM POSSIBLE RECALL

	a		*b*	
Condition	*M*	%	*M*	%
Group 1 (4/8)	4.3	53.1	5.9	74.2
Group 2 (8/8)	5.5	68.8	7.1	88.5

The marked preponderance of *b* items over *a* items in a test of free recall offers strong support for the assumption that they are—under the usual conditions of paired associate learning—differentially available for recall.

The bulk of the data of table 1 comes from complete recalls of pairs, which was to be expected; this simply indicates that associative learning took place. The differences just described between *a* and *b* terms comes necessarily from partial recalls. Since these included only those members of a pair that were recalled in the absence of their "partner" (e.g., recall of *a* in the absence of *b*, and vice versa), they may be regarded as "pure" instances of free recall, viz., recall without the aid of association between the recalled item and its corresponding pair member. Table 2 gives the frequencies of partial and paired recalls in each of the two groups.

The data on partial recall clearly show that *a* and *b* terms were differentially available for recall. For Group 1 the *b* terms were about three times as numerous as the *a* terms; Group 2 gave a still greater preponderance of *b* recalls.

3. *Effects of Differential Practice on Recall of* a *and* b *Terms.* The results obtained with Group 1 tell us that the advantage in recall of *b* terms occurs relatively early in learning. The effect of the

Table 2

PARTIAL AND PAIRED RECALLS OF *a* AND *b* TERMS: MEAN NUMBER RECALLED AND PERCENTAGE OF TOTAL RECALL

Conditions	*Paired recalls (a with b)*		*Partial recall (a alone)*		*Partial recall (b alone)*		*Total recall (Total a + b)*	
	M	%	M	%	M	%	M	%
Group 1 (4/8)	6.8	66.3	.8	8.6	2.6	25.1	10.2	100
Group 2 (8/8)	10.2	80.8	.4	3.3	2.0	15.9	12.6	100

additional practice received by Group 2 was to increase significantly the recall of *a* and *b* terms, respectively (a comparison of *b* terms yielded a t of 3.56, $p < .01$; for *a* terms $t = 2.05$, $p = .05$). The added practice in addition maintained the relation between *a* and *b* terms at about the same level as in Group 1. (Of all items recalled by Group 1, *a* terms were given 42.2 per cent of the time, *b* terms 57.8 per cent; for Group 2 the respective percentages were 43.6 and 56.4.)

Conclusion

The implications of these findings for the problem of backward association are evident. The presence of appreciable and significant differences in the recall of *a* and *b* terms under standard conditions of paired associate learning by the method of anticipation lends strong support to the conclusion that the customary technique of testing for backward association is structured so as to favor the measure of forward association. It appears that tests of forward and backward association have been derived from the recall of terms differing in availability.

III. EXPERIMENTAL ANALYSIS OF ITEM AVAILABILITY AND BACKWARD ASSOCIATION

In the present section we shall report an investigation of the empirical bases of backward association. The principal intention is to trace the contribution of the process of recall, or more particularly, of the availability of items, to the phenomena of association.

A. Symmetry under Conditions of Simultaneity

Theory and investigation have not encompassed the range of questions that must be considered in connection with the directionality of functional connections. Investigation, which has been confined to the verbal sphere, has concentrated almost entirely on the role of temporal successiveness. The problem of directionality is, however, relevant to different modalities and conditions, and needs to be placed in broader perspective. Indeed, the issue of symmetry must be considered with reference to functional connections generally, whether these are associative or not.

As a first step we chose to investigate the problem of direction in the visual modality, and under conditions of simultaneity. The stimuli were visual forms, and the perceptual relations between the connected terms were systematically varied. (The relations in question have been previously studied, and were shown to exert strong effects on the ease of connections; see Asch, Ceraso and Heimer, 1960; Asch and Ceraso, unpublished.) Under these conditions the temporal distinction disappears, but the issue of directionality remains. The question is whether the connections between stationary stimulus distributions would be established more strongly in one direction than another as the relations between them are varied.

In the light of the analysis of the preceding section, it is necessary to add that, in the experiments now to be described, the terms that were connected were equally available to recall (Asch, Ceraso, and Heimer, 1960). The respective terms were of approximately equivalent difficulty, and the conditions of learning did not favor some appreciably over others. In brief, we shall study the question of symmetry in stationary visual patterns under conditions of nearly equal availability.

Experiment II. The Constitutive Relation

The starting point of the present inquiry was the discovery of an instance of symmetry in the course of the study of a different problem (*ibid.*). The problem concerned the properties of connections between visual forms when they belonged to the same perceptual unit. We found that the terms in question were equipotential in arousing recall of each other. It is necessary to give a brief account of the procedure and the finding.

The stimuli were visual figures, the contours of which were delineated by means of discontinuous smaller forms (see fig. 1). Each pattern thus had two clearly distinguishable properties: the overall form (F), and its constitutents or modes (M). The relation between form and modes, which may be designated as constitutive, created percepts that were phenomenally unitary. (For a fuller account of the constitutive relation, see *ibid.*, 3–4).

A test of aided recall came after one learning trial. There were two comparable groups. For the test one group was given form alone (drawn in continuous contour), and the second group was shown the modes (drawn in linear array), under instructions to reproduce the missing aspect (see fig. 1). Under these conditions form and mode were equivalent in eliciting recall of each other (see *ibid.*, table 2, experiments 2 and 3).

This finding, which was based on the comparison of group performances, failed to establish, however, whether individual S's did equally well in both directions; the group data might be compatible with the presence of opposed trends in different (or the same) individuals. The following experiment, which was designed to answer this question, tested each S for recall both of forms and modes.

The conditions of learning were those of the previous investigation. The series consisted of ten patterns (see *ibid.*, fig. 3, column 1); they were shown singly, and once, each for four seconds. The S's were instructed to anticipate a test of free recall. The test came three minutes following the exposure of the last stimulus; the interval was occupied with a side task. S's were sixteen undergraduates. For the test of recall all forms were drawn, as before, in continuous contour, and all modes as a set of linear arrays. S's were first shown, singly and in random sequence, the forms of five stimuli and the modes of the other five stimuli, under instructions to draw the missing term on a blank sheet. Subsequently they were shown the modes corresponding to the forms they saw previously, and the forms corresponding to the earlier modes. Thus, during the first part of the recall test, S saw the forms of one half of the series and the modes of the other half; in the second part of the test, the entire series was tested in the other direction. S's were divided into two subgroups; the order in which they were shown the two sets of ten stimuli was reversed.

We shall consider first the results obtained in the first half of the test. Since the results of the two subgroups were closely similar, they were combined. Recall of missing forms was 28, of missing modes 25. The corresponding values in the second half of the test were 26 and 35. The two halves of the test did not differ significantly in recall either of forms or modes ($p > .05$ by the Wilcoxon paired replicates test). On this basis the data of both halves of the test were combined, and the recall of forms and modes across the entire series was compared. There was no significant difference between the

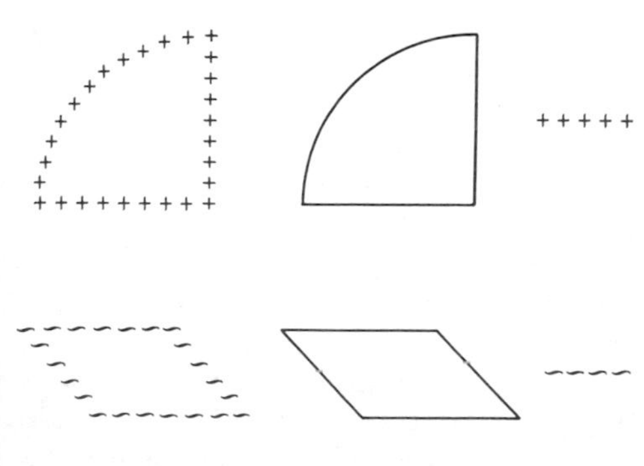

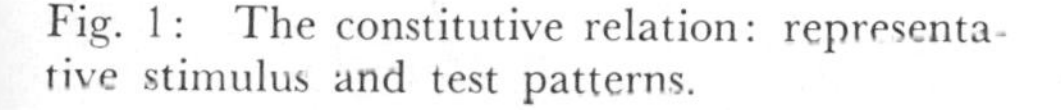

Fig. 1: The constitutive relation: representative stimulus and test patterns.

two kinds of recall in the performance of individual subjects; forms were recalled as frequently as modes ($p > .05$ by the Wilcoxon test).

Although forms and modes were recalled equally, it is necessary to test for the presence of directional effects in individual stimulus patterns. Since each *S* was tested separately for both aspects (form and mode) of each stimulus pattern, it is possible to determine the presence of directionality within a given stimulus pattern. The distribution of correct and incorrect recalls of form (*F*) and modes (*M*) of the same pattern are presented in table 3.

Recall of forms with either a wrong or no mode occurred 16 times; there were 22 instances of correct recall of a mode with either no form or a wrong form. The Wilcoxon test again yielded no significant difference. It is clear, therefore, that there was no consistent directional preference for either forms or modes.

Under the conditions of this experiment (and of those to be described in this section) higher overall recall of one term would be an index of directionality (provided irrelevant conditions, such as differential availability, did not play a part).[6] Instances of correct recall of both terms of a stimulus pattern (the $+F+M$ category of table 3) do, however, raise a question of interpretation. It might appear that such complete recalls are due simply to ease of connection, that they are therefore neutral to the issue under examination, and that a conclusion should rest on the relative frequencies of incomplete recalls (viz., categories 2 and 3 of table 3). This reasoning is, we believe, incorrect. Even the extreme instance, not here realized, of perfect learning would be strong evidence for equidirectionality, since a high level of recall in one direction would not coincide with a high level of recall in the other direction unless symmetry were a fact. Complete recalls are entirely compatible with equidirectionality, while a strong directional preference would necessarily reduce their occurrence. Thus the notion of "ease of connection" cannot explain away equidirectionality. Recall in both directions becomes all the more significant as evidence for symmetry when the level is far from the maximum, as was the case in this experiment.

Table 3

FREQUENCY OF CORRECT RECALL OF FORM (*F*) AND MODE (*M*) OF THE SAME STIMULUS PATTERN

$+F$ $+M$	$+F$ $-M$	$-F$ $+M$	$-F$ $-M$	Total
38	16	22	84	160

[6] Previous experiments (Asch, Ceraso, and Heimer, 1960) have shown that under conditions of free recall, form and mode are reproduced with approximately equal frequency. The possibility of differential availability is, therefore, highly doubtful.

Experiment III. The Relation of Inclusion

The equivalence of form and mode in eliciting recall of each other admits of a number of interpretations. There is, for example, the possibility that membership in one unit is the responsible condition. In order to settle this question we undertook the following experiment.

The stimuli were pairs of visual forms, one included within the boundary of the other (see fig. 2). The pairs selected were heterogeneous; that is, they did not form a unit, the relation between them being that of mere inclusion.

Six patterns were employed. The learning procedure and the method of testing for the two parts of each pattern were identical with those of the previous experiment; the order of testing for inner and outer figures was again counterbalanced. In addition, the use of a given figure in the inner and outer positions was also counterbalanced. There were sixteen *S*'s.

Table 4 gives the distribution of recalls of inner and outer forms corresponding to the same stimulus pattern. Of a

Table 4

FREQUENCY OF CORRECT RECALL OF INNER (I) AND OUTER (O) PARTS OF THE SAME STIMULUS PATTERN

$+I+O$	$+I-O$	$-I+O$	$-I-O$	Total
51	7	14	24	96

total of 123 correct recalls, 65 were of outer and 58 were of inner figures; these were recalled with approximately equal frequency. Fifty-one of the 96 patterns (53 per cent) were correctly completed in both directions, whereas only 21 (about 22 per cent) were partially completed. The preponderance of outer over inner recalls (14 vs. 7 instances) is small when considered in relation to total recall; further, only seven *S*'s contributed to this trend. That most correct recalls (82.9 per cent) came from patterns completed in both directions is, we believe, evidence for equidirectionality. As stated earlier, a clear directional preference should have produced a greater incidence of partial recalls, especially when the total level of recall was not unduly high (65.4 per cent of possible recall). We conclude that there is little evidence for a directional preference when the relation between terms is that of inclusion.

Experiment IV. The Part-Whole Relation

We now sought another perceptual relation that might be more likely to produce asymmetry—the relation of part to whole. The stimuli, illustrated in figure 3, were closed visual units, each containing two clearly distinguished parts—a main part comprising most of the figure, and a smaller, subsidiary part at the right, which completed it. Perceptually the small part appears to belong to the larger, or to qualify it, rather than the reverse.

There were six stimuli, each drawn in India ink on white cardboard. They were shown singly and once, each for a period of four seconds, with no interval between exposures. Again, the instructions were to anticipate a test of free recall. The sequence of stimuli was systematically shifted from *S* to *S*. The *S*'s were twelve Swarthmore undergraduates.

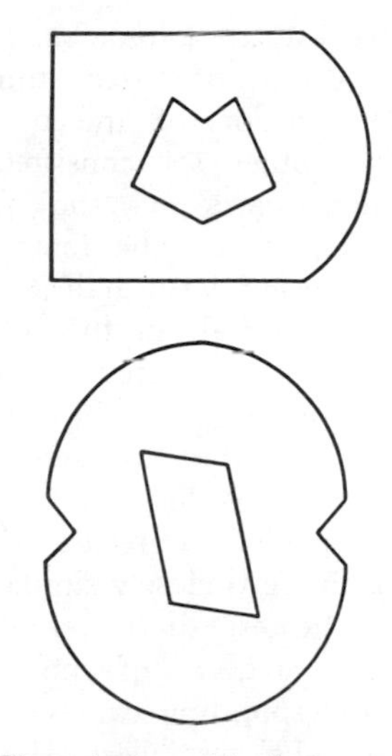

Fig. 2: The relation of inclusion: representative stimulus patterns.

The test of recall, which came after three minutes, followed the pattern of the preceding experiments. The procedure was again that of aided recall; the two parts of each stimulus were drawn on separate cards (see fig. 3). Two sets of recall

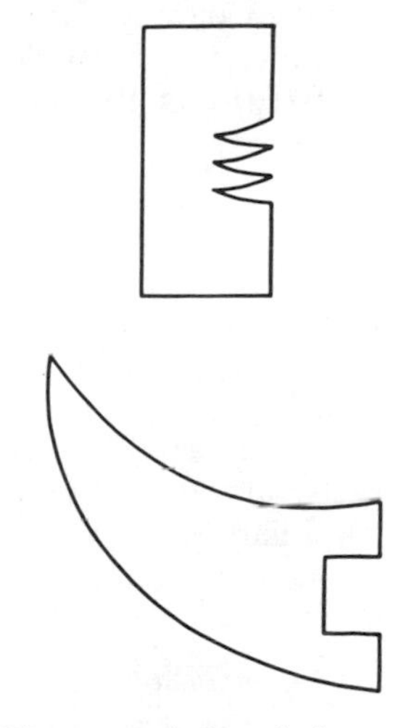

Fig. 3: The part-whole relation: representative stimulus patterns.

stimuli were prepared. One set contained the main portion of three stimuli, and the smaller portion of the other three stimuli. The other set consisted of the corresponding parts of the preceding stimuli. Thus, during the first part, the subject was tested with half the stimuli in one way and half in the other way; the series was then tested in the other direction. Again there were two subgroups, who were given the two sets of recall stimuli in reverse order.

Again we pooled the results of the subgroups, which were closely similar. In the first half of the test, there were 19 recalls of the main part, 16 of the subsidiary part; the corresponding values in the second half of the test were 16 and 19. According to the method of paired replicates, there was no significant difference between the respective recalls in individual *S*'s ($p > .05$).

Since recall for each stimulus was tested twice, once with each part, one can again inquire how often recall in one direction went with, or failed to correspond to, recall in the other direction. The results, summarized in table 5, give the frequencies of each of the possible combinations.

Table 5

FREQUENCY OF CORRECT RECALL OF MAIN (*M*) AND SUBSIDIARY (*S*) PARTS OF THE SAME STIMULUS PATTERN

$+M+S$	$+M-S$	$-M+S$	$-M-S$	Total
27	8	8	29	72

The respective parts of the stimulus distributions elicited recall of each other with equal frequencies. Of the total of 72 stimuli (6×12), 27 produced correct recalls from each part; partial recalls of the main and subsidiary parts were identical in frequency. Again we found no evidence for directionality.

Conclusion

Symmetry or equidirectionality was the rule in each of the preceding experiments. This was the case for the relation of constitution, of inclusion, and for the part-whole relation.[7]

It is evident that the property of unity was not a condition of symmetry; equidirectionality was the prevailing result whether the percepts were unitary or not. These findings are of consequence for a further reason. It is problematic whether connections between the members of a single unit (such as those formed by the relations of constitution and of part and whole) are associative, or whether they differ in process from connections between one unit and another (such as those represented by the relation of inclusion). The present results suggest that functional connections are symmetrical under conditions of simultaneity, whether these are associative or not. (For a discussion of the relation between association and unity, see Asch, Ceraso and Heimer, 1960: 39–43.)

It may seem that symmetry was an obvious and necessary consequence of the given conditions. The patterns appeared simultaneously, so that the observer could

[7] An earlier (unpublished) experiment with Dr. J. Ceraso provides similar evidence for the relation of figure and ground. The stimuli were distributions of the kind illustrated in figure 4; figure and ground differed in color.

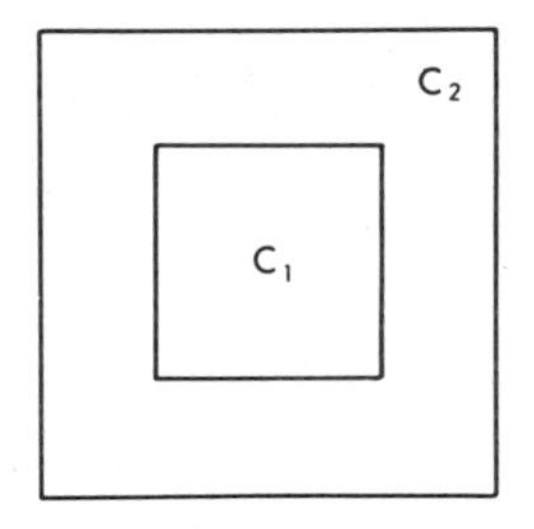

Fig. 4: The figure-ground relation.

The conditions of learning were incidental, the task being to compare the attractiveness of figure and ground colors. A test of matching followed. One group of *S*'s was shown the figure colors singly, and instructed to match them with an array of colors that had belonged to the ground; a second group matched the ground colors against an array of figure colors. The two sets of performances were closely similar and insignificantly different.

move freely between the respective parts or aspects in either direction. This reasoning misses, we believe, an essential point. The perceptual relations in question were not those of equality; they provided definitely ordered modes of perception, which we are apt to describe by giving more emphasis to one of the terms than to the other. The outcome was not obvious; evidence alone could decide whether the given relations might produce directionality.

We have shown that symmetry of connections is, under certain conditions, beyond question. The situations here studied were free of differential availability, but further evidence is needed before concluding that availability alone accounts for the findings. In particular, it is necessary to study those conditions that contain in clear form the relation of temporal succession. This will be the object of the experiments that follow.

B. Availability and Directionality

The rationale of the experiments in this and the succeeding sections grows out of the earlier analysis of the relation of recall to association (see pp. 138–141). We proposed that a decision concerning the presence and magnitude of backward association can be obtained only when availability is controlled. Further, it should be possible to demonstrate that tests of backward association are a function of the level of availability. This was the purpose of the experiment to be now described. Briefly, we varied the conditions of availability for two groups in a paired associate learning situation, and we compared the resulting backward associations. We employed verbal materials, thus reintroducing the distinction between forward and backward association.

Experiment V

Procedure:

Two groups of twelve *S*'s each learned a list of eight pairs of syllables. The pairs, and the method of counterbalancing left and right members of a pair within each group, were identical with those of Experiment I. The other procedures had the aim of equalizing the availability of both members of a pair for one group (Group 1), and of maintaining the standard anticipation conditions for paired associate learning in the other group (Group 2). *S*'s were assigned to Groups 1 and 2 alternately, on the basis of the order in which they appeared for the experiment.

Group 2. The technique of anticipation was that of Experiment I (see pp. 139–140). To repeat briefly, *S* was presented with the *a* item in the memory drum for three seconds followed by a three-seconds exposure of the *a*—*b* pair. He pronounced the *a* item on its appearance and anticipated the *b* item before the exposure of the full pair. The inter-trial interval was six seconds. Except for the final test of recall, the procedure was identical with that of Group 2 of Experiment I.

Group 1. The technique followed with Group 1, which was designed to equalize availability for all items, needs to be elaborated in detail.

(1) *Item Learning.* Prior to associative learning the syllables were learned as items in the following way. The sixteen syllables composing the pairs to be subsequently learned were arranged in three different sequences. Each was presented to *S* on a memory drum for three seconds. during which time he recited the syllable aloud. After each recitation of the sixteen items, *S* was allowed one minute in which to recall as many syllables as possible, and in any order. A different order of syllable presentation was used on each trial within a block of three trials; at the fourth trial the first trial order was repeated. This procedure continued until six recall tests had been completed. The aim was to equalize the recall of items that were subsequently to become *a* and *b* terms.

(2) *Pair Learning.* Since the method of anticipation learning was likely to re-

establish a difference of availability between *a* and *b* terms, a free recall method of pair learning was adopted. Eight pairs of syllables were arranged in the memory drum in three different sequences. (Care was taken to insure that the order existing between members of a pair, as well as between the second member of one pair and the first member of a succeeding pair, did not correspond to any of the three sequences employed during the previous item learning stage.) Each pair was exposed for three seconds; *S* was instructed to recite the pair aloud. Following each recitation trial, *S* was allowed one minute in which to recall the pairs in any order. Learning was to a criterion of one errorless recitation plus two additional learning and test trials.

The eight pairs of syllables ranged from zero to 47 per cent in the Glaze (1928) list of association values. One-third of the group was started on each of the three learning orders respectively.

(3) *Test.* The test of backward association was identical for both groups. It came within one minute after learning to criterion.

To evaluate the magnitude of backward association one must have a measure of forward association obtained under identical conditions. Further, both tests of each pair should ideally be obtained at the same point in time. Since this cannot be achieved practically, the following technique was adopted. All sixteen items were presented to *S* one at a time for three seconds each. *S* was instructed to recite the item out loud and to try to complete the pair, viz., to give the syllable that previously appeared with it. Immediately before the test *S* was informed that some items would come from the left side of a pair, others from the right side, and that he was to complete the pair in either case. The test followed immediately, so that *S* had little or no time in which to rehearse. The sixteen test items appeared in a sequence that differed from those used either in pair-learning or in the initial item learning situation. Left and right items alternated in the test sequence. Of the first eight items, four were *a* terms and four were *b* terms; none of these eight items, however, came from the same pair. The second set of eight items consisted of syllables that had not appeared among the first set of eight. Thus, if an *a* member of a given pair appeared in the first half of the test, its *b* member came in the second half of the test. In this manner each *S* was given the opportunity to respond in both the forward and backward directions with the same pair. The first and second sets of eight test items were exchanged for half the group, so that the order of testing for forward and backward association was equated for all pairs.

Results:

(1) *Item Learning of Group 1.* Of a possible sixteen items, *S*'s recalled on the average 12.7 syllables on the last (viz., sixth trial) of the item training task. No *S*'s scored lower than 10 correct recalls; two *S*'s recalled all items. The training procedure was quite effective in producing high item availability.

(2) *Pair Learning.* Group 1 required a mean of 9.4 trials to errorless recall. Since none of the syllable pairs had a Glaze association value higher than 47 per cent, the relative ease of mastery probably reflects the effectiveness of the initial item training task upon subsequent pair learning.

Group 2 required an average of 15.9 trials to complete mastery of all eight pairs on a single trial by the method of anticipation. The difference between the groups is significant ($t = 3.10$, $p < .01$). Since they were randomly constituted out of the same population, it is highly likely that this difference reflects the changed conditions of learning rather than actual differences in learning ability.

The mean numbers of correct anticipations for all learning trials were 62.6 and

58.3 for Groups 1 and 2, respectively; the difference is not significant ($t = .59$, $p > .5$).[8]

(3) *Test of Forward and Backward Association.*

a. The data for forward (*F*) and backward (*B*) associations of Groups 1 and 2 appear in table 6. Inspection reveals that the order in which a given pair was tested, that is, whether the test came in the first or second half, did not alter the frequency of recall. On this basis we are justified in pooling the data for both halves of the test sequence.[9]

b. The difference between the means of forward and backward recalls of Group 1 is not significant ($t = .71$, $p > .05$). The difference between the Group 2 means, however, favors forward recall and is highly significant ($t = 5.21$, $p < .001$). The ratio of forward to backward recall for Group 2 was 1.56:1, a value comparable to those recently reported (Feldman and Underwood, 1957; Jantz and Underwood, 1958). We conclude that when availability of the members of a pair is equated (as in Group 1), the difference between backward and forward association virtually disappears. On the other hand, conditions of learning (such as those of Group 2) that produce a higher availability of the *b* response members of a pair, produce significant decrements in the measure of backward association.[10]

Table 6

MEAN NUMBER CORRECT FORWARD (*F*) AND BACKWARD (*B*) RECALLS ACCORDING TO THE ORDER IN WHICH THE PARTICULAR DIRECTIONS WERE TESTED

Order of test	*Group 1 Direction required in test*		*Group 2 Direction required in test*	
	F	*B*	*F*	*B*
First	3.0	2.7	3.4	2.2
Second	2.7	2.8	3.6	2.2
Total	5.7	5.4	7.0	4.5

c. The following analysis of individual pairs throws further light on the main question. The recall data for each pair can be categorized in one of three ways:

(1) $+F$ $+B$ represents pairs whose members were correctly recalled in both the forward (*F*) and backward (*B*) direction.

(2, 3) $+F$ alone or $+B$ alone. These represent pairs that were recalled only in the forward ($+F$) or only in the backward ($+B$) direction.

(4) $-F$ $-B$ represents the category of pairs that were not recalled in either direction. The data appear in table 7.

Categories 1 and 3 represent pairs that produced backward associations; categories 1 and 2 are from pairs that produced

[8] Since *S*'s of Group 1 had the advantage of item learning, we anticipated that they would reach the same criterion after fewer anticipations than Group 2, and thus come to the final test with associations of weaker average strength than *S*'s of Group 2. In that case the interpretation of differences between them could become equivocal. This was the reason that *S*'s of Group 1 continued learning and test trials for two trials beyond the point of complete list mastery. This procedure, we see, succeeded in equating the groups in terms of overlearning practice at the point of test for forward and backward association.

[9] In the course of learning, four *S*'s of Group 1 recalled a total of seven pairs in an order opposite to the usual left-right direction. Since these might constitute "backward" practice that would favor correct backward recall in the test, these pairs were excluded from analysis of the test data. Inclusion of these pairs, however, in no way changes the outcome to be reported.

[10] A similar experiment involving six pairs of conjunctions and prepositions failed to show significant differences in backward and forward recall. This was true regardless of whether original learning was by the method of anticipation or by free recall technique. We interpret these findings as effects of the high level of item availability that conjunctions and prepositions enjoy. Thus free recall training could be expected to add little to the already high recall level of these terms.

Table 7

FREQUENCY OF PAIRS YIELDING EVIDENCE OF BACKWARD (B) AND FORWARD (F) ASSOCIATION. THE MEANS AS A PERCENTAGE OF THE TOTAL NUMBER OF PAIRS TESTED ARE ALSO PRESENTED

	1. $+F$ $+B$		2. $+F$ alone		3. $+B$ alone		4. $-F$ $-B$		5. Total pairs*	
	M	%	M	%	M	%	M	%	M	%
Group 1	4.4	59.6	1.3	16.8	1.0	13.5	.8	10.1	7.5	100.0
Group 2	4.1	51.0	2.9	36.4	.4	5.2	.6	7.3	8.0	100.0

*The difference in total pairs between Group 1 and Group 2 is due to the elimination of seven pairs from Group 1 (see p. 146, fn. 9).

forward associations. In Group 1, 73.1 per cent of the pairs gave correct backward association and 76.4 per cent of the pairs gave correct forward association; 10.1 per cent showed no evidence of either forward or backward association. The comparable percentages for Group 2 are 56.2, 87.4 and 7.3. Thus, for Group 1 the proportions of pairs producing backward and forward associations, respectively, were virtually equal, whereas a difference of over 30 per cent existed in Group 2. The present analysis clearly supports the conclusion that decrements in backward association are artifacts of differential item availability.

d. The following analysis (see table 8) brings to the fore another aspect of the findings. Group 1 recalled 74.7 per cent and Group 2, 71.9 per cent of all possible items. That is, total recall was much the same in both groups. The groups differed, however, as we saw, in relative recall of forward and backward items. (The percentages of all possible forward and backward recalls, respectively, were 76.4 and 73.0 for Group 1; the corresponding values for Group 2 were 87.5 and 56.2.) Comparing the two groups, it is apparent that the higher recall of *a* items (backward associations) in Group 1 occurred at the expense of forward recalls. Since the groups did not differ significantly in the number of correct anticipations on original learning, it is unlikely that the poorer recall of forward associates (viz., of *b* terms) in Group 1 can be attributed to differences in original learning. Rather it appears as though total recall were subject to a limiting function of memory, whereby the number of items that can be elicited in an aided recall situation approaches an asymptote.

Table 8

TOTAL RECALL, FORWARD AND BACKWARD RECALL AS A PERCENTAGE OF TOTAL POSSIBLE RECALL

	Group 1	*Group 2*
Total recall	74.7	71.9
Forward recall	76.4	87.5
Backward recall	73.0	56.2

If there were no compensating function of this sort, forward recall, we may assume, would have been identical for both groups (at the level of 87.5 per cent). In this hypothetical situation, Group 1 could exhibit equality of forward and backward association only by eliciting additional backward recalls to the same level. That this was not the case suggests that the process of item recall may follow its own laws, and that its properties may be only indirectly related to the presence of associative connections.

(4) *A Comparison Between Aided and Free Recall.* The difference between backward and forward recall under standard conditions of learning (of Group 2) is, we saw, a function of differential availability. The following analysis goes a step further, and attempts to determine

whether the apparent weakness of backward association under these conditions can be wholly accounted for on the basis of the relative availability of *a* and *b* terms.

To this end we compared Group 2 of the present experiment with Group 2 of Experiment I. Both groups learned identical paired associate lists by the method of anticipation to the criterion of one errorless trial. The treatment of the two groups differed in no way except at the point of final test. Group 2 of Experiment I was tested for free recall of both *a* and *b* terms; Group 2 of the present experiments was tested by the method of aided recall; that is, one of the terms of a pair was given, and recall of the other term was requested. Further, both *a* and *b* terms of the same pair were elicited in the tests; in this manner both groups were given the opportunity to recall all terms. Let us refer to them as Group A-R (Aided Recall) and Group F-R (Free Recall). Since the two groups were run at different times as parts of two different experiments, it is necessary to establish whether they were equivalent in rate of learning. The mean number of trials to reach the criterion of eight correct responses on a single trial was 17.4 ± 7.7 for Group F-R and 15.9 ± 5.7 for Group A-R. The difference is not significant ($t = .52$, $p > .05$). We may conclude that the two groups were equated with respect to learning.

The recall data appear in table 9. (1) Both groups recalled approximately seven out of eight *b* items; the difference is of course not significant.[11] (2) Groups A-R and F-R recalled a mean number of 4.5 and 5.5 *a* items. respectively. The mean difference of 1.0 was not significant ($t = 1.56$, $p. > .1$).[12]

Table 9

ITEMS ELICITED AS A PERCENTAGE OF TOTAL POSSIBLE CORRECT AND MEAN NUMBER CORRECT

	a Terms		*b Terms*		*Total recall*	
	M	%	M	%	M	%
Group A-R	4.5	56.2	7.0	87.5	11.5	71.9
Group F-R	5.5	68.8	7.1	88.5	12.6	78.6

It is of consequence that Group F-R did not differ significantly from Group A-R in recall of *a* items. This finding indicates that the level of backward association obtained in aided recall was essentially equivalent to the recall of the same items as measured by free recall. This evidence is suggestive of the possibility that both outcomes are manifestations of the same underlying process.

Decrements in recall of *a* items under free recall conditions cannot be attributed to a directional associative process.[13] Since

[11] Group A-R shows a loss of 12.5 per cent in recall at this point, which may be due either to failure of the forward association or to loss of the *b* item at the point of recall. That group F-R exhibits a like amount of loss suggests that the decrement of A-R may be attributed to loss of items rather than to a failure in association.

[12] The obtained mean difference of one item may be attributed at least in part to the fact that Group F-R was allowed two minutes in which to recall all sixteen items, while the A-R Group had three seconds in which to anticipate each item. Thus, items having latencies greater than three seconds would not be elicited under A-R conditions, whereas F-R conditions would be more favorable to high latency items.

[13] That free recall of items is not directly related to associative connections between the members of pairs is evidenced by the fact that large numbers of *a* and *b* items are recalled singly (see Groups 1 and 2, Experiment I). To say that free recall is contingent upon the usual associative relation between stimulus and response terms becomes absurd, since an item must first be recalled in order to elicit its corresponding pair member. Once it is admitted that some items may be recalled without the benefit of a stimulus, the door is opened for the possibility that all items are recalled in the same manner. This is not to suggest that free recall occurs in the absence of any associative aid. Rather we suggest that the usual model of aided recall is not appropriate to the free recall situation.

the magnitude of such recall was equivalent under free and aided recall conditions, the possibility that decrements in backward association are themselves not due to a unidirectional associative process must be seriously entertained.

Summary

Under standard conditions of anticipation learning, backward association was significantly weaker than forward association (Experiment V, Group 2). These were also the conditions that produced a greater availability of *b* terms (Experiment I). Thus the standard procedure of anticipation learning favors the measure of forward recall.

Differences of recall of items due to availability were virtually of the same magnitude as the differences between forward and backward association (see Group 2 of Experiments I and V). When the availability of *a* and *b* terms was equalized, forward and backward recall became insignificantly different (Experiment V, Group 1). These results strongly suggest that differences between forward and backward association can be completely accounted for on the basis of differences in availability of items.

C. Successiveness and Directionality

In the preceding experiments the terms to be associated were given simultaneously. To be sure, a factor of direction was present in the verbal learning conditions. Despite their objective simultaneity, there was a distinct temporal difference between the activity upon the first term (the recitation of *a*) and upon the second term (the reading or anticipation of *b*). The simultaneous presence of *a* and *b* may, however, have depressed the effects of directionality, by allowing silent rehearsal, and thus incidental learning, in the backward direction. It seemed appropriate to introduce a condition that would maximize the likelihood of obtaining unidirectional association and minimize contrary tendencies. To this end we devised the following experiment.

Experiment VI

The terms to be associated, which were learned by the method of anticipation, were now presented in strict temporal succession, i.e., they never appeared simultaneously. Further, the items were arranged in triplets (represented as *a—b—c*)—not in pairs, as is customarily the case. By permitting associations to be formed among three terms, it becomes possible to raise the following question. Assuming learning to have taken place in such a manner that, given *a, S* anticipates *b*, and given *b*, he anticipates *c*, what is the effectiveness of *b* in eliciting *c* relative to its effectiveness in eliciting *a*? This, of course, is the question of the relative effectiveness of forward (*b—c*) and backward (*b—a*) association. In the present context, however, forward and backward do not refer to the identical association but to separate associations that share the same term. The present design carries yet other implications for the problem of directionality that will be mentioned later.

Procedure:

There were three phases to the experimental procedure. In order to reduce differences of availability, the items were learned prior to the associative task. They were then associated in triplets. Thereupon comparable groups of *S*'s were tested for forward and backward recall in several ways to be described below.

1. *Item Learning*. Twelve syllables, with Glaze (1928) associative values ranging from zero to 40 per cent, were presented in the memory drum singly with a three-second exposure time, *S* reciting each syllable as it appeared. There were ten such trials; after each trial *S* attempted free recall of all syllables. The interval between trials was eighteen seconds. The sequence of twelve syllables was arranged in three different orders, which were alternated on succeeding trials.

No syllables appeared in the same order that they subsequently had when arranged in triplets.

2. *Learning of Triplets* (a—b—c). The twelve syllables were divided into four sets of three syllables each. Each syllable was presented successively at a three-second presentation rate; the inter-trial interval was eighteen seconds. Learning was by the method of anticipation, with *S* pronouncing (rather than spelling) each item. *S* was instructed to pronounce the first member of each triplet when it appeared, and to anticipate the second member; similarly, the appearance of the second member was the signal to the anticipation of the third member. All incorrect anticipations were corrected by having *S* recite the proper item when it appeared; if an anticipation was correct, *S* did not recite the syllable when it subsequently appeared. This procedure insured that each syllable was recited only once on any given trial.

A horizontal line beneath the third member of each triplet indicated to *S* that the next item to appear would be the first member of a different triplet. To prevent serial effects in the learning of the entire list the sequence of triplets was varied from trial to trial. The order of the triplets for one half of the group was reversed for the other half. The sequence of syllables within the same triplet was varied from *S* to *S*. There were six such orders; each of six *S*'s learned one of the six arrangements of a given triplet. Thus, for the entire group of *S*'s, all three members of a triplet occupied each place in the triplet an equal number of times.

The syllables composing a triplet had the same Glaze association value; the values of the four triplets were zero, 20, 27, and 40 per cent, respectively. Learning was to a criterion of one errorless trial (eight correct anticipations) plus two additional trials. Thereupon the *S*'s were divided into three groups; these differed in the kind of test to which they were exposed. Assignment to these groups was on the basis of learning performance of the same within-triplet sequences. There were twelve *S*'s in Groups 1 and 2, and twenty *S*'s in Group 3.[14]

3. *Tests of Forward and Backward Recall.* There were three conditions of recall; these came immediately after the last learning trial.

(*a*) *Forward Recall* (a—b—c). Group 1 was presented with the first member of a triplet in the memory drum and requested to anticipate the second member before its appearance. At the end of three seconds the second item appeared, and *S* was requested to supply the last item. This procedure was repeated for each triplet separately, with a six-second pause between triplets.

(*b*) *Backward Recall* (c—b—a). Group 2 was tested in a manner similar to Group 1, except that recall was required in the backward direction. The third member of each triplet was the first to appear, followed by the second.

(*c*) *Forward and Backward Recall* (b—c; b—a). *S*'s of Group 3 were presented with the middle item and requested to anticipate the following and preceding syllables. One half of the *S*'s were shown the middle item and were asked to give the last item; after three seconds the identical middle item again appeared, and this time *S* was requested to respond with the first member of the triplet. The other half of Group 3 was requested to respond in opposite order, first with the *a* item and then with the *c* item.

Results:

A. Original Learning. The three groups were essentially equated in the learning of the triplets as a whole, and also in the learning of *a—b* and *b—c* associations, respectively. The mean numbers of trials to criterion were 19.3, 19.6 and 18.8 for Groups 1, 2, and 3, respectively. A

[14] After the initial group of thirty-six *S*'s was completed, eight additional *S*'s were added to Group 3 on account of the high variability manifested in this condition.

simple analysis of variance of the three groups, in terms of number of trials to reach criterion, was insignificant ($F = .28$, $p > .05$). Similarly, the groups did not differ significantly in rate of *a—b* or *b—c* learning, respectively. This was demonstrated by a χ^2 test, which compares the obtained values with those that would occur by chance alone. Thus the median test for the number of errors in *a—b* learning yielded a χ^2 of .53 ($p > .70$); for the number of errors in *b—c* learning χ^2 was 2.06 ($p > .30$). On this basis, the error data in the learning of *a—b* associates for all three groups were combined and compared with the combined data for *b—c* associates; the respective mean numbers of errors were 34.6 and 27.9. This difference is highly significant ($t = 2.16$; $p < .05$) and indicates that there was more overlearning of *b—c* than of *a—b* pairings.

B. Forward and Backward Recall.

a. Groups 1 and 2. The number of correct *a—b* and *b—c* pairings in Groups 1 and 2 are presented in table 10.

Inspection revealed no difference in the number of correct recalls between the two types of pairings within each group (viz., *a—b* vs. *b—c* for Group 1 and *b—a* vs. *c—b* for Group 2).[15] The total number of correct recalls for each group was therefore combined, and the two groups were compared with each other on this basis.

Table 10

MEAN NUMBER CORRECT RESPONSES: GROUPS 1 AND 2

	Group 1			*Group 2*	
	M	S.D.		M	S.D.
$a \to b$	3.4	.62	$b \to a$	3.0	.57
$b \to c$	3.6	.66	$c \to b$	2.9	.85

The mean numbers of total correct recalls were 7.0 and 5.9 for Groups 1 and 2, respectively; this difference was not significant ($t = 1.38$, $p > .1$).

Although the difference lacked significance, forward recall was somewhat higher than backward recall. The percentages of total possible correct recalls were 87.5 and 73.8 for Groups 1 and 2, respectively. The occurrence of some loss in performance in Group 1 at the time of test, relative to the last learning trial, suggests that the test situation itself may be responsible for some disturbance. The greater loss in backward recall of Group 2 might be accounted for, at least partially, if one assumes that the amount of disturbance is a function of the degree to which the test and learning situations differ.

b. Group 3. Forward *b—c* and backward *b—a* recall within Group 3 yielded means of 3.0 and 2.4, respectively. This difference in favor of forward recall is significant ($t = 2.14$, $p < .05$). The percentages of total possible recall were 75.0 in the forward, and 60.0 in the backward direction.

Table 11, which includes the corresponding data from the other experiments, indicates that the level of correct recall was depressed in Group 3. The difference between the means for backward recall in Groups 2 and 3 is significant ($t = 2.00$, $p = .05$); the difference in forward recall in Groups 1 and 3 lacked in forward recall in Groups 1 and 3 lacked significance ($t = 1.93$, $p > .05$). Both comparisons are, however, in the same direction. This finding suggests that the test situation of Group 3 may have produced some general

[15] All *S*'s received initial free recall practice with individual terms. This was done in an effort to equate the terms for item availability. It is quite possible, however, that the method of learning produced a bias that favored recall of *b* and *c* terms over *a* terms, since *a* items were never anticipated in the course of learning, whereas *b* and *c* items were frequently anticipated. Unfortunately we do not have an independent test of this possibility (such as a free recall test). The test results reported above showed no apparent difference in recall of *a* and *b* terms for Group 2; however, reference to table 11 indicates that for Group 3, *c* terms were more frequently recalled than *a* terms. Whether the latter represents the favoring of forward over backward association or higher availability of *c* items remains ambiguous.

Table 11

FORWARD AND BACKWARD ASSOCIATION AS A PERCENTAGE OF TOTAL POSSIBLE CORRECT RESPONSES. THE MEAN NUMBER CORRECT FOR EACH CONDITION IS ALSO INCLUDED

	Group 1		*Group 2*		*Group 3*	
	%	M	%	M	%	M
Forward ($b \rightarrow c$)	89.6%	3.6	—	—	75.0%	3.0
Backward ($b \rightarrow a$)	—	—	75.0%	3.0	60.0%	2.4

interference specific to that situation, but it is not clear why there was greater disruption of backward than of forward recall in the same test situation.

Is the superiority of forward association in Group 3 characteristic of all or most subjects? Of all or most triplets?

a. To start with the latter question, we tallied the number of triplets showing (*a*) a preference for forward over backward associations; (*b*) equality of forward and backward associations; and (*c*) a preference for backward over forward associations. Table 12 gives the results as proportions of all 80 triplets (4×20). Two-thirds of the triplets were equivalent in both directions; triplets favoring the forward direction exceeded those favoring the backward direction by 15 percentage points. By far the greater number of triplets failed to show an advantage in the forward direction.

b. We now tallied the number of correct forward and of backward recalls for each *S*. Of the total sample of twenty *S*'s, ten showed a clear preference for forward recall, eight *S*'s recalled equally in both directions, and two *S*'s favored the backward direction. If directionality were a significant property of the associative process, one might expect a greater proportion of *S*'s to favor the forward direction. The finding that *S*'s manifesting a preference for forward association are equal in number to all others is in direct opposition to the assumption of a unidirectional associative process.[16]

c. Fifty per cent of all *S*'s (of Group 3) favored forward association. We ask now whether this preference extended to all or most triplets. Table 12 gives the results for each half of Group 3. *S*'s with predominantly forward associations exhibited this preference in less than half (42 per cent, or less than two out of four) of the triplets. This analysis offers little evidence for consistent superiority of forward association in any one *S*. Those ten *S*'s who showed no forward preference did so with 95 per cent of all triplets. In all, the results strongly suggest that superiority of

Table 12

PREFERENCE FOR FORWARD AND BACKWARD ASSOCIATIONS (IN PER CENT)

	Triplets		
	F > B	F = B	F < B
Ten *S*'s showing forward preference	42.5%	55.0%	2.5%
Ten *S*'s showing no forward preference	5.0%	80.0%	15.0%
All *S*'s	23.7%	67.5%	8.7%

[16] It may be suggested that a more convincing argument for the absence of a directional process would have been obtained had the number of *S*'s showing a higher frequency of forward over backward associations been equal to the number of *S*'s yielding a greater frequency of backward over forward associations. This suggestion has merit; however, one must note that the eight *S*'s manifesting equivalence of directionality represent negative instances of the assumption of a directional process favoring forward association. The *S*'s falling into the category of directional equivalence cannot therefore be disregarded.

forward association was not a function of specific characteristics of learners or materials.

Summary

Forward and backward associations were compared in sets of three terms (*a—b—c*), when these appeared in temporally successive order and were preceded by practice in recall of the items. There was a tendency for forward recall to be superior; of two major comparisons, one reached and the other fell short of statistical significance. The difference in favor of forward association was of the order of 15 per cent. Detailed analysis showed that the preponderance of forward associations was not a consistent characteristic of the learners.

D. Backward Learning and Directionality

The measure of backward association on which we have relied in the preceding experiments consisted of a test obtained on a single trial following a period of learning. In the following experiment we shall employ a more inclusive measure of backward association, namely, reversal learning up to a criterion. This procedure will permit us to focus in greater detail upon the two alternative explanations of backward association effects: (1) that backward learning literally requires the formation of a new set of associations, in addition to those already formed in the forward direction; and (2) that backward learning does not require the formation of new associations (but rather an increase in the availability of the original *a* terms). According to the latter alternative, reversal learning should be rapid; the first alternative must predict a slow rate of reversal acquisition.

Since there is no exact specification of what constitutes slow and rapid backward learning, a test of the alternatives stated above cannot be made directly. We can, however, compare the rate of reversal learning with the rate of continued forward learning by an equivalent group.

Experiment VII

Procedure:

There were two groups of twelve *S*'s each. Item availability practice preceded paired associate learning in both groups. After reaching identical levels of performance on *a—b learning, S*'s of Group 1 began *b—a* learning for a period of ten trials; *S*'s of Group 2 continued with ten trials of *a—b* learning. This procedure permits a comparison of forward and reverse learning for groups matched in terms of original *a—b* practice. Upon completion of the final ten *a—b* trials, *S*'s of Group 2 also learned the reversed (*b—a*) pairs to a criterion of one perfect recitation. Comparison of the rates of reverse learning in Groups 1 and 2 will allow a determination of the effect of differential amounts of *a—b* learning on the rate of reverse learning. The sequence of steps is summarized in table 13.

The materials consisted of twelve nonsense syllables; each of the Glaze (1928) association values of zero, 7, 20, 33, 40, and 47 per cent was represented by two syllables.

1. *Item Learning.* The twelve syllables were arranged on a Stoelting memory drum in three separate sequences. Each syllable was presented for three seconds, with a negligible inter-item interval. *S* recited each syllable aloud with the intention of retaining each for a free recall test that followed each trial. After each complete recitation of the list, *S* was given one minute in which to recall as many items as possible, and in any order. This procedure was followed for ten trials.

As noted above, the item sequence was varied on three successive trials, whereupon the first sequence was repeated. Special care was taken to eliminate the successive occurrence of items which were to appear as pairs on the subsequent paired associate task.

2. *Initial Paired Associate Learning.* The twelve syllables were formed into six pairs. The members composing a pair

Table 13

SCHEDULE OF FORWARD AND BACKWARD LEARNING

	1.	*2.*	*3.*	*4.*
Group 1	Item learning: 10 trials	*a—b* learning: One errorless recitation plus 2 trials	*b—a* learning: 10 trials	
Group 2	Item learning: 10 trials	*a—b* learning: One errorless recitation plus 2 trials	*a—b* learning: 10 trials	*b—a* learning: One errorless recitation

were of identical association values. As stated earlier, no pair of syllables had appeared in immediate succession during the preceding period of item practice.

The procedure was a modified form of paired associate learning. To reduce the likelihood of specific backward practice in *a—b* learning, the members of a pair were never exposed jointly. The *a* term always appeared alone in the left portion of the memory drum window, followed by the *b* term, which also appeared alone, in the right portion of the window. Each syllable was exposed for three seconds with negligible inter-item intervals. The inter-trial interval was eighteen seconds.

S pronounced the *a* syllable on its appearance and attempted to anticipate the *b* syllable. If he anticipated the *b* term correctly, he did not again recite it on its appearance; he did so, however, when he either failed to anticipate or did so incorrectly.

The pairs were presented in three different orders. In each group the *a* and *b* terms were interchanged for one-half of the *S*'s. Thus, for each group as a whole, each term appeared equally often in the *a* and *b* positions.

Both groups learned to a criterion of one errorless recitation of all six pairs, plus two additional trials.

3. *Subsequent Paired Associate Learning.* (*a*) After reaching criterion, Group 1 *S*'s were told to relax for a moment; they were informed that the order of appearance of the pair members would be reversed and that the learning procedure would remain the same in all other respects. There followed ten trials of reverse (*b—a*) learning. This completed the experiment for *S*'s of Group 1. (*b*) Upon reaching criterion *S*'s of Group 2 were also told to relax for a moment, and were informed that they were to continue learning in exactly the manner they had been following up to that point. There followed ten additional trials of *a—b* learning. The time interval, including instructions, between the end of original pair learning and the beginning of subsequent *a—b* or *b—a* learning was approximately thirty seconds for both groups. (*c*) *S*'s of Group 2 began *b—a* learning thirty seconds after reaching their final *a—b* learning trial. This continued to the point of one errorless recitation of all six pairs.

Results:

1. *Item Learning.* Groups 1 and 2 were equivalent in the recall of items during the phase preceding paired associate learning. The mean number of correct recalls per subject per trial was 7.8 for Group 1, and 7.2 for Group 2. These two groups were also equivalent in recall of *a* and *b* terms, respectively. The mean numbers of *a* items correctly recalled per subject per trial were 3.9 and 3.6 for Groups 1 and 2, respectively; the corresponding means for the *b* terms were identical, viz., 3.9 and 3.6. The latter result is relevant in

the light of evidence (Feldman and Underwood, 1957) that familiarity with *b* items facilitates subsequent paired associate learning more than familiarity with *a* items.

2. *Initial a—b Learning.* The mean numbers of trials to a criterion of six correct anticipations on a single trial were 12.5 and 15.0 for Groups 1 and 2, respectively. The corresponding means for the number of correct anticipations to the criterion here employed (one errorless trial plus two trials) were 44.6 and 53.2. In neither case was the difference significant as measured by *t*-tests, ($p > .05$ in each case). We may conclude that the groups did not differ in rate of *a—b* learning.

3. *Comparison of Forward and Backward Learning.* The following four indices will be used in comparing reverse and forward learning (at stage 3): number of correct responses on trial 1; number of trials to criterion; number of errors to criterion; and number of errors per trial per *S*. The obtained values appear in table 14.

The differences between each set of means of Groups 1 and 2 were significant at the .05 level or better. The results are uniform in indicating the superiority of forward over backward learning after comparable stages of *a—b* practice have been reached.

Table 14

Comparison of Backward and Forward Learning (Stage 3)

	Mean correct: trial 1	*Mean trials to criterion*	*Mean errors to criterion*	*Mean errors per trial per subject*
Group 1: backward learning	3.7	4.9	7.6	1.4
Group 2: forward learning	4.8	2.7	3.2	.7

To evaluate the findings it is necessary to examine the magnitude of the obtained differences.

(1) Backward association was at a level of 61 per cent (3.7 correct recalls out of a possible 6) within one minute after completion of forward learning. Forward association at the same point of time was at a level of 80 per cent (4.9 correct recalls out of 6). Thus, prior to specific reversal learning, backward and forward association differed by 20 per cent. This difference is statistically significant, but in absolute terms it is indeed small. We have to conclude that forward practice is extremely efficient in producing backward association. By far the greater amount of reversal had been achieved before specific reversal learning.

(2) The mean number of trials to reach criterion was 4.9 and 2.7 for the *b—a* and *a—b* conditions, respectively. The difference of 2.2 trials represents the amount of practice necessary to produce complete *b—a* learning, beyond the point at which *a—b* learning would be complete. Although this difference is statistically sig-

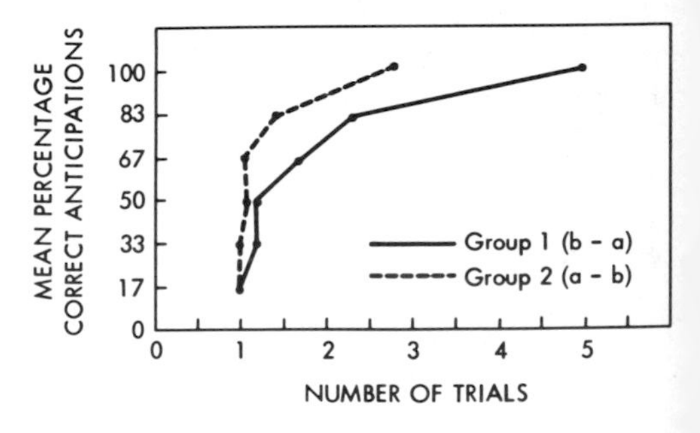

Fig. 5: Comparison of the rates of forward (*a—b*) and backward (*b—a*) learning: mean percentage correct as a function of trials. Groups 1 and 2 received approximately the same amount of prior practice preceding backward learning. The horizontal distance between points indicates differences in rate of acquisition between the two groups. For example, in order to reach the level at which 83 per cent of all *b* items were correctly anticipated, Group 1 required a mean of 2.3 trials, whereas Group 2 reached this level in 1.4 trials.

nificant, it is again noteworthy that so few trials sufficed to overcome the initial difference. The acquisition curves plotted in figure 5 illustrate this point. Interpolation indicates that when forward learning was at a level of 100 per cent, *b—a* learning was slightly above the 83 per cent mark. Thus, comparison with a suitable control measure shows that backward association was remarkably high.

(3) The error scores tell much the same story. Errors to criterion at stage 2 were expressed as a percentage of errors to criterion at stage 1. The mean per cent values were 29.6 for Group 1, and 10.8 for Group 2. Thus both groups showed a large reduction in errors during stage 2 acquisition, the greater reduction occurring with continued forward learning.

4. *The Effect of* a—b *Overlearning on* b—a *Acquisition.* Group 2 continued with *a—b* learning for ten additional trials; all but two *S*'s subsequently learned the *b—a* pairs to criterion. Groups 1 and 2 thus differed substantially in amount of *a—b* practice prior to *b—a* learning. A comparison between the groups may thus permit an estimate of the effect of *a—b* overlearning on *b—a* learning.

The two groups did not differ in original *a—b* learning, as measured by number of trials to criterion or number of correct anticipations. Mean trials to criterion for Groups 1 and 2 were 14.5 and 16.0, respectively ($t = .58$, $p > .5$); the corresponding mean correct anticipations were 44.6 and 51.1 ($t = 1.08$, $p > .2$). They differed markedly, of course, in amount of *a—b* practice. Group 1 averaged 44.6 correct forward anticipations before *b—a* learning commenced; the corresponding value for Group 2 was 106.2.

The acquisition curves for the two groups appear in figure 6. Group 1 required an average of 4.9 trials to criterion; Group 2 reached the same criterion in 3.0 trials. The difference in 1.9 trials is significant ($t = 2.40$, $p < .05$).

Increasing *a—b* practice thus had some effect upon the rate of *b—a* learning.

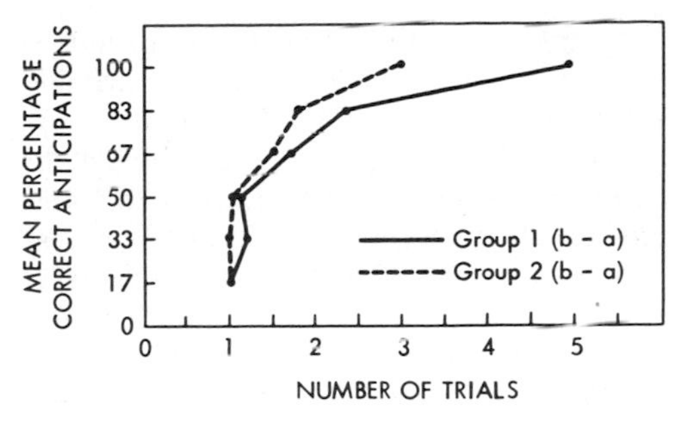

Fig. 6: Comparison of rates of backward (*b—a*) learning after two degrees of forward practice: mean percentage correct as a function of trials. Group 1 ($N=12$) had a mean number of 44.6 correct anticipations on forward learning (*a—b*) prior to the backward practice. The horizontal distance between points indicates differences in rate of acquisition between the two groups. For example, in order to reach the level at which 83 per cent of all *b* items were correctly anticipated, Group 1 required a mean of 2.3 trials, whereas Group 2 reached this level in 1.8 trials.

However, in view of the large differences in such practice between the two groups, the total effect appears rather small.[17] Indeed, the mean number of correct anticipations on the first trial of *b—a* learning was 3.7 for Group 1 and 4.4 for Group 2; this difference was not significant ($t = 1.4$, $p > .1$). The effect of prior practice is apparently most evident at the later stages of list mastery.

Summary

The results of the present experiment do not permit an unequivocal conclusion concerning the identity of forward and backward association. Nevertheless, the high level of backward association which is present immediately after forward prac-

17 The slight effectiveness of *a—b* overlearning on *b—a* acquisition is commensurate with the thesis that backward learning is a function of item availability.

The results also suggest that sheer frequency of recitation may serve to increase the availability of *a* terms for subsequent backward recall, but that this procedure is probably not as efficient as direct recall practice with the items.

tice, and the rapid rate of acquisition in subsequent backward learning, provide substantial support for the identity hypothesis. To account for the absence of complete equality between forward and backward performance it is again necessary to consider the role of availability. Although the procedure of item learning tended to equalize the availability of *a* and *b* terms, subsequent anticipation practice may well have reinstated it to some degree. It is for further investigation to decide whether this was the case, or whether differential availability can account completely for the moderate amount of asymmetry here obtained.

IV. DISCUSSION

Associations, we have found, are completely symmetrical over a wide range of conditions (Experiments II-V). Under certain other conditions (Experiments VI and VII) there was evidence of some asymmetry in favor of the forward direction, but so limited in amount as not to obscure the substantial equivalence of directions. Even if one accepts the latter findings without question, a point to which we shall return, the trend of the results compels a revision of current conceptions about associative directionality.

A. The Authenticity of Backward Association

These findings must first meet certain frequently raised general objections against the validity of backward association.

(1) One is the assertion, mentioned earlier, that backward association is a product of direct backward practice. Our observations furnish no support for this interpretation. In all present experiments employing the method of anticipation, the *S*'s were carefully questioned at the conclusion regarding the possibility of silent rehearsal in a direction opposite to that in which the items were presented during learning. No *S* reported rehearsal of backward associations. Most *S*'s were surprised to hear the instructions that preceded the backward association tests, and expressed doubts of their ability to produce backward recall. The evidence we were able to obtain fails to give any indication in support of direct backward practice. There remains the possibility that such practice did occur but was not detectable by the *S*'s. It is evidently difficult to rule out this eventuality; if it did occur, it is most unlikely that such practice, which would necessarily be incidental, could account for the high levels of backward association obtained between nonsense syllables. We must conclude that direct backward practice had little or no effect on backward association.

(2) When the associative task is intentional, the learner frequently rehearses a pair repeatedly to himself in the forward direction. In such rehearsal the *b* item precedes as well as follows the *a* item (e.g., *a*—*b*—*a*—*b*) in close contiguity. We may not conclude, though, that such forward practice could account for the present results. Woodworth (1915), and subsequently Thorndike (1932), showed that the "belongingness" of members in the same unit is essential in the formation of an association, and that the effect of sheer contiguity is strikingly weak. Forward practice of the present kind is perhaps best represented as (*a*—*b*) (*a*—*b*). If forward associations were formed between *b* and *a* under these conditions, they were weaker than associations within the pair, and cannot account adequately for the obtained backward effects.

(3) There is a kind of backward recall that cannot be taken as evidence of backward association. When, for example, one tries to recite backward a series of numbers that one has heard, one keeps the series mentally in the order in which one heard it, only "reading it off" in the reverse order. In that case the reversal of direction depends on an intellectual operation that does not touch the associative question. We need to ask whether such

operations entered in the present experiments. It should be evident at once that this could not easily occur under the conditions here studied, if for no other reason than that the task required the recall not of one set but of items from a number of different sets (or pairs). No *S* attempted to run through the pairs in memory, and thus to find the *a* that had been paired with a given *b*. Even if they had tried, the time limits would have nullified such efforts. But further, *S*'s uniformly reported upon questioning that the *b* term brought up the *a* term without intermediation.

(4) What of the further possibility that backward recall consisted of a movement from the *b* term to the beginning of the pair? This was the proposal of Müller and Pilzecker (1900), who suggested the operation of an "initial reproductive tendency," or a tendency for each part of an associated sequence to reproduce first the initial member and subsequently the other members in their proper order. The evidence for this interpretation was derived from the learning and recall of nonsense syllable triples (*a—b—c*). Following a period of practice the last syllable of each triplet was given as the stimulus, under instructions to respond with the first syllable that came to mind. Under these conditions, the *a* member was recalled first in the majority of instances (56 per cent), the *b* syllable was recalled first far less frequently (17 per cent). More recently, G. Meyer (1939), who repeated and extended the investigation of Müller and Pilzecker, obtained very similar results.

Concerning the interpretation of Müller and Pilzecker, one can say simply that it presupposes backward association, since it implies the capacity to find one's way from a later to an earlier part of a sequence. In a subsequent discussion Koffka questioned the associationistic bias of the Müller and Pilzecker interpretation, proposing instead that part of an associated series "tends to establish the whole process that gave rise to the whole trace" (1935: 567). In illustration he cited the tendency to recall an entire expression when a part is given (e.g., Hesperus → The Wreck of the Hesperus). In effect, Koffka proposed that recall takes the form of a part-whole contact (e.g., $c \rightarrow abc$), and that the reference to backward association may be misleading. This was also the interpretation adopted by Meyer. The evidence Koffka offered is not decisive for the present problem. His illustrations are convincing because they were mainly drawn from meaningful contents. In such instances the terms in question are associated with each other via a meaning; consequently each term could well produce recall of the meaning, and thus of the missing terms in the order that corresponds to the meaning.

What shall we say, though, of the findings of Müller and Pilzecker, and of Meyer, with nonsense syllables? In this connection Meyer has argued forcibly that the usual associative interpretation would imply the paradoxical conclusion that remote backward associations are stronger than immediate backward associations. The findings of these investigators are, we believe, not conclusive. They imposed particular rhythms on the sequence during learning, in contrast to the procedure we followed. Meyer explicitly recognized that "the temporal organization is as much a part of the complex as are the syllables themselves" (1939: 279), and that it was probably reinstated during recall, thus contributing to the recall of the items. There is reason to hold that temporal organization is not an associative phenomenon, at least not of the same order as associations between syllables. If so, temporal organization may have played a role analogous to that of meaning. Still a further question must be raised concerning the technique of these investigations. They asked repeatedly for the recall of the members of sequences in the order in which they came to mind, when these were learned in the same rhythm. Under these conditions it was quite probable that attitudinal factors played a decisive role. The subjects may have assumed that it was preferable to respond in an orderly way, or in accordance with the original sequence. Even if this was not their initial assumption, they may well have followed this procedure once they hit upon it.

Our own findings were based on systematic comparisons of forward and backward recall. As far as could be ascertained, there was no detectable difference between the movement from *b* to *a* and from *a* to *b*. The available evidence provides no support for the view that the operation of backward recall is in any respect different from that of forward recall.

B. Conditions Favoring Forward Recall

In several of the preceding experiments there was no difference between forward and backward recall. Other experiments continued to show a superiority of forward recall, although of limited amount. Generally, when a difference did develop between the two directions, it favored forward recall. It is therefore necessary to outline some of the possible reasons for the latter effect.

One obvious interpretation is that under certain, as yet unspecified, conditions, associations are moderately stronger in the forward direction. One must also consider the role of nonassociative, or performance, factors.

(1) The procedure here adopted for equating item availability was to practice recall of items prior to paired associate learning. Two methods of paired associate learning were then employed, which produced different final results. When pairs were learned by the method of free recall, forward and backward recall were equivalent (Experiment V, Group 1). However, paired associate learning by the method of anticipation continued to show an advantage for forward recall (Experiments VI and VII). These results follow consistently, we believe, from the analysis underlying this investigation. Although item learning equalized item availability, subsequent anticipatory learning established a higher availability of *b* terms. Under these conditions the advantage in favor of forward recall tended to persist although its magnitude was reduced. On the other hand, free recall learning, which directed *S*'s to the anticipation of both *a* and *b* items, maintained equal availability up to the final test.

(2) Many *S*'s viewed the backward recall task as very difficult and, as noted earlier, were doubtful of their success with it. These attitudinal circumstances may have acted to depress backward recall.

(3) Yet another circumstance that may have favored forward association has to do with mnemonic devices and other approaches to paired associate learning. To illustrate, occasionally an *S* might associate only a portion of the *a* term with its partner. Thus, he might associate the letter *P* of the syllable FIP with NUV. In the test for backward recall, he may indeed offer *P* as the response, which would be scored as wrong.

Although the preceding factors have not been investigated directly in the present context, they must be taken into account in any evaluation of backward and forward association. We consider it reasonable to suppose that they account for the residue of differences that we have found.

Conditions of Availability

There is, we noted earlier, a considerable lack of consistency in the literature concerning the relative strength of forward and backward association (see p. 138). The interpretation here advanced demands that variations in the level of backward associations be a function of differences in the level of item availability. It should therefore be possible to demonstrate this relation by an examination of the body of investigations of backward association. Unfortunately, this cannot be done exhaustively, mainly because there are diverse conditions of availability, and adequate accounts of them are often lacking. Below we shall attempt to outline some of the determinants of availability that might affect measures of backward association.

1. *Item Familiarity.* It is probable that the more familiar an item the more available it is to recall. Backward recall should therefore increase with familiarity.[18] On this basis we may deduce certain more particular conclusions. (*a*) Meaningful materials, which we assume to be highly available, should produce high backward recall. The results reported earlier with paired conjunctions and prepositions are in accord with this formulation (see fn. 10). Going in the same direction are findings of an experiment by Thornton (reported by Feldman and Underwood, 1957) with adjective pairs. Under these conditions of high familiarity, backward recall was 83 per cent of maximum.[19] (*b*) Jantz and Underwood (1958) and Hunt (1959) have reported that backward recall increases with increase in association value of the terms. Item availability may underlie this relationship. At present we know of no evidence bearing on this point; it should be possible to demonstrate whether association value is a function of availability. (*c*) It follows necessarily that backward recall will be superior to forward recall if the former items are more available than the latter. At least one investigation (Stoddard, 1929) has reported such results for associations between English words and their French equivalents. This finding serves to underline further the necessity of the distinction between association and recall. In the absence of this distinction, the paradoxical conclusion would follow that backward association can be stronger than forward association.

Each of the preceding proposals follows from the general proposition that measures of association are a function of availability. The more particular conclusion is that variations in availability will, regardless of their cause, produce corresponding variations in measures of backward association.

2. *Conditions of Learning.* Since we have dwelt on this point extensively, it will suffice to say that availability is a function of methods of learning. The method of anticipation virtually insures the higher availability of *b* terms (see Experiments I and V). Free recall learning of pairs, on the other hand, tends to equate *a* and *b* terms for availability (see Experiment V).

3. *Conditions of Recall.* Forward and backward recall may differ in latency, the latter requiring more time. Thus, studies allowing more time for recall should show relatively high degrees of backward recall and closer equality with forward recall. According to Feldman and Underwood (1957), unlimited recall time increased backward recall measurably. It has been customary to consider latency an index of associative strength, an interpretation that supports the accepted accounts of forward and backward association. This is to slight the possibility that response latency is a function of item availability, and as such is independent of strength of association. There is need of a direct study of this proposition.

[18] Familiarity refers to a range of experimental conditions that may affect availability differentially. The preceding experiments with paired associate learning employing the method of anticipation provided one demonstration. Although *a* and *b* items were seen and pronounced with equal frequency, the *b* items, which were also anticipated, were more recallable (Experiment I). There was also evidence of increased availability of *a* items with an increase of trials, an indication of the effect of recitation (Experiment I, Groups 1 and 2).

[19] A somewhat separate question concerns the effect of a *relation* of meaning between associated terms on directionality. If, as we have proposed, associative symmetry is the general rule, a relation of meaning is not a further condition of symmetry. However, such a relation does provide an additional important means of recall, namely, from the given term to the meaning in question, and thus to the missing term (see p. 156).

It is in order to mention at this point another source of error at times encountered in the measurement of backward association. A statement of the magnitude of backward association makes sense only when the level of forward association can also be given. Further, these measures must be obtained at the same point of time. Consequently the comparison of forward association on the criterion trial with a subsequent test of backward association is open to question. This is particularly so in the light of the well-known fact that when a test of forward association follows directly after criterion, there is usually a decrement relative to the criterion score (Hilgard, 1951; Underwood, 1954). It is at once apparent that the procedure of testing first for forward association and subsequently for backward association exaggerates the level of the former.[20]

4. *Temporal Successiveness and Directionality.* The two experimental conditions that produced a somewhat weaker level of backward than of forward associations enforced a strictly successive mode of presentation of the stimuli (Experiments VI and VII). It is not certain that temporal directionality was responsible for this outcome; earlier we suggested that the procedure of learning in these experiments may have tended to produce differential availability in favor of the forward direction. Unfortunately we have no evidence to compare these findings with those that employ the more traditional procedure of simultaneous exposure of pairs. If temporal directionality did play a part, it would also be necessary to conclude that it failed to prevent a strikingly high level of backward association. There is need of further investigation, especially of the possibility that temporal order is effective insofar as it determines the degree of organization of units (see pp. 160–161).

C. Associative Symmetry and Direction

The present findings establish that direction is not carried by the associative process. Association provides the conditions for going from either term to the other; it does not prescribe the direction that will be followed in a given instance. The direction in which one will actually proceed cannot therefore come from symmetrical associations. It follows from the principle of associative symmetry that association and order have distinct sources, and that the processes underlying direction must be sought outside the associative bond.

The separation that this investigation has established between facts of order or direction and association proper is in contradiction with the central postulate of associationism that all cognitive processes are associative. It has a direct bearing on the scope of associative functions, and on their relation to other forms of cognition. It now becomes necessary, for example, to consider the proposition that, in general, phenomena of order—spatial, temporal, or logical—are not products of association.[21] The failure to distinguish between association and direction is clearly traceable to the central postulate just referred to.

The symmetry of associations should increase notably the possibilities of cognitive functioning. However, investigators

[20] Experiment V (Group 2) illustrates this point. Backward association following the criterion trial was 56.2 per cent of maximum possible recall; if forward recall had been assumed to be at the level of 100 per cent, it would be correct to state that backward association was 56 per cent of forward association. Actually the level of forward association following the criterion trial was 87.5 per cent; the latter value alone qualifies as the basis for an estimate of backward association. When the proper base line is used to measure the magnitude of backward association, the latter will be more substantial than if this necessary precaution is omitted.

[21] An investigation by Dr. B. Kutner (1947) and the first author provided evidence for recall of the temporal order of a sequence of events when these were not associatively connected.

in the associative tradition drew the opposite conclusion when they considered the possibility of associative symmetry, tending to see departure from unidirectionality as a source of disorganization or maladaptiveness. Thus McGeoch stated: "If forward and backward connections [in serial learning] were formed in equal degree, series would function with equal readiness in either direction and might become a battleground of associative interference" (1942: 90). The basis of this statement is the assumption that specific chaining of connections alone provides for orderly functioning, and that there are no other cognitive operations that secure order.

Cognitive operations (and actions) must, to be sure, occur in a specific order if they are to be appropriate. It does not, however, follow that the ability to think of them in any other order obscures our knowledge of the order in which they did or should occur. One can entertain the thought that the punishment precedes the crime without the risk of becoming confused about the actual sequence of such events. The association experiment itself provides evidence relevant to this point. Associations can be recalled backward and forward, yet the learner has a remarkably good knowledge of their actual past order. To cite one instance from the present investigation, *S*'s in one experiment (Experiment I, Group 1) were asked to state, after learning and a test of free recall, whether the items they recalled had been left or right members of their pair. Of a total of 163 recalls, 160 (98 per cent) were correctly identified. There is, to say the least, no incompatibility between the ordering of mental events and associative symmetry.

The conclusion we draw is that symmetrical associations increase the latitude of psychological functioning without necessarily incurring the danger of confusion. In this respect associations share a general property of cognitive processes. In thinking, too, we traverse the available terrain in different and opposed directions. The cause recalls the effect, but the effect also brings the cause to mind. In working on a geometrical problem the succeeding steps bring us to the goal, but we also work back from the goal to the required steps. Associative operations are far more limiting than thinking operations; within these limits, however, they possess a flexibility that characterizes cognitive functioning in general.

D. Directionality in Conceptual Relations

Psychological symmetry may be a function of many processes, not of association alone. In what follows we shall consider briefly the problem of symmetry in connection with conceptual relations, and we shall confine ourselves to a particular and simple relation.

Let R stand for a given relation between two terms, a and b, in that order; we may designate the proposition "a stands in relation R to b" as aRb. The latter implies the converse relation between b and a, which may be expressed as $bR'a$. Our concern is with the psychological step from R to R'. When the relation is that of equality, R and R' are identical, both logically and psychologically, as in the statement "a and b are friends." Is the converse also given psychologically when R is asymmetrical?[22] The answer is, we believe, in the affirmative. To assert that "a is taller than b" is to imply, both logically and psychologically, that b is shorter than a; similarly, "Brutus killed Caesar" implies that "Caesar was killed by Brutus." Indeed, the ability to infer the converse is the criterion for deciding whether the relation R was understood. To be sure, the relation and its converse

[22] The reader must distinguish between psychological symmetry and symmetry as a logical property of aRb. The latter may be symmetrical (e.g., a equals b), asymmetrical (e.g., a is taller than b), or nonsymmetrical (e.g., a is a brother of b). The property of logical symmetry does not decide whether the corresponding psychological process is symmetrical; the relation between these is the question under discussion.

place the emphasis differently, but each is available to us when we make either assertion, and the choice we make is according to the context. The conclusion is that symmetrical and asymmetrical relations of the form *aRb* are psychologically reversible. This is a consequence of the fact that *R* mutually implicates the terms in question, that the relation cannot be asserted for either of the terms alone.

There are instances that are apparently contradictory. A child will call a given man his uncle, but be at a loss to state his own relationship to him. In this case, however, the term "uncle" functions in part as a proper name, to which the preceding assertions do not apply. If the child knows how the uncle is related to him, he knows in what relation he stands to the uncle. To turn to a far different region, one-sided relations are well known in the interpersonal sphere. One may be strongly sensitive to the unfriendliness of another person without realizing one's own contribution to it. The point of view is here of importance, and obviously it often fails to do justice to all the parties. In such instances, too, it is clear that "he is hostile to me" also asserts "I am the object of his hostility." The example involves, in addition, correlative relations, which we do not here consider; the hostility of the other may arouse distrust or hurt. A proper analysis requires finally a distinction between the objective relations in question and those that are phenomenally represented. The latter would, we believe, offer no contradiction to the main point. We conclude that logically asymmetrical (and symmetrical) relations of the form *aRb* are psychologically reversible.[23]

[23] It may be well to note finally that associative and logical relations raise quite different issues. The associative task concentrates on the noting and subsequent recovery of particular terms; in the logical relation the terms are subsidiary. Similarly, the conversion of a logical relation requires an inference, not so a backward association.

E. Identity of Forward and Backward Association

The principle of unidirectionality asserts that an association between *a* and *b* and between *b* and *a* are distinct events, that they are two associations. Cason has correctly seen this, stating that where there is backward association "the practice has been in *two* directions, and *two* associations have been formed" (1926: 226). What conclusion follows on this score from the principle of associative symmetry? The latter asserts that forward and backward associations are inseparable, that they are formed as part of one process, and that they are of equal strength. In short, it states a relation of equivalence between them. Equivalence is not necessarily, however, identity.

The last experiment reported in this investigation (Experiment VII) represented an effort to deal with this problem. We reasoned that a certain additional output of associative work must be necessary for backward learning if backward association requires the formation of associations over and above those established in the forward direction. In this connection we also considered the advisability of the following experiment. It involves the comparison of paired associate learning under two conditions: once, under instructions to form *a—b* associations; and second, under instructions to form associations in both directions.[24] Again we reasoned that, if the latter task required more work of association, the results should make this evident. It is at once apparent, though, that a conclusion would be clear only in the case of asymmetry, and that the confirmation of symmetry would veil the answer.

In the absence of an operation that would specify the difference between one and two associations, one might be in-

[24] In the second procedure, the learner would be presented with identical *a—b* and *b—a* pairs, thus overtly practicing them in both directions.

clined to dismiss the question as semantic. Of what consequence is it whether we correct all associative results reported in the literature by a factor of two, or let them stand as is? To proceed in this way would, however, be to break with the principle guiding this investigation, which insists on the necessity of distinguishing between the operations that can be performed at a given time and the task of theoretical analysis. The issue may well be of consequence for an eventual physiological model of the associative process. In the meantime one must leave the question open.

F. Reversible and Irreversible Processes

We must now note an important restriction of the preceding analysis. Forward and backward association have, by tacit agreement, referred to the relation between units, and have strictly excluded the reversal of relations within a unit. In the study of backward association one compares recall from *a* to *b* with recall from *b* to *a;* the terms themselves remain intact. This restriction in the customary definition of the problem has escaped the attention it merits, because the concepts of unit and organization have been largely lacking in the analysis of associations.

These observations require us to consider directionality within units. Relations between units are, we have found, reversible. On the other hand, the character of many units is given in an essential way by their direction. This is the case with movements, such as a person's gait, or the motion of an athlete, and generally with acts of skill. It holds for units such as melodies. Direction belongs to these events in the sense that their identity and their functional value is destroyed when the internal relations are altered or reversed. We also find it difficult or impossible to think of these in any but the forward direction. There are irreversible psychological events.

The problem would receive a simple solution if one could conclude that reversal occurs between units, and that units are irreversible. However, stationary visual units, such as were studied in the present investigation, pose a difficulty for this proposal. Although the relation of forward and backward, and therefore the notion of reversibility, does not strictly apply to them, the presence of complete equidirectionality between their parts (or aspects) is of note. It seems necessary, therefore, to distinguish between units that are and those that are not directional. A more promising lead derives from the observation that directional units, such as melodies and movements, are, in contrast to others, extended in time. Is the determining difference one between stationary and temporal organization, the former represented most prominently by visual distributions given simultaneously and the latter by auditory and kinesthetic events?

There is need at this point for further analysis, since there appears to be evidence for a degree of symmetry also within temporally extended events. Thus there is no difficulty in recalling that the slow part of a movement was preceded by an agitated phase. This suggests that there is reversibility when the parts of a unit are differentiable. On the other hand, it is far harder to visualize the reversal of a stroke in tennis, when the components of the movement are less differentiable. At this point there are unsolved problems. Clearly the question of directionality does not arise at all unless the parts are differentiable; differentiability must be present both in directional and nondirectional units. One might suppose that in an irreversible unit, such as a melody, there is an extreme determination of the parts by their place in the organization. Do we have reason to hold, though, that the part-whole organization of visual units, which are not directional, is less unitary? This brings us back to the possibility that there is an ultimate difference between stationary and temporal organization. A solution awaits a deeper understanding of the concepts of unit, of part and subpart, and of degree of organization.

In illustration of some of the preceding questions one may cite the analysis by Thorndike (1932) of the "polarity" of associations. Thorndike implicitly treats relations between and within units as psychologically equivalent. In the main he found that it is markedly easier to complete the missing second half of a familiar sentence or expression than the missing first half; and similarly for the completion of the beginnings and ends of words. On this basis he concluded that forward association is stronger than backward association.

Since words are highly distinguishable the directionality of a sentence may appear to contradict the preceding conclusions. To reason in this way ignores the role of meaning, which doubtless guides recall in the forward direction, while reversal must proceed without reference to meaning. In addition, an ordinary sentence possesses a syntactical structure. The reversal of a word raises a still different question. A word is both a visual entity and an auditory-kinesthetic unit with a definite temporal structure. In its latter aspect a word is directional according to the preceding analysis, but it has not been established that it is directional as a visual pattern. Analysis must consider quite directly the properties of the respective modalities.[25]

V. CONCLUSIONS

The present inquiry provides evidence for a principle of associative symmetry, or for the equality of backward and forward association.

The results offer support for the conclusion that the relative weakness of backward association frequently reported in the literature is an artifact of differential availability of items. Measures of forward and backward association can be adequately compared only when the conditions of availability are equal, a requirement that investigation has frequently failed to observe. The usual procedures of investigation have produced differential availability that favored the measures of forward association. Equalization of item availability abolishes the difference between forward and backward association, or reduces it to a small amount. The evidence for the preceding statements may be summarized as follows: (*a*) When the paired terms are stationary (and simultaneously given) visual forms of approximately equal availability, no evidence of a favored direction is obtained. This result holds as the geometrical relations between the terms are varied (Experiments II, III, IV). (*b*) The standard anticipation method of verbal paired associate learning produces unequal availability of the members of a pair. As measured by free recall, the first member of a pair is more poorly recalled than its partner which was anticipated during learning (Experiment I). Backward association under these conditions is markedly weaker than forward association (Experiment V, Group 1). Further, there is a direct correspondence between the degree of differential availability and the relative weakness of backward association (Experiments I and V). (*c*) When a procedure that equalizes item availability is employed, the difference between forward and backward association disappears (Experiment V, Group 2). Thus backward association can be made to vary by controlling item availability. (*d*) Under certain conditions forward association continues to be slightly stronger than backward association (Experiments VI and VII). The absence of complete equivalence may be a function of nonassociative factors, among them the reinstatement of differential availability in the course of anticipation learning. The

[25] We would also account similarly for the comparative difficulty in reciting the alphabet backward. The advantage of forward reproduction may derive from the fact that recitation has constituted the alphabet into an auditory-motor unit.

conclusion follows that directionality is not a property of the association.

The large amounts of backward association obtained under the varied experimental conditions of this investigation cannot be understood as a product of incidental learning, or of uncontrolled factors.

The preceding conclusions apply to associations between units. Directionality obtains only between parts of units but not all relations internal to a unit are directional. Stationary visual units are not directional; as a rule temporal units are.

Associative symmetry permits the transition in recall from one term to another in more than one way. In this respect association resembles other cognitive processes. This increase of latitude is not a source of interference or disorder, a supposition that rests on an analogy between the associative process and a stimulus-response action sequence. The capacity to recall events in more than one order does not interfere with a knowledge of the actual order in past experience.

Associative symmetry and knowledge of order or direction are distinct operations. The principle of associative symmetry cannot account for direction; it requires the conclusion that direction is carried by processes other than association. The failure to draw this conclusion rests on the axiom that association is the fundamental cognitive process.

Psychological symmetry is a function of different processes, of which association is only one. It was suggested that logical relations of the form *aRb* are psychologically symmetrical.

The question was left open whether forward and backward association are to be understood as two associations or as one.

The distinction here advanced between association and recall reveals a basic ambiguity in the body of knowledge accumulated in the area of human learning and forgetting. All the available evidence concerning associative processes rests on data of recall. As long as the properties of the recall process are unknown or not taken into account, the existing evidence concerning associative functioning remains questionable. The present investigation has examined one consequence of this confusion. Several other consequences follow, of which a few may be mentioned. For example, this study may be said to demonstrate that identical associations are formed between terms differing in familiarity. It reopens the more general question whether association is a function of familiarity. Similarly, latency of response, which has been considered an index of the strength of association, may be a function rather of item availability. Finally, the concept of associative strength itself must be re-examined in the light of the present analysis. Investigation of some of these questions is now in progress.

The distinction between association and recall illustrates the difficulties of a scientific attitude that defines the properties of a process in terms of measuring operations. This procedure tends to slight those properties of the underlying process that are not included in the measuring operations, and to attribute to the process properties that may be peculiar to the measuring operations.

References

Asch, S. E., J. Ceraso, and W. Heimer. 1960. Perceptual conditions of association. *Psychol. Monogr.* 57 (3).

Asch, S. E., and J. Ceraso. The part-whole relation in the formation of associations. (Unpublished.)

Cason, H. 1924. The concept of backward association. *Amer. Jour. Psychol.* 35: 217–221.

Cason, H. 1926. Specific serial learning; a study of backward association. *Jour. Exp. Psychol.* 9: 195–227.

Feldman, S. M., and B. J. Underwood. 1957. Stimulus recall following paired-associate learning. *Jour. Exp. Psychol.* 53: 11–15.

Glaze, J. A. 1928. The association value of nonsense syllables. *Jour. Genet, Psychol.* 35: 255–267.

Guthrie, E. R. 1933. Association as a function of time interval. *Psychol. Rev.* 40: 355–367.

Hermans, T. G. 1936. A study of the relative amounts of forward and backward association of verbal material. *Jour. Exp. Psychol.* 19: 769–775.

Hilgard, E. R. Methods and procedures in the study of learning. Ch. 15, Handbook of experimental psychology, S. S. Stevens (ed.), New York, John Wiley, 1951.

Hunt, R. G. 1959. Meaningfulness and articulation of stimulus and response in paired associate learning and stimulus recall. *Jour. Exp. Psychol.* 57: 262–267.

Jantz, E. M., and B. J. Underwood. 1958. R-S learning as a function of meaningfulness and degree of S-R learning. *Jour. Exp. Psychol.* 56: 174–179.

Koffka, K. 1935. The principles of Gestalt psychology. New York, Harcourt.

Kutner, B. 1947. The recall of temporal order. M. A. Thesis, New School for Social Research.

McCormack, P. D. 1961. Backward mediated positive transfer in a paired-associate task. *Jour. Exp. Psychol.* 61: 138–141.

McGeoch, John A. 1942. The psychology of human learning. New York, Longmans, Green.

Meyer, G. 1939. Temporal organization and the initial reproductive tendency. *Jour. Psychol.* 7: 269–282.

Müller, G. E., and A. Pilzecker. 1900. Experimentelle Beiträge zur Lehre vom Gedächtnis. *Z. Psychol.* Ergbd. 1.

Murdock, B. B., Jr. 1956. "Backward" learning in paired associates. *Jour. Exp. Psychol.* 51: 213–215.

—— 1958. "Backward" associations in transfer and learning. *Jour. Exp. Psychol.* 55: 111–114.

Primoff, E. 1938. Backward and forward association as an organizing act in serial and paired associate learning. *Jour. Psychol.* 5: 375–395.

Stoddard, G. D. 1929. An experiment in verbal learning. *Jour. Ed. Psychol.* 20: 452–457.

Storms, L. H. 1958. Apparent backward association: a situational effect. *Jour. Exp. Psychol.* 55: 390–395.

Thorndike, E. L. 1932. Fundamentals of learning. New York: Bureau of Publications, Teachers College.

Trowbridge, M. H. 1938. A study of backward and remote forward association. *Jour. Exp. Psychol.* 22: 319–337.

Underwood, B. J. 1954. Speed of learning and amount retained: a consideration of methodology. *Psychol. Bull.* 51: 276–282.

Wohlgemuth, A. 1912. On memory and the direction of associations. *Brit. Jour. Psychol.* 5: 447–465.

Woodworth, R. S. 1915. A revision of imageless thought. *Psychol. Rev.* 22: 1–27.

Young, R. K. 1959. A comparison of two methods of learning serial associations. *Amer. Jour. Psychol.* 72: 554–559.

On the Relation Between the Probability of a Word as an Association and in General Linguistic Usage

DAVIS HOWES

The word-association experiment, developed primarily as a clinical tool, is now being used extensively as a method for the quantitative analysis of linguistic behavior (1, 3, 5, 6). Its value in such investigations depends to a considerable degree upon the extent to which results of the experiment can be generalized to language emitted under other, more natural conditions. The criticism is often advanced, for example, that the specialized nature of the instructional set and other conditions attendant upon the experimental situation invalidates the association experiment as a technique for studying general linguistic usage.

The question can be resolved empirically only by comparing specific properties of language produced in the association experiment with corresponding properties of language produced under conditions free of the constraints of the experimental situation. One property that has been studied is the distribution of word-association frequencies, which Skinner (7) has shown to approximate Zipf's law as closely as do the distributions of word frequencies taken from samples of continuous discourse (11). The comparison is here extended from the form of the distributions to the actual frequencies with which individual words occur in both types of sample.

To perform this comparison we need a listing of all different words with their frequencies of occurrence in general usage in one column and their over-all frequencies of occurrence as responses in the word-association experiment in a second parallel column. If the correlation between the frequencies in the two columns is perfect, the language of the word-association experiment may be said to be *stochastically equivalent* to the language of general usage. In that event we could conclude that the special conditions in-

Davis Howes, "On the Relation Between the Probability of a Word as an Association and in General Linguistic Usage," *Journal of Abnormal and Social Psychology*, 54 (1957), 75–85. Reprinted by permission of the author and publisher.

troduced by the association experiment do not affect a person's selection of words. The effect of a stimulus word in the association experiment, on this hypothesis, is merely to redistribute the factors underlying the emission of words without changing them. If, on the other hand, the frequencies in the two parallel columns are so disparate that it is impossible to predict one set of frequencies from the other, we would be forced to conclude that the experimental situation introduces fundamental changes into the processes underlying a person's selection of words. An empirical determination of the correlation between the two columns will permit us to decide which of these two conceptions of the association experiment applies.

DEFINITIONS

An explicit statement of the problem requires more careful definition of concepts than has been traditional in this field. In this section the concept of stochastic equivalence of language samples is developed from definitions based upon certain idealized linguistic experiments.

We restrict ourselves to the written language produced by some specified population of persons O. It is assumed that the written language emitted by O can be decomposed into sequences of occurrences of a set of discrete spatial patterns or *letters*. Any permutation of letters bounded by spaces is a *word*, and the set of all possible words for a given set of letters is the *vocabulary*. Thus for English the vocabulary is the denumerable set of words *A, B, . . ., Z, AA, AB, . . ., ZZ, AAA, AAB, . . ., ZZZ, ...*

A word is said to be emitted *in the free situation* if at the time of its emission the behavior of O is in no way affected by the experimenter. An occurrence of the jth word of the vocabulary is written w_j if it is emitted in the free situation.

Consider a fixed time interval T, called the *base interval*, during which a random sample from the population O emits words in the free situation. The probability of obtaining an occurrence of the jth word in a random draw from the sample of words emitted in T is the *base probability* of that word, $P(w_j)$. The base probabilities of all words in the vocabulary define a vector $\mathbf{P}$,

$$\mathbf{P} = [P(w_1), P(w_2), \cdots, P(w_j) \cdots], \qquad \Sigma_j P(w_j) = 1, \qquad [1]$$

which is called the *base probability vector*. This vector is fixed uniquely by a population O and a base interval T.

Similar definitions apply to the written language produced in a word-association experiment. Let another random sample from the same population O be given a standard association experiment (4, p. 38) during randomly-selected segments of the interval T. The symbol r_j will be used to represent an occurrence of the jth word as a response (association) in such an experiment in order to distinguish it from a word emitted in the free situation. A stimulus presentation of the ith word by the experimenter is denoted by s_i. The probability of obtaining an occurrence of the jth word in a random draw from the sample of associations given in response to a stimulus presentation of the ith word is the *associative probability* of the jth following the ith word, $p_{s_i}(r_j)$. The associative probabilities of all words in the vocabulary following presentation of the ith word define a vector $\mathbf{p}_i$, called the *associative probability vector* for the ith word,

$$\mathbf{p}_i = [p_{s_i}(r_1), p_{s_i}(r_2), \cdots, p_{s_i}(r_j), \cdots], \qquad p_{s_i}(r_i) = 0, \qquad \Sigma_j P_{s_i}(r_i) = 1. \qquad [2]$$

The ith term of this vector, $p_{s_i}(r_i)$, is always zero, since the standard experimental procedure does not permit the subject to give the stimulus word as his response.

To establish the connection between the associative vector $\mathbf{p}_i$ and the base vector $\mathbf{P}$ we consider the vector of conditional probabilities of words emitted in the free situation,

$$\mathbf{P}_i = [P_{w_i}(w_1), P_{w_i}(w_2), \cdots, P_{w_i}(w_j), \cdots], \quad \sum_j P_{w_i}(w_j) = 1 \quad [3]$$

Since

$$P(w_j) = \sum_i P(w_i)P_{w_i}(w_j), \quad [4]$$

the base vector $\mathbf{P}$ represents the weighted average of the vectors $\mathbf{P}_i$,

$$\mathbf{P} = \bar{\mathbf{P}}_i = \sum_i P(w_i)\mathbf{P}_i. \quad [5]$$

In order to obtain a comparable quantity for words emitted in the association experiment we define a *base associative probability vector* as the identically weighted average of the vectors p_i,

$$\mathbf{p} = \bar{\mathbf{p}}_i = \sum_i P(w_i)\mathbf{p}_i. \quad [6]$$

One can think of the base associative probabilities as the frequencies of occurrence of words as responses in an association experiment in which the stimulus words represent a random sample of the words the experimental subjects would have emitted during the same interval of time had they been left in the free situation. In practice, no word is presented as a stimulus more than once in a given association experiment. Each associative probability vector $\mathbf{p}_i$ therefore has to be estimated from responses made to a single experimental presentation of the ith word. It is therefore convenient to compute the base associative vector from the product of the matrix of associative probabilities $[\mathbf{p}_1, \mathbf{p}_2, \ldots, \mathbf{p}_i, \ldots]$ postmultiplied by the column vector $\mathbf{P}$

$$\mathbf{p} = \bar{\mathbf{p}}_i = [\mathbf{p}_1, \mathbf{p}_2, \cdots, \mathbf{p}_i, \cdots]\mathbf{P}. \quad [7]$$

The concepts introduced at the outset of the paper can now be given more precise definition. *Stochastic equivalence* between the language emitted in the association experiment and the language emitted in the free situation is defined by equality of the vectors $\mathbf{P}$ and $\mathbf{p}$. When these vectors are defined as in Equations 5 and 6 the equivalence is said to be of the *first order*. First-order stochastic equivalence thus implies that, for every pair (i, j) of words in the vocabulary,

$$\sum_i P(w_i)P_{w_i}(w_j) = \sum_i P(w_i)P_s(r_j). \quad [8]$$

Stochastic equivalence of any higher order can be defined by substituting conditional and associative probabilities of a higher order for those of the first order in Equations 2 and 3. Stochastic equivalence of the second order, for example, would imply in analogy to Equation 8 that

$$\sum_{ij} P(w_{ij})P_{w_{ij}}(w_k) = \sum_{ij} P(w_{ij})\, p_{s_{ij}}(r_k) \quad [9]$$

for all triples (i, j, k) of words in the vocabulary. In the present study we shall be concerned exclusively with first-order relationships. It is important, however, to recognize the possibility that the results obtained for the first order may not apply to higher-orders.

The equation $\mathbf{P} = \mathbf{p}$ is trivial if the associative probabilities of all word pairs are equal to their corresponding conditional probabilities, i.e., if for all pairs (i, j) of words,

$$\begin{aligned} p_{s_i}(r_j) &= P_{w_i}(w_j), \\ p_{s_k}(r_k) = 0, &\quad \sum_j p_{s_i}(r_j) = 1, \quad [10] \\ P_{w_k}(w_k) = 0, &\quad \sum_j P_{w_j}(w_j) = 1. \end{aligned}$$

Now, there are no data from which the conditional probabilities $P_{w_i}(w_j)$ can be estimated accurately. But inspection of the data from any word-association experiment is alone sufficient to show that in fact associative probabilities differ greatly from conditional probabilities for at least some word pairs. To cite one example, the associative probability of the word *light* following the stimulus word *dark* is found experimentally to be about 0.4, while the probability that *light* follows *dark* in the free situation (i.e., the probability of the sequence *dark light* over the probability of *dark*) is clearly of a lower order of magnitude. Thus the real question at issue is whether the average associative probabilities are equal to the average conditional probabilities even though the individual associative and conditional probabilities differ greatly.

The method used here to test for stochastic equivalence is to calculate the coefficient of correlation between empirical estimates of $P(w_j)$ and $\sum_i P(w_i) p_{s_i}(r_j)$ for as large a sample of words as possible. A correlation coefficient of one implies perfect stochastic equivalence; a correlation of zero, perfect stochastic independence. The square of the correlation coefficient measures the proportion of the variance of the empirical data that is due to the relationship between the two sets of frequencies. It is thus a measure of the extent to which the hypothesis of stochastic equivalence accounts for those data. The square of the correlation also indicates the precision with which the probabilities of words in the free situation can be estimated from the laboratory situation of the association experiment. In this sense, it may be interpreted as an index of the potential value of the association experiment as a general laboratory method for the statistical analysis of language.

MEASUREMENTS

Measurements of base probabilities and associative probabilities for the same population of subjects have not been published. For base probabilities the most extensive set of data published is the Lorge magazine count (8). This is an analysis of 4.6 million words of text from five popular American magazines issued during the period 1927–1938. For associative probabilities the standard tables are still those published by Kent and Rosanoff in 1910 (4), which list the associations spoken to each of 100 stimulus words by a population of 1,000 subjects, including 500 hospital workers, 200 professional persons and 150 high school students. Since the two sets of data differ with respect to population of subjects, time when measured, and mode of response (written or spoken), an estimate of the correlation between base probability and base associative probability based on these tables cannot be expected to approach unity even in the case of stochastic equivalence.

The Kent-Rosanoff tables list each combination of letters as a separate word, but the published version of the magazine count combines the entries for certain inflected forms (e.g., plurals ending in *s*, verb forms ending in *ed* or *ing*) with the root forms. The corresponding entries in the Kent-Rosanoff tables have been combined in the present analysis to make the two sets of frequencies comparable.

The stimulus words used in the Kent-Rosanoff study constitute a very unrepresentative sample of the set of all possible words. All are nouns and adjectives, for example, and all are words of medium frequency (their median log frequency is 2.6 with a standard deviation of 0.5 log unit). Weighting each associative frequency by the magazine-count frequency of the stimulus word appears to be of limited value in such a case. On the other hand, the weighting procedure greatly increases computational labor. Computation of base associative probabilities has therefore been simplified by using the approximation

$$\sum_i P(w_i) p_{s_i}(r_j) \simeq 0.01 \sum_i p_{s_i}(r_j) \qquad [11]$$

in which the 100 stimulus words receive equal weights.

The notation may be simplified somewhat for the purpose of describing the data by dropping the indicators *w*, *s*, and *r* which distinguish the various functions of words in the experiments. The base probability is then denoted by $P(j)$ and the base associative probability by

$\sum_i P(i) p_i(j)$. The empirical estimates of these theoretical quantities will be referred to as the *magazine-count frequency* $F(j)$ and the *summed Kent-Rosanoff frequency* $\Sigma f_i(j)$, respectively.

ANALYSIS OF DATA

Fig. 1 is a plot of the relation between magazine-count frequency and summed Kent-Rosanoff frequency on logarithmic coordinates. The numbers bordering the scatter plot represent the numbers of words having frequencies of zero, whose logarithms are therefore negative infinite. A significant positive correlation is evident from the figure, but the relationship is by no means rectilinear over the entire range. The form of the regression lines, as well as the magnitude of the correlation, is therefore of interest. Both types of analysis, in turn, require that the form of the conditional distribution functions be known.

Variation of base associative probability with base probability constant. Consider first the conditional distributions in the vertical dimension of Fig. 1. These distributions show what proportion of words having a given magazine-count frequency occur 0, 1, 2, . . . times as responses in the Kent-Rosanoff tables. Fig. 2-A presents several such distributions on logarithmic-normal coordinates. A straight line on these coordinates indicates that the logarithms of the variable plotted on the abscissa are normally distributed with a mean indicated by the intercept of the line and a standard deviation inversely proportional to its slope. The sets of points in Fig. 2-A are well described by a set of lines that are both straight and parallel, indicating that the conditional distributions of log base associative probability for given base probability are both normal and homoscedastic. (Actually, there is a slight increase in the standard deviation of log $\Sigma f_i(j)$ at the highest magazine-count frequencies, but this is due to the use of wider class-intervals in that range in order to obtain distributions of more than 100 cases.)

The regression of summed Kent-Rosanoff frequency on magazine-count frequency is shown by the solid circles in Fig. 3-A. The coordinates are logarithmic. Medians have been substituted for means in the regression analysis because the distributions include zero frequencies the logarithms of which are infinite. The regression line has a maximum at a magazine-count frequency of about 800 and falls off sharply on both sides of that point.

It may be observed that the regression line in Fig. 3-A covers only about half the total range of log $F(j)$. Words that are rare in the magazine count tend not to occur at all in the Kent-Rosanoff tables, which comprise a much smaller sample. When the magazine-count frequency is small (< 150), the median summed Kent-Rosanoff frequency is therefore zero and the median log $\Sigma f_i(j)$ is negative infinite. At the very highest magazine-count frequencies more than half the words again fail to occur in the Kent-Rosanoff tables, so that the median log $\Sigma f_i(j)$ is negative infinite in that range too.

An estimate of the regression line over the full range can be found by using a theorem which states that the line connecting a given fractile of each of a set of normal, homoscedastic distributions is parallel to a line connecting any other fractile of the same set of distributions.[1] Since the highest fractiles of the conditional distributions of log $\Sigma f_i(j)$ are finite

[1] A proof may be indicated for a set of normal distribution functions $G_1(x)$, $G_2(x)$, . . . , $G_n(x)$ having standard deviations $\sigma_1 = \sigma_2 = \sigma_n = \sigma$. Let a and b be two proportions, $0 \leq a < b \leq 1$, for which the fractiles of the various distribution functions are $x_1(a)$, $x_2(a)$, . . . , $x_n(a)$ and $x_1(b)$, $x_2(b)$, . . . , $x_n(b)$, respectively. If $h(a)$ and $h(b)$ are the corresponding fractiles of the standardized normal distribution function, we can write $x_1(b) - x_1(a) = [h(b) - h(a)]\,\sigma = x_2(b) - x_2(a) = x_n(b) - x_n(a)$. A line connecting the points $x_1(a)$, $x_2(a)$, . . . , $x_n(a)$ will therefore lie $[h(b) - h(a)]\,\sigma$ units of x below a line connecting the points $x_1(b)$, $x_2(b)$, . . . , $x_n(b)$. Hence the two lines will be parallel.

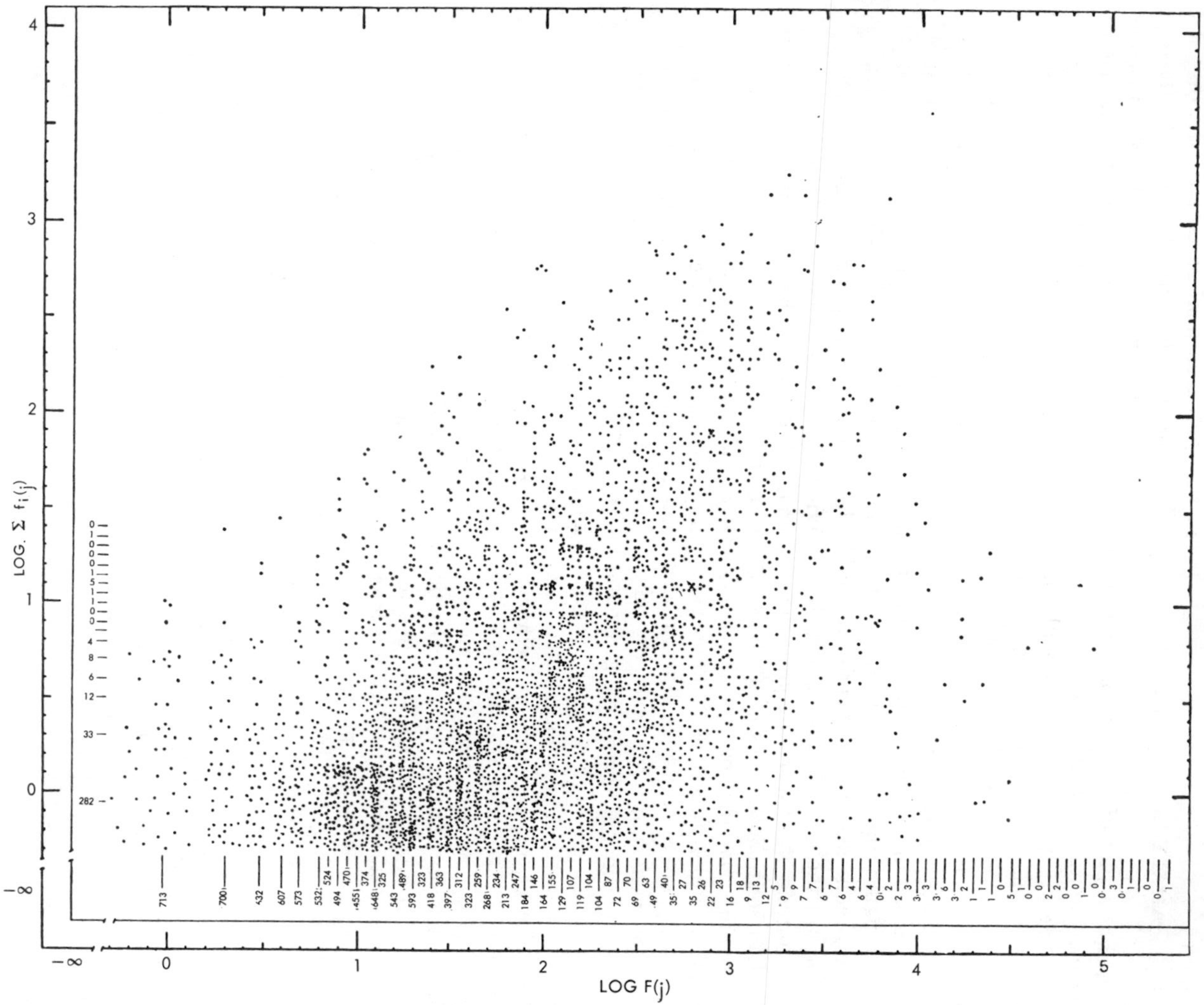

Fig. 1: Scatterplot showing the relationship between summed Kent-Rosanoff frequency, $\Sigma f_i(j)$, and magazine-count frequency, $F(j)$. Logarithmic coordinates.

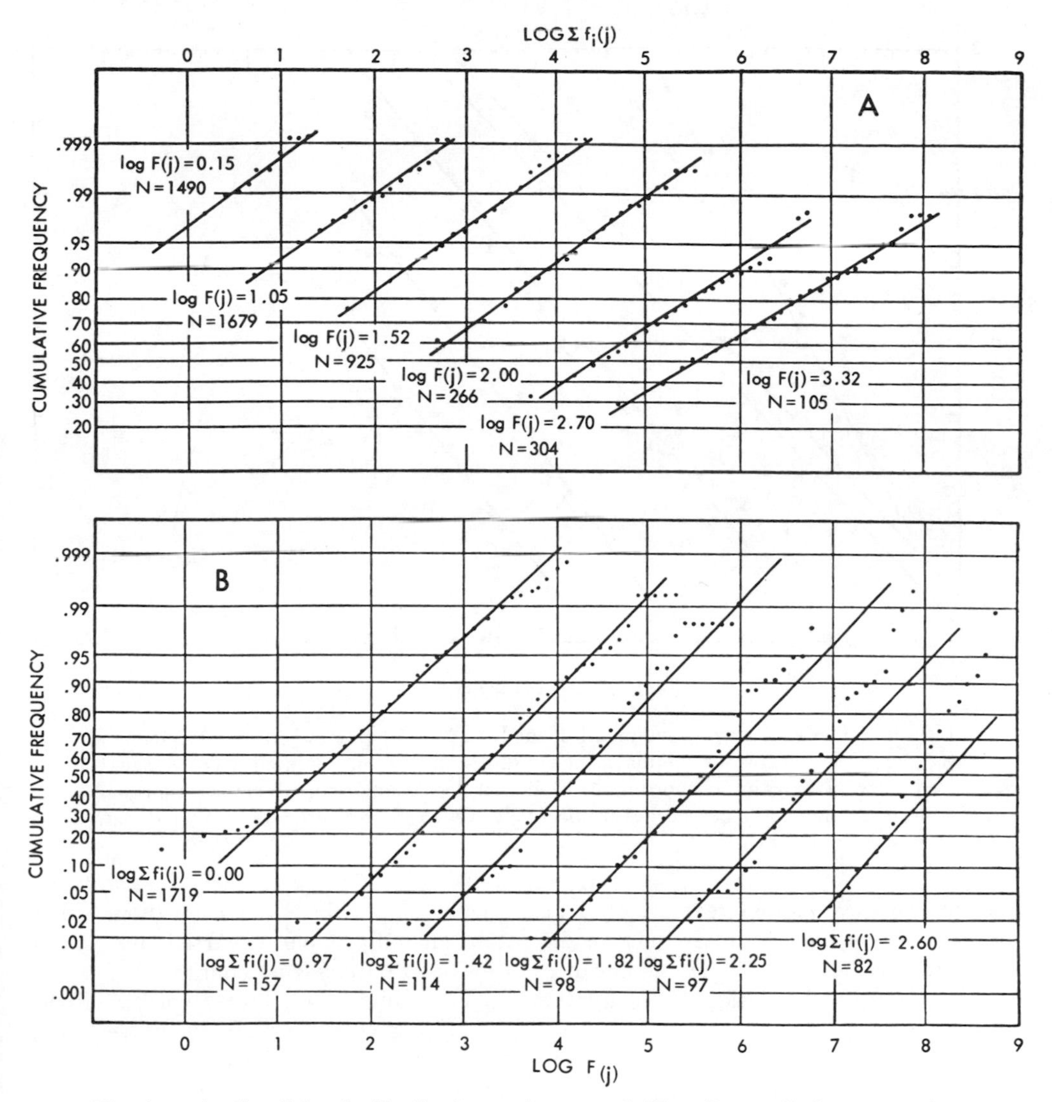

Fig. 2: *A*. Conditional distributions of summed Kent-Rosanoff frequency for selected values of magazine-count frequency. *B*. Conditional distributions of magazine-count frequency for selected values of summed Kent-Rosanoff frequency (Ordinate is proportional to the normal deviate, abscissa is logarithmic. The distributions have been separated by displacing each one to the right one log unit).

for all magazine-count frequencies, the slope of the regression line can be estimated from the slope of a line connecting one of those fractiles. In Fig. 3-A the 95th and 75th percentiles of the log $\Sigma f_i(j)$ distributions are indicated by crosses and triangles, respectively. These data indicate a regression line that is rectilinear and positive for magazine-count frequencies of less than 800 (log $F(j) < 2.9$). (The leveling-off of the 95th percentiles for log $F(j) < 1$ is due to an artifact explained in the following paragraph.) Above that point the regression

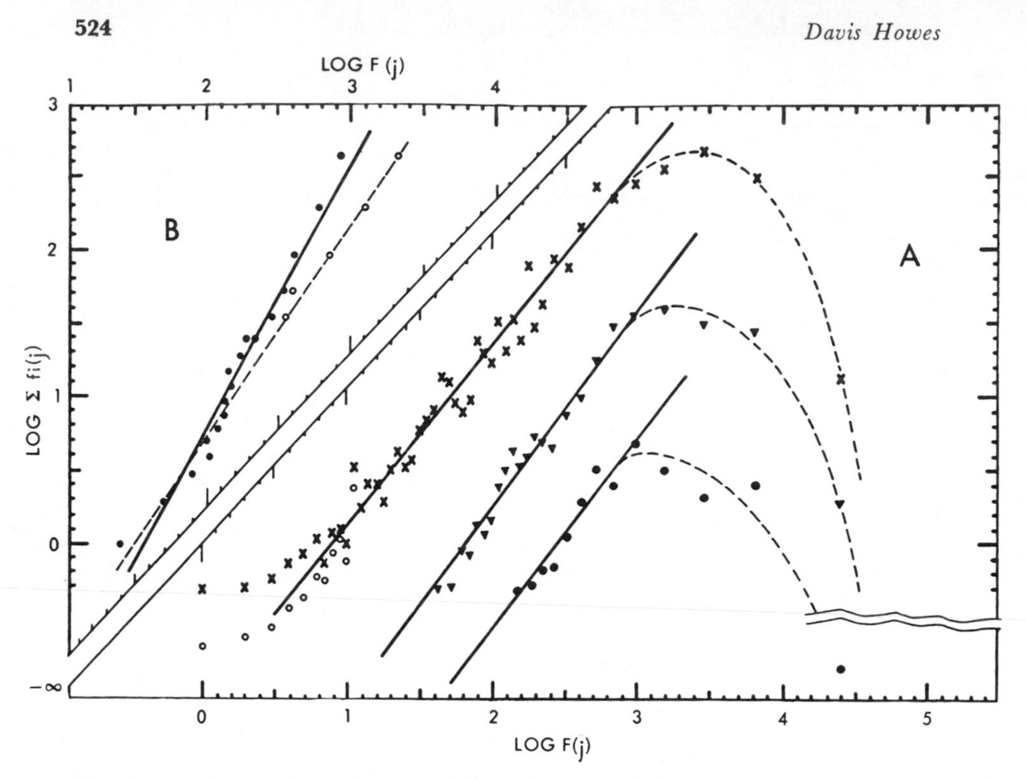

Fig. 3: *A*. Regression of summed Kent-Rosanoff frequency on magazine-count frequency. *B*. Regression of magazine-count frequency on summed Kent-Rosanoff frequency (Logarithmic coordinates. Solid circles, triangles, and crosses represent 50th, 75th, and 95th percentiles, respectively. Open circles indicate corrected data as described in text).

line undergoes a sudden reversal until at the highest magazine-count frequencies its slope approaches $-\infty$. The significance of this reversal will be taken up in a later section.

The leveling-off of the 95th percentiles for log $F(j) < 1$ is due to the omission of a number of words in that range. The magazine count is published as one of four word counts in the Thorndike-Lorge tables (8). These tables do not list the frequency of a word in each count if the combined frequency of the word in all four counts is less than 18. Moreover, the combined frequency itself is given only if it is greater than 3. In the data of Fig. 1 only magazine-count frequencies specifically listed in the tables are used. Words with combined frequencies of less than 18 are thus assigned a magazine-count frequency of zero in Fig. 1 even though they may actually have occurred up to 17 times in the magazine count.

The number of these words actually having a given magazine-count frequency can be estimated approximately by assuming that the occurrences making up the combined frequency of a word are distributed randomly among the four equal component counts.[2] The summed Kent-

[2] Let Q be the combined frequency of a word in all four counts and q_1, q_2, q_3, and q_4 the unknown component frequencies, any one of which may be chosen to represent the magazine-count frequency. Then $\Sigma_i q_i = Q$ by definition and the limits $4 \leq Q \leq 17$ and $0 \leq q_i \leq 17$ follow from the nature of the Thorndike-Lorge tables. The number of possible arrangements of the four component frequencies that satisfy these conditions for given Q may be denoted by A_Q, and the number of

Rosanoff frequency can be found for each word with a known combined frequency and assigned on a proportionate basis to the estimated magazine-count frequencies. In this way the words omitted from the published tables can be assigned values of $F(j)$ and $\Sigma f_i(j)$. These data can be used to correct Fig. 1.

The 95th percentiles of the $\Sigma f_i(j)$ distributions for these corrected data are shown by the open circles in Fig. 3-A (no correction is indicated for magazine-count frequencies of 12–17 where the change was not appreciable). The corrected data fall quite close to the theoretical straight line except for magazine-count frequencies of three or less ($\log F(j) \leq 0.5$). In that range the correction is only partial because the published tables do not report words with combined frequencies of less than 4. The partial correction has a large enough effect, however, to indicate that complete correction would eliminate the remaining deviations of these points from the rectilinear regression line.

Variation of base probability with base associative probability constant. Consider next the conditional distributions in the horizontal dimension of Fig. 1, which show the proportion of words with a given frequency in the Kent-Rosanoff tables that occur 0, 1, 2, . . . times in the magazine count. Figure 2-B shows several of these distributions on logarithmic-normal coordinates. In this case the sets of points do not describe parallel straight lines as in Fig. 2-A. Two artifacts, however, affect these data: the omission of words with magazine-count frequencies of less than 18, described in the preceding paragraphs; and the reversal of the regression line for $\log \Sigma f_i(j)$ on $\log F(j)$, shown in Fig. 3-A. When the effects of these two factors are taken into account, the theoretical distributions of log base probability, indicated by the straight lines in Fig. 2-B, turn out to be normal and homoscedastic.

The first factor is responsible for the leveling-off at the lower ends of the distributions of Fig. 2-B (the effect does not show up in the two right-hand distributions because they contain no points in the affected range). It has been pointed out that words with combined frequencies of less than 18 in the four word counts of the Thorndike-Lorge tables had to be assigned a frequency of zero in Fig. 1 although their true magazine-count frequencies may be as high as 17. This produces an excess of words in the interval $F(j) \leq 0.5$ and a corresponding deficiency in the interval $0.5 < F(j) \leq 17.5$. In the cumulative plot of Fig. 2-B, therefore, the points for $F(j) = 0.5$ (-0.3 on the logarithmic abscissa) lie well above their true values, while those for $F(j) = 17.5$ ($+1.2$ on the logarithmic abscissa) are correct. The correction procedure described in connection with Fig. 3-A eliminates this type of deviation altogether.

The second factor, the reversal of the regression line of Fig. 3-A, is responsible for the deviations at the upper ends of the distributions of Fig. 2-B. The effect of the reversal is to lower the positions of points at the extreme right of Fig. 1 from the positions they would occupy if the regression line of Fig. 3-A were rectilinear over its entire range. At $\log F(j) = 3.0$ the median point is lowered about 0.1 log unit; at $\log F(j) = 3.5$, about 1 log unit; and at $\log F(j) = 4.0$, about 2 log units. Consequently, a horizontal slice through the upper part of Fig. 1 has a large proportion of its points in the range log

these arrangements that assume a frequency m in the component representing the magazine count, $A_{m|Q}$. The probability that a word with a combined frequency Q has a magazine-count frequency m may be estimated from the ratio $A_{m|Q}/A_Q$. Suppose N_Q words are listed with combined frequencies of Q in the Thorndike-Lorge tables. Then $n_{m|Q} = N_Q (A_{m|Q}/A_Q)$ estimates the number of words with combined frequencies of Q that have magazine-count frequencies of m. The estimated number of words with magazine-count frequency m that are omitted from the published Thorndike-Lorge tables is therefore $n_m = \Sigma_Q n_{m|Q} = \Sigma_Q N_Q (A_{m|Q}/A_Q)$.

$F(j) \geq 3.0$ removed by the reversal of the regression line. A distribution of log $F(j)$ at this level therefore has the form of a truncated normal distribution (2, §6.9). Distributions of log $F(j)$ taken at successively lower levels of Fig. 1 have proportionately fewer points removed by the reversal. The degree of truncation should decrease accordingly. At the very lowest levels of Fig. 1, in fact, the reversal actually adds more points from higher levels than it removes to still lower levels. The net effect at these levels is thus to add a small number of points in the affected range.

In Fig. 2-B, distributions of log $F(j)$ for successively lower levels of log $\Sigma f_i(j)$ are arranged from right to left. All six sets of data can be brought into accord with the theoretical straight lines by replotting them for the following assumed degrees of truncation (reading from right to left): 55%, 35%, 18%, 9%, 0%, and − 10% (negative truncation indicates the addition of points instead of their removal). For each set of data the degree of truncation that gives the best fit to the theoretical line is of the order of magnitude required by the data of Fig. 1.

The medians of both empirical and theoretical distributions are used in Fig. 3-B to indicate the regression of magazine-count frequency on summed Kent-Rosanoff frequency. Solid circles represent medians of the empirical (truncated) distributions, open circles the medians of the theoretical (normal and homoscedastic) distributions. (For log $\Sigma f_i(j) \leq 1.3$ the solid circles represent both sets of medians.) Each set of data is well described by a straight line, the slope for the empirical medians (solid line in Fig. 3-B) being slightly steeper than the slope for the theoretical medians (dashed line).

Since the medians of the theoretical distributions have to be estimated from the theoretical lines of Fig. 2-B, their accuracy is open to question. As a test of their validity, the slope of the line fitted to the theoretical medians can be estimated by a second procedure. The truncation of the empirical distributions of log $F(j)$ does not extend to the lowest fractiles. Hence a line passed through a low fractile of the empirical distributions should have the same slope as the dashed line of Fig. 3-B representing the medians of the theoretical distributions.[2] The line of best fit to the 25th percentiles of the empirical distributions has a slope of 1.45 ± 0.1, compared to 1.40 ± 0.1 for the dashed line of Fig. 3-B. By way of comparison, the dashed line of Fig. 3-B, representing the medians of the empirical distributions, has a slope of 1.85 ± 0.1.

Correlation between base probability and base associative probability. Only a small proportion of the words represented in Fig. 1—perhaps 0.5%—are involved in the reversal of the regression line in Fig. 3-A. The behavior of all other words is described by the rectilinear regression lines of Fig. 3-A and 3-B (dashed line). For these data, which satisfy the assumptions of a normal correlation surface (2, p. 585), the product-moment correlation coefficient ρ can be used to measure the degree of association between base probability and base associative probability. Numerical computation of ρ is impossible because of the presence of infinite scores. The correlation can be determined from the angle θ between the two regression lines, however, since

$$\tan \theta = \frac{(1-\rho^2)\,\sigma_1\sigma_2}{\rho\,(\sigma_1^2+\sigma_2^2)}.$$

(2, Equation 19.7.12). For the present data, θ is 3.5 degrees (Figs. 3-A and 3-B), σ_1 is 1.10 log units (Fig. 2-A), and σ_2 is 0.75 log unit (Fig. 2-B). The corresponding estimate of ρ is $+0.937 \pm 0.001$.

This correlation must be interpreted in the light of several adverse factors affecting the data: the difference of 30 years between the dates of the two sets of data; the different composition of the two populations of subjects; the contrasts between the written language of the magazine count and the spoken language of the Kent-Rosanoff experiment; the small number of stimulus words tested in the Kent-Rosanoff study; and the use of the approximation to base associative probability instead of its exact definition. All these factors can be expected to introduce uncorrelated variance into the results. The true correlation between base probability and base associative probability, uncontaminated by these sources of error, must therefore be close to 1.0. Stochastic equivalence thus appears to apply to the words considered in this section.

The reversal of regression at high magazine-count frequencies. The words having the highest magazine-count frequencies are the ones that are responsible for the inversion in the regression line of Fig. 3-A. Table 1 lists the 25 words having the highest magazine-count frequencies along with their summed Kent-Rosanoff frequencies. Without exception, the high magazine-count frequencies of these words are matched with very low summed Kent-Rosanoff frequencies. The average summed Kent-Rosanoff frequency is only 0.2% of the average magazine-count frequency, after correction for the difference in size of sample.

Study of Table 1 discloses that all the words listed there are of a characteristic type. They are words whose primary function is to connect other words in continuous discourse: articles, conjunctions, auxiliaries, prepositions, pronouns. These may be called *interstitial* words. The low frequencies of such words in the Kent-Rosanoff tables could be expected on two grounds. First, the subjects in the association experiment are instructed to emit only one-word utterances. The absence of continuous discourse eliminates the principal function of interstitial words, thereby reducing the number of occasions on which they are called forth. Second, it has been well established that subjects tend to give associations of the same part of speech as the stimulus words (10, p. 347). The complete absence of interstitials among the 100 Kent-Rosanoff stimulus words would therefore result in low frequencies for those words as associations. The former interpretation of the result implies that interstitial words represent a special type of word to which the property of stochastic equivalence does not apply, while the latter interpretation holds that the exceptional behavior of these words is merely an artifact of the particular association experiment that has been analyzed.

Table 1

SUMMED ASSOCIATIVE FREQUENCIES FOR THE 25 WORD CLASSES WITH THE HIGHEST MAGAZINE-COUNT FREQUENCIES

	$F(j)$	$\sum f_i(j)$	
Word	*Magazine Count* $N=$ 4,591,125	*Kent-Rosanoff* $N=$ 100,000	*Jenkins* $N=$ 19,100
1. the	236472	0	28
2. and	138672	0	54
3. a	117222	0	12
4. to	115358	0	126
5. of	112601	0	38
6. I	89489	6	84
7. in	75253	0	29
8. was	58732	0	44
9. that	55667	0	73
10. it	52107	0	196
11. he	49268	0	82
12. you	42581	13	219
13. for	39363	6	54
14. had	34341	0	42
15. is	33404	0	135
16. with	32903	0	42
17. her	31824	1	60
18. she	31087	0	70
19. his	30748	0	104
20. as	30693	0	10
21. on	30224	1	64
22. at	26250	0	61
23. have	24456	19	47
24. but	23704	0	27
25. me	23364	14	242
Sum	1,535,783	54	1943
Sum/N	0.33451	0.00054	0.10171

The best evidence on the question is found in a recent association experiment by Jenkins[3] in which over 50 interstitials, including all but three of the words in Table 1 (*in, her, as*), were among the 200 stimulus words. Table 1 shows the frequencies, summed over all 200 stimulus words, with which the words listed there occurred as responses in the Jenkins study. The effect is striking: there is a 200 to 1 increase in frequency over the Kent-Rosanoff experiment. The 25 words of Table 1, while they constitute only 0.05% of the Kent-Rosanoff responses, make up 10% of the Jenkins responses and 33% of the magazine count. Inclusion of interstitial words in the list of stimulus words thus goes a long way toward closing the gap between the summed associative frequencies and the magazine-count frequencies of interstitial words. Use of the complete formula for base associative probability instead of the approximation would narrow the gap even more.

The Jenkins experiment, based on fewer than 100 subjects, is not extensive enough to warrant a more elaborate analysis. But it shows clearly that the particular selection of stimulus words used by Kent and Rosanoff is chiefly responsible for the reversal of the regression line in Fig. 3-A. The sharpness of the contrast between the Jenkins results and those of Kent and Rosanoff further suggests the possibility that stochastic equivalence may apply to interstitial words as well as to noninterstitial ones. A large and carefully designed experiment would be required, however, in order to test this possibility adequately.

SUMMARY AND CONCLUSIONS

The summed associative probability of a word, measured by its total frequency in the Kent-Rosanoff tables, is considered in relation to the probability of emission of the word in general linguistic usage, measured by its frequency in the Lorge magazine count. Two features stand out in the data: a high positive correlation (.94) for magazine-count frequencies of less than 800; and a sharp reversal in this relationship for higher magazine-count frequencies. Perhaps neither result, taken singly, is as striking as the fact that both appear so clearly in the same set of data.

The inverse relationship for high magazine-count frequencies is produced by a fairly small number of words of a special type, called *interstitial* words because their chief function is to connect other words in continuous discourse (i.e., conjunctions, articles, prepositions, auxiliaries, pronouns). Such words were systematically excluded from the list of stimulus words used by Kent and Rosanoff. As a consequence, they were rarely emitted as associations despite their high magazine-count frequencies. Data from another association experiment, in which interstitial stimulus-words were included, indicate that the reversal of correlation found in the Kent-Rosanoff data can largely, if not completely, be eliminated by an unbiased selection of stimulus words.

The high correlation found for all other words indicates that the average probability that a given word will be emitted as a response in the word-association experiment is the same as its probability in general discourse. The language of association can therefore be said to be *stochastically equivalent* to the language of general discourse. This relationship implies that a person's selection of words is not affected by the artificial laboratory situation required for the association experiment. Hence the effect of a given stimulus word upon a subject's response must be due to a redistribution of the set of factors governing emission of words in general discourse. The results thus serve to validate the association experiment as a method for studying under laboratory

[3] I wish to thank Dr. J. J. Jenkins of the University of Minnesota for generously placing his data at my disposal and Miss Evelyn Segal for preparing the computations.

control the processes governing the emission of words in general discourse.

References

1. Cofer, C. N., & Shevitz, R. Word-association as a function of word-frequency. *Amer. J. Psychol.,* 1952, 65, 75–79.
2. Hald, A. *Statistical theory with engineering applications.* New York: Wiley, 1952.
3. Howes, D., & Osgood, C. E. On the combination of associative probabilities in linguistic contexts. *Amer. J. Psychol.,* 1954, 67, 241–258.
4. Kent, G. H., & Rosanoff, A. J. A study of association in insanity. *Amer. J. Insanity,* 1910, 67, 37–96; 317–390.
5. O'Neil, W. M. The effect of verbal association on tachistoscopic recognition. Univer. of Minnesota Stud. on Verbal Behavior, Tech. Rep. No. 4, 1953.
6. Russell, W. A., & Storms, L. H. Implicit verbal chaining in paired-associate learning. *J. exp. Psychol.,* 1955, 49, 287–293.
7. Skinner, B. F. The distribution of associated words. *Psychol. Rec.,* 1937, 1, 71–76.
8. Thorndike, E. L., & Lorge, I. *The teacher's word book of 30,000 words.* New York: Teachers College, Columbia Univer., 1944.
9. Thumb, A., & Marbe, K. *Experimentelle Untersuchungen über die psychologischen Grundlagen der sprachlichen Analogiebildung.* Leipzig: Engelmann, 1901.
10. Woodworth, R. S. *Experimental psychology.* New York: Holt, 1938.
11. Zipf, G. K. *Human behavior and the principle of least effort.* Cambridge, Mass.: Addison-Wesley, 1949.

Changes with Age in the Verbal Determinants of Word-Association

SUSAN M. ERVIN-TRIPP

The earliest investigators of word-association noted that adult associations were usually in the same grammatical class as the stimulus-words, and that such responses had especially short latencies.[1] These findings challenge an explanation of the learning of word-associations through simple contiguity in overt speech. On this basis, the most frequent response to transitive verbs would be *the*.

A paradigmatic response—that is, a response in the same grammatical class—might arise through similarity of referents, common affixes, or common past verbal contexts.[2] The last determinant has the

* These data were collected as part of a project on children's reasoning sponsored by the Higgins Fund, The assistance of Edith Kaplan and Roseanne Mandler is gratefully acknowledged.

[1] Gustav Aschaffenburg, Experimentelle Studien über Assoziationen: I. Die Assoziation im normalen Zustande, *Psychol. Arbeit.* 1, 1895, 209–299; B. B. Bourdon, Observatives sur la reconnaissance, la discrimination et l'association, *Rev. Phil. France et l'Etranger,* 40, 1895, 153–185; C. G. Jung, *Studies in Word Association,* 1919, 234–235; Paul Menzerath, Die Bedeutung der sprachlichen Geläufigkeit oder der formalen sprachlichen Beziehung für die Reproduktion, *Z. Psychol.,* 48, 1908, 1–95; Friedrich Schmidt, Experimentelle Untersuchungen zur Assoziationslehre, *Z. Psychol.,* 28, 1902, 65–95; Albert Thumb and Karl Marbe, *Experimentelle Untersuchungen über die psychologishen Grundlagen der sprachlichen Analogiebildung,* 1901, 1–87; Arthur Wreschner, Die Reproduktion und Assoziation von Vorstellungen, *Z. Psychol. Ergbd.,* 3, 1907, 329–599.

[2] The syntagmatic-paradigmatic distinction was made in discussion of word-association by J. J. Jenkins, in C. E. Osgood and T. A. Sebeok (eds.) *Psycholinguistics, Supplement, J. abnorm. soc. Psychol.* 52, 1954, 114–116; Sol Saporta, Linguistic structure as a factor and as a measure in word association, Minnesota Conference on Associative Processes in Verbal Behavior, 1955, 210–213.

Susan M. Ervin-Tripp, "Changes with Age in the Verbal Determinants of Word-Association," *The American Journal of Psychology,* **74,** No. 3 (September, 1961), 361–372. Reprinted by permission of the author and publisher.

greatest generality. Even the isolated words offered in an association-test have been encountered before in verbal contexts. Two words may be said to be contextually similar to the degree that their past verbal environments overlap. Contextual similarity thus includes both grammatical and semantic similarity between the stimulus-word and response-word, to the extent that the totality of verbal contexts defines meaning.

Two models could account for the learning of association between contextually similar words. A forward association would predict that repetition of *a cup of coffee* and *a cup of tea* would lead to the association of *coffee* with *tea* and of *tea* with *coffee,* due to their contiguity during competition of the response. A reverse, or mediated association, would be learned with practice of *front door* and *back door.* In this case, though, since *door* mediates the association of *front* and *back,* it would be the most likely response in free association. Savings in paradigmatic responses would be expected only in a condition of constrained response. It has been shown that both of these conditions do produce learning.[3]

In the following study, differences with age in the frequency of different types of word-association will be examined with reference to an analysis of learning. The following changes with age are expected.

(1) Decrease in syntagmatic responses. Syntagmatic (sequential) associations are more probable where the variety of contexts following the stimulus-word is low relative to its frequency, reducing the number of competing associates. With age, there is an increase in the length and variety of sentences,[4] so that the relative strength of the average syntagmatic association is less.

Syntagmatic associations refer here to any sequential associate, not necessarily the immediately contiguous one. Since determiners (*the, my*), pure prepositions (*of, from*), copulas (*is, become*), nominative pronouns, and coördinate conjunctions virtually never occur in utterances of one word,[5] they would not be expected as responses on an association-test,[6] and may be eliminated in calculation of the sequential probabilities of stimulus- and potential response-words.

(2) Increase in paradigmatic responses. Paradigmatic associates are more likely when the variety of verbal contexts of a stimulus-term is high relative to its frequency. In addition, as vocabulary increases, children have more contextually similar responses in antonyms, synonyms, and words drawn from the abstraction-hierarchy of the stimulus-word.

(3) Differential shift toward paradigmatic responses. If a word occurs frequently in the final position of a sentence, it has relatively weak syntagmatic associations. Such words are nouns, adverbs,

[3] Evidence for the model of forward association was offered by W. E. Jeffrey and R. J. Kaplan, Semantic generalization with experimentally induced associations, *J. exp. Pyschol.,* 54, 1957, 336–338, and P. M. Kjeldergaard and D. L. Horton, An experimental analysis of associative factors in stimulus equivalence, response equivalence and chaining paradigms, Studies in Verbal Behavior, 1960, No. 3 (University of Minnesota), 21–34. Response-competition is less likely in a speaker than in a listener anticipating speech sequences. David McNeill has ingeniously suggested that children's slower verbal responses may not create the conditions for paradigmatic contiguity through anticipation.

[4] M. C. Templin, Certain language skills in children, *Univ. Minn. Child Welf. Monogr.,* 1957, No. 26, 76–96.

[5] In an unpublished tally of a day's conversational speech transcribed by W. F. Soskin, functions-words were rare, except for question-words, in single-word utterances.

[6] While many functional-words would not appear in isolation in either a text- or conversational-count, they are sometimes produced by students as isolated responses in school-exercises. If they occur in isolation as stimulus-words in the association-test itself, their subsequent probability as an isolated response may be increased as has been reported by Davis Howes, On the relation between the probability of a word as an association and in general linguistic usage, *J. abnorm. soc. Psychol.,* 54, 1957, 84.

adjectives, and intransitive verbs. On the other hand, adverbs of frequency (*always, seldom*), transitive verbs, and question-words (*when, who*) occur less often in final positions. They would be expected to elicit syntagmatic responses at later ages than other categories.

(4) Decrease in clang-responses. Since children have less practice than adults in both verbal and non-verbal associations with words, they are more likely to respond to the immediate sound-properties of verbal stimuli, as if the words were nonsense. Indeed, children are known to display more generalization between words that sound alike.[7]

Earlier research partially supports these generalizations. Wreschner, using German words, found that age and education were both related to paradigmatic dominance, and that children preferred concrete nouns as responses regardless of the class of the stimulus-word.[8] Inflectional affixes in German confound clang-responses and paradigmatic responses.

Reanalysis of Woodrow and Lowell's data for English reveals that paradigmatic responses increased and syntagmatic responses decreased with age.[9] The range of form-classes included was limited, however, and the list was not confined to cases where the adult primary response was present in children's vocabularies. Age-changes may be merely due to specific changes in vocabulary in such cases, though it is true that these alone should not produce the bias in the direction of change which the data indicate.

METHOD

Materials

The list of associative words, 46 in number, was chosen from a variety of grammatical classes. Since the work was done in conjunction with a study on learning antonyms, 39 of the items were so chosen that the primary response of adults was coördinate or antonymous. All stimulus-words and primary responses of adults were, according to Rinsland, probably within the vocabulary of the youngest children.[10] The form-classes were alternated within the list and the same order of presentation was used for all *S*s.

The *closed-alternative test* was composed of 35 items, the last 10 being omitted for the third-graders. Three kinds of items were alternated on the list to test the relative strength of syntagmatic, paradigmatic, and antonymous responses. In one set the words were grammatically alike (*snow, winter, summer*), but contained an antonym. In a second set, an antonym was contrasted with a syntagmatic associate, (*pillow, soft, hard*). In the third group, syntagmatic and paradigmatic associates were contrasted, (*fire, hot, warm*).

Subjects

Twenty-three *S*s were chosen from the kindergarten, 10 from the first grade, 52 from the third grade, and 99 from the sixth grade. In the last two grades, the entire class was tested in a group; in the first two, the children were tested individually.

Procedure

The *S*s in the kindergarten and first grade were tested orally; those in the third and sixth grades gave their responses in writing. To keep speed uniform and to help slow readers, *E* read the words aloud to the older children.

Instructions. The following instructions were given for the word-association test.

7 B. F. Riess, Genetic changes in semantic conditioning, *J. exp. Psychol.*, 36, 1946, 143–152.

8 Wreschner, *op. cit.*, 70.

9 Herbert Woodrow and Frances Lowell, Children's association frequency tables, *Psychol. Monogr.*, 22, 1916 (No 97), 81.

10 H. D. Rinsland, *A Basic Vocabulary of Elementary School Children*, 1954.

When you hear a word, sometimes it makes you think of another word. If you heard *cat* you might think of *milk,* or *purr*, or *dog,* or *black*—almost anything. What does *cat* make you think of? What does *eat* make you think of? Anything else?

All single-word answers were accepted.

For the closed-alternative form also given, the children were told to say or to draw a line showing with which word the middle word of three seemed to go best. An example was given: "Does *brother* go better with *sister* or with *father*?"

Response-analysis of Free Associates

Both the stimulus-words and the response-words were classified by a method of defining grammatical class derived from Fries.[11] Test-frames or contexts were established; a word was assigned to a class if it could fit into the frames altered by substitutions from the same grammatical classes as the words in the frame. The same word might fall in several classes—*walk* is both noun and verb, for instance. In addition, coders were instructed to try to judge probable contexts according to children's usage. Thus *people* was not classified as a verb.

In the following list of some of the principal classes used in the analysis, the numbers indicate the agreement scores among the coders' obtained by computing the probability that an item coded in the given class by one coder would also be coded in that class by another coder. Disagreements largely stemmed from cases where one coder thought a usage too rare to include.

(1) Nouns, including verbs with '*-ing*', if they could be preceded by adjectives but not adverbs; 0.97.

(2) Pronouns, excluding possessives; 0.96.

(3) Transitive verbs; 0.87.

[11] C. C. Fries, *The Structure of English,* 1952, 65–109.

(4) Intransitive verbs; 0.87. Since most transitive verbs also occur in intransitive contexts (*he likes to eat*), coders were instructed not to code as intransitive any verbs which could be made transitive merely by adding an object.

(5) Adjectives, including verbs with *-ing* and *-ed* if they can be preceded by modifiers or by both adjectives and adverbs of manner; 0.92.

(6) Adverbs; 0.90.

(7) Nominal adverbs; 0.79. This is a subgroup of adverbs which can occur after certain prepositions, *e.g. now, here.*

The above comprise Fries' parts of speech. Below are several classes of functional words, most of which cannot occur alone in an utterance without the presence of some other parts of speech.

(8) Modifiers, which precede adverbs or adjectives; 0.85. Examples are *quite, really, too, just, very.*

(9) Determiners, which include the traditional articles and possessive pronouns; 0.97. Examples: *most, the, my, that, some.*

(10) Prepositions; 0.99.

(11) Interrogative words and *subordinate conjunctions* which were pooled for this analysis because of the large overlap in composition of the classes; 0.87.

Sequential Analysis

As an approximation to the sequences of grammatical classes in children's speech, children's books were subjected to an analysis of grammatical sequences. One hundred or more cases of items in each class were tallied in sequence from the texts to yield an estimate of the probability of each class given another class, and the probability of occurrence of the class in final position. Tallies were discontinued when it appeared that the probabilities for the given class were stable. Two tallies were noted for each item, one of the class of the word immediately following in the text, and the other of the class of the next word omitting functional words. The only major deviation from Fries' categories was that copulas (*is, seems*) were treated as functional words.

RESULTS

Closed-alternative Test

Of the 9 items where there were no antonyms so that only form-class was at issue, there were 5 showing significant increase with age in the selection of the paradigmatic alternative (Table 1). On the 11 items where antonyms were compared with syntagmatic choices, there were 5 significant increases with age. In all, two cases of marked decrease appeared, both involving the smallest sample, where the proportions are least reliable.

Paradigmatic Responses in Free-association

In counting paradigmatic associates on the free-association test, coders used a simple criterion to isolate the purest instances of paradigmatic responses. Responses were called paradigmatic only (a) if they can occur in the same class as the stimulus-word even if each also occurs in other classes, and (b) if they do not occur in immedate sequence or separated only by a determiner in ordinary continuous speech. Thus, though all are nouns, *front-door* and *table-spoon* were not tallied as paradigmatic, nor was *game-play*. The second restriction was not generalized to

Table 1

PROPORTIONAL CHOOSING SAME GRAMMATICAL CLASS ON CLOSED ALTERNATIVE TEST

Stimulus-sets (with correct pair marked)	*Kindergarten and first grade* ($N = 33$)	*Third grade* ($N = 95$)	*Sixth grade* ($N = 56$)
fire hot —warm	61	30	48†
witch wicked—bad	42	35	56‡
up —high sky	39	42	56†
lie —cheat bad	36	47	72‡
black —dark night	27	40	48
trees —grass green	17	—*	18
ball —bat play	66	—	96§
supper eating —drinking	37	—	36
write desk —table	83	—	73
pillow soft —hard	21	15	32†
sad —happy fun	15	37‡	52†
dark night —day	39	39	45
fast run —walk	36	26	34
go —come here	42	58	70**
behind back —front	39	47	48
to —from away	27	41	54**
he him —her	70	42	48
light float —sink	67	63	66
softer —harder stone	24	—	50†
played—worked hard	34	—	50

* Some items were omitted at the end of the test in the third grade.
† Higher proportion than in next youngest group, $p < 0.05$.
‡ $p < 0.01$. § $p < 0.001$.
**Higher than youngest group, $p < 0.01$, but not different from middle group.

all function-words rather than merely determiners, because such a rule would include conjunctions. Almost any pair of words in the same grammatical class might, of course, occur in sequence linked by a conjunction. The restrictive rule was pragmatic in origin and in practice successfully excluded the cases which appeared ambiguous as to paradigmatic or syntagmatic status.

One-tailed tests of significance were made of the increases, and are presented only for adjacent groups except when there was a gradual increase that was not sharply inflected. Of the eight nouns, six showed significant increases between the youngest *S*s and those in the third grade (Table 2). The remaining two stimulus-words, *moon* and *winter*, had a very high proportion of paradigmatic responses in the youngest group. Five of six verbs, and all of the prepositions, adverbs, pronouns, and comparative adjectives showed increases with age. *When* produced a low proportion of paradigmatic responses at all ages.

Table 2

PROPORTION OF PARADIGMATIC RESPONSES ON FREE-ASSOCIATION TEST

Stimulus-word	*Response-class tallied*	*Kindergarten and first grade* ($N = 33$)	*Third grade* ($N = 98$)	*Sixth grade* ($N = 52$)
table	N	18	69§	79
moon	N	69	80	71
boy	N	69	92‡	98
front	N	57	85‡	77
night	N	57	74*	83
winter	N	69	77	83
hand	N, TV	48	74†	79
game	N	15	33*	34
build	TV	15	18	48§
give	TV	15	34*	63‡
float	TV, IV	33	46	81§
worked	TV, IV	39	55	58
come	IV	33	71§	75
walking	TV, IV	30	52*	81‡
from	P	12	15	44§
across	P, Adv	12	41†	54
over	P, Adv	36	60†	65
up	P, Adv	63	81*	77
out	P, Adv	42	78§	77
before	P, Adv, SC	33	78§	85
always	Adv	12	49§	75†
there	Adv	18	67§	58
yesterday	N, Adv	63	90‡	94
him	Pro	30	76§	71
these	Pro, D	18	64§	71
when	Q	12	14	21
softer	A	42	69†	73
hotter	A	51	71*	62
slower	A	57	79†	81
worse	A, Adv	42	86§	87

* Higher proportion than in next youngest group, $p < 0.05$.
† $p < 0.01$. ‡ $p < 0.001$. § $p < 0.0001$.

The primary responses of adults for most of the stimulus-words was a coördinate or antonymous response. It could be argued that the increase in paradigmatic responses simply represents a learning of a particular type of paradigmatic response, or that it merely represents a culturally stereotyped learning of the primary response or training with conjunctive phrases. There are two tests of this explanation. One consists of examining the words which do not have high-frequency primary responses in the oldest group; namely, *game, build, across, when.* Three of the four showed age-increases.

A more stringent test consists of examining only responses other than those that are primarily adult, thus reducing the sample size in each grade. Fourteen items remain with sufficient cases for a statistical analysis, and of these eight showed significant increases with age in paradigmatic responses.

Thus the shift to paradigmatic responses cannot be regarded simply as due to increased learning of the adult primary and peculiar to coördinate or contrast responses.

Since the number of multiple-word responses decreased with age, it could be argued that the change between the youngest *S*s and those in the third grade is largely a result of learning to isolate single words. The phrase-responses were retained in the tallies on the grounds that these were the younger child's version of a syntagmatic response, most often consisting of the stimulus-word embedded in a phrase. For the older children the response was often merely the main, or modified, term of the phrase. Thus, in young children *across* might elicit *across the street;* in the third-graders simply *street.*

If only the single-word responses be tallied as a stringent test, a few of the age-changes disappear and all are of course reduced in magnitude. It remains substantially true even of the single-word responses that paradigmatic frequencies increase.

Syntagmatic Responses

The fact that paradigmatic responses increase with age does not demonstrate that the remaining responses bear a systematic relation to the stimulus-words. They might be randomly selected from all grammatical classes regardless of the stimulus-class.

If the response-words in association were a function of immediate succession in texts, 45% of associations to transitive verbs would be determiners, and 51% of associations to intransitive verbs would be prepositions. The actual associative probabilities are, in each case, 2%.

When functional words are omitted from the textual count, on the grounds that functional words rarely occur in isolation and will, therefore, be improbable as associative responses, then the text-sequential probabilities are as shown in Table 3. The associative responses shown below them correspond closely, when corrected so that the probabilities of responses in the same form-class as the stimulus-word are based on the expectations if the responses are syntagmatic.

Since there is no way of knowing from inspection which of these responses were based on substitution and which on sequence, an arbitrary correction was made. The probabilities of same-form-class associative responses were assumed to equal those in the texts.

This table is distorted by two factors. One is not easily modified—double coding was used for many responses, and influenced particularly strongly the classes of nouns and verbs. The second difficulty is that there is a difference in the basal probability of each form-class, regardless of antecedents, in texts and in association. This is to be expected because of the difference between textual frequency and occurrence in single-word utterances.

Table 3

PROBABILITY OF GRAMMATICAL CLASSES IN TEXTS AND WORD-ASSOCIATION FOLLOWING SPECIFIED ANTECEDENT CLASSES*

	Noun, Pronoun		*Intrans. Verb*		*Trans. Verb*		*Adjective*	
Response-class	text	word assoc.	text	word assoc.	text	word assoc.	text	word assoc.
Noun, pronoun	.31	(.70)	.68	.35	.92	.75	.79	.56
Intransitive verb	.19	.21	.01	(.46)	.03	.02†	.01	.06
Transitive verb	.33	.27	.05	.09†	01	(.46)	—	.13
Adjective	.13	.17	.06	.18	.02	.02	.16	(.71)
Adverb	.03	.02	.20	.28	.02	.07	.03	.03

* Word-association probabilities include function-words and therefore do not add to unity. Parenthesized values represent uncorrected responses in paradigmatic classes.

† When a verb-response to a verb-stimulus was double-coded as both transitive and intransitive, only the paradigmatic code was counted, thus decreasing the values in these cells. Other double coding was not adjusted.

It may be noted that the difference was greatest for nouns and pronouns, chiefly because the latter were much less common in associations than in texts.[12] A correction may be made by transforming the table into deviations from row-means, omitting the diagonal cells. Table 3 has been presented here in uncorrected form because the correction could be made if desired, yet the raw form may be more useful to other investigators. The product-moment correlation between contingent probabilities in texts and in associations after these corrections was 0.87. This correlation may be interpreted as a measure of the dependence of associations on the class of the stimulus-word, once corrections for paradigmatic probabilities and for differential probabilities of offering a response in text and in isolation have been applied. Thus, most of the variance remaining in the word-associations was due to training in textual sequences.

A few examples may clarify the character of syntagmatic responses. The most common response of changed form-class to *across* was *street,* to *float* was *boat,* to *come* was *here,* to *build* was *house,* to *game* was *play,* to *table* was *eat,* to *when* was *now.* The last may be regarded as syntagmatic in the sense that it represents a response to a question.

Some of these responses seem to indicate backward associations, but the question of associational direction cannot be solved readily with these data, and backward associations undoubtedly confound the data of Table 3.

There were very similar distributions of probabilities in the three age-groups when contingent associations were separately examined. There was a significant change with age in the direction of increasing frequencies of transitive verbs as responses to nouns and decreasing adjectival responses to nouns. Possibly this change reflects a change in speech away from descriptive sentences.

Sentence-final Position

It was expected that words which can occupy the final position in a sentence may have less strong subsequent syntagmatic responses. In terms of the proportion in final position in texts, adverbs

12 In a day's conversational transcript kindly supplied by W. F. Soskin, pronouns occurred in single-word utterances proportionally less often than any other class except functional words. In proportion to their total frequency, nouns were 7.6 times as probable.

were highest (0.36), next nouns (0.20), and intransitive verbs and adjectives (0.14). The probability of occurrence in final position of transitive verbs and function-words was less than 0.03. On these grounds we would expect that *build, give, from,* and *when* would have strong syntagmatic associations, and thus less paradigmatic dominance. In addition, *always,* while classed as an adverb, occurs most typically in a pre-verbal position or before an adjectival predicate. It may be seen in Table 2 that these words all showed late development of paradigmatic dominance, there being a significant increase between the third and sixth grade in paradigmatic responses to *build, give, from,* and *always.* The proportion of paradigmatic responses to *from* and *when* remained low even in the sixth grade. The proportion of paradigmatic responses in the youngest group was highest for nouns, and next for adjectives.

Clang-associates

Clang-associations are interpreted most broadly as all responses with the same initial consonants, with rhyming vowels, or with similar syllables included. Two exclusions were made from the tally—stimulus-words which had clang-antonyms or inflectional affixes such as *-ing, -er,* and *ed.* With these restrictions, the average number of clang-associates per child decreased from 8.33 in the youngest group, to 2.73 in the third grade and 1.62 in the sixth grade. When only clang-responses which were nonsense words or bore no meaningful link with the stimulus-word were considered, the difference was more marked, the frequencies being 4.39, 0.36, and none, respectively.

DISCUSSION

The marked increase in paradigmatic responses with age might be a result of several factors other than the relative strength of conflicting syntagmatic responses. Older children may have more practice in single-word responses than the youngest. The youngest were tested by an oral technique while the older groups wrote their responses. Yet in the controlled-choice test, all 14 sets showed increases in written paradigmatic responses between the third and sixth grades.

Perhaps the change as a function of age reflects educational experience. First-graders in the schools sampled were using exercise-books practicing substitutions of antonyms and synonyms in sentences. Such exercises were not in use at the time of the study of Woodrow and Lowell, in which the children 9–12 yr. of age showed as high syntagmatic predominance as the kindergarteners in the current study. The widespread use of such materials in this country might account both for the increase in common (usually paradigmatic) responses found by Jenkins and Russell over a 30-yr. period in college students,[13] and for the lower degree of commonality of response in Europeans.[14] Yet this explanation does not suffice completely. Woodrow and Lowell's adult sample did show many paradigmatic responses, and non-literate Navaho adults also markedly prefer paradigmatic primaries.[15] Formal educational practices merely hasten changes which occur with experience even without schooling.

Associational Direction

The analysis by classes clearly supports the assumption of predominance of forward associations. There was no evidence, for example, of an increment to noun-adjective or to intransitive verb-noun associative responses arising from backward

[13] W. A. Russell and J. J. Jenkins, The complete Minnesota norms for responses to 100 words from the Kent-Rosanoff test, Technical Report 11, University of Minnesota, 1954.

[14] M. R. Rosenzweig, Comparisons among word-association responses in English, French, German, and Italian, this JOURNAL, 74, 1961, 347–360.

[15] Sample of 38 Navahos collected for the Southwest Project in Comparative Psycholinguistics by Arnold Horowitz and Susan Ervin.

association, when the textual probabilities are compared to the associative responses.[16]

There is some evidence also for this directional bias in English usage. If a word rarely occurs in the final position of a sentence, it also rarely occurs alone. These classes—nominative pronouns, copulas, and function-words—seem to be the most structurally dependent, apparently because some syntagmatic association is very strong. Thus nouns, intransitive verbs, adjectives, adverbs, and accusative pronouns, which can occur in the final position of a sentence, also appear alone in answers to questions. When, however, questions seem to demand a response in a structurally dependent class, two kinds of answers are given. The answer may be longer than a single word: *who's coming? I am. We are.* Or the respondent chooses a class that can occur alone: *Who's coming? me; whose is it? mine. I, we,* or *my* did not occur alone as a response in spoken texts. The only exception to this pattern is the interrogative-word.

A full test of the hypothesis that frequency of final position is related to an earlier increase in paradigmatic responses should be conducted with stimulus-words which can occur in isolation. Verbs with known positional probabilities would be good candidates for such a study, as would subclasses of adverbs. Adverbs of frequency of occurrence typically precede the verb whereas adverbs of place, manner and absolute time more often occupy sentence-final position.

Of the two models presented earlier, the results of the present study conform to the learning model for forward associations. Can this model also account for other forms of verbal behavior showing similar age-changes? The norms of the Stanford-Binet test and Werner and Kaplan's study of nonsense-words both showed age-changes in definitions.[17] The younger children offered sentences as definitions; the older offered synonyms. Brown and Berko have shown that there is a high correlation between paradigmatic dominance in associations and synonymous definitions, for various grammatical classes.[18] The simple model of forward-association does not seem adequate to account for synonymous definitions of nonsense-words such as those found by Werner and Kaplan, but experimental evidence is not available on this point.

SUMMARY

Children in kindergarten, first, third, and sixth grades were given free- and two-choice associative-tests. It was found that there was a significant increase with age in the proportion of responses in the same grammatical class as the stimulus-word, with an earlier increase in words occurring more often in final position in sentences than in words typically medial in sentences. There was a decrease with age in clang-associations. When paradigmatic associates were removed, there was a correlation of 0.87 between the transitional probabilities of five grammatical classes in word-association, and the five classes in texts with the function-words or connective words eliminated. The functional-words do not ordinarily occur in isolation in speech and virtually never occurred as response-words in association.

These findings support a theory of associations based on training by forward contiguity in speech. Responses in the same grammatical class as the stimulus

[16] If the data in Thumb and Marbe, *op. cit.*, 56–63, are retabulated separately for intransitive and transitive verbs, verb-responses dominate for the former, and nouns for the latter.

[17] Heinz Werner and Edith Kaplan, The acquisition of word meanings: A developmental study, *Soc. Res. Child Developm. Monogr.*, 15 1952 (No. 51), 84.

[18] R. W. Brown and Jean Berko, Word association and the acquisition of grammar, *Child Development*, 31, 1960, 1–14. This study also replicated the findings on change with age reported here.

can be learned on the basis of occurrence in the same preceding verbal contexts. Their predominance over sequential associations from speech could derive from the relative variety of the contexts of the stimulus-word, and from the relative strength of substitutable terms. Both contextual variety and size of vocabulary increase with age and hence responses should come increasingly to correspond in grammatical class to the stimulus-word.

Mediated Generalization and the Interpretation of Verbal Behavior: I. Prolegomena[1, 2]

CHARLES N. COFER
and JOHN P. FOLEY, JR.

Looking at the mediated generalization and the free recall papers together leads to a realization of how much change there has been, over the almost quarter-century that elapsed between their publication dates, in our knowledge, sophistication, and awareness of how complex are problems of language behavior. I still think that stimulus equivalence between or among stimuli that are not physically similar, the problem to which the concept of mediated generalization was applied, is an important matter. And I think that Foley and I left the mediating mechanism, conceptualized as an implicit, fractionalized, kinesthetic r_x *with stimulus properties, vague enough to fit with a number of possible processes. Yet, it is clear that we conceived the mediating mechanism as a* response-like process, *peripheral in character, in the Hullian tradition. The trend since 1942 has been to postulate more centrally located mechanisms—hypotheses, codes, strategies, plans, and the like. Peripheral response processes as mediators no longer seem adequate; yet they had the virtue of anchoring our postulated*

Charles N. Cofer and John P. Foley, Jr., "Mediated Generalization and the Interpretation of Verbal Behavior: I. Prolegomena," *The Psychological Review,* **49**, No. 6 (November, 1942), 513–540. Reprinted by permission of the authors and publisher.

[1] The present paper represents the theoretical background for research being conducted by the writers under a grant-in-aid from the American Association for the Advancement of Science.

[2] The writers wish to express their appreciation to the following persons who read and criticized a preliminary copy of the present paper: Professor C. H. Graham, Professor E. R. Guthrie, Professor C. L. Hull, Professor J. McV. Hunt, Professor W. S. Hunter, Dr. Margaret Keller, Dr. F. A. Mote, Professor Harold Schlosberg.

mediating mechanisms to events which, if not directly observable are at least observable in principle. This is much less the case with central processes. In the free recall paper I can see myself wavering between a desire to be concrete about organization as mediated by specific associations, category names, and the like and a realization that such denotable mediators are difficult to find and often clearly unlikely to be present.

Foley and I were concerned with transfer from one stimulus to other stimuli, and we proposed that there are many possible dimensions over which such transfer can be accomplished. Important as this problem is, it is an analytic or, even, an atomistic formulation of the problem. It ignores contextual features in which verbal units are embedded; this context can be either instructional, semantic, or syntactic. We said nothing about any kinds of context in the mediated generalization paper; the free recall paper does show, at least implicitly, some awareness of the importance of all kinds. Perhaps this is a significant difference between 1942 and 1965—in 1942 we could use a conditioned response model and ignore context because little was known or had been thought about context, but in 1965 this was no longer possible. We still know little about context or how it works, but we can no longer ignore it.

I wonder, now, that Foley and I could imply, as I think we did, that our paper treated language. *Our paper shows little recognition of the complex, hierarchical character of the system that a language is. Of course, the free recall paper doesn't deal with language in this sense, either. But it is concerned with* memory *and explicitly so.*

The years since 1942 have seen major developments in our understanding of the bases on which words can be interrelated. I think Foley and I were concerned mainly with referential meaning, although we didn't say so. Certainly the use of synonyms in our later experimental work implies that we saw the mechanism of mediating responses as explaining transfer among synonyms, and synonyms, by definition, are related to one another by meaning. We also wrote about interword associations, but I think we had no clear idea that possibly we were talking about something different from meaning. The research of the last decade or so has brought interword associations to the fore as the basis for interword transfer in many situations and has also shown the close relationship that often obtains between interword meaning, on the one hand, and interword association, on the other. It is still perhaps a moot question as to which is basic or primary, but at least we now know enough to ask this question rather than not to think of it as was the case in 1942.—CHARLES N. COFER

Since Watson's epoch-making hypothesis relating thinking to sub-vocal speech, psychologists have emphasized, to a greater or lesser degree, the important rôle which language mechanisms (verbal, manual, postural, etc.) play in complex human behavior. Although there has been much speculation regarding the nature and function of linguistic behavior, relatively few experimental data are available as the basis for systematized theory in this area. In fact, language mechanisms have often been regarded as 'uncontrolled variables' in psychological investigations.

The present paper reports an attempt (1) to extend the objective principles derived from conditioned response experimentation to certain aspects of linguistic behavior, and (2) to show how such an interpretation of language behavior throws light on other psychological phenomena in which language plays an important rôle. It should be emphasized at the outset that not only are the conditioned response principles (*e.g.*, reinforcement, generalization) here employed well established and generally accepted, but their validity as principles of linguistic behavior has been determined by direct experimentation, as will be noted from the survey of related experiments below, although the implications of such experiments for psychological theory do not appear to have been fully recognized.

Language is here regarded as a form of conditioned behavior—both on the part of the speaker and on the part of the person spoken to. This objective psychological approach to language behavior differs considerably from the philological and related approaches in which the major interest is in language morphology, *i.e.*, language as things—isolated words or syllables. It also differs fundamentally from the logical discipline of semiotics (*cf.* Morris, 16), which is concerned with the systematic elaboration of the meta-language in terms of which all sign situations may be classified and discussed. And it should be further emphasized that the study of language-as-conditioned behavior has no traffic with mentalistic theories which regard language as a means of 'expressing ideas.' For a comparison of these different approaches to language as well as for an objective psychological treatment of grammar, the reader is referred to Kantor (8).

I. EXPERIMENTAL BACKGROUND AND OPERATIONAL ANALYSIS

In the following paragraphs, we shall begin with a brief consideration of the phenomenon of generalization, followed by a discussion of the distinction between mediated and nonmediated (physical) generalization. Attention will then be directed to the problem of mediated verbal generalization,[3] after which the experiments in this field will be classified and the more relevant ones briefly summarized. The present section will conclude with a theoretical analysis of mediated generalization as a specific conditioned response phenomenon.

The phenomenon of generalization or irradiation of conditioned responses refers to the empirically determined fact that if a conditioned response is established to a given stimulus (S_1), other stimuli (S_{2-n}) of the same dimension will elicit the response without reinforcement, the magnitude of the generalized response varying inversely with the distance of S_{2-n} from S_1 along the given dimension.[4] Such stimulus equivalence or gradients of generalization have been experimentally demonstrated in the case of various stimulus dimensions, such as the pitch or loudness of tones, as determined by psychophysical experiments, and the spatial distance of tactual stimuli applied to the body surface.

Several investigators have recently shown that generalization occurs along a *semantic gradient,* although the mechanisms involved need to be clarified and extended by theoretical implication. If we omit all other experiments in which conditioned responses have been formed to verbal stimuli[5] and consider only those

[3] We recognize the possibility of linguistic mediated generalization gradients of a non-verbal nature, as in the case of sign and gesture languages. Mediated generalization in some form undoubtedly occurs in such instances, and it would be interesting to study the generalization gradients in these language systems.

[4] We are not concerned here with the phenomenon of response equivalence, or response generalization.

[5] Noteworthy among such studies have been those on the conditioned acquisition of voluntary control of previously involuntary responses, as well as those on the effect of positive and negative attitudinal factors on conditioning. Although both of these areas of investigation are relevant to the present problem of semantic generalization, no attempt will be made to consider them here. Similarly, the experiments

directly concerned with semantic generalization, we may classify the investigations into three major categories.[6] The first of these comprises *experiments in which a conditioned reaction has been established to a stimulus object (denotatum) and generalization obtained to its name (sign).* Positive results of this type have been reported by Kapustnik (9), Keller (10), Kotliarevsky (11, 12), Nevsky and Levin (17), Razran (19), Smolenskaya (27), Traugott (29), and Traugott and Fadeyeva (30). Conversely, Kapustnik (9) and Shastin (25), have described *experiments in which conditioned reactions have been established to a word (sign) and generalization obtained to its object (denotatum).* A third type of experiment has been concerned with the *establishment of a conditioned reaction to one word (sign) and generalization to other semantically and phonetically related words (signs).* Experiments by Diven (3), Keller (10), Razran (20, 21, 22), Riess (23, 24), and Wylie (32) are concerned with this problem. Since they are most relevant to the present paper, these experiments may be briefly described.

Razran (20) measured the amount of saliva secreted while he thought of 'saliva' in English, Russian, German, French, Spanish, and Polish. As controls he used the Gaelic word for saliva, with which he was unfamiliar, a pair of nonsense syllables, and a period of 'blank consciousness.' A quantitative index of his familiarity with these languages was obtained through his speeds of reading and of association in each. The results indicated that the largest amount of saliva[7] was secreted for the Russian word, the language of his childhood and adolescence, in spite of the fact that he is now more fluent in English. The German, French, Spanish, Gaelic, and Polish words yielded decreasing amounts of saliva in this order, which was the order of his familiarity with the languages, except for a reversal between Gaelic and Polish. Thus the degree of generalization appeared to vary as a function of his knowledge of or frequency of use of the specific languages, although the results, obtained on a single subject, are tentative.

A quantitative study of semantic conditioning in three adult human subjects is elsewhere reported by Razran (21). An attempt was made to separate the semantic or meaning-content factor from the phonetic or visual-auditory form of the word by the use of synonyms and homophones. Four stimulus words *(style, urn, freeze, surf)* were flashed on a screen while the subjects were eating, the amount of salivation to each of the stimulus words and subsequently to each of the homophones *(stile, earn, frieze, serf)* and synonyms *(fashion, vase, chill, wave)* being tested.[8] The mean generalization was 59 per cent to the synonyms and 37 per cent to the homophones, thus indicating that the verbal conditioning was largely semantic.

Riess (23) has repeated Razran's experiment, using the same stimulus and test words but employing the galvanic skin reaction (GSR) to a loud buzzer as a substitute for the salivary technique. The number of subjects varied from 4 to 9 in the case of the four stimulus words.

on indirect or mediated conditioning (Shipley, N. E. Miller, Lumsdaine) are arbitrarily omitted from the present discussion, owing to the fact that the mediated generalization is not semantic in character.

[6] In his description of methods for studying conditioned reflexes in man, Ivanov-Smolensky (7) includes a discussion of verbal conditioning, but neither the original monograph nor a complete abstract was available to the writers. References to two other volumes edited by Ivanov-Smolensky, and presumably including a summary of experiments on verbal conditioning and semantic generalization performed by students in his laboratory, are cited by Razran (21, p. 90, footnotes 1 and 2).

[7] Measured by means of Razran's 'cotton technique,' which consists in ascertaining the increment in weight of an absorbent dental cotton roll inserted under the subject's tongue for a period of one minute.

[8] *Ibid.*

Riess also found generalization to be greater to the synonyms than to the homophones, the mean percentage gain from conditioning being 94.5 for the homophones and 141.0 for the synonyms. In a recent unpublished study Riess (24) has included antonyms and has studied generalization at different age levels. Results appear to indicate that in young children generalization is greater to the homophones than to the synonyms, with the antonyms intermediate between the two, thus suggesting the relatively greater importance of phonetic as compared with semantic factors in the behavior of young children. With adults, however, the relationship is reversed, the order of increasing amount of generalization being: homophones, antonyms, synonyms.

Wylie (32) repeated the experiment performed by Razran and Riess, conditioning the GSR (elicited by shock) to certain words and testing generalization not only to homophones and synonyms of these words but also to other words (controls) bearing no relationship to the conditioned words. She found evidence of greater generalization to the homophones and to the synonyms than to the control words, but her results indicated greater generalization to the homophones than to the synonyms. This variation from the findings of Razran and Riess may, perhaps, result from the fact that her subjects said they expected shock on the words that sounded like the conditioned words but not on the synonyms of those words. Had her subjects been misled as to the nature of the experiment, this result might not have occurred. Wylie further studied semantic generalization by using nonsense syllables. Her subjects learned several pairs of syllables by the paired associates method, and the first members of two of these pairs were then conditioned. Generalization was found to be much greater to the syllables associated with the conditioned syllables than to those syllables associated with non-conditioned syllables.

Another experiment by Razran (22) followed the same general method as that described three paragraphs above. For single-word conditioning, semantic factors were again found to be the most important determiners of the amount of salivary generalization in the adult subject, although 'phonetographic' relationships (sound-spelling, *e.g., dark, mark*) were also very significant, especially at the beginning of the conditioning and after long continued pairings. Syntactic generalization was also studied by conditioning a salivary reaction to a 3-word sentence (consisting of subject, copula, and predicate) and then testing for generalization to other 3-word sentences in which one or more of the three words was reversed —giving rise to 7 verbal variations and to 4 contradictory and 3 concordant statements (*e.g., Poverty is degrading: Wealth is degrading, Poverty is not degrading, Poverty is not uplifting, Wealth is uplifting, etc.*) Results indicated that the amount of generalization obtained depended upon the following factors (in decreasing order of strength of generalization): general agreement of statement, agreement of copula, predicate, subject; but reversals of copulas interfered more with transfer than general reversals of statements. Razran also reported that conditioned single words lost some of their generalization-strengths when combined in sentences, and that subjects' opinions regarding the truth of the statement influenced the conditioning as well as the generalization value of the sentence.

In a study designed to investigate the conditioning of anxiety reactions (GSR) to words, Diven (3) found generalization spreading 'by meaningful relation' to other words in the series. For example, from the reinforced word *barn*, generalization occurred to other words in a 'rural' category.

In a somewhat different experiment, still in its preliminary stages, Keller (10) has found that when the GSR is conditioned to the picture of an object, there is generalization to the name of the object.

She has also shown that a conditioned response established to one picture of an object (*e.g.,* a hat) will be generalized to the picture of another object in the same category (*e.g.,* another hat). In part, this last result might be attributed to physical similarity of the pictures of the objects, but there may also be a factor of conceptual identity in the different pictures which is in part responsible for the generalization.

Let us now turn to a consideration of mediated as compared with non-mediated generalization. It will be noted that *the dimension along which generalization occurs in the experiments described above is not a dimension characteristic of the physical attributes of the stimuli.* The classical formulation of generalization principles presupposes naive organisms (*cf.* Hull, 5), whereas *mediated (e.g., semantic) generalization depends upon previously conditioned (usually language) behavior.* Razran (19, pp. 70–71) implies this distinction in his 'polymodal concept' of human conditioning, according to which the mean amount of conditioning is held to be a function of (1) a *physiological factor* dependent upon the 'biological potency' of the stimulus and its correlated 'physiological reaction-change' and (2) a *psychological factor* resulting from the associational history and patterning of the stimulus. A similar distinction has been made by Hull (6) in a discussion of the problem of stimulus equivalence in behavior theory.[9] Hull suggests that the three mechanisms mediating stimulus equivalence are: (1) the *partial physical identity* of the stimulus compounds, (2) *primary or physiological generalization* (irradiation), and (3) *secondary or indirect generalization* through the arousal of a reaction previously conditioned to the same stimulus continuum. Hilgard and Marquis (4, p. 201, italics ours) summarize the problem of generalization and the definition of stimulus similarity as follows:

> There are a number of types of equivalence between stimuli (and the responses which they evoke) which cause the stimuli to be reacted to *as* similar, so that conditioned responses formed to one of the stimuli will be generalized to the other. Among these may be mentioned: *partial identity* (whereby stimulus A—B is similar to A—C); *sensory similarity* (so that two colors are more alike than a color and a tone); *formal similarity* (for example, two patterns of ascending pitch); *affective similarity* (equivalence mediated by emotionally flavored processes, as in the "dark brown taste" or "blue Monday"); and *mediated similarity* (as in the equivalence of words of different sounds, but of common meanings). Of these relationships, only the first (partial identity) may be conceived of as physical similarity. The second (sensory similarity) may be mediated by relatively primitive physiological processes, as represented in the classical experiments on generalization within a sensory modality. The others all depend upon relatively complex processes, many of which require previous learning in order that the stimuli involved may be responded to as similar.

It is with this final type of 'mediated' generalization that we are here concerned. It is clear that semantic generalization would not take place in the case of a subject who did not know the meaning of the words or who saw no conceptual identity or similarity in the pictures of the hats in Keller's experiment. The mediated or semantic generalization in such experiments thus presupposes and depends upon the pre-experimental formation of conditioned responses or associations, *i.e., the gradient of generalization is a gradient along a dimension of conditioned stimulus functions.* The stimuli need be similar only in so far as they have been previously conditioned to the same (or similar) response.

A simplified schema of such mediated or semantic generalization is suggested in Fig. 1. At some pre-experimental time, the subject has become conditioned, either by direct reinforcement or by higher order

[9] Many of these distinctions bear a resemblance to Kantor's interbehavioristic 'stimulus function.'

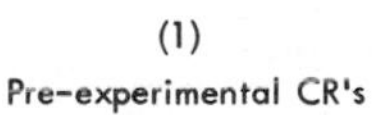

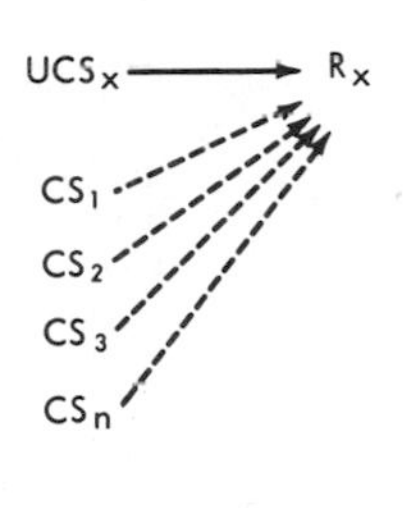

(2)
Experimental CR's for testing mediated generalization

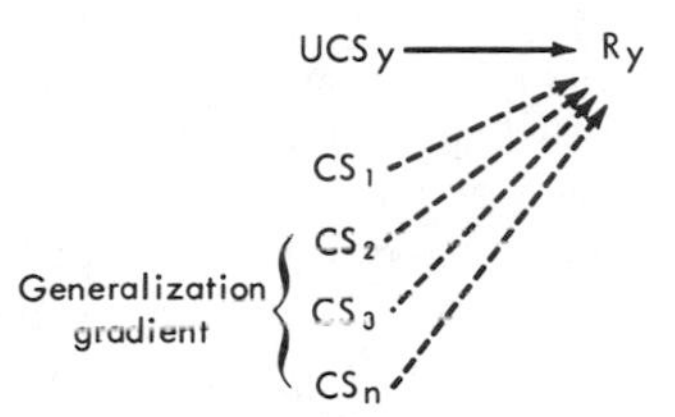

Fig. 1: Simplified descriptive schema for the development of mediated generalization.

conditioning, to make R_x *to* CS_1, CS_2, $CS_3 \ldots CS_n$. The subject is next experimentally conditioned by reinforcing CS_1 with UCS_y, setting up a conditioned response, R_y. Generalization is now found to $CS_2 \ldots CS_n$, the magnitude of the generalized response presumably depending upon the relative strengths of the pre-experimental conditioning of $CS_1 \ldots CS_n$ to R_x.

It should be emphasized that the schema in Fig. 1 is an operational account of what descriptively occurs in mediated generalization. Hypotheses regarding further, non-observable mechanisms could be introduced with reference to the manner in which generalization may be said to occur along the previously-conditioned stimulus-response continuum. Thus one might assume, following the theoretical analysis of Guthrie, Hull, and others, that upon the pre-experimental conditioning of $CS_1 \ldots CS_n$ to R_x, each of these stimuli is also conditioned to an implicit, fractional, kinesthetic r_x, which invariably occurs with each pre-experimental reinforcement of R_x. In the later, experimental situation, CS_1 is conditioned to R_y. But during each reinforcement of this conditioning, CS_1 evokes r_x, the proprioceptive stimulation (s_x) from which also becomes conditioned to R_y. Now, when $CS_2 \ldots CS_n$ is presented alone for testing mediated generalization, it will evoke r_x, whose s_x will in turn elicit R_y.[10] Thus, from a purely molar or descriptive point of view, $S_2 \ldots S_n$ will lead directly to R_y. A diagrammatic representation and more detailed discussion of these inferred mechanisms are presented by Hull (6, pp. 27–28).

II. FORMAL ILLUSTRATION, METHODS OF EXPERIMENTAL DEMONSTRATION, AND IMPLICATIONS FOR BEHAVIOR THEORY

In this section an attempt will be made to extend the previous analysis and to illustrate its application to various psychological situations. More specifically, the

[10] Evidence concerning the rôle of such mediating responses is found in a series of different experiments by Miller (13, 14), designed to test the influence of past experience upon the transfer of subsequent training. Although both rodent and human subjects were used in different experiments, our present interest is in the verbal behavior of the latter. One such experiment made use of numbers and letters as different material categories pre-experimentally acquired and inter-associated by the subjects. A conditioned GSR differentiating between a specific number and a specific letter was set up, and differential generalization was found to other numbers and letters which had not been subject to direct reinforcement (*cf.* 13, p. 70). In further series of experiments, "controlled patterns of association were established through the learning of nonsense syllables. Possible effects of original similarities between pairs of syllables were eliminated by the systematic use of the same syllables in different patterns of association for different subjects. Differential conditioned galvanic reactions were established to a pair of stimuli by shock and non-shock combinations, after which the previous associates of the shock and non-shock pair were presented without shock. Photographic records of the

section will begin with the discussion of a formal system of notation for designating mediated (*i.e.,* synonym) and non-mediated (*i.e.,*. homophone) generalization gradients, after which the discussed synonym and homophone relationships will be illustrated by application to an hypothetical subject. A number of other gradients (other than synonym and homophone) along which mediated generalization might be expected to occur will next be suggested. A minimum number of formal concepts essential to the present theory will then be presented, followed by a discussion of methods for experimental check or demonstration of the expected relationships in the case of a given subject. The paper will conclude with the suggested application of the theory to various fields of psychological investigation.

The implications of semantic generalization for behavior theory, especially when combined with non-semantic or physical (*e.g.,* phonetic) generalization, appear not to have been adequately recognized. The relationships explicated in Fig. 1 may be regarded as a generalized statement of the nature of mediated stimulus equivalence. We are here interested in one form of mediated generalization, *viz.,* that involved in verbal language behavior; we are also concerned with non-mediated generalization insofar as it plays a part in these problems.

In Fig. 2 we have suggested certain formal relationships which might be expected to obtain in the case of an organism whose language behavior is highly developed. Mediated generalization is here depicted in terms of synonymity of words and non-mediated generalization in terms of homophonymity of words. The following set of definitions will explain the system of notation used in this figure:

P refers to the original, reinforced stimulus (presentation) word.

S refers to a synonym of *P*.

H refers to a homophone of *P*.

N refers to a neutral word.

Numbers in parentheses designate the number of semantic or phonetic transformations removed from *P*.

S_s refers to a synonym of the preceding synonym.

S_h refers to a synonym of the preceding homophone.

H_s refers to a homophone of the preceding synonym.

(No notation is required for a homophone

---

responses showed contrasting reactions to the syllables associated to the shock and non-shock elements of the primary conditioning pair" (13, 'Digest,' inserted in front of 'Table of Contents').

"Additional experiments on human subjects demonstrated that (*a*) galvanic reactions may be conditioned to the stimuli involved in the subject's own verbal responses; (*b*) conditioned reactions of this type are subject to experimental extinction; (*c*) under certain circumstances, the functional activity of the verbal response previously associated with both members of a pair of stimuli may be essential to the subsequent transfer of conditioning from one of these stimuli to the other; and (*d*) under certain circumstances this crucial rôle of the mediating verbal response may be demonstrated—with dynamically opposite effect—for the transfer of either the positive or the negative aspects of a differential conditioned galvanic response" (13, p. 70). Miller thus concludes that the evidence (from both human and rodent subjects) in his series of experiments "demonstrates the influence of previous associations upon the generalization of subsequent conditioning and indicates that mediating responses can play an important rôle in this transfer" (13, 'Digest').

Miller and Dollard (15, p. 77) report an unpublished dissertation by Birge (1) in which behavioral generalization in children was found to be mediated by verbal responses. Birge found that "if young children are taught to call two very different stimulus objects by the same name, other responses (such as reaching for the objects) are more likely to generalize from one to the other than when the two objects have been given different names." Birge likewise noted that "such generalization is much more likely to occur when the children say the name aloud, so that it is certain that the cue-producing response is actually present, than when they do not say the name aloud" (15, p. 77). Miller and Dollard (15, pp. 74–78) also discuss the rôle of the mechanism of mediated generalization in various forms of adult social behavior.

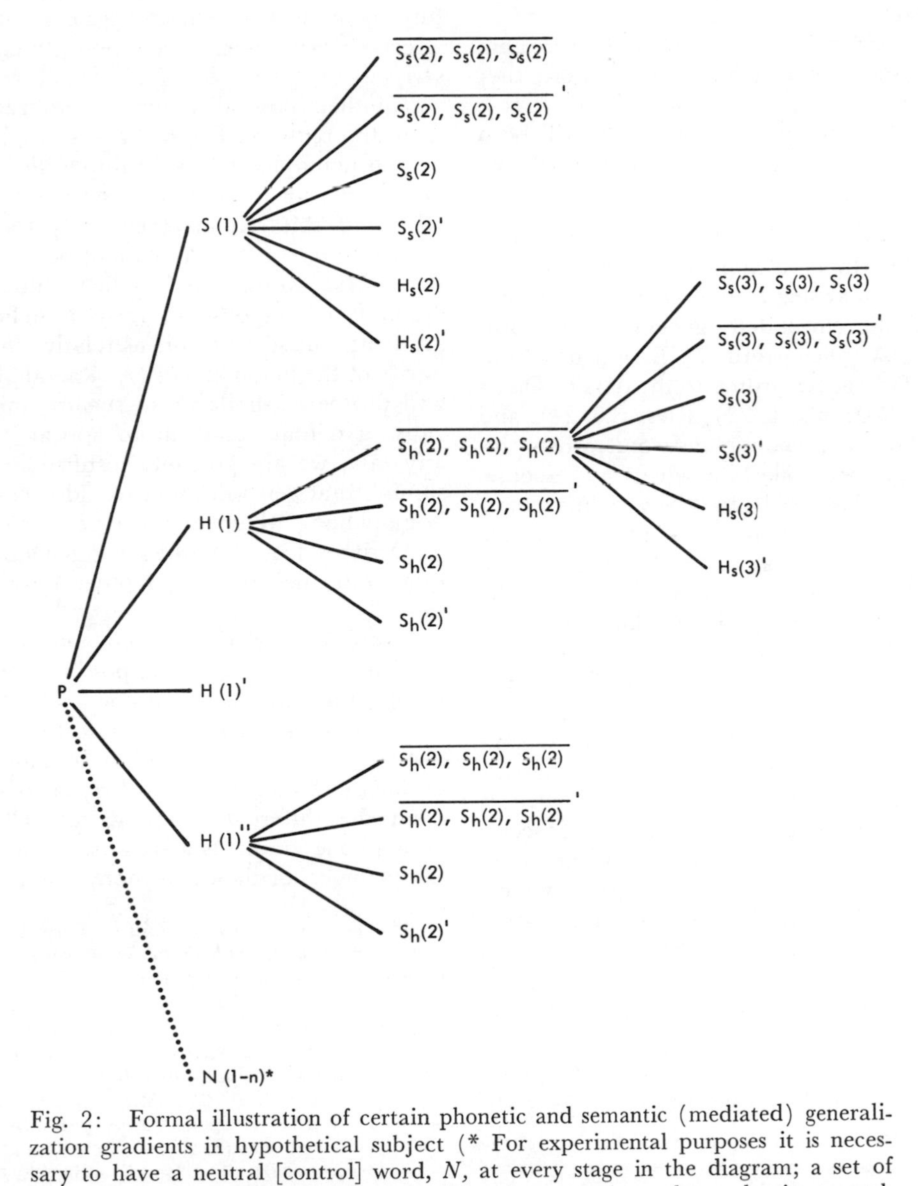

Fig. 2: Formal illustration of certain phonetic and semantic (mediated) generalization gradients in hypothetical subject (* For experimental purposes it is necessary to have a neutral [control] word, *N*, at every stage in the diagram; a set of such neutral words bearing the relationship of synonymity or homophonity to each other could also be utilized as additional controls).

of a preceding homophone. *Cf.* below.)

A prime ($'$), or primes ($''$or$'''$), is used to differentiate various words or various sets of words which are synonyms or homophones of the preceding word but not synonyms or homophones of each other.

A long bar (——) is used to cover a set of words (synonyms) which are also synonyms of each other. It is extremely unlikely that there will be a set of homophones which are synonyms of each other.

It is evident that if two or more words are homophones of a preceding word they will be homophones of each other. It is extremely unlikely that there will be a set of synonyms which are homophones of each other.

It will be noted that Fig. 2 is a formal representation of some of the possible relationships arising from certain phonetic and semantic (mediated) generalization gradients. A given word, *P*, is presented and reinforced. According to the data of Diven (3), Razran (21, 22), Riess (23, 24), and Wylie (32), synonomous words, when presented, will likewise elicit a response, though less in degree. Now *P* may have only one synonym or it may also have several synonyms; in the latter case these several synonyms may not bear to *P* the same degree of semantic relationship, *i.e.*, one word (synonym) may be more completely interchangeable with *P* than the others although all must bear some degree of interchangeability with *P*. (In this connection it should be noted that language authorities seldom assert that two words have precisely the same meaning. It seems likely, therefore, that the foregoing statement is sound.[11]) Therefore, we may have a series of words, varying in semantic similarity to *P*, which would be likely to elicit different degrees of response as a function of the degree of their similarity to *P*.[12]

Furthermore, *P* may have more than one meaning; *e.g.*, the word *vain* has both the meaning of *conceited* and of *fruitless*. Hence, it is possible to conceive the reinforcement of *P* as causing generalization effects along more than one semantic series.

Another possibility for generalization from the reinforced word (*P*) is provided by the homophone relationship.[13] For example, if *vain* is the reinforced word, the effects of this reinforcement may spread to *vein* and to *vane*. We cannot be certain that these words would elicit different amounts of response to form a definite gradient, but such factors as relative familiarity of the homophones (*cf*. Razran, 20) and degree of similarity in spelling might cause a definite gradient to appear.[14] At any rate, we are probably justified in assuming that generalization would occur to homophones, whatever the type of curve.

Deriving from the foregoing generalization gradients are several other possibilities:

1. From each of the synonyms of the original word there will be possible homophone gradients. Also, in the event that any of these synonyms has more than one distinct meaning, there will be in addition gradients formed by the synonyms arising from the different meaning, as well as homophone gradients arising from each of the members of the new synonym series.

11 It is necessary to remember that the relation of synonymity in the language behavior of persons is dependent upon previous associations (conditioning). Hence, we cannot expect generalization gradients to picture the dictionary semantic relationships but should expect them to vary with the particular individual in the light of his language history. *Cf., e.g.,* Mosier, C. I., A psychometric study of meaning. *Psychol. Bull.,* 1939, 36, 607–608, and *J. soc. Psychol.,* 1941, 13, 123–140.

12 *Ibid.*

13 There are many possibilities here. In the text we are chiefly concerned with words, conventionally designated as homonyms or homophones, which are alike in sound but not in spelling and meaning. Homographs could also be considered, both when the words have the same sound and spelling but different meanings (*e.g., fair, beautiful* and *fair, market*) and when the words are spelled alike but differ in both sound and meaning (*e.g., bow, knot* and *bow, forward part of a vessel*). Likewise, we have said nothing concerning the place of the antonym in this picture. Generalization along each of these (and other) continua could readily be investigated.

14 It should also be noted that partial identity in sound or spelling might be adequate for some generalization to appear. For example, if *lamp* be the reinforced word, generalization might appear to such words as *tramp, cramp, camp,* etc. *Cf.* Razran (22).

2. Each of the homophones arising from the synonyms described above in 1 also may have synonyms, causing additional synonym gradients to appear; these synonyms may have homophones, more than one meaning, etc. The number of possible gradients is thus extended to a very large number.

3. Each of the members of the series of words homophonous with respect to *P* may have synonyms,—several sets of synonyms in the cases of words having more than one meaning. Each of these synonyms may have homophones, and so on.

With these statements and comments as an introduction, we may now examine Fig. 3, which illustrates the application of the relationships discussed in Fig. 2 to a concrete but hypothetical example. In discussing this diagram, certain important considerations must be kept in mind. The semantic and phonetic gradients portrayed are *limited* to synonym and homophone relationships, and for purposes of clarity, only *certain* of these relationships have been suggested. Moreover, the relationships or dimensions shown are purely formal, whereas those involved in the case of actual subjects would be distinctly idiosyncratic—varying as the result of the individual subject's particular linguistic biography. Fig. 3 thus pictures certain formal relationships, or generalization gradients, which, it is assumed, may be *simultaneously* activated (strengthened) upon the reinforcement of *P*. In the following descriptive text, the italicized words are the words found in Fig. 3, and the symbols indicate where they would appear in Fig. 2.[15]

The presentation word *vane* (P) is taken as the original, reinforced stimulus from which generalization would be expected to occur along the synonym gradient leading to *weathercock* ($S_{(1)}$) and along homophone gradients leading to *vain* ($H_{(1)}$) and to *vein* ($H_{(1)}'$). The word *four* ($N_{(1)}$) is inserted as a neutral or control word. From *vain,* three different synonym gradients are shown, the first leading to *fruitless* (S_h (2)), another to *conceited, egotistical, proud or pompous* ($\overline{S_h(2), S_h(2), S_h(2), S_h(2)}$), and a third to *trifling* or *foolish* ($\overline{S_h(2), S_h(2)'}$). *Pompous* bears a quasi-homophonic relationship to *pampas* ($H_s(3)$), from which alternate synonym and homophone gradients lead consecutively to *steppes* ($S_h(4)$), *steps* ($H_s(5)$), *stairs* ($S_h(6)$), *stares* ($H_s(7)$), and *looks* ($S_h(8)$). Two synonym gradients are depicted from *fruitless.* The one to *sterile* or *barren* ($\overline{S_s(3), S_s(3)}$), leads from *barren* to its synonym, *dull* or *stupid* ($\overline{S_s(4), S_s(4)}$), and to its homophone, *baron* ($H_s(4)$), whose synonym is *nobleman* or *lord* ($\overline{S_h(5), S_h(5)}$). The other synonym gradient from *fruitless* leads to *useless, unprofitable, worthless* or *idle* ($\overline{S_s(3), S_s(3), S_s(3), S_s(3)'}$), the homophone gradients from *idle* leading to *idol* ($H_s(4)$) and to *idyll* ($H_s(4)'$); whereas the synonym gradient from *idol* leads to *god* ($S_h(5)$). It is of some theoretical significance to note, as shown by the broken line in Fig. 3, that *god* is a synonym of *lord* ($H_s(5)$), whose associative strength is derived through *baron* ($H_s(4)$) and *barren* ($S_s(3)$) (*cf.* above); thus a circularity is achieved in the suggested semantic and phonetic gradients, and the words *god* and *lord* would be expected to show intensified magnitudes owing to algebraic summation of their reaction potentials (*cf.* below).

From *vein* ($H_{(1)}'$), another homophone of the original presentation word *vane* (P), three different synonym gradients are represented in Fig. 3. One leads to *bed, fissure* or *lode* ($S_h(2)$, $S_h(2)$, $S_h(2)''$), with *lode* furnishing the homophone, *load* ($H_s(3)$) and the synonyms, *path, road* or *way* ($\overline{S_s(3), S_s(3), S_s(3)}$), the last named leading to its homophone,

[15] To a certain extent the relationships suggested in Fig. 3 have also been suggested by Woodworth (31, pp. 36–37), although less systematically, in his discussion of 'mediate' or 'indirect recall.' *Cf.* a later section of this paper.

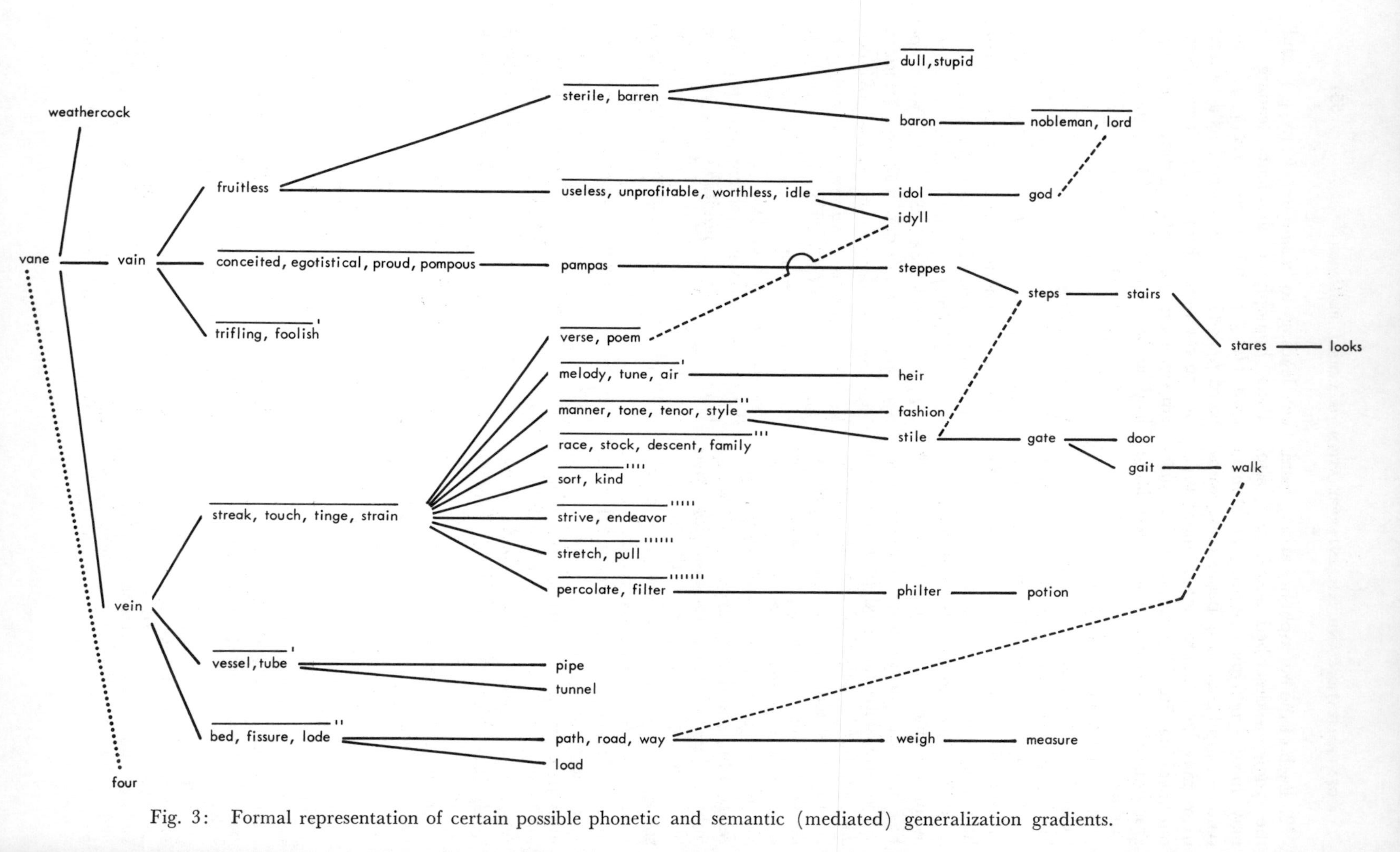

Fig. 3: Formal representation of certain possible phonetic and semantic (mediated) generalization gradients.

weigh ($H_s(4)$) and thence to the latter's synonym, *measure* ($S_h(5)$). A second gradient from *vein* leads to *vessel* or *tube* ($S_h(2)$, $S_h(2)'$), the latter having the two additional synonym gradients terminating in *pipe* ($S_s(3)$) and *tunnel* ($S_s(3)'$), respectively. The third synonym gradient represented from *vein* leads to *streak, touch, tinge* or *strain* ($S_h(2)$, $S_h(2)$, $S_h(2)$, $S_h(2)$), from the last word of which the following eight synonym gradients (all $S_s(3)$) are derived: *verse* or *poem; melody, tune* or *air*—leading to the last's homophone *heir* ($H_s(4)$); *manner, tone, tenor* or *style*—leading to the last's synonym, *fashion* ($S_s(4)$), and homophone *stile* ($H_s(4)$), with its own synonym, *gate* ($S_h(5)$) and its homophone, *gait* ($H_s(6)$) and the latter's synonym, *walk* ($S_h(7)$); *race, stock, descent* or *family; sort* or *kind; strive* or *endeavor; stretch* or *pull;* and *percolate* or *filter*—leading to the latter's homophone, *philter* ($H_s(4)$), and its own synonym, *potion* ($S_h(5)$). Attention is also called to the fact that *poem* ($S_s(3)$) is a possible synonym of *idyll* ($H_s(4)'$), as indicated by the broken line in Fig. 3, which fact illustrates another case of circular or double reinforcement along different semantic and phonetic generalization gradients. Similarly, *stile* ($H_s(4)$) is a synonym of *steps* ($H_s(5)$), and *way* ($S_s(3)$) is a synonym of *walk* ($S_h(7)$). These examples of circular generalization gradients differ from the *god-lord* relationship discussed in the preceding paragraph in that in the present instances the reaction potentials of the two words (*poem* and *idyll; stile* and *steps; way* and *walk*) are of different theoretical magnitudes, since they differ in the number of semantic and phonetic transformations removed from the original, reinforced presentation word, *vane*.

As was previously pointed out, the above gradients suggested in Figs. 2 and 3 have been limited to *certain of the formal synonym and homophone relationships* assumed to obtain in the case of the original, experimentally reinforced presentation word. In the actual experimental situation, many additional gradients will obviously operate concurrently. The following list of such formal gradients,[16] or formal dimensions along which generalization may be expected to occur, may serve to indicate this semantic and phonetic multiplicity: egocentric (*success—I must*); egocentric predicate (*lonesome—never*); evaluation (*rose—beautiful*); matter-of-fact predicate or substance-attribute (*spinach—green*); attribute-substance (*green—spinach*); subject-relation, including agent-action (*dog—bite*) and action-agent (*bite—dog*); object-relation, including verb-object (*shoot—deer*) and object-verb (*deer—shoot*); causality, including cause-effect (*joke—laughter*) and effect-cause (*laughter—joke*); coordination (*cow—horse*); subordination or genus-species (*fruit—apple*); supraordination or species-genus (*table—furniture*); contrast, opposites, or antonym (*black—white*); coexistence or contiguity (*Sunday—church*); identity or synonym (*blossom—flower*); diminutives (*man—boy*), and their converse (*boy—man*); phrase completing (*forward—march*); word completing or compounding (*black—board*); assonance, partial identity, or rhyme (*pack—tack*); syntactic change (*deep—depth*); homonym, including homophone (*vane—vain*) and homograph *a* (*fair, beautiful—fair, market*) as well as homograph *b* (*bow, weapon—bow, forward part of vessel*). In addition, generalization may be expected to occur along dimensions relating to other formal aspects of the words,[17] such as

[16] This list follows, with modification, the classification of response in the free association experiment, as suggested by Jung and adapted by Wells, F. L., A preliminary note on the categories of association reactions, Psychol. Rev., 1911, 18, 229–233.

[17] Skinner (26, p. 96) refers to certain of these mediated generalization gradients, although from a different point of view and in a less systematic manner. He writes: "Perseveration is a figurative way of saying that when a member of a group is elicited, all

number of syllables, presence of prefix or suffix, presence and particular location of particular letters (*e.g.,* initial letter, as in the case of alliteration), as well as words associated with national, political, economic, 'racial,' social, occupational, fraternal, recreational, or purely 'personal' matters. In the case of the actual subject, of course, the existing mediated verbal generalization gradients will be idiosyncratic—the result of the individual's particular past conditioning. The above, formal gradients are thus hypothetical abstractions illustrative of some of the possible logical and philological relationships.

The foregoing discussion has been designed to suggest some of the possible interpretations of verbal behavior in the light of a systematic application of the concept of generalization to at least a part of this field. It is, of course, necessary to check, experimentally, the relationships postulated above; we shall deal with this matter in a later section of this paper. It first seems necessary, however, to outline a minimum number of formal concepts which might somewhat simplify the application of the previous analysis to areas of behavior in which language plays a part. At this stage in the development of our analysis, we have not thought it essential to set down a number of definitions and rigorously worded postulates, although we recognize both the desirability and the necessity for doing so ultimately. Therefore, we are here introducing only the most vital concepts which we regard as important to the further explication of the present theoretical and experimental analysis.

1. *Reaction potential.*—When an organism is introduced into a given stimulating situation, there may, originally, be no especial response apparent. Subsequent to the reinforcement of some *S-R* sequence, however, the organism, in the presence of this situation, will respond in a predictable way. Thus we may say that the organism has a *reaction potential.*[18]

2. *Strength of reaction potential.*—If two reactions are possible in a given situation and one is made instead of the other, the former may be said to have possessed a greater strength of reaction potential than the latter. Within the framework of the present schema, the reaction made by the organism at any given time will depend upon the relative strengths of the existing reaction potentials, the strongest reaction potential evoking its response if its strength is above the reaction threshold. If two reaction potentials of equal or approximately equal strength are present, there will be no response (inhibition, blocking) until spontaneous recovery or some other process causes one reaction potential to become stronger than the other.[19]

The strength of a given reaction potential at any moment may be assumed to depend upon the number of experimental reinforcements of *P,* the number of semantic and phonetic transformations it (the given word) is removed from *P,*[20]

members of the group are temporarily strengthened relative to their normal latent strengths. Thus, if I say *hire,* all my responses which resemble that response are temporarily strengthened—particularly the response *hire* itself, which is likely to be elicited again sooner than its resting strength would dictate, and *higher,* which leads me to pun. Also strengthened are all words beginning with *h* (hence alliteration) and all ending in *ire* (hence rhyme). As to perseveration of theme, my response *hire* strengthens all responses associated with its referent, and I am likely to 'go on' to speak of labor, wages, and so on."

18 This term is similar in many respects to such terms as response tendency, reaction tendency, response potential, behavior tendency, behavior potential, excitatory potential, etc., used by other writers.

19 For completeness, it would be necessary to assume a liminal difference between the strengths of two reaction potentials before one could evoke its reaction in the presence of the other.

20 We may assume, for the sake of simplicity, a constant decrement in the generalization of reaction potential from *P* for each of the transformations a given word is removed from *P.* We recognize that this assumption may be too simple and that the amount of generaliza-

and the number of pre-experimental reinforcements of the given word (*cf.* Fig. 2). It is also possible that to the reaction potential of a given word would be added the pre-experimental reaction potential of *P* and that of each of the word preceding it along the continuum from *P*. Whether this is the case is a question for empirical determination.

Further, if a given reaction potential be derived from reaction potentials present as a result of the simultaneous activation of two or more gradients arising directly or indirectly from the reinforcement of *P*, as in the case of the god-lord, idyll-poem, gate-steps, and way-walk examples cited above, the strength of the reaction potential of this response will be intensified, since the positive reaction potentials from the different gradients may summate.[21]

3. *Reaction threshold.*—It may be assumed that for a response to occur, the strength of its reaction potential must reach a certain magnitude (and that positive potentials must exceed negative ones by this amount). This magnitude may be designated as the *reaction threshold* and for purposes of convenience may be regarded as equal for all verbal responses.

The application of the principle of generalization to language behavior is based upon the experimental evidence and logical inferences summarized above. The evidence thus far available has been secured by studying the subject's reactions without any especial effort to control or to secure information about his previous language history. In other words, the investigations have proceeded without a systematic attempt to discover the relative strengths of different reaction potentials at the moment of experimentation. In some ways this is an unsatisfactory situation. For this reason, as well as to indicate the manner in which we might go about determining whether Fig. 2 (or its special case, Fig. 3) is an adequate representation of the way in which generalization operates in the case of language behavior, we wish now to mention briefly four possible procedures for giving the experimenter some degree of knowledge concerning or control over the relative strengths of the verbal reaction potentials in the subject with whom he expects to work.

(1) The first method involves the pre-experimental reinforcement of certain verbal reactions, such that when the experimental session itself begins, the experimenter will have reason to expect that certain reaction potentials will be stronger than others.

(2) The second method involves the pre-experimental determination of the present strength of reaction potentials either statistically through Kent-Rosanoff frequencies, for example, or by actual measurements of word association tendencies in the subjects in question.[22]

(3) The third method, similar in some respects to the second, involves securing information concerning the subject's language biography, as was the case in Razran's experiment (20) cited above, in which the experimenter was able to assess the relative familiarity of the subject with different languages.

(4) The fourth method involves setting up an artificial situation in which

tion of reaction potential may be a function, for example, of the pre-experimental reaction potential of the given word. Similarly, we have assumed that all reaction potentials at a given number of transformations from *P* will be incremented by a constant amount upon the reinforcement of *P*. This, also, may be too simple an assumption.

[21] We recognize that inhibitory gradients arising from the negative reinforcement (punishment) of *P* are possible. It may be assumed that the negative reaction potentials of members of such series will sum algebraically with such positive reaction potentials as may exist.

[22] The verbal summator, described by Skinner (26), could likewise be employed for this purpose. This method consists in the repeated presentation of skeletal speech samples which, through summation and 'imitation,' elicit the strongest latent speech responses of the subject.

symbols (*e.g.*, nonsense syllables) having small (minimal) amounts of reaction potential could be used and differentially strengthened in a manner similar to that employed in Wylie's experiment (32, *vide supra*).

By employing such methods as these along with an involuntary response, such as the GSR, one should be able to determine fairly accurately whether the picture given in our theoretical diagrams resembles that present in an actual subject, or whether there are certain major inadequacies in our analysis.

On the basis of the foregoing analysis, it seems possible to integrate certain diverse phenomena ordinarily regarded in psychological writings as more or less unrelated. We have chosen a few such examples for brief comment. Although these examples have been selected from various traditional 'fields,' it is to be noted that the distinctions between these fields are somewhat arbitrary (and from our standpoint unsatisfactory).

1. *Perception.*—Perception is usually defined as the response to the 'meaningful character' of a stimulus in terms of past experience or in terms of the 'structural properties' of the field. From the point of view of the present writers, a perceptual response is a conditioned response; the response may have originated through direct or higher order conditioning or may have resulted from generalization. Undoubtedly much of this generalization arises from physical similarity of stimuli, although it may likewise occur frequently through semantic and related gradients (*cf.* above). Thus, for example, in certain experiments on the perception of tachistoscopically presented forms, the subjects' reports evidence modification of the original figure in the direction of a familiar (often verbalized) object. Perhaps many instances of the *'déjà vue'* phenomenon as well as other cases of recognition may also be accounted for through the processes of mediated generalization, although the factor of partial physical identity of the situations must also be recognized as important.

2. *'Set' or Einstellung.*—When a given performance is modified by events which precede it in time, this modification is often attributed to the 'set' of the subject, and the set is said to have resulted from the prior events. Many instances of 'set' are alleged to involve muscular adjustments, but other instances, particularly those involving verbal processes, are left unexplained (unless naming may be said to constitute an explanation!).[23]

It seems possible that the mechanism of mediated generalization may be operative in some of these cases. The writers are currently attempting to test this possibility by determining the number of words from a given list which can be reported by subjects after a single exposure; sometimes the test list is preceded by experience with synonyms of its members, whereas the control condition involves pre-test experience with unrelated words. A 'set' is thus built up in the one case, or, as we have phrased it, the activation of semantic gradients through the presentation of the synonyms should result in a superior performance on the related list. A practical example of this sort is found in the memory span test, in which the results might be influenced by the pre-test verbal behavior of both subject and examiner. Thus, the memory span for disconnected words might be greatly modified if some of their synonyms chanced to be employed before the actual administration of the test or if different words in the series fell on the same or mutually reinforcing gradients.

3. *Learning.*—Many problems in the psychology of learning may likewise be clarified by this analysis, at least in the case of problems in which meaningful

23 The importance of 'set,' attitudinal factors, and the like has been demonstrated in a number of conditioning experiments; such factors undoubtedly operate though instructions, 'sophistication,' and implicit self-administered stimulation, both before and during the course of many other kinds of experiments.

words—discrete or connected—are employed. One of us (2) has previously suggested that gradients of the sort described above may operate to cause at least some of the errors made in prose learning.[24]

4. *Memory* (*Indirect recall*).—One example will perhaps suffice to illustrate the application of the present theory of mediated verbal generalization to memory behavior. In his discussion of memory, Woodworth (31, pp. 36–37) has described a process which he has called indirect or mediated recall. Thus in recalling the second of two paired associates, the subject may report the use of intermediary steps such as meaningful relation. For instance, in the case of the pair, *above-conceal,* the word *ceiling* may intervene, being similar in meaning to *above* and similar in sound to *conceal.* These relationships would seem explicable in terms of semantic gradients in the first step and in terms of quasi-phonetic gradients in the second. Other memory phenomena, such as perseveration, might also be clarified by this type of analysis.

5. *Intelligence.*—While a detailed analysis has not been attempted, it seems possible that the gradients here described may be important in differentiating various degrees of 'intelligence,' as measured by the usual verbal intelligence tests. Thus, the level of performance on such tests may well be influenced by the number and type of semantic transformations which a subject, by virtue of his previous learning, is able to accomplish.

6. *Reasoning.*—Success in reasoning situations is often regarded as a function of the number of modes of attack with which a subject may approach the problem, or as related to the variety of approaches he exhibits in discovering a solution. It may perhaps be suggested that in the verbal sphere, at least, the number and type of semantic transformations, which the subject is able to accomplish is an important determinant of the reasoning process.

7. *Free association.*—Free association, whether in laboratory or everyday life situation, offers an obvious illustration of mediated verbal generalization. Beginning with a stimulus word or other stimulus material, the course of the responses may be regarded as determined by the language relationships peculiar to a given subject (according to the dimensions above indicated) and by the different strengths of the existing reaction potentials. Other language relationships not strictly determined by phonetic and formal or institutionalized semantic factors (*i.e.,* those associations peculiar to any one individual's reaction history) likewise play a part.[25] A similar statement may be made with respect to reverie and other imaginative behavior. Non-verbal stimulation, such as pictures, scenes, and the like, may well initiate a series of vocal (or sub-vocal) reactions in these instances.

8. *Emotional behavior.*—A suggestion may also be made as to the possible importance of the mechanisms here described in the case of emotional behavior. If a traumatic experience (to take a relatively simple example) be accompanied by a chance event, *e.g.,* the lighting of a cigarette, a whole series of words may subsequently cause anxiety or fear (neurotic) behavior. Thus, generalization could occur from *match* to such words as *wedding,*

[24] *Cf.* also Thorndike's (28) analysis of the possible rôle of phonetic and semantic factors in producing errors during the learning of English equivalents of French words.

[25] In this connection it is important to note that even if one assumes a fixed number of semantic and phonetic dimensions and a purely formal language history, the individual may give consecutive verbal responses which bear no relationship *to each other* along any of these dimensions. Such consecutive apparently unrelated responses frequently occur in continuous free association experiments. From our discussion of the theoretical basis of semantic and phonetic generalization, it will be apparent that such superficially unrelated responses (*e.g. load* and *baron* in Fig. 3) might lawfully occur provided their reaction potentials were of sufficient strength at consecutive intervals of time.

marriage, wedlock, nuptial; from *light,* generalization might take place to *lamp,* and, through assonance or partial identity, to *tramp* and finally to *hobo.* In the last instance the individual would probably be unable to report the reasons for his fear of hoboes ('unconscious anxiety,' *sic*) and a lengthy investigation at best might be necessary to get at the basis for the fear.[26] From this point of view, the free association technique may be regarded as a diagnostic method for studying the patient's particular semantic gradients in order to determine the biographical events leading to his aberrant conditioning. It is interesting to note that other so-called psychoanalytic mechanisms and techniques might perhaps be treated in a similar manner.

We could multiply indefinitely these instances of the type of psychological inquiry to which the application of the theory here advanced would seem to promise fruitfulness. And it should be noted that most of these questions are capable of direct experimental test, at least in principle. Indeed, many relevant data are already available in the literature, and need only be summarized in the light of the present systematization in order to bring considerable clarity and unity into otherwise disparate and unsystematized areas of investigation.

References

1. Birge, J. S. The rôle of verbal responses in transfer. Ph.D. dissertation, Yale University, 1941. Pp. 76.
2. Cofer, C. N. An analysis of errors made in the learning of prose material. *Psychol. Bull.* 1941, 38, 726.
3. Diven, K. Certain determinants in the conditioning of anxiety reactions. *J. Psychol.,* 1937, 3, 291–308.
4. Hilgard, E. R. & Marquis, D. G. *Conditioning and learning.* New York: Appleton-Century, 1940. Pp. 429.
5. Hull, C. L. The goal gradient hypothesis applied to some 'field-force' problems in the behavior of young children. Psychol. Rev., 1938, 45, 271–299.
6. ——. The problem of stimulus equivalence in behavior theory. Psychol. Rev., 1939, 46, 9–30.
7. Ivanov-Smolensky, A. G. (Methods of studying conditioned reflexes in man.) Moscow: Medgiz, 1933. Pp. 104. (*Cf. Psychol. Abstracts,* 1934, 8, 18, No. 152.)
8. Kantor, J. R. An objective psychology of grammer. Bloomington, Ind.: *Indiana Univ. Pubs., Science Series,* 1935, No. 1. Pp. 344.
9. Kapustnik, O. P. (The interrelation between direct conditioned stimuli and their verbal symbols). *Trudy Laboratorii Fiziologii Vysshey Nervnoy Deyatel'nosti Rebyonka pri Leningradskom Pedagogicheskom Institute Gertzena,* 1930, 2 11–22. (*Cf. Psychol. Abstracts,* 1934, 8, 18, No. 153.)
10. Keller, M. Personal communication to the writers.
11. Kotliarevsky, L. I. (The formation of pupillary conditioned reflexes and a differentiation in response to both direct and verbal stimuli.) *Arkhiv Biologicheskikh Nauk* (*Arch. Sci. Biol.*), 1935, 39 (2), 477–489. (*Cf. Biol. Abstracts,* 1937, 11, 1462, No. 13724).
12. ——. (Cardio-vascular conditioned reflexes to direct and to verbal stimuli.) *Fiziol. Zh. S.S.S.R.,* 1936,

[26] A fascinating field for investigation is here suggested in connections with Mowrer's discussion of the motivational value of anxiety in learning. This problem, however, is beyond the scope of the present paper. *Cf.* Mowrer, O. H. A stimulus-response analysis of anxiety and its rôle as a reinforcing agent. Psychol. Rev. 1933, 46, 553–565.

20, 228–242. (*Cf. Psychol Abstracts,* 1939, 13, 411–412, No. 4046.)

13. Miller, N. E. The influence of past experience upon the transfer of subsequent training. Ph.D. dissertation, Yale University, 1935. Pp. 73 and 4 appendices.

14. Miller, N. E. The influence of past experience upon the manner in which new training is generalized: an analytical study employing the conditioned response technique. *Unpublished manuscript.* Read at meeting of Eastern Psychological Association, New York City, April 1, 1938, under the title, The conditioning of galvanic responses to verbal reactions of the subject and the rôle of patterns of association learned prior to this conditioning upon its subsequent generalization. *Psychol. Bull.*, 1938, 35, 531.

15. ——, & Dollard, J. *Social learning and imitation.* New Haven, Conn.: Yale Univ. Press, 1941. Pp. 341.

16. Morris, C. W. Foundations of the theory of signs. *Internat. Ency. Unified Sci.*, 1938, I, No. 2. Pp. 59.

17. Nevsky, I. M., & Levin, S. L. (Unconditioned and conditioned secretory activity in children during hypnosis.) *Kazansky Meditzinsky Zhurnal,* 1932, 28, 344–351. (*Cf.* Razran, G. H. S., 18, pp. 30–32, paragraphs 40–41.)

18. Razran, G. H. S. Conditioned responses in children: a behavioral and quantitative critical review of experimental studies. New York: *Archives of Psychol.*, 1933, No. 148. Pp. 120.

19. ——. Conditioned responses: an experimental study and a theoretical analysis. New York: *Archives of Psychol.*, 1935, No. 191. Pp. 124.

20. ——. Salivating, and thinking in different languages. *J. Psychol.*, 1935–1936, 1, 145–151.

21. ——. A quantitative study of meaning by a conditioned salivary technique (semantic conditioning). *Science,* 1939, 90, 89–90.

22. ——. Semantic, syntactic, and phonetographic generalization of verbal conditioning. *Psychol. Bull,* 1939, 36, 578.

23. Riess, B. F. Semantic conditioning involving the galvanic skin reflex. *J. exp. Psychol.,* 1940, 26, 238–240.

24. ——. Personal communication to the writers.

25. Shastin, N. R., summarized by Krasnogorski, N. I. Bedingte und unbedingte Reflex im Kindesalter und ihre Bedeutung für die Klinik. *Ergeb. d. Inner. Mediz. und Kinderhk.,* 1931, 39, 613–730. (*Cf.* Razran, G. H. S., 18, p. 23, paragraph 28.)

26. Skinner, B. F. The verbal summator and a method for the study of latent speech. *J. Psychol.,* 1936, 2, 71–107.

27. Smolenskaya, E. P. (Verbal symbols of conditioned and differential stimuli.) *Na Putyakh k Izuch. vysshykh Form Neirodin. Reb.,* 1934, 304–315. (*Cf. Psychol. Abstracts,* 1935, 9, 131, No. 1163.)

28. Thorndike, E. L. Mental dynamics shown by the abbreviation and amelioration of words in hearing and remembering. *Amer. J. Psychol.* 1941, 54, 132–133.

29. Traugott, N. N. (The interrelations of immediate and symbolic projections in the process of the formation of conditioned inhibition.) *Na Putyakh k Izuch. vysshykh Form Neirodin. Reb.,* 1934, 273–303. (*Cf. Psychol. Abstracts,* 1935, 9, 131, No. 1166.)

30. ——, & Fadeyeva, V. K. (The effect

of difficult extinction of food-procuring reflexes upon the general and speech behavior of children.) *Na Putyakh k Izuch. vysshykh Form Neirodin. Reb.*, 1934, 316–403. (*Cf. Psychol. Abstracts,* 1935, 9, 131–132, No. 1167).

31. WOODWORTH, R. S. *Experimental psychology*. New York: Holt, 1938. Pp. 889.

32. WYLIE, R. C. Generalization of semantic conditioning of the galvanic skin response. Unpublished M.A. thesis, University of Pittsburgh, 1940. Pp. 40.

Mediation in Paired-Associate Learning

NAN E. McGEHEE
and RUDOLPH W. SCHULZ

Russell and Storms (1955) have shown that language habits inferred from free-association norms are presumably capable of mediating the learning of verbal paired associates. Their *S*s learned to associate a word (B) with a nonsense syllable (A) in learning the first of two lists. The response unit B was the first word of an associative-chain (B-C-D) inferred from the norms. Following A-B learning, *S*s learned a test list consisting of A-D and A-X pairs. The A-D pairs were learned significantly faster than the A-X control pairs. However, as Russell and Storms (1955) hasten to point out, "The mere demonstration of mediational influences in learning. . . does not explain how the effect is achieved" (p. 292). One main purpose of the present experiments was to attempt to provide this explanation for the above situation.

As pointed out recently (Underwood & Schulz, 1960), it is analytically fruitful to conceive of verbal learning as a two-phase process. The first phase consists of a response-acquisition or response-recall phase where *S* is concerned with learning or recalling the response units per se. The second phase, the associative phase, involves learning to associate the response units with their appropriate stimulus units.

The usual interpretation of the Russell and Storms (1955) result has been the one that the associative phase of test-list acquisition was facilitated via the specific associative chains linking the A and D items of the respective pairs. An alternative interpretation, made apparent by the two-phase conception, is that facilitation occurred because the B items on the first list enhanced the availability of the D items during A-B learning by raising them in *S*'s response hierarchy. Moreover, this enhanced availability could facilitate test-list acquisition in the absence of any specific associative link between A and D. That is, the increased ease of response recall which would accompany heightened availability should facilitate test-list acquisition. The latter expectation is consistent with the results of a recent study in which it was found that the acquisition of paired-adjective lists was facilitated when the availability of the response units was enhanced by deliberate pretraining (Underwood, Runquist, & Schulz, 1959). The

Nan E. McGehee and Rudolph W. Schulz, "Mediation in Paired-Associate Learning," *Journal of Experimental Psychology,* **62**, No. 6 (1961), 565–570. Reprinted by permission of the authors and publisher.

availability hypothesis was tested in Exp. I.

A second purpose of Exp. I was to compare performance under Russell and Storms' (1955) mediated and nonmediated conditions with performance under a condition in which first and test lists were unrelated (i.e., the practice control of transfer experiments). This was done to determine, in somewhat more absolute terms, the amount of facilitation which results from mediation in this situation.

The third purpose of Exp. I was to extend the generality of the Russell and Storms' (1955) results by replicating them with a design consisting of independent random groups and homogeneous lists as well as including *S*s of both sexes.

The results of Exp. I failed to support the availability hypothesis. However, for reasons too lengthy to detail here, we remained skeptical as to whether the failure of the availability hypothesis necessarily implied that mediation had taken place via specific associative chains. Therefore, Exp. II was undertaken to investigate the matter further. Namely, if there is specific linkage, then a test list in which the A and D items are inappropriately paired (i.e., the analogue of the S_1-R_1, S_1-R_r paradigm of conventional transfer terminology) should be more difficult to learn than the nonmediated test list. Put another way, there should be mediated interference. Indeed, Norcross and Spiker (1958) have demonstrated just such mediated interference for associative links acquired entirely in the laboratory. In Exp. II an attempt was made to demonstrate mediated interference in the present situation.

A second purpose of Exp. II was that of determining the "criticalness" of the free-association norms as predictors of the mediation effects obtained in Exp. I. That is, while the B and D items were selected so as to minimize the possibility of a *direct* free-associative link between them, the method of selection *did not* preclude the possibility of a meaningful relationship between these items (e.g., Thief-Take, Wish-Need, etc.). Similarly, it did not prevent the occurrence of interlist relationships between response units in terms of formal similarity (e.g., Smell-Stem, Memory-Matter, etc.). Hence, if the interlist relationships between response units, along dimensions *not* predictable from free-association norms, were stronger in the mediated condition than in the nonmediated condition, then the interpretation of the superior performance in the mediated condition would require revision. Therefore, Exp. II included a condition in which the first and test lists were learned in reverse order (A-D, A-B). The logic of this arrangement is based on the assumption that the associative linkage defined by the free-association norms is unidirectional (i.e., B-C-D, but not D-C-B). Thus, making A-D the first list and A-B the test list, should reduce substantially, or even eliminate, the facilitation presumed to be mediated by habits inferred from free-association norms. Contrariwise, a relationship between B and D based on interlist response similarity should be unaffected by the reversal of the lists because it would be expected to be a bidirectional relationship. Storms (1958) has proposed and tested a similar hypothesis for a situation involving a single mediating term. He found clear evidence for bidirectionality with normatively unidirectional materials.

METHOD

Lists: Exp. I.—The relationships between first and test lists define the conditions of Exp. I, and are summarized in Table 1. The first-list designations shown in Table 1 will be used as abbreviations in subsequent references to the various conditions (e.g., the mediated condition will be called Cond. A2-B, the nonmediated condition will be Cond. A2-X, etc.).

The stimulus designations A1 and A2 are used to distinguish between the two sets of 10 nonsense syllables required by the design of Exp. I. The syllables were selected so that inter- and intralist similarity would be at a minimum. Their association values ranged from 0% to 27% according to Glaze (Underwood & Schulz, 1960, Appendix A). In minimizing similarity it was impossible, with one exception, to retain the syllables used by Russell and Storms.

The B, D, and X response units were the same words as those used by Russell and Storms (1955) and are shown in Table 3 of their article (p. 290). The details regarding the selection of these words may also be found there. In brief, C was the most frequent free-association response to B, and D the most frequent free-associate of C, but D was not among the 10 most frequent responses to B, e.g., B (Trouble), C (Bad), D (Good). The members of the X-Y-Z chain are related to one another in the same manner as the members of the B-C-D chain; however, the members of the two respective chains were not related, and must not be related, to each other. Each list consisted of 10 paired associates.

Conditions A2-B and A2-X correspond to Russell and Storms' (1955) chained (A-D) and unchained (A-X) conditions, respectively. The availability hypothesis would be supported if test-list performance in Cond. A1-B is superior to that in Cond. A1-X. Similarly, comparison of A2-B with A1-X will determine if absolute positive transfer resulted from mediation.

Lists: Exp. II.—Conditions A2-B and A2-X of Exp. 1 were replicated. The lists of Cond. A2-D were the same as those of Cond. A2-B in Table 1 except that A2-D was the first list and A2-B the test list. Condition A2-Br is most easily described as follows. Let A_1-B_1, A_2-B_2, etc. represent the syllable-word pairings of the first list. Similarly, B_1 is the beginning of the free-association chain B_1-C_1-D_1. The test list represents a random re-pairing of the respective A and D items: A_1-D_4, A_3-D_{10}, A_5-D_1, etc. This test list was List A2-D—the same one used in Exp. I and in Cond. A2-B and A2-X of this study.

Mediated interference will be demonstrated if performance in Cond. A2-Br is inferior to that in Cond. A2-X. If mediation in these materials is unidirectional, performance in Cond. A2-D and A2-X should not differ.

Procedure: Exp. I and II.—Each *S* was read standard instructions for paired-associate learning prior to learning the first list. This list was then learned to a criterion of three consecutive errorless recitations. Following the completion of first-list learning all *S*s rested for 4 min. After brief instructions to proceed as before, *S*s were

Table 1

RELATIONSHIPS BETWEEN FIRST AND TEST LISTS DEFINING CONDITIONS OF EXP. I

Condition	*First List*	*Mediation Chain*	*Test List*	*Inferred Action*
Mediated	A2-B	B-C-D	A2-D	A2 ↗ B → C ↘ D; A2 ··········· D
Nonmediated	A2-X	X-Y-Z	A2-D	A2 ↗ X → Y → Z; A2 ··········· D
Availability	A1-B	B-C-D	A2-D	A2 ↗ ?; A2 ··········· D
Practice control	A1-X	X-Y-Z	A2-D	A2 ↗ ?; A2 ··········· D

presented the test list for 10 anticipation trials. For those *S*s not reaching a criterion of one errorless recitation during the first 10 trials, test-list acquisition was continued until this criterion was reached. The lists were presented on a memory drum at a 2:2-sec. rate with a 4-sec. intertrial interval. The 10 pairs in each list were presented in five random orders to prevent serial learning of the response units. The experimental session was limited to 50 min. for all *S*s.

Subjects.—The *S*s, Northwestern University undergraduates, were randomly assigned to conditions, with 30 and 24 *S*s per condition in Exp. I and II, respectively. The *S*s were naive with respect to the materials used, although most of them had served in other verbal learning experiments prior to their present service. When an *S* did not complete the experiment he was replaced by the next *S* appearing at the laboratory. There was no relationship between failure to complete the experiment and conditions.

RESULTS AND DISCUSSION

First-list acquisition: Exp. I and II. —Performance, in terms of mean number of trials to reach the criterion of three consecutive perfect recitations, did not differ significantly under the four respective conditions of either experiment (Exp. I: $F=1.77$, $P>.10$; Exp. II: $F<1$). In Exp. I the means were 18.33, 19.23, 18.90, and 15.43 for Cond. A2-B, A2-X, A1-B, and A1-X, respectively. The respective means for Cond. A2-B, A2-D, A2-X, and A2-Br of Exp. II were 13.62, 14.75, 14.71, and 15.87. The comparable difficulty of Lists A2-B and A2-D as first lists permits direct comparisons of test-list performance under Cond. A2-D with the other conditions of Exp. II, since the test list for this condition was List A2-B while List A2-D served as test list for the other conditions.

Test-list acquisition: Exp. I.—Test list performance is shown in Fig. 1. It is apparent from Fig. 1 that performance under Cond. A2-B, A1-B, and A1-X was essentially equivalent. Performance under Cond. A2-X was consistently inferior to performance under the other three conditions. The mean total number of correct responses during Trials 1–10 was 78.23, 65.43, 79.50, and 81.30 for Cond. A2-B, A2-X, A1-B, and A1-X, respectively. The standard error of these means ranged from 1.64 to 2.75. The only reliable ($P<.01$) differences among these means are those involving a comparison between Cond. A2-X and each of the other three conditions. The results for mean number of trials to reach the criterion of one perfect recitation were in complete agreement with those for total correct responses.

From these results it seems clear that Russell and Storms' (1955) findings were reliable and of some generality. The significantly ($t=3.79$, $P<.01$) superior performance under mediated as contrasted with nonmediated conditions in the present study represents a reproduction of their results. The interlist relationship in these two conditions—S_1-R_1, S_1-R_2—is such that negative transfer would ordinarily be expected. Hence, the failure

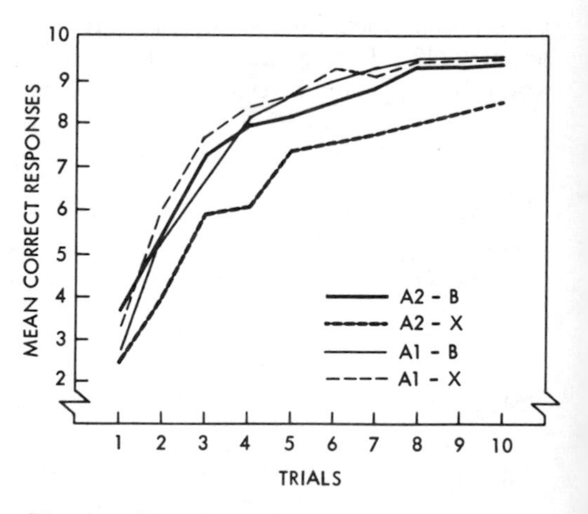

Fig. 1: Test-list performance in Exp. I as a function of various relationships between the stimulus and response units of the first and test lists. (See text for a complete description of these relationships.)

to find negative transfer under the mediated condition and the presence of a substantial amount of negative transfer in the nonmediated condition indicates that the inhibitory effects of the interlist relationship were somehow overcome in the mediated condition. However, comparison of performance under mediated and practice-control conditions makes it clear that the facilitation produced by mediation was not of sufficient magnitude to produce absolute positive transfer (see Fig. 1).

Finally, it is apparent that the availability hypothesis was not supported by the results of the present study. That is, had the availability of the D units of the test list in Cond. A1-B been enhanced during first-list acquisition, then test-list performance under Cond. A1-B should have been superior to performance under Cond. A1-X. As can be seen from Fig. 1, it was not. Moreover, an analysis of overt errors failed to adduce any evidence indicating enhanced response availability in Cond. A1-B. Therefore, mediation effects, at least in the present situation, cannot be attributed to facilitation of the response-recall phase of test-list acquisition via enhanced response availability.

Test-list acquisition: Exp. II.—The performance on the test list for Trials 1–10 is shown in Fig. 2. The means for the total number of correct responses over the 10 trials were 83.04, 66.37, 71.62, and 61.54 for Cond. A2-B, A2-X, A2-D, and A2-Br, respectively. The standard error of these means ranged from 1.75 to 2.57. The overall differences among means are highly reliable ($F=10.55$, $P<.01$).

Significant ($t=5.12$, $P<.01$) superiority of performance in Cond. A2-B over Cond. A2-X again replicates Russell and Storms' (1955) results along with those of Exp. I.

As can be seen from Fig. 2, performance was initially comparable in Cond. A2-X and A2-Br, but after Trial 3 the curves diverge with performance under Cond. A2-X remaining consistently su-

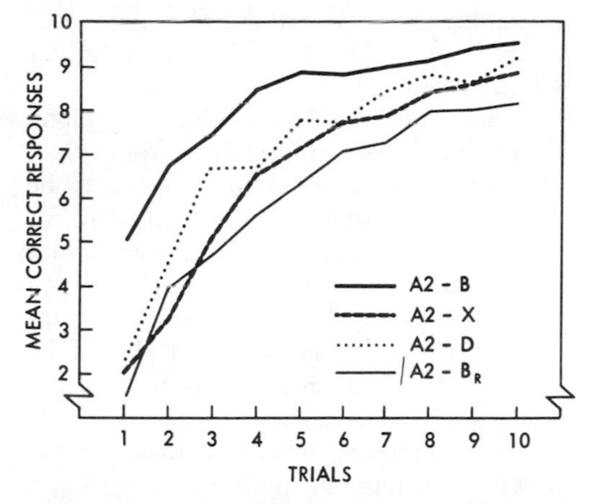

Fig. 2: Test-list performance in Exp. II as a function of various relationships between the stimulus and response units of the first and test lists. (See text for a complete description of these relationships.)

perior on Trials 4 through 10. The conditions did not differ significantly ($t=1.45$, $P>.10$) in terms of total correct over Trials 1–10. However, the difference in mean performance is clearly in the expected direction. Furthermore, consistent with the divergence in the curves of Fig. 2 for these conditions, the means for the number of trials to reach the criterion of one perfect recitation were 8.92 for Cond. A2-X and 11.87 for Cond. A2-Br. This difference in trials to reach criterion is highly significant ($t=2.65$, $P<.01$). It appears justifiable to conclude that mediated interference has been demonstrated in Cond. A2-Br. This result agrees with the one obtained by Norcross and Spiker (1958) with associative chains learned in the laboratory.

Inspection of Fig. 2 reveals a trend toward slightly better performance, at least initially, in Cond. A2-D than in Cond. A2-X. However, when the means for total correct on the 10 test-list trials for Cond. A2-D and A2-X were compared they failed to differ significantly ($t=1.61$, $P>.10$). Indeed, in terms of mean trials to criterion Cond. A2-D was slightly inferior to Cond. A2-X. Furthermore, performance under Cond. A2-D was reliably poorer ($t=3.51$, $P<.01$) than under Cond. A2-B.

Thus interlist response similarity along dimensions not predictable from free-association norms does not appear to be a major contributor to the facilitation of test-list performance in the present situation. This result appears to conflict with the one described earlier, which Storms (1958) obtained. However, it should be recalled that his situation differed from the present one in that it involved only a single mediating term in contrast to the present two-term mediating link. Perhaps, the potency of the "recency" effect to which he attributes his results varies inversely with the length of mediating chain. If this is the case, the present contradiction would be resolved easily.

In short, the results of Exp. I and II seem to provide fairly conclusive evidence that mediation in the Russell and Storms (1955) situation can be explained in terms of the facilitation of the associative phase of test-list acquisition via specific unidirectional associative chains linking the respective A and D items of the test-list pairs. Moreover, this interlist response relationship is associated with previously acquired language habits reflected by free-association norms.

SUMMARY

Two experiments were conducted to determine, among other things, how language habits inferred from free-association norms might mediate the learning of verbal paired associates in the Russell and Storms' (1955) situation. Their general procedure was replicated except that independent random groups and homogeneous lists as well as *S*s of both sexes were used. The interlist relationship between the stimulus syllables and response words of the first and test lists were appropriately varied to define the various conditions under which the 216 *S*s of the present experiments learned the 10-item lists on a memory drum at a 2:2-sec. rate.

From the results it was concluded that: (*a*) The response-recall phase of test-list acquisition is not facilitated in the mediated condition. (*b*) Mediated interference can be produced with the Russell and Storms' (1955) materials. (*c*) Under the mediated condition, the associative phase of test-list acquisition is facilitated via the specific associative chains linking the stimulus and response units of the respective pairs. (*d*) The free-association norms are "critical" in defining these associative chains. (*e*) Russell and Storms' (1955) results are reproducible and of considerable generality even though the facilitation produced by mediation does not result in absolute positive transfer.

References

Norcross, K. J., & Spiker, C. C. Effects of mediated associations on transfer in paired-associate learning. *J. exp. Psychol.*, 1958, 55, 129–133.

Russell, W. A., & Storms, L. H. Implicit verbal chaining in paired-associate learning. *J. exp. Psychol.*, 1955, 49, 287–293.

Storms, L. H. Apparent backward association: A situational effect. *J. exp. Psychol.*, 1958, 55, 390–395.

Underwood, B. J., Runquist, W. N., & Schulz, R. W. Response learning in paired-associate lists as a function of intralist similarity. *J. exp. Psychol.*, 1959, 58, 70–78.

Underwood, B. J., & Schulz, R. W. *Meaningfulness and verbal learning.* Chicago: Lippincott, 1960.

Words, Meanings and Concepts

JOHN B. CARROLL

I wrote this article in an attempt to show how the psychology of language and concept formation could be applied to practical teaching problems. It was not intended as a precise statement of relations among words, meanings, and concepts, nor as a contribution to the theory of language. If I were to rewrite the article, I suppose I might attempt to go more deeply into some of these matters, for example, to discuss the difference between meaning *and* reference, *which might be important for the teacher to know about. And I still feel somewhat uneasy about the treatment of "relational" concepts like* mass *and* weight; *psychologists have not yet adequately conceptualized the status of such concepts, much less shown how they are learned and understood. I hope this article will stimulate its readers to delve more deeply—either by the formulation of a more adequate theory or by empirical research—into the exploration of these problems.*

—JOHN B. CARROLL

The teaching of words, and of the meanings and concepts they designate or convey, is one of the principal tasks of teachers at all levels of education. It is a concern of textbook writers and programmers of self-instructional materials as well. Students must be taught the meanings of unfamiliar words and idioms; they must be helped in recognizing unfamiliar ways in which familiar words may be used; and they must be made generally aware of the possibility of ambiguity in meaning and the role of context in resolving it. Often the task that presents itself to the teacher is not merely to explain a new word in familiar terms, but to shape an entirely new concept in the mind of the student.

Whether the teaching of words, meanings, and concepts is done by the teacher, the textbook writer, or the programmer, it is generally done in an intuitive, unanalytic way. The purpose of this article is to sketch, at least in a first approximation, a more analytical approach to this task. One would have thought that volumes would have been written on the subject, but apart from such brief treat-

John B. Carroll, "Words, Meanings and Concepts," *Harvard Educational Review*, 34 (1964), 178–202. Reprinted by permission of the author and publisher.

ments as those of Brownell and Hendrickson[1], Serra[2], Levit[3], and Vinacke[4], for example, one searches the literature in vain for any comprehensive treatment of concept teaching. One is reassured that there are gaps to be filled.

There is, in the first place, an unfortunate hiatus between the word "meaning" and the very word "concept" itself. *Meaning* and *concept* have usually been treated as quite separate things by different disciplines. *Meaning,* for example, has been considered the province of a somewhat nebulous and insecure branch of linguistics called *semantics.*[5] *Concept* is almost anybody's oyster: it has continually been the concern of the philosopher, but has received generous attention from psychology. While the meanings of these two terms can be usefully distinguished in many contexts, it is also the case that a framework can be made for considering their intimate interconnections.

[1] William A. Brownell and Gordon Hendrickson, "How Children Learn Information, Concepts, and Generalizations" *Forty-Ninth Yearbook, National Society for the Study of Education, Part I,* ed. N. B. Henry (Chicago: University of Chicago Press, 1950), 92–128.

[2] Mary C. Serra, "How to Develop Concepts and Their Verbal Representations," *Elem. Sch. J.,* LIII (1953), 275–285.

[3] Martin Levit, "On the Psychology and Philosophy of Concept Formation," *Educ. Theory,* III (1953), 193–207.

[4] W. Edgar Vinacke, "Concept Formation in Children of School Ages,," *Education,* LXXIV (1954), 527–534.

[5] Even if a technical science of "semantics" is a comparatively modern invention,—dating, say, from Bréal's article on the subject published in a classical journal in 1883,—the field might be said to have been thoroughly discussed. The classic work of Ogden and Richards (C. K. Ogden and I. A. Richards, *The Meaning of Meaning* (3rd ed.; New York: Harcourt, Brace, 1930).), the somewhat faddish writings stemming from Korzybski's doctrines of "general semantics" (A. Korzybski, *Science and Sanity; an Introduction to Non-Aristotelian Systems and General Semantics* (8th ed.; Lakeville, Conn.: 1948).), and the recent work in psychology of Osgood *et al.* (Charles E. Osgood, George J. Suci, and Percy Tannenbaum, *The Measurement of Meaning* (Urbana, Illinois: Univ. of Illinois Press, 1957).), Brown (Roger Brown, *Words and Things* (Glencoe, Illinois: The Free Press, 1958).), and Skinner (B. F. Skinner, *Verbal Behavior* (New York: Appleton-Century-Crofts, 1957).) might be said to have disposed of most of the general problems of a science of meaning. On the other hand, Stephen Ullmann's recent book (Stephen Ullmann, *Semantics, an Introduction to the Science of Meaning* (Oxford: Basil Blackwell, 1962).) claims only to be in the nature of a "progress report," pointing to the "revolution" that has taken place in modern linguistics and the "advances in philosophy, psychology, anthropology, communication engineering and other spheres" that have had "important repercussions in the study of meaning."

There has been a rash of papers on the implications of linguistics for the teaching of English, the teaching of reading, the teaching of foreign languages, and so on. In fact, the idea that linguistics has much to contribute to educational problems in the "language arts" has become almost embarrassingly fashionable. One's embarrassment comes from the fact that despite certain very definite and positive contributions that linguistics can make to these endeavors, these contributions are of relatively small extent. Once we accept such fundamental tenets of linguistics as the primacy of speech over writing, the structure of the language code as a patterning of distinctive communicative elements, and the arbitrariness of standards of usage, and work out their implications in detail, we find we are still faced with enormous problems of methodology in the teaching of such subjects as English, reading, and foreign languages. The position is particularly difficult in connection with the study of meaning, because most branches of linguistics have paid little attention to this study; some linguists have seemed to go out of their way to exclude the study of meaning from their concerns as linguists. Although there are recent attempts (Paul Ziff, *Semantic Analysis* (Ithaca, N. Y.: Cornell Univ. Press, 1960) and Jerrold J. Katz and Jerry A. Fodor, "The Structure of a Semantic Theory," *Language,* XXXIX (1963), 170–210.) to systematize semantic studies, these efforts may be less than completely successful if they fail to take account of the fundamentally psychological problem of how individuals attain concepts and how these individually-attained concepts are related to word meanings. The treatment of this problem offered in the present paper is exceedingly sketchy and must be regarded as only a first approximation.

Second, there is a gap between the findings of psychologists on the conditions under which very simple "concepts" are learned in the psychological laboratory and the experiences of teachers in teaching the "for real" concepts that are contained in the curricula of the schools. It is not self-evident that there is any continuity at all between learning "DAX" as the name of a certain geometrical shape of a certain color and learning the meaning of the word "longitude." Even if such a continuity exists, it is not clear how the relative difficulty or complexity of concepts can be assessed.

Third, a problem related to the second arises when we ask whether there is any continuity, with respect to psychological "processes," between the inductive, nonverbal type of learning studied in the psychological laboratory under the guise of "concept learning" and the usually more deductive, verbal-explanatory type of teaching used in the classroom and in typical text materials Take, for example, the kind of concept learning that has been explored so fruitfully by Bruner and his associates.[6] The experimental setting they employed is essentially a game between the experimenter and the subject: the experimenter says he is thinking of a concept—and perhaps he shows an example of his "concept," whereupon the subject's task is to make guesses about other possible instances of the concept in such a way that he will eventually be able to recognize the concept as defined by the experimenter. But in every case, one feels that the experimenter could have "taught" the subject the concept by a very simple verbal communication like "three circles" (for a "conjunctive" concept in which two attributes must occur together) or "any card that has either redness or two borders" (for a "disjunctive" concept) or "any card with more figures than borders" (for a "relational" concept). Teaching a concept in school is usually not all that simple.

In an effort to fill these gaps, we will sketch out a framework for conceptualizing problems of Meaning and Concept. For reasons that will eventually become clear, we must start with the notion of Concept.

THE NATURE OF CONCEPTS

In a totally inorganic world there could be no concepts, but with the existence of organisms capable of complex perceptual responses, concepts become possible. In brief, concepts are properties of organismic experience—more particularly, they are the abstracted and often cognitively structured classes of "mental" experience learned by organisms in the course of their life histories. There is evidence that animals other than human beings behave with regard to concepts in this sense, but we shall confine our attention to human organisms. Because of the continuity of the physical, biological, and social environment in which human beings live, their concepts will show a high degree of similarity; and through language learning, many concepts (classes of experience) will acquire names, that is, words or phrases in a particular language, partly because some classes of experience are so salient and obvious that nearly every person acquires them for himself, and partly because language makes possible the diffusion and sharing of concepts as classes of experience. We use the term "experience" in an extremely broad sense—defining it as any internal or perceptual response to stimulation. We can "have experience of" some aspect of the physical, biological, or social environment by either direct or indirect means; we can experience heat, or light, or odor directly, while our experiences of giraffes or atoms, say, may be characterized as being indirect, coming only through verbal descriptions

[6] Jerome S. Bruner, Jacqueline J. Goodnow, and George A. Austin, *A Study of Thinking* (New York: Wiley. 1956).

or other patterns of stimuli (pointer readings, etc.) that evoke these concepts.

One necessary condition for the formation of a concept is that the individual must have a series of experiences that are in one or more respects similar; the constellation of "respects" in which they are similar constitutes the "concept" that underlies them. Experiences that embody this concept are "positive instances" of it; experiences that do not embody it may be called "negative instances." A further necessary condition for the formation of a concept is that the series of experiences embodying the concept must be preceded, interspersed, or followed by other experiences that constitute negative instances of the concept. As the complexity of the concepts increases (i.e., as there is an increase in the number of interrelations of the respects in which experiences must be similar in order to be positive instances), there is a greater necessity for an appropriate sequencing of positive and negative instances in order to insure adequate learning of the concept.[7] At least this is true when the concept has to be formed from *non-verbal* experiences only, i.e., from actual exemplars or referents of the concept as contrasted with non-exemplars. But concept learning from verbal explanation, as will be noted below, must, as it were, put the learner through a series of vicarious experiences of positive and negative instances. For example, in telling a child what a lion is, one must indicate the range of positive and negative instances—the range of variations that could be found in real lions and the critical respects in which other animals—tigers, leopards, etc.—differ from lions.

We have been describing what is often called the process of abstraction. We have given a number of *necessary* conditions for the formation of a concept; exactly what conditions are *sufficient* cannot yet be stated, but in all likelihood this will turn out to be a matter of (a) the number, sequencing, or timing of the instances presented to the individual, (b) the reinforcements given to the individual's responses, and (c) the individual's orientation to the task. The evidence suggests that the learner must be oriented to, and attending to, the relevant stimuli in order to form a concept. The public test of the formation of a concept is the ability to respond correctly and reliably to new positive and negative instances of it; we do not wish to imply, however, that a concept has not been formed until it is put to such a test.

The infant acquires "concepts" of many kinds even before he attains anything like language. One kind of concept that is acquired by an infant quite early is the concept embodied in the experience of a particular object—a favorite toy, for example. As the toy is introduced to the infant, it is experienced in different ways—it is seen at different angles, at different distances, and in different illuminations. It is felt in different positions and with different parts of the body, and experienced with still other sense-modalities—taste, smell. But underlying all these experiences are common elements sufficient for the infant to make an identifying response to the particular toy in question—perhaps to the point that he will accept only the particular specimen that he is familiar with and reject another specimen that is in the least bit different. The acceptance or rejection of a specimen is the outward sign of the attainment of a concept—as constituted by the class of experiences associated with that particular specimen. The experiences themselves are sufficiently similar to be their own evidence that they constitute a class—a perceptual invariant, therefore, together with whatever affective elements that may be present to help reinforce the attainment of the concept (pleasure in the sight, taste, smell, and feel of the toy, for example).

Even the concept contained in a par-

[7] Earl B. Hunt, *Concept Learning: An Information Processing Problem* (New York: Wiley, 1962).

ticular object represents a certain degree of generality—generality over the separate presentations of the object. But preverbal infants also attain concepts which from the standpoint of adult logic have even higher degrees of generality. A further stage of generality is reached when the infant comes to recognize successive samples of something—e.g., a particular kind of food—as equivalent, even though varying slightly in taste, color, temperature, etc. Because the different samples of food are about equally reinforcing, the infant gradually learns to overcome the initial tendency to reject a sample that is experienced as not quite the same as one previously experienced. That is, what seems to be initially a negative instance turns out to be a positive instance because it provides the same reinforcement as the earlier instance—the reinforcement being in this case a "sign" that the new experience is to be taken in the same class as former ones. An even higher stage of generality is achieved when the child will accept and make a common response to any one of a number of rather different stimuli—for example, any one of a number of different foods. In adult terms, he has attained the concept of "food" in some elementary sense. The explanation of this phenomenon may indeed draw upon the usual primary reinforcement theory (the equivalence of different foods in satisfying a hunger drive) but it also depends upon various secondary reinforcements, as when the parent punishes the child for eating something not considered "food," like ants or mud. This is an elementary case in which culture, as represented by parents, provides signs as to what the positive and negative instances of a concept are.

Direct experience, i.e., the recognition of experiences as identical or similar, allows the infant to attain concepts that in adult language have names such as redness, warmth, softness, heaviness, swiftness, sweetness, loudness, pain, etc. In some cases, the infant's concepts of sensory qualities may be rather undifferentiated. For example, because big things are generally experienced as heavy and strong, and small things are generally experienced as lightweight and weak, the infant's concept of size may not be adequately differentiated from his concepts of weight and strength. Without any social reinforcement to guide him, his concept of "redness" may range over a rather wide range of the color spectrum, and if he happens to have been born into a culture which pays little attention to the difference, say, between what we would call "red" and "orange," his concept of "redness" may remain relatively undifferentiated even after he has learned a language—just as it has been demonstrated that different varieties of blue are not well coded in everyday English.[8]

Furthermore, we can infer from various investigations of Piaget[9] that the child's concepts of size, weight, and other physical attributes of objects do not contain the notion of "conservation" that his later experiences will teach him. For all the infant or young child knows of the physical universe, objects can change in size, weight, etc., in quite arbitrary ways. It is only at a later stage, when the child has had an opportunity to form certain concepts about the nature of the physical universe that his concepts of size, weight, and number can incorporate the notion of constancy or conservation that mature thinking requires. Experience with objects that can expand or contract through stretching or shrinking gives the child a concept of size that can properly explain the fact that a balloon can be blown up to various sizes. Indeed, this explanation may involve the concepts of "expansion" and "contraction." At a still

[8] Roger W. Brown and Eric H. Lenneberg, "A Study in Language and Cognition," *J. Abnorm. Soc. Psychol.*, XLIX (1954), 454–462.

[9] John H. Flavell, *The Developmental Psychology of Jean Piaget* (Princeton: Van Nostrand, 1963).

later stage, the child may learn enough about the relation of heat to expansion to explain why it is necessary to have seams in concrete roads, or why one allows for expansion in the building of large bridges. And it will be relatively unlikely that even as an adult he will learn enough about the concept of size to understand the concept of relativity—that the size of a body is relative to the speed at which it is traveling and the system in which it is measured.

Thus, concepts can in the course of a person's life become more complex, more loaded with significant aspects. Concepts are, after all, essentially idiosyncratic in the sense that they reside in particular individuals with particular histories of experiences that lead them to classify those experiences in particular ways. My concept of "stone" may not be precisely your concept of "stone" because my experiences with stones may have included work with pieces of a peculiar kind of vitreous rock that you have seldom seen. To a large extent, how I sort out my experiences is my own business and may not lead to the same sortings as yours.

Nevertheless, I can specify the way I sort out my experiences by noting the *critical attributes* that differentiate them. I can specify what sensory qualities and attributes are necessary before I will classify an experience as being an experience of what I call a stone. But it is not even necessary for a person to be able to specify such attributes. A child who has learned a certain concept—who has learned to recognize certain experiences as being similar—may not necessarily be able to verbalize what attributes make them similar; he may not even be aware of the fact that he has attained a certain concept, since it may be the case that only his behavior—the fact that he consistently makes a certain response to a certain class of stimuli—indicates that he has formed a concept. Such would be the case, for example, for the classic instance where the child is afraid of the barber because he wields instruments (scissors) that look like those of the doctor whom he has already learned to fear, and because he wears a similar white smock.

Indeed, this last instance exemplifies the fact that concepts may include affective components. Because concepts are embodied in classes of experiences they include all the elements of experiences that may occur in common—perceptual and cognitive elements as well as motivational and emotional elements. My concept of "stone" may reflect, let us say, my positive delight in collecting new varieties of minerals, whereas your concept may reflect the fact that you had unpleasant experiences with stones—having them thrown at you in a riot, or finding lots of them in your garden. Osgood's "semantic differential,"[10] in which one is asked to rate one's concepts on scales such as good-bad, strong-weak, fast-slow, active-passive, light-heavy, pungent-bland, etc., is a way of indexing certain relatively universal cognitive and affective components of individual experiences as classed in concepts; it would perhaps more properly be called an "experiential differential" than a "semantic differential." The fact that fairly consistent results are obtained when concept ratings from differnt people are compared or averaged implies that people tend to have generally similar kinds of experiences, at least within a given culture.

It has already been suggested earlier that since man lives in an essentially homogeneous physical and biological environment and a partially homogeneous social environment, it is inevitable that a large number of concepts arrived at by individual people should be the same or at least so nearly identical in their essential attributes as to be called the same; these concepts we may call *conceptual invariants.* We can be sure that through-

[10] Charles E. Osgood, George J. Suci, and Percy H. Tannenbaum, *The Measurement of Meaning* (Urbana, Illinois: Univ. of Illinois Press, 1957).

out the world people have much the same concepts of *sun, man, day, animal, flower, walking, falling, softness,* etc. by whatever names they may be called. The fact that they have names is incidental; there are even certain concpts that for one reason or another (a taboo, for example) may remain nameless.

It is probably when we enter into the realms of science and technology and of social phenomena that the concepts attained by different people will differ most. In science and technology concepts vary chiefly because of differences, over the world, in the levels of scientific and technological knowledge reached; and in the social sphere they will differ chiefly because of the truly qualitative differences in the ways cultures are organized. Nevertheless, within a given community there will be a high degree of commonality in the concepts recognized and attained, in the sense that there will be relatively high agreement among people as to the attributes that are criterial for a given concept. For example, even though types of families vary widely over the world, the concept of *family* within a given culture is reasonably homogeneous. At the same time, differences in intellectual and educational levels will account for differences in the sheer number of concepts attained by individuals within a given culture.

WORDS AND THEIR MEANINGS

In the learning of language, words (and other elements in a linguistic system, including phonemes, morphemes, and syntactical patterns) come to be perceived as distinct entities, and in this sense they form one class of perceptual invariants along with the perceptual invariants that represent common objects, feelings, and events. The child must learn to perceive the various instances of a given sound or word as similar, and eventually to differentiate the several contexts in which a given sound or sound pattern is used. (We know of an instance of a very young child who somehow learned to react violently to the word "no," but she would react just as violently to the word "know," even when it was embedded in a sentence. The process of differentiation took a considerable time.)

Many words or higher units of the linguistic system come to stand for, or name, the concepts that have been learned pre-verbally. Certainly this is true for a long list of words that stand for particular things or classes of things, qualities, and events. For the English language, these categories correspond roughly to proper and common nouns; adjectives; and verbs of action, perception, and feeling. It is perhaps less clear that "function words" like prepositions and conjunctions, or grammatical markers like the past tense sign can represent concepts, but a case can be made for this. For example, prepositions like *in, to, above, below, beside, near* correspond to concepts of relative spatial position in a surprisingly complex and subtle way; and conjunctions like *and, but, however, or* correspond to concepts of logical inclusion and exclusion, similarity and difference of propositions, etc.

The processes by which words come to "stand for" or correspond to concepts can best be described in psychological terms. Without going into the details here, we can only say that in every case there is some sort of reinforcing condition that brands a word as being associated with a given concept. This is true whether the word is learned as what Skinner[11] calls a *mand* (as when a child learns the meaning of *water* as a consequence of having water brought whenever he says "water") or as a *tact* (as where the child is praised or otherwise reinforced for saying "water" when he sees or experiences water), because in either case the word is paired contiguously with the concept

11 B. F. Skinner, *Verbal Behavior* (New York: Appleton-Century, Crofts, 1957).

as an experience. The connection between a word and the concept or experience with which it stands in relation must work in either direction: the word must evoke the concept and the concept must evoke the word.

As a physical symbol, a word is a cultural artifact that takes the same, or nearly the same, form throughout a speech community. It is a standardized product on which the speech community exercises a considerable degree of quality control. Not so with concepts, which as we have seen may vary to some extent with the individual, depending on his experiences of the referents of the words. Society does, however, maintain a degree of "quality control" on the referential meaning of words. The conditions under which the use of words is rewarded or not rewarded—either by successful or unsuccessful communication or by direct social approval or disapproval—can be looked upon as constituting the "rules of usage" of a word, and these rules of usage define the *denotative meaning* of a term. Thus, there is a rule of usage such that the noun *mother* can be used only for a certain kind of kinship relation. One thinks of denotative meaning as something that is socially prescribed. Connotative meaning, however, banks heavily on those aspects of concepts that are widely shared yet non-criterial and perhaps affective (emotional) in content. "Mother" as a noun might evoke various emotional feelings depending upon one's experience with mothers.

Perhaps it is useful to think of words, meanings, and concepts as forming *three* somewhat independent series. The words in a language can be thought of as a series of physical entities—either spoken or written. Next, there exists a set of "meanings" which stand in complex relationships to the set of words. These relationships may be described by the rules of usage that have developed by the processes of socialization and communication. A "meaning" can be thought of as a standard of communicative behavior that is shared by those who speak a language. Finally, there exist "concepts"; the classes of experience formed in individuals either independently of language processes or in close dependence on language processes.

The interrelations found among these three series are complex; almost anyone can give instances where a word may have many "meanings," or in which a given "meaning" corresponds to several different words. The relationships between societally-standardized "meanings" and individually-formed "concepts" are likewise complex, but of a somewhat different nature. It is a question of how well each individual has learned these relationships, and at least in the sphere of language and concepts, education is largely a process whereby the individual learns either to attach societally-standardized words and meanings to the concepts he has already formed, or to form new concepts that properly correspond to societally-standardized words and meanings. A "meaning" of a word is, therefore, a societally-standardized concept, and when we say that a word stands for or names a concept it is understood that we are speaking of concepts that are shared among the members of a speech community.

To the extent that individual concepts differ even though they possess shared elements, misunderstandings can arise. My concept of "several" may correspond to the range "approximately three to five," where yours may correspond to "approximately five to fifteen." Speech communities may differ, too, in the exact ranges in which they standardize meanings. The word *infant* seems to include a higher age range in Great Britain (in the phrase "infants' schools") than it does in the United States, and in legal contexts the word may even refer to anyone who has not attained some legal age like twenty-one years.

The fact that words vary in meaning according to context has given rise to one form of a "context theory of meaning" which seems to allege that the meaning of a word is to be found in its context; this is only true, however, in the sense that the context may provide a *clue* as to the particular meaning (or standardized concept) with which a word is intended to be associated. In fact, the clue usually takes the form of an indication of one or more elements of a concept. For example, in the phrase *A light load* the context suggests (thought it does not determine absolutely) that *light* is to be taken as the opposite of heavy because loads vary more importantly in weight than in their color, whereas the context in *A light complexion* suggests the element of color because complexions can vary in color but only very improbably in weight. It is not surprising that normal language texts have been found to have redundancy, for the elements of concepts suggested by the words in a sentence are often overlapping.

Frequently context is the key to the fact that a word is being used in an archaic or unusual sense. A student who cannot square the usual meaning of *smug* with its use in the following lines from Shakespeare's *Henry IV* (*Part I*):

> "And here the smug and silver
> Trent shall run
> In a new channel, fair and evenly"

had better resort to a dictionary, where he will find that an earlier meaning of *smug* is *trim, neat*. We cannot dwell here on the interesting ways in which words change in meaning historically, often in response to changes in emphasis given to the various criterial attributes embodied in the concepts corresponding to words. Just as one example, though, consider the historical change of meaning of "meat" from (originally) "any kind of food" to "edible part of animal body, flesh," where the criterial attribute "part of animal body" gradually came to be reinforced alongside the attribute "edible thing."

DEFINITIONS

What, by the way, is the function of a dictionary definition in the light of the system of ideas being presented here? Aside from the few instances where dictionary definitions present pictures or drawings of the items being defined, two main techniques are used in dictionary entries: (1) the use of verbal equivalents, and (2) the use of formal definition by stating *genus et differentia*. The use of verbal equivalents, as where we are told that *smug* can mean "trim, smooth, sleek," has the function of evoking either a (hopefully) previously known concept to which both the defined word and the defining word stand in the same relation, or a series of (hopefully) previously known concepts from whose common elements the reader can derive the concept to which the defined word properly stands in relation. The use of a formal definition, on the other hand, literally "marks off the boundaries of" the concept by first indicating what it has in common with other experiences (*genus*) and then indicating in what respects or attributes (*differentia*) it differs from other experiences. For example, if we are told that *tarn* is a small mountain lake or pool, we know that in many respects it is similar to other lakes or pools—that it is an enclosed, contained body of water, but that it is a special kind of lake of a given size and location. One could, therefore, presumably acquire the concept named *tarn* by learning to make this response only in connection with the criterial attributes defining it. What could be simpler, particularly if one is verbally told what the criterial attributes are? The only kind of intellectual mishap would occur, one would think, when one of the attributes is misunderstood or overlooked. Calling Lake George (in the Adirondacks) a *tarn* would be grossly to neglect or misunderstand the element of small size.

CONCEPT FORMATION RESEARCH

We are now in a position to inquire into the possible relevance of concept formation research to the learning of the meanings and concepts associated with words in a language.

Practically all concept formation research since the days of Hull[12] has been concerned with essentially the following task: the subject is presented with a series of instances which are differentiated in some way; either the task is finding out in what way the several instances match up with one of a small number of names, or (in the simpler case) it is one of discovering why some instances are "positive" (i.e., instances of the "concept" the experimenter has in mind) or "negative" (not instances of the "concept"). Typically the stimulus material consists of simple visual material characterized by a number of clearly salient dimensions—e.g., the color of the figures, the geometrical shape of the figures, the number of figures, the number of borders, the color of the background, etc. Occasionally the critical characteristics of the concept are not clearly in view—as in Hull's experiment where the critical stroke elements of Chinese characters tended to be masked by the rest of the figures, or as in Bouthilet's[13] experiment where the critical feature was the inclusion of letters found in the stimulus word. Sometimes the critical elements are semantic elements of words, as in Freedman and Mednick's experiment[14] in which the task was to find the common semantic element in a series of words such as *gnat, needle, stone,* and *canary.*

Thus, there are two elements to be studied in any concept-formation task: (1) the attributes which are criterial to the concept—their nature and number, the number of values each attribute has and the discriminability of these values, and the salience of the attributes themselves—that is, whether the attributes command attention and are readily perceivable, and (2) the information-handling task required of the subject in view of the order in which positive and negative instances are presented and the amount of information concerning the concept that is furnished by each presentation. Most of what we know about this kind of concept attainment task can be summarized in the following statements:

1. Concept attainment becomes more difficult as the number of relevant attributes increases, the number of values of attributes increases, and the salience of the attributes decreases.

2. Concept attainment becomes more difficult as the information load that must be handled by the subject in order to solve the concept increases, and as the information is increasingly carried by negative rather than positive instances.

3. Various strategies for handling the information load are possible, and some are in the long run more successful than others.

CONCEPT LEARNING IN SCHOOL

I suspect that anyone who has examined the concept formation literature with the hope of finding something of value for the teaching of concepts in school has had cause for some puzzlement and disappointment, because however fascinating this literature may be, as it wends its way through the detailed problems posed by the methodology itself, its relevance to the learning of concepts in the various school subjects is a bit obscure.

[12] C. L. Hull, "Quantitative Aspects of the Evolution of Concepts," *Psychol. Monogr.,* No. 123, (1920).

[13] L. Bouthilet, "The Measurement of Intuitive Thinking" (unpublished Ph. D. Thesis Univ. of Chicago, 1948).

[14] J. L. Freedman and S. A. Mednick, "Ease of Attainment of Concepts as a Function of Response Dominance Variance," *J. Exp. Psychol.,* LV (1958), 463–466.

Let us look at the major differences between concept learning in school and in the laboratory.

(1) One of the major differences is in the nature of the concepts themselves. A new concept learned in school is usually a genuinely "new" concept rather than an artificial combination of familiar attributes (like the concept "three blue squares" such as might be taught in a psychological experiment).

(2) New concepts learned in school depend on attributes which themselves represent difficult concepts. In more general terms, concepts learned in school often depend upon a network of related or prerequisite concepts. One cannot very well learn the concept of derivative, in the calculus, until one has mastered a rather elaborate structure of prerequisite concepts (e.g., slope, change of slope, algebraic function, etc.). Further, the attributes on which school-learned concepts depend are frequently verbal, depending on elements of meaning that cannot easily be represented in terms of simple sensory qualities as used in concept formation experiments.

(3) Many of the more difficult concepts of school learning are of a relational rather than a conjunctive character; they deal with the relations among attributes rather than their combined presence or absence. Concept formation experiments have thus far revealed little about the acquisition of relational concepts.

(4) An important element in school learning is the memory problem involved in the proper matching of words and concepts. Thus, the problems of paired-associate memory are added to those of concept learning itself. For example, a student in biology or social studies has to learn not only a large number of new concepts, but also a large number of unfamiliar, strange-looking words to be attached to these concepts. The rate at which new concepts can be introduced is probably limited, just as the rate at which foreign language words can be acquired is limited.

(5) The most critical difference between school concept learning and concept learning in psychological experiments is that the former is for the most part deductive and the latter is generally inductive. It would be relatively rare to find a concept taught in school by the procedure of showing a student a series of positive and negative instances, labeled as such, and asking him to induce the nature of the concept with no further aid. Such instances could be found, of course; perhaps they would exemplify a pure "discovery method," and perhaps there should be more use of this method than is the case. The fact is that a pure discovery method is seldom used, because it is rather slow and inefficient. Even if a teaching procedure incorporates "discovery" elements, it is likely to be combined with deductive elements. The concept to be taught is described verbally—perhaps by a rule or definition—and the student is expected to attain the concept by learning to make correct identification of positive and negative instances. For example, he is told what an "indirect object" is and then is given practice in identifying the indirect objects (positive instances) among other words (negative instances). Many simple concepts can be taught by a wholly deductive procedure. For most students, the dictionary definition of *tarn* will be a sufficient stimulus for attainment of the concept. On the other hand, it is well known that purely deductive, verbal procedures are frequently insufficient to help learners attain concepts. Concept formation experimentation would be more relevant to school learning problems if it could give more attention to examining the role of verbalization and other deductive procedures in concept attainment.

Nevertheless, there are certain similarities between concept attainment in school and concept formation in psychological experiments. These arise chiefly from the fact that not every concept is learned *solely* in a formalized, prearranged school setting. The school environment is in many ways continuous with the out-of-school environment; concepts are learned partly in school, partly out of school. The process whereby the elementary concepts of a language are learned closely parallels that of the psychological concept formation experiment. A child learns the concept "dog" not by having the concept described to him but by learning to restrict his usage of the word *dog* to instances regarded as positive by the speech community. In this process there are many false responses—either false positives (calling a non-dog a dog) or false negatives (believing a dog to be a non-instance), before an appropriate series of reinforcements produces correct concept attainment. Similar phenomena occur with concepts in the school curriculum. A child who has been told that his cousins visiting him from Peoria are "tourists" may not realize that tourists do not need to be relatives, and when he is told that the Germans who have settled in his town are "immigrants," he may believe that all foreigners visiting his town are immigrants. Concept formation experiments yield information as to the range and variety of instances that have to be furnished for efficient and correct concept formation in the absence of formal instruction.

But if the foregoing statement is true, concept formation studies should also yield insights as to what information has to be furnished for *deductive* concept formation, e.g., from a formal definition. Obviously, a formal definition is successful only to the extent that it correctly identifies and describes all the criterial attributes that are likely to be relevant for a concept, and to the extent that it communicates the proper values and relationships of these to the learner. The burden is both on the definition itself and on the learner. A student may fail to learn the concept *tarn* from the definition previously cited either because it omits some essential criterial attribute (e.g., that a tarn must contain *water* rather than, say, *oil* or *lava*), or because the student fails to comprehend the meaning of its elements (for example, how small is "small"?).

What is actually going on in most school learning of concepts is a process that combines in some way deductive and inductive features.

Descriptions and definitions provide the deductive elements of the process. The several parts of a description or definition specify the attributes and relationships that are criterial for the concept. The order in which these specifications are arranged in the description and presented to the student may have something to do with the ease of concept attainment, particularly in the case of complex concepts with many attributes and complex interrelationships (like the case of *tort* discussed below). As yet we have no well-founded generalizations about the order in which the criterial attributes for a concept should be presented.

At the same time, inductive procedures entail the citing of positive and negative instances of the concept. We know from concept attainment research that learning is facilitated more by positive than by negative instances, even though the "information" conveyed by these instances is the same in a given experimental context. But in real-life concept learning, the number of dimensions that may possibly be relevant is less limited; the function of positive instances is as much to show *which* dimensions are relevant as it is to show what values of them are critical. We may speculate that the real value of what we are calling inductive procedures in concept learning is to afford the learner an opportunity to test his understanding of and memory for the elements of verbal descriptions and definitions. This testing may even involve the construction and testing of alternative hypotheses.

For example, consider the following verbal statement of what a "paradigm" (for research on teaching) is:

"Paradigms are models, patterns, or schemata. Paradigms are not theories; they are rather ways of thinking or patterns for research that, when carried out, can lead to the development of theory."[15]

As a verbal statement, this is hardly adequate; fortunately, Gage proceeds to exhibit a number of positive instances of "paradigms" by which his readers can test out their notions of what this concept might be. Many readers will still have difficulty, however, because he fails to exhibit *negative* instances of paradigms.

What is needed, eventually, is a scientific "rhetoric" for the teaching of concepts—assembled not only from the traditional rhetoric of exposition but also from whatever scientific experiments on concept teaching can tell us. We will be better off, however, if concept-attainment studies begin to give attention to the manner in which real-life, non-artificial concepts can be taught most efficiently—presumably by combination of both deductive and inductive procedures.

ILLUSTRATIONS OF CONCEPT TEACHING PROBLEMS

To suggest the kinds of problems that arise in the teaching of concepts or that might be investigated through formal research, I propose to analyze a small number of concepts of various types, at several levels of difficulty.

Tourist vs. Immigrant

A fourth grade teacher reported difficulty in getting her pupils to understand and contrast the meanings of the words *tourist* and *immigrant*. Neither word appears in Dale and Eichholz's[16] list of words known by at least sixty-seven percent of children in the fourth grade, although *tour* (as a sight-seeing trip) was known by seventy percent. In the sixth-grade list, *immigrant* was known by seventy percent and *tourist* by seventy-seven percent; the figures are ninety-seven percent (for *immigration*) and ninety-six percent (for *tourist*) in the 8th-grade list.

To an adult, the differentiation between the concepts designated by *tourist* and *immigrant* looks almost trivially simple. Aside from the sheer memory problem in learning and differentiating the words themselves, what are the sources of confusion for the child? In specific cases, a tourist and an immigrant might have many common characteristics: both might be from a foreign country, or at least from some distance away from the local community; both might be of obviously non-native culture because of dress, complexion, speech, and behavior; both might be doing what would appear to be "sight-seeing," though possibly for different purposes. The differences between a tourist and an immigrant might not be very apparent, being primarily differences of motivation. Indeed, a tourist might become an immigrant overnight, just by deciding to be one.

As we have seen, there is a sense in which the concept-attainment experimental literature is relevant to the child's problem in learning the meanings of the words *tourist* and *immigrant*. If the child is presented with various instances of people who are either tourists or immigrants, properly labeled as such, but with no further explanation, it will be the child's task to figure out what attributes or characteristics are relevant to the differentiation of these concepts. This might occur either in school or outside of school. Most likely the instances of tourists and immigrants will be relatively sporadic over time, and the instances may not vary in such a way as to show what attributes are truly relevant. For example, all the tourists may be obviously American whereas all the immigrants may be obviously Mexican, let us say. The tourists may all be well-dressed, the im-

[15] N. L. Gage, "Paradigms for Research on Teaching." *Handbook of Research on Teaching,* ed. *N. L. Gage* (Chicago: Rand McNally, 1963), 94–141.

[16] Edgar Dale and Gerhard Eichholz, *Children's Knowledge of Words* (Columbus: Bureau of Educational Research and Service, Ohio State University, 1960).

migrants poorly dressed, and so on. If the natural environment is like a grand concept-formation experiment, it may take the child a long time to attain the concepts *tourist* and *immigrant;* indeed, the environment may not be as informative as the usual experimenter, since the child may not always be informed, or reliably informed, as to the correctness of his guesses. No wonder a child might form the concept that a tourist is any well-dressed person who drives a station-wagon with an out-of-state license plate!

The purpose of teaching is to short-cut this capricious process of concept attainment within the natural environment. Through the use of language, there should be relatively little difficulty in explaining to a child that an immigrant is one who moves from one country or region to another in order to change his permanent residence, while a tourist is one who travels around for pleasure without changing his permanent residence. One can use simple explanations like: "He's going to stay here, have his home here..." or "He's just traveling around for the fun of it while he's on vacation, and someday he'll get back home." There should be no difficulty, at any rate, if the child has already mastered certain prerequisite concepts. Among these prerequisite concepts would be: the concept of home or permanent residence and all that it implies; the concept of the division of world territory into different countries and those in turn into regions; and the concept of traveling for pleasure or curiosity. It is very likely that the child who is having trouble understanding the concept of tourist vs. the concept of immigrant has not got clearly in mind these prerequisite notions that constitute, in fact, the criterial attributes upon which the distinction hangs.

Alternatively, a child might be having trouble because he has not dispensed with irrelevant aspect of these concepts: he might think that a tourist has to be always an American, whereas an immigrant must be a foreigner, because he has seen *American* tourists and *foreign* immigrants, no *American* immigrants nor *foreign* tourists. The ingenious teacher will think of the possible misunderstandings that could arise through the influence of irrelevant attributes of tourists and immigrants.

Time

K. C. Friedman[17] pointed out that elementary school children have much trouble with various time concepts. A child sees no incongruity, for example, in saying, "My older brother was born a long time ago." According to Friedman, it was not until Grade VI that all children in his school could state the date or list the months in perfect order. They had difficulty, he reports, in forming a concept of the "time line" and then in recognizing the placement of various historical events on such a time line. It is easy to see why the child would have these difficulties; even as adults it is difficult for us to appreciate the significance of the fantastically long periods implied by geological time. It should be noted that our concept of a time line is essentially a *spatial* concept whereby we translate temporal succession in terms of spatial order and distances. For a child, times does not flow in a straight line nor in any other particular direction, unless it is around the clock, in a circular or spiral dimension! How can the child form a concept of time and its units? Is time a class of experiences? Does it have criterial attributes? The paradigms of concept-formation experiments do not seem to apply here readily. But let us examine the situation more closely. How can the child have experiences of time and generate the concept of a time line? Certainly there can be experiences of intervals of time—watching a second hand

[17] Kopple C. Friedman, "Time Concepts of Elementary-school Children," *Elem. Sch. J.*, XLIV (1944), 337–342.

of a clock move through the second-markings, or experiencing the succession of night and day, noticing the change of seasons or waiting for the end of the school year. Moving from one time period to another could be likened to moving from one square of a sidewalk to the next. It should be an easy transition to thinking of the time line as a sidewalk of infinite extent in both directions—toward the past and toward the future. Marking off the days on the calendar and naming the days and months should help to reinforce this cognitive structure. Extrapolation of the time line is like generalizing these time experiences to all possible such experiences.

One of the difficulties comes, presumably, from the fact that the far reaches of the past and the future cannot be immediately experienced, and one immediately has trouble if one attempts to show a time line that includes historical events in the distant past along with a representation of the relationship between today, yesterday, and the day before yesterday. (Incidentally, it is hard to believe Pistor's[18] claim that young children cannot tell the difference between the present and the past, in view of the fact that they can correctly use the present tenses of verbs in simple situations.) Time lines of different scales must be used, and the concept of scale will itself be hard for children to understand unless it is carefully explained —perhaps by showing maps of the immediate environment in different scales. Only after such ideas have been mastered will it be possible for the child to have any appreciation of such concepts as *year, century, 1492* (as a date), *B.C., generation. Generation* and *eon,* by the way, would have to be introduced as somewhat flexible, arbitrary units of time, as contrasted with fixed, measureable units such as *year* and *century.*

[18] Frederick Pistor, "Measuring the Time Concepts of Children," *J. Educ. Res.,* XXX (1939), 293–300.

Quantitative expressions like "many," "few," "average"

Ernest Horn[19] pointed out that certain quantitative concepts like *many, few,* and *average* are often so difficult that children do not give reasonable interpretations of them. It is very likely that the source of the difficulty is that children tend not to be able to think in relative terms. Children (and perhaps their teachers) would like to be able to assign definite ranges of numbers for such words as *many, few, average, a sizable amount,* etc., when actually they are all relative terms. There has even been a psychological experiment to demonstrate this: Helson, Dworkin, and Michels[20] showed that adult subjects will consistently give different meanings to a word like "few" when it is put in different contexts. For example, "few" meant about twelve percent on the average, in relation to 100 people, whereas it meant four percent, on the average, in relation to 1,728,583 people.

In teaching a child these relational concepts the problem would be to exhibit or describe numerous instances in which the absolute base varies but in which the actual numbers of quantities meant would at the same time vary sufficiently to give the impression that these words do not indicate anything like exact amounts. It should be pointed out that 100 things might be "many" in some situations and "few" in others. The use of "average" in such a context as "There was an average number of people in church today" can be taught by drawing attention to its relation to the probable extremes of the numbers of people that might be in church, generalizing the concept to other situations like "I caught an average num-

[19] Ernest Horn, *Methods of Instruction in Social Studies* (New York: Scribner, 1937).

[20] Harry Helson, Robert S. Dworkin and Walter C. Michels, "Quantitative Denotations of Common Terms as a Function of Background," *Amer. J. Psychol.,* LXIX (1956), 194–208.

ber of fish today." This might lead to the introduction of the average as a statistic or number that gives information about the "central tendency" of some frequency distribution. It may help to use an unfamiliar or unusual context to bring out this concept in sharp relief. For example, I like to illustrate the utility of the statistical mean or arithmetic average by asking students to imagine that the first space men to reach Mars discover human-like creatures there whose average height is—and this is where the mean becomes really informative—3 inches!

The basic concept of the mean arises in the context of experiences in which there is a plurality of objects measured in some common way. As a first approximation, as far as a child is concerned, the average is a number that is roughly halfway between the highest and lowest measurements encountered, and in some way "typical" of these measurements. Only at some later stage does the child need to learn that the mean is a number that can be computed by a formula and that it has certain properties.

Longitude

It is difficult to understand why E. B. Wesley[21] says that concepts related to the sphericity of the earth, like latitude and longitude, are not easily taught to the average child before Grades VI and VII. Wesley was writing before the advent of the space age when every child knows about space capsules traveling around the globe. Though it may still be difficult to get a child to see how the flatness of his immediate environment is only apparent and that the immediate environment corresponds to just a small area on the globe, it can certainly be done, well before Grade VI, through suitable demonstrational techniques. Having established the sphericity of the earth, one should be able to teach latitude and longitude as concepts involved in specifying locations on the globe. Their introduction should properly be preceded by simpler cases in which one uses a system of coordinates to specify location—e.g., equally spaced and numbered horizontal and vertical lines drawn on a blackboard with a game to locate letters placed at intersection of lines, a map of one's town or city in which marginal coordinates are given to help locate given streets or places of interest, and finally a Mercator projection map of the world with coordinates of latitude and longitude. Children exposed to the "new math" with its number lines and coordinates should have no trouble with this. Then let us show children by easy stages how a Mercator projection corresponds to the surface of the Earth (certainly an actual globe marked off with latitude and longitude should be used), then how it is necessary to select a particular line (that passes through the Greenwich Observatory) as the vertical coordinate from which to measure, and how the circumference of the earth is marked off in degrees—180° West and 180° East from the Greenwich meridian.

The object is to build for the child a vivid experience of the framework or cognitive structure within which the concept of longitude is defined. The further complications introduced by the use of other kinds of world projections or by the use of regional or even local maps could then be explored. Easily-obtained U.S. Geological Survey maps of one's locality would concretize the meanings of further concepts, e.g., the division of degrees into minutes and seconds, and the fact that a degree of longitude will gradually shrink in length as one moves northward from the equator.

Tort

The concept of *tort* is very likely to be unfamiliar or at least vague to the average

[21] E. B. Wesley and Mary A. Adams, *Teaching Social Studies in Elementary Schools* (Rev. ed.: Boston: D. C. Heath, 1952), p. 307.

reader. Even a dictionary definition[22] may not help much in deciding whether arson, breach of contract, malicious prosecution, or libel are positive instances of torts. The case method used in many law schools, whereby students examine many positive and negative instances of torts in order to learn what they are, is somewhat analogous to a concept formation experiment of the purely inductive variety.

A study[23] of the various laws and decisions relating to torts yields the following approximate and tentative characterization of the concept as having both conjunctive and disjunctive aspects:

$$\text{TORT} = (A + B + C + D + E + F + G + H)\ (I + J)\ (K)\ (-L)\ (-M)\ (-N)\ (-O)$$

where A = battery
B = false imprisonment
C = malicious prosecution
D = trespass to land
E = interference to chattels
F = interference with advantageous relations
G = misrepresentation
H = defamation
I = malicious intent
J = negligence
K = causal nexus
L = consent
M = privilege
N = reasonable risk by plaintiff
O = breach of contract

Within a parenthesis, terms joined by the sign + are mutually disjunctive attributes; a minus sign (−) within a parenthesis signifies "absence of"; the full content of each parenthesis is conjunctive with the content of every other parenthesis. Thus, we can read the formula as follows: "A tort is a battery, a false imprisonment, a malicious prosecution, a trespass to land, . . . , or a defamatory act which is done either with malicious intent or negligently, which exhibits a causal nexus with the injury claimed by the plaintiff, *and* which is done without the plaintiff's consent, *or* without privilege on the part of the defendant, *or* without a reasonable risk by the plaintiff, *or* which is not a breach of contract."

Thus, *tort* turns out to be a concept very much on the same order as *tourist* —a collocation of criterial attributes with both conjunctive and disjunctive features. Deciding whether an act is a tort requires that one check each feature of a situation against what can be put in the form of a formula (as done above). Presumably, a person presented with a properly organized series of positive and negative instances of torts could induce the concept, provided he also understood such prerequisite concepts as *battery, misrepresentation*, etc.

Mass vs. weight

One of the more difficult concepts to teach in elementary physics is that of *mass*. What kind of concept is it and how can one learn it and experience it? How can it be distinguished from the concept of weight? Actually, if we ignore certain subtle questions about mass, such as that of whether inertial and gravitational mass are demonstrably identical, the concept of mass is not as difficult as it might seem; the real difficulty is to teach the sense in which it is different from weight. In fact, weight is perhaps the more difficult concept, because the weight of an object can vary to the point that it can become "weightless."

The concept of mass, one would think, ought to develop for the learner (be he a child or an adult) in much the same way that concepts of other properties of the physical world develop—analogously, that

22 The *American College Dictionary* defines *tort* as "a civil wrong (other than a breach of contract or trust) such as the law requires compensation for in damages; typically, a willful or negligent injury to a plaintiff's person, property, or reputation."

23 For helping me in my treatment of the concepts of *tort* and *mass* I am indebted to my student, Mr. Edward A. Dubois.

is, to concepts of color, number, and volume. For mass is a property of objects that differentiates them in our experience: there are objects with great mass (like the earth, or a large boulder) and there are objects with small mass (like a feather or a pin or the air in a small bottle), and our experiences of objects with respect to mass can differ enormously, particularly in our proprioceptive senses. Further, mass is a property of objects that is *conserved* regardless of whether the object is in motion or at rest; conservation of mass is learned through experience just as conservation of other properties is learned. Even the physical definition of mass as that property of things which accounts for the relative amount of force which has to be applied to produce a certain amount of acceleration is perceived in common-sense terms as the property of objects that determines the amount of force or effort that one would have to exert to move or lift it. The well-known "size-weight" illusion (in which, for example, we exert an undue amount of effort to lift or push some large but relatively light object) illustrates the fact that our perceptions of an object typically include some impression of its mass. The physical operation of measuring mass by determining the ratio of force to acceleration is an operational extension of the kind of behavior we exhibit when we see how much force it will take to move a heavy trunk.

The real trouble comes in the fact that we are too prone to equate mass with weight, mainly because equal masses also have equal weights when compared by means of a balance, or when measured with a spring balance at the same point on the earth's surface (at least, at the same distance from the earth's center). If we were more easily able to experience the fact that the weight of an object of given mass changes as acceleration due to gravity changes—for example by going to the moon and observing the "weight" of objects there, or by experiencing "weightlessness" in an orbital flight around the earth, weight and mass might be just as easy to distinguish as size and mass. Since such experiences would be rather hard to come by, to put it mildly, we have to be content with the imaginal representation of weight as a *variable* property of objects that really depends upon a relation between the gravitational force exerted on an object and its mass (actually, the product of these two). A child might be made to understand how objects of different masses could have equal "weight" –a relatively large object on the moon and a relatively small one on the earth, for example, as measured by a spring balance which is sensitive to the pull of gravity; or how an object of constant mass would have different weights at different distances from the earth (the pull of gravity thus varying). We would have to conclude that weight, properly speaking, is a relational concept that can only be understood when the total framework in which weight can be defined is described. Mass, on the other hand, is a concept that corresponds much more directly to immediate perceptions of reality.

It will be noted that the teaching of mass and weight concepts involves several prerequisite concepts—e.g., the pull of gravity, the relation between the mass of an object like the earth or the moon and the gravitational force it exerts, and the concept of acceleration. The pull exerted by a magnet could be used for illustrating certain aspects of the concept of gravitational force; a large magnet and a small magnet could represent the respective gravitational pulls of earth and moon; the concept of acceleration can be introduced verbally as "how fast something gets started" and later as an accelerating curve of velocity.

Without really meaning to do so, this discussion of mass and weight has turned out to be a consideration of how such concepts might be taught at relatively early stages—say, somewhere in the elementary school. Nevertheless, some of the same teaching techniques might not be amiss even at high school or college levels. At these levels the chief problem is to give meaning to mathematical formulas such as

$$\text{mass} = \frac{\text{force}}{\text{acceleration}}$$

The implication of this formula, that mass is constant for a given object, can be illustrated by showing with actual physical materials that as force is increased, acceleration is increased proportionately. The effect of increasing mass could be shown by demonstrating that acceleration (roughly indicated by distance traveled against friction) under a constant force diminishes. To a large extent, such experiments can be considered as yielding in precise mathematical terms the relationships that are perceived in every-day experience and that lead to our intuitive understanding of such a concept as mass.

Above all, it should be noted that *mass* is a relational concept, a constant property of objects that reveals itself through the relation between the forces applied to the object and the resultant acceleration. Negative instances can only be properties of objects like weight, size, etc., that are not revealed in this way.

SUMMARY

The basic concern of this paper has been with the teaching of concepts and the relevance of psychological and psycholinguistic theory and experimentation in guiding such teaching.

It has been necessary, first, to point out that concepts are essentially non-linguistic (or perhaps better, *a*linguistic) because they are classes of experience which the individual comes to recognize as such, whether or not he is prompted or directed by symbolic language phenomena. Because the experiences of individuals tend to be in many respects similar, their concepts are also similar, and through various processes of learning and socialization these concepts come to be associated with words. The "meanings" of words are the socially-standardized concepts with which they are associated. One of the problems in teaching concepts is that of teaching the associations between words and concepts, and this is analogous to a paired-associate learning task.

At the same time, new concepts can be taught. One procedure can be called inductive: it consists of presenting an individual with an appropriate series of positive and negative instances of a concept, labeled as such, and allowing him to infer the nature of the concept by noticing invariant features or attributes. This is the procedure followed in the usual concept formation experiment: although our present knowledge allows us to specify several *necessary* conditions for the formation of a concept, we still do not know what conditions are *sufficient*.

Another procedure for concept teaching may be called deductive, and it tends to be the favored procedure in school learning (and, in fact, in all expository prose). It is the technique of presenting concepts by verbal definition or description. This technique has received relatively little attention in psychological experimentation, but it seems to parallel inductive concept attainment in the sense that verbal descriptions are specifications of criterial attributes that can enable the individual to shortcut the process of hypothesis, discovery, and testing that typically occurs in the inductive concept-attainment procedure. Nevertheless, it is not known how relevant our knowledge of critical factors in inductive concept formation is for the guidance of deductive teaching procedures.

It is pointed out, however, that the efficient learning of concepts in school probably involves both inductive and deductive procedures. An analysis of typical concepts of the sort taught in school shows that they do indeed follow the models studied in psychological experimentation, but that they are more likely to involve complex relationships among prerequisite concepts. The difficulties that learners have in attaining a concept are likely to be due to their inadequate mastery of prerequisite concepts and to errors made by the teacher in presenting in proper sequence the information intrinsic to the definition of the concept.

On Some Factors in the Organizational Characteristics of Free Recall[1]

CHARLES N. COFER

In recent years, much of my research has been concerned with the free-learning or free-recall situation. This is the case in which a list of words of some length is presented to a subject, and he is asked to recall the items in any order in which they occur to him. Interest in the recall performance has centered on two of its features and the variable related to them. One of these features is the total number of words correctly recalled, and the other one, which I shall emphasize here, is the order or *organization* of the recall as compared to the organization present among the items as originally presented. The general procedure was first developed by Bousfield and reported in 1953, and has been extensively explored by him and his students as well as by Jenkins and Russell (1952) and their associates. In this paper I shall review interpretations which have been made of clustering, data which pertain to these analyses, and suggest a formulation which I now find plausible.

Perhaps the major reason for studying this situation arises from the finding that subjects do, in fact, reorganize the material so that the recalls differ in sequential properties from those of the original list. My attention was first engaged by this phenomenon because of its seeming rela-

[1] Address of the retiring President, Eastern Psychological Association, presented at Philadelphia, April 17, 1964. Much of the work reported here was supported by contracts Nonr 595(04), Nonr 285(47) and Nonr 656(30) between the Office of Naval Research and the University of Maryland, New York University, and the Pennsylvania State University, respectively. This paper is Technical Report No. 1, under contract Nonr 656(30). Reproduction in whole or in part is permitted for any purpose of the United States Government. Assistance was also provided by a faculty research grant from the University of California, Berkeley, during 1962–1963. I am indebted to the following colleagues and students for reading and criticizing a draft of this paper: David Palermo, John Hall, Lowell Schipper, James J. Jenkins, David Wicklund, Darryl Bruce, and John Robinson.

Charles N. Cofer, "On Some Factors in the Organizational Characteristics of Free Recall," *American Psychologist,* 20 (1965), 261–272. Reprinted by permission of the author and publisher.

tion to the changes found in the recall of complex materials by Bartlett (1932). It appeared to offer a more convenient and simpler experimental situation for the study of such changes than the ones he used. In addition, however, and equally important, is the fact that features of verbal organization seem to be reflected in the ways in which subjects order their recalls in this free situation.

The first experiments by Bousfield employed lists which contained categorized subgroups of words. For example, a list of 40 items might be composed of 10 animals, 10 weapons, 10 cities, and 10 articles of clothing. These 40 items were presented to the subject in a random order, and the extent to which, in his recall, the subject put together the animals, the cities, and so on, represents a reorganization or *clustering* of categorized items. I shall refer to this procedure as *category clustering*. Jenkins and Russell (1952; see also Jenkins, Mink, & Russell, 1958) selected pairs of items from their standardization (Russell & Jenkins, 1954) of the Kent-Rosanoff Word Association Test. They took stimuli, say TABLE and MOUNTAIN, and frequent responses to the stimuli, e.g., CHAIR and HILL, respectively. Words selected in this manner were presented in a random order to subjects for recall. What I shall call *associative clustering* was found when in their recalls the subjects put together in sequence the stimuli and their responses which had been separated at list presentation. Category clustering and associative clustering represent operational definitions of the terms "organization" or 'reorganization" in recall, as I shall use them here.

The interpretation which Bousfield at first gave to category clustering involved the activation of superordinates by the instances which were presented. Thus, the occurrence of various items, such as DOG, CAT, LION, MONKEY, would activate the superordinate "animal." This superordinate, in combination with other factors, controlled the emission of items in recall so that they appeared in clusters; the number of words recalled, also, was augmented by the superordinate. Jenkins and Russell, on the other hand, did not use superordinate concepts. Since the clustering they obtained was based on and related to preexperimental associative strength between the members of the pairs, they had no need to go beyond the associative factor to account for the clustering they obtained.

My first experiment on clustering (Cofer, 1959) represented an attempt to show that logical relations in the language would mediate clustering. My list of 40 words consisted of eight groups of 5 words each, each group being composed of synonymous words. The words were taken from Haagen's (1949) materials which provide groups of items whose degree of synonymity to another item was rated. For example, the items REGAL, SCEPTERED, STATELY, and KINGLY are all to some degree synonyms of the word ROYAL, and these five items made up one of the word groups. When I scrambled the 40 words and, after presentation, obtained recall, I did get clustering, but it was unexpectedly minimal. Synonymity, in other words, did not provide a very good basis for clustering, at least as measured. This was a puzzling finding, but it seemed to clear up when associational data on these items were examined.

For other purposes, a set of single-response free associations to each of a number of words in Haagen's list was obtained. Following a method invented by Patricia Jenkins (Jenkins & Cofer, 1957), and later independently developed by Bousfield, Whitmarsh, and Berkowitz (1960), I computed the associative overlap between the members of each pair of synonyms (Cofer, 1957). This overlap score is, in essence, the proportion of associations which two words have in common. Plotting associative overlap against degree of rated synonymity yields the curve shown in Figure 1. It is clear that associative overlap is highest when

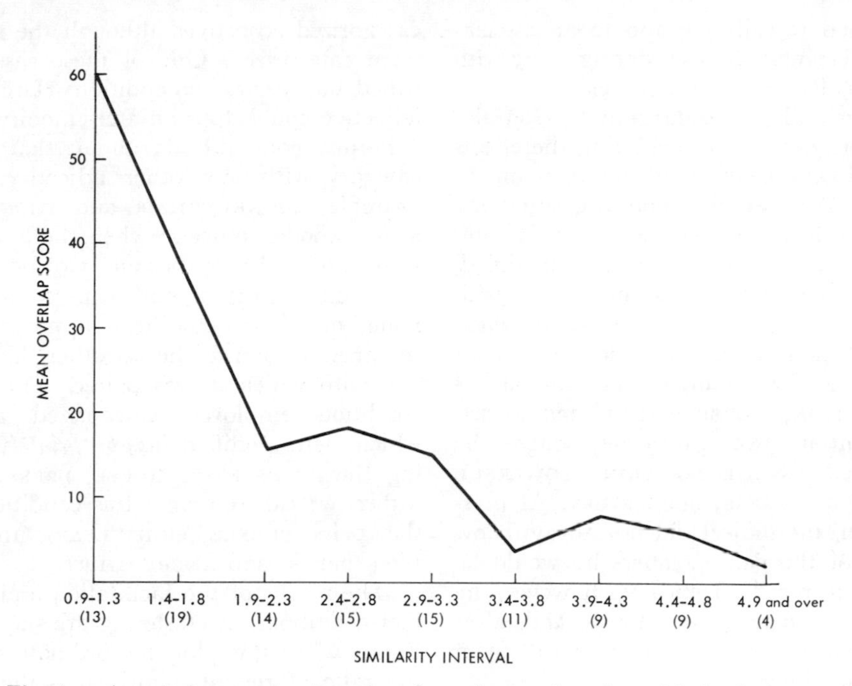

Fig. 1: Associative overlap in pairs of words as a function of judged synonymity between the members of the pair. (Synonymity ranges from high—0.9–1.3—to low—4.9+. The numbers in parentheses along the abscissa indicate the number of pairs represented in the mean overlap score for the synonymity interval.)

synonymity is close (low numbers to the left of the figure) and decreases abruptly as synonymity decreases (to the right of the graph). Since many of my synonyms, for example, REGAL and STATELY, or SCEPTERED and KINGLY, are not very close synonyms, it seemed reasonable to interpret the low clustering values as paralleling the low degree of associative relation which characterizes these synonyms.

At about the same time, Cohen, Bousfield, and Whitmarsh (1957) had set about to collect associations to the names of categories. For example, they presented their subjects with a category name, such as a four-legged animal or an article of clothing, and asked for instances of the category. This is a kind of controlled association, i.e., the acceptable responses are restricted to a given class. Tabulation of the responses showed a frequency distribution such that some responses occur very frequently in a group of subjects, and others infrequently. Thus to ANIMAL, DOG and CAT are frequent responses, whereas PLATYPUS, AARDVARK, and VICUÑA are infrequent. Bousfield, Cohen, and Whitmarsh (1958) then studied clustering for lists in which the items were high-frequency associates of category names and for lists in which the items were low-frequency associates of the same names. The differences were striking, with the high-frequency associates showing marked clustering and the low-frequency lists relatively little. This finding (and other data), I think, shifted Bousfield away from superordinates to associations as responsible for the mechanics of clustering. The success of Deese (1959) in predicting free-recall scores for lists of words differing in interitem associative strength may also have been a factor. The synonym data, Bousfield's findings, and Deese's success combined to shift me also to an associative interpretation of clustering along with Jenkins, Russell, and Bousfield.

Meanwhile, Gonzalez and I (Gonzalez & Cofer, 1959) were exploring the effects of modifiers on the tendency of nouns to cluster. We used the following situation: A list of 40 nouns, representing four categories, was selected which, unmodified, showed significant clustering. Then, with other subjects, we presented lists in which each of these nouns was modified by an adjective. For example, the unmodified nouns, LION, HORSE, DRESS, and SHIRT, representing two categories, might be presented as STRONG LION, POWERFUL HORSE, RED DRESS, BLUE SHIRT. At presentation, the subject did not always know which of the pair members he would be asked to recall. Typically, however, he was asked to recall the nouns, and, after a 5-minute, filled interval, to recall them a second time.

We set up four conditions, as follows. In two, the adjectives, as well as the nouns, were categorized. One of these we called the facilitation condition, in which nouns of a given category were always modified by adjectives from one category. The example I just gave was one in which all animals were modified by adjectives indicating strength (STRONG and POWERFUL modifying LION and HORSE) and all articles of clothing were modified by color adjectives (RED and BLUE modifying DRESS and SHIRT). This illustrates the arrangement of modifiers in the facilitation condition. The second condition, the *conflict* condition, used the same words but here the nouns of a category were modified by adjectives drawn from all the categories used. For example, HORSE might still be modified by POWERFUL but LION by TAWNY; DRESS might be modified by a size adjective like LONG and perhaps SHIRT by STRONG, a strength-class adjective. The adjective categories were distributed *across* the noun categories in the conflict condition.

The other two conditions did not use categorized adjectives although the nouns were categorized. One of these cases we called the *specificity* condition. Here each adjective could appropriately modify only 1 noun among the 40, and it shared no category with any other adjective. For example, CABINET, CHAIR, and STICK may all be wooden objects; when the 3 words were modified they became LIQUOR CABINET, ROCKING CHAIR, and WALKING STICK; none of these modifiers appropriately modified a noun in the list other than the one with which it was paired. The final condition employed categorized nouns which were modified *inappropriately*. Using the nouns LION, HORSE, DRESS, and SHIRT, we can represent this condition by the pairs PURPLE LION, LEAFY HORSE, WISE DRESS, and ANGRY SHIRT.

The results of the facilitation and conflict conditions on clustering are shown in Figure 2. In this plot, the ordinate shows the ratio of repetition, which is the proportion of words recalled which are recalled in clusters. The graph shows, in order along the abscissa, the mean values for the facilitation (F) condition for both immediate and delayed recall (after 5-minute, filled interval), the conflict condition (C), and the unmodified (control) condition (C_N).

Figure 2 shows an increment in clustering for the facilitation condition for both

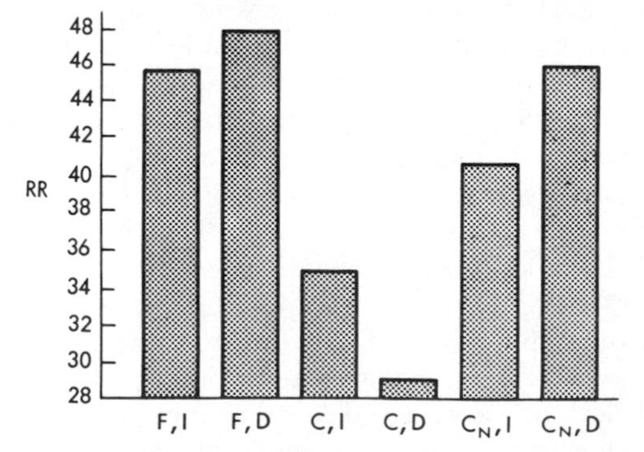

Fig. 2: Mean ratio of repetition recall scores for facilitation and conflict conditions. (F refers to facilitation, C to conflict, and C_N to control conditions; I and D refer to immediate and delayed—5-minute—recalls, respectively.)

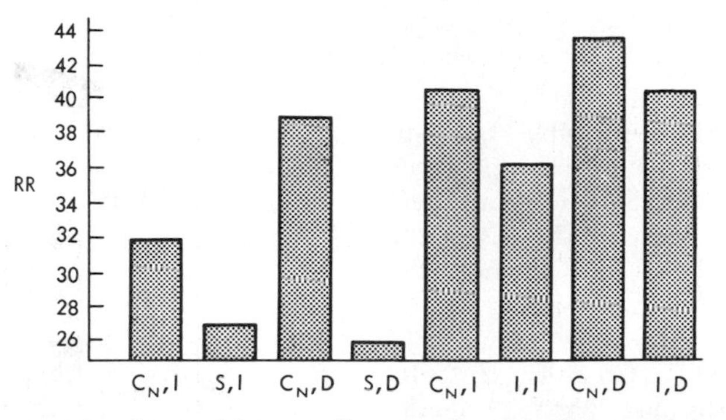

Fig. 3: Mean ratio of repetition recall scores for specificity and inappropriate-modification conditions. (The I which follows a comma and the D refer to immediate and delayed—5-minute—recalls, respectively. The four bars to the left represent the control—C_N—and the specificity—S—conditions of the specificity experiment. The four bars to the right represent the control—C_N—and the inappropriate-modification (I before the comma) conditions of the inappropriate-modification experiment. The two experiments employed different materials, so the four bars to the left cannot be compared directly to the four on the right.)

recalls, as compared to the controls; the conflict condition is inferior to the control at immediate recall and becomes more inferior at delayed recall. Remember that these two lists contained identical words but in different pairings. Figure 3 presents results for the specificity and inappropriate-modification conditions. It shows a marked reduction of clustering for both specificity (S,I) and inappropriate-modification (I,I) conditions (in comparison with their controls, first C_N,I and second C_N,I), with no recovery for the specificity condition (S,D) at the second recall. Rises in clustering at second recall are often seen in other cases. Word recall, not shown in these figures, was augmented under the facilitation condition but suppressed under the other conditions, relative to their controls.

These results showed marked effects of modification in the arrangements we employed. In order to have a further basis for their interpretation, I (Cofer, 1960) then collected single-word free-association data for the nouns alone, the adjectives alone, and the adjective-noun pairs. The associational findings for the specificity, conflict, and inappropriate-modification conditions were relatively clear. For example, the unmodified nouns CABINET, CHAIR, and STICK all elicit WOOD with some frequency in free association. These common associations, however, drop out when the associations to the word *combinations* LIQUOR CABINET, ROCKING CHAIR, and WALKING STICK are compared. One might say, for the specificity and also the inappropriate modifications, that the modifiers had eliminated the associational basis for clustering which the unmodified nouns possessed. A similar but somewhat different effect was seen in the conflict condition. As indicated, CHAIR, alone, may elicit WOOD as a response. But the phrase BROKEN CHAIR might yield response like OLD—responses similar to some of those yielded by a pair like TATTERED DRESS. Thus, associationally, CHAIR and DRESS, modified by these adjectives, might cluster together rather than with other wooden objects and with articles of clothing, respectively. That is, clustering might occur on the basis of the categories of the modifiers rather than on the basis of the noun categories. We do not actually know that this happened enough here to account for the decline of clustering under the conflict condition, but it is a distinct possibility, and another experiment shows clearly that it can happen. I will mention it in a moment.

While associational changes due to modification offer a plausible basis for the effect of the conflict, specificity, and inappropriate-modification conditions, there were *no* aspects of the association data which paralleled the augmentation of clustering and recall seen in the facilitation condition.

Gonzalez and I (Gonzalez & Cofer, 1959) also performed an investigation which was concerned with whether a clustering effect present in either adjectives or nouns would carry over through pairing to other nouns or adjectives which, by themselves, do not cluster. We prepared four lists of words: a list of categorized adjectives, a list of uncategorized adjectives, a list of categorized nouns, and a list of uncategorized nouns. In one half of the experiment, the categorized adjective list was set to modify the uncategorized nouns; nouns were recalled, and clustering was scored for the nouns on the basis of the categories of the adjectives which had modified the nouns during presentation. Recalls for a control group which was given the uncategorized nouns were also scored for clustering on this basis. The other half of the experiment represented the reverse case: Uncategorized adjectives modified categorized nouns; adjectives were recalled, and clustering among the adjectives was scored on the basis of the categories of the nouns they had modified during presentation. Recalls of a control group for the uncategorized adjectives alone were scored in the same way. The results are shown in Figure 4.

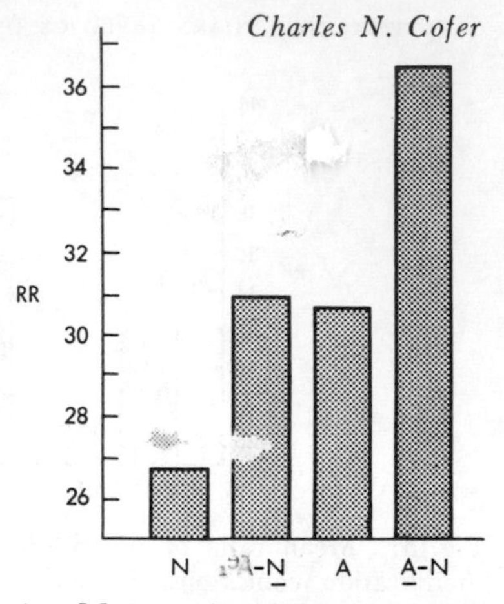

Fig. 4: Mean ratio of recall scores in the mediation effect. (The bar A-N represents the clustering obtained in the recalls of uncategorized nouns when clustering was scored on the basis of the categories of the adjectives which modified the nouns at presentation; the bar N gives the values for the same nouns, not modified at presentation, scored in the same way. A-N indicates clustering in the recall of adjectives on the basis of the nouns they modified during presentation; A is the control for the A-N group.)

Clearly, the uncategorized nouns clustered on the basis of the categories of the adjectives which had modified them at presentation (A-N), as compared to the noun control (N), and the uncategorized adjectives clustered more highly on the basis of the categories of the nouns they had modified at presentation (A-N), relative to the adjective control (A). These findings, which we have called the *mediation effect,* seem difficult to account for on the basis of simple transfer of associations between pair members, and, together with the data from the facilitation condition in the previous experiments, constitute a limitation on obvious associational interpretations of clustering. The name, mediation effect, is a descriptive one, indicating that the clustering occurs through categories not well represented in the list in which clustering is found.

Another problematic finding concerning the associational mechanism of clustering comes from the comparison of high-frequency and low-frequency associates to the category names. We have done several experiments on the hypothesis that low-frequency associates, which, as I have said before, do not cluster very strongly, should be more affected by conditions which impair clustering than high-frequency associates. We have compared the effects of modifiers on the clustering of low-frequency and high-frequency associ-

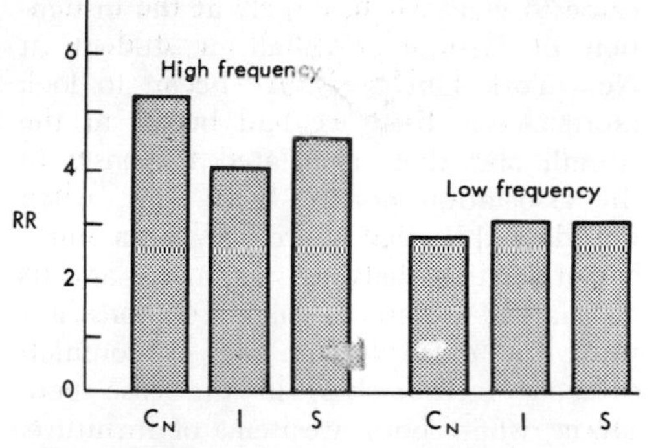

Fig. 5: Mean ratio of repetition immediate-recall scores for high-frequency and low-frequency associates of category names under inappropriate (I) and specificity (S) conditions. (The two control conditions are designated C_N.)

ates to the same category names but in different lists (Cofer & Segal, 1959b). Figure 5 shows the results. The surprising outcome here is that clustering is not significantly different for the low-frequency associates in the control (C_N, unmodified) condition from what it is for the specificity (S) and inappropriate-modification (I) conditions. On the other hand, there is a clear effect for high-frequency associates, comparable to the results which I showed in Figure 3. A similar finding emerged when the context effects were achieved by embedding categorized nouns in sentences at presentation, and the subjects were asked to recall only the nouns (Cofer, 1961a). As Figure 6 shows, clustering in high-frequency nouns was reduced by this context (S), and this effect has been achieved in several experiments employing slightly different conditions (Cofer, 1961b; Cofer & Segal, 1959a). However, with the low-frequency associates of category names no effect of sentence context (S) has been observed.

An alternative approach for the comparison of high-frequency and low-frequency associates is to use conditions designed to augment clustering. We have not used the facilitating modification condition as yet to achieve these effects, but last year, at Berkeley, Reicher and I (Cofer & Reicher, 1963) employed a different method of presentation designed to facilitate clustering. This method we have called the *block* method. In this procedure, all the items belonging to a category occur one after another, i.e., together, during list presentation, rather than being randomized with items from other categories. Our hypothesis was that block presentation would augment clustering, and that the augmentation would be greater for low-frequency than for high-frequency associates of the category names. We expected this result on the ground that high-frequency items might cluster maximally after random presentation. In other words, we were expecting to find an interaction between the frequency level of the nouns and the method of presentation—block or random. Figure 7 shows that block presentation did augment clustering for items from both frequency levels, but there was no significant interaction. Block presentation affected both types of items to about the same degree, rather than affecting one more than the other. Yet to be evaluated is a possible ceiling effect on the high-frequency associates. Perhaps I should also observe that these

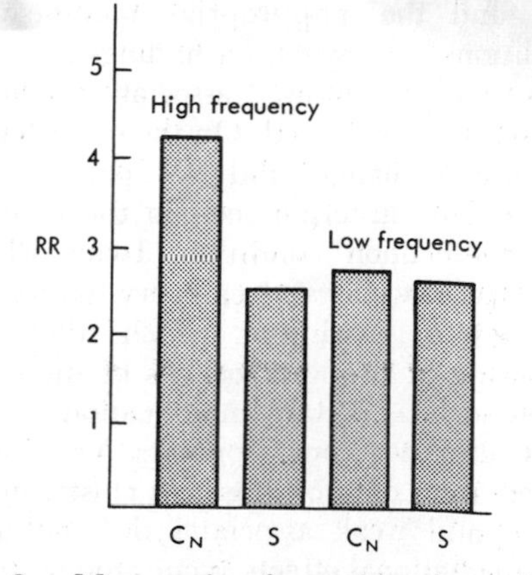

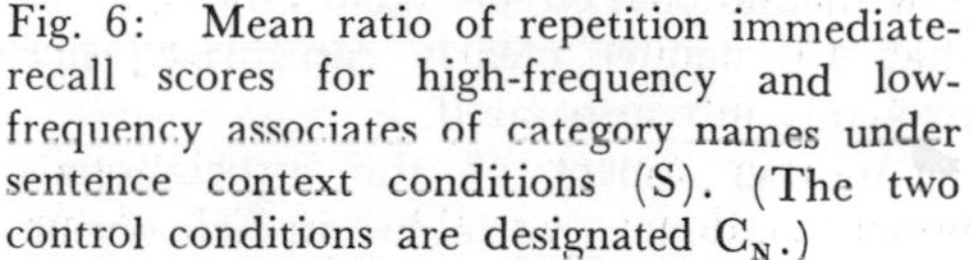
Fig. 6: Mean ratio of repetition immediate-recall scores for high-frequency and low-frequency associates of category names under sentence context conditions (S). (The two control conditions are designated C_N.)

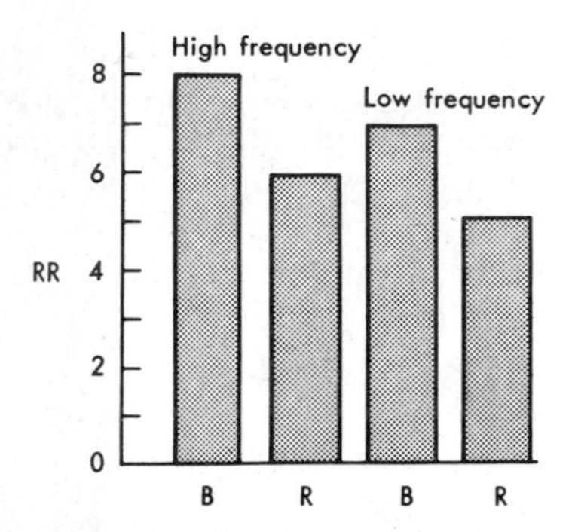

Fig. 7: Mean ratio of repetition immediate-recall scores for high-frequency and low-frequency associates of category names under block (B) and random (R) presentation procedures.

findings can be said to represent a failure by the subject to show as much clustering in his recall as the list provides (RR of .92). This failure is greater for low-frequency than for high-frequency associates.

Let me summarize so far. Measured association seems to explain associative clustering as Jenkins and Russell (and also Bousfield) have studied it, and category clustering in the work of Bousfield. Alteration of within-category associational relations by means of adjective modification reduced clustering in the specificity, conflict, and the inappropriate-modification conditions. The synonym findings are consistent with the limited associative overlap among the words used. On the other hand, associative changes did not parallel the increase in clustering seen in the facilitative-modification condition. Items which are weak associates of category names are resistant to conditions which alter the clustering of strong associates of the categories such as certain modification conditions and sentence context. Yet block presentation did not augment clustering of strong and weak associates differentially. The mediational effects occur among items that are neither clearly categorized nor probably interassociated.

Another aspect of the associational-nonassociational variable in clustering came to view when, largely at the instigation of George Marshall, a student at New York University, we began to look more closely than we had before at the stimuli and their associated responses in the association norms. It is clear, when one does this, that there may be a number of relations between a stimulus and its associated responses. Such relations appear, for example, as one of common category membership, in the case BED-CHAIR, where both are items of furniture, in contrast to cases in which a common category is not easy to see. BED-SLEEP or BED-DREAM would illustrate this latter situation. Let me put it this way: It is not as easy to find a concise, specific category to link BED with SLEEP, or with DREAM, as it is in the case of BED and CHAIR. The question may be raised, of course, whether this difference matters. Marshall and I (Marshall & Cofer, 1961) and, then, Marshall (1963) for his dissertation, conducted several experiments to find out.

What we wished to do was to compare clustering for categorized words with clustering for uncategorized words, with strength of normative association between the pair members equated. To do this, we obtained free associations on a variety of stimuli (Marshall & Cofer, in press), and then we were able to select categorized pairs and uncategorized pairs with equal or nearly equal associative overlap scores. The score here was the mutual relatedness index, or MR, which includes all of the associations which two words have in common expressed as a proportion of all of their associations. For example, if BED and DREAM both elicit SLEEP, NIGHT, and NIGHTMARE as associates, these would figure in their overlap (see Marshall & Cofer, 1963). However, CHAIR, which BED might elicit, would probably not be evoked by DREAM; CHAIR would count as one of the associates in the total given to BED, but not as a common or overlapping associate. The direct elicitation of one item by the other, as in the case BED→DREAM or DREAM→BED, would be counted in the overlap score.

An experiment was performed with six groups of subjects (Marshall, 1963, pp. 23–70). Each group was presented a scrambled list of 24 words. In the list were six categorized pairs and six uncategorized pairs at a given MR level, and there were six such lists, one per group, each representing an MR level, from low to high. Clustering was scored when the pair members appeared together in the recalls. Figure 8 shows the clustering score over four trials (the items were rescram-

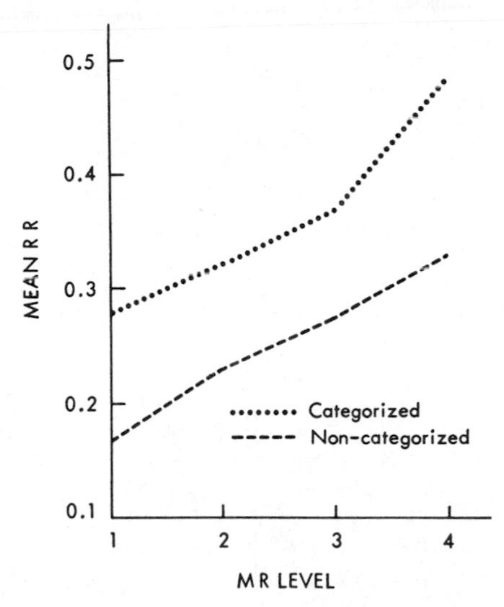

Fig. 9: Mean ratio of repetition scores for recall at each of four successive trials for pairs with equal associative overlap, but classified as either categorized or noncategorized.

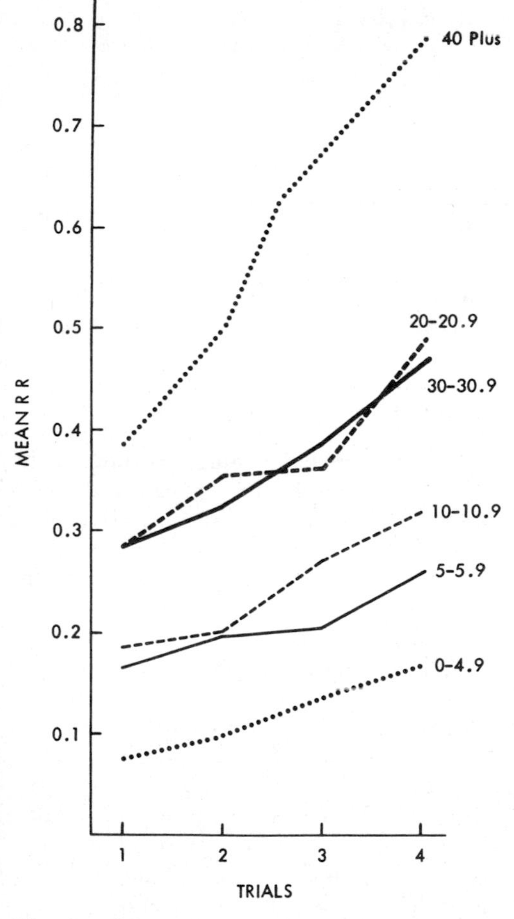

Fig. 8: Mean ratio of repetition scores for recall at each of four successive trials of lists composed of pairs varying in degree of associative overlap from 0–4.9 to 40+.

bled each time they were presented) with MR level as the parameter. It is clear that MR level is a very potent variable so far as clustering is concerned. Figure 9 shows clustering over trials for the categorized and uncategorized pairs, and the superiority of the categorized pairs at each trial is evident. There is no interaction with trials, however.

Figure 10 shows clustering for categorized and uncategorized pairs plotted against MR level. Remember that associative overlap is balanced here. What the figure suggests is an interaction of the categorization factor with MR level. At high MR levels categorization makes no difference to clustering, but at intermediate and to some extent at low values there is a difference in favor of the categorized pairs. This interaction is signicant.

As a part of the experiment which I have just summarized, Marshall gave his subjects, after they had finished their learning trials, what he called a Recognition Association Test. This test consisted of the 24 items with which the subject had just been working, randomly arranged in a 6×4 matrix. The subject was asked

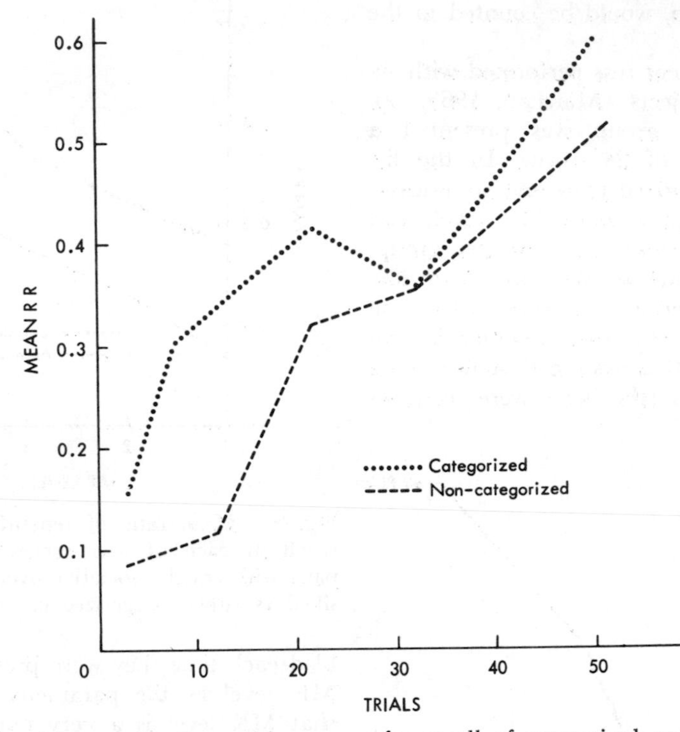

Fig. 10: Mean ratio of repetition scores for recall of categorized and noncategorized pairs as a function of associative overlap (MR level).

to select and to designate pairs of words which he felt were related in some way. Marshall then tabulated these designations into three groups: One represented the categorized pairs which Marshall had put into the list. The second represented the uncategorized but associated pairs which had been placed in the list. The third consisted of pairings which had not been placed in the list—they were inventions by the subjects and were called *idiosyncratic* pairs. (They *are* idiosyncratic in that few common pairings are achieved by more than two subjects.) Figure 11 shows the number of these three kinds of pairs as a function of MR level. It is clear that at the three lowest MR levels idiosyncratic pairings are "recognized" frequently by the subjects but that, as MR increases, these pairings drop out. The "recognition" of uncategorized pairs provides almost a mirror image of the curve for the idiosyncratic pairs, being infrequent at first and rising rapidly as MR level increases above intermediate values. Although the recognition scores for categorized pairs start fairly high, even at low MR levels, they do show a substantial rise with MR value to the point where the curve for these pairs is virtually identical to the one for uncategorized pairs.

We can also ask, do the idiosyncratic pairs cluster? This question was answered by searching the recall protocols for each subject for instances of clustering involving the idiosyncratic pairs he had designated on the Recognition Association Test. Figure 12 shows a plot of the proportion of the clustering obtained at each MR level which is attributable to each kind of pair—categorized, uncategorized, and idiosyncratic. As could be expected, the idiosyncratic pairs account for from 20% to 40% of the clustering obtained

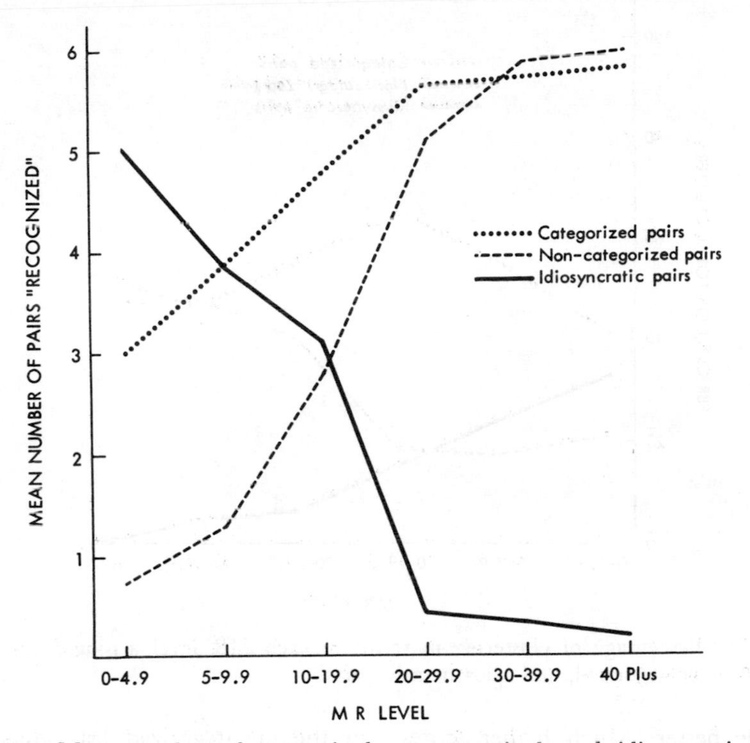

Fig. 11: Mean number of categorized, noncategorized, and idiosyncratic pairs "recognized" as a function of MR level of the pairs.

at the three lowest MR levels, but account for virtually none of it at the higher MR values. The other curves show that the categorized pairs account for much more clustering at low and intermediate MR levels than the uncategorized pairs, a fact with which we are already familiar.

Another experiment of Marshall's (1963, pp. 71–95) adds some further information both concerning categorized and uncategorized pairs and concerning idiosyncratic pairings. In this experiment, a further associative factor was included: the extent to which the associative overlap of pair members is due to their elicitation of each other as associates (what we call direct) or to their joint elicitation of other responses as associates in common (nondirect). For example, DOCTOR and LAWYER each elicits the other as an associate, and these direct associates account for 74% of their common associations. ROBIN and PARROT, on the other hand, do not elicit each other as associates, but achieve their substantial associative overlap by eliciting BIRD as a common (nondirect) associate. For this experiment, two lists were made up, equal in MR index (mean about that of the third level in the prior experiment). One of them was composed of directly and nondirectly associated *categorized* pairs, the other of directly and nondirectly *uncategorized* pairs. Thus, the lists here were homogeneous as to the presence of categorized or uncategorized pairs, whereas in the prior experiment all lists were mixed, containing both categorized and uncategorized pairs.

Figure 12 shows clustering over trials for the four types of pairs the two lists contained. It is clear that uncategorized, nondirectly associated pairs show little clustering over the trials and that the directly associated, uncategorized pairs do

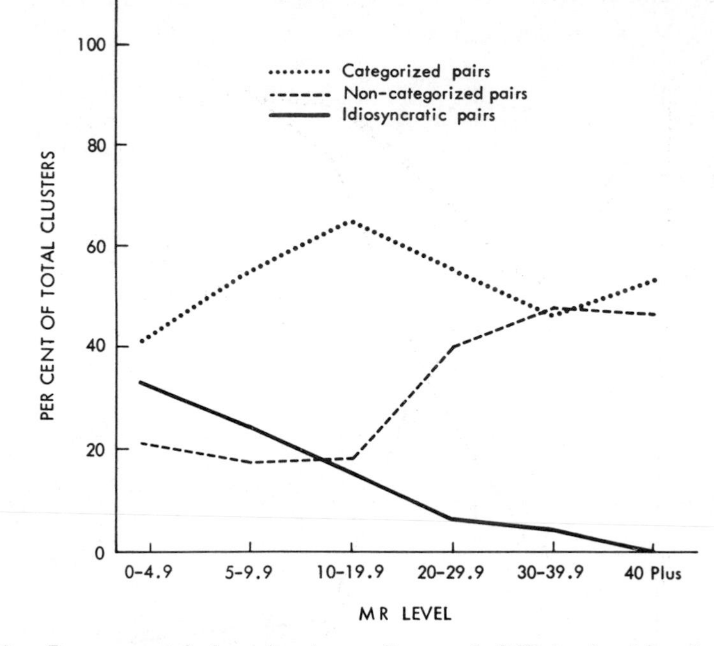

Fig. 12: Percentage of clustering in recall at each MR level arising from categorized, noncategorized, and idiosyncratic pairs.

only a little better. Much higher scores occur with categorized pairs of both types, and the improvement over trials is marked. There is a significant interaction of the categorization-noncategorization variable with trials for these homogeneous lists, whereas there was no interaction of these variables for a mixed list of about the same MR level in the preceding experiment.

Results from the Recognition Association Test show that the categorized pairs are clearly recognized here—in fact the mean number of idiosyncratic pairings for the homogeneous categorized list is only .52. For the uncategorized pair list, however, 4.63 of the pairings are idiosyncratic, and this is a substantially higher value than was obtained for either type of categorized pair. Direct comparison of these values for the comparable mixed list of the prior experiment is not possible, but it seems likely that the homogeneity of the lists made the categorization factor more salient in the categorized pair list, and the uncategorized pairings less salient in the uncategorized list, than was true in the mixed lists. This may be why an interaction of categorization and trials appears with homogeneous lists and does not do so with mixed lists.

I believe that there is some parallel between the idiosyncratic pairings we have found under certain conditions and Tulving's (1962) notion of subjective organization in free recall. Tulving has used a list of unrelated words presented in different orders over a number of trials. Free-recall instructions were used, but Tulving has found that the same sequences of words do appear, despite these instructions, over a number of the recalls. He suggests that these sequences among words, which the experimenter has selected as unrelated, indicate that subjects can find bases for organization in such unrelated items and that recall scores rise as these sequences become more pronounced. Perhaps our idiosyncratic pairings represent the subjects' identification of relationships among the words which they use to achieve clustering. But it is worth noting that when strong, measured associative relations are prominent, as they are at high MR levels, these associations are used, and idiosyncratic pairings drop out. Similarly, categorical relations also provide an alternative to subjective or idiosyncratic pairings and are effective over a wide range of MR levels. What we perhaps have here may be stated as follows: Subjects will, themselves, find relationships among items which will confer organization on recall. But when certain relationships among items in the list are prominent, as they are among categorized words and among highly associated items, the subject uses the ones provided, and subjective organization falls to low levels.

We have a little data (Marshall & Cofer, 1961, Exp. III), presented in Figure 14, which appear to be consistent with this interpretation. In this experiment, mixed lists of categorized and uncategorized word pairs at two levels of MR were presented under either a set or a no-set condition. The set was induced by telling the subjects that they might notice relations among some of the words, and that such relations would help in the recall of the words. The data show that the set augmented clustering for both the categorized and uncategorized pairs at the high MR level but had no differential effect on these kinds of pairs at the low MR level used. Given word relations of some prominence, then, set, so far as these results go, guides the subject to identify and use them in his recall.

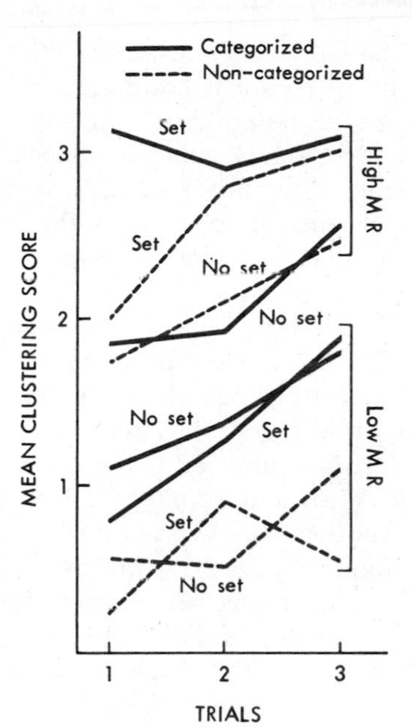

Fig. 14: Mean ratio of repetition values for the recalls at successive trials of categorized and noncategorized pairs of words with high and low associative overlap (MR) under set and no-set conditions.

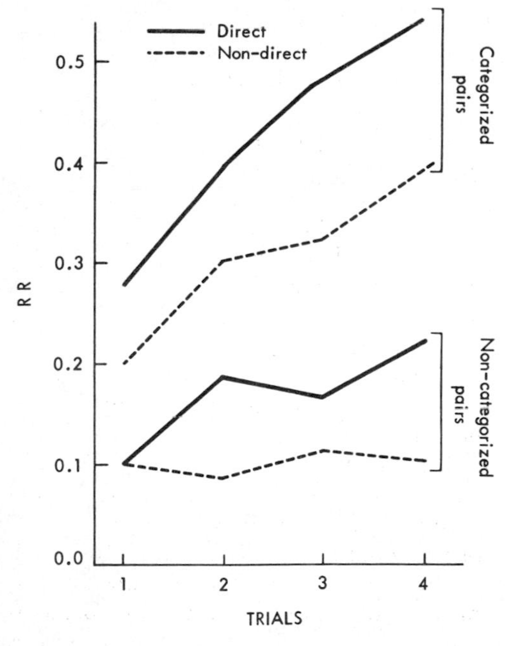

Fig. 13: Mean ratio of repetition scores for recall at successive trials of categorized and noncategorized pairs, directly or nondirectly associated.

Resulting from the experiments with word pairs, an interpretation which makes some sense is as follows: Category relations and, in uncategorized pairs, strong associative tendencies may operate to exclude idiosyncratic bases of organization. Probably, a word tends to suggest other words to subjects. When one of the suggested words is also on the list, as is the case with highly associated pair members, and the subject discovers the other word, a "unit" is completed and a selection from among the alternatives which the first word suggests is achieved, blocking out the other alternatives. Such a mechanism is consistent, at least, with the repeated finding that intrusions are infrequent in immediate free recall. But when the pair on the list represents a low-strength association the subject may not respond to the other word as related to the one he hears or sees first; the items provided do not form a unit and the subject goes about constructing units of his own devising. Another way of saying this might be that highly associated words are integrated units (Underwood & Schulz, 1960) or are structures (Mandler, 1962).

The same things may be said for categorized words. They appear to function as integrated units or as structures, but do so over a wide range of associative levels. How do they do this? One possibility is that the category name serves to unite them. However, free-association data to each member of a categorized pair do not always support this interpretation. The words EAGLE and CROW do individually elicit in common the response BIRD, and this category name may link them into a unit or structure for the subject. But VIOLIN and PIANO do not elicit INSTRUMENT often, and are linked, associatively, through words like MUSIC and PLAY neither of which is as precise or restrictive a category designation as BIRD is for EAGLE and CROW. There may, however, be a more restricted *domain* of associations between categorized words than is the case with uncategorized words of equal associative overlap. The uncategorized words SMOOTH and SILK, for example, are linked mainly by SOFT. It is perhaps less likely that one would get back to either SMOOTH or SILK if he had coded them as SOFT than it is that he would get back to VIOLIN and PIANO from code words like PLAY or MUSIC. This is, however, entirely a matter of conjecture at the present time.

It should not be forgotten that in our recall experiments with pairs *both* words are always presented, though not together. This is a condition which may affect the ways in which the words are related. Dolinsky (1963) has shown that when subjects are presented with two words and are asked to write in another word that logically connects the two, the word written is not typically one which is a dominant association of both the words. Often the word the subject supplies is not an association to either word at all (7 of 17 cases), sometimes it is a dominant response to one of the words (3 instances), and sometimes it is a nondominant association to one or both of the words (7 cases). It may be that, in the process of list presentation or at recall, the occurrence of the two categorized words instigates a linking response on the part of the subject, a response which is not high in associational frequency to either word alone. Or it may be that some process like "priming" of low-strength associations (Segal, 1962; Storms, 1958) may be involved. We do not know, although the findings for the set condition and for homogeneous lists, which I have already mentioned, suggest that clustering is augmented when the subject is directed to look for relationships. Whatever the value of associational or categorical relations for predicting characteristics of recall, we need much more information than we have on how such factors function to affect recall in the way they seem to do.

I have formulated the proposition that: When sufficiently prominent, experimenter-provided associational and categorical relations between members of a word pair provide a basis for clustering in free recall alternative to the bases—associational or otherwise—the subject will use to effect subjective organization or idiosyncratic pairing. Does this proposition apply as well to the other instances of clustering I have discussed? Let me try to answer this question in a few brief statements.

1. The associative clustering reported by Jenkins and Russell seems to fit; relatively highly associated pairs probably carried most of the clustering they found (Jenkins, Mink, & Russell, 1958), though category relations were also present, in all likelihood.

2. So far as category clustering is concerned, there seems to be no problem, as both prominent category and associational relations are present to provide bases for clustering.

3. The synonyms possessed few associations in common and did not represent effective categorical groups. The limited clustering obtained is consistent with these characteristics.

4. With modifiers in the specificity, conflict, and inappropriate-modification designs it seems likely that both associational and category relationships are disrupted, thus decreasing clustering.

5. I have said that the augmented clustering in the facilitation condition was not accompanied by consistent associative changes. Perhaps the subject in this case constructed units, like strong animals and colored clothing, as codes by which to organize and augment his recall.

6. That low-frequency associates of category names are resistant to conditions disruptive of clustering remains a puzzle. Recall is not as high for such items as it is for high-frequency associates. Perhaps because the number of the recalled units here is small they can somehow withstand disruption when some relations, categorical or associational, are recognized. This may be consistent with the failure of the low-frequency items to be augmented more by block presentation than they were.

7. The mediational effects are even less tractable to interpretation than are other phenomena I have listed. Somehow the subject must achieve noun units in terms of adjective categories or, in the other case, adjective units on the basis of the noun categories. We need more information to decide how he accomplishes this.

I have, throughout this paper, contrasted associational and categorical bases for clustering. It now seems to me, and this represents a change of heart, that such a contrast is neither useful nor heuristic. In free recall, our evidence suggests, subjects will use either or both of these bases to accomplish their recalls and will find ways to organize recalls even though the experimenter has not provided means in the list he presents. Free recall can tell us something of the way verbal organization is set up, but we are largely in the dark as to how this organization acts to bring related items together whatever the basis of their relationship. How do associations and category relations lead the subject to put this with that?

This is perhaps a different way of asking the same question the Würzburgers raised 60 years ago. But an approach which it suggests, at least to me, is an exhaustive study of situations and tasks (Jenkins, 1963) in an effort to uncover the variables which augment and those which diminish the effects of preestablished association and category relations on intellectual processes. Tasks can vary from discrimination learning, on the one hand, to free recall, on the other, in terms of the opportunity they give for interword relationships to display their effects. We have seen that an induced set and the factor of homogeneity of lists can apparently influence the use of certain interword relations. We should examine the entire range of this "intentionality" variable—from incidental learning to specific, induced sets—in interaction with task and materials variables, in order, by a kind of triangulation, to fix precisely the conditions under which preestablished associations and categories will work and will not work. Thomas Hobbes said, in a discussion of trains of association around 300 years ago, that 'the mind can lead from almost anything to anything." We have learned, in this discussion, that the word *almost* is a critical term in this quotation, and the work of the future can best be described, perhaps, as the search for its further explication.

References

BARTLETT, F. C. *Remembering.* New York: Cambridge Univer. Press, 1932.

BOUSFIELD, W. A. The occurrence of clustering in the recall of randomly arranged associates. *Journal of General Psychology,* 1953, 49, 229–240.

BOUSFIELD, W. A., COHEN, B. H., & WHITMARSH, G. A. Associative clustering in the recall of words of different taxonomic frequencies of occurrence. *Psychological Reports,* 1958, 4, 39–44.

BOUSFIELD, W. A., WHITMARSH, G. A., & BERKOWITZ, H. Partial response identities in associative clustering. *Journal of General Psychology,* 1960, 63, 233–238.

COFER, C. N. Associative commonality and rated similarity of certain words from Haagen's list. *Psychological Reports,* 1957, 3, 603–606.

COFER, C. N. A study of clustering in free recall based on synonyms. *Journal of General Psychology,* 1959, 60, 3–10.

COFER, C. N. An experimental analysis of the role of context in verbal behavior. *Transactions of the New York Academy of Sciences,* 1960, 22(Ser. 2), 341–347.

COFER, C. N. Further studies of clustering in the recall of nouns embedded during presentation in sentences. Technical Report No. 2, 1961, New York University, Contract Nonr 285(47), Office of Naval Research. (a)

COFER, C. N. Some effects of modifiers on the clustering of nouns embedded during presentation in sentences. Technical Report No. 6, 1961, New York University, Contract Nonr 285(47), Office of Naval Research. (b)

COFER, C. N., & REICHER, G. M. The effects of grouping during presentation and of an immediate recall on clustering in free recall. Paper read at Western Psychological Association, Santa Monica, California, April 1963.

COFER, C. N., & SEGAL, E. Certain modifier effects with nouns varying in degree of clustering tendency. Technical Report No. 29, 1959, University of Maryland, Contract Nonr 595(04), Office of Naval Research. (a)

COFER, C. N., & SEGAL, E. An exploration of clustering in the recall of nouns embedded during presentation in sentences. Technical Report No. 27, 1959, University of Maryland, Contract Nonr 595 (04), Office of Naval Research. (b)

COHEN, B. H., BOUSFIELD, W. A., & WHITMARSH, G. A. Cultural norms for verbal items in 43 categories. Technical Report No. 22, 1957, University of Connecticut, Contract Nonr 631(00), Office of Naval Research.

DEESE, J. Influence of inter-item associative strength upon immediate free recall. *Psychological Reports,* 1959, 5, 305–312.

DOLINSKY, R. Word association, mediation, and conceptual category. Paper read at Eastern Psychological Association, New York City, April 1963.

GONZALEZ, R. C., & COFER, C. N. Exploratory studies of verbal context by means of clustering in free recall. *Journal of Genetic Psychology,* 1959, 95, 293–320.

HAAGEN, C. H. Synonymity, vividness, familiarity, and association value ratings of 400 pairs of common adjectives. *Journal of Psychology,* 1949, 27, 453–463.

JENKINS, J. J. Mediated associations: Paradigms and situations. In C. N. Cofer & B. S. Musgrave (Eds.), *Verbal behavior and learning.* New York: McGraw-Hill, 1963. Pp. 210–245.

JENKINS, J. J., MINK, W. D., & RUSSELL, W. A. Associative clustering as a function of verbal association strength. *Psychological Reports*, 1958, 4, 127–136.

Jenkins, J. J., & Russell, W. A. Associative clustering during recall. *Journal of Abnormal and Social Psychology*, 1952, 47, 818–821.

Jenkins, Patricia M., & Cofer, C. N. An exploratory study of discrete free association to compound verbal stimuli. *Psychological Reports*, 1957, 3, 599–602.

Mandler, G. A. From association to structure. *Psychological Review*, 1962, 69, 415–427.

Marshall, G. R. The organization of verbal material in free recall: The effects of patterns of associative overlap on clustering. Unpublished doctoral dissertation, New York University, 1963.

Marshall, G. R., & Cofer, C. N. Associative, category and set factors in clustering among word pairs and triads. Technical Report No. 4, 1961, New York University, Contract Nonr 285(47), Office of Naval Research.

Marshall, G. R., & Cofer, C. N. Associative indices as measures of word relatedness: A summary and comparison of ten methods. *Journal of Verbal Learning and Verbal Behavior*, 1963, 1, 408–421.

Marshall, G. R., & Cofer, C. N. Single-word free association norms for 328 responses from the Connecticut Cultural norms for verbal items in categories. In L. Postman (Ed.), *Norms of word association*. New York: Academic Press, in press.

Russell, W. A., & Jenkins, J. J. The complete Minnesota norms for responses to 100 words from the Kent-Rosanoff Word Association Test. Technical Report No. 11, 1954, University of Minnesota, Contract N8 onr 66216, Office of Naval Research.

Segal, S. J. *The effect of different contextual conditions on the priming of free and continued word associations.* (Doctoral dissertation, New York University) Ann Arbor, Mich.: University Microfilms, 1962. No. 2223.

Storms, L. H. Apparent backward association: A situational effect. *Journal of Experimental Psychology*, 1958, 55, 390–395.

Tulving, E. Subjective organization in free recall of "unrelated" words. *Psychological Review*, 1962, 69, 344–354.

Underwood, B. J., & Schulz, R. W. *Meaningfulness and verbal learning.* Chicago: Lippincott, 1960.

Verbal Mediating Responses and Concept Formation[1]

ALBERT E. GOSS[2]

During the several years subsequent to the appearance of "verbal mediating responses and concept formation," at least three different issues have arisen that were not dealt with explicitly or that were not anticipated therein. These issues are: (a) assessment of initial strengths and derivative patterns of relationships between initiating stimuli and mediating responses, and factors that change such relationships; (b) the complexity of mediational analyses of concept formation; and (c) interpretations of concept formation that are sometimes presumed to be appreciably different from, often in contrast to, mediational analyses.

Assessment of and Changes from Initial Strengths and Derivative Patterns of Relationships

Precision of prediction or postdiction by means of theories of conceptual behavior based, in part, on either nonmediational or mediational analyses requires accurate assessment of initial strengths and derivative patterns of relationships between initiating stimuli and terminating responses or of relationships involving initiating stimuli, mediating responses and stimuli, and terminating responses. Of particular concern here are assessment of strengths and derivative patterns of initial relationships between initiating

[1] An earlier version of this paper was presented as part of a symposium on Mediating Processes in Transfer at the 1958 meetings of the American Psychological Association in Washington, D. C.

[2] The proposals in this paper own much to the ideas and experimental work of Janice E. Carey, James D. Fenn, Harvey Lacey, Marie C. Moylan, and Alvin J. Simmons. An opportunity to read an analysis by Arnold H. Buss aided development of the present treatment of reversal and nonreversal shifts. In their readings of earlier drafts, Barbara S. Musgrave and Charles N. Cofer offered many useful suggestions. Finally, Mary E. W. Goss, though not responsible for the infelicities of presentation which remain, was responsible for the elimination of many others.

Albert E. Goss, "Verbal Mediating Responses and Concept Formation," *Psychological Review,* **68**, No. 4 (1961), 248–274. Reprinted by permission of the author and publisher.

stimuli and mediating responses, and the specification of factors that change such relationships.

Initial relationships. *The set of stimuli of Rosen and Goss's (1965) experiment were 16 blocks exemplifying the combinations of black and white, tall or short, and square or circular top and bottom areas that were large or small. For the task of acquiring new verbal responses in terms of height-size, they obtained direct evidence that the presumptive relationships of greatest initial strength between those initiating stimuli and mediating responses involved verbal responses that were the names of the values of the color, shape, or both of each block. For the task of sorting by height-size subsequent to pretraining in the form of seeing and discriminating among the blocks, they obtained parallel evidence of the same presumptive relationships.*

For some (e.g. Bower & Trabasso, 1964; Spiker 1960), the relationships between initiating stimuli and what Rosen and Goss considered mediating responses are the "original" concepts. Acquisition of additional responses that are isomorphic with some among the many "original" concepts is considered concept discovery, concept identification, or concept attainment rather than concept formation or concept learning. Whether treated as potential or actual mediating responses and stimuli or as the responses of the relationships that are called "original" concepts, accurate assessment of the initial strengths and derivative patterns of relationships between initiating stimuli and (mediating) responses of naming each of the members of a specific set of stimuli of a particular type is important for several reasons. First, such assessment provides the estimates of the initial state requisite to any derivation of strengths and patterns of the relationships involving these and any additional stimulus-response relationships during subsequent trials. Second, when the objective of an experiment is to add further responses that are isomorphic with some among the original responses or that replace those original responses, such assessment can guide the specification of isomorphisms designed either to assure the occurrence of chaining, replacement or both at varying rates. Third, such assessment also constitutes a point of departure for investigations to determine the manner in which the particular initial state was established. Finally, such assessment may contribute to the specification of factors that change the initial stimulus-response relationships.

Factors that change initial relationships. *The primary concern of most investigations of conceptual behavior has been changes in strengths and derivative patterns of relationships between initiating stimuli and new terminating responses. Such changes have sometimes been in part the bases for inferences of changes in strengths and derivative patterns of relationships between initiating stimuli and mediating responses or the "original" concepts. Such specification of changes in relationships between initiating stimuli and mediating responses or of "original" concepts is indirect. But these changes are conceived as being in large measure the basis of the changes in strengths and derivative patterns of relationships between initiating stimuli and terminating responses. Accordingly, more direct data are desirable on factors involved both in formation of and changes in initial strengths and derivative patterns of relationships between initiating stimuli and potential mediating responses. Such research will almost certainly have to begin with young children and work upward to increasingly older* Ss. *Of particular importance is the extent to which instructions from* E *or that are self-induced alter strengths and derivative patterns of those relationships. Use of sets of stimuli of a particular type that are relatively exotic may be an alternative or supplementary approach.*

Complexity

A frequent objection to mediational analyses of behavioral phenomena, in general, and to the proposed mediational analyses of conceptual behavior, in particular, is the complexity of such analyses. Three comments are germane to this objection. They concern kinds of complexity, orientative and analytical structures, and problems of more complex behavioral situations.

Kinds of Complexity. *Two kinds of complexity must be distinguished. One is complexity of structures, patterns, or paradigms of observed and presumed stimulus-response relationships of various classes of situations. The other is complexity of basic or general laws of the strengthening, maintenance, generalization, weakening of those relationships.*

Complexity of structure. *Structures of observed and presumed stimulus-response relationships may be complex in terms of the number and dimensions or characteristics of the initiating stimuli in a specific set of a particular type, and in terms of the number of responses in the specific set of terminating responses to those initiating stimuli. These structures may also be complex in terms of the number of indispensable stimulus-response relationships, units, links in the sequence(s) from several initiating stimuli to one or more of the terminating responses. Often both types of complexity are involved.*

For concept-formation situations involving specific sets of particular different types of initiating stimuli, each of the figures in "verbal mediating responses and concept formation" illustrates the structure of observed and presumed stimulus-response relationships of both one-stage and two-stage paradigms. These structures are complex primarily because of the numbers of initiating stimuli and numbers of terminating responses of the specific sets. In one-stage paradigms—which may be reasonably representative of the behavior of animals, young children, and well-practiced adults—these structures might be reduced to the n_s *relationships between each initiating stimulus of a subset and one among the terminating responses. However, even with occurrences of mediating responses and stimuli, both initially and upon attainment of criterion, most if not all of the sequences from each initiating stimulus of a subset to a terminating response are likely to involve only a few relationships, units, links. Such structures, in Gustav Bergmann's phrase, "are complex, but not profound."*

None of the figures of verbal mediating responses involves complexity in terms of sequence(s) from several initiating to one or more terminating responses that entail from a few to many indispensable stimulus-response relationships, units, links. Such complexity has been dealt with, in general, elsewhere (Goss, 1961). It is not pertinent here.

In order to achieve relatively complete representation of the stimulus-response relationships on Trial i *with a concept-formation situation constituted of a specific set of several initiating stimuli of a particular type and a specific set of two or more terminating responses, complexity of structure in terms of numbers of relationships is unavoidable in one-stage paradigms and, even more so, in two-stage paradigms. Simplification can be achieved by devices such as omission of many or most of the initiating stimuli, unrealistic or no assumptions regarding initial states, or an assumption of homogeneity of units with respect to changes in strengths. But these simplifying devices may sometimes work against adequate theoretical or empirical analyses. Regardless, the simplicity they suggest is misleading.*

For analyses of various situations at a behavioral level, complex structures may have been and may still be relatively rare in psychology. But, even for simple situations, complex structures are hardly new (e.g. Hull, 1935; Lewin, 1946, p. 798). Moreover, in analyses of various situations that involve both behavioral and neural levels, complex structures are commonplace. Finally, in other sciences such as physics and chemistry, and in all engineering specialties, complex structures are also commonplace. In fact, the relatively complete representation of some specific structure with particular functional properties may require elaborate schemas that extend through many pages. A substantial proportion of psychologists, however, apparently do not understand the ultimate indispensability of complex structures that provide relatively complete representation of behavioral situations, have not had the requisite exposure to such structures to be comfortable with them, or lack the patience to work through them to reasonable comprehension of the component relationships.

Complexity of laws. *In physics, a relatively small number of basic, general, or fundamental laws—often with the functional status of a set of axioms or postulates—permits deduction of a large number of less general laws or theorems. In order to extend a particular set of laws to situations consisting of more "bodies" or "particles" than are subsumed in the set of basic laws or axioms, one or more composition rules may be required. To the extent that such rules hold, the relatively small number of basic laws or axioms can be extended to those more complex situations or structures for prediction or for explanation of both less general laws and singular events.*

In psychology, as in other sciences and technologies, relatively complete, frequently complex representation of behavioral situations is often desirable for, is ultimately indispensable to specification of the initial state of some behavioral situation or, more generally, of the state for that situation on Trial i. *Relatively complete, frequently complex representation is often desirable, is ultimately indispensable to demonstrating that only a few general laws suffice to explain observed changes in that situation. The traditional general laws include contiguity, frequency, and similarity. They may be supplemented by a few composition rules such as those for competing responses and for chaining. Complexity of structure may be indispensable to attainment of simplicity of general laws. That this may be the case is also frequently unrecognized or ignored.*

Orientative and analytical paradigms. *Orientative, or what might be labeled didactic or classificatory structures, patterns, or paradigms for particular situations, must be distinguished from analytical or explanatory structures, patterns, or paradigms for those same situations. Orientative structures, as illustrated by various traditional paradigms for classical conditioning and for instrumental conditioning (e.g. Keller & Schoenfeld, 1950, p. 51) may be sufficient for introducing undergraduate students to the content being considered under those headings and for initial, superficial differentiation among those situations. But these paradigms are rarely, if ever, sufficient for analytical or explanatory purposes. For example, should conceptions of instrumental conditioning such as Spence's (1956, pp. 49–51) be approximately correct, the independence of these situations suggested by traditional paradigms of classical and operant or instrumental conditioning is completely misleading.*

The figures of "verbal mediating responses and concept formation" were conceived as sufficiently analytical for most present experimental and theoretical treatments of concept formation. In order to provide the necessary, relatively complete representation of observed and presumed stimulus-response relationships for concept-formation situations involving different types and specific sets of initiating stimuli, the structures must be more complex than structures whose purpose is orientative. For the latter purpose a simple, one-stage n_s*:1 representation may suffice.*

Problems of complexity. *In part because of the relative overemphasis on classical and instrumental conditioning situations of the past three decades, many psychologists have not often been exposed to problems of analyses and explanation of many of the more complex behavioral situations. Moreover, when they have been exposed, the proposed analyses are likely to have involved misleading simplifications. Then, too, many psychologists have apparently not been exposed to various of the more complex analyses of classical and, particularly, operant or instrumental conditioning situations such as those of Spence (1956, pp. 49–51). Again, when they have been exposed to materials on operant or instrumental conditioning, the almost exclusive preoccupation with parameters of reinforcement, especially different schedules, has deflected attention from variables whose* modus operandi *must be developed in terms of complex structural considerations.*

Interpretations Sometimes Presumed to be Different than, in Contrast to Mediational Interpretations

As suggested elsewhere (Goss, 1964), mediational analyses of concept formation are introduced when certain observational and theoretical conditions obtain. The purpose of their introduction is to provide a description of observed and presumed stimulus-response relationships, both initially and subsequently, that is extensive enough and detailed enough to permit explanation of changes in those relationships. Of particular concern are the criterion relationships between initiating stimuli and terminating responses. Such mediational analyses are not different from or in contrast to various other proposed interpretations of concept formation. Among such other interpretations are those that use the "statistics" of information theory as well as those that use various other terms of or suggestive of information theory in seemingly explanatory fashion. Also among those other interpretations are stimulus-adaptation notions, certain all-or-none proposals, and computer simulation.

With respect to use of the "statistics" of information theory, nothing unique or explanatory is introduced by transforming the number of values along dimensions into "bits." In general, it suffices both to describe and to

quantify the stimuli as combinations of n *values along each of* m *dimensions. Moreover, providing the requisite information about proportions of occurrences of stimuli, of responses, of stimulus-response events is available, relationships between initiating stimuli and terminating responses on Trial* i *of any concept-formation situation can always be expressed "in uncertainty terms" (Garner, 1962, pp. 310–337). Uncertainty terms are just descriptive constants, descriptive statistics; they are neither unique to some theory nor explanatory.*

As numbers of relevant and irrelevant dimensions increase, the number of observed and presumed stimulus-response relationships increases. Such an increase can be described as greater "storage load" that requires more time and effort for "information retrieval," and the like. These terms add nothing. They merely give other names to what can be described, is described adequately in terms of relationships involving values along component dimensions of initiating stimuli and terminating responses or involving initiating stimuli, mediating responses and stimuli, and terminating responses.

Noted elsewhere (Rosen & Goss, 1965) is the possibility that "stimulus adaptation" (Bourne & Restle, 1959) is a misleading way of referring to what are probably changes in stimulus-response relationships, more specifically, in relationships between initiating stimuli and verbal mediating responses.

Also noted there is the possibility that some results presumably supportive of an all-or-none conception of the course of formation of associations (Bower & Trabasso, 1964) can be reinterpreted easily as consequences of changes in relationships between initiating stimuli and mediating responses. Regardless of the specific instance of purported all-or-none associations thus reinterpreted, mediational analyses are neutral with respect to most or all specific conceptions of the nature and course of strengthening, maintenance, generalization, weakening of stimulus-response relationships.

Mediational analyses are also neutral with respect to reinforcement or informative feedback interpretations (e.g. Bourne & Bunderson, 1963). Viewed manipulatively, reinforcing or informative events constitute some of the conditions of the strengthening, maintenance, and weakening of stimulus-response relationships. Viewed more analytically, reinforcement or informative events may determine the nature and extent of Ss' *responses to the particular initiating stimulus that was presented primarily during the interval between such events and presentation of the next stimulus. Viewed manipulatively, analytically, or both, a reinforcement or informative feedback interpretation may apply both to nonmediational and to mediational analyses.*

Sometimes, what is at least prospectively a theory is stated by words-within-diagrams that suggest the graphic schemes used to summarize the nature and sequences of major steps of some computer programs (Hunt, 1962, pp. 232, 236). But these words-within-diagrams can be replaced by concepts and principles regarding the nature and sequences of stimulus-response relationships. Indeed, these words-within-diagrams are usually devices to represent, with varying degrees of completeness, the pertinent concepts and principles. Furthermore, these words-within-diagrams schemes for computer programs should not be confused with the actual programs.

Whatever the merits of computer simulation of the processes involved in concept formation, such simulation is also neutral with respect to non-mediational or mediational analyses.

Hunt's (1962, pp. 234–235) decision trees can be regarded as part of a theory to be translated into a computer program. Decision trees represent one way of specifying possible combinations and sequences of mediating responses and stimuli that precede terminating responses of saying or otherwise indicating that a particular stimulus is or is not an example of a particular concept.

Computer simulation is simply one means of carrying out the calculations necessary for prediction or postdiction with any theory. Thus, the better description would be computer calculation. Precision of the predictions or postdictions generated by computer calculations is contingent on the extent to which pertinent variables are incorporated in mathematical formulation of a theory, and on the adequacy of statements of relationships among those variables. Computer calculation does not assure meeting either of these requirements, particularly the latter. Moreover, nothing in any non-mediational or mediational analysis precludes mathematical formulation or representation of laws of changes in the component relationships and, subsequently, computer calculation of resultant derivations. Of course, in either nonmediational or mediational analyses, inability to specify initial strengths and derivative patterns of stimulus-response relationships, and other difficulties, may preclude derivation of predicted values that agree satisfactorily with obtained values. Computer calculation does not assure such agreement.—Albert E. Goss

References

Bourne, L. E., Jr., and C. V. Bunderson, "Effects of delay of informative feedback and length of postfeedback interval on concept identification," *J. exp. Psychol.,* 65 (1963), 1–5.

Bourne, L. E., Jr., and F. Restle, "Mathematical theory of concept identification," *Psychol. Rev.,* 66 (1959), 278–296.

Bower, G., and T. Trabasso, "Concept identification," in *Studies in Mathematical Psychology,* ed. R. C. Atkinson. Stanford: Stanford Univer. Press, 1964.

Garner, W. R., *Structure and Uncertainty as Psychological Concepts,* New York: John Wiley & Sons, Inc., 1962.

Goss, A. E., "Acquisition and use of conceptual schemes," in *Verbal Learning and Verbal Behavior,* ed. C. N. Cofer. New York: McGraw-Hill Book Company, 1961.

————, "Verbal mediation," *Psychol. Rec.,* 14 (1964), 363–382.

Hull, C. L., "The mechanism of the assembly of behavior segments in novel combinations suitable for problem solution," *Psychol. Rec.* 42 (1935), 219–245.

Hunt, E. B., *Concept Learning.* New York: John Wiley & Sons, Inc., 1962.

Keller, F. S., and W. N. Schoenfeld, *Principles of Psychology.* New York: Appleton-Century-Crofts, 1950.

LEWIN, K. "Behavior and development as a function of the total situation," in *Manual of Child Psychology,* ed. L. Carmichael New York: John Wiley & Sons, Inc., 1946.

ROSEN, D. E., and A. E. GOSS, "Pre-experimentally acquired verbal responses during acquisition and subsequent use of experimentally acquired verbal responses in conceptual block sorting," *J. genet. Psychol.,* **107** (1965), 313–335.

SPENCE, K. W., *Behavior Theory and Conditioning.* New Haven: Yale Univer. Press, 1956.

SPIKER, C. C., "Research methods in children's learning," in *Handbook of Research Methods in Child Development,* ed. P. H. Mussen New York: John Wiley & Sons, Inc., 1960.

Over the past five decades, verbal mediating responses and stimuli have figured as important elements in a number of stimulus-response analyses of concept formation. This paper briefly reviews these analyses as a prelude to carrying out its main purpose, which is the further explication of the role of verbal mediating responses in conceptual behavior. More specifically, spelled out first are criteria for concept formation tasks, particularly as compared with those for conventional paired-associates tasks. Then described in considerable detail are some paradigms of presumed stimulus-response relationships in concept formation. Finally, the paradigms are considered in conjunction with certain variables and learning principles, and sample predictions are generated.

Probably the earliest explicit stimulus-response analysis of the role of verbal mediating responses in conceptual behavior is that which Max Meyer illustrated with the concept "food" in his *Fundamental Laws of Human Behavior* (1911, pp. 213–214). The same example of the essential features of concepts was used subsequently by Weiss (1925), Dashiell (1928), and Gray (1931). Although Watson (1920, p. 102) chose a different example, his treatment of conceptual behavior also emphasized verbal mediating responses. The primary purpose of these early analyses was to show that conceptual phenomena—which had previously been thought to be impervious to behavioristic treatment—could be dealt with in stimulus-response terms. Understandably for the time, such analyses were only incidentally combined with learning principles to derive predictions about the effects of potentially significant variables on conceptual behavior, and none of the predictions was tested experimentally.

Early in the forties, Birge (1941), Miller and Dollard (1941), and Cofer and Foley (1942) made suggestions concerning the possible significance of verbal mediating responses for conceptual behavior. These treatments, however, were more concerned with defining and applying the mechanism of response-mediated similarity and generalization than with analyzing in detail the role of this mechanism in concept formation. The same is true of Gibson's (1940) development and use of the somewhat parallel notion of internal generalization and its complement, internal differentiation.

A decade later, Osgood (1953) offered *post factum* analyses of the conceptual tasks and results described by Hull (1920), Smoke (1932), Heidbreder (1946a, 1946b), and Reed (1946). These analyses, along with those of Baum (1951) and Mandler (1954), emphasized the mechanism of response-mediated similarity and generalization to the virtual exclusion of the complementary mechanism of response-mediated dissimilarity and discrimination. During the same period, Goss and his students extended their studies of the latter mechanism (e.g., Goss & Greenfeld, 1958) to the analysis and investigation of the effects of experimentally controlled verbal pretraining on conceptual sorting (e.g., Fenn & Goss, 1957), conceptual naming (Lacey, 1959), and animistic thinking (e.g., Simmons & Goss, 1957).

Hypotheses about the role of verbal mediating processes in reversal and nonreversal shifts of conceptual phenomena have been proposed and tested by Kendler and his students (e.g., Kelleher, 1956; Kendler & D'Amato, 1955), as well as by Buss (1956), Gormezano and Grant (1958), and Harrow and Friedman (1958). These proposals apparently evolved primarily from the considerable body of data and theory concerning the simple discriminative behaviors of infrahuman and preverbal human organisms to which Spence (1936) has been the major contributor, rather than from existing hypotheses and data concerning response-mediated similarity and dissimilarity. Of similar origin is Wicken's (1954) analysis of the strengthening of discriminative responses to values along one dimension of multidimensional stimuli, and his subsequent more explicit hypotheses as to how verbal mediating responses might be the vehicles of "perceptual sets" (Wickens & Eckstrand, 1954).

Pavlov's "second signal system" is essentially equivalent to mediating responses and stimuli, and it has been the basis for recent analyses of "higher nervous activity" by Soviet psychologists (e.g., Elkonin, 1957). Within this framework, Liublinskaya (1957) has described theoretical and experimental work on the role of the second signal system in the conceptual behaviors of preschool children.

Of the many analyses and studies that bear directly or indirectly on the role of verbal mediating responses and stimuli in concept formation, some have been supported solely by informal examples rather than by experimental data and principles. Those which do refer to experimental materials have often been limited to one or two relatively specific situations. And there has been a tendency to consider the nature and implications of only a few of the many possible patterns of relationships that can exist among initiating stimuli, mediating responses and stimuli, and terminating responses (Goss, 1955, 1956).[3] There is clearly need for a more comprehensive yet experimentally rooted analysis; within the limitations to be

[3] A temporal sequence of stimulus-response events in which a mediating response and stimulus may be distinguished can be represented as $S_{Initiating}$-$R_{Mediating}$~$S_{Mediating}$-$R_{Terminating}$. Social situations or experimental tasks are conceived as beginning with or initiated by some stimulus "element" or "compound" and as terminating with a response which is reinforced or punished; is instrumental in altering a subject's environment; or, more generally, has simply been designated the terminating, reference, or criterion response. Any stimulus event or receptor activation might be the initiating stimulus of a sequence, though usually and practically such stimuli are social and physical events.

Ideally, two criteria must be met in order for responses and the stimuli they produce to be considered mediating responses and stimuli. The first criterion is the observation of or grounds for inferring the occurrence of one or more responses subsequent to the initiating stimulus and before the terminating response. The second criterion is the demonstration that such temporally intermediate responses and stimuli have actual or potential facilitative or inhibitory effects on one or more measures of the occurrence and strength of the terminating response. Relative covertness and some particular topography as additional criteria seem unnecessarily restrictive. However, because of the presumed greater functional significance for most complex behaviors of postverbal humans of mediating responses originally or presently involving the vocal musculature, the focus of the analyses developed here will be on such responses and the stimuli they produce—verbal mediating responses and stimuli. A more exhaustive treatment of the definition of mediating responses and stimuli and of the bases for inferring or confirming their occurrences and effects and effect can be found in Goss (1956).

described, such an analysis is offered in this paper.

CRITERIA FOR CONCEPT FORMATION TASKS

General specification of the nature of concept formation tasks is a logical starting point. Because many concept formation tasks have much in common with conventional paired-associates learning tasks, differentiation of the two types of tasks is also required.

General Criteria

Fundamental to the definition of concept formation tasks (conceptual behaviors) are patterns of relationships between initiating stimuli and terminating responses. More particularly, such tasks involve patterns in which two or more independently presented initiating stimuli evoke the same terminating response. It is the independent presentation of stimuli that distinguishes concept formation tasks from convergent stimulus-compound situations. Thus crudely characterized, of course, the simplest concept formation tasks are essentially identical to phenomena more often labeled primary stimulus generalization and response-mediated generalization (Dollard & Miller, 1950; Goss, 1955). Indeed, the latter phenomena might be looked on as limiting cases of the former.

Those situations *commonly* regarded as concept formation tasks, however, are more complex. Sets of initiating stimuli are partitioned into two or more subsets, at least one of which has two or more independently presented members. Usually each of the subsets has two or more members, and the learning requirement is acquisition of the same response to all members of a particular subset and of a different response for each subset.

At a descriptive level, the sets of initiating stimuli in concept formation studies have been markedly heterogeneous. Because some sets apparently require paradigms different from those for other sets, and also for simplicity, sets of initiating stimuli are divided here into three types. These three types seem sufficient both for the development of adequate one-stage and two-stage paradigms and for the representation of all sets of initiating stimuli.

In the first type of set, all members are either variations in values along one physical or psychophysical dimension, or they are combinations of values along two or more dimensions. The dimensions may be primary or derived; the combinations may be completely or incompletely orthogonal. Illustrative of such sets are four squares which are red-small, red-large, blue-small, and blue-large.

Initiating stimuli in the second type of set can be partitioned into two or more subsets on the basis that all stimuli of each subset have some physically specifiable element or relation in common. The stimuli within each of these subsets differ from each other with respect to additional features. Thus, the stimuli of each subset consist of both common and variable features, neither of which has been (or perhaps could be) completely reduced to combinations of physical or psychophysical dimensions. Four stimuli, two of which have an S-shaped form in common and two of which have a sword-shaped form in common, but whose other features differ, are representative of this type of set of initiating stimuli.

Sets of initiating stimuli which are less readily or not at all reducible to combination of values along dimensions, or to subsets defined by common elements or relations, constitute the third type of set. Illustrative of this type are sets of words for objects, properties, or relations. Subsets of words are usually, but not necessarily, specified on the basis of observations or assumptions that all of the stimuli of each subset evoke one or more common responses, some of which differ from the common responses evoked by the stimuli of each of the other subsets. An example of such sets of initiating stimuli is provided subsequently.[4]

With this type of initiating stimuli the bases for partitioning into subsets and for assigning responses to those subsets might be entirely arbitrary or random. For example, eight consonant-vowel-consonant initiating stimuli, none of which has any letters in common, might be randomly partitioned into four subsets of two members each. As stimuli for responses, a different one of four two-digit numbers, none of which has any digit in common, might then be randomly assigned to each of the subsets of initiating stimuli, with the requirement that a different response be conditioned to each subset of initiating stimuli.

Paired-Associates Learning Tasks and Concept Formation Tasks

Paired-associates learning can be regarded as referring either to a particular kind of task or to a more general *procedure* for establishing and changing stimulus-response associations. Many concept formation *tasks,* however, have employed the paired-associates *procedure* for strengthening associations between stimulus members and responses elicited by response members. Both conventional paired-associates tasks and such concept formation tasks may therefore be regarded as complementary special cases of patterns of stimulus-response associations which are strengthened by the paired-associates procedure (Metzger, 1958; Richardson, 1958).

There is only one essential difference between conventional paired-associates learning tasks and concept formation tasks in which stimulus-response associations are established by the paired-associates procedure. That difference is in the ratio of stimulus members to responses which are to be conditioned to those stimuli. For conventional paired-associates learning tasks, the ratio of stimulus members to response members has been 1:1: i.e., separate associations are established between each of mn_s different stimulus members and each of the mn_r different responses elicited by mn_r response members.

For the formation of concepts by the paired-associates procedure, however, the ratio of stimulus members to the responses which are conditioned to those stimuli has been greater than 1:1: i.e., for at least one, and usually for all of m subsets of stimulus members, $n_{s_j} > 1$, where n_{s_j} is the number of stimuli in the jth subset. Regardless of the type of sets of initiating stimuli, by increasing the numbers of responses to equal the number of initiating stimuli, concept formation tasks in which stimulus-response associations are established by the paired-associates procedure can be transformed into conventional paired-associates learning tasks. Conversely, by decreasing the number of responses from equality with the number of initiating stimuli the latter can be transformed into concept formation tasks.

[4] The first and possibly the second of the three types of sets of initiating stimuli distinguished here and the relationships with terminating responses into which these types of stimuli enter are equivalent to what have been labeled elsewhere as conjunctive categories or concepts (Bruner, Goodnow, & Austin, 1956, pp. 41–43, 244–245). The third of the present types seems approximately equivalent to Bruner, Goodnow, and Austin's disjunctive categories or concepts. From Bruner, Goodnow, and Austin's definition of relational concepts or categories and the accompanying examples, it cannot be determined whether such relational categories overlap with the first and second of the types noted here or whether such categories involve some additional type of initiating stimuli not distinguished here.

PARADIGMS

The role of verbal mediating responses in concept formation tasks can be developed most easily and clearly by means of two-stage paradigms of presumed relationships among initiating stimuli, mediating responses and stimuli, and terminating responses for each of the three types of initiating stimuli which were distinguished in the preceding section. Inferences regarding mediating responses and stimuli are usually based on characteristics of relationships between initiating stimuli and terminating responses. Accordingly, in the first part of this section, the two-stage paradigms are developed within the framework of one-stage paradigms which involve only initiating stimuli and terminating responses. Noted in connection with the description of these paradigms are some explanatory consequences, in particular, for reversal and nonreversal shifts.

Concept formation tasks are usually complex, and mediating responses and stimuli are commonly inferred rather than observed directly. Two-stage paradigms of conceptual behaviors should, therefore, be proposed cautiously. Emphasized in the second part of this section are some precautions in the development and use of two-stage paradigms.

"Abstract set or attitude," "hypotheses," and "strategies" are notions often advanced as central to any explanations of conceptual behaviors. Moreover, they are often regarded as opposed to stimulus-response analyses of concept formation tasks. The thesis elaborated in the last part of this section, however, is that these are not opposing notions, but rather are already embodied or can be readily assimilated within the one-stage and two-stage paradigms of the present analysis.

One-Stage and Two-Stage Paradigms

One-stage paradigms of conceptual situations and behaviors involve relationships between initiating stimuli and terminating responses. Such paradigms provide baselines for the development of two-stage paradigms, which introduce verbal mediating responses and stimuli. One-stage paradigms are not merely stepping stones, however; they are useful in themselves, in that they appear to represent adequately some of the conceptual behaviors of infrahuman organisms, of preverbal humans, and of humans under conditions which preclude or short circuit verbal mediating responses.

Combinations of Values along Dimensions

One-stage paradigms. A set of stimuli consisting of combinations of two values along each of two dimensions is the simplest case of possible sets of stimuli containing complete orthogonal combinations of m values along each of n dimensions. The four initiating stimuli of the one-stage paradigm shown in Figure 1 are combinations of two values (x_1, x_2) along an X dimension, and of two values (y_1, y_2) along a Y dimension. For example, x_1 and x_2 might be the values giving rise to the colors red and blue, respectively, along a dimension of wave length; y_1 and y_2 might be small and large areas, respectively, along a (derived) dimension of size.

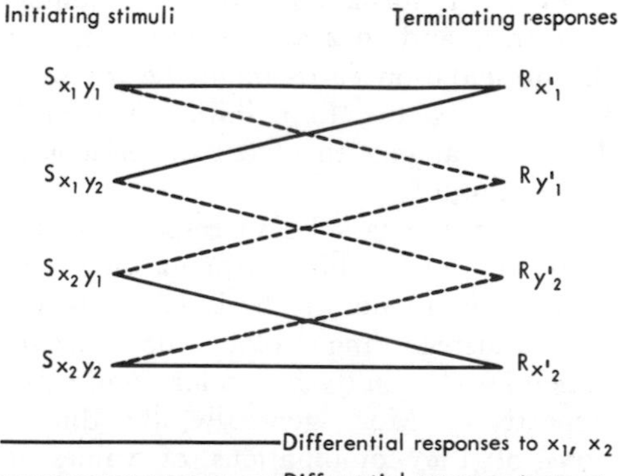

Fig. 1: One-stage paradigm of relationships involving initiating stimuli which are combinations of two values, x_1, x_2 along an X dimension and two values, y_1, y_2 along a Y dimension. (The differential terminating responses $R_{x'_1}$, $R_{x'_2}$ are to x_1, x_2, while $R_{y'_1}$, $R_{y'_2}$ are to y_1, y_2. The X dimension might be color with values of red, x_1, and blue, x_2, and the Y dimension might be size with values of small, y_1, or large, y_2.

The two terminating responses could be naming by means of familiar words, nonsense syllables, or manipulanda representing two different names. Or they could be sorting by placing the stimuli in groups, matching them with other stimuli, or approaching-avoiding. The two patterns of relationships between initiating stimuli and terminating responses depict the associations whose strengthening or occurrence are referred to here as concept formation. That both animals and humans can acquire such differential responses to one or some of the dimensions of multidimensional stimuli has been amply demonstrated (Kelleher, 1956; Kendler & D'Amato, 1955; Woodworth, 1958).

Determinants of the actual and potential patterns of relationships that will be learned include the number of fixed, relevant, and irrelevant dimensions presented, as well as the number of values selected along the relevant and irrelevant dimensions. A *fixed* dimension is exemplified by but one value along the dimension for all of the members of the set of initiating stimuli. For the stimuli shown in Figure 1, form dimensionality, number of forms, and location of the forms on the presentation cards might be the same for each of the four initiating stimuli. They are among the fixed dimensions of those stimuli.

Should the task be to respond on the basis of red or blue, disregarding size, or to respond on the basis of small and large, disregarding color, the relevant dimensions would be color and size, respectively. More generally, the dimensions of the combinations of values to which discriminative responses are to be conditioned are the *relevant* dimensions. *Irrelevant* dimensions are those which, in the formation of some particular concept(s), involve values which must be disregarded. Such dimensions—or, more precisely, the values along such dimensions—may be completely or incompletely orthogonal with respect to combinations of values along the relevant dimensions.[5]

Once the component associations of particular patterns of relationships, such as those in Figure 1, are at a given level of strength, changes may occur either *singly* or *jointly,* in the initiating stimuli, the terminating responses, and the stimulus-response relationships. Such changes are important, because they are the bases for concept generalization and for reversal and nonreversal shifts.

The initating stimuli can be changed by adding or shifting to new values along the original dimensions of the stimuli, or by adding or subtracting dimensions and values along those dimensions. The degree of occurrence of previously learned differential responses to altered sets of stimuli is the measure of *concept generalization.* Except where concept generalization has been used as a criterion of concept formation (e.g., Heidbreder, 1946a, 1946b), however, this phenomenon has not been of great experimental interest. For this reason, to elaborate on concept generalization here is considered premature.

Both the initiating stimuli and the terminating responses can remain the same, but their relationships, or the relevant and irrelevant dimensions and values, can be changed by reversal or nonreversal shifts. The effects of such shifts on conceptual behaviors, and explanations of those effects, have been among the major concerns of many recent studies of concept formation (e.g., Kendler & Kendler, 1959). It is important, therefore, to describe reversal and nonreversal shifts within one-stage paradigms for this type of initiating stimuli. Also, such description is prerequisite to the subsequent analysis of the role of verbal mediating responses and

[5] As is suggested by the overlap of the terminology employed here and that employed in classifying analysis of variance designs (e.g., Federer, 1955), such designs provide models of some of the many possible relationships between terminating responses and sets of initiating stimuli which are combinations of values along dimensions.

stimuli in reversal and nonreversal shifts.

With reversal shifts the values or combinations of values to which differential responses are learned remain the same, but the responses to values or combinations of values are interchanged. In Figure 1, for example, $R_{x'_1}$ might be shifted from $S_{x_1y_1}$ and $S_{x_1y_1}$ to $S_{x_2y_1}$ and $S_{x_2y_2}$; and $R_{x'_2}$ would become the reinforced response to $S_{x_1y_1}$ and $S_{x_1y_2}$ instead of to $S_{x_2y_1}$ and $S_{x_2y_2}$ Specifically, the response to red-small and red-large would be shifted to blue-small and blue-large, and the response to blue-small and blue-large would be made to red-small and red-large.

A complete nonreversal shift entails a change from differential pairings of responses with combinations of values along one or more dimensions to differential pairings of those responses with combinations of values along one or more entirely different dimensions. Thus, the pattern of relationships in Figure 1 might be changed from responding in terms of x_1 and x_2 along X, disregarding y_1 and y_2, along Y, to responding differentially to y_1 and y_2, disregarding x_1 and x_2. Only the relationships of the two responses to the initiating stimuli and not the responses themselves are changed. The relationship between $S_{x_1y_1}$ (red-small) and $R_{x'_1}$ would remain the same but that response would be changed from $S_{x_1y_2}$ (red-large) to $S_{x_2y_1}$ (blue-small). The relationship between $S_{x_2y_2}$ (blue-large) and $R_{x'_2}$ would remain the same but that response would be changed from $S_{x_2y_1}$ (blue-small) to $S_{x_1y_2}$ (red-large).

New terminating responses can be introduced. Should the old and the new responses have the same topography and, because of time limitations imposed by the task, be prohibited from occurring in sequence, the old responses must be inhibited for the new responses to occur. Such a state of affairs has been described as a condition, if not the optimum condition, for *negative transfer*. What results is simply a shift from one one-stage paradigm to another one-stage paradigm. But if the old and new responses do not interfere with each other (have separate topographies or can occur in sequence), the old responses may not drop out but instead constitute relatively stable links—mediating responses and stimuli—between initiating stimuli and the new terminating responses. Thus, a two-stage paradigm would have emerged. This is, of course, the sequence of events which has been presumed in investigations of the effect of verbal pretraining on subsequent conceptual sorting and naming (e.g., Fenn & Goss, 1957).

Despite the usefulness and greater simplicity of one-stage paradigms, there are considerations which suggest that such paradigms are less adequate than two-stage paradigms for explanation and prediction of the conceptual behavior of verbal humans in many concept formation tasks and even, perhaps, of some of the conceptual behaviors of infrahuman organisms and nonverbal humans. These considerations include: (*a*) observations of positive transfer from verbal pretraining to subsequent conceptual sorting or naming and of facilitation due to instructions or instruction induced sets (Carey & Goss, 1957; Fenn & Goss, 1957; Gelfand, 1958; Goss & Moylan, 1958; Hunter & Ranken, 1956; Lacey & Goss, 1959), (*b*) the relatively greater ease of reversal than of nonreversal shifts for human adults (Buss, 1956; Gormazano & Grant, 1958, Harrow & Friedman, 1958; Kendler & D'Amato, 1955; Kendler & Mayzner, 1956) and for children who are fast learners (Kendler & Kendler, 1959) in contrast to the superiority of nonreversal shifts for animals (Kelleher, 1956) and for children who are slow learners (Kendler & Kendler, 1959) and (*c*) verbal humans' reports of the occurrence and use of names for dimensions and values of stimuli in the conceptual sorting of stimuli (e.g., Lacey & Goss, 1959). An additional consideration rests primarily on the results of studies employing the third type of sets of stimuli (e.g., Reed, 1946). Without the postulation of common verbal or other responses to subsets of stimuli whose members are highly dissimilar physically, generalization of a common terminating response from one stimulus of a subset to other stimuli of the subset would be precluded. Each of the associations between initiating stimuli and terminating responses would have to be strengthened separately, with a consequent increase in difficulty of mastering the task.

Two-stage paradigms. Shown in Figure 2 are some of the possible stimulus-response relationships in a two-stage expansion of the one-stage paradigm presented in Figure 1. The four subsets of these relationships which should be distinguished are those: between initiating stimuli and mediating responses; between mediating stimuli and mediating responses or, more simply, between mediating responses; between mediating stimuli and terminating responses; and between initiating stimuli and terminating responses.

Within the first of these subsets of relationships, variations in the strength of two subpatterns of relationships between initiating stimuli and mediating responses may have somewhat different effects on conceptual behaviors. The first subpattern represents relationships in which responses of naming the dimensions occur. These are the associations between the initiating stimuli and R_X, R_Y. The second subpattern represents responses of naming the specific values along the dimensions. The responses of these associations are R_{x_1} for x_1; R_{x_2} for x_2; R_{y_1} for y_1; and R_{y_2} for y_2.

When the relationships between mediating stimuli and mediating responses are added, variations in the strengths of three more subpatterns of relationships can be distinguished. The first of these subpatterns is sequences of responses of naming the dimensions. These appear in the lower half of Figure 2 under "Dimensions" as

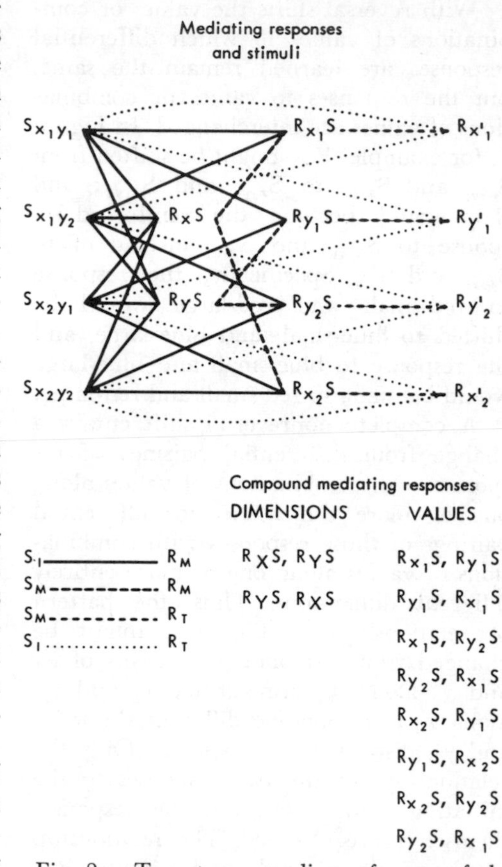

Fig. 2: Two-stage paradigm of some of the relationships possible between initiating stimuli and mediating responses, between mediating stimuli and mediating responses, between mediating stimuli terminating responses, and between initiating stimuli and terminating responses. (In order to simplify the possible relationships of the diagram, relationships involving compound mediating responses for dimensions and compound mediating responses for values along dimensions are listed separately.) The mediating responses might be differential with respect to x_1, x_2 along the X dimension or to y_1, y_2 along the Y dimension which is also the case for the terminating responses.

$R_X S$, $R_Y S$ and $R_Y S$, $R_X S$. The second subpattern is sequences of responses of naming values along dimensions. The eight sequences of combinations and orders of two of such responses are shown in the lower half of Figure 2 under "Values." The third of these subpatterns is sequences of responses of naming both dimensions and values along dimensions. For example, combining one of the two responses of naming a dimension with one of the four responses of naming a value would generate 16 permutations of a particular dimension response with a particular value response.

Variation in the strength of each of these five subpatterns of relationships between initiating stimuli and mediating responses might have somewhat different effects on the direction and degree of: extralist response interference with both mediating responses and terminating responses, trial-to-trial variability of the stimulus patterns immediately prior to the terminating responses, response-mediated similarity, and response-mediated dissimilarity. In turn, these conditions should influence direction and degree of transfer to acquisition of associations between initiating stimuli and terminating responses. Table 1 summarizes assumptions about the effects of each of the first four subpatterns on extralist response interference, trial-to-trial variability of stimulus patterns, response-mediated similarity, and response-mediated dissimilarity. Table 1

Table 1

SPECIFIC PATTERNS OF STIMULUS-RESPONSE RELATIONSHIPS

Specific Patterns Involving	*Extralist Response Interference*	*Stimulus Variability*	*Response-Mediated Similarity*	*Response-Mediated Dissimilarity*
Dimensions:				
R_X, R_Y	Reduce (+)	Reduce (+)	Increase (—)	Decrease (—)
R_XR_Y, R_YR_X	Reduce (+)	Reduce (+)	Increase (—)	Decrease (—)
Values along single dimensions:				
R_{x_1}, R_{x_2}	Reduce (+)	Reduce (+)	Increase for $S_{x_1y_1}$, $S_{x_1y_2}$ and for $S_{x_2y_1}$, $S_{x_2y_2}$ (+ for $R_{x'_1}$, $R_{x'_2}$ and — for $R_{y'_1}$, $R_{y'_2}$)	Increase for $S_{x_1y_1}$, $S_{x_1y_2}$ in relation to $S_{x_2y_1}$, $S_{x_2y_2}$ (+ for $R_{x'_1}$, $R_{x'_2}$ and — for $R_{y'_1}$, $R_{y'_2}$)
R_{y_1}, R_{y_2}	Reduce (+)	Reduce (+)	Increase for $S_{y_1x_1}$, $S_{y_1x_2}$ and for $S_{y_2x_1}$, $S_{y_2x_2}$ (+ for $R_{y'_1}$, $R_{y'_2}$ and — for $R_{x'_1}$, $R_{x'_2}$)	Increase for $S_{y_1x_1}$, $S_{y_1x_2}$ in relation to $S_{y_2x_1}$, $S_{y_2x_2}$ (+ for $R_{y'_1}$, $R_{y'_2}$ and — for $R_{x'_1}$, $R_{x'_2}$)
Combination of values along dimensions: $R_{x_1}R_{y_1}$, $R_{y_1}R_{x_1}$, etc.	Reduce (+) to Increase (—)	Reduce (+) to Increase (—)	No differential effects among initiating stimuli	

Note.—The direction of these effects are shown along with whether they are expected to have facilitative (+) or inhibitory (—) consequences. In the case of responses to values along single dimensions, whether particular initiating stimulus-mediating response relationships are facilitative or inhibitory is contingent on the relationships between initiating stimuli and terminating responses which are to be acquired.

also indicates whether these four consequences of each of the four subpatterns considered separately are expected to be facilitative (+), inhibitory (−), or neutral with respect to the formation of particular concepts. At present there is no way of combining the separate presumed facilitative, inhibitory, or neutral effects into a net facilitative, inhibitory, or neutral effect.

Except where precluded by prior training in the experimental situation, by selection on the basis of associations to the same or similar sets of initiating stimuli, or by instructions, each of these four subpatterns might occur both within trials and in successive trials during a good part of the course of acquiring associations between the initiating stimuli and the terminating responses. Their relative strengths at any point in learning—and, therefore, their effects on acquisition of initiating stimulus-terminating response associations—will be contingent on factors which include the following: their initial relative strengths, the values or combinations of values along one or more dimensions to which the differential terminating responses are being strengthened, time permitted to make the terminating responses, and degree of mastery of the terminating responses.

The fifth subpattern, which involves sequences of mediating responses of naming the dimension and of naming values along the dimension, may also influence acquisition of terminating responses. For example, fairly strong bidirectional associations might exist or be established between R_XS and R_{x_1}, R_{x_2}, and between R_YS and R_{y_1}, R_{y_2}. Should R_X be stronger than R_Y, R_{x_1} and R_{x_2} would occur and be available for mediating discriminative terminating responses to $S_{x_1y_1}$, $S_{x_1y_2}$ and to $S_{x_2y_1}$, $S_{x_2y_2}$ rather than to $S_{x_1y_1}$, $S_{x_2y_1}$, and $S_{x_1y_2}$, $S_{x_2y_2}$. Contingent on the relationships between initiating stimuli and terminating responses which were being differentially reinforced, facilitation or inhibition of these associations might be occasioned.

The remaining two subsets of relationships, those between mediating stimuli and terminating responses and those between initiating stimuli and terminating responses, are of primary importance here because of their presumed roles in reversal and nonreversal shifts. The upper diagram of Figure 3 shows the relationships among initiating stimuli, mediating responses and stimuli, and terminating responses which might exist at appreciable levels of strength upon attainment of differential responses to the x_1 and x_2 values along the X dimension. Should there be introduction of differential reinforcement of R_{x_2} to $S_{x_1y_1}$, $S_{x_1y_2}$, and of R_{x_1} to $S_{x_2y_1}$, $S_{x_2y_2}$ to bring about a reversal shift, six associations might be changed: the four between the initiating stimuli and the terminating responses, and the two between the mediating stimuli and the terminating responses. In contrast, 14 association might be affected by a nonreversal shift to the differential reinforcement of responses to the y_1 and y_2 values of Y. These are the four between initiating stimuli and R_{x_1}, R_{x_2}, which might be weakened; the four between those stimuli and R_{y_1}, R_{y_2}, which might be strengthened; the two between S_{x_1} and S_{x_2} and the terminating responses which might be extinguished while the two between S_{y_1} and S_{y_2} and those responses are established and strengthened; and the two associations between initiating stimuli and terminating responses ($S_{x_1y_1}$ and $R_{x'1}$; $S_{x_2y_1}$ and $R_{x'2}$), which must be reversed.

If equal weights are assumed for the component associations of two-stage paradigms, and if shifting is inversely related to the number of associations which must or may have to be changed, reversal shifts should be accomplished more rapidly than nonreversal shifts. Within one-stage paradigms, reversal shifts will affect more associations and therefore be more difficult than nonreversal shifts. Thus, as Kendler

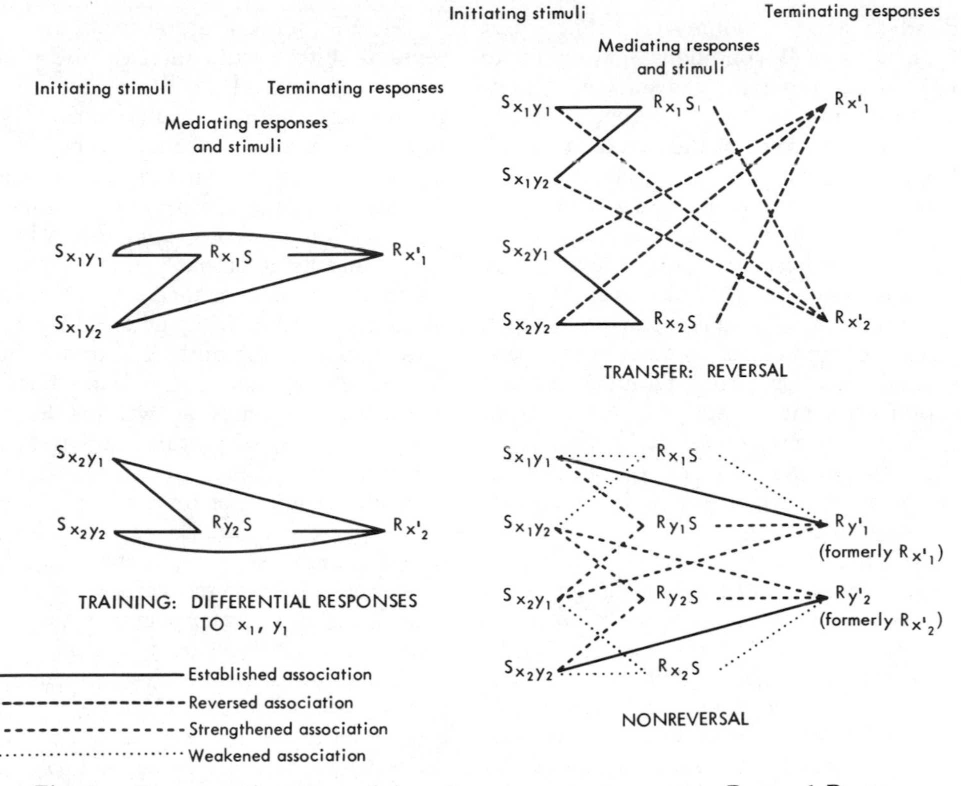

Fig. 3: The paradigm for training show conceptual response, $R_{x'_1}$ and $R_{x'_2}$ to $S_{x_1y_1}$, $S_{x_1y_2}$ and $S_{x_2y_1}$, $S_{x_2y_2}$, respectively, after whose strengthening to some criterion level, reversal and nonreversal shifts are made. (As shown in the two paradigms for transfer, a reversal shift requires changes in only 6 associations, while a nonreversal shift may affect up to 14 associations. The terminating responses remain the same with respect to general topography and specific form—only the stimulus-response relationships into which they may enter are altered. $R_{y'_1}$ and $R_{y'_2}$ of the nonreversal shift are the same responses as $R_{x'_1}$ and $R_{x'_2}$, respectively. However, the subscripts were changed to indicate that differences along the *Y* dimension, y_1, y_2, are the new bases for differential responses.)

and his associates (Kendler & D'Amato, 1955) have suggested, but without detailed development of the basis for this proposal, one-stage and two-stage paradigms generate opposing predictions about the relative ease of reversal and nonreversal shifts.

In general, as the number of dimensions and values increases, the number of associations involved in nonreversal shifts becomes increasingly greater than the number altered by reversal shifts. Other factors equal, therefore, with greater numbers of dimensions and values, the relative disadvantage of nonreversal shifts should become greater. Other factors, however, are not likely to be equal. As Buss (1956) has noted, with nonreversal shifts responses on the basis of the previously reinforced values along the no-longer-relevant dimension continue to be reinforced on 50% of the trials. The weakening of such differential responses will, therefore, be retarded, and will further contribute to the disadvantage of nonreversal shifts. But four additional conditions may serve to reduce the relative disadvantage of nonreversal shifts.

First, once some of the initiating stimuli begin to elicit the new mediating responses, when other initiating stimuli are presented these mediating responses should generalize extensively among those stimuli. One basis of such generalization would be the presence of stimuli common to each trial: i.e., those arising from the experimental situation, from postural and receptor-orienting responses, and from responses to instructions other than those aspects referring to more specific associations between initating stimuli and mediating responses.

Second, because each of the values along the new dimension of the nonreversal shift is an element common to a subset of stimuli, the new mediating response for a subset of initiating stimuli should generalize among the members of the subset. Simultaneously, of course, the same two conditions should result in the generalization of inhibition of the relationships between initiating stimuli and the old mediating responses.

Third, though not included in the paradigms of Figure 3, the response R_X, which represents the response of naming the *X* dimension, might be replaced by the comparable response, R_Y, for the *Y* dimension. The increased frequencies of occurrence of stimuli produced by R_{y_1} and R_{y_2}, which are presumably already associated with R_Y, would be the bases of the initial evocations of R_Y. Because R_Y is only one response, however, its strengthening and generalization among the initiating stimuli should be even faster and more extensive than the strengthening and generalization of R_{y_1} and R_{y_2}. Therefore, R_Y should begin to occur first and, because of the preestablished associations between the stimuli it produced and R_{y_1} and R_{y_2}, their probabilities of occurrence relative to R_{x_1} and R_{x_2} should be increased markedly.

Fourth, successive reversal or nonreversal shifts should increase the probabilities of occurrence of mediating responses referring to a change in task. With successive reversal and nonreversal shifts, number of trials to learn the new concepts of each shift usually decreases. Some of this increasingly more rapid formation of new concepts is probably due in part to warm up or performance set in the form of familiarization with mode and rate of presentation of the initiating stimuli. Such familiarization should eliminate irrelevant competing responses as well as lead to greater stability of postural and receptor-orienting responses to thus assure more effective reception of the initiating stimuli and lower the variability of response-produced stimuli. Also, with experience, subjects should learn to recognize with greater confidence and greater accuracy that they have reached perfect or near perfect performance of discriminative responses to some subsets of stimuli. Consequently, any error then made would serve as a cue that the experimenter has shifted the concepts rather than the concepts have not yet been learned. Further, subjects will be increasingly familiar with whether the shifts are reversal or nonreversal shifts and, if the latter, with how many dimensions have probably been shifted and even to what dimensions the shifts have probably been made. Thus, mediating responses of the form "He's changed the task" or "Something has changed" should come to control whole sets of further mediating responses which name dimensions and values along dimensions. These four conditions should reduce the net disadvantage of nonreversal to reversal shifts to margins which are much less than those suggested by simply counting the numbers of equally weighted associations which such shifts might affect.

Common Elements or Relations

One-stage paradigms. Figure 4 is a one-stage paradigm for concept formation with sets of stimuli, such as those constructed by Hull (1920), in which each subset requiring a common response consists of a common element accompanied by other features which vary unsystematically from instance to instance. Furthermore, the common elements are neither completely nor incompletely orthogonal combinations of values along one or more discernible physical or psychophysical dimensions. If common "relations" among the parts of complex forms are regarded as separable from the features which vary among instances exemplifying the same relation, Smoke's (1932) set of initiating stimuli and other sets that resemble his can also be represented by this paradigm.

Two-stage paradigms. The two-stage paradigm for the second type of initiating stimuli is shown in Figure 5. The letters or word subscripts of the mediating responses are possible specific pre-established mediating responses to the indicated initiating stimuli. Worth noting, because of their predictive consequences, are three major differences between this paradigm and the two-stage paradigm for sets of stimuli composed of combinations of values along dimensions shown in Figure 2.

First, no responses of naming the component dimensions are present. However,

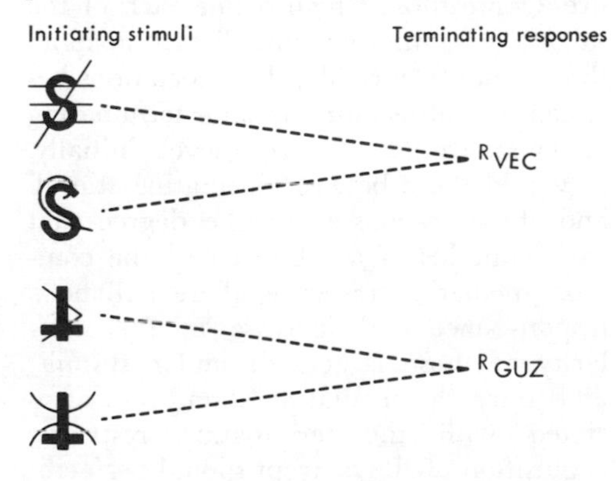

Fig. 4: One-stage paradigm of relationships between nonsense syllable terminating responses and initiating stimuli which consist of two different common elements each of which is accompanied by features which differ from figure to figure.

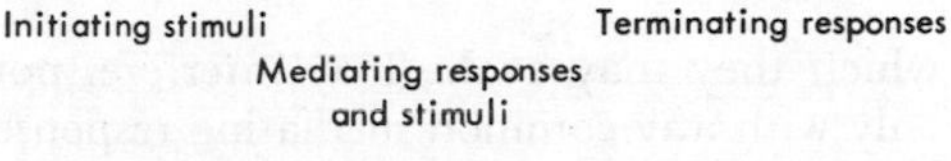

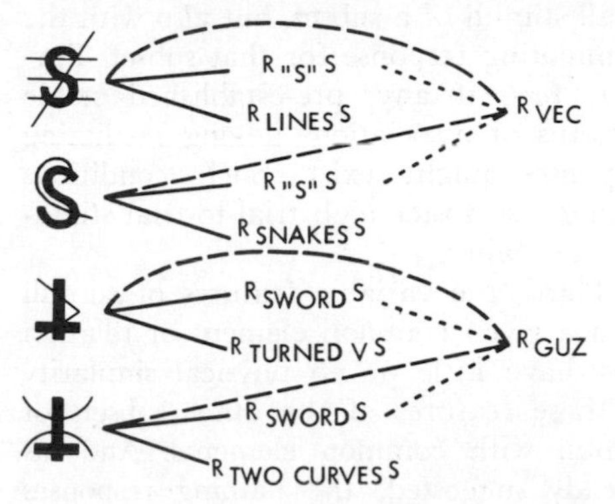

Fig. 5: Two-stage paradigm of the relationships possible between initiating stimuli, which consist of two different common elements and variable features, and both mediating and terminating responses and also between mediating stimuli and terminating responses.

should the common elements of two or more subsets be at the same spatial position, responses of orienting-toward and naming that position might occur and be strengthened. Although such responses and the stimuli they produce would be nondifferential with respect to the relationships between initiating stimuli and terminating responses, their occurrence might reduce extralist intrusions and stimulus variability as well as assure more frequent reception of the elements which distinguish one subset of figures from another.

Second, both the common element of members of a subset and the variable features of those members are likely to be made up of a fairly large number of discriminable features, each of which elicits naming responses. If the common element or relation which defines a particular subset of stimuli does elicit some response which is the same for all members of the subset, that response to each member is likely to have considerable competition from the responses to other parts of the common element as well as from responses to the variable features of each member. Such responses and the further responses which they may evoke may interfere, not only with any common mediating response to all stimuli of a subset, but also with the terminating response for that subset. Further, few, if any, pre-established stable patterns of associations among mediating responses might exist. Such conditions should also foster high trial-to-trial stimulus variability.

Third, the variable features of stimuli with a given common element or relation may have little or no physical similarity to those features of the other subsets of stimuli with common elements. And, as already suggested, the naming responses evoked by one subset may have little overlap with those evoked by the other subsets. While reversal shifts could be instituted, such characteristics of the stimuli would severely limit or obviate nonreversal shifts.

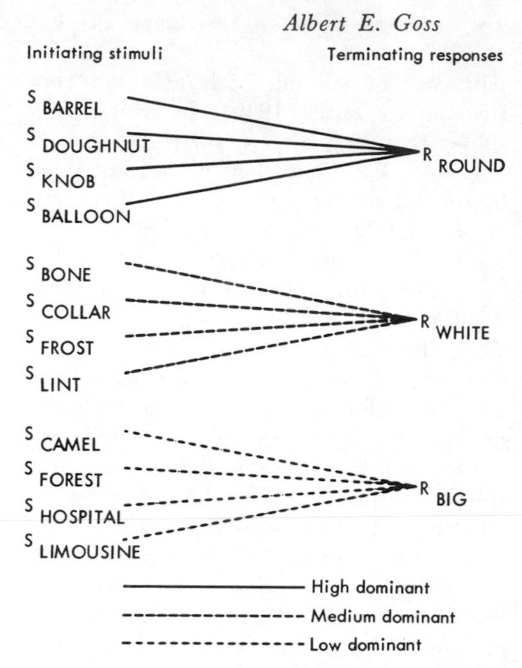

Fig. 6: One-stage paradigm of relationships between subsets of initiating stimuli each of which is defined by elicitation of a common terminating response by the stimuli. (The words used are from Underwood and Richardson's—1956—first list and are of three levels of dominance with respect to their elicitation of the terminating responses.)

Elicitation of Common Responses

One-stage paradigms. The third kind of stimuli are those whose subsets are distinguished from each other on the basis of their members' elicitation of some common response that differs from the common responses defining each of the other subsets. Figure 6 is a one-stage paradigm and Figure 7 is a two-stage paradigm of the stimulus-response relationships presumed to be involved in the formation of concepts with such stimuli.

In the one-stage paradigm, increased frequency of arousal of each one of the common terminating responses by the stimuli of the subset is viewed as strengthening of the concept. The stronger the initial associations between the stimuli of subsets and their terminating response, and the higher the variance of those associations, the more rapid the formation of concepts (Freedman & Mednick, 1958; Underwood & Richardson, 1956). The limiting case of the formation of such concepts is the acquisition, from zero levels of initial strength, of common responses which have each been assigned to a different subset of physically dissimilar stimuli.

Two-stage paradigms. The mediating responses of the two-stage paradigm (Figure 7) are those which define each of the subsets of initiating stimuli. In general, though not necessarily, the associations between initiating stimuli and terminating responses would be at zero levels initially, as would those between mediating stimuli and those responses. To the degree that each stimulus of a subset elicits the common mediating response, there will be a response-mediated increase in the similarity of those largely dissimilar stimuli; and, once the mediating stimulus is associated with the terminating response, acquisition of the concept should be facilitated by response-mediated generalization. Griffith and Spitz (1958) and Griffith, Spitz, and Lipman (1959) obtained direct relationships between correct abstractions made by normal and mentally retarded

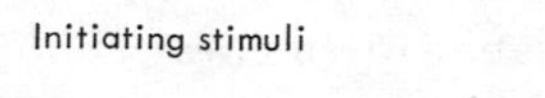

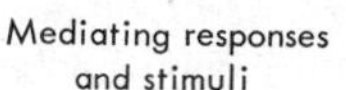

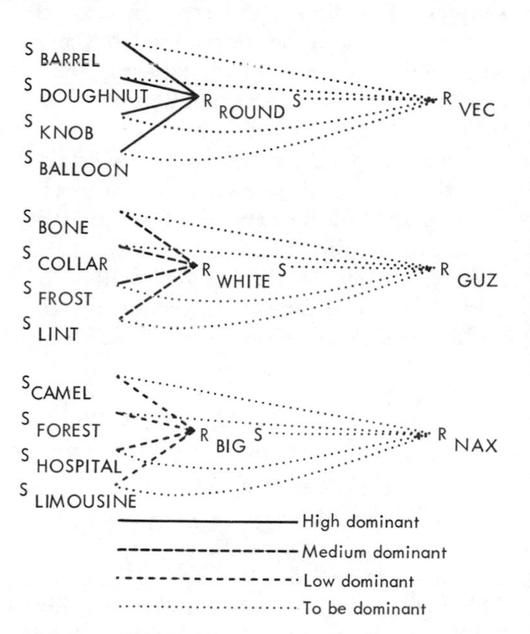

Fig. 7: Two-stage paradigm of relationships possible between subsets of initiating stimuli defined by the elicitation of common responses which now function as mediating responses and stimuli in the acquisition of new associations between each of the subsets of initiating stimuli and their common nonsense syllable terminating responses. (The mediating responses should increase the similarity of stimuli within subsets and decrease the similarity of stimuli of each subset to those of other subsets.)

children and number of words defined by the same possible common abstractions. From these relationships they inferred that the common definition mediated the common abstractions.

The presence of different mediating response-produced stimuli, each associated with a different terminating response, might also increase the response-mediated dissimilarity and discrimination of stimuli which are members of different subsets (Fenn & Goss, 1957). Such an increase would counteract any generalization of terminating responses among subsets due to fortuitous physical resemblances among stimuli belonging to different response-defined subsets.

The relationships between initiating stimuli and terminating responses which are to be strengthened need not be isomorphic with the relationships between initiating stimuli and mediating responses. With increasing departures from isomorphism, the acquisition of terminating responses might be retarded, possibly to a degree sufficient to produce some negative transfer. Because the mediating responses might also reduce extralist response interference and stimulus variability, however, the net transfer might still be positive.

If each of the initiating stimuli belongs to two or more response-defined subsets, each stimulus would be expected to evoke two or more different mediating responses, at least during the initial trials. Unless each terminating response is then isomorphic with the two or more responses defining each of the other combinations of subsets, multiple mediating responses to initiating stimuli can be expected to increase generalization among subsets; thus some retardation of the learning of terminating responses would be occasioned. Because of greater trial-to-trial variability in stimulation preceding terminating responses, multiple mediating responses to initiating stimuli may always produce some retardation relative to the maximum positive transfer that is achievable with a single mediating response to each initiating stimulus.

Use of Two-Stage Paradigms

Each of the preceding two-stage paradigms represents a different general case of relationships among the particular type of sets of initiating stimuli, mediating responses and stimuli, and terminating responses. The members of each of these types of sets of initiating stimuli may differ with respect to their complexity, their similarity and other properties, their number, and their probabilities of occurrence (Goss, 1955). Thus, it should be obvious that each particular concept formation task and its attendant conditions requires detailed analysis in terms of presumed stimulus-response elements and initial relationships among these elements, and also in terms of the changes in those elements and relationships which are expected to occur. The nature and strengths of both initial and changed relationships should be expressed as completely and precisely as possible. Association techniques or training controlled by the experimenter are the means of specifying the strengths of initial relationships. It should also be remembered that—except when isolated and controlled—changes in many or all of the stimulus-response relationships present probably occur, if not simultaneously, within rather small blocks of trials.

Finally, some subjects who have formed concepts correctly may not provide verbal reports of the bases for their conceptual behaviors which correspond to experimenters' specifications of the bases for forming particular concepts. When verbal mediating responses do not occur, or occur only partially, sporadically, or during the earlier phases of concept formation, appropriate verbal reports would not be expected. Should the words which constitute subjects' mediating responses differ from the labels preferred by experimenters, subjects' reports might be considered wrong or incomplete. Further, during the course of acquisition the sets of verbal mediating responses may have changed. Should subjects have failed to distinguish such changes or to indicate when they took place, their reports would seem inaccurate and confused. In addition, if subjects described the terminating responses or both mediating and terminating responses as bases for their conceptual behaviors, while experimenters' specifications were only in terms of verbal mediating responses, subjects' verbal reports would seem unsatisfactory. This would also be the case were the subjects' mediating responses nonverbal.

Differences between the labels used by subjects and those preferred by experimenters can only be determined by careful, detailed analyses of the labeling habits of subjects from a given population. Confusions between mediating and terminating responses can be minimized by ascertaining the temporal sequences of subjects' responses. Only by careful observation of locomotor-manipulative responses (and even this may be inadequate) will it be possible to determine the presence of nonverbal mediating responses.

PLACE OF "ABSTRACT SET OR ATTITUDE," "HYPOTHESES," AND "STRATEGIES" IN THE FRAMEWORK OF THIS ANALYSIS

"Abstract set or attitude" (Goldstein & Scheerer, 1941; Hanfmann & Kasinin, 1942), "hypotheses" (Woodworth, 1958), and "strategies" (Bruner, Goodnow, & Austin, 1956) are terms frequently used to label some aspects of the behavior involved in acquiring concepts as well as to explain success or failure in this process. Unfortunately, these notions have certain features that limit both their experimental usefulness and their explanatory power. In general, their presence or absence is ordinarily determined on the basis of characteristics of the conceptual behaviors observed. Thus, they are post hoc descriptions which usually cannot be used predictively. Often, too, the notions are treated as primary or sole explanations of conceptual behavior when, in fact, other factors—such as types of sets of initiating stimuli, specific attributes of each type of stimuli, and amount and conditions of practice—appear to be of equal or greater importance. And, on the whole, the relationship of these terms to more general theories of behavior is tenuous at best.

In the face of such shortcomings, one

course for a stimulus-response analysis of concept formation consists of ignoring the terms entirely. Another course, followed here, is to attempt to assimilate what is meaningful and useful about the terms within the rather rigorous framework that this paper has presented. More specifically, it is suggested that the most meaningful and useful aspects of such notions as abstract set or attitude, hypotheses, and strategies are in part already present in this analysis, and that what is valuable but not present requires only certain translations in order to be assimilated. These aspects are considered below under the following headings: verbal mediating responses and stimuli, strengths of reactions to occurrences and extent of reversal or nonreversal shifts, sequences in which verbal mediating responses occur on single and successive trials, sequences of receptor-orienting responses, and prior habits and persistence of covert or overt verbalization and rehearsal.

Verbal Mediating Responses and Stimuli

Following Fenn and Goss (1957), perhaps the simplest as well as the most common meaning of abstract set or attitude and hypotheses in concept formation is, conceived narrowly, the occurrence of verbal mediating responses and stimuli. Conceived more broadly, this meaning subsumes the largely pre-experimentally established patterns of relationships: (*a*) between initiating stimuli and mediating responses, where the latter are names for dimensions and values as well as for common elements or variable features, or where they are common responses or meanings that define subsets of initiating stimuli; (*b*) between such mediating responses and other mediating responses; and (*c*) between such mediating responses and terminating responses. The first part of this section on paradigms was largely devoted to an analysis of the role of these patterns of relationships in concept formation. The functional significance for concept formation of this meaning of abstract set or attitude and hypotheses has, therefore, already been considered.

Reactions to Shifts

Also considered earlier were mediating responses that identify shifts in the task. Such responses, it was suggested, should increase in strength with successive reversal or nonreversal shifts and thus mediate changes in whole sets of further mediating responses which name dimensions and values along dimensions. These changes might be called shifts in hypotheses or strategies. And their occurrence could be taken as evidence of the presence of an abstract or attitude.

Sequences in Which Verbal Mediating Responses Occur

Bruner, Goodnow, and Austin (1956, pp. 81–103, 126–147) have suggested that conditions of presentation of initiating stimuli influence trial-to-trial sequences of choice and "guess" responses. Thus, when subjects could select each successive initiating stimulus, the four sequences or strategies which were distinguished logically were simultaneous scanning, successive scanning, conservative focusing, and focus gambling. When the successive occurrences of initiating stimuli were controlled by the experimenter, they distinguished wholist (whole, focusing) and part-scanning (part) strategies or sequences. Under the condition of presentation in which subjects could select each successive initiating stimulus, the responses which were recorded were terminating responses, first in the form of a choice and then as a guess. Presumably these choices and guesses were preceded, most immediately, by mediating responses consisting of names for the combinations of values of the stimulus selected and the names of the consequent guess of the correct concept. Therefore, the sequences or strategies they distinguished, and which were found to occur to some degree in various subjects, could be regarded as providing some information about sequences of mediating responses through successive selections of stimuli. Under the condition of presentation in which the experimenter determined each successive initiating stimulus, each hypothesis written during the 10-second period following each initiating stimulus could be regarded as congruent with the just preceding mediating response. The sequences of such hypotheses, therefore, probably reflected trial-to-trial sequences of the last mediating response of each trial. No information about intratrial sequences was reported.

The two-stage paradigms of the first part of this section show each initiating stimulus as eliciting only one mediating response which is either the name for a dimension or value along a dimension, or a single combination of names for dimensions or values. Contingent on both the time subjects have to respond and on subjects' prior experiences with the same or similar stimuli, each initiating stimulus may elicit not one name or combination of names, but a sequence of names or combinations of names. For example, the subject might respond to a particular initiating stimulus with the sequence "red, small, color, size," in which "size" was the last response to occur prior to the appearance of the stimulus eliciting the terminating response to be conditioned to the initiating stimulus. Because of the shorter time interval, the terminating response might be more strongly conditioned to stimuli produced by size than to stimuli produced by the earlier mediating responses. More generally, should terminating responses be most strongly conditioned to stimuli produced by mediating responses which occurred just prior to elicitation of the terminating responses, the sequences with which mediating responses occur and whether those responses are names of values or of dimensions might have marked effects on concept formation.

Whether the effects are facilitative or inhibitory will be contingent on particular conditions. Thus, were size the relevant dimension and large and small the two values along that dimension, the sequence "color, red (or blue), size, large (or small)" should produce greater facilitation than the sequence "size, large (or small), color, red (or blue)." Similarly, sequences in which the last mediating responses were names for common elements of the initiating stimuli rather than names for their variable features should facilitate acquisition of different terminating responses to each subset of initiating stimuli with common features. Inhibitory consequences would be predicted for sequences ending with mediating responses which were names for variable features rather than for common elements. Also, occurrence of the common response to a subset of initiating word stimuli, after more specific associations to those words rather than before such associations, should facilitate; the opposite sequence should inhibit.

A further consideration would be whether the same sequence or different sequences of mediating responses occurred on each presentation of each initiating stimulus or of each member of particular subsets of initiating stimuli. With the sequence, "color, red (or blue), size, large (or small)," for example, constancy of the sequence should be most facilitative, were size the relevant dimension, and most inhibitory, were color the relevant dimension. A reduction in the percentage of times "size, large (or small)" occurred last, and a concomitant increase in the percentage of times "color, red (or blue)" occurred last, should be relatively less facilitative or less inhibitory in the formation of size or color concepts, respectively.

Modes of systematic variation of the components of sequences and of the order in which the components occur can be learned. Therefore, subjects can be expected to differ in the degree to which they have learned to vary the nature and sequences of mediating responses through successive trials. As a result subjects will not only differ with respect to the abstract set or attitude, hypotheses, and strategies with which they began but also with respect to those which are present through successive trials. Whether particular sequences or ways of varying such sequences are facilitative or inhibitory will be contingent on the particular concepts to be formed.

Sequences of Receptor-Orienting Responses

Receptor-orienting responses and their consequences may sometimes be functionally equivalent to mediating responses and stimuli (Goss, 1955). For this reason, abstract set or attitude, hypotheses, or strategies may also be conceived as sequences of receptor-orienting responses.

When initiating stimuli which are relatively small in size are presented at the same place, one at a time, receptor-orienting responses may be of little importance. Possible exceptions are initiating stimuli composed of combinations of common elements or relations and variable features for which the common element or relation of all members of a particular subset have the same location. Should there be some favored point of initial fixation for individual subjects, or for groups of subjects, whether the common element or relation of a particular subset was at that location or at other locations might influence acquisition of the concepts.

Simultaneous presentation of all initiating stimuli or groups thereof, however, might increase the importance of sequences of receptor-orienting responses. Both arrangement of initiating stimuli on the display, and the subjects' pre-experimental and subsequent experimental experiences, should determine the particular sequence of receptor-orienting responses on a given trial. The initial and subsequent fixation points might maximize focusing on successive stimuli whose combinations of values and changes in those combinations were optimal for the formation of particular concepts. If so, such sequences of receptor-orienting responses should facilitate concept formation. For other arrangements of initiating stimuli the same sequences might be inhibitory.

Prior Habits of Verbalization, Rehearsal, and Persistence Therein

Included in Dollard and Miller's (1950, pp. 118–119) set of factors in "social training in the use of higher mental processes" is "training to stop and think." Adolescent and adult subjects explicitly instructed to use verbal mediating responses may differ little, if at all, in the degree to which such responses are activated. However, without such explicit instructions—and therefore largely dependent on the subjects' past experiences with similar tasks—they may or may not stop and think: i.e., they may or may not make overt or covert verbal mediating responses prior to occurrences of terminating responses to the initiating stimuli. Furthermore, some subjects may rehearse such responses between trials while others may think of other things; the latter subjects may in other words, fail to attend to the task continuously. Finally, in the face of initial failures, some subjects may persist in stopping and thinking and in rehearsing while other subjects may temporarily or permanently stop both activities. Up through adolescence the strengths of such habits should be directly related to age. Awaiting detailed determination, however, are both the nature of the relationships of habits of verbalization and rehearsal to age and the effects of such habits on probabilities of occurrence of verbal mediating responses.

In summary, conceived analytically rather than simply as names for certain instructions or for certain changes in terminating responses, the notions of abstract set or attitude, hypotheses, and strategies apparently refer to one or more of the preceding classes of relationships among the stimuli and responses of concept formation tasks. Some of the classes of relationships include mediating responses and stimuli; those which do not can be expected to have indirect effects on relationships that do involve mediating responses and stimuli.

PRINCIPLES AND PREDICTIONS

Though referred to occasionally—and always assumed—in the preceding section, little direct attention has yet been given to the classes of variables and of general principles involving those variables which enter into explanations of the strengthening, generalization, and weakening of the stimulus-response associations entailed in the one- and two-stage paradigms that have been described. Of obvious relevance are the classes of principles that concern effects on associations or on performance of classes of variables such as: schedules of practice and reinforcement-punishment, the number and both absolute and relative strengths of conflicting responses, the number of stimuli associated with the same response and the strengths of those associations, and the degree of similarity among initiating stimuli and among mediating stimuli. Setting limits to the operation of these classes of variables are the patterns of relationships among initiating stimuli, mediating responses and stimuli, and terminating responses and also conditions of stimulus presentation, such as whether initiating stimuli are presented simultaneously or successively (Bruner et al., 1956) and whether they are all positive, negative, or both positive and negative (Hovland, 1952; Hovland & Weiss, 1953).

It is not the purpose of this paper to make an exhaustive enumeration of the consequences predicted by the application of each class of potentially relevant variables and the principles involving them to the several paradigms or to the various patterns of relationships the paradigms contain. In order to show explicitly how such variables and principles may be profitably combined with the paradigms, however, this final section deals with certain aspects of predictions of the effects of three important classes of variables for which some data are available. These are: strength of associations between initiating stimuli and mediating responses; patterns of relationships among initiating stimuli, mediating responses and stimuli, and terminating responses; and similarity of initiating stimuli. In each case, pertinent experimental studies are described.[6]

Strengths of Associations between Initiating Stimuli and Mediating Responses

The strengths of associations between initiating stimuli and verbal mediating responses will be determined by conditions of practice such as the number and distribution of trials or degree of mastery of those relationships prior to undertaking transfer or criterion tasks. In general, any condition of practice and reinforcement-punishment known to increase or decrease the strengths of stimulus-response associations of multiunit tasks are, through their effects on strengths of associations between initiating stimuli and mediating responses, potential determinants of subsequent performance on transfer or criterion tasks.

[6] Not considered, however, are those studies of the relative effects of reversal and nonreversal shifts which were noted in the first part of the second section. Also ignored are studies (Bensberg, 1958; Carey & Goss, 1957; Fenn & Goss, 1957; Hunter & Ranken, 1956; Wickens & Eckstrand, 1954) which were primarily demonstrations of positive transfer from verbal pretraining to subsequent conceptual behaviors; these demonstrations served as bases for inferences about the functional significance of verbal mediating responses in conceptual behaviors. Several additional experiments (Attneave, 1957; Rhine & Silun, 1958; Shepard & Shaeffer, 1956; Sigel, 1953, 1954; Solley & Messick, 1957; Staats & Staats, 1957; Wulff & Stolurow, 1957) have been excluded because they did not involve either experimentally controlled verbal pretraining or conventional concept formation criterion tasks.

In Figures 2 and 7, the relationships between initiating stimuli and mediating responses, and between the initiating stimuli in combination with mediating stimuli and terminating responses, can be described as isomorphic. Put another way, for each different mediating response to a subset of initiating stimuli, there is one and only one terminating response, each of which is different from the terminating response paired with any other mediating response. For such isomorphic patterns of relationships, it is predicted that rate of acquisition of associations between initiating stimuli and terminating responses would be a direct function of strengths of associations between initiating stimuli and mediating responses. Because of generalized responses (errors of generalization, confusions, intralist intrusions), trials to learn associations between initiating stimuli and terminating responses should be related to trials in learning associations between initiating stimuli and mediating responses by an ogival function or by curves showing some slight initial negative transfer rather than being negatively accelerated throughout (Goss, 1955).[7]

Pertinent to this prediction are two recent investigations (Goss & Moylan, 1958; Lacey & Goss, 1959) of the relationship between transfer to conceptual behaviors and strengths of associations between initiating stimuli and presumed verbal mediating responses. In both investigations, the initiating stimuli were 16 blocks, each of which was tall or short, black or white, in combination with top and bottom areas which were large or small, square or circular. In the Goss and Moylan study, nonsense syllable responses or familiar word responses were conditioned to subsets of tall-large, tall-small, short-large, and short-small initiating stimuli. Lacey and Goss used only nonsense syllable responses. The transfer task of both studies was sorting by height-size, and in both the number of blocks sorted by height-size was directly related to degree of mastery of associations between initiating stimuli and presumed mediating responses, as well as to numbers of trials in learning those associations. Unfortunately the resultant curves were not adequate for more precise specification of functions relating direction and degree of transfer to degree of mastery of associations between initiating stimuli and mediating responses, or to trials in learning these associations.[8] As suggested elsewhere for paired-associates learning tasks (Goss, 1955), such specifications are further complicated by the likelihood that the functions are contingent on parameters such as patterns of relationships among initiating stimuli, mediating responses and stimuli, and terminating responses, as well as on the degree of similarity of initiating stimuli.

Patterns of Relationships

Within two-stage paradigms, regardless of the type of sets of initiating stimuli, it is useful to distinguish four extreme patterns of relationships among subsets of initiating stimuli, mediating responses and stimuli, and terminating responses, because each pattern should result in somewhat different conceptual behaviors involving the terminating responses. Figure 8 shows these four patterns. In Patterns *A* and *B*, the relationships between mediating responses and subsets of initiating stimuli are isomorphic with those between terminating responses and subsets of initiating stimuli plus mediating stimuli. This isomorphism does not hold for Patterns

[7] Murdock (1958) argues that with appropriate allowance for generalization responses, the function is negatively accelerated throughout.

[8] An alternative suggestion (Lacey & Goss, 1959) is that greater mastery of experimentally established associations between initiating stimuli and nonsense syllable responses increases the likelihood of arousal of pre-experimentally established associations between initiating stimuli and names for dimensions and values along dimensions. Such names might then serve as the actual verbal mediating responses of the transfer or criterion task.

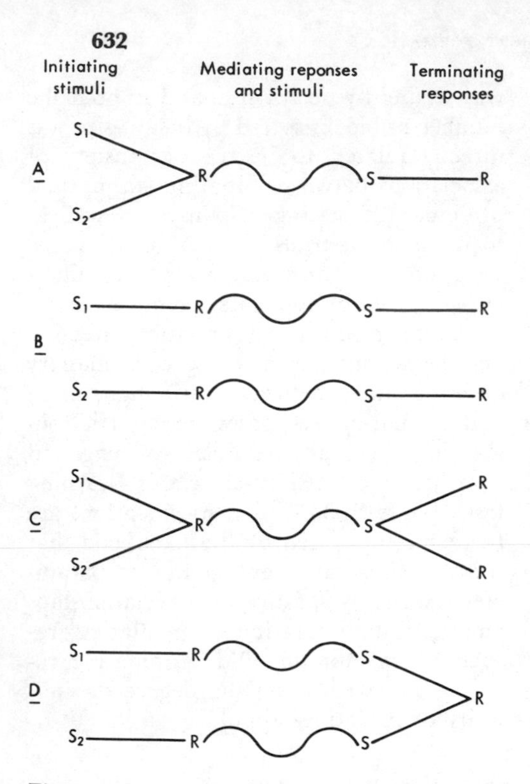

Fig. 8: Four possible extreme patterns of relationships among subsets of initiating stimuli, mediating responses and stimuli, and terminating responses.

C and *D*. Pattern *C* is characterized by a common mediating response to both subsets of initiating stimuli and by two terminating responses, one of which is to stimulus compounds consisting of stimuli from the first subset plus the mediating stimulus, and the other of which is to stimulus compounds consisting of stimuli from the second subset plus the mediating stimulus. Pattern *D* is characterized by a different mediating response to each subset of initiating stimuli, and by a common terminating response both to compounds consisting of the stimuli in the first subset plus the stimulus produced by the mediating response to those stimuli, and to compounds consisting of the stimuli in the second subset plus the stimulus produced by the mediating response to those stimuli.

For concept formation tasks involving the relationships of Patterns *A* and *B*, prior acquisition of the associations between subsets of initiating stimuli and a common mediating response should facilitate acquisition of associations between the subsets of initiating stimuli and a common terminating response; prior acquisition of different mediating responses should facilitate acquisition of associations between initiating stimuli subsets and different terminating responses. Greater response-mediated similarity and generalization is the basis for the prediction for Pattern *A*, and greater response-mediated dissimilarity and discrimination is the basis for the prediction for Pattern *B*.

For Pattern *C*, in contrast, the greater similarity of the subsets of initiating stimuli (based on the presence of a common mediating stimulus) should retard acquisition of a different terminating response to each subset. For Pattern *D*, greater dissimilarity of the subsets of initiating stimuli (based on the presence of a different mediating stimulus for the stimuli of each subset) should slow the learning of a common terminating response to each subset.

Lacey (1959) tested each of these predictions. His stimuli were eight line drawings of faces or houses, each of which was printed on pink, light blue, light yellow, and light green paper. Eight to 11 year old children first learned either a common or different nonsense syllable mediating response to two subsets of initiating stimuli. The transfer or criterion task was acquisition of a new set of nonsense syllable responses as either a common or different terminating response to those same subsets of initiating stimuli. Thus the relationships of terminating responses to initiating stimuli and to mediating responses and stimuli were those of Patterns *A*, *B*, *C*, or *D*.

Measured against the performance of control groups, whose prior training controlled for facilitation due to warm up and receptor-orienting responses, positive transfer was obtained with Patterns *A* and *B* and negative transfer occurred with

Patterns *C* and *D*. Therefore, as predicted, the pattern of relationships among subsets of initiating stimuli, mediating responses and stimuli, and terminating responses determined whether positive or negative transfer occurred. Lacey's results also suggested that Pattern *B* might produce greater relative positive transfer, though no greater absolute positive transfer, than Pattern *A*. Patterns *C* and *D*, however, did not seem to differ with respect to either relative or absolute amounts of negative transfer.

Similarity of Initiating Stimuli

For Patterns *A*, *B*, *C*, and *D*, similarity of sets of initiating stimuli might influence amount and perhaps direction of transfer from verbal pretraining to subsequent conceptual behaviors. For Patterns *A* and *D*, disregarding mediating responses and stimuli, similarity within and between subsets of initiating stimuli should be directly related to ease of learning associations between those stimuli and a common terminating response. Patterns *B* and *C* involve acquisition of discriminative terminating responses to initiating stimuli. Rate of acquisition of those associations should be directly related to similarity of stimuli within subsets of initiating stimuli and inversely related to similarity between those subsets. When verbal mediating responses and stimuli are considered, similarity of initiating stimuli might modify the expected positive transfer with Patterns *A* and *B* and the expected negative transfer with Patterns *C* and *D*.

Present data and theory do not warrant attempts to develop more exact predictions of the influence of similarity of initiating stimuli on direction and amount of transfer. However, since the second variable of Lacey's (1959) experiment was two degrees of similarity of the members of the sets of face and house stimuli, some pertinent data are available.

For Patterns *A* and *D* together, disregarding verbal mediating responses and stimuli, similarity was directly related to mastery of associations between iniating stimuli and terminating responses; inverse relationships were obtained with Patterns *B* and *C* together. For Pattern *A*, while absolute amount of positive transfer was directly related to similarity, an inverse relationship was obtained for relative amount of transfer. For Pattern *D*, both absolute and relative amounts of positive transfer were inversely related to similarity. For Patterns *B* and *C*, both absolute and relative amounts of positive transfer were directly related to similarity. However, since most of the relationships for each pattern separately were not statistically significant, at best they provide hypotheses for replicatory investigations.

In general, for concept formation tasks involving prior strengthening of presumed mediating responses, the findings presently available suggest that conceptual behaviors involving terminating responses are influenced by: strengths of associations between initiating stimuli and mediating responses; patterns of relationships among initiating stimuli, mediating responses and stimuli, and terminating responses; and similarity of initiating stimuli. Furthermore, these findings are reasonably consistent with predictions based on two-stage paradigms in combination with principles of the role of these and other classes of variables in the strengthening, generalization, and weakening of stimulus-response associations.

SUMMARY

The purpose of this paper was to analyze the role of verbal mediating responses in concept formation. First summarized was the historical development of stimulus-response analyses of conceptual behaviors which have emphasized the role of mediating responses and stimuli, particularly verbal mediating responses. The influence of Max Meyer and Watson on the behavioristic analyses of the 1920s was noted. Although Birge, Miller and Dollard, Cofer and Foley, and Gibson furthered such analyses in the early 1940s, only the more detailed recent analyses of Baum, Osgood, Mandler, Goss, Kendler, and others have led to hypotheses which have been tested experimentally.

The first section provided a general specification of concept formation tasks and described the relationship between concept formation and conventional paired-associates tasks. The second section first described the structures and some explanatory consequences of one-stage and two-stage paradigms of conceptual behaviors with each of three types of sets of initiating stimuli. Some precautions in the use of these paradigms were then noted, and assimilation within the present analysis of the notions of abstract set or attitude, hypotheses, and strategies was proposed. The third section showed the complementary relationship between the one-stage and two-stage paradigms and classes of variables and principles involving those variables which enter into explanations of the strengthening, generalization, and weakening of the component stimulus-response associations. Two-stage paradigms in combination with some of these principles were then used to generate sample predictions of effects on concept formation of: strengths of relationships between initiating stimuli and mediating responses; some patterns of relationships among initiating stimuli, mediating responses and stimuli, and terminating responses; and relative similarity of initiating stimuli.

References

ATTNEAVE, F. Transfer of experience with a class-schema to identification-learning of patterns and shapes. *J. exp. Psychol.*, 1957, 54, 81–88.

BAUM, M. H. A study in concept attainment and verbal learning. Unpublished PhD dissertation, Yale University, 1951.

BENSBERG, G. J., JR. Concept learning in mental defectives as a function of appropriate and inappropriate "attention sets." *J. educ. Psychol.*, 1958, 49, 137–143.

BIRGE, J. S. The role of verbal responses in transfer. Unpublished PhD dissertation, Yale University, 1941.

BRUNNER, J. S., GOODNOW, J. J., & AUSTIN, G. A. *A study of thinking.* New York: Wiley, 1956.

BUSS, A. H. Reversal and nonreversal shifts in concept formation with partial reinforcement eliminated. *J. exp. Psychol.*, 1956, 52, 162–166.

CAREY, J. E., & GOSS, A. E. The role of verbal labeling in the conceptual sorting behavior of children. *J. genet. Psychol.*, 1957, 90, 69–74.

COFER, C. N., & FOLEY, J. P., JR. Mediated generalizations and the interpretation of verbal behavior: I. Prolegomena. *Psychol. Rev.*, 1942, 49, 513–540.

DASHIELL, J. F. *Fundamentals of objective psychology.* Boston: Houghton Mifflin, 1928.

DOLLARD, J., & MILLER, N. E. *Personality and psychotherapy.* New York: McGraw-Hill, 1950.

ELKONIN, D. B. The physiology of higher nervous activity and child psychology. In B. Simon (Ed.), *Psychology in the Soviet Union.* Stanford: Stanford Univer. Press, 1957.

FEDERER, W. T. *Experimental design: Theory and application.* New York: Macmillan, 1955.

FENN, J. D., & GOSS, A. E. The role of mediating verbal responses in the conceptual sorting behavior of normals and schizophrenics. *J. genet. Psychol.*, 1957, 90, 59–67.

FREEDMAN, J. L., & MEDNICK, S. A. Ease of attainment of concepts as a function of response dominance variance. *J. exp. Psychol.*, 1958, 55, 463–466.

GELFAND, S. Effects of prior associations

and task complexity upon the identification of concepts. *Psychol. Rep.*, 1958, 4, 568–574.

GIBSON, E. J. A systematic application of the concepts of generalization and differentiation to verbal learning. *Psychol. Rev.*, 1940, 47, 196–229.

GOLDSTEIN, K., & SCHEERER, M. Abstract and concrete behavior: An experimental study with special tests. *Psychol. Monogr.*, 1941, 53(2, Whole No. 239).

GORMEZANO, I., & GRANT, D. A. Progressive ambiguity in the attainment of concepts on the Wisconsin Card Sorting Test. *J. exp. Psychol.*, 1958, 55, 621–627.

GOSS, A. E. A stimulus-response analysis of the interaction of cue-producing and instrumental responses. *Psychol. Rev.*, 1955, 62, 20–31.

GOSS, A. E. University of Massachusetts conference on problem solving. Amherst, Massachusetts, June 19–21, 1956.

GOSS, A. E., & GREENFELD, N. Transfer to a motor task as influenced by conditions and degree of prior discrimination training. *J. exp. Psychol.*, 1958, 55, 258–269.

GOSS, A. E., & MOYLAN, M. C. Conceptual block-sorting as a function of type and degree of mastery of discriminative verbal responses. *J. genet. Psychol.*, 1958, 93, 191–198.

GRAY, J. S. A behavioristic interpretation of concept formation. *Psychol. Rev.*, 1931, 38, 65–72.

GRIFFITH, B. C., & SPITZ, H. H. Some relationships between abstraction and word meaning in retarded adolescents. *Amer. J. ment. Defic.*, 1958, 63, 247–251.

GRIFFITH, B. C., SPITZ, H. H., & LIPMAN, R. S. Verbal mediation and concept formation in retarded and normal subjects. *J. exp. Psychol.*, 1959, 58, 247–251.

HANFMANN, E., & KASININ, J. Conceptual thinking in schizophrenia. *Nerv. ment. dis. Monogr.*, 1942, No. 67.

HARROW, M., & FRIEDMAN, G. B. Comparing reversal and nonreversal shifts in concept formation with partial reinforcement controlled. *J. exp. Psychol.*, 1958, 55, 592–598.

HEIDBREDER, E. The attainment of concepts: I. Terminology and methodology. *J. gen. Psychol.*, 1946, 35, 173–189. (a)

HEIDBREDER, E. The attainment of concepts: II. The problem. *J. gen. Psychol.*, 1946, 35, 191–223. (b)

HOVLAND, C. I. A "communication analysis" of concept learning. *Psychol. Rev.*, 1952, 59, 461–472.

HOVLAND, C. I., & WEISS, W. Transmission of information concerning concepts through positive and negative instances. *J. exp. Psychol.*, 1953, 45, 175–182.

HULL, C. L. Quantitative aspects of the evolution of concepts. *Psychol. Monogr.*, 1920, 28(1, Whole No. 123).

HUNTER, G. F., & RANKEN, H. B. Mediating effects of labeling on sorting behavior and judgments of similarity. Paper presented at Eastern Psychological Association, Atlantic City, March 1956.

KELLEHER, R. T. Discrimination learning as a function of reversal and nonreversal shifts. *J. exp. Psychol.*, 1956, 51, 379–384.

KENDLER, H. H., & D'AMATO, M. F. A comparison of reversal shifts and nonreversal shifts in human concept formation behavior. *J. exp. Psychol.*, 1955, 48, 165–174.

KENDLER, H. H., & KENDLER, T. S. Reversal and nonreversal shifts in kindergarten children. *J. exp. Psychol.*, 1959, 58, 56–60.

KENDLER, H. H., & MAYZNER, M. S., JR. Reversal and nonreversal shifts in card-sorting tests with two and four categories. *J. exp. Psychol.*, 1956, 51, 244–248.

LACEY, H. Mediating verbal responses and

stimulus similarity as factors in conceptual naming by school-age children. Unpublished PhD dissertation, University of Massachusetts, 1959.

LACEY, H., & GOSS, A. E. Conceptual block sorting as a function of number, pattern of assignment, and strength of labeling responses. *J. genet. Psychol.*, 1959, 94, 221–232.

LIUBLINSKAYA, A. A. Development of children's speech and thought. In B. Simon (Ed.), *Psychology in the Soviet Union*. Stanford: Stanford Univer. Press, 1957.

MANDLER, G. Response factors in human learning. *Psychol. Rev.*, 1954, 61, 235–244.

METZGER, R. A comparison between rote learning and concept formation. *J. exp. Psychol.*, 1958, 56, 226–231.

MEYER, M. F. *The fundamental laws of human behavior*. Boston: Gorham, 1911.

MILLER, N. E., & DOLLARD, J. *Social learning and imitation*. New Haven: Yale Univer. Press, 1941.

MURDOCK, B. B., JR. Intralist generalization in paired-associate learning. *Psychol. Rev.*, 1958, 65, 306–314.

OSGOOD, C. E. *Method and theory in experimental psychology*. New York: Oxford Univer. Press, 1953.

REED, H. B. Factors influencing the learning and retention of concepts: I. The influence of set. *J. exp. Psychol.*, 1946, 36, 71–87.

RHINE, R. J., & SILUN, B. A. Acquisition and change of a concept attitude as a function of consistency of reinforcement. *J. exp. Psychol.*, 1958, 55, 524–529.

RICHARDSON, J. The relationship of stimulus similarity and numbers of responses. *J. exp. Psychol.*, 1958, 56, 478–484.

SHEPARD, W. O., & SHAEFFER, M. The effect of concept knowledge on discrimination learning. *Child Develpm.*, 1956, 26, 173–178.

SIGEL, I. Developmental trends in the abstraction ability of children. *Child Develpm.*, 1953, 24, 131–144.

SIGEL, I. The dominance of meaning. *J. genet. Psychol.*, 1954, 85, 201–207.

SIMMONS, A. J., & GOSS, A. E. Animistic responses as a function of sentence contexts and instructions. *J. genet. Psychol.*, 1957, 91, 181–189.

SMOKE, K. L. An objective study of concept formation. *Psychol. Monogr.*, 1932, 42(4, Whole No. 191).

SOLLEY, C. M., & MESSICK, S. J. Probability, learning, the statistical structure of concepts, and the measurement of meaning. *Amer. J. Psychol.*, 1957, 70, 161–173.

SPENCE, K. W. The nature of discrimination learning in animals. *Psychol. Rev.*, 1936, 43, 427–449.

STAATS, C. K., & STAATS, A. W. Meaning established by classical conditioning. *J. exp. Psychol.*, 1957, 54, 74–80.

UNDERWOOD, B. J., & RICHARDSON, J. Verbal concept learning as a function of instructions and dominance level. *J. exp. Psychol.*, 1956, 51, 229–238.

WATSON, J. B. Is thinking merely the action of language mechanisms? Part V. *Brit. J. Psychol.*, 1920, 11, 87–104.

WEISS, A. P. *A theoretical basis of human behavior*. Columbus, Ohio: Adams, 1925.

WICKENS, D. D. Stimulus-response theory as applied to perception. In, *Kentucky symposium: Learning theory, personality theory, and clinical research*. New York: Wiley, 1954.

WICKENS, D. D., & ECKSTRAND, G. A. Transfer of perceptual set. *J. exp. Psychol.*, 1954, 47, 274–278.

WOODWORTH, R. S. *Dynamics of behavior*. New York: Holt, 1958.

WULFF, J. J., & STOLUROW, L. M. The role of class-descriptive cues in paired-associates learning. *J. exp. Psychol.*, 1957, 53, 199–206.